Developmental Neuropsychiatry

Developmental Neuropsychiatry

Edited by

MICHAEL RUTTER

University of London Institute of Psychiatry

THE GUILFORD PRESS

New York • London

A Division of Guilford Publications, Inc.
200 Park Avenue South, New York, N.Y. 10003

Printed in the United States of America

Second printing, June 1984

LIBRARY OF CONGRESS CATALOGING IN PUBLICATION DATA

Main entry under title:

Developmental neuropsychiatry.

Includes bibliographies and indexes.

1. Brain-damaged children. 2. Minimal brain dysfunction in children. I. Rutter, Michael. [DNLM: 1. Brain damage, Chronic—In infancy and childhood. 2. Child development disorders. 3. Hyperkinetic syndrome. 4. Learning disorders. WS 350.6 D489206]

RJ496.B7D48 1983 618.92'8589 83-1633

ISBN 0-89862-621-8

Contributors

Hansook Ahn, PhD, Brain Research Laboratories, Department of Psychiatry, New York University Medical Center, New York, New York

Ramiro Arrieta, MD, Instituto Nacional de Ciencias y Tecnología de la Salud del Niño–DIF, Sistema Nacional Para el Desarrollo Integral de la Familia, Mexico City, Mexico

Dirk J. Bakker, PhD, Subfaculty of Psychology, Department of Developmental, Educational, and Physiological Neuropsychology, Pedological Institute and Free University, Amsterdam, The Netherlands

Lynette Bradley, PhD, Department of Experimental Psychology, University of Oxford, Oxford, England

Peter E. Bryant, PhD, Department of Experimental Psychology, University of Oxford, Oxford, England

Oliver Chadwick, PhD, G. H. Sergievsky Center, College of Physicians and Surgeons, Columbia University, New York, New York; Institute for Basic Research in Developmental Disabilities, Staten Island, New York

Barton Childs, MD, Department of Pediatrics, Johns Hopkins University School of Medicine, Baltimore, Maryland

Donald J. Cohen, MD, Departments of Pediatrics and Psychiatry, and the Yale Child Study Center, Yale University School of Medicine, New Haven, Connecticut

John A. Corbett, MB, FRCPsych, MRCP, DCH, DPM, The Bethlem Royal and Maudsley Hospitals, London, England

Joaquín Cravioto, MD, MPH, DSc, Instituto Nacional de Ciencias y Tecnología de la Salud del Niño–DIF, Sistema Nacional Para el Desarrollo Integral de la Familia, Mexico City, Mexico

Virginia I. Douglas, PhD, Department of Psychology, McGill University, Montreal, Quebec, Canada; Department of Psychology, The Montreal Children's Hospital, Montreal, Quebec, Canada

H. Bruce Ferguson, PhD, Department of Psychology, Carleton University, Ottawa, Ontario, Canada

Joan M. Finucci, PhD, Department of Pediatrics, Johns Hopkins University School of Medicine, Baltimore, Maryland

Uta Frith, DipPsych, PhD, Medical Research Council Developmental Psychology Unit, London, England

Rachel Gittelman, PhD, College of Physicians and Surgeons, Columbia University, New York, New York; New York State Psychiatric Institute, New York, New York

Philip J. Graham, FRCP, FRCPsych, Department of Child Psychiatry, University of London Institute of Child Health, London, England; Department of Child Psychiatry, Hospital for Sick Children, London, England

Margaret E. Hertzig, MD, Department of Psychiatry, Cornell University Medical Center, New York, New York

E. Roy John, PhD, Brain Research Laboratories, Department of Psychiatry, New York University Medical Center, New York, New York

Herbert Kaye, PhD, Department of Psychology, State University of New York at Stony Brook, Stony Brook, New York

Patricia A. O'Connor, PhD, Department of Child Psychiatry, College of Physicians and Surgeons, Columbia University, New York, New York; New York State Psychiatric Institute, New York, New York

Leslie Prichep, PhD, Brain Research Laboratories, Department of Psychiatry, New York University Medical Center, New York, New York

Sheri Prupis, BA, Department of Child Psychiatry, New York State Psychiatric Institute, New York, New York

Judith L. Rapoport, MD, Section on Child Psychiatry, National Institute of Mental Health, Bethesda, Maryland

Byron P. Rourke, PhD, Department of Psychology, University of Windsor, Windsor, Ontario, Canada; Department of Neuropsychology, Windsor Western Hospital Centre, Windsor, Ontario, Canada

Michael Rutter, MD, FRCP, FRCPsych, Department of Child and Adolescent Psychiatry, University of London Institute of Psychiatry, London, England

Paul Satz, PhD, Neuropsychiatric Institute, University of California at Los Angeles, Los Angeles, California

Steven Schonhaut, PhD candidate, Department of Clinical Psychology, J. Hillis Miller Mental Health Center, University of Florida, Gainesville, Florida

Stephen Q. Shafer, MD, MPH, Departments of Public Health (Epidemiology) and Neurology, College of Physicians and Surgeons, Columbia University, New York, New York; Epidemiology of Developmental Brain Disorders Department, New York State Psychiatric Institute, New York, New York

David Shaffer, MB, MRCP, FRCPsych, DPM, Departments of Child Psychiatry, Clinical Psychiatry, and Pediatrics, College of Physicians and Surgeons, Columbia University, New York, New York; New York State Psychiatric Institute, New York, New York

Bennett A. Shaywitz, MD, Departments of Pediatrics and Neurology, Yale University School of Medicine, New Haven, Connecticut

Sally E. Shaywitz, MD, Department of Pediatrics, Yale University School of Medicine, New Haven, Connecticut

Robert L. Sprague, PhD, Institute for Child Behavior and Development, University of Illinois at Urbana-Champaign, Champaign, Illinois

Ann Stewart, MB, ChB, DCH, Department of Paediatrics, University College Hospital Medical School, London, England

Cornelis J. Stokman, PhD, Department of Child Psychiatry, New York State Psychiatric Institute, New York, New York

John D. Strang, PhD, Department of Psychology, University of Windsor, Windsor, Ontario, Canada; Department of Neuropsychology, Windsor Western Hospital Centre, Windsor, Ontario, Canada

Eric Taylor, MA, MB, MRCP, MRCPsych, Department of Child and Adolescent Psychiatry, University of London Institute of Psychiatry, London, England

Michael R. Trimble, MPhil, BSc, MB, ChB, MRCP, MRCPsych, The National Hospital for Nervous Diseases, London, England

Gabrielle Weiss, MD, Department of Psychiatry, The Montreal Children's Hospital, Montreal, Quebec, Canada

J. Gerald Young, MD, Yale Child Study Center, Yale University School of Medicine, New Haven, Connecticut

Acknowledgments

This book was planned and the writing begun during my tenure of a Fellowship at the Center for Advanced Study in the Behavioral Sciences, Stanford, California. I am most grateful to the Grant Foundation, the Foundation for Child Development, the Spencer Foundation, and the National Science Foundation (BNS 78-24671) for support during my period at the Center. The original concept of the volume derived from discussions with Erwin and Helen Witkin of the Society for Continuing Medical Education, Inc., Baltimore, and with Rachel Gittelman and Byron Rourke; I much appreciate all the help that they provided.

Portions of my chapters derive from articles published in the *American Journal of Psychiatry* (1981, *138*, and 1982, *139*), the *Journal of Clinical Neuropsychology* (1982, *4*), and *Psychological Medicine* (1980, *10*, and 1981, *11*); thanks are due to the editors of all three journals for permission to use that material.

M. R.

Preface

It is curious that the neuropsychiatry of adult life and of childhood have remained so remarkably separate from one another. Indeed, it is striking that the several authoritative textbooks on neuropsychiatry, or organic psychiatry as it is termed sometimes, have had very little to say about children. Rather, almost all the writings about childhood have approached the topic from the perspective of the behavioral concept of "minimal brain dysfunction"—a controversial syndrome that has little to do with neurological disease or damage as ordinarily understood. In fact, many recent commentators have questioned whether there is any justification for the concept at all. Yet it would be wrong to assume that the neuropsychiatric findings on adults can be extended to children without modification. It is known that the early years of infancy are marked by large and important changes in brain structure and functioning and that the effects of damage may be greatly modified by whether or not the organ is mature or immature, slowly or rapidly developing. Moreover, it cannot be assumed that trauma or disease will influence skills yet to develop in the same way as those already well established. There is a need to consider the field of developmental neuropsychiatry as a major topic in its own right.

That is the purpose of this volume, which comprises a series of essays on different facets of the topic; each seeks to summarize what is known and to outline the conceptual and empirical issues that remain to be resolved. As is appropriate for a subject that constitutes a crossroads of interests, the authors represent a range of disciplines—spanning psychology, psychiatry, and pediatrics. They have been selected both for their research leadership in one or another aspect of developmental neuropsychiatry and for their clinical experience in the care of patients with neuropsychiatric disorders. The objective throughout has been to provide a bridge between research and clinical practice, and the book is intended for those who approach the topic from either viewpoint.

Most traditional medical texts tackle their subject matter by means of a systematic coverage of all the various syndromes and diseases that fall within the purview of some speciality or subspeciality. That is not the strategy followed here; hence, there are a few conditions, such as infantile autism, in many ways epitomizing developmental neuropsychiatry, which are not considered in detail. Their omission was deliberate on the grounds that they have been well covered in other books. Rather, the purpose of this volume was to consider the basic principles that apply in any consideration of neuropsychiatric associations arising during the period of development. The topics to be considered were chosen to portray the conceptual and methodological issues that pervade developmental neuropsychiatry, in order to differentiate the many areas of agreement from the few that are subject to controversy.

Following an introductory chapter that introduces some of the key issues, the first major section of the volume is concerned with the psychological sequelae associated with some of the more common conditions of childhood that involve brain disease or injury. If we are to understand the possible disorders that may stem from subtle or covert brain dysfunction, we must first appreciate the effects of overt damage. However, that immediately raises the issue of how brain function or dysfunction is to be assessed or measured. That constitutes the focus of the second major section of the book.

The third and fourth sections consider two groups of disorders in some detail in order to exemplify the neuropsychiatric issues that arise with respect to clinical conditions not obviously caused directly by brain disease or damage, but in which there are pointers to possible organic brain dysfunction. Between them, these two groups—hyperkinetic/attentional deficit disorders and learning disabilities—cover the range of syndromes usually considered to fall into the general category of "minimal brain dysfunction." Whether or not that description constitutes a useful diagnostic category is reconsidered in the last chapter of the book, which seeks to appraise the present state of the art in the light of the findings and ideas discussed in the previous chapters.

Contents

Developmental Neuropsychiatry

Introduction: Concepts of Brain Dysfunction Syndromes

MICHAEL RUTTER

It has long been recognized that damage or disease of the brain in childhood may result in intellectual impairment and behavioral disturbance. That observation is scarcely surprising, of course. After all, the brain is the organ of the mind, and it might well be supposed that injury to that organ would have consequences for the behavioral and cognitive functions that it serves. One would have thought that the basic association between brain *tissue* pathology and the phenomena of *psycho*pathology could be taken for granted. As Karl Jaspers (1963) put it: "Insight into the aetiology of psychic events cannot be achieved at all without some knowledge of somatic function, more particularly the physiology of the nervous system . . . the unity of soma and psyche seems indisputable" (p. 4). With that basic assumption accepted, it might seem that interest would have turned to the specifics—to the various particular ways in which different types of pathology in different parts of the brain lead to specific psychiatric syndromes. Just as the neurologist has sought to link particular disorders, such as aphasia, with the specifics of focal brain pathology or of diseased brain systems, so the neuropsychiatrist might seek to do the same with psychic phenomena.

However, that has not been the course of medical or psychological history over this century. Jaspers (1963) expressed the dilemma eloquently:

> Investigation of somatic function, including the most complex cortical activity, is bound up with the investigation of psychic function. . . . Yet we must remember that neither line of enquiry encounters the other so directly that we can speak of some specific psychic event as directly associated with some specific somatic event or of an actual parallelism. The situation is analogous with the exploration of an unknown continent from opposite directions, where the explorers never meet because of impenetrable country that intervenes. We only know the end links in the chain of causation from soma to psyche and vice versa, and from both these terminal points we endeavour to advance. *Neurology* has discovered that the cortex with the brain stem provides the organ most closely associated with psychic function, and its researches have reached their highest peak so far in the theory of aphasia, agnosia, and apraxia. It seems, however, as if the further neurology advances, the further the psyche recedes; *psychopathology* on the other hand explores the psyche to the limits of consciousness but finds at these limits no

Michael Rutter. Department of Child and Adolescent Psychiatry, University of London Institute of Psychiatry, London, England.

somatic process directly associated with such phenomena as delusional ideas, spontaneous affects and hallucinations. In many cases, which increase in number as we gain in knowledge, the primary source of psychic change is found to lie in some cerebral disorder. Yet we always find that no one specific psychic change is characteristic for any one of these disorders. The facts seem to be that cerebral disorders may be responsible for almost all possible psychic changes though the frequency with which they appear may vary in different disorders. (p. 4)

Subsequent research findings have amply confirmed the wisdom of Jasper's admonitions. Nevertheless, in apparent disregard of these complexities, the literature has become strewn with a motley collection of sweeping claims and counterclaims on the behavioral consequences of brain damage and dysfunction in childhood. Thus, it has been asserted that "the behavioral manifestations of cerebral damage, whatever the etiology, are fairly uniform and characteristic" (Bakwin & Bakwin, 1967, p. 567) and "the behavior pattern associated with MBD [minimal brain dysfunction] is rather distinct [and] is easily identified" (Wender, 1971, p. 3). Necessarily, statements such as these have involved a great mixing of concepts. As Birch (1964) pointed out in a critique that antedated the growth industry of "minimal cerebral dysfunction," the concept of the "brain-damaged child" refers to a pattern of behavior and not to any known pathologic alteration in the tissues of the brain; moreover, "attaching the adjective 'minimal' . . . does not increase the descriptive accuracy of the term or add either to its scientific validity or its usefulness" (p. 5). Others have noted that the changes from "damage" to "dysfunction" and from "brain" to "cerebral" also fail to give either precision or nosological justification (Rie, 1980).

The pathognomonic significance for CNS [central nervous system] impairment of given symptoms or categories of symptoms requires greater empirical support or an explicit theoretical rationale that is consistent with knowledge in the neurosciences. For definitions of "minimal brain dysfunctions" to be convincing and to have relevance for practice and research, the consequences of such dysfunctions must be distinguishable from the consequences of other determinants of adaptation. . . . In the absence of a syndrome, it is illogical to continue to use a designation that represents one. (Rie, 1980, p. 14)

It is all too easy to mock and cast scorn on the terms and concepts. Yet a vast literature has grown up around the nature of behavioral syndromes of "MBD," and vigorous controversies continue on just what are the psychological sequelae of brain damage in childhood. In part, the terms and concepts arose as a reaction against some of the more extreme views on the psychodynamics of behavior and as a recognition of the growing empirical evidence on the importance of "organic" factors in etiology. Thus, in arguing for the importance of MBD as a cause of behavioral disorders and learning disabilities, Clements and Peters (1962) criticized the unwarranted tendency "to weave a complete causative fabric out of the fragile threads of stereotypes such as sibling rivalry, rejecting parents, repressed hostility, Oedipal conflict, repressed sexuality, etc., much of which may well be secondary and epiphenomenal rather than primary" (p. 185). It now seems that the pendulum swung too far, with neuromythologies replacing psychomythologies. Nevertheless, behind the fog of obfuscating dogma lies the reality of children with disturbances of behavior or educational difficulties that stem, at least in part, from abnormalities in brain function deriving from disease, damage, or genetic factors rather than from experiential influences or internal conflicts. Although, certainly, it appears that "all too often speculations about minimal brain dysfunction have given rise to postures of certainty when only ignorance exists" (Rutter, 1982), and although the terms and concepts used have added confusion rather than clarification, many distinguished investigators have nevertheless been involved in the process of reifying MBD. Before turning to the present state of the art and to the issues facing clinicians and researchers today, there is a need to look back at the historical development of ideas so that the way forward may be seen more clearly.

THE DEVELOPMENT OF THE CONCEPT OF MINIMAL CEREBRAL DYSFUNCTION

There have been several accounts of the history of the concept of MBD (Kalverboer, 1978; Kessler, 1980; Rutter, 1982; Rutter, Graham, & Yule, 1970; Strother, 1973; Werry, 1979). The origins of the interest in behavioral syndromes of brain dysfunction in childhood are probably to be found in the reports during the 1920s that hyperactivity, antisocial behavior, and emotional instability commonly developed following encephalitis (cf., e.g., Bond & Partridge, 1926; Ebaugh, 1923; Hohman, 1922). Rather similar symptoms were said to occur after head injury (Blau, 1936; Strecker & Ebaugh, 1924), and it came to be believed that, as Bond and Partridge (1926) put it, "The intensively hyperkinetic form of reaction . . . seems the most conclusively organic." A few years later, Kahn and Cohen (1934), in a seminal paper, coined the term "organic drivenness" to describe this type of hyperkinesis. Shortly afterward, Bradley (1937) reported that overactivity often responded to stimulant medication. The accounts of postencephalitic behavior disorders were clinical, nonquantitative, and lacking in appropriate controls, so that it is not possible to determine from the published reports how often similar syndromes occurred in the absence of brain damage and hence how far the clinical picture was pathognomonic. Nevertheless, the scene was set for acceptance of the concept that there was a distinctive brain damage syndrome.

The view that the presence of hyperkinesis might itself be used as an indication of damage to the brain drew further strength from Strauss's very influential studies of what he regarded as "brain-injured" children (Strauss & Kephart, 1940, 1955; Strauss & Lehtinen, 1947). In essence, he and his colleagues claimed that various characteristics—including hyperactivity, disinhibition, and distractability—differentiated "brain-injured" mentally retarded children from those who were not "brain-injured." On this basis, they argued that all brain lesions were followed by a similar kind of behavioral disturbance and, moreover, that this type of behavior was always due to brain damage. Not only is that logic quite seriously faulty, but also the signs and symptoms of brain injury on which it was based were of dubious validity. In particular, it was assumed that it was acceptable to make a neurological diagnosis solely on the presence of perceptual difficulties as shown by psychological test findings. In spite of these grave deficiencies, the "Strauss syndrome" rapidly came to be accepted as one that involved organic brain dysfunction. In addition, it came to be held by many clinicians that hyperkinesis was a secondary consequence of underlying perceptual problems (Bender, 1975) and that perceptual–motor training was the treatment of choice for brain-injured children, although there continued to be little empirical support for the efficacy of this method of intervention (Hallahan & Cruickshank, 1973).

The next landmark in the story of MBD is provided by Pasamanick and Knobloch's studies in the 1950s and early 1960s of the associations between pregnancy complications and a range of outcomes extending from cerebral palsy and mental retardation to hyperactivity and reading disorders (Knobloch & Pasamanick, 1966; Pasamanick & Knobloch, 1960, 1966; Rogers, Lilienfeld, & Pasamanick, 1955). They postulated a "continuum of reproductive casualty" in which the effects of damage to the brain during the perinatal period and the birth process were thought to vary according to the extent of the damage. When the damage was severe, clear-cut neurological disorders resulted, but when it was mild there was a predisposition to behavioral or learning difficulties that was unaccompanied by any overt signs of neurological abnormality. Thus, they hypothesized the existence of minimal brain injury that was similar in kind, but not in degree, to the injury that gave rise to cerebral palsy and mental retardation.

Subsequent research has confirmed the notion of *covert* brain damage through the demonstration that a careful clinical neurological examination may show no abnormalities, in spite of the presence of indisputable structural brain damage. Thus, Solomons, Holden, and Denhoff (1963) observed that children who have obvious neurological abnormalities in infancy may appear neurologically normal when examined some years later. Similarly, Meyer and Byers (1952) noted that the neurological sequelae of encephalitis may clear up completely as the affected children grow older. Also, in Shaffer, Chadwick, and Rutter's (1975) study of children with gross traumatic damage to the brain substance confirmed at neurosurgical operation, only a third showed definite neurological signs at follow-up a few years later, and a third showed no signs whatever of neurological abnormality, dubious or definite. Or again, in a prospective study of children with closed head injuries, Rutter, Chadwick, Shaffer, and Brown (1980) found that only half of those with a posttraumatic amnesia of at least 1 week showed any type of neurological abnormality. All these findings, together with others, indicate that there are some children with definite brain damage who show no abnormalities on clinical neurological examination (Rutter & Chadwick, 1980). To that extent the "continuum" hypothesis of brain injury has been substantiated.

However, the specific application of that idea to reproductive casualty has proved more problematic, as shown in the several reviews of the topic from varying viewpoints (Birch & Gussow, 1970; Neligan, Kolvin, Scott, & Garside, 1976; Sameroff & Chandler, 1975; Werner, 1980). One of the major difficulties in any assessment of the long-term sequelae of perinatal brain injury is the uncertainty as to whether any such injury has actually occurred. Low birth weight, maternal toxemia, and the like carry an increased risk of brain damage; however, it is a risk, not an actuality, and furthermore the risk is quite low. As a consequence, very weak associations between perinatal complications and brain damage syndromes are to be expected, simply because the few children with true brain injuries resulting from perinatal factors will be diluted by the much larger number who experienced perinatal hazards but who escaped cerebral damage. There is also the further problem that pregnancy complications and low birth weight tend to be much more frequent in socially disadvantaged groups, so that such sequelae as do occur may be a consequence of the psychosocial adversities rather than any form of brain injury, minimal or maximal. Indeed, most large-scale studies, such as the British National Child Development Study (Davie, Butler, & Goldstein, 1972) or the American Collaborative Perinatal Project (Broman, Nichols, & Kennedy, 1975; Nichols & Chen, 1981) show that the overall level of cognitive and behavioral deficits following perinatal complications is quite low in the general population of children who do not have overt cerebral palsy or mental retardation, once statistical controls for social variables have been introduced. However, several investigations have also shown an *interactional* effect, such that the outcome for children at perinatal risk is worse for those reared in social disadvantage (Drillien, 1964; Sameroff & Chandler, 1975; Werner, 1980). It seems that biological hazards are most likely to lead to adverse sequelae later when they are combined with psychosocial adversity.

Finally, during the last two decades, the term "MBD" has come to be applied increasingly to a broad group of behavioral and learning disabilities in childhood (Clements, 1966), in which the main features are based on the hyperkinetic syndrome but with the addition of perceptual, cognitive, and specific learning disabilities (Peters, Davis, Goolsby, Clements, & Hicks, 1973; Satz & Fletcher, 1980). The extension of this diagnosis to a wider and wider segment of the child psychiatric population is illustrated by Wender's (1971) estimate that it applies to about half of all clinic cases and by Gross and Wilson's (1974) use of the term for a majority of their child psychiatric patients. As they themselves comment, "It is surely remarkable that three-quarters of over a thousand child patients were found to have this disorder." It is indeed remarkable, and it is necessary to ask what grounds there are for supposing that most children presenting with psychiatric problems have some form of organic brain dysfunction. The answer is that the basis for the claim is the controversial belief that the *form* of the behavioral disorder itself indicates brain dysfunction.

CONCEPTS OF MINIMAL BRAIN DYSFUNCTION

The evidence on the claim made above is considered in later chapters of this volume. However, first the different types of MBD hypotheses to be examined must be noted. It would be wrong to suppose that clinicians and researchers are now dealing with a single concept of MBD, for they are not. Many finer distinctions could be drawn, but perhaps the most basic division is that between the view of MBD as a lesser variant of gross traumatic or infective brain damage, and the view of MBD as something that is quite different and in which the organic origin probably lies in a genetic abnormality rather than in any form of injury to the brain (Rutter, 1982; Werry, 1979).

The former view sees brain damage in *quantitative* terms as a unitary continuum variable that produces a characteristic set of deficits, the nature of which depends on the *amount* of brain damage, rather than on its site or etiology. The argument for this concept of MBD was expressed by Gross and Wilson (1974) as follows: "The most compelling evidence for the existence of MBD as an entity is (1) the similarity . . . between its symptoms and symptoms of children with proven brain disease; and (2) the remarkable response to certain medications, a response not found in non-MBD children." The empirical research findings on both these issues are discussed in later chapters. However, it should be noted at this stage that the current concerns that subclinical lead intoxication may lead to impaired intelligence and hyperactive behavior (Bryce-Smith & Waldron, 1974a, 1974b; Needleman, Gunnoe, Leviton, Reed, Peresie, Mather, & Barrett, 1979; Rutter, 1980) constitute an extension of that concept from pre- and perinatal hazards to postnatal toxins and poisons—an issue discussed in Chapter 3.

The latter view of MBD as a *qualitatively* different type of disorder is epitomized by Wender's (1971, 1973, 1978) concept of it as a condition involving a diminished capacity for positive and negative affects and abnormalities in cortical arousal. The clinical phenomena of this hypothesized diagnostic category are said to approximate to those of the hyperkinetic syndrome. Thus, Wender (1978) stated that Laufer and Denhoff's (1957) description of the hyperkinetic behavior syndrome provided "as good a summary as any." The etiology is thought to lie in genetically determined abnormalities in the metabolism of serotonin, dopamine, and norepinephrine—with, perhaps, underactivity of dopaminergic systems as the basic biochemical "lesion" (Wender, 1978). As with Gross and Wilson (1974), Wender relies on a distinctive response to stimulants as one of the hallmarks of the syndrome, but he also invokes family history findings in support of a genetic basis (Wender, 1971; Wender, Reimherr, & Wood, 1981).

Although these two hypotheses (regarding a continuum of brain injury and a qualitatively distinct behavioral syndrome of genetic/biochemical origin) have constituted the main views dominating the field, recently a third approach has become more prominent. This view rejects the notion of any *single* brain syndrome and, instead, takes as its starting point the knowledge that the brain is a complex organ serving many different functions. Contrasting patterns of neurophysiological or neuropsychological test performance are used to identify right- or left-hemisphere dysfunction and, within each hemisphere, to differentiate frontal lobe deficits from, say, parieto-occipital lobe deficits (cf., e.g., Flor-Henry, 1979; Golden, Osmon, Moses, & Berg, 1981; Tucker, 1981; Wexler, 1980). In this way, there have been attempts to link *focal* abnormalities of brain function with particular types of learning disability or with specific psychiatric syndromes. There is no doubt that the delineation of different types of learning disability on the basis of psychological test performance is already proving useful (see Chapter 23). However, the link between neuropsychological test performance and localized brain injury or dysfunction remains more speculative.

STRATEGIES OF INVESTIGATION AND PLAN OF THIS VOLUME

As Benton (1973) noted, all these concepts of MBD involve the use of "a behavioral concept with neurological implications." This means that the validity of that concept and of its neurological implications must be tested. All the remaining chapters of this book are concerned with one or other aspect of that rather complicated issue.

The first section of the book has as its starting point identified brain pathology or overt brain dysfunction—as caused by severe perinatal hazards, malnutrition, poisoning, various specific medical syndromes, or head injury, or as associated with epilepsy and the use of anticonvulsants. These chapters tackle the question of the behavioral and cognitive consequences of known brain injury in its various forms. The most basic issue here is whether there are any identifiable psychological sequelae of brain damage. At first sight, that would seem to be a very straightforward matter. After all, it has been well demonstrated that very gross brain lesions can cause severe mental retardation. Indeed, it is known that severe retardation is virtually always due to some identifiable structural brain abnormality (Crome, 1960). Similarly, disintegrative psychoses occurring as a consequence of widespread brain disease are also recognized (Corbett, Harris, Taylor, & Trimble, 1977). It would appear that it is just a matter of determining similar associations with some of the less devastating varieties of brain pathology. But, in fact, the matter is considerably more complicated.

The problems arise from at least five different sources (Rutter, 1981a), most of which were identified as long ago as 1902 by Still in his classic paper, "Some Abnormal Psychical Conditions in Children." Firstly, both psychiatric disorder and intellectual impairment have many causes, including psychosocial stresses as well as constitutional factors. Disorder or impairment in a brain-injured child may be a consequence of factors that are quite unconnected with brain pathology (such as psychosocial adversity, life stresses, or genetic factors). As a consequence, it is essential to compare rates of disorder in brain-damaged groups with rates in the general population. Only in this way will it be possible to be sure that the frequency of psychiatric, or cognitive, problems is above base level. Secondly, however, many brain-damaged children are also physically handicapped, and it could be that the psychological sequelae stem from the physical handicap rather than from the brain lesion. Again, comparative studies are called for in order to check which is the crucial variable. In addition, in order to assess whether the associations with brain injury are likely to represent a *causal* influence, it is necessary to determine whether there is a consistent relationship between the severity of the brain pathology and the severity of psychiatric disorder or intellectual impairment (Rutter, 1981b).

Thirdly, brain damage often leads to *both* intellectual impairment and psychiatric disorder, and it could be that the emotional and behavioral problems in brain-injured children stem from low IQ rather than brain damage—an important possibility, as intelligence may be low for a host of reasons other than brain damage. The implication is that IQ controls are crucial in order to determine whether the high rates of disorder in brain-damaged children are just a function of low IQ.

Fourthly, attention must be paid to the causes of the brain injury, because they could also constitute the causes of the psychological difficulties. Thus, disruptive children of limited intelligence may be more likely to receive head injuries (see Chapter 5), or to develop lead intoxication as a result of pica (Rutter, 1980). The need is for longitudinal studies of change *following* brain injury.

Fifthly, brain-damaged children are often disadvantaged in many other ways, so that their problems may stem as much from the associated psychosocial adversity as from the brain pathology. Careful study of, and control for, psychosocial variables is essential.

These issues are considered in relation to various different types of brain pathology in the chapters that follow, with the conclusion that the presence of brain injury *is* associated with a markedly increased risk of both intellectual impairment and psychiatric disorder. Moreover, the evidence also indicates that this association represents a *causal* influence of brain injury.

These conclusions apply to the consequences of *overt* brain damage. Further considerations arise with respect to the continuum notion of *covert* damage—that is, with the suggestion that there can be subclinical brain damage that gives rise to behavioral and cognitive sequelae. In essence, this involves five questions:

1. Can there be brain damage without abnormalities on a neurological examination? (As we have seen, there can be.)
2. If so, does such damage give rise to psychological sequelae?
3. What is the threshold of severity of brain injury above which such sequelae can be detailed?
4. Under what circumstances can subclinical brain damage occur?
5. How may organic brain dysfunction be recognized if the clinical neurological examination is normal?

The last question constitutes the explicit focus of the second section of the book, which deals with the measurement of brain function and dysfunction. Neurological "soft signs," temperamental variables, neuropsychological techniques, and the neurophysiological approaches sometimes termed "neurometrics" are among the tactics considered.

The rather different concept of MBD as a qualitatively distinct syndrome that is thought to be due to a genetically determined biochemical abnormality rather than to any form of brain damage, major or minor, raises quite separate issues. The most basic question here is whether there is evidence for the existence of a meaningfully distinctive behavioral syndrome that differs from other psychiatric conditions. This question, of course, is fundamental in the nosological identification of any diagnostic entity (Rutter, 1978). The point is that to have any validity, the syndrome must be shown to differ from other conditions in some features *other than the behaviors that define it.* Such features could include such varied items as prediction to other behaviors or to specific psychological characteristics, course and outcome, response to treatment, biochemical correlates, or genetic origins. These issues are discussed in the third section of the book, which deals with the hyperkinetic/attentional deficit syndrome. There is continuing controversy over the diagnostic criteria to be used for this syndrome (or group of syndromes). Originally, most attention was focused on the poorly modulated, socially inappropriate overactivity—hence the term "hyperkinetic syndrome." In recent years, many investigators have come to consider that the fundamental defining characteristic of the condition may lie in some form of attentional deficit, rather than any motor abnormality. In view of the great importance of that issue, the concepts and findings are considered in detail by Virginia Douglas in Chapter 14.

As is evident from the differing views expressed, the question of whether there is a nosologically distinct hyperkinetic or attentional deficit syndrome remains unresolved. There is no doubt, of course, that severely overactive and inattentive children exist. That is not the issue. Rather, the question is whether overactivity, inattention, or social disinhibition serve to define a disorder or group of disorders that can be validly differentiated from the broad run of behavioral and conduct disturbances of childhood. Also, if such a syndrome can be shown to exist, there is then the secondary question of whether or not it has an organic etiology and, if it has, what specific deficits or abnormalities are involved. Whatever the nature of overactivity and attentional deficits, and whatever the resolution of the classification issue, there remains the important matter of how best to treat children presenting with these problems. That topic is considered in several further chapters, with particular reference to the use of stimulant drugs, behavioral methods, and special educational treatments.

Quite apart from the issues concerning the hyperkinetic/attentional deficit syndrome, there is a further set of questions concerning learning disorders, as these, too, have been linked with MBD. They are dealt with in the fourth section of the book. The first issue here concerns the subdivision of learning disorders. Chapters 22, by Uta Frith, and 23, by Byron Rourke and John Strang, clearly indicate the importance of differentiating among arithmetical disabilities, "pure" spelling difficulties (without accompanying reading retardation), and reading disorders. However, there are also strong indications that reading disorders themselves need to be further subdivided. Much of the confusion and contradictions in the literature stem from treating as homogeneous a group that, in actuality, is heterogeneous. As with the hyperkinetic/attentional deficit syndrome, beyond the classification issues lie questions on etiology, prognosis, and treatment—topics considered in the remaining chapters in this section. The final chapter of the volume reassesses the concepts of MBD in the light of the preceding chapters.

References

Bakwin, H., & Bakwin, R. M. *Clinical management of behavior disorders in children* (3rd ed.). Philadelphia: W. B. Saunders, 1967.

Bender, L. A career of clinical research in child psychiatry. In E. J. Anthony (Ed.), *Explorations in child psychiatry*. New York: Plenum Press, 1975.

Benton, A. L. Minimal brain dysfunction from a neuropsychological point of view. *Annals of the New York Academy of Science*, 1973, *205*, 29–37.

Birch, H. G. The problems of "brain damage" in children. In H. G. Birch (Ed.), *Brain damage in children: The biological and social aspects*. Baltimore: Williams & Wilkins, 1964.

Birch, H. G., & Gussow, J. D. *Disadvantaged children: Health, nutrition and school failure*. New York: Grune & Stratton, 1970.

Blau, A. Mental changes following head trauma in children. *Archives of Neurology and Psychiatry*, 1936, *35*, 723–769.

Bond, M., & Partridge, C. E. Post-encephalitic behavior disorders in boys and their management in a hospital. *American Journal of Psychiatry*, 1926, *6*, 25–103.

Bradley, C. The behavior of children receiving benzedrine. *American Journal of Psychiatry*, 1937, *94*, 577–585.

Broman, S. H., Nichols, P. L., & Kennedy, W. A. *Preschool IQ: Prenatal and early development correlates*. Hillsdale, N.J.: Erlbaum, 1975.

Bryce-Smith, D., & Waldron, H. A. Lead, behavior and criminality. *Ecologist*, 1974, *4*, 367–377. (a)

Bryce-Smith, D., & Waldron, H. A. Blood-lead levels, behavior and intelligence. *Lancet*, 1974, *1*, 1166–1167. (b)

Clements, S. D. *Minimal brain dysfunction in children* (NINDS Monograph No. 3, U.S. Public Health Service Publication No. 1415). Washington, D.C.: U.S. Government Printing Office, 1966.

Clements, S. D., & Peters, J. E. Minimal brain dysfunctions in the school-age child. *Archives of General Psychiatry*, 1962, *6*, 185–197.

Corbett, J., Harris, R., Taylor, E., & Trimble, M. Progressive disintegrative psychosis in childhood. *Journal of Child Psychology and Psychiatry*, 1977, *18*, 211–219.

Crome, L. The brain and mental retardation. *British Medical Journal*, 1960, *1*, 897–904.

Davie, R., Butler, N., & Goldstein, H. *From birth to seven: A report of the National Child Development Study*. London: Longman, 1972.

Drillien, C. M. *Growth and development of the prematurely born infant*. Edinburgh: Livingstone, 1964.

Ebaugh, F. G. Neuropsychiatric sequelae of acute epidemic encephalitis in children. *American Journal of Diseases of Children*, 1923, *25*, 89–97.

Flor-Henry, P. On certain aspects of the localization of the cerebral systems regulating and determining emotion. *Biological Psychiatry*, 1979, *14*, 677–698.

Golden, C. J., Osmon, D. C., Moses, J. A., & Berg, R. A. *Interpretation of the Halstead–Reitan Neuropsychological Test Battery: A casebook approach*. New York: Grune & Stratton, 1981.

Gross, M., & Wilson, W. C. *Minimal brain dysfunction: A clinical study of incidence, diagnosis and treatment in over 1000 children*. New York: Brunner/Mazel, 1974.

Hallahan, D. P., & Cruickshank, W. M. *Psychoeducational foundations of learning disabilities*. Englewood Cliffs, N.J.: Prentice-Hall, 1973.

Hohman, L. B. Post-encephalitic behavior disorders in children. *Johns Hopkins Hospital Bulletin*, 1922, *33*, 372–375.

Jaspers, K. [*General psychopathology*] (7th ed.) (J. Hoenig & M. W. Hamilton, trans.). Manchester, England: Manchester University Press, 1963.

Kahn, E., & Cohen, L. H. Organic drivenness—a brain stem syndrome and an experience—with case reports. *New England Journal of Medicine*, 1934, *210*, 748–756.

Kalverboer, A. F. MBD: Discussion of the concept. *Advances in Biological Psychiatry*, 1978, *1*, 5–17.

Kessler, J. W. History of minimal brain dysfunction. In H. E. Rie & E. D. Rie (Eds.), *Handbook of minimal brain dysfunctions: A critical view*. New York: Wiley, 1980.

Knobloch, H., & Pasamanick, B. Prospective studies on the epidemiology of reproductive casualty: Methods, findings, and some implications. *Merrill–Palmer Quarterly*, 1966, *12*, 27–43.

Laufer, M. W., & Denhoff, E. Hyperkinetic behavior syndrome in children. *Journal of Pediatrics*, 1957, *50*, 463–474.

Meyer, E., & Byers, R. K. Measles encephalitis: A follow-up study of sixteen patients. *American Journal of Diseases of Children*, 1952, *84*, 543–579.

Needleman, H., Gunnoe, C., Leviton, A., Reed, M., Peresie, H., Mather, C., & Barrett, P. Psychological performance of children with elevated lead levels. *New England Journal of Medicine*, 1979, *300*, 689–695.

Neligan, G. A., Kolvin, I., Scott, D. McI., & Garside, R. F. *Born too soon or born too small* (Clinics in Developmental Medicine No. 61). London: Spastics International Medical Publications/Heinemann Medical Books, 1976.

Nichols, P. L., & Chen, T. -C. *Minimal brain dysfunction: A prospective study*. Hillsdale, N.J.: Erlbaum, 1981.

Pasamanick, B., & Knobloch, H. Brain damage and reproductive casualty. *American Journal of Orthopsychiatry*, 1960, *30*, 298–305.

Pasamanick, B., & Knobloch, H. Retrospective studies on the epidemiology of reproductive casualty: Old and new. *Merrill–Palmer Quarterly*, 1966, *12*, 7–26.

Peters, J. E., Davis, J. S., Goolsby, C. M., Clements, S. D., & Hicks, T. J. *Physicians' handbook: Screening for MBD*. London: Ciba Medical Horizons, 1973.

Rie, H. E. Definitional problems. In H. E. Rie & E. D. Rie (Eds.), *Handbook of minimal brain dysfunctions: A critical view*. New York: Wiley, 1980.

Rogers, J., Lilienfeld, A., & Pasamanick, B. Pre- and para-natal factors in the development of childhood behavior disorders. *Acta Psychiatrica et Neurologica Scandinavica*, 1955, *102* (Suppl.).

Rutter, M. Diagnostic validity in child psychiatry. *Advances in Biological Psychiatry*, 1978, *2*, 2–22.

Rutter, M. Raised lead levels and impaired cognitive/behavioral functioning: A review of the evidence. *Developmental Medicine and Child Neurology*, 1980, *22* (Suppl. 42, No. 1).

Rutter, M. Psychological sequelae of brain damage in children. *American Journal of Psychiatry*, 1981, *138*, 1533–1544. (a)

Rutter, M. Epidemiological/longitudinal strategies and causal research in child psychiatry. *Journal of the American Academy of Child Psychiatry*, 1981, *20*, 513–544. (b)

Rutter, M. Syndromes attributed to "minimal brain dysfunction" in childhood. *American Journal of Psychiatry*, 1982, *139*, 21–33.

Rutter, M., & Chadwick, O. Neuro-behavioural associations and syndromes of 'minimal brain dysfunction.' In F. C. Rose (Ed.), *Clinical neuroepidemiology*. Tunbridge Wells, England: Pitman Medical Publishing, 1980.

Rutter, M., Chadwick, O., Shaffer, D., & Brown, G. A prospective study of children with head injuries: I. Design and methods. *Psychological Medicine*, 1980, *10*, 633–645.

Rutter, M., Graham, P., & Yule, W. *A neuropsychiatric study in childhood* (Clinics in Developmental Medicine Nos. 35–36). London: Spastics International Medical Publications/Heinemann Medical Books, 1970.

Sameroff, A. J., & Chandler, M. J. Reproductive risk and the continuum of caretaking casualty. In F. D. Horowitz (Ed.), *Review of child development research*, (Vol. 4). Chicago: University of Chicago Press, 1975.

Satz, P., & Fletcher, J. M. Minimal brain dysfunctions: An appraisal of research concepts and methods. In H. E. Rie & E. D. Rie (Eds.), *Handbook of minimal brain dysfunctions: A critical view*. New York: Wiley, 1980.

Shaffer, D., Chadwick, O., & Rutter, M. Psychiatric outcome of localized head injury in children. In R. Porter & D. FitzSimons (Eds.), *Outcome of severe damage to the central nervous system* (Ciba Foundation Symposium No. 34). Amsterdam: Elsevier–Excerpta Medica–North Holland, 1975.

Solomons, G., Holden, R. H., & Denhoff, E. The changing picture of cerebral dysfunction in early childhood. *Journal of Pediatrics*, 1963, *63*, 113–120.

Still, G. F. Some abnormal psychical conditions in children. *Lancet*, 1902, *1*, 1008–1012, 1077–1082, 1163–1168.

Strauss, A. A., & Kephart, N. C. Behavior differences in markedly retarded children measured by a new behavior rating scale. *American Journal of Psychiatry*, 1940, *96*, 1117–1124.

Strauss, A. A., & Kephart, N. C. *Psychopathology and education of the brain-injured child* (Vol. 2, *Progress in theory and clinic*). New York: Grune & Stratton, 1955.

Strauss, A. A., & Lehtinen, V. *Psychopathology and education of the brain-injured child* (Vol. 1). New York: Grune & Stratton, 1947.

Strecker, E., & Ebaugh, F. Neuropsychiatric sequelae of cerebral trauma in children. *Archives of Neurology and Psychiatry*, 1924, *12*, 443–453.

Strother, C. R. Minimal cerebral dysfunction: A historical overview. *Annals of the New York Academy of Science*, 1973, *205*, 6–17.

Tucker, D. M. Lateral brain function, emotion, and conceptualization. *Psychological Bulletin*, 1981, *89*, 19–46.

Wender, P. *Minimal brain dysfunction in children*. New York: Wiley, 1971.

Wender, P. Some speculation concerning a possible biochemical basis of minimal brain dysfunction. *Annals of the New York Academy of Science*, 1973, *205*, 18–28.

Wender, P. Minimal brain dysfunction: An overview. In M. A. Lipton, A. DiMascio, & K. F. Killam (Eds.), *Psychopharmacology: A generation of progress*. New York: Raven Press, 1978.

Wender, P., Reimherr, F. W., & Wood, D. R. Attention deficit disorder ("minimal brain dysfunction") in adults: A replication study of diagnosis and drug treatment. *Archives of General Psychiatry*, 1981, *38*, 449–456.

Werner, E. E. Environmental intraction in minimal brain dysfunction. In H. E. Rie & E. D. Rie (Eds.), *Handbook of minimal brain dysfunctions: A cricital view*. New York: Wiley, 1980.

Werry, J. S. Organic factors. In H. C. Quay & J. S. Werry (Eds.), *Psychopathological disorders in childhood* (2nd ed.). New York: Wiley, 1979.

Wexler, B. E. Cerebral laterality and psychiatry: A review of the literature. *American Journal of Psychiatry*, 1980, *137*, 279–291.

SECTION ONE

Brain Traumata and Disorders: Psychological Sequelae

CHAPTER ONE

Severe Perinatal Hazards

ANN STEWART

INTRODUCTION

Although childbirth always has been regarded as potentially dangerous to mothers, it is only in recent years that consideration has been given to the hazards the infants have to overcome if they are to survive. By the early 1960s, enough was known about fetal and neonatal physiology to allow speculation on the nature of these hazards. It was concluded that, in the absence of gross congenital defects, physiological derangements such as hypoxia were largely responsible for deaths in infants; and that it was those same conditions that caused central nervous system damage among infants who survived. Due to immaturity of all organ systems, infants born early in gestation were particularly liable to these abnormalities; hence the high mortality in low-birth-weight infants and the large incidence of neurological and mental handicaps among the few who survived (Stewart, 1977).

Based on physiological considerations, new regimes of management for the perinatal period were introduced in the mid-1960s for infants at greatest risk of death or handicap. These regimes were designed to prevent the occurrence of potentially lethal abnormalities in the perinatal and neonatal periods; or, if that was not possible, to allow the prompt detection and treatment of any identifiable abnormality.

Fundamental to the design of these methods was the belief that the majority of the infants were potentially normal and that any damage, whether it be lethal or compatible with survival, was likely to occur in the perinatal period. Nevertheless, centers in Europe and North America, such as our own at University College Hospital (UCH), London, which have been actively engaged in these developments since the basic physiological knowledge became available in the 1960s, considered it mandatory to monitor the progress of the treated infants.

If the proposition that death and handicaps in sick and immature infants were often due to physiological derangements occurring around the time of birth was correct, many of the data collected for this purpose by the specialist centers developing intensive methods of management are of relevance to the etiology of brain damage. At UCH we studied the outcome of the highest risk group of infants treated—namely, those with a birth weight of 1500 g or less.

Ann Stewart. Department of Paediatrics, University College Hospital Medical School, London, England.

The principal objective of this study was to discover the incidence of serious handicapping conditions among the survivors. We defined these conditions as ones that, in the long term, would seriously interfere with the individual's ability to lead a satisfactory life (Agerholm, 1975; Court, 1976). These conditions included problems that required special educational provision or treatment throughout the child's schooling and might influence his or her employment later. They did not include lesser problems that required only limited periods of remedial treatment. Although the main objective of the study was to identify major handicaps, it has been possible to examine the data for information concerning the relationship between perinatal events and the long-term development of the survivors.

POPULATION AND METHODS

During the 12 years 1966–1977, 694 infants of birth weights from 500 to 1500 g were admitted to the neonatal unit at UCH. This total included all 338 infants born in UCH whose birth weights fell within the range, and 342 infants who were admitted shortly after birth from many other hospitals within a radius of about 100 miles. In addition, 14 infants were admitted from their homes where they had been born unexpectedly.

All the infants were managed intensively in the perinatal period, using methods described in detail elsewhere (Reynolds, 1978). In brief, they included a high standard of obstetric care, with particular emphasis on the early identification of pregnancies at risk of premature delivery; prompt resuscitation of the infants at birth and subsequently; the mechanical support of breathing when necessary; the provision of adequate warmth and nutrition; and the prevention as far as possible of biochemical derangements such as hypoxia, hypoglycemia, and hyperbilirubinemia. Although all these facilities were available as of 1966, refinements such as continuous blood gas monitoring and total parenteral nutrition have been added in more recent years.

After leaving the hospital, the children were seen regularly in the follow-up clinic for clinical, developmental, and auditory assessments, including a posterior auricular muscle response test (PAM) (Fraser, Conway, Keene, & Hazell, 1978) at 6 months and an audiogram at 3.5 to 5 years. At 3.5 years, the children were seen by a clinical psychologist for cognitive evaluation using the Stanford–Binet IQ test, Form L-M, standardized in 1962 (Terman & Merrill, 1961); items from the Merrill–Palmer test (Stutsman, 1931); and, for children born since 1973, the Reynell Developmental Language Scales (Reynell, 1969). The children born from 1966 to 1970 were reexamined both medically and by the clinical psychologist at 8 years. Detailed assessments were made in the hospital clinic and in school on all children living in the United Kingdom and on children living near major centers abroad. Tests used at 8 years included the Wechsler Intelligence Scale for Children (WISC) (Wechsler, 1949); Neale Analysis of Reading Ability (Neale, 1966); and the Bender–Gestalt test of visuomotor perception (scored according to the method described by Koppitz, 1964). The children's teachers were asked to complete the Bristol Social Adjustment Guide (Stott & Marston, 1971).

During the first 5 years of life, the children's ages were adjusted to take account of the number of weeks that they had been born before 40 weeks of gestation.

RESULTS

Mortality

During the 12-year study period, 276 (39%) of the 694 infants admitted to the neonatal unit died within the first 28 days of life. The mortality rate, however, was not constant throughout the period. There was a highly significant ($p < .001$) downward trend in the rate for infants born in UCH (Reynolds & Stewart, 1979). For example, the rate was 48% in 1966 and only 25% in 1977. Improvements were noted also in the rates for referred infants (Blake, Pollitzer, & Reynolds, 1979). A total of 36 infants died after the neonatal period, aged 29 days to 2 years—the majority from complications of neonatal respiratory illnesses. The remaining 382 infants survived.

Of the 382 surviving infants, 198 were born in UCH; the remaining 184 were referred infants. There were 166 males and 216 females. A total of 299 infants resulted from singleton pregnancies, 60 from twin pregnancies, and 23 from triplet, quadruplet, quintuplet (one set), and sextuplet (one set, five survivors) pregnancies. Ninety infants (24%) had birth weights below the 10th percentile, according to the data of Lubchenco and coworkers (Lubchenco, Hansman, Dressler, & Boyd, 1963), and were considered to be "small for gestational age" (SGA). The mean birth weight of the group was 1209.5 g (range of 638–1500), and the mean period of gestation was 30.2 weeks (range of 24–42). There were 121 infants (32%) requiring mechanical ventilation for respiratory failure, due primarily to hyaline membrane disease in 40, preterm apnea in 42, failure to establish satisfactory respiration at birth in 18, and a variety of causes (including necrotizing enterocolitis) in the remaining 21 infants. Twenty-five infants had one or more exchange transfusions, usually to treat abnormalities of clotting. Of 285 infants born between 1971 and 1977, 77 received total parenteral nutrition, including 37 who were given Intralipid.

Follow-Up: Major Handicaps

At follow-up, aged 2 years or more, 335 (88%) of the children had no major handicap; 41 (11%) had major handicaps, including 24 (6%) whose handicaps were severe enough to require attendance at a special school or unit. Six (2%) infants were lost to follow-up. Of the 41 handicapped children, 22 (55%) had cerebral palsy; 15 (38%) had mental retardation (defined as an IQ of more than 2 standard deviations below the mean); 14 (35%) had sensory neural hearing losses; 4 had hydrocephalus; 3 had retrolental fibroplasia; and 1 had congenital cataracts. In only two cases among these 41 children was the handicap attributable to congenital defect, including one child with cataracts and another with an odd physique and mental retardation, similar to the conditions of her mother and elder sibling. Common metabolic abnormalities had been excluded in this family, but access for further investigation was refused.

Within this group of 376 children, the incidence of major handicaps did not differ significantly between the 196 infants born in UCH and the 180 who were referred from other hospitals; nor between the 163 males and the 213 females; nor between the 286 infants whose birth weights were "appropriate for gestational age" (AGA) and the 90 who were SGA. Although there were fewer handicapped children among those from professional- and managerial-class families, the difference between the proportions with handicaps in the various

Table 1-1. Proportion of handicap among 376 children with birth weights of 1500 g or less, by socioeconomic states; birth weight; period of gestation; neonatal complications; and presence of neonatal convulsions and treatment with mechanical ventilation

	n	HANDICAPS	
SOCIOECONOMIC STATUS			
Social class[a]			
I–II	120	9 (7%)	
III	109	17 (15%)	
IV	79	8 (11%)	
Single-parent family	63	7 (11%)	
No record	5	nil	
Total	376	41 (10%)	
BIRTH WEIGHT			
501–750 g	6	2 (33%)	
751–1000 g	57	11 (19%)	
1001–1250 g	139	14 (10%)	
1251–1500 g	174	14 (8%)	
Total	376	41 (11%)	
Overall significance		$p < .01$	
PERIOD OF GESTATION			
26 weeks or less	18	8 (44%)	
27–28 weeks	80	9 (11%)	
29–30 weeks	130	16 (12%)	
31–32 weeks	91	5 (5%)	
33 weeks or more	57	3 (5%)	
All gestations	376	41 (11%)	
Overall significance		$p < .001$	
NEONATAL COMPLICATIONS			
No convulsions	343	24 (7%)	$p < .001$
Convulsions	33	16 (48%)	
Not mechanically ventilated	257	14 (5%)	$p < .001$
Mechanically ventilated	119	27 (23%)	
Serum bilirubin			
Less than 170 μmol/liter	257	18 (7%)	$p < .01$
170 μmol/liter or more	119	22 (18%)	
No parenteral nutrition	203	16 (8%)	$p < .02$
Total parenteral nutrition	77	15 (19%)	
PRESENCE OF NEONATAL CONVULSIONS AND TREATMENT WITH MECHANICAL VENTILATION			
No mechanical ventilation			
No convulsions	238	11 (5%)*	ns
Convulsions	19	3 (16%)**	
Mechanical ventilation			
No convulsions	101	14 (14%)*	$p \ll .001$
Convulsions	18	13 (72%)**	
Total	376	41 (11%)	

[a]According to the *Registrar General's Classification of Occupations* (1970).

*$p < .02$, ventilation versus no ventilation; no convulsions.

**$p < .01$, ventilation versus no ventilation; convulsions.

socioeconomic groups did not achieve statistical significance. In contrast, the incidence of major handicap was very significantly related to birth weight ($p < .01$) and to the period of gestation ($p < .001$).

The incidence of handicaps varied according to the presence of perinatal complications. For example, there were 45 infants whose perinatal periods were completely uneventful, and none of these had major handicap. In contrast, almost half of the children (48%) who had convulsions in the neonatal period ($p < .001$), 23% of the infants who required mechanical ventilation for respiratory failure ($p < .001$), 18% of the children who were jaundiced with an indirect serum bilirubin greater than 170 μg/ml ($p < .01$), and 19% of the children who were so ill that they required total parenteral nutrition ($p < .02$) had handicaps.

Within the mechanically ventilated group, there were other interesting findings. For example, the incidence of major handicaps varied according to the underlying condition thought to be responsible for respiratory failure. Only 8% of the children ventilated for hyaline membrane disease alone were handicapped, whereas 40% of the children ventilated because of preterm apnea and 28% of those ventilated from birth because of perinatal asphyxia had major handicaps. Among the ventilated children, the difference in handicap rate between those who had convulsions in the neonatal period (72%) and those who did not (14%) was very highly significant ($p < .001$). In contrast, there was no significant difference in the proportion of handicapped children among infants who were neither ventilated nor had convulsions (5%) and those who had convulsions but were not ventilated.

Early Cognitive Development

A total of 288 infants were aged 3.5 years or more at their last assessment. The majority (222) of the children were tested on the Stanford–Binet IQ Scale, but in order to accommodate the varying skills of these young children, including children from families where English was not the first language, 66 children were tested on the Merrill–Palmer Scale, the Wechsler Pre-School and Primary Scale of Intelligence (Wechsler, 1967), the McCarthy Scales of Children's Abilities (McCarthy, 1970), or the Griffiths Test (Griffiths, 1954). The distribution of the scores obtained at this first assessment, using one of the five tests on each child, is shown in Table 1-2. The distribution of the scores from the 222 children tested on the Stanford–Binet Scale is shown in Table 1-3. The mean of the IQ scores was 107.7 ($SD \pm 15.3$), but it must be noted that in addition to children whose standard-deviation ranking on one of the other tests fell throughout the distribution, 15 of the 16 children whose standard-deviation ranking was more than 2 standard deviations below the mean could not be tested on the Stanford–Binet Scale, so their score could not be included in the calculation of this mean value.

The distribution of test scores among children with and without major handicaps is shown in Table 1-4. They differed very significantly, with scores much lower in those with major handicaps ($p < .001$). The distribution of scores of the handicapped children with cerebral palsy also differed significantly from those among children without handicap, being lower in the cerebral-palsied group ($p < .001$). However, it should be noted that just over half of the children with cerebral palsy scored within or above the average range. The distribution of test scores also differed according to birth weight, with scores

Table 1-2. Distribution of scores from a test of cognitive functioning at 3.5 years, among 288 children with birth weights of 1500 g or less

STANDARD DEVIATIONS	n	%	%
− 3 or below	8	2.8	
− 2 to − 2.99	8	2.8	12.8
− 1 to − 1.99	21	7.3	
0 to − 0.99	65	22.6	61.4
0 to + 0.99	112	38.9	
+ 1 to + 1.99	61	21.2	25.6
+ 2 to + 2.99	13	4.5	
Total	288	100	100

being lower in the children with birth weights of 1000 g or less ($p < .01$); they also differed according to year of birth, with scores being lower in those born before July 1971 ($p < .001$). These same differences were reflected in the mean scores on the Stanford–Binet; the 74 children born before July 1971 had a mean IQ of 102.3 (±14.7), compared with that of 110.4 (±15.0) for those born after that date ($n = 148$); those ($n = 28$) with birth weights of 501 to 1000 g had a mean IQ of 99.5 (±16.4), compared with 108.8 for those with birth weights of 1001 to 1500 g ($n = 194$); those with a major handicap ($n = 12$) had a mean IQ of 98.3 (±22.2), compared with 108.2 (±14.7) for those without a major handicap ($n = 210$). Differences according to socioeconomic class were less striking, the only significant difference being between the mean IQ for social classes I and II (106) and that for classes IV and V (92).

Language Development

Because of suggestions made by other workers (Fitzhardinge, 1976) of specific speech defects in infants born early in gestation, in 1973 we added the Reynell Developmental Language Scales to our assessment program for follow-up at 3.5 years. It was not possible to test 13 children—seven because of major

Table 1-3. Distribution of Stanford–Binet IQ values at 3.5 years, among 222 children with birth weights of 1500 g or less

STANFORD–BINET IQ	n	%	%
67 or less	1	0.4	6.3
68–83	13	5.8	
84–99	52	23.4	63.9
100–115	90	40.5	
116–131	55	24.7	
132–147	10	4.5	29.7
148 or more	1	0.4	
Total	222	100	100

Note. Mean IQ = 107.7 ± 15.3.

handicaps, including two with sensory neural hearing losses, and six children because they did not speak English. In addition, there were five children who were tested before 3 years of age because of concern about their early acquisition of language skills. As a result of these assessments, interventions were arranged, and it was not considered appropriate to include the scores from any subsequent tests of these children in the analysis.

Among the 90 other children available for testing, at a modal age of 3 years 10 months (range 2 years 8 months to 4 years 6 months), the mean standard score on the expressive scale was −0.31 ($SD \pm 1.0$) and on the comprehension scale it was +0.29 ($SD \pm 1.33$). These results indicated that as a group the children were functioning as expected for a normal population on both the expressive and comprehension scales. There were, however, 15 (17%) children who scored more than 1.5 standard deviations below the mean on one (9) or both scales (6). Three of these 15 children had significant sensory neural hearing losses, and six had conductive losses secondary to secretory otitis media that required surgical intervention, leaving six (6.6%) with evidence of a delay in the learning of language not due to hearing loss. Three out of these six children and

Table 1-4. Distribution of scores from a test of cognitive functioning at 3.5 years, among 288 children with birth weights of 1500 g or less, by presence of handicaps; presence of cerebral palsy or other handicaps; birth weight; date of birth; and socioeconomic status

STANDARD DEVIATIONS	VARIABLES		
PRESENCE OF HANDICAPS			
	NO HANDICAPS	HANDICAPS	
− 1 or below	16 (6%)	21 (62%)	
− 0.99 to + 0.99	168 (66%)	9 (26%)	
+ 1 or above	70 (28%)	4 (12%)	
Totals	254 (100%)	34 (100%)	
	$p < .001$		
PRESENCE OF CEREBRAL PALSY OR OTHER HANDICAPS			
	NO HANDICAPS	CEREBRAL PALSY	OTHER HANDICAPS
− 1 or below	16 (6%)	8 (47%)	13 (76%)
− 0.99 to + 0.99	168 (66%)	6 (35%)	3 (18%)
+ 1 or above	70 (28%)	3 (18%)	1 (6%)
Totals	254 (100%)	17 (100%)	17 (100%)
BIRTH WEIGHT			
	501–1000 g	1001–1500 g	
− 3 or below	2 (4.5%)	6 (2.5%)	
− 2 to − 2.99	4 (9.2%)	4 (1.6%)	
− 1 to − 1.99	7 (15.9)%	14 (5.7%)	
0 to − 0.99	10 (22.7%)	55 (22.6%)	
0 to + 0.99	14 (31.8%)	98 (40.2%)	
+ 1 to + 1.99	7 (15.9%)	54 (20.1%)	
+ 2 to + 2.99	0	13 (5.3%)	
Totals	44 (100%)	244 (100%)	
	$p < .01$		

(continued)

Table 1-4. (Continued)

STANDARD DEVIATIONS	VARIABLES		
	DATE OF BIRTH		
	JAN. 1, 1966–JUNE 30, 1971		JULY 1, 1971–DEC. 31, 1976
− 3 or below	5 (5%)		3 (1.6%)
− 2 to − 2.99	2 (2%)		6 (3.2%)
− 1 to − 1.99	14 (14%)		7 (3.7%)
0 to − 0.99	30 (30%)		35 (18.6%)
0 to + 0.99	32 (32%)		80 (42.6%)
+ 1 to + 1.99	16 (16%)		45 (23.9%)
+ 2 to + 2.99	1 (1%)		12 (6.4%)
Totals	100 (100%)		188 (100%)
		$p < .001$	
	SOCIOECONOMIC STATUS		
		SOCIAL CLASS[a]	
	I, II	III	IV, V, UNCLASSIFIED
− 1 or below	4 (12%)	1 (6%)	12 (30%)
− 0.99 to + 0.99	22 (67%)	11 (69%)	24 (60%)
+ 1 or above	7 (21%)	4 (25%)	4 (10%)
	ns	ns	
Mean Stanford–Binet IQs	106 ± 13* (n = 28)	104 ± 13.5 (n = 18)	92 ± 22.5* (n = 30)
	ns	ns	

[a]According to the *Registrar General's Classification of Occupations* (1970).

*Differences between I, II and IV, V, unclassified = $p < .001$.

all of the five children identified early with significant language delays came from seriously disadvantaged homes, including five where one parent was psychiatrically disturbed.

Later Cognitive Development at 8 Years

Of the 98 oldest children in the study, born during 1966–1970, one healthy child died at age 4 in a domestic accident, and three were lost to follow-up; these occurrences left 94 children available for study. At 8 years, 74 (76%) of these children were attending regular classes in normal schools and were functioning normally both at home and at school. Fourteen (14%) children, although attending normal schools, were receiving additional help either because they were "slow learners" (nine) or because of hearing losses (three), or because they required physiotherapy for cerebral palsy (two). Only five (5%) children were attending special schools for the mentally or physically handicapped (Table 1-5). The remaining child was living in the United States and was known to be attending a normal school, but the mother refused to cooperate with colleagues who attempted to obtain more information. No child was attending a school for the maladjusted. As a result of our assessment, we considered that one boy from a disturbed home would benefit from such a placement, and the local authority accepted our recommendation and transferred him.

Of the 94 children available, 80 were living either in the United Kingdom or near major centers abroad and were assessed in detail. Three children were Greek-speaking and could only be assessed on performance items, and two children were so retarded that a satisfactory estimate of their IQs could not be made. Educational testing of these two children was impossible. The proportions who were in normal schools with or without help and who were in special schools were the same as those in the total group.

Among the 75 children who were fully assessed, the mean value of the full-scale WISC IQ was 100 (±17). The mean value for the language subscale was 99.5 (±19) and the value for the performance subscale was 100 (±14). Inclusion of the results of the performance subscale for the three Greek-speaking children did not alter the mean value for this subscale. Subdivision of these 75 children according to sex, place of birth, birth weight, and the presence of handicap resulted in subgroups of small numbers, which made comparisons difficult. For example, there were only five children who had birth weights of less than 1001 g. The mean value of their WISC full-scale IQ was 90, which was lower than the value of 100 for the heavier infants. However, this difference did not achieve statistical significance. The only statistically significant finding was a lower mean value (80) among the children with major handicaps when compared with those without (102).

The mean reading age of the group ranged from 7 years 10 months on the comprehension scale of the Neale Analysis of Reading to 8 years 2 months on the accuracy scale, at a mean chronological age of 8 years 3 months. Although not optimal, these results did not suggest an excess of children with learning difficulties, which is confirmed by the proportions of children with significant delay (24 months below the chronological age), which ranged from 8% to 11%, according to the subscale. What is more, none of the children with significant delay had a WISC IQ above the mean.

Nine children (12%) were considered to have perceptuomotor disorders (a score of more than 1 standard deviation below the mean on the Koppitz scoring of the Bender–Gestalt test). This proportion was similar to that found among a group of 60 8-year-old children in two local schools. Four children (5%) scored

Table 1-5. School placement at 8 years of 98 children with birth weights of 1500 g or less, born in 1966–1970

PLACEMENT	*n*	%
In normal schools		
Require no help	74	76
Require special help	14	14
Cerebral palsy	2	
"Slow learners"	9	
Hearing loss	2	
Hearing loss + cerebral palsy	1	
No detailed information	1	1
In special schools	5	5
Mentally retarded	3	
Cerebral palsy (IQ normal)	1	
Partially sighted (IQ normal)	1	
Died, aged 4 years	1	1
Lost to follow-up	3	3
Total	98	100

in the maladjusted range on teachers' ratings of the Bristol Social Adjustment Guide. This proportion did not differ from that (11%) reported by Stott (Stott & Marston, 1971) among the unselected group of inner-city children that he used to standardize the test. However, it was significantly lower than the proportion (22%) reported by Drillien (1961) among a group of very-low-birth-weight infants born in the 1950s.

PREDICTIONS

The results of this study indicated that certain perinatal variables were associated with an increased risk of handicap. These same variables appeared to affect cognitive development. In order to try to discover the relative importance of these associations, analysis of variance with multiple-inclusion stepwise regression was carried out using programs from the Statistical Packages for the Social Sciences (SPSS) (Nie, Hadlaihull, Jenkins, Steinbrenner, & Bent, 1975). Independent variables were chosen either because they were known to affect the dependent variables (e.g., social class) or because significant associations with the incidence of handicaps or the rate of cognitive development have been found. The 12 variables that were used are shown in Table 1-6, and the results are tabulated in Table 1-7.

Convulsions and respiratory failure were the most important independent predictors of overall major handicap, as they were of cerebral palsy. Convulsions were also the most important predictors of level of cognitive functioning at 3.5 years for the group as a whole. In contrast, social factors were the most important predictors among the children who did not have major handicaps. Likewise, they were the most important predictors of IQ value at both 3.5 and 8 years and of teachers' behavioral ratings at 8 years. The Bender–Gestalt test is thought to assess intact visuomotor functioning rather than to give a measure of the level of functioning, and it requires certain minimum skills that eliminate its use in the severely handicapped. Jaundice, respiratory failure, and apnea were all independent predictors of the scores obtained among the 74 children tested at 8 years. Although the relative importance of the 12 variables included in the analysis varied according to the dependent variable under consideration, the majority of the perinatal variables contributed to the variance of all the outcome factors used as measures of the quality of functioning of these very-low-birth-weight survivors at follow up.

DISCUSSION

For many years, until the early 1960s, it was generally believed that most low-birth-weight infants were born prematurely or of low birth weight because they were abnormal. Abnormalities included those of genetic origin or resulting from intrauterine infections or other disasters of early embryonic life. This view appeared to be confirmed by the reports of early attempts at improving survival of the very-low-birth-weight infant, which resulted only in the salvage of handicapped survivors (Drillien, 1958; Lubchenco, Horner, Reed, Hix, Metcalf, Cohig, Elliott, & Bourg, 1963). It was not until 1968 that Davies and Russell (Davies & Russell, 1968) reported the preliminary results of a follow-up study of 100 infants with birth weights of 2000 g or less born after the introduction of

Table 1-6. Twelve social and perinatal independent variables used in analysis of variance with multiple-inclusion stepwise regression

Socioeconomic status of the family
Mode of delivery (three variables)
Gestation
Intrauterine growth (SGA)
Condition at birth
Apneic spells in the neonatal period
Hyaline membrane disease
Respiratory failure (treated with mechanical ventilation)
Convulsions in the neonatal period
Jaundice (serum bilirubin of 170 μg/liter or more)

early feeding techniques, and showed that the proportion of handicap was low among the survivors. Less than 10% of these infants were handicapped, in contrast to proportions in excess of 30% that had been reported from specialist centers in the preceding 10 years (Drillien, 1967; Stewart, 1977). These authors suggested that much of the handicap reported among low-birth-weight infants, at least in the recent past, was due to dehydration, hypoglycemia, and hyperbilirubinemia, consequent on the practice of withholding feeding from tiny or sick infants. Three years later, Rawlings, Reynolds, Stewart, and Strang (1971) in London, and Calâme and Prod'hom (1972) in Lausanne, reported similar results among even smaller infants who weighed 1500 g or less at birth; both groups of authors drew conclusions similar to those of Davies and Russell.

Since that time, there have been many reports of low incidences (10% or less) of handicaps among very-low-birth-weight survivors cared for with methods designed to prevent potentially harmful biochemical derangements in the perinatal period (Stewart, Reynolds, & Lipscomb, 1981). The authors have inferred that the results were due to modern attitudes toward perinatal management and implied that any handicap that did occur was due to hazards that these methods failed to control. A few studies attempted to relate handicaps to specific perinatal factors. In general, they showed that handicaps were commonest in the sickest infants (Stewart & Reynolds, 1974; Stewart, Turcan, Rawlings, Hart, & Gregory, 1978), particularly those with respiratory failure requiring mechanical ventilation (Fitzhardinge, 1978) and those with clinical evidence of brain insult (Nelson & Ellenberg, 1979). Some workers, impressed by the apparent association between abnormalities in the perinatal period and unfavorable outcome, have devised "risk scores" (Parmalee, 1977; Wu, 1977). Although this approach confirmed the association between adverse perinatal events and handicap (Stennert, Schulte, Vollrath, Brunner, & Fravenrath, 1978) it tended to mask more precise associations that were likely to lead to the identification of causal relationships (Abramovich, Gregory, Slemick, & Stewart, 1979).

All these reports have one thing in common: The data that were analyzed and from which authors drew their conclusions concerned vulnerable infants born since about 1963 and cared for with modern methods of perinatal care, using modern technology. The main objective of these methods was homeostasis, so it was very likely that deviations could be and were measured and recorded, thus giving a reasonably accurate estimate of the hazards that individual infants overcame in order to survive. Results of this kind were not reported in the earlier studies because, apart from anything else, the technological facilities to

Table 1-7. Results of analysis of variance with multiple-inclusion stepwise regression

DEPENDENT VARIABLE	*n*	TOTAL VARIABLES	INDEPENDENT PREDICTORS	VARIANCE (%)
Major handicap	376	12	4	23
			Convulsions	
			Respiratory failure	
			Jaundice	
			Hyaline membrane disease	22
Cerebral palsy	376	12	2	16
			Convulsions	
			Respiratory failure	13
Cognitive functioning at 3.5 years				
Total group	288	11	4	18
			Convulsions	
			Social class	
			Breech delivery	
			SGA	14.5
Without handicap	254	13	4	13
			Social class	
			Gestation	
			SGA	
			Breech delivery	11
Handicapped	34	10	0	44
		Convulsions		
		Mode of aelivery (2)		
		Condition at birth		
		Social class		
		Gestation		
		SGA		
		Apnea (2)		
		Jaundice		44
Stanford–Binet IQ at 3.5 years	222	11	2	9
			Social class	
			Convulsions	5
Cognitive functioning at 8 years	80	11	3	32.5
			Social class	
			Convulsions	
			Jaundice	25
WISC IQ at 8 years	75	12	2	25
			Social class	
			Jaundice	16
Neale Analysis of Reading Ability	75	12	3	31
			Social class	
			Mode of delivery	
			Jaundice	16
Comprehension	74	11	1	29
			Mode of delivery	6
Bender–Gestalt	74	10	3	30
			Jaundice	
			Respiratory failure	
			Apnea	21
Teachers' behavioral ratings	78	11	1	29
			Social class	9

make the measurements were not available. Unfortunately, this fact was not recognized by some recent workers, who examined the work of others for evidence of the cause of handicap among vulnerable infants (Sameroff & Chandler, 1975) and who concluded that there was no evidence that perinatal illnesses affected long-term outcome.

The use of IQ values and levels of educational achievements as measures of the effects of perinatal hazards introduced additional difficulties for interpretation. Results from the most severely handicapped children are inaccurate or even, as in the case of educational tests, unobtainable. These profoundly affected children, therefore, are often excluded from the analysis, and yet they offer the strongest evidence for or against the influence of perinatal hazards on long-term outcome. Not surprisingly, analysis of these types of data indicated that social factors predicted outcome (Sameroff & Chandler, 1975), but they did not provide evidence, as has been suggested (Chalmers, 1979), that perinatal events had no influence on outcome.

The results of the study reported here concern a prospectively enrolled group of infants selected because they were admitted to a neonatal intensive care unit during the 12 years 1966–1977 and because they weighed less than 1501 g at birth. During that period, the mortality among these infants fell and the proportion of healthy survivors increased, while the proportion of handicapped survivors remained constant at about 5% of the total population or 10% of the survivors. Fewer than 1% of the survivors were handicapped by congenital defects. Within the group, the proportion of handicaps depended upon birth weight, period of gestation, and the presence of serious perinatal illness, particularly respiratory failure and those illnesses complicated by convulsions. For example, the incidence of handicaps was highest among infants who weighed less than 751 g or who were born before completing 27 weeks of gestation. None of the infants with an uncomplicated perinatal history were handicapped. In contrast, over 20% of the infants who required treatment for respiratory failure with mechanical ventilation and almost half of the infants who had convulsions in the neonatal period had handicaps at follow-up. Statistical analysis indicated that these two factors were the most important independent predictors both of major handicaps in general and of cerebral palsy in this group of infants. Convulsions were the most important independent predictors of the level of cognitive functioning at 3.5 and 8 years, when the total group was considered. In contrast, social factors were more important in predicting level of cognitive functioning among the children without handicaps, the IQ value among infants who could be tested at 3.5 and 8 years, and the teachers' perception of the children's behavior at 8 years. Perhaps most important, however, was the observation that perinatal factors contributed to the variance of all the variables used to indicate quality of outcome among these very-low-birth-weight infants. The numbers in this study were relatively small and the measures of the children's functioning were crude, but these data do imply causal associations between serious perinatal hazards and major defects of neurological and cognitive functioning among very-low-birth-weight children as they grow older.

Consideration of the influence of perinatal hazards on lesser difficulties, such as those relating to learning, is much more difficult. Populations of the most vulnerable intensive care survivors are small, and matched controls do not exist. It is possible to test and assign scores or values to results only on children who have sufficient skills to attempt the tests; and these tests cannot be applied until the children are older and therefore strongly affected by their environment.

In our own study group, for example, the incidence of unexplained delay in the learning of language was probably not different from that in a normal population. However, the children were selected by their ability to hear, co-operate, and concentrate sufficiently to do the test! Likewise, among the older children tested at age 8, the results of the educational tests did not indicate an excess of children with significant learning difficulties or perceptuomotor problems, and there were no children with large discrepancies between IQ scores and results obtained from educational testing. Nevertheless, perinatal factors, as already mentioned, did contribute to the variance of these variables.

It could be argued from these data, that perinatal factors had little effect on later cognitive and behavioral development in this study of very-low-birth-weight intensive care survivors, and that the main influences were social ones. This, however, ignores the fact that the most seriously compromised children were excluded from the analysis because of the methods of assessment used. An alternative explanation, and one that appears more logical, is that the measurement of achievements such as reading skills indicates the degree to which a child has compensated for any disability he or she may have, but it does not measure the extent of the original disability, supposing that one were present. Optimum compensation occurs in optimum social conditions; hence the apparent effect of social factors if measures of cognitive functioning, achievement, and behaviour are the only ones considered. In this context, the observation that the IQ scores improved at the same time as the mortality rates did suggests that the numbers of children with disabilities were decreasing.

New technology is allowing clinicians and researchers to examine the problem much more directly. Recently, techniques for ultrasound imaging of the brain became available (Pape, Blackwell, Cusick, Sherwood, Houang, Thorburn, & Reynolds, 1979; Lipscomb, Blackwell, Reynolds, Thorburn, Cusick, & Pape, 1979). Hemorrhage into the germinal layer or ventricles can be identified with certainty, as can changes in structure such as hydrocephalus. As the imaging is real-time, vascular pulsations can be seen, and it is likely that clinicians will be able in due course to make estimates of cerebral blood flow.

Intraventricular hemorrhages are commonly found in the brains of very-low-birth-weight infants who die, particularly among infants who die after hyaline membrane disease (Pape & Wigglesworth, 1979). It is likely, from neuroanatomical considerations, that the brain damage that may result if bleeding extends into brain substance could cause cerebral palsy if the infant survives (MacDonald, 1967; Pape & Wigglesworth, 1979). Cerebral palsy was the commonest abnormality found in the present study of very-low-birth-weight infants, affecting over half of the handicapped children. Now that clinicians and researchers can identify germinal layer and intraventricular hemorrhages in the early days of life, it should be possible to study the circumstances in which they occur and so to discover the factor—or more likely, the set of factors—that causes them. It should also be possible to determine the relationship between these structural changes in the brain and eventual outcome for neurological and cognitive functioning.

In 1979 we started to study, prospectively, the most vulnerable infants born before 33 weeks of gestation. A total of 38% of these infants had germinal-layer or intraventricular bleeds when studied within 8 days of birth. Within the group, the incidence of hemorrhage depended on birth weight, length of gestation, and the presence of serious respiratory illnesses, in the same way that handicaps depended on these variables in our earlier very-low-birth-weight study. Convulsions in the neonatal period were also frequently associated with evidence of bleeding on ultrasound scanning (Thorburn, Lipscomb, Blackwell, Cusick, Pape, Stewart, & Reynolds, 1980).

The follow-up study of these prospectively enrolled infants who had ultrasound scans in the newborn period is still at a very early stage. During the first 6 months of the study, there were 26 survivors. When they were examined at 9–12 months of age (after correction for preterm birth), 15 of the 16 infants with normal scans were progressing normally. In contrast, half of the infants who had hemorrhages or cerebral atrophy diagnosed within 8 days of birth were abnormal (Thorburn *et al.*, 1980).

These are preliminary results based on small numbers of very young children. However, they do suggest that objective methods of brain imaging in the neonatal period will confirm the causal relationship between adverse perinatal events and abnormalities of neurological functioning in childhood, which was deduced from the earlier analysis. As more information becomes available, it should be possible to identify both the etiology of the lesions and their penalty in terms of neurological and cognitive functioning if a child survives. It should also be possible to design strategies to prevent these abnormalities—or to define criteria on which to base decisions for the ethical withdrawal of care from severely compromised infants.

Addendum

More recent ultrasound brain scan results have confirmed the finding that very low birth weight, very short period of gestation, and serious respiratory illness are associated with hemorrhage in the periventricular region (PVH), including intraventricular hemorrhage (Thorburn, Lipscomb, Stewart, Reynolds, & Hope, 1982); follow-up studies have shown that these scan abnormalities are associated with neurodevelopmental sequelae (Palmer, Dubowitz, Levene, & Dubowitz, 1982; Stewart, Thorburn, Hope, Goldsmith, Reynolds, & Lipscomb, 1982; Thorburn, Lipscomb, Stewart, Reynolds, Hope, & Pape, 1981). Such abnormalities were infrequent in preterm infants with normal scans and in those with PVH not complicated by ventricular enlargement or extension of blood into brain tissue. In contrast, infants with ventricular enlargement, whether accompanied by PVH or not, generally had a poor prognosis; the prevalence of adverse sequelae seemed to depend upon the cause and extent of the ventricular enlargement.

It appears that adverse sequelae are more often due to hypoxic damage to brain tissue than to hemorrhage itself. Mental retardation was only seen in infants with extensive bilateral cerebral atrophy thought to be due to extensive hypoxic damage.

PVH recognized by ultrasound may be a good marker of perinatal insult to the preterm infant's brain, but there is little correspondence between the size of the hemorrhage and the extent of permanent damage. PVH does not occur in the brains of mature infants. Hypoxic damage itself can only be diagnosed indirectly from ultrasound by the recognition of loss of brain tissue due to atrophy. These changes do not become apparent until many days after the original insult; and only extensive loss of tissue can be recognized. Animal studies using topical nuclear magnetic resonance indicate that biochemical changes accompanying cellular hypoxic damage in the brain may be detectable (Delpy, Gordon, Hope, Parker, Reynolds, Shaw, & Whitehead, 1982; Devel, 1982). Preliminary findings on asphyxiated mature infants indicate that hypoxic damage can be recognized in the human brain when or very shortly after it occurs (Cady, Costello, Dawson, Delpy, Hope, Reynolds, Tofts, & Wilkie, 1983).

Acknowledgments

This work was supported by a grant from the British Department of Health and Social Security.

Many colleagues have contributed to the study described in this chapter and I should like to thank them. In particular, I am very grateful for the unfailing support of Anthea Blake, Jo March, Grace Rawlings, and E. O. R. Reynolds, as well as for the endless cooperation of the children and their families.

References

Abramovich, S. J., Gregory, S., Slemick, M., & Stewart, A. L. Hearing loss in very-low-birth-weight infants treated with intensive care. *Archives of Disease in Childhood*, 1979, *54*, 421–426.

Agerholm, M. Handicaps and the handicapped. *Royal Society of Health Journal*, 1975, *95*, 3–8.

Blake, A. M., Pollitzer, M. J., & Reynolds, E. O. R. Referral of mothers and infants for intensive care. *British Medical Journal*, 1979, *2*, 414–416.

Cady, E., Costello, A. de L., Dawson, J., Delpy, D. T., Hope, P. L., Reynolds, E. O. R., Tofts, P., & Wilkie, D. Personal communication, 1983.

Calâme, A., & Prod'hom. L. S. Prognostic vital et qualité de survie des prématurés pesant 1500 g et moins à la naissance soignés en 1966–1968. *Schweizerische Medizinische Wochenschrift*, 1972, *102*, 65–70.

Chalmers, I. Search for indices. *Lancet*, 1979, *2*, 1063–1065.

Court, S. D. M. *Fit for the future: Report of the Committee on Child Health Services*. London: Her Majesty's Stationery Office, 1976.

Davies, P. A., & Russell, H. Later progress of 100 infants weighing 1000 to 2000 g at birth fed immediately with breast milk. *Developmental Medicine and Child Neurology*, 1968, *10*, 725–735.

Delpy, D. T., Gordon, R. E., Hope, P. L., Parker, D., Reynolds, E. O. R., Shaw, D., & Whitehead, M.D. Non-invasive investigation of cerebral ischemia by phosporus nuclear magnetic resonance. *Pediatrics*, 1982, *70*, 310–313.

Devel, R. K. Pathophysiology, live. *Pediatrics*, 1982, *70*, 650–652.

Drillien, C. M. Growth and development in children of very low birth weight. *Archives of Disease in Childhood*, 1958, *33*, 10–18.

Drillien, C. M. Incidence of mental and physical handicaps in school-age children of very low birth weight. *Pediatrics*, 1961, *27*, 452–464.

Drillien, C. M. The long-term prospects for babies of low birth weight. *British Journal of Hospital Medicine*, 1967, *1*, 937–944.

Fitzhardinge, P. M. Follow-up studies on the low-birth-weight infant. *Clinics in Perinatology*, 1976, *3*, 503–516.

Fitzhardinge, P. M. Follow-up studies on infants treated by mechanical ventilation. *Clinics in Perinatology*, 1978, *5*, 451–461.

Fraser, J. G., Conway, M. J., Keene, M. H., & Hazell, J. W. P. The postauricular myogenic response. *Journal of Laryngology and Otology*, 1978, *92*, 293–303.

Griffiths, R. *The abilities of babies*. London: University of London Press, 1954.

Koppitz, E. M. *The Bender-Gestalt Test for Young Children*. New York: Grune & Stratton, 1964.

Lipscomb, A. P., Blackwell, R. J., Reynolds, E. O. R., Thorburn, R. J., Cusick, G., & Pape, K. E. Ultrasound scanning of brain through anterior fontanelle of newborn infants. *Lancet*, 1979, *2*, 39.

Lubchenco, L. O., Hansman, C., Dressler, M., & Boyd, E. Intrauterine growth as estimated from live-born birth-weight data at 24 to 32 weeks of gestation. *Pediatrics*, 1963, *32*, 793–800.

Lubchenco, L. O., Horner, F. A., Reed, L. H., Hix, I. E., Metcalf, D., Cohig, R., Elliott, H. C., & Bourg, M. Sequelae of premature birth. *American Journal of Diseases of Children*, 1963, *33*, 101–115.

MacDonald, A. D. *Children of very low birth weight*. London: Heinemann, 1967.

McCarthy, D. *McCarthy Scales of Children's Abilities*. New York: Psychological Corporation, 1970.

Neale, M. D. *Neale Analysis of Reading Ability*. London: Macmillan, 1966.

Nelson, K. B., & Ellenberg, J. H. Neonatal signs as predictors of cerebral palsy. *Pediatrics*, 1979, *64*, 225–232.

Nie, N. H., Hadlaihull, C., Jenkins, J. G., Steinbrenner, K., & Bent, D. H. *Statistical package for the social sciences*. New York: McGraw-Hill, 1975.

Palmer, P., Dubowitz, L. M. S., Levene, M. I., & Dubowitz, V. Developmental and neurological progress of preterm infants with intraventricular hemorrhage and ventricular dilatation. *Archives of Disease in Childhood*, 1982, *57*, 748–753.

Pape, K. E., Blackwell, R. J., Cusick, G., Sherwood, A., Houang, M. T. W., Thorburn, R. J., & Reynolds, E. O. R. Ultrasound detection of brain damage in the preterm infant. *Lancet*, 1979, *1*, 1261–1264.

Pape, K. E., & Wigglesworth, J. S. *Haemorrhage, ischaemia, and the perinatal brain.* London: Spastics International Medical Publications, 1979.

Parmalee, A. H. Early identification of cerebral palsy in preterm infants. *Pediatric Research*, 1977, *11*, 381. (Abstract)

Rawlings, G., Reynolds, E. O. R., Stewart, A., & Strang, L. B. Changing prognosis for infants of very low birth weight. *Lancet*, 1971, *1*, 516–519.

Registrar General's classification of occupations, Office of Population Censuses and Surveys. London: Her Majesty's Stationery Office, 1970.

Reynell, J. *Reynell Developmental Language Scales.* Windsor, England: National Foundation for Educational Research, 1969.

Reynolds, E. O. R. Neonatal intensive care and the prevention of major handicap. In K. Elliott & M. O'Connor (Eds.), *Major mental handicap: Methods and costs of prevention* (Ciba Foundation Symposium No. 59, new series). Amsterdam: Elsevier, 1978.

Reynolds, E. O. R., & Stewart, A. L. Intensive care and the very-low-birth-weight infant. *Lancet*, 1979, *2*, 254.

Sameroff, A. J., & Chandler, M. J. Reproductive risk and the continuum of caretaking casualty. In F. D. Horowitz, M. Hetherington, S. Scarr-Salapatek, & G. Siegal (Eds.), *Review of child development research* (Vol. 4). Chicago: University of Chicago Press, 1975.

Stennert, E., Schulte, F. J., Vollrath, M., Brunner, E., & Fravenrath, C. The etiology of neurosensory hearing defects in preterm infants. *Archives of Oto-Rhino-Laryngology*, 1978, *221*, 171–182.

Stewart, A. L. The survival of low-birth-weight infants. *British Journal of Hospital Medicine*, 1977, *18*, 182–189.

Stewart, A. L., & Reynolds, E. O. R. Improved prognosis for infants of very low birth weight. *Pediatrics*, 1974, *54*, 724–735.

Stewart, A. L., Reynolds, E. O. R., & Lipscomb, A. P. Outcome for infants of very low birth weight: Survey of world literature. *Lancet*, 1981, *1*, 1038–1041.

Stewart, A. L., Thorburn, R. J., Hope, P. L., Goldsmith, M., Reynolds, E. O. R., & Lipscomb, A. P. Relation between ultrasound-appearance of the brain in very preterm infants and neurodevelopmental outcome at 18 months of age. *Second Perinatal Intracranial Conference, Washington, D.C.* Columbus, Ohio: Ross Laboratories, 1982.

Stewart, A. L., Turcan, D., Rawlings, G., Hart, S., & Gregory, S. Outcome for infants at high risk of major handicap. In K. Elliott & M. O'Connor (Eds.), *Major mental handicap: Methods and costs of prevention* (Ciba Foundation Symposium No. 59, new series). Amsterdam: Elsevier, 1978.

Stott, D. H., & Marston, N. C. *The child in school* (Bristol Social Adjustment Guide Nos. 1 & 2, 4th ed.). London: University of London Press, 1971.

Stutsman, R. *Mental measurement of preschool children.* New York: Harcourt, Brace and World, 1931.

Terman, L. M., & Merrill, M. A. *Stanford–Binet Intelligence Scale.* London: Harrup, 1961.

Thorburn, R. J., Lipscomb, A. P., Blackwell, R. J., Cusick, G., Pape, K. E., Stewart, A. L., & Reynolds, E. O. R. Personal communication, 1980.

Thorburn, R. J., Lipscomb, A. P., Stewart, A. L., Reynolds, E. O. R., & Hope, P. L. Timing and antecedents of periventricular hemorrhage and of cerebral atrophy in very preterm infants. *Early Human Development*, 1982, *7*, 221–238.

Thorburn, R. J., Lipscomb, A. P., Stewart, A. L., Reynolds, E. O. R., Hope, P. L., & Pape, K. E. Prediction of death and major handicap in very preterm infants by brain ultrasound. *Lancet*, 1981, *1*, 1119–1121.

Wechsler, D. *Manual of Wechsler Intelligence Scale for Children.* New York: Psychological Corporation, 1949.

Wechsler, D. *Wechsler Preschool and Primary Scale of Intelligence.* New York: Psychological Corporation, 1967.

Wu, P. Y. K. Discussion. In A. Anderson, R. Beard, M. Brudenell, & P. M. Dunn (Eds.), *Preterm labour.* London: Royal College of Obstetricians and Gynaecologists, 1977.

CHAPTER TWO

Malnutrition in Childhood

JOAQUÍN CRAVIOTO / RAMIRO ARRIETA

"Infantile protein–calorie malnutrition" is a generic term used to group the whole range of mild to severe clinical and biochemical signs present in infants and children as a consequence of a deficient intake and/or utilization of foods of animal origin, accompanied by variable intakes of rich carbohydrate foods. "Kwashiorkor" and "marasmus" are the names given in the U.S. and British Commonwealth literature to the two extreme clinical varieties of the syndrome. The appearance of marasmus or kwashiorkor is related to the age of the child; the time of full weaning; the time of introduction of food supplements to breast milk; the caloric density and protein concentration of the supplements the child actually ingests; and the frequency and severity of infectious diseases present, particularly during weaning.

In all latitudes, the syndrome presents the same basic biochemical and clinical features. The regional variations described are generally associated with other concomitant nutritional deficiencies, the pattern of weaning, and the infectious pathology prevalent in the area.

At the community level, protein–calorie malnutrition is a man-made disorder characteristic of the poorer segments of society, particularly of preindustrial societies, where the social system consciously or unconsciously creates malnourished individuals, generation after generation, through a series of social mechanisms that includes limited access to goods and services, limited social mobility, and restricted experiential opportunities at crucial points in the lives of children.

The prevalence of protein–calorie malnutrition (i.e., the number of cases in relation to the population at risk at a given point in time) is not fully known. Estimates for severe protein–calorie malnutrition in different preindustrial regions of the world vary from .5 to 7% in children below 5 years of age. In general, marasmus predominates in urban settlements while kwashiorkor prevails in the rural areas, with a tendency to be replaced by marasmus as breast feeding declines and both micro- and macroenvironmental conditions continue unchanged.

Bengoa's (1974) data indicate that about 10 million Latin American children aged less than 5 years suffer protein–calorie malnutrition of various degrees of

Joaquín Cravioto and Ramiro Arrieta. Instituto Nacional de Ciencias y Tecnología de la Salud del Niño–DIF, Sistema Nacional Para el Desarrollo Integral de la Familia. Mexico City, Mexico.

severity at any one time. Incidence (i.e., number of new cases diagnosed during a period given of time per unit of population studied) of severe malnutrition in preschool children born and living in a representative community of central Mexico during their first 5 years of life was 7.5%. The proportion of kwashiorkor to marasmus was 2:1, with the number of kwashiorkor girls twice as high as for boys. The proportion of marasmus in girls and boys was 4:3 (Cravioto & DeLicardie, 1974). The higher incidence in girls than in boys seems to be associated with the lower social value attached to females in these social groups (Cravioto, Lindoro, & Birch, 1971).

The problem of severe malnutrition should be looked at from the viewpoint of how long how many children have suffered, rather than considering just how many are affected (McLaren, 1966). In this context, marasmus with its earlier age of appearance and its prolonged course might be more important than kwashiorkor in terms of its possible long-term consequences.

SOME OF THE DIFFICULTIES IN ASSESSING THE ROLE OF MALNUTRITION IN MENTAL DEVELOPMENT IN YOUNG CHILDREN

Since protein–calorie malnutrition in children is an ecological outcome of a life style, it can be easily understood that the interpretation of the role played by malnutrition in causing alterations in mental development, behavior, and learning ability is complicated by the presence of a large number of other variables, which themselves are able to produce such disturbances.

Some of the main variables found in multiple combinations in the macro- and microenvironment of the social groups where malnutrition is prevalent include the following: illiteracy or poor general educational level; traditional, unsuitable modes of child care; importance attached to and attitude toward basic education; low economic resources; poor living conditions with inadequate sanitation; overcrowding; and insufficient experiences for the stimulation of child growth and development. This ecological system clearly complicates assessment of the possible role of nutritional deficiency in growth and developmental disturbances in children with current or previous malnutrition.

The mental sequelae of malnutrition during lactation and the preschool period can rarely be assessed completely at the time of the pathological nutritional process, particularly with regard to intellectual functions, school performance, and (possibly) economic and social competence. For a satisfactory assessment to be made, a certain time interval must elapse between the period of primary risk and the one in which these functions may be measured properly. During this interval, many other environmental factors may affect development of a child's mental ability. To evaluate the effect of the nutritional variable, it is essential to understand and interpret the additive or synergistic contribution of all the other environmental variables that play a role in this intervening period.

It would be erroneous to think that the delay between the period of malnutrition and that in which its possible consequences can be measured has only negative effects. In fact, except in very rare cases, any effect of malnutrition on the functioning of the central nervous system is unlikely to be expressed by alterations of simple reflexes and adaptive behavior. As long as 54 years ago, Lashley (1929) reported that up to 20% of the rat cerebral cortex could be extirpated without any consequences for the animal's behavior in a maze. On the other hand, Maier and Schneirla (1935) showed that only 3% of the cortex had to be destroyed to produce marked alterations in more complex learning processes. Consequently, retarded differentiation (or even diffuse lesions) produced by malnutrition in the central nervous system should not be expected to become apparent until long after the age at which the nutritional insult occurs. At these later ages, when more complex processes should become established to achieve functional integration, there are greater possibilities for increasing the sensitivity of signs indicating brain dysfunction.

In this context, it is useful to bear in mind that the results of general psychological tests in infancy are of little or no predictive value for later ages. Nevertheless, when the intelligence quotients (IQs) obtained at slightly older ages (e.g., between 1.5 and 2.5 years of age) are correlated with those obtained between 8 and 18 years, the predictive value is seen to increase considerably. In a study of the relationship between the IQ at school age and tests made between 19 and 30 months, McCall, Hogarty, and Hulbert (1972) found a correlation coefficient of .49, which means that almost 25% of the variance in the IQs obtained between 8 and 18 years of age could be explained by the results observed in infancy. In contrast, a complete lack of correlation was found between the IQ at school age (8 to 18 years) and tests made between 1 and 6 months for age (correlation coefficient = .01).

A delay in assessing the consequences of malnutrition is thus essential if one wishes to measure the entire impact of the potential deficit. Once again, the need to account for the possible qualitative and quantitative influences of social and other variables on mental development during this interval is crucial.

A further problem in interpreting the possible mental sequelae of malnutrition is related to the criteria used for measuring mental development, behavior, and learning ability. Pollitt and Thomson (1977), in their authoritative review, emphasize the conceptual and methodological problems that arise in applying intelligence tests to societies (or groups) with cultural or other factors modulating mental development that differ from those of the society or population for which the test was designed. At present, there are sufficient data to support the view that similar activities or behavior in culturally different populations may not be functionally equivalent, while certain different activities and behavior may be entirely equivalent.

This focuses attention on the care needed to differentiate the "standard" validity from the validity that is inherent to the theoretical basis of the test. In other words, methods for standardizing the tests must be obtained, and, in addition, the degree to which the functions under investigation (memory, attention, perception, etc.) explain the results must be known. The latter point is of prime importance, since the difference in performance between the study population and that for which the test was originally designed might have different meanings for different functions.

In summary, our interpretation of the role played by malnutrition in the production of disorders of development is complicated by the presence of associated variables. These variables include infection, social disadvantage, the time of life at which malnutrition is experienced, the dates at which more sensitive evaluation of its consequences for adaptive functioning may take place, and the tests employed to measure the performance of the individuals or populations under study.

INFLUENCE OF AGE ON OUTCOME

In 1920 Jackson and Stewart reported that nutritional deficiency imposed shortly after birth had permanent effects on the subsequent somatic growth of animals of several species, while transient malnutrition occurring after weaning depressed growth only for the duration of the deprivation period without effect on ultimate size. The age at which a young animal ceased to be vulnerable to permanent impairment varied considerably among the species studied. In the rat, it appeared to occur shortly after the end of the normal suckling period.

In spite of early findings, subsequent research has almost always used weaning or adult animals. Such research has led to claims that, although nearly all the organs and tissues of chronically starved rats are markedly reduced in weight, the brain is unaffected in terms of both size and chemical composition. However, the so-called "invulnerability" of the brain to nutritional deprivation was put into perspective by Dobbing and Kersley (1963), who showed that the apparent immunity of the *adult* brain to starvation was not shared by the *developing* brain, which at certain periods during its development could be adversely and permanently affected by even a mild dietary restriction.

Now it is widely accepted that during its development the brain has at least one postembryonic phase when it passes through a transient period of rapid increase ("brain growth spurt"). This period is very important because it means that the *timing* of etiological factors in relation to the growth spurt sequence is of even greater significance than their duration and their severity are. Moderate growth restriction of a degree commonly seen in human populations, if present during the period of the brain growth spurt, results in permanent structural and functional modifications. A similar degree and duration of growth restriction imposed either before or after the brain growth spurt is without lasting effects. For the human, the period from about the 30th week of gestation until at least the end of the second year of life is one in which there seems to be a very high risk of permanent impairment if there are inadequate conditions for brain growth (Dobbing, 1976).

Until about 1962, the concept of invulnerability of the brain to environmental factors was widely held. The work of Keys and associates (Keys, Brozek, Henschel, Mickelson, & Taylor, 1950) had shown that severe malnutrition led to only transient impairments of psychological performance. Normal adults who voluntarily had reduced their body weight to 70–80% of their normal weight through severe restriction of food intake showed below-normal psychological test performance. But during rehabilitation mental performance improved, and by the time the subjects were considered as recovered from malnutrition, their scores were normal. Also, Kugelmass, Poull, and Samuel (1944) reported an increment of 18 points in the IQs of a group of malnourished children following a marked improvement in their diet. Thus, it came to be accepted that malnutrition had only a transient effect on mental development and learning.

In the field of developmental biology, researchers are accustomed to consider that results obtained in adult subject and in older children are not always applicable to fast-growing organisms. Since available data, both in human infants and in experimental animals, were consistent with the idea that severe protein–calorie malnutrition affected the normal pattern of biochemical maturation (Cravioto, 1962), it was considered improbable that the central nervous system could not participate in this general deceleration of growth and development. Accordingly, it was hypothesized that the effect of malnutrition on mental development would vary as a function of the period of life at which malnutrition would be experienced.

To test the hypothesis, all severely malnourished children admitted to the Nutrition Ward of the Hospital Infantil de México during 1959 were selected for study. Immediately after successful treatment of any infectious diseases and correction of electrolyte disturbances, if present, the behavior of the children was assessed by the Gesell method. Tests were repeated at regular intervals of 2 weeks during the entire period the children were hospitalized. In all, serial information was obtained on 20 children: six infants below 6 months of age, nine between 15 and 29 months, and five between the ages of 37 and 42 months.

The results of the first test session confirmed previous reports, since all children were noted to have below-age-norm scores in all fields of behavior. As recovery from malnutrition occurred, developmental quotients increased in most of the patients, and the gap between normal age expectation and the actual performance of the children progressively diminished, except in the group of infants whose age on admission was less than 6 months. These younger malnourished infants showed no tendency to "catch up" and thus increased in developmental age only by a figure equal to the number of months they remained in the hospital. In older children, not all spheres of behavior exhibited the same speed of recovery. Language, which in general was the function most affected, showed the slowest rate of return to normal age expectancy.

When the serial data for each child were plotted against days of hospitalization, the rate of behavioral recovery from the initial deficit varied in direct relation to age at admission: The older the group, the greater the value of the slope. The slopes were sufficiently steep, and progress in the first 2 weeks of treatment was so rapid, that it appeared unlikely (at that time) that the differences between initial test performance and level of functioning during nutritional rehabilitation could be due to the extra care and attention the children had received in the hospital (Cravioto & Robles, 1963, 1965).

To test the hypothesis that the effects of malnutrition are greater the younger the age of the affected child, Hoorveg and Standfield (1972) selected from the records of a rural clinic near Kampala, Uganda, three groups of 20 survivors of severe malnutrition ages 11 to 17 years, who had been treated for a combination of marasmus and kwashiorkor suffered before 27 months of age. Group 1 consisted of former cases treated before 16 months of age; Group 2 consisted of former patients who had been admitted between the ages of 16 and 21 months; and Group 3 was constituted of former patients whose ages on admission were between 22 and 27 months. Psychological test performance was assessed in terms of general intelligence, verbal abilities, spatial and perceptual abilities, visual memory, short-term memory, learning and incidental learning, and motor development. Significant differences were found in memory for designs, on which Group 3 performed better than Groups 1 and 2, and in the learning task, on which Group 2 did better than Group 1. In two other tests, incidental learning and short-term memory, the differences as a function of age at which malnutrition was treated reached a significant level of confidence of

.10. The findings were in the expected direction in which those children who suffered younger did more poorly.

Guillen-Alvarez (1971), in a group of 14 survivors of severe protein–calorie malnutrition suffered at ages 3 to 19 months, found a significant correlation between the ages at which malnutrition occurred and IQs obtained from a battery of tests, which included Raven Progressive Matrices, Koch Test, and Goodenough Test applied at ages 10 to 12 years.

Stein, Susser, Saenger, and Marolla (1975) in their comprehensive epidemiological study of the Dutch Hunger Winter of 1944–1945, found no relation between the mental performance of young men at military induction and their prenatal exposure to famine. The measures of mental performance included Raven Progressive Matrices, Language Comprehension, Arithmetic, Clerical Aptitude, Bennet Test of Mechanical Comprehension, and a score combining the results of all these tests. All the scores obtained failed to show any effect of the famine on performance at age of induction into military service. No evidence was found of interaction of prenatal famine exposure with indexes of social environment (social class, religious affiliation, family size, and birth order) that might have influenced compensatory learning opportunities and subsequent mental development. Similarly, no evidence was found that selected survival might have masked or distorted an association of prenatal famine exposure with mental performance at the age of military induction. It is of interest that a higher prevalence of congenital anomalies of the central nervous system was related to prenatal famine exposure.

The finding that nutritional deprivation confined to the prenatal period may be too brief to produce a detectable effect on postnatal mental performance seems in agreement with the report of DeLicardie, Vega, Birch, and Cravioto (1971) that mild–moderate malnutrition suffered only during the neonatal period affected body size but not mental performance, at least during the first year of life of the infants studied.

Hertzig, Birch, Richardson, and Tizard (1972) have approached the issue of age and outcome in searching for a correlation between children's ages at hospitalization for treatment of severe malnutrition and IQs (Wechsler Intelligence Scale for Children) at school age. Pearson correlations were calculated for the full-scale, verbal, and performance IQs in a sample of 74 cases. The respective coefficients of −.13, −.13, and −.14 indicate a random relationship between the age of a severely malnourished child at the time of admittance for treatment and his or her IQ at school age. This was confirmed when the IQs of 74 survivors of severe malnutrition were divided into three subgroups according to the age of admission for treatment: before 8 months of age; between 8 and 12 months; and between 13 and 24 months. An analysis of variance showed that the means for the subgroups were not statistically different at the .05 level of confidence. However, the IQ mean values in the survivors of malnutrition are misleading, due to the significant number of children who scored at the floor level of the Wechsler. Accordingly, before accepting the authors' conclusion of no relationship between the time at which severe malnutrition occurs and the severity of mental outcome, it might be convenient to test for performance differences in children's age groups using nonparametric techniques.

Nwuga (1977), too, found no systematic relationship between the age during the first 3 years of life at which the children had kwashiorkor and the level of intellectual performance at school age, but it was noted that the onset of kwashiorkor is not always synonymous with admission to a hospital. In our experience, a child with kwashiorkor or marasmus is not taken into a hospital unless he or she also suffers from acute infection or shows symptoms of a disorder that may threaten life. Even severe malnutrition is rarely a sufficient cause for medical consultation.

There are very few human investigations on the influence of duration of malnutrition on later mental performance. Chase and Martin (1970) have reported that in a follow-up study of 19 infants who had been in the hospital for treatment of severe malnutrition at ages of less than 1 year, those who had suffered the syndrome for more than the first 4 months of their lives had the lowest developmental quotients (Yale Revised Developmental Examination) at 3.5 years after discharge. Performance in all areas of development tested was significantly lower than was the performance of children admitted with malnutrition before the age of 4 months. The development of the children with a shorter duration of malnutrition did not differ from that found in a control group also examined at a mean age of 3.5 years. At this time all the survivors of malnutrition lasting only for the first 4 months of life had developmental quotients above 80, whereas 9 of 10 children suffering from malnutrition for periods longer than the first 4 months of life had developmental quotients below 80. Once again, these findings are in agreement with the report of DeLicardie *et al.* (1971); this group found that a group of infants who, for no apparent reason, had a body weight at 15 days of life below their birth weight continued to weigh less than did controls matched for size at birth throughout the 1st year of life, and also to lag behind the controls in total body length, head circumference, chest circumference, arm circumference, and skin fold thickness—without, however, showing a significant difference in the course of behavioral development.

Srikantia, Sastry, and Naidu (1975) compared Indian children rehabilitated from kwashiorkor (suffered between the ages of 18 and 36 months) with matched controls at ages of 8 to 11 years. Intersensory organization was poorer in the index cases than in the control subjects, with differences highly significant. When these children were again tested 5 years later, the differences between the two groups had considerably decreased. Although the survivors of severe protein–calorie malnutrition still made more errors than the control children did, the difference was not statistically significant. After another 2 years, the performance of both groups of children was errorless.

The apparent catch-up of the originally malnourished group has to be considered carefully. When applying a test with a clear developmental course, the point at which the asymptotic performance is reached might be the only difference between a group with normal development and a group with a developmental delay. If a child has already reached the maximal level of performance, and another child obtains that same level later in time, it cannot properly be said that the second child has "caught up" with the first, although both children now have the same score. Moreover, in societies where demands are specific to chronological age, the importance of a delay in development might be fundamental for the future role and status of those affected. This is true in spite of the fact that later in life, such as in adulthood, the test performance of these individuals may not differ at all from that obtained by their more fortunate counterparts.

INFLUENCE OF NONNUTRITIONAL VARIABLES ON OUTCOME

Since nutritional status is an outcome of the social and cultural reality of a family and a community, individuals who are at the greatest and most persistent nutritional risk tend to cluster in the lowest socioeconomic segments of society. These segments differ from the remainder in a host of other disadvantages. They tend to have poorer housing, higher morbidity rates, lower levels of formal education, and greater degrees of outmoded patterns of child care; in short, they tend to live in circumstances that are less conducive to the optimal development of technological and educational competence. The presence of these associations makes it inevitable that any consequences for mental development and learning deriving from nutritional conditions of risk will be associated with socioeconomic status and the variables attaching to it.

There has been some tendency to view the relationship between nutritional status and socioeconomic status as circular and to conclude that the abnormal outcomes in development and learning can be accounted for by social status per se. This is unfortunate, since it substitutes a truism for an analysis. Given the associations between lower socioeconomic standing and suboptimal mental outcomes, the task of the analysis is to identify the effective variables that mediate these outcomes.

If "intelligence" is operationally defined as the process through which a child learns the use of the tools of his or her culture in order to know and to manipulate the environment, it seems apparent that, at each stage of development, mental performance will be directly related to both the genetic endowment of the individual and the several environments in which the child has lived so far. Heredity and environment do not summate as additive combinations; rather, the quantitative effect of either one is dependent on and interacts with the contribution given by the other factor. Thus, the contribution of heredity to the variance of a certain characteristic or trait is not a constant, but rather is a variable the magnitude of which depends on the environment in which the individual was and is located. Similarly, with different genetic makeups, the same environment would contribute in different proportions to the expression of a trait. Accordingly, mental growth would be modified to the degree to which conditions of life associated with depressed social position function directly to modify the growth and differentiation of the central nervous system and indirectly to affect the opportunity for obtaining, and the motives for profiting from, experience. For example, social class as such does not determine physical stature; rather, individuals are stunted when their social positions provide an environment (in terms of nutrition, morbidity, habits, etc.) that influences the biological processes involved in growth in body length. The study of child development across the gradient of disadvantage would permit the assessment of the contribution of early malnutrition, either along or in combination with other environmental factors, to suboptimal growth and performance in the human species.

In trying to sort out the contributory effects of the so-called "nonnutritional variables," one of the strategies used has been the comparison of children who have survived a severe episode of infantile malnutrition with their own siblings raised in the same family environment but not experiencing the same severity of nutritional insult. The assumption behind this strategy is that the use of siblings as controls cancels out the majority of the demographic or macroenvironmental variables, leaving those related to the specific microenvironment of each child within his or her own family to be accounted for by other means or study.

From data published in four studies that have used the sibling strategy (Birch, Piñeiro, Alcalde, Toca, & Cravioto, 1971; Cravioto, Piñeiro, Arroyo, & Alcalde, 1969; Hertzig *et al.*, 1972; Nwuga, 1977), it is apparent that the environment in which children at risk of severe malnutrition live is highly negative in its effects on mental development. Irrespective of the diagnosis of severe malnutrition, children developing in this habitat have a high probability of exhibiting not only poor performance on intelligence testing but also low scores in intersensory organization and perceptual–visual competence. The presence of a superimposed episode of severe malnutrition occurring early in life and resulting in hospital admission is associated with intellectual performance at an even lower level than that characteristic of these children's poor psychosocial environment.

Demographic data strongly indicate that having a child hospitalized for severe clinical malnutrition in fact identifies a family in which *all* children are at risk for significant mild–moderate malnutrition on a chronic basis. Therefore, survivors of severe malnutrition and their siblings are similar in sharing a common exposure to subnutrition on a lifelong basis and differ in this nutritional background only in that the index cases have a superimposed episode of acute exacerbation. Consequently, the comparison of siblings and index children does not provide a full picture of the overall effects of nutritional inadequacy on mental performance. Rather, it indicates the additional consequence for maldevelopment that may attach to the superimposed episode of acute exacerbation. The use of siblings as controls also means that the children compared have shared a generally disadvantageous social and family environment, several features of which can in themselves significantly contribute to the depression of the intellectual performance levels. This factor, too, should result in the minimizing of differences between survivors of severe malnutrition and their siblings and provides further support to the significance of the differences found in development.

Among the families with a high prevalence of severe malnutrition, cognition is seldom identified as a powerful tool for individual achievement. This is more often seen during infancy and the preschool years. Faced with a low purchasing power resulting directly from the lack of modern technology and actual information, parents are preoccupied with the more pressing needs of survival. Problems related to housing, sufficient food, employment, transportation, acute disease, physical energy, family conflict, and economic and physical safety take the highest priority. Under this load, there is often neglect of the infants' manipulatory and exploratory play activities and a failure to introduce into that play the auditory, visual, and tactile stimuli that constitute the precursors of symbols. In these homes, there is seldom time to play with, talk to, or read to a child. In many of these families, too, there is a lack of awareness of the importance of these activities for the child's development.

Cravioto and DeLicardie (1973) sought to assess the influence of environment on the occurrence of early severe malnutrition through a comparison of the environmental characteristics of two groups: a group of 22 children who developed severe protein–energy malnutrition, and a group of children selected from the same birth cohort who were never diagnosed as severely malnourished and who were matched at birth for sex, gestational age, season of birth, body weight, body length, and psychomotor behavior. Three kinds of macroenvironmental factors that had been longitudinally recorded, starting at birth, received consideration: (1) the parents as biological and social organisms; (2) the family structure; and (3) objective circumstances such as sources of family income, income per capita, and sanitary facilities available in the household.

The age, height, or weight of either parent; the mother's number of pregnancies; and the number of live children in the family all failed to distinguish between families with and without severely malnourished children. Moreover, no significant relationship was found between the presence or absence of severe clinical malnutrition and the variables of personal cleanliness, literacy, and educational level.

The parents' contact with mass media was assessed in terms of radio listening and (in literate parents) newspaper reading. The two groups did not differ with respect to the proportion of newspaper readers among either mothers or fathers. Similarly, the number of fathers who listened regularly to the radio was similar in both the malnourished group and the control group. But the situation with the mothers was different. There were almost equal numbers of radio listeners and nonlisteners in the malnourished group, but the number of listeners among the matched control group was more than three times the number of nonlisteners (the difference between groups was significant at the .05 level).

No significant differences between the malnourished and control groups were found with respect to family size or type of family (nuclear or extended). The socioeconomic status of the families was estimated by using four indicators: main source of family income, sanitary facilities in the household, annual income per capita, and percentage of total income spent on food. No significant associations were found between any of these factors and the presence or absence of severe malnutrition.

In summary, from all features of the macroenvironment, the only differential between severely malnourished children and controls matched at birth for gestational age, body weight, and total body length was the mother's contact with the world outside the village through regular radio listening. None of the other characteristics of the parents (biological, social, or cultural) or family circumstances (including per capita income, main source of income, and family size) was significantly associated with the presence or absence of severe malnourishment.

Because of the lack of association between the features of the *macro*environment and the presence of severe malnutrition, attention was directed toward the analysis of the *micro*environment of the two groups of children. The potential stimulation of the children's homes, as a general indicator of the quality of child care, and the mother's psychological characteristics (as the principal stimulating agents for the children) were selected as the focus of the analysis. The Caldwell (1967) home stimulation inventory was used to assess key aspects of the quantity and/or quality of social, emotional, and cognitive stimulation available to the children. Maternal transactions with the children were recorded using an adaptation of the Maternal Behavior Profile developed by Nancy Bayley (1964), which contains 20 variables describing a mother's transactions during testing. The analysis of group differences was based on a summary measure of the mothers' habitual responses during the first 12 consecutive monthly examinations.

It was evident that, even before the appearance of the first case of severe malnutrition, available home stimulation scores were markedly lower in the malnourished group. Thus, at 6 months of age one of every four "future malnourished" children had a home with a score of 30 or fewer points on a scale with a range from 27 to 41, and none scored higher than 36 points. None of the control children had a home with a score of less than 32 points, and at least one of every four homes scored above 36 points. Similarly, at 58 months of age, when the malnourished children had been rehabilitated, almost one-half of the survivors of severe malnutrition were in homes with scores below 104 points on a scale with a range from 55 to 124, and one-fourth of their homes did not exceed 84 points. In contrast, the homes of the control children had a minimum of 100 points, with almost one-half above 110 points.

The behavioral responses of mothers of infants who later developed severe malnutrition were also different from the responses observed in the mothers of the control children. The greatest difference between the two groups was obtained in the behavior displayed by mothers when, in a test situation, their children performed adequately and easily; in the overt signs of sensitivity toward the children; and in the mothers' response to the interview.

Significant differences were also observed for interest in the children's performance, response to children's needs, the mothers' view of their role in the test situation, and emotional involvement of the mothers with their children ($p < .01$). The amount of verbal communication with and the expressions of affection toward the children also showed significant differences between the groups ($p < .02$). Mothers' reactions when their children performed extremely well, their status consciousness, and their cooperation with the examiners during the test also significantly differentiated the groups ($p < .05$).

The mothers' behavioral responses when the children had difficulty with test items, their affective response to the entire situation, and their control of the children during the test showed similar but nonsignificant ($p < .10$) trends. The amount of physical contact with the children, the mothers' overall general evaluation of the children, their tolerance of their children's behavior, the type of physical contact with the children, and their hostility toward the children all failed to differentiate the groups (Cravioto & DeLicardie, 1975).

Srikantia and Sastry (1972) have shown that mothers of children with or without kwashiorkor, even when matched for variables such as age, parity, family size, income, religion, caste, and urban or rural setting, differed not only in their specific knowledge and concepts of food values, weaning practices, and timing of supplementary foods, but also in their attitudes on general health care and in their concern for their children's health. The mothers of kwashiorkor children also performed at a lower level on a battery of intelligence tests devised for their cultural setting. A low level of measured intelligence was also found by Martinez, Ramos-Galván, and De La Fuente (1951) in a group of mothers of severely malnourished children in Mexico.

In a study conducted in a preindustrial bilingual village of Guatemala (Cravioto, Birch, DeLicardie, & Rosales, 1967) it was observed that, in addition to radio listening by mothers, the language spoken to children at home separated infants with significantly different weight increments in the first 6 months of their lives. Mothers who addressed their children in the local dialect of the village had infants whose weight increments were significantly lower than the increments of infants whose mothers talked to them in the national language.

Perhaps listening regularly to the radio and the use of the national language rather than the local dialect represent a breaking away from traditional patterns. Mothers showing these characteristics may take more chances with innovative ideas; may be more likely to provide their children with a more diversified and stimulating home environment; and may view their own role as a continuous series of affective, engaging and gratifying transactions between mother and child, and not simply as one of passive traditional status to be taken for granted and carried on with a minimum of gratifying interaction and novelty.

It is clear that a low level of home stimulation and the presence of a passive traditional mother, unaware of the cognitive needs of her child and responding to him or her in a minimal way as if unable to decode the infant's signals, are two features of the poor microenvironment of the potentially malnourished child that in themselves are capable of influencing mental growth and development.

Yatkin and McLaren (1970), in Lebanon, compared two groups of severely malnourished children paired for sex and age. Mental performance during nutritional recovery was evaluated by the Griffiths Mental Development Scale. One of these groups was provided with a rich environment consisting of a colorful hospital ward with pictures, toys, and music where nurses deliberately played with and sang to the children and established a warm nurse–child relationship. The nonstimulated group stayed in a place of about the same size, but one that was not colorful and lacked toys and music. Both the stimulated and unstimulated children received the same medical and dietary treatment. The initial difference in developmental quotients between the groups was not significant. With nutritional recovery, both groups increased their mental performance to a similar and significant degree. However, toward the end of the 4-month observation period, the stimulated group showed higher quotients as a result of a drop in the mean performance of the nonstimulated children. Also, it is most important to note that at the end of successful treatment with physical recovery, both groups remained below age norms, with the greatest deficits evident in the area of language and communication.

At 3 to 4 years after discharge from the hospital, the children, together with two further groups consisting of their healthy young siblings and a healthy control group of unrelated children of the same low socioeconomic class, were reexamined on the Stanford–Binet intelligence test. The children rehabilitated from malnutrition had significantly lower IQs than those of both their siblings and the unrelated healthy controls. The children who had received stimulation during their hospitalization period had lower scores than did those who lacked added stimulation. Yatkin and McLaren considered that this lower performance of the previously stimulated group might be related to their lower socioeconomic conditions.

Through the inclusion in the study of a fifth group, consisting of children with malnutrition not severe enough to require hospitalization, Yatkin and McLaren found that hospitalization plays a minor role as a cause of depressed mental function in malnutrition. Similarly, Richardson (1976) found that although the IQs of Jamaican school-age children who had suffered severe protein–energy malnutrition in infancy correlated with the presence of the episode of severe malnutrition, there were also correlations with total body length at the time of intelligence testing and with a measure of the children's social background. The percentage of explained variance was lowest for the episode of malnutrition and greatest for the social attribute; body height gave an intermediate value.

Cravioto and Arrieta (in press) have attempted to assess the role of stimulation as a nonnutritional variable through the study of groups of severely malnourished infants below the age of 6 months, comparing the rates of mental development obtained with and without systematic stimulation added to the dietary and medical treatment of 36 infants. On admission, all infants showed arrested growth and development, with body weights and lengths comparable to those of a normal newborn or at most to a well-nourished 2-month-old infant in the vast majority of the patients. Developmental achievement was below 50% of age norms.

The program of systematic stimulation included several elements. First, the psychologist and the nurses attending the infants learned to provide a reproducible model of mother–child interaction based on the scales developed by Ainsworth, Bell, and Stayton (no date) for the measurement of mother–child transactions occurring during the first year of life. Second, the microenvironment of each stimulated infant was reconstructed to provide a high rating on the Caldwell home stimulation inventory. Third, based on the performance of each infant on the Gesell and the Uzgiris–McHunt Scales of Development, a detailed individual program was devised to stimulate the child to acquire the next behavioral step in each particular scale. Social reinforcement was the only type of reward given to the infants and staff. Nondesirable behaviors were not reinforced.

At the end of 6 months of treatment, it was apparent that infants who received systematic cognitive, language, and emotional stimulation in addition to the medical and dietary management, within the context of a good mother–child interaction, brought the majority of nutritionally rehabilitated infants (70–90%) back to the normal age-expected levels of performance on the Gesell Scales of Development. As a contrast, only 30% of the infants who received the dietary and medical treatment without systematic stimulation reached the levels of performance accepted as normal. A subgroup of these latter infants who were capable of eliciting from the staff actions that were considered as stimulating in themselves also presented more substantial gains than did the group that was only given the medical and dietary treatment currently in use in modern pediatric hospitals.

Preliminary results have shown that those infants whose mothers learned to carry on the program of systematic stimulation at home, and whose attitudes changed so that they took an active, engaging, and satisfying interactive role with their infants, have continued to present normal performance levels at each age tested. Mental scores and physical measurements appear to be independent of whether or not stimulation was provided during the children's hospital stay.

In a study of malnutrition and language development in a cohort of children followed from birth to 46 months of age, an analysis of the intercorrelations among variables was undertaken in order to separate the possible influences of stimuli deprivation from those of chronic protein–energy malnutrition (Cravioto & DeLicardie, 1973). The correlation between body height and language measures remained significant after partialing out the effect of home stimulation (.23 compared with .26 before partialing). This finding suggests that the association between height (as an indicator of nutritional status) and language is to a large extent independent of the effect of home stimulation. When the relationship between home stimulation and language was partialed out for body height, the correlation dropped from .20 to .15; and when the language measures were "held constant," the correlation between home stimulation and body height changed from .23 to .19. These results could be interpreted as meaning that home stimulation contributes relatively more to body height than it does to language, while body height contributes more than home stimulation does to the variance language.

In children rehabilitated from malnutrition, Klein, Lester, Yarbrough, and Habitch (1972) have reported that the level of prediction of cognitive function given by sociocultural factors such as quality of dwelling, father's formal education, mother's dress, mother's personal cleanliness, task instruction, and social contacts is significantly increased with the inclusion of body height and head circumference.

As a part of their longitudinal study on growth and development, DeLicardie and Cravioto (1974) analyzed the behavioral styles of response of children with and without a documented episode of severe clinical malnutrition. In order to control for level of measured intelligence, a comparison group of children of the same sex and IQ as the survivors of malnutrition was included, as well as a group of children without antecedents of severe malnutrition whose body weight, height, head, chest, and arm circumferences at birth were equal to those of the malnourished children. Significant differences were found between the styles of response according to the presence or absence of the antecedent of severe malnutrition. Differences in IQ could not account for differences in the style in which the children approached the task given by the examiner.

Since the survivors of malnutrition differed from the control children in the amount and type of stimulation available in their homes, survivors and controls with equal scores in home stimulation were compared in order to separate the effects of early malnutrition from those of stimuli deprivation. Controls, matched at birth, expressed their verbal network responses mainly in terms of rationalizations of competence; survivors of severe malnutrition expressed their responses predominantly as requests for aid. Controls matched with the survivors for sex and IQ had similar proportions of rationalizations of competence, requests for aid, and substitution of the task. These findings seem to indicate that besides the effect of stimuli deprivation on the style of response, severe malnutrition also modulates the style of behavior elicited.

In the attempt to separate the influences of social environment from those that may derive from malnutrition as such, studies on children from middle or high socioeconomic classes who suffered secondary malnutrition due to congenital pyloric stenosis or cystic fibrosis are relevant.

General intelligence (on the Peabody Picture Vocabulary Test and Raven Progressive Matrices) was assessed in 50 children—44 boys and 6 girls, aged from 5 to 14 years—who had been treated for congenital pyloric stenosis (Klein, Forber, & Nader, 1975). This disease involves a brief period of minimal to gross starvation during the period from birth to 3 months of life. Almost immediately after surgical correction, the child is able to consume an adequate diet with a rapid recovery of a normal nutritional status. The severity of starvation, for the purposes of the study, was determined as a percentage difference between an infant's weight on admission to the hospital and the expected weight for age, extrapolated from weight at birth. Two groups of children were used for comparison. The first consisted of the 44 siblings closest in age to the patient; the second had 50 children matched for age, sex, and father's level of education on a case-by-case basis.

There was a significant negative intragroup correlation between degree of severity of starvation and measured intelligence ($r = -.323$; $p < .05$), and also a significant correlation between severity of starvation and scores on a scale that measured parental evaluation of a child's intellectual development and expected educational potential ($r = .367$; $df = 49$; $p < .01$). However, there were no consistent differences in global intelligence among the index cases, siblings, and matched controls.

In a group of Swedish adults who had suffered from inanition starting between the ages of 6 and 20 days due to pyloric stenosis, Berlung and Rabo (1974) found a significant correlation between their height attained at adulthood and the weight loss and duration of the episode of starvation. Nonetheless, performance on an intelligence test administered at the time of induction into military service did not correlate with the antecedent of severe malnutrition in early infancy.

Intellectual performance, sensory–motor abilities, and social adaptation were studied by Lloyd-Still, Hurwitz, Wolff, and Schwachaman (1974) in a group of 41 patients, aged 2 to 21 years, who had suffered from severe malnutrition in the first 6 months of life but who came from an adequate socioeconomic environment. Of these patients, 34 had cystic fibrosis, 3 had ileal atresia, and the other 4 had protracted diarrhea. Their intellectual performance (on the Merrill–Palmer test) at ages 18 to 72 months was significantly lower than that of their siblings of similar age. However, in the patients 5 years or older, mean IQ values on the Wechsler Intelligence Scale for Children or Wechsler Adult Intelligence Scale were not significantly different between index cases and siblings. Neither motor abilities nor social adaptation, measured by the Lincoln–Oseretzky Test and the Vineland Scale, respectively, gave significantly different values in patients and siblings.

Winick, Meyer, and Harris (1975) have reported the effects of environmental enrichment by early adoption in three groups of Korean children who were adopted by North American families before their third year of life: (1) a "severely malnourished" group whose weights and heights at the time of adoption were below the 3rd percentile of Korean norms; (2) a "moderately nourished" group with both height and weight between the 3rd and the 25th percentiles; and (3) a "well-nourished" group with height and weight above the 25th percentile. At follow-up 4 to 13 years later, there were no differences in body weight among these three groups. Height, however, was significantly lower in the malnourished than in the well-nourished group, but not different from that of the moderately nourished group. The same pattern was found for both IQ and current achievement, with the added finding of a significant difference in achievement scores between the malnourished and the moderately nourished groups. The IQ and achievement scores in all three groups had values equal to or above the mean values for North American children. Similarly, all three groups had mean heights above the 50th percentile of the Korean standard. These findings show that an enriched environment can counteract the effects of early deprivation, but nevertheless that early nutritional deprivation is associated with later differences in intellectual performance within the normal range.

Recently (Cravioto, 1980), we have had the opportunity of analyzing the visual–kinesthetic and auditory–visual development of children with known nutritional histories during their first 7 years of life. Performance levels at ages 66, 73, 78, and 86 months, obtained in survivors of severe chronic malnutrition before 36 months of age, were compared with the levels attained by children from the same birth cohort and similar socioeconomic conditions, matched at birth for physical size and sensory–motor organization, who never had severe malnutrition.

In both neurointegrative aspects of development, the patterns of improvement in performance as a function of age exhibited by survivors of malnutrition and controls approximated the form of a growth function, with a marked difference in the value of the intercept and the age at which asymptotic values were attained. The longitudinal data clearly showed evidence of a marked delay in intersensory integration in the survivors in both visual–kinesthetic and auditory–visual development.

When the survivors of malnutrition were matched with well-nourished controls for total (low) stimulation available in the home, their lower levels of competence persisted in the visual–kinesthetic abilities. The picture for the development of auditory–visual integration was markedly different. At all ages tested, the proportions of low and high performers were about the same in both groups.

Data from previous studies on visual–kinesthetic integration (Champakam, Srikantia, & Gopalan, 1968; Cravioto, DeLicardie, & Birch, 1966; Cravioto, Birch, & DeLicardie, 1967; Cravioto, DeLicardie, Piñeiro, Lindoro, Arroyo, Alcalde, 1971; Srikantia *et al.*, 1975) are in agreement with our longitudinal results in the sense that severe malnutrition, independently of the characteristics of the stimulation available at home, is per se strongly associated with the levels of competence in the visual–kinesthetic task. Since the quality and quantity of the stimulation available at home also shows a significant correlation with the intersensory task, the developmental lag observed in survivors of malnutrition appears to be the result of the effects of earlier malnutrition in association with certain microenvironmental factors related to child care.

The findings for auditory–visual integration, as noted, give a totally different picture. The performance of the survivors was at the same (low) level observed in control children, when the effects of home stimulation were partialed out. The disappearance of the developmental lag in the survivors points to a strong association between stimulation available in the home and competence in auditory–visual integration, and to a lack of association between a previous history of severe malnutrition and auditory–visual competence.

The importance of sorting out specific mental abilities as a function of the macro- and microenvironmental factors that would exert a more powerful influence on them is obvious from both the practical and theoretical viewpoints.

Barnes and his associates, on the basis of their results from a large series of studies on experimental animals, prefer to speak of the interaction between malnutrition and environmental stimulation (Barnes, 1968; Barnes, Moore, & Pond, 1970; Frankova & Barnes, 1968; Levistky & Barnes, 1972, 1973). These authors have considered that the physiological mechanisms that may be responsible for the long-term beneficial effects of early stimulation may not be operative if a concurrent state of malnutrition is present during a critical period of development. Malnutrition may thus change environmental experiences by physiologically rendering an animal less capable of receiving or integrating information about the environment. Even in the absence of biochemical alterations of the brain, malnutrition may elicit behavior (particularly apathy and social withdrawal in humans; see DeLicardie & Cravioto, 1974) that is incompatible with the incorporation of environmental information necessary for optimum cognitive development.

Recently, Morgan and Winick (1980b) have reported that early stimulation of rat pups during the first 3 weeks of life reduces the change in open-field behavior caused by malnutrition at 21 days postnatally. The improved behavior was associated with a significantly higher ganglioside and glycoprotein *N*-acetylneuraminic acid (NANA) in the cerebrum and cerebellum. After 6 months of nutrition rehabilitation, early stimulation continued to be associated with better performance on a Y maze. The biochemical changes in the cerebrum also persisted into adulthood.

Searching for the importance of these biochemical findings, in a second study, Morgan and Winick (1980a) injected NANA into rat pups, while controls received glucose injections. The administration of NANA was associated with an increase in cerebral and cerebellar ganglioside and glycoprotein NANA concentrations. There was also a concomitant reduction in the expected behavioral abnormalities secondary to malnutrition. After 6 months of nutrition rehabilitation, rats treated with NANA from the 14th to the 21st day of life learned a Y maze more quickly than controls did, and the biochemical changes in brain persisted. The results point toward the possibility that early stimulation might affect behavior through changes in NANA concentration.

The similarity of the biochemical changes produced in the brain by either malnutrition or stimuli deprivation (Castilla, Cravioto, & Cravioto, 1979) is of primary importance, since it leads to the consideration that most probably no single disadvantage plays a major part in lowering human achievement in malnourished populations. As Dobbing (1976) has emphasized, the human may have an outstanding capacity to compensate for one disadvantage by utilizing an advantage of another type.

The main questions for further research in the field of nutrition, mental development, learning, and behavior should concern the description and documentation of the mechanisms of action of malnutrition per se or in conjunction with other features of the unfavorable environment in which malnutrition thrives.

Findings in humans and in experimental animals lead to a concept of an ecological "spiral effect." A low level of adaptive capacity, ignorance, social custom, infection, or environmental paucity of foodstuffs and stimuli all appear to result in malnutrition, which may produce a large pool of individuals who come to function in suboptimal ways. Such persons are themselves more ready to be victims of ignorance and less effective than otherwise would be the case in their social adaptation. In turn, they may rear children under conditions and in a fashion designed to produce a new generation of malnourished individuals.

References

Ainsworth, M., Bell, S. M., & Stayton, D. J. *Four scales for rating maternal behavior*. Unpublished manuscript, no date.

Barnes, R. H. Behavioral changes caused by malnutrition in the rat and the pig. In D. C. Glass (Ed.), *Environmental influences*. New York: Rockefeller University Press and Russell Sage Foundation, 1968.

Barnes, R. H., Moore, A. V., & Pond, W. G. Behavioral abnormalities in young adult pigs caused by malnutrition in early life. *Journal of Nutrition*, 1970, *100*, 145–155.

Bayley, N. *Maternal psychological profile*. Unpublished manuscript, 1964.

Bengoa, J. M. The problem of malnutrition. *WHO Chronicle*, 1974, *28*, 3–7.

Berlung, G., & Rabo, E. A long-term follow-up investigation of patients with hypertrophic pyloric stenosis, with special reference to the physical and mental development. *Acta Paediatrica Scandinavica*, 1947, *62*, 125–129.

Birch, H. G., Piñeiro, C., Alcalde, E., Toca, T., & Cravioto, J. Relation of kwashiorkor in early childhood and intelligence at school age. *Pediatric Research*, 1971, *5*, 579–585.

Caldwell, B. M. Descriptive evaluation of child development and of developmental settings. *Pediatrics*, 1967, *40*, 46–54.

Castilla, L., Cravioto, A., & Cravioto, J. Efectos a corto plazo de la interacción estimulación–desnutrición proteíco–calorica sobre el desarrollo bioquímico. *Gaceta Médica de México*, 1979, *115*, 225–233.

Champakam, S., Srikantia, S., & Gopalan, C. Kwashiorkor and mental development. *American Journal of Clinical Nutrition*, 1968, *21*, 844–852.

Chase, P. H., & Martin, H. P. Undernutrition and child development. *New England Journal of Medicine*, 1970, *282*, 933–976.

Cravioto, J. Appraisal of the effect of nutrition on biochemical maturation. *American Journal of Clinical Nutrition*, 1962, *11*, 484–492.

Cravioto, J. Intersensory development in survivors of early malnutrition and stimuli deprivation. In P. B. Pearson & J. R. Greenwell (Eds.), *Nutrition, food, and man*. Tucson: University of Arizona Press, 1980.

Cravioto, J., & Arrieta, R. The effect of added systematic stimulation on the mental recovery of severely malnourished infants less than six months old. *The Pediatrician*, in press.

Cravioto, J., Birch, H. G., & DeLicardie, E. R. Influencia de la desnutrición sobre la capacidad de aprendizaje del niño escolar. *Boletín Médico Hospital Infantil de México*, 1967, *24*, 217–233.

Cravioto, J., Birch, H. G., DeLicardie, E. R., & Rosales, L. The ecology of infant weight gain in a preindustrial society. *Acta Paediatrica Scandinavica*, 1967, *56*, 71–84.

Cravioto, J., & DeLicardie, E. R. Mental performance in school-age children: Findings after recovery from early severe malnutrition. *American Journal of Diseases of Children*, 1970, *120*, 404–410.

Cravioto, J., & DeLicardie, E. R. Environmental correlates of severe clinical malnutrition and language development in survivors from kwashiorkor or marasmus. *Boletín Oficina Sanitaria Panamericana* (English edition), 1973, *7*, 50–70.

Cravioto, J., & DeLicardie, E. R. Size at birth and preschool severe malnutrition. *Acta Paediatrica Scandinavica*, 1974, *63*, 577–580.

Cravioto, J., & DeLicardie, E. R. Mother–infant relationship prior to the development of clinical severe malnutrition in the child. In P. L. White & N. Selvey (Eds.), *Proceedings, VI Western Hemisphere Nutrition Congress*. Acton, Massachusetts: Publishing Sciences Group, 1975.

Cravioto, J., DeLicardie, E. R., & Birch, H. G. Nutrition, growth and neurointegrative development: An experimental and ecologic study. *Pediatrics*, 1966, *38*, 319–372.

Cravioto, J., DeLicardie, E. R., Piñeiro, C., Lindoro, M., Arroyo, M., & Alcalde, E. Neurointegrative development and intelligence in school children recovered from malnutrition in infancy. *Proceedings of the Nutrition Society of India*, 1971, *10*, 192–215.

Cravioto, J., Lindoro, M., & Birch, H. G. Sex differences in I.Q. pattern of children with congenital heart defects. *Science*, 1971, *174*, 1042–1043.

Cravioto, J., Piñeiro, C., Arroyo, M., & Alcalde, E. Mental performance of school children who suffered malnutrition in early age. In Swedish Nutrition Foundation (Ed.), *Nutrition in preschool and school age*. Uppsala: Almquist & Wiksells, 1969.

Cravioto, J., & Robles, B. The influence of protein–calorie malnutrition on psychological test behavior. In Swedish Nutrition Foundation (Ed.), *Mild-moderate forms of protein-calorie malnutrition*. Uppsala: Almquist & Wiksells, 1963.

Cravioto, J., & Robles, B. Evolution of adaptive and motor behavior during rehabilitation from kwashiorkor. *American Journal of Orthopsychiatry*, 1965, *35*, 449-464.

DeLicardie, E. R., & Cravioto, J. Behavioral responsiveness of survivors of clinical severe malnutrition to cognitive demands. In J. Cravioto, L. Hambraeus, & B. Valhquist (Eds.), *Early malnutrition and mental development*. Uppsala: Almquist & Wiksells, 1974.

DeLicardie, E. R., Vega, L., Birch, H. G., & Cravioto, J. The effect of weight loss from birth to fifteen days on growth and development in their first year. *Biologia Neonatorum*, 1971, *17*, 249-259.

Dobbing, J. Vulnerable periods in brain growth and somatic growth. In D. F. Roberts & A. M. Thomson (Eds.), *The biology of human fetal growth*. London: Taylor & Francis, 1976.

Dobbing, J., & Kersley, J. B. The vulnerability of the developing brain. *Journal of Physiology*, 1963, *166*, 34.

Frankova, S., & Barnes, R. H. Effect of malnutrition in early life on avoidance conditioning and behavior of adult rats. *Journal of Nutrition*, 1968, *96*, 485-493.

Guillen-Alvarez, G. Influence of severe marasmic malnutrition in early infancy on mental development at school age. In Wienner Medizinischen Akademic (Ed.), *Proceedings, XII International Congress of Pediatrics*. Vienna: 1971.

Hertzig, M. E., Birch, H. G., Richardson, S. A., & Tizard, J. Intellectual levels of school-age children severely malnourished during the first two years of life. *Pediatrics*, 1972, *49*, 814-824.

Hoorveg, J., & Standfield, P. The influence of malnutrition on psychologic and neurologic development: Preliminary communication. In Pan-American Health Organization (Ed.), *Nutrition, the nervous system and behavior* (PAHO Scientific Publication No. 251). Washington, D.C.: Pan-American Health Organization, 1972.

Jackson, C. M., & Stewart, C. A. The effect of inanition in the young upon the ultimate size of the body and of the various organs in the albino rat. *Journal of Experimental Zoology*, 1920, *30*, 97-128.

Keys, A., Brozek, J., Henschel, A., Mickelson, O., & Taylor, H. L. *The biology of human starvation* (Vol. 2). Minneapolis: University of Minnesota Press, 1950.

Klein, P. S., Forber, G. B., & Nader, P. R. Effects of starvation in infancy (pyloric stenosis) on subsequent learning abilities. *Pediatrics*, 1975, *87*, 8-15.

Klein, R. E., Lester, B. M., Yarbrough, C., & Habitch, J. P. On malnutrition and development: Some preliminary findings. In A. Chávez, H. Bourges, & S. Basta (Eds.), *Proceedings, IX International Congress of Nutrition, México*. Basel: Karger, 1972.

Kugelmass, I. N., Poull, L. E., & Samuel, E. L. Nutritional improvement of child mentality. *American Journal of Medical Sciences*, 1944, *204*, 631-633.

Lashley, K. S. *Brain mechanisms and intelligence*. Chicago: University of Chicago Press, 1929.

Levistky, D. V., & Barnes, R. H. Nutritional and environmental interactions in the behavioral development of the rat: Long-term effects. *Science*, 1972, *176*, 68-71.

Levistky, D. V., & Barnes, R. H. Malnutrition and animal behavior. In D. J. Kallen (Ed.), *Nutrition, development and social behavior* (Publication No. NIH73-242). Washington, D.C.: U.S. Government Printing Office, 1973.

Lloyd-Still, J. D., Hurwitz, I., Wolff, P. H., & Schwachaman, H. Intellectual development after malnutrition in infancy. *Pediatrics*, 1974, *54*, 306-311.

Maier, N. R. R., & Schneirla, T. C. *Principles of animal behavior*. New York: McGraw-Hill, 1935.

Martínez, P. D., Ramos-Galván, R., & De La Fuente, R. Los factores ambientales en la pelagra de los niños de México. *Boletín Médico del Hospital Infantil de México*, 1951, *6*, 743-749.

McCall, R. B., Hogarty, P. S., & Hulburt, N. Transitions in infant sensorimotor development and the prediction of childhood I.Q. *American Psychologist*, 1972, *27*, 728-748.

McLaren, D. S. A fresh look at protein-calorie malnutrition. *Lancet*, 1966, *2*, 485-488.

Morgan, B. L. G., & Winick, M. Effects of administration of *N*-acetylneuraminic acid (NANA) on brain NANA content and behavior. *Journal of Nutrition*, 1980, *110*, 416-424. (a)

Morgan, B. L. G., & Winick, M. Effects of environmental stimulation on brain *N*-acetylneuraminic acid content and behavior. *Journal of Nutrition*, 1980, *110*, 425-432. (b)

Nwuga, V. C. B. Effect of severe kwashiorkor on intellectual development among Nigerian children. *American Journal of Clinical Nutrition*, 1977, *30*, 1423-1430.

Pollitt, E., & Thomson, C. Protein-calorie malnutrition and behavior: A view from psychology. In R. G. Wurtman & J. J. Wurtman (Eds.), *Nutrition and the brain* (Vol. 2). New York: Raven Press, 1977.

Richardson, S. A. The relation of severe malnutrition in infancy to the intelligence of school children with differing life histories. *Pediatric Research*, 1976, *10*, 57–61.

Srikantia, S. G., & Sastry, C. Y. Effect of maternal attributes on malnutrition in children. *Proceedings, I Asian Congress of Nutrition*, India, 1972.

Srikantia, S. G., Sastry, C. Y., & Naidu, A. N. Malnutrition and mental function. *Proceedings, X International Congress of Nutrition*, Kyoto, Japan, 1975.

Stein, Z., Susser, M. W., Saenger, G., & Marolla, F. *Famine and human development: The Dutch hunger winter 1944–1945*. London: Oxford University Press, 1975.

Winick, M., Meyer, K. K., & Harris, R. C. Malnutrition and environmental enrichment by early adoption. *Science*, 1975, *190*, 1173–1175.

Yatkin, U. S., & McLaren, D. S. The behavioral development of infants recovering from severe malnutrition. *Journal of Mental Deficiency Research*, 1970, *14*, 25–32.

CHAPTER THREE

Poisoning in Childhood

PHILIP J. GRAHAM

In the modern world, children's brains are exposed to a wide variety of toxins arising in different ways from a variety of sources. Classification can be achieved in a number of ways, but perhaps the most obviously appropriate for psychiatric purposes involves initial separate consideration of acute and chronic poisoning.

Symptoms attributable to acute central nervous system (CNS) involvement that can be produced by toxic agents include coma, delirium, and mental disturbances (especially temporary psychotic states); convulsions; headaches; muscle spasms; and general or partial paralysis (Arena, 1970). Such acute symptomatology is produced by literally dozens of different poisons, and, although a few produce characteristic symptoms and signs, most do not.

Chronic CNS involvement can result in a rather wide range of effects, including fluctuating levels of consciousness, general or specific deficits of cognitive functioning (especially memory impairment), chronic psychotic states, and a range of emotional and behavioral disorders, as well as disorders of nerve or muscle function.

Both acute and chronic poisoning can be produced accidentally or nonaccidentally. The source of accidental poisoning may be the home (where a child may be exposed to a range of drugs and domestic products as well as poisoned food), school or work, and the atmosphere. The motivation underlying nonaccidental poisoning is varied. Thus children and adolescents may poison themselves with suicidal intent, or they may show parasuicidal behavior, intending to harm but not to kill themselves. They may poison their own brains for hedonistic reasons, with substances such as alcohol and amphetamines. They may be poisoned by others who have homicidal intention or who, by analogy with parasuicide, apparently intend to harm but not to kill them. Finally, they may be poisoned accidentally by agents such as antidepressants, anticonvulsants, and tranquilizers that have been given to them with therapeutic intentions.

ACUTE ACCIDENTAL POISONING

Although it is certain that in Western society and even in many developing countries (Bannerjee & Battachariya, 1978) acute accidental poisoning is very

Philip J. Graham. Department of Child Psychiatry, University of London Institute of Child Health, London, England; Department of Child Psychiatry, Hospital for Sick Children, London, England.

common, it is difficult to state with any precision just how common it is. Reports from poison centers established to advise on management, especially management of severe or unusual forms of poisoning, will only provide an incomplete picture. Statistics from hospital accident and emergency departments provide a better source, particularly as it is known that family physicians tend to refer to such departments virtually all cases about which they are contacted. However, much accidental poisoning of a mild nature must be dealt with in the home without the help of professional advice.

Statistics from accident and emergency departments may also be misleading, however, because they tend to include children who have been brought because of a worry that they *might* have ingested a harmful agent when in fact this has not been the case. Calnan, Dale, and de Fonseka (1976), for example, studying an English population, found the rate of suspected poisoning (an episode requiring medical attention) in children under the age of 15 years to be 3.4 per 1000 per year and 8.7 per 1000 per year in children under the age of 5 years. However, intensive interviewing of parents who had sought medical advice for the problem, together with an examination of casualty department records, revealed that in 65% of the cases the children had not in fact ingested the suspected materials or had ingested innocuous substances. Even in the remaining 35%, in about a third of the cases the children had in fact suffered no symptoms that could be attributed to toxic effects. It is thus necessary to treat with some caution findings such as those of Silva, Buckfield, Spears, and Williams (1978), who found, in a total population of 3-year-olds living in Dunedin, New Zealand, that 78% of them had ingested poison in a sufficiently worrying manner to result in the seeking of medical advice. Nevertheless, the figures for accidental poisoning are impressively high, and Deeths and Breeden (1971) quote their own work and the work of others to suggest that in the U.S. population of children under 5 years of age, there are approximately 2 million poisoning episodes and 400 deaths per year. Most studies on the subject suggest that boys are involved in accidental poisoning rather more commonly than girls and that the peak age of incidence is around 18 months to 2.5 years. A fatal outcome for children who accidentally poison themselves is apparently less common in the United Kingdom, and an average of about 30 deaths per year in children under 10 years of age occurred in England, Wales, and Scotland between 1958 and 1977 (Fraser, 1980).

The type of substance ingested by young children when they are accidentally poisoned will, of course, vary with what is available. In most Western homes self-prescribed drugs, and particularly aspirin in one or other of its forms, usually head the list of poisons accidentally taken. Thus, studying admissions to a pediatric hospital, Deeths and Breeden (1971) found that drugs accounted for 58% of poisoning episodes, with aspirin compounds responsible in about three-fifths of the drug cases. Hydrocarbons used as distillates or solvents accounted for 18%. Most drug studies suggest that, after aspirin compounds, psychotropic drugs—especially minor tranquilizers and antidepressants—are the most common type of pharmacological agent involved. By contrast, in Calcutta, India, in an area serving both an urban and a rural population, Bannerjee and Battachariya (1978), studying the statistics of a pediatric ward for 1968 and 1976, found kerosene oil to be the most common toxin ingested in both these years. Ominously, medical agents that caused only 3.8% of accidental poisoning episodes in 1968 in Calcutta were responsible for 12.3% by 1976. In the United

States, the most common nonmedicinal household products ingested by children and leading to admission in poisoning centers are, in order of descending importance, cosmetics, pesticides, petroleum products, soaps and cleaners, bleaches, disinfectants and deodorizers, polishers and waxes, and lye and other corrosives (Done, 1970).

Patterns of drugs responsible for fatal overdoses have varied over the years and, in the 1970s, tricyclic antidepressants became the leading fatal poisons (Fraser, 1980). Children who are accidentally poisoned differ in background from those who are not. Sobel (1970) noted that previous investigations, such as that by Baltimore and Meyer (1968), had failed to demonstrate that parental ignorance regarding the effect of drugs or the care with which drugs were stored away explained accident proneness in young children. Rather, they had suggested that the nature of family relationships was more important than cognitive factors were in etiology. In an investigation of 122 poisoned children under 5 years of age identified in the community and compared to 278 randomly selected controls, Sobel found no relationships on a "hazard" scale measuring the degree to which substances were left around. There were also no relationships with socioeconomic status. By contrast, significant differences between the groups were found in the quality of struggle for power within the home, marital disharmony, parental mental illness, and family stress. Psychopathological factors within a child, such as childhood neuroticism, were also significantly related to accidental poisoning. The possible importance of the factors within the child is also suggested by the findings of Stewart, Thach, and Freidin (1970) that children who had been accidentally poisoned at a mean age of 2.6 years were found to show more hyperkinetic behavior than children in a control group were when followed up on average 6 years later. Further, a group of hyperactive children were reported by their parents to have a history of more frequent accidents in the past than those of a nonhyperkinetic control group. Shaw (1977) compared 50 preschool children thought to have ingested poison with 50 controls and found that the poisoned children had had more changes of accommodation during their lives. Their fathers had had more jobs and had themselves a more frequent history of involvement in accidents of different types. The homes from which these children came were rated as less stimulating, and the children's explorative tendencies were more developed. On the basis of these findings, Shaw pointed to the similarities between the background of accidentally poisoned children and those subject to nonaccidental injury.

Many of these studies of background factors in acute accidental poisoning are retrospective, and one possible confounding factor that must be considered is that the behavioral and cognitive differences within the children, such as differences in IQ and hyperkinesis, are the result of the poisoning rather than exclusively related to etiology. This issue is considerably clarified by the study of Angle, McIntire, and Meile (1968), who compared 41 children admitted to a poisoning center with acute CNS intoxication with a similar number of paired controls also hospitalized for accidental poisoning but free of CNS symptomatology. The controls were matched closely for age, sex, race, and socioeconomic background, and the follow-up examinations carried out in ignorance of the type of poisoning originally suffered 18 months to 14 years after the poisoning occurred. There were no differences in IQ as assessed on the Stanford–Binet, in electroencephalogram (EEG) abnormalities, in visuomotor performance, or in the rate of behavior disturbance. Behavior disturbance was very common (40%) in both groups. The only adverse sequelae were found in a subgroup of children mainly poisoned by insecticides, who had repeated convulsions at the time of their original admission. These had lower than expected IQ scores and deficits on visuomotor performance. As, overall, the group of acutely poisoned children with CNS involvement did not show impairment of cognitive performance and behavioral problems when compared to non-CNS-affected children, it seems likely that retrospective studies of background factors are likely to be valid in their conclusions, provided that other methodological conditions of such studies are met satisfactorily.

ACUTE NONACCIDENTAL POISONING

Although homicidal poisoning of children and poisoning them with intent to injure but not to kill them does occur, it seems to be very rare. The most common forms of acute nonaccidental poisoning, therefore, are motivated by self-injury or by the desire to achieve pleasure in one form or another.

In the United Kingdom and the United States, suicide rates are very low indeed up to the age of 15 years (Shaffer, 1974), when they show a sharp increase, though there are grounds for thinking that in Japan, the United Kingdom, and the United States, suicide in the preadolescent child may be becoming less rare. In the 15- to 19-year age group, suicide is largely achieved by self-poisoning. Parasuicide, defined by Kreitman (1977) as a nonfatal act in which an individual deliberately causes self-injury or ingests a substance in excess of any prescribed or generally recognized therapeutic dosage, is also unusual before the age of 14 years; although anecdotal reports, especially from the West Coast of the United States, suggest that the rates of parasuicide are rising rapidly even in preadolescent and pubescent children, they are still relatively low compared with those in the later teenage years. However, in the 15- to 19-year age group, rates rise sharply, and this trend has increased over recent years. Thus in Edinburgh (Kreitman, 1977), rates in males rose from 39 per 100,000 population in 1962–1963 to 471 per 100,000 in 1974. In females the rates for the same age group over the corresponding period rose from 288 per 100,000 to 1006 per 100,000. The proportion of parasuicidal activity that is due to self-poisoning is very high.

The acute toxic effects of the various drugs involved are well known and depend on the nature of the medication (Teitelbaum, 1970). Stimulants or analeptics and dysleptic (consciousness-distorting) agents produce hyperactivity, restlessness, seizures, and psychotic manifestations. The subject may, in an irrational, restless phase, attempt to harm himself or herself further. Depression of consciousness, sometimes leading to coma and death, results from ingestion of sedatives and neuroleptic drugs. Assuming survival from the suicidal attempt, long-term cognitive or behavioral effects arising from the acute insult to the brain do not appear to be recorded. If prolonged anoxia occurs as a result of the depression of centers controlling vital functions, then this can lead to permanent brain damage, with consequent paralysis and intellectual deterioration. The distinction between acute and chronic poisoning, when poisoning occurs in teenagers taking drugs for the purposes of pleasure or the extension of life experience and sometimes leads to addiction, is not easy to make. Consequently, the discussion of the effects of toxins ingested or inhaled in this manner is postponed to the section on chronic nonaccidental poisoning.

CHRONIC ACCIDENTAL POISONING

Food Additives

It has been suggested (Feingold, 1975) that food additives such as tartrazine and salicylates are a potent cause of hyperactivity in children. If this is indeed the case, and controlled trials cast considerable doubt on the validity of this hypothesis except perhaps in a small minority of young children (Goyette, Conners, Petti, & Curtis, 1976; Weiss, Williams, Margen, Abrams, Caan, Citron, Cox, McKibben, Ogar, & Schultz, 1980), the mode of action is uncertain—it could be toxic, or it could constitute some form of idiosyncratic response. However, Augustine and Levitan's (1980) demonstration that the food dye erythrosine impairs neurotransmitter release in isolated neuromuscular synapses in the frog suggests a direct toxic mechanism. This issue, which has been well reviewed elsewhere (Conners, 1980; Taylor, 1979) is not considered further here.

Lead

If food additives are excluded from consideration, the only major cause of chronic nonaccidental poisoning is exposure to heavy metals. Of these, lead, mercury, thallium, arsenic, and cadmium have been described as causing the occasional and unusual cases seen in poisoning centers. Lead, however, is still not an unusual cause of serious poisoning in the United States; it has also been suggested (and this is a matter of considerable controversy) that exposure to moderate or even low levels of lead in the environment may produce adverse cognitive and behavioral effects. For this reason, and because most recent work on toxic effects on children concentrates on this issue, most attention in this review is given to this problem.

Sources

Lead occurs naturally in the earth, but Patterson (1965) has calculated that, because of man-made industrial sources, existing rates of lead absorption in inhabitants of the United States not exposed to undue amounts of the substance are about 30 times the natural rates. He has claimed that existing body burdens of lead are about 100 times the natural burden so that, whereas an average body burden would be in the region of .2 $\mu\%$, existing actual body burdens are reflected in mean rates of 15–25 $\mu\%$. Such estimates of the importance of industrial contamination are not uncontested. Fosse and Justesen (1978), for example, estimating lead in teeth, probably currently the most accurate measure of chronic lead exposure, found that the mean level of deciduous teeth from individuals living in Bergen in the Middle Ages (1.24 μg) was virtually the same as that in rural Norway today. However, teeth taken from children in urban Norwegian areas had levels three to four times those in medieval Bergen.

Although it seems certain that human industrial activity has contributed to the level of lead in the environment, the relative contributions from different sources are unclear. Diet is said to be a major source (Needleman & Piomelli, 1978), with some lead being incorporated from soil into vegetables as they grow and more being added in the process of canning. However, lead may enter into the diet because particulate matter from the atmosphere has settled upon and contaminated food. Atmospheric lead may therefore contribute indirectly through diet as well as directly through the inhalation of small particles (1–5 μm). Probably lead enters the atmosphere mainly from emissions from automobiles, as currently (in the United Kingdom) lead additives are added to petrol (gasoline) in the process of refinement. Waldron (1975) found that the mean blood level of people living near a newly opened British motorway intersection showed an increase of 5.3 μg (males) and 4.0 μg (females) over the 1-year period after the motorway had opened. On the other hand, Ter Haar and Aronow (1975), utilizing the fact that a radioactive isotope of lead (Pb 210) occurs naturally in the atmosphere but hardly at all in lead from other sources, concluded on the basis of their findings, though these have been strongly challenged, that dust and air-suspended particles are not important sources of lead in urban children. Although Stephens (1978) claims that a convincing case has been made for the importance of gasoline emissions in contributing to total lead body burden, probably it is still true (Department of the Environment, 1974) that it is very difficult to assess the relative importance of all the pathways of lead into human beings. The evidence on this point has been well summarized (Department of Health and Social Security, 1980). It is well established that children living near sources of unduly high quantities of lead show high levels of lead in their bodies, no matter how this is measured. Lansdown, Shepherd, Clayton, Delves, Graham, and Turner (1974), for example, found a significant (although weak—.18) positive correlation between lead levels in children living near a lead smelter factory and distance of children from the factory.

Metabolic Effects of Lead

Lead may affect the CNS in a number of different ways. Thus the presence of lead has been shown in rats to affect the activity of a brain enzyme, cerebellar adenyl cyclase, which is necessary for the transmission of nervous impulses (Nathanson & Bloom, 1975). As well as its effect on enzyme activity, and probably mediated by its affinity for amino acids containing sulphur, lead also binds itself to cell mitochondria and thus affects the transport of oxygen in cell metabolism (Needleman & Piomelli, 1978). In rats succumbing to lead poisoning, gross anatomical changes have been shown, in addition to widespread cellular damage to the brain, which tends to be most marked in the cerebellum. Blackman (1937) demonstrated capillary necrosis and thrombosis in the brains of children dying of lead poisoning several decades ago. Lead is not thought to be a necessary constituent of any normal metabolic process.

Animal Studies

A variety of experiments in animals has demonstrated adverse effects of lead on learning tasks. Young pups born to adult rats who were dosed with lead before conception (Brady, Herrera, & Zenick, 1975) showed deficits in a black–white discrimination learning task. The effect of preconception lead administration to the paternal rat was as great as that to the maternal rat, suggesting a gametotoxic effect. Carson, van Gelder, Karas, and Buck (1975) showed retarded discrimination learning in lambs whose mothers were experimentally exposed to lead in pregnancy. Silbergeld and Goldberg (1974) have produced hyperactive behavior in mice by dosing their mothers' milk with lead, and Bushnell and Bowman (1979) produced similar reversal learning deficits by administering lead to rhesus monkeys in the first year of life.

Animal work, therefore, has demonstrated that adverse effects occur when lead is administered at any stage of development, that such effects may involve both learning and behavior, and that they appear dose-related. The usual problems of generalizing from animal work to human behavior and learning exist in this area of study. It is unclear, for example, how far blood lead levels can really be equated, and in one experiment a number of animals died, suggesting that the workers were exposing animals to encephalopathogenic doses. It is also sometimes uncertain whether reported effects are due to toxicity or to associated undernutrition.

Methods of Estimating Body Lead in Children

Blood lead is the most common measure for estimating lead in the body. This can be reliably assessed in a variety of ways, but because lead is relatively rapidly cleared from the blood, it only provides an estimate of the level of absorption over the previous few days. In children who have been living in the same environment for many years, it can be assumed that repeated blood estimations probably provide a good indicator of the level of chronic exposure. Single blood levels may be misleading with respect to the individual child, though they will provide reasonable indications of exposure if groups of children are examined. In general, groups of children living in urban environments not usually contaminated by lead may be expected to have mean blood lead levels in the region of 10 to 25 μg/100 ml. Children living in mildly contaminated environments will have levels in the range of 26 to 40 μg/100 ml; in moderately contaminated environments, 40 to 60 μg/100 ml; and in severely contaminated environments, more than 60 μg/100 ml.

More recently, it has become generally accepted that estimates of lead in deciduous teeth provide a potentially better index of chronic lead exposure. Lead is stored in teeth, but in general is not mobilized from this store, so that tooth lead should provide a satisfactory picture of cumulative exposure. Again, reliable methods of estimation have been demonstrated, although there are large differences among laboratories' results and sometimes between studies published by the same laboratory in levels found, depending on the methods used and the part of the tooth examined. Thus Needleman and Shapiro (1974) initially reported mean dentine lead levels of 84 μg/g using one method of estimation, whereas later studies from the same or a closely adjacent area using another method appear to have found mean levels in the region of 12 μg/g. By contrast, Winneke (1979) found a mean of 4.57 μg/g in children living in Duisberg, West Germany—a moderately contaminated city. Explanation of the differences may lie in variations in method (e.g., dentine lead versus whole-tooth estimations), but comparison of findings is often made more difficult by unexplained discrepancies. Further, it is not yet possible to compare with any confidence levels of tooth lead with repeated levels of blood lead. Presumably, a chronically elevated blood lead level may be expected to be linked to a raised tooth lead level. Needleman's findings suggest that tooth lead differences of at least 18 μg were preceded 3 or 4 years earlier by mean blood lead differences of only 11.4 μg/100 ml. Winneke (1979) suggests differences of 2 μg tooth lead reflect differences of 5 μg/100 ml blood lead. The relationship between tooth lead and blood lead estimations is therefore quite unclear.

Finally, Pueschel, Kopito, and Schwachmann (1972) and Pihl and Parkes (1977) have reported studies examining lead in hair. Clearly hair is a readily available source of material for analysis, but until further information is available on the reliability of estimation, the relationship to other estimates of lead body burden, and the effect of environmental contaminants on levels found, it would seem unwise to rely exclusively on this method of analysis.

Cognitive–Behavioral Sequelae of High Lead Body Burdens

In general, high lead body burdens may be said to be reflected in blood lead levels of more than 60 μg/100 ml. It can be assumed that children who have been suffering from overt symptoms and signs of lead poisoning fall into this group. Byers and Lord (1943) reported the outcome in 20 children who had shown nonencephalopathic symptoms of lead poisoning between the ages of 1 and 3 years when examined later between the ages of 6 and 12 years. The study was uncontrolled, but the severity of the deficits over a wide range of intellectual and behavioral variables was considerable. Thirty-five years later, Sachs, Krall, McCaughran, Rozenfeld, Yongsmith, Growe, Lazar, Novar, O'Connell, and Rayson (1978) reported on a group of children who had been treated for lead poisoning at ages ranging from 14 to 72 months. At that time, their lead levels were estimated at between 50 and 365 μg/100 ml. When compared later with their siblings next in age who had had mean blood levels less than 40 μg/100 ml, no significant differences were found over a wide range of measures, except for the arithmetic subtest. However, examination of the results reveals reasonably consistent nonsignificant differences in the expected direction, especially in the tests of visuomotor integration.

Finally, the work of Kotok (1972) and Kotok, Kotok, and Heriot (1977) should be mentioned. In the earlier of these two papers, a group of children with elevated (mean 58 μg/100 ml) blood lead levels were found not to differ on the Denver developmental screening test from a group of children with normal levels. This work was criticized because of the relative crudity of the measure of cognitive development used, and in the later paper a much wider range of variables was assessed. A group of 31 children (mean age 43 months), with blood lead levels of 61 μg/100 ml to 200 μg/100 ml, was matched with a group of 36 children of similar age, sex, and social class. Results favored the control group on tests of social maturity, spatial ability, spoken vocabulary, information, comprehension, and auditory memory, although the results only reached a significant level in the case of spatial ability and in most instances the differences found were in the region of 1 to 6 points.

Rummo, Routh, Rummo, and Brown (1979) studied 45 4- to 8-year-old children who had been exposed to lead in their domestic environment. A group of 10 children who had a mean blood lead level of 64 μg/100 ml and had suffered encephalopathic symptoms was found to be significantly different from a normal control group on a range of measures (e.g., a 10-point difference on a test of perceptual performance, and an 11-point difference on a memory scale). These results suggest that a high or severe lead body burden is inconsistently associated with small 2- to 5-point differences over a range of cognitive measures unless encephalopathic symptoms have occurred, in which cases the differences found are generally greater.

Cognitive–Behavioral Sequelae of Moderately Raised Lead Body Burdens

De la Burdé and Choate (1975) compared 67 children with a history of eating plaster and paint at 1 to 3 years of age and mean blood levels of 40 μg/100 ml with a control group of 70 children living in domestic circumstances where such behavior was less possible, but controlled for sex, race, and several socioeconomic variables. The comparisons were made when the children were 7 to 8 years old. Lead-exposed children were significantly more likely to be borderline or mentally defective, though the mean full-scale Wechsler Intelligence Scale for Children (WISC) IQ difference was only 3.5 points. The lead-exposed children were more timid and showed shorter attention spans, although there were no differences in levels of activity. Landrigan, Whitworth, Baloh, Stashling, Barthel, and Rosenblum (1975) examined 46 symptom-free children living near a lead smelter in a relatively lead-free environment. The mean blood level of the exposed group was 48 μg/100 ml (range 40–68 μg/100 ml). The lead-exposed children generally performed somewhat more poorly than the control group, and there was an 8-point significant difference in performance IQ. The high-lead children were also significantly slower on the test of finger–wrist tapping. Other differences tended to be in the 1- to 4-point range in the expected direction. Needleman (1977) and Perino and Ernhart (1974) obtained positive findings of about the same magnitude with children of similar lead body burdens. By contrast, McNeil, Ptasnik, and Croft (1975), studying children drawn from the same population as that studied by Landrigan *et al.* and living near the same lead smelter, found a group of children with mean blood lead levels of 50.3 μg/100 ml to be closely similar in psychological test performance to a nonexposed group (mean blood lead level 20.2 μg/100 ml). Indeed, the lead-exposed group performed significantly better on the Oseretsky test of motor coordination.

Rummo *et al.* (1979), whose findings in relation to an encephalopathic group have already been quoted, also compared 4- to 8-year-old children exposed to lead to a more moderate degree and with mean blood lead levels of 55.7 μg/100 ml and 50.2 μg/100 ml. These children, in marked contrast to the encephalopathic group, hardly differed at all from those in the control group (mean blood lead level 21.2 μg/100 ml) on the McCarthy Intelligence Scales or the Werry–Weiss–Peters Parent Rating of Hyperactivity. Ratcliffe (1977) found no differences on a range of reliable behavioral and cognitive measures between two groups of 5-year-olds who had been shown to vary in their mean blood lead levels at 2 years (44.4 μg/100 ml vs. 28.2 μg/100 ml). Baloh, Sturm, Green, and Gleser (1975) and Gregory and Mohan (1977) also obtained findings in children with blood levels in this range that, although not statistically significant, nevertheless suggested slight associations. Again, one must conclude that in children with moderate lead body burdens, there are small inconsistently found deficits equivalent to between 2 and 5 IQ points and a slight excess of behavioral problems.

Probably the most thorough study yet reported in this area of work is that of Needleman, Gunnoe, Leviton, Reed, Peresie, Maher, and Barrett (1979). A group of 6- to 7-year old children with high lead levels (greater than 24 μg) were compared with a group of children having low lead dentine levels (less than 6 μg) on a wide range of behavioral and cognitive measures. The groups, or at least a proportion of the children in the groups, had been previously found to have mean blood levels of 35.5 and 23.8 μg/100 ml, respectively. The groups differed when examined in their intellectual level, in attention span, speech processing, and various other factors. After correction had been made for expected differences in socioeconomic status, parental education, and maternal vocabulary scores, differences were relatively small—in the region of 4 to 5 IQ points—but nevertheless were statistically significant. Winneke (1979), examining lead concentration in whole deciduous teeth from children in Duisberg, also compared high-lead (mean 9.2 μg) and low-lead (mean 2.4 μg) groups matched on a variety of social measures. The mean blood lead levels of children in the city were assessed at about 18μg/100 ml, and the blood lead levels of the high-lead group were therefore mainly in the 30–40 μg/100 ml range, with the controls mainly in the 10–20 μg/100 ml range. Differences in the expected direction were found in the verbal, performance, and full-scale IQs. These differences were of 5 to 7 points in magnitude.

The studies of David should perhaps be mentioned, although methodologically these are rather less than satisfactory because of biases in selection. In a recent paper, David (David, Hoffman, & Kagey, 1978) reports finding positive correlations between blood lead levels (mean 18.3 μg/100 ml) and a variety of behavioral deficits, including inattentiveness, fearfulness, hyperactivity, and academic problems in a population of American black, Puerto Rican, and other Caribbean children.

Recently Yule, Lansdown, Millar, and Urbanowicz (1981) have investigated a group of 166 children aged 6 to 12 years with blood lead levels ranging from 7 to 33 μg/100 ml, using a variety of intelligence and education tests. There was a significant negative association between performance on most of the tests and the level of lead in the blood, even after social class had been taken into account. These studies again suggest that mild lead body burdens are inconsistently related to IQ differences of 5 to 7 points and a slight excess of behavioral problems.

Implications

The implications of these studies have been thoroughly considered by Rutter (1980). Among the more methodologically sound studies that have been published, there is a reasonable amount of consistency in the findings. At all levels of blood lead from 20 μg/100 ml up to 80 μg/100 ml, there are either small differences on the verge of statistical significance or no differences between high- and low-lead groups, both on a wide range of cognitive measures and in behavioral deficits. No specific cognitive or behavioral defect has been identified. Verbal and performance IQ are linked with lead toxicity to a rather similar degree; also, antisocial, emotional, and hyperactive problems are all tenuously linked. It is notable that the strengths of the relationships found were almost exactly the same, whether the blood levels examined were within the thresholds usually defined as beyond the upper limit of normal levels (36–40 μg/100 ml) or well within that limit—although of course, lead encephalopathy has been well documented and has undeniable long-term effects.

The explanation of this series of findings is not straightforward. It is difficult to explain them in terms of a direct effect of lead on brain function, though Burchfiel, Duffy, Bartels, and Needleman (1980) have in fact described increased widespread low-frequency delta activity in spontaneous EEGs recorded from 22 children with high tooth lead levels when compared with a group of controls. However, it seems likely that a direct effect of lead on brain function would lead to a clear-cut dose effect, with children with the highest levels suffering most severely. The only study in nonencephalopathic children to show a dose effect is that of Needleman *et al.* (1979), where dentine lead over a wide range was very consistently related to teachers' ratings of behavior, but in this study social factors were not controlled at all. This is the only example of a dose effect, though a number of workers have attempted to demonstrate such a finding. It seems to me somewhat more probable that uncontrolled social factors underlie the tendency of some children both to ingest or inhale rather large quantities of lead than others and to demonstrate intellectual and behavioral deficits. Such factors might be expected to operate with roughly the same power, regardless of the level at which the children were exposed to environmental lead. It is notable that the two studies in which low- and high-lead groups have been most satisfactorily controlled for pica (Baloh *et al.*, 1975; Kotok *et al.*, 1977) have both come up with generally negative findings. Control of relevant social factors is not easy, and although most studies reported here do control for parental socioeconomic status (and, in some cases, for parental intelligence), the findings from accidental poisoning—for example, Sobel's (1970)—suggest that more subtle intrafamilial factors may be more relevant, especially as far as behavior disturbance is concerned. Nevertheless, most authorities would now accept that there is a serious possibility that low-level lead exposure may well produce at least a modest deficit in cognitive performance. The issue is, however, far from finally resolved. In view of the importance of the findings, because of their relevance to the issue of lead in gasoline, it is important to stress that further research in this area is needed. The findings so far are reasonably clear-cut; the implications are by no means straightforward.

Other Heavy Metals

In the 1930s and 1940s, "pink disease" or acrodynia was commonly seen in infants in the first 2 to 3 years of life. This condition, characterized by signs of cerebral irritability, restlessness, and fretfulness as well as by puffy, peeling hands and feet, was first recognized to be caused by mercurial compounds in teething powders by Hubbard in 1945 (see Warkany & Hubbard, 1948). Subsequent case reports, such as that by Dathan (1954), confirmed this impression. In the early 1950s, mercurial compounds were removed from teething powders, and the condition has virtually disappeared. Thallium sulfate was a common constituent of pesticides in the 1950s, and Reed, Crawley, and Faro (1963) described 72 children seen with acute or chronic accidental overdosage over a 6-year period. Nine of the children died. Follow-up 4 years after diagnosis revealed neurological abnormalities to be common in the remainder. The authors also reported a high proportion (58%) showing unspecified mental abnormalities. The use of thallium in pesticides was firmly controlled in the late 1950s, and again no further cases appear to have been reported.

TOXIC EFFECTS OF SUBSTANCES TAKEN FOR PLEASURE

Although the average age of chronic alcoholism is declining and although most teenagers experience the effects of alcohol (J. O'Connor, 1977), problem drinking extending beyond drunkenness is an unusual occurrence in the United Kingdom (Stacey & Davies, 1970). Alcoholic blackouts are rare and abstinence symptoms are extremely uncommon, except perhaps in the newborn when the pregnant mother has been addicted. However, this picture may well be changing. Rutter (1979) and Ritson (1981) have reviewed evidence that suggests that there has been a particularly marked increase in drunkenness offenses among the young since 1968, and it appears that the rate of cirrhosis of the liver in the 15–24 age group is also rising (Donnan & Haskey, 1977).

The pattern of toxic effects after ingestion or inhalation of other drugs in childhood is similar to that occurring in adulthood, and this has been readably summarized as far as cannabis is concerned by Edwards (1976). Thus, Kolansky and Moore (1971) described 38 adolescents and young adults who developed severe psychiatric problems as a result of marijuana intake. The syndromes developed were poor social judgment, poor attention span, anxiety, depression, apathy, and indifference. Eight of their patients showed psychotic reactions with chronic delusional ideation, and a further 18 showed "borderline" psychotic states. In a later publication (Kolansky & Moore, 1972), the authors provide the significant information that reactions persist for 3 to 24 months after cessation of drug usage and that in a high proportion of their patients marijuana was the only drug taken. Although clearly marijuana usage is only rarely accompanied by such severe and prolonged psychiatric disorders, it seems well established that it does occasionally produce such reactions in the young.

The toxic effects of amphetamine, barbiturates, and lysergic acid diethylamide (LSD) have been well described elsewhere and do not appear to have any special features when occurring in the young. Glue sniffing (D. J. O'Connor, 1979) does appear to be a type of addiction occurring specifically in the young, and it is on the increase in the United Kingdom, especially among teenagers living in deprived areas with high levels of delinquency and unemployment. The substance is obtained in the form of gasoline, paint thinner, adhesives, and a variety of other substances. The mild excitement and euphoria may be followed by illusions and hallucinations. Spraying aerosol directly into the nose and mouth has been reported as causing sudden death (Watson, 1977). Long-term effects are more likely to be mediated by liver or kidney damage, and it is uncertain whether there are long-term toxic effects on brain function, though a recent report (King, Day, Oliver, Lush, & Watson, 1981) suggests that long-term neurological impairment following solvent encephalopathy may occur.

CHRONIC NONACCIDENTAL POISONING

The deliberate administration of toxic substances by parents to their own children constitutes an unusual form of child abuse. Rogers, Tripp, and Bentovim (1976) reported six cases of this type in which the substances administered were salt, a diuretic, tuinal, mandrax, dihydrocodein, phenformin, and chloral. The presenting symptoms were frequently neurological, with fits, faints, and ataxia. The symptoms and findings on investigation are characteristically inexplicable in terms of known pathology and symptomatology, and they tend to occur after parental visits to hospitalized children or on the children's return home. The diagnosis is made by detection of the drug in the blood, urine, or gastric contents. Family background is similar to that occurring in physically abused children, and, once a diagnosis has been made, management should follow similar principles.

The side effects of prescribed medication, especially anticonvulsants and psychotropic drugs, also constitute a common form of poisoning, but they are beyond the scope of this review. The effect of anticonvulsants is discussed in Chapter 6 of this volume. The hazards to children from toxic substances remain widespread; in view of the potential hazards of environmental pollution and the greater availability of drugs and synthetic substances for self-administration, there is a need for careful monitoring and sometimes for greater control.

CONCLUSION

Poisoning in childhood, whether accidental or deliberately self-induced, is a common phenomenon. The availability of different toxins and the pattern of their usage to relieve pain or produce pleasure varies from culture to culture and from decade to decade. It is therefore necessary for the competent child and adolescent psychiatrist to ensure that he or she is aware of the most recent trends in the use of drugs and the characteristic patterns of behavior they produce.

References

Angle, C. R., McIntire, M. S., & Meile, R. L. Neurological sequelae of poisoning in children. *Journal of Pediatrics*, 1968, *73*, 531–539.

Arena, J. M. *Poisons: Toxicology, symptoms and treatment* (2nd ed.). Springfield, Ill.: Charles C Thomas, 1970.

Augustine, G. J., & Levitan, H. Neurotransmitter release from a vertebrate neuromuscular synapse affected by a food dye. *Science*, 1980, *207*, 1489–1490.

Baloh, R., Sturm, R., Green, B., & Gleser, G. Neuropsychological effects of chronic asymptomatic lead absorption. *Archives of Neurology*, 1975, *32*, 326–330.

Baltimore, C., & Meyer, R. J. A study of storage, child behavioral traits, and mother's knowledge in 52 poisoned families and 52 comparison families. *Pediatrics*, 1968, *42*, 312–317.

Bannerjee, P., & Battachariya, S. Changing pattern of poisoning in children in a developing country. *Journal of Tropical Paediatrics*, 1978, *24*, 136–139.

Blackman, S. S. The lesion of lead encephalitis in children. *Johns Hopkins Hospital Bulletin*, 1937, *61*, 1–43.

Brady, K., Herrera, Y., & Zenick, H. Influences on parental lead exposure on subsequent learning ability of offspring. *Pharmacology, Biochemistry and Behavior*, 1975, *3*, 561–565.

Burchfield, J., Duffy, F., Bartels, P. H., & Needleman, H. L. Combined discriminating power of quantitative electroencephalography and neurophysiologic measures in evaluating CNS effect of lead at low levels. In H. L. Needleman (Ed.), *Low level lead exposure*. New York: Raven Press, 1980.

Bushnell, P. J., & Bowman, R. E. Reversal learning deficits in young monkeys exposed to lead. *Pharmacology, Biochemistry and Behavior*, 1979, *10*, 733–742.

Byers, R. K., & Lord, E. E. Late effects of lead poisoning on mental development. *American Journal of Diseases of Children*, 1943, *66*, 471–494.

Calnan, M. W., Dale, J. W., & de Fonseka, C. P. Suspected poisoning in children: Study of the incidence of true poisoning and poisoning scare in a defined population. *Archives of Disease in Childhood*, 1976, *51*, 180–185.

Carson, T. L., van Gelder, G. A., Karas, G. C., & Buck, W. B. Slowed learning in lambs prenatally exposed to lead. *Archives of Environmental Health*, 1974, *29*, 154–156.

Conners, C. K. *Food additives and hyperactive children*. New York: Plenum Press, 1980.

Dathan, J. G. Acrodynia associated with excessive intake of mercury. *British Medical Journal*, 1954, *1*, 247–249.

David, O. J., Hoffman, S., & Kagey, B. *Sub-clinical lead effects*. Paper presented at Conservation Society symposium, London, April 6, 1978.

Deeths, T. M., & Breeden, J. T. Poisoning in children: A statistical study of 1057 cases. *Journal of Pediatrics*, 1971, *78*, 299–305.

De La Burde, B., & Choate, M. S. Early asymptomatic lead exposure and development at school age. *Journal of Pediatrics*, 1975, *87*, 638–642.

Department of the Environment. *Lead in the environment and its significance to man* (Pollution Paper No. 2). London: Her Majesty's Stationery Office, 1974.

Department of Health and Social Security. *Lead and health*. London: Her Majesty's Stationery Office, 1980.

Done, A. K. Poisoning from common household products. *Pediatric Clinics of North America*, 1970, *17*, 569–581.

Donnan, S., & Haskey, J. Alcoholism and cirrhosis of the liver. *Popular Trends*, 1977, *7*, 18–24.

Edwards, G. Cannabis and the psychiatrist's position. In J. D. P. Graham (Ed.), *Cannabis sativa*. London: Academic Press, 1976.

Feingold, G. *Why your child is hyperactive*. New York: Random House, 1975.

Fosse, G., & Justesen, N. P. Lead in deciduous teeth of Norwegian children. *Archives of Environmental Health*, 1978, *33*, 166–175.

Fraser, N. C. Accidental poisoning deaths in British children 1958–77. *British Medical Journal*, 1980, *280*, 1596–1598.

Goyette, C. H., Conners, C. K., Petti, T. A., & Curtis, L. E. Effects of artificial colors on hyperactive children: A double-blind challenge study. *Psychopharmacology Bulletin*, 1978, *14*, 39–40.

Gregory, R. J., & Mohan, P. J. Effect of symptomatic lead exposure on childhood intelligence: A critical review. *Intelligence*, 1977, *1*, 381–400.

King, M. A., Day, R. E., Oliver, J. S., Lush, M., & Watson, J. Solvent encephalopathy. *British Medical Journal*, 1981, *283*, 633–665.

Kolansky, H., & Moore, W. T. Effects of marijuana on adolescents and young adults. *Journal of the American Medical Association*, 1971, *216*, 486–492.

Kolansky, H., & Moore, W. T. Toxic effects of chronic marijuana use. *Journal of the American Medical Association*, 1972, *222*, 35–41.

Kotok, D. Development of children with elevated blood lead levels. *Journal of Pediatrics*, 1972, *80*, 57–61.

Kotok, D., Kotok, R., & Heriot, J. T. Cognitive evaluation of children with elevated blood lead levels. *American Journal of Diseases of Children*, 1977, *131*, 791–793.

Kreitman, N. *Parasuicide*. London: Wiley, 1977.

Landrigan, P. J., Whitworth, R. H., Baloh, R. W., Stashling, N. W., Barthel, W. F., & Rosenblum, B. F. Neurophysiological dysfunction in children with chronic low-level lead absorption. *Lancet*, 1975, *1*, 708–712.

Lansdown, R. G., Shepherd, J., Clayton, B. E., Delves, H. T., Graham, P. J., & Turner, W. C. Blood lead levels, behaviour and intelligence: A population study. *Lancet*, 1974, *1*, 538–541.

McNeil, J. L., Ptasnik, J. A., & Croft, D. B. Evaluation of long-term effects of elevated blood lead concentration in asymptomatic children. *Archives of Industry, Hygiene, and Toxicology*, 1975, *26* (Suppl.), 97–118.

Nathanson, J., & Bloom, F. Lead-induced inhibition of brain adenyl cyclose. *Nature*, 1975, *255*, 419–420.

Needleman, H. *Studies in subclinical lead exposure* (Environmental Protection Agency Publication No. 600/1-77-037). Springfield, Va.: National Technical Information Service, 1977.

Needleman, H., Gunnoe, C., Leviton, A., Reed, R., Peresie, H., Maher, C., & Barrett, P. Deficits in psychologic and classroom performances of children with elevated dentine lead levels. *New England Journal of Medicine*, 1979, *300*, 689–695.

Needleman, H., & Piomelli, S. *The effects of low-level lead exposure*. New York: Natural Resources Defense Council, 1978.

Needleman, H., & Shapiro, I. Dentine lead levels in asymptomatic Philadelphia schoolchildren: Subclinical exposure in high and low risk groups. *Environmental Health Perspective*, 1974, *7*, 27–31.

O'Connor, D. J. A profile of solvent abuse in schoolchildren. *Journal of Child Psychology and Psychiatry*, 1979, *20*, 365–368.

O'Connor, J. Annotation: Normal and problem drinking among children. *Journal of Child Psychology and Psychiatry*, 1977, *18*, 279–284.

Patterson, C. Contaminated and natural environments of man. *Archives of Environmental Health*, 1965, *11*, 344–360.

Perino, J., & Ernhart, C. B. The relation of sub-clinical lead level to cognitive and sensorimotor impairment in black preschoolers. *Journal of Learning Disabilities*, 1974, *7*, 26–30.

Pihl, R. O., & Parkes, M. Hair element content in learning disabled children. *Science*, 1977, *198*, 204–206.

Pueschel, S. M., Kopito, L., & Schwachmann, H. Children with an increased lead burden: A screening and follow-up study. *Journal of the American Medical Association*, 1972, *222*, 462–466.

Ratcliffe, J. M. Developmental and behavioural functions in young children with elevated blood levels. *British Journal of Preventative and Social Medicine*, 1977, *31*, 258–264.

Reed, D., Crawley, J., & Faro, S. N. Thallotoxicosis. *Journal of the American Medical Association*, 1963, *183*, 516–522.

Ritson, B. Alcohol and young people. *Journal of Adolescents*, 1981, *4*, 92–100.

Rogers, D., Tripp, J., & Bentovim, A. Non-accidental poisoning: An extended syndrome of child abuse. *British Medical Journal*, 1976, *1*, 793–796.

Rummo, J. H., Routh, D. K., Rummo, N. J., & Brown, J. F. Behavioural and neurological effects of symptomatic and asymptomatic exposure in children. *Archives of Environmental Health*, 1979, *34*, 120–124.

Rutter, M. *Changing youth in a changing society: Patterns of adolescent development and disorder*. London: Nuffield Provincial Hospital Trust, 1979.

Rutter, M. Raised lead levels and impaired cognitive behavioural functioning: A review of the evidence. *Developmental Medicine and Child Neurology*, 1980, *22*(Suppl. 1).

Sachs, H. K., Krall, V., McCaughran, D. A., Rozenfeld, I. H., Yongsmith, N., Growe, G., Lazar, B. S., Novar, L., O'Connell, L., & Rayson, B. IQ following treatment of lead poisoning on mental development. *Journal of Pediatrics*, 1978, *93*, 428–431.

Shaffer, D. Suicide in childhood and early adolescence. *Journal of Child Psychology and Psychiatry*, 1974, *15*, 275–292.

Shaw, M. T. Accidental poisoning in children: A psychosocial study. *New Zealand Medical Journal*, 1977, *85*, 269–272.

Silbergeld, E., & Goldberg, A. Hyperactivity: A lead-induced disorder. *Environmental Health Perspective*, 1974, *7*, 227–232.

Silva, P. A., Buckfield, P., Spears, G. F., & Williams, S. Poisoning, burns, and other accidents experienced by a thousand Dunedin three year olds: A report from the Dunedin multidisciplinary child development study. *New Zealand Medical Journal*, 1978, *87*, 242–244.

Sobel, R. Psychiatric implications of accidental poisoning in childhood. *Pediatric Clinics of North America*, 1970, *17*, 653–685.

Stacey, B., & Davies, J. Drinking behaviour in childhood and adolescence: An evaluative review. *British Journal of Addiction*, 1970, *65*, 203–212.

Stephens, R. *The total relationship between airborne lead and body-lead burden*. Paper presented to Conservation Society, London, 1978.

Stewart, M. A., Thach, B. T., & Freidin, M. R. Accidental poisoning and the hyperactive child syndrome. *Diseases of the Nervous System*, 1970, *31*, 403–407.

Taylor, E. Food additives, allergy, and hyperkinesis. *Journal of Child Psychology and Psychiatry*, 1979, *20*, 357–363.

Teitelbaum, D. T. Poisoning with psychoactive drugs. *Pediatric Clinics of North America*, 1970, *17*, 557–567.

Ter Haar, G., & Aronow, R. Tracer studies of ingestion of dust by urban children. In T. B. Griffin & J. H. Knelson (Eds.), *Environmental quality and safety* (Vol. 2, Suppl., *Lead*). London: Academic Press, 1975.

Waldron, H. A. Lead levels in blood of residents near the M6-A38 (M) interchange, Birmingham. *Nature*, 1975, *253*, 345–346.

Warkany, J., & Hubbard, D. M. Mercury in the urine of children with acrodynia. *Lancet*, 1948, *1*, 829–830.

Watson, J. M. Glue sniffing in profile. *Practitioner*, 1977, *218*, 255–259.

Weiss, B., Williams, J. H., Margen, S., Abrams, B., Caan, B., Citron, L. J., Cox, C., McKibben, J., Ogar, D., & Schultz, S. Behavioral responses to artificial food colors. *Science*, 1980, *207*, 1487–1488.

Winneke, G. *Neurophysiological studies in children with elevated tooth lead levels.* Paper presented at the symposium "Toxic Effects of Environmental Lead," Conservation Society, London, May 10, 1979.

Yule, W., Lansdown, R., Millar, I. B., & Urbanowicz, M. A. The relationship between blood lead concentration, intelligence and attainment in a school population: A pilot study. *Developmental Medicine and Child Neurology*, 1981, *23*, 567–576.

CHAPTER FOUR

Specific Medical Syndromes

PHILIP J. GRAHAM

INTRODUCTION

Opportunities to study the anatomical, physiological, and metabolic substrate of psychiatric and psychological disorders are rare. Most of the patients seen by psychologists and psychiatrists never come to postmortem, nor do physical investigations offer much promise of illumination. However, a small minority of children do provide the opportunity for pathological study; they are those with frank neurological disorders who suffer in addition from psychiatric syndromes. Of course, researchers and clinicians need to be cautious in generalizing findings from this atypical group. If, for example, clinicians assume the presence of hyperuricemia in every self-destructive child they see, they are doomed to disappointment. Yet a search for brain mechanisms in the genesis of psychiatric disorder in children with neurological disease could be fruitful if applicable more generally. In any case, it is of vital importance to the group of children specifically afflicted. My review of the topic mainly focuses on those medical syndromes for which specific cognitive or behavioral correlates have been claimed, but I do not discuss those conditions (namely, brain trauma, nutritional deficiencies, perinatal damage, and epilepsy) covered in other chapters.

CHROMOSOMAL ANOMALIES

Down Syndrome

Of a large number of conditions now known to be produced by autosomal anomalies, Down syndrome remains by far the most common and accounts for about one-third of the mentally handicapped population with IQs below 50. The neuropathological basis of mongolism has been extensively investigated, but not satisfactorily defined. Changes found are usually diffuse and nonspecific (Crome, 1965; Crome, Cowie, & Slater, 1966). The brain is smaller than normal, averaging about 76% of normal size. The simplification of gyral pattern and the infrequency of cells in cortical layer III, which have been

Philip J. Graham. Department of Child Psychiatry, University of London Institute of Child Health, London, England; Department of Child Psychiatry, Hospital for Sick Children, London, England.

described as characteristic, do not appear to be invariably present. It is interesting that in older patients with mongolism, early signs of presenile dementia of Alzheimer's type have frequently been described (e.g., Olsen & Shaw, 1969).

The IQs of children with mongolism vary from below 25 to above 70 (G. F. Smith & Berg, 1976). Various factors influence intellectual outcome. Thus the age of the children at the time they are tested appears important. In children under the age of 3 years, an IQ over 70 is not uncommon, and indeed about a quarter of afflicted young children show intelligence at this level. As Down syndrome children get older, however, IQ tends to decrease. This is probably not an artifact of the tests used, as it has been demonstrated over a range of intelligence tests, including the Stanford–Binet, Wechsler, Merrill–Palmer, Cattell, and Leiter (G. F. Smith & Berg, 1976). Carr (1970) found a striking decline on the Bayley scale of motor and mental development between 6 weeks and 2 years, with a mean developmental age declining from 81 to 35. Although there is no evidence that they have any marked characteristic pattern of intellectual skills, Down syndrome children, in comparison with other retarded children, do tend to show poor visuomotor skills (as shown by their capacity to reproduce patterns) and poor tactile discrimination (Hermelin & O'Connor, 1961; O'Connor & Hermelin, 1961). IQ levels seem to remain stable from 5 to 19 years, but there is some suggestion that dementing, which parallels the neuropathological changes of aging, may occur with this condition much earlier than is usual in adults. In line with the findings on personality, described below, social quotients are generally higher than IQs so that the children often appear brighter than in fact they are.

There is uncertainty regarding a link between cell type of mongolism and intellectual level. Penrose (1967) reported mosaic mongols to have higher IQs than other varieties. However, in a large study of institutionalized mongol individuals, Johnson and Abelson (1969b) found the mean IQ of translocation cases to be highest (38), trisomy cases intermediate (32), and mosaic lowest (29). In general there is rather poor correlation between physical findings on examination (e.g., number of stigmata) and IQ, although this finding may be misleading, as it is based on the more handicapped group of Down syndrome children found in institutions. Studies based on total groups of such children might give a different result.

Children reared at home seem to fare better than children reared in institutions (Carr, 1970), although the fact that mentally retarded children of very low ability and with multiple disabilities are more likely to be institutionalized makes the evidence difficult to evaluate (Tizard & Grad, 1961). There is anecdotal evidence that children of those parents such as teachers who take a firm educational line from an early age tend also to have a somewhat more favorable outcome. Populations of institutionalized mongols score less highly than do those in the general population (Shipe & Shotwell, 1965). Early stimulation programs enhance mental development, but do not elevate IQ levels above 70.

Since Langdon Down's original description of the syndrome, it has been thought that mongol children show characteristic personality features—they are said to be lively, good-natured, affectionate, socially adaptable, placid, and relatively free of behavior problems. There is indeed a certain amount of confirmation of this stereotype. Although Baron (1972) found no differences in temperament between mongol and nonmongol toddlers, Domino (1965) found that institutionalized mongols were significantly more often rated by naïve observers as clownish, content, good-natured, and warm, compared with institutionalized nonmongol retarded children of the same age. Silverstein (1964) also found that mongols were rated higher by ward personnel on the Petersen scale of general adjustment than nonmongols, although there were no significant differences in measures of extraversion–introversion.

In general, therefore, the personality stereotype of mongol children has some validity, although exceptions are not uncommon. The evidence for low rates of behavior disturbance is less certain. Menolascino (1965) found 13% of 86 Down syndrome children less than 8 years of age to have significant psychiatric problems, a rate that he calculated to be similar to that of the general population. He found a high rate of abnormal electroencephalograms (EEGs) (50%) among the disturbed group when compared to the rate among the behaviorally normal (13%). Johnson and Abelson (1969a) found that translocation cases, who were the most intelligent, also were more active and aggressive than children with trisomy and mosaic variants of the same syndrome. This suggests the possibility of a physical basis for some of the behavior problems.

Ovarian Dysgenesis (Turner Syndrome)

Turner syndrome, occurring in females, is characterized by short stature, webbing of the neck, failure of development of secondary sexual characteristics at puberty, and a wide range of congenital abnormalities. These women have 45 chromosomes instead of the usual complement of 46, with only one X and no other X or Y chromosome present. The chromosomal cell structure may be homogenous, but about half the patients show a mosaic chromosomal pattern, with some cells containing XO and others XX chromosomal material.

Schaffer (1962) demonstrated a specific cognitive defect in spatial function in patients with this condition, and it has sometimes been suggested that they also show a higher than expected rate of general mental retardation. However, Garron (1977) compared 67 Turner syndrome females, aged between 6 and 31 years, with a closely matched control group and found no excess in the probands of severe or moderate mental retardation. Turner syndrome patients did significantly worse on most nonverbal tests of the Wechsler Intelligence Scale for Children (WISC) and Wechsler Adult Intelligence Scale (WAIS) with a mean verbal IQ of 104 (mosaic Turner syndrome patients also averaged 104) and performance IQ 86 (mosaics 92). Probands also did worse on some verbal tests, especially those requiring numerical skills, but this may not involve a separate cognitive deficit, as mathematical skill is known to relate to spatial ability. These spatial deficits occur with equal severity in both mosaic and nonmosaic types of Turner syndrome, and Garron suggests that they are best understood with reference to the cognitive processes involved rather than by consideration of the stimulus attributes. Silbert, Wolfe, and Lilianthal (1977) attempted to analyze the processes involved by comparing 13 phenotypic females possessing the karyotype abnormalities with controls on tests of spatial perception and organization, sensorimotor sequencing, automatization, rhythm, tonal memory, and auditory figure–ground abilities. They concluded that the probands showed a specific disability in tasks requiring spatial integration into synthetic wholes but were nevertheless able to analyze spatial configurations into their component parts. They attributed this cognitive deficit to right-hemisphere dysfunction. Although studies of the psychosocial development of patients with Turner syndrome have been conducted, there do not appear to be any psychiatric studies of personality or of rates and types of psychiatric disorder.

XYY Syndromes

Since the first description of the XYY chromosomal abnormality (Sandberg, Koepf, Ishihara, & Hauschka, 1961) there has been much controversy regarding its behavioral implications. Although the condition only occurs in .1% of the population, 3% of the men in special-security hospitals have been shown to possess the anomaly. Nevertheless the risk of an XYY individual entering a special-security hospital is only 1 to 3.5%. The crucial information regarding the likelihood of affected individuals showing violent behavior of a serious type, but not so grave as to require admission to a special hospital, is not yet available. Preliminary findings from a longitudinal study conducted in Edinburgh (Ratcliffe, Axworthy, & Ginsborg, 1979) suggest that most XYY individuals may not show this type of problem. Out of the 11 XYY babies followed up into early childhood, four showed significant behavior problems (not of a particularly aggressive type), as compared to two out of 18 controls. The mean IQ of the affected children was 98, compared to 116 in the controls. In a review of 43 infants with the XYY syndrome, followed prospectively, Robinson, Lubs, Nielsen, and Sorensen (1979) concluded that about a third of the children showed delayed speech or language development, and that there was a slight shift to the left in IQ distribution. These findings, incidentally, make it uncertain how best to counsel mothers in whom a fetus has been detected as showing the XYY anomaly in the early antenatal period.

METABOLIC DISORDERS

Metabolic disorders affecting the central nervous system can be classified according to whether they arise from defects in amino acid metabolism; amino acid transport; carbohydrate or lipid metabolism; or a miscellaneous variety of other metabolic processes, involving, for example, copper and uric acid (Menkes, 1974).

Phenylketonuria

Probably the most common of these disorders is phenylketonuria, a disorder of amino acid metabolism, in which there is a deficiency in phenylalanine hydroxylase, an enzyme responsible for converting dietary phenylalanine to tyrosine. Instead, phenylalanine is converted into phenylpyruvic acid, phenylacetic acid, and phenylacetylglutamine. Effects of the enzymatic defect on the anatomy of the central nervous system include interference with maturation of grey matter, defective myelination, and cystic degeneration of grey and white matter (Menkes, 1974).

Clinical manifestations of the untreated condition include severe mental retardation, fits, severe behavioral disturbances (perhaps especially autism), and rough, dry, sometimes eczematous skin. It is likely, however, that the phenotype varies with the nature of the enzymatic defect, as some children with apparently classical phenylketonuria from a metabolic point of view show a normal mental development.

Whereas most of the diagnosed cases used to be found to have IQs in the below-50 range, the advent of treatment in the form of a low-phenylalanine diet has drastically altered the prognosis. There can now be no reasonable doubt that it is indeed highly effective. I. Smith, Lobascher, and Wolff (1973) reported the results of follow-up of 24 children whose treatment was started early (between 4 and 135 days from birth). Their IQ range was 77 to 127, with a mean of 93. This was lower than expected from the results of assessment of other members of the family (mean IQ of siblings equaled 110; mean IQ of parents equaled 101), but nevertheless it was markedly higher than had previously been reported in untreated cases. Poor results were related both to early overstarvation in dietary phenylalanine and to later poor control resulting in a hyperphenylalaninemia. O'Grady, Berry, and Sutherland (1970) demonstrated that higher IQ figures are most likely to be due to treatment by showing that the mean IQ of 108 for patients treated early (107 for unaffected siblings) compared with a mean IQ of untreated affected siblings of 71.

It has remained uncertain how long it is necessary to maintain children on treatment in order to ensure safety from intellectual deterioration. I. Smith, Lobascher, Stevenson, Wolff, Schmidt, Grubel-Kaiser, and Bickell (1978) reported on 47 patients treated at the Hospital for Sick Children, London, and showed a rather consistent and statistically significant 6-point IQ deterioration in a before-and-after assessment when treatment was stopped between 5 and 15 years. By contrast, in a group of 22 children treated in Germany reported in the same paper, IQ falls were not demonstrable when children of this age were placed on a relaxed low-phenylalanine diet rather than a normal diet. The age at which it is safe for affected children to go on a normal diet remains uncertain, but present clinical impressions suggest that midadolescence, when maturation of the central nervous system is complete, may be a more appropriate time. On the other hand, it is important to remember that phenylketonuric girls on a normal diet stand a high risk, if they become pregnant, of giving birth to congenitally deformed and mentally handicapped children because of the exposure of the fetus to high levels of maternal phenylalanine.

Although intellectual development in treated cases of phenylketonuria is relatively normal, rates of behavioral deviance in treated children are unusually high. Thus Stevenson, Hawcroft, Lobascher, Smith, Wolff, and Graham (1979) compared teacher behavior ratings (Rutter, 1967) of 99 early-treated children with 197 classroom controls in a sample drawn from the U.K. National Phenylketonuria Register. The rate of deviance was 20% in the control group and 40% in the cases—a highly significant difference. There was a particularly high rate of neurotic-type deviance in the affected boys. In girls, high rates of deviance were especially common in those with IQs below 70, but in boys all ranges of intelligence were affected. It was suggested that high deviance rates might be due to a direct continuing effect of high blood phenylalanine, to the enduring effect of early exposure to high phenylalaninemia, to the psychological effects of an unpalatable and restrictive diet, or to a genetic factor predisposing to both phenylketonuria and an increasing vulnerability to psychiatric disorder. Further research from the large sample of affected children available from the U.K. National Register may clarify this issue.

Galactosemia

Galactosemia is a disorder of carbohydrate metabolism, arising as a result of a deficiency in galactose-1-phosphate uridyl transferase. The elevated levels of reducing substance that circulate as a result of this enzyme deficiency stimulate the production of insulin so that the brain is exposed to persistent hypoglycemia. It is the hypoglycemia that is thought to result in brain damage and dysfunction. The condition (which is transmitted in an autosomal recessive manner) is very rare and results in damage to the liver and spleen as well as in early cataract formation. Over the past 25 years, children diagnosed with this condition have been treated with galactose-free or low-galactose diets, and this has minimized the brain damage. Whereas pretreatment IQ levels were mainly in the region of 50 to 70, treated cases tend to achieve average levels of ability. Thus Fishler, Koch, Donnell, and Graliker (1966) identified 34 affected children and assessed them at ages 2 months to 17 years. The mean IQ of the boys was 96 and of the girls 91. This contrasted with a mean IQ for unaffected male siblings of 105 and for females of 99, suggesting that an 8- or 9-point IQ decrement is associated with the condition. These authors also pointed to a high incidence of specific visual perceptual retardation in the older children. Komrower and Lee (1970), assessing 60 affected children aged between 2 and 17 years, also found some suggestion of visuospatial problems with the Bender–Gestalt Test, but these could not be regarded as specific defects as, in general, they were commensurate with the depressed IQ levels. These workers obtained a mean IQ of 80, with a tendency of the IQ to decline with age. It is possible that this occurred as a result of less effective treatment being provided in the early days when it was at a more experimental stage.

Both Fishler *et al.* (1966) and Komrower and Lee (1970) found younger children with this condition to be unduly anxious and fearful, and older children tense, aggressive, and antiauthority. In the latter study, the children assessed by teachers on the Bristol Social Adjustment Guide were found to score high on the dimensions of "unforthcomingness," "hostility to adults," and "depression." In both groups, restlessness and lack of concentration were common. As in phenylketonuria, therefore, the improvement in intelligence level achieved by appropriate dietary treatment does not quite result in attainment of full intellectual potential, and behavioral abnormalities remain relatively common.

Lesch–Nyhan Syndrome

This very rare condition, occurring as a result of a defect in the enzyme hypoxanthine–guanine phosphoribosyl transferase, is mentioned because of its possible significance in an understanding of the genesis of self-abusive behavior. The metabolic disorder is characterized by hyperuricemia; in addition to choreaathetosis and moderately severe mental retardation, the children show quite unusually severe self-destructive behavior and self-mutilation. Nyhan (1976) pointed to differences between the self-destructive behavior shown in this syndrome and that manifested in autism and mental retardation. In this condition, self-destruction is of a different order of severity, with biting commonly producing gross loss of tissue. In other conditions, head banging and skin picking are more frequent. The child with the Lesch–Nyhan syndrome is more likely to show aggression directed outward, and his or her self-destructiveness is much more difficult to modify. Dizmang and Cheatham (1970), in a psychiatric study of five children aged 9 to 15 years suffering from this condition, reported that self-destructive behavior began when the children were aged 1 to 5 years and seemed to be triggered off by some form of fairly minor accidental injury. The patients were incapable of explaining their own destructiveness and dissociated themselves from it. One said "I don't bite myself—it's my teeth." The children experienced pain as a result of their self-mutilation and were happier when physically restrained, becoming anxious when restraints were removed. These authors postulated that external trauma serves for these children as a fixating and locating stimulus forming the basis of an internalized compulsive repetitive tendency to inflict pain on themselves and others. They suggested that this mechanism might also be operating in physically abused children, who also have a tendency to harm themselves. It seems more likely, however, that the existence of a specific biochemical lesion is more crucial to the development of the self-destructiveness. Anderson, Dancis, Alpert, and Herrmann (1977) suggested, on the basis of experimental studies, that while Lesch–Nyhan children are incapable of learning from aversive stimulation, they can learn from positive reinforcement. This specific learning disability could be related to the presence of an identifiable gene.

As far as treatment is concerned, Nyhan (1976) reported some success with the use of carbidopa and tryptophan, but the findings are as yet preliminary. He also, incidentally, reported mildly encouraging results with behavior modification programs aimed at extinguishing self-destructive behavior by withdrawing attention from it, but he suggested that continuing serious problems occurred if attempts were made to remove physical restraints. Gilbert, Spellacy, and Watts (1979) review problems in the behavior modifications of the self-destructive behavior, especially the difficulty in achieving generalization of improvement to the home situation.

Hypothyroidism

The relatively recent introduction of screening programs with early treatment of hypothyroidism has raised interest in the psychological aspects of this condition. McFaul, Dorner, Brett, and Grant (1978) reported psychological findings in 30 patients aged 2.7 to 21 years, all of whom were treated before the age of 2 years. The mean IQ was 92.4; the rate of behavior disorders, as assessed by teacher questionnaires, was probably elevated, though the lack of a control group makes this uncertain. There were no clear-cut differences in intelligence between early-treated (between 4 and 10 weeks) and later-treated cases. However, routine screening will make it possible to institute treatment even earlier, and it will be informative to note the results of follow-up studies in this condition in the future.

TUMORS OF THE BRAIN

After the tumors of the blood-forming tissues, brain tumors are the most common type of malignancy occurring in childhood. It has been calculated that approximately 600 new cases occur in childhood each year in the United States and 180 to 200 in the United Kingdom (Till, 1975). Approximately 60% of childhood brain tumors occur in the subtemporal part of the brain, and, of these, most are either medulloblastomas or cerebellar astrocytomas. The remainder consist of supratentorial tumors and tumors of the brain stem and adjacent structures. Only 3% of brain tumors are metastatic—a marked contrast to the situation in adults. It is unusual for brain tumors in childhood to present with symptoms of intellectual deterioration or behavioral change. Headache and vomiting are by far the most common presenting symptoms, and, although there may be some accompanying irritability, this does not usually result in any diagnostic confusion (Till, 1975). One clear exception to this rule is the mode of presentation of pontine gliomata. Cairns (1950), Arseni and Goldenburg (1959), and Lassman and Arjona (1967) have all described striking personality changes occurring with this type of tumor. Characteristically, a period of withdrawal, apathy, and lethargy is followed by aggression, overactivity, temper tantrums, and physical violence. Presentation occurs between 3 and 13 years, and the outcome is uniformly fatal even with treatment by irradiation, though the course may last several years. Other types of brain stem tumor (Panitch & Berg, 1970) are more likely to present with disturbance of gait and symptoms such as squint that are referable to cranial nerve involvement, but behavioral changes involving lethargy, irritability, inability to concentrate, enuresis, and sleep disturbance do also occur.

The prognosis of brain tumors in childhood is somewhat gloomy, even with the best available treatment (surgery and irradiation). Clearest information is available on the most common type of tumor, the medulloblastomas. Two studies (Bloom, Wallace, & Henk, 1969; Hope-Stone, 1970) suggest that the survival rate at 5 years is between 40 and 75% and at 10 years between 30 and 50%. In the 22 survivors reported by Bloom *et al.*, 82% were reported to be without serious disability. Two of those followed up had some partial disability, and two were seriously intellectually deteriorated. It is of interest that the two demented cases were those who had presented at the youngest age (11 and 15 months), as more recent findings (Eiser, 1979; Meadows, Massari, Fergusson, Gordon, Littman, & Moss, 1981) suggest that very young children are sensitive to irradiation and may, when treated in this way for a leukemic condition, also suffer significant intellectual loss. There is also a need for further work to clarify whether apparently unscathed survivors show deficits of a less obvious type, as follow-up investigations so far have tended to rely on fairly crude indicators of psychological functioning. Matson and Crigler (1969), for example, reporting on treated cases of craniopharyngioma, describe no particular psychological or behavioral problems, even though the survivors were often partially sighted and required replacement hormone therapy. However, no systematic studies of behavioral status following surgery for brain tumors in childhood appear to have been carried out, and these negative findings must be treated with caution. Surgical reports of lack of psychological disability in tumor follow-up series do not accord with my own clinical experience but, of course, this is of a selected nature.

INFECTIONS OF THE CENTRAL NERVOUS SYSTEM

The outbreak of epidemic encephalitis following on World War I resulted in high mortality among children (though not apparently among adults) and a high frequency of subsequent psychiatric morbidity. Ebaugh (1923), Kennedy (1924), and Strecker (1929) all reported series of children followed up for some years after the initial acute illness. This acute phase is characterized by sleepiness, fever, and other signs of localized central nervous system involvement. It was followed by the gradual onset of significant personality changes, especially of an antisocial type. Ebaugh (1923), however, described a wide range of behavioral and emotional sequelae, involving insomnia with nocturnal agitation, affective disorders of depressive type, hysterical reaction, and undue fearfulness, as well as mental retardation. Reading these reports, it is difficult to be certain whether at least some of the phenomena described might not have been due to underlying chronic social stress, the acute stress of the illness and associated hospitalization, and other factors not directly related to the encephalitic process. However, the presence of associated neurological sequelae, such as parkinsonism, and the apparent absence of such stresses in the reports provided, do make it likely that a direct brain damage effect on behavior occurred not infrequently and resulted in serious personality problems, though doubtless these may have been compounded by inappropriate institutional management.

Since the 1920s, reports of epidemic encephalitis and of subsequent behavioral sequelae have been sporadic, and there seems general though not universal agreement that encephalitis is a most uncommon cause of childhood psychiatric disorder. In an article somewhat misleadingly entitled "Post-Encephalitic Behavior Disorder—A Forgotten Entity," Levy (1959) described 100 children with hyperkinetic and antisocial behavior disorders, virtually all apparently successfully treated with dextroamphetamine sulfate. However, the etiology of these cases seems to be largely nonencephalitic, with high forceps delivery, frequent attacks of hypthermia, and severe infectious disease in early infancy given as the main etiological factors. Further, in the case examples cited, the disorganization of social background shown by affected children is often striking. Levy's claim that "a great many cases labeled as behavior disorder and juvenile delinquency are caused by an unrecognized organic brain disorder usually . . . in the form of a post-encephalitic behavior disorder" seems unsubstantiated.

Nevertheless, isolated outbreaks of well-documented encephalitic disorder do continue to occur. Sabatino and Cramblett (1968) reported on 14 children who had suffered from California encephalitis virus (CEV) disease between the ages of 5 and 14 years. The acute illness, which lasted 4 to 15 days, was characterized by fever, lethargy, headaches, and impairment of consciousness. When followed up 7 months to 2 years after the initial illness, the mean IQ of the children was just below average (verbal 94, performance 97). Ten of the children were said to have auditory perceptual problems, and others deficits in visual perception. The children were said to have a variety of emotional and behavioral problems, especially nervousness, hyperactivity, restlessness, and disruptive behavior, together with learning problems, but the absence of controls and the lack of information regarding family background make the follow-up information difficult to evaluate.

Meningitic infections also have been considered to have possible adverse effects on subsequent behavioral functioning. However, this impression is not strongly confirmed by the most comprehensive study so far available (Lawson, Metcalfe, & Pampiglione, 1965). A total of 99 children whose infections had been contracted between the ages of 2 months and 15 years were followed up 1 to 8 years afterward. Their mean IQ on the WISC was 105, and there was no unusual excess of children with verbal–performance discrepancies, nor were any specific deficits identified. Only one child was thought to have developed a significant degree of mental retardation as a result of the infection. There was some suggestion that children who contracted the infection before the age of 1 year had a more adverse intellectual outcome. A high proportion of the children developed emotional and behavioral problems as described by their parents, and an additional number were reported to be showing learning problems in school, but the absence of a control group makes this information of uncertain significance. There was, however, some suggestion that those children who had contracted nonbacterial infections were more likely to show learning difficulties than those who had had bacterial illnesses. About 21% of the children had EEG abnormalities reported as "definitely abnormal," but there was no correlation between EEG findings and intellectual, behavioral, or learning deficits. In a smaller-scale study of 18 children following aseptic meningitis, Fee, Mariss, Kardash, Reite, and Seitz (1970) noted that the only definitely adverse outcomes occurred in the few children who had seizures in the acute phase of their illness.

OTHER SYNDROMES

Spina Bifida

Spina bifida (of which the following description is largely derived from Menkes, 1974) arises from a failure of fusion of the vertebral column. As a result, spinal cord tissue protrudes, forming a meningocele or meningomyelocele, depending on the contents of the herniated tissues. Defects in bone closure are in fact secondary to a defect in neural tube closure; the cause for this defect is unknown at the present time, though it is generally thought that both genetic and environmental factors are involved. Posterior defects in the lumbar and lumbosacral regions are the most common type, with about three-quarters of infants presenting with myelomeningocele and one-quarter with meningocele. In 95% of children with defects at these low levels, however, there is an associated abnormality (the Chiari malformation) of the fourth ventricle and spinal cord, frequently with some degree of atrophy of central nervous tissue. Cellular defects in the cerebral hemisphere may also occur, although these are less commonly found. Mechanical distortion accompanies these cellular defects, giving rise to kinking of the fourth ventricle and spinal canal, thus producing obstruction of the flow of cerebrospinal fluid and hydrocephalus.

Spina bifida occurs at a variable rate between .2 and 4.2 per 1000 births, and has a recurrence rate in siblings of 5%. Primary neurological defects comprise motor and sensory deficits, depending on the level of the lesion, and partial or complete paralysis of the bladder and bowel, together with sexual dysfunction. Disturbances of brain function occur as a result of hydrocephalus (present in 90% of cases and in 50 to 75% at birth), defects in brain cell formation, and ascending infection. Prognosis depends to a considerable degree on the nature of treatment undertaken. Untreated, 84% of cases die by the age of 2, whereas with early surgical repair of the spinal defect and shunt correction of the hydrocephalus, mortality is reduced to 36%. In universally treated series, the mortality depends upon the nature of the anatomical defect. Lorber (1971), reporting on 524 unselected treated cases of myelomeningocele, found that of those with hydrocephalus, only 37% survived to the age of 7 years, whereas 89% of those without hydrocephalus survived. In 323 children followed up for 7 to 12 years, Lorber found only 4 with no handicap, 20 with moderate handicaps, 66 with severe physical handicaps but IQs in the normal range, and 44 with severe physical and mental handicaps. The study suggested that improvements in surgical and medical management did not specifically reduce the proportion of children with serious intellectual and physical handicaps. Poor prognosis was associated with extensive paralysis at birth, head circumference exceeding the 90th percentile by 2 cm, and severe kyphosis or other associated congenital defects. These prognostic factors are now used by the majority of surgeons as an indication for a more conservative approach to surgery, with vigorous attempts being made to treat only those who stand a reasonable chance of survival without gross handicaps.

Spain (1974) examined verbal and performance ability in a group of 129 affected children, and found that 58% had a developmental quotient of less than 80 on the Griffiths eye–hand coordination and performance scale. Lorber (1971), in the series already quoted, which consisted largely of rather older children, found that about two-thirds had IQs below 80. Hunt and Holmes (1976), in a series of 83 survivors, examined anatomical and surgical factors associated with level of intelligence. They found that children who contracted an infection of the central nervous system (ventriculitis, meningitis, or septicemia) had significantly lower IQs. In those children without infection but with shunts inserted, the IQ was closely correlated with the level of sensory impairment recorded at birth; the lower the level recorded, the higher the subsequent IQ. There was no correlation between IQ and occipital–frontal circumference, nor between IQ and the age at which the shunt was inserted. However, the thickness of the pallium below the right parietal eminence (measured at the time of the insertion of the shunt) was significantly related to IQ level if the shunt was inserted before the age of 4 weeks. If the shunt was subsequently inserted, there was no such relationship. There appears, incidentally to be a surprisingly good relationship between early infant assessment and later IQ in the spina bifida children. Fishman and Palkes (1974) found a correlation of .82 in a group of 21 children with congenital malformation of the central nervous system who had been tested on the Cattell Intelligence Scale at 18 months and the Stanford–Binet at 5 years.

Spina bifida does not appear to be associated with any specific cognitive deficits. However, children suffering from this condition have been reported to show excessive verbal facility, hyperverbalism, or, more picturesquely, the "cocktail party syndrome" (Tew, 1979). Swisher and Pinsker (1971) compared 11 children with spina bifida and hydrocephalus and the same number of children with limb deformities matched in other respects. Children with spina bifida used more words in an unstructured conversational setting, though not in a more formal situation. On the Illinois Test of Psycholinguistic Ability, the spina bifida children also scored generally lower than the controls, except, as predicted, on the test tapping automatic levels of oral language. These authors suggest that the hyperverbalism or "cocktail party syndrome" possibly arises as a result of differential social reinforcement of superficial verbal utterances, but it is difficult to see why this should occur particularly in spina bifida; it is perhaps more probable that specific brain mechanisms are involved.

There are rather few studies of psychiatric disorder in children with spina bifida, but Dorner (1976) interviewed 46 teenagers aged 13 to 19 years (mean 16.4 years) and found that 85% reported feeling miserable and unhappy to the point of being tearful and wanting to "get away from it all," compared to below 50% with these feelings in the general population. About a quarter of the affected girls had suicidal ideas and, in the girls, depression and misery were quite closely linked with social isolation. No attempt has been made to disentangle organic from social factors in the genesis of psychiatric disorder in this group, but insofar as hydrocephalus has not been found to relate to the frequency of disorder once IQ is controlled, it may be presumed that social factors are probably of greater importance.

Prader–Willi Syndrome

A large number of other syndromes, at least partly genetically determined, are associated with mental handicap and associated behavioral deviance. Menkes (1974) lists 12 such syndromes in which short stature is associated with mental retardation. Prader–Willi syndrome is characterized by hypotonia in early infancy, the early development of obesity, and mild to moderate growth deficiency (Zellweger & Schneider, 1968). It occurs as a familial condition, as Clarren and Smith (1977) have demonstrated, and these authors also suggest that the condition may be produced by a single localized defect in early brain development leading to a small frontal brain, muscle hypotonia, and hypothalamic dysfunction producing appetite disturbance and obesity. The voracity of the appetite may bring such a child to psychiatric attention, and it is for this reason that the condition has been singled out for consideration here. However, apart from the unusual severity of the craving for food, and the length to which a Prader–Willi child will go to obtain it, there are no specific features in the appetite disturbance, and the mechanism of its development is not understood. No specific treatment is available.

NEUROLOGICAL CONDITIONS PRESENTING AS PSYCHIATRIC DISORDERS

Finally, in any discussion of the psychiatric aspects of organic neurological syndromes, some attention must be given to the fact that disorders of the brain may sometimes present with features more suggestive of purely psychiatric disorders. Rivinus, Jamison, and Graham (1975) described 12 patients referred over a period of 1 year to the inpatient service of a pediatric neurological department for whom psychiatric diagnoses had been made, though a definite neurological disorder was eventually diagnosed. The various psychiatric diagnoses made included anxiety state, hysterical reaction, child psychosis, and conduct disorder. There were characteristic features of symptomatology in these patients, especially *deteriorating* school performance, visual loss, and postural disturbance, which are unusual in the normal run of children attending psychiatric departments. The range of neurological disorders involved was also wide and included cerebral tumors, subacute sclerosing panencephalitis, metachromatic leukodystrophy, and dystonia musculorum deformans. In neurological outpatient departments, epilepsy is probably the condition most commonly presenting with features suggestive of psychological disorder (see Chapter 6 of this volume).

CONCLUSION

In this selected review of specific medical syndromes associated with cognitive and/or behavioral deficits, most attention has been given to those syndromes for which either more recent work has been carried out or in which I have personally had some clinical or research experience. Even so, the range of associations described makes it clear that the psychiatry of pediatric neurological disorders is diagnostically challenging and that further study of the subject could be potentially fruitful both for the patients with the types of conditions involved, and for others without overt neurological handicaps but with psychological problems in which study of neurological function might yet be illuminating.

References

Anderson, L., Dancis, J., Alpert, M., & Herrmann, L. Punishment, learning and self-mutilation in Lesch–Nyhan disease. *Nature*, 1977, *265*, 461–463.

Arseni, C., & Goldenburg, M. Psychic disturbances in infiltration of the brain stem. *Acta Neurochirurgica*, 1959, *7*, 292–300.

Baron, S. Temperament profile of children with Down's syndrome. *Developmental Medicine and Child Neurology*, 1972, *14*, 640–643.

Bloom, H. J. G., Wallace, E. N. K., & Henk, J. M. The treatment and prognosis of medulloblastoma in childhood. *American Journal of Roentgenology*, 1969, *105*, 43–62.

Cairns, H. Mental disorders with tumours of the pons. *Folia Psychiatrica, Neurologica, Neurochirurgica Neerlandica*, 1950, *53*, 193–203.

Carr, J. Mental and motor development in young mongol children. *Journal of Mental Deficiency Research*, 1970, *14*, 205–220.

Clarren, S. K., & Smith, D. W. Prader–Willi syndrome: Variable severity and recurrence risk. *American Journal of Diseases of Children*, 1977, *131*, 798–800.

Crome, L. The pathology of Down's disease. In L. T. Hilliard & B. H. Kirman (Eds.), *Mental deficiency*. London: Churchill Livingstone, 1965.

Crome, L., Cowie, V., & Slater, E. A statistical note on cerebellar and brain stem weight in mongolism. *Journal of Mental Deficiency Research*, 1966, *10*, 69–72.

Dizmang, L. H., & Cheatham, C. F. The Lesch–Nyhan syndrome. *American Journal of Psychiatry*, 1970, *127*, 671–677.

Domino, G. Personality traits in institutionalized mongoloids. *American Journal of Mental Deficiency*, 1965, *69*, 568–570.

Dorner, S. Adolescents with spina bifida: How they see their situation. *Archives of Disease in Childhood*, 1976, *51*, 439–444.

Ebaugh, F. Neuropsychiatric sequelae of acute epidemic encephalitis in children. *American Journal of Diseases of Children*, 1923, *25*, 89–97.

Eiser, C. Intellectual development following treatment for childhood leukaemia. In J. M. A. Whitehouse & H. E. M. Kay (Eds.), *CNS complications of malignant disease*. London: Macmillan, 1979.

Fee, W. E., Mariss, M. I., Kardash, S., Reite, M., & Seitz, C. The long-term prognosis of aseptic meningitis in childhood. *Developmental Medicine and Child Neurology*, 1970, *12*, 321–329.

Fishler, K., Koch, R., Donnell, G., & Graliker, B. V. Psychological correlates in galactosemia. *American Journal of Mental Deficiency*, 1966, *71*, 116–125.

Fishman, M., & Palkes, H. The validity of psychometric testing in children with congenital malformations of the central nervous system. *Developmental Medicine and Child Neurology*, 1974, *16*, 180–185.

Garron, D. C. Intelligence among persons with Turner's syndrome. *Behavioral Genetics*, 1977, *7*, 105–127.

Gilbert, S., Spellacy, E., & Watts, R. W. E. Problems in the behavioural treatment of self-injury in the Lesch–Nyhan syndrome. *Developmental Medicine and Child Neurology*, 1979, *21*, 795–800.

Hermelin, B., & O'Connor, N. Shape, perception and reproduction in normal children and mongol and nonmongol imbeciles. *Journal of Mental Deficiency Research*, 1961, *5*, 67–71.

Hope-Stone, H. F. Results of treatment of medulloblastomas. *Journal of Neurosurgery*, 1970, *32*, 83–88.

Hunt, G. M., & Holmes, A. E. Factors related to intelligence in treated cases of spina bifida cystia. *American Journal of Disease of Children*, 1976, *130*, 823–827.

Johnson, R. C., & Abelson, R. B. The behavioral competence of mongoloid and non-mongoloid retardates. *American Journal of Mental Deficiency*, 1969, *73*, 856–857. (a)

Johnson, R. C., & Abelson, R. B. Intellectual, behavioral, and physical characteristics associated with trisomy, translocation and mosaic types of Down's syndrome. *American Journal of Mental Deficiency*, 1969, *73*, 852–855. (b)

Kennedy, R. Prognosis of sequelae of epidemic encephalitis in children. *American Journal of Diseases of Children*, 1924, *29*, 158–172.

Komrower, G. M., & Lee, D. H. Long-term follow-up of galactosaemia. *Archives of Disease in Childhood*, 1970, *45*, 367–373.

Lassman, L., & Arjona, V. E. Pontine gliomas of childhood. *Lancet*, 1967, *1*, 913–915.

Lawson, D., Metcalfe, M., & Pampiglione, G. Meningitis in childhood. *British Medical Journal*, 1965, *1*, 557–562.

Levy, S. Post-encephalitic behavior disorder—a forgotten entity: A report of 100 cases. *American Journal of Psychiatry*, 1959, *115*, 1062–1067.

Lorber, J. Results of treatment of myelomeningocoele: An analysis of 524 unselected cases. *Developmental Medicine and Child Neurology*, 1971, *13*, 279–303.

Matson, D. D., & Crigler, J. F. Management of craniopharyngioma in childhood. *Journal of Neurosurgery*, 1969, *30*, 377–390.

McFaul, R., Dorner, S., Brett, E. M., & Grant, D. B. Neurological abnormalities in patients treated for hypothyroidism from early life. *Archives of Disease in Childhood*, 1978, *53*, 611–619.

Meadows, A. T., Massari, D. J., Fergusson, J., Gordon, J., Littman, P., & Moss, K. Declines in IQ scores and cognitive dysfunctions in children with acute lymphocytic leukaemia treated with cranial irradiation. *Lancet*, 1981, *2*, 1015–1018.

Menkes, J. H. *Textbook of pediatric neurology*. Philadelphia: Lea & Febiger, 1974.

Menolascino, F. J. Psychiatric aspects of mongolism. *American Journal of Mental Deficiency*, 1965, *69*, 653–660.

Nyhan, W. L. Behavior in the Lesch–Nyhan syndrome. *Journal of Autism and Childhood Schizophrenia*, 1976, *6*, 235–242.

O'Connor, N., & Hermelin, B. Visual and stereognostic shape recognition in normal children and mongol and non-mongol imbeciles. *Journal of Mental Deficiency Research*, 1961, *5*, 63–66.

O'Grady, D. J., Berry, W. K., & Sutherland, B. S. Phenylketonuria: Intellectual development and early treatment. *Developmental Medicine and Child Neurology*, 1970, *12*, 343–347.

Olsen, M., & Shaw, C. Pre-senile dementia and Alzheimer's disease in mongolism. *Brain*, 1969, *92*, 147–156.

Panitch, H. S., & Berg, B. O. Brain stem tumors of childhood and adolescence. *American Journal of Diseases of Children*, 1970, *119*, 465–472.

Penrose, L. Studies of mosaicism in Down's anomaly. In G. A. Jervis (Ed.), *Mental retardation*. Springfield, Ill.: Charles C Thomas, 1967.

Ratcliffe, S. G., Axworthy, D., & Ginsborg, A. The Edinburgh study of growth and development in children with sex chromosome abnormalities. In A. Robinson, H. A. Lubs, & D. Bergsma (Eds.), *Sex chromosome aneuploidy: Prospective studies on children*. New York: Alan Liss, 1979.

Rivinus, T., Jamison, D., & Graham, P. Childhood organic neurological disease presenting as psychiatric disorder. *Archives of Disease in Childhood*, 1975, *50*, 115–119.

Robinson, A., Lubs, H. A., Nielsen, J., & Sorensen, K. Summary of clinical findings: Profile of children with 47 XXY, 47 XXX, and 47 XYY karyotypes. In A. Robinson, H. A. Lubs, & D. Bergsma (Eds.), *Sex chromosome aneuploidy: Prospective studies on children.* New York: Alan Liss, 1979.

Rutter, M. A children's behaviour questionnaire for completion by teachers. *Journal of Child Psychology and Psychiatry*, 1967, *8*, 1–11.

Sabatino, D., & Cramblett, H. Behavioural sequelae of Californian encephalitis virus infection in children. *Developmental Medicine and Child Neurology*, 1968, *10*, 331–337.

Sandberg, A. A., Koepf, G. F., Ishihara, T., & Hauschka, T. S. An XYY human male. *Lancet*, 1961, *2*, 488–489.

Schaffer, J. W. A specific cognitive deficit observed in gonadal aplasia (Turner's syndrome). *Journal of Child Psychology*, 1962, *18*, 403–406.

Shipe, D., & Shotwell, A. M. Effects of out of home care on mongoloid children: A continuation study. *American Journal of Mental Deficiency*, 1965, *69*, 649–652.

Silbert, A., Wolff, P. H., & Lilienthal, J. Spatial and temporal processing in patients with Turner's syndrome. *Behavior Genetics*, 1977, *7*, 11–21.

Silverstein, A. B. An empirical test of the mongoloid stereotype. *American Journal of Mental Deficiency*, 1964, *68*, 493–497.

Smith, G. F., & Berg, J. M. *Down's anomaly*. Edinburgh: Churchill Livingstone, 1976.

Smith, I., Lobascher, M., Stevenson, J. E., Wolff, O., Schmidt, H., Grubel-Kaiser, S., & Bickel, H. Effect of stopping low-phenylalanine diet on intellectual progress of children with phenylketonuria. *British Medical Journal*, 1978, *2*, 723–726.

Smith, I., Lobascher, M., & Wolff, O. Factors influencing outcome in early treated phenylketonuria. In J. Seakins, R. Saunders, & C. Toothill (Eds.), *Treatment of inborn errors of metabolism*. London: Churchill Livingstone, 1973.

Spain, B. Verbal and performance ability in pre-school children with spina bifida. *Developmental Medicine and Child Neurology*, 1974, *16*, 773–780.

Stevenson, J., Hawcroft, J., Lobascher, M., Smith, I., Wolff, O. H., & Graham, P. J. Behavioural deviance in children with early-treated phenylketonuria. *Archives of Disease in Childhood*, 1979, *54*, 14–18.

Strecker, E. Behaviour problems in encephalitis. *Archives of Neurology and Psychiatry*, 1929, *21*, 137–144.

Swisher, L. P., & Pinsker, E. J. The language characteristics of hyperverbal hydrocephalic children. *Developmental Medicine and Child Neurology*, 1971, *13*, 746–755.

Tew, B. The "cocktail party syndrome" in children with hydrocephalus and spina bifida. *British Journal of Disorders in Communication*, 1979, *14*, 89–101.

Till, K. *Paediatric neurosurgery*. Oxford: Blackwell Scientific Publications, 1975.

Tizard, J., & Grad, J. C. *The mentally handicapped and their families*. London: Oxford University Press, 1961.

Zellweger, H., & Schneider, H. J. Syndromes of hypotonia, hypomentia, hypogonadism, obesity (HHHO): The Prader–Willi syndrome. *American Journal of Diseases of Children*, 1968, *115*, 588–598.

CHAPTER FIVE

Head Injury

MICHAEL RUTTER / OLIVER CHADWICK / DAVID SHAFFER

INTRODUCTION

Epidemiology of Head Injuries in Childhood

Head injuries in childhood are relatively frequent occurrences (Field, 1976) and constitute one of the most common causes of brain damage among school-age children (Swinyard, Swansen, & Greenspan, 1963). Moreover, at least in the United Kingdom, the number of children treated in hospitals for head injuries has risen steadily since the 1950s (Craft, Shaw, & Cartlidge, 1972), although it is uncertain how far this represents more head injuries and how far a more liberal admissions policy. Of the children with severe injuries, the increased availability of more successful treatment methods has probably resulted in a decrease in deaths (Field, 1976). What effect this has had on the number of disabled survivors is unknown (Jennett, 1975b).

The circumstances in which children sustain head injuries have been noted in several different reports of consecutive series of cases. Among preschool children, accidents in the home account for a significant proportion of cases, but, in school-age children, falls constitute the commonest cause of milder head injuries treated in hospitals (Burkinshaw, 1960; Comninos, 1979; Hendrick, Harwood-Nash, & Hudson, 1964; Klonoff, 1971), with road traffic accidents as the most frequent source of severe head injuries—as they are for all levels of injury in adults (Heiskanen & Kaste, 1974; Hjern & Nylander, 1964; Rowbotham, MacIver, Dickson, & Bousfield, 1954; Rutter, Chadwick, Shaffer, & Brown, 1980). In addition, however, parental assault constitutes an important minority of cases—4% in Craft's series (Craft *et al.*, 1972). Boys outnumber girls in rate of head injuries sustained, particularly during the primary-school years, which constitute the peak age period for head injuries in childhood (Field, 1976).

Michael Rutter. Department of Child and Adolescent Psychiatry, University of London Institute of Psychiatry, London, England.

Oliver Chadwick. G. H. Sergievsky Center, College of Physicians and Surgeons, Columbia University, New York, New York; Institute for Basic Research in Developmental Disabilities, Staten Island, New York.

David Shaffer. Departments of Child Psychiatry, Clinical Psychiatry, and Pediatrics, College of Physicians and Surgeons, Columbia University, New York, New York; New York State Psychiatric Institute, New York, New York.

Characteristics of Children Experiencing Head Injury

It is important to recognize that children experiencing head injury are far from a random sample of the general population. As a consequence, the lack of a control group in most studies showing intellectual impairment and behavioral difficulties following head injury (Black, Jeffries, Blumer, Wellner, & Walker, 1969; Black, Blumer, Wellner, & Walker, 1971[1]; Blau, 1936; Bowman, Blau, & Reich, 1974; Brink, Garrett, Hale, Woo-Sam, & Nickel, 1970; Burkinshaw, 1960; Fabian, 1956; Flach & Malmros, 1972; Gaidolfi & Vignolo, 1980; Harris, 1957; Heiskanen & Kaste, 1974; Hjern & Nylander, 1964; Otto, 1960; Richardson, 1963; Rowbotham *et al.*, 1954; Strecker & Ebaugh, 1924) means that it is not possible to determine how far the problems resulted from cerebral trauma, how far they resulted from other nonneurological consequences of the accident, and how far they resulted from preexisting difficulties that *ante*dated the injury.

Studies comparing children who have experienced accidental head injuries with control groups of various sorts have consistently shown differences in both the children and their families (Backett & Johnston, 1959; Burton, 1968; Craft *et al.*, 1972; Manheimer & Menninger, 1967; Partington, 1960). However, these differences are much more characteristic of children suffering mild head injuries from falls than those sustaining severe injuries following road traffic accidents (Klonoff, 1971; Rutter *et al.*, 1980). Thus, as measured by teacher or parent questionnaires or by interview data, children with head injuries have tended to be impulsive, aggressive, attention-seeking, and behaviorally disturbed. It is not that the children show a homogeneous personality pattern, but, rather, that they exhibit a variety of behaviors that lead them into dangerous situations giving rise to accidents. The families of children experiencing accidents also differ from the general population in showing more parental illness and mental disorder, more social disadvantages of various kinds, and less adequate supervision of the children's play activities. Thus, Rune (1970) and Hjern and Nylander (1964) both found more mental disturbance among the mothers of injured children than among many mothers in comparison groups. Marital instability and broken homes have also been reported as more frequent in the families of children sustaining head injuries (Klonoff, 1971; Rune, 1970). The same pattern of associations has been found through studies focusing on parents rather than children. Thus, G. W. Brown and Davidson (1978) found that the children of depressed mothers were more likely to experience accidents. It is evident, then, that children suffering head injuries are at psychiatric risk for a variety of reasons quite separate from the brain trauma resulting from the injury. Obviously, these risk variables must be taken into account in any assessment of the psychological sequelae that stem directly from cerebral damage.

Pathophysiology of Brain Injury

Before turning to the behavioral and cognitive consequences of brain injury, a consideration of the pathophysiology involved is in order. Pathophysiology is rather different with closed and with open head injuries. With closed head

1. Black, Blumer, Wellner, Shepard, and Walker (1981) have provided data on sibling controls for some purposes, but the findings were not analyzed in a manner that adequately deals with these issues.

injuries, there tends to be contusion and laceration, not only at the site of impact but also at the opposite pole, with the latter (so-called "contrecoup effects") often more severe than the former, and with a tendency to be particularly marked in the temporal and orbital regions (Bloomquist & Courville, 1947; Löken, 1959). In addition, there is often widespread interruption and degeneration of nerve fibers as a result of shearing injuries (Strich, 1969). Subdural bleeding is usual, and generally there is acute cerebrovascular congestion and hyperemia (Bruce, Raphaely, Goldber, Zimmerman, Bilaniuk, Schut, & Kuhl, 1979).

In contrast, in open injuries involving skull fracture and tearing or penetration of the dura mater, contrecoup damage is minimal or even absent (Löken, 1959). The energy of the trauma is expended locally, with the fractured bones acting as a sort of buffer. However, there is often extensive local laceration, with intracranial hematomas, venous sinus involvement, and infection as the chief complications (Braakman, 1972; Miller & Jennett, 1968). Frequently there is no loss of consciousness (unlike severe closed head injuries, where it is almost invariable), but the risk of epilepsy is much higher than with closed injuries (Jennett, 1975a; Lishman, 1978).

However, it should be noted that the effects of head injury in childhood, especially infancy and early childhood, differ in some respects from those in adult life (Cummins & Potter, 1970). The skull of a young person is less rigid than that of an adult, so that there is greater cushioning and less frequent contrecoup damage (Courville, 1965); on the other hand, there is likely to be greater distortion of the brain and hence more marked generalized shearing damage.

Age Differences in Response to Brain Injury

Although the empirical findings are somewhat contradictory and the theoretical concepts a matter of controversy (see Geschwind, 1974; Goldman, 1974; St. James Roberts, 1979), it seems likely that there are important age differences in the ways in which the brain responds to injury. However, several rather different processes are operating, with the consequence that it is not possible to conclude that, overall, the effects are "worse" or "better" in early childhood (Rutter, 1982). Firstly, it has been found that very young infants are more likely to have serious intellectual impairment following infections or irradiation of the brain (see Eiser, 1978; Rutter, Graham, & Yule, 1970; Sells, Carpenter, & Ray, 1975; Witelson, 1977). The reason for this apparently greater vulnerability in early infancy probably lies in the general observation that immature organs tend to be more susceptible to injury than mature ones are, and that organs are most liable to damage at the time of their most rapid growth—which, in the case of the brain, consists of the prenatal period and the first 2 years or so after birth (Dobbing & Smart, 1974).

Secondly, there are the contrary consequences of the greater "plasticity" of functioning and the greater potential for interhemispheric transfer of functions in the immature brain. This is most obvious in the results of the early studies showing that left-hemisphere damage in infancy is less likely to lead to permanent language impairment than are similar lesions occurring in later childhood or adult life (Lenneberg, 1967; Rutter *et al.*, 1970). This observation initially led to claims that the two hemispheres are equipotential in infancy

(Basser, 1962); but more recent research findings indicate that this is an overstatement (Isaacson, 1975; St. James Roberts, 1979; Witelson, 1977). Even in infancy there is substantial hemispheric specialization, and the powers of recuperation after brain damage in adult life have been found to be greater than used to be supposed. Even so, it does seem that there is somewhat greater versatility of functioning in infancy, and in particular it is more readily possible for the right hemisphere to take over language functions. But this effect applies to *inter*hemisphere transfer, and not to transfer of functions *within* one hemisphere. Evidence is lacking on the latter, but it does not seem that it is generally greater in young children, and hence it may well be that the greater potential for recovery in infancy applies only to *unilateral*, and not bilateral, lesions.

Thirdly, there are probable age differences in the extent of neuronal or glial regrowth; the immature brain possessing greater regenerative and reparative potential (Ebels, 1980; Lynch & Gall, 1979). Bishop (1981) has suggested that, with the exception of the striate cortex, there is a fairly strong inverse relationship between the plasticity of a function (i.e., the degree to which recovery is possible after brain injury) and the myelination of cortical neurons subserving that function. However, it should not be assumed that this necessarily leads to better restoration of *function* (Geschwind, 1974; Goldberger, 1974; Goldman, 1974). The regrowth may lead to an *interference* with function as well as to improvements. The late onset of epilepsy is perhaps a case in point. Also, it should be noted that mature neurons may also be capable of forming new synaptic connections; some modification of structure can take place in the mature as well as in the immature brain (see Lynch & Gall, 1979).

In this connection, too, it should be emphasized that functional recovery is not necessarily a result of structural change. Improved functioning may be a result of a variety of quite different processes, including (1) vicarious functioning of undamaged neural tissues (i.e., a part or a side of the brain deals with a function for which it would not ordinarily have responsibility); (2) behavioral substitution (i.e., undamaged systems become more efficient but do not alter the role); and (3) the use of alternative strategies or "tricks" to circumvent handicaps; as well as (4) functional reorganization (either through collateral sprouting or biochemical changes); (5) recovery of functioning impaired (but not destroyed) by vascular constriction, edema, or similar processes; and (6) the beneficial effects of neuronal degeneration, as by the death of a neuron with an inhibitory function (Geschwind, 1974; Goldberger, 1974; Goldman, 1974).

Assessment of the Severity of Head Injury

The duration of posttraumatic amnesia (PTA) has been found to constitute the most generally useful measure of the severity of diffuse brain damage. One of the most immediate consequences of generalized injury to the brain is a disturbance of consciousness, which may vary from a slight reduction in alertness to deep coma. After recovery of consciousness, there usually remains a more prolonged period during which recent events are not remembered reliably, consistently, or accurately. This period of PTA is usually measured up to the point at which the memory for ongoing events of daily life becomes continuous (Brooks, 1976). Its duration can be assessed reasonably reliably (but only if it lasts an hour or more—Gronwall & Wrightson, 1980); it allows rough quantification along a single continuum for both mild and severe injuries; and it constitutes a reasonably good predictor of long-term mental and physical recovery (Bond, 1975; Brooks, Aughton, Bond, Jones, & Rizvi, 1980; Jennett, 1975b; Russell, 1971).

However, the duration of PTA is a less satisfactory measure of severity in open head injuries with fracture of the skull, which often involve no loss of consciousness (Jennett, 1975a, 1975b; Lishman, 1978). In particular, it provides no guide to the extent of localized brain damage. Although there is no very satisfactory measure of the amount of local trauma, some guidance is provided by the occurrence of late posttraumatic epilepsy and the presence of abnormalities on neurological examination (Chadwick, Rutter, Thompson, & Shaffer, 1981; Jennett, 1975a).

BRAIN INJURY AS A CAUSE OF BEHAVIORAL OR COGNITIVE DYSFUNCTION

With these considerations in mind, it needs to be considered how far brain injury actually *causes* psychiatric disorder or intellectual impairment (as distinct from just being associated with these problems as a result, perhaps, of the kinds of children who sustain injuries). Intellectual and psychiatric sequelae are best discussed separately. However, with both, we refer to our prospective study of 5- to 14-year-old children who experienced head injuries of sufficient severity to give rise to a PTA of 7 days or more (G. Brown, Chadwick, Shaffer, Rutter, & Traub, 1981; Chadwick, Rutter, Brown, Shaffer, & Traub, 1981; Chadwick, Rutter, Shaffer, & Shrout, 1981; Rutter *et al.*, 1980). The sample was obtained from regional neurosurgical units in southeast England and consisted of consecutive admissions to these units of children fulfilling our selection criteria. An individually matched control group of hospital-treated children also suffering severe accidents, but with orthopedic rather than cranial injuries, was studied in the same way. This served to control not only for disorders arising as a result of hospital admission or other accident-related stresses not involving brain injury, but also for changes that were consequent upon the passage of time or repeated testing rather than upon trauma-related recovery or deterioration. In order to determine the threshold of severity of brain damage above which either transient or persistent sequelae might occur, we also studied a third group of children with less severe head injuries—namely, those that resulted in a PTA of less than 7 days, but of at least 1 hour's duration. The children were seen for detailed individual psychological testing immediately after the accident and then again 4 months, 1 year, and 2¼ years after the injury. The parents were systematically interviewed at the same times, and behavioral questionnaires were completed by the children's class teachers at school.

Cognitive Sequelae

The question of whether the cognitive deficit shown by the children who suffered head injuries was actually *caused* by the brain trauma may be approached by considering whether cognitive recovery took place during the follow-up period. It is a general rule with acute damage to the brain that the intellectual deficit is greatest immediately after the damage and that progressive improvement occurs during the following months. The presence of this pattern of recovery, therefore, provides a strong indication that the initial deficit was a consequence of the brain damage. Conversely, the absence of any recovery phase would provide strong circumstantial evidence that the initial deficit was *not* due to brain injury. Figure 5-1 provides a graphic presentation of the findings on the Wechsler Intelligence Scale for Children (WISC) performance subscale. It is evident that there *was* a marked cognitive recovery phase in the severe-head-injury group (with a PTA of at least 7 days) but *none* in the mild-injury group (with a PTA in the range of 1 hour to 1 week. We conclude that *severe* head injuries did indeed *cause* intellectual impairment, but equally that mild injuries did not. The findings from other prospective studies are similar in showing substantial cognitive recovery during the year after injury (Black *et al.*, 1969; Black *et al.*, 1971; Klonoff, Low, & Clark, 1977; Klonoff & Paris, 1974).

A second way of approaching the same problem is provided by the scrutiny of possible "dose–response" relationships—that is, by determining whether there is a consistent association between the severity of the brain injury and the extent of the intellectual deficit *within* the head-injury group. Figure 5-2 summarizes the findings of that analysis. For this purpose, "transient" intellectual impairment was deemed to be present when there was significant recovery but no final deficit. "Recovery" was operationally defined as an increase in performance IQ score between the initial testing and the 1-year follow-up that was of a magnitude found in fewer than 5% of controls (24 points or more). The lack of a final deficit was defined as a 2¼-year follow-up score that was within one standard deviation (*SD*) of the control-group mean. "Persistent impairment" was deemed to be present when there was initial cognitive recovery (as already defined) but when the final follow-up score was at least 1 *SD* below the

Figure 5-1. Head injury and cognitive recovery. From "A Prospective Study of Children with Head Injuries: II. Cognitive Sequelae" by O. Chadwick, M. Rutter, G. Brown, D. Shaffer, and M. Traub, *Psychological Medicine*, 1981, 49–61. Copyright 1981 by Cambridge University Press. Reprinted by permission.

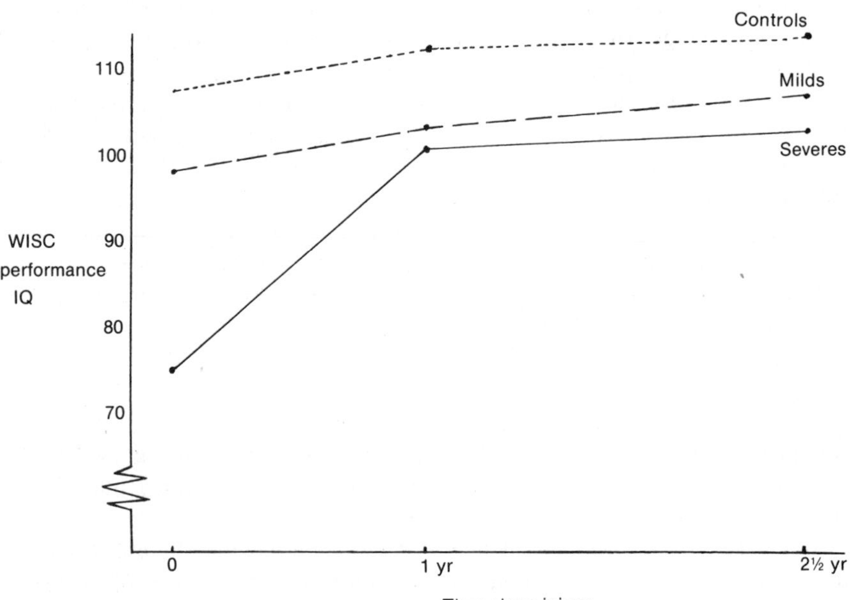

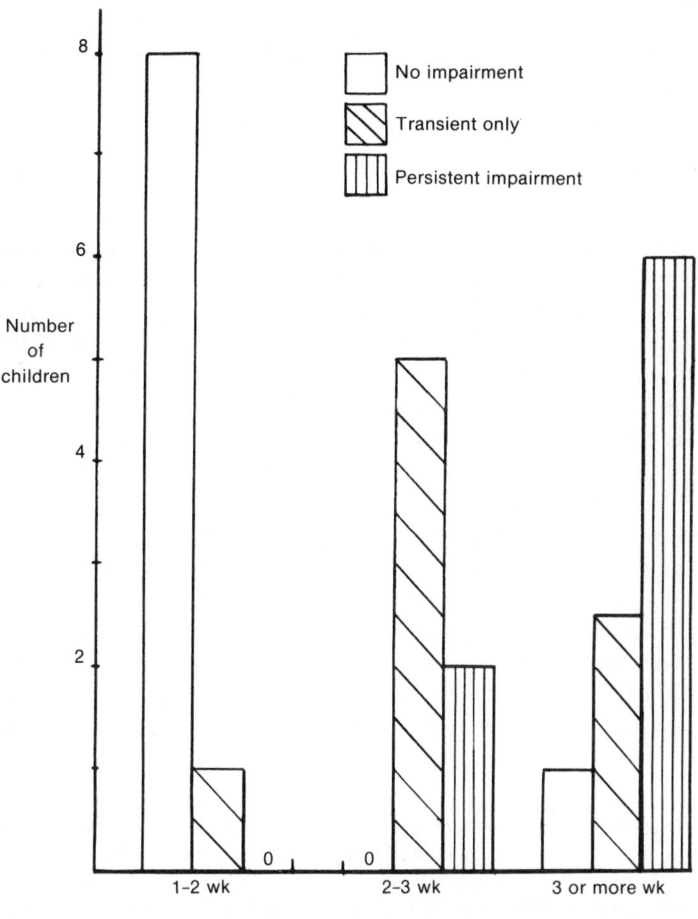

Figure 5-2. Intellectual impairment and posttraumatic amnesia (PTA). Data from Chadwick, Rutter, Brown, Shaffer, and Traub (1981).

control-group mean. Figure 5-2 shows the cross-tabulation, within the severe-head-injury group, between these measures of intellectual impairment and the duration of PTA (which serves as an index of the severity of brain injury). It is clear that the two are strongly associated. The majority of children with PTAs of at least 3 weeks showed persistent intellectual impairment; transient impairment was more characteristic of the subgroup with PTAs of 2 to 3 weeks; whereas most of the children with PTAs of less than 2 weeks showed no impairment, transient or persistent. Again, the results of other investigations are similar. Thus, Brink and her colleagues (1970) and Levin and Eisenberg (1979) both found a direct correlation between duration of coma and postinjury IQ level; Stover and Zeiger (1976) noted a relationship between duration of coma and residual functional impairment; and Heiskanen and Kaste (1974) showed that subsequent school performance was worse in children with prolonged unconsciousness. In adults, too, the duration of PTA has been found to predict both cognitive sequelae (Brooks *et al.*, 1980) and social recovery (Oddy,

Humphrey, & Uttley, 1978). The strong dose–response relationship provides a powerful indication that the intellectual deficits seen in children with severe head injuries are indeed due to brain injury.

Psychiatric Sequelae

The parallel question of whether brain injury caused psychiatric disorder needed to be tackled in a somewhat different way, in that there cannot be the same presupposition of recovery. Here, the crucial need was to obtain a measure of the children's behavior *before* the accident. Of course, this could not be done prospectively, but it could be done (and was done) immediately after the injury. Because this information was gathered *before* a child's postinjury psychiatric state could be known, it constituted as unbiased a measure of preaccident behavior as could be obtained. The findings are summarized in Figure 5-3. The severe-head-injury children and their controls were closely comparable in their preinjury behavior, but the rate of psychiatric disorder in the severe-head-injury group had greatly increased by the time of the 4-month follow-up and remained at a level more than double that in the control group for the whole of the rest of the follow-up period. The implication is that the risk of psychiatric disorder had been greatly increased by the head injury.

However, the question of cause may be examined more directly by confining attention to those disorders that arose only *after* the injury in children without psychiatric disorder prior to the accident. The level of disorders un-

Figure 5-3. Psychiatric disorder before and after accident in children with severe head injuries and in controls. From "Neurobehavioural Associations and Syndromes of 'Minimal Brain Dysfunction'" by M. Rutter and O. Chadwick, in F. C. Rose (Ed.), *Clinical Neuroepidemiology*, London: Pitman Medical Publishing, 1980. Copyright 1980 by Pitman Medical Publishing. Reprinted by permission.

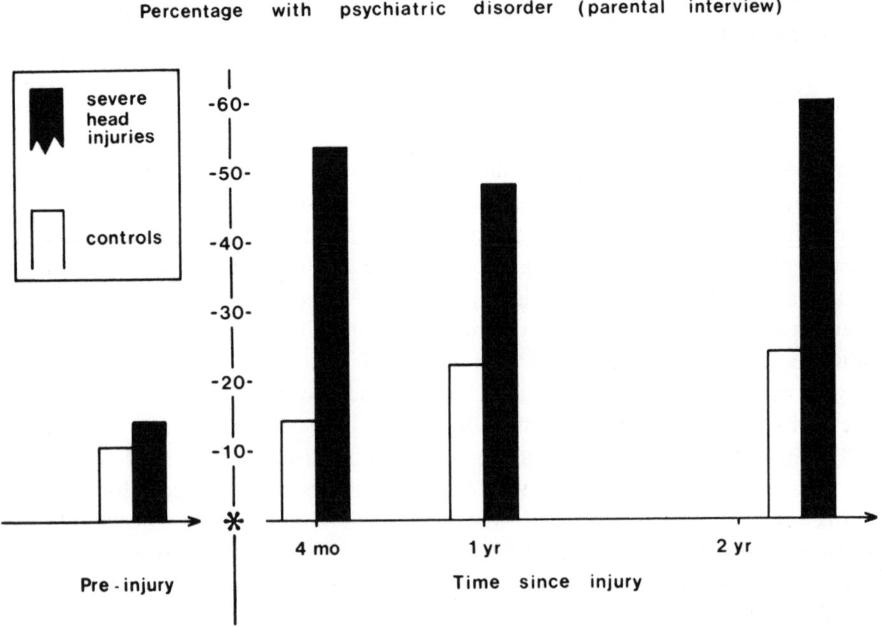

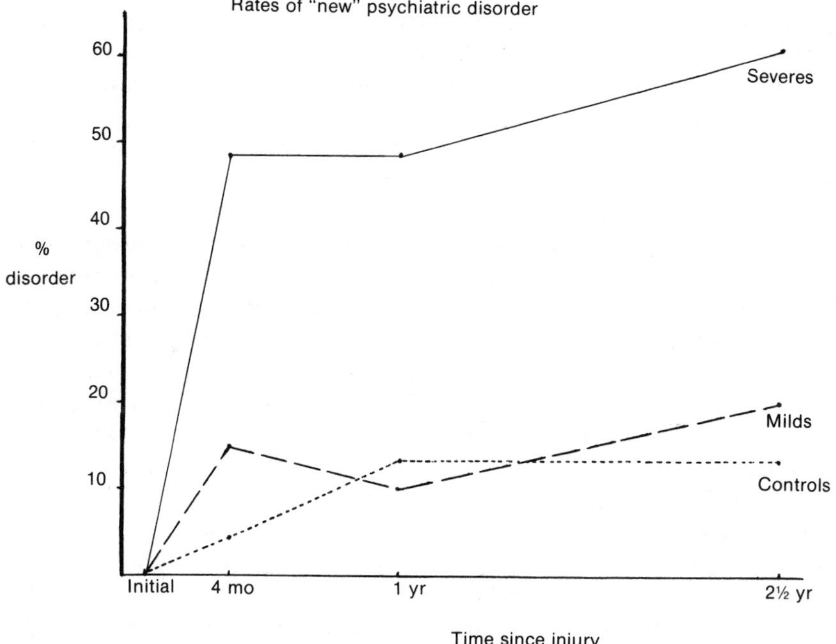

Figure 5-4. Psychiatric disorder arising after accident in children with orthopedic or head injuries. Data from Brown, Chadwick, Shaffer, Rutter, and Traub (1981).

connected with brain trauma but resulting either from the passage of time and the experience of stresses that this may have involved, or from the nonspecific stresses of the accident and of hospital admission, is given by the rate of new psychiatric disorders arising during the course of the follow-up period in controls. The rate of disorders specifically due to brain injury is represented by the *difference* between the head-injury children and their controls. As is evident from the findings shown in Figure 5-4, the rate of new disorders in the severe-head-injury group was much increased, but that in the mild-injury group was no different from that in the controls. As with intellectual deficits, the results show a causal influence with severe head injuries, but not with mild injuries.

Threshold of Injury

These findings raise another question—namely, that of the threshold of injury above which psychological sequelae can be found. We have indicated already that in our own study both cognitive and behavioral sequelae could be identified only with head injuries of sufficient severity to give rise to a PTA of at least 1 week. More detailed analyses broadly confirmed this observation (Chadwick, Rutter, Brown, Shaffer, & Traub, 1981). There was no indication of deficits of any kind in the case of injuries resulting in a PTA of less than 24 hours. With injuries in the group with PTAs of from 2 to 7 days, again most analyses showed *no* intellectual deficit and *no* psychiatric sequelae. However, it was not possible entirely to rule out the possibility of occasional very minor deficits of a transient kind, although the bulk of the evidence was against their occurrence. Definite psychological sequelae could only be identified with certainty when there was a PTA of at least 7 days. Persistent psychiatric sequelae were quite common with all durations of PTA above that level, but, although transient intellectual deficits were also common in this severity range, cognitive impairments lasting as long as 2¼ years were mainly found in the group of children with PTAs lasting 3 weeks or longer. In short, it seemed from this investigation that the threshold of severity of brain injury is quite high with respect to psychological sequelae.

Of course, at best, PTA provides only a very rough-and-ready guide to the severity of brain injury. Penetrating injuries or traumata giving rise to compound depressed skull fractures are less likely to result in prolonged unconsciousness (Braakman, 1972; Miller & Jennett, 1968). Thus, in our parallel follow-up study of children with localized head injuries involving dural tears and visible damage to the underlying cortex (Shaffer *et al.*, 1975; Chadwick, Rutter, Thompson, & Shaffer, 1981), nearly two-thirds were unconscious for less than 30 minutes, and half did not lose consciousness at all. The relative severity of head injuries was shown in other ways—for example, by the fact that more than a fifth developed epileptic seizures and that a fifth were left with clear-cut neurological handicaps of one sort or another. Cognitive impairment (as reflected in both intellectual deficit and reading backwardness) was most frequent in the children with the most severe injuries—as judged by unconsciousness lasting more than 3 days, by the presence of cerebral edema needing treatment during the immediate postinjury period, and by the late onset of fits (Chadwick, Rutter, Thompson, & Shaffer, 1981; Shaffer, Bijur, Chadwick, & Rutter, 1980). Psychiatric disabilities, on the other hand, although somewhat more frequent in children with late-onset fits (Shaffer *et al.*, 1975) did not show the same direct relationship to the severity of injury (Shaffer, Bijur, Chadwick, & Rutter, 1982). This has also been the case with studies of head injury in adults (Bond, 1975; Lishman, 1972), although psychiatric disorders more frequently arise when there has been a prolonged PTA (Lishman, 1968).

The same pattern applied again in our prospective study. While psychiatric disorder showed a significant dose–response relationship with duration of PTA, it was both weaker and less consistent than that found in the case of intellectual impairment. Moreover, as shown in Figure 5-5, although psychiatric disorder was most frequent among the children showing neurological abnormalities at the 2¼-year follow-up, the rate was still substantially raised in the subgroup, with no abnormalities on a systematic and thorough clinical neurological examination (G. Brown *et al.*, 1981).

It should be added that the relationship between cognitive impairment and psychiatric disorder was also quite weak, as demonstrated in Figure 5-6. It should not be assumed that there will be the same threshold for the two types of sequelae, nor should it be assumed that the mechanisms involved are the same.

Although other investigations have not focused directly on the question of threshold, their findings nevertheless point to the probability of a fairly high threshold. Thus, investigations in which most of the head injuries have been relatively minor have usually noted the rather low level of serious sequelae and infrequency of the postconcussional syndrome so common in adults (Burkinshaw, 1960; Dillon & Leopold, 1961; Harris, 1957; Rune, 1970). Similarly, attention has been drawn to the extent to which disorders in children with mild head injuries were already present before the accident or developed as a consequence of chronic home stresses rather than brain damage (Fabian, 1956;

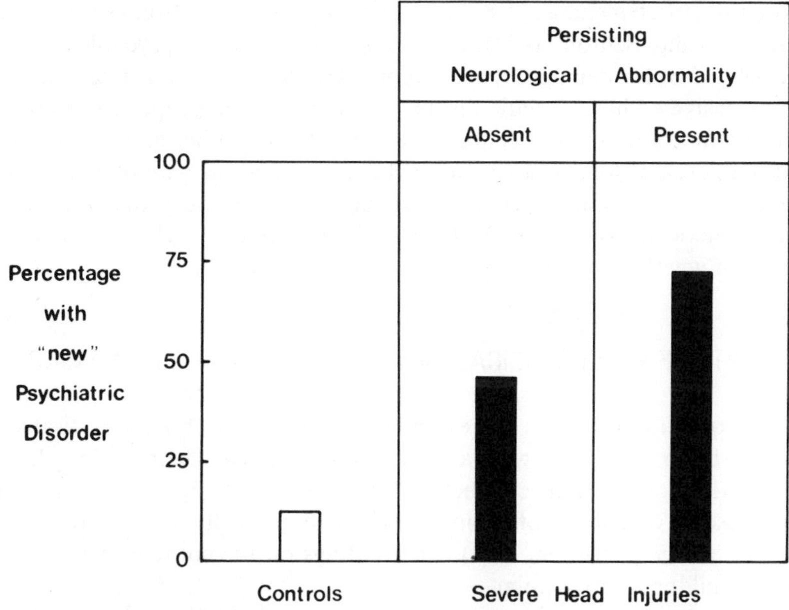

Figure 5-5. Psychiatric disorder in relation to the presence or absence of neurological abnormality in children with severe head injuries. From "Neurobehavioural Associations and Syndromes of 'Minimal Brain Dysfunction'" by M. Rutter and O. Chadwick, in F. C. Rose (Ed.), *Clinical Neuroepidemiology*, London: Pitman Medical Publishing, 1980. Copyright 1980 by Pitman Medical Publishing. Reprinted by permission.

Figure 5-6. Psychiatric disorder in relation to the presence or absence of intellectual impairment in children with severe head injuries. From "Neurobehavioural Associations and Syndromes of 'Minimal Brain Dysfunction'" by M. Rutter and O. Chadwick, in F. C. Rose (Ed.), *Clinical Neuroepidemiology*, London: Pitman Medical Publishing, 1980. Copyright 1980 by Pitman Medical Publishing. Reprinted by permission.

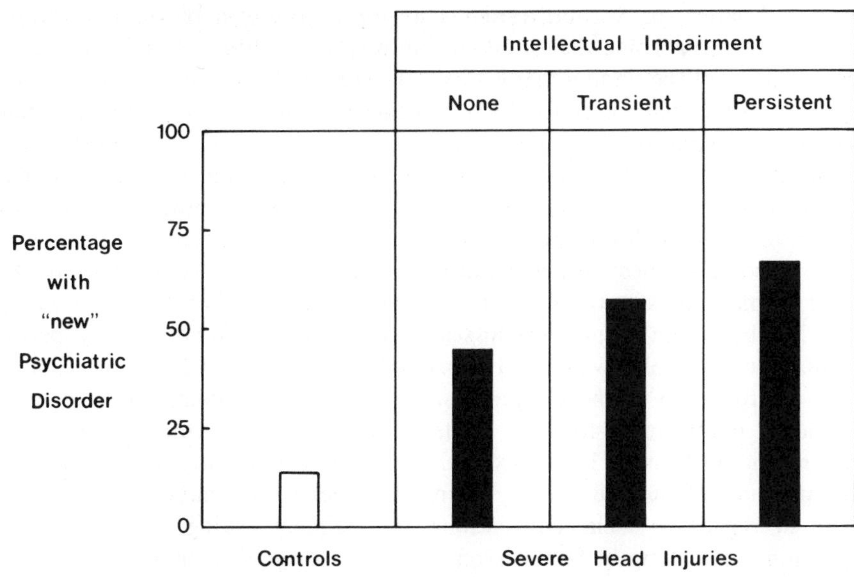

Harrington & Letemendia, 1958; Hjern & Nylander, 1964; Otto, 1960). We may conclude, as did Benton (1973) in an earlier review of the psychological consequences of brain damage, that "cerebral lesions in children must either be quite extensive or have specific disorganizing functional properties in order to produce important behavioral abnormalities." On the other hand, it should be noted that, even as long as a year after the trauma, adults with quite mild head injuries may show subtle deficits in vigilance and memory that are evident during hypoxic stress (Ewing, McCarthy, Gronwall, & Wrighbury, 1980). It is not known whether the same applies to children.

SPECIFICITY OF PSYCHOLOGICAL IMPAIRMENTS DUE TO BRAIN INJURY

The next question concerns the extent to which the psychological disabilities caused by brain injury follow a pathognomonic pattern. There is a long history of attempting to isolate specific behaviors or specific cognitive disabilities that are supposedly diagnostic of brain injury—with generally negative results (see Rutter *et al.*, 1970; Rutter, 1981). The findings on the consequences of brain injury in childhood are similar.

Thus, in our prospective study of head injuries (Chadwick, Rutter, Brown, Shaffer, & Traub, 1981; Chadwick, Rutter, Shaffer, & Shrout, 1981), we found that timed visuospatial and visuomotor tests tended to show more impairment than verbal tests did, as reflected in the recovery phases for the verbal and performance scores on the WISC (shown in Figure 5-7). Similar findings have been reported for adults with head injuries (Mandleberg & Brooks, 1975). However, that aside, no pattern of deficit specific to head injury could be identified. A wide range of specialized tests dealing with variables such as paired associate learning, immediate and delayed recall, attentiveness, distractibility, verbal fluency, and speed of information processing was used in an attempt to isolate subtle or specific deficits in children without global intellectual impairment, but, apart from a tendency for speed of visuomotor and visuospatial functioning to be particularly impaired, none was found (Chadwick, Rutter, Shaffer, & Shrout, 1981). This was partially a result of cognitive patterns varying somewhat among children, but more especially it was a consequence of the finding that it was rather unusual to get marked deficits on specific tests of narrow functions unless there was also some degree of global intellectual impairment. A wide-range intelligence test, such as the WISC, picks up most intellectual deficits that result from head injury, and extensive batteries of neuropsychological tests do not do much better. On the other hand, specific tests concerned with the speed of visuomotor or visuospatial functioning do pick up some intellectual deficits attributable to head injury in children who have normal scores on the WISC (Chadwick, Rutter, Shaffer, & Shrout, 1981).

Much the same applies to our search for behavioral abnormalities specific to brain injury (G. Brown *et al.*, 1981). On the whole, the patterns of psychiatric disorder found in the head-injury children were closely comparable to those found in controls, or for that matter in any group of young people with psychiatric problems. The one exception to that generally negative picture was the presence of marked socially disinhibited behavior: undue outspokenness without regard to social conventions, the frequent asking of embarrassing questions or making of very personal remarks, or getting undressed in social

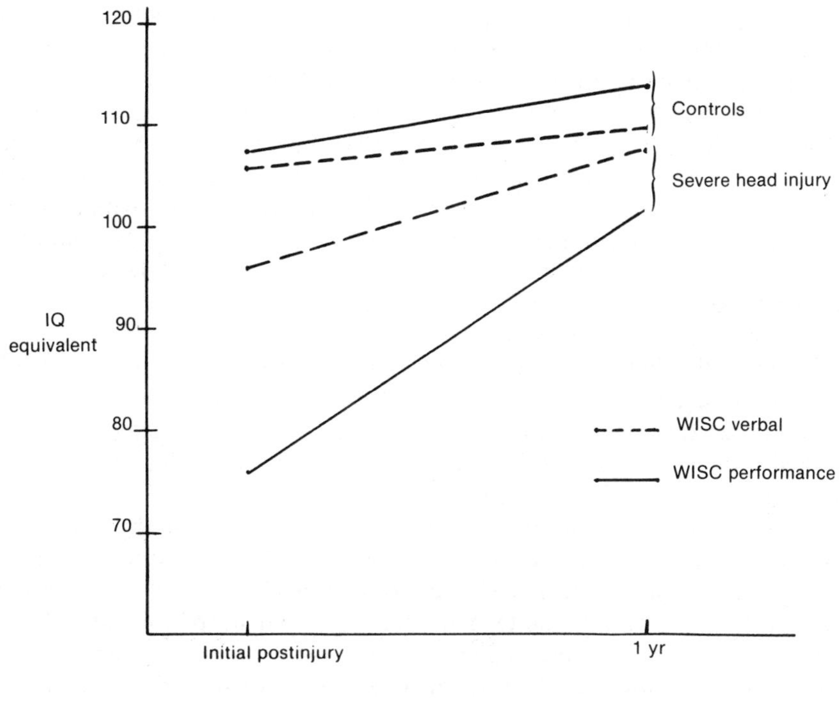

Figure 5-7. Cognitive recovery during the year after head injury. Data from Chadwick, Rutter, Brown, Shaffer, and Traub (1981).

situations in which this would usually be regarded as unacceptable behavior. Sometimes this was also associated with forgetfulness, overtalkativeness, carelessness in personal hygiene and dress, and impulsiveness. This pattern of gross social disinhibition applied to only a minority of disorders, and it was present only in those arising after rather severe head injuries. It is reasonable to conclude that this particular pattern (with its resemblance to the so-called "frontal lobe syndromes" seen in adults—see Lishman, 1978) was a fairly direct result of brain injury, but it constituted the only behavior specific to brain injury that was found. Although some clinical reports in the 1920s and 1930s (Blau, 1936; Strecker & Ebaugh, 1924) suggested that hyperactivity and resistance to discipline was particularly distinctive of the behaviors consequent upon head injury; this has not been confirmed by the more systematic later investigations utilizing control groups (Klonoff *et al.*, 1977; Klonoff & Paris, 1974; Shaffer *et al.*, 1975).

Locus of Injury and Patterns of Cognitive Deficits

Of course, the notion that there might be a specific pattern of psychological impairment characteristic of all forms of brain damage is a somewhat unlikely one, in view of the very varied functions served by the brain. Although it tends to function as a coordinated whole, it is a far from homogeneous organ. Accordingly, it might be supposed that the cognitive and behavioral sequelae would vary according to the hemisphere or lobe affected. In adults, that has indeed been found to be the case, to a limited but nevertheless important extent.

It is accepted that the pattern of cognitive deficits after unilateral cerebral lesions in adults tends to differ, according to which hemisphere is damaged (Chadwick, Rutter, Thompson, & Shaffer, 1981; Lishman, 1978; McFie, 1975a; Newcombe, 1969). In general, verbal impairment is most characteristic of left-hemisphere lesions (even in the absence of dysphasia) and visuospatial impairment of right-hemisphere lesions. This differential pattern is evident even when there is no general intellectual loss, but also it seems that overall decreases in IQ are most likely after left parietotemporal damage, and possibly after frontal lesions on either side. The effects of laterality are probably most marked in the period immediately following the acquisition of the lesion (Fitzhugh, Fitzhugh, & Reitan, 1962), but, nevertheless, they have been found to persist for as long as 20 years afterward (Newcombe, 1969). It also appears that the effects are most marked with deep intrinsic lesions and may not be evident at all with superficial external trauma to the cortex (Newcombe, 1969).

The findings in children have been less clear-cut than this, although, insofar as there has been a tendency, it has run in the same direction. Thus, McFie (1961) found that memory for designs was worse with right-sided lesions but that there was only a mild tendency for verbal deficits to be worse with left-hemisphere lesions. His preliminary findings (McFie, 1975b) from a larger series of children with head injuries, hematomas, abscesses, or tumors showed much the same results. There was no consistent tendency for the verbal IQ to be lower in left-sided lesions, although learning of new words was more impaired. Laterality effects seemed to be more marked in older adolescents than in younger children.

The matter was investigated further in our follow-up study of children who had sustained unilateral compound depressed fractures of the skull resulting in tears in the dura mater and with gross damage to the underlying brain observed at operation (Chadwick, Rutter, Thompson, & Shaffer, 1981). All the children had been 12 years of age or less at the time of injury and were of school age at the time of follow-up at least 2 years later. Cognitive deficits tended to be slightly more marked with visuospatial and visuomotor skills than with verbal skills, regardless of which hemisphere was damaged. Also, intellectual impairment was significantly associated with the overall severity of generalized brain damage, and probably also with the severity of local trauma, as reflected in late post-traumatic epilepsy or motor abnormalities contralateral to the side of the injury. The possible effects of laterality and locus of injury were examined both before and after excluding cases with generalized damage. They were also studied in the subgroup of 20 children with more severe local lesions resulting in persisting neurological signs of motor abnormalities but no detectable contrecoup effects (as determined by the absence of ipsilateral motor signs). But, however analyzed, we could find no significant laterality or locus effects with respect to the pattern of cognitive functioning as shown on either the WISC or more specific tests (such as those assessing learning of new words, verbal fluency, or motor impersistence). There was, however, a slight but consistent tendency for all tests of scholastic attainment to show greater impairment with left-hemisphere lesions. This tendency was somewhat more marked in the children who were under 5 years of age at the time of injury. We may conclude that the evidence, when considered as a whole, suggests that the cognitive deficits associated with lateralized brain injuries in childhood are of a broadly similar type to those associated with adult injuries, but that the effects tend to be less specific and less differentiated in children. The consequence is that the pattern of cognitive functioning following head injury provides no useful guide to the locus of the brain lesion in the individual child.

Locus of Lesion and Behavioral Sequelae

The effects of locus of brain injury on psychiatric sequelae in adults were systematically studied by Lishman (1968) in his investigation of 670 patients with penetrating injuries who had been treated at the Oxford emergency head-injury unit. Of these, 144 were judged to have severe psychiatric disabilities during the course of a 5-year follow-up. Affective disorders, behavioral abnormalities (lack of judgment, disinhibition, etc.), and somatic complaints all tended to be more frequent after right-hemisphere damage; also, all were most strongly associated with frontal lobe lesions than with lesions in other lobes (apart from depression and irritability, which were linked with parietal as well as frontal lobe damage). Thus, it appeared that, in contrast to intellectual deficits (which were strongly associated with left-hemisphere damage), psychiatric sequelae were most apparent with right-sided damage. Similarly, whereas intellectual deficits were most associated with lesions in the tempero- and parieto-occipital regions, all forms of psychiatric sequelae tended to be associated with frontal lobe lesions.

Possible associations between the locus of brain damage and specific forms of psychiatric disturbance in adults have also been examined by a variety of other techniques, including the correlates of epileptic foci in different loci, the effects of unilateral electroconvulsive therapy, EEG patterns, unilateral carotid injections of a barbiturate, presentation of films to visual half-fields, and neuropsychological patterns in different psychiatric states (see Flor-Henry, 1979; Gainotti, 1979; Lishman, 1978; Tucker, 1981; Wexler, 1980). Much of this evidence is indirect and open to varying interpretations; nevertheless, it is generally in keeping with the notion that the right hemisphere is particularly concerned with the processing of emotions, and that right-sided lesions tend to be particularly associated with depression. Rather different loci are associated with schizophrenia; left-sided temporal lobe epilepsy constitutes the type of brain dysfunction most strongly associated with schizophrenia.

The question of whether the locus of brain injury influences the type of psychiatric symptomatology in childhood was examined in our study of 98 children with localized head injuries (Shaffer *et al.*, 1982). The results were somewhat equivocal in that the site of injury was not associated with the overall psychiatric diagnosis or with the type of emotional or behavioral disturbance, as indicated by the pattern of scores on the teachers' questionnaire. On the other hand, when individual symptom clusters (based on the combination of information from mothers, teachers, and the children themselves) were considered separately, a significant association was found between depression and lesions in the right frontal and left posterior regions. More detailed analyses showed that this association was maintained even after controlling for age, sex, and psychosocial factors. However, no relationship was found between site of injury and symptoms of overactivity, inattention, aggression, or antisocial behavior.

The findings with respect to locus of lesion and depression are provocative in their implications and are in keeping with Flor-Henry's (1979) suggestion of a functional link between the right frontal and left parieto-occipital lobes. Nevertheless, that link has yet to be adequately established, and the association between these loci and depressive symptomatology needs to be replicated before it can be accepted as valid.

NONNEUROLOGICAL MODIFYING FACTORS

Age at Injury

Although there are several reasons why it might be expected that a child's age at the time of injury should influence the psychological sequelae of head injury, there is little evidence on the extent to which this does in fact occur. In our own study of children with severe generalized brain trauma (defined in terms of a PTA exceeding 3 weeks), there was some suggestion that cognitive recovery during the first year after injury might be slightly more rapid in those aged 5 to 10 years than in those over 10 years of age, but the differences were small and well short of statistical significance (Chadwick, Rutter, Brown, Shaffer, & Traub, 1981). Klonoff *et al.* (1977), too, found that the child's age at injury was not a major variable in the determination of persistent cognitive impairment. Woo-Sam, Zimmerman, Brink, Uyehara, & Miller (1970), on the other hand, found that intellectual impairment several years after head injury was more frequent in children aged below 8 years at the time of the accident than in those aged over 10. It could be that although younger children recover more rapidly, they do so less completely. However, two other possibilities must be considered as well. Firstly, it may be that the effects of age are minimal during the school-age years, but that they are greater during the very early years of life. Secondly, the age at injury may influence the type of cognitive deficit. There is some limited empirical support for both suggestions. Thus, Woods (1980) compared unilateral perinatal and infantile brain lesions with those arising after a child's first birthday, all the lesions being thought to be frontal or frontoparietal in location. Lesions arising during the first year of life tended to be associated with somewhat greater intellectual deficits that involved both verbal *and* performance abilities, regardless of the side of the lesion. In contrast, the effects of lesions after the first birthday depended on the side of the lesion. The later left-hemisphere lesions were associated with lowered verbal and performance scores, whereas the right-hemisphere lesions led to impaired performance scores only. The findings are limited by uncertainty on whether the lesions were of comparable severity at different ages, by uncertainty on whether the lesions were strictly unilateral, and by the fact that the etiology of postnatal lesions differed from that of the perinatal disorders. Nevertheless, the findings from our study of localized head injuries provide some support for the suggestion that very early brain lesions may have somewhat different effects from those following trauma in later childhood (Chadwick, Rutter, Thompson, & Shaffer, 1981; Shaffer *et al.*, 1980). There was a fairly consistent tendency among those with left-sided injuries for cognitive scores to be lower in the children who were aged under 5 years at the time of injury. Even more strikingly, scholastic attainments were more severely impaired in the younger children.

The findings so far on age effects are too few and too contradictory for any firm statements. But it may be concluded tentatively that the main difference probably lies between the effects of lesions in infancy and those later in childhood, with only minimal age effects during the school-age years. Furthermore, it may be that age effects differ with respect to *speed* of cognitive recovery, the *pattern* of cognitive deficit, and the ultimate *extent* of intellectual impairment. It should also be emphasized that the short-term and long-term sequelae may not be the same and that the consequences reflect age-related changes in intellectual requirements as well as developmental alterations in brain plasticity. Insofar as brain damage has its greatest impact on *new* learning (Hebb, 1942), it is likely to lead to greater impairment in young children just because they have more new learning to undertake and less accumulated knowledge and established skills on which to rely (Rutter, 1981). But also (regardless of age at injury), intellectual deficits may be more apparent in later childhood just because the intellectual demands and the need for autonomy and cognitive flexibility are greater then than in the early years of life (Bowman *et al.*, 1974).

While little is known on age effects with respect to cognitive deficits, even less is known on their role regarding psychiatric sequelae. In our studies of both generalized (G. Brown *et al.*, 1981) and localized head injuries (Shaffer *et al.*, 1975), we could detect no relationship between the child's age at injury and the risk of psychiatric disorder following head injury. However, the matter needs to be studied further, and the available data are not sufficient to rule out more subtle effects.

Sex of Child

There are major sex differences in rates of psychiatric disorder and in children's responses to various forms of psychosocial stress or adversity (Rutter, 1982). However, both the cognitive and behavioral sequelae of head injury have been found to be broadly similar in boys and girls in the very few studies that have examined the matter (G. Brown *et al.*, 1981; Chadwick, Rutter, Brown, Shaffer, & Traub, 1981; Shaffer *et al.*, 1980). This has also been the case with brain damage due to causes other than trauma (Rutter *et al.*, 1970). The possible role of sex differences in children's responses to head injury requires further investigation, but, on the evidence to date, it does not appear to be an important modifying factor. Conversely, however, this negative finding also means that severe brain injury tends to reduce, or even to eliminate, the sex differences in psychiatric disorder that are so striking in the general population.

Social Class

In children without brain damage, social class is consistently associated with intelligence, the intercorrelation being about .5 (Rutter & Madge, 1976). In brain-injured children, too, social class correlates with IQ (Chadwick, Rutter, Brown, Shaffer, & Traub, 1981). However, such evidence as is available indicates that social class is of little importance in predicting cognitive recovery following head injury (Chadwick, Rutter, Brown, Shaffer, & Traub, 1981; Woo-Sam *et al.*, 1970). There is some suggestion that recovery may be marginally better in children from socially more advantaged homes, but differences have been well short of statistical significance and quite minor compared with the effects of severity of injury.

Family Reactions

Few data are available on the manner in which families react to their children's head injuries, or on how these reactions might influence psychiatric sequelae. However, in our prospective study (G. Brown, 1982), we found that the initial impact in the group with severe injuries was considerable. Thus, a third of the parents whose children had PTAs exceeding 1 week in length had doubted at some point whether their children would survive (this never occurred with the parents of children experiencing orthopedic or mild head injuries). After the anxieties engendered by the children's remaining in coma, there were further worries created by their unusual behavior as they regained consciousness. Not surprisingly, more parents of children with severe head injuries (13 out of a group of 28) than of those with orthopedic injuries (4 out of 28) showed emotional disturbances from which they took a long time to recover. There was also a tendency for the parents of head-injured children to become more overprotective (doing more for their children and allowing them less autonomy and independence), and to be less strict in their discipline (parents being particularly afraid to use physical punishment when their children were taking anticonvulsants). Although a head injury tended to be followed by some initial increase in marital tensions, it was unusual for these to continue for more than a few months.

The sample size was rather small for an analysis of the role of these family reactions as modifying factors in relation to psychiatric sequelae. Nevertheless, it was evident that the children whose parents showed most changes in their behavior (in terms of their own emotional disturbance, an increase in overprotection, or a decrease in discipline) tended to have an increased risk of psychiatric disorder following head injury. It seemed that these alterations in parental behavior were reactive to the injury and its meaning to them, rather than to changes in their children's behavior. Also, the overall pattern of findings suggested that the form of parental reaction played some part in protecting the children from or rendering them more vulnerable to psychiatric sequelae.

Psychosocial Adversity

In our studies of both localized (Shaffer *et al.*, 1975) and generalized brain injuries (G. Brown *et al.*, 1981), psychosocial factors have proved to be important predictors of psychiatric sequelae. In the investigation of children with cortical lesions resulting from unilateral compound depressed fractures of the skull with associated dural tears, psychiatric disorders were significantly more frequent in children from broken homes or discordant family environments; in children whose mothers or fathers had psychiatric disorders; or from large families in which there were four or more siblings. Similar associations were evident in our prospective study of children with generalized brain injuries.

A summary measure of psychosocial adversity was created by summing the scores on six separate indexes (giving a score of 1 when the item was present): anomalous or discordant family; large family size or overcrowding; admission to foster care or a children's home because of family difficulties; psychiatric disorder in the mother; paternal criminality; and low social status (G. Brown *et al.*, 1981). The rate of new psychiatric disorders arising *after* severe head injury was still raised above that in controls (children with orthopedic injuries) even in the absence of psychosocial adversity, but psychiatric disorder was most frequent of all when a severe brain injury was combined with psychosocial adversity (see Figure 5-8).

Temperament and Preinjury Behavior

There have been difficulties in the assessment of the possible importance of a child's temperament or preinjury behavior in modifying his or her response to brain injury, in that necessarily the measurements have had to be retrospective. However, in our prospective study, it was possible greatly to reduce the potential biases that are inherent in retrospective measures, by obtaining information

Figure 5-8. Psychosocial adversity and the development of "new" psychiatric disorders after injury. Data from Brown, Chadwick, Shaffer, Rutter, and Traub (1981).

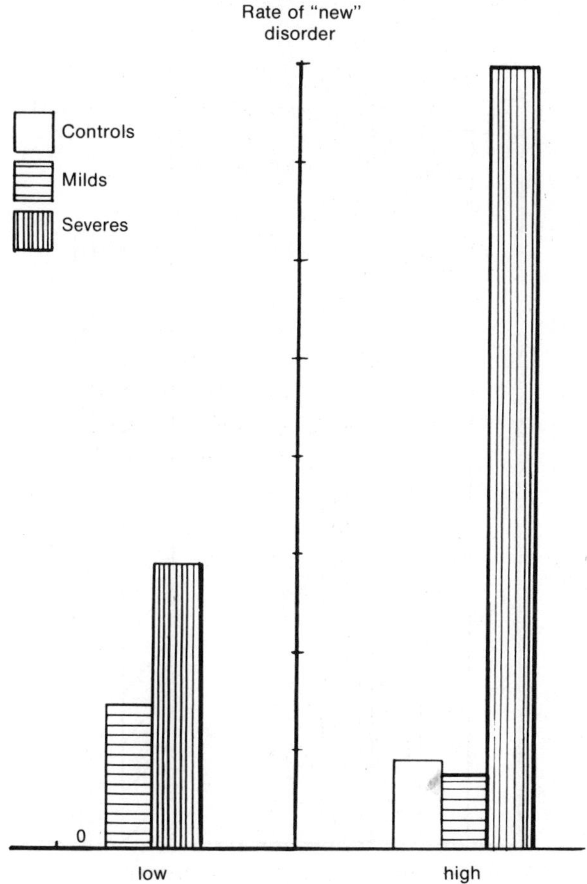

on the preaccident period from parents and teachers very soon after the accident and before the informants could know whether there would be any behavioral sequelae of the injury (G. Brown *et al.*, 1981). Preaccident behavior was categorized as (1) normal or showing no significant abnormality; (2) showing minor emotional or behavioral problems not sufficient to warrant a rating of psychiatric disorder; and (3) showing overtly handicapping psychiatric disorders. In order to focus on children whose psychiatric disabilities were specifically due to head injury, the last group (with disorders antedating the accident) was eliminated from further analyses. Then, the role of the children's preaccident behavior in predisposing to psychiatric sequelae could be assessed by means of a comparison of the first two groups with respect to the rate of psychiatric disorders arising de novo after the accident (see Figure 5-9). Whereas only a quarter of the group with normal preaccident behavior developed disorder by the time of the 1-year follow-up, over half of those with preinjury abnormalities did so. It was evident that even in children with severe brain injuries, the development of psychiatric sequelae was in part a function of their preaccident behavior. While this was not apparent in Black *et al.*'s (1971) follow-up study,

Figure 5-9. Children's behavior before head injury and psychiatric state 1 year after injury. Data from Brown, Chadwick, Shaffer, Rutter, and Traub (1981).

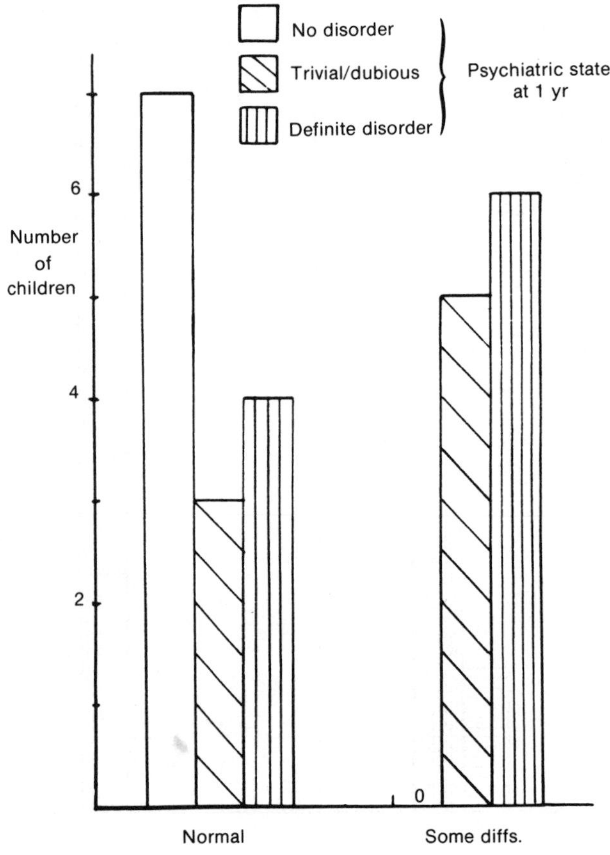

their behavioral assessments were unstandardized and did not differentiate between preaccident *disorders* and preaccident behavioral *traits*.

Harrington and Letemendia (1958) approached the same question in a different way—through a comparison of an unselected group of children treated for head injury with a group of children with head injuries referred to a psychiatric clinic. The latter group showed a similar severity of head injury but differed in terms of adverse personality features and family characteristics. The authors concluded that nonneurological factors played the major role in the genesis of the psychiatric problems. However, it should be noted that this conclusion applied to a group with generally rather mild head injuries, so that the relative importance of brain damage could well be greater in children with more severe injuries (as it was in our own studies).

Cognitive Impairment

In studies of children with brain lesions due to factors other than head injury, usually it has been found that psychiatric disorder is more frequent in those with either a low level of general intelligence or severe reading difficulties (Rutter *et al.*, 1970; Seidel, Chadwick, & Rutter, 1975). There has been a similar trend in studies of children with head injuries, although the associations have been neither as strong nor as consistent (G. Brown *et al.*, 1981; Shaffer *et al.*, 1980). Thus, in our prospective study of children with generalized brain injury, there was a trend for children with psychiatric disorder arising after the injury to have somewhat lower performance IQs (G. Brown *et al.*, 1981). However, this was most marked in relation to the IQ scores obtained soon after the accident (this constituted the only difference to reach statistical significance), indicating that the association between psychiatric disorder and IQ was most marked when the IQ level strongly reflected the results of brain injury. Moreover, even this immediate postaccident IQ score only predicted psychiatric disorder during the first year of follow-up—suggesting that the later occurring psychiatric disorders were less directly due to brain injury.

Modifying Factors and Cognitive Sequelae

It is evident that, with the exception of a child's age at injury, nonneurological factors play a negligible role in modifying the cognitive sequelae of severe head injuries. Taken in conjunction with the evidence of a strong dose–response relationship with the severity of the injury (as judged by duration of PTA), this gives rise to the strong inference that when there is intellectual impairment it arises as a fairly direct result of brain trauma.

Modifying Factors and Psychiatric Sequelae

The findings with respect to psychiatric sequelae, however, are quite different. Although, as argued above, there is good evidence that brain injury constitutes a specific etiological influence, its effects are more indirect and less consistent than with cognitive sequelae. This is shown both by the weaker dose–response relationship with severity of injury and by the much greater importance of nonneurological modifying factors, such as psychosocial adversity, family reactions, and preaccident behavior or temperamental features. The etiology of psychiatric disorders arising after head injury is more complex than the origins of intellectual impairment. Brain injury per se plays an important role, but it constitutes, not *the* cause, but rather one element in a multifactorial etiology involving both neurological and nonneurological variables.

COURSE OF RECOVERY

Studies in adults (Bond, 1975; Bond & Brooks, 1976; Fahy, Irving, & Millac, 1967; Mandleberg & Brooks, 1975) have indicated that most intellectual recovery takes place during the first 6 months after injury, although, especially in the case of more severe injuries, intellectual gains may continue at a slower pace for much longer. In addition, there is some suggestion that verbal skills recover more quickly than do visuospatial skills, but that the latter may go on improving for a longer time, with some improvement continuing for as long as 2 years after injury. However, isolated cases of late recovery several years after head injury have been reported (J. C. Brown, 1975). Much the same has been found with children (although there is some indication that there may be a later fall-off in verbal skills—see Black *et al.*, 1971).

The course of cognitive recovery in our prospective study of children with severe head injuries is shown in Figure 5-10, which gives the degree of deficit on the coding subtest of the WISC (expressed in terms of the difference in *SD*s between the cases and their individually matched controls). Although the difference is a slight one, it appears that the recovery slope continues on a steeper gradient for longer in the children with the most severe injuries.

Figure 5-11 shows a different examination of the same matter, provided by splitting the group, not according to duration of PTA, but rather according to

Figure 5-10. The course of cognitive recovery after head injury according to the severity of the injury. From "A Prospective Study of Children with Head Injuries: II. Cognitive Sequelae" by O. Chadwick, M. Rutter, G. Brown, D. Shaffer, and M. Traub, *Psychological Medicine*, 1981, 49–61. Copyright 1981 by Cambridge University Press. Reprinted by permission.

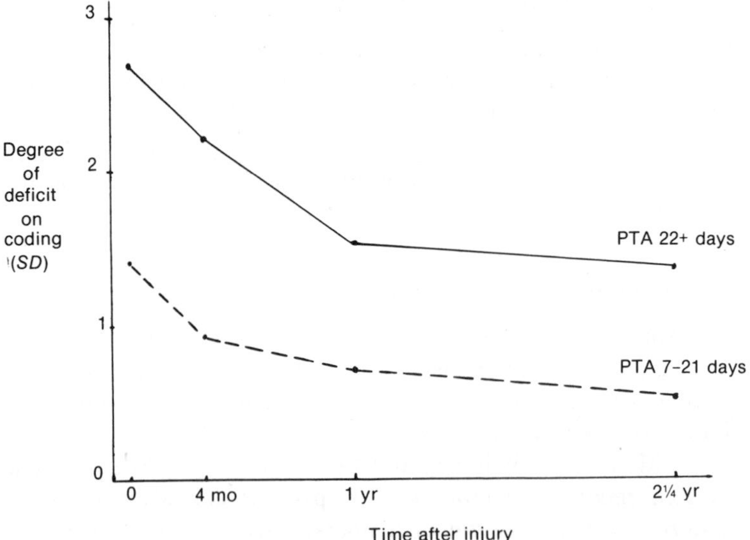

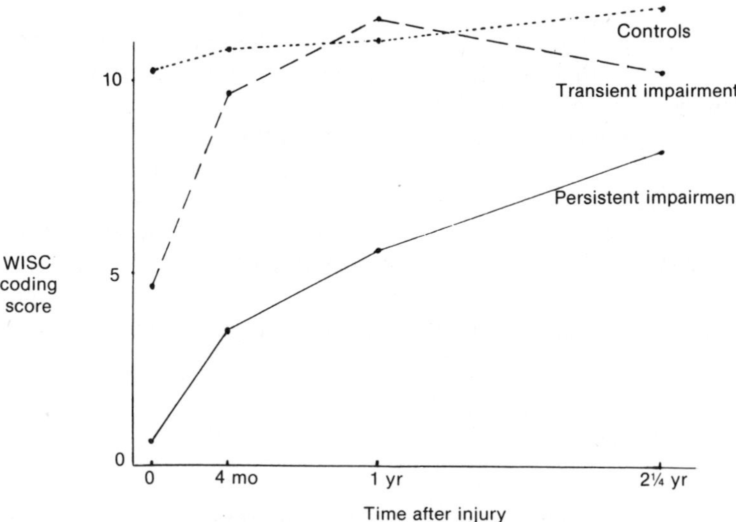

Figure 5-11. The course of cognitive recovery after head injury according to the severity of intellectual impairment. From "A Prospective Study of Children with Head Injuries: II. Cognitive Sequelae" by O. Chadwick, M. Rutter, G. Brown, D. Shaffer, and M. Traub, *Psychological Medicine*, 1981, 49–61. Copyright 1981 by Cambridge University Press. Reprinted by permission.

whether there was transient or persistent cognitive impairment. The children whose impairment was only transient improved their scores on coding during the year after injury but improved no further thereafter. In contrast, the persistent-impairment group showed a substantial continuing improvement during the second year after injury. As all follow-up ceased at that point, we do not know whether there was any further recovery after that. However, combining all findings, we may conclude that cognitive recovery is most marked immediately after head injury; that substantial intellectual improvement continues throughout the first year after brain trauma; and that much smaller gains may occur during the second year, perhaps especially in those children with the most severe injuries.

The pattern of findings with respect to psychiatric disability are much less clear-cut. Black *et al.* (1969, 1971) reported that hyperkinesis reached a peak some 3 months after injury and that poor control of emotions persisted at a high level for about 2 years, whereas conduct problems did not show a major increase until 4 or 5 years after the head injury. Unfortunately, findings from a sibling control group (Black *et al.*, 1981) have not yet been presented in sufficient detail to show which (if any) of these changes were specific to head injury (as distinct from being a consequence of increasing age). Klonoff (Klonoff *et al.*, 1977; Klonoff & Paris, 1974), on the other hand, reported a marked tendency for all symptoms to subside during the course of the follow-up. However, it is difficult to know how much weight to attach to this finding in view of the large loss of cases and the inadequate reporting of methodology.

In our own prospective study, the main increase in psychiatric disturbance took place during the months immediately following the injury, and it was then that social disinhibition was at its peak. Thereafter there was no substantial fall-off in psychiatric problems during the 2¼-year follow-up, but there was a tendency for the characteristic pattern of socially embarrassing behavior to diminish, so that the disorders in the severe-head-injury group at the final follow-up were less clearly distinctive. The only symptom to show a consistent increase during the later period of follow-up was overeating, but this occurred in too few children for much weight to be attached to the finding. Perhaps the main conclusion to draw is that, whereas cognitive deficits following head injury had become much attenuated by 2¼ years after the accident, psychiatric disorders continued to be a persistent problem. Although the data are not as strong as one would like, it is probably also the case that scholastic problems continue long after deficits have ceased to be apparent on standard tests of general intelligence.

PREVENTIVE ACTION

The issues of the rehabilitation of children suffering head injuries and of the steps that may be taken to prevent the various cognitive and behavioral sequelae have received surprisingly little attention. Although it is clear that there are various potentially useful ways in which recovery might be facilitated, it has to be admitted that very little is known about how much can in fact be achieved by any form of intervention. However, at least four different types of action need to be considered. Firstly, there are the medical and surgical steps needed immediately following the injury in order to prevent or deal with the complications of injury (Bruce, Schut, Bruno, Wood, & Sutton, 1978). While these are important, they are outside the scope of this chapter. Secondly, there is the role of counseling the parents on the effects of brain injury. Hjern and Nylander's (1964) findings suggest that psychiatric sequelae are less frequent when parents are told that concussion of the brain is usually a fairly trivial condition, that most sequelae tend to be transient, and that active reintroduction of a child to normal activities is appropriate and helpful. Our own findings also suggest that it is desirable that parents be advised against being unduly protective. Thirdly, there is the possible value of active programs of rehabilitation with speech therapy, occupational therapy, and the like. There is some indication from studies with adults that this may be helpful (Bond & Brooks, 1976; Relander, Troupp, & Bjorkensten, 1972), although whether the same results apply with children is not known. Fourthly, there are the actions that may be taken to ameliorate maladaptive family responses, to remedy scholastic difficulties, and to deal with emotional and behavioral problems. No evidence is available on what can be achieved in this connection, but it is evident that a broad-based approach is likely to be required.

CONCLUSION

Severe head injuries constitute an important cause of both cognitive impairment and psychiatric disability in children. However, in assessing the sequelae that follow head injury, it is important to take into account the fact that, compared with the general population, children experiencing head injuries more often come from families experiencing psychosocial adversities. Nevertheless, even so, it is clear that brain injury substantially increases the risk of psychological difficulties. The effect with respect to intellectual deficits is a fairly direct one, with the extent of the deficit a function of the severity of generalized brain damage. In contrast, the effects of head injury on behavior are less straightforward. Undoubtedly, brain injury makes a specific impact in increasing the psychiatric risk, but in addition both temperamental features and psychosocial variables play important roles. Brain injury in childhood tends to have a greater effect on the speed of visuospatial and visuomotor functioning than on verbal skills, but otherwise there is little that is specific in the pattern of cognitive deficit. Similarly, psychiatric problems are varied in type, with marked social disinhibition as the only feature specific to brain injury. Very considerable cognitive recovery takes place during the 2 years after head injury, but scholastic and psychiatric disabilities more often tend to be long-lasting. There is a potential for various forms of preventive intervention, but little is known about their efficacy.

References

Backett, E. M., & Johnston, A. M. Social patterns of road accidents to children: Some characteristics of vulnerable families. *British Medical Journal*, 1959, *1*, 409–413.

Basser, L. S. Hemiplegia of early onset and the faculty of speech with special reference to the effects of hemispherectomy. *Brain*, 1962, *85*, 427–460.

Benton, A. L. Minimal brain dysfunction from a neuropsychological point of view. *Annals of the New York Academy of Science*, 1973, *205*, 29–37.

Bishop, D. V. M. Plasticity and specificity of long range localization in the developing brain. *Developmental Medicine and Child Neurology*, 1981, *23*, 251–255.

Black, P., Blumer, D., Wellner, A. M., & Walker, A. E. The head-injured child: Time-course of recovery, with implications for rehabilitation. In *Head injuries* (Proceedings of an international symposium held in Edinburgh and Madrid, April 2–10, 1970). Baltimore: Williams & Wilkins, 1971.

Black, P., Blumer, D., Wellner, A. M., Shepard, R. H., & Walker, A. E. Head trauma in children: Neurological, behavioral, and intellectual sequelae. In P. Black (Ed.), *Brain dysfunction in children: Etiology, diagnosis and management*. New York: Raven Press, 1981.

Black, P., Jeffries, J., Blumer, D., Wellner, A., & Walker, A. E. The post-traumatic syndrome in children: Characteristics and incidence. In A. E. Walker, W. F. Caveness, & M. Critchley (Eds.), *The late effects of head injury*. Springfield, Ill.: Charles C Thomas, 1969.

Blau, A. Mental changes following head trauma in children. *Archives of Neurology and Psychiatry*, 1936, *35*, 723–769.

Bloomquist, E. R., & Courville, C. B. The nature and incidence of traumatic lesions of the brain. *Bulletin of the Los Angeles Neurological Societies*, 1947, *12*, 174–183.

Bond, M. R. Assessment of the psychosocial outcome after severe head injury. In R. Porter & D. FitzSimons (Eds.), *Outcome of severe damage to the central nervous system* (Ciba Foundation Symposium No. 34, new series). Amsterdam: Elsevier–Excerpta Medica–North Holland, 1975.

Bond, M. R., & Brooks, D. N. Understanding the process of recovery as a basis for the investigation of rehabilitation for the brain injured. *Scandinavian Journal of Rehabilitation Medicine*, 1976, *8*, 127–133.

Bowman, K. M., Blau, A., & Reich, R. Psychiatric states following head injury in adults and children. In E. H. Feiring (Ed.), *Brock's injuries of the brain and spinal cord and their coverings*. New York: Springer, 1974.

Braakman, R. Depressed skull fracture: Data, treatment and follow-up in 225 consecutive cases. *Journal of Neurology, Neurosurgery, and Psychiatry*, 1972, *35*, 395–402.

Brink, J. D., Garrett, A. L., Hale, W. R., Woo-Sam, J., & Nickel, V. C. Recovery of motor and intellectual function in children sustaining severe head injuries. *Developmental Medicine and Child Neurology*, 1970, *12*, 545–571.

Brooks, D. N. Wechsler Memory Scale performance and its relationship to brain damage after severe closed head injury. *Journal of Neurology, Neurosurgery, and Psychiatry*, 1976, *39*, 593–601.

Brooks, D. N., Aughton, M. E., Bond, M. R., Jones, P., & Rizvi, S. Cognitive sequelae in relationship to early indices of severity of brain damage after severe blunt head injury. *Journal of Neurology, Neurosurgery, and Psychiatry*, 1980, *43*, 529–534.

Brown, G. Unpublished data, 1982.

Brown, G., Chadwick, O., Shaffer, D., Rutter, M., & Traub, M. A prospective study of children with head injuries: III. Psychiatric sequelae. *Psychological Medicine*, 1981, *11*, 63–78.

Brown, G. W., & Davidson, S. Social class, psychiatric disorder of mother, and accidents to children. *Lancet*, 1978, *1*, 378–381.

Brown, J. C. Late recovery from head injury: Case report and review. *Psychological Medicine*, 1975, *5*, 239–248.

Bruce, D. A., Raphaely, R. C., Goldber, A. I., Zimmerman, R. A., Bilaniuk, L. T., Schut, L., & Kuhl, D. E. Pathophysiology: Treatment and outcome following severe head injury in children. *Child's Brain*, 1979, *5*, 174–191.

Bruce, D. A., Schut, L., Bruno, L. A., Wood, J. H., & Sutton, L. N. Outcome following severe head injuries in children. *Journal of Neurosurgery*, 1978, *48*, 679–688.

Burkinshaw, J. Head injuries in children: Observations on their incidence and causes with an enquiry into the value of routine skull x-rays. *Archives of Disease in Childhood*, 1960, *35*, 205–214.

Burton, L. *Vulnerable children*. New York: Schocken, 1968.

Chadwick, O., Rutter, M., Brown, G., Shaffer, D., & Traub, M. A prospective study of children with head injuries: II. Cognitive sequelae. *Psychological Medicine*, 1981, *11*, 49–61.

Chadwick, O., Rutter, M., Shaffer, D., & Shrout, P. A prospective study of children with head injuries: IV. Specific cognitive deficits. *Journal of Clinical Neuropsychology*, 1981, *3*, 101–120.

Chadwick, O., Rutter, M., Thompson, J., & Shaffer, D. Intellectual performance and reading skills after localized head injury in childhood. *Journal of Child Psychology and Psychiatry*, 1981, *22*, 117–139.

Comninos, S. C. Early prognosis of severe head injuries in children. *Acta Neurochirurgica*, 1979, *28*(Suppl.), 144–147.

Courville, C. B. Contrecoup injuries of the brain in injury. *Archives of Surgery*, 1965, *90*, 157–165.

Craft, A. W., Shaw, D. A., & Cartlidge, N. E. Head injuries in children. *British Medical Journal*, 1972, *3*, 200–203.

Cummins, B. H., & Potter, J. M. Head injury due to falls from heights. *Injury*, 1970, *2*, 61–64.

Dillon, H., & Leopold, R. C. Children and the post-concussion syndrome. *Journal of the American Medical Association*, 1961, *175*, 86–92.

Dobbing, J., & Smart, J. L. Vulnerability of developing brain and behaviour. *British Medical Bulletin*, 1974, *30*, 164–168.

Ebels, E. J. Maturation of the central nervous system. In M. Rutter (Ed.), *Scientific foundations of developmental psychiatry*. London: Heinemann Medical Books, 1980.

Eiser, C. Intellectual abilities among survivors of childhood leukaemia as a function of CNS irradiation. *Archives of Disease in Childhood*, 1978, *53*, 391–395.

Ewing, R., McCarthy, D., Gronwall, D., & Wrighbury, A. P. Persisting effects of minor head injury observable during hypoxic stress. *Journal of Clinical Neuropsychology*, 1980, *2*, 147–155.

Fabian, A. A. Prognosis in head injuries in children. *Journal of Nervous and Mental Disease*, 1956, *123*, 428–431.

Fahy, T. J., Irving, M. H., & Millac, P. Severe head injury. *Lancet*, 1967, *2*, 475–479.

Field, J. H. *Epidemiology of head injury in England and Wales*. London: Her Majesty's Stationery Office, 1976.

Fitzhugh, K. B., Fitzhugh, L. C., & Reitan, R. M. Wechsler–Bellevue comparison in groups with "chronic" and "current" lateralized and diffuse brain lesions. *Journal of Consulting and Clinical Psychology*, 1962, *26*, 306–310.

Flach, J., & Malmros, R. A long-term follow-up of children with severe head injury. *Scandinavian Journal of Rehabilitation Medicine*, 1972, *4*, 9–15.

Flor-Henry, P. On certain aspects of localization of the cerebral systems regulating and determining emotion. *Biological Psychiatry*, 1979, *14*, 677–698.

Gaidolfi, E., & Vignolo, L. A. Closed head injuries of school-age children: Neuropsychological sequelae in early adulthood. *Italian Journal of Neurological Sciences*, 1980, *2*, 65–73.

Gainotti, G. The relationship between emotions and cerebral dominance: A review of the clinical and experimental evidence. In J. Gruzelier & P. Flor-Henry (Eds.), *Hemispheric asymmetries of function in psychopathology*. Amsterdam: Elsevier–North Holland, 1979.

Geschwind, N. Late changes in the nervous system: An overview. In D. G. Stein, J. J. Rosen, & N. Butters (Eds.), *Plasticity and recovery of function in the central nervous system*. New York: Academic Press, 1974.

Goldberger, M. E. Recovery of movement after CNS lesions in monkeys. In D. G. Stein, J. J. Rosen, & N. Butters (Eds.), *Plasticity and recovery of function in the central nervous system*. New York: Academic Press, 1974.

Goldman, P. S. An alternative to developmental plasticity: Heterology of CNS structures in infants and adults. In D. G. Stein, J. J. Rosen, & N. Butters (Eds.), *Plasticity and recovery of function in the central nervous system*. New York: Academic Press, 1974.

Gronwall, D., & Wrightson, P. Duration of post-traumatic amnesia after mild head injury. *Journal of Clinical Neuropsychology*, 1980, *2*, 51–60.

Harrington, J. H., & Letemendia, F. J. Persistent psychiatric disorders after head injuries in children. *Journal of Mental Science*, 1958, *104*, 1205–1218.

Harris, P. Head injuries in childhood. *Archives of Disease in Childhood*, 1957, *32*, 488–491.

Hebb, D. O. The effect of early and late brain injury upon test scores, and the nature of normal adult intelligence. *Proceedings of the American Philosophical Society*, 1942, *85*, 275–292.

Heiskanen, D., & Kaste, M. Late prognosis of severe brain injury in children. *Developmental Medicine and Child Neurology*, 1974, *16*, 11–14.

Hendrick, E. B., Harwood-Nash, D. C. F., & Hudson, A. R. Head injuries in children: A survey of 4465 consecutive cases at the Hospital for Sick Children, Toronto, Canada. *Clinical Neurosurgery*, 1964, *11*, 46–65.

Hjern, B., & Nylander, I. Acute head injuries in children: Traumatology, therapy, and prognosis. *Acta Paediatrica Scandinavica*, 1964 (Suppl. 152).

Isaacson, R. L. The myth of recovery from early brain damage. In N. Ellis (Ed.), *Aberrant development in infancy*. London: Wiley, 1975.

Jennett, W. B. *Epilepsy after non-missile head injuries*. London: Heinemann Medical Books, 1975. (a)

Jennett, W. B. Scale, scope, and philosophy of the clinical problem. In R. Porter & D. FitzSimons (Eds.), *Outcome of severe damage to the central nervous system* (Ciba Foundation Symposium No. 34, new series). Amsterdam: Elsevier–Excerpta Medica–North Holland, 1975. (b)

Klonoff, H. Head injuries in children: Predisposing factors, accident conditions, and sequelae. *American Journal of Public Health*, 1971, *61*, 2405–2417.

Klonoff, H., Low, M. D., & Clark, C. Head injuries in children: A prospective five year follow-up. *Journal of Neurology, Neurosurgery, and Psychiatry*, 1977, *40*, 1211–1219.

Klonoff, H., & Paris, R. Immediate, short-term, and residual effects of acute head injuries in children: Neuropsychological and neurological correlates. In R. M. Reitan & C. A. Davison (Eds.), *Clinical neuropsychology: Current status and applications*. New York: Halstead Press, 1974.

Lenneberg, E. H. *Biological foundations of language*. New York: Wiley, 1967.

Levin, H. S., & Eisenberg, H. M. Neuropsychological outcome of closed head injury in children and adolescents. *Child's Brain*, 1979, *5*, 281–292.

Lishman, W. A. Brain damage in relation to psychiatric disability after head injury. *British Journal of Psychiatry*, 1968, *114*, 373–410.

Lishman, W. A. The psychiatric sequelae of head injury: A review. *Psychological Medicine*, 1972, *3*, 304–318.

Lishman, W. A. *Organic psychiatry*. Oxford: Blackwell Scientific Publications, 1978.

Löken, A. C. The pathologic–anatomical basis for late symptoms after brain injuries in adults. *Acta Psychiatrica Neurologica Scandinavica*, 1959, *34*(Suppl. 137), 30–42.

Lynch, G., & Gall, C. Organization and reorganization in the central nervous system: Evolving concepts of brain plasticity. In F. Falkner & J. M. Tanner (Eds.), *Human growth* (Vol. 3: *Neurobiology and nutrition*). London: Balliere Tindall, 1979.

McFie, J. Intellectual impairment in children with localized postinfantile cerebral lesions. *Journal of Neurology, Neurosurgery, and Psychiatry*, 1961, *24*, 361–365.

McFie, J. *Assessment of organic impairment*. London: Academic Press, 1975. (a)

McFie, J. Brain injury in childhood and language development. In N. O'Connor (Ed.), *Language, cognitive deficits, and retardation*. London: Butterworths, 1975. (b)

Mandleberg, I. A., & Brooks, D. N. Cognitive recovery after severe head injury: I. Serial testing on the Wechsler Adult Intelligence Scale. *Journal of Neurology, Neurosurgery, and Psychaitry*, 1975, *38*, 1121–1126.

Manheimer, D. I., & Menninger, G. D. Personality characteristics of the child accident repeater. *Child Development*, 1967, *38*, 491–513.

Miller, J. D., & Jennett, W. B. Complications of depressed skull fracture. *Lancet*, 1968, *2*, 991–995.

Newcombe, F. *Missile wounds of the brain: A study of psychological deficits*. London: Oxford University Press, 1969.

Oddy, M., Humphrey, M., & Uttley, D. Subjective impairment and social recovery after closed head injury. *Journal of Neurology, Neurosurgery, and Psychiatry*, 1978, *41*, 611–616.

Otto, U. The post-concussion syndrome in children. *Acta Paedopsychiatrica*, 1960, *27*, 6–20.

Partington, M. W. The importance of accident-proneness in the aetiology of head injuries in childhood. *Archives of Disease in Childhood*, 1960, *35*, 215–223.

Relander, M., Troupp, H., & Bjorkensten, G. Controlled trial of treatment for cerebral concussion. *British Medical Journal*, 1972, *4*, 777–779.

Richardson, R. Some effects of severe head injury: A follow-up study of children and adolescents after protracted coma. *Developmental Medicine and Child Neurology*, 1963, *5*, 471–482.

Rowbotham, G. F., MacIver, I. N., Dickson, J., & Bousfield, N. E. Analysis of 1,400 cases of acute injury to the head. *British Medical Journal*, 1954, *1*, 726–730.

Rune, V. Acute head injuries in children. *Acta Paediatrica Scandinavica*, 1970 (Suppl. 209).

Russell, W. R. *The traumatic amnesias*. London: Oxford University Press, 1971.

Rutter, M. Psychological sequelae of brain damage in children. *American Journal of Psychiatry*, 1981, *138*, 1533–1544.

Rutter, M. Developmental neuropsychiatry: Concepts, issues and problems. *Journal of Clinical Neuropsychology*, 1982, *4*, 91–115.

Rutter, M., & Chadwick, O. Neurobehavioural associations and syndromes of "minimal brain dysfunction." In F. C. Rose (Ed.), *Clinical neuroepidemiology*. London: Pitman Medical Publishing, 1980.

Rutter, M., Chadwick, O., Shaffer, D., & Brown, G. A prospective study of children with head injuries: I. Design and methods. *Psychological Medicine*, 1980, *10*, 633–645.

Rutter, M., Graham, P., & Yule, W. *A neuropsychiatric study in childhood* (Clinics in Developmental Medicine Nos. 35–36). London: Spastics International Medical Publications/Heinemann Medical Books, 1970.

Rutter, M., & Madge, N. *Cycles of disadvantage: A review of research*. London: Heinemann Educational Books, 1976.

St. James Roberts, I. Neurological plasticity, recovery from brain insult and child development. In H. W. Reese & L. P. Lipsitt (Eds.), *Advances in child development and behavior* (Vol. 14). New York: Academic Press, 1979.

Seidel, U. P., Chadwick, O., & Rutter, M. Psychological disorders in crippled children: A comparative study of children with and without brain damage. *Developmental Medicine and Child Neurology*, 1975, *17*, 563–573.

Sells, C. J., Carpenter, R. L., & Ray, C. G. Sequelae of central-nervous-system enterovirus infections. *New England Journal of Medicine*, 1975, *293*, 1–4.

Shaffer, D., Bijur, P., Chadwick, O., & Rutter, M. Head injury and later reading disability. *Journal of the American Academy of Child Psychiatry*, 1980, *19*, 592–610.

Shaffer, D., Bijur, P., Chadwick, O., & Rutter, M. *Localized cortical injury and psychiatric symptoms in childhood*. Manuscript submitted for publication, 1982.

Shaffer, D., Chadwick, O., & Rutter, M. Psychiatric outcome of localized head injury in children. In R. Porter & D. FitzSimons (Eds.), *Outcome of severe damage to the central nervous system* (Ciba Foundation Symposium No. 34, new series). Amsterdam: Elsevier–Excerpta Medica–North Holland, 1975.

Stover, S. L., & Zeiger, H. E. Head injury in children and teenagers: Functional recovery correlated with duration of coma. *Archives of Physical Medicine and Rehabilitation*, 1976, *57*, 201–205.

Strecker, E. A., & Ebaugh, F. G. Neuropsychiatric sequelae of cerebral trauma in children. *Archives of Neurology and Psychiatry*, 1924, *12*, 443–453.

Strich, S. J. The pathology of brain damage due to blunt head injuries. In A. E. Walker, W. F. Caveness, & M. Critchley (Eds.), *The late effects of head injury*. Springfield, Ill.: Charles C Thomas, 1969.

Swinyard, C. A., Swansen, J., & Greenspan, L. An institutional survey of 143 cases of acquired cerebral palsy. *Developmental Medicine and Child Neurology*, 1963, *6*, 615–625.

Tucker, D. M. Lateral brain function, emotion, and conceptualization. *Psychological Bulletin*, 1981, *89*, 19–46.

Wexler, B. E. Cerebral laterality and psychiatry: A review of the literature. *American Journal of Psychiatry*, 1980, *137*, 279–291.

Witelson, S. F. Early hemispheric specialization and interhemispheric plasticity: An empirical and theoretical review. In S. J. Segalowitz & F. A. Gruber (Eds.), *Language development and neurological theory*. London: Academic Press, 1977.

Woods, B. T. The restricted effects of right-hemisphere lesions after age one: Wechsler test data. *Neuropsychologia*, 1980, *18*, 65–70.

Woo-Sam, J., Zimmerman, I. L., Brink, J. D., Uyehara, K., & Miller, A. R. Socio-economic status and post-trauma intelligence in children with severe head injuries. *Psychological Reports*, 1970, *27*, 147–153.

CHAPTER SIX

Epilepsy and Anticonvulsant Medication

JOHN A. CORBETT / MICHAEL R. TRIMBLE

Epilepsy usually occurs as a condition existing independently of any gross underlying disease state, but in some cases the seizures arise as a result of some structural brain pathology. As the latter may give rise to both cognitive and behavioral sequelae that are unrelated to seizures, it is important to differentiate these two broad groups of epilepsies when considering their psychiatric implications. A further consideration is that epilepsy is usually treated by means of anticonvulsant drugs, which themselves may have effects on behavior and on intellectual functioning. In this chapter we pay particular attention to that issue, but before doing so we discuss the empirical findings on the extent to which epilepsy itself is accompanied by an increase in psychiatric disability and/or cognitive impairment.

EPILEPSY AND EMOTIONAL-BEHAVIORAL DISORDERS

Most authorities agree that emotional-behavioral disorders are more common among children with epilepsy, but estimates vary widely. This is largely due to factors of selection and to methods of assessment. For example, some studies have been concerned with specialized samples that may be quite unrepresentative of epileptic children in the general population; some lack any kind of control group; and most have used unstandardized measures of behavior of unknown reliability and validity. For these reasons, early studies such as that of Bridge (1949) in the United States, who considered that 46% of 742 children attending an epileptic clinic showed personality disorders, must be considered of historical interest only. Similarly, Henderson (1953), interviewing parents, teachers and school doctors of 365 educable children from 16 towns and areas of England, reported that 44 (12%) were described as disturbed or badly behaved, but little reliance can be placed on these subjective impressions of behavior disorder.

In their survey of epilepsy in 14 general practices in the London area, Pond and Bidwell (1960) were among the first investigators to utilize an epidemiological approach. They found that 10 out of 39 (26%) epileptic schoolchildren had behavioral problems as determined by a psychiatric social worker's interview,

John A. Corbett. The Bethlem Royal and Maudsley Hospitals, London, England.

Michael R. Trimble. The National Hospital for Nervous Diseases, London, England.

Table 6-1. Studies of the prevalence of behavior disorders in children with epilepsy

AUTHOR(S)	SAMPLE	FREQUENCY OF BEHAVIOR DISORDER
Bridge (1949)	742 children attending an epileptic clinic	46%
Price (1950)	50 epileptic schoolchildren	56%
Henderson (1953)	Representative sample of schoolchildren	12%
Pond & Bidwell (1960)	39 schoolchildren from a general practice study	25%
Rutter, Graham, & Yule (1970)	86 schoolchildren from total population study in Isle of Wight	29%
Mellor, Lowit, & Hall (1971)	308 schoolchildren from north-east Scotland	27%
Richman (1964)	171 children attending special school for epilepsy	48%
Corbett & Trimble (1977)	312 children attending special school for epilepsy	67%

but there was no attempt to confirm the reliability or validity of the measures, and there was no control group.

These problems were overcome by Rutter and colleagues (Rutter, Graham, & Yule, 1970) and by Mellor (Mellor, 1977; Mellor, Lowit, & Hall, 1971), who carried out epidemiological studies on the Isle of Wight and in northeast Scotland, respectively, using the same standardized rating scales to assess behavior. On the Isle of Wight, 29% of 63 children suffering from epilepsy uncomplicated by other neurological disorders were found to have suffered from psychiatric disorders, compared with only 7% in the general population sample of 2189 school children. The rate of psychiatric disorder in 308 children with epilepsy from schools in northeast Scotland was 27%, compared with 15% in matched controls.

It is clear from these studies that the rates of emotional–behavioral disorders are even higher in children with complicated epilepsy. This is also confirmed by studies of children attending special schools for epilepsy, using the same standardized measures (Corbett & Trimble, 1977; Richman, 1964).

Difficulty arises over the distinction between complicated and uncomplicated epilepsy. Rutter *et al.* (1970) used the former term quite specifically to include only "those with associated structural brain disorder" (as we do, too, in this chapter), but this distinction has not been made in many other studies. In some reports a distinction has been made between "organic" and "nonorganic" epilepsy, which tends to beg the question, while in others the term has been used to describe the complexity of different seizure types occurring in the same child.

Finally, there is a considerable literature on the relationship between epilepsy and mental retardation in children, reviewed by Corbett, Harris, and Robinson (1975). Most studies suggest that the intelligence of children with uncomplicated epilepsy is usually within the normal range. The proportion of children having seizures (in the previous year) is of the order of .7% for the general population of school children. This figure rises markedly with the degree of retardation so that among 155 severely retarded children (IQ < 50), in an epidemiological study carried out by Corbett and Harris (1974), 32% had a history of seizures at some time during their lives, while 19% had had at least one seizure during the previous year. In this study, the frequency of epilepsy in children with gross brain abnormality or cerebral palsy was even greater.

Types of Psychiatric Disorders

Much has been written about the so-called "epileptic personality" in childhood, and while a number of studies have suggested an increase in symptoms such as irritability, temper outbursts, and aggression (Keating, 1961), there seems little evidence to support the concept of a typical epileptic personality (Tizard, 1962). The evidence against a specific behavioral syndrome of brain damage in childhood has recently been reviewed by Rutter (1977), who emphasized that most of the neuroepileptic children in the Isle of Wight study (Rutter *et al.*, 1970) showed the usual mixture of emotional and conduct disorders found in children without brain damage. A few children showed the rarer syndromes of hyperkinesis and psychosis, and although these were more common than in non-brain-damaged children with psychiatric disorder, both were closely related to low IQ, so that these diagnoses were mainly made in mentally retarded children with brain damage.

There are a few psychiatric conditions, such as acute confusional states, dementia, and ictal disorders such as petit mal status, that are consistently associated with organic brain dysfunction. These are important in their own right, but constitute a small proportion of cases of child psychiatric disorder and do not account for the greatly increased rates of behavioral disturbance seen in children with epilepsy. It seems clear that, on the whole, although children with seizure disorders have an increased rate of psychiatric problems, the disorders they develop are of a similar nature to those found in nonepileptic children (Bagley, 1972; Graham & Rutter, 1968; Pond, 1961; Verduyn, 1980).

EPILEPSY AND COGNITION

Early reviews of the topic (e.g., Keating, 1960) suggested a relatively high rate of intellectual impairment in epileptic children. However, most studies utilized highly selected samples (often with institutionalized subjects) and did not differentiate between complicated and uncomplicated epilepsy.

General Intelligence

Studies of outpatient samples that have avoided some of these problems have found that children with uncomplicated seizures have significantly higher scores on psychological testing (Zimmerman, Burgmeister, & Putnam, 1951) and a lower rate of mental retardation (Keith, Ewart, Green, & Gate, 1955) than those with symptomatic epilepsy associated with structural brain abnormalities had. Rodin (1968), reviewing the relationship between intelligence and epilepsy, concluded that lowered intelligence occurred in children with "organic" epilepsy and that children with "nonorganic" epilepsy usually have abilities within the normal range, although there may be a tendency for the lower end of the normal range to be overrepresented.

This was confirmed in the Isle of Wight general population study (Rutter *et al.*, 1970), where impairment of intelligence was found in children whose fits were associated with cerebral palsy or other brain disorders, but not those with uncomplicated epilepsy. The 64 children in the latter group showed a normal distribution of full-scale IQ scores on the Wechsler Intelligence Scale for Children (WISC), with a mean of 102. However, variability in the IQ pattern was much greater than normal: there was an increase in large verbal-performance discrepancies on the WISC, and 18% of the children showed significant reading retardation on the Neale test. These findings suggest the existence of subtle cognitive disabilities among children with uncomplicated epilepsy.

It has long been recognized that global measures, such as the IQ, are inappropriate for the identification of specific cognitive deficits, but there is less agreement on what measures should be used (Brittain, 1980).

Educational Attainment

It is only recently that educational attainment has been examined systematically in a fashion that allows differentiation from overall intellectual ability. Most epileptic children attend ordinary day schools, and often their condition appears not to be known to their teachers (Gregoriades, 1972; Holdsworth & Whitmore, 1974)—a finding that has been used to imply that they experience only minimal educational handicaps (Gulliford, 1971).

On the other hand, 16% of the 85 children studied by Holdsworth and Whitmore (1974) were regarded as having fallen seriously behind educationally, and about half had been referred to the school psychological service because of their scholastic difficulties. Reviewing his own studies on the Isle of Wight—together with those of Bagley (1970), Hartlage and Green (1972), Stores and Hart (1976), and Long and Moore (1979)—Yule (1980) concluded that, as a group, children with uncomplicated epilepsy are likely to be of average intelligence, but to be reading about 1 year behind their chronological age level by the age of 10 to 11 years. This masks the more serious finding that about one in five such children are likely to show severe specific reading retardation and that children with complicated epilepsy have even higher rates of reading retardation (Corbett & Trimble, 1977).

Intellectual Deterioration

The early studies of Fox (1924), and later that of Yarcorzynski and Arieff (1942), suggested that, at least in some patients, intellectual deterioration could occur in individuals with severe epilepsy. In contrast, Pond (1974) has argued that the proportion of deteriorated patients does not appear to increase with age and that deteriorated adult patients had shown early signs of this phenomenon in childhood. Rodin (1968), measuring performance on the Wechsler Adult Intelligence Scale (WAIS) at 5- to 9-year intervals, reported a small but significant decrease in IQ among individuals with seizures; this appeared to be more evident in those with initially high IQ scores.

It can be concluded that while most children, particularly those with uncomplicated epilepsy, show no evidence of intellectual deterioration, a small minority show a progressive fall in intellectual ability (Chaudhry & Pond, 1961; Trimble & Corbett, 1980a).

ORIGINS OF PSYCHIATRIC AND COGNITIVE SEQUELAE

A number of factors have been incriminated as possible causes for behavior disturbance and cognitive impairment. As these often interact, it may be difficult to identify the relative contribution of each in an individual case. They include seizure frequency and chronicity, seizure type, the site and extent of underlying neurophysiological disturbance as shown on the electroencephalogram (EEG), the child's age at the onset of the seizures, underlying brain damage, psychosocial influences, and drug therapy. One of the problems of evaluating studies that have examined these factors is that often the factors have been looked at in isolation, with no attempt to control for (or sometimes even to consider) other variables.

Seizure Frequency

Early studies of the effect of seizure frequency on behavior and learning yielded conflicting results. Yarcorzynski and Arieff (1942), for example, failed to find any correlation between seizure frequency and intellectual deterioration. In contrast, Keith *et al.* (1955) reported that patients with a high frequency of grand mal attacks were more likely to be mentally retarded; Halstead (1957), too, reported an inverse relationship between the frequency of grand mal attacks and IQ levels. In many studies it is difficult to disentangle the effects of frequent seizures from other factors, such as brain damage, with which they may be associated. But Chaudhry and Pond (1961) found that high-frequency seizures (more than two per month) were significantly more common in a group of epileptic children with deterioration in IQ than they were in a control group of children who also had brain damage and epilepsy but no intellectual deterioration. The control group, however, also showed a better response to medication and less focal and generalized abnormality on the EEG.

More recent studies have shown an effect of seizure frequency on learning ability both in humans (Goode, Penry, & Driefuss, 1970) and in animals with

Table 6-2. Factors that may give rise to behavioral and emotional disturbance in children with epilepsy

1. Neurological
   - Brain damage—extent and site
   - Cerebral dysrhythmia
2. Social
   - Family and community attitudes toward epilepsy
   - Restriction of activities
   - Family disturbance
   - Labeling
3. Psychological
   - Intellectual retardation
   - Specific learning disorders
   - Child's perception of seizures (e.g., change in body image)
4. Pharmacological
   - Anticonvulsant drugs
   - Other drugs

experimental epilepsy (Wyler & Lockhard, 1977). Frequent seizures, particularly when combined with an early age of onset, seem to constitute a risk factor for cognitive difficulties (Dikmen & Matthews, 1977; Dikmen, Matthews, & Harley, 1977; Dodrill & Wilkins, 1976; Holdsworth & Whitmore, 1974).

There is less evidence on the effects of seizure frequency on behavior. Hartlage and Green (1972) reported a significant negative relationship between seizure frequency and social maturity in their sample of 6- to 16-year-olds. On the other hand, Pond and Bidwell (1960) reported a close relationship between early age of onset of seizures (not febrile in origin), poor seizure control (i.e., seizures daily or weekly), and emotional problems in childhood. This was confirmed by Holdsworth and Whitmore (1974), who reported that behavior problems in children with epilepsy were more likely to occur in girls with frequent major seizures who also had educational problems.

Age of Onset of Seizures

Although early studies (Rodin, 1968) found little evidence for a relationship between age of onset of seizures and cognitive impairment, more recent studies of children with different types of seizures (Dikmen *et al.*, 1977; Kløve & Matthews, 1974) have found an association between intellectual impairment and the age at which either brain damage was sustained or seizures first occurred. In general, an early age of onset, particularly when seizures are associated with perinatal brain injury (Bagley, 1972; Gudmunsson, 1966) or take the form of infantile spasms (Corbett *et al.*, 1975), tends to be associated with cognitive impairment. However, febrile convulsions occurring later in infancy tend to be benign unless there has been status epilepticus (Ounsted, 1971).

Brain Damage

It seems likely that the presence or absence of brain damage may underly the links between seizure frequency and age of onset with intellectual or behavioral impairment. For example, Kløve and Matthews (1974), comparing epileptic patients with and without brain damage, showed that those with brain damage were more impaired than were those with epilepsy of unknown origin. The argument for brain damage as a pervasive underlying influence linking epilepsy and behavior disorder has been cogently argued by Graham and Rutter (1968).

Site of Origin and Type of Epilepsy

Although there is a clearly established link between temporal lobe epilepsy and schizophrenia in adults, reviews of the association of temporal lobe epilepsy and personality disorder are less conclusive (Pond, 1974; Stevens, 1975). Some studies suggest that psychiatric problems are more common in individuals with temporal lobe or psychomotor epilepsy (Gudmunsson, 1966; Rutter *et al.*, 1970) or with minor seizures of other types (Bagley, 1971). Also, the hyperkinetic syndrome has been reported to be particularly frequent in children with temporal lobe epilepsy (Lindsay, Ounsted, & Richards, 1979; Ounsted, Lindsay, & Norman, 1966). One recent study of children with epilepsy attending normal schools showed that boys with left-temporal-spike abnormalities, compared with those with other EEG findings, were more disturbed, more often overactive, more inattentive, and more frequently socially isolated (Stores, 1977). Other findings on the relationship between EEG findings and behavior disturbance are, however, conflicting. For example, Nuffield (1961a, 1961b), who examined the EEGs of epileptic children attending a psychiatric clinic, noted a significant relationship between spike and wave abnormalities of the temporal lobe and aggressive behavior, and 3 c/sec spike and wave discharges with neurotic behavior. On the other hand, Ritvo, Arnitz, and Walter (1970) found no significant relationship between clinical diagnosis and EEG findings in 184 hospitalized child psychiatry patients.

In a more carefully controlled study, Kaufman and his coworkers (Kaufman, Harris & Schaffer, 1980) point out that most of the studies that reported an association between specific types of behavioral problems and particular EEG abnormalities have "included heterogeneous groups of children within apparently homogeneous categories." They suggest that the reported correlations may be mere chance associations. Reviewing 946 patients seen over a 12-year period, they failed to replicate Nuffield's findings. Although 350 children had spike abnormalities on their EEGs, only 22 had "pure" EEG patterns (unilateral temporal-lobe spikes; generalized 3 c/sec spike and wave; or generalized irregular spike and wave). Of these, 11 had just a single EEG, and the authors emphasize the importance of considering only carefully defined EEG patterns that are consistent over time.

Early investigations of the effect of seizure type on cognitive performance suggested that people with more than one seizure type were more impaired intellectually than those exhibiting just one type of seizure (Lennox & Lennox, 1960). Halstead (1957) found that children with grand mal seizures alone had Stanford–Binet IQ scores superior to those with both grand mal and petit mal seizures. Kløve and Matthews (1974), comparing groups of patients with different types of seizures, found the greatest impairment in those with major motor seizures who had evidence of specific identifiable neurological insult, and least impairment in those with minor seizures without other evidence of brain damage.

Psychosocial Factors

The burden of living under the threat of convulsions was summed up by Bridge (1949) as follows: "The most serious handicap to happy and satisfactory living that most epileptic children have to face is not their seizures, but the failure to adapt themselves psychologically to their disease and its accompanying circumstances."

Many writers have emphasized the family and social rejection experienced by the child with epilepsy (de Haas, 1962). It has been found that the epileptic child suffers from social isolation, has few friends, and reports being teased at school (Golding, Perry, Margolin, Stotsky, & Foster, 1971; Mulder & Sourmeijer, 1977). Kleck (1968) found that secrecy and a fear of exposure among people with epilepsy constituted a major problem; he suggested that the feelings of shame were learned from parents. Long and Moore (1979) found that parents were less optimistic about epileptic children's future achievements than about those of their nonepileptic siblings. These findings were linked to greater parental restrictiveness and to epileptic children's lower self-esteem and academic achievement.

The impact of the seizures on a family also has been reviewed by Lindsay (1972), Ward and Bower (1978), and Sillanpäa (1973). The last author, in his study of the social prognosis of children with epilepsy in Finland, found a higher incidence of marital breakdown and divorce among parents of children with epilepsy than in the normal population. However, there are few studies that indicate whether the disturbed social life of children with epilepsy is primarily a result of the seizures, or whether social factors are responsible for the secondary behavior and disturbance.

Grunberg and Pond (1957), studying a psychiatric clinic population, found a significant relationship between conduct disturbance and adverse factors in the family and social background of children with epilepsy—emphasizing the important interaction between family and social factors and epilepsy in the genesis of psychiatric disorders.

While children with epilepsy are probably more vulnerable to the social stress that causes psychiatric disorders in nonepileptic children, there have been few studies of the effects of specific forms of stress. However, Rutter *et al.* (1970) suggested that "prejudice probably played little part in the development of psychiatric disorder" in epileptic children.

ANTICONVULSANT DRUGS

Anticonvulsant drug studies fall into three main groups: those that have not distinguished among different drugs, those examining the effects of specific drugs, and those that have included the measurement of serum anticonvulsant levels.

Lennox (1942), assessing the causes of mental deterioration in 1245 patients with epilepsy, incriminated anticonvulsant drugs in 15% of cases, although 18 years later he reduced this figure to 5% (Lennox & Lennox, 1960). Relatively few studies of the effect of multiple drugs in children have been carried out, and even these few have produced conflicting results. Chaudhry and Pond (1961), examining the causes of intellectual deterioration in 28 epileptic children, found no evidence to implicate anticonvulsants and suggested that the deterioration was related to seizure frequency. Holdsworth and Whitmore (1974), in a study of 117 epileptic children in normal schools, found no difference in educational attainment according to whether or not phenobarbitone was being prescribed. These findings are supported by the study of Loveland, Smith, and Forster (1957), who assessed psychological performance over a period of 3 months in 26 patients, using a battery of tests. They concluded that anticonvulsant drugs had little effect on total adjustment to the environment. There were no controls in this study, and most of the patients had been receiving anticonvulsant drugs for some years prior to the study. Thus, it is not altogether surprising that no deterioration was detected.

On the other hand, several studies of multiple drugs have reported impairment in learning, with particular effects on visuospatial performance (Kerfriden, 1970; Rayo & Martin, 1959; Tchicaloff & Gaillard, 1970).

Phenobarbitone

As far as studies of the effects of specific anticonvulsant drugs are concerned, early reports suggested few adverse effects. Somerfeld-Ziskind and Ziskind (1940) and Wapner, Thurston, and Holowack (1962) found no effects on learning after several weeks of treatment with phenobarbitone. Most of the studies that have shown a deterioration in psychological functioning have been with adult patients or volunteers (Hutt, Jackson, Belsham, & Higgins, 1968; Tchicaloff & Gaillard, 1970).

Unfavorable behavioral changes have been estimated to occur in 20 to 75% of children receiving phenobarbitone as prophylaxis for febrile convulsions in infancy (Heckmatt, Houston, & Dodds, 1976; Thorn, 1975; Wolf & Forsythe, 1978). Although Camfield, Chaplin, Doyle, Shapiro, Cummings, and Camfield (1979) found no significant differences in IQ between groups of toddlers treated with phenobarbitone or with a placebo after 8 to 12 months, there were effects on memory that were related to serum levels, and effects on comprehension that were related to duration of treatment. Hyperactivity, which has been a feature in other studies (Wolf & Forsythe, 1978), was not seen, although 15 out of the 315 children on phenobarbitone showed an increase in daytime fussiness and irritability.

Phenytoin

Acute intoxication with phenytoin leads to a confusional state, sometimes referred to as "encephalopathy," which is associated with neurological signs of toxicity, especially nystagmus and ataxia. It has become apparent that a chronic picture of progressive degenerative disorder may also occur without classical cerebellar signs, and also that this may occur with relatively low dosages (Logan & Freeman, 1969; Vallarta, Bell, & Reichert, 1974). Rosen (1968) and Stores (1975) have both reported impaired intellectual performance in children on long-term treatment with phenytoin.

Ethosuximide

Guey, Charles, Coquery, Roger, and Soulayrol 1967), studying the effects of ethosuximide in 25 children with petit mal epilepsy, reported both speech and memory impairment and affective disturbance. However, 15 of the 25 patients in this study were mentally retarded and were receiving other drugs at the time of the trial. Soulayrol and Rogers (1970) reported impaired intellectual functioning in children treated with ethosuximide, but this has not been confirmed in other controlled studies (Brown, Dreifuss, Dyken, Goode, Penry, Porter, White, & White, 1975; Smith, Philipus, & Gaurd, 1968).

Carbamazepine

Carbamazepine has been reported to have psychotropic effects, and Schain, Ward, and Guthrie (1977) reported that improvement in cognitive functioning in children changed when this drug was substituted for conventional anticonvulsants, although this finding was not confirmed in a study of a smaller number of patients by Rett (1976). In spite of these findings, it is difficult to be certain to what extent the improvement noted with carbamazepine is due to the removal of more sedative anticonvulsant drugs. At least one study, while reporting improvement in most patients on the drug treated over long periods, has shown a deterioration in behavior in some subjects (Dalby, 1975).

Other Anticonvulsants

There have been no studies of the effects of primidone on behavior in children, although adults have occasionally been reported to develop a florid confusional state on doses within the normal therapeutic range (Booker, 1972), and it is well recognized that the drug may initially cause drowsiness and have similar effects to phenobarbitone in causing restlessness in some children.

Sulthiame probably has only a weak anticonvulsant effect when used on its own, although it has been reported to have a beneficial effect on behavior disorders in mentally retarded patients (Al-Kaisi & McGuire, 1974; Moffatt, Siddiqui, & Mackay, 1970).

Finally, there are few data on the behavioral effects of valproate sodium, although uncontrolled trials suggest that it may improve visuomotor coordination (Schlack, 1974) and improve alertness and school performance (Barnes & Bower, 1975).

The measurement of serum drug levels has been a major advance in the study of anticonvulsants. Almost all the studies so far have been on adults, but from these it is clear that with phenobarbitone and phenytoin there is a close correlation between clinical signs of intoxication and serum levels (Kutt, Winters, Kokenge, & McDowell, 1964). Nevertheless, there is also considerable individual variation, and not all patients with toxic blood levels exhibit clinical signs of toxicity (Reynolds, 1970a; Reynolds & Travers, 1974). Evidence of psychological impairment without obvious clinical signs of toxicity may be found in subjects with relatively low serum levels of phenytoin and phenobarbitone (Hutt *et al.*, 1968; Ideström, Schalling, Calquist, & Sjoquist, 1972), but there have been no systematic studies in children of the relationship between anticonvulsant levels and behavior.

Folate Metabolism

Over recent years there has been increasing recognition of the many different metabolic complications of chronic therapy with anticonvulsant drugs. In particular, attention has been focused on observations that subnormal levels of serum folic acid are found in patients with epilepsy, particularly in those taking phenytoin. Low serum and red cell folate levels are found, but only rarely is there frank megaloblastic anemia. However, in view of the probable importance of folic acid in cerebral metabolism, it has been suggested that such folate deficiency may lead to neuropsychiatric problems (Reynolds, 1970b).

Supporting evidence comes from the observation that psychiatric disorders may be seen in nonepileptic patients with folate deficiency, from clinical reports of anticonvulsant-induced folate deficiency, and from clinical reports of anticonvulsant-induced folate deficiency and dementia (Melmed, Reckes, & Hersko, 1975) or schizophrenia-like psychosis (Reynolds, 1967) that respond to folic acid therapy. Furthermore, it has been established that adult patients with psychiatric illness are more likely to have folate deficiency (Reynolds, Preece, &

Chanarin, 1969; Snaith, Mehta, & Raby, 1970), with the lowest levels seen in psychotic and demented patients. In spite of these findings, there is no evidence from the trials that have been carried out (reviewed by Trimble & Corbett, 1980b) of improvement following the administration of folic acid; also, the effect on seizure frequency has been variable.

It is relevant that there has only been one study of the administration of folic acid in children with folate depletion; this failed to show any effect on either seizure or behavior (Bowe, Cornish, & Dawson, 1971).

Anticonvulsant and Folate Levels in Children

Corbett and Trimble studied the relationship between anticonvulsant drug levels and the behavior and cognitive performance of 312 epileptic children attending a special school (Corbett & Trimble, 1977; Trimble & Corbett, 1980a, 1980b; Trimble, Corbett, & Donaldson, 1980). Case-note information was gathered on age, sex, seizure onset and type, and the drugs prescribed. An estimate of seizure frequency was provided by the number of seizures in the month prior to examination. A clinical neuropsychiatric examination assessed gross neurological abnormalities above the brain stem. Psychomotor slowing, drowsiness, irritability, and distractability were assessed on a 4-point scale, using criteria modified from Rutter *et al.* (1970). A score of 2 or 3 indicated a moderate or severe abnormality. A pilot study with 40 children showed that interobserver reliability was 80% or better on each of the items.

Psychological assessments were available for all the children, and, in many cases, there were separate assessments of verbal and performance IQ. Most of the children had received two or more IQ assessments while at the school, so that it was possible to detect a group of children whose IQ had deteriorated over time (as defined by a fall in IQ of more than 10 points between two estimates done over a year apart). These data were not provided to the clinical investigators.

Behavior was rated using the Rutter "A" scales (completed by the houseparents) and "B" scales (completed by the children's teachers). These were scored in the standard way, and by taking established cutoff points it was possible to detect children who were "deviant." Behavioral abnormalities in the group with "deviant" scores were classified into either "emotional" or "conduct" disorders, depending on analysis of the items scored.

Blood was taken from the children in the early morning, in the fasting state, as near as possible to their neuropsychiatric examination. Serum anticonvulsant estimates were carried out for phenytoin, phenobarbitone, primidone, and in most cases, carbamazepine. Additionally, serum and red cell folic acid were estimated. The pilot study had indicated that blood levels of phenobarbitone, primidone, and phenytoin remained constant for those children who received the same dose of the drug over the previous 12 months, and the problem of compliance that has been noted in some outpatient studies was thus minimized.

Of the 312 children, 219 were males, and the great majority (267) were between 10 and 16 years of age. The drug most commonly prescribed was phenytoin (68%), followed by carbamazepine (42%) and valproate sodium (42%), and then by primidone (28%), sulthiame (18%), and phenobarbitone (15%). Other drugs were prescribed to a smaller percentage of children but were not assessed in detail in this study. A total of 11% of the children had gross neurological disorders above the brain stem.

A fall in IQ was found in 15 percent of the 204 children who had two or more estimates of IQ. The mean IQ of the total population of children was 66 (±19) and verbal–performance IQ estimates were available in 244 children. The means were 72 (±16) and 74 (±20), respectively. For those with a fall in IQ, this was greater than 15 points in the majority, and in some the fall was considerable (range 10–48 points).

Figure 6-1 shows the mean serum anticonvulsant levels in children with deterioration in IQ and psychomotor slowing, compared with the remainder of the population. The children with falls in IQ had significantly higher mean phenytoin and primidone levels ($p < .05$) than did the remainder of the population. Although the mean levels of phenytoin and primidone were higher in the children with psychomotor slowing, this did not reach statistically significant levels.

Pearson correlation coefficients between the serum anticonvulsant levels and IQ were calculated for children with IQs above 70. By omitting children with low IQs, it was hoped to eliminate some of the difficulties of measurement of IQ at the lower end of the scale and to minimize the effects of gross brain damage. These data indicated significant negative correlations between phenobarbitone and phenytoin levels and the performance IQ ($p < .05$), and a trend toward significance with primidone ($p < .1$). No relationship with the verbal scale of the IQ was noted.

In order to reduce the effect of factors such as seizure frequency and brain damage, which might be influencing these results, the mean serum levels of anticonvulsants were reassessed after excluding children with more than 10 seizures a month. These results again indicate significantly greater levels of

Figure 6-1. Mean serum levels of drugs in patients with cognitive disabilities (striped bars: side effects present).

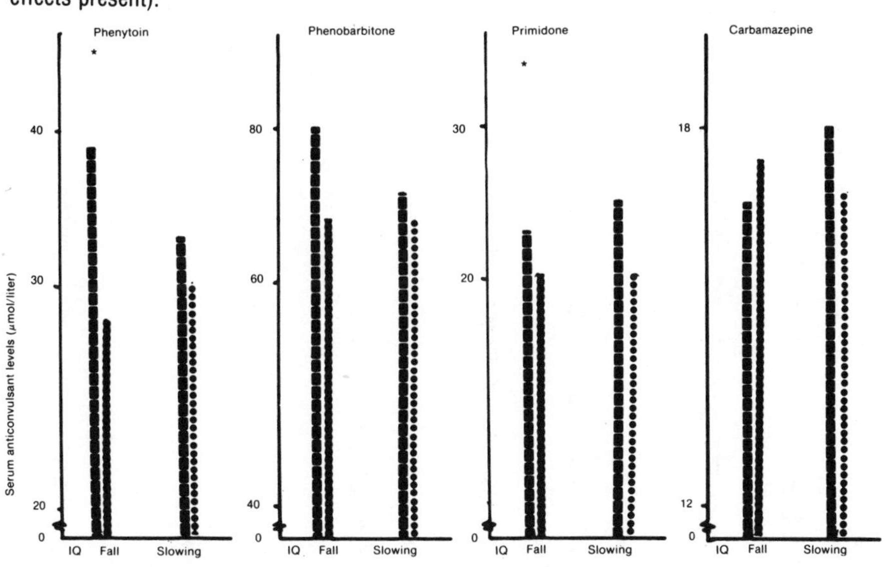

phenytoin in the population with a fall in IQ. No relationship was found between seizure frequency and the fall in IQ, although psychomotor slowing was significantly and positively related to seizure frequency.

Figure 6-2 shows no significant relationship between behavioral deviance and the levels of individual drugs, although the overall rate of deviance was high, with 67% of the children scoring above the cutoff point on either the houseparents' or teachers' scale. The folate levels were significantly lower in those children rated as neurotic by teachers or houseparents, and this also applied to those children rated as depressed on clinical examination ($p < .05$)—see Figure 6-3). Again, there was a highly significant association ($p < .01$) between serum folate levels and intellectual deterioration, children with deterioration having low serum and red cell folate levels. These results suggest that anticonvulsant drug levels are related to impairment in cognitive function in children with epilepsy, and that this may be reflected in their serum anticonvulsant levels.

It must be acknowledged that the population studied here is a highly selected one, containing children with complicated epilepsy, usually receiving multiple drugs. Nevertheless, in order to collect such information, it was necessary to define a population where abnormalities were likely to be frequent; in any case, it is often the patients such as the ones studied here who present with problems that are therapeutically most difficult to manage.

The findings in adult patients (Reynolds & Travers, 1974) that cognitive deterioration and psychomotor slowing may occur in association with raised anticonvulsant levels that are still within the normally accepted therapeutic range is supported in children. The actual mechanisms whereby anticonvulsant drugs produce an effect on cognitive processes has not been adequately explored, but the finding in this study that the group of children with low folate levels (less than 2 ng/ml) contained significantly more children who were

Figure 6-2. Mean serum levels of drugs in patients with behavior disturbances (striped bars: side effect present).

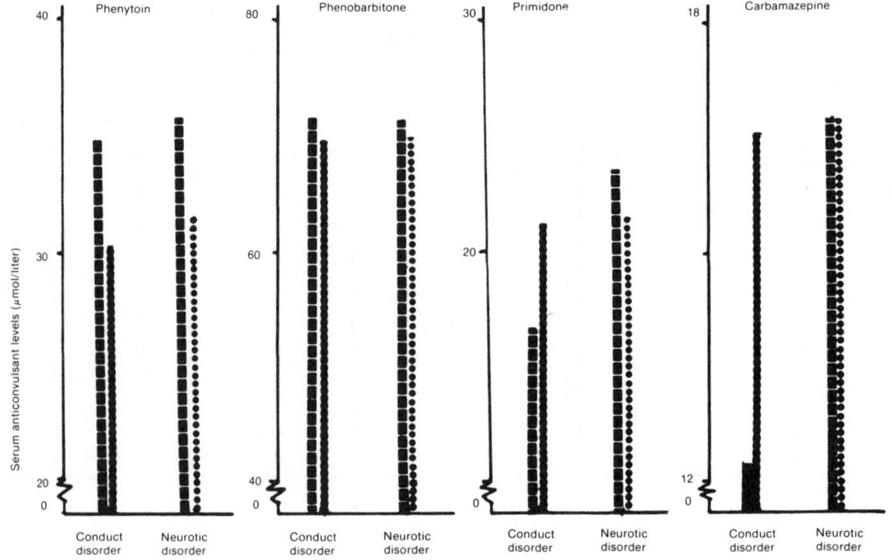

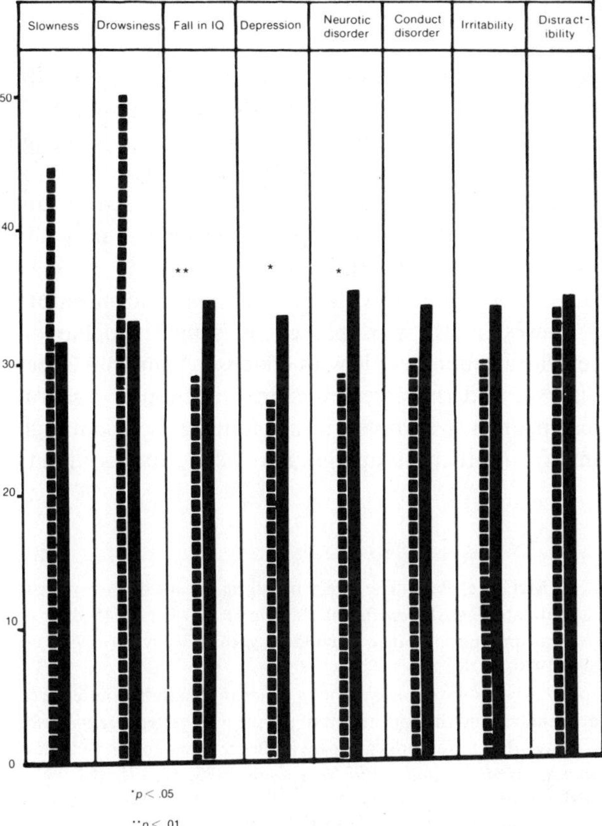

Figure 6-3. Serum folic acid levels (ng/ml) and side effects (striped bars: side effect present).

currently receiving phenytoin ($p < .001$) lends support to the suggestion (from studies of adult patients) that anticonvulsant-induced disorders of folic acid metabolism may be implicated in both cognitive deterioration and behavior disorder in children.

Unfortunately, little is known about normal red cell and serum levels in children, and it is clearly necessary to repeat this investigation using a normal control group. When the red cell folate levels of the children in this study were compared with a group of 96 patients without epilepsy or known disorders of folate metabolism attending a general medical clinic, they were found to be significantly lower ($p < .001$) (Trimble *et al.*, 1980).

The children studied here had complex epilepsy and were usually receiving more than one anticonvulsant drug. The fact that significant associations were found between serum anticonvulsant and folate levels on the one hand, and cognitive and behavioral measures on the other, suggests that the effects of long-term anticonvulsant administration in children with epilepsy requires further investigation. The lack of clear-cut associations with psychiatric disorders is not surprising in view of the multiplicity of factors that might be incriminated in such a population. With an increasing trend toward monotherapy for epilepsy, there is a clear need to evaluate further the effects of anticonvulsants using similar measures.

CONCLUSIONS

One of the main difficulties in evaluating the relative contributions of anticonvulsant therapy and of the multiple other factors reviewed earlier in this chapter lies in the difficulty in assessing the behavioral and cognitive status of children with epilepsy. Corbett (1980), reviewing some of the methodological issues, concluded that the measures that have been used in most studies have been derived from studies of nonepileptic children and may not necessarily be appropriate for research in this area.

Recent advances in anticonvulsant treatment and monitoring have led to an increased interest in the part played by drugs in behavioral change and intellectual deterioration in people with epilepsy. There have been relatively few studies in children, and those reviewed in this chapter illustrate some of the methodological problems involved in attempting to disentangle the effects of anticonvulsants from other factors that may be incriminated in this association.

References

Al-Kaisi, A. M., & McGuire, R. J. The effect of sulthiame on disturbed behaviour in mentally subnormal patients. *British Journal of Psychiatry*, 1974, *124*, 45–49.

Bagley, C. The educational performance of children with epilepsy. *British Journal of Educational Psychology*, 1970, *40*, 82–83.

Bagley, C. *The social psychology of the child with epilepsy* London: Routledge & Kegan Paul, 1971.

Bagley, C. Social prejudice and the adjustment of people with epilepsy. *Epilepsia*, 1972, *13*, 33–38.

Barnes, S. E., & Bower, B. D. Sodium valproate in the treatment of intractable childhood epilepsy. *Developmental Medicine and Child Neurology*, 1975, *17*, 175–181.

Booker, H. E. Primidone toxicity. In D. M. Woodbury, J. K. Penry, & R. P. Schmidt (Eds.), *Antiepileptic drugs*. New York: Raven Press, 1972.

Bowe, J. C., Cornish, E. J., & Dawson. M. Evaluation of folic acid supplements in children taking phenytoin. *Developmental Medicine and Child Neurology*, 1971, *13*, 343–354.

Bridge, E. M. *Epilepsy and convulsive disorders in children.* New York: McGraw-Hill, 1949.

Brittain, H. Epilepsy and intellectual functions. In B. M. Kulig, H. Meinhardi, & G. Stores (Eds.), *Epilepsy and behaviour*. Lisse, The Netherlands: Swets & Zeitlinger, 1980.

Brown, T. R., Dreifuss, F. E., Dyken, P. R., Goode, D. J., Penry, J. K., Porter, R. J., White, B. J., & White, P. T. Ethosuccimide in the treatment of absence (petit mal) seizures. *Neurology*, 1975, *25*, 515–525.

Camfield, C. S., Chaplin, S., Doyle, A. B., Shapiro, S. H., Cummings, C., & Camfield, P. R. Side effects of phenobarbitone in toddlers: Behavioral and cognitive effects. *Journal of Pediatrics*, 1979, *95*, 361–365.

Chaudhry, M. R., & Pond, D. A. Mental deterioration in epileptic children. *Journal of Neurology, Neurosurgery, and Psychiatry*, 1961, *24*, 213–219.

Corbett, J. A. Methodological issues underlying the assessment of the behaviour in children with epilepsy. In B. M. Kulig, H. Meinhardi, & G. Stores (Eds.), *Epilepsy and behaviour*. Lisse, The Netherlands: Swets & Zeitlinger, 1980.

Corbett, J. A., & Harris, R. Epilepsy in children with severe mental retardation. In P. Woodford (Ed.), *Epilepsy and mental handicap* (Report of Symposium No. 16). London: Institute for Research into Mental and Multiple Handicap, 1974.

Corbett, J. A., Harris, R., & Robinson, R. G. Epilepsy. In J. Wortis (Ed.), *Mental retardation and developmental disabilities* (Vol. 7). New York: Brunner/Mazel, 1975.

Corbett, J. A., & Trimble, M. *Neuropsychiatric aspects of anticonvulsant treatment in children with epilepsy*. Paper presented at IV World Congress of Psychiatry, Honolulu, Hawaii, 1977.

Dalby, M. A. Behavioral effects of carbamazepine. In J. K. Penry & D. D. Daley (Eds.), *Advances in neurology* (Vol. 11). New York: Raven Press, 1975.

Dikmen, S., & Matthews, C. G. Effects of major motor seizures frequency upon cognitive–intellectual functions in adults. *Epilepsia*, 1977, *18*, 21–29.

Dikmen, S., Matthews, C. G., & Harley, J. P. Effects of early versus late onset of major motor epilepsy on cognitive–intellectual performance: Further considerations. *Epilepsia*, 1977, *18*, 31–35.

Dodrill, C. B., & Wilkins, R. J. Relationship between intelligence and electroencephalographic epileptiform activity in adult patients. *Neurology*, 1976, *26*, 525–531.

Fox, J. T. Response of epileptic children to mental or educational tests. *British Journal of Medical Psychology*, 1924, *4*, 235–248.

Golding, J., Perry, S. L., Margolin, R. J., Stotsky, B. A., & Foster, J. C. *The rehabilitation of the young epileptic: Dimensions and dynamic factors.* Lexington, Mass.: Lexington Books, 1971.

Goode, D. J., Penry, J. K., & Dreifuss, F. E. Effects of paroxysmal spike-wave on continuous visuomotor performance. *Epilepsia*, 1970, *11*, 241–254.

Graham, P., & Rutter, M. Organic brain dysfunction and child psychiatric disorder. *British Medical Journal*, 1968, *3*, 695–700.

Gregoriades, A. D. A medical and social survey of 231 children with seizures. *Epilepsia*, 1972, *13*, 13–20.

Grunberg, F., & Pond, D. A. Conduct disorders in epileptic children. *Journal of Neurology, Neurosurgery, and Psychiatry*, 1957, *20*, 65–68.

Gudmunsson, G. Epilepsy in Iceland. *Acta Neurologica Scandinavica*, 1966, *43* (Suppl. 25).

Guey, J., Charles, C., Coquery, C., Roger, J., & Soulayrol, R. Study of the psychological effects of ethosuccimide on 25 children suffering from petit mal epilepsy. *Epilepsia*, 1967, *8*, 129–141.

Gulliford, D. R. *Special educational needs.* London: Routledge & Kegan Paul, 1971.

de Haas, A. M. L. Social aspects of epilepsy in childhood. *Epilepsia*, 1962, *8*, 44–55.

Halstead, H. Abilities and behaviour of epileptic children. *Journal of Mental Science*, 1957, *103*, 28–47.

Hartlage, L. C., & Green, J. B. The relation of parental attitudes to academic and social achievement in epileptic children. *Epilepsia*, 1972, *13*, 21–26.

Heckmatt, J., Houston, A., & Dodds, K. Failure of phenobarbitone to prevent febrile convulsions. *British Medical Journal*, 1976, *1*, 559–561.

Henderson, P. Epilepsy in school children. *British Journal of Preventative and Social Medicine*, 1953, *1*, 9–14.

Holdsworth, L. & Whitmore, K. A study of children with epilepsy attending ordinary schools. *Developmental Medicine and Child Neurology*, 1974, *16*, 746–758.

Hutt, S. J., Jackson, P. M., Belsham, A., & Higgins, G. Perceptual motor behaviour in relation to blood phenobarbitone levels: A preliminary report. *Developmental Medicine and Child Neurology*, 1968, *10*, 626–632.

Ideström, C. M., Schalling, D., Calquist, U., & Sjoquist, F. Acute effects of diphenyldantoin in relation to plasma levels: Behavioral and psychological studies. *Psychological Medicine*, 1972, *2*, 111–120.

Kaufman, K. R., Harris, R., & Schaffer, R. D. Problems of categorisation of child and adolescent EEGs. *Journal of Child Psychology and Psychiatry*, 1980, *21*, 333–342.

Keating, L. E. A review of the literature on the relationship of epilepsy and intelligence in schoolchildren. *Journal of Mental Science*, 1960, *106*, 1042–1059.

Keating, L. E. Epilepsy behaviour disorders in schoolchildren. *Journal of Mental Science*, 1961, *107*, 161–180.

Keith, H. M., Ewart, J. C., Green, M. N., & Gate, R. P. Mental status of children with convulsive disorders. *Neurology*, 1955, *5*, 419–492.

Kerfriden, P. Effets physiques de favourable des medicacions anticonviliales. *Revue de Neuropsychiatrie*, 1970, *18*, 605–609.

Kleck, R. *Self-disclosure patterns among epileptics.* Hanover, N.H.: Dartmouth University Press, 1968.

Kløve, H., & Matthews, C. G. Neuropsychological studies of patients with epilepsy. In R. M. Reitan & L. A. Davidson (Eds.), *Clinical neurophysiology: Current status and applications.* New York: Wiley, 1974.

Kutt, H., Winters, W., Kokenge, R., & McDowell, F. Diphenylhydantoin metabolism: Blood levels and toxicity. *Archives of Neurology*, 1964, *11*, 642–648.

Lennox, W. G. Brain injury, drugs, and environment as a cause of mental decay in epilepsy. *American Journal of Psychiatry*, 1942, *99*, 174–180.

Lennox, W. G., & Lennox, M. A. *Epilepsy and related disorders.* Boston: Little, Brown, 1960.

Lindsay, J. The difficult epileptic child. *British Medical Journal*, 1972, *3*, 283–285.

Lindsay, J. Ounsted, C., & Richards, P. Long-term outcome in children with temporal lobe seizures: III. Psychiatric aspects in childhood and adult life. *Developmental Medicine and Child Neurology*, 1979, *21*, 631–636.

Logan, W. J., & Freeman, J. M. Pseudodegenerative diseases due to diphenylhydantoin intoxication. *Archives of Neurology*, 1969, *21*, 631–637.

Long, C. G., & Moore, J. R. Parental expectations of their epileptic children. *Journal of Child Psychology and Psychiatry*, 1979, *20*, 299–312.

Loveland, N., Smith, B., & Forster, F. Mental and emotional changes in epileptic patients on continuous anticonvulsant medication. *Neurology*, 1957, *7*, 856–865.

Mellor, D. *A study of epilepsy with particular reference to behaviour disorder*. Unpublished M.D. thesis, University of Leeds, 1977.

Mellor, D. H., Lowit, I., & Hall, D. J. *Are epileptic children different from other children*? Paper presented at Annual Meeting of British Group of Paediatric Neurologists, Oxford, 1971.

Melmed, E., Reckes, A., & Hersko, C. Reversible cerebral nervous dysfunction in folate deficiency. *Journal of Neurological Sciences*, 1975, *25*, 93–98.

Moffatt, W. R., Siddiqui, A. R., & Mackay, D. N. The use of sulthaime with disturbed mentally subnormal patients. *British Journal of Psychiatry*, 1970, *117*, 673–678.

Mulder, H. C., & Sourmeijer, P. B. M. Families with a child with epilepsy: A sociological contribution. *Journal of Biosocial Science*, 1977, *9*, 13–24.

Nuffield, E. J. A. Electroclinical correlations in childhood epilepsy. *Epilepsia*, 1961, *2*, 178–196. (a)

Nuffield, E. J. A. Neurophysiology and behavioural disorders in epileptic children. *Journal of Mental Science*, 1961, *107*, 438–458. (b)

Ounsted, C. Some aspects of seizure disorders. In R. Gardner & D. Hill (Eds.), *Recent advances in paediatrics*. London: Churchill Livingstone, 1971.

Ounsted, C., Lindsay, J., & Norman, R. *Biological factors in temporal lobe epilepsy* (Clinics in Developmental Medicine No. 22). London: Spastics International Medical Publications/Heinemann Medical Books, 1966.

Pond, D. A. Psychiatric aspects of epileptic and brain damaged children. *British Medical Journal*, 1961, *2*, 1378–1382.

Pond, D. A. Epilepsy and personality disorders. In P. J. Vinken & G. W. Bruyn (Eds.), *Handbook of clinical neurology* (Vol. 15). New York: Elsevier, 1974.

Pond, D. A., & Bidwell, B. H. A survey of epilepsy in 14 general practices: II. Social and psychological aspects. *Epilepsia*, 1960, *1*, 285–299.

Rayo, D., & Martin, F. Standardized psychometric tests applied to the analysis of the effects of anticonvulsant medication on the proficiency of young epileptics. *Epilepsia*, 1959, *1*, 189–207.

Rett, A. The so-called psychotropic effect of tegretol in the treatment of convulsions of cerebral origin in children. In W. Birkmayer (Ed.)., *Epileptic seizures–behaviour–pain*. Stuttgart: Hans Huber, 1976.

Reynolds, E. H. Schizophrenia-like psychoses of epilepsy and disturbances of folate and B-12 metabolism induced by anticonvulsant drugs. *British Journal of Psychiatry*, 1967, *113*, 911–919.

Reynolds, E. H. Iatrogenic disorders in epilepsy. In D. Williams (Ed.), *Neurology* (Vol. 5). London: Butterworths, 1970. (a)

Reynolds, E. H. Neurological aspects of folate and B12 metabolism. *Clinics in Haematology*, 1970, *5*, 661–694. (b)

Reynolds, E. H., Preece, J., & Chanarin, I. Folic acid and anticonvulsants. *Lancet*, 1969, *1*, 1264–1265.

Reynolds, E. H., & Travers, R. Serum anticonvulsant concentrations in epileptic patients with mental symptoms. *British Journal of Psychiatry*, 1974, *124*, 440–445.

Richman, N. *The prevalence of psychiatric disturbance in a hospital school for epileptics*. Unpublished D.P.M. thesis, University of London, 1964.

Ritvo, E., Arnitz, E. M., & Walter, R. D. Correlations of psychiatric disorders and EEG findings: A double blind study of 184 hospitalized children. *American Journal of Psychiatry*, 1970, *126*, 988–996.

Rodin. E. *The prognosis of patients with epilepsy*. Springfield, Ill.: Charles C Thomas, 1968.

Rosen, J. A. Dilantin dementia. *Transactions of the American Neurological Association*, 1968, *93*, 273–277.

Rutter, M. Brain damage syndromes in childhood: Concepts and findings. *Journal of Child Psychology and Psychiatry*, 1977, *18*, 1–21.

Rutter, M., Graham, P., & Yule, W. *A neuropsychiatric study in childhood* (Clinics in Developmental Medicine Nos. 35–36). London: Spastics International Medical Publications/ Heinemann Medical Books, 1970.

Schain, R. J., Ward, J. N., & Guthrie, D. Carbamazepine as an anticonvulsant in children. *Neurology*, 1977, *27*, 476–480.

Schlack, H. G. Ergenye in the treatment of epilepsy. *Therapiewoche*, 1974, *24*, 39–42.

Sillanpäa, M. Medico-social prognosis of children with epilepsy. *Acta Paediatrica Scandinavica*, 1973, *62* (Suppl. 237).

Smith, W. L., Phillipus, M. J., & Gaurd, H. L. Psychometric study of children with learning problems and positive-spike EEG patterns, treated with ethosuccimide and placebo. *Archives of Disease in Childhood*, 1968, *43*, 616–619.

Snaith, R. P., Methta, S., & Raby, A. H. Serum folate and vitamin B12 in epileptics with and without mental illness. *British Journal of Psychiatry*, 1970, *116*, 179–183.

Somerfeld-Ziskind, E., & Ziskind, E. Effect of phenobarbital on the mentality of epileptic patients. *Archives of Neurology and Psychiatry*, 1940, *43*, 70–79.

Soulayrol, R., & Roger, J. Effets psychiatriques défavorables des médications antiépileptiques. *Revue de Neuropsychiatrie Infantile*, 1970, *18*, 599–603.

Stevens, J. R., Interictal clinical manifestations of complex partial seizures. In J. K. Penry, & D. D. Daley (Eds.), *Advances in neurology* (Vol. 11), New York: Raven Press, 1975.

Stores, G. Behavioural effects of anticonvulsant drugs. *Developmental Medicine and Child Neurology*, 1975, *17*, 647–658.

Stores, G. Behavior disturbance and type of epilepsy in children attending ordinary schools. In J. K. Penry (Ed.), *Epilepsy: Proceedings of the VIII International Symposium*. New York: Raven Press, 1977.

Stores, G., & Hart, J. A. Reading skills in children with generalised or focal epilepsy attending ordinary school. *Developmental Medicine and Child Neurology*, 1976, *18*, 705–716.

Tchicaloff, M., & Gaillard, F. Quelques effets indésirables des médicaments antiépileptiques sur les rendements intellectuels. *Revue de Neuropsychiatrie Infantile*, 1970, *18*, 599–603.

Thorn, I. A controlled study of prophylactic longterm treatment of febrile convulsions with phenobarbital. *Acta Neurologica Scandinavica*, 1975, *60* (Suppl.), 67–70.

Tizard, B. The personality of epileptics: A discussion of the evidence. *Psychological Bulletin*, 1962, *59*, 196–210.

Trimble, M. R., & Corbett, J. A. Behavioural and cognitive disturbances in epileptic children. *Irish Medical Journal*, 1980(Suppl.), *73*, 21–28. (a)

Trimble, M. R., & Corbett, J. A. Anticonvulsant drugs and cognitive function. In J. A. Wada & J. K. Penry (Eds.), *Advances in epileptology: The X International Symposium*. New York: Raven Press, 1980. (b)

Trimble, M. R., Corbett, J. A., & Donaldson, D. Folic acid and mental symptoms in children with epilepsy. *Journal of Neurology, Neurosurgery, and Psychiatry*, 1980, *43*, 1030–1034.

Vallarta, J. M., Bell, D. B., & Reichert, A. progressive encephalopathy due to chronic hydantoin intoxication. *American Journal of Diseases of Children*, 1974, *128*, 27–34.

Verduyn, C. Social factors contributing to poor emotional adjustment in children with epilepsy. In B. M. Kulig, M. Meinhardi, & G. Stores (Eds.), *Epilepsy and behaviour*. Lisse, The Netherlands: Swets & Zeitlinger, 1980.

Ward, F., & Bower, B. D. A study of certain social aspects of epilepsy in childhood. *Developmental Medicine and Child Neurology*, 1978, *20* (Suppl. 39).

Wolf, S. M., & Forsythe, A. Behavior disturbance, phenobarbital, and febrile seizures. *Pediatrics*, 1978, *61*, 728–730.

Wapner, T., Thurston, D. L., & Holowack, J. Phenobarbital: Its effects on learning in epileptic children. *Journal of the American Medical Association*, 1962, *182*, 937–939.

Wyler, A. R., & Lockhard, J. S. Seizure severity and acquisition and performance of operant tasks in a monkey model. *Epilepsia*, 1977, *18*, 109–116.

Yarcorzynski, G. K., & Arieff, A. J. Absence of deterioration in patients with nonorganic epilepsy with especial reference to bromide therapy. *Journal of Nervous and Mental Disease*, 1942, *95*, 687–697.

Yule, W. Educational achievement. In B. M. Kulig, M. Meinhardi, & G. Stores (Eds.), *Epilepsy and behaviour*. Lisse, The Netherlands: Swets & Zeitlinger, 1980.

Zimmerman, F. T., Burgmeister, B. B., & Putnam, T. J. Intellectual and emotional makeup of the epileptic. *Archives of Neurology and Psychiatry*, 1951, *65*, 545–556.

SECTION TWO

The Measurement of Brain Function and Dysfunction

CHAPTER SEVEN

Hard Thoughts on Neurological "Soft Signs"

STEPHEN Q. SHAFER / DAVID SHAFFER / PATRICIA A. O'CONNOR / CORNELIS J. STOKMAN

In childen of normal IQ without focal neurological signs, poor performances on various tasks elicited in neurological examination—so-called "soft signs"—have been found to be associated with psychological abnormalities such as learning difficulties and psychiatric disorders (see Chapter 8 of this volume). "Soft signs" include such phenomena as dysdiadochokinesia, mirror (contralateral associated) movements, dysgraphesthesia, astereognosis, and "the choreiform twitch" which elicited from subjects without discrete neurological deficit or mental retardation. Despite the impressive literature documenting their correlates, "soft signs" are held by some to be of little value: "Soft signs are diagnostic of soft thinking" (Ingram, 1973). This chapter discusses some of the methodological issues that may interfere with clinicians' understanding of the meaning of the association between "soft signs" and psychological dysfunction.

The first set of issues concern problems in classification; that is, in the unbiased identification of both signs and their psychological correlates. A common criticism of the finding that "soft signs" correlate with cognitive or emotional abnormalities centers on their presumed unreliability. In fact, this criticism is not logical, for unreliability would be expected to diminish any association, not to inflate it. Furthermore, as is soon noted, many measurements of "soft signs" are in fact quite reliable. However, both misclassification effects and reliability assessment (see Table 7-1) warrant more discussion.

Stephen Q. Shafer. Departments of Public Health (Epidemiology) and Neurology, College of Physicians and Surgeons, Columbia University, New York, New York; Epidemiology of Developmental Brain Disorders Department, New York State Psychiatric Institute, New York, New York.

David Shaffer. Departments of Child Psychiatry, Clinical Psychiatry, and Pediatrics, College of Physicians and Surgeons, Columbia University, New York, New York; New York State Psychiatric Institute, New York, New York.

Patricia A. O'Connor. Department of Child Psychiatry, College of Physicians and Surgeons, Columbia University, New York, New York; New York State Psychiatric Institute, New York, New York.

Cornelis J. Stokman. Department of Child Psychiatry, New York State Psychiatric Institute, New York, New York.

Table 7-1. Summary of major methodological problems that must be considered in assessing the "soft signs" literature

PROBLEMS	FINDINGS IN LITERATURE
Misclassification of phenomena due to between-rater disagreement.	Adequate reliability shown. Unreliability unlikely to create false association.
Misclassification due to fluctuating states in subject.	Conflicting results which in general point to stability. Variations unlikely to create false association.
Signs of focal neuropathology misinterpreted as soft signs.	Occur in minority of studies. Usually controlled.
Impaired cognitive ability leading to poor neurological test performance.	Poorly or not at all controlled in most studies. Probably accounts for some of observed association with behavior.
Multiple statistical comparisons.	No results corrected for multiple comparisons, but association too consistent to be fortuitous.
Selection bias.	Possibly strong in minority of studies, minimal or absent in most.
Examiner bias.	Unquantifiable. The foremost suspect for creating a mountain from a molehill.

MISCLASSIFICATION EFFECTS

Imperfect raters blind to a subject's status would be expected to misclassify subjects in one subgroup at the same probability with which they misclassify subjects in another. The expected effect of such *nondifferential* misclassification is to reduce the size of an observed measure of positive association (Copeland, Checkoway, McMichael, & Holbrook, 1977). If imperfect measures consistently lead to the conclusion that a specific problem group does worse than a control group, there are three possible explanations: (1) There is a true difference between the groups, and it is even greater than that which is observed; (2) the reported associations are due to some other bias; (3) negative studies are not being reported.

Errors in rating neurological performance can cause two quite different types of mistakes. Random errors in measurements will serve to *underestimate* the size of an effect, for any of the reasons listed above. This may lead to the conclusion that the effect is negligible (a Type II error). In contrast, systematic biases may tend to *overestimate* the size of an effect (Type I error). Clinically, this may occur when a child who is referred to a specialized clinic is given an incorrect (positive) diagnosis because of knowledge about the association. An example would be when "soft signs," behavior disturbance, and an adverse family environment coexist in the same child who has been referred to a pediatric neurology clinic. The psychiatric disturbance may be attributed to the "soft signs," with a resulting diagnosis of "minimal brain dysfunction", whereas in reality the disorder may have been a consequence of family difficulties and would have arisen irrespective of the child's neurological status.

These errors, however, are different from a dismissal of the association as factitious, an argument that cannot be supported on the grounds of poor measurement alone.

Two types of reliability—interrater agreement and test–retest stability—are of concern here. Neither has been extensively reported on in the "soft sign" literature. The most useful study until recently was that by Rutter, Graham, and Birch (1966), who tested interrater agreement for a number of different items. Their samples varied in size and composition, and were large in relation to those in most reliability studies. Looking at choreiform movements in 79 children aged 10 to 11 from the Isle of Wight study group (mostly referred for learning problems or retardation), two examiners reached an overall agreement rate of 57%, with 71% agreement on "absent," 34% agreement on "slight," and 53% agreement on "marked" (Rutter *et al.*, 1966). Interrater agreement between the same two examiners on some 40 other tasks and summary items was detailed in a later book (Rutter, Graham, & Yule, 1970). Concordance varied with the sample that was tested. For example, reliability for stretch reflexes was very low in the Isle of Wight sample, but better in a separate group of 26 physically handicapped children. For mirror movements, elicited during rapid clamp squeezing, Pearson *r* was .56 in the Isle of Wight sample, and .78 in the physically handicapped test group. Pearson *r* in the latter group was .71 for touching fingers with thumb; .57 for finger–nose test; .86 for hopping on one foot; and .88 for overall judgment on cerebellar dysfunction. In other studies, Wolff and Hurwitz (1966) established 93% overall agreement between themselves in replicate observations for choreiform twitches in 2631 subjects aged 9 to 12. Werry, Minde, Guzman, Weiss, Dogan, and Hoy (1972) examined reliability with an independent simultaneous rater sitting in on 10 of 60 examinations. On only 3 of 140 items was there less than 80% agreement.

Percentage of agreement depends heavily on the frequency of the categorized trait in the sample and hence has been challenged as a measure of interobserver consistency by the κ statistic. Like the intraclass correlation coefficient, to which it is analogous, κ takes into account *both* random error and systematic threshold differences between or among observers. However, it does not distinguish between these sources of error. One can imagine a data set in which all subjects are ranked identically by each of several judges, but in which the average score for subjects varies by judge. Here a reliability measure based on ranks would have a maximum value of 1.0, but the intraclass correlation, taking threshold differences into account, could be much lower. In most studies involving two or more raters, the raters share a training background that minimizes threshold differences (which may be large among separate institutions). However, we believe that when prevalences are to be compared among samples or when categories have diagnostic implications, threshold differences cannot be overlooked as a source of error. Thus, the advantage of κ (and its analogous intraclass correlation) in correcting for chance may be lost in its inability to distinguish between random error and error due to threshold differences.

The issue of delineating the effect of threshold differences is particularly salient in the "soft sign" literature. In the Collaborative Perinatal Project, the assessment of the presence of "soft signs" among subjects in 14 institutions yielded very discrepant rates, with fairly consistent rates within each institution (Nichols & Chen, 1981). An analysis-of-variance procedure would be needed to separate out the components of variance, permitting the calculation of the interrater within-institution and the interrater between-institution components. Thus, one could test the significance of the between-institution effect as a measure of threshold differences. Similarly, a κ statistic could be calculated within an institution and, separately, across institutions. The difference between these would be a measure of the effect of threshold differences for categorical data.

Among mutually trained raters of "soft signs," random error is likely to be more important than threshold differences; hence, the κ statistic does not exact an undue penalty.

The imprecise boundaries of what distinguishes "good" from "less than satisfactory" reliability, together with the rarity of purely coincidental agreement, make the case for κ more elegant than overwhelming. This controversial issue is concisely discussed by Fleiss (1981).

The interrater studies of Rutter *et al.* (1966, 1970) are informative, for cross-tabulated data are shown, allowing calculation of κ. For choreiform movements in the Isle of Wight sample, κ for "none or slight" versus all others was .47. More solid values of κ exceeding .6 would surely emerge for other signs, in that there were many comparisons in which percentage of agreement was higher than it was for choreiform movements.

Quitkin, Rifkin, & Klein (1976) were the only "soft sign" investigators to use the κ statistic. In their reliability study, two raters simultaneously scored 25 hospitalized subjects on 16 signs that had been observed in at least 1% of the 298 patients from whom the 25 came. Of these, 11 signs were found during the simultaneous sessions by at least one examiner. The κ coefficient was significantly different ($p < .01$) from its null value for 10 of the 11 signs. Perfect agreement ($\kappa = 1.00$) emerged for 9 items, including speech, coordination, finger–thumb mirror movement, pronation–supination, and tandem walking. We conclude from these reports that acceptable, even exemplary, interrater agreement is possible.

Observations in some important studies have been made by a single neurological examiner (Kennard, 1960; Peters, Romine, & Dykman, 1975). This eliminates interobserver disagreement. But intraobserver variability, which may be considerable, is nowhere quantified in these reports or elsewhere. The use of a single examiner does not remove examiner error, and, of course, it does not test or describe that error.

SHORT-TERM STABILITY

The next, and equally important, aspect of reliability in the measurement of "soft signs" is stability over time. Assuming that there is one rater who re-examines the same subject, stability may be affected by variation in the rater, by variation in the subject, and by error. When two or more raters take part, interrater disagreement also contributes to variability. There is as yet no study to compare intrarater with interrater agreement over time. The test–retest designs we have reviewed do not distinguish within-rater or between-rater from within-subject variability. Nevertheless, repeated measure studies of "soft signs" have tended to see test–retest variability as largely due to subjects, neglecting the examiner component.

Among studies that have examined stability, Peters *et al.* (1975) recalled 10 boys up to 6 months later. One specific reexaminer (not the first rater) agreed with the original rating 84% of the time overall on 79 items, including dysgraphesthesia, mirror movements, and dysdiadochokinesia. However, the overall percentage of agreement cannot be interpreted without knowing the frequency of these findings. Denckla (1973) observed high correlations of .78 and .81 for speed of successive finger touches in each hand at a 3-week retest. McMahon and Greenberg (1977) cast doubt on the stability of "soft sign" recordings. They reported examinations, five times in 8 weeks, on a group of 44 boys aged 6 to 11 years on treatment for hyperactivity. Only 12 subjects held a steady score on the dysdiadochokinesia measure. For the other 32, the sign was inconsistently present, with no trend toward loss or gain over the series. Since examiner variability was not estimated, the conclusion that the behaviors being measured were themselves inconsistent cannot be confirmed or denied.

Shapiro, Burkes, Petti, and Ranz (1978) describe "general consistency of 'nonfocal' neurological signs." A total of 80 successive pediatric psychiatric admissions aged 6 to 12 were seen on days 1, 2, and 7, each by one of four participating physicians. The items covered included three series of left–right discrimination items, one hand–foot–eye preference, double simultaneous stimuli, assessment of extraocular muscles and muscle tone, whirling test, and extension test, but did not include dysgraphesthesia, synkinesis, or dysdiadochokinesia. These investigators reported "consistent relationships" in scores across the three dates for all nine items, although no statistics were provided.

Foster, Margolin, Alexander, Benitez, and Carr (1978) found a subject practice effect on repeatedly testing 10 unmedicated psychiatric inpatients aged 7 to 12. Every subject was tested on a battery of five tests—finger approximation, tandem gait, one-eyed winking, nystagmus, and plantar response—six or more times over the course of 37 days. During the administration of each battery of tests, every subject was observed by a pair of examiners. For each successive administration, the two examiners were rotated from a team of three. Subjects improved significantly on all items except one-eyed winking. This short report suggests that frequent repetitions can alter what most researchers would like to believe is a representative sampling of a child's behavior in carrying out fixed tasks. The authors contrast this situation to that in IQ testing, where a vast universe of test items can be drawn on to mitigate practice effects. However, examiner effects (interrater and intrarater reliability) were not assessed, so that the imputed practice effects cannot be confirmed.

Only Quitkin *et al.* (1976) have examined both test–retest and between-rater agreement using a separate within-subject, over-time design. One of the two examiners who had participated in an initial examination reexamined each of 16 patients within 2 days of that examination. The Pearson r for total number of signs for time 1 and time 2 was .96. The κ statistics on the 15 most common signs showed that five having significant ($p < .05$) κ coefficients of 1.0, .76, .63, 1.0, and .53 persisted. The between-rater correspondence was even greater.

These reports support the view that some signs elicited in certain ways are not ephemeral, and Quitkin *et al.*'s study suggests that short-term within-subject or within-rater variability may contribute more to total variance than does interrater variability.

LONG-TERM STABILITY

Long-term persistence is another aspect of "soft sign" measurement. If the time course of the signs–behaviors relationship is charted, stability over long periods must be documented. Menkes, Rowe, and Menkes (1969) traced 14 of 18 subjects who, 24 years earlier, had had hyperactivity or learning disability and one or more of the following: clumsiness of fine movements, visual motor deficits, and impaired or delayed speech. Of these subjects, 11 had had a neurological exam, with 8 showing "definite evidence" of neurological dysfunction. Functional outcomes in this group were very bad and certainly do not represent all children with learning disability. Hertzig (1982) reexamined 53 out of a group of 156 children in special educational placement after a 4-year interval. All 53 had initially been found to have "soft signs" but to be free of localizable neurological signs. The mean age at the first examination was 10.5 years. The mean number of signs per subject declined significantly, from 4.8 to 2.5. The proportion of first-exam positives and negatives identically classed at the follow-up varied greatly by task (see Table 7-2).

CONFOUNDING EFFECTS

Stability of "soft signs" would be spuriously increased by sampling persons with fixed focal findings, and it should be noted that the test–retest studies quoted above appear to have had few or no such subjects.

There is a consensus in the "soft sign" literature that individuals with a known neuroanatomical lesion such as cerebral palsy should be distinguished from those without such a lesion. Failure to make this distinction might result in the referral problem group having a higher proportion of subjects with a specific brain lesion, which could be both a cause of poor neurological test performance and of disturbed thought or behavior. The relationship of *focal*

Table 7-2. Percentage of subjects scoring the same at 4-year follow-up as at first test, by original classification and test item

	ORIGINAL CATEGORY	
ITEM	+	−
Astereognosis	70	79
Double simultaneous stimulation	67	95
Balance	61	76
Choreiform movements	50	84
Imitative movements	50	94
Speech	38	97
Coordination	32	95
Tone	31	70
Gait	30	75
Dysgraphesthesia	00	94

Note. Data from Hertzig (1982).

neurological deficit to behavior change is an important area of research but is quite separate from the study of the relationship of behavior to *neurological test performance dysfunction* in persons whose brains are presumed to be anatomically intact. The latter is our only concern in this chapter. How, in fact, have investigators operationally defined who is eligible to be studied? How have they restricted entrance into their samples?

Hertzig, Bortner, and Birch (1969) looked separately at 26 children with and 64 children without associated focal stigmata when comparing both groups with normal schoolchildren. Kennard (1960) did not separate those groups. She specified that some children had had encephalitis and that 23 of 69 had epilepsy. Several studies involving problem and comparison groups (Lerer & Lerer, 1976; Peters *et al.*, 1975; Werry *et al.*, 1972) specified that neurological exclusion criteria were used, but did not define them. Owen, Adams, Forrest, Stolz, and Fisher (1971) found "definitive" neurological signs" in three educationally handicapped subjects. Prechtl and Stemmer (1962) gave examples of exclusion diagnoses: "Children with other obvious neurological signs (e.g., cerebral palsy or microcephaly) . . . were excluded." Routh and Roberts (1972) excluded children with "overt cerebral palsy or epilepsy." The greatest detail about inclusions and exclusions comes from the report of Gubbay, Ellis, Walton, and Court (1965). These investigators started with 24 individuals (mean age 12 years) whose presenting symptom was "severe clumsiness." All had verbal IQs higher than 80. Three children were excluded "when their clumsiness was found to be due solely to pyramidal or extrapyramidal disease." Seven more were included in a special group because they had "minimal evidence of dysfunction in pyramidal or cerebellar pathways, insufficient to contribute significantly to their fundamental clumsiness." Of this subgroup, three had "suffered major cerebral illness in the past." Carey, McDevitt, and Baker (1979) were prepared to include subjects with focal signs who had been referred to a neurologist for behavioral problems, but not for "nonbehavioral problems such as seizures, retardation, cerebral palsy, or headaches."

Since one examiner's "obvious" may be another's "subtle" and one history's "major" may be another history's "mild," it is hard to tell what proportion of potential subjects for a "soft sign" study have been excluded from observation or analysis in each study. There is thus an unknown amount of "noise" confounding the "soft signs"—behavior association by a presumed cerebral injury–behavior relationship. Nevertheless, the latter certainly does not account for the whole "soft signs"–behavior relationship; an association is also evident in cross-sectional studies of mainstream schoolchildren (Adams, Kocsis, & Estes, 1974; Stine, Saratsiotis, & Mosser, 1975), among whom specific neurological deficits are uncommon. Stine *et al.* (1975), for example, found just one child in 575 with such a deficit.

Cognitive ability is another potential confounder. The selection of study subjects may lead to confounded estimates of the signs–behavior relationship if "problem" or "referred" subject groups have lower IQs than control groups do. The construct validity of neurological "soft signs" has never been established by design or statistical control over either IQ or attention, except in that most studies have excluded retarded subjects. It is notable, however, that Quitkin *et al.* (1976) found mean IQs of 94 and 96 in their high-sign-prevalent groups, compared to 102 for one group of nonsign patients and greater than 107 in three other nonsign patient groups. Kennard (1960) remarks that her cases all had IQs greater than 79, while IQs of the controls all exceeded 90. Other published studies that compared a problem group to a control group did not, however, specify the distribution of IQ by group. Instead, a lower limit of IQ was set, which every subject in any group must have exceeded. Either performance or verbal IQ of 90 or above is a typical cutoff point (Denckla & Rudel, 1978; Peters *et al.*, 1975). These findings suggest that other psychological (cognitive) constructs may cause the observed signs–behavior association to look stronger than it really is.

ERRORS OF INFERENCE

In a body of reports, each covering many neurological and several behavioral–emotional states, multiple statistical comparisons can be made. If a study's overall significance rides on finding one or more "differences significant at the $p < .05$ level," the overall probability of a Type I error should be adjusted for the number of comparisons (by, say, the Bonferroni method). When, however, a high proportion of all comparisons made achieve the nominal significance level in the hypothesized direction, overall Type I error seems unlikely. Although not a single report adjusted significance levels to account for the number of comparisons, the proportion of all reported comparisons within and across studies significant at $p < .05$ or better is far too high to be fortuitious.

Peters *et al.* (1975), for example, made 79 comparisons, of which 44 were positive and significant at the .05 level or better. Stine *et al.* (1975) had a Type I error probability less than .05 for 11 of 156 comparisons. Adams *et al.* (1974) made 60 comparisons (10 items, 3 groups, 2 sexes) of which only 4 were significant. Lucas, Rodin, and Simson (1965) made 23,000 comparisons in a correlation matrix, of which 1031 reached significance. While this is only a chance level, virtually all were positive—a distribution incompatible with chance.

However, one cannot tell from published reports whether whole groups of comparisons were made, found insignificant, and shelved without mention; furthermore, the proportion of tests that are "significant" can be inflated by treating closely related measures as if they were independent. In doing so, one is essentially repeating the same test. The interrelationships of variables need to be made explicit in the "soft sign" literature to guard against this threat to sound inference. Likewise, there should be formal accounting for all comparisons, especially those suggested by a look at the data. These require a more rigorous multiple-comparison procedure, such as Scheffe's test.

SELECTION BIAS

Internal validity reflects the strength of the evidence that the apparent effect of the independent variable (e.g., treatment, exposure, risk category) on the outcome variable is due to a real relationship between them, not to some process that would have operated even without the independent variable (Cook & Campbell, 1979). "Selection bias" is a major threat to internal validity. Sackett (1979) suggests the term "admission-rate bias," because this problem was first remarked upon by Berkson in hospitalized patients. "Berkson's paradox" is that even when there is no association in the source population, a sample may show a "significant" difference. This would occur if subjects with some combination of factors are more likely to enter a study group than those with only one or the other factors are. Such a sample could arise in patients from a neurology clinic if, for instance, a disturbed child who is also very clumsy is more likely to be sent for neurological assessment than a child who is equally disturbed but who does not seem neurologically inept. This spectre is always difficult to document (see Brown, 1976). Roberts, Spitzer, Delmore, and Sackett (1978) contend that Berkson's paradox is unlikely to operate unless the suspected factor can lead to admission, referral or eligibility for sampling in its own right.

The wide variety of settings and routes to referral series and the presence of the association in unreferred samples make it unlikely that this form of bias has been a major contributor to inflated measures of association between "soft signs" and behavior.

EXAMINER BIAS

"Examiner bias" is an examiner's tendency to base ratings on clues pertaining to other ratings that should be independent. This form of bias has never been quantified in the "soft signs" literature. Hatfield and Landers (1979) demonstrated it for gross motor performance on a balancing board. Even the most rigid research protocol cannot prevent spontaneous disclosure or behavior by the subject that may favor a rater's judgment. For example, a squirmy or impulsive subject might be classed "positive" for a slightly dysrhythmic motor performance that the same examiner would call "normative" in a quiet, relaxed subject. Likewise, an earlier finding may color a later decision on the same subject.

This form of bias will be least in brief screening, or when all examinees are expected to act deviantly. It will be most serious in long, detailed examinations meant to test, for example, whether referred children are neurologically distinct from controls. To attempt that differentiation without bias requires great care that nothing about setting, demeanor, or clothing tip off the neurological examiner to a subject's status. Even these precautions may be wasted if the subject keeps taking a watch off the table and playing with it, or needs several repetitions of simple instructions. The degree to which reported associations are distorted by this bias cannot be quantified. Little about the testing environment is usually described. Werry *et al.* (1972) candidly noted that conversation often revealed a subject's status. We believe this bias has inflated all estimates of the sign–behavior association to varying degrees, simply because it cannot be fully controlled.

CONCLUSION

No short review of the "soft signs" literature can hope to weigh sampling procedures, technical variations, and errors of inference as sources of unreliable variability across the findings of different studies. Still less could any single chapter rule on exactly which tests done exactly which way are the most valid measures of a domain that belongs solely not to classical neurologists nor to cognitive psychologists nor only to psychiatrists. Reviewing the many studies calls attention to the need for a longitudinal study that can address all or many of these issues simultaneously.

Acknowledgments

This work was made possible by grants from NIMH Center Grant #MH30906-01A and #MH30906-03, NIMH Education Grant #2T01 MH07715-17, and by the Research Associate Program created by the New York State Legislature, Office of Mental Hygiene, Division of Research.

References

Adams, R. M., Kocsis, J. J., & Estes, R. E. Soft neurological signs in learning-disabled children and controls. *American Journal of Diseases of Children*, 1974,*128*, 614–618.

Brown, G. W. Berkson fallacy revisited: Spurious conclusions from patient surveys. *American Journal of Diseases of Children*, 1976, *130*, 56–60.

Carey, W. B., McDevitt, S. C., & Baker, D. Differentiating minimal brain dysfunction and temperament. *Developmental Medicine and Child Neurology*, 1979, *21*, 765–772.

Cook, T. D., & Campbell, D. T. *Quasi-experimentation.* Chicago: Rand-McNally, 1979.

Copeland, K. T., Checkoway, H., McMichael, A. J., & Holbrook, R. H. Bias due to misclassification in the estimation of relative risk. *American Journal of Epidemiology*, 1977, *105*, 488–495.

Denckla, M. B. Development of speed in repetitive and successive finger movements in normal children. *Developmental Medicine and Child Neurology*, 1973, *15*, 635–645.

Denckla, M. B., & Rudel, R. G. Anomalies of motor development in hyperactive boys. *Annals of Neurology*, 1978, *3*, 231–233.

Fleiss, J. L. *Statistical methods for rates and proportions* (2nd ed.). New York: Wiley, 1981.

Foster, R. M., Margolin, L., Alexander, C., Benitez, O., & Carr, F. Equivocal neurological signs, child development, and learned behavior. *Child Psychiatry and Human Development*, 1978, *9*, 28–32.

Gubbay, S. S., Ellis, E., Walton, J. N., & Court, S. D. M. Clumsy children: A study of apraxic and agnosic defects in 21 children. *Brain*, 1965, *88*, 295–312.

Hatfield, B. D., & Landers, D. M. Observer expectancy effects upon appraisal of gross motor performance. *Research Quarterly*, 1979, *49*, 53–61.

Hertzig, M. E. Stability and change in nonfocal and neurological signs. *Journal of the American Academy of Child Psychiatry*, 1982, *21*, 231–236.

Hertzig, M. E., Bortner, M., & Birch, H. G. Neurologic findings in children educationally designated as "brain-damaged." *American Journal of Orthopsychiatry*, 1969, *39*, 437–446.

Ingram, T. T. S. Soft signs. *Developmental Medicine and Child Neurology*, 1973, *15*, 527–530.

Kennard, M. A. Value of equivocal signs in neurological diagnosis. *Neurology*, 1960, *10*, 753–764.

Lerer, R. J., & Lerer, M. P. The effects of methylphenidate on the soft neurological signs of hyperactive children. 1976, *Pediatrics*, *57*(4), 521–525.

Lucas, A. R., Rodin, E. A., & Simson, C. B. Neurological assessment of children with early school problems. *Developmental Medicine and Child Neurology*, 1965, *7*, 145–156.

McMahon, S. A., & Greenberg, L. M. Serial neurologic examination of hyperactive children. *Pediatrics*, 1977, *59*(4), 584–587.

Menkes, M., Rowe, J., & Menkes, J. A twenty-five year follow-up study on the hyperkinetic child with minimal brain dysfunction. *Pediatrics*, 1969, *39*, 393–399.

Nichols, P., & Chen, T. *Minimal brain dysfunction: A prospective study*. Hillsdale, N.J.: Erlbaum, 1981.

Owen, F. W., Adams, P. A., Forrest, T., Stolz, L. M., & Fisher, S. Learning disorders in children: Sibling studies. *Monographs of the Society for Research in Child Development*, 1971, *36*(4, Serial No. 144).

Peters, J. E., Romine, J. S., & Dykman, R. A. A special neurological examination of children with learning disabilities. *Developmental Medicine and Child Neurology*, 1975, *17*, 63–78.

Prechtl, H. F. R., & Stemmer, C. H. The choreiform syndrome in children. *Developmental Medicine and Child Neurology*, 1962, *4*, 119–127.

Quitkin, F., Rifkin, A., & Klein, D. F. Neurologic soft signs in schizophrenia and character disorder. *Archives of General Psychiatry*, 1976, *33*, 845–853.

Roberts, R. S., Spitzer, W. D., Delmore, T., & Sackett, D. An empirical demonstration of Berkson's bias. *Journal of Chronic Diseases*, 1978, *31*, 119–128.

Routh, D. K., & Roberts, R. D. Minimal brain dysfunction in children: Failure to find evidence for a behavioral syndrome. *Psychological Reports*, 1972, *31*, 307–314.

Rutter, M., Graham, P., & Birch, H. G. Interrelations between the choreiform syndrome, reading disability and psychiatric disorder in children of 8–11 years. *Developmental Medicine and Child Neurology*, 1966, *8*, 149–159.

Rutter, M., Graham, P., & Yule, W. *A neuropsychiatric study in childhood* (Clinics in Developmental Medicine Nos. 35–36). London: Spastics International Medical Publications/Heinemann Medical Books, 1970.

Sackett, D. Bias in analytic research. *Journal of Chronic Diseases*, 1979, *32*, 51–63.

Shapiro, T., Burkes, L., Petti, T. A., & Ranz, J. Consistency of "nonfocal" neurological signs. *Journal of the American Academy of Child Psychiatry*, 1978, *17*, 70–79.

Stine, O. C., Saratsiotis, J. B., & Mosser, R. S. Relationship between neurological findings and classroom behavior. *American Journal of Diseases of Children*, 1975, *129*, 1036–1040.

Werry, J., Minde, K., Guzman, A., Weiss, G., Dogan, K., & Hoy, E. Studies on the hyperactive child: VII. Neurologic status compared with neurotic and normal children. *American Journal of Orthopsychiatry*, 1972, *42*, 441–451.

Wolff, P. H., & Hurwitz, I. The choreiform syndrome. *Developmental Medicine and Child Neurology*, 1966, *8*, 160–165.

CHAPTER EIGHT

Neurological "Soft Signs": Their Origins and Significance for Behavior

DAVID SHAFFER / PATRICIA A. O'CONNOR / STEPHEN Q. SHAFER / SHERI PRUPIS

INTRODUCTION

In this chapter, we define a neurological "soft sign" as nonnormative performance on a motor or sensory test identical or akin to a test item of the traditional neurological examination, but a performance that is elicited from an individual who shows none of the features of a fixed or transient localizable neurological disorder. This definition is in line with that proposed by Bender (1956). Specifically:

1. The origins of a neurological "soft sign" as so defined cannot be related to any serious postnatal neurological insult of the sort that might be expected to leave residual neurological signs (e.g., severe head injury, intoxication, infection or tumor).

2. Groupings of "soft signs" found in an individual should *not* have a pathognomonic pattern of a kind that would usually indicate one or more clearly localized structural lesions, generalized encephalopathy, or central nervous system (CNS) involvement. There is, of course, no reason why nonnormative performances on certain items should not coexist with separate pathognomonic or localizing signs. Indeed, the two will be found in the same subject (Hertzig, Bortner, & Birch, 1969). When they are, however, their meaning is quite different. For example, poor rapid alternating movements with the right forearm in someone with mild distal weakness, widened palpebral fissure,

David Shaffer. Departments of Child Psychiatry, Clinical Psychiatry, and Pediatrics, College of Physicians and Surgeons, Columbia University, New York, New York; New York State Psychiatric Institute, New York, New York.

Patricia A. O'Connor. Department of Child Psychiatry, College of Physicians and Surgeons, Columbia University, New York, New York; New York State Psychiatric Institute, New York, New York.

Stephen Q. Shafer. Departments of Public Health (Epidemiology) and Neurology, College of Physicians and Surgeons, Columbia University, New York, New York; Epidemiology of Developmental Brain Disorders Department, New York State Psychiatric Institute, New York, New York.

Sheri Prupis. Department of Child Psychiatry, New York State Psychiatric Institute, New York, New York.

absent abdominal reflexes, increased stretch reflexes, and an extensor plantar response all on the right side would be evidence of a lesion of the left pyramidal tract. The identical motor performance in someone with no associated findings would be called a "soft sign."

3. We have not regarded as "soft signs" nonnormative execution of such highly specialized procedures as the mimicking of specific auditory or visual rhythms (Birch & Belmont, 1965; Wolff & Cohen, 1980); inaccurate responses to questions of left–right orientation (Belmont & Birch, 1965), the face–hand test (Bender, Fink, & Green, 1951); postrotatory nystagmus (Ayres, 1972); "whirling" (Bender, 1956), nor any of the standardized test batteries such as the Purdue Formboard, the Halstead–Reitan, or the Lincoln–Ozeretsky, although performance on these measures may well be related to the presence of "soft signs" as we have defined them.

The interest of "soft signs" defined in this way, therefore, does not lie in any supposed reflection of a known disease or as a cause of marked physical disability. Rather, *if* "soft signs" are of clinical interest, it will be because they serve as an index for some other cognitive or behavioral dysfunction. If this is the case, then it is important to determine their origins and their cause. We set out to examine these questions in this chapter.

LITERATURE REVIEW

The relationship between neurological "soft signs" and psychiatric disturbance in adults has been reviewed by Shaffer (1978). Here we review sound studies of the relationships between "soft signs" and *children's* behavior and cognition. Most studies can be grouped into one of the following categories, according to their sampling procedures.

1. A comparison of prevalence of signs in a *clinically referred group* (e.g., children attending a psychiatric, learning disorder, or developmental disorder clinic) and *normal controls.* Chapter 7 of this volume has pointed to potential sources of bias in studies carried out among clinically referred populations, the main concern being that bias will lead to the differential referral of children with a conjunction of abnormalities. This is most likely to be the case for developmental disorder clinics or pediatric neurology clinics that specialize in the evaluation and management of children with learning or behavior problems. Also, studies in a referred population cannot provide information about the extent to which, say, behavior or learning difficulties in the population at large are related to soft signs, and so cannot be used to demonstrate the specificity or sensitivity of signs and their usefulness as a marker.

2. *Comparisons within groups* of psychiatrically disturbed, learning-disordered, or delinquent subjects that examine the differential prevalence of "soft signs" in diagnostic subcategories. This type of study is in some ways more satisfactory, because any referral bias is likely to be shared by the different groups. In studies of this kind, it is important that the diagnostic groupings be established reliably, that they be described in a way that permits replication, and that the problem of multiple diagnoses be dealt with in a consistent and explicit fashion.

3. Studies in *populations unselected for any of the variables of interest* (i.e., neurological, psychiatric, or cognitive and learning disorders). Clearly these avoid some of the problems outlined above.

Regardless of design, study features that need to be taken into account in reviewing this area of research are these:

1. Whether subjects with a presumptive "hard" neurological disorder or subjects who are currently taking drugs that might affect neurological function are treated separately for the purpose of analysis.
2. The reliability and validity of the neurological, psychiatric, and cognitive measures.
3. The blindness of the examiners of one dimension to the child's status on any other dimension.
4. Whether account has been taken of IQ and age (both of these measures appear to be related to "soft signs" and may also be related to both the prevalence and the form of psychiatric disorder).

Patients and Normal Controls

Several studies have compared the neurological status of children with a psychiatric disturbance with that of controls. Larsen (1964) examined 129 institutionalized disturbed adolescents and 71 age- and sex-matched well-adjusted controls. A large number of comparisons were carried out, and it was concluded that the institutionalized boys performed less well on virtually all neurological measures. However, the patient sample included subjects with mental retardation and organic brain syndrome, and neither the neurological examination nor the psychiatric diagnoses were standardized or predefined. A more satisfactory study looking at children with mixed disorders was that carried out by Peters, Romine, and Dykman (1975), who compared 82 male child guidance clinic patients and 45 normal controls. The mean age of the group was near 10 years, and the neurological examination was standardized and reliable. Account was taken of age at examination, and it was noted that 11 out of 20 neurological variables occurred more often in the patient group than in the controls. These measures included dysdiadochokinesia, dysgraphesthesia, finger agnosia, and overflow movements. Three studies have compared children with hyperkinetic disorder and controls. McMahon and Greenberg (1977) noted that two-thirds of a group of 102 children with a referral diagnosis of hyperactivity had neurological "soft signs." The study was uncontrolled, and no diagnostic criteria for either the neurological signs or hyperactivity were provided. Camp, Bialer, Sverd, and Winsberg (1978) studied a small sample of 32 male hyperactives seen at a special psychiatric clinic. The diagnosis was confirmed using the David, Clark, and Voeller (1972) behavioral rating scale. These were compared with 111 normal boys attending a summer camp. Neurological status was assessed on the Physical and Neurological Examination for Soft Signs (PANESS) scale of "soft signs" (Close, 1973). Unfortunately, evaluations were not blind. Children with gross neurological abnormalities were excluded, and only subjects functioning in the normal IQ range were included. Comparisons were made within age groups. No significant differences were noted between the hyperactives and the control group.

Within-Group Comparison

Certain studies have examined subgroups within a total patient population to see whether children with neurological "soft signs" differ from those without, or whether one diagnostic group has more or fewer signs than another. Kennard (1960) examined 123 consecutive adolescent psychiatric inpatients, excluding children with psychosis, low IQ, inadequate records, and very disturbed family backgrounds. The patient group had significantly more "soft signs" than did a noninstitutionalized control group, and within the patient sample, adolescents with thought disorder and a diagnosis of organic mental disorder had significantly more "soft signs" than other diagnostic groups. "Soft signs" were also related to IQ. However, the sample included a number of children with frank neurological disease ("some" who had had encephalitis, 23 with "frank epileptic seizures"); the exclusionary criteria were likely to lead to the selective underrepresentation of certain disorders; and the psychiatric diagnoses were assigned in an unstandardized way without diagnostic criteria and without provision for dealing with diagnostic overlap. Boshes and Myklebust (1964) compared the behavioral and cognitive characteristics of 44 children with, and 41 children without, neurological "soft signs" attending a learning disability clinic. This study has variously been described as showing no differences between the groups and as indicating an interaction among "soft signs," age, and IQ, with the older neurologically impaired children showing lower IQ and more dependent behavior than the older nonimpaired group, there being no differences between the two young groups. However, the neurological evaluation was not standardized, and the description of the statistical methods used is too sparse or obscure to permit appraisal.

Paulsen (1978) and Paulsen and O'Donnell (1979) examined the relationship between neurological "soft signs" and different dimensions of behavior measured on a variety of standardized instruments within a group of 76 black boys in a residential treatment center. They found no relationship between "soft signs" and antisocial or withdrawn behavior, but signs were found significantly more often in impulsive children who scored high on an "immaturity factor," derived from the Deveraux scale, which included such behaviors as distractibility, dependency, and sloppiness.

Hyperactivity has been the subject of a number of "soft sign" studies. Lucas, Rodin, and Simson (1965) examined 72 third-grade children referred to or eligible for attendance in a special class for the learning disabled. The neurological examination was standardized, and the examiners were blind to the assigned psychiatric diagnosis. No relationship was found between signs and IQ, and antisocial and withdrawing behavior, although hyperkinesis was noted to be associated with poor coordination, synkinesis, choreiform movements, and dysdiadochokinesia. However, diagnostic criteria were not given, and the authors examined a very large number of correlations. Although one may have some confidence in the failure to find a relationship with antisocial disorder (which does not usually pose a diagnostic criterion problem), the very large number of correlations examined and the absence of criteria for the more-difficult-to-define diagnosis of hyperactivity leads to caution in interpreting the positive findings that emerge from this study.

Hertzig *et al.* (1969) also studied "soft signs" and hyperactivity in 90 10- to 12-year-olds randomly selected from a school for children with presumed brain damage and educational or behavioral difficulties, as well as 15 controls. Both "hard" and "soft signs" were elicited during a standardized evaluation by examiners blind to each child's psychiatric state. Comparisons were made between children who showed evidence of hyperkinetic behavior during examination and the remainder. Significantly more "soft signs" were found in the hyperkinetics than in the other diagnostic groups or in the controls. However, the study included children with frank neurological disorder, and the sample of behavior upon which the diagnosis of hyperactivity was made was a narrow one.

Wikler, Dixon, and Parker (1970) studied 24 consecutive referrals to a child psychiatry outpatient clinic with school behavior problems, excluding all cases with organic conditions and low IQs. Comparisons were made with age-, sex-, and IQ-matched controls. Neurological status was recorded in a standardized way, and cases were categorized on the basis of predefined criteria into those with and without hyperactivity. There were significantly more signs in the clinic than in the control group, but not between hyperactives and other diagnoses. Using a somewhat different strategy, Werry, Minde, Guzman, Weiss, Dogan, and Hoy (1972) compared the prevalence of neurological signs in 20 hyperactive children of normal intelligence and without evidence of neurological disorder with a similar number of "neurotic" and 40 control children. A scale-score criterion was applied for the diagnosis of hyperactivity, and the neurological evaluation was standardized and reliable, although not blind. Ten out of 17 signs occurred more often in the hyperactive than in either comparison group, most of these being signs of motor coordination.

Lewis, Shanok, Pincus, and Glaser (1979) examined the relationship between neurological "soft signs" and the degree of aggressiveness in the histories of 97 incarcerated delinquent boys. "Soft signs" and choreiform movements were significantly related to the degree of aggression. However, the sample included subjects with CNS disorders, and the role of IQ in the study is unclear. This is because the relationships between IQ and aggressive behavior fell just short of significance and the relationship between neurological "soft signs" and IQ was unexplored, which, given its frequently noted association in other studies, required an appropriate analysis to take IQ into account.

Finally, examining a somewhat different dimension of behavior, Carey, McDevitt, and Baker (1979) classified 61 3- to 7-year-old children referred to a pediatric neurology clinic for behavior and learning difficulties into those with and without neurological signs. A temperamental profile of these children was derived from the Behavioral Style Questionnaire (McDevitt & Carey, 1978). The neurologically impaired children scored significantly more often in the deviant range on the dimensions of adaptibility, persistence, high activity, and negative mood. However, the reliability of the neurological examination was not tested, criteria for neurological abnormality are not given, and neither age nor IQ differences have been taken into account, so that the possibility exists for there being a spurious relationship.

Unselected Populations

There have been few population-based studies carried out to examine the relationship between neurological "soft signs" and either cognitive or behavioral difficulties. Of these, two have examined the correlates of choreiform movements, which were reported by Prechtl and Stemmer (1962) to be a component of a "choreiform syndrome" consisting of involuntary movements, behavior difficulties, and learning difficulties. Rutter, Graham, and Birch (1966), in an exemplary study, examined three unreferred groups of 7- to 9-year-old children chosen randomly from total populations of normal school children, as well as children with mental retardation and reading retardation. A further group of children, chosen because they were likely to show significant psychiatric and learning problems, was also examined. The neurological, cognitive, and psychiatric evaluations were standardized, reliable, and carried out blind. Although choreiform movements were found to be more common in children of low intelligence, they were not otherwise found to be related to learning difficulties or psychiatric disorder.

Wolff and Hurwitz (1966) determined the prevalence of choreiform movements in unselected populations of normal children and adolescents in both the United States and Japan, and in selected institutionalized groups of delinquent and disturbed children in both countries. Significantly higher rates were found in the disturbed and delinquent populations in both countries. There were consistent sex differences, with the excess of signs being more marked in boys. A partial follow-up was carried out on a random subsample of the unselected U.S. population (Wolff & Hurwitz, 1973), who had originally been identified as sign-positive, and age- and sex-matched controls from the same sample. Existing school records were standardized to obtain measures of achievement and behavior. Retrieval rates were satisfactory. Boys in the choreiform-movement group were found to have similar IQs to the controls, but they had significantly more spelling and reading difficulties, and had been referred significantly more often for psychiatric care. An analysis of teachers' comments suggested that they were more likely to be labeled as immature, unmotivated, and uncooperative than were members of the control group. There were no differences in comments about hyperactivity or inattention between the two groups.

Owen, Adams, Forrest, Stolz, and Fisher (1971) carried out a population-based study with a wider range of neurological variables. A total school population was screened to obtain a group of educationally handicapped children of normal IQ, all of whom had same-sex siblings of school age, and an IQ- and sex-matched control group without learning difficulties. The groups were compared, along with their same-sexed siblings, on a range of neurological variables. The educationally handicapped group differed from the control group (but not from their siblings) in rates of dysdiadochokinesia. There were no significant differences for choreiform or overflow movements. Adams, Kocsis, and Estes (1974) studied a total school population of 368 fourth-grade children with IQs above 85 and without any significant physical disabilities. The mean age of the population was 10 years. The population was then classified on the basis of the Myklebust Learning Quotient (Myklebust, 1968) into those with significant learning disabilities, an intermediate group, and normals. The learning disability group differed from the others only in their scores of dysgraphesthesia and dysdiadochokinesia, but the overlap between the learning disabled and the nondisabled groups was such that the authors concluded that the signs could not be used usefully for clinical purposes.

In summary, a set of very diverse studies on differently constituted samples and using very different criteria for disorder show some consistencies in finding signs to be related to IQ and to be more prevalent in psychiatric patients and in children with learning difficulties. The relationships between signs and hyperkinesis are somewhat inconsistent, and this may reflect the measurement problems that confound this diagnosis (see Sandberg, Wieselberg, & Shaffer, 1980; Shaffer & Greenhill, 1979). There are also some consistent findings of a relationship between emotional immaturity and dependency and "soft signs." The relationship to antisocial disorder and aggression is obscured by selection bias in those few studies that have examined that dimension.

SAMPLE: THE COLLABORATIVE PERINATAL PROJECT

An opportunity for examining some of the relationships in a fashion that meets many of the desired criteria cited above exists in a study of the children included in the Collaborative Perinatal Project (CPP).

The CPP was initiated by the National Institute of Neurological and Communicative Disorders and Stroke (NINCDS) for the purpose of investigating "pregnancy wastage" (Berendes, 1966). A large sample was collected from 12 universities and their 14 affiliated hospitals, including the Columbia–Presbyterian Medical Center, a subsample of which we investigated. A consecutive sampling procedure was adopted, with only declared adoption donors and women who presented too late for repeated prenatal care at the respective centers being excluded (Niswander & Gordon, 1972). In all, about 53,000 women were enrolled in the CPP between 1959 and 1965.

Data collection began with the initial registration of each mother at the time of her visit to the participating medical center. Information was obtained at each subsequent prenatal visit, at the time of labor and delivery, and at regular intervals in the child's life until age 7 (age 8 at six of the participating institutions).

At age 7, subjects received a comprehensive physical and neurological examination, which included testing for 18 neurological "soft signs" (see Table 8-1). These can be broadly grouped within the constructs of involuntary movements, coordination difficulty, and abnormality of sensory integration. The reliability of the original neurological examination has not been well documented, although precise instructions in how to elicit signs were provided in a standard manual. The number of raters per institution was also large, thus

Table 8-1. Frequency of specified neurological findings at age 7 exam by sex

FINDINGS	M ($n=231$)	F ($n=225$)	TOTAL ($n=456$)	χ^2	p
Movements					
Spontaneous tremor	0	1	1	ns	—
Tic	1	1	2	ns	—
Mirror movements	15	5	20	3.99	.05
Other	3	4	7	ns	—
Coordination					
Dysmetria	4	1	5	ns	—
Dysdiadochokinesia	44	22	66	7.18	.01
Awkwardness not otherwise classified	54	25	79	11.13	.001
Other	3	4	7	ns	—
Sensory integration					
Astereognosis—fine	12	2	14	5.76	.01

reducing the possibility of systematic bias. The rate of positive findings at Columbia was higher than at other centers. Method studies conducted at the time suggested that between-center differences were consistent during the whole period of the study. This suggests that the source of those differences is variation in threshold level at different study centers, rather than variation within centers (Nichols & Chen, 1981). The Columbia sample may thus have a low specificity. If this error were present, it would tend to decrease the chances of detecting true relationships.

During the cognitive assessment at age 7, a psychologist who was blind to all other information about each child observed and rated the child for 15 different behaviors (see Appendix). Reliability data for these ratings are not available, although Nichols and Chen (1981) report that the behavior ratings are similarly distributed across the 14 participating institutions, which can be taken as a weak indirect indicator of their reliability.

Subjects

We have examined the relationship between "soft signs" and behavior in a subsample of children enrolled in this study at Columbia–Presbyterian Medical Center. The target sample was 576 black and white subjects born in 1962 and 1963. A total of 17 subjects with definite neurological impairment manifest up to age 7 have been excluded for the analyses that follow (see Table 8-2).

The actual sample analyzed here consisted of the 456 (82%) of the target subjects who were present at the 7-year examination. A number of demographic and family variables obtained at the prenatal information were examined to determine whether those who did not attend at age 7 differed from those who did. There were no differences in age or education of parents, mother's employment status, presence of father in the home, person–room ratio, or length of gestation at birth. Subjects did differ in length of gestation at the initial preregistration. Those not attending at age 7 had been registered significantly later in pregnancy than those who did (not seen at 7: $\bar{x} = 22.0$ weeks; seen at 7: $\bar{x} = 20.3$ weeks; $t = 2.23$, $p < .02$). The race and sex characteristics of the remaining 456 subjects are shown in Table 8-3.

Table 8-2. Exclusions from analyses

NUMBER OF CASES	RACE/SEX	REASON FOR EXCLUSION
4	2 B/M, 2 W/M	Microcephaly
1	B/M	Cerebral palsy, microcephaly
6	2 B/M, 1 W/M, 1 B/F, 2 W/F	Seizures, other than febrile
1	B/M	Lead intoxication, seizure
1	B/M	Herpes simplex meningoencephalitis and seizure
1	B/M	Febrile convulsion with focal feature
1	W/M	Anterior horn cell disease
1	W/M	Mild cerebral palsy and seizures
1	B/F	Obtundation and transient bilateral extensor plantar responses following car accident (age 5)
Total 17		

Table 8-3. Race-by-sex distribution of subjects included in analysis

RACE	SEX MALE	FEMALE
Black	175	164
White	116	104

Rates for each neurological "soft sign" assessed at age 7 are given in Table 8-1. A total of 127 subjects (28% of the 456 seen) were noted to have one or more of the signs. There were no differences by race, but significantly more males than females were scored positive on one or more items (see Table 8-4).

Subjects were grouped on the basis of their "soft sign" status at age 7 (none positive/one or more positive). No differences were found for the two groups on a range of social, demographic, and family factors, which included mother working during pregnancy or at age 7, father absent at either of these times, mean maternal and paternal ages, duration of mother's and father's educations, person–room ratio, and family income.

Behavior and "Soft Signs"

Approximately one-third of the Columbia subjects were not scored on one of the behavior items ("separation from mother"); therefore this has been omitted from our analyses. All items were originally rated on a 5-point scale. We judged 7 of the items to be bipolar, with deviant behavior at each extreme. New items were therefore developed to represent each unipolar behavior, yielding a total of 21 items (see Appendix). Scoring was reduced to a 3-point scale: 0—"not a problem"; 1—"possible problem"; 2—"definite problem."

A priori scales were devised to represent three domains of behavior: Hyperactivity, Aggression, and Dependency/Withdrawal (see Table 8-5). The internal consistency of each was tested using coefficient α (Nunnally, 1978). Four items were dropped to increase reliability, one each from Aggression and Dependency/Withdrawal, and two from Hyperactivity. The final scales had satisfactory α reliabilities, with 3 to 10 items each. Intercorrelations among the scales (Table 8-6) indicate that relatively separate behavioral domains are represented by the three scales; some overlap is present between Hyperactivity and Aggression, with the modest correlation of .40.

An analysis-of-covariance procedure was used to examine the differences between the "signs present at 7" and "signs absent at 7" groups on each of the behavioral scales while covarying for sex (see Table 8-7). The groups did not

Table 8-4. Distribution of signs present versus absent by sex

SEX	NO SIGNS PRESENT *n*	%	ONE OR MORE SIGNS PRESENT *n*	%
Male	150	45.6	81	63.8
Female	179	54.4	46	36.2

Note. $\chi^2 = 11.4$, 1 *df*, $p < .001$.

Table 8-5. Item numbers for each behavioral scale

SCALE	ITEM NUMBERS	COEFFICIENT α
Hyperactivity	8, 9, 10, 11	.75
Dependency/ Withdrawal	1, 2, 3, 4, 6, 7, 8, 10, 11, 12	.71
Aggression	5, 13, 14	.78

Note. Item descriptions in Appendix.

Table 8-6. Intercorrelation of behavior scales

	DEPENDENCY/WITHDRAWAL	AGGRESSION
Hyperactivity	−.01	.40*
Dependency/Withdrawal	—	.05

*$p < .001$.

Table 8-7. Means and standard deviations of behavior scales by sign status at age 7 by sex

		SIGN STATUS AT AGE 7			
		PRESENT		ABSENT	
SCALE (RANGE)	SEX	$\bar{x}$	*SD*	$\bar{x}$	*SD*
Hyperactivity (0–8)	M	1.0	1.46	.76	1.24
	F	.71	1.44	.61	1.09
Dependency/Withdrawal (0–20)	M	3.10	2.38	2.65	1.98
	F	2.81	2.38	2.29	1.74
Aggression (0–6)	M	.20	.70	.17	.75
	F	.07	.33	.08	.52

differ on Hyperactivity or Aggression. However, subjects with signs at 7 scored significantly higher on the Dependency/Withdrawal scale after covarying for sex ($F(1, 437) = 5.08$, $p < .025$).

The examination detailed above had at least two limitations. First, the reliability of the neurological examination has not been extensively examined. Secondly, the behaviors studied are limited to those demonstrated by the children during psychological testing. The validity of such a narrow sample of behavior is clearly open to question.

In order to address this problem, we carried out a 10-year follow-up of black male subjects from the Columbia sample of the CPP. Subjects were selected on the basis of their positive "soft sign" status at 7, along with controls matched for race, sex, age, and lack of signs. Social and family characteristics of the groups were examined at the time of the 17-year follow-up, and no differences were found between the signs and the control groups on any of the following variables: parents' marital status, level of education of mother and father, class of employment of mother and father, mother or father's age, and number of full and half siblings.

An initial analysis of the findings obtained from a direct mental status interview of the boys when aged 16–18 (see Shaffer, Stokman, O'Connor, Shafer,

Table 8-8. Psychiatric diagnostic category and early "soft sign" status

DIAGNOSTIC CATEGORY	EARLY "SOFT SIGNS" PRESENT	EARLY "SOFT SIGNS" ABSENT	STATISTICAL SIGNIFICANCE χ^2	STATISTICAL SIGNIFICANCE p
No diagnosis	39	40		
Antisocial disorder	6	8		
Depression	12	3	5.4	.02
Other diagnosis (including 1 schizophrenic)	4	4		

Barmack, Hess, Spalten, & Schonfeld 1982) indicate that while the "soft signs at age 7" group showed no excess of antisocial or conduct disorders, they had a significant excess of affective diagnoses (see Table 8-8). A single subject had received inpatient treatment for a psychiatric illness, and was also in the group with soft signs at age 7. Those findings at ages 16–18 are therefore broadly consonant with those that we report in this chapter (i.e., that "soft signs" are associated with emotional rather than with behavioral problems). It should be understood that these represent preliminary findings based on an evaluation of the adolescent alone. Further data on the subjects, derived from a variety of sources, are currently being examined.

Cognitive Measures and Soft Signs

An opportunity to examine the question of the relationship between "soft signs" and cognitive functioning has also arisen in the data available from the CPP. The examination at age 7 included the administration of the Wechsler Intelligence Scale for Children (WISC) and subscales of the Wide-Range Achievement Test (WRAT) (reading, spelling, and math) (Jastak & Jastak, 1965).

Differences at age 7 between subjects with and without signs were examined using an analysis-of-covariance procedure to control for the effect of sex. Results indicate a consistent and significant pattern of lower scores by the "soft signs present" group (see Table 8-9). However, when IQ was partialed out, differences between the groups in reading and spelling were not significant.

Table 8-9. Cognitive measures by "soft sign" status at age 7 by sex

COGNITIVE MEASURE	SEX	SIGNS AT AGE 7 PRESENT $\bar{x}$	PRESENT n	ABSENT $\bar{x}$	ABSENT n	t	F^a	p
Full-scale IQ at 7 (WISC)	M	91.7	(8)	99.4	(147)	4.38		.001
	F	96.9	(45)	99.6	(176)	1.48		ns
							9.65	.001
Reading (WRAT)	M	31.4	(77)	34.1	(146)	1.75		ns
	F	33.9	(45)	36.9	(175)	2.56		.01
							9.69	.001
Spelling (WRAT)	M	22.1	(78)	23.9	(147)	1.65		ns
	F	24.2	(45)	25.0	(177)	1.09		ns
							9.44	.001

[a] F ratio tests the significance of the effect of sign status on the cognitive variables, controlling for sex.

We have noted in a large group of children unselected for either cognitive or psychiatric problems and examined in a standardized fashion that neurological "soft signs" are related to both low IQ and certain behavioral abnormalities. However, low IQ and behavior disorder are also related to each other (Rutter, Tizard, & Whitmore, 1970/1981). Correlations between the 7-year-olds' behavioral measures (Hyperactivity, Dependency/Withdrawal, and Aggression) and the cognitive measures (IQ and WRAT reading, spelling, and arithmetic) (see Table 8-10) indicate a moderately strong linear relationship between those factors. It was therefore felt to be important to examine whether the children who had "soft signs" *and* deviant behavior were the same as the children who had "soft signs" and low IQs.

To examine this overlap, we have defined "deviant behavior" as a score of more than one standard deviation above the sex appropriate mean. This analysis among the males (Table 8-11) revealed that rates of deviant behaviors in boys of normal IQ were similar in boys with and without "soft signs." However, a combination of *both* low IQ and "soft signs" significantly increased the risk for several very different behaviors. Examination among females (Table 8-11) was not possible because of the very small numbers.

THE ORIGINS OF NEUROLOGICAL "SOFT SIGNS"

Both the review of the literature and the data presented above suggest that neurological "soft signs" are significant predictors of behavior and cognitive functioning. It is, therefore, of interest to examine their possible etiology. Four different possibilities are examined here.

The first is that the neurological signs result from some early-acquired lesion (i.e., are a feature of brain disease). This suggestion was first made by Prechtl and Stemmer (1962), who, in their uncontrolled retrospective study of neurology clinic referrals, reported that a high proportion of patients with choreiform syndrome had a past history of obstetric difficulties. The hypothesis was also advanced by Gubbay, Ellis, Walton, and Court (1965), who compared two small groups of children referred to a pediatric neurology clinic because of clumsiness. One group had uncomplicated apraxias ($n = 14$); the second group

Table 8-10. Intercorrelations of behavioral and cognitive measures by sex

MEASURE	SEX	IQ	READING	SPELLING
Hyperactivity	M	−.43	−.23	−.34
	F	−.33	−.31	−.41
Dependency/Withdrawal	M	−.42	−.26	−.27
	F	−.49	−.31	−.30
Aggression	M	−.23	−.18	−.22
	F	−.18	−.16	−.19
IQ	M	—	.53	.60
	F	—	.51	.56
Reading	M	—	—	.85
	F	—	—	.86

Note. All intercorrelations are significant at $p < .001$.

Table 8-11. Frequency of subjects with "soft signs," IQ less than 80, and deviant behavior

BEHAVIOR	"SOFT SIGN" STATUS	IQ < 80 n	IQ < 80 (%)	p^a	IQ > 80 n	IQ > 80 (%)	TOTAL
MALES							
Hyperactivity	SS +	5	(6)		7	(9)	80
	SS −	1	(.6)		13	(9)	147
				$p < .05$			
Dependency/Withdrawal	SS +	5	(6)		14	(18)	79
	SS −	3	(2)		26	(15)	145
				ns			
Aggression	SS +	3	(3)		5	(6)	81
	SS −	1	(.6)		10	(7)	147
				ns			
FEMALES							
Hyperactivity	SS +	0	(0)		3	(6)	45
	SS −	1	(.1)		14	(8)	176
				ns			
Dependency/Withdrawal	SS +	2	(5)		7	(16)	44
	SS −	0	(0)		26	(15)	172
				ns			
Aggression	SS +	0	(0)		2	(4)	45
	SS −	1	(.05)		6	(3)	176
				ns			

[a]Probabilities determined using Fisher's exact test.

($n = 7$) had apraxias with associated features suggestive of cerebellar or pyramidal involvement. The groups did not differ in IQ or learning ability. The authors regarded the second patient group as being patients with mild cerebral palsy, and because of the lack of IQ and learning differences between the groups, suggested that by analogy the first group should also be regarded as being on a spectrum with cerebral palsy. However, Prechtl and Stemmer's data are not presented in a satisfactory format, and Gubbay *et al.*'s study is clearly inferential, has small numbers and a biased sample, and does not deal directly with etiological factors.

In their study of a total sample of retarded children in Aberdeen, for whom good obstetric records were available, Rutter *et al.* (1966) found no relationship between choreiform movements and birth weight, length of gestation, or other gross complications of pregnancy, such as preeclamptic toxemia or bleeding.

We have examined the same questions in the CPP sample, using the comprehensive obstetric records, and have set out to examine whether there was a greater prevalence of neurological "soft signs" among children who had traumatic deliveries, who were asphyxiated or hyperbilirubinemic in the period immediately after birth, or in whom the pregnancy was complicated by prenatal hemorrhage or preeclamptic toxemia. Also, we determined whether "soft signs" were overrepresented in children of short gestation and of low weight for gestation dates. These are all factors that are held to be related to cerebral palsy.

The prevalence of a series of factors commonly associated with cerebral palsy in the groups who had and did not have signs at age 7 are set out in Table 8-12.

In preparing this analysis, "antepartum hemorrhage" was defined as any uterine, cervical, or vaginal bleeding occurring during pregnancy. "Short gesta-

Table 8-12. Prenatal, delivery, and neonatal events by "soft sign" status at age 7

VARIABLES	SS +	SS −	SIGNIFICANCE
Prenatal			
Toxemic during pregnancy			
No	95	257	
Yes	30	64	ns
Hemorrhage during pregnancy			
No	86	219	
Yes	41	110	ns
Delivery			
Premature			
No	105	294	
Yes	22	35	ns
Low birth weight for date			
Males			
No	72	144	$\chi^2 = 4.25$
Yes	9	5	$p < .04$
Females			
No	43	164	
Yes	3	15	ns
Birth weight ($\bar{x}$)	3103 g	3186 g	ns
Gestation at date ($\bar{x}$)	39.4 wk	39.4 wk	ns
Neonatal			
Bilirubin			
No (less than 16)	112	317	
Yes (16 or more)	5	12	ns

tion" was defined as gestation less than 36 weeks. "Low weight for gestation dates" was defined as being below the 10th percentile for gestational age, using Lubchenco, Hansman, Dressler, and Boyd's (1963) growth standards.

There was a significant excess of low weights for gestation dates among males with soft signs at 7. However, as only 9 out of 81 "soft sign" males had low weights for gestation dates, we also need to look for other causes.

A second possibility is that neurological "soft signs" are developmental phenomena (i.e., that they are transient phenomena that pass with neurological maturation). This has been suggested by certain data from cross-sectional studies (e.g., Peters *et al.*, 1975), in which a negative correlation between age and signs has been noted. However, it is of interest that Peters *et al.* found different relationships between signs and age in the control and in the patient groups, suggesting that age-relatedness is not a uniform process. Another source of error is that not all studies analyze age prevalence data separately for each sex. Signs are nearly always found to be less prevalent in girls. If this factor is not taken into account, different age-standardized rates may reflect variations in the sex composition of each cohort. Wolff and Hurwitz (1966) failed to show any decline in prevalence with age for a number of signs after sex was taken into account.

In the follow-up study that we have described here, more than half of the children who had shown dysdiadochokinesia and mirror movements at age 7 still showed these signs 10 years later. Similarly, Hertzig (1982), in a 5-year follow-up study of children who were previously shown to have neurological signs found that *all* still had neurological signs of one sort or another, although the stability for any one sign was only moderate (i.e., children who had shown one sign at the time of the first examination might no longer show that sign and might then be showing a different sign at the time of the second examination).

A third possibility is that neurological "soft signs" of the type described above are best regarded as a heritable individual difference. There have been few studies into the genetics of "soft signs." However, Owen *et al.* (1971) found that educationally handicapped children with a mean age of 10 did not differ from their normally achieving siblings with respect to certain tests (double simultaneous sensation, rhythmic tapping) that are sometimes regarded as "soft signs," both groups doing less well on these tests than a group of unrelated normally achieving children of the same age, sex, and IQ and their siblings. Of greatest interest in this regard are Nichols and Chen's (1981) findings of concordance for neurological soft signs among twins and siblings examined in the CPP. Eight out of 12 monozygotic twins are concordant for "soft signs," which was significantly more common than the 1.36 that would be expected. Concordance was also significantly greater than expectation in same-sex dizygotic twins and in siblings.

Another study of related interest suggests that signs might be transmitted in tandem with other determinants of psychiatric vulnerability. Rieder and Nichols (1979) studied the neurological and behavioral status of 45 7-year-old offspring of schizophrenics—a disease with a strong genetic basis—and a closely matched control group drawn from the Boston subsample of the CPP. Significantly more of the schizophrenics' offspring had either signs or a combination of signs and deviant behavior than members of either control group had.

Finally, it is important not to overlook the possibility that neurological soft signs may be behavioral epiphenomena that, like social behavior, can be influenced by learning, motivation, attention, and stress. The evidence on this count is scanty. Prechtl and Stemmer (1962) anecdotally report that stress increases choreiform movements. Foster, Margolin, Alexander, Benitez, and Carr (1978), in a small study without controls and under nonblind conditions, noted that performance on the neurological examination improved with practice. Although this suggests that children can learn to improve their performance on the neurological examination, other explanations such as rater bias and regression to the mean cannot be ruled out. Similarly, because of the short duration of the study, it is not known whether the reported improvement was maintained. Lerer and Lerer (1976) have reported that neurological signs became less prevalent in disturbed children treated with methylphenidate than in placebo-treated controls. Retest conditions were similar for both groups, so that improvement could not be a function of practice. However, the possibility exists that the stimulant drugs have a direct effect on motor and sensory performance, rather than an indirect one mediated through behavior. This is supported by the ancillary finding that 10 of 11 children who showed *no* neurological improvement *did* show a marked behavioral improvement. On the other hand, our finding that neurological status was more likely to be deviant in low-IQ, hyperactive children (i.e., children with the behaviors we might expect to be related to poor compliance during examination) cannot rule out this possibility.

CONCLUSION

Both a review of the literature and our own studies among children in the CPP suggests that neurological "soft signs" are related to cognitive dysfunction, learning difficulties, and psychiatric disturbance. The relationship of "soft signs" to specific psychiatric syndromes is less certain. Thus the examination of our data on subjects at age 7 suggests that "soft signs" are more likely to be associated with hyperactive behavior in low-IQ males, whereas our follow-up in adolescent males suggests a relationship to affective symptomatology that is independent of IQ (Shaffer *et al.* 1982). Although both the literature and our own studies suggest somewhat inconsistent relationships at different ages, methodological variation is so considerable that judgment on this issue probably needs to be deferred. However, nonspecificity of psychiatric correlates of "soft signs" could be taken as consistent with the view that minimal brain dysfunction, of which "soft signs" may be an indicator, should best be regarded as a nonspecific etiological influence that increases vulnerability to psychiatric disorder but does not necessarily result in any specific, behaviorally defined psychiatric syndrome.

"Soft signs" probably have many origins. In some children, they may be a consequence of mild brain damage; in others, they will represent a genetically determined individual difference that may also be related to the biological determinants of psychiatric disorder. Either of these origins is compatible with their showing a developmental course in which the signs become more difficult to elicit with increasing age.

In general, the base rate of neurological "soft signs" in children who do not show problems is so high as to make these phenomena of only limited clinical value for such exercises as screening, prediction, and so forth. However, the task of delineating their relationship to psychiatric disturbance remains an important task in increasing clinicians' understanding of the biological determinants of psychiatric disturbance.

APPENDIX: BEHAVIOR ITEMS—AGE 7 EXAMINATION

ORIGINAL ITEM (range: 1–5)	ITEMS DEVELOPED AS UNIPOLAR (range: 0–2)	A PRIORI SCALE (item dropped)
Fearfulness	*Fearful*	Dependent/Withdrawn
1. Completely unafraid	1–3 = 0	
2. Very little fear evidenced	4 = 1	
3. Normal caution	5 = 2	
4. Inhibited and uneasy		
5. Very fearful and apprehensive		
Rapport with examiner	*Shy*	Dependent/Withdrawn
1. Exceptionally shy, withdrawn	3–5 = 0	
2. Shy; very little social interaction	2 = 1	
3. Initial shyness; feels at ease	1 = 2	
4. Very friendly		
5. Extreme friendliness		
Self-confidence	*Unconfident*	Dependent/Withdrawn
1. Extremely self-critical	3–5 = 0	
2. Distrusts own ability	2 = 1	
3. Adequately self-confident	1 = 2	
4. Usually satisfied with performance		
5. Very self-confident; can tackle anything		

ORIGINAL ITEM (range: 1–5)	ITEMS DEVELOPED AS UNIPOLAR (range: 0–2)	A PRIORI SCALE (item dropped)
Emotional reactivity	*Unreactive*	Dependent/Withdrawn
1. Extremely flat	3–5 = 0	
2. Little change in emotional tone	2 = 1	
3. Affect appropriate to situation	1 = 2	
4. Mood more variable than average	*Labile*	(Hyperactive)
5. Extreme instability of emotional responses	1–3 = 0	
	4 = 1	
	5 = 2	
Degree of cooperation	*Negative*	Aggressive
1. Extreme negativism	3–5 = 0	
2. Resistive to directions	2 = 1	
3. Mostly responds well to directions	1 = 2	
4. Eager to conform	*Suggestible*	(Dependent/Withdrawn)
5. Extremely suggestible/conforming	1–3 = 0	
	4 = 1	
	5 = 2	
Level of frustration tolerance	*Frustrated/Withdrawn*	Dependent/Withdrawn
1. Withdraws completely	3–5 = 0	
2. Occasional withdrawal with difficulty	2 = 1	
	1 = 2	
3. Attempt to cope with difficult situation	*Frustrated/Aggressive*	(Aggressive)
	1–3 = 0	
4. Upset by difficulty, some anger	4 = 1	
5. Acting out/crying; uncontrolled	5 = 2	
Degree of dependency	*Dependent*	Dependent/Withdrawn
1. Very self-reliant; refuses help	1–3 = 0	
2. Rarely needs reassurance	4 = 1	
3. Appropriately dependent	5 = 2	
4. Needs frequent help/approval		
5. Constant need for attention/help		
Duration of attention span	*Distractible*	Hyperactive
1. Attends very briefly; highly distractible	3–5 = 0	
	2 = 1	
2. Easily distractible	1 = 2	
3. Adequate time on task	*Persevering*	Dependent/Withdrawn
4. More than average time on tasks	1–3 = 0	
5. Unable to shift attention	4 = 1	
	5 = 2	
Goal orientation	*Lack of persistence*	Hyperactivity
1. No effort to reach goal	3–5 = 0	
2. Mostly content to sit still	2 = 1	
3. Able to keep goal in mind	1 = 2	
4. Continues effort beyond necessary		
5. Compulsive absorption in task		

ORIGINAL ITEM (range: 1–5)	ITEMS DEVELOPED AS UNIPOLAR (range: 0–2)	A PRIORI SCALE (item dropped)
Level of activity	*Overactive*	Hyperactive
1. Placid, sluggish, passive	1–3 = 0	
2. Mostly content to sit still	4 = 1	
3. Normal amount of activity	5 = 2	
4. Very seldom able to sit quietly	*Inactive*	Dependent/Withdrawn
5. Constantly in motion	3–5 = 0	
	2 = 1	
	1 = 2	
Nature of activity	*Rigid*	Dependent/Withdrawn
1. Unable to shift activity	3–5 = 0	
2. Tends to be inflexible	2 = 1	
3. Flexible behavior patterns	1 = 2	
4. Behavior frequently impulsive	*Impulsive*	Hyperactive
5. Extremely impulsive	1–3 = 0	
	4 = 1	
	5 = 2	
Nature of communication	*Verbal fluency*	Dependent/Withdrawn
1. Little or no verbal communication	3–5 = 0	
2. Only answers directed questions	2 = 1	
3. Answers questions; may initiate	1 = 2	
4. Answers freely; sometimes	*Verbal organization*	(Hyperactive)
illogical	1–3 = 0	
5. Difficult to follow thinking	4 = 1	
	5 = 2	
Assertiveness	*Asssertive*	Aggressive
1. Dominating, aggressive approach	3–5 = 0	
2. Quite forceful, unnecessarily	2 = 1	
rough	1 = 2	
3. Self-assertive but accepts situation		
4. Passive acceptance		
5. Extreme passivity, malleability		
Hostility	*Hostile*	Aggressive
1. Overt physical/verbal attacks	3–5 = 0	
2. Very uncooperative, may become	2 = 1	
angry	1 = 2	
3. Appropriate negative affect/behavior		
4. Very agreeable, rarely shows hostility		
5. Ingratiating child		

Acknowledgments

This work was made possible by NIMH Center Grants #MH30906-01A and #MH30906-03, NIMH Education Grant #2T01 MH07715-17, and the Research Associate Program created by the New York State Legislature, Office of Mental Hygiene, Division of Research.

References

Adams R. M., Kocsis, J. J., & Estes, R. E. Soft neurological signs in learning-disabled children and controls. *American Journal of Diseases of Children*, 1974, *128*, 614–618.

Ayres, A. J. Types of sensory integrative dysfunction among disabled learners. *American Journal of Occupational Therapy*, 1972, *26*, 13–18.

Belmont, L., & Birch, H. Lateral dominance, lateral awareness, and reading disability. *Child Development*, 1965, *36*, 57–71.

Bender, L. *Psychopathology of children with organic brain disorders.* Springfield, Ill.: Charles C Thomas, 1956.

Bender, M., Fink, M., & Green, M. Patterns in perception on simultaneous tests of face and hand. *Archives of Neurology and Psychiatry*, 1951, *66*, 355–362.

Berendes, H. W. The structure and scope of the Collaborative Project on cerebral palsy, mental retardation, and other neurological and sensory disorders of infancy and childhood. In S. S. Chipman, A. M. Lilienfeld, B. G. Greenberg, & J. F. Donnelly (Eds.), *Research methodology and needs in perinatal studies.* Springfield, Ill.: Charles C Thomas, 1966.

Birch, H. G., & Belmont, L. Auditory–visual integration, intelligence, and reading ability in school children. *Perceptual and Motor Skills*, 1965, *20*, 295–305.

Boshes, B., & Myklebust, H. R. A neurological and behavioral study of children with learning disorders. *Neurology*, 1964, *14*, 7–12.

Camp, J. A., Bialer, I., Sverd, J., & Winsberg, B. G. Clinical usefulness of the NIMH physical and neurological examination for soft signs. *American Journal of Psychiatry*, 1978, *135*, 362–364.

Carey, W. B., McDevitt, S. C., & Baker, D. Differentiating minimal brain dysfunction and temperament. *Developmental Medicine and Child Neurology*, 1979, *21*, 765–772.

Close, J. Scored neurological examination in pharmacotherapy of children. *Psychopharmacology Bulletin*, 1973, *9*, 142–148.

David, O., Clark, J., & Voeller, K. Lead and hyperactivity. *Lancet*, 1972, *2*, 900–903.

Foster, R. M., Margolin, L., Alexander, C., Benitez, O., & Carr, F. Equivocal neurological signs, child development and learned behavior. *Child Psychiatry and Human Development*, 1978, *9*, 28–32.

Gubbay, S. S., Ellis, E., Walton, J. N., & Court, S. D. M. Clumsy children: A study of apraxic and agnosic defects in 21 children. *Brain*, 1965, *88*, 295–312.

Hertzig, M. E. Stability and change in nonfocal neurological signs. *Journal of the American Academy of Child Psychiatry*, 1982, *21*, 231–236.

Hertzig, M. E., Bortner, M., & Birch, H. G. Neurologic findings in children educationally designated as "brain-damaged." *American Journal of Orthopsychiatry*, 1969, *39*, 437–446.

Jastak, J. F., & Jastak, S. R. *The Wide-Range Achievement Test.* Wilmington, Del.: Guidance Associates, 1965.

Kennard, M. A. Value of equivocal signs in neurological diagnosis. *Neurology*, 1960, *10*, 753–764.

Larsen, V. L. Physical characteristics of disturbed adolescents. *Archives of General Psychiatry*, 1964, *10*, 55–58.

Lerer, R. J., & Lerer, M. P. The effects of methylphenidate on the soft neurological signs of hyperactive children. *Pediatrics*, 1976, *57*, 521–525.

Lewis, D. O., Shanok, S. S., Pincus, J. H., & Glaser, G. H. Violent juvenile delinquents. *Journal of the American Academy of Child Psychiatry*, 1979, *18*, 307–319.

Lubchenco, L. O., Hansman, C., Dressler, M., & Boyd, E. Intrauterine growth as estimated from liveborn birth-weight data at 24 to 42 weeks of gestation. *Pediatrics*, 1963, *32*, 793–800.

Lucas, A. R., Rodin, E. A., & Simson, C. B. Neurological assessment of children with early school problems. *Developmental Medicine and Child Neurology*, 1965, *7*, 145–156.

McDevitt, S. C., & Carey, W. B. The measurement of temperament in 3–7 year old children. *Journal of Child Psychology and Psychiatry*, 1978, *19*, 245–253.

McMahon, S. A., & Greenberg, L. M. Serial neurologic examination of hyperactive children. *Pediatrics*, 1977, *59*, 584–587.

Myklebust, H. R. Learning disabilities: Definition and overview. In H. R. Myklebust (Ed.), *Progress in learning disabilities* (Vol. 1) New York: Grune & Stratton, 1968.

Nichols, P., & Chen, T. *Minimal brain dysfunction: A prospective study.* Hillsdale, N.J.: Erlbaum, 1981.

Niswander, K. R., & Gordon, M. *The women and their pregnancies: The Collaborative Perinatal Study of the National Institute of Neurological Diseases and Stroke* (DHEW Publication No. (NIH) 73-379). Washington, D.C.: U.S. Government Printing Office, 1972.

Nunnally, J. C. *Psychometric theory.* (2nd ed.). New York: McGraw-Hill, 1978.

Owen, F. W., Adams, P. A., Forrest, T., Stolz, L. M., & Fisher, S. Learning disorders in children: Sibling studies. *Monographs of the Society for Research in Child Development*, 1971, *36*(4, Serial No. 144)

Paulsen, K. Reflection-impulsivity and level of maturity. *Journal of Psychology*, 1978, *99*, 109–112.

Paulsen, K., & O'Donnell, J. P. Construct validation of children's behavior problem dimensions: Relationship to activity level, impulsivity, and soft neurological signs. *Journal of Psychology*, 1979, *101*, 273–278.

Peters, J. E., Romine, J. S., & Dykman, R. A. A special neurological examination of children with learning disabilities. *Developmental Medicine and Child Neurology*, 1975, *17*, 63–78.

Prechtl, H. F. R., & Stemmer, C. H. The choreiform syndrome in children. *Developmental Medicine and Child Neurology*, 1962, *4*, 119–127.

Rieder, R. O., & Nichols, P. L. Offspring of schizophrenics: III: Hyperactivity and neurological soft signs. *Archives of General Psychiatry*, 1979, *36*, 665–674.

Rutter, M., Graham, P., & Birch, H. G. Interrelations between the choreiform syndrome, reading disability and psychiatric disorder in children of 8–11 years. *Developmental Medicine and Child Neurology*, 1966, *8*, 149–159.

Rutter, M., Tizard, J., & Whitmore, K. (Eds.). *Education, health, and behaviour.* London: Longmans, 1970. (Reprinted, Huntington, N.Y.: Krieger, 1981.)

Sandberg, S., Wieselberg, M., & Shaffer, D. Hyperkinetic and conduct problem children in a primary school population. Some epidemiological considerations. *Journal of Child Psychology and Psychiatry*, 1980, *21*: 293–312.

Shaffer, D. "Soft" neurological signs and later psychiatric disorder: A review. *Journal of Child Psychology and Psychiatry*, 1978, *19*, 63–65.

Shaffer, D. & Greenhill, L. A critical note on the predictive validity of "the hyperkinetic syndrome." *Journal of Child Psychology and Psychiatry*, 1979, *20*, 61–72.

Shaffer, D., Stokman, C. J., O'Connor, P. A., Shafer, S., Barmack, J. E., Hess, S., Spalten, D., & Schonfeld, I. Early soft neurological signs and later psychopathology. In N. Erlenmeyer-Kimling & B. S. Dohrenwend (Eds.), *Lifespan research on the prediction of psychopathology.* New York: Columbia University Press, 1982.

Werry, J., Minde, K., Guzman, A., Weiss, G., Dogan, K., & Hoy, E. Studies on the hyperactive child: VII. Neurologic status compared with neurotic and normal children. *American Journal Orthopsychiatry*, 1972, *42*, 441–451.

Wikler, A., Dixon, J. F., & Parker, J. B., Jr. Brain function in problem children and controls: Psychometric, neurological, and electroencephalographic comparisons. *American Journal of Psychiatry*, 1970, *127*, 94–105.

Wolff, P. H., & Cohen, C. Dual task performance during bimanual coordination. *Cortex*, 1980, *16*, 119–133.

Wolff, P. H., & Hurwitz, I. Functional implications of the minimal brain damage syndrome. *Seminars in Psychiatry*, 1973, *5*, 105–115.

Wolff, P. H., & Hurwitz, J. The choreiform syndrome. *Developmental Medicine and Child Neurology*, 1966, *8*, 160–165.

CHAPTER NINE

Temperament and Neurological Status

MARGARET E. HERTZIG

INTRODUCTION

Current interest in the study of temperament can perhaps be said to date from the initiation of the longitudinal studies of Thomas, Chess, and their coworkers in the mid-1950s (Thomas & Chess, 1977; Thomas, Chess, & Birch, 1968; Thomas, Chess, Birch, Hertzig, & Korn, 1963). Although numerous observations of individual differences among infants and young children had been reported prior to this date (Bergman & Escalona, 1949; Fries & Woolf, 1953; Gesell & Ames, 1937; Shirley, 1931, 1933), the New York Longitudinal Study (NYLS) investigative group specifically delineated the systematic exploration of the *how* rather than the *what* (abilities and content) or the *why* (motivations) of behavior as its primary area of concern. The methods of investigation permitted information with respect to activity level, rhythmicity, initial responses to new situations, adaptability, threshold of responsiveness, quality of mood, distractibility, and attention span and persistence to be reliably obtained over time.

During the past 20 years, as interest in the study of temperament has grown, these attributes have been identified and their distributions described in many children living in a wide variety of social and cultural circumstances (Thomas & Chess, 1977). While the organization of temperament has been examined in some groups of handicapped children—for example, those with mild mental retardation or with congenital rubella (Chess & Korn, 1970; Chess, Korn, & Fernandez, 1971)—there has been a paucity of studies of temperament in children at increased risk of cerebral injury, or of relationships between temperament and brain damage (Rutter, 1977; Shaffer, 1977).

What information is available tends to suggest that although brain damage may well be associated with an increased rate of "difficult" or poorly adaptive characteristics, the temperamental attributes of affected children vary widely (Rutter, 1977). The question continues to be of considerable importance, however, because of the frequency with which overactivity, inattentiveness, and distractibility are considered as behavioral manifestations of neurological impairment (Wender, 1971).

Margaret E. Hertzig. Department of Psychiatry, Cornell University Medical Center, New York, New York.

The present report addresses this question in the course of the examination of data deriving from a longitudinal study of temperament in low-birth-weight infants. Numerous studies have repeatedly confirmed that low birth weight may have deleterious effects on physical and mental development (Abramowicz & Kass, 1966; Davis & Tizard, 1975; Drillien, 1961, 1967; Drillien, Thomson, & Burgoyne, 1980; Fitzhardinge & Ramsay, 1973; Francis-Williams & Davis, 1974; Janus-Kukulska & Liss, 1966; Kitchen, Ryan, Rickards, McDougall, Billson, Keir, & Naylor, 1980). Thus a sample of low-birth-weight children represents one in which the risk of central nervous system (CNS) disorder is relatively high. However as the consequences of low birth weight are not uniform, ranging from profound physical and mental handicap to no discernable disability, there is an opportunity to compare the temperamental attributes of neurologically defined subgroups of children.

DESCRIPTION OF STUDY AND METHODS

Subjects

This sample consists of 66 children in 63 families, born between 1962 and 1965. Initially, 71 children were enrolled in the study, but five were lost to follow-up. Of these, two died; one succumbed to "crib death" at 4 weeks of age, and one died as a consequence of congenital heart disease at 2 months. An additional three families moved to distant areas when their children were 3 months, 5 years, and 6 years old, respectively.

All of the children came from families that were intact at the time of their birth, and that were socially and economically well situated. All but two of the fathers had graduated from high school; 43 (65%) had attended college, 28 (42%) had graduated from college, and 18 (27%) had attended graduate school. All but one of the mothers had graduated from high school; 27 (41%) had attended college, 14 (21%) had graduated, and 8 (12%) had attended graduate school. Thirty (46%) of the fathers had occupations at the executive or professional level: these included accountants, engineers, physicians, and professors. Thirteen (20%) had clerical, sales, or lower-management jobs, and 23 (35%) were skilled workers, artisans, or policemen. Twenty-seven (44%) of the children had mothers who returned to work before their fifth birthdays. Of these, 13 were employed fulltime and 14 part-time. The occupational distribution of these women was similar to that of their husbands.

All of the low-birth-weight children weighed between 1000 g (2 pounds 3 ounces) and 1750 g (3 pounds 14 ounces) at birth. The sample included three sets of twins. An additional two children were surviving members of twin pairs, while one child was a twin whose sibling weighed more than 1750 g. Four children (5%) derived from pregnancies that were complicated by first-trimester bleeding; 16 other pregnancies (24%) were complicated by third-trimester bleeding and five (7%) by preeclampsia. Four children (5%) were delivered by cesarean section; three of these were repeat sections with the mother in active labor, and one was necessitated by the presence of a placenta previa.

Gestational age, based on a mother's report of her last menstrual period, ranged from 26 to 39 weeks, with a mean of 32.30 $\pm$ 3.19 weeks. Gestational age was estimated to be over 37 weeks in six cases. Twenty-eight of the children

(42%) were small for their gestational dates when the Tanner and Thompson (1970) standards for intrauterine growth were applied. For 20%, active resuscitation for the initiation of respiration was required. Postnatal course was complicated by severe respiratory distress, frequent and prolonged periods of apnea, seizures, systemic infections, or jaundice requiring exchange transfusions in 30% of cases. In an additional 45%, less severe complications including mild respiratory distress, brief and infrequent apneic episodes, or superficial infections of the eyes or umbilicus were noted.

All children were initially nursed in isolettes. Ambient oxygen was monitored frequently and maintained at the lowest concentration possible to prevent cyanosis. Prolonged and severe apnea was treated by manual bag and mask resuscitation. Positive-pressure respirators were not used. Bilirubin levels were determined on all jaundiced infants, and exchange transfusions were performed for an indirect bilirubin of 20 mg/100ml or over. Only one infant received intravenous fluids. Oral feedings were started as soon as possible and consisted of standard formulae administered in strengths of 25 calories per ounce of weight for the first 2 or 3 weeks of life and then reduced to 20 calories per ounce. Antibiotics used were penicillin, streptomycin, and chloramphenicol. Length of stay in the nursery ranged from 16 to 86 days, with a median of 41 days. Weight gain per day was determined by dividing the difference between discharge weight and birth weight by the number of days in the nursery and was found to range from 12.75 g to 68.12 g, with a median of 20.01 g. Visiting was confined to prescribed hours, and parents were not permitted to handle their infants until they had graduated from the isolettes.

Methods

The methods used for the collection of data on temperament were identical to those employed in the NYLS (Thomas & Chess, 1977; Thomas *et al.*, 1963, 1968). Parents were the primary source of information with respect to the behavioral characteristics of their children. Interviews were conducted at 6-month intervals during the first 2 years of life and again at 3 years of age. The interview was designed to elicit detailed descriptions of behavior in everyday-life situations. During infancy, these included the routines of feeding, sleeping, dressing, bathing, and diaper changing, as well as contact with people. Later interviews focused also on problem-solving behavior, play preferences, and social interactions. Throughout, emphasis was placed on what and how the children did what they did. Interim reports were obtained annually until 8 years of age and again at 12 years. Changes in familial organization were inquired after, and descriptions of the children's behavioral responses to these and other special events were recorded. In addition, full reports of medical and/or psychiatric consultation and treatment as well as progress in school were noted. Wechsler Intelligence Scale for Children (WISC) IQs, as well as Wide-Range Achievement Test (WRAT) scores in reading and arithmetic, were obtained on each child in the eighth year of life.

Procedures for the analysis of temperament followed those developed in the course of the NYLS. The methods of scoring, together with measures of reliability and validity, are fully described in previous publications (Thomas *et al.*, 1963, 1968). In summary, nine categories of temperament were established by an inductive content analysis of the parent interview protocols, covering the

Table 9-1. Nine categories of temperament

CATEGORY	WEIGHTED SCORE
Activity	
High	0
Moderate	1
Low	2
Rhythmicity	
Regular	0
Variable	1
Irregular	2
Adaptability	
Adaptive	0
Variable	1
Nonadaptive	2
Approach–withdrawal	
Approach	0
Variable	1
Withdrawal	2
Threshold	
High	0
Moderate	1
Low	2
Intensity	
Intense	0
Variable	1
Mild	2
Mood	
Positive	0
Variable	1
Negative	2
Distractibility	
Distractible	0
Variable	1
Nondistractible	2
Persistence	
Persistent	0
Variable	1
Nonpersistent	2

first year of life of the first 22 children enrolled in that study. Each record was item-scored to a 3-point scale established for each category.

To avoid contamination by "halo effects," no successive interviews of a given child were scored contiguously. As the number of scorable items varied from interview protocol to interview protocol, it was necessary to develop a standard method of scaling before quantitative comparisons of temperamental attributes could be undertaken. Standard scores were calculated by converting the raw score in each category to a weighted score, which ranged from 0 to 2. The categories, together with their weighted-score points, are summarized in Table 9-1.

The categories are defined as follows:

1. Activity level: The motor component present in a given child's functioning and the diurnal proportion of active and inactive periods.

2. Rhythmicity: The predictability and/or unpredictability in time of such functions as sleep–wake behavior, hunger, feeding pattern, and elimination schedule.

3. Approach–withdrawal: The nature of the initial response to a new stimulus, be it new food, new toy, or new person. Approach responses are positive, whether displayed by mood expression, verbalizations or motor activity, while withdrawal responses are negative.

4. Adaptability: Responses to new or altered situations over time. In this category, attention is directed toward the ease with which responses can be modified in a desired direction, not on the nature of the initial response.

5. Threshold of responsiveness: The intensity level of stimulation that is necessary to evoke a discernible response, irrespective of the specific form the response may take or the sensory modality affected.

6. Intensity of reaction: The energy level of response, irrespective of its quality or direction.

7. Quality of mood: The amount of pleasant, joyful, and friendly behavior, as contrasted with unpleasant, crying, and unfriendly behavior.

8. Distractibility: The effectiveness of extraneous environmental stimuli in interfering with or in altering the direction of the ongoing behavior.

9. Attention span and persistence: Two categories that are related. "Attention span" concerns the length of time a particular activity is pursued by the child. "Persistence" refers to the continuation of an activity in the face of obstacles to the maintenance of the activity direction.

Validity of the NYLS parents' reports of their children's behavioral characteristics was assessed by subjecting narrative protocols (obtained in the course of two direct 4-hour observations, conducted at different times within 1 week of the parents' interviews) to be the same scoring procedures. Each direct observation was found to agree with the parents' interview at the 1% level of confidence. In addition, high levels of both intra- and interscorer reliability at the 90% level of confidence were achieved. No separate assessments of validity and reliability were made in the course of the collection and analysis of information obtained from the parents of the low-birth-weight children, as the two studies were conducted during overlapping time periods by the same personnel.

The neurological examinations were complete, age-appropriate, and included the assessment of both localizing and nonfocal signs. At all ages, localizing signs included standard measures of CNS damage, such as abnormalities in cranial nerves, lateralized dysfunctions, and the presence of pathological reflexes. Between infancy and 5 years of age, nonfocal signs included disturbances in muscle tone, generalized hyperreflexia, clumsiness of gait, and poor fine motor coordination. The assessment of nonfocal signs at 8 years of age was more complex and was conducted in accordance with procedures developed by Lawrence Taft for a total-population study of mentally retarded school children in Aberdeen, Scotland (Birch, Richardson, Baird, Horobin, & Illsley, 1970). Performance on individual tasks was rated as "within normal limits," "mildly impaired," or "markedly impaired." Tasks were then grouped to permit the development of judgments about the integrity of broader functional areas. As the examination was viewed as a clinical and not a psychometric assessment, no attempt was made to standardize the number of tasks within each area. The following criteria were employed:

1. Speech. Each child was engaged in sufficient informal conversation to permit the assessment of clarity and intelligibility. Word sound production was rated in accordance with the examiner's difficulty in comprehension. Marked impairments were required for the designation of speech as a nonfocal sign.

2. Balance. Balance was designated as a nonfocal sign if performance on at least two of the following three tasks was markedly impaired:

a. Standing balance: The child was required to stand still with eyes closed, feet together, arms extended, and fingers spread apart for 30 seconds. Marked impairment was reflected in three or more back-and-forth movements of the body exceeding 1 inch in both directions during the observation period.

b. Hopping: The child was asked to hop 10 consecutive times on each foot. Marked impairment reflected a failure to hop at least five consecutive times on both feet.

c. Walking a line in tandem: The child was asked to take 10 steps, placing the heel directly in front of the toe of the other foot (as in walking on a tightrope), with arms at sides. Marked impairment reflected a failure to approximate heel and toe for at least five consecutive steps.

3. Coordination. Coordination was designated as a nonfocal sign if performance on at least two of the following four tasks was markedly impaired:

a. Finger-to-nose: The child was required to extend each arm laterally and touch the index finger to the tip of the nose five times with each hand with eyes open. The sequence was repeated with the eyes closed. Marked impairment reflected a failure to touch the tip of the nose at least three times with both hands with eyes closed.

b. Alternating pronation–supination: This test was performed with the child standing, one arm relaxed at the side. The other elbow was flexed 90° with the hand pointing forward. The child was requested to pronate and supinate the extended hand quickly five times and to repeat the task using the other hand. Marked impairment was reflected by the movement of both elbows a distance of 4 or more inches during execution of the alternating hand movements.

c. Foot taps: The child was seated in a straight chair and asked to tap the toe of each foot in succession a total of 10 times while maintaining the heel on the floor. He or she was then asked to tap both feet together an additional 10 times. Marked impairment reflected a failure to sustain at least five simultaneous toe taps.

d. Heel–shin: This task was performed with the child seated in a straight chair with legs extended. He or she was required to move one heel down the shin of the opposite leg from the knee to the big toe without losing contact. The task was repeated two times with each leg. Marked impairment reflected two or more losses of contact on each of the four trials.

4. Gait. Gait was observed as the child walked back and forth a distance of 20 feet. Designation as a nonfocal sign required the presence of at least two of the following: a base of more than 10 inches, a failure to alternate flexion and extension of the knees smoothly, absence of a heel–toe gait, or immobility of the arms.

5. Sequential finger–thumb opposition. This task required the child to imitate the examiner in the opposition of thumb to fingers in the following

sequence; index, fourth, middle, pinky, pinky, middle, fourth index. The child was requested to repeat each movement before the next was illustrated. The performance of both hands was assessed. Imitative movements were designated as a nonfocal sign if at least two errors (not spontaneously corrected) occurred on each hand.

6. Muscle tone. Muscle tone was assessed in accordance with the procedure described by Rutter, Graham, and Yule (1970). All four extremities were examined as follows: Tone of the upper limbs was tested by (a) flapping the hand while holding the lower forearm, (b) planta- and dorsiflexion of the wrist, (c) flexing and extending the elbow, and (d) dorsiflexing the wrist and bending the fingers back. Tone of the lower limb was tested by (a) holding the thigh above the knee with the leg hanging down and flapping the knee, and (b) testing the range of motion of the ankle. In order to insure that these movements were carried out while the extremity was limp, the child was engaged in conversation about something else to divert his or her attention from the examiner's manipulation. Tone was recorded separately for all extremities. A finding of marked hypo- or hypertonia in all four extremities was required for tone to be designated as a nonfocal sign.

7. Graphesthesia. The child was seated with eyes closed and hands positioned vertically facing the examiner, and asked to name the letters or numbers he or she felt being written. A ball point pen with the point retracted was used to trace the following symbols: Right hand, *3*, *a*, *2*; left hand, *8*, *c*, *R*. If errors were made, the child was asked to identify the symbols visually. Graphesthesia was designated as a nonfocal sign if at least two failures on each hand occurred in the face of accurate visual identification.

8. Astereognosis. The child was requested to identify the following objects by feeling them with each hand in turn, keeping eyes closed: a pocket comb, a key, a quarter, and a penny. Manipulation was permitted, but not transfer. After the entire sequence was administered, visual identification was required. Astereognosis was classified as a nonfocal sign if three failures in the face of accurate visual identification were observed.

9. Choreiform movements. The assessment of choreiform movements was based on the procedure developed by Prechtl (Prechtl & Stemmer, 1966). The child was asked to assume the position previously described for the assessment of standing balance while the examiner watched for small jerky twitches occurring in the fingers, wrist, joints, arms, and shoulders. Choreiform movements were designated as a nonfocal sign if 10 or more twitches were observed within a 30-second period.

All responses were recorded on a specially designed protocol during the course of the examination. Decisions with respect to clinical neurological status were made following review of the entire set of examination protocols by the examiner after an interval of at least 6 months. Between infancy and 5 years of age, neurological status was characterized as either "within normal limits" or "abnormal." Abnormalities during this period reflected the presence of any localizing findings and/or any nonfocal signs. More stringent criteria were applied to the examinations conducted at 8 years of age. Children of this age were judged to be neurologically abnormal (1) if any localizing signs of CNS abnormality were present or (2) if two or more nonlocalizing signs were found. The results of the neurological examinations conducted on 66 children in their

Table 9-2. Neurological findings at 8 years of age

TYPE OF FINDING	M	F	TOTAL
Localizing signs	7	6	13
Quadriplegia, severe disability	2	2	4
Quadriplegia, moderate disability	0	1	1
Right hemiplegia, moderate disability	0	1	1
Right hemiplegia, mild disability	1	0	1
Left hemiplegia, mild disability	2	0	2
Diplegia, moderate disability	0	1	1
Diplegia, mild disability	1	0	1
Left upper limb monoplegia, mild disability	0	1	1
Athetosis, mild disability	0	1	1
Two or more nonlocalizing signs	13	7	20
Balance	7	6	13
Coordination	7	3	10
Choreiform movements	8	0	8
Muscle tone	4	4	8
Gait	3	4	7
Graphesthesia	5	1	6
Finger–thumb opposition	3	2	5
Speech	3	0	3
Astereognosis	2	1	3
Normal	11	22	33
Balance	1	1	2
Finger–thumb opposition	0	2	2
Tone	0	2	2
Gait	1	0	1
Speech	1	0	1
Coordination	0	1	1
Graphesthesia	0	1	1
None	8	15	23

eighth year of life are summarized in Table 9-2, where it may be seen that 13 children (7 boys and 6 girls) were found to have localizing findings; 20 children (13 boys and 7 girls) were found to have two or more nonlocalizing signs; and 33 children (11 boys and 22 girls) were found to be neurologically normal.

In the analyses that follow, subgroups of low-birth-weight children are defined in terms of their neurological status at 8 years of age. This decision was based upon the following considerations: (1) 93% of the original sample of 71 children were examined at this point in time, as compared with 75% during the first 6 months of life, 70% at 1 year, 80% at 2 years, 87% at 3 years, and 89% at 5 years; and (2) the more stringent criteria used to define neurological abnormality at 8 years permitted a clear distinction to be made between children who displayed localizing and those who displayed nonlocalizing signs. Furthermore, as the data of Table 9-3 indicate, with the exception of examinations conducted during the first year of life, the predictive value of earlier assessments for neurological status at 8 years of age was significant at better than 5% level of confidence.

RESULTS

Three aspects of the relationship of temperament to neurological status in low-birth-weight children are addressed here. The first is concerned with the exploration of similarities and differences among three neurologically defined subgroups

Table 9-3. Stability and change in neurological status

	STATUS AT 8 YEARS					
AGE	NORMAL	ABNORMAL	TOTAL	χ^2	*df*	*p*
6 months						
Abnormal	13	23	36			
Normal	11	6	17	3.8106	1	<.05
Total	24	29	53			
1 year						
Abnormal	5	11	16			
Normal	20	14	34	3.088	1	<.10
Total	25	25	50			
2 years						
Abnormal	4	15	19			
Normal	25	13	38	10.1433	1	<.01
Total	29	28	57			
3 years						
Abnormal	8	16	24			
Normal	24	14	38	5.2392	1	<.05
Total	32	30	62			
5 years						
Abnormal	7	23	30			
Normal	24	9	33	15.3395	1	<.001
Total	31	32	63			

along each of nine temperamental dimensions during the first 3 years of life. The second focuses upon the relation of neurological status to a particular combination of temperamental attributes—the "difficult child." Interest in this latter question derives from the clinical observation of Thomas and Chess (1977) that children who were simultaneously irregular in biological functioning, withdrawing in new situations, tending toward intense and negative expressions of mood, and nonadaptable or slowly adaptable had an increased risk for the later emergence of behavior disorder. In the final section of the chapter, the relationship between neurological status, behavior disorder, and "difficulty" in low-birth-weight children is explored.

Temperament and Neurological Status

The means and standard deviations of the weighted scores for each of the three neurologically defined subgroups of low-birth-weight children, and for the group as a whole at 1, 2, and 3 years of age, are presented in Table 9-4. The possibility of differences among the subgroups was explored by means of multivariate techniques. Thus, a single statistical test was employed to examine simultaneously the relation of neurological status and of age to each of the nine temperamental attributes. This multivariate analysis of variance (MANOVA) utilizes a nine-dimensional measure, the "profile of temperament," as the dependent variable. The independent variables are neurological status, age, and the interaction between age and neurological status. The effect of each of these independent variables on "temperamental profile" can be assessed by means of a multivariate equivalent of the F test, such as Wilks's criterion. It was found that neurological status had no significant effect on "temperamental profile" (see Table 9-5). This finding of no difference with respect to the nine-

Table 9-4. Mean weighted scores for nine categories of temperament in low-birth-weight children at 1, 2, and 3 years of age

		YEAR 1			YEAR 2			YEAR 3		
VARIABLE	GROUP[a]	*n*	*M*	*SD*	*n*	*M*	*SD*	*n*	*M*	*SD*
Activity	Neg.	33	.85	.12	33	.73	.14	31	.73	.20
	LF	13	.88	.18	12	.81	.17	11	.90	.24
	NL	20	.82	.10	19	.70	.19	20	.64	.20
	TS	66	.85	.13	64	.73	.16	62	.73	.22
Rhythmicity	Neg.	33	.55	.20	33	.59	.40	31	.59	.50
	LF	13	.69	.37	12	.67	.33	11	.52	.41
	NL	20	.66	.33	19	.57	.31	19	.72	.55
	TS	66	.54	.29	64	.57	.36	61	.62	.50
Adaptability	Neg.	33	.64	.19	33	.71	.23	31	.62	.23
	LF	13	.80	.16	12	.85	.22	11	.73	.28
	NL	20	.62	.23	19	.82	.19	20	.72	.28
	TS	66	.67	.21	64	.77	.22	62	.67	.25
Approach–withdrawal	Neg.	33	.64	.24	33	.42	.32	31	.40	.43
	LF	13	.70	.27	12	.69	.57	11	.54	.44
	NL	20	.64	.34	19	.60	.42	20	.43	.41
	TS	66	.65	.28	64	.52	.41	62	.43	.42
Threshold	Neg.	33	1.12	.19	33	1.18	.29	31	1.17	.56
	LF	13	1.15	.15	12	1.19	.26	10	1.51	.41
	NL	20	1.06	.11	19	1.13	.35	18	1.24	.59
	TS	66	1.02	.19	64	1.18	.30	59	1.25	.54
Intensity	Neg.	33	.99	.19	33	.80	.21	31	.97	.25
	LF	13	.92	.23	12	.77	.18	11	1.03	.32
	NL	20	.89	.16	19	.79	.14	20	.89	.25
	TS	66	.95	.19	64	.79	.18	62	.96	.27
Mood	Neg.	33	1.06	.18	33	1.07	.17	31	1.05	.27
	LF	13	1.13	.18	12	1.15	.19	11	1.04	.24
	NL	20	1.11	.18	19	1.15	.17	20	1.06	.17
	TS	66	1.09	.18	64	1.06	.18	62	1.05	.24
Distractibility	Neg.	33	.44	.24	33	.36	.38	25	.24	.50
	LF	13	.59	.31	10	.36	.31	11	1.06	.75
	NL	20	.49	.20	18	.44	.47	18	.50	.70
	TS	66	.48	.25	61	.38	.39	54	.49	.69
Persistence	Neg.	33	.33	.19	33	.46	.22	31	.64	.45
	LF	13	.28	.17	12	.41	.26	11	.47	.48
	NL	20	.34	.20	19	.42	.28	20	.53	.40
	TS	66	.32	.19	64	.44	.24	62	.57	.44

[a]LF, localizing findings; NL, nonlocalizing signs of CNS dysfunction; TS, total sample of low-birth-weight children.

Table 9-5. MANOVA relating "temperamental profile" to neurological status and age in low-birth-weight children

HYPOTHESIS	*F*	*df*	*p*[a]
No neurological effect	1.55	18, 112	ns
No age effect	4.95	18, 196	.001
No neurological × age effect	1.29	36, 368	ns

[a]Wilks's criterion.

dimensional "profile of temperament" renders further examination of the relationship of individual temperamental attributes to neurological status unwarranted.

However, it should be noted (see Table 9-4) that the overall "profile of temperament" did change significantly with age. Table 9-6 summarizes the F values obtained when analyses of variance (ANOVAs) comparing the mean weighted scores obtained for each of the nine temperamental attributes at 1, 2, and 3 years were performed. Rhythmicity and mood are the only characteristics that did not change significantly over time (see Table 9-6). As the mean weighted scores for the group as a whole (see Table 9-1) indicate, activity level was lower during the second and third years of life than during the first. Children were less adaptive and more intense at 2 years than at either 1 or 3. Increasing age was accompanied by a decrease in initial withdrawal reactions to new situations, a decrease in sensory threshold, and a decrease in persistence. However, distractibility was greater at 2 years than at either 1 or 3. Moreover, as the statistical interaction between age and "temperamental profile" was not significant (see Table 9-5), these changes were independent of neurological status.

The "Difficult Child"

Although overall temperamental organization was found not to differ in low-birth-weight children of differing neurological status, the possibility still remained that neurologically impaired children might be more likely to display combinations of "difficult" temperamental attributes than those who are neurologically intact might. Thomas and Chess's (1977) clinical description of the "difficult child" has provided the basis for the construction of an "index of difficulty," which is the linear combination of the following five tempermental attributes: rhythmicity, adaptability, approach–withdrawal, intensity, and mood. The higher the numerical value of this index, the more "difficult" the child. The means and standard deviations for the group as a whole and for each of the neurologically defined subgroups at 1, 2, and 3 years are presented in Table 9-7, and the results of an ANOVA relating "difficulty" to neurological status and age are presented in Table 9-8.

Neurological status was found to have a significant effect on "difficulty." Moreover, degree of "difficulty" was significantly different at different ages in

Table 9-6. ANOVA relating temperament and age in low-birth-weight children

TEMPERAMENTAL ATTRIBUTE	*df*	*F*	*p*
Activity	2, 63	8.18	$< .001$
Rhythmicity	2, 63	.07	ns
Adaptability	2, 63	4.93	$< .01$
Approach–withdrawal	2, 63	3.77	$< .01$
Threshold	2, 63	3.09	$< .05$
Intensity	2, 63	10.37	$< .001$
Mood	2, 63	1.46	ns
Distractibility	2, 63	4.75	$< .01$
Persistence	2, 63	6.22	$< .01$

Table 9-7. "Index of difficulty" in neurologically defined subgroups of low-birth-weight children

	YEAR 1			YEAR 2			YEAR 3		
FINDINGS	*n*	*M*	*SD*	*n*	*M*	*SD*	*n*	*M*	*SD*
Localizing findings	13	2.40	.66	13	2.59	1.05	11	1.79	.82
Nonlocalizing findings	20	2.14	.90	19	2.34	.48	19	2.02	.90
Negative findings	33	1.91	.72	33	1.99	.70	31	1.69	.98
Total	66	2.07	.78	64	2.21	.76	61	1.81	.93

each of the neurologically defined subgroups. However, the statistical interaction between "degree of difficulty" and age was not significant, indicating that trends over time were similar in all three neurologically defined subgroups. Thus all children, whether they had localizing neurological findings, had two or more nonlocalizing signs of CNS dysfunction, or were without evidence of abnormality in clinical examination conducted at 8 years of age, were more "difficult" during the second year of life than at any other time during the preschool period. The increase in "degree of difficulty" during the second year is a reflection of the tendency exhibited by children in each of the neurologically defined subgroups to become increasingly intense and nonadaptive in their responses at this point in time (see Table 9-4).

Behavior Disorder, Neurological Status, and "Difficulty"

The fact that changes in "degree of difficulty" during the first 3 years of life were essentially independent of neurological status makes it possible to consider the entire preschool period as a unit when examining the relations between behavior disorder, neurological status, and difficulty. For simplicity of presentation, this strategy was adopted. The analyses that follow are based upon a composite "index of difficulty" that was obtained by determining the average of each child's "difficulty" scores at 1, 2, and 3 years of age.

Psychiatric consultation was requested for 18 of the 66 low-birth-weight children prior to 12 years of age. Presenting complaints, neurological status, and age at which consultation was requested are summarized in Table 9-9. Children who came to psychiatric notice were significantly more likely to be neurologically impaired ($\chi^2 = 6.1155$, $df = 1$, $p < .05$). However, the frequency with which consultation was requested did not differ significantly among children with localizing and nonlocalizing findings ($\chi^2 = 1.086$, $df = 1$, p ns).

Table 9-8. ANOVA relating "index of difficulty" to neurological status and age in low-birth-weight children

SOURCE	SUM OF SQUARES	MEAN SQUARE	*df*	*F*	*p*
Neurological status	74186.86	37093.43	2	3.85	$< .05$
Year	45872.79	22936.40	2	4.59	$< .01$
Neurological status × year	8681.53	2170.38	4	.43	ns
Subject (neurological)	606493.01	9626.87	63		
Residual error	594480.66	4995.64	119		
Total	1324341.73				

Children who came to psychiatric notice were also found to be significantly more "difficult" during the first 3 years of life. The mean composite "index of difficulty" among those for whom psychiatric consultation was requested was 2.20 ± 0.39, as contrasted with 1.93 ± 0.64 for the remainder ($t = 2.07$, $df = 64$, $p < .05$). This finding was not unexpected, in view of the previously determined relationship between "difficulty" and neurological status. However, within the group of neurologically impaired children, those who came to psychiatric notice were no more "difficult" than those who did not. The mean composite "index of difficulty" for the 13 children in this group for whom psychiatric consultation was requested was 2.23 ± 0.44, as contrasted with 2.26 ± 0.77 for the remaining 20 children in the neurologically impaired group ($t = .14$, $df = 31$, p ns). Beyond this, within the group of 33 neurologically impaired children, those who came to psychiatric notice did not differ significantly with respect to any of the nine dimensions of temperament when considered individually.

DISCUSSION

The individual temperamental attributes of the neurologically impaired children of the present study closely resemble those of children with similar birth histories and early life experiences, deriving from comparable social circum-

Table 9-9. Presenting complaints in low-birth-weight children who came to psychiatric notice

			PRESENTING COMPLAINT[a]										
CASE NO.	AGE AT NOTICE (YR)	NEUROLOGICAL STATUS	IDL	OA	TT	A/D	IPC	O	OD	PPR	PSP	RB	A
102	4	Localized	+	+									
106	5	Localized		+	+						+		
332	3	Localized	+		+								
103	6	Nonlocalized	+	+			+				+		
108	7	Nonlocalized	+				+				+		
114	3	Nonlocalized	+									+	
116	6	Nonlocalized			+		+				+		
122	5	Nonlocalized		+		+	+				+		
130	4	Nonlocalized		+	+	+							
131	2.5	Nonlocalized	+	+	+								
324	7	Nonlocalized	+		+					+	+		
331	6	Nonlocalized	+	+			+				+		
334	2.5	Nonlocalized		+	+	+	+						
111	6	Negative							+				
321	8	Negative							+	+	+		
323	11	Negative								+			+
326	8	Negative									+		
333	4.5	Negative						+					

[a]IDL, immaturity, developmental lag; OA, overactivity; TT, temper tantrums; A/D, aggressive/destructive; IPC, inattentive, poor concentration; O, oppositional; OD, overly demanding; PPR, poor peer relations; PSP, poor school performance; RB, ritualistic behavior; A, anxious.

stances, who were neurologically intact. The absence of difference with respect to such characteristics as activity, persistence, and distractibility during the first 3 years of life is of interest in the light of the commonly held view (Wender, 1971) that brain-injured children deviate systematically from the norm along these dimensions. Thus the individual temperamental attributes of the neurologically impaired children of the present study to not conform to the stereotype of the child with cerebral damage.

These results are consistent with and expand upon Thomas and Chess's (1977) clinical descriptions of the temperamental characteristics of the three brain-injured subjects of the NYLS. Activity level in these three children was noted to range from moderate to high, distractibility from moderately nondistractible to highly distractible, and persistence from moderately persistent to moderately impersistent. Similar variability was noted in relation to the other categories as well.

Nevertheless, the neurologically defined subgroups of the low-birth-weight children were found to differ systematically in relation to that constellation of temperamental attributes that Thomas and Chess (1977) have labeled the "difficult child." The mean "index of difficulty" reflecting a temperamental pattern of irregularity in biological functioning occurring in conjunction with an increased tendency to withdraw in new situations, slow adaptability to change, and intense and negative mood was significantly higher among those children who were neurologically impaired.

Furthermore, as would be expected in the light of the previously reported association between degree of difficulty and behavioral disturbance (Thomas & Chess, 1977), the children of the present sample who came to clinical notice were significantly more "difficult" during the first 3 years of life than were those whose behavior did not lead their parents to request psychiatric consultation. In addition, children with both localizing and nonlocalizing signs of CNS dysfunction were significantly more likely to be brought for evaluation than were those who were without clinical evidence of CNS abnormality or dysfunction.

These two sets of findings would appear to suggest that the increased risk of psychiatric disorder among children with neurological impairment (Rutter, 1977; Rutter *et al.*, 1970) might well be a consequence of the increased risk of "difficulty" exhibited by those children. Carey (Carey, McDevitt, & Baker, 1979), in a cross-sectional study, has also found that the most "difficult" children among those referred because of behavioral and/or school learning problems were those with clinical neurological findings. Among the neurologically impaired children of the present sample, however, "difficulty" during the first 3 years of life was not predictive of later behavioral disturbance.

"Temperament," however, whether defined in terms of nine individual dimensions or as a combination of particularly "difficult" attributes is not static, but varies significantly over time (cf. Tables 9-5 and 9-8). Although no systematic relation between age and neurological status was found, it should be noted that individual children make a differential contribution to group trends. This point is illustrated by the data of Table 9-10, in which the Pearson product–moment correlations for each of the nine temperamental attributes and the "index of difficulty" are presented. Of the 20 correlations, only 12 were significant at better than the 5% level, and the maximum amount of variance accounted for was 18%. Thus, group trends are of limited value in defining changes in the behavior patterns of individual children over time. It is entirely

Table 9-10. Interyear correlations of temperamental attributes in low-birth-weight-children

	YEAR 1–YEAR 2			YEAR 2–YEAR 3		
ATTRIBUTE	n	r	p	n	r	p
Activity	64	.3517	$<.01$	61	.3607	$<.01$
Rhythmicity	64	.3904	$<.001$	60	.3585	$<.01$
Adaptability	64	.4072	$<.001$	61	.1614	ns
Approach–withdrawal	64	−.0450	ns	61	.4090	$<.001$
Threshold	64	.4184	$<.001$	58	.1394	ns
Intensity	64	.0905	ns	61	.2131	$<.05$
Mood	64	.2599	$<.05$	61	.3205	$<.01$
Distractibility	61	−.1699	ns	51	.1685	ns
Persistence	64	.1930	ns	61	.0961	ns
Index of difficulty	64	.2432	$<.05$	61	.2441	$<.05$

possible that, although the neurologically impaired children who came to later psychiatric notice were no more difficult during the preschool period than those who did not, at least some of them may well have become so by the time consultation was sought. It is also likely, however, that a family's decision to seek psychiatric consultation is also influenced by factors other than their child's particular constellation of temperamental attributes.

The mean IQ of those neurologically impaired children who came to clinical notice was 92.54 ± 24.73, as compared with 100.70 ± 24.67 for the remainder of the neurologically impaired group. Although this difference did not reach statistical significance, the trend toward lower IQ among those children whose parents sought psychiatric evaluation is reflected in the frequency with which generalized immaturity or specific development lags were included among the presenting complaints. Moreover, poor school performance was reported in all of the neurologically impaired children who came to notice during the school years (see Table 9-9).

Although the association between type of neurological impairment and requests for psychiatric consultation did not reach statistical significance, a smaller proportion of children with localizing findings (23%) than with non-localizing signs of CNS dysfunction (50%) came to clinical notice. This trend suggests the possibility that parents are better able to tolerate more "difficult" temperamental attributes when they occur in association with visible physical handicap. This is consistent with Seidel's finding (Seidel, Chadwick, & Rutter, 1975) of a greater frequency of psychiatric disorder in mildly, as contrasted with severely, crippled children.

The importance of parental tolerance for particular behavior patterns in contributing to a decision to seek psychiatric consultation is further illustrated by the fact that, despite the frequency with which overactivity was listed as a complaint by the parents who brought their children for evaluation, the mean activity score of the clinical cases was not found to differ from the remainder of the neurologically impaired group.

Rutter (1977), too, has suggested that, in addition to its effect on temperament and personality, brain damage may lead to psychiatric disturbance through its impact on cognitive capacity as well as on the organization of familial patterns of response. The data of the present study are entirely consistent with this view, and in addition underscore the importance of evaluating the interaction between temperament and other characteristics both of the child and the environment in which growth and development takes place (Thomas & Chess, 1977).

Acknowledgments

Appreciation is expressed to Alexander Thomas, with whom earlier drafts of this chapter were discussed, and to Mary Middleman, for statistical consultation.

References

Abramowicz, M., & Kass, E. A. Pathogenesis and prognosis of prematurity. *New England Journal of Medicine*, 1966, *275*, 878–885, 938–943, 1001–1007, 1053–1059.

Bergman, P., & Escalona, S. Unusual sensitivities in very young children. *Psychoanalytic Study of the Child*, 1949, *34*, 33–47.

Birch, H. G., Richardson, S. A., Baird, D., Horobin, G., & Illsley, R. *Mental subnormality in the community: A clinical and epidemiologic study*. Baltimore; Williams & Wilkins, 1970.

Carey, W. B., McDevitt, S. C., & Baker, D. Differentiating minimal brain dysfunction and temperament. *Developmental Medicine and Child Neurology*, 1979, *21*, 765–772.

Chess, S., & Korn, S. Temperament and behavior disorders in mentally retarded children. *Archives of General Psychiatry*, 1970, *23*, 122–127.

Chess, S., Korn, S., & Fernandez, P. *Psychiatric disorders of children with congenital rubella*. New York: Brunner/Mazel, 1971.

Davis, P. A., and Tizard, J. P. M. Very low birthweight and subsequent neurological defect. *Developmental Medicine and Child Neurology*, 1975, *17*, 3–17.

Drillien, C. M. The incidence of mental and physical handicaps in school age children of very low birthweight. *Pediatrics*, 1961, *27*, 452–464.

Drillien, C. M. The incidence of mental and physical handicaps in school age children of very low birthweight: II. *Pediatrics*, 1967, *39*, 238–247.

Drillien, C. M., Thomson, A. J. M., & Burgoyne, K. Low birthweight children at early school age: A longitudinal study. *Developmental Medicine and Child Neurology*, 1980, *22*, 26–47.

Fitzhardinge, P. M., & Ramsay, M. The improving outlook for the small premature infant. *Developmental Medicine and Child Neurology*, 1973, *15*, 497–459.

Francis-Williams, J., & Davis, P. A. Very low birthweight and later intelligence. *Developmental Medicine and Child Neurology*, 1974, *16*, 709–728.

Fries, M., & Woolf, P. Some hypotheses on the role of congenital activity types in personality development. *Psychoanalytic Study of the Child*, 1953, *8*, 48–57.

Gesell, A., & Ames, L. G. Early evidence of individuality in the human infant. *Journal of Genetic Psychology*, 1937, *47*, 339–346.

Janus-Kukulska, A., & Liss, S. Developmental peculiarities of prematurely born children with birth weight below 1250 grams. *Developmental Medicine and Child Neurology*, 1966, *8*, 285–295.

Kitchen, W. H., Ryan, M. M., Rickards, A., McDougall, A. B., Billson, F. A., Keir, E. H., & Naylor, F. D. A longitudinal study of very low birthweight infants: IV. An overview of performance at eight years of age. *Developmental Medicine and Child Neurology*, 1980, *22*, 172–188.

Prechtl, H., & Stemmer, C. The choreiform syndrome in children. *Developmental Medicine and Child Neurology*, 1966, *8*, 149–159.

Rutter, M. Brain damage syndromes in childhood: Concepts and findings. *Journal of Child Psychology and Psychiatry*, 1977, *18*, 1–21.

Rutter, M., Graham, P., & Yule, W. *A neuropsychiatric study in childhood* (Clinics in Developmental Medicine Nos. 35–36). London: Spastics International Medical Publications/Heinemann Medical Books, 1970.

Seidel, U. P., Chadwick, O. F. D., & Rutter, M. Psychological disorders in crippled children: A comparative study of children with and without brain damage. *Developmental Medicine and Child Neurology*, 1975, *17*, 563–573.

Shaffer, D. Brain injury. In M. Rutter & L. Hersov (Eds.), *Child psychiatry: Modern approaches*. Oxford: Blackwell Scientific Publications, 1977.

Shirley, M. M. *The first two years: A study of twenty-five babies.* Minneapolis: University of Minnesota Press, 1931 and 1933.

Tanner, J. M., & Thompson, A. M. Standards for birth weight at gestation periods from 32 to 42 weeks, allowing for maternal height and weight. *Archives of Disease in Childhood*, 1970, *45*, 566–569.

Thomas, A., & Chess, S. *Temperament and development.* New York: Brunner/Mazel, 1977.

Thomas, A., Chess, S., & Birch, H. G. *Temperament and behavior disorders in children.* New York: New York University Press, 1968.

Thomas, A., Chess, S., Birch, H. G., Hertzig, M. E., & Korn, S. *Behavioral individuality in early childhood.* New York: New York University Press, 1963.

Wender, P. H. *Minimal brain dysfunction in children.* New York: Wiley, 1971.

CHAPTER TEN

Neuropsychological Assessment

OLIVER CHADWICK / MICHAEL RUTTER

INTRODUCTION

At one time neuropsychological assessments tended to be largely concerned with the diagnosis of "brain damage" or "organicity." Between the 1940s and 1960s, there was an outpouring of reports on supposed specific tests for brain damage. As Herbert (1964) noted in a review of the concepts and findings, most of these tests utilized an implicit model of brain function "which assumes a homogeneous response to tests by heterogeneous groups of brain-injured children." Increasingly, this view came to be criticized both on the grounds that it represented a misleading, inadequate, and oversimplified theory of brain functioning, and on the grounds that the empirical findings failed to provide an adequate rationale for diagnostic tests of "brain damage" (see, e.g., Graham & Berman, 1961; Herbert, 1964; Meyer, 1957). As a consequence, this approach has been virtually abandoned by neuropsychologists (Boll & Barth, 1981). Nevertheless, as some of these measures of "organicity" continue to be popular in clinical practice outside teaching centers, they are briefly discussed in this chapter.

As investigators became increasingly aware of the variability in neurological disorders and in the psychological sequelae of organic brain conditions, there came to be an increasing reliance on neuropsychological batteries that included tests designed to assess a diverse range of brain functions. Halstead (1947) and Reitan (1964, 1968; Reitan & Davison, 1974) were the pioneers of this approach, and probably the majority of the test batteries in use today (at least in North America) have their origins in the Halstead–Reitan Neuropsychological Test Battery (see Boll, 1981). Most of the earlier work utilizing a test battery approach continued to focus on a simple differentiation of patients into those with and those without brain damage. This differentiation has continued as an important objective as attention has shifted to the study of children with questionable brain disorders (Tsushima & Towne, 1977) or with supposed

Oliver Chadwick. G. H. Sergievsky Center, College of Physicians and Surgeons, Columbia University, New York, New York; Institute for Basic Research in Developmental Disabilities, Staten Island, New York.

Michael Rutter. Department of Child and Adolescent Psychiatry, University of London Institute of Psychiatry, London, England.

"minimal brain dysfunction" (MBD). The observation that such children show lesser cognitive abnormalities of the same type as those that characterize children with overt and indisputable brain pathology has been used to validate the MBD concept.

However, in recent years there has been a growing interest in the use of the neuropsychological examination to lateralize or localize brain lesions (see, e.g., Reitan, 1964). Some of the strongest claims regarding this use of test batteries stem from Golden (1981) in his application of the Luria–Nebraska Neuropsychological Battery. The findings with adults have been said to confirm its usefulness "in the detection, lateralization and localization of discrete brain lesions that are typically seen in the neurological setting" (Golden, Moses, Fishburne, Engum, Lewis, Wisniewski, Conley, Berg, & Graber, 1981). It has been argued that neuropsychological tests are diagnostically useful in identifying the errors that can occur even with computerized tomography (CT) scans (Filskov & Goldstein, 1974; Golden, Moses, Fishburne, *et al.*, 1981). The validity of these claims are considered, and the possible application of this approach to the assessment of children is discussed.

Quite apart from these (perhaps controversial) diagnostic potentialities, the whole field of research represented by the work with test batteries is of interest through the light it may throw on the general question of brain–behavior relationships. It is clear, for example, that children with learning disabilities exhibit a variety of cognitive deficits. As shown by the work of Rourke (1981) and his associates (Petrauskas & Rourke, 1979; see also Chapters 23 and 29 of this volume), different types of reading, spelling, and arithmetic disabilities can be defined in terms of patterns of neuropsychological abilities and deficits. This research is important in terms of its potential contribution to syndrome definition and to treatment planning, as well as in the possible (and disputed) use of test findings to yield information on the functional integrity (or otherwise) of the two cerebral hemispheres.

A rather different use of neuropsychological tests is represented by their contribution to the accurate description of a patient's handicaps (see, e.g., Rutter, Graham, & Yule, 1970). Tests for this purpose cover a wide range of cognitive, motor, perceptual, and language functions. In many cases, they measure functions (such as motor coordination, right–left differentiation, or constructional abilities) that constitute essential elements in any adequate neurological examination of children. However, the tests differ from a neurological assessment in their focus on the precise *quantification* of developmental functions, rather than on a qualitative appraisal of the nature or meaning of the deficit. As such, the tests are of value not only in defining the pattern of a child's handicap, but also in measuring progress during and after treatment.

Finally, neuropsychological tests can be employed as part of an experimental approach to the investigation of individual cases, an approach pioneered by Shapiro (1951, 1970). He argued that the best way to understand a psychological deficit was to find a way of measuring it, to bring the variable under experimental control, and hence to determine by means of a "cognitive–functional" analysis (Meichenbaum, 1976) which aspects of functioning are leading to impaired performance. Curiously, this aspect of neuropsychology has received little attention in recent years. Nevertheless, its potential value in rehabilitation and remediation is evident (Diller & Gordon, 1981).

Rationale for Tests of Brain Damage

As numerous reviewers have made clear, much of the earlier work on the development of "tests of brain damage" was based on simplistic and outmoded notions of "organicity" (cf. Boll, 1978; Herbert, 1964; Meyer, 1957). Indeed, the conceptual and methodological problems that are involved in the psychological diagnosis of brain impairment are so great that many psychologists have suggested that it would be preferable for the whole enterprise to be dropped and replaced by an entirely different approach to neuropsychological assessment (cf. Herbert, 1964; Yule, 1978).

Four main conceptual criticisms have been leveled against the "tests of brain damage" approach. First, it is naive to suppose that an organ as complex as the brain could give rise to any single, uniform indicator of dysfunction. This is perhaps a valid criticism of the single-test approach, but it is not applicable to the use of multitest batteries explicitly designed to identify the *several* patterns of psychological dysfunction that may stem from brain injury. Moreover, there are numerous parallels in other branches of medicine of tests that serve as satisfactory general indicators of the overall efficiency of particular body organs. The batteries of biochemical tests for liver function constitute one obvious example.

Secondly, it has been argued that, as the test findings can give rise only to an undifferentiated diagnosis of "something wrong with the brain," the results are of no theoretical or practical value. However, that criticism relies on a misleading concept of diagnosis as a one-step procedure giving rise to a precise etiological and anatomical/physiological designation of the causative lesion. Again, there are plenty of examples in medicine where such general measures have indeed proved to be of practical importance both in the identification of malfunction requiring more detailed diagnostic appraisal and also in the monitoring of progress following treatment. The various tests of cardiac function and of pulmonary efficiency constitute well-known applications of this kind. However, it should be noted that the latter usage requires that the test findings *quantify* the efficiency of organ functioning, as well as just noting the presence of malfunction.

Thirdly, it has been observed that the identification of brain injury does not necessarily mean that that injury has caused the psychological or psychiatric problem with which the patient presents. Such a specific linkage requires a knowledge of brain–behavior relationships that is so far largely lacking. Furthermore, in practice, the linkage is made difficult because many types of brain damage represent static conditions with few functional sequelae, and also because psychiatric conditions can arise from psychosocial stresses as well as from structural brain pathology. Boll (1978) cites the example of a well-functioning college graduate with a static lesion in the right parietal lobe caused by a perinatal event. The man showed normal adjustment until he became acutely depressed following two bereavements in his immediate family, which led to increased financial and personal responsibilities as well as to the loss of important relationships. He was referred to the psychologist for testing to "rule out organicity." Testing showed performance in the range characteristic of brain-damaged individuals. This "confirmed" the presence of the brain lesion already identified on other criteria. But, as Boll points out, the finding in no way contributed to diagnostic assessment or therapeutic planning because of the lack of evidence linking the perinatal lesion with his recent onset of depression. It is apparent that the identification of brain pathology, and the demonstration that that pathology has caused the presenting clinical problem, constitute two very different issues. However, again, that is no different from the diagnostic situation in medicine generally. The laboratory finding of impaired liver or kidney function does not mean that such malfunction has caused the patient's signs or symptoms; nevertheless, the finding constitutes an important item of information that needs to be taken into account in any overall diagnostic formulation. Neuropsychological test findings should be used in the same way.

Fourthly, it has been argued (e.g., Herbert, 1964) that the major weakness of all tests of brain damage is the lack of any adequate theory of brain function upon which they can be based. Golden (1981) maintains that his battery *is* based on such a theory—namely, Luria's theory of higher cortical functions. However, the validity of this claim seems questionable (Spiers, 1981), and certainly it is evident that most neuropsychological tests rest on a rather shaky theoretical base. As a consequence, the finding of an "abnormal" score on some test rarely leads to a clear understanding of the nature of the hypothesized brain malfunction that it is supposed to reflect. There is no doubt that that lack of knowledge constitutes a severe limitation to the clinical inferences that can be drawn from neuropsychological test findings. But, of course, that very lack reflects the early state of the art with respect to knowledge on higher cortical functions as much as weaknesses in the neuropsychological approach. Not only is further neuropsychological research indicated in order to further our understanding of brain–behavior relationships, but also, even at present, test findings may serve to alert the clinician to impaired brain function, although they fail to elucidate the precise nature of that impairment.

Clearly, there are serious conceptual limitations in current approaches to neuropsychological assessment. Nevertheless, in our view, these have been overstated by many critics who have failed to appreciate that the limitations are shared by many other special investigations in current medical usage. Provided that a neuropsychological assessment could give rise to a valid measure of organic brain malfunction, that would be a useful element in a diagnostic appraisal. Just as tests of liver and kidney function and of cardiopulmonary efficiency are in routine clinical use for the identification of malfunction requiring more detailed diagnostic appraisal and for the monitoring of progress following treatment, so, similarly, it is reasonable to suppose that comparable tests of brain function might be equally useful. As discussed in other chapters of this volume, chronic malnutrition (see Chapter 2) and lead poisoning (see Chapter 3) both constitute examples of treatable conditions that may sometimes result in brain damage, which often is mainly manifest in the form of mild cognitive impairment. Clearly, if a neuropsychological assessment could alert the clinician early to the occurrence of "subclinical" brain damage, that would be of great value. The point is that medical treatments such as those used to reduce levels of body lead are not free of risk, and there is a need to know when mild or moderate increases in lead are *actually* causing damage or dysfunction that warrant individual treatment. Also, psychological symptoms may sometimes constitute the first manifestation of intracranial tumors or of other progressive neurological diseases where the need for early detection is obvious and often vital. Unfortunately, the symptoms of organic and of functional mental disorders can be very similar (see Lezak, 1976; Lishman, 1978), and often it is difficult to know when to embark on extensive neurological investigations. A test that could aid the clinician in this decision would be helpful. With neurological conditions, psychological tests might also provide accurate and objective baseline measures against which to assess the benefits of treatment, as well as to monitor the damage that may come as an unintended side effect of interventions (Smith, 1975), such as prophylactic irradiation for leukemia (Eiser, 1980). However, for that to be possible, it would be necessary that the tests *quantify*, as well as detect, brain malfunction.

Of course, too, it is true that although the identification of brain damage may be crucially important with some conditions, it is not necessarily so with all. For example, at present there is little evidence that the classification, treatment, or outcome of reading retardation is influenced by the presence or absence of neurological abnormalities (see Benton & Pearl, 1978). Nor has evidence of such abnormalities been of much value in predicting the drug response of hyperkinetic children (see Chapter 16 of this volume). It is obvious that the identification of unspecified brain damage will be of greater importance in some circumstances than in others—and of no importance at all in some. Nevertheless, there is no doubt that, *if* neuropsychological tests could accurately identify brain damage, this could be of great practical use (as well as an aid to the better theoretical understanding of brain dysfunction).

Validation of Tests of Brain Damage: Methodological Considerations

The key question, of course, lies in the proviso. That is, can a neuropsychological assessment provide a valid measure of organic brain malfunction? In approaching this issue, it is important to bear in mind the circumstances in which the assessment might be used for that purpose. As Cronbach (1970) has emphasized, it is inappropriate to ask the general question, "Is this test valid?" Instead, we need to enquire, "How valid is this test for the decision I wish to make?" or "How valid is the interpretation I propose for the test?" (p. 122).

Generally speaking, when a new measure is developed, its validity is best assessed by testing it in relation to some more established index of the condition that it is supposed to measure. For this reason, the usual strategy employed in the examination of the validity of tests of brain damage has been a comparison of the performance of children with a known neurological disorder with that of neurologically normal controls. In most cases, the two groups have been found to differ in their neuropsychological test scores. However, this comparison is not applicable to the clinical situation in which tests of brain damage are most likely to be employed. If a child is already known to have cerebral palsy, it would be quite superfluous to ask for a neuropsychological assessment to determine if there is any brain malfunction. Rather, the tests are most needed when the neurological findings are ambiguous in their implications, or are normal in spite of other reasons for suspecting the presence of organic brain malfunction. Furthermore, the contrast between "brain damage" and "normality" used in most validation studies does not test the alternatives that face the clinician in most circumstances. More typically, the patient will have presented with some disorder; the query does not concern the presence of the disorder, but rather, which of a number of possible factors might account for it. Thus, it may be that the child shows a language delay, which could be due to perinatal brain injury, to a genetically determined specific developmental disorder, to an extreme normal variation in the age of language acquistion, or to sociocultural privation—to mention but four possibilities. The question, then, is whether the test can aid in the differentiation among these alternatives. Alternatively, the problem may be a fall in scholastic performance, and the question is whether the fall is due to a loss of interest, poor teaching, depression, or some acquired brain disease. Again, the problem is one in which there is a *known* deficit in some aspect of cognitive performance, but an uncertainty as to whether or not that deficit reflects organic brain dysfunction.

For all these reasons, the tests cannot be concerned solely with an impairment in some neuropsychological function, if that function can be impaired through causes other than brain damage. Rather, the tests must show functioning that is abnormal in *type*, in *pattern*, or of such a *degree* that the impairment is unlikely to be due to other causes.

It will be appreciated that these considerations raise two rather different methodological issues. Firstly, there is the need to determine whether "abnormal" neuropsychological test findings can arise from causes other than brain damage. There have been surprisingly few attempts to examine this issue. However, the few studies that have done so show that the matter is crucial. Thus, in adults, both Prigatano and Parsons (1976) and Finlayson, Johnson, and Reitan (1977) found that level of education had a significant effect on scores on the Halstead–Reitan battery. The effect of brain damage was generally greater than that of education, and in most cases the tests differentiated brain-damaged subjects from controls within educational categories. However, in a few cases the scores of poorly educated controls were more abnormal than those of university-educated brain-damaged subjects, and, often, the brain-damaged–control differentiation was weakest in the case of poorly educated individuals. As Prigatano and Parsons (1976) conclude, "The overall implication of the findings is that the clinical neuropsychologist would be well advised to know how performance on the Halstead Test battery related to non-brain-damage factors in the patients seen for clinical evaluation." Or, as Finlayson *et al.* (1977) put it, there is a "need for the clinician to consider other methods of inference than level of performance in rendering clinical judgments."

Similarly, with children, Knights and Tymchuk (1968) found that performance on the category test of the Halstead–Reitan battery was significantly correlated with IQ, and that the tests appeared to be sensitive to impairment, regardless of whether the impairment was due to a brain lesion or to some other factor.

Of course, it could be suggested that the way to deal with this problem is to standardize the scores for IQ and education (as well as for age, which has a major effect in childhood of course, but also in later adult life). Such standardization would be an advantage, but it would not resolve the difficulty. This is because (1) it is likely that there are additional factors other than IQ and education that affect test performance (not only have these factors yet to be identified, but there would be immense practical problems in standardizing on many factors simultaneously); and (2) brain damage in children (perhaps unlike that in adults) tends to have its main effect on general intelligence (Davison, 1974).

Accordingly, if the "effect" of IQ is partialed out statistically, it is likely to remove the main effect of brain damage also.

But the problem in this connection is far from restricted to the substantial correlation between overall IQ measures and neuropsychological test battery findings (McKay, Golden, Moses, Fishburne, & Wisniewski 1981). Often, the need is to differentiate between "organic" and "functional" psychiatric disorders (Lishman, 1978). This need arises because (perhaps more in adults than in children) some functional disorders may show features suggestive of organic brain disease. For example, acute schizophrenia may result in disorientation and minor impairments of consciousness, and severe depression may lead to disordered cognitive functioning. Conversely, some organic diseases may have an insidious onset, with various apparently "neurotic" symptoms as the first indication that anything is wrong. The question is whether neuropsychological testing can help make the "organic–functional" differentiation in these cases. The matter has been investigated in adults (see Heaton & Crowley, 1981), but scarcely at all in children. The adult studies suggest that the tests make most "errors" in the differentiation between organic states and schizophrenia—but the interpretation of this finding is made uncertain by the recent evidence from computerized axial tomography (CT scans) that some schizophrenic patients may have cerebral atrophy. At present, all that can be said with regard to children is that it is not known whether neuropsychological test findings can correctly identify organic brain dysfunction in the presence of marked psychiatric disorder. In view of the importance of this issue, it is crucial that the matter be investigated.

The second methodological issue is of a rather different kind. If it is accepted that the tests will be most used clinically when neurological findings are ambiguous or normal, then it is not enough to show that they differentiate clear-cut cases of brain damage or neurological disorder. Obviously, there could be no confidence in a test that failed to make such differentiations, but it is essential to go on to show that it *also* identifies cases without neurological handicaps. The implication is that cases of overt neurological disorder must be excluded from this second critical validation exercise. This is necessary because an abnormal neuropsychological assessment may reflect defects in motor coordination or language function that are part of the same disability evident on a clinical neurological examination; and also because it cannot be assumed that the higher cortical functions that are abnormal in the presence of a hemiparesis or aphasia will also be abnormal when there is no motor or language deficit. But if cases of overt brain damage are excluded from the validation exercise, there is the very serious problem of knowing what to put in their place. One alternative has been to use children with abnormal electroencephalograms (EEGs), on the grounds that such a group is likely to include children with covert brain damage. However, in a well-controlled study by Tymchuk, Knights, and Hinton (1970), this comparison led to the unexpected result that the normal-EEG group had more abnormal neuropsychological test findings than the abnormal-EEG group. Of course, this paradoxical result underlines the fallibility of the EEG—not only may the EEG be normal to visual inspection in children with known brain damage, but also many apparently normal children have EEGs reported as showing abnormalities (Harris, 1977). Variants of the same strategy are the use of children with "questionable" brain disorders, as ascertained through clinical history and examination (Tsushima & Towne, 1977) or the use of learning disability as a proxy for uncertain brain damage (Selz & Reitan, 1979). Such studies have usually shown that these groups differ from normals on neuropsychological test performance (as they did in the two studies cited), but most comparisons (including these two) have failed to equate the groups for IQ. Not surprisingly, the "uncertain-damage" groups have had a lower mean IQ, and it may well be that the difference in IQ accounts for most or all of the differences on other items in the test battery. As already noted, the IQ test is particularly sensitive to brain damage in children (Davison, 1974), and for this reason it is advisable (if not essential) to include tests of general intelligence in any neuropsychological battery. However, it may be the very fact of lowered intelligence that has led to the query regarding possible brain damage. It would be circular reasoning of the worst kind to use evidence of low IQ to demonstrate that the low IQ was due to brain damage! Moreover, mild "impairments" of intelligence (such as shown by an IQ of, say, 85) are usually *not* due to brain damage, and hence it is crucial to have a test that can determine which impairments are and which are not a result of organic brain malfunction. Also, of course, all studies using "uncertain-damage" groups (by definition) employ a validating criterion that is itself uncertain. Accordingly, the interpretation of any differences found, or not found, must also remain somewhat speculative.

The main difficulty in attempting to validate psychological tests of brain dysfunction is that of reconciling the need to examine children who are *known* to have suffered brain injury with the need to exclude those with current neurological abnormalities on a clinical examination. One possible solution to this dilemma is to focus on individuals for whom the clinical evidence of brain damage lies entirely in the past. Our own study of children with severe head injuries resulting in a posttraumatic amnesia (PTA) of at least 1 week provided such an opportunity. Their course over the 2 to 3 years following the injury was compared with that of children suffering orthopedic injuries not associated with any damage to the head (see Chapter 5 of this volume). It may be supposed that 1 week's PTA indicates that some damage to the brain took place. Nevertheless, only half the group showed neurological abnormalities at follow-up (Rutter, Chadwick, Shaffer, & Brown, 1980), and less than a third showed persisting intellectual impairment (Chadwick, Rutter, Brown, Shaffer, & Traub, 1981). One key group consisted of those who suffered transient intellectual impairment (defined in terms of a significant deficit initially after the injury followed by recovery without final deficit). There were only eight children who met these criteria and, by definition, they were of normal intelligence (Chadwick, Rutter, Shaffer, & Shrout, 1981). Most of the items in the neuropsychological test battery used failed to show any difference in scores compared with the individually matched orthopedic control group—indicating that children usually show specific cognitive deficits only if they also exhibit general cognitive impairment (a finding evident on multivariate analyses with the group as a whole, as well as with this small subgroup). However, the head-injured children were significantly impaired on a few timed tests requiring fast motor responses. This showed that sometimes there may be specific cognitive deficits that are not picked up by broad-range intelligence tests. On the other hand, only half of this small group of eight were entirely free of neurological abnormalities on a systematic neurological examination. Accordingly, it remains uncertain how well neuropsychological test batteries would fare in detecting brain damage in children without either neurological abnormalities or intellectual impairment. Obviously four children form far too small a sample for such an analysis, but the strategy remains one worth exploring further.

Single Tests for Brain Damage

With these conceptual and methodological considerations in mind, we may now turn to some of the findings on different approaches to the neuropsychological assessment of brain damage. Early studies tended to focus on the results of various single tests supposed to be sensitive to the effects of brain damage. For example, the Bender Visual–Motor Gestalt Test (Bender, 1938) examined the subject's ability to copy designs, with a special emphasis on rotational errors; Graham and Kendall's (1960) Memory-for-Designs Test assessed immediate memory of line drawings of geometric figures; and the Goldstein–Scheerer Color-Form Sorting Test (Goldstein & Scheerer, 1941) was designed to detect difficulties in forming abstract concepts. The results of these efforts were generally disappointing (Graham & Berman, 1961), and, as Herbert (1964) noted in his critical review, most studies had serious limitations, with the great majority of tests being of unknown reliability and inadequately standardized and validated. It is true that many of the tests showed statistically significant group differences between brain-damaged and normal samples, but the considerable overlap in scores usually meant that the misclassification rates were unacceptably high when applied to individual cases. It is important to note that the problem of unacceptably high misclassification rates applies even when developmentally appropriate scoring systems (such as the Koppitz system for scoring the Bender test; see Koppitz, 1975) are employed, or when complex statistical adjustments are made (Tymchuk & Nishihara, 1976). The diminishing popularity of single tests of brain damage during the last two decades may be attributed not only to their general lack of success as diagnostic instruments and their lack of independence from developmental level or mental age, but also to the unsatisfactory theoretical assumptions and formulations on which they were based.

Intellectual Patterns

Rather than utilize special tests, another approach has been to study the pattern of scores on tests of general intelligence. Two main features have been used as indexes of brain damage: (1) visuospatial skills that are markedly inferior to verbal skills; and (2) a wide disparity in cognitive skills, as reflected by a large verbal–performance discrepancy on the Wechsler Intelligence Scale for Children (WISC) or by wide scatter across the subtests. With both features there is consistent empirical evidence to indicate that they are indeed more often found in brain-damaged than in normal populations. For example, in the Isle of Wight epidemiological study (Rutter, Graham, & Yule, 1970), twice as many children with some form of neuroepileptic disorder had a WISC verbal score that exceeded the performance score, than the other way round. Similarly, in our prospective study of children with head injuries (Chadwick, Rutter, Brown, Shaffer, & Traub, 1981), we found that visuospatial skills were impaired more seriously and more lastingly than verbal skills. Or again, in their recent study of 78 hydrocephalic children, Dennis and her colleagues found the mean WISC performance scale IQ to be some 10 points below the verbal IQ, with a mean verbal–performance discrepancy score of the same size (Dennis, Fitz, Netley, Sugar, Harwood-Nash, Hendrick, Hoffman, & Humphreys, 1981). These findings are of interest in terms of the light they throw on the manner in which different brain functions are affected by injury. However, they are of no use for the diagnosis of brain damage in individuals.

Three main problems may be identified (Rutter *et al.*, 1970; Yule, 1978). First, subtests or small groups of subtests always tend to be less reliable than the overall scores on broad-range intelligence tests. This is mainly because the subtests measure a smaller sample of cognitive behavior. The *difference* between two subscores or the *ratio* between them will, of course, be even more unreliable (as it will involve the unreliability of two tests rather than one). The consequence is that verbal–performance discrepancies (or discrepancies between any two other scores) have to be quite large to be at all reliable in the sense that the same discrepancy would be found on repeated testing. Secondly, although more brain-damaged than normal children show deviant intellectual test patterns, nevertheless such patterns are found in only a *minority* of brain-damaged children. Children with brain injury show quite varied patterns of cognitive test performance, and, as a result, all of the discrepancy indexes fail to identify most of the children with known organic brain malfunction. Thirdly, many normal children also show the supposedly "abnormal" discrepancy or cognitive test pattern. Although, *relatively* speaking the deviant patterns are less common in normal children, in *absolute* terms they are more common. This follows from the effects of the markedly differing base rates for "brain damage" and for "normality," an effect well discussed by Meehl and Rosen (1955). As Yule (1978) points out, this means that although a performance score 25 points below tne verbal score on the WISC is *twice* as common in brain-damaged subjects as in normal children, nevertheless the odds *against* a child with such a verbal–performance discrepancy having brain injury are in the region of 500 to 13! It should be noted that these odds apply to the general population as a whole. It may well be that the odds are more in favor of brain damage among patients referred with symptoms that raise the possibility of some brain disorder. Nevertheless, the general point on the need to take base rates into account remains valid and important.

For all these reasons, intellectual patterns or discrepancy indexes are of no value for the individual diagnosis of brain damage. A fourth problem applies to many other types of test profile analysis. The Wechsler scales have the major advantage that there are published tables (e.g., Field, 1960) indicating the frequency with which discrepancies of any given magnitude are to be expected in the general population. As a result, it is easy to determine how unusual any discrepancy is, and hence how likely it is to be a reliable or (statistically) abnormal finding. But with most tests utilized for profile analysis, such data are not available. The consequence is that claims about clinically meaningful test patterns lack substance and may well be based on findings that are either unreliable or so common in the general population as to be of little note.

Neuropsychological Test Batteries

The advantages of including measures of several different aspects of neuropsychological functioning were clearly indicated by the series of longitudinal investigations of preschool children with definite brain injury carried out in St. Louis 20 years ago (Ernhart, Graham, Eichman, Marshall, & Thurston, 1963; Graham, Ernhart, Craft, & Berman, 1963; Graham, Ernhart, Thurston, & Craft, 1962). Compared with uninjured children, the brain-damaged group was impaired on verbal and conceptual skills as well as on perceptuomotor tasks. It was apparent that a *range* of measures was needed to identify all types of cognitive deficit.

Considerations such as these have led to the increasing use of composite batteries of neuropsychological tests. Most of those used with children stem from the work of Reitan (see Boll, 1974, 1981; Reitan, 1974) whose approach has its origins in Halstead's (1947) studies with brain-damaged adults and in his search for a battery of procedures that would tap the whole range of cognitive functions that may be impaired by brain injury. Initially, most emphasis was placed on tests thought to be particularly sensitive to the effects of frontal-lobe injury: "The frontal lobes, long regarded as silent areas, are the portion of the brain most essential to biological intelligence" (Halstead, 1947, p. 149). Since Halstead's original work, efforts have been made to improve the original 10-test battery by dropping tests that failed to meet the criteria for statistical validation (Boll, 1974; Reitan, 1955) and by adding tests to cover functions not adequately assessed by the original battery (see Boll, 1981). In addition, since 1951, the assessment procedures have been adapted for use with children. This has resulted in the emergence of two broadly comparable test batteries—one for use with 9- to 14-year-olds, and the other for 5- to 8-year-olds. The two sets of tasks are based on the same general principles, and some of the same specific tests are included in both. Age-specific norms for some of the tests in the children's batteries have been presented by Spreen and Gaddes (1969), but these were derived from a predominantly middle-class sample, and population-based normative data are not yet available. However, the batteries are still in the developmental stage, and new tests continue to be added, with others occasionally falling into disuse. As a consequence, slightly different combinations of tests have been employed by different workers (see Reitan & Davison, 1974).

The batteries include a category test designed to tap abstract concept formation and current learning skills; a tactual performance test based on a modification of the Seguin formboard, designed to assess motor speed, the use of tactile and kinesthetic cues, and incidental memory; the Seashore rhythm test for nonverbal auditory perception and attention; the trail-making test that requires speed, visual scanning, and the ability to progress in sequence; an assessment of strength of grip by a hand dynamometer; an aphasia screening test; and various procedures to evaluate sensory perception. The tests of rhythm, perception of speech sounds, and trail making are not administered to children under age 9. The WISC and the Wide-Range Achievement Test (WRAT) are usually included as "allied procedures" used with the test battery.

Several studies have shown that, as a group, children with clear evidence of overt brain injury have scores on the test battery that differ significantly from those of neurologically normal comparison groups (Boll, 1974; Klonoff, Robinson, & Thompson, 1969; Reed, Reitan, & Kløve, 1965; Reitan, 1974). Davison (1974) has collated the data obtained by Reitan (1974), Boll (1974), Reed *et al.* (1965), and Klonoff and Low (1974) in order to determine the relative sensitivity of the separate tests included in the Halstead–Reitan assessment. The results were consistent in showing that the WISC full-scale IQ, verbal IQ, and performance

IQ were among the most sensitive of all measures used. This finding, of course, in part reflects the fact that the Wechsler scales were deliberately designed to tap a wide range of cognitive functions, so that it is not surprising that most children with cognitive deficits showed a greater or lesser degree of impairment on either their verbal or performance IQ (or both). Not all deficits were reflected in a lowered IQ, but most were (Klonoff & Low, 1974), and once the IQ differences between groups were partialed out there remained only a few, much reduced, differences on the more specialized tests in the battery. This finding for children is somewhat different from that for adults, in whom specific cognitive deficits in the absence of general intellectual impairment are more frequent following brain injury. The reasons for this age difference in the cognitive sequelae of brain damage are not adequately understood, but it is likely that, in part, it reflects the fact that intelligence is still in the process of development in childhood. Hence, deficits in new learning skills or in particular aspects of cognition are liable to impede intellectual development in childhood, whereas established intelligence in adult life is less likely to show a decrement with the same cognitive deficits. Reed and Fitzhugh (1966), for example, found that children with brain injury tended to show greater impairment on tasks (such as the information and vocabulary subtests of the WISC) that depended on knowledge normally acquired during the growing years. Individuals suffering brain damage during adult life already had that knowledge and instead were more likely to show deficits on problem-solving tasks, such as the category test of the Halstead–Reitan battery.

These empirical findings were adumbrated by Hebb (1942) in a seminal work that considered the possible effects of age in determining the cognitive sequelae of brain injury. He argued that such sequelae would tend to be more severe and more generalized when damage occurred in early infancy rather than in later life, and that brain damage may hinder the acquisition of new abilities while having less effect on skills already learned. As we have noted, to some extent the empirical research findings support Hebb's suggestion. However, it is clear that brain lesions can have quite varied effects and that any simple generalization on the types of skills affected is bound to have numerous exceptions. Moreover, comparisons of the effects of brain lesions in childhood and in adult life have been bedevilled by the fact that the *types* of brain lesions in childhood tend not to be the same as those in adult life (St. James Roberts, 1979). Accordingly, it has proved difficult to compare like with like across different age periods, and conclusions on age differences in the effects of brain injury can only be tentative and provisional on the basis of the limited available data.

However, quite apart from these important theoretical considerations, there remains the crucial practical point that if groups of brain-damaged and neurologically normal children are equated for IQ, it is likely that rather few differences will be detected on the more specialized and specific tests of the Halstead–Reitan battery. The question then is, if there cannot be reliance on an overall difference in *levels* of performance, can brain-damaged individuals be picked out on the basis of a distinctive *pattern* of scores that differentiates them from normals? No adequate answer to that question is yet available. Knights and Tymchuk (1968) showed that the category test of the Halstead–Reitan battery did not differentiate children with brain damage from those with serious social adjustment difficulties (but no neurological impairment), when the groups were matched for age and WISC IQ. The finding casts doubt on the notion that individual test scores can be used as an index of brain damage, but, of course, it does not deal with the possibility of differences in overall pattern attributable to brain injury.

The possible importance of pattern criteria was supported by the findings of a recent study with adults (Heaton, Grant, Anthony, & Lehman, 1981), which showed that on two out of three prediction tasks, clinicians' independent ratings of the Halstead–Reitan battery findings were more accurate than was an automated quasi-actuarial system. Both were equally successful in recognizing normal controls (89–92% accuracy), but the clinicians were more successful (87–91% versus 75%) in identifying brain-damaged individuals. They were also more accurate in lateralizing lesions. The findings are particularly striking in that most other research favors actuarial over clinical prediction (Meehl, 1954; Sawyer, 1966). However, the situation is one that seems to have some of the characteristics of tasks thought to be most suitable for clinical prediction. Meehl (1973) suggested that clinicians might be better in the evaluation of highly configural relationships between predictor and criterion, and in weighing highly unusual specific findings that would be too uncommon to be adequately represented in actuarial formulas. The actuarial approach in the Heaton *et al.* (1981) study was relatively crude, and it may well be that the clinicians' superiority reflected the inadequacies of the "rules" used in producing a statistical prediction, rather than any inherent superiority of the clinical approach. However, that underlines the paucity of knowledge at present on just which are the crucial features of neuropsychological test performance that characterize brain-damaged patients.

So far, there have been rather few attempts to evaluate the accuracy of the Halstead–Reitan battery for the identification of *individual* children with brain injury, although that possibility was explored by Reitan and Boll (1973) in relation to clinical judgments based on test scores. More recently, Selz and Reitan (1979) have provided a set of 37 formal "rules" to permit the more objective classification of children as "brain-damaged," "learning-disabled," or "normal," solely on the basis of their test performance. They found that when cutoff scores were chosen post hoc so as to minimize misclassification, 73% of their 75 cases could be correctly diagnosed as belonging to one of their three criterion groups. Most misclassifications were in the learning-disabled group. There was 87% correct classification for the normal versus brain-damaged discrimination, when classification as learning disabled was treated as half correct. No control child was classified as brain-damaged (one was categorized as learning-disabled), but four of the 25 brain-damaged children were classified as controls on the basis of their test scores, and a further four were classified as learning-disabled.

The study represents a useful attempt to assess the value of the test battery for individual diagnosis, but, unfortunately, the investigation suffers from several shortcomings. Firstly, the controls were volunteers rather than a random or representative sample of the general population. Secondly, the cutting points for classification were chosen post hoc to minimize misclassification (hence, errors are likely to be more frequent when the rules are applied to a new population). Thirdly, the three groups were not equated for IQ, and it is likely that many of the test battery findings simply reflected these group differences in general intelligence (the findings were not presented in sufficient detail for any assessment of the extent to which this was the case).

We may conclude that, so far, the Halstead–Reitan battery has not been shown to provide a sufficiently sensitive or accurate means of detecting brain damage for its use to be recommended for individual diagnosis. Further research into the cognitive functions tapped by the battery may be fruitful in producing a better understanding of brain–behavior relationships, and, in turn, that knowledge may allow the development of a valid diagnostic instrument based on a neuropsychological assessment. However, that day remains some time away.

The Halstead–Reitan battery has been considered in some detail because its widespread use has resulted in substantial experience regarding its scope and potential. The Luria–Nebraska Neuropsychological Battery (Golden, 1981) represents a more recent addition which, at least in adults, seems to give rise to generally comparable findings (Golden, Kane, Sweet, Moses, Cardellino, Templeton, Vicente, & Graber, 1981). Both aim to provide a *standard* means of assessment for use in research and clinical practice, with the advantage of facilitating comparisons between centers. So far we have considered its use as a composite measure (with serious reservations about its value). But, of course, its prime purpose is not (or should not be) to obtain an overall index of brain function, but rather to provide a standard set of measures for the assessment of a representative range of clinically relevant functions. This use of neuropsychological assessment is discussed later, but it should be noted here that there are many functions that are *not* adequately tapped by these batteries. It would be most unwise to restrict neuropsychological assessment to the use of any of the currently available batteries (see Satz & Fletcher, 1981), although they may contribute to such an assessment.

LATERALIZATION AND LOCALIZATION OF BRAIN LESIONS

The initial basis for the use of neuropsychological test batteries to provide evidence on the lateralization and localization of brain lesions came from the repeated observations that the pattern of cognitive deficits after unilateral cerebral lesions in adults differed according to which hemisphere was damaged (see, e.g., McFie, 1975a; McFie & Piercy, 1952; Newcombe, 1969; Reed & Reitan, 1963). In general, it has been found that verbal impairment is most characteristic of left-hemisphere lesions (even in the absence of dysphasia), and that visuospatial impairment follows right-hemisphere lesions. This pattern may be evident in the verbal and performance IQ scores on the Wechsler scales. However, in an attempt to provide better differentiated and more precise measures of different aspects of verbal and visuospatial skills, other tests have been added to the test batteries. For example, a new-word learning test (Walton & Black, 1959), in which the person has to learn and memorize the meaning of 10 unfamiliar words; a verbal fluency test (Borkowski, Benton, & Spreen, 1967), designed to quantify word-searching difficulties; and the Aphasia Screening Test (Halstead & Wepman, 1949) have all been used to assess different aspects of language functioning. Similarly, tests designed to assess the abilities to draw and to recognize forms and shapes have been utilized to quantify visuospatial skills.

On the whole, this differential pattern of cognitive skills and deficits has been found to differentiate right-hemisphere from left-hemisphere lesions in adults with a fair degree of accuracy (see Boll & Barth, 1981). Moreover, the pattern seems to hold even when there is no general intellectual loss. However, although the laterality patterns may persist for as long as 20 years after injury (Newcombe, 1969), they are most striking in the period immediately following the time the lesion was incurred (Fitzhugh, Fitzhugh, & Reitan, 1962). It also appears that the effects are most marked with deep intrinsic lesions and may not be evident at all with superficial external trauma to the cortex (Newcombe, 1969).

The findings on localization of lesions within a hemisphere are less clear-cut. It seems that overall decreases in IQ are most likely after left parieto-temporal damage (Weinstein & Teuber, 1957) and possibly also after frontal lesions on either side (Lishman, 1978). However, most of the other findings on localization rely heavily on clinical judgments concerning test score patterns and do not lend themselves to succinct summaries of which types of deficits are to be expected from lesions in particular parts of the brain (see Filskov & Goldstein, 1974; Golden, 1981; Golden, Moses, Fishburne, *et al.*, 1981; Reitan, 1964).

One of the earliest attempts to evaluate the sensitivity of a neuropsychological test battery to cognitive differences stemming from lateralized or localized lesions was provided by Reitan (1964). Four groups, each consisting of 16 adult patients with right or left, anterior or posterior, focal brain lesions, were selected for this study. Using written case reports, with identifying and neurological information deleted, Reitan came to a categorical clinical decision on localization. His proportion of correct classifications in the four groups ranged from 7 out of 16 to 15 out of 16, with an overall accuracy rate of 42 out of 64 (66%) correct. Interestingly, however, when analyzed statistically rather than clinically, only eight variables showed significant intergroup differences on an analysis of variance. Furthermore, all eight differences stemmed from two procedures, the tactual performance test and the finger-tapping test. In essence, this meant that differences simply reflected greater clumsiness in the hand contralateral to the lesion. In other words, the tests were picking up motor deficits rather than cognitive impairments as such. Reitan (1964) argued that impressionistic clinical assessments were of greater relevance to the differentiation of localized cerebral lesions than single statistical comparisons of test score means.

More recently, Golden and his colleagues have reported a cross-validation study of the use of the Luria–Nebraska Neuropsychological Battery to lateralize and localize brain lesions in adults (Golden, Moses, Fishburne, *et al.*, 1981). Their approach differed from Reitan's in two key respects. Firstly, the neuropathological localization was based on CT scans; secondly, the neuropsychological localization was derived from scale scores, with diagnoses based on numerical rules rather than clinical judgment. The results showed locus agreement in 65 out of 87 (75%) cases. It is not clear from the published paper which tests contributed to the correct psychological diagnoses, but it is evident that the battery included many tests of motor function as well as of cognition. While the results show a usefully high correct "hit" rate from the test battery, in drawing conclusions on the meaning of the findings it should be noted that (1) the injuries were acute rather than chronic; (2) the testing was not fully blind, in that most of the subjects were patients previously seen by the raters (thus introducing the possibility of bias); (3) the localization was undertaken only for patients known to have a brain lesion (hence there are no data on how many controls would have been incorrectly diagnosed as having a focal brain lesion; (4) no patient had a psychiatric disorder; (5) the patients presented to a neurological clinic (and presumably most had obvious neurological abnormalities); and (6) 6 out of 30 controls were incorrectly diagnosed as having brain damage. The last point inevitably means that in the general population, most diagnoses of brain damage would be *wrong* simply because the base rate for normality is far higher than that for brain damage (see discussion above on discrepancy indexes).

The findings can be considered from several different points of view. Firstly, and most importantly, they might be used to provide information on brain–behavior relationships. Undoubtedly, it would be useful to know more about the contrasting patterns of cognitive deficits that result from lesions in different parts of the brain. Unfortunately, as published, the results do not contribute to this issue, in that no findings are given on the particular test findings associated with lesions in different parts of the brain. Of course, the presentation of such findings is no easy matter, because insofar as the test battery findings do differentiate lesions in different loci, it is likely to be the overall *pattern* that is important rather than the scores on individual tests (Boll, 1981; Rourke, 1981). Nevertheless, it is only by producing the findings on specific tests (and not just overall "hit" rates) that brain–behavior relationships can be better understood.

Secondly, the results can be considered as an evaluation of the utility of neuropsychological test findings in the neurological diagnosis of patients known to have some form of brain lesion. It is claimed by the proponents of this usage that the accuracy is as good as (or better than) most of the standard clinical and radiological investigative procedures used in neurological practice (Filskov & Goldstein, 1974; Golden, Moses, Fishburne, *et al.*, 1981). However, it seems premature to draw this conclusion, both because truly blind evaluations have yet to be undertaken and because it is not yet known in which circumstances psychological findings can, and in which they cannot, be relied upon for lateralization and localization.

Thirdly, the findings may bear on the question of using neuropsychological patterns to draw inferences about brain dysfunction in individuals *without* any known neurological condition—as in the case of individuals with learning disabilities (Rourke, 1981). This is an important issue, but it is also one that involves immense problems. In the first place it relies on specific knowledge about brain–behavior relationships—knowledge that is so far lacking. In the second place, it assumes that the findings on individuals with overt neurological abnormalities can be generalized to those without such abnormalities. The main difficulty here concerns the uncertainty on the extent to which the diagnostic success of the test batteries depends on the *motor* abnormalities in the patients studied. Finally, there is the implicit assumption that because known brain lesions lead to particular psychological deficits, the presence of such deficits can be used to diagnose brain lesions. Of course, that does not follow logically, unless such deficits never occur in the absence of brain lesions (which obviously is not the case).

The findings considered so far all concern adults, and it is necessary to ask whether the patterns in children are similar or different. It seems that the hemisphere differences are less clear-cut, although the general pattern has tended to be in roughly the same direction. Thus, McFie (1961) found that memory for designs was worse for right-sided lesions, but that there was only a mild tendency for verbal deficits to be worse with left-hemisphere lesions. The preliminary findings (McFie, 1975b) from a larger series of children with head injuries, hematomas, abscesses, or tumors showed much the same. There was no consistent tendency for verbal IQ to be lower with left-sided lesions, although learning of new words was more impaired. Laterality effects seemed to be more marked in adolescents aged 15 years or above than in younger children. Woods and Teuber (1973) found that lesions in the left hemisphere lowered both verbal and performance IQ scores in relation to those of sibling controls, whereas lesions of the right hemisphere primarily affected performance IQ scores. More recently, Woods (1980) compared the effects of unilateral cerebral lesions (diagnosed on the basis of clinical, EEG, CT scan, or angiography findings) according to whether or not the lesion was incurred before or after the child's first birthday. He found that (1) very early lesions of the right hemisphere resulted in significantly low verbal and performance IQ scores; (2) later childhood lesions of the right hemisphere had significant effects only on performance IQ; and (3) both early and late lesions of the left hemisphere led to impairment of both verbal and performance IQ. In short, it appeared that right-hemisphere lesions in infancy affected verbal intelligence, whereas this was not so in later childhood.

Lehmkuhl, Kotlarek, and Schieber (1981) used a range of neuropsychological tests to study 24 cerebral-palsied children, six with localized cortical or subcortical lesions in the left hemisphere (as diagnosed by CT scans), six with similar lesions in the right hemisphere, six with unilateral ventricular enlargement on the right, and six with such enlargement on the left. The two former groups had lower IQs than those with ventricular enlargement, but no laterality effects could be detected.

Wedell (1960), in a study of cerebral-palsied children, found a somewhat inconsistent pattern in which left-hemisphere lesions were associated with more impaired performance on three-dimensional spatial tasks, and right-hemisphere lesions with impairment on most perceptual tasks. In Annett's (1973) study of hemiplegic children, WISC verbal scores did not differ according to the side of the lesion, but speech delay was much more frequent with left-hemisphere damage. It may be relevant, however, that both these groups of cerebral-palsied children included many with global intellectual impairment, so that the general deficit may have concealed more specific losses. Kershner and King (1974) examined this possibility in a small study of seven left-hemiplegic and seven right-hemiplegic children of normal intelligence. There was some tendency for verbal skills to be more impaired with left-hemisphere damage and for visuospatial skills to be more impaired with right-sided lesions, but most of the differences were quite small, and on some tests from the Reitan battery the findings went in the reverse direction. Scholastic attainment did not differ according to the side of the lesion.

In our own studies of possible localization and lateralization effects in childhood, we utilized unilateral compound depressed fractures of the skull involving a tear in the dura and damage to the underlying brain as the source of focal injuries (Chadwick, Rutter, Thompson, & Shaffer, 1981). Within the age group studied (the children were aged 12 years or less at the time of injury), there were very few significant hemisphere or locus effects. In particular, the hemisphere damaged did not affect the pattern of verbal and performance IQ scores. Nor, perhaps surprisingly, were there any hemisphere effects with respect to specific measures, such as new faces learning or verbal fluency, that have shown laterality effects in adults. However, there was a tendency for all tests of scholastic achievement to show greater impairment with left-hemisphere lesions. Although the age by hemisphere interaction fell far short of statistical significance, this tendency was most marked in children who were under the age of 5 years at the time of the head injury. Also, with most WISC subtests and with reading, there was a consistent trend for scores to be lowest in the children injured when younger—a finding in keeping with that of Woods (1980), already noted.

It might be argued that the largely negative findings in this study were an artifact of either the mildness of the injuries or the presence of contrecoup damage. In order to deal with these objections, attention was focused on the subgroup of 20 children who showed a strictly unilateral neurological disorder with motor abnormalities contralateral to the side of the injury. Still, no hemisphere effects on patterns of cognitive deficit could be detected (other than those slight tendencies already mentioned). Moreover, the negative findings applied to a range of seven specialized neuropsychological tests as well as to the results on the WISC.

Kohn and Dennis (1974) studied the same issue by comparing findings in four individuals who had undergone left hemidecortication and in four with right hemidecortication. Both groups had had symptoms from the first year of life, and in both the mean age at testing was 21 to 22 years. The full-scale and verbal IQs tended to be closely similar, regardless of the hemisphere removed by surgery; however, there was a nonsignificant tendency for the performance IQ to be lower (76 vs. 82) in the case or right hemidecortication. On half of the specific tests employed, the performance of the two groups was indistinguishable, but on the WISC mazes, the Porteus Maze test, and the road-map test of direction sense and extrapersonal orientation, the right-hemisphere group were consistently inferior to the left-hemisphere group.

Gott (1973) investigated possible age differences in the effects of laterality of lesions on patterns of cognitive functioning by comparing three cases of hemispherectomy for acquired disease—one at age 10, one at age 7, and one at age 28 (the first being a left hemispherectomy and the latter two being right hemispherectomies, with the testing carried out at 12, 16, and 34 years, respectively). The child who had a left hemispherectomy did not show the verbal deficits characteristic of adults with extensive left-hemisphere damage. Thus, her verbal IQ was 8 points above her performance IQ, and compared with the two right-hemispherectomy cases she actually obtained lower scores on several nonverbal tests (the Hooper Visual, the Bender–Gestalt, and the Arthur Stencil design), although she performed better on others (such as the Porteus Maze). Comparison of the two right-hemispherectomy cases showed that the discrepancy between verbal and nonverbal skills was greater for the individual who had had the hemispherectomy in adult life than for the one who had had it in middle childhood. It was concluded that hemispherectomy in childhood results in a less differentiated loss of cognitive skills than is the case in adult life. However, it also appeared that hemispherectomy in childhood results in a greater general impairment of intelligence.

Fedio and Mirsky (1969) examined laterality effects in a different fashion by comparing epileptic children who had left temporal abnormalities on the EEG with those showing focal abnormalities in the right temporal area. The two groups did not differ significantly with respect to verbal or performance IQ, but there was a just-significant tendency for verbal scores to be lower than performance scores in a higher proportion of children with left-hemisphere lesions. The groups did not differ in memory span or in copying of designs, but the left-temporal-focus group showed worse supraspan memory, more perseveration errors, and worse verbal learning. Pennington, Galliani, and Voegele (1965) found no association between the side of EEG dysrhythmia and WISC pattern. However, the children were not epileptic, and the significance of the EEG focus as an indication of any kind of brain lesion must be considered rather dubious.

On the face of it, these results suggest that differential hemisphere effects on cognitive functioning are less evident in childhood than in adult life. In part, this may be a function of the fact that the greatest laterality and locus effects in adults have been found with relatively *acute* brain lesions, whereas nearly all the studies of children have concerned *chronic* lesions. On the other hand, it seems unlikely that the lack of effects in childhood is entirely a consequence of attentuation, since laterality effects in adults persisted for 20 years in Newcombe's (1969) study of penetrating head injuries. Also, it could be argued that greater hemisphere effects in childhood would be found with deep lesions than with the largely cortical lesions in some of the studies (such as our own). But, again, that does not seem to be an adequate explanation, as McFie (1975b) reported that the cognitive features found with space-occupying lesions in children were similar to those associated with localized head injuries.

We may conclude that the evidence, when considered as a whole, suggests that the cognitive deficits associated with lateralized brain injuries tend to be less specific in childhood than in adult life. There is only a very slight and inconsistent tendency for early left-hemisphere lesions to lead to verbal deficits, although probably such lesions are more likely to result in scholastic difficulties. The reasons for an apparently greater effect of early lesions (especially of the left hemisphere) on scholastic attainment remain obscure. It could reflect a greater biological vulnerability during the preschool years, but, equally, it could mean that the brain injury is more likely to impair the acquisition of new skills than to result in the loss of well-established skills (Hebb, 1949). Preschool children have yet to learn to read, spell, and perform arithmetical operations, whereas older children are likely to have already acquired the basic skills in these operations. Visuospatial abilities tend to be affected by lesions in either hemisphere, but there is a slight tendency for them to be somewhat more impaired by right- than by left-hemisphere lesions when the lesions are acquired in the postinfancy period. Generalized impairment of intelligence tends to be greatest with lesions (of either hemisphere) very early in life, but whether this simply means that early lesions tend to involve greater brain damage is uncertain.

It is clear that the study of lateralized and localized brain lesions in childhood carries the potential for increasing our understanding of developmental trends in brain–behavior relationships. However, on the evidence to date, neuropsychological findings are of very limited use in the diagnosis of the locus of chronic brain lesions (it is not known whether they are of greater value in the localization of acute lesions). For the same reasons, the inference of focal brain dysfunction in individuals without known neurological disease from patterns of cognitive test performance remains a highly speculative enterprise resting on a very shaky empirical base.

DELINEATION OF COGNITIVE AND OTHER DEFICITS

Up to this point, we have considered neuropsychological assessments in terms of their use in drawing inferences about localized and generalized brain lesions. As we have indicated, there are serious limitations to their use for that purpose. However, although much research has been directed toward this aim (motivated by an interest in brain–behavior relationships as much as by the desire to develop a diagnostic instrument), the identification of brain lesions is not the chief value of neuropsychological assessment in routine clinical practice. Rather, its main contribution lies in the accurate delineation of cognitive and other deficits. This field of work is most conveniently discussed in terms of its various different applications.

Psychometric Assessment of "Neurological" Features

The neurological examination of children differs from that of adults in terms of the need to take into account the person's developmental level and the need to assess a range of functions that alter with age (Touwen & Prechtl, 1970). Thus, children's coordination skills increase as they grow older; associated movements (so-called "mirror movements") decrease with age; and choreiform activity is normal in young children but constitutes an atypical feature when observed in adolescents. With developmental features of this type, to a large extent any judgment on whether or not a child's performance is abnormal depends on a *quantitative* assessment of the degree of impairment in relation to age norms, rather than on qualitative considerations. It is for this reason that a range of tests have been devised for the psychometric assessment of neurodevelopmental characteristics (Rutter *et al.*, 1970). Such tests are superior to the clinical neurological examination in two crucial respects: (1) They provide a detailed objective quantification of performance that is not dependent on clinical judgment; and (2) tables are available to indicate the precise extent to which a child's scores depart from those obtained by normal children of the same age. Such precision is crucial both in the initial assessment of whether or not there is any neurodevelopmental abnormality and in the monitoring of progress. However, psychometric assessment is less satisfactory than the clinical neurological examination for the assessment of the *quality* and *type* of neurodevelopmental dysfunction—items that are crucial in the diagnostic appraisal of the meaning of any abnormalities found. Neurological and psychometric assessments of incoordination, language deficits, and sensory disturbance fulfill rather different functions; both types of assessments are needed and complement each other. Tests of motor coordination, motor impersistence, and language constitute three somewhat different examples of this use of neuropsychological assessment.

The Oseretsky Test of Motor Proficiency (Oseretsky, 1931) was primarily intended as an overall index of motor development. A major revision was published by Sloan in 1955; Stott (1966) produced another modification a decade later; and Rutter *et al.* (1970) developed a shortened version of the test suitable for use with 10- to 12-year-old children. Each of these versions comprises a battery of short tests involving both gross motor control (such as balancing on one leg or walking backward in a straight line) and fine motor control (such as picking up matchsticks one at a time from one box and placing them in another). Scoring depends on both accuracy and speed of performance. The test has been shown to have satisfactory reliability; it agrees reasonably well with neurological findings; and it differentiates groups of neurologically abnormal and mentally retarded children from normals (Rutter *et al.*, 1970). It correlates significantly with age but not with IQ within the normal range of intelligence. Briefer tests of aspects of coordination are also available in Annett's manual dexterity task (1970), Denckla's finger-movement test (1973), and the Purdue Pegboard (Costa, Scarola, & Rapin, 1964; Costa, Vaughn, Levita, & Farber, 1963; Rapin, Tourk, & Costa, 1966).

Fisher (1956) coined the term "motor impersistence" to describe an inability to carry out purposive movements on command. Benton and his coworkers (Benton, Garfield, & Chiorini, 1964; Garfield, 1964; Garfield, Benton, & MacQueen, 1966; Joynt, Benton, & Fogel, 1962) developed a short battery of nine tests to assess this phenomenon. Subjects are required to sustain a variety of voluntarily initiated motor acts (such as closing eyes, protruding the tongue, or keeping the mouth open) for specified time periods. Their findings, and those of others (Rutter *et al.*, 1970) have shown that motor impersistence is a developmental phenomenon that improves with age and which can be reliably measured. Persistence is impaired in children of very low IQ, and even more so in children with cerebral disorders. It remains uncertain exactly what physiological function is assessed by the test, but the findings suggest that the impersistence may reflect impaired cortical control of motor activity.

Numerous tests of language and speech skills have been developed (see Mittler, 1972). For some years the Illinois Test of Psycholinguistic Abilities (Kirk, McCarthy, & Kirk, 1968) dominated the field, but it has fallen into disfavor because of its complexity and reliance on an outmoded model of communication, as well as the lack of validating evidence for the utility of the profiles of language skills that it generates. Instead, two rather different types of language tests are in current usage. Firstly, there are the scales designed to quantify speech or language retardation; these are primarily of value in the assessment of children presenting with some form of developmental delay. The Reynell Developmental Language Scales (Reynell, 1969) are the most generally useful in this connection because of their ability to differentiate between *comprehension* of language and language *expression* or production. Articulation may be assessed by means of the Edinburgh Articulation Test (Anthony, Bogle, Ingram, & McIsaac, 1971) and symbolic play through the Lowe and Costello (1976) test. Secondly, there are the tests designed to assess more subtle language deficits not manifest in the form of a delay in language development. Oldfield and Wingfield's (1964) object-naming test, Borkowski *et al.*'s (1967) word fluency test, and the variety of auditory–perceptual and language related tests in the Halstead–Reitan battery (Boll, 1981) and in Rourke's (1981) neuropsychological test battery for use with learning-disabled children constitute examples of this kind. Unlike the developmental delay scales, many of this latter group of tests lack adequate normative data. They provide a potentially useful means of investigating some of the higher-level language functions that may be associated with learning difficulties or with organic brain syndromes, but most are not yet at a stage when they can be recommended for routine clinical use.

Complex Cognitive Functions

For many years, much neuropsychological work has been concerned with the development of tests to assess different types of complex cognitive functions of a kind not ordinarily included in a clinical neurological examination. A review of many of the procedures that have been usefully employed to assess neuropsychological functioning in adults has been provided by Lezak (1976). At present, the range of standardized tests available for use with children is much narrower.

The majority of these tests can be seen as more or less direct attempts to detect, quantify, or delineate forms of cognitive impairment that present as clinical problems. Thus, deficits in learning and memory may be assessed by means of Walton and Black's (1959) modified new-word learning test, in which the child is required to learn and remember the meaning of a list of unfamiliar words (White, 1959); by various paired-associate learning tests (e.g., Wechsler, 1945); and by tests that measure the child's ability to memorize and recall various word lists, sentences, or passages. A variety of visual retention tests are available to examine recall and recognition of material that is less susceptible to verbal encoding. These include the Binet Memory for Designs and the Benton Visual Retention Test, for which children's norms are available (Benton, 1974b). Even though these tests may provide useful information about learning and memory, their results frequently leave doubts about the precise nature and significance of any deficit found. For example, it will often be uncertain whether impairment on a memory test reflects a deficit in the storage or the retrieval of information. Perhaps more importantly, it is generally unclear how far specific cognitive difficulties in the course of everyday life are reflected in poor performance on short formal tests of this kind.

The measurement of attention has been the subject of particularly extensive research, because of its importance in theories of information processing (see, e.g., Broadbent, 1958, 1971; Hale & Lewis, 1979); its central role in concepts of hyperactivity (see Chapter 14 of this volume); the frequency with which poor concentration is said to be associated with psychiatric disorder and with learning problems (Rutter, Tizard, & Whitmore, 1970/1981; Taylor, 1980); its link with schizophrenia (Garmezy, 1977); and its association with organic brain dysfunction (Fedio & Mirsky, 1969; Rosvold, Mirsky, Sarason, Bransome, & Beck, 1956). Of the many tests measuring various aspects of the ability to attend, the continuous performance test (Rosvold *et al.*, 1956) has been particularly widely used. The child is presented with a series of stimuli that follow one another in rapid succession, and is required to respond whenever a particular prespecified (and infrequent) target stimulus appears. The test has a high face validity for the measurement of sustained attention, but, in view of its very wide usage, there is a surprising paucity of data on its psychometric properties (Taylor, 1980).

Dichotic-listening tasks were used originally to examine a person's ability to attend *selectively* to one of two simultaneously presented messages. In recent years they have been employed extensively to examine hemispheric specialization or the functional integrity of the two hemispheres (see Chapter 25 of this volume).

Other tests have been designed to assess different aspects of attention, and it is now clear that the original (rather naïve) notion that attention constitutes a unitary process must be abandoned. As the concepts involved in the measurement of attention are fully discussed by Douglas in Chapter 14, they are not considered further here.

Reaction times may be assessed through tasks that require the child to press particular keys every time a particular light signal is given (Gronwall & Sampson, 1974). The complexity of the task may be varied by increasing the number of choices available and by reversing the linkages (so that, for example, the key furthest to the left must be pressed whenever the light stimulus on the extreme right is presented).

The Matching Familiar Figures Test (Kagan, Rosman, Day, Albert, & Phillips, 1964) has been widely employed as a measure of "impulsivity." This is a visual matching test in which the child is asked to select from a set of six similar figures the one that is identical with a simultaneously presented test figure. Impulsivity is thought to be indicated by a rapid reaction time and a high number of errors (Kagan, 1965, 1966). However, there is only a modest correlation between errors and reaction time, and, although both measures appear useful, there are problems in the overall concept of impulsivity as originally proposed (Ault, Mitchell, & Hartmann, 1976).

Numerous other tests have been reported in the literature, but these examples provide an indication of the types of functions that may be assessed. There is no doubt that this approach is a useful one in terms of its potential for defining more accurately the specific patterns of cognitive deficit shown by individual children. However, many problems remain in the interpretation of test findings. Firstly, the tests vary greatly in the extent to which adequate norms are available. Secondly, as indicated in the discussion of the tests mentioned, there is continuing uncertainty both about the concepts involved and about the particular skills tapped by each test. Thirdly, it is not uncommon for the test scores to appear relatively unimpaired when clinical observations suggest the presence of significant cognitive problems.

Various steps have been taken in an attempt to make the tests more sensitive. For example, tasks may be made more complex, or distractions may be introduced, or the task may be extended in time with the demand of good performance under self-paced and relatively unstructured conditions. While it cannot be said that any of these variations has been adequately assessed, the results so far available do not suggest that they provide meaningful gains in sensitivity (see, e.g., Blackburn & Benton, 1955; Chadwick, Rutter, Shaffer, & Shrout 1981). Nevertheless, studies of adults suggest that the approach may have promise. For example, Gronwall and Sampson (1974) found that impairments after head injury were somewhat more marked on the most complex forms of their reaction-time task (see above). It seemed that the deficit was a result of a slowness in processing information at a central level. The findings of van Zomeren (1981) support this view, but they also suggest that head injury probably has to be rather severe before increases in the complexity of the task can be expected to result in improved differentiation between cases and controls.

The demands of a task may also be altered by manipulating the environmental conditions under which it is carried out. Thus, a recent study of young men one year after they sustained mild head injuries indicated that experimentally induced hypoxia (through reduction of oxygen in a hypobaric chamber) may reveal covert difficulties in information processing (Ewing, McCarthy,

Gronwell, & Wrightson, 1980). The possibility that appropriate manipulation of the task requirements or conditions may increase the sensitivity of neuropsychological tests warrants further exploration.

Single-Case Study

Not infrequently, standardized tests identify the presence of a cognitive deficit and indicate something of its characteristics and components, but yet fail to show the mechanisms involved and hence fail to provide an adequate guide to the form of remediation required. Some 30 years ago, Shapiro (1951, 1970) outlined an experimental approach to the investigation of single cases, in which the strategy requires the clinician to formulate explicit hypotheses, to devise means to measure the variables relevant to the hypotheses, and then to attempt to bring the variable under experimental control in order to determine whether it functions in the manner hypothesized. More recently, Diller and Gordon (1981) have indicated the importance of this approach in the rehabilitation of neurologically disabled individuals. Systematic manipulations of the task and of the task conditions are required in order to determine *why* the task is difficult for that individual, and *how* the remediation program may be planned in order to help the person make the most of his assets and circumvent the problems that stem from his deficits. Berger (1977) provided an example of this approach with the study of a boy with a reading and spelling disability associated with motor coordination difficulties. The hypothesis tested was that a defect in eye movement control was interfering with the acquisition of the appropriate left–right scanning skill used in reading. Meichenbaum and Goodman (1971) used a comparable "cognitive–functional" approach (Meichenbaum, 1976) to determine whether a small group of impulsive children made many errors on the Matching Familiar Figures Test because they were too fast or because they were too careless. The finding that a lengthening of their decision time in itself failed to reduce their error rate ruled out the first hypothesis as a sufficient explanation. Of course, there are a variety of problems in this method of study but, as Shallice (1979) has argued, not only may the technique be clinically useful, but also the case study approach constitutes a promising neuropsychological technique for providing more general information on the functional organization of cognitive subsystems.

Monitoring Progress

Another important function of neuropsychological assessment is that of monitoring cognitive change—either in the form of recovery following acute brain injury (such as after trauma to the head) or following neurosurgery; or in the form of possible deterioration, either as a result of excessive medication (as with multiple anticonvulsants—see Chapter 6 of this volume) or as a consequence of some suspected degenerative brain disease. Because psychometric testing can provide detailed quantitative measures of a wide range of cognitive skills, potentially they offer considerable advantages over other forms of clinical assessment as a means of detecting relatively small changes or trends over time. Moreover, because the tests are administered in a standard manner, using explicit criteria for quantifying performance, they are likely to be reasonably reliable even if subsequent testing has to be undertaken by different psychologists.

Nevertheless, in practice, there are considerable difficulties in using tests to monitor cognitive change. Firstly, if the same tests are used on more than one occasion, improvements in performance are to be anticipated as a result of prior exposure and practice. On the WISC, for example, a rise of 3½ points in verbal IQ and 9½ points in performance IQ is normal when the test is readministered after an interval of 1 month (Wechsler, 1974). The practical importance of this was evident in our 2- to 3-year follow-up of children suffering mild or severe head injuries (Chadwick, Rutter, Brown, Shaffer, & Traub, 1981). The children with mild head injuries showed a gain of 5 IQ points over the first year of follow-up. This might well have been interpreted as recovery from brain injury, had the control group not shown the same gain in IQ. The severe-head-injury group, in contrast, showed a gain of 20 points, most of which clearly *was* a function of cognitive recovery.

Secondly, if different tests are used (either to avoid a practice effect or because the change in the child's age has taken him or her out of the age range of the test first used), a change in score may simply reflect the imperfect correlation between cognitive tests designed to assess the same functions. In effect, each test samples cognitive behavior and, as with any other form of sampling, it is inevitable that no two samples will be identical.

Thirdly, if the child has been receiving specific remediation, any improvement in scores may simply reflect practice on those tasks that are common to the remediation program and to the tests used in monitoring progress. When this is an issue, it is essential to plan the neuropsychological assessment in such a way that it taps the relevant skills while at the same time it avoids the specific tasks employed in rehabilitation.

Fourthly, any change in scores may be due to changes in the child's motivational state or psychiatric condition, or to minor changes in task conditions. For example, one study (Clark & Rutter, 1979) showed that autistic children achieved better overall cognitive scores when first given easier items on which they could succeed than when the first items led to failure. Initial failure seemed to lead to stereotyped pattern of response associated with lack of appropriate task involvement.

No particular group of tests provide an answer to these (and other) difficulties, which are inherent in any assessment of cognitive change. Rather, there is a need for a systematic case study approach, in which a range of tasks and of task conditions are systematically varied in an attempt to test competing hypotheses on the explanation for the findings obtained.

Testing the Handicapped Child

Lastly, there remain the issues involved in the neuropsychological assessment of handicapped children. Throughout this chapter, there has been an emphasis on the techniques that are special to neuropsychology, rather than on those that are shared with general clinical psychology. However, in order to correct the perspective, it is necessary to emphasize that a broad-range IQ assessment such as that provided by the WISC, together with standardized tests of reading, spelling, and arithmetic, constitute the backbone of any neuropsychological appraisal. As already noted, intelligence tests such as the Wechsler scales are among those most sensitive to brain injury (Benton, 1974a; Smith, 1975). Moreover, the availability of good age-standardized normative data for the IQ scores provides an essential frame of reference for the interpretation of the child's performance on unstandardized and more specialized tests (Milner, 1969).

Nevertheless, as Berger and Yule (1972) have pointed out, tests developed for use with nonhandicapped children may yield inappropriate conclusions when applied to handicapped individuals. They emphasize the importance of choosing tasks that will arouse and maintain the children's interest; of starting at a level that ensures success; and of avoiding tests in which the child's general test performance is impeded by specific handicaps irrelevant to the skills being assessed. Thus, it is essential to avoid tests that rely on the understanding of spoken instructions if the child is deaf or has a severe deficit in language comprehension; to avoid performance tests that require sight if the child is blind; and to avoid timed tests that require a motor response if the child has coordination problems. The most generally useful test of cognition for young language-impaired children is the Merrill–Palmer scale (Stutsman, 1948). It has the advantages of being interesting to young chidren, of requiring the minimum of spoken instructions, of having a wide range of items requiring no speech from the child, and of a procedure for dealing with items refused rather than failed. The Arthur adaptation of the Leiter International Performance Scale (Leiter & Arthur, 1955) requires no spoken instructions or responses and is particularly appropriate for deaf children or children with receptive language difficulties. However, the test is bulky, and its standardization is less than optimal (also a limitation of the Merrill–Palmer). For school-age children, the WISC continues to be the most generally satisfactory, providing a differentation between "verbal" and "performance" IQs, as well as the opportunity to use the verbal scale alone with blind children or with those suffering gross physical handicaps. Raven's Progressive Matrices (Raven, 1960) may also provide a useful guide to intellectual level. The test consists of patterns and geometrical figures with one piece missing, which the child has to choose from among a group of possible answers. A board form of the test can also be created, and this may be preferable for some handicapped children (see Clark & Rutter, 1979). It is designed to test reasoning skills not involving speech, but performance is also strongly dependent on visual perception.

With all tests, it is important to appreciate that the neuropsychological assessment is not complete without a systematic account from the child's parents of what he or she can do *outside* the test situation. Moreover, it is never acceptable to leave discrepancies between test findings and parental reports unexplained. The existence of a discrepancy is *always* an indication for the examination of possible reasons for the discrepancy (Berger & Yule, 1972).

CONCLUSIONS

The whole field of neuropsychological assessment in childhood is in a stage of transition. Two decades ago it was apparent that the attempts to devise single diagnostic tests for "brain damage" were both conceptually unsound and practically unworkable. As a result, that aspect of neuropsychology came into some degree of disrepute, although the use of psychometric procedures to delineate and investigate both general and specific cognitive deficits remained an essential part of good clinical practice. However, pioneers continued to study brain–behavior relationships, and batteries of neuropsychological tests came to be used increasingly with adults. Their value has still to be adequately established; opinions differ on the extent to which it is warranted to use them as individual diagnostic instruments; and the claims of some of their more enthusiastic exponents have somewhat outstripped the empirical evidence that might justify them. Nevertheless, as it became clear that the batteries might have some utility, their use was extended from adults to children, with a particular interest in their application to the study of learning disabilities. Cognitive tests have proved useful in the differentiation of different types of learning disability, but it remains uncertain just which brain functions the test scores reflect. There are indications that the cognitive sequelae of brain injury in childhood may not be identical to those in adult life, and hence that the identification of "lesions" on the basis of test findings may be a somewhat hazardous enterprise. Nevertheless, the study of brain–behavior relationships in childhood is still a young science, and it is too early to know what can be achieved through a skilled neuropsychological assessment. Certainly, it is already much more than was the case 20 years ago, but still many of the most interesting and promising approaches remain research procedures rather than established tools for routine clinical use.

References

Annett, M. The growth of manual preference and speed. *British Journal of Psychology*, 1970, *61*, 545–558.

Annett, M. Laterality of childhood hemiplegia and the growth of speech and intelligence. *Cortex*, 1973, *9*, 4–33.

Anthony, A., Bogle, D., Ingram, T. T. S., & McIsaac, M. W. *The Edinburgh Articulation Test.* Edinburgh: Churchill Livingstone, 1971.

Ault, R. L., Mitchell, C., & Hartmann, D. P. Some methodological problems in reflection–impulsivity research. *Child Development*, 1976, *47*, 227–231.

Bender, L. *A Visual–Motor Gestalt Test and its clinical use*. New York: American Orthopsychiatric Association, 1938.

Benton, A. L. Clinical neuropsychology of childhood: An overview. In R. M. Reitan & L. A. Davison (Eds.), *Clinical neuropsychology: Current status and applications.* New York: Wiley, 1974. (a)

Benton, A. L. *The Revised Visual Retention Test* (4th ed.). New York: Psychological Corporation, 1974. (b)

Benton, A. L., & Pearl, D. (Eds.). *Dyslexia: An appraisal of current knowledge.* New York: Oxford University Press, 1978.

Benton, A. L., Garfield, J. C., & Chiorini, J. C. Motor impersistence in mental defectives. In J. Oster (Ed.)., *Proceedings of the International Copenhagen Conference on the Scientific Study of Mental Retardation.* Copenhagen: Statens & Andssvageforsorg, 1964.

Berger, M. Psychological testing. In M. Rutter & L. A. Hersov (Eds.), *Child psychiatry: Modern approaches.* Oxford: Blackwell Scientific Publications, 1977.

Berger, M. and Yule, W. Cognitive assessment in young children with language delay. In M. Rutter & J. A. M. Martin (Eds.), *The child with delayed speech.* (Clinics in Developmental Medicine No. 43). London: Spastics International Medical Publications/Heinemann Medical Books, 1972.

Blackburn, H. L., & Benton, A. L. Simple and choice reaction time in cerebral disease. *Confinia Neurologia*, 1955, *15*, 327–338.

Boll, T. J. Behavioral correlates of cerebral damage in children aged 9 through 14. In R. M. Reitan & L. A. Davison (Eds.), *Clinical neuropsychology: Current status and applications.* New York: Wiley, 1974.

Boll, T. J. Diagnosing brain impairment. In B. B. Wolman (Ed.), *Clinical management of mental disorders: A handbook*. New York: Plenum Press, 1978.

Boll, T. J. The Halstead–Reitan Neuropsychology Battery. In S. B. Filskov & T. J. Boll (Eds.), *Handbook of clinical neuropsychology*. New York: Wiley, 1981.

Boll, T. J., & Barth, J. T. Neuropsychology of brain damage in children. In S. B. Filskov & T. J. Boll (Eds.), *Handbook of clinical neuropsychology*. New York: Wiley, 1981.

Borkowski, J. G., Benton, A. L., & Spreen, O. Word fluency and brain damage. *Neuropsychologia*, 1967, *5*, 135–140.

Broadbent, D. E. *Perception and communication*. Oxford: Pergamon Press, 1958.

Broadbent, D. E. *Decision and stress*. London: Academic Press, 1971.

Chadwick, O., Rutter, M., Brown, G., Shaffer, D., & Traub, M. A prospective study of children with head injuries: II. Cognitive sequelae. *Psychological Medicine*, 1981, *11*, 49–61.

Chadwick, O., Rutter, M., Shaffer, D., & Shrout, P. E. A prospective study of children with head injuries: IV. Specific cognitive deficits. *Journal of Clinical Neuropsychology*. 1981, *3*, 101–120.

Chadwick, O., Rutter, M., Thompson, J., & Shaffer, D. Intellectual performance and reading skills after localized head injury in childhood. *Journal of Child Psychology and Psychiatry*, 1981, *22*, 117–139.

Clark, P., & Rutter, M. Task difficulty and task performance in autistic children. *Journal of Child Psychology and Psychiatry*, 1979, *20*, 271–285.

Costa, L. D., Scarola, L. M., & Rapin, I. Purdue Pegboard scores for normal grammar school children. *Perceptual and Motor Skills*, 1964, *18*, 748–752.

Costa, L. D., Vaughn, H. G., Levita, E., & Farber, N. Purdue Pegboard as a predictor of the presence and laterality of cerebral lesions. *Journal of Consulting Psychology*, 1963, *27*, 133–137.

Cronbach, L. J. *Essentials of psychological testing* (3rd ed.). New York: Harper International Editions, 1970.

Davison, L. A. Current status of clinical neuropsychology. In R. M. Reitan & L. A. Davison (Eds.), *Clinical neuropsychology: Current status and applications*. New York: Wiley, 1974.

Denckla, M. B. Development of speed in repetitive and successive finger movements in normal children. *Developmental Medicine and Child Neurology*, 1973, *15*, 635–645.

Dennis, M., Fitz, C. R., Netley, C. T., Sugar, J., Harwood-Nash, D. C. F., Hendrick, E. B., Hoffman, H. J., & Humphreys, R. P. The intelligence of hydrocephalic children. *Archives of Neurology*, 1981, *38*, 607–615.

Diller, L., & Gordon, W. A. Rehabilitation and clinical neuropsychology. In S. B. Filskov & T. J. Boll (Eds.), *Handbook of clinical neuropsychology*. New York: Wiley, 1981.

Eiser, C. Effects of chronic illness in childhood: A comparison of normal children with those treated for childhood leukaemia and solid tumours. *Archives of Disease in Childhood*, 1980, *55*, 766–770.

Ernhart, C. B., Graham, F. K., Eichman, P. L., Marshall, J. M., & Thurston, D. Brain injury in the preschool child: Some developmental considerations. II. Comparison of brain-injured and normal children. *Psychological Monographs*, 1963, *77*, (11, Whole No. 574), 17–33.

Ewing, R., McCarthy, D., Gronwall, D., & Wrightson, P. Persisting effects of minor head injury observable during hypoxic stress. *Journal of Clinical Neuropsychology*, 1980, *2*, 147–155.

Fedio, P., & Mirsky, A. F. Selective intellectual deficits in children with temporal lobe or centrencephalic epilepsy. *Neuropsychologia*, 1969, *7*, 287–300.

Field, J. G. Two types of tables for use with Wechsler's intelligence scales. *Journal of Clinical Psychology*, 1960, *16*, 3–7.

Filskov, S. B., & Goldstein, S. G. Diagnostic validity of the Halstead–Reitan Neuropsychological Battery. *Journal of Consulting and Clinical Psychology*, 1974, *42*, 382–388.

Finlayson, M. A. J., Johnson, K. A., & Reitan, R. M. Relationship of level of education to neuropsychological measures in brain-damaged and non-brain-damaged adults. *Journal of Consulting and Clinical Psychology*, 1977, *45*, 536–542.

Fisher, M. Left hemiplegia and motor impersistence. *Journal of Nervous and Mental Disease*, 1956, *123*, 201–218.

Fitzhugh, K. B., Fitzhugh, L. C., & Reitan, R. M. Wechsler–Bellevue comparison in groups with "chronic" and "current" lateralized and diffuse brain lesions. *Journal of Consulting Psychology*, 1962, *26*, 306–310.

Garfield, J. C. Motor impersistence in normal and brain-damaged children. *Neurology*, 1964, *14*, 623–630.

Garfield, J. C., Benton, A. L., & MacQueen, J. C. Motor impersistence in brain damaged and cultural-familial defectives. *Journal of Nervous and Mental Disease*, 1966, *142*, 434–440.

Garmezy, N. The psychology and psychopathology of attention. *Schizophrenia Bulletin*, 1977, *3*, 360–369.

Golden, C. J. A standardized version of Luria's neuropsychological tests: A quantitative and qualitative approach to neuropsychological evaluation. In S. B. Filskov & T. J. Boll (Eds.), *Handbook of clinical neuropsychology*. New York: Wiley, 1981.

Golden, C. J., Kane, R., Sweet, J., Moses, J. A., Cardellino, J. P., Templeton, R., Vicente, P., & Graber, B. Relationship of the Halstead–Reitan Neuropsychological Battery to the Luria–Nebraska Neuropsychological Battery. *Journal of Consulting and Clinical Psychology*, 1981, *49*, 410–417.

Golden, C. J., Moses, J. A., Fishburne, F. J., Engum, E., Lewis, G. P., Wisniewski, A. M., Conley, F. K., Berg, R. A., & Graber, B. Cross-validation of the Luria–Nebraska Neuropsychological Battery for the presence, lateralization and localization of brain damage. *Journal of Consulting and Clinical Psychology*, 1981, *49*, 491–507.

Goldstein, K., & Scheerer, M. Abstract and concrete behavior: An experimental study with special tests. *Psychological Monographs*, 1941, *53* (2, Whole No. 239), 1–151.

Gott, P. S. Cognitive abilities following right and left hemispherectomy. *Cortex*, 1973, *9*, 266–274.

Graham, F.K., & Berman, P. W. Current status of behavior tests for brain damage in infants and pre-school children. *American Journal of Orthopsychiatry*, 1961, *31*, 713–727.

Graham, F. K., Ernhart, C. B., Craft, M., & Berman, P. W. Brain injury in the preschool child: Some developmental considerations: I. Performance of normal children. *Psychological Monographs*, 1963, *77* (10, Whole No. 573), 1–16.

Graham, F. K., Ernhart, C. B., Thurston, D., & Craft, M. Development 3 years after perinatal anoxia and other potentially damaging newborn experiences. *Psychological Monographs*, 1962, *76* (3, Whole No. 522), 1–53.

Graham, F. K., & Kendall, B. S. Memory-for-Designs Test: Revised general manual. *Perceptual and Motor Skills* 1960, *11* (Monograph Supplement No. 2-VII), 147–188.

Gronwall, D. M. A., Sampson, H. *The psychological effects of concussion*. Auckland: Auckland University Press/Oxford University Press, 1974.

Hale, G. A., & Lewis, M. (Eds.). *Attention and cognitive development*. New York: Plenum Press, 1979.

Halstead, W. C. *Brain and intelligence*. Chicago: University of Chicago Press, 1947.

Halstead, W. C., & Wepman, J. M. The Halstead–Wepman Aphasia Screening Test. *Journal of Speech and Hearing Disorders*, 1949, *14*, 9–13.

Harris, R. The EEG. In M. Rutter & L. Hersov (Eds.), *Child psychiatry: Modern approaches*. Oxford: Blackwell Scientific Publications, 1977.

Heaton, R. K., & Crowley, T. J. Effects of psychiatric disorders and their somatic treatments on neuropsychological test results. In S. B. Filskov & T. J. Boll (Eds.), *Handbook of clinical neuropsychology*. New York: Wiley, 1981.

Heaton, R. K., Grant, I., Anthony, W. Z., & Lehman, R. A. W. A comparison of clinical and automated interpretation of the Halstead–Reitan battery. *Journal of Clinical Neuropsychology*, 1981, *3*, 121–142.

Hebb, D. O. The effect of early and late brain injury upon test scores, and the nature of normal adult intelligence. *Proceedings of the American Philosophical Society*, 1942, *85*, 275–292.

Hebb, D. O. *The organization of behavior*. New York: Wiley, 1949.

Herbert, M. The concept and testing of brain damage in children: A review. *Journal of Child Psychology and Psychiatry*, 1964, *5*, 197–216.

Joynt, R. J., Benton, A. L., and Fogel, M. L. Behavioral and pathological correlates of motor impersistence. *Neurology*, 1962, *12*, 876–881.

Kagan, J. Impulsive and reflective children: Significance of conceptual tempo. In J. D. Krumboltz (Ed.), *Learning and the educational process*. Chicago: Rand McNally, 1965.

Kagan, J. Developmental studies in reflection and analysis. In A. H. Kidd & J. L. Rivoire (Eds.), *Perceptual development in children*. New York: International Universities Press, 1966.

Kagan, J., Rosman, B. L., Day, D., Albert, J., & Phillips, W. Information processing in the child: Significance of analytic and reflective attitudes. *Psychological Monographs*, 1964, *78*(1, Whole No. 578), 1–37.

Kershner, J. R., & King, A. J. Laterality of cognitive functions in achieving hemiplegic children. *Perceptual and Motor Skills*, 1974, *39*, 1283–1289.

Kirk, S., McCarthy, J., & Kirk, W. *The Illinois Test of Psycholinguistic Abilities* (Rev. ed.). Urbana: University of Illinois Press, 1968.

Klonoff, H., & Low, M. Disordered brain function in young children and early adolescents: Neuropsychological and electroencephalographic correlates. In R. M. Reitan & L. A. Davison (Eds.), *Clinical neuropsychology: Current status and applications.* New York: Wiley, 1974.

Klonoff, H., Robinson, G. C., & Thompson, G. Acute and chronic brain syndromes in children. *Developmental Medicine and Child Neurology*, 1969, *11*, 198–213.

Knights, R. M., & Tymchuk, A. J. An evaluation of the Halstead–Reitan category tests for children. *Cortex*, 1968, *4*, 403–414.

Kohn, B., & Dennis, M. Patterns of hemispheric specialization after hemidecortication for infantile hemiplegia. In M. Kinsbourne & W. L. Smith (Eds.), *Hemispheric disconnection and cerebral function.* Springfield, Ill.: Charles C Thomas, 1974.

Koppitz, E. M. *The Bender–Gestalt Test for Young Children* (Vol. 2, *Research and application, 1963–1973*). New York: Grune & Stratton, 1975.

Lehmkuhl, G., Kotlarek, F., & Schieber, P. M. Neurologische und neuropsychologische Befunde bei Kindern mit angeborenen umschriebenen Hirnläsionen. *Zeitschrift für Kinder und Jugendpsychiatrie*, 1981, *9*, 126–138.

Leiter, R. G., & Arthur, G. *Leiter International Performance Scale.* New York: C. H. Stoelting, 1955.

Lezak, M. D. *Neuropsychological assessment.* New York: Oxford University Press, 1976.

Lishman, W. A. *Organic psychiatry: The psychological consequences of cerebral disorder.* Oxford: Blackwell Scientific Publications, 1978.

Lowe, M., & Costello, A. J. *The Symbolic Play Test.* Windsor, England: National Foundation for Educational Research, 1976.

McFie, J. Intellectual impairment in children with localized postinfantile cerebral lesions. *Journal of Neurology, Neurosurgery, and Psychiatry*, 1961, *24*, 361–365.

McFie, J. *Assessment of organic intellectual impairment.* London: Academic Press, 1975. (a)

McFie, J. Brain injury in childhood and language development. In N. O'Connor (Ed.), *Language, cognitive deficits and retardation.* London: Butterworths, 1975. (b)

McFie, J., & Piercy, M. Intellectual impairment with localized cerebral lesions. *Brain*, 1952, *75*, 292–311.

McKay, S. E., Golden, C. J., Moses, J. A., Fishburne, F., & Wisniewski, A. Correlation of the Luria–Nebraska Neuropsychological Battery with the WAIS. *Journal of Consulting and Clinical Psychology*, 1981, *49*, 940–946.

Meehl, P. E. *Clinical versus statistical prediction.* Minneapolis: University of Minnesota Press, 1954.

Meehl, P. E. *Psychodiagnosis: Selected papers.* Minneapolis: University of Minnesota Press, 1973.

Meehl, P. E., & Rosen, A. Antecedent probability and the efficiency of psychometric signs, patterns, or cutting scores. *Psychological Bulletin*, 1955, *52*, 194–216.

Meichenbaum, D. Cognitive–functional approach to cognitive factors as determinants of learning disabilities. In R. M. Knights & D. J. Bakker (Eds.), *The neuropsychology of learning disorders: Theoretical approaches.* Baltimore: University Park Press, 1976.

Meichenbaum, D., & Goodman, J. Training impulsive children to talk to themselves: A means of developing self-control. *Journal of Abnormal Psychology*, 1971, *77*, 115–126.

Meyer, V. Critique of psychological approaches to brain damage. *Journal of Mental Science*, 1957, *103*, 80–109.

Milner, B. Residual intellectual and memory deficits after head injury. In A. E. Walker, W. F. Caveness, & M. Critchley (Eds.), *The late effects of head injury.* Springfield, Ill.: Charles C Thomas, 1969.

Mittler, P. Psychological assessment of language abilities. In M. Rutter & J. A. M. Martin (Eds.), *The child with delayed speech* (Clinics in Developmental Medicine No. 43). London: Spastics International Medical Publications/Heinemann Medical Books, 1972.

Newcombe, F. *Missile wounds of the brain: A study of psychological deficits.* London: Oxford University Press, 1969.

Oldfield, R. C., & Wingfield, A. The time it takes to name an object. *Nature*, 1964, *202*, 1031–1032.

Oseretsky, N. Psychomotorik Methoden zur untersuchung der Motorik. *Zeitschrift angewandt Psychologie*, 1931, *17*, 1–58.

Pennington, H., Galliani, C. A., & Voegele, G. E. Unilateral electroencephalographic dysrhythmia and children's intelligence. *Child Development*, 1965, *35*, 539–546.

Petrauskas, R. J., & Rourke, B. P. Identification of subtypes of retarded readers: A neuropsychological multivariate approach. *Journal of Clinical Neuropsychology*, 1979, *1*, 17–37.

Prigatano, G. P., & Parsons, O. A. Relationship of age and education to Halstead Test performance in different patient populations. *Journal of Consulting and Clinical Psychology*, 1976, *44*, 527–533.

Rapin, I., Tourk, L. M., & Costa, L. D. Evaluation of the Purdue Pegboard as a screening test for brain damage. *Developmental Medicine and Child Neurology*, 1966, *8*, 45–54.

Raven, J. C. *Guide to the Standard Progressive Matrices*. London: H. K. Lewis, 1960.

Reed, H. B. C., & Fitzhugh, K. B. Patterns of deficits in relation to severity of cerebral dysfunction in children and adults. *Journal of Consulting Psychology*, 1966, *30*, 98–102.

Reed, H. B. C., & Reitan, R. M. Intelligence test performances of brain-damaged subjects with lateralized motor deficits. *Journal of Consulting Psychology*, 1963, *27*, 102–106.

Reed, H. B. C., Reitan, R. M., & Kløve, H. Influence of cerebral lesions on psychological test performance of older children. *Journal of Consulting Psychology*, 1965, *29*, 247–251.

Reitan, R. M. An investigation of the validity of Halstead's measures of biological intelligence. *Archives of Neurology and Psychiatry*, 1955, *73*, 28–35.

Reitan, R. M. Psychological deficits resulting from cerebral lesions in man. In J. M. Warren & K. Akert (Eds.), *The frontal granular cortex and behavior*. New York: McGraw-Hill, 1964.

Reitan, R. M. Psychological assessment of deficits associated with brain lesions in subjects with normal and subnormal intelligence. In J. L. Khanna (Ed.), *Brain damage and mental retardation: A psychological evaluation*. Springfield, Ill.: Charles C Thomas, 1968.

Reitan, R. M. Psychological effects of cerebral lesions in children of early school age. In R. M. Reitan & L. A. Davison (Eds.), *Clinical neuropsychology: Current status and applications*. New York: Wiley, 1974.

Reitan, R. M., & Boll, T. J. Neuropsychological correlates of minimal brain dysfunction. *Annals of the New York Academy of Science*, 1973, *205*, 65–88.

Reitan, R. M., & Davison, L. A. (Eds.). *Clinical neuropsychology: Current status and applications*. New York: Wiley, 1974.

Reynell, J. *Reynell Developmental Language Scales*. Slough, England: National Foundation for Educational Research, 1969.

Rosvold, H. E., Mirsky, A. F., Sarason, I., Bransome, E. D., & Beck, L. H. A continuous performance test of brain damage. *Journal of Consulting Psychology*, 1956, *20*, 343–350.

Rourke, B. P. Neuropsychological assessment of children with learning disabilities. In S. B. Filskov & T. J. Boll (Eds.), *Handbook of clinical Neuropsychology*. New York: Wiley, 1981.

Rutter, M., Chadwick, O., Shaffer, D., & Brown, G. A prospective study of children with head injuries: I. Design and methods. *Psychological Medicine*, 1980, *10*, 633–645.

Rutter, M., Graham, P., & Yule, W. *A neuropsychiatric study in childhood* (Clinics in Developmental Medicine Nos. 35–36). London: Spastics International Medical Publications/Heinemann Medical Books, 1970.

Rutter, M., Tizard, J., & Whitmore, K. (Eds.). *Education, health, and behavior*. New York: Krieger, 1981. (Originally published 1970.)

St. James Roberts, I. Neurological plasticity, recovery from brain insult, and child development. In H. W. Reese & L. P. Lipsitt (Eds.), *Advances in child development and behavior* (Vol. 14). New York: Academic Press, 1979.

Satz, P., & Fletcher, J. M. Emergent trends in neuropsychology: An overview. *Journal of Consulting and Clinical Psychology*, 1981, *49*, 851–865.

Sawyer, J. Measurement and prediction, clinical and statistical. *Psychological Bulletin*, 1966, *66*, 178–200.

Selz, M., & Reitan, R. M. Rules for neuropsychological diagnosis: Classification of brain function in older children. *Journal of Consulting and Clinical Psychology*, 1979, *47*, 258–264.

Shallice, T. Case study approach in neuropsychological research. *Journal of Clinical Neuropsychology*, 1979, *1*, 183–211.

Shapiro, M. B. An experimental approach to diagnostic psychological testing. *Journal of Mental Science*, 1951, *97*, 748–764.

Shapiro, M. B. Intensive assessment of the single case: An inductive–deductive approach. In P. Mittler (Ed.), *Psychological assessment of mental and physical handicaps*. London: Methuen, 1970.

Sloan, W. The Lincoln–Oseretsky motor development scale. *Genetic Psychology Monographs*, 1955, *51*, 183–252.

Smith, A. Neuropsychological testing in neurological disorders. In W. J. Friedlander (Ed.), *Advances in neurology* (Vol. 7). New York: Raven Press, 1975.

Spiers, P. A. Have they come to praise Luria or to bury him?: The Luria–Nebraska battery controversy. *Journal of Consulting and Clinical Psychology*, 1981, *49*, 331–341.

Spreen, O. J., & Gaddes, W. H. Development norms for 15 neuropsychological tests age 6 to 15. *Cortex*, 1969, *5*, 171–191.

Stott, D. H. A general test of motor impairment for children. *Developmental Medicine and Child Neurology*, 1966, *8*, 523–531.

Stutsman, R. *Guide for administering the Merrill–Palmer Scale of Mental Tests.* New York: Harcourt, Brace & World, 1948.

Taylor, E. Development of attention. In M. Rutter (Ed.), *Scientific foundations of developmental psychiatry.* London: Heinemann Medical Books, 1980.

Touwen, B. C. L., & Prechtl, H. F. R. *The neurological examination of the child with minor nervous dysfunction.* (Clinics in Developmental Medicine No. 38). London: Spastics International Medical Publications/Heinemann Medical Books, 1970.

Tsushima, W. T., & Towne, W. S. Neuropsychological abilities of young children with questionable brain disorders. *Journal of Consulting and Clinical Psychology*, 1977, *45*, 757–762.

Tymchuk, A. J., Knights, R. M., & Hinton, G. C. Neuropsychological test results of children with brain lesions, abnormal EEGs and normal EEGs. *Canadian Journal of Behavioural Science*, 1970, *2*, 322–329.

Tymchuk, A. J., & Nishihara, A. Scoring system. *Journal of Pediatric Psychology*, 1976, *1*, 15–17.

van Zomeren, A. H. *Reaction time and attention after closed head injury.* Lisse, The Netherlands: Swets & Zeitlinger, 1981.

Walton, D. W., & Black, D. A The validity of a psychological test of brain damage. *British Journal of Medical Psychology*, 1959, *105*, 270–279.

Wechsler, D. A standardized memory scale for clinical use. *Journal of Psychology*, 1945, *19*, 87–95.

Wechsler, D. *Wechsler Intelligence Scale for Children* (revised). New York: Psychological Corporation, 1974.

Wedell, K. Variations in perceptual ability among types of cerebral palsy. *Cerebral Palsy Bulletin*, 1960, *2*, 149–157.

Weinstein, S., & Teuber, H.-L. Effects of penetrating brain injury on intelligence test scores. *Science*, 1957, *125*, 1036–1037.

White, J. G. Walton's modified word-learning test with children. *British Journal of Medical Psychology*, 1959, *32*, 221–225.

Woods, B. T. The restricted effects of right-hemisphere lesions after age one: Wechsler test data. *Neuropsychologia*, 1980, *18*, 65–70.

Woods, B. T., & Teuber, H.-L. Early onset of complementary specialization of cerebral hemispheres in man. *Transactions of the American Neurological Association*, 1973, *98*, 113–115.

Yule, W. Diagnosis: Developmental psychological assessment. *Advances in Biological Psychiatry*, 1978, *1*, 35–54.

CHAPTER ELEVEN

Neurometrics: Quantitative Evaluation of Brain Dysfunction in Children

LESLIE PRICHEP / E. ROY JOHN / HANSOOK AHN / HERBERT KAYE

Childhood can be a period of frustration and alienation for children who have difficulties in school. In many cases, learning disabilities may be due to deviations from "normal" brain function. Estimates of the prevalence of learning disability due to brain dysfunction vary from 5 to 15% of the school-age population (Benton & Pearl, 1978; Eisenberg, 1966; HEW National Advisory Committee, 1969; Minskoff, 1973; Myklebust & Boshes, 1969; Silverman & Metz, 1973; Wender, 1971). The learning-disabled (LD) population is obviously heterogeneous; many different causes may underlie particular behavior or psychometric performance. The dysfunctional process in any one case cannot be inferred from the deficient product. We believe that a critical element in the attempt to aid a child with learning difficulties is the ability to clearly establish the presence or absence of brain dysfunctions and, if present, to specify the anatomical location and functional implications of the disorder as completely as possible.

A review of the literature reveals abundant evidence establishing that the electroencephalogram (EEG) and cortical evoked potential (EP) can be used to assess the anatomical integrity, functional status, and maturational development of the brain, and to evaluate information processing related to sensory, perceptual, and cognitive functions. Numerous detailed reviews of this evidence are available (Callaway, Tueting, & Koslow, 1978; Desmedt, 1977; John, 1977; John, Karmel, Corning, Easton, Brown, Ahn, John, Harmony, Prichep, Toro, Gerson, Bartlett, Thatcher, Kaye, Valdes, & Schwartz, 1977; Otto, 1978; Regan, 1972; Satterfield, 1973; Shagass, 1977). To date, however, clinical application of electrophysiological methods to the evaluation of LD children (or, more generally, to patients with cognitive impairment) has been greatly limited by the qualitative nature of feature extraction based on visual inspection of data. Consequently, results have often been suggestive but inconclusive. With the advent of economical and powerful minicomputers, many investigators have

Leslie Prichep, E. Roy John, and Hansook Ahn. Brain Research Laboratories, Department of Psychiatry, New York University Medical Center, New York, New York.

Herbert Kaye. Department of Psychology, State University of New York at Stony Brook, Stony Brook, New York.

turned their attention to the problem of devising methods to extract and quantify features of diagnostic utility from electrophysiological data (Dolce & Kunkel, 1975; John, 1977; John *et al.*, 1977; Kellaway & Petersén, 1973; Rémond, 1972).

This chapter describes "neurometrics," a technology that is intended to increase the sensitivity and to extend the utility of electrophysiological assessment into the domain of sensory, perceptual, and cognitive functions. This assessment quantifies features objectively extracted from both EEG and multimodal EPs elicited in a variety of standardized test conditions, and describes brain dysfunctions in terms of statistically significant deviations from age-related normative values.

NEUROMETRIC DATA ACQUISITION SYSTEM

This system combines high-performance amplifiers, software to deliver a standardized test battery using microprocessor-controlled stimulators, and accurate digital recording equipment. Data are gathered from the 19 channels of the International 10/20 Electrode System (Jasper, 1958), recorded monopolar referenced to linked earlobes. Transorbital electrodes are used to record the electro-oculogram (EOG), which allows the monitoring of eye movement. The system includes computer software that tests the impedance of each electrode and calibrates each amplifier. On-line artifact rejection algorithms are used to assess the quality of data and to allow the computer to reject data contaminated by eye or body movement. Data acquisition continues, by combining artifact-free segments of data, until an adequate sample for data analysis has been gathered. In this way, it is routinely possible to obtain reliable data from uncooperative patients in categories often considered refractory to testing (e.g., from children who are yery young, hyperactive, or mentally retarded; from psychotic patients; and from patients with senile dementia).

The Neurometric Test Battery, delivered by the microprocessor system that automatically controls the stimulator, provides a set of standardized conditions that constitute tests or "challenges" of a wide variety of brain functions. The data are stored in digital format, accompanied by digitally encoded protocols to permit subsequent automatic retrieval and data analysis. Upon retrieval, any desired monopolar or bipolar derivations can be reconstructed by the computer.

NEUROMETRIC TEST BATTERY

Each of the conditions included in the Neurometric Test Battery is based upon results described in the literature related to electrophysiological measures, reflecting brain functions that seem likely to be critically important for a child to learn efficiently and therefore potentially relevant to objective identification and diagnosis of brain dysfunction in LD children. Rather than using intuition to select some subset of these procedures, electrode placements, and measures, we were comprehensive in our construction of the initial Neurometric Test Battery. We included in this battery examples of every type of potentially informative assessment that seemed feasible to achieve by EEG and EP methods. The only restraint on condition selection was our commitment to designing a test that would have broad general applicability, regardless of age, culture, intellectual level, or cooperativeness of the patient. This approach provides a common standardized evaluation, applicable across the entire developmental spectrum as well as to the widest possible range of patients. To accomplish this, we used passive "challenges" of brain function that do not require the patient to respond behaviorally to any item, to solve problems, or to follow complex instructions. The patient need only observe stimuli presented under different conditions. Functional status is inferred by comparing responses elicited under these different conditions.

Each condition included in the battery is considered a test item and yields several different kinds of scores, which quantify separate features of the electrical activity. Composite conditions or "challenges" are constructed by computer, in which information obtained under one condition is evaluated relative to that obtained under another condition. Table 11-1 shows the test items included in the initial battery. This battery and the background literature are described in detail elsewhere (see John, 1977; John *et al.*, 1977).

Evaluation of the data set constructed with this extensive initial battery, from approximately 1000 cases (mostly children between the ages of 6 and 16), led to development of two modified batteries. These reduced redundancy and also emphasized items found to be maximally useful in discriminating between normally functioning and dysfunctioning populations. The Clinical Battery includes a minimum set of conditions to assess eyes-closed EEG, sensory acuity, and general visual and auditory processing capabilities. The Research Battery expands the Clinical Battery to include additional items from the initial battery that may be useful in identifying subgroups in the dysfunctional population, as well as new items suggested by progress in the field and experience with neurometrics that may be useful in differential diagnosis. The items in these new batteries are indicated in Table 11-1.

NEUROMETRIC DATA ANALYSIS SYSTEM

From the digital record constructed by the data acquisition system, quantitative analytical programs automatically extract various features of the EEG and EPs that our experience and the literature indicate to be of diagnostic utility. Each feature extracted from the data is subject to a Z transformation relative to age-appropriate normative values. This statistical evaluation yields the objective probability that the observed measure might be obtained from a normally functioning person of the same age as the patient. The individual's overall neurometric profile is presented in a clinic report. Any statistically deviant features are summarized in head diagrams that show the anatomical region(s) in which they were found, and the most probable behavioral implications of these findings are discussed.

Background for Selection of EEG Measures and Features

The neurometric measures and features extracted from the spontaneous electrical activity of the brain (EEG) are based upon previous results that correlate them with learning disabilities, neurological disorders, and other cognitive dysfunctions.

Table 11-1. Contents of initial complete Neurometric Test Battery with a brief indication of the intended purpose of each item

NEUROMETRIC TEST ITEM	INTENDED PURPOSE
EEG CONDITIONS AND CHALLENGES	
Conditions	
1. Eyes-open, spontaneous EEG, beginning of test[a]	Baseline measures for eyes-open EEG.
2. Eyes-closed, resting EEG, beginning of test[b]	Baseline measures for eyes-closed EEG.
3. Eyes-open, spontaneous EEG, end of test	Replication of initial measures.
4. Eyes-closed, spontaneous EEG, end of test	Replication of initial measures.
5. Photic driving at 2.5, 5, 10, and 18 Hz	Driving EEG at the normally dominant frequencies, delta, theta, alpha, and beta.
6. Sinusoidal flicker at 1 Hz	Response to meaningless stimulation over a 2-minute period.
Challenges	
7. Eyes-open minus eyes-closed EEG, beginning of test[b]	Effect of removal of visual input.
8. Eyes-open minus eyes-closed EEG, end of test	Replication of initial challenge.
9. Eyes-open, beginning, minus eyes-open, end 10. Eyes-closed, beginning, minus eyes-closed, end	Estimate of effects due to state, such as anxiety about test or fatigue due to testing, versus characteristic individual features displayed across states.
11. Photic driving at each frequency minus eyes-closed baseline EEG	Yields reactivity in delta, theta, alpha, and beta ranges.
12. Initial period of response to sinusoidal flicker minus last period	Habituation of EEG.
EP CONDITIONS AND CHALLENGES	
Sensory Acuity	
Conditions	
13. 65 lines per inch, 50% transmission[a]	Perceived as blank flash.
14. 27 lines per inch, 50% transmission[a]	Seen as checkerboard if visual acuity is approximately 20/20.
15. 7 lines per inch, 50% transmission[a]	Seen as checkerboard unless visual acuity is worse than 20/200.
16. 45-db click[a]	Elicits auditory EP unless hearing loss is sufficiently severe to interfere with language acquisition.
Challenges	
17. Blank minus 7 lines/inch[a]	Effects of change in visual contrast—significant differences in EP should be seen unless visual acuity is worse than 20/200.
18. Blank minus 27 lines/inch[a]	Effects of change in visual contrast—significant differences in EPs should be seen unless visual acuity is worse than 20/20.
19. 7 lines/inch minus 27 lines/inch[a]	Effects of change in visual contrast.
Prediction of Temporal Order	
Conditions	
20. Regular (a) flash, (b) click,[a] and (c) tap	Regular presentation of stimuli (flash, click, and tap) at 1-sec intervals. EPs reflect response to predictable temporal event.
21. Random (a) flash, (b) click,[a] and (c) tap	Random presentation of stimuli (flash, click, and tap). EPs reflect response to unpredictable temporal event.
Challenges	
22. Random versus regular flash 23. Random versus regular click[a] 24. Random versus regular tap	Change in EP wave shape reflects diminished response to predictable stimuli, indicates recognition of repeated temporal sequence. Late component in EP to random stimuli reflects uncertainty of random event.

Pattern Perception

Conditions	
25. Large square[b] 26. Small square 27. Large diamond[b] 28. Small diamond	Each contributes to an estimate of perception of differences in geometric forms.
29. *b*[a] 30. *d*[a] 31. *p*[b] 32. *q*	Each contributes to estimates of central discrimination between shapes of letters most commonly reversed.
Challenges	
33. Large square minus small square 34. Large diamond minus small diamond	Estimate of preservation of shape invariance, independent of size.
35. Large square minus large diamond[b] 36. Small square minus small diamond	Estimate of perception of differences in geometric form.
37. *b* minus *d*[a] 38. *p* minus *q*	Evaluation of EPs to laterally reversed letters.
39. *b* minus *p*[b] 40. *d* minus *q*	Evaluation of EPs to vertically reversed letters.

Figure–Ground Relations

Conditions	
41. Silent video program presented simultaneously with regular alternations of (a) flash, (b) click, and (c) tap[b]	Interaction between meaningful visual input (figure, consisting of scenes on a video screen) and meaningless visual, auditory, or somatosensory input (ground).
42. Musical recording presented simultaneously with regular alternations of (a) flash, (b) click, and (c) tap[b]	Interaction between meaningful auditory input (figure, consisting of a tape recording of a musical selection or story) and meaningless visual, auditory, or somatosensory input (ground).
Challenges	
43. Flash in the presence of video minus (a) flash alone, repeated for (b) click and (c) tap[b]	Reflects dynamic structuring of figure–ground relationships that require discrimination between relevant visual "signal" and irrelevant "noise," which may be either ipsimodal (video–visual) or cross-modal (video–auditory or video–somatosensory).
44. Click in the presence of music minus (a) click alone, repeated for (b) flash and (c) tap[b]	Reflects dynamic structuring of figure–ground relationships requiring discrimination between relevant auditory "signal" and irrelevant "noise," which may be either ipsimodal (music–auditory) or cross-modal (music–visual or music–somatosensory).

Habituation–Rehabituation

Conditions	
45. Simultaneous presentation of flash, click, and tap, 25 times/set for five sequential sets	Baseline for rate and degree of habituation, averaged separately for sets 1–5.
46. Repeat of #45, following interruption by presentation of random stimuli (#21)	Baseline for rate and degree of rehabituation, averaged separately for sets 1–5.
Challenges	
47. Phasic habituation: phasic habituation set 1, minus sets 2, 3, 4, and 5 separately. 48. Rehabituation: rehabituation minus rehabituation (for sets 1–5 separately)	Reveals rate and amount of suppression of information input about a meaningless monotonous event; reflects attention and short-term memory.
49. Habituation–rehabituation (for five sets separately)	Memory of initial habituation by comparison with initial phasic habituation reveals whether suppression of meaningless input is facilitated by memory of previous experience.

(continued)

Table 11-1. (Continued)

Conditioned Response Evaluation	
Conditions	
50. Regular (a) flash, (b) click, and (c) tap (control)	Baseline control measures.
51. Flash followed by click 250 msec later	Sensory–sensory conditioning with visual conditioned stimulus (flash) and auditory unconditioned stimulus (click).
52. Click followed by flash 250 msec later	Sensory–sensory conditioning with auditory conditioned stimulus (click) and visual unconditioned stimulus (flash).
Challenges	
After sensory–sensory conditioning with visual conditioned stimulus and auditory unconditioned stimulus:	
53. Postconditioning flash minus control flash	Reflects effects of conditioning as specific changes in response to conditioned stimulus.
54. Postconditioning click minus control click	Control for "sensitization," revealed as generalized change to unconditioned as well as conditioned stimulus.
55. Postconditioning tap minus control tap	Control for "pseudoconditioning," revealed as generalized change to any stimulus.
After sensory–sensory conditioning with auditory conditioned stimulus and visual unconditioned stimulus:	
56. Postconditioning flash minus control flash	Control for sensitization.
57. Postconditioning click minus control click	Estimate of specific conditioning effect.
58. Postconditioning tap minus control tap.	Control for pseudoconditioning.

[a]Item included in the present Clinical Battery.

[b]Item included in the present Research Battery (in addition to all items in the Clinical Battery).

Published normative data on the frequency composition of the EEG as a function of age (Hagne, Persson, Magnusson, & Petersén, 1973; Matoušek & Petersén, 1973) reveal a systematic evolution with maturation. In fact, we have found that in normally functioning children, the developmental characteristics of the EEG are accurately described by a series of polynomial equations discussed below in more detail (John, Ahn, Prichep, Trepetin, Brown, & Kaye, 1980). These equations permit objective evaluation of whether or not a particular child shows a maturational lag or a developmental deviation in the frequency composition of the EEG in any region(s). In general, with maturation there is a steady decrease in the amount of slow activity in each region. Quantitative frequency analysis in LD children has revealed an unusually high incidence of excessive slow-wave activity, possibly indicating a maturational lag (Ahn, Prichep, John, Baird, Trepetin, & Kaye, 1980; Capute, Niedermeyer, & Richardson, 1968; Cohn & Nardini, 1958; Kinsbourne, 1973; Pavy & Metcalfe, 1965; Satterfield, 1973; Satterfield, Cantwell, Lesser, & Podosin, 1972; Wikler, Dixon, & Parker, 1970). Quantitative frequency analysis has also been used to aid detection of certain neuropathologies and psychopathologies (Gotman, Skuce, Thompson, Gloor, Ives, & Ray, 1973; Harmony, 1983; Harmony, Otero, Ricardo, Valdes, & Fernandez, 1975; John *et al.*, 1977; Kellaway & Petersén, 1973; Matoušek & Petersén, 1973; Walter & Brazier, 1969).

Quantitative evaluation of symmetry between EEGs recorded from bilaterally symmetrical regions of the brain has also been found to be important in describing deviations from "normal" brain functions. Asymmetry has been shown to be correlated with learning disabilities, as well as many types of neuropathology and psychopathology (Hanley & Sklar, 1976; Harmony, 1983; John, 1977; John *et al.*, 1977; Muehl, Knott, & Benton, 1965; Otero, Harmony, & Ricardo, 1975a, 1975b; Rebert, Sproul, & Wexler, 1978).

The findings above suggest that quantitative definition of the frequency composition and symmetry characteristics of the EEG have great utility in diagnostic evaluation of the EEG.

Measures and Features Extracted from the EEG

Neurometric quantitative analysis of the EEG includes the following: (1) Frequency analysis. Absolute and relative power is computed in four frequency bands (delta, 1.5–3.5 Hz; theta, 3.5–7.5 Hz; alpha, 7.5–12.5 Hz; beta, 12.5–25 Hz) for each of eight bipolar derivations (C_3C_z, C_4C_z, T_3T_5, T_4T_6, P_3O_1, P_4O_2, F_7T_3, F_8T_4). (2) Percentage of power asymmetry. Differences in the amplitude of the EEG between these bilateral derivations are computed for each frequency band. (3) Coherence. Percentage of coherence, reflecting the degree of wave-shape symmetry and synchrony between bilateral derivations, is computed for each freqeuency band.

Background for Selection of EP Measures and Features

When any stimulus is presented, a transient oscillating electrical potential occurs in the ongoing EEG, which is called the "evoked potential" (EP). Using computer techniques, a series of evoked potentials time-locked to a stimulus can be averaged, permitting the EP to be extracted from the background EEG, which bears no consistent relationship to the stimulus. In this way, the anatomical distribution, wave shape, and latency characteristics of the electrical responses of various brain regions to different stimulus conditions can be determined.

Since EP features can reflect maturation (Dustman & Beck, 1969; Ellingson, 1967a, 1967b; Rhodes, Dustman, & Beck, 1969; Rose & Ellingson, 1970; Schenkenberg & Dustman, 1970), sensory acuity (Barnet, 1972; Graziani & Weitzman, 1972; Harter & White, 1968, 1970), perceptual processes (Clynes, Kohn, & Gradijan, 1967; Fields, 1969; Herrington & Schneidau, 1968; John, 1974; John, Herrington, & Sutton, 1967; Pribram, Spinelli, & Kamback, 1967), and cognitive processing of information (see review by John, 1977), they are uniquely well suited for the study of LD children, whose problems may stem from dysfunctions at any or all of these levels.

EP studies have been carried out on large groups of patients with a variety of neurological disorders and on children with learning disabilities. A high proportion of neurological patients display abnormal EP morphology or asymmetry, especially in response to visual stimuli. Children with learning disabilities often display EP abnormalities such as poor signal-to-noise ratio, marked asymmetries, poor reactivity, and abnormal morphology of EPs. This literature is reviewed by Harmony (1983) and John (1977).

Measures and Features Extracted from the EPs

A neurometric examination includes EPs elicited by a variety of visual and auditory stimuli. Under each of these standardized test conditions, averaged EPs are obtained from each electrode in the 10/20 System. The variance within each averaged sample of EPs is computed to 10-msec latency intervals across the analysis epoch, which is usually 500 msec long. From these raw data, the following quantitative features are extracted: (1) The signal strength and signal-to-noise ratio (average signal value divided by variance at each latency band) is computed for the early, middle, and long latency intervals, which approximate the periods within which primarily sensory, perceptual, and cognitive processes are believed to occur. (2) The asymmetry and consistency of asymmetry between EPs from symmetrically located electrodes, as reflected by the signal strength and signal-to-noise ratio of the bilateral difference wave is determined. (3) A morphology descriptor, which evaluates the accuracy with which the individual EPs can be reconstructed as a combination of standard-factor wave shapes (which usually describes EPs from healthy persons very well) is constructed. (4) The signal-to-noise ratio of the difference wave between stimulus conditions is computed to assess the significance of differences between EPs elicited from the same electrode by different visual stimuli or different sound patterns.

These various EP features provide objective measures of the strength of the electrophysiological response in each monitored region to each class of sensory stimulus, the consistency of the response, the wave shape of the response, and the differential response of the region to differences between stimuli. These measures permit quantitative estimation of the way that each brain region processes different types of information.

Normative Data Base and *Z* Transformation of All Extracted EEG and EP Features

We have constructed a normative data base that contains neurometric test data on approximately 600 normally functioning children aged 6 to 16 years. Using criteria like those of Matoušek and Petersén (1973), we selected from this group 306 "nonrisk" children on which to calculate age "norms" for all EEG and EP measures and extracted features in each region. (Details of this "norming" procedure are reported elsewhere; see John *et al.*, 1980; John, Prichep, Ahn, Easton, Fridman, & Kaye, 1983.)

In neurometric quantitative analysis, EEG and EP measures are subjected to logarithmic or other transforms to achieve Gaussian distributions. All measures are then *Z*-transformed relative to the means and standard deviations of these age-related normative data. This permits the estimation of the probability of obtaining the observed value by chance in that anatomical derivation in a normally functioning healthy child the same age as any patient. Another advantage of using Z transformations is that indexes describing disparate univariate dimensions are transformed into a common metric of probability and can therefore be compared and/or combined in multivariate or composite indexes. In our experience, such composite indexes often possess substantially more powerful utility for differential diagnosis than their univariate constituents. Information about such indexes is to be provided elsewhere first (John *et al.*, 1983).

VALIDITY OF THE ARTIFACT REJECTION ALGORITHM

Since all neurometric analyses are based on data gathered using a computer program for automatic artifact rejection, it was important to test the validity of this algorithm. The frequency distribution of the EEG is the most likely measure to be distorted by artifacts. A total of 10 records of eyes-closed EEG from "normal" children and 10 records from LD or hyperactive children were selected for study. The two groups were balanced for age. Frequency and symmetry analyses were carried out using the full 1-minute record accepted as valid by the computer acquisition system. The EEG records were then subjected to visual editing by an experienced EEG technician. All EEG segments considered to be contaminated by artifacts were removed, and the data excluding these portions were reanalyzed. The correlation coefficients and the significance of differences between the two sets of computer- and human-artifacted data were computed for both the spectral estimators and the symmetry and coherence measures, separately for each derivation, and separately for the normal and LD groups. Consistent high correlations were found between the computer-artifacted data with and without subsequent human editing. Most correlations between these two sets of data were above .93 for spectral measures and above .90 for coherence and power asymmetry measures. As can be seen in Tables 11-2a and 11-2b, the lowest correlations (with few exceptions) were found in the frontotemporal derivations, probably reflecting effects of eye movements smaller than the threshold levels set by the computer. Thus, it appears that meticulous and stringent visual editing (removing an average of approximately 30% of the computer-artifacted records) had little effect on the quantitative measures. In spite of these encouraging findings, we maintain a conservative position and continue to visually inspect and edit all our EEG records before analyses are performed.

TEST-RETEST RELIABILITY

The replicability of measures extracted from the EEG was studied for both short (within-session) and long (between-session) intervals. One minute of eyes-closed and 1 minute of eyes-open EEG, collected at the beginning and end of

Table 11-2a. Correlation coefficients between spectral estimators from unedited and edited eyes-closed EEG samples in normal ($n = 10$) children

	FREQUENCY							
	DELTA		THETA		ALPHA		BETA	
REGION	NORMAL	LD	NORMAL	LD	NORMAL	LD	NORMAL	LD
C_3C_Z	.961	.980	.988	.998	.990	.992	.998	.998
C_4C_Z	.976	.991	.990	.999	.995	.953	.998	.997
T_3T_5	.980	.959	.998	.989	.999	.994	.999	.985
T_4T_6	.981	.974	.997	.988	.994	.993	.996	.928
P_3O_1	.989	.955	.986	.987	.998	.984	.999	.994
P_4O_2	.996	.960	.987	.988	.996	.991	.999	.970
F_7T_3	.881	.931	.969	.945	.990	.985	.982	.984
F_8T_4	.888	.903	.977	.950	.996	.985	.988	.930

Note. Average length of EEG sample:

	NORMAL	LD
Unedited	59.77	54.24
Edited	42.36	39.70
% removed	29.13	26.81

Table 11-2b. Correlation coefficients between coherence and power asymmetry measures from unedited and edited samples of eyes-closed EEG data (same children as Table 11-2a)

	FREQUENCY							
	DELTA		THETA		ALPHA		BETA	
REGION	NORMAL	LD	NORMAL	LD	NORMAL	LD	NORMAL	LD
COHERENCE								
C	.977	.965	.982	.985	.903	.995	.912	.963
T	.786	.922	.929	.976	.998	.981	.983	.962
PO	.765	.911	.957	.958	.975	.980	.976	.914
FT	.874	.753	.982	.840	.989	.988	.822	.881
POWER ASYMMETRY								
C	.635	.927	.910	.978	.962	.989	.959	.991
T	.924	.927	.982	.994	.977	.988	.996	.923
PO	.928	.948	.983	.991	.937	.992	.944	.976
FT	.393	.943	.915	.940	.902	.934	.969	.890

Note. Average length of EEG sample:

	NORMAL	LD
Unedited	59.77	54.24
Edited	42.36	39.70
% removed	29.13	26.81

each test session (1–2 hours apart), were quantitatively analyzed and compared for each of 23 normal children. The correlation coefficients between eyes-closed relative power in EEGs at beginnings and ends of sessions, for monopolar derivation, are shown in Table 11-3. All test–retest correlations were excellent, significant at .001 level or better, as assessed by Fischer's Z. Data obtained in the eyes-open condition were significantly less reliable than in the eyes-closed condition, and absolute power measures were found to be much less reliable than measures of relative power. In view of these results, we focused our attention on eyes-closed relative power measures in our subsequent work.

Short- and long-term test–retest reliability of spectral measures for relative power was assessed in LD children for periods up to 4 years. Seventy-five children were divided into three groups with increasing intertest intervals: (1) 1–2 hours between tests (i.e., comparing beginning to end of test sessions) ($n = 15$);

Table 11-3. Test–retest reliability: Correlation coefficients between relative power in eyes-closed EEG at beginning and end of session ($n = 23$)

	REGION								
FREQUENCY	F_3	F_4	C_3	C_4	P_3	P_4	O_1	O_2	AVERAGE ACROSS LEADS
Delta	.740	.845	.769	.693	.787	.847	.801	.861	.793
Theta	.811	.713	.885	.817	.865	.771	.779	.871	.814
Alpha	.904	.908	.867	.827	.907	.854	.853	.918	.880
Beta	.842	.894	.777	.689	.893	.823	.863	.791	.822
Average across bands	.824	.840	.825	.757	.863	.824	.824	.860	.827

Table 11-4. Test–retest reliability correlation coefficients for frequency measures in eyes-closed EEG over varying intertest intervals (ITIs) for independent learning-disabled samples

				TEST–RETEST CORRELATION COEFFICIENTS BASED ON Z VALUES				TEST–RETEST CORRELATION COEFFICIENTS BASED ON RELATIVE POWER VALUES			
n	MEAN AGE	MEAN ITI	FREQUENCY	LC	LT	L PO	L FT	LC	LT	L PO	L FT
15	11.7	1.5 hr	Delta	.60	.83	.76	.85	.86	.92	.78	.79
			Theta	.63	.88	.95	.73	.79	.89	.91	.52
			Alpha	.94	.94	.86	.96	.86	.97	.88	.80
			Beta	.56	.86	.48	.88	.86	.86	.62	.90
			Delta + theta	.76	.80	.86	.88	.86	.85	.88	.79
			Average across bands	.70	.86	.78	.86	.85	.90	.81	.76
30	10.1	.6 yr	Delta	.79	.80	.76	.54	.81	.82	.74	.52
			Theta	.74	.74	.94	.44	.84	.58	.75	.51
			Alpha	.93	.79	.88	.61	.92	.88	.71	.87
			Beta	.86	.69	.49	.51	.87	.45	.47	.42
			Delta + theta	.93	.78	.71	.57	.93	.73	.80	.46
			Average across bands	.85	.76	.76	.53	.87	.69	.69	.56
30	9.4	2.5 yr	Delta	.40	.55	.49	.60	.42	.74	.57	.63
			Theta	.83	.55	.60	.54	.90	.66	.79	.57
			Alpha	.88	.87	.84	.56	.77	.77	.81	.67
			Beta	.82	.53	.46	.46	.75	.61	.63	.54
			Delta + theta	.85	.63	.71	.57	.80	.67	.76	.65
			Average across bands	.76	.63	.62	.55	.73	.69	.71	.61
Regional average across ITIs and bands				.77	.75	.72	.65	.82	.76	.74	.64

Note. Values are given separately for correlations based on *Z* values for frequency and relative power values in the left central (LC), left temporal (LT), left parieto-occipital (L PO), and left fronto-temporal (L FT) regions. Comparative values were found for right-hemisphere derivations. Overall reliability across frequency bands for all regions for increasing intertest intervals was .80, .73, and .64 for *Z* values, and .83, .70, and .69 for relative power.

(2) 1–24 months between tests ($n = 30$); (3) 24–48 months between tests ($n = 30$). The correlations between relative power and *Z* values for frequency estimates for eight bilateral derivations in the first and second tests were computed for the three groups. The average test–retest correlation for relative power was .83, .70, and .69, for the shortest to longest intertest intervals respectively. Similar results were found for *Z* values. Table 11-4 shows the test–retest correlations for left-hemisphere derivations for all three intervals. These values indicate that reliability of the EEG quantitative features is quite good, even in a dysfunctional group and over a long period of time.

DEVELOPMENTAL EQUATIONS FOR EEG

In order to develop valid statistical criteria for evaluation of EEG values from individual children, we studied the distribution of relative power values in the four frequency bands, in bilateral frontotemporal, temporal, central, and parieto-occipital bipolar derivations, in large samples ($n = 600$) of normally functioning children aged 6 to 16. These distributions were found to be approximately Gaussian after logarithmic transformation ($\log [x/100 - x]$) and could therefore be legitimately subjected to parametric evaluation.

The large volume and orderly nature of our bank of data from normally functioning children, in conjunction with the systematic changes evident in previously published normative tables based on data from 561 Swedish children (Matoušek & Petersén, 1973), encouraged us to construct regression equations to describe maturational changes in the EEG. First, we transformed those previously published normative tables to obtain relative (percentage of) power in each band and then log-transformed these values. Regression equations were then computed for each measure, separately for each derivation. Fourth-degree polynomial functions yielded a satisfactory fit for all measures across the 1–21 age range. These equations were reduced to the form $\bar{Y} = C_0 + C_1t + C_2t^2 + C_3t^3 + C_4t^4$, where t is age in years minus one.

Z transformation of an EEG frequency measure from a child, based on the value predicted from these regression equations, permits estimation of the probability of obtaining the observed value by chance in a normally functioning healthy child of that age. We tested the precision with which such measurements fell within the predicted distributions, derived from data originally obtained from Swedish children, in an independent group of "normally" functioning U.S. children ($n = 140$). The "false-positive" *Z* values (significant at the $p \leq .05$ level) were found to be quite low, and compared favorably with the 12–30% reported using subjective analysis of EEGs from normal children (Eeg-Olafsson, 1970; Gibbs & Gibbs, 1964).

Second, a group of 306 U.S. normal children, aged 6 to 16, was divided into split-half subgroups, balanced for chronological age and date of test. An independent set of regression equations was then derived using data from the first half of this population of U.S. normal children and tested on the second half. First-order linear equations, of the form $\bar{Y} = C_0 + C_1t$, where t is age in years, were found to describe the U.S. data with high accuracy in the 6–16 age range. The incidence of false positives at the $p \leq .05$ level in the second half was found to be 6.7%. The two halves were then merged, and final regression equations were computed for each of the 32 EEG parameters for the total sample.

In order to compare regression equations independently derived using data from U.S. and Swedish populations, new regression equations were computed from the published Swedish data across the restricted age range used in the regression equations for our U.S. data (6–16 years). It was found that both sets of data could be fit by first-order linear equations, of the form $\bar{Y} = C_0 + C_1t$, where t is age in years. The striking similarity between the two sets of regression equations computed independently on EEG features extracted from groups of healthy U.S. and Swedish children can be seen in Figure 11-1. The corresponding sets of coefficients, C_0 and C_1, are presented in Table 11-5, separately for each derivation. The close correspondence between these two independent descriptions of the developmental evolution of these quantitative EEG parameters, from two different cultures, suggests that they constitute a first approximation to a description of the rules governing the maturation of these EEG parameters in the normal healthy human brain. Details of this study are reported elsewhere (John *et al.*, 1980).

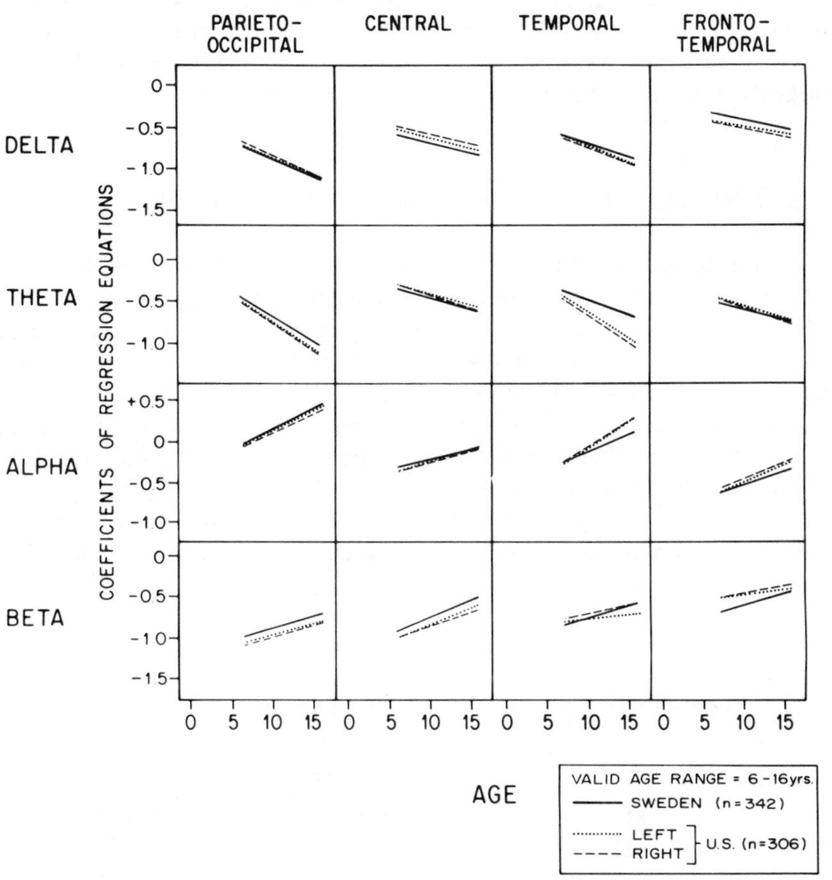

Figure 11-1. Regression equations for data from U.S. children ($n = 306$) and Swedish children ($n = 342$) for each frequency band and derivation. From "Developmental Equations for the Normal Human EEG" by E. R. John, H. Ahn, L. Prichep, M. Trepetin, D. Brown, and H. Kaye, *Science*, 1980, *210*, 1255–1258. Copyright 1980 by the American Association for the Advancement of Science. Reprinted by permission.

CULTURALLY FAIR NATURE OF MEASURES

Our sample included urban, suburban, rural, black, white, male, and female subgroups. No significant differences in the distribution of the EEG parameters were found among any of these subgroups and the normative data, nor between any two subgroups. These findings indicated that the extracted EEG features were independent of cultural or ethnic background, socioeconomic status, and sex.

Further, Z values for relative power in all frequency bands also conformed closely to the distributions predicted by our regression equations in an independent group of normally functioning children from Barbados ($n = 91$). In this group, false positives (at the $p = .05$ level) were 9%. In addition, there were no differences between the distributions of Z values in normal children from the U.S. and Barbados in 31 of the 32 EEG measures. These findings further establish the generality of the neurometric equations and provide more reassurance that they define developmental rules applicable to children who live in markedly different cultural environments (Ahn *et al.*, 1980).

DEVELOPMENTAL EQUATIONS REFLECT BRAIN DYSFUNCTION

The incidence of significant EEG spectral deviations from the values predicted by the neurometric equations were also studied in three groups of dysfunctional children: (1) patients "at risk" for neurological disorders and examined in a pediatric neurology service ($n = 474$); (2) LD children with borderline normal intelligence who exhibited generalized learning disabilities and poor achievement in one or more areas ($n = 143$); (3) specifically learning-disabled (SLD) children of normal intelligence who exhibited specific learning difficulties with poor achievement in at least one area ($n = 163$).

In addition, the significance of differences in the distribution of Z values between a group of normally functioning children and each of these other

Table 11-5. Coefficients of regression equations describing EEG spectra of healthy U.S. ($n = 306$) and Swedish ($n = 324$) children, for log ($x/100 - x$)

	DELTA				THETA				ALPHA				BETA			
	RELATIVE POWER		*SD*		RELATIVE POWER		*SD*		RELATIVE POWER		*SD*		RELATIVE POWER		*SD*	
DERIVATION	C_0	C_1	C_0	C_1	C_0	C_1	C_0	C_1	C_0	C_1	C_0	C_1	C_0	C_1	C_0	C_1
Parieto-occipital																
U.S. P_3O_1	−.41	−.043	.28	−.01	−.06	−.063	.31	−.01	−.34	.047	.41	−.02	−1.24	.029	.23	−.01
U.S. P_4O_2	−.37	−.046	.29	−.01	−.06	−.063	.31	−.01	−.37	.049	.43	−.02	−1.25	.030	.29	−.01
Sweden[a]	−.44	−.040			−.12	−.055			−.38	.050			−1.24	.029		
Central																
U.S. C_3C_Z	−.33	−.026	.25	−.01	−.11	−.028	.21	.00	−.52	.028	.40	−.02	−1.25	.036	.19	−.01
U.S. C_4C_Z	−.33	−.025	.20	.00	−.10	−.030	.22	−.01	−.52	.027	.34	−.01	−1.22	.035	.20	−.01
Sweden[a]	−.35	−.024			−.14	−.026			−.38	.023			−1.20	.042		
Temporal																
U.S. T_3T_5	−.31	−.039	.26	−.01	.00	−.060	.30	−.01	−.72	.062	.38	−.01	−.086	.008	.46	−.02
U.S. T_4T_6	−.35	−.036	.25	−.01	.01	−.061	.36	−.01	−.67	.059	.43	−.02	−0.91	.011	.38	−.02
Sweden[a]	−.41	−.029			−.13	−.043			−.55	.043			−1.04	.027		
Frontotemporal																
U.S. F_7T_3	−.31	−.018	.25	−.01	−.25	−.028	.31	−.01	−.89	.040	.27	−.01	−0.60	.010	.55	−.03
U.S. F_8T_4	−.31	−.019	.24	−.01	−.24	−.030	.25	−.01	−.81	.035	.28	−.01	−0.61	.012	.45	−.02
Sweden[a]	−.30	−.020			−.28	−.025			−.83	.032			−0.80	.029		

Note. x denotes relative power in each frequency band. No valid estimate of standard deviation of the relative power can be computed from the published Swedish data (Matoušek & Petersén, 1973). The data are valid for children aged 6 to 16 years. From "Developmental Equations for the Normal Human EEG" by E. R. John, H. Ahn, L. Prichep, M. Trepetin, D. Brown, and H. Kaye, *Science*, 1980, *210*, 1255–1258. Copyright 1980 by the American Association for the Advancement of Science. Reprinted by permission.

[a]These equations are based on pooled data from left and right sides, as published by Matoušek and Petersén (1973).

groups was tested by computing the exact probabilities of the chi-square on the actual distributions for every measure.

The neurological "at risk" patients and both LD groups showed a marked incidence of deviant Z values for each of these measures (ranging from 4 to 44%). For each group, significant "hits" were diffusely distributed across all head regions as well as across the delta, theta, and alpha bands. This diffuse distribution of "hits" in all three groups suggests that dysfunctions in any cerebral region can contribute to a wide variety of performance or behavioral deficiencies.

Since false-positive conclusions about brain dysfunction can have far-reaching consequences, we considered it desirable to define the threshold for inferring probable dysfunction as approximately twice the number of significant values expected by chance, or "hits" (i.e., 4 hits at the $p \leq .05$ or 2 hits at the $p \leq .01$ level). Using this criterion, the overall incidence of children with hits beyond threshold at the $p \leq .05$ level was 58% in neurological patients, 57% in LDs, and 54% in SLDs. If we restricted the criterion to one in which we considered only cases with twice the number of hits expected by chance at the $p \leq .01$ level, the false-positive rate was reduced to 4% in groups of normals, while 48% of the neurological patients, 46% of the LDs, and 47% of the SLDs still displayed hits beyond threshold.

Table 11-6 and Figure 11-2 show the percentage of deviant Z values for U.S. normal children, Barbados normal children, patients at risk for neurological disorders, LDs, and SLDs. It can be seen that the neurometric developmental equations, previously shown to be stable and culturally fair, yield few hits in normal healthy children and detect a substantial incidence of significant deviations from normal values in heterogeneous groups of children "at risk" for a wide variety of neurological diseases or learning disabilities.

NEUROMETRIC CORRELATES OF DIFFERENT BEHAVIORAL DYSFUNCTIONS

The above results show that neurometrics can reveal significant brain dysfunctions in a large proportion of children with behavioral or learning difficulties and, thus, can assist the clinician in distinguishing between problems of primarily neurological and psychological origins. However, the utility of neurometric assessments for differential diagnosis requires demonstration of differential behavioral correlates of different neurometric profiles. In relation to this, we here briefly describe three studies that have investigated the correlation between neurometric indexes and different learning disabilities.

Neurometric Evaluation of Children with Different Types of Underachievement

The first of these studies and its replication used neurometrics to investigate the electrophysiological correlates of school achievement and underachievement in children of normal intelligence (Ahn, 1977; Ahn & John, 1980). In both studies, the children were divided into four groups: (1) normal school achievers who had arithmetic, spelling, and reading skills all at grade level or better (total n in both studies = 72); (2) verbal underachievers (VUAs) who had reading and spelling at least two levels below grade, but arithmetic skills at grade level or better (total n in both studies = 19); (3) arithmetic underachievers (AUAs)

Table 11-6. Percentage distribution of "hits" for Z-transformed EEG measures for five groups

	GROUP 1, U.S. NORMALS ($n = 306$)			GROUP 2, BARBADOS NORMALS ($n = 91$)			GROUP 3, NEUROLOGICAL "AT RISK" ($n = 474$)			GROUP 4, LEARNING DISABLED ($n = 143$)			GROUP 5 SPECIFICALLY LEARNING DISABLED ($n = 163$)		
DERIVATION	NS	$p \leq .05$	$p \leq .01$	NS	$p \leq .05$	$p \leq .01$	NS	$p \leq .05$	$p \leq .01$	NS	$p \leq .05$	$p \leq .01$	NS	$p \leq .05$	$p \leq .01$
Delta															
LPO	96	4	0	96	4	2	69	31	19	70	30	21	73	27	17
RPO	96	4	1	99	1	0	70	30	18	66	34	20	75	25	16
LC	97	3	1	97	3	1	87	13	5	77	23	10	80	20	7
RC	97	3	1	99	1	0	87	13	6	78	22	8	86	14	5
LT	96	4	1	99	1	0	79	21	11	76	24	10	71	29	18
RT	97	3	0	99	1	0	78	22	14	76	24	10	80	20	13
LFT	97	3	0	89	11	2	78	22	11	85	15	6	82	18	9
RFT	97	3	0	88	12	5	75	25	14	89	11	6	77	23	6
Theta															
LPO	98	2	0	96	4	0	72	28	17	77	23	14	73	27	12
RPO	98	2	0	97	3	0	68	32	18	77	23	13	76	24	12
LC	97	3	0	97	3	0	87	13	6	87	13	3	88	12	5
RC	97	3	0	98	2	0	86	14	5	87	13	5	87	13	4
LT	96	4	1	93	7	1	76	24	13	82	18	6	81	19	6
RT	95	5	1	98	2	0	72	28	16	80	20	10	83	17	10
LFT	96	4	0	97	3	0	83	17	12	89	11	3	87	13	6
RFT	97	3	1	98	2	1	83	17	9	85	15	8	83	17	7

Alpha															
LPO	95	5	1	95	5	0	62	38	28	64	36	26	69	31	23
RPO	94	6	1	98	2	0	56	44	31	62	38	27	66	34	21
LC	96	4	1	100	0	0	81	19	8	78	22	13	79	21	12
RC	94	6	0	97	3	0	83	17	8	80	20	10	80	20	9
LT	95	5	1	98	2	0	68	32	19	71	29	15	71	29	19
RT	95	5	0	99	1	0	66	34	20	70	30	19	70	30	20
LFT	97	3	0	98	2	1	76	24	12	74	26	15	80	20	10
RFT	97	3	0	97	3	2	80	20	10	75	25	12	76	24	12
Beta															
LPO	98	2	2	100	0	0	91	9	7	87	13	6	89	11	7
RPO	96	4	2	100	0	0	90	10	7	80	20	8	88	12	7
LC	96	4	1	97	3	2	90	10	8	90	10	5	88	12	6
RC	97	3	1	98	2	1	90	10	8	88	12	6	88	12	7
LT	95	5	2	98	2	0	87	13	9	77	23	13	83	17	7
RT	96	4	2	96	4	1	89	11	7	77	23	13	84	16	12
LFT	94	6	3	97	3	0	94	6	3	82	18	10	88	12	6
RFT	97	3	1	99	1	0	96	4	2	84	16	8	90	10	6

Note. n is the number of subjects. We classified a child as dysfunctional if we found more than twice the number of significant values that would be expected by chance. By this criterion, at the $p \leq .05$ level, 10% of Group 1, 6.9% of Group 2, 58% of Group 3, 57% of Group 4, and 54% of Group 5 would be classified as dysfunctional. At the $p \leq .01$ level, 4% of Group 1, 2% of Group 2, 48% of Group 3, 46% of Group 4, and 47% of Group 5 would be considered dysfunctional. Abbreviations: L, left; R, right; PO, parieto-occipital; C, central; T, temporal; and FT, frontotemporal; NS, not significant. From "Developmental Equations Reflect Brain Dysfunctions" by H. Ahn, L. Prichep, E. R. John, H. Baird, M. Trepetin, and H. Kaye, *Science,* 1980, *210,* 1259–1262. Copyright 1980 by the American Association for the Advancement of Science. Reprinted by permission.

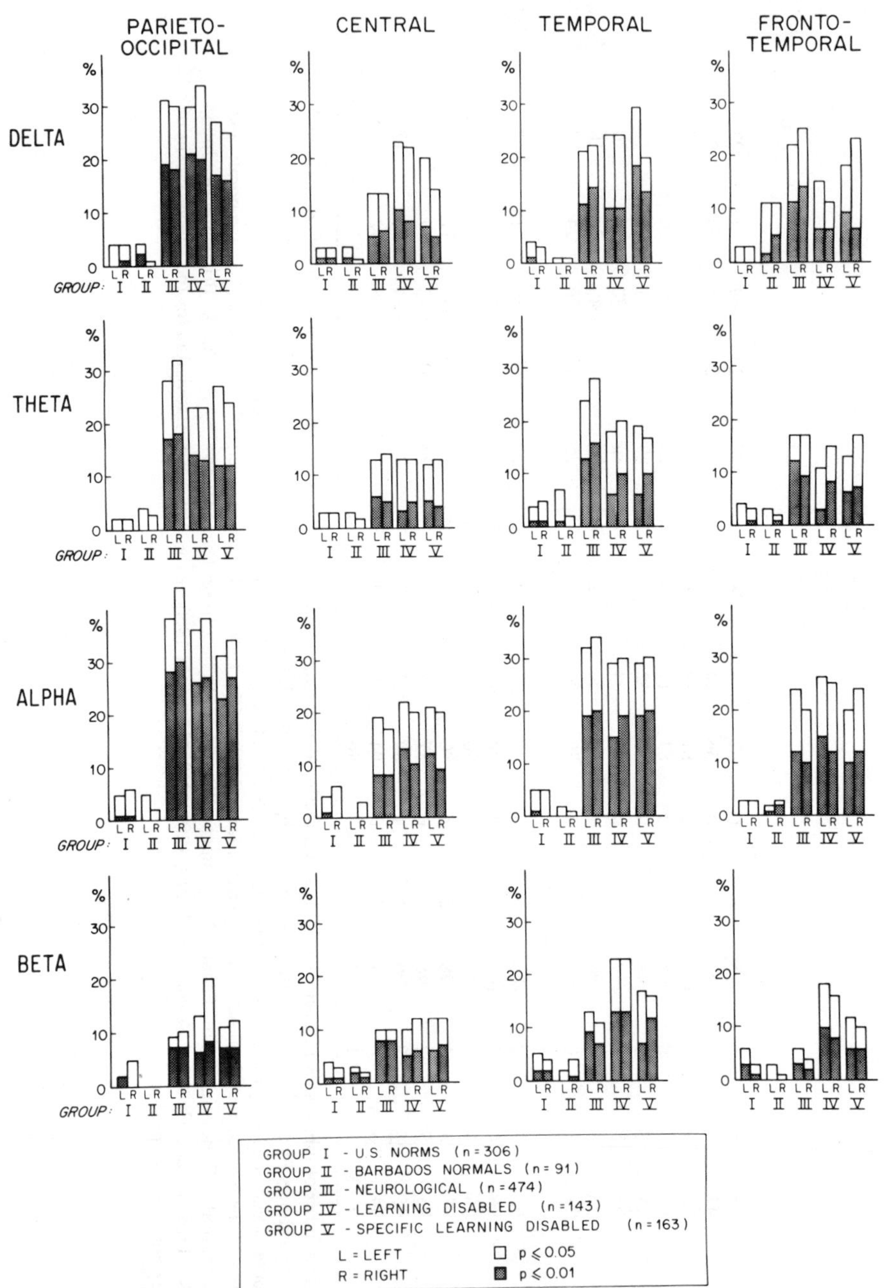

Figure 11-2. Percentage distribution of hits for the five groups. From "Developmental Equations Reflect Brain Dysfunctions" by H. Ahn, L. Prichep, E. R. John, H. Baird, M. Trepetin, and H. Kaye, *Science*, 1980, *210*, 1259–1262. Copyright 1980 by the American Association for the Advancement of Science. Reprinted by permission.

who had arithmetic skills at least two levels below grade but with reading and spelling skills at grade level or better (total *n* in both studies = 29); (4) mixed underachievers (MUAs) who had reading, spelling, and arithmetic skills at least two levels below grade (total *n* in both studies = 41). A separate group of normal children was matched for age, sex, handedness, and full-scale IQ to each of the three underachieving groups.

EEGs and visual evoked potentials (VEPs) were obtained using the Neurometric Test Battery. Group grand-average EPs were computed, and normal minus underachiever difference waves were derived between grand averages for each group of underachievers and its corresponding matched controls. The significance of the difference waves were computed as a function of latency, using the variances within each subgroup. These data clearly showed that children with different patterns of underachievement have different neurometric profiles. The VUAs had VEP amplitude differences from achievers at approximately 200–350 msec, predominantly in the left hemisphere (P_3, C_3). The AUAs showed excess theta in the posterior regions (P_3O_1, P_4O_2) and had VEP amplitude differences at about 200–350 msec, predominantly in the right hemisphere (P_4, C_4). MUAs showed excess delta and theta in the posterior regions and had VEP amplitude differences at about 100–200 msec, bilaterally but markedly in the left hemisphere (C_3, T_3). The VEP differences among group grand averages were obtained consistently in most or all of 11 different visual stimulus conditions, showing that the observed effects were independent of the specific information content of the different visual stimuli.

The overwhelming majority of significant differences between homogeneous subgroups of specifically or multiply LD children and age-matched control groups appeared in two latency domains: 100–200 msec and 200–300 msec (the first presumably related to perceptual and the second to cognitive processes). Taking into account the different latencies and different leads at which significant intergroup differences emerged, it seems probable that a stepwise multiple discriminant function could be constructed, using VEP amplitude at different latencies (especially the 100–200 and 200–300 msec latency regions) in different leads, which might differentially and accurately classify members of VUA, AUA, and MUA subgroups. If this proves possible, it could provide a basis for early identification of underachievement and earlier intervention.

Behavioral Correlates of Neurometric Profiles

In a second study, the behavioral, attentional, and psychometric concomitants of children, separated on the basis of neurometric profiles, were evaluated with primary focus on theta-excess effects on attentional behavior (Whiteside, 1979). Children were selected who were characterized by various specific neurometric patterns and learning capabilities, as follows:

1. Theta excess only, in two or more cortical regions; LD ($n = 22$).
2. Delta excess only, in two or more cortical regions; LD ($n = 12$).
3. Auditory evoked potential (AEP) asymmetries only, in two or more regions; LD ($n = 12$).
4. Neurometrically normal; LD ($n = 9$).
5. Neurometrically normal; normally functioning ($n = 22$).

These 77 children were examined in a series of five behavioral tasks, adapted from the Asarnow, Steffy, Maccrimmon, and Cleghorn (1977) Attention Battery by Whiteside (1979). This procedure included the Digit Span and Cancellation (Digit/Symbol Substitution Test) from the Wechsler Intelligence Scale for Children, Revised (WISC-R), the Stroop Color Naming Test, the Spokes (Trail-Making) Test, and a simple reaction-time key-press task. In addition, all children received a full-scale WISC-R and Wide-Range Achievement Test (WRAT) reading, spelling, and arithmetic test.

Results showed that, while the WISC-R differentiated between LD and normally functioning children, it could not differentiate between neurometrically normal and neurometrically abnormal LD children. Neurometrically normal and neurometrically abnormal groups of LD children could be differentiated on the basis of WRAT scores (the poorer performance being related to the presence of neurometric abnormalities, but not to the different patterns of abnormal neurometric profiles distinguishing the group compared in this study).

Performance on the behavioral tasks, however, separated the children along lines correlated with neurometric abnormality. Different subgroups showed different patterns of deficit on the subtests; in particular, the theta-excess group showed poor performance on those tasks that required sustained attention. In terms of the specific behavioral tasks, the theta-excess group showed significant differenital deficits in reaction time and digit span, as well as Stroop Test errors. The delta-excess group showed significant differential deficits in digit span and errors on Spokes Test. The EP asymmetry group showed proportionately more errors on the Spokes and Stroop Tests, and longer digit span times.

Neurometric Evaluation of Epileptic Achievers and Underachievers

In a third study, we investigated the electrophysiological correlates of school achievement and underachievement in groups of epileptic and nonepileptic children, all of normal intelligence (Baird, John, Ahn, & Maisel, 1980). The epileptic children were divided into two groups: Group I had a history of successful performance in school ($n = 12$); Group II had a history of school failure ($n = 11$). The nonepileptic "healthy" children were also divided into two groups, one with demonstrated school success ($n = 22$) and the other with school failure ($n = 19$). The epileptic children were matched for duration of medication and degree of seizure control.

Both visual inspection and quantitative analysis of the EEG and VEP show many abnormal features in epileptic children whose seizures have been well controlled for a long time by medication. Comparison of epileptic children who have learning difficulties with epileptic children who perform well in school reveals some similarities and numerous differences. Almost all of these children display abnormal sharp waves; these are as frequent, severe, and anatomically widespread in those who do well as in those who do poorly. The poor school performance of some epileptic children does not, therefore, seem to be due to the physiological processes that produce occasional sharp waves in the EEG. The incidence of beta bursts was twice as frequent in Group II, suggesting that paroxysmal activity of that sort may have greater functional significance than occasional sharp waves. The most salient features characterizing the epileptic children with school problems were excessive activity in theta and beta bands, especially in the central, temporal, and frontotemporal regions, and hyperreactivity of evoked responses in the frontal and frontopolar regions.

These observations may be related to previous reports of attention problems in epileptic children with learning difficulties (Holdsworth & Whitmore, 1974; Stores & Hart, 1976). Excessive theta activity may be an EEG correlate of hippocampal activation during orientation reflexes to irrelevant stimuli inappropriate to the classroom situation. The abnormal activity in frontal regions, reflected both in the beta excesses and the hyperreactive AEPs, may be correlated wth difficulty in controlling impulsive behavior and focusing attention. These epileptic children may have problems primarily in attention, rather than in learning per se.

Comparison of epileptic achievers with healthy achievers shows more asymmetry and lower coherence than normal in the EEGs of the medicated epileptic children, but only theta abnormality in the frequency spectrum. The treatment of these children, therefore, seems to have been more successful in normalizing the electrical activity of their brains, as well as their behavior.

ADDITIONAL NEUROMETRIC STUDIES

Although space does not permit detailed discussion, it is important to mention briefly a number of additional studies that further demonstrate the utility of neurometrics in studying patients with cognitive dysfunction.

In one such study the neurometric characteristics of children who consistently reversed letters such as *b* and *d* were investigated (Clark, 1981). It was found that "reversers" could be classified into four general groups depending upon the type of letter reversal errors they made: lateral errors (*b–d*), vertical errors (*b–p*), errors in verbal response to a visual stimulus, and errors in written response to an auditory stimulus. In addition, "reversers" could be identified on the basis of classroom teacher observation, or on the basis of time for task completion across all timed tasks.

Although each of these groups showed some dysfunction in the parieto-occipital region, distinct differences in neurometric profiles in this region were found among groups. Patterns of abnormalities in the relative power within various frequency bands, the presence or absence of asymmetries, and the additional involvement of frontotemporal or temporal regions were found to be correlated with specific types of errors in letter reversal.

These differences suggest that letter and word reversal by LD children is not a unitary or singular behavioral problem related to a unique neurological dysfunction. Rather, there are differential neurometric EEG profiles correlated with various types of reversal problems.

Neurometric correlates of cognitive dysfunctions have also been found in our studies of groups of adult patients suffering from a variety of neurological or psychiatric disturbances. In these studies, we have examined patients with memory deficits persisting long after head injury, patients during recovery from trauma-induced coma, elderly persons with mild or severe impairment of capacities due to memory loss, manic–depressive patients with and without cognitive impairment after long-term lithium medication, and chronic alcoholics with mild to severe cognitive deficits. Within each of these groups, certain common features of neurometric abnormality can be discerned. Some of these features are similar in patients suffering from different disorders, but some seem more characteristic of particular disorders. These findings are to be published in articles currently in preparation.

MATURATIONAL LAG, DEVELOPMENTAL DEVIATION, *Z*-REGION

At present, several new measures are being evaluated that are discussed briefly here because we expect them to add useful new insights to evaluation of LD children. Measures of "maturational lag" and "developmental deviation" are two such measures. For each head region, the square root of the sum of squares of the Z scores for relative power in the four frequency bands is calculated. This is called the "vector sum." The distribution of vector sums has been determined for each derivation as a function of age, in our sample of normal children. When a significantly large vector sum is obtained in any region ($p \leq .05$), an algorithm computes the vector sum that the same set of measures of relative power would yield when different values of age are inserted into the EEG regression equations. If there is some age for which the vector sum yielded by the observed measures of relative power would be within the normal distribution, this is defined as the "physiological age" of the region. The difference between the physiological age and the chronological age of the patient is defined as the "maturational lag" for that region. If there is no age for which the observed relative power measures would yield a vector sum within normal limits, that region is defined to show a "developmental deviation." Preliminary studies with these measures indicate that LD populations may be characterized by maturational lag, whereas neurological patients are more often characterized by developmental deviations. Being able to describe brain dysfunction in this way may add a novel diagnostic and prognostic dimension to the evaluation of learning disabilities.

"Z region" is a weighted regional summary Z score that describes the probability of deviation from normally expected values for a region across all EEG measures. This is a multivariate measure that shows very few false positives ($p \leq .05$) in normals (averaging approximately 49) and identifies significantly deviant regions in a great number of LD and neurologically at-risk children. For example, 34% of the children in the neurological population were significantly deviant in the left parieto-occipital region. Power summary statistics such as this have potentially important implications for mass screening of, and early intervention in, at-risk populations.

Finally, we are studying the functional implications of the findings and gathering information relevant to the etiology of these various dysfunctions. We are also beginning to study the effectiveness of different prescriptive treatments in remediation of the behavioral problems associated with specific neurometric profiles.

SUMMARY

Neurometrics is an objective, reliable method for the recording and analysis of brain electrical activity. Neurometric measures have been shown to be independent of cultural or ethnic background, socioeconomic status, and sex.

Features of diagnostic utility in the EEG and EP are extracted and quantified. For each feature, the probability of deviation from normal is statistically determined. An individual neurometric profile is constructed for each patient, describing all statistically deviant measures, the regions in which they deviate from normative values, and the implications for dysfunction based on these findings. Using neurometric measures, very few normally functioning children are found to have statistically significant deviations from expected values, whereas there is a high incidence of significant deviations in children with learning disabilities and those at risk for various neurological disorders. Finally, and most important with respect to differential diagnosis of the heterogeneous group called "learning-disabled," a variety of specific neurometric profiles have been shown to be correlated with specific behavioral dysfunctions.

Acknowledgments

Data presented in this chapter were gathered at several sites and supported by a number of research grants.

The majority of the "normally" functioning U.S. children were examined at the James E. Allen Learning Center, Dix Hills, New York, and at the Brain Research Laboratories, New York University Medical Center, New York, New York, in a project supported by National Science Foundation Grant #DAR 78-18772 (formerly APR 76-25662), intended to provide part of the data base for construction of EEG/EP discriminant function capable of separating LD from normal children. Additional data on "normally" functioning children were collected at the Rockland Psychological and Educational Center in Spring Valley, New York, and the Early Childhood Resource Center, University of Maryland, Eastern Shore, Princess Anne, Maryland.

The study of Barbados children was conducted in collaboration with F. Ramsey, J. Galler, and G. Solimano and was supported by the Ford Foundation, Grant #770-0471. Data were collected on a sample of 129 children who were exposed to malnutrition in the first year of life. They were matched by age, grade, gender, and handedness to a control sample of 129 children who had not suffered from malnutrition. The full results of this study are to be published elsewhere. Only a subset of the control population is used in the analyses reported in the current chapter and is referred to as "Barbados normals" ($n = 91$).

The majority of the LD and SLD children were attending the James E. Allen Learning Center of the Board of Cooperative Educational Services (BOCES) District III. These children were examined in a project supported by the Office of Education, Bureau of Education for the Handicapped, Grant #G007604516, intended to use neurometric methods to diagnose and help remediation of the LD child.

Children "at risk" for neurological disorders were studied at the Pediatric Neurology Service Handicapped Children's Unit, St. Christopher's Hospital for Children, Philadelphia, Pennsylvania, and supported in part by National Institutes of Health General CRC Grant RR-75. The data acquisition terminal was constructed by Neurometrics, Inc., under license from New York University Medical Center.

Studies involving adult patient populations are currently in progress in collaboration with the Departments of Psychiatry and Neurosurgery at New York University Medical Center. These studies are supported in part by Grants #MH 32577 and NS 07366.

References

Ahn, H. *Electroencephalographic evoked potential comparisons of normal children and children with different modes of underachievement.* Unpublished doctoral dissertation, University of Iowa, 1977.

Ahn, H., & John, E. R. *Neurometric characteristics of different types of underachievers.* Manuscript submitted for publication, 1980.

Ahn, H., Prichep, L., John, E. R., Baird, H., Trepetin, M., & Kaye, H. Developmental equations reflect brain dysfunctions. *Science*, 1980, *210*, 1259–1262.

Asarnow, R. F., Steffy, R., Maccrimmon, D., & Cleghorn, J. M. An attentional assessment of foster children at-risk for schizophrenia. *Journal of Abnormal Psychology*, 1977, *86*, 267–275.

Baird, H. W., John, E. R., Ahn, H., & Maisel, E. Neurometric evaluation of epileptic children who do well and poorly in school. *Electroencephalography and Clinical Neurophysiology*, 1980, *48*, 683–693.

Barnet, A. Sensory evoked response recording. In A. Rémond (Ed.), *Handbook of electroencephalography and clinical neurophysiology* (Vol. 15B, *Hereditary congenital and perinatal diseases*). Amsterdam: Elsevier, 1972.

Benton, A. L., & Pearl, D. (Eds.). *Dyslexia: An appraisal of current knowledge.* New York: Oxford University Press, 1978.

Callaway, E., Tueting, P., & Koslow, S. (Eds.). *Event related potentials in man.* New York: Academic Press, 1978.

Capute, A. J., Niedermeyer, E. F. L., & Richardson, F. The electroencephalogram in children with minimal cerebral dysfunction. *Pediatrics*, 1968, *41*, 1104–1114.

Clark, P. *Neurometric correlates of reading reversals in learning disabled children.* Unpublished doctoral dissertation, State University of New York at Stony Brook, 1981.

Clynes, M., Kohn, M., & Gradijan, J. Computer recognition of the brain's visual perception through learning the brain's physiological language. *IEEE International Conference Record,* 1967, *9*, 125–142.

Cohn, R., & Nardini, J. The correlation of bilateral occipital slow activity in the human EEG with certain disorders of behavior. *American Journal of Psychiatry*, 1958, *115*, 44–54.

Desmedt, J. (Ed.). *Visual evoked potentials in man.* Oxford: Clarendon Press, 1977.

Dolce, G., & Kunkel, H. (Eds.). *CEAN: Computerized EEG analysis.* Stuttgart: Gustav Fischer Verlag, 1975.

Dustman, R. E., & Beck, E. C. The effects of maturation and aging on the waveform of visually evoked potentials. *Electroencephalography and Clinical Neurophysiology*, 1969, *26*, 2–11.

Eeg-Olafsson, O. The development of electroencephalogram in normal children and adolescents from the age 1–21 years. *Acta Paediatrica Scandinavica*, 1970 (Suppl. 208).

Eisenberg, L. The epidemiology of reading retardation and a program of preventive intervention. In J. Money (Ed.), *The disabled reader: Education for the dyslexic child.* Baltimore: John Hopkins University Press, 1966.

Ellingson, R. J. Methods of recording cortical evoked responses in the human infant. In A. Minkowski (Ed.), *Regional development of the brain in early life.* Oxford: Blackwell Scientific Publications, 1967. (a)

Ellingson, R. J. The study of brain electrical activity in infants. In L. P. Lipsitt & C. C. Spiker (Eds.), *Advances in child development and behaviour* (Vol. 3). London: Academic Press, 1967. (b)

Fields, C. Visual stimuli and evoked responses in the rat. *Science*, 1969, *165*, 1377–1379.

Gibbs, F. A., & Gibbs, E. L. *Atlas of encephalography* (Vol. 3, *Neurological and psychological disorders*). Cambridge, Mass.: Addison-Wesley, 1964.

Gotman, J., Skuce, D. R., Thompson, C. J., Gloor, P., Ives, J. R., & Ray, W. F. Clinical applications of spectral analysis and extraction of features from electroencephalograms with slow waves in adult patients. *Electroencephalography and Clinical Neurophysiology*, 1973, *35*, 225–235.

Graziani, L. J., & Weitzman, E. D. Sensory evoked responses in the neonatal period and their application. In A. Rémond (Ed.), *Handbook of electroencephalography and clinical neurophysiology* (Vol. 15B, *Hereditary congenital and prenatal diseases*). *Amsterdam:* Elsevier, 1972.

Hagne, I., Persson, J., Magnusson, R., & Petersén, I. Spectral analysis via fast fourier transform of waking EEG in normal infants. In P. Kellaway & I. Petersén (Eds.), *Automation in clinical electroencephalography.* New York: Raven Press, 1973.

Hanley, J., and Sklar, B. Electroencephalic correlates of developmental reading dyslexics: Computer analysis of recordings from normal and dyslexic children. In G. Leisman (Ed.), *Basic visual process and learning disability.* Springfield, Ill.: Charles C Thomas, 1976.

Harmony, T. *Functional neuroscience* (Vol. 3, *Neurometric diagnosis of neuropathology*), Hillsdale, N.J.: Erlbaum, 1983.

Harmony, T., Otero, G., Ricardo, J., Valdes, P., & Fernandez, G. (Chairs). *Application of computation in the study of the nervous system.* Symposium presented at annual meetings of Centro Nacional de Investigaciones Científicas de Cuba, Havana, October 1975.

Harter, M. R., & White, C. T. Effects of contour sharpness and check-size on visually evoked cortical potentials. *Vision Research*, 1968, *8*, 701–711.

Harter, M. R., & White, C. T. Evoked cortical response to checkerboard patterns: Effect of check-size as a function of visual acuity. *Electroencephalography and Clinical Neurophysiology*, 1970, *28*, 48–54.

Herrington, R. N., & Schneidau, P. Effects of imagery on wave shape of visual evoked response. *Experientia*, 1968, *24*, 1136–1137.

HEW National Advisory Committee on Dyslexia and Related Reading Disorders. *Reading disorders in the United States.* Washington, D.C.: U.S. Department of Health, Education and Welfare, 1969.

Holdsworth, L., & Whitmore, K. A. Study of children with epilepsy attending ordinary schools: I. Their seizure patterns, progress and behavior in school. *Developmental Medicine and Child Neurology*, 1974, *16*, 746–758.

Jasper, H. H. The 10/20 Electrode System of the International Federation. *Electroencephalography and Clinical Neurophysiology*, 1958, *10*, 371–375.

John, E. R. Assessment of acuity, color vision and shape perception by statistical evaluation of evoked potentials. *Annals of Ophthalmology*, 1974, *6*, 55–56.

John, E. R. *Functional neuroscience* (Vol. 2, *Neurometrics: Clinical applications of quantitative electrophysiology*). Hillsdale, N.J.: Erlbaum, 1977.

John, E. R., Ahn, H., Prichep, L., Trepetin, M., Brown, D., & Kaye, H. Developmental equations for the normal human EEG. *Science*, 1980, *210*, 1255–1258.

John, E. R., Herrington, R. N., & Sutton, S. Effects of visual form on the evoked response. *Science*, 1967, *155*, 1439–1442.

John, E. R., Karmel, B. Z., Corning, W. C., Easton, P., Brown, D., Ahn, H., John, M., Harmony, T., Prichep, L., Toro, A., Gerson, I., Bartlett, F., Thatcher, R., Kaye, H., Valdes, P., & Schwartz, E. Neurometrics: Numerical taxonomy identifies different profiles of brain functions within groups of behaviorally similar people. *Science*, 1977, *196*, 1393–1410.

John, E. R., Prichep, L., Ahn, H., Easton, P., Fridman, J., & Kaye, H. Neurometric evaluation of cognitive dysfunctions and neurological disorders in children. *Progress in Neurobiology*, 1983.

Kellaway, P., & Petersén, I. (Eds.). *Automation of clinical electroencephalography.* New York: Raven Press, 1973.

Kinsbourne, M. Minimal brain dysfunction as a neurodevelopmental lag. In F. de la Cruz, B. H. Fox, & R. H. Roberts (Eds.), *Minimal brain dysfunction. Annals of the New York Academy of Sciences*, 1973, *205*.

Matoušek, M., & Petersén, I. Frequency analysis of the EEG in normal children and adolescents. In P. Kellaway & I. Petersén (Eds.), *Automation of clinical electroencephalography.* New York: Raven Press, 1973.

Minskoff, J. G. Differential approaches to prevalence estimates of learning disabilities. In F. de la Cruz, B. H. Fox, & R. H. Roberts (Eds.), *Minimal brain dysfunction. Annals of the New York Academy of Sciences*, 1973, *205*.

Muehl, S., Knott, J., & Benton, A. EEG abnormality and psychological test performance in reading disability. *Cortex*, 1965, *1*, 434–440.

Myklebust, H. R., & Boshes, B. *Minimal brain damage in children.* (Final report to U.S. Public Health Service). Washington, D.C.: U.S. Department of Health, Education and Welfare, 1969.

Otero, G., Harmony, T., & Ricardo, J. Polarity coincidence correlation coefficient and signal energy ratio of ongoing EEG activity: II. Brain tumor. *Activitas Nervosa Superior*, 1975, *17*, 120–126. (a)

Otero, G., Harmony, T., & Ricardo, J. Polarity coincidence coefficient and signal energy ratio of ongoing EEG activity: III. Cerebral vascular lesions. *Activitas Nervosa Superior*, 1975, *17*, 127–130. (b)

Otto, D. (Ed.). *Multidisciplinary perspectives in event-related brain potential research.* Washington, D.C.: U.S. Government Printing Office, 1978.

Pavy, R., & Metcalfe, J. The abnormal EEG in childhood communication and behavior abnormalities. *Electroencephalography and Clinical Neurophysiology*, 1965, *19*, 414.

Pribram, K. H., Spinelli, D. N., & Kamback, M. C. Electrocortical correlates of stimulus response and reinforcement. *Science*, 1967, *157*, 94–95.

Rebert, C. S., Sproul, A., & Wexler, B. N. EEG asymmetry in educationally handicapped children. *Electroencephalography and Clinical Neurophysiology*, 1978, *45*, 436–442.

Regan, D. *Evoked potentials in psychology, sensory physiology, and clinical medicine.* New York: Wiley–Interscience, 1972.

Rémond, A. (Ed.). *Handbook of electroencephalography and clinical neurophysiology* (Vol. 15B, *Hereditary congenital and perinatal diseases*). Amsterdam: Elsevier, 1972.

Rhodes, L. E., Dustman, R. E., & Beck, E. C. Visually evoked potentials of bright and dull children. *Electroencephalography and Clinical Neurophysiology*, 1969, *26*, 237.

Rose, G. H., & Ellingson, R. J. Ontogenesis of evoked potentials. In W. A. Himwich (Ed.), *Developmental neurobiology.* Springfield, Ill.: Charles C Thomas, 1970.

Satterfield, J. H. EEG issues in children with minimal brain dysfunction. In S. Walzer & P. H. Wolff (Eds.), *Minimal cerebral dysfunction in children.* New York: Grune & Stratton, 1973.

Satterfield, J. H., Cantwell, D. P., Lesser, L. I., & Podosin, R. L. Physiological studies of the hyperkinetic child. *American Journal of Psychiatry*, 1972, *128*, 1418–1424.

Schenkenberg, T., & Dustman, R. E. Visual, auditory and somatosensory evoked response changes related to age, hemisphere and sex. *Proceedings of 78th Annual Convention, American Psychological Association*, 1970, 183–184.

Shagass, C. (Ed.). *Psychopathology and brain dysfunction.* New York: Raven Press, 1977.

Silverman, L. J., & Metz, A. S. Numbers of pupils with specific learning disabilities in local public schools in the United States: Spring 1970. In F. de la Cruz, B. H. Fox, & R. H. Roberts (Eds.), *Minimal brain dysfunction.* New York: New York Academy of Science, 1973.

Stores, G., & Hart, J. Reading skills in school children with generalized or focal epilepsy. *Developmental Medicine and Child Neurology*, 1976, *18*, 705–716.

Walter, D. O., & Brazier, M. A. B. Advances in EEG analysis. *Electroencephalography and Clinical Neurophysiology*, 1969 (Suppl. 27).

Wender, P. H. *Minimal brain dysfunction in children.* New York: Wiley–Interscience, 1971.

Wikler, A., Dixon, J. F., & Parker, J. B. Brain function in problem children and controls: Psychometric, neurological, and electroencephalographic comparisons. *American Journal of Psychiatry*, 1970, *127*, 634–645.

Whiteside, B. *Theta excess relates to difficulties on tasks requiring sustained attention.* Unpublished master's thesis, State University of New York at Stony Brook, 1979.

CHAPTER TWELVE

Measurement Issues and Approaches

ERIC TAYLOR

There is at present a jumble of different approaches to the assessment and treatment of "neuropsychiatric disorder." Even the phrase defines different conditions in different places. Are problems such as learning disability and hyperactivity to be seen as reflections of a physically disordered brain, or as behavior patterns to be understood only at a psychological level of analysis? The uncertainty that surrounds such questions emphasizes that there is no general consensus on the criteria that could be used for the presence of minor degrees of physical dysfunction of the brain. This review, therefore, considers the adequacy of some current measures applied to children, and takes account of different levels of measurements—from the attempts to find behavioral or psychometric patterns that predict neurological abnormality, to the electrical and chemical measures that seem closer to the actions of neurons within the brain. The first consideration is whether researchers and clinicians can recognize a good measure if they meet one.

WHAT WOULD GOOD MEASURES BE LIKE?

Measures of brain function are required for many different purposes. A researcher interested in the relationships between brain and behavior may wish for a convenient index of overall biological impairment of the central nervous system (CNS) that will successfully differentiate between groups of subjects. Other researchers seek measures that usefully describe a physical basis of specific psychological functions—or even explain them. The clinician who wants to make diagnoses and predict the future for individual children will need a test that accurately classifies *individuals* into those with damaged brains and those whose biological equipment is intact. The therapist whose main concern is to describe and treat a child's problems effectively will require tests of psychological functions that can generate or monitor programs of intervention; for him or her, it is of only secondary interest whether the tests truly mirror the brain's integrity. It is not reasonable to expect a measure to be good in every respect. The validation of measures of brain function will therefore be different ac-

Eric Taylor. Department of Child and Adolescent Psychiatry, University of London Institute of Psychiatry, London, England.

cording to the ways in which they are intended to be used. Confusion has resulted when evidence from one area is used to support inferences in another.

Nevertheless, some criteria will apply to all proposed measures. Naturally, it is essential that they have adequately high reliability. Even in this, however, the level of reliability that is considered adequate will vary with the purpose. For instance, the goal of monitoring progress in treatment will not require a test with very high stability over time; the need for sensitivity to changes in the state of the subject is likely to imply a need for only moderate test–retest "reliability."

Requirements of a Group Test for Brain Dysfunction

One necessary quality of an adequate test of brain function will be its ability to discriminate sharply between children known to have damaged brains and children known to be neurologically normal. For some of the tests to be considered below (e.g., the Halstead–Reitan psychometric batteries), this discrimination is the core of the argument for their validity; for others (e.g., John's Neurometric Test Battery), it has played a minor part in their development.

When a test has been shown to be sensitive to the effects of known brain damage, its development as a neurological tool is by no means complete. Ideally, it should also be shown to be unaffected by variables other than those determining the biological state of the brain. This step is necessary because of the likely inferences to be based upon the test. Much research is based upon the strategy of identifying neuropsychological measures that will prove more sensitive than the conventional assessment of the neurologist, and one aim is to apply such measures to populations without overt neurological impairment. For example, one might seek to infer that learning disorders are based upon a biological impairment of brain function by showing that children who are slow to learn get abnormal scores on a test that distinguishes between head-injured children and their normal controls. Evidently, however, this inference will only have much strength if one also knows that abnormal scores cannot be caused by other factors, such as psychiatric disorder, low motivation, or adversity in the psychological environment. In general, this further step in validation will require more attention than it has received. It is not enough to show that one's measure yields normal scores for a control group of normal children, unless the control group is so very large that it is unlikely not to contain members on whom other kinds of pathogenic influences are acting. This need to demonstrate the absence of associations where none is predicted is in line with Campbell and Fiske's (1959) emphasis on discriminant, as well as convergent, validation for tests of individual differences. In practice, of course, it is unlikely that absolutely pure measures will be found; this will make it all the more important that contaminating factors are identified so that they can be controlled experimentally or allowed for clinically.

Further problems arise in the attempt to find indexes of brain function that are more sensitive than the clinical neurological assessment. The inference from the definitely brain-damaged to the more subtly affected makes the assumption that minor degrees of brain dysfunction will show only quantitative differences from grosser impairments. This assumption is in line with Pasamanick and Knobloch's (1960) conception of "the continuum of reproductive casualty"; it has a little support—for example, from Reitan and Boll (1973) and Selz and Reitan (1979), in whose studies a group of children with doubtful brain dysfunction scored intermediately between brain-damaged and control groups. However, it is not an assumption that is universally made. There might equally be a *qualitative* difference between overt brain damage and minimal brain dysfunction (MBD) (Wender, 1971). Indeed, some accounts of MBD make it clear that the syndrome being described is very different from any recognizable neurological condition. While many studies (Rutter, 1977) indicate that brain damage is associated with the whole range of psychiatric disorders, MBD is supposed to be more specifically linked to hyperactivity, learning disorders, and aggression (Clements, 1966). Whereas brain damage is evidenced by localizing neurological signs, regardless of age, the signs of MBD are described as age-dependent and nonlocalizing. While the behavioral symptoms of brain damage are often difficult to treat (by drugs, at any rate), MBD is supposed to be responsive to stimulant medication. In sum, it is not always clear just what is meant by MBD, but it does not always mean the same thing as a mild degree of brain damage. Accordingly, criterion-referenced instruments will not necessarily be enough to test the hypotheses about the condition.

The establishment of measures will therefore need to be based in part on their construct validity. A good measure will show a pattern of associations with other measures related to brain function, with tests of the structural integrity of the brain (such as radiological investigations), and with indexes of such insults to the brain as an abnormal perinatal history or (speculatively) the presence of minor congenital anomalies. It will also *not* show associations with extrinsic factors such as social class or parental education. Furthermore, a good test must add something to existing measures. Its association with indexes of dysfunction should therefore be greater than can be accounted for by psychopathology's or a low IQ's being associated with both.

So far, I have spoken of brain function as though it were a unitary function. This is, of course, not so, and it is not probable that any single test of psychological function will by itself be a good guide to CNS integrity. This is a familiar situation in clinical neurology. An extensor plantar response is a highly specific test of one kind of brain damage, but a very insensitive test of brain function as a whole. Sensitivity, in this instance, is achieved by using a wide range of items in the clinical examination. Batteries of neuropsychological tests have therefore been constructed with the aim of allowing few false negatives.

Requirements for a Diagnostic or Prescriptive Test

Individual diagnosis is more exacting in its demands for sensitivity and specificity than is discrimination between groups. A test may distinguish very significantly between groups, but still give very high rates of false positives and false negatives. Any set of measures that is referenced against an external criterion of CNS integrity will be judged by the proportion of children that it classifies correctly. The apparently normal children who are classified by the test as mildly or questionably brain-damaged will be the key group in validation, for they will be different from their fellows in other ways if the set of measures is valid.

In principle, clinical diagnosis should be an admirable measure of brain dysfunction, since it allows for the differential weighting of different kinds of evidence. It is possible for diagnosis to be operationalized and replicable. In practice, unfortunately, this has not been achieved. The diagnostic category of

"MBD" has been abused so harshly that it no longer conveys a meaning. There is no evidence that the diagnosis has been validated in any of the ways that I am considering here for more specific tests: in particular, diagnosed children have not been shown to be different from their fellows in any biological variable that was not part of the original definition.

Good measures of brain function will have other properties. They must be practicable and convenient. It may be hoped in addition that they will be psychologically meaningful, and give robust and useful accounts of psychopathology in those with brain dysfunction. Indeed, many would argue (e.g., Yule, 1978) that their primary purpose is to give helpful descriptions of psychological problems. The different goals are compatible: Researchers and clinicians need both to detect brain dysfunction and to describe it; but it is not essential that the same test should do both. Indeed, it is so unlikely that the same tests will be good for both purposes that it may not be an efficient strategy to try to combine the two. Certainly evidence relating to one purpose does not validate a test for another.

In summary, then, ideal measures are convenient, reliable, yet sensitive to change; they are highly successful in identifying children with neurological disorders, and they converge upon other measures of CNS integrity; they are not sensitive to other factors; yet they clearly describe psychologically meaningful processes, and they give an educationally useful profile of strengths and weaknesses. Mere reality is unlikely to match them! I now consider briefly how far behavioral, neurological, psychometric, and physiological measures have progressed toward the ideal.

BEHAVIORAL MEASURES

There is a long and unhappy history of using behavioral abnormalities as indexes of neurological disorder. The danger of circularity is obvious when the behavior is the evidence for the brain dysfunction that is supposed to explain it. Several studies (reviewed by Cantwell, 1980; Rutter, 1977; and Shaffer, 1977) have therefore investigated the behavior of children with known brain damage. The evidence is clear that brain damage does indeed give rise to psychiatric abnormalities, but that there is nothing very specific about the symptoms. There is no single brain damage syndrome. Accordingly, there is no overall behavioral measure of brain dysfunction. There are, however, some rare kinds of psychiatric problem that point strongly to a physical cause: The unusual pattern of self-injury in the Lesch–Nyhan syndrome is specifically related to a recessively inherited deficiency of purine metabolism (Nyhan, 1976). Much of the debate concerning the expression of brain dysfunction in behavior has revolved around the behaviors and syndrome of hyperactivity. As I point out, however, measures of hyperactivity do not meet the requirements for a neurological test.

Firstly, when children with illnesses affecting the brain are compared with other children, they are indeed found to have higher rates of problems diagnosed as hyperkinetic (Rutter, Graham, & Yule, 1970; Seidel, Chadwick, & Rutter, 1975). They more often show the symptom of overactivity as rated by adults, but there is nothing specific about this. They also have higher rates of underactivity and unduly persistent attention (Chess & Hassibi, 1970). Furthermore, overactive and restless behavior is not uncommon in children without neurological disease. Since normal children are much more numerous than the brain-damaged, an individual with overactivity is much more likely to be normal than to be a neurological case. This need to take differences in base rates into account when interpreting test results from clinically defined groups is of great importance (Meehl & Rosen, 1955) and recurs throughout the present discussion.

Secondly, studies of children attending clinics give some evidence that there is no association between measures of overactivity, impulsiveness, and inattention on the one hand and neurological measures on the other (Sandberg, Rutter, & Taylor, 1978; Schulman, Kaspar & Throne, 1965; Werry, 1968). Shaffer, McNamara, and Pincus (1974) compared children with and without brain damage and with and without conduct disorder; they found that measures of increased and impersistent activity were associated with conduct disorder rather than with brain damage per se. This study should not be overinterpreted, as their design implied that the brain-damaged children seen were not a representative group: accordingly, the positive conclusion (of the association between overactivity and conduct disorder) is more securely founded than is the negative conclusion that overactivity is not a feature of brain damage. The general conclusions of all these studies are limited by the nature of their measures. For present purposes, however, they demonstrate clearly how inadequate these measures are to index the functioning of the brain.

Thirdly, there is no reason to believe that illness affecting the brain is the only association of hyperactivity. Psychological and social factors are associated with impulsive, overactive, and inattentive behaviors, and in some situations are likely to be causative (Taylor, 1980c; Tizard & Hodges, 1978; Tizard & Rees, 1974).

Fourthly, it is not established that measures of hyperactivity converge on other measures of dysfunction or evidence of structural damages. Many studies have compared children with the diagnosis of hyperactivity to normal controls, in the hope of establishing a biological validation and etiology for the condition. While differences are sometimes shown, they are diagnostically nonspecific. If anything is validated by such tests, it is a general concept of psychopathology of conduct—and this is, of course, in line with the diagnostically nonspecific effects of overt brain damage. Weak and inconsistent associations have been shown between hyperactive behavior and minor congenital abnormalities (Rapoport, Pandoni, Renfield, Lake, & Ziegler, 1977; Waldrop, Pederson, & Bell, 1968), neurological signs (Nichols & Chen, 1981; Werry, Minde, Guzman, Weiss, Dogan, & Hoy, 1972), electroencephalogram (EEG) abnormalities (Taylor, 1980b), the effect of ingested food additives (Conners, 1980; Taylor, 1979), the effect of stimulant drugs (see Chapter 16 of this volume), and monoamine metabolism (Cohen & Young, 1977; see also Chapter 15 of this volume). However, for none of these has any specificity to hyperkinesis been demonstrated (see also Chapter 17).

One must conclude that measures of overactive and inattentive behavior cannot yet even define a group of children characterized by organic dysfunction of the brain; much less do they allow for identification of brain-damaged children.

How do they fare as tools in the assessment of children with neurological disease or handicap? Some, at any rate, of the available behavioral measures have been very successful in discriminating between the effects of drug and placebo treatment (Conners, 1977); and there is some evidence that hyperkinetic behaviors are important for the prognosis of children with temporal lobe epilepsy (Lindsay, Ounsted, & Richards, 1979). However, these behaviors constitute only one kind of disturbance among the many that need to be assessed, and should not be overemphasized. The simplest kinds of measures are those of activity level, recorded mechanically or electronically or by analysis of videotape or by observers' counts of movements made. The conceptual simplicity of these measures is misleading, for they have not achieved good distinctions between hyperactives and others, nor have they been particularly drug-sensitive. Qualitative measures of activity, which can include judgments about the relevance of the movements being recorded, have been necessary. Such judgments are presumably included in the ratings of behaviors, made by people who know the child well, that constitute the scales (e.g., Conners, 1969, 1970b; Patterson, 1964; Quay, 1977) that have been the backbone of pharmacological research. However, these ratings are all rather global, and much more detailed analysis of behaviors such as "distractibility," "impulsiveness," "persistence," and "disruptiveness" will be necessary before these scales can take a part in a neuropsychological analysis of a child's problems (see Chapter 13 of this volume). It also remains to be demonstrated that these behaviors are in fact the core difficulties. It may well be that they can improve without any overall change in psychological functioning (Gittelman-Klein & Klein, 1975), and that important therapeutic progress can be achieved in children whose activity level is unaffected.

Finally, an important qualification must be entered about the conclusions I have arrived at concerning the lack of validity of behavioral measures as indexes of brain function. They are all confined to current measures, and should not be seen as disqualifying all possible concepts of hyperkinesis, or indeed of MBD. These issues are dealt with elsewhere in this volume. Indeed, there are substantial hints in the research literature that rigorous and narrow definitions of hyperkinesis result in groups of children with evidence of biological dysfunction over and above that to be expected in any psychopathological group. Pervasive overactivity (Campbell, Endman, & Bernfeld, 1977; Sandberg *et al.*, 1978; Schachar, Rutter, & Smith, 1981) and gross overactivity (Taylor, 1980a) may be valid in this way, and these constitute more valuable concepts than broader definitions (see Chapter 13); they are likely to require further development of behavioral measures.

PSYCHOMETRIC APPROACHES

Neuropsychological tests, from the start, have been developed for the purposes of individual diagnosis. Research has not yet established any single test to be a useful indicator of brain damage. Clinicans, however, continue to base diagnostic decisions upon such tests. Furthermore, debate continues upon the value of collections of tests such as the Reitan–Indiana Neuropsychological Test Battery (see Chapter 10). I therefore consider validation with this example in mind.

It is clear that significant differences are to be found between the psychological test scores of some groups of brain-damaged children and normal controls. This applies to the Halstead–Reitan battery (Reed, Reitan, & Kløve,

1965; Reitan & Boll, 1973). Indeed, it also applies to tests (such as the Wechsler Intelligence Scale for Children, or WISC) that are not designed for this purpose and are less time-consuming to administer (Chadwick, Rutter, Brown, Shaffer, & Traub, 1981; Rutter *et al.*, 1970). It may well be that the longer battery discriminates more efficiently, although it is hard to compare different studies in which the subjects are selected in different ways. It is not yet clear that the increase in discriminating power is large enough to justify the greater cost. Nor is it clear whether any particular "profile" of test scores is specifically associated with brain damage. Indeed, the history of interpreting test profiles is particularly discouraging. Yule (1978) has given a damning critique of the attempts to base any useful conclusions about the brain upon the differences between subtests in such measures as the Illinois Test of Psycholinguistic Ability (Kirk, McCarthy, & Kirk, 1968), the Frostig Developmental Test of Visual Perception (Frostig, Lefever, & Whittlesey, 1964), or the WISC (including the hallowed verbal–performance discrepancy).

More to the present purpose, it seems that such a battery of tests can yield a rather sharp distinction between neurological cases and controls, with none of the controls in Selz and Reitan's (1979) study showing "definite" neuropsychological deficits on a discriminant function that identified three-quarters of the "brain-damaged." To be sure, any test of general intelligence has something of this power. An IQ of less than 50, for example, implies very strongly that structural damage is to be found in the brain (Crome, 1960); we know this because the scores have been associated with the external criterion of postmortem pathological change.

The pitfalls in interpretation appear in those who show intermediate levels of impairment. The Selz and Reitan study cited above did not find that learning-disabled children scored in the "definite" range of impairment. Most obtained scores in the "borderline" range (which also characterized 8% of normal children). It is wrong to regard those with "borderline" scores as *necessarily* showing a less marked effect of the same factors that caused the "definitely impaired" scores. The point may be clearer by analogy with the IQ: The majority of those with "mildly retarded" scores (50–70) do not have neurological disease, but represent simply the lower range of the normal variation, determined by the same factors that operate in the general population (Clarke & Clarke, 1974). For this reason, it would be highly misleading to regard the borderline intellectually retarded as showing brain damage—or brain dysfunction in any useful sense. It may be equally unsound to consider borderline "neuropsychological" impairment as evidence of organic abnormalities. The onus will fall upon the test developers to demonstrate that children identified as impaired, but for whom conventional neurological assessment is normal, nevertheless show evidence of cerebral insults or damage or physiological dysfunction or genetic vulnerability.

It could of course turn out—as it could for the behavior measures considered above—that some particular ability might prove to be closely linked to the physical functioning of the brain. For example, the inability to focus and sustain attention has been regarded as central to the problem of learning disorders (Ross, 1976) and hyperactivity (Douglas, 1972); and also as reflecting neurological responsiveness (Dykman, Ackerman, Clements, & Peters, 1971). However, it is clear that while neurological damage *can* cause inattention, often it does not; and that many other factors can impair the various abilities that are called "attention" (Taylor, 1980c). It would be illegitimate, therefore, to use the presence of attention deficit as a good argument for brain abnormality. Other examples may be more promising. Ojemann (1979) has recently presented striking evidence for the localization within the brain of specific functions such as short-term memory and word recognition. Direct electrical stimulation of very small areas of the brain of adults undergoing psychosurgery seems to affect quite specific cognitive processes. Yet even this suggestion that small physical lesions in the brain *can* impair psychological function does not give any support to the view that psychological dysfunction is *only* (or even usually) caused in this way.

Ojemann's experiments, however, do underline some potential problems in the development of psychological measures. There seem to be consistent changes in the biological location of function, depending on experimental details—apparently minor—in the design of the psychological test. The possible number of different kinds of brain damage and compensation may therefore be exceedingly high. The chances then of standardized group tests' giving useful accounts of basic difficulties would be very low. It is therefore not surprising that available measures have been so useless in describing deficits or guiding treatment. At present, there is no point in basing prescriptive educational teaching on supposed impairments of particular neuropsychological processes (Farnham-Diggory, 1980). Advances in this area are more likely to come from an experimental approach to individual cases.

In summary, available psychometric tests have a limited, but promising, ability to discriminate brain-damaged children from normal controls. They are not yet competent for the diagnosis of borderline or doubtful cases on their own, and are only weak guides to therapeutic practice. Nothing is to be gained from trying to use a single test battery for all clinical purposes, and much is to be lost. Present ability to detect brain dysfunction seems most likely to be improved by studies addressing the validity of standardized group tests. By contrast, improvement in knowledge of how to describe dysfunction and prescribe treatments is likely to require development of single-case methodology and of psychological tests that take account of subtle changes in the details of the task.

Neurological Examination

Measures of neuromuscular coordination have a high face validity because of their similarity in form to the localizing signs of brain disease used by the neurologist. The similarity may, however, be more apparent than real. Rutter *et al.*, (1970) have pointed out that the term "soft signs" has confused several different kinds of signs. Mild forms of localizing signs (such as an equivocal plantar response) are seldom used, and have a rather different status from signs (such as strabismus or weakness of grip) that can also be produced by non-neurological factors, and also from developmental signs representing a lack of coordination that would be normal at a younger age. The last kind forms the bulk of the signs used in schemes of developmental neurological assessment. Their age dependency can be handled by requiring a judgment from the examiner on normality for children of that age, or by confining the instrument to a narrow age range of children, or by recording absolute performance and treating the results as a psychometric test score (as in the Lincoln–Oseretsky test battery). One may, however, doubt how far the judgment of the examiner is (or should be) successful in allowing for the influence of age, since it is a rather consistent finding that the number of children with abnormal scores falls with increasing age. Furthermore, the judgment of the examiner is by no means constant among experienced clinicians. Nichols and Chen (1981), in an American perinatal collaborative study, found that different centers showed a 10-fold difference in the proportion of children diagnosed as neurologically abnormal. Nevertheless, it is possible to achieve interrater reliability in such tests (Rutter *et al.*, 1970).

It is not only the major requirement for age-related judgments that distinguishes the developmental neurological examination from the classical skills of the neurologist. The performances tested are often better seen as skills than as uncomplicated responses. Table 12-1 shows selected data from a battery of neurological tests adminstered to children with disorders of behavior and learning, and to normal controls. The items that best discriminated the children with psychological problems from their controls were complex indeed. Dysgraphesthesia, poor balance, and ataxia in fine rapid movements were the best discriminators. These tests have in common the requirement for a complex processing of information in the guidance of movement. They invite experimental psychological analysis, which might well lead to useful progress in understanding the nature of certain kinds of brain dysfunction. But certainly they do not share the validity of the classical neurological examination, based as it is upon correlations with structural neuropathology.

Developmental neurological signs are therefore not exempt from the requirements for validation set out in the first part of this chapter; yet all too

Table 12-1. Neurological examination in hyperactive and control children

SIGN	HYPERACTIVE ($n = 62$)	CONTROL ($n = 38$)
Poor articulation of consonants	50%	5%
Dysgraphesthesia	32%	5%
Poor balance (on one foot)	39%	8%
Inaccuracy in finger opposition	40%	16%
Choreiform movements	47%	11%
Finger–nose test	31%	16%
Dysdiadochokinesia (finger–thumb)	23%	5%
Impaired hopping	19%	0%
Impersistence of outstretched hands	18%	0%
Mirror movements of hands	42%	26%
Impaired two-point discrimination	34%	37%
Unequal ankle reflexes	5%	5%
Equivocal plantar response	21%	11%
Increased tone in lower limbs	3%	0%
Mild facial weakness	0%	5%
Abnormal jaw jerk	3%	3%

Note. The table shows the percentages of children in whom each sign was definitely present. The items are selected from a lengthier examination applied to 62 children referred for treatment of restlessness/inattention and 38 normal children who were free of problems but classmates of children referred. The examiner was blind to the diagnostic status of the children. Unpublished data from a series reported by Conners and Taylor (1980).

often they have not been examined in this way. However, it does appear that such sets of tests signficantly discriminate between the brain-damaged and the normal (Rutter *et al.*, 1970; Touwen & Kalverboer, 1973; Touwen & Prechtl, 1970).

Indeed, it would be surprising if they did not, given the extent to which motor abnormalities are presenting features of neurological disease. It is perhaps more noteworthy that there is substantial overlap, so that use of this test alone would lead to a rather high rate of misclassification. Thus, one score derived from the examination used in the Isle of Wight studies (Rutter *et al.*, 1970) classified 1 child out of 125 normals as brain-damaged and about 60% of neurologically diagnosed children. This is a clear distinction, but even so it is still a shaky basis for diagnosis. Consider, for the sake of argument (although of course the numbers are far too small for satisfactory extrapolation), a population of 2500 children, including 50 brain-damaged. On this basis, there will be about 40 children with abnormal examinations—20 of them brain-damaged and 20 of them normal. The test score above would therefore give a 50% false-positive rate and a 40% false-negative rate. The unusual feature about this test is not that it is poor at classification, but that it has been sufficiently well researched for judgments of this kind. It is also important to note that this score discussed above did *not* differentiate the intellectually retarded or the reading-delayed from normals. Individual items may be more discriminating, as shown in Table 12-1. It is therefore possible to construct a series of items that does predict both brain damage and psychological abnormalities, and further development of such tests is in order.

Other steps in validation will need more attention (see also Chapters 7 and 8 of this volume). Researchers and clinicians need to know more about the extent to which factors other than brain damage can affect examination scores. Chronological age, sex, and IQ are associated with test scores (Adams, Kocsis, & Estes, 1974; Myklebust, 1973; Peters, Romine, & Dykman, 1975), so that they must be interpreted developmentally; further, cooperation and motivation may also play a part.

Indeed, it is not clear that the neurological examination retains predictive power when the confounding effects of IQ are allowed for. It may be, for instance, that the higher frequency of neurological "soft signs" in the hyperkinetic than the neurotic is attributable, not to brain damage, but to lower IQ in the hyperkinetic group. In Sandberg *et al.*'s (1978) clinic study, such signs were related *only* to IQ among all the measures taken. The presence of this association in children within the normal range of intelligence implies that the point is not answered simply by excluding the retarded from one's studies.

The lack of other kinds of validation means that one must carefully consider how much congruity there is between the neurological examination and other ways of investigating the brain. Unfortunately, the importance of the question has not generated very much in the way of empirical research. Advocates of the examination must content themselves as best they can with such crumbs as the weak or absent association with an abnormal history—for example, the finding on the association with potentially damaging perinatal events (Nichols & Chen, 1981; Werry, 1968); the unreplicated finding of an association with a psychophysiological pattern of diminished response of the autonomic nervous system to novel or signal stimuli (Taylor, 1981); the inconsistent findings on any association with EEG abnormalities (Werry, 1968); and the high frequency of abnormalities in specific patterns of schizophrenia and character disorder (Quitkin, Rifkin, & Klein, 1976). At the same time, advocates must avert their gaze from the lack of any demonstrated association with drug response (Barkley, 1976) or the sequelae of head injury (Shaffer, Chadwick, & Rutter, 1975). At the most optimistic, one must reckon with the need thoroughly to include the developmental status of children in any interpretation of their examinations; at worst, one must be prepared to regard such an examination as an index only of motor learning, susceptible to the same influences as other kinds of learning, and like them bearing only a remote relationship to the integrity of the brain.

If I have stressed the present uncertainty rather than the potential of measures of neuromuscular coordination, it is because clinical and administrative practice often exaggerates the structure of interpretation that these measures can bear. Developmental screening of preschool children is now widely practiced in the United Kingdom, and is of course very valuable for the early identification of handicapping illnesses and sensory impairments. However, one of the purposes of the massive program is to detect the minor developmental neurological signs reviewed above in the expectation of making a preventive impact on later educational problems (Drillien & Drummond, 1977). It is not yet known that identifying children in this way is efficient or useful—or even safe.

NEUROPHYSIOLOGICAL MEASURES

Physiological measures, like the neurological tests I have considered, give at first glance a high promise that they can measure organic cerebral events. This promise may be illusory; it is all too easy to be trapped into a fallacy of physiological primacy. This fallacy asserts that a physically recorded event is determined by physical factors. In fact, however, many of the events recorded physiologically are best seen as forms of behavior. It is obvious that lacrimation is better seen as reflecting misery than as reflecting localized cerebral activity. Less obviously, changes in the form of the evoked potential (EP) wave can just as well be the consequences of altered attention as the causes of it. The question of validation therefore must be approached systematically.

There is of course no doubt that some EEG findings are more common in damaged brains. It is equally clear that there is a rich association between learning disorders and other sorts of EEG abnormalities (Taylor, 1980b). What is not established is whether these two kinds of EEG abnormalities are similar. The first kind of pattern—with unequivocal, often localizing, signs of abnormal physiological activity (such as spikes)—is useful for neurological diagnosis, but it is seldom encountered in the hyperactive or learning-disordered populations for whom evidence of brain dysfunction is most eagerly sought. Visual inspection of ink-and-paper records has given a rather conflicting set of findings, from which one cannot conclude even that such abnormalities are more common in groups with psychopathology (Harris, 1977). Though valid, these measures are not particularly useful for the detection of minor dysfunction.

The second kind of EEG abnormality is a quantitative deviation in function, whose detection often requires very sophisticated instrumentation and analysis. EP and power spectrum measures are the most used. These have proved most promising in their ability to show robust differences between learning-disordered children and normals. Those with learning disabilities show, for instance, a smaller amplitude of late components of the averaged visual evoked response (Conners, 1970a; Preston, Guthries, & Childs, 1974); a smaller contingent negative variation (Dykman *et al.*, 1971); more power at most frequencies of the EEG (Maxwell, Fenwick, Fenton, & Dollimore, 1974), but a deficit in the high-frequency, 40-Hz component (Sheer, 1976) and possibly in other frequencies too (Shaw, 1976); diminished autonomic reactions to signal stimuli (Dykman *et al.*, 1971); and diminished attenuation of the alpha rhythm by mental activity (Fuller, 1977). Measures such as these—particularly unresponsiveness to stimuli—also discriminate between hyperactive children and normal controls (Cohen & Douglas, 1972; Prichep, Sutton, & Hakerem, 1976; Satterfield & Dawson, 1971; Taylor, 1981), though it is unclear whether this is due to the high frequency of conduct disorder in both, or some other pattern of clinical features. It is also unclear whether these high-level abnormalities are pointers to brain damage, or rather whether they reflect dysfunction only at the psychological level.

The most ambitious and consistent approach to these issues has been that of "neurometrics" as developed by John and his associates (John, Karmel, Corning, Easton, Brown, Ahn, John, Harmony, Prichep, Toro, Gerson, Bartlett, Thatcher, Kaye, Valdes, & Schwartz, 1977; see Chapter 11 of this volume). A very extensive (and expensive) set of EEG measures yields a rich harvest of abnormalities in "learning-disordered" groups. This does not, of course, validate the Neurometric Test Battery as a measure of brain damage. The best evidence on that point is that the battery differentiated children at a pediatric neurology clinic from normals; but this is not enough. The neurological characteristics of the referred group are not clear, and one must suspect that many of them had problems of learning or behavior alone, and were referred for an opinion on neurological status. As a result, the question of brain dysfunction is largely begged. I do not mean to argue that the tests are valueless, but only that they must not be uncritically accepted as tools for establishing the presence or absence of organic abnormalities. Further development will be needed before they can be used for that purpose.

Indeed, a substantial amount of development will be necessary before they can usefully give that information in an individual case. If we take the figures that 4% of a normal population is ascertained by the Neurometric Test Battery, while 50% of patients "at risk" for neurological illness are also ascertained; and if we make the rather generous assumption that as many as 5% of children are "at risk"; then the difference in base rates implies that a child ascertained by the Neurometric Test Battery is twice as likely *not* to be "at risk" as he or she is to be so. This is a better level of prediction than that allowed for by many psychological tests, but it does not allow for strong diagnostic conclusions.

The absence of effect of social class, sex, and culture upon these measures is a welcome part of the development of the Neurometric Test Battery. The relationships with IQ and mental age remain to be tested. It is not to be expected that the effect of IQ is removed merely by excluding intellectually retarded children, for it is likely that important associations between evoked potentials and IQ exist within the normal range (Callaway, 1973; Eysenck, 1981). The suggestion that this method shows different anatomical foci in different categories of underachievement is most interesting—and also rather surprising, in view of the crude nature of these categories. Of course, the use of this test battery to detect underachievement would be rather cumbersome and costly. It would only be justifiable if children identified by the battery, but not identified by psychological testing, proved to be very prone to school failure on follow-up. It would be quite unacceptable to exclude educationally retarded children who are neurometrically normal from qualifying for remedial programs or special aid. Neither should anyone be tempted to think that these unsupported measures, if abnormal in a group of children failing educationally, would show that there was "really" something wrong with the children. They might still be neurologically normal victims of psychosocial adversity.

Indeed, in the current state of knowledge, it would not be right to make any educational decisions on the basis of inferences about neurophysiological status. Some of the features of current physiological measures suggest that they do not contain very much information about complex psychological processes. The averaged EP, for instance, is derived from recordings of the responses to a stimulus presented very many times. It is therefore confined inescapably to those events after a stimulus that follow an absolutely consistent time course. Any process whose latency or localization varies with changes in the stimulus or the subject is likely to be excluded from analyses so far available. There are many other biological measures that also relate to aspects of brain function. In general, however, there is still very little information on how they are associated with psychological functioning in children.

In principle, biochemical approaches can be used as indexes to the activity of systems of neurons within the brain. For example, one can assay the concentration in cerebrospinal fluid (CSF) of the metabolites of neurotransmitters. The beginnings of biochemistry–behavior correlations have suggested that, among autistic children, those with most stereotypy and hyperactivity have most CSF homovanillic acid (Cohen, Caparulo, Shaywitz, & Bowers, 1977); and that some children with "MBD" may show reduced levels of this metabolite of dopamine (Shaywitz, Cohen, & Bowers, 1977). Biochemical measures can also be a guide to the activity of peripheral neuronal systems; the concentration of the enzyme dopamine-β-hydroxylase in blood and urine has been regarded as an index of autonomic nervous system activity, and altered levels have been noted in some children with hyperactivity (Rapoport *et al.*, 1977) and in young adults with attentional deficits (Spring, Nuechterlein, Sugarman, & Matthysse, 1977). However, biochemical studies so far are scanty and inconclusive. While such measures can be altered by the activity of neurones, they are susceptible to many other influences, such as diet, and methodological pitfalls abound (Cohen & Young, 1977). This kind of abnormality can be the result as well as the cause of psychological events.

Other promising biological measures, such as regional cerebral blood flow and positron emission tomography, deserve application. A few of them (such as indexes of lead intoxication) should be regarded as signs of potential insults to the brain rather than as measures of brain function. Some (such as the pharmacological dissection of behavior) are considered in Chapter 16 of this volume. Others, primarily investigations of brain structure (such as computerized axial tomography) may have strong implications for function. Hier, Le May, Rosenberger, and Perlo (1978), for example, have used evidence of a structural difference in "dyslexic" children—a reversal of the normal pattern of asymmetry in cerebral fissures—as the basis for interpretations about functioning (in this case, that reading delay results when the processes involved are carried on in the hemisphere less well suited to them).

There is, in sum, high promise of important advances from the relating of physiological measures to psychological processes. This enterprise is in its infancy, with the exception of the quantitative analysis of surface EEGs, which can perhaps be said to have reached early childhood. For the present, the gap between the behavioral and the neurophysiological levels of discourse remains unbridged. Much research will be necessary before physiological measures are valuable as evidence of damaged brain functioning or as guides to intervention.

CONCLUSIONS: OUTSTANDING ISSUES

I have argued that the detection of minor degrees of neurological abnormality is an uncertain business. None of the measures reviewed is wholly satisfactory for this purpose, according to the standards outlined at the beginning of this chapter. To say this is not to be nihilistic, but to emphasize the research work that still has to be done. Many of the criticisms made apply chiefly to the uncritical use of single tests; the combination of abnormalities on different kinds of tests may well be a very much more powerful means of identifying minor dysfunction. One of the outstanding issues is the need for adequate validation of instruments for this purpose. When they have been validated, they will be useful for etiological research, for forensic purposes, and perhaps for prognosis. They should not be expected to be equally useful for suggesting and guiding treatment or education. The second outstanding issue is therefore the need for the development of descriptive tests and methods of analysis for individuals.

Another outstanding major issue, which is bound up with both the other two, is that of the interrelations of different measures. The search for biological correlates of psychological symptoms has been rather unrewarding; if any pathological concepts have been firmly supported in this way, they are only the very general notion of behavior disorder and the more restricted idea of childhood psychosis. There are, however, suggestions that the refinement of psychological description should allow for more specific associations to be found, as in the case of pervasive hyperkinesis. The other strategy, of examining the meaningfulness of biological measures, has been little pursued. We are far indeed from understanding the nature of the links between the activity of neurons and the behavior of children. There is a major need for the encouragement of research by teams with expertise in both the psychological and biological domains. Without this, clinical practice is likely to remain the prey of controversy and dogma.

References

Adams, R. M., Kocsis, J. J., & Estes, R. E. Soft neurological signs in learning-disabled children and controls. *American Journal of Diseases of Children*, 1974, *128*, 614–618.

Barkley, R. A Predicting the response of hyperkinetic children to stimulant drugs: A review. *Journal of Abnormal Child Psychology*, 1976, *4*, 327–348.

Callaway, E. Correlations between average evoked potentials and measures of intelligence. *Archives of General Psychiatry*, 1973, *29*, 553–558.

Campbell, D. T., & Fiske, D. W. Convergent and discriminant validation by the multitrait–multimethod matrix. *Psychological Bulletin*, 1959, *56*, 81–105.

Campbell, S. B., Endman, M. W., & Bernfeld, G. A three-year follow up of hyperactive preschoolers into elementary school. *Journal of Child Psychology and Psychiatry*, 1977, *18*, 239–249.

Cantwell, D. P. Brain damage and psychiatric disorder in childhood. In C. F. Purcell, (Ed.), *Psychopathology of children and youth: A cross-cultural perspective*. New York: Josiah Macy, Jr., Foundation, 1980.

Chadwick, O., Rutter, M., Brown, G., Shaffer, D., & Traub, M. A prospective study of children with head injuries: II. Cognitive sequelae. *Psychological Medicine*, 1981, *11*, 49–61.

Chess, S., & Hassibi, M. Behavior deviations in mentally retarded children. *Journal of the American Academy of Child Psychiatry*, 1970, *9*, 282–297.

Clarke, A. M., & Clarke, A. D. B. The changing concept of intelligence. In A. M. Clarke & A. D. B. Clarke (Eds.), *Mental deficiency: The changing outlook* (3rd ed.). London: Methuen, 1974.

Clements, S. *Minimal brain dysfunction in children* (NINDS Monograph No. 3, U.S. Public Health Service Publication NO. 1415). Washington, D.C.: U.S. Government Printing Office, 1966.

Cohen, D. J., Caparulo, B. K., Shaywitz, B. A., & Bowers, M. B. Jr. Dopamine and serotonin in neuropsychiatrically disturbed children. *Archives of General Psychiatry*, 1977, *34*, 545–550.

Cohen, D. J., & Young, J. G. Neurochemistry and child psychiatry. *Journal of the American Academy of Child Psychiatry*, 1977, *16*, 353–411.

Cohen, N., & Douglas, V. Characteristics of the orienting response in hyperactive and normal children. *Psychophysiology*, 1972, *9*, 238–246.

Conners, C. K. A teacher rating scale for use in drug studies with children. *American Journal of Psychiatry*, 1969, *126*, 152–156.

Conners, C. K. Cortical visual evoked response in children with learning disorders. *Psychophysiologyd*, 1970, *7*, 418–428. (a)

Conners, C. K. Symptom patterns in hyperkinetic, neurotic and normal children. *Child Development*, 1970, *41*, 667–682. (b)

Conners, C. K. Methodological considerations in drug research with children. In J. M. Wiener (Ed.), *Psychopharmacology in childhood and adolescence*. New York: Basic Books, 1977.

Conners, C. K. *Food additives and hyperactive children*. New York: Plenum Press, 1980.

Conners, C. K., & Taylor, E. Pemoline, methylphenidate, and placebo in children with minimal brain dysfunction. *Archives of General Psychiatry*, 1980, *37*, 922–930.

Crome, L. The brain and mental retardation. *British Medical Journal*, 1960, *1*, 897–904.

Douglas, V. Stop, look and listen: The problem of sustained attention and impulse control in hyperactive and normal children. *Canadian Journal of Behavioural Science*, 1972, *4*, 259–282.

Drillien, C. M., & Drummond, M. B. (Eds.). *Neurodevelopmental problems in early childhood: Assessment and management*. Oxford: Blackwell Scientific Publications, 1977.

Dykman, R., Ackerman, P., Clements, S., & Peters, J. Specific learning disabilities: An attentional deficit syndrome. In H. Mykelbust (Ed.), *Progress in learning abilities* (Vol. 2). New York: Grune & Stratton, 1971.

Eysenck, H. J. Biological measurement of IQ. In H. J. Eysenck & L. Kamin (Eds.), *Intelligence: The battle for the mind*. London: Macmillan, 1981.

Farnham-Diggory, S. Learning disabilities: A view from cognitive science. *Journal of the American Academy of Child Psychiatry*, 1980, *19*, 570–578.

Frostig, M., Lefever, D. W., & Whittlesey, J. R. B. *The Marianne Frostig Developmental Test of Visual Perception*. Palo Alto, Calif.: Consulting Psychologists Press, 1964.

Fuller, P. W. Computer-estimated alpha attenuation during problem solving in children with learning disabilities. *Electroencephalography and Clinical Neurophysiology*, 1977, *42*, 149.

Gittelman-Klein, R., & Klein, D. Are behavioral and psychiatric changes related in methylphenidate-treated, hyperactive children? *International Journal of Mental Health*, 1975, *4*, 182–198.

Harris, R. The EEG. In M. Rutter & L. Hersov (Eds.), *Child psychiatry: Modern approaches*. Oxford: Blackwell Scientific Publications, 1977.

Hier, D. B., LeMay, M., Rosenberger, P. B., & Perlo, V. P. Developmental dyslexia: Evidence for a subgroup with a reversal of cerebral asymmetry. *Archives of Neurology*, 1978, *35*, 90–92.

John, E. R., Karmel, B. Z., Corning, W. C., Easton, P., Brown, D., Ahn, H., John, M., Harmony, T., Prichep, L., Toro, A., Gerson, I., Bartlett, F., Thatcher, R., Kaye, H., Valdes, P., & Schwartz, E. Neurometrics. *Science*, 1977, *196*, 1393–1410.

Kirk, S. A., McCarthy, J. J., & Kirk, W. *The Illinois Test of Psycholinguistic Abilities* (*Rev. ed*). Urbana: University of Illinois Press, 1968.

Lindsay, J., Ounsted, C., & Richards, P. Long-term outcome in children with temporal lobe seizures: III. Psychiatric aspects in childhood and adult life. *Developmental Medicine and Child Neurology*, 1979, *21*, 630–636.

Maxwell, A. E., Fenwick, P., Fenton, G. W., & Dollimore, J. Reading ability and brain function: A simple statistical model. *Psychological Medicine*, 1974, *4*, 274–280.

Meehl, P., & Rosen, A. Antecedent probability of the efficiency of psychometric signs, patterns, or cutting scores. *Psychological Bulletin*, 1955, *52*, 194–216.

Myklebust, H. R. Identification and diagnosis of children with learning disabilities: An interdisciplinary study of criteria. *Seminars in Psychiatry*, 1973, *5*, 55–77.

Nichols, P. L., & Chen, T.-C. *Minimal brain dysfunction: A prospective study*. Hillsdale, N.J.: Erlbaum, 1981.

Nyhan, W. L. Behavior in the Lesch–Nyhan syndrome. *Journal of Autism and Childhood Schizophrenia*, 1976, *6*, 235–252.

Ojemann, G. Individual variability in cortical localisation of language. *Journal of Neurosurgery*, 1979, *50*, 164–169.

Pasamanick, B., & Knobloch, H. Brain damage and reproductive casualty. *American Journal of Orthopsychiatry*, 1960, *30*, 298.

Patterson, G. R. An empirical approach to the classification of normal disturbed children. *Journal of Clinical Psychology*, 1964, *20*, 326–337.

Peters, J. E., Romine, J. S., & Dykman, R. A. A special neurological examination of children with learning disabilities. *Developmental Medicine and Child Neurology*, 1975, *17*, 63–78.

Preston, A., Guthries, J. J., & Childs, B. Visual evoked responses in normal and disabled readers. *Psychophysiology*, 1974, *11*, 452–457.

Prichep, L., Sutton, S., & Hakerem, G. Evoked potentials in hyperkinetic and normal children under certainty and uncertainty. *Psychophysiology*, 1976, *13*, 419–428.

Quay, H. C. Measuring dimensions of deviant behavior: The behavior problem checklist. *Journal of Abnormal Child Psychology*, 1977, *5*, 277–289.

Quitkin, F., Rifkin, A., & Klein, D. F. Neurological soft signs in schizophrenia and character disorders. *Archives of General Psychiatry*, 1976, *33*, 845–853.

Rapoport, J. L., Pandoni, C., Renfield, M., Lake, C. R., & Ziegler, M. G. Newborn dopamine-β-hydroxylase, minor physical anomalies, and infant temperament. *American Journal of Psychiatry*, 1977, *134*, 676–679.

Reed, H. B. Jr., Reitan, R. M., & Kløve, H. Influence of cerebral lesions on psychological test performances of older children. *Journal of Consulting Psychology*, 1965, *29*, 247–251.

Reitan, R., & Boll, T. Neuropsychological correlates of minimal brain dysfunction. *Annals of the New York Academy of Science*, 1973, *205*, 65–88.

Ross, A. O. *Psychological aspects of learning disabilities and reading disorders.* New York: McGraw-Hill, 1976.

Rutter, M. Brain damage syndromes in childhood: Concepts and findings. *Journal of Child Psychology and Psychiatry*, 1977, *18*, 1–22.

Rutter, M., Graham, P., & Yule, W. *A neuropsychiatric study in childhood* (Clinics in Developmental Medicine Nos. 35–36). London: Spastics International Medical Publications/Heinemann Medical Books, 1970.

Sandberg, S., Rutter, M., & Taylor, E. Hyperkinetic disorder in psychiatric clinic attenders. *Developmental Medicine and Child Neurology*, 1978, *20*, 279–299.

Satterfield, J., & Dawson, D. Electrodermal correlates of hyperactivity in children. *Psychophysiology*, 1971, *8*, 191–197.

Schachar, R., Rutter, M., & Smith, A. The characteristics of situationally and pervasively hyperactive children: Implications of syndrome definition. *Journal of Child Psychology and Psychiatry*, 1981, *22*, 375–392.

Schulman, J., Kaspar, J., & Throne, F. *Brain damage and behavior: A clinical–experimental study.* Springfield, Ill.: Charles C Thomas, 1965.

Seidel, U. P., Chadwick, O. F. D., & Rutter, M. Psychological disorders in crippled children: A comparative study of children with and without brain damage. *Developmental Medicine and Child Neurology*, 1975, *17*, 563–573.

Selz, M., & Reitan, R. M. Rules for neuropsychological diagnosis: Classification of brain function in older children. *Journal of Consulting and Clinical Psychology*, 1979, *47*, 258–264.

Schaffer, D. Brain injury. In M. Rutter & L. Hersov (Eds.), *Child psychiatry: Modern approaches.* Oxford: Blackwell Scientific Publications, 1977.

Shaffer, D., Chadwick, O., & Rutter, M. Psychiatric outcome of localised head injury in children. In R. Porter & D. FitzSimons (Eds.), *Outcome of severe damage to the central nervous system.* Amsterdam: Elsevier–Excerpta Medica–North Holland, 1975.

Shaffer, D., McNamara, N., & Pincus, J. H. Controlled observations on patterns of activity, attention, and impulsivity in brain damaged and psychiatrically disturbed boys. *Psychological Medicine*, 1974, *4*, 4–18.

Shaw, J. C. Cerebral function and the EEG in psychiatric disorder: A hypothesis. *Psychological Medicine*, 1976, *6*, 307–311.

Shaywitz, B. A., Cohen, D. J., & Bowers, M. B. Jr. CSF amine metabolites in children with minimal brain dysfunction. (MBD). *Journal of Pediatrics*, 1977, *90*, 67–71.

Sheer, D. E. Focused arousal and 40 Hz EEG. In R. Knights & D. Bakker (Eds.), *The neuropsychology of learning disabilities.* Baltimore: University Park Press, 1976.

Spring, B., Nuechterlein, K. H., Sugarman, J., & Matthysse, S. The "new look" in studies of schizophrenic attention and information processing. *Schizophrenia Bulletin*, 1977, *3*, 470–482.

Taylor, E. Food additives, allergy, and hyperkinesis. *Journal of Child Psychology and Psychiatry*, 1979, *20*, 357–363.

Taylor, E. Brain damage: Evidence from measures of neurological function in children with psychiatric disorder. In E. F. Purcell (Ed.), *Psychopathology of children and youth: A cross-cultural perspective.* New York: Josiah Macy, Jr., Foundation, 1980. (a)

Taylor, E. Childhood disorders. In H. M. Van Praag, M. H. Lader, O. J. Rafaelson, & E. J. Sachar (Eds.), *Handbook of biological psychiatry.* New York: Dekker, 1980. (b)

Taylor, E. Development of attention. In M. Rutter (Ed.), *Scientific foundations of developmental psychiatry.* London: Heinemann Medical Books, 1980. (c)

Taylor, E. Neurophysiologische Grundlagen abnormen verhaltens. *Zeitschrift für Kinder und Jugendpsychiatrie*, 1981, *9*, 53–71.

Tizard, B., & Hodges, J. The effect of early institutional rearing on the development of eight-year-old children. *Journal of Child Psychology and Psychiatry*, 1978, *19*, 99–118.

Tizard, B., & Rees, J. A comparison of the effects of adoption, restoration to the natural mother, and continued institutionalization on the cognitive development of four-year-old children. *Child Development*, 1974, *45*, 92–99.

Touwen, B. C. L., & Kalverboer, A. F. Neurologic and behavioral assessment of children with "minimal brain dysfunction." *Seminars in Psychiatry*, 1973, *5*, 79–94.

Touwen, B. C. L., & Prechtl, H. F. R. *The neurological examination of the child with minor dysfunction* (Clinics in Developmental Medicine No. 38). London: Spastics International Medical Publications/Heinemann Medical Books, 1970.

Waldrop, M., Pederson, F., & Bell, R. Q. Minor physical anomalies and behavior in preschool children. *Child Development*, 1968, *39*, 391–400.

Wender, P. *Minimal brain dysfunction in children.* New York: Wiley, 1971.

Werry, J. Studies on the hyperactive child: IV. An empirical analysis of the minimal brain dysfunction syndrome. *Archives of General Psychiatry*, 1968, *19*, 9–16.

Werry, J., Minde, K., Guzman, A., Weiss, G., Dogan, K., & Hoy, E. Studies on the hyperactive child: VII. Neurological status compared with neurotic and normal children. *American Journal of Othopsychiatry*, 1972, *42*, 441–450.

Yule, W. Diagnosis: Developmental psychological assessment. In A. F. Kalverboer, H. M. Van Praag, & J. Mendlewiecz (Eds.), *Minimal brain dysfunction: Fact or fiction?* Basel: Karger, 1978.

SECTION THREE

Hyperkinetic/Attentional Deficit Syndrome

CHAPTER THIRTEEN

Behavioral Studies: Questions and Findings on the Concept of a Distinctive Syndrome

MICHAEL RUTTER

DIAGNOSTIC CONCEPTS

Most of the chapters in this section of the book assume the existence of a nosologically valid and clinically distinct hyperkinetic or attentional deficit syndrome. Some writers, wishing to emphasize the "constitutional" nature of the condition and its "medical" basis, have gone further in using the term "minimal brain dysfunction" (MBD) to include these postulates in the diagnostic label. The arguments in favor of this view have been expressed most fully, and most forcefully, by Wender (1971, 1978), who suggested that MBD constitutes a valid and meaningful psychiatric syndrome in which hyperactivity and attention deficits are the most prominent clinical features, but where there are the additional attributes of deficits in impulse control, altered interpersonal relations, altered emotionality, perceptual–cognitive abnormalities and congenital anatomical stigmata. However, he went on to add that the exact boundaries of the syndrome are unclear and that it is not known which symptoms are either necessary or sufficient for the diagnosis. There is the additional supposition that the hypothesized syndrome is due to a genetically transmitted biochemical abnormality, which probably involves a disorder of monoamine metabolism (See Chapter 15 of this volume). Other investigators have put the issues in a slightly different way but have concurred in the view that it constitutes a valid syndrome (e.g., Cantwell, 1977; Weiss & Hechtman, 1979)—a view reflected in its inclusion, together with operational criteria for diagnosis, in the most recent edition of the American Psychiatric Association's (1980) *Diagnostic and Statistical Manual of Mental Disorders* (DSM-III). On the other hand, systematic appraisals of the empirical research findings by a variety of reviewers have raised serious questions as to whether such validity has yet been established (Loney, 1980; Rapoport & Ferguson, 1981; Rie & Rie, 1980; Ross & Ross, 1976; Rutter, 1982a; see also Chapter 17 of this volume).

However, before considering the extent to which behavioral studies support the concept of a distinctive syndrome, it is necessary to outline in greater detail the characteristics of the syndrome whose validity is to be evaluated. DSM-III

Michael Rutter. Department of Child and Adolescent Psychiatry, University of London Institute of Psychiatry, London, England.

indicates that the onset is typically before age 3 years and invariably before 7; that developmentally inappropriate inattention (as shown by a failure to finish tasks, being easily distracted, not seeming to listen, or having difficulty concentrating), and impulsivity (as shown, for example, by difficulty organizing work, acting before thinking, or calling out in class) are the two crucial features; but that hyperactivity (as shown, for example, by excessive running about, difficulty staying seated, or restlessness while asleep) may not be present, that academic difficulties are common, and that there are a variety of associated features such as negativism, bullying, temper outbursts, and lack of response to discipline. This description is generally in line with those put forward by Wender (1971), Safer and Allen (1976), Weiss and Hechtman (1979), and other writers on the topic.

Because the behaviors said to be characteristic of the syndrome sound gross and easily distinctive, and because there is general agreement on the characteristic symptoms, it might be supposed that there would be high reliability in the diagnosis of the syndrome. However, this has not been found to be the case. Not only have several studies in the United States shown relatively low levels of agreement among parents, teachers, and clinicians on which children should be regarded as hyperkinetic (Kenny, Clemmens, Hudson, Lentz, Chicci, & Nair, 1971; Lambert, Sandoval & Sassone, 1978); but the syndrome also tends to be diagnosed nearly 50 times as often in North America as in Britain. In the former, the syndrome constitutes up to half (or sometimes even more than half) of all children referred to psychiatric clinics (Gross & Wilson, 1974; Huessy & Gendron, 1970; Safer & Allen, 1976; Wender, 1971), whereas in the United Kingdom the diagnosis is made in only about 1 or 2% of child patients of normal intelligence (Rutter, Shaffer, & Shepherd, 1975; Taylor, 1980).

Of course, it is possible (although unlikely) that this huge cross-national difference in diagnostic usage *could* reflect real differences in the prevalence of the syndrome—perhaps related to variations in environmental lead, food additives, genetic predisposition, or one of the other factors hypothesized to be causal. Direct international comparisons to examine this possibility have not yet been undertaken, although they are much needed. However, it seems fairly clear already that, whether or not there is some true difference in prevalence, there must also be differences between clinicians in the ways in which the diagnosis is made. This is strongly suggested by the finding that scores on the hyperactivity factor of the Conners scale (which shows good agreement with the diagnosis of the hyperkinetic syndrome in the United States) do not vary between countries in the directions expected on the basis of the syndrome diagnosis (Glow, 1979; Sandberg, Wieselberg, & Shaffer, 1980; Sprague, Cohen, & Eichlseder, 1977; Taylor & Sandberg, 1982; Trites, 1979). Thus, the mean hyperactivity score for boys in South London was .84 in the Taylor and Sandberg (1982) study, compared with a mean of .56 for boys in Pittsburgh (Goyette, Conners, & Ulrich, 1978) and the midwestern United States (Werry, Sprague, & Cohen, 1975), and a mean of 1.07 for boys in New Zealand (Werry & Hawthorne, 1976). Although the diagnosis of hyperkinetic or attentional deficit syndrome is made only infrequently in Britain, the behaviors of restlessness, fidgetiness, inattention, and disruptiveness are commonly noted in school classrooms. It is necessary to ask how such major differences in diagnostic practice could arise and what implications they carry for the concept of a coherent, valid biological syndrome.

Possible explanations for the differences in the frequency with which the syndrome is diagnosed need to be sought in the concept, in the epidemiological features, and in the findings on measurement. So far as the first is concerned, DSM-III points out that "because the symptoms are typically variable, they may not be observed directly by the clinician," and "typically the symptoms of this disorder in any given child vary with situation and time," and also "it is the rare child who displays signs of the disorder in all settings or even in the same setting at all times." The problem immediately arises as to which reports or which settings or which times or which measures should be given priority in coming to a diagnosis. While good empirical data on diagnostic practice are lacking, it would seem from a reading of clinical papers that clinicians in the United Kingdom tend to reserve the diagnosis for the very few children who are markedly overactive and inattentive in nearly all situations (Ingram, 1956; Ounsted, 1955), whereas, as is evident from the DSM-III criteria, the U.S. practice does not demand that the behaviors be pervasive.

Epidemiological findings highlight another issue: namely, that anything from a sixth to a half of children, according to a variety of general population surveys, are reported by their parents or teachers to be markedly overactive or inattentive (Lapouse & Monk, 1958; Rutter, Tizard, & Whitmore, 1970/1981; Werry & Quay, 1971). Even when combinations of symptoms are required, the prevalence is still quite high. Thus, if a cutoff point of 1.5 *SD* above the mean on the Conners scale is used, some 10 to 20% of children in the general population are identified as "hyperactive," and even if a 2.1 *SD* cutoff is used, still some 5% of children are selected (Trites, 1979). Of course, the figure obtained depends on the cutoff point used, but that immediately raises the question of how "severe" the behavior must be in order to be regarded as clinically significant. No satisfactory answer to the question is available, but clearly an answer is needed in that the behaviors that make up the syndrome are extremely common in the general population of elementary-school children.

A further feature that is evident from epidemiological data is the rather low level of agreement between teacher and parent reports (Campbell, Schleifer, & Weiss, 1978; Goyette *et al.*, 1978; Langhorne, Loney, Paternite, & Bechtoldt, 1976; Sandberg, 1981). The correlations on the hyperactivity factor scores between parent and teacher versions of the Conners scale have ranged from .18 to .36, with an across-study average of .26 (Sandberg, 1981). A similar lack of agreement between parents and teachers has been found with other questionnaires, with the consequence that whereas many children have high scores on *either* the parent or teacher scales, rather few have high scores on both. For example, the figures in the Isle of Wight study for hyperactivity as assessed on the Rutter scales were 16% and 2% respectively (Schachar, Rutter, & Smith, 1981). Several questions arise from these observations, but the most basic is whether the lack of agreement is a function of low reliability of the scale or of different concepts or perceptions of hyperactivity, or whether it is the case that many children are indeed overactive in some situations but not others. If the last proves to be correct, then of course there are the further questions of what characteristics of situation influence hyperactivity or inattention, whether deviant children respond to situational factors in the same way as do normal children, and whether there are clinically important differences between children who show situation-specific hyperactivity and those who are pervasively overactive.

Retest Reliability

Several different approaches have been followed in examining the reliability and validity of different measures of overactivity and inattention (Sandoval, 1977; Taylor, 1980). Firstly, retest reliability has been used as an index of the consistency and short-term temporal stability of measures. Not unexpectedly, this is high for questionnaires (see, e.g., Conners, 1973; Zentall & Barack, 1979), but interrater agreement provides a better test of reliability for this type of measure. However, retest assessments for standardized tests, for quantitative mechanical devices, and for observational measures have often shown surprisingly *low* levels of agreement. For example, Klein and Young (1979) found that *none* of their 17 observational variables measured on the morning of one school day correlated significantly with the same variables on the afternoon of the following day. The authors suggested that this was likely to be due to situational effects, as the morning lessons were academic and the afternoon lessons arts and crafts.

Montagu (1975) found a near-zero retest reliability (over a period of a few days) for motor activity as assessed from an ultrasonic system using the Doppler effect (although a much higher reliability for the children's noise level). Plomin and Foch (1981) found poor retest reliability (.33) for errors of omissions on the continuous-performance test assessment of sustained attention, but slightly better reliability (.47) for errors of commission. The free-play observational measures of activity level in the same study had a near-zero retest reliability over a 1- to 2-month period. In that the test–retest situations in these two studies were comparable (although nonstandard and unstructured), this suggests that there are sources of variation other than "situation" effects—at least as defined in terms of the supposed format and content of activities.

But, to a considerable extent, these very weak retest reliabilities are likely to be a function of taking very short samples of behavior (an hour or so) to measure enduring attributes. Numerous studies of variables of several different kinds have shown that this is a general problem. From moment to moment and from situation to situation, there is great variability in how any one person behaves (see Mischel, 1979), but this is in no way incompatible with the fact that there is also substantial consistency over time (Eysenck & Eysenck, 1980; Olweus, 1979, 1980). As Epstein (1979) showed in his general review of the issue, there is much greater temporal stability when the behavioral measures are averaged over a sufficient number of occurrences. Bell and Waldrop (1982) have made the same point with specific reference to hyperactivity, arguing that some half-dozen observational sessions are needed to obtain a valid differentiation of hyperkinetic children. Given this adequate range of sampling, measures of activity and attention may show quite good retest reliability, and indeed quite substantial stability over rather long periods of time. For example, Plomin and Foch (1981) found a test–retest reliability of .67 over a 1- to 2-month period for pooled 1-week pedometer scores (the pedometer being worn at the waist to record up and down movements of the trunk); Campbell *et al.* (1978) showed a correlation of .67 between preschool hyperactivity at 4½ years and the hyperactivity score on the Conners parent questionnaire at 6½; and Buss, Block, and Block (1980) found that actometer scores (an actometer is a modified self-winding watch that measures limb movement) at 3 years averaged over three 2-hour occasions a week or so apart correlated .44 with those at 4 years, with observer-based indexes showing even higher consistency (.75) over this 1-year period.

Interrater Reliability

Interrater reliabilities have usually been moderately high for questionnaire measures. Thus, the agreement between mothers and fathers on the hyperactivity factor score for the Conners scale was .55 in the Goyette *et al.* (1978) study, and the agreement among three child care workers in the Stevens, Kupst, Suran, and Schulman (1978) study ranged from .58 to .73. The agreement between teachers has tended to be of the same magnitude, or sometimes rather higher (e.g., .70 in Glow & Glow, 1980; .53 in Trites, Blouin, Ferguson, & Lynch, 1980). These levels of agreement are sufficient to justify the use of the scales, but they fall far short of unity, and it is necessary to ask why that is the case (a point considered further below).

Interrater reliability has usually been considerably higher for observational techniques. For example, Copeland and Weissbrod (1978) had interobserver agreements in the 93–97% range; Jacob, O'Leary, and Rosenblad (1978) found an average κ of .86 for interobserver agreement pooled over categories, groups, and settings; Blunden, Spring, and Greenberg (1974) had interrater correlations between .76 and .90; and Abikoff, Gittelman-Klein, and Klein (1977) showed a mean ψ coefficient of .76 for all observation categories, with similarly high reliability in a later replication study (Abikoff, Gittelman, & Klein, 1980).

The consistently greater interrater reliability (but *lower* retest reliability) of observational measures compared with questionnaire measures is striking and raises important questions as to possible reasons for the difference. At least four possibilities are immediately apparent: variations over time, situation specificities, types of overactivity, and disparities in people's concepts of hyperkinesis.

Interobserver agreement is calculated on the basis of multiple operationally defined items of molecular behavior as seen by two people at the same place and at the same (very brief) time. In sharp contrast, interrater agreement on questionnaires refers to rather broad behavioral attributions for children seen over lengthy periods of time in a variety of different situations. Thus, with questionnaires, there is more room for variations in the way in which the behavioral items are interpreted by the rater, as well as resulting from situational influences.

Little is known about the effects of altering the wording of questionnaires to increase their behavioral specificity. However, Sandoval's (1981) findings suggest that changes in the format of scales may make some difference, with advantages in the use both of more precise behavioral descriptions rather than judgmental items and of an admixture of positive and negative descriptors (for example, "does not sit still at desk during set work or regular class activities" and "stays calmly seated during school assemblies or other programs," rather than "restless or overactive"). Other studies, too, have provided evidence on the extent to which different questionnaire measures of hyperactivity agree with one another. For example, Sandberg *et al.* (1980) found that hyperactivity scores on the Rutter teacher scale correlated only .46 with hyperactivity scores on the Conners scale, even though both scales had been rated by the same teachers with reference to the same time period. The explanation lies in the fact that rather different behaviors are assessed by the hyperactivity factor on the two scales. On the Conners scale, the factor includes a variety of items on disruptive behavior (e.g., "demands attention," "disturbs," "excitable," "teases," "anxious to please"), whereas these are excluded from the hyperactivity factor on the Rutter scale. Not surprisingly, questionnaires such as the David and the Conners, with a greater overlap between the items assessing "hyperactivity," show greater agreement (Zentall & Barack, 1979).

Agreement across Measures and Settings

The possible importance of situational effects, of differences in rating perspectives, and of consistency among different aspects of hyperactivity and inattention can be considered through an examination of the empirical findings on the extent of agreement across measures and across settings. As already noted, most studies have shown quite low correlations between parent and teacher ratings of hyperactivity. All findings show *some* agreement between parent and teacher ratings (usually at a statistically significant level), but the generally low level indicates either marked situational effects or differences in the concepts used or behaviors tapped.

Various studies have tackled this issue by determining the level of agreement between questionnaire scores and systematic observation measures. The general finding has been that there is at best only a moderate level of agreement (Abikoff *et al.*, 1977; Blunden *et al.*, 1974; Copeland & Weissbrod, 1978; Klein & Young, 1979; Rapoport & Benoit, 1975; Whalen, Collins, Henker, Alkus, Adams, & Stapp, 1978), but all investigations have suffered from the limitation that the behaviors observed and the behaviors rated were not the same. In particular, the observations usually dealt with highly specific items, such as children leaving their chairs or being off task, whereas the ratings have been both more general and more judgmental. A further reason for expecting low agreement is that the two have not dealt with the same period of time—the observation scores applied strictly to the hour or so of observation, whereas the teacher or parent ratings were made on the basis of observations of children's behavior over many months. Moreover, as already noted, low agreement would also be expected on the basis of the low retest reliability of most observational measures.

Rather more light is thrown on the matter by studies looking at the *pattern* of agreements across measures and situations. Thus, Stevens *et al.* (1978), in a study of 13 boys in a day hospital program, found that actometer scores of children varied markedly among settings (the classroom, the gymnasium, the woodshop, and a group therapy session). Moreover, questionnaire ratings generally showed a substantial correlation with actometer counts in the *same* setting, but a much lower correlation with counts in other settings. Similarly, Schulman, Kaspar, and Throne (1965) found only a .26 correlation between the total actometer score for the day as a whole and scores for structured task activity, and only a .15 correlation between waking activity levels and sleeping activity levels. As these measures were strictly objective and quantified, it may be concluded that children's levels of activity do indeed truly vary across situations and, hence, that part of the explanation for the low agreement between parents and teachers is likely to lie in the situation specificity of some children's overactive behavior. However, the Stevens *et al.* (1978) study also brings out another point: namely, that mothers' ratings correlated best with the children's activity level in *unstructured* rather than structured settings. That raises the issues of which setting best reflects those elements of hyperactivity most relevant to the diagnosis.

Glow and Glow (1980) compared self-ratings, peer ratings, teacher ratings, and parent ratings for 20 normal children. The findings showed substantially greater overlap between peer and teacher ratings (which applied to fairly comparable situations) than between peer and parent ratings (which did not), suggesting the importance of situational effects. However, the results also showed that the various ratings tended to reflect different *aspects* of behavior. Thus, when peer and teacher ratings were pooled to produce an overall factor matrix, the peer rating of hyperactivity loaded on an attention deficit factor, whereas the teacher rating loaded on an unsocialized behavior factor. The findings were even more complex when peer and parent ratings were pooled, in that the peer rating of hyperactive loaded on the attention-getting factor; whereas the parent rating of hyperactive–impulsive showed no strong relationship with any factor (although it had the strongest loading on shy–sensitive!), and the rating of immature–inattentive had a strong negative loading on the social competence factor.

The findings indicate that there may be more than one type of overactivity, and certainly that hyperactivity is not a unitary variable. Klein and Young (1979), for example, suggested that there may be anxious hyperactives, conduct-problem hyperactives, inattentive hyperactives, and hyperactive children with little in the way of problems. As usually conceived, hyperactivity involves a range of behaviors that include squirmy fidgetiness while stationary, gross motor activity such as rushing around or repeatedly getting up and down out of one's chair, impulsiveness, socially inappropriate behavior, socially disruptive behavior, and inattention. In this connection, it should be appreciated that it is not self-evident which aspect of hyperactivity is most valid or relevant for syndrome identification. It could well be the case that the most important feature for diagnostic differentiation is not the sheer amount of limb movement, but rather the inappropriate or inadequate *modulation* of activity level (Whalen *et al.*, 1978). If so, the issue of situation variability in hyperactivity may be crucial—a point discussed in greater detail below.

Much the same issues and conclusions apply to the measurement of inattention—a concept that is probably even more complex and multifaceted than activity (Berlyne, 1970; Keogh & Margolis, 1976; Taylor, 1980; see also Chapter 14 of this volume). Children need not only to direct and sustain their attention to tasks, maintaining appropriate vigilance, but also to divide their attention, selectively responding to some cues but ignoring others. A variety of tests have been shown to have reasonable retest reliability and predictive validity. However, although the different measures tend to intercorrelate positively, they do so at a quite low level (Keogh & Margolis, 1976). Thus, Stores, Hart, and Piran (1978), in a study of epileptic children, found generally low intercorrelations between a continuous-performance test and a measure of distractibility, and between both of these and a teacher rating of inattentiveness. Similarly, in a study of both normally achieving and educationally handicapped boys in third through eighth grades, Keogh and Margolis (1976) found that the correlations between attentional measures based on the Children's Embedded Figures Test, the Matching Familiar Figures Test, and the Children's Checking Task, were only moderate (.01 to .50) and of similar magnitude to the correlations with reading achievement (although much greater than those with IQ). Similarly, Plomin and Foch (1981) found no significant correlation between perceptual-speed tests (in which children must seek a balance between speed and accuracy) and measures of sustained attention and selective attention. The former differentiated pediatrician-diagnosed hyperactive children from normals, whereas the latter two did not in this study. On the other hand, somewhat different findings have emerged from other investigations (see below). The question of which of these attentional measures are most relevant to the concept of an attention deficit syndrome remains unresolved (but see also Chapter 14).

SITUATION EFFECTS

It seems, then, that quite apart from differences between measures and between raters, children truly do vary in their activity and attentiveness across different situations. The next issue is what characteristics of the situations and of the children determine this variability. So far, there have been only a very few investigations that have tackled the problem, but they provide some useful pointers. Whalen and her colleagues (Whalen *et al.*, 1978; Whalen, Henker, Collins, Finck, & Dotemoto, 1979) have compared hyperactive boys, both on and off medication, with normal boys in experimentally manipulated classrooms during a naturalistic summer school program. They found that all groups showed the lowest levels of task attention when given a difficult task at which they had to work at a pace set by the teacher rather than by themselves. However, the effects were greatest for the nonmedicated hyperactive boys, and indeed there were no differences between the hyperactive and control groups in the self-paced, easy-materials condition. A further study showed similar findings with respect to the effects of noise (a radio tuned to a rock music station). Jacob *et al.* (1978) also used systematic observational techniques to compare hyperactive and normal children in different types of classrooms—the situational variable in their case being the degree of "formality" (meaning whether they were expected to remain in their seats and do assigned work or to choose among various educational games that often required cooperation with other children). Overall, the hyperactive children were somewhat less affected than the controls by the difference in settings, but the differences between the two groups of children were most striking in the formal setting. Whereas the hyperactive children did not differ from controls in "changes in position" (a measure of motor restlessness) or in their production of "weird sounds" in the *informal* classroom, they showed markedly higher scores on both in the *formal* classroom. The hyperactive children actually showed less daydreaming than did controls in the informal classroom, but again they showed more in the formal setting. Zentall (1980) examined the same issue with 31 matched pairs of hyperactive and normal children studied in six classroom settings. Like Jacobs *et al.* (1978), he found that the differences between the two groups were influenced by the setting, the hyperactive children being most clearly differentiated in familiar, structured settings. Interestingly, hyperactive children were not behaviorally distinctive in novel settings—a finding that perhaps explains why overactivity in the pediatrician's office is not a particularly good predictor (Sleator & Ullman, 1981).

It may be concluded that, at least as usually diagnosed, abnormal hyperactivity is likely to be most readily apparent in the classroom at times when the children are being expected to be involved in formal work. Normal children are more overactive in free-play settings, but, although hyperkinetic children are too, the differences between them are least apparent in those circumstances. It may well be that it is hyperkinetic children's limited ability to modify their behavior according to the needs and demands of the situation that is most diagnostically characteristic. If so, one might predict that pervasive overactivity should differ from situational overactivity, and that, within the latter group, overactivity at school may be more important diagnostically than overactivity at home.

SITUATIONAL VERSUS PERVASIVE HYPERACTIVITY

The next issue, then, is whether there is any utility to the distinction between children who are hyperactive in only some situations ("situational hyperactivity") and those who are hyperactive in most ("pervasive hyperactivity"). Schleifer and his colleagues (Schleifer, Weiss, Cohen, Elman, Cvejic, & Kruger, 1975) were probably the first investigators to make systematic use of this distinction, and a 2-year follow-up study of the preschoolers in that project showed that the pervasively hyperactive children requested more feedback from their mothers, talked more in a problem-solving situation, and made more immature moral judgments (Campbell, Schleifer, Weiss, & Perlman, 1977). A further follow-up a year later (Campbell, Endman, & Bernfeld, 1977) confirmed the prognostic validity of the differentiation between situational and pervasive hyperactivity. Other classroom observations showed that the pervasive hyperactives were more often out of their seats and more often off task than were either situational hyperactives or classroom controls. Teacher ratings on the Conners scale showed no differences between the situational and pervasive hyperactives on either the hyperactivity or conduct problem factors, but the pervasive hyperactives were significantly more inattentive. In short, the results suggest that the pervasive hyperactives not only showed a significantly worse prognosis, but also that the difference was most striking with respect to the attention deficits supposed by many clinicians to be basic to the hyperkinetic syndrome.

The possible importance of the situational versus pervasive distinction was further investigated by Schachar, Rutter, and Smith (1981), using data from the Isle of Wight follow-up study to age 15 of all children living on the island at age 10. Scores at age 10 on the hyperactivity factors of the Rutter parent and teacher scales were used to divide the population into the 2% with pervasive hyperactivity (i.e., high scores on both), the 14% with situational hyperactivity (i.e., a high score on one only), and the remainder. The results showed that pervasive hyperactivity was strongly associated with cognitive deficits and (independently of cognitive impairment) with overall behavioral disturbance, whereas situational hyperactivity was not. It was also found that the pervasive group had a worse prognosis over the next 4 years. Situational hyperactivity did not differ from other forms of disturbance with respect to either cognitive correlates or prognosis—a finding that suggests that hyperactivity in only one situation may be of little diagnostic importance. The results pointed to the importance of the distinction between pervasive and situational hyperactivity. However, it could be that the association with impaired cognition, overall behavioral disturbance, and poor prognosis was a function of pervasive deviance of any type, rather than of pervasive hyperkinesis as such. This possibility was examined by comparing pervasive and situational overactivity with pervasive and situational "unsociability." The results showed that the distinctive correlations applied specifically to *pervasive hyperkinesis* and not to other pervasive forms of abnormal behavior.

Further support for the suggestion that pervasive hyperkinesis may constitute a meaningful syndrome is provided by the findings on the very small subgroup of children in Sandberg, Rutter, and Taylor's (1978) clinic study who showed overactivity not only at home and at school, but also when systematically observed in a standard setting at the clinic. Even when matched with other clinic children for age and IQ, they showed significantly more anomalies on a neurodevelopmental examination, made more errors on the Matching Familiar Figures Test, and were significantly more likely to have been overactive from the preschool years.

Taylor (1980) has recently compared the very few (5%) Maudsley Hospital children rated as showing "gross hyperactivity" with other psychiatric clinic patients. The "grossly overactive" children (although the term is not explicitly defined as such, it probably means pervasive overactivity) were significantly more likely to have IQs below 70, clumsiness, specific developmental delays, and symptoms with a duration exceeding 3 years. Further research is needed into the situational versus pervasive distinction, but the rather few findings so far available point to the possible diagnostic validity of pervasive overactivity and the probable lack of possible nosological meaning in overactivity that is manifest in only one situation.

HYPERACTIVITY AND INATTENTION

In the discussion thus far, I have considered hyperactivity and inattention without focusing explicitly on the question of the extent to which, either singly or together, they constitute truly distinct dimensions or clusters of behavior. Achenbach and Edelbrock (1978) and Quay (1979) have reviewed factor-analytic studies, and both note that a hyperactivity dimension has been apparent in most studies, although it has not appeared in all. Since these reviews, Loney, Langhorne, and Paternite (1978), in an analysis of psychiatric clinic chart ratings, have shown a clear factor that loads on judgment deficits, hyperactivity, and inattention; Soli, Nuechterlein, Garmezy, Devine, and Schaefer (1981) demonstrated a somewhat similar factor, using problem checklists completed by the parents of children attending a child guidance clinic; and Schachar *et al.* (1981) found a hyperactivity factor (loading on "very restless, often jumping up and down, hardly ever still"; "squirmy, fidgety child"; and "cannot settle to anything for more than a few moments") that was consistent across age and sex in their reanalysis of the Isle of Wight general population data. Taylor and Sandberg (1982) found the same in their study of London school children. It seems that there is reasonable agreement on the presence of an identifiable dimension of behavior that usually includes gross overactivity, fidgetiness, and inattention. However, for several different reasons the finding says little about the meaningfulness of separating out hyperactivity and/or attention deficits as a separate diagnostic group. In the first place, the intercorrelations are likely to reflect the conceptions of the raters as much as the clustering of the behaviors (especially as many of the items are highly judgmental); in the second place, the correlations reflect associations across the whole range from normality to abnormality, whereas the associations may be different at the extremes (which possibly are most relevant for the testing of diagnostic hypotheses); thirdly, it is behaviors that are being correlated rather than *individuals* who are being clustered (although, of course, statistical techniques can be used for that purpose, too); and fourthly, the analyses have usually been conducted within a single instrument. The same intercorrelations and the same factors do *not* necessarily emerge if different instruments are pooled (Langhorne *et al.*, 1976). But most important of all, the analyses test neither the independence of the behavioral dimension nor its validity in terms of predicting to some other variable.

The extent to which hyperactivity and attention deficits are associated remains an important question that requires study. So far, the findings are rather inconclusive. The factor-analytic studies vary as to whether attentional deficits are included in the hyperactivity factor or constitute a separate dimension (Achenbach & Edelbrock, 1978; Lahey, Green, & Forehand, 1980; Quay, 1979), but, either way, intercorrelational data do not show whether the two are linked in children with extreme deviance. Certainly, there are many children who show attentional deficits but not hyperactivity, and the converse. Indeed, Ullman, Barkley, and Brown (1978), using a series of objective measures of activity and inattention, found that the two disabilities overlapped surprisingly little in their study of hyperactive children. On the other hand, Levy and Hobbes (1981) found that attentional measures derived from a continuous-performance test and the Draw-a-Line-Slowly Test provided a good differentiation between hyperkinetic and normal children. Clearly, there is *some* association between hyperactivity and inattention, in that most (but not all) investigators have found that hyperactive children performed poorly on measures of attention (Rosenthal & Allen, 1978). But this finding could be tautological in part, in that inattention is usually included in the criteria for the diagnosis.

Moreover, both the hyperactivity and the attention deficits could simply reflect aspects of overall disturbance. The data from Firestone and Martin's (1979) comparison of hyperactive, behavior problem, asthmatic, and normal children suggest that, at least to some extent, this may be the case. Clinically diagnosed hyperkinetic children were indeed much more active than the others, as shown by the stabilimetric cushion findings. However, they did not make more errors than the behavior problem group on the Matching Familiar Figures Test (although they had considerably longer latencies, suggesting that their cognitive style might be distinctive). On the other hand, the particular pattern found was inconsistent with that in other reports (Campbell, Douglas, & Morgenstern, 1971; Sandberg *et al.*, 1978).

These results allow no firm conclusions. What needs to be determined is whether attentional deficits (either in general or of a particular type) are more frequently found in children selected purely for hyperactivity than they are in nonhyperactive children with a similar degree of overall behavioral disturbance.

Furthermore, in terms of the hypothesis that attentional deficits constitute the "true" basis of the syndrome, there is the further question of whether children with hyperactivity associated with attentional deficits differ systematically from those with hyperactivity alone. These comparisons have not yet been made.

HYPERACTIVITY AND OTHER CLINICAL SYNDROMES

Hyperactivity and Learning Disorders

A further issue concerns the differentiation between the hyperkinetic/attention deficit syndrome and learning disorders. Usually these have been regarded as quite separate conditions (as reflected in their having separate sections in this volume). However, clinical studies have shown that the two sets of problems overlap very frequently (Silver, 1981). On the one hand, children identified as clinically hyperactive have been found to have rates of learning difficulties well above those in the general population. In Lambert and Sandoval's (1980) study, over a third of hyperkinetic children had some type of learning disability, a rate three times that of controls. Children with *non*hyperkinetic behavior disorders had an intermediate rate of learning disabilities. Not only is the overall academic achievement of hyperkinetic children usually below normal (Keogh, 1971), but also the rate of specific reading difficulties has been found to be substantially increased in most studies (Cantwell & Satterfield, 1978; Minde, Lewin, Weiss, Lavigueur, Douglas, & Sykes, 1971). As already noted, these cognitive and learning deficits are most frequently associated with pervasive hyperactivity (Schachar *et al.*, 1981), the link with situational overactivity being quite weak.

On the other hand, children identified as having specific learning disabilities have been found to have increased rates of attentional deficits, hyperactive behavior, and impulsivity (Rutter & Yule, 1977), although the association with specific features of hyperactivity/attention deficit seems no greater than that with measures of general behavioral disturbance (Aman, 1979). Because children with reading difficulties have seemed to show attentional deficits on tasks not involving reading (Malmquist, 1958; Rutter *et al.*, 1970/1981), and because hyperactive behavior has been found to predict reading difficulties (DeHirsch & Jansky, 1966), some writers have considered that the attentional difficulties predisposed such children to learning disabilities. On the other hand, there are also reasons for supposing that academic failure may generate inattention and hyperactivity (Cunningham & Barkley, 1978).

It is evident, then, that there is a substantial overlap between hyperactivity and learning disabilities. However, there are plenty of children with learning disabilities who do *not* show hyperactivity or attentional deficits, and there are hyperactive children whose learning and scholastic achievement is normal. It remains unclear whether these "pure" groups differ from the overlap group. Moreover, it is equally uncertain how far the link is specific to hyperactivity/attention deficit disorders and how far it is common to conduct disturbances as a whole. This issue is apparent in Delamater, Lahey, and Drake's (1981) comparison of hyperactive and nonhyperactive children with learning disabilities, in that the groups differed as much on conduct problems as they did on hyperactivity and inattention (as judged by their Conners scale scores). Nevertheless, it was striking that the hyperactive group had markedly lower IQ scores (a mean of 87 compared with 99 on the full scale of the Wechsler Intelligence Scale for Children, or WISC), and were more likely to have experienced "psychosocial stress"—although the groups did not differ on psychophysiological variables.

Nichols and Chen (1981) compared hyperactive and learning-disabled children, using data from the Collaborative Perinatal Project. In many respects, the two groups were similar. For example, both showed a male preponderance, an association with maternal smoking during pregnancy, perinatal problems and early developmental difficulties, cognitive deficits, attentional difficulties, impaired right–left differentiation, and the presence of retarded siblings. On the other hand, there were also important differences. Thus, the learning-disabled children tended to come from large families of low socioeconomic status, whereas the hyperkinetic children did not. Also, the family history findings were different, with the familial associations applying mainly to like disorders, with rather few links across the two conditions (i.e., hyperkinesis was associated with a family history of hyperactivity rather than of learning disorders, and vice versa). Neither showed a particularly strong association with neurological "soft signs," but the association was somewhat stronger in the case of hyperactivity. Of course, the children in the Nichols and Chen project were identified on relatively crude indexes, and it is highly likely that both the learning-disabled and hyperactive groups were heterogeneous in composition. Nevertheless, their findings suggest that the overall links between learning disabilities, hyperactivity, and neurological "soft signs" are too weak to justify the concept of a cohesive MBD syndrome. If there is such a syndrome, it will need to be based on more precise defining characteristics. That will require not only a clearer differentiation of what types of learning disorders and of hyperactivity are to be included, but also a better differentiation within the broad group of disturbances of conduct.

Hyperactivity and Conduct Disturbances

One of the central questions with regard to the validity of the hyperkinetic syndrome category is whether it shows any meaningful difference from general disorders of conduct. The question arises because of the huge overlap between hyperactivity and attentional deficits on the one hand, and disturbances of conduct on the other (Cantwell, 1980). Not only do several factor-analytic studies show that the two forms of behavior are included in the same factor, but even when they appear in different factors, hyperactivity and conduct disturbance measures tend to be highly intercorrelated in practice, in spite of the factors having been constructed to be orthogonal (Achenbach & Edelbrock, 1978; Lahey *et al.*, 1980; Quay, 1979). Moreover, the correlates of hyperactivity and the correlates of conduct disorder are closely similar as shown by a comparison of studies of the two syndromes (Sandberg *et al.*, 1978). It has been found in both general population (Sandberg *et al.*, 1980) and clinic studies (Sandberg *et al.*, 1978) that most children with disorders of conduct are also hyperactive, and (to a lesser extent) vice versa. On the other hand, there are some children with one set of behaviors but not the other, and several investigators have sought to determine whether they differ in any meaningful way.

Sandberg *et al.* (1978) compared psychiatric clinic children according to the presence or absence of hyperactivity on either the parent or teacher version of the Conners scale. No differences were found except (as noted above) in the case of the few children with pervasive hyperkinesis. Stewart and colleagues (Stewart, Cummings, Singer, & de Blois, 1981; Stewart, de Blois, & Cummings, 1980) also compared clinic children with hyperactivity alone, children with unsocialized aggression alone, and those with both. The "pure" hyperactives tended to have fewer symptoms of behavioral disturbance but a higher rate of learning difficulties than the other children did. Parental disorder (particularly antisocial personality and alcoholism) was associated with hyperactivity in the absence of aggression. Loney and her colleagues (Langhorne & Loney, 1979; Loney *et al.*, 1978) have made somewhat similar comparisons within a group of children *all* diagnosed as having the hyperkinetic or MBD syndrome. The exclusive hyperactives differed in terms of showing more errors on the Bender–Gestalt test and a better initial drug response; while both the exclusive aggressives and the hyperactive aggressives differed in coming from homes of lower socioeconomic status and in having less loving parents, fewer neurological "soft signs," and more aggression at follow-up. Interestingly, the hyperactive aggressives appeared to constitute a more extreme version of the aggressive group, so that in many instances they differed more markedly from the pure hyperactives than did the pure aggressives.

Prinz, Connor, and Wilson (1981) examined the links between hyperactivity and aggression by a different strategy. Using teacher ratings, they selected a group of disruptive hyperactive children whom they compared with a control group from the same classrooms. As expected, the hyperactive group showed much more aggressive behavior, as assessed on a daily behavior checklist. However, in addition, the occurrence of specific aggressive behaviors predicted the *same-day* occurrence of hyperactive behaviors, although the converse was not the case. The findings suggest a close intertwining of hyperactive and aggressive behaviors such that most aggressive children were also hyperactive (24 out of 26) and that there was strong conditional relationship between the two on a day-to-day basis. In contrast, there was a sizable group of hyperactive children who were not aggressive (50 out of 74).

More data are required before firm conclusions could be warranted. However, the pointers are that hyperactive aggressive children tend to be generally similar to nonhyperactive aggressive children, but that a "pure" hyperactive group may turn out to be somewhat distinctive in terms of a stronger association with cognitive problems.

Hyperactivity and "Psychopathy"

Disorders of conduct that involve socially disruptive, aggressive, or antisocial behavior constitute some half of the conditions seen by child psychiatrists at their clinics and also about half the disorders identified in general population surveys (Rutter *et al.*, 1970/1981; Graham, 1979). Most clinicians agree that conduct disorders constitute a heterogeneous group of problems, but there is far less agreement on the basis for subclassification (Rutter & Giller, 1983). The main interest with respect to disorders in childhood has centered on the notion of hyperkinetic or attentional deficit disorders as the key subgroup. However, in adulthood, the main thrust of research has been directed toward "psychopathy" (Hare, 1970; Hare & Schalling, 1978). The concept of psychopathy has proved at least as elusive and difficult to define as that of hyperactivity or attentional deficits. Nevertheless, there is a substantial body of evidence suggesting that psychopaths differ from nonpsychopathic criminals in their psychophysiological functioning, with psychopaths tending to show reduced anxiety and an impairment in passive avoidance learning following punishment. The evidence on children is very much more limited, but there are pointers suggesting that refractory delinquents tend to be differentiated by lower skin conductance reactivity with a longer recovery time (Borkovec, 1970; Davies & Maliphant, 1971a, 1971b; Siddle, Mednick, Nicol, & Foggitt, 1976; Siddle, Nicol, & Foggitt, 1973) and possibly by impaired passive avoidance learning (Davies & Maliphant, 1974). The parallels with the findings on hyperactivity are striking in that, although the research results are somewhat contradictory, there has been a general tendency for hyperactive children to be slower to respond to stimulation and to show reduced autonomic responses (Hastings & Barkley, 1978).

Some years ago, Quay (1965, 1977a, 1977b) proposed that psychopaths were motivated by an abnormally great need for stimulation. There have been rather few studies that have tested this suggestion, but the findings of the few that have done so (DeMyer-Gapin, & Scott, 1977; Orris, 1969; Whitehill, DeMyer-Gapin, & Scott, 1976) have been interpreted by the authors as confirmatory. On the other hand, equally, the behaviors found to be characteristic of "refractory" delinquents could be said to indicate restlessness, inattention, and boredom with externally imposed tasks—the features of hyperactivity and attention deficits.

There has been no research directed at the differentiation of the hyperactivity/attentional deficit syndrome from the syndrome of psychopathy, in that the two notions have stemmed from rather different theoretical orientations. Nevertheless, it is clear that both concepts have much in common, and that both are concerned with the general issue of whether there is a distinctive and meaningful subgroup of socially disruptive children that differs from the remainder of those with conduct disturbances.

CONCLUSIONS

It is all too obvious from this review of behavioral studies that researchers are far from having achieved a validated concept of a hyperkinetic/attentional deficit syndrome. The host of studies showing differences between hyperkinetic children (as diagnosed either by clinical judgment or questionnaire scores) and normal children are irrelevant to the issue of classification. However, they *do* negate the rather silly notion that the whole thing is a myth, involving no more than a "medical" label invented to justify giving drugs to children whose behavior is annoying to adults (Schrag & Divoky, 1975). It is quite clear that the phenomena of overactivity and inattention are real enough; observational studies show that these are *not* synonymous with disruptive behavior, and follow-up studies indicate that these behaviors are both socially handicapping and persistent (see Chapter 20 of this volume). The issue is *not* whether hyperactivity/attentional deficit syndromes differ from normality (which obviously they do), but rather whether they differ in any meaningful way from *other* psychiatric conditions.

For a diagnostic category to have scientific meaning, it must be shown to be distinctive in terms of etiology, course, response to treatment, or some variable *other than the symptoms that define it* (Rutter, 1978). Thus, it is of no avail to assert that what differentiates the hyperkinetic syndrome is the presence of hyperactivity, or that what differentiates the attentional deficit syndrome is the presence of attentional deficits! That is no more than a tautology. Rather, the key issue is whether the constellation of hyperkinetic or attentional deficit behaviors constitute a syndrome (or syndromes) that differ(s) from conduct disorders, depression, schizophrenia, sociopathy, and the like. The evidence on this issue is discussed in later chapters of this volume and is brought together by Ferguson and Rapoport in Chapter 17, with an essentially negative conclusion.

In my own review of the same issues (Rutter, 1981), I, too, have observed that the claims for the existence of a qualitatively distinct syndrome have far outrun the empirical findings that could justify them. But I have also noted that much of the research has been rather tangential to the issue of syndrome definition and that it is only now that some of the crucial investigations are being undertaken. Moreover, most studies have been concerned with rather broad, often ill-defined, and almost certainly heterogeneous groups of fidgety, restless, disruptive, and inattentive children. It may be that real differences have been concealed by the unhelpfully global nature of the categories studied. Accordingly, it was necessary to have recourse to the Scottish-style judicial verdict of "not proven."

In this chapter, I have focused on the behavioral evidence that provides pointers on the conceptual and methodological issues that need to be taken into account in deriving more homogeneous and valid diagnostic groups. It is apparent that there are a variety of methods available for the assessment of activity, attention, and related behaviors. It is quite feasible to develop accurate measures for the relevant features, and, indeed, to a very considerable extent such measures are ready to hand. However, it is also evident that activity and attention are themselves complex concepts that include several rather disparate characteristics. It is not yet clear precisely which types of hyperactivity or inattention are most relevant for syndrome definition. A further issue of great importance concerns the situational and temporal variability of these behaviors. This variability is great enough to make observational measures based on just one observational session highly suspect. If hyperactive or inattentive children are to be selected on the basis of observations, it will be essential to use composite measures pooled over several sessions. Moreover, it seems that free-play situations are inappropriate for this purpose and that familiar, structured task situations may be most suitable.

Questionnaire measures have the advantage of being much more economical in time and resources, as well as automatically covering children's behavior over a substantial period of time. On the other hand, they suffer from greater difficulties in the differentiation of overactive, inattentive, and socially disruptive behaviors. It is not that these three types of behavior involve the same concept, for they do not. Most factorial studies have shown a "hyperactivity" factor that is distinct from a factor characterized by socially disruptive, aggressive, and antisocial behavior (although studies differ on whether or not inattention is part of or separate from the hyperactivity factor—see Taylor & Sandberg, 1982). But, in practice, although the factors may be constructed to be orthogonal to one another, the behaviors that make up the factors have proved to be highly intercorrelated. As a result, it has not been easy to differentiate between hyperactive and nonhyperactive children with conduct disorders.

A further limitation of questionnaires is that, necessarily, they are based only on the behavior manifest in the presence of the rater. As much hyperactive inattentive behavior is situation-specific, this may mean that the questionnaire scores reflect a child's interaction pattern with the rater as much as they reflect an enduring behavioral characteristic (a problem shared with measures of temperamental style—see Rutter, 1982b). Accordingly, if questionnaires are to be used, it may be desirable to define the syndrome on the basis of abnormal scores on scales completed by at least two individuals who see the child in different situations. These could be a parent and a teacher (as usually it has been in previous attempts to identify *pervasive* hyperactivity), but it might also be two teachers or a teacher and a peer. In that connection, however, it should be noted that questionnaire measures of overactivity are probably more satisfactory than those of inattention. It may well be that inattention of some type will turn out to be the key element in the syndrome (see Chapter 14 of this volume), but research has not yet reached the stage where this can be reliably detected by questionnaire screening instruments.

When the evidence is considered as a whole, it is clear that there is no good support for the very broad notion of a hyperkinetic or attentional deficit syndrome, which is so frequent that it accounts for half the cases seen at child psychiatric clinics. But there are pointers that there may be a less common, valid syndrome, definable in terms of overactivity and inattention, that is manifest across a range of situations and circumstances. So far, the evidence in support of this hypothesis is too slender to consider it validated, but it remains a possibility well worth further investigation.

References

Abikoff, H., Gittelman-Klein, R., & Klein, D. F. Validation of a classroom observation code for hyperactive children. *Journal of Consulting and Clinical Psychology*, 1977, *45*, 772–783.

Abikoff, H., Gittelman, R., & Klein, D. F. Classroom observation code for hyperactive children: A replication of validity. *Journal of Consulting and Clinical Psychology*, 1980, *48*, 555–565.

Achenbach, T. M., & Edelbrock, C. S. The classification of child psychopathology: A review and analysis of empirical efforts. *Psychological Bulletin*, 1978, *85*, 1275–1301.

American Psychiatric Association. *Diagnostic and statistical manual of mental disorders* (3rd ed.). Washington, D.C.: Author, 1980.

Aman, M. G. Cognitive, social, and other correlates of specific reading retardation. *Journal of Abnormal Child Psychology*, 1979, *7*, 153–168.

Bell, R. Q., & Waldrop, M. F. Temperament and minor physical anomalies. In R. Porter & G. Collins (Eds.), *Temperamental differences in infants and young children* (Ciba Foundation Symposium No. 89). London: Pitman Books, 1982.

Berlyne, D. E. Attention as a problem in behavior therapy. In D. Mostofsky (Ed.), *Attention: Contemporary theory and analysis*. New York: Appleton-Century-Crofts, 1970.

Blunden, D., Spring, C., & Greenberg, L. M. Validation of the classroom behavior inventory. *Journal of Consulting and Clinical Psychology*, 1974, *42*, 84–88.

Borkovec, T. D. Autonomic reactivity to sensory stimulation in psychopathic, neurotic, and normal juvenile delinquents. *Journal of Consulting and Clinical Psychology*, 1970, *35*, 217–222.

Buss, D. M., Block, J. H., & Block, J. Preschool activity level: Personality correlates and developmental implications. *Child Development*, 1980, *51*, 401–408.

Campbell, S., Douglas, V., & Morgenstern, G. Cognitive styles in hyperactive children and the effect of methylphenidate. *Journal of Child Psychology and Psychiatry*, 1971, *12*, 55–67.

Campbell, S. B., Endman, M. W., & Bernfeld, G. A three-year follow-up of hyperactive preschoolers into elementary school. *Journal of Child Psychology and Psychiatry*, 1977, *18*, 239–249.

Campbell, S. B., Schleifer, M., & Weiss, G. Continuities in maternal reports and child behaviors over time in hyperactive and comparison groups. *Journal of Abnormal Child Psychology*, 1978, *6*, 33–45.

Campbell, S. B., Schleifer, M., Weiss, G., & Perlman, T. A 2-year follow-up of hyperactive preschoolers. *American Journal of Orthopsychiatry*, 1977, *47*, 149–162.

Cantwell, D. Hyperkinetic syndrome. In M. Rutter & L. Hersov (Eds.), *Child psychiatry: Modern approaches.* Oxford: Blackwell Scientific Publications, 1977.

Cantwell, D. Hyperactivity and antisocial behavior revisited: A critical review of the literature. In D. Lewis (Ed.), *Biophysical vulnerabilities to delinquency*. New York: Spectrum, 1980.

Cantwell, D. P., & Satterfield, J. H. The prevalence of academic underachievement in hyperactive children. *Journal of Pediatric Psychology*, 1978, *3*, 163–171.

Conners, C. K. Rating scales for use in drug studies with children. *Psychopharmacology Bulletin*, 1973, 24–29.

Copeland, A. P., & Weissbrod, C. S. Behavioral correlates of the hyperactivity factor of the Conners teacher questionnaire. *Journal of Abnormal Child Psychology*, 1978, *6*, 337–343.

Cunningham, C. E., & Barkley, R. A. The role of academic failure in hyperactive behavior. *Journal of Learning Disabilities*, 1978, *11*, 15–21.

Davies, J. G. V., & Maliphant, R. Autonomic responses of male adolescents exhibiting refractory behaviour in school. *Journal of Child Psychology and Psychiatry*, 1971, *12*, 115–118. (a)

Davies, J. G. V., & Maliphant, R. Refractory behaviour at school in normal adolescent males in relation to psychopathy and early experience. *Journal of Child Psychology and Psychiatry*, 1971, *12*, 35–42. (b)

Davies, J. G. V., & Maliphant, R. Refractory behaviour in school and avoidance learning. *Journal of Child Psychology and Psychiatry*, 1974, *15*, 23–32.

DeHirsch, K., & Jansky, J. J. Early prediction of reading, writing, and spelling ability. *British Journal of Disorders of Communication*, 1966, *1*, 99–107.

Delamater, A. M., Lahey, B. B., & Drake, L. Toward an empirical subclassification of "learning disabilities": A psychophysiological comparison of "hyperactive" and "nonhyperactive" subgroups. *Journal of Abnormal Child Psychology*, 1981, *9*, 65–77.

DeMyer-Gapin, S., & Scott, T. J. Effect of stimulus novelty on stimulation seeking in antisocial and neurotic children. *Journal of Abnormal Psychology*, 1977, *86*, 96–98.

Epstein, S. The stability of behavior: I. On predicting most of the people much of the time. *Journal of Personality and Social Psychology*, 1979, *37*, 1097–1126.

Eysenck, M. W., & Eysenck, H. J. Mischel and the concept of personality. *British Journal of Psychology*, 1980, *71*, 191–204.

Firestone, P., & Martin, J. E. An analysis of the hyperactive syndrome: A comparison of hyperactive behavior problem, asthmatic and normal children. *Journal of Abnormal Child Psychology*, 1979, *7*, 261–273.

Glow, R. A. A validation of Conners TQ and a cross-cultural comparison of prevalence of hyperactivity in children. In G. Burrows & J. Werry (Eds.), *Advances in human psychopharmacology*. Greenwich, Conn.: JAI Press, 1979.

Glow, R. A., & Glow, P. H. Peer and self-rating: Children's perception of behavior relevant to hyperkinetic impulse disorder. *Journal of Abnormal Child Psychology*, 1980, *8*, 471–490.

Goyette, C. H., Conners, C. K., & Ulrich, R. F. Normative data on revised Conners parent and teacher rating scales. *Journal of Abnormal Child Psychology*, 1978, *6*, 221–236.

Graham, P. J. Epidemiological studies. In H. C. Quay & J. S. Werry (Eds.), *Psychopathological disorders of childhood* (2nd ed.). New York: Wiley, 1979.

Gross, M., & Wilson, W. C. *Minimal brain dysfunction.* New York: Brunner/Mazel, 1974.

Hare, R. D. *Psychopathy: Theory and research.* New York: Wiley, 1970.

Hare, R. D., & Schalling, D. (Eds.). *Psychopathic behaviour: Approaches to research.* Chichester, England: Wiley, 1978.

Hastings, J. E., & Barkley, R. A. A review of psychophysiological research with hyperkinetic children. *Journal of Abnormal Child Psychology*, 1978, *6*, 413–448.

Huessy, H. R., & Gendron, R. A. Prevalence of the so-called hyperkinetic syndrome in public school children in Vermont. *Acta Paedopsychiatrica*, 1970, *37*, 243–248.

Ingram, T. T. S. A characteristic form of overactive behaviour in brain-damaged children. *Journal of Mental Science*, 1956, *102*, 550–558.

Jacob, R. G., O'Leary, K. D., & Rosenblad, C. Formal and informal classroom settings: Effects on hyperactivity. *Journal of Abnormal Child Psychology*, 1978, *6*, 47–59.

Kenny, T. J., Clemmens, R. L., Hudson, B. W., Lentz, G. A., Chicci, R., & Nair, P. Characteristics of children referred because of hyperactivity. *Journal of Pediatrics*, 1971, *79*, 618–622.

Keogh, B. K. Hyperactivity and learning disorders: Review and speculation. *Exceptional Children*, 1971, *38*, 101–107.

Keogh, B. K., & Margolis, J. S. A component analysis of attentional problems of educationally handicapped boys. *Journal of Abnormal Child Psychology*, 1976, *4*, 349–359.

Klein, A. R., & Young, R. D. Hyperactive boys in their classroom: Assessment of teacher and peer perceptions, interactions and classroom behaviors. *Journal of Abnormal Child Psychology*, 1979, *7*, 425–442.

Lahey, B. B., Green, K. D., & Forehand, R. On the independence of ratings of hyperactivity, conduct problems, and attention deficits in children: A multiple-regression analysis. *Journal of Consulting and Clinical Psychology*, 1980, *48*, 566–574.

Lambert, N. M., & Sandoval, J. The prevalence of learning disabilities in a sample of children considered hyperactive. *Journal of Abnormal Child Psychology*, 1980, *8*, 33–50.

Lambert, N. M., Sandoval, J., & Sassone, D. Prevalence of hyperactivity in elementary school children as a function of social system definers. *American Journal of Orthopsychiatry*, 1978, *48*, 446–463.

Langhorne, J. E., Jr., & Loney, J. A four-fold model for subgrouping the hyperkinetic/MBD syndrome. *Child Psychiatry and Human Development*, 1979, *9*, 153–159.

Langhorne, Jr., J. E., Loney, J., Paternite, C. E., & Bechtoldt, H. P. Childhood hyperkinesis: A return to the source. *Journal of Abnormal Psychology*, 1976, *85*, 201–209.

Lapouse, R., & Monk, M. A. An epidemiologic study of behavior characteristics in children. *American Journal of Public Health*, 1958, *48*, 1134–1144.

Levy, F., & Hobbes, G. The diagnosis of attention deficit disorder (hyperkinesis) in children. *Journal of the American Academy of Child Psychiatry*, 1981, *20*, 376–384.

Loney, J. Hyperkinesis comes of age: What do we know and where should we go? *American Journal of Orthopsychiatry*, 1980, *50*, 28–42.

Loney, J., Langhorne Jr., J. E., & Paternite, C. E. An empirical basis for subgrouping the hyperkinetic/minimal brain dysfunction syndrome. *Journal of Abnormal Psychology*, 1978, *87*, 431–441.

Malmquist, E. *Factors related to reading disabilities in the first grade of the elementary school.* Stockholm: Almquist & Wiksell, 1958.

Minde, K., Lewin, D., Weiss, G., Lavigueur, H., Douglas, V., & Sykes, E. The hyperactive child in elementary school: A 5-year, controlled follow-up. *Exceptional Children*, 1971, *38*, 215–221.

Mischel, W. On the interface of cognition and personality: Beyond the person–situation debate. *American Psychologist*, 1979, *34*, 740–754.

Montagu, J. D. The hyperkinetic child: A behavioural, electrodermal, and EEG investigation. *Developmental Medicine and Child Neurology*, 1975, *17*, 299–305.

Nichols, P. L., & Chen, T.-C. *Minimal brain dysfunction: A prospective study*. Hillsdale, N.J.: Erlbaum, 1981.

Olweus, D. Stability of aggressive reaction patterns in males: A review. *Psychological Bulletin*, 1979, *86*, 852–875.

Olweus, D. The consistency issue in personality psychology revisited, with special reference to aggression. *British Journal of Social and Clinical Psychology*, 1980, *19*, 377–390.

Orris, J. B. Visual monitoring performance in three subgroups of male delinquents. *Journal of Abnormal Psychology*, 1969, *74*, 227–229.

Ounsted, C. The hyperkinetic syndrome in epileptic children. *Lancet*, 1955, *2*, 303–311.

Plomin, R., & Foch, T. T. Hyperactivity and paediatrician diagnoses, parental ratings, specific cognitive abilities, and laboratory measures. *Journal of Abnormal Child Psychology*, 1981, *9*, 55–64.

Prinz, R. J., Connor, P. A., & Wilson, C. Hyperactive and aggressive behaviors in childhood: Intertwined dimensions. *Journal of Abnormal Child Psychology*, 1981, *9*, 191–202.

Quay, H. C. Psychopathic personality as pathological stimulation-seeking. *American Journal of Psychiatry*, 1965, *122*, 180–183.

Quay, H. C. Psychopathic behavior: Reflections on its nature, origins, and treatment. In I. C. Uzgiris & F. Weizmann (Eds.), *The structuring of experience*. New York: Plenum Press, 1977. (a)

Quay, H. C. The three faces of evaluation: What can be expected to work. *Criminal Justice and Behavior*, 1977, *4*, 341–354. (b)

Quay, H. C. Classification. In H. C. Quay & J. S. Werry (Eds.), *Psychopathological disorders of childhood* (2nd ed.). New York: Wiley, 1979.

Rapoport, J. L., & Benoit, M. The relation of direct home observations to the clinic evaluation of hyperactive school-age boys. *Journal of Child Psychology and Psychiatry*, 1975, *16*, 141–147.

Rapoport, J., & Ferguson, H. B. Biological validation of the hyperkinetic syndrome. *Developmental Medicine and Child Neurology*, 1981, *23*, 667–682.

Rie, H. E., & Rie, E. D. (Eds.). *Handbook of minimal brain dysfunctions: A critical view*. New York: Wiley, 1980.

Ross, D. M., & Ross, S. A. *Hyperactivity: Research, theory, and action*. New York: Wiley, 1976.

Rosenthal, R. H., & Allen, T. W. An examination of attention, arousal, and learning dysfunctions of hyperkinetic children. *Psychological Bulletin*, 1978, *85*, 689–715.

Rutter, M. Diagnostic validity in child psychiatry. *Advances in Biological Psychiatry*, 1978, *2*, 2–22.

Rutter, M. Psychological sequelae of brain damage in childhood. *American Journal of Psychiatry*, 1981, *138*, 1533–1544.

Rutter, M. Syndromes attributed to "minimal brain dysfunction" in children. *American Journal of Psychiatry*, 1982, *139*, 21–33. (a)

Rutter, M. Temperament: Concepts, issues and problems. In R. Porter & G. Collins (Eds.), *Temperamental differences in infants and young children* (Ciba Foundation Symposium No. 89). London: Pitman Books, 1982. (b)

Rutter, M., & Giller, H. *Juvenile delinquency: Trends and perspectives*. Harmondsworth. England: Penguin Books, 1983.

Rutter, M., Shaffer, D., & Shepherd, M. *A multiaxial classification of child psychiatric disorders*. Geneva: World Health Organization, 1975.

Rutter, M., Tizard, J., & Whitmore, K. (Eds.). *Education, health and behaviour*. Huntington, N.Y.: Krieger, 1981. (Originally published, 1970.)

Rutter, M., & Yule, W. Reading difficulties. In M. Rutter & L. Hersov (Eds.), *Child psychiatry: Modern approaches*. Oxford: Blackwell Scientific Publications, 1977.

Safer, D., & Allen, R. *Hyperactive children: Diagnosis and management*. Baltimore: University Park Press, 1976.

Sandberg, S. On the overinclusiveness of the diagnosis of hyperkinetic syndrome. In M. Gittelman (Ed.), *Intervention strategies with hyperactive children*. New York: Sharpe, 1981.

Sandberg, S., Rutter, M., & Taylor, E. Hyperkinetic disorder in psychiatric clinic attenders. *Developmental Medicine and Child Neurology*, 1978, *20*, 279–299.

Sandberg, S., Wieselberg, M., & Shaffer, D. Hyperkinetic and conduct problem children in a primary school population: Some epidemiological considerations. *Journal of Child Psychology and Psychiatry*, 1980, *21*, 293–311.

Sandoval, J. The measurement of the hyperactive syndrome in children. *Review of Educational Research*, 1977, *47*, 293–318.

Sandoval, J. Format effects in two teacher rating scales of hyperactivity. *Journal of Abnormal Child Psychology*, 1981, *9*, 202–213.

Schachar, R., Rutter, M., & Smith, A. The characteristics of situationally and pervasively hyperactive children: Implications for syndrome definition. *Journal of Child Psychology and Psychiatry*, 1981, *22*, 375–392.

Schrag, P., & Divoky, D. *The Myth of the hyperactive child, and other means of child control*. New York: Pantheon, 1975.

Schleifer, M., Weiss, G., Cohen, N., Elman, M., Cvejic, H., & Kruger, E. Hyperactivity in preschoolers and the effect of methylphenidate. *American Journal of Orthopsychiatry*, 1975, *45*, 38–50.

Schulman, J. L., Kaspar, J. C., & Throne, F. M. *Brain damage and behavior: A clinical experimental study*. Springfield, Ill.: Charles C Thomas, 1965.

Siddle, D. A. T., Mednick, S. A., Nicol, A. R., & Foggitt, R. H. Skin conductance recovery in anti-social adolescents. *British Journal of Social and Clinical Psychology*, 1976, *15*, 425–428.

Siddle, D. A. T., Nicol, A. R., & Foggitt, R. H. Habituation and overextinction of the GSR component of the orienting response in anti-social adolescents. *British Journal of Social and Clinical Psychology*, 1973, *12*, 303–308.

Silver, L. A. The relationship between learning disabilities, hyperactivity, distractibility and behavioral problems: A clinical analysis. *Journal of the American Academy of Child Psychiatry*, 1981, *20*, 385–397.

Sleator, E. K., & Ullman, R. K. Can the physician diagnose hyperactivity in the office? *Pediatrics*, 1981, *67*, 13–17.

Soli, S. D., Nuechterlein, K. H., Garmezy, N., Devine, V. T., & Schaefer, S. M. A classification system for research in childhood psychopathology: I. An empirical approach using factor and cluster analyses and conjunctive decision rules. In B. A. Maher (Ed.), *Progress in experimental personality research* (Vol. 10). New York: Academic Press, 1981.

Sprague, R. L., Cohen, M. N., & Eichlseder, W. *Are there hyperactive children in Europe and the South Pacific?* Paper presented at the American Psychological Association Symposium, "The Hyperactive Child: Fact, Fiction and Fantasy," San Francisco, August 1977.

Stevens, T. M., Kupst, M. J., Suran, B. G., & Schulman, J. L. Activity level: A comparison between actometer scores and observer ratings. *Journal of Abnormal Child Psychology*, 1978, *6*, 163–173.

Stewart, M. A., Cummings, C., Singer, S., & de Blois, C. S. The overlap between hyperactive and unsocialized aggressive children. *Journal of Child Psychology and Psychiatry*, 1981, *22*, 35–46.

Stewart, M. A., de Blois, C. S., & Cummings, C. Psychiatric disorder in the parents of hyperactive boys and those with conduct disorder. *Journal of Child Psychology and Psychiatry*, 1980, *21*, 283–292.

Stores, G., Hart, J., & Piran, N. On attentiveness in schoolchildren with epilepsy. *Epilepsia*, 1978, *19*, 169–175.

Taylor, E. Development of attention. In M. Rutter (Ed.), *Scientific foundations of developmental psychiatry*. London: Heinemann Medical Books, 1980.

Taylor, E., & Sandberg, S. *Classroom behaviour problems and hyperactivity: A questionnaire study in English schools.* Manuscript submitted for publication, 1982.

Trites, R. L. *Hyperactivity in children: Etiology, measurement, and treatment implications.* Baltimore: University Park Press, 1979.

Trites, R. L., Blouin, A. G. A., Ferguson, H. B., & Lynch, G. The Conners' teacher rating scale: An epidemiologic inter-rater reliability and follow-up investigation. In K. Gadow & J. Loney (Eds.), *Psychological aspects of drug treatment for hyperactivity*. Boulder, Colo.: Westview Press, 1980.

Ullman, D. G., Barkley, R. A., & Brown, H. W. The behavioral symptoms of hyperkinetic children who successfully responded to stimulant drug treatment. *American Journal of Orthopsychiatry*, 1978, *48*, 425–437.

Weiss, G., & Hechtman, L. The hyperactive child syndrome. *Science*, 1979, *205*, 1348–1354.

Wender, P. *Minimal brain dysfunction in children.* New York: Wiley–Interscience, 1971.

Wender, P. Minimal brain dysfunction: An overview. In M. A. Lipton, A. DiMascio, & K. F. Killam (Eds.), *Psychopharmacology: A generation of progress*. New York: Raven Press, 1978.

Werry, J., & Hawthorne, D. Conners' teacher questionnaire—norms and validity. *Australian and New Zealand Journal of Psychiatry*, 1976, *10*, 259–262.

Werry, J., & Quay, H. The prevalence of behavior symptoms in younger elementary school children. *American Journal of Orthopsychiatry*, 1971, *41*, 136–143.

Werry, J. S., Sprague, R. L., & Cohen, M. N. Conners' teacher rating scale for use in drug studies with children: An empirical study. *Journal of Abnormal Child Psychology*, 1975, *3*, 217–229.

Whalen, C. K., Collins, B. E., Henker, B., Alkus, S. R., Adams, D., & Stapp, J. Behavior observations of hyperactive children and methylphenidate (Ritalin) effects in systematically structured classroom environments: Now you see them, now you don't. *Journal of Pediatric Psychology*, 1978, *3*, 177–187.

Whalen, C. K., Henker, B., Collins, B. E., Finck, D., & Dotemoto, S. A social ecology of hyperactive boys: Methylphenidate (Ritalin) effects and medication by situation interactions in systematically structured classroom environments. *Journal of Applied Behavior Analysis*, 1979, *12*, 65–81.

Whitehill, M., DeMyer-Gapin, S., & Scott, T. J. Stimulation seeking in antisocial preadolescent children. *Journal of Abnormal Psychology*, 1976, *85*, 101–104.

Zentall, S. S. Behavioral comparisons of hyperactive and normally active children in natural settings. *Journal of Abnormal Child Psychology*, 1980, *8*, 93–109.

Zentall, S. S., & Barack, R. S. Rating scales for hyperactivity: Concurrent validity, reliability and decisions to label for the Conners and David abbreviated scales. *Journal of Abnormal Child Psychology*, 1979, *7*, 179–190.

CHAPTER FOURTEEN

Attentional and Cognitive Problems

VIRGINIA I. DOUGLAS

INTRODUCTION

The past decade has marked a period of intense interest in childhood hyperactivity, culminating in the adoption of a new diagnostic label, "attention deficit disorder" (ADD), in the most recent revision of the American Psychiatric Association's *Diagnostic and Statistical Manual of Mental Disorders* (1980). The change in the label was influenced by research findings demonstrating that these children's inappropriate activity and disruptive behaviors are accompanied by more subtle, but equally important, deficits in cognitive processes.

Although the new label refers only to attentional problems, research findings suggest that attentional difficulties represent one of a constellation of closely related deficits, all of which have far-reaching effects on the children's behavior, academic achievement, and cognitive functioning. A tentative list of the defective processes includes (1) the investment, organization, and maintenance of attention and effort; (2) the inhibition of impulsive responding; (3) the modulation of arousal levels to meet situational demands; and (4) an unusually strong inclination to seek immediate reinforcement (Douglas, 1980a; Douglas & Peters, 1979).

A number of investigators have emphasized one or more of these processes (e.g., Conners, 1975; Douglas, 1972; Douglas & Peters, 1979; Dykman, Ackerman, Clements, & Peters, 1971; Rosenthal & Allen, 1978; Ross, 1976; Swanson & Kinsbourne, 1979; Wender, 1971). There are marked differences, however, in the manner in which writers have defined the processes, as well as considerable confusion regarding the nature of the relationships among them.

Progress in understanding and treating hyperactivity/ADD also has been hampered by several other sources of ambiguity and confusion. These include a lack of adequate diagnostic procedures for identifying ADD children and a failure of investigators to discriminate between primary and secondary deficits and to differentiate between possible reasons for poor performance on cognitive tasks.

Virginia I. Douglas. Department of Psychology, McGill University, Montreal, Quebec, Canada; Department of Psychology, The Montreal Children's Hospital, Montreal, Quebec, Canada.

THE ISSUE OF SUBJECT SELECTION

Diagnostic Criteria

Barkley (1982) has suggested that the following criteria be used to identify ADD children:

1. Parental/teacher complaints of inattention, impulsivity, restlessness, and poor compliance and self-control.
2. A score on a standardized rating scale of hyperactive behavior of at least two standard deviations above the mean for normal children.
3. Reported age of onset of symptoms by 5 years of age.
4. Duration of symptoms of at least 12 months.
5. Pervasiveness of symptoms across at least 50% of the situations on the Home Situations Questionnaire.
6. An IQ estimate of at least 70.
7. Exclusion of autism, psychosis, severe language delay, blindness, deafness, or gross neurological disease.

Depending on one's research goals, additional criteria may be desirable. Much of our own work at McGill University, for example, has been directed toward discovering the processes underlying hyperactivity. For this reason, we have been particularly anxious to establish subject groups that are as homogeneous and "pure" as possible. Thus, to avoid contamination with the symptoms of mental retardation, we have set the lower IQ limit for our samples at 80 rather than 70. For similar reasons, we have been more stringent than some investigators have been in screening out children from disrupted or economically deprived families. Our practice of avoiding cases in which serious problems within a family might be contributing to a child's symptoms has, we believe, helped avoid misdiagnosis of children who exhibit "fidgeting" behavior associated with anxiety. It also may explain why we have found less evidence of aggressivity in our subjects than other investigators have reported. Although we recognize that family factors assume great importance in the long-term adjustment of hyperactive children (Loney, Langhorne, & Paternite, 1978; Milich & Loney, 1979), our own emphasis has been on the somewhat more subtle cognitive and social consequences of ADD that are likely to occur even when the children are reared in a reasonably benevolent environment.

Hyperactivity, Academic Problems, and Learning Disabilities

As Barkley (1982) and other reviewers (Douglas & Peters, 1979; Ross & Pelham, 1981) have stressed, an important unresolved issue in subject selection involves the problem of differentiating between hyperactive and learning-disabled (LD) children. Several obstacles, including the global nature of the learning disability concept and the failure to differentiate between primary and secondary deficits, make a successful resolution of this problem difficult.

There have been two opposing developments in the literature on learning disabilities. On the one hand, some researchers are seeking to delineate relatively specific learning disabilities and to develop diagnostic techniques to assess them (Boder, 1977; Mattis, French, & Rapin, 1975). Other investigators, however, have extended use of the LD label to include all children who demonstrate poor academic performance that is not attributable to such factors as mental retardation, emotional problems, lack of adequate schooling, or various physical causes (gross organic damage, visual or hearing impairment).

This broad application of a "wastebasket" LD label has contributed greatly to the existing confusion between hyperactivity and learning disability, because it frequently leads to inclusion within the LD category of hyperactive children who develop academic problems as a result of their more basic attentional and inhibitory problems. We (Douglas & Peters, 1979) have emphasized the importance of differentiating between primary deficits in hyperactive and LD children and deficits that develop out of the children's original constitutional predispositions. In the case of LD children, we have postulated that the children are born with a constitutional predisposition toward one or more specific learning disabilities, such as language-processing problems or visual–perceptual problems. It is suggested that failure experiences resulting from these original deficiencies may then lead to secondary concentration problems, restlessness, and impulsivity.

When these sources of possible confusion are considered, it is not surprising to find reports of considerable overlap between hyperactive and LD samples on both academic and behavioral measures (Ain, 1980; Benezra, 1980; Lambert & Sandoval, 1980; Tant, 1978). In addition, there are, in all probability, some children who are constitutionally predisposed toward both learning and hyperactivity problems. Nevertheless, it should be noted that, even in studies that fail to take account of the above methodological and conceptual problems, the overlap reported is far from complete (Anderson, Halcomb, & Doyle, 1973; Douglas, 1972; Douglas & Peters, 1979; Doyle, Anderson, & Halcomb, 1976; Dykman *et al.*, 1971).

Some investigators have adopted the strategy of studying only "pure" examples of hyperactive and LD children (Ackerman, Elardo, & Dykman, 1979; Dykman, Ackerman, & Oglesby, 1979). Indeed, Ross and Pelham (1981) have suggested that, unless children with learning problems are screened out of hyperactive samples, the samples must be considered "contaminated" and the studies suspect. However, if the argument regarding the long-term effects of hyperactive symptoms on the children's academic functioning is correct, this approach could lead to highly selected subject samples that are unrepresentative of the general population of hyperactive children.

We (Douglas & Peters, 1979) have suggested some ways of coping, at least partially, with this dilemma. A careful history regarding the duration and pervasiveness of symptoms associated with hyperactivity can be extremely helpful. One usually would not expect an LD child to develop these symptoms until he (a majority of hyperactives are boys) is old enough to have experienced school failure; also, the hyperactive-like symptoms of an LD child should not be as prevalent in social settings as in the academic environment. We have found, too, that diagnostic testing and teaching by skilled examiners can help establish whether a child has simply failed to learn a particular skill or whether he has a genuine learning impairment. Simple measures of attention, such as vigilance tasks, may also prove helpful (Anderson *et al.*, 1973; Doyle *et al.*, 1976; Dykman *et al.*, 1971), as may specially designed teacher rating scales (Lahey, Stempniak, Robinson, & Tyroler, 1978). Much work is still needed, however, to validate and standardize such instruments and procedures, and then to find ways of combining them so as to provide optimal criteria for assigning the ADD and LD diagnoses.

THE MECHANISMS AND THEIR EFFECTS

Speculations regarding the underlying mechanisms of ADD have developed out of investigations directed toward defining the cognitive weaknesses and strengths of these children, and from studies designed to evaluate the effects of a variety of manipulations on task performance. These studies suggest that defective attentional, inhibitory, arousal, and reinforcement mechanisms can account for all of the deficits reported thus far (Douglas, 1980a; Douglas & Peters, 1979). These processes are very closely related. Indeed, depending on one's viewpoint, the same deficit often can be attributed to several of these proposed mechanisms.

Secondary Effects

Early speculations about the nature of hyperactive children's deficits were based mainly on behavioral observations and data from comparatively simple laboratory measures. However, studies of the children's performance on higher-level tasks suggested that the postulated mechanisms exert a secondary and spiraling effect on the development of cognitive abilities and on the children's motivation and style of coping with complex cognitive problems (Douglas, 1980a; Douglas & Peters, 1979; Tant & Douglas, 1982). Hypothesized effects include impaired development of metacognition; a lowered level of effectance (mastery) motivation; and less complex and enriched neural representations ("schemata") of perceptual and cognitive experiences.

There is also some evidence suggesting that the gap between the cognitive abilities of ADD and normal children may widen as the youngsters grow older (Douglas, 1980a; Douglas & Peters, 1979). ADD children would be expected to fall further behind their age-mates over time for at least two reasons. First, later learning often requires more deliberate, active, and conscious effort than early learning. Secondly, later learning is heavily dependent upon early learning. Thus, if a child spends his early years processing the events of his environment carelessly and superficially, he will have less information available to guide and motivate future learning.

Causes of Task Failure: Can't, Don't, or Won't?

Whenever hyperactive children perform poorly on a test, it is essential to discover the reasons for their poor performance. Sometimes they are genuinely incapable of completing the task. On the other hand, hyperactive children are notorious for failing to make consistent use of information and skills they are known to possess. Investigations have revealed a wide range of manipulations and conditions that are effective in eliciting evidence of such "hidden" knowledge. These have included, for example, having an authority figure present while the children work; administering tests individually; increasing the interest value of tasks; delivering auditory stimuli through earphones; treating the children with stimulant medication; and using rewards or response costs to encourage correct performance. Such manipulations appear to combat or compensate for the effects of the children's attentional, inhibitory, and arousal problems (Douglas & Peters, 1979).

Developmental psychologists (Brown, 1975; Flavell, 1970; Meacham, 1972) also have stressed the importance of distinguishing among possible reasons for a child's failure to perform a task successfully. Flavell has suggested that the term "production deficiency" be applied when a child can be induced to use a mediator that he did not produce spontaneously. As Brown (1975) explains, Flavell considers a "mediation deficiency" to be present "when the subject is unable to use a potential mediator (strategy) efficiently, even when he is specifically instructed and trained to do so" (Brown, 1975, p. 135).

The differentiation between production and mediation deficiencies is usually not difficult when simple operations are involved. In the case of more complex processes, however, it is advisable to apply a number of manipulations in an effort to elicit successful performance. If these attempts fail, the investigator must then explore possible causes. For example, a child may not have had the opportunity to acquire the necessary knowledge, or he may have intellectual limitations that make the task too difficult to accomplish. It is also possible, however, that attentional and related problems have prevented a child from acquiring the information needed to perform the task.

Since the effects of such gaps in learning are likely to spiral, a developmental perspective is essential if researchers are to understand the origins of poor task performance in ADD children. A developmental perspective also is needed when therapists and clinicians attempt to teach the children knowledge or skills they have failed to acquire. This frequently means returning to very basic operations and building the subsequent steps in the learning process carefully, in order to ensure that gaps in knowledge resulting from the children's self-regulatory problems are filled. If this painstaking approach is ignored, stimulant medication or contingency management may help correct production deficiencies, but they could hardly be expected to have much impact on failures that result from earlier failures to utilize learning opportunities effectively.

DEFINING THE DEFECTIVE MECHANISMS AND THEIR RELATIONSHIPS

Although many investigators have referred to possible attentional, inhibitory, arousal, or reinforcement problems in ADD children (e.g., Conners, 1975; Dykman *et al.*, 1971; Douglas, 1972; Douglas & Peters, 1979; Rosenthal & Allen, 1978; Ross, 1976; Swanson & Kinsbourne, 1979; Wender, 1971), there has been considerable confusion in the ways in which these terms are used.

Attentional Deficits

A multiplicity of labels have been devised to designate different aspects of attention (Berlyne, 1970; Douglas, 1974; Douglas & Peters, 1979; Kahneman, 1973; Moray, 1969; Posner & Boies, 1971; Rosenthal & Allen, 1978; Solley & Murphy, 1969; Swets & Kristofferson, 1970). At McGill, we have adopted a two-stage approach in order to discover the nature of the attentional deficits of hyperactive children. First, tasks thought to assess particular aspects of attention are administered to hyperactive and control subjects. Second, the effects of a variety of conditions and manipulations on performance are investigated to clarify the nature of the hyperactive children's deficits further (Douglas, 1980a; Douglas & Peters, 1979). In spite of such efforts, difficulties still stem from confusions surrounding terminology. In particular, a variety of meanings are being assigned to the terms "sustained" and "selective" attention (Rosenthal & Allen, 1978; Ross & Pelham, 1981).

Sustained Attention

Some authors equate the term "sustained attention" with "vigilance" (Ross & Pelham, 1981). This usage reflects the fact that attentional problems in hyperactive children were first demonstrated on vigilance tasks. However, the children's performance on more complex tasks reveals three related aspects of their attentional problems, all involving self-regulation: (1) the maintenance of attention over time; (2) the extent to which attention is self-directed and organized; and (3) the amount of effort that is invested (sometimes referred to as the "intensive" aspect of attention). Sometimes "sustained attention" has been used as a shorthand term to apply to all three of these dimensions (Douglas, 1974, 1975, 1976, 1980a, 1980b; Douglas & Peters, 1979). In order to avoid confusion, however, it appears advisable to limit "sustained attention" to the maintenance of attention over time.

Although a few theorists have stressed the importance of effort in attention (Broadbent, 1977; Kahneman, 1973; Posner, 1978), there has been insufficient emphasis on individual differences in the investment and organization of effort, and on factors within tasks that make concentration easy or difficult for particular individuals. On relatively simple vigilance tasks, effort is usually assessed by maintenance of performance over time, although even here equal emphasis must be placed on the controlled quality of the effort required to remain alert to the demands of these dull, repetitive tasks, and to hold back impulsive responding.

In the case of more complex tasks requiring careful, organized, perceptual search strategies, or an exhaustive analysis of possible solutions to a logical problem (Douglas, 1980a; Douglas & Peters, 1979), this emphasis on self-regulatory processes, involving the investment of effort and the inhibition of impulsive responding, becomes even more important. A distinction between attentional strategies involving *exploration* and those involving *search* becomes critical (Douglas, 1980a, 1980b; Douglas & Peters, 1979). Developmental studies have shown that the attention of young children is frequently controlled by salient, curiosity-producing features of stimuli and by reinforcement-correlated features in the environment. In older children, these diffuse, exploratory behaviors tend to be replaced by self-governed, organized search strategies that enable the children to extract the particular information from their environment that is required for task solution. This differentiation between exploration and search helps explain why observers can sometimes be confused by the amount of attention hyperactive children seem to pay in such "high-interest" situations as watching TV (Ross & Pelham, 1981). The interest of the children may be "captured" in such situations, but they may actually extract less information from the available perceptual stimuli than normal children do. It is unfortunate that developmental psychologists sometimes use the term "selective attention" to refer to the directed, organized quality of search strategies; this usage is likely to be misleading.

Selective Attention and Distractibility

The terms "selective attention" and "distractibility" have been used with a variety of meanings. Most frequently the terms are used to refer to a subject's ability to focus on critical target stimuli while "ignoring" nontarget stimuli. Typically, a good deal of emphasis is placed on the "ignoring" aspect of this definition, while the "focusing" or "concentrating" aspect tends to be underemphasized. Also underemphasized is the possibility that responses to incorrect stimuli may result, not from a failure to ignore these stimuli, but from a failure to inhibit strong response tendencies raised in some individuals by the tasks typically used in studies of selective attention.

Confusion also has arisen because authors who use the terms may (implicitly or explicitly) have different explanatory principles in mind to explain why subjects fail to ignore extraneous stimuli. This explanation often involves a "defective filter mechanism," or a discrimination problem that is manifested in a failure to differentiate between critical and noncritical stimuli (Cruikshank, Bentzen, Ratzeburg, & Tannhauser, 1961; Laufer, Denhoff, & Solomons, 1957; Rosenthal & Allen, 1978; Ross, 1976). Other investigators have explored the possibility that problems with concurrent processing may be implicated in apparent deficits in selective attention (McIntyre, Blackwell, & Denton, 1978). The explanation for this interpretation rests on the assumption that both target and nontarget stimuli must be processed to a level necessary for making the required discrimination between relevant and irrelevant stimuli.

Even simple attentional tasks reveal the difficulties involved in delineating the mechanism responsible for inattention. For example, although vigilance tasks are usually considered measures of sustained attention, they also involve a large "selectivity" component; the subject must respond only to certain stimuli. If a child "misses" correct stimuli, can the researcher or clinician be sure that the presence of incorrect stimuli played an important role in the poor performance? If the child responds to incorrect stimuli, should this be attributed to a failure to ignore these stimuli, a failure to discriminate between correct and incorrect stimuli, or a failure to inhibit an ongoing response tendency to push the lever? Problems of interpretation become even more difficult when experimenters employ complex selective-attention paradigms, such as dichotic-listening tasks involving the delivery of different kinds of target and nontarget stimuli to the two ears. It is also necessary to make a clear differentiation between two kinds of reaction to the presence of extraneous stimuli (Douglas & Peters, 1979). First, a subject may "pay attention" to nontarget stimuli, as by looking up at them. More important, however, is the effect of the intended distractors on task performance. Does their presence result in impaired performance?

Partial answers to these questions are discussed later in this chapter, but a few general statements can be made here. First, a surprising number of attempts to prove that hyperactive children are abnormally distractible have been unsuccessful (Douglas & Peters, 1979). Since there have been several studies in which potentially distracting stimuli were placed in close proximity to a task or were integrally related to it, I do not believe that it is possible to argue that these efforts failed because of experimental paradigms in which "the distracting stimulus has not been a part of the task in any way" (Rosenthal & Allen, 1978, p. 711).

Secondly, in considering studies in which decreased performance of ADD children in the presence of extraneous stimuli *has* been found, it is essential to explore possible causes of the performance decrement. It is my opinion that these causes seldom implicate defective filters, discrimination problems, or difficulties with concurrent processing. Rather, the reason for the children's poor performance often can be traced to concentration, inhibitory, arousal, or reinforcement problems. Thus, in some "distraction" studies, it has been shown that neither hyperactive nor control children ignored extraneous stimuli (i.e., both groups processed the irrelevant information). The performance differences that were found appeared to result from the fact that the control children were better able to *inhibit responding* to the nontarget stimuli. In other studies, a strong case can be made for the hypothesis that hyperactive subjects attended to extraneous events in order to avoid tasks they found difficult or boring; in these examples, concentration, inhibitory, and/or stimulus-seeking explanations might be evoked. A stimulus-seeking hypothesis also could explain why ADD children have sometimes been drawn to the salient dimensions of a task configuration, even when these aspects were not central to the task. Alternatively, one could argue that both normal and hyperactive children process the most compelling dimensions of a task first, but that the superior concentration abilities of normal children enable them to process *beyond* these more salient dimensions. As a final example, hyperactives may be more vulnerable than control children to extraneous stimuli because they are experiencing greater difficulty with the central task. Hyperactives have been found to perform poorly on a wide range of simple and complex tasks requiring sustained, organized concentration. If they are experiencing difficulty *before* distractors are introduced, they would be highly vulnerable to any manipulations that place additional processing burdens on them, including the addition of extraneous stimuli. This last example underlines the importance of including a nondistraction condition in research designs of studies investigating distractibility in ADD children.

In view of the many complications surrounding the terms "selective attention" and "distractibility," it would be desirable to eliminate the terms from future research reports. The labels are in such widespread use, however, that this is not likely to happen. Thus, it may only be possible to insist that investigators define their use of the terms as clearly as possible. In addition, they should state explicitly whether they have underlying causal mechanisms in mind, and, if so, the nature of the mechanisms being postulated should be described.

Inhibitory Control

As Ross (1976) has pointed out, terms like "impulsivity," "inhibitory control," and "disinhibition" have been used with a variety of meanings. According to Gorenstein and Newman's (1980) definition, disinhibition refers to "human behavior that has been interpreted as arising from lessened controls on response inclinations" (p. 302). The degree of inhibitory control demonstrated by a child will depend upon a number of interacting task, condition, and subject variables. In the case of ADD children, it may be argued that inhibitory problems are likely to be particularly evident when external controls are lacking and when the children have developed a strong response set toward stimuli or activities they find reinforcing.

As with concentration difficulties, impulsive tendencies can be observed throughout a wide range of cognitive tasks, varying from simple to complex. On simple tasks, inhibitory difficulties may be manifested in an inability to withhold responding until target stimuli appear, or as a tendency to respond repeatedly to a single target stimulus. On more complex tasks, the children's impulsivity may be reflected in an inclination to act before they have understood a problem clearly, or before they have given sufficient thought to possible solutions.

Relationship between Inhibition, Attention, Stimulus Seeking, and Response to Reward

Unlike Ross (1976), I do not think that theorists should stress attentional problems in ADD children while minimizing emphasis on inhibitory processes. While I agree that preventing children from responding quickly does not guarantee that they will reflect productively on problems before making their responses, inhibition of impulsive responding often is a necessary, though insufficient, step in teaching ADD children to approach problems in a reflective, reasoned manner. Thus, both the facilitatory and the inhibitory aspects of self-regulation must be emphasized.

There has been a confusing tendency to equate impulsivity with fast responding, arising from Kagan's (1966) work on the cognitive style of reflection–impulsivity. However, recent studies have shown that ADD children often use time in an inefficient manner, even when they appear to be attending and well motivated. This means that latency (response-time) measures may be influenced by both the children's typical rate of responding and the efficiency with which they process available information. Consequently, theories that fail to take the interaction between time and quality of processing into account are likely to be misleading.

Some authors have taken an opposite approach from Ross (1976) and have emphasized the inhibitory problems of hyperactive children, while downplaying the role of attention. Gorenstein and Newman (1980) argue that hyperactivity, together with psychopathy, hysteria, antisocial and impulsive personality, and alcoholism, belong to a class of disorders that they label "disinhibitory psychopathology." They suggest that the syndrome produced in animals by lesions in the septal–hippocampal–frontal (SHF) system can serve as a "functional research model" of human disinhibitory psychopathology, and they review a number of experimental paradigms in which similar abnormalities have been found in psychopaths and septal animals. The results of the studies have been variously interpreted as reflecting an avoidance deficit, a tendency to seek stimulation, or hypersensitivity to reward. Gorenstein and Newman then present a compelling argument against the tendency of clinicians to focus on the apparent avoidance deficit of psychopaths, while neglecting the inclination of these individuals to seek immediate gratification. They point to the "irresistible and exaggerated hold" that immediate reward gains in SHF animals and argue that a similar phenomenon is evident in human psychopathy.

After reviewing several studies in which the effect of a variety of reinforcement contingencies on the task performance of hyperactive children were investigated, we (Douglas & Peters, 1979) reached a similar conclusion regarding the impact of reinforcers on hyperactive children. In discussing possible reasons for the impaired performance of hyperactives under some reinforcement schedules, we suggested:

> One reason . . . seems to be that the reinforcers become a highly salient aspect of the learning situation for the hyperactive child. Consequently he may be paying more attention to the reinforcers themselves (or the reinforcing person) than to the particular behavior being reinforced, or to the specific stimuli associated with it. In addition, hyperactive children appear to be unusually sensitive to the loss of reinforcement and to the failure of expected reinforcers to appear. (Douglas & Peters, 1979, p. 209)

Arousal Differences

Recent reviews (Ferguson & Pappas, 1979; Feuerstein, Ward, & Le Baron, 1979; Hastings & Barkley, 1978; Rosenthal & Allen, 1978) reveal wide disagreement regarding the nature of hyperactive children's arousal problems, as well as serious theoretical and methodological difficulties in the concept of arousal.

Much of the early theorizing was guided by the intuitively appealing notion that ADD children's general level of arousal seemed to differ from that of normal children. However, most findings suggest that "hyperactive children are probably not under- or overaroused in their resting levels on autonomic functions, although some children may display resting cortical underarousal" (Hastings & Barkley, 1978, p. 431). The major positive findings have come from studies of the impact of stimuli on measures of autonomic and central functioning. The results from these investigations have rather consistently pointed to an *underreactivity* to environmental stimulation. Following this lead, investigators have begun to concentrate on a variety of evoked response measures, frequently employing paradigms in which subjects are required to make behavioral responses to particular stimuli. Thus, the emphasis appears to be shifting away from general levels of activation toward measures reflecting alertness to specific stimuli. Stated differently, the recent studies appear to be dealing mainly with psychophysiological correlates of attentional processes.

It is important to stress, however, that an individual's alertness to stimuli is strongly influenced, not just by his or her general state of arousal, but by what he or she has learned from past experiences. A number of recent cognitive and neuropsychological theories, such as those of Bindra (1976), Gibson (1969), Hebb (1949), and Neisser (1976), emphasize the role of experience in developing "expectancies" or readiness to respond to particular aspects of a situation (Douglas, 1980a; Douglas & Peters, 1979). As Gibson and Rader (1979) have so succinctly stated, "attention is much more than alertness."

It is tempting, in view of these empirical and theoretical developments, to downplay the concept of general arousal and to concentrate on attentional differences in hyperactive children. Concomitant physiological measures, such as evoked responses or orienting responses, could be monitored, but they would be treated as psychophysiological correlates of attentional processes. Experience with these combined psychological and psychophysiological procedures would ultimately reveal whether the central and autonomic measures associated with "arousability" provide insights about attentional mechanisms beyond those to be gained from task performance measures alone.

Nevertheless, not enough is known about the effects of the motivational states of ADD children on attentional and other behaviors to abandon measures of general arousal entirely. Their behaviors suggest that hyperactive children frequently are functioning outside an optimal range of arousal (Douglas, 1980a; Douglas & Peters, 1979). Sometimes they are not sufficiently alert to the demands of a task, particularly if it is dull and repetitive, while at other times they become too excited to perform effectively. Whatever the mechanism involved, it appears that hyperactives are less able than normal children are to control or modulate their own arousal levels in accordance with task or situational demands. In addition, there is modest evidence that they may have an abnormal tendency to seek stimulation, a phenomenon that may be related to their unusual sensitivity to reward.

Although most of the psychophysiological findings point only to *low* arousability in ADD children, the attentional tasks and experimental procedures typically used in psychophysiological studies tend to be dull and uninteresting, particularly after the first few trials. Thus, it is possible that these experimental paradigms are inadequate for testing the hypothesis that, in addition to "underarousability" in situations that do not capture their attention, the children can be more readily "triggered" than normal children can be into supraoptimal states of arousal (Douglas & Peters, 1979). Interestingly, most of the studies suggesting this phenomenon have involved the *administration of rewards* during vigilance and problem-solving tasks. In one of the investigations (Firestone & Douglas, 1975), autonomic measures, taken while the children were receiving positive feedback for fast responses on a reaction-time task, revealed that the administration of rewards was accompanied by unusually high arousal in the hyperactive sample; in addition, impulsive responding increased. Although the technical problems are considerable, it would be most interesting to obtain parallel behavioral, psychophysiological, and task performance data from hyperactive and control subjects, while varying both the level of task novelty and the incentive value of reinforcers. Such studies might yield valuable insights into the relationships between attention, impulsivity, arousal, and responsivity to reinforcement in hyperactive children.

SCOPE OF THE PRESENT REVIEW

The review that follows focuses on several goals that arise out of the preceding discussion. These include (1) defining the nature of hyperactive children's attentional deficits; (2) evaluating the evidence for primary attentional, inhibitory, arousal, and reinforcement problems and exploring the relationships among them; (3) ruling out other possible explanations for the children's deficits; (4) differentiating between production deficits and deficits that result from other causes; and (5) determining the long-term effects of the primary defective mechanisms on the children's cognitive development.

Because much of the relevant literature has been covered in previous reviews (Douglas, 1980a; Douglas & Peters, 1979), recent studies are stressed here. Emphasis is placed on investigations in which the performance of hyperactive and control subjects have been compared, and the focus is on underlying psychological rather than neurological mechanisms.

In evaluating research findings, comparisons are made between the performance of hyperactive children and one or more control groups on a number of measures. Inferences sometimes are drawn, based on comparisons that yield statistical significance as opposed to those that do not. Whenever this approach is taken, there is a danger that the differences found may result from psychometric properties of the instruments employed, rather than from real differences between the samples. When researchers go further and compare the relative effects of task, drug, or environmental manipulations on different subject samples, the problems of interpretation become even more confounded. Chapman and Chapman (1973) have discussed a number of factors that make such comparisons difficult: They include differences in the discriminating power of tasks because of differences in reliability; shape of the distribution of scores; and mean, variance, and shape of the distribution of item difficulty. We (Douglas & Peters, 1979) have pointed to possible effects of statistical artifacts arising from the fact that the variance of scores obtained from hyperactive samples often is unusually large.

Clearly, interpretation of the findings to be discussed must be made with caution. Nevertheless, I would argue that the *pattern* of weaknesses and strengths that emerges from these comparisons points consistently to the underlying attentional, inhibitory, arousal, and reward-seeking mechanisms that I have proposed.

"DISTRACTIBILITY"

I have argued that ADD children's most basic attentional problems are related to the investment, organization, and maintenance of attention and effort (Douglas & Peters, 1979). Although extraneous stimuli may disrupt the performance of hyperactive children more than that of normal children under *some* conditions, the children's "distractibility" appears to be secondary to the more central problems just discussed.

The Effects of Extraneous Stimuli

In an earlier discussion of this controversy, we (Douglas & Peters, 1979) questioned assumptions that hyperactive children are impaired in the ability to filter out extraneous stimuli, to discriminate between central and irrelevant stimuli, or to perform concurrent analyses on stimuli. We concluded that attempts to improve the children's academic performance by placing them in stimulus-reduced environments had proved unsuccessful; moreover, in some studies, an increase in activity level occurred when the children were deprived of normal environmental stimulation.

Findings from 11 studies employing a wide range of tasks and task-irrelevant stimuli were reviewed. In several of the investigations, the intended distractors were placed in close proximity to task stimuli or formed an integral part of the task to be performed (e.g., drawings placed among words to be read, color words printed in contradictory colors, or nontarget words spoken simultaneously with target words). There was little evidence that the performance of hyperactive children was more disrupted than that of control children by the presence of extraneous stimuli. Interestingly, in two of the studies (Bremer & Stern, 1976; Steinkamp, 1974), hyperactive children seemed to pay more attention to the "distractors," but their task performance was no more impaired than that of the controls.

Two "incidental memory" studies by Peters (1977) are also relevant. In the first, a modified version of Hagen's (1967) Incidental Memory Task was used. The design included a nondistraction condition in which only the "central" stimuli (pictures of animals which the subjects were instructed to remember) appeared on cards presented to the children. In the distraction condition, both the animal to be remembered and an irrelevant picture of a household object (the "incidental" stimulus) appeared on each card. Somewhat surprisingly, Peters found that central memory scores in the distraction and nondistraction conditions did not differ significantly. In addition, there was no evidence from either the central or incidental memory measures that the hyperactive subjects had processed the irrelevant pictures more than the control children, or that their performance was more influenced by the presence of the extraneous pictures. Peters's second study involved a "selective listening" task. Children were required to repeat and remember words spoken by a male voice and to ignore words being spoken simultaneously by a female voice. Again, Peters included both a distraction and a nondistraction condition. He found that the hyperactive children remembered fewer of the target words than the control children did in *both* the distraction and the nondistraction conditions. In addition, there was no evidence that the ability of the hyperactive subjects to remember the target words was more susceptible than that of the controls to the distracting influence of the task-irrelevant words.

It should be noted that, although the studies reported provide little support for hypotheses involving faulty filtering mechanisms, discrimination problems, or difficulties with concurrent processing, there were several indications of underlying concentration and inhibitory problems. One of the distraction studies (Peters, 1977), for example, involved a color-naming task; again, both a distraction and a nondistraction condition were included. Although Peters found no evidence that irrelevant form cues affected hyperactives more than controls, he did find that the performance of the hyperactives was worse the *second time* they took the task, regardless of whether the second administration occurred in the distraction or nondistraction condition. The flagging attention of ADD children on dull, routine tasks is a common phenomenon. Peters's finding underscores the importance of controlling for order effects in "distraction" studies. Our subsequent review (Douglas & Peters, 1979) indicated that investigators frequently fail to observe this precaution.

Several recent studies have utilized tasks recommended by Ross and Pelham (1981) as suitable instruments for investigating the controversy surrounding "selective attention." In the discussion to follow, tasks are designated as meaures of "concurrent listening" if subjects are required to process information originating from two sources and presented simultaneously. The term "selective listening" is used when subjects are instructed to pay attention to information from one source and to ignore simultaneously presented information from another source.

Several experimenters have used the "dichotic listening" method to evaluate concurrent and selective listening; this method involves the simultaneous presentation of different, but relatively simple, stimuli (such as digits) to the two ears through earphones. Simultaneously presented stimuli are matched on loudness or intensity and sometimes on other dimensions. Instructions given to the subjects vary. For example, they may be told to report everything they hear as soon as they hear it; they may be directed before each trial to report only the information from a particular ear; or they may be directed to report all of the information they can remember from one ear before reporting information from the other ear.

Davidson and Prior (1978) used a format involving the presentation of a series of pairs of single words to hyperactive and normal children under two conditions. In the first condition (concurrent listening), they were required to report everything they heard as soon as they heard it; in the second condition (selective listening), they were precued by a light on either their left or their right side to report only the stimulus presented to that ear. The investigators report no significant group effects or group × ear interactions in either of the conditions. There also were no group differences on a score based on number of intrusions from the nondesignated ear. Thus, there was no evidence of problems with either concurrent or selective listening in the hyperactive children.

Loiselle, Stamm, Maitinsky, and Whipple (1980) used a dichotic task in which the stimuli were 60 synchronized and matched pairs of speech syllables (*pa*, *ta*, *ka*, etc.), presented in brief, discrete trials, at constant intervals. Subjects were instructed to name the syllables they heard after the presentation of each pair. Thus the task assessed concurrent listening. Loiselle *et al.* found "only moderate deficiencies" in the hyperactive sample. Differences between the hyperactive and normal groups on number of syllables identified correctly approached significance for right-ear stimuli and were not significant for left-ear stimuli. The authors stress that these differences were considerably less than those obtained on two other listening tasks (discussed below).

It perhaps could be argued that the above paradigms, involving pairs of single stimuli, are too simple to elicit evidence of filtering difficulties. However, a study by Hiscock, Kinsbourne, Caplan, and Swanson (1979) suggests that hyperactive children have no particular difficulty coping with the paired presentation of groups of three digits. Although the basic design of Hiscock *et al.*'s study involved a comparison of the effects of stimulant medication on the ability of drug-responsive and nonresponsive hyperactive children to perform dichotic-listening tests, the authors also compared the dichotic-listening data obtained from hyperactive subjects in their placebo condition with data obtained previously from a large sample of normal children. They found no significant differences between the normal and hyperactive groups and concluded that "perhaps the best explanation for the [dichotic] task's insensitivity to the medication condition is that most hyperactive children are not deficient in performance on this task, at least when it is of brief duration" (p. 30).

More data are needed, however, before an accurate evaluation of the performance of hyperactive children on dichotic-listening tasks can be made. As Hiscock *et al.* mention, task duration may affect hyperactive–control comparisons. In addition, in a pilot study carried out in 1964 in our laboratory at

McGill, Campbell (1964) found that the occurrence of statistically significant differences between hyperactive and control groups depended on the number of digits administered. Thus, interpretation of any hyperactive–control differences found with more demanding versions of the task will have to take account of task manipulations that place extra burden on the maintenance of attention and effort.

Loiselle *et al.*'s study (1980) is of particular interest, because they investigated the performance of the same group of 12- and 13-year-old hyperactive boys on three tasks, chosen to tap different aspects of attention. One of these, a dichotic-listening task, is described above. Their second was a vigilance task in which a series of brief tone pips was presented binaurally over a 10-minute period at a constant rate of 40 per minute. The majority of pips were at 1500 Hz, but several signal pips at 1560 Hz were randomly interspersed among them. The subject was instructed to press a response button whenever he thought he heard a signal tone.

For their third task, a selective-listening task, the stimuli were two independent, dichotically presented series of tone pips at 800 Hz for one ear and at 1500 Hz for the other. Each series also contained several randomly interspersed signal pips (840 Hz for the 800-Hz series and 1560 Hz for the 1500-Hz series). The subject was instructed to listen and count the number of signal pips presented to one ear and ignore those presented to the other. Although the authors do not make this point, it should be noted that the nature of the stimuli being presented to each of the two ears was very similar to those used in the vigilance task just described. The additional "selectivity" factor was associated with the instructions to attend to the signal stimuli to one ear and ignore those to the other ear.

During the selective-listening task, Loiselle *et al.* monitored auditory evoked response potentials (ERPs) from the series of tone pips for each ear. The authors obtained data on two ERP components thought to be related to attention, N $\overline{100}$ and P $\overline{300}$. Comparisons between the hyperactive and normal samples on the task performance measures revealed that the hyperactive boys had considerable difficulty with both the vigilance task and the selective-attention task. The authors also found hyperactive–normal differences on both the N $\overline{100}$ and the P $\overline{300}$ components of the ERP. The comparisons were based on "enhancement scores" reflecting enhancement of amplitude of the components to the attended channel as opposed to the nonattended channel. There were large differences between the subject groups on the N $\overline{100}$ amplitude-enhancement score (43.8% for the control group and 13.7% for the hyperactive group). Similarly, the amplitude score for the control group on the P $\overline{300}$ measure was over three times greater to the attended than to the nonattended signals, whereas the clinical group showed no significant increase to the attended signals. In addition, the latency of the P $\overline{300}$ component increased significantly to the attended signals for the control group but not for the hyperactive boys. (The authors point out that it takes longer to detect, process, and respond to the signal pips.)

It is important to note, however, that no significant group differences were found to nonattended channels for N $\overline{100}$ or P $\overline{300}$ amplitudes or latencies. This suggests that the ERP differences obtained between hyperactive and normal samples are caused, not so much by unusual responsivity on the part of the hyperactive boys to the stimuli reaching the nonattended ear, as to a failure to *invest extra effort* in order to concentrate on the signal stimuli to the attended ear. These findings are reminiscent of one of our studies (Cohen & Douglas, 1972), in which we used skin conductance orienting-response measures (ORs) to assess the response of hyperactive children to signal and nonsignal stimuli. We found no group differences on the ORs to nonsignal stimuli. While responding to the signal stimuli, however, controls exhibited a significantly greater increase than hyperactives in both tonic and phasic ORs. The similarity between the two studies rests in the failure of hyperactive children to *extend the additional effort* required by demanding task instructions.

In discussing their results, Loiselle *et al.* stress that minimal group differences were found on the dichotic-listening task (discussed earlier), which involved concurrent listening. They point to the large group differences found on the vigilance and selective-attention tasks and interpret these, together with the ERP findings, as indicating "severe dysfunction by the clinical boys for selective attention, involving both stimulus and response sets" (p. 193). As mentioned earlier, however, vigilance tasks have traditionally been classified as measures of sustained attention and effort, although they certainly can be seen as having a "selectivity" component. It is of interest to compare the mean response scores reported by Loiselle *et al.* from their data on the vigilance and selective-attention tasks. In the case of the "mean response correct" scores, for example, the hyperactives received a mean score of 59.4% as opposed to 87.9% for the normal sample, while on the selective-attention tasks the comparable figures are 45.7% versus 81.3%. It is difficult, of course, to make direct comparisons between the two tasks, particularly since the method of presentation (random intervals in the selective task vs. regular intervals in the vigilance task) differ. Nevertheless, the similar patterns and magnitude of difficulty experienced by the hyperactive and control children on the two tasks is noteworthy; together with the lack of significant ERP differences on the nonattended channel, these findings raise the question as to how much of the hyperactive children's difficulties on the selective-attention task can be attributed to the delivery of a set of tone blips to the second ear. That is, we might question the impact of the intended "selectivity" manipulation over and above the impact of the vigilance requirements involving stimuli to the attended ear.

Defining the Conditions That Elicit Distractibility in Hyperactives

Two recent studies help define the conditions under which high distractibility *can* be elicited in hyperactive children. In the first, Rosenthal and Allen (1980) used a speeded classification task to test the effects of irrelevant stimulus dimensions on task performance. The task stimuli represented four stimulus values of each of three dimensions (form, color, and position), the salience for each child having been assessed on Odom and Guzman's (1972) procedure. There were no differences between their hyperactive and control groups on the classification task when the irrelevant dimensions appearing on task stimuli were low on individual children's salience hierarchies. However, the hyperactives exhibited greater distraction effects than controls did (one-tailed t test) when the salience of the irrelevant dimension was high. These findings are reminiscent of the description of "exploratory strategies" presented earlier and could also be interpreted as supporting a stimulus-seeking hypothesis.

In the second study in which distractibility was reported in hyperactives, Radosh and Gittelman (1981) investigated the effects of appealing distractors (colorful pictures or fragments of abstract art) on the performance of hyperactive and normal children on a task in which arithmetic problems were shown for up to 3 seconds on a teaching machine. The presence of both types of distractors resulted in greater impairment in their hyperactive children than in the normal sample. The authors refer to two propositions on distractibility advanced earlier by Klein and Gittelman-Klein (1975). They suggest that distractibility represents "in part, exploratory behavior in the service of appetitive interests" and "in part, a response to mental effort and therefore mental fatigue" (p. 11). Not surprisingly, Radosh and Gittelman report that many of their subjects found the arithmetic task aversive; the children complained about the amount of work (there were 300 trials) and were frustrated by the fast pacing of the tasks.

Thus, some of the factors that elicit "distractibility" in hyperactive children include the degree of boredom, distaste, or difficulty associated with a particular task; the salience or novelty of potential distractors; the disinclination of hyperactive children to process beyond the more obvious or salient aspects of a task; and the children's failure to inhibit overt responses to task-irrelevant stimuli. It should be noted that all of these factors can be related to faulty self-regulatory processes and/or unusually strong approach tendencies in situations the children find rewarding.

SPECULATIONS REGARDING THE BASIC DEFICIT

Because the pattern of deficits that has been observed in ADD children points to several overlapping hypotheses regarding the nature of the mechanisms involved, it is difficult at this time to decide whether one of the postulated mechanisms is more basic than the others. One could argue, for example, that the basic deficit involves a strong inclination to seek immediate gratification and reinforcement. Hypotheses regarding stimulation-seeking behaviors might be included within this explanation. Alternatively, it is possible to stress the children's apparent lack of self-control. In this case, the central problem would be seen as involving a defective inhibitory mechanism. It also is possible to circumvent the issue of which of these processes is more central by positing an imbalance between approach and inhibitory forces.

These different hypotheses lead to slightly differing explanations of reported phenomena. An explanation involving a faulty control mechanism could be advanced, for example, to explain the apparent failure of hyperactive children to modulate their own arousal levels to meet situational demands. On the other hand, their tendency to become overly excited in reward-associated situations could result from an unusual sensitivity to reinforcement. Similarly, their impaired attention on dull or difficult tasks and the accompanying "underarousability" that has been reported could be attributed to the low level of stimulation or reinforcement these tasks afford. In conditions such as these, one might expect the children to find the necessity for concentrated effort particularly distasteful and unpleasant. Alternatively, it is possible to speak of the necessity for exerting both inhibitory and facilitory control in order to persevere on such tedious or demanding tasks.

It is evident that there is considerable concurrence between these interrelated hypotheses and the "exploratory versus search" distinction discussed earlier. Central to these formulations is an emphasis on a child's inclination to seek salience, novelty, and immediate reinforcement, as opposed to an ability to regulate behavior in accordance with more indirect and long-term goals.

Ruling Out Other Explanations for Observed Deficits

Several of the findings to be discussed help rule out hypotheses that have been advanced to account for observed deficits in hyperactive children. First, it is not necessary to posit either a basic avoidance deficit or an insensitivity to punishment (Freeman, 1978; Kinsbourne, 1977; Wender, 1971, 1974). Although the children fail to avoid negative consequences in many situations, these failures could be attributable to unusually strong approach tendencies and/or a relatively weak capacity to control response inclinations. It also seems unlikely that ADD children are incapable of forming appropriate associations or mediational responses in aversive situations (Gorenstein & Newman, 1980; Kinsbourne, 1977), although again, it is clear that they frequently fail to do so. A more probable explanation is that their approach inclinations are so powerful, and/or their inhibitory powers are so weak, that they are prevented from reflecting about causal relationships.

Two other hypotheses, a visual–perceptive deficit and a memory deficit (Aman, 1978; Sandoval, 1977), also can be eliminated as likely explanations for the children's performance deficits. As in the earlier discussion of distractibility, I do not suggest that hyperactive children never demonstrate deficits on perceptual or memory tasks. I do argue, however, that there is no basic deficiency in their capacity to perceive visual or auditory stimuli accurately, or to encode, store, and retrieve such information. When deficits are found on perceptual or memory tasks, I believe they can be attributed to a failure to invest sufficient effort in such activities as processing visual or auditory information carefully and deeply, committing the information to memory, and retrieving information that has been successfully processed and stored.

An alternate explanation for the reported "perseveration" problems of hyperactive children (Ross, 1976) is also considered here. Although examples of situations are presented in which hyperactive subjects have persisted in inappropriate behaviors, it is equally important to note that there are several reported examples of their abandoning correct solutions of problems prematurely to embark upon new approaches. Thus, the children do not appear to have a basic deficit in the ability to "change set." It seems more likely that they persist in inappropriate approach behaviors they find rewarding and that the frequently reported erratic and unpredictable quality of their performance is due to a similar inclination to seek novelty and avoid boredom. As in previous examples, it also could be argued that faulty self-regulatory processes fail both to inhibit inappropriate approach behaviors and to facilitate the onerous effort required to remain with a task until acceptable performance has been achieved. In either case, the proposed mechanisms could account for both "perseveration" in situations the children find reinforcing and a failure to persist in situations that they do not.

Effects of Treatment Manipulations

Changes resulting from treatment interventions seldom yield definitive answers about the nature of the processes underlying defective performance, as evidenced by the plethora of "explanations" that have been advanced to account for the effects of stimulant medication and contingency management. Nevertheless, such findings can contribute to researchers' understanding of the causes of performance deficits. If, for example, a child successfully performs a task he or she previously failed when an intervention is introduced, the researcher knows that the child possesses the knowledge or skills assessed by the task, and that a process influenced by the manipulation has prevented him or her from displaying this knowledge. Often, of course, the matter is not so clear. As Brown (1975) cautions, the production–mediation deficiency distinction is not absolute, but involves a continuum extending from overlearned skills to ones that a child is incapable of mastering.

Sometimes a given intervention seems to affect hyperactive and control children differently. As I have mentioned, this appears to be true of some reward schedules. In the case of stimulant medication, there is some evidence of parallel effects on ADD and control children (see Chapters 16 and 18 of this volume). This does not negate the possibility, however, that hyperactive children may have a greater need than normal children have for stimulant medication or judiciously applied reinforcers in order to perform within acceptable limits. It also appears that some manipulations fail to bring hyperactive samples up to the levels obtained by control samples receiving the same treatment. Thus, relatively speaking, the deficits remain.

The effects of cognitive training on hyperactives also can be informative, especially when researchers are trying to discover the limits of these children's competence and the factors that have prevented them from acquiring particular skills or problem-solving strategies. I have argued that this approach may be particularly appropriate for combating the secondary effects of ADD children's attentional, inhibitory, arousal, and reinforcement deficits (Douglas, 1980b). Cognitive training can be used to provide the children with information and problem-solving strategies that their basic deficits have prevented them from acquiring. It also can be used to teach the kinds of mediating behaviors that seem to be lacking in the disinhibitory pathologies (Gorenstein & Newman, 1980). These might include helping the children to become more aware of causal relationships between their own behaviors and events that follow, to gain better control over their own arousal levels and response tendencies, and to bridge delays in need gratification.

Cognitive-training programs of this kind have proved more successful than stimulant medication or contingency management in promoting generalization and maintenance of treatment effects on cognitive, social, and academic measures (Douglas, 1980b, in press-a, in press-b). This suggests that the effects have extended beyond temporary alleviation of production deficiencies. It also shows that when special care is taken to combat the children's basic deficits, their capacity for learning new skills is considerable.

Effects of Task Parameters and Conditions

A good deal also can be learned from examining the effects of a variety of task parameters and conditions on the performance of hyperactive children. Under naturally occurring circumstances the children's performance is unusually variable and often appears unpredictable (Douglas, 1972; Douglas & Peters, 1979). It may be revealing, therefore, to discover factors that influence the apparent inconsistency. As mentioned earlier, a number of factors serving to lower the demands for self-governed effort and concentration result in improved performance levels in the children. There are, as well, several examples of the complimentary phenomenon: When the requirement for self-directed, cautious effort is increased, their performance deteriorates. Manipulations having detrimental effects include extending the time they are asked to work on dull, unpopular tasks, or subjecting them to repeated administrations of the same boring task.

Interestingly, however, ADD children may behave quite differently when they are assigned colorful or moderately challenging tasks and when feedback is consistently available. ADD subjects seem to "settle in" to such situations after an erratic start. Examples are discussed below where they have shown surprisingly good transfer on challenging but interesting tasks. One might speculate that they become overly aroused or impulsive when they first meet these situations; thus the subsequent improvement in performance may be associated with adaptation, accompanied by a lowering of arousal to more optimal levels.

The method of presenting task stimuli also seems to have important consequences. There are examples where ADD children have responded poorly to materials presented automatically at a pace set by the experimenter, but have improved their performance when they were able to set their own pace. A likely explanation is that a higher price is paid in the experimenter-paced paradigm for lapses of attention.

TASKS ON WHICH DEFICITS APPEAR

Differences between samples of hyperactive and control subjects have been found on a number of tasks (Aman, 1978; Barkley, 1977; Douglas, 1972; Douglas & Peters, 1979; Messer, 1976; Rosenthal & Allen, 1978; Ross & Ross, 1976; Ross & Pelham, 1981; Sandoval, 1977; Whalen & Henker, 1976). These include relatively simple tasks, traditionally considered as measures of attention or vigilance; complex cognitive tasks requiring perceptual and logical search strategies; tasks involving motor control; measures of academic performance; and tests and situations assessing social awareness and judgment. Emphasis here is placed on the "attentional" and cognitive measures.

Vigilance and Reaction-Time Tasks

Much of the early work with hyperactive children involved vigilance or reaction-time tasks. Although a variety of vigilance paradigms have been used, most share a number of common properties. Subjects are required to pay close attention to relatively simple visual or auditory stimuli, often over extended periods of time, so that they will be able to respond in a designated manner to certain stimuli or configurations of stimuli when they appear. An additional requirement involves withholding responses to nonsignal stimuli. Because of the extended and constant nature of the demands made on subjects, the tasks sometimes have been referred to as "continuous-performance tests" (CPTs) (Rosvold, Mirsky, Sarason, Bransome, & Beck, 1956).

Simple reaction-time tasks, as well as reaction-time tasks involving delay (DRT tasks), have also been employed in studies with hyperactive samples. In the simple versions, stimuli are delivered at either constant or random intervals, and the subject must respond as quickly as possible. In DRT tasks, the child receives a warning signal, followed by a delay period, which is terminated by a reaction signal to which he is required to respond as quickly as possible. Like vigilance tasks, reaction-time tasks are experimenter-paced, require constant monitoring on the part of the subject over a period of several minutes, and necessitate withholding of inappropriate responses.

On vigilance measures, hyperactives generally have been found to make more errors of omission (failing to respond to correct stimuli) and of commission (responding to incorrect stimuli) than normal controls. On reaction-time tasks, mean latencies are generally slower in hyperactive subjects. Variability of reaction times is also greater, reflecting the frequently reported erratic quality of the children's performance. Hyperactives also make more inappropriate responses on DRT tasks; these errors include pushing the response button before the reaction signal appears, responding to the warning signal, and pushing more than once in response to the reaction signal. Thus, both types of tasks reveal a failure on the part of the children to react effectively and consistently to target stimuli, as well as a failure to withhold inappropriate responses (Barkley, 1977; Douglas, 1972; Douglas & Peters, 1979; Rosenthal & Allen, 1978; Ross & Ross, 1976; Sandoval, 1977; Whalen & Henker, 1976).

These findings have been interpreted as evidence for concentration and inhibitory problems in hyperactive children. It should be noted, however, that it is difficult within these paradigms to separate the effects of attentional and impulsivity difficulties. This problem is particularly obvious in early studies, in which investigators apparently did not delete trials on which impulsive responses were made when computing reaction times. Even when this precaution is taken, however, the disruptive effects of making an incorrect response might influence performance on adjacent trials. On the other hand, many of the inappropriate responses made by ADD children on these tasks are *not* associated with incorrect or misleading stimuli. Thus, errors of this kind provide relatively clear evidence of inhibitory problems, provided it is remembered that they appear within the general context of tasks making heavy attentional demands.

These early findings have held up relatively well in recent studies. Loiselle *et al.* (1980) obtained highly significant group differences on their vigilance paradigm (discussed above). The study is of particular interest because, as well as scoring omission and commission errors, the investigators computed reaction-time scores based only on correct responses. Since their experimental and control subjects differed on all three of their measures (percentage of correct responses, commission errors, and mean reaction times), it probably can be concluded that the hyperactives demonstrated both attentional and inhibitory problems.

Hoy, Weiss, Minde, and Cohen (1978) measured sustained attention with a checking test in which hyperactive and normal adolescents were required to tap only when they heard words containing an *s*. The hyperactives differed from controls only on the measure reflecting incorrect responses. There is evidence, therefore, that at least the impulsivity problems of hyperactives continue into adolescence. Hoy *et al.* also report that their hyperactive adolescents were *not* more affected than control subjects were by a distraction condition consisting of a voice reading a passage about heroin, presumably a highly "meaningful" topic for this age group.

A few recent investigators have included a nonhyperactive "clinical" control group in their designs. Using a DRT task, Firestone and Martin (1979) found that the mean reaction time of their hyperactive group was significantly slower than that of both an asthmatic and a normal control sample. The hyperactive children also made more interstimulus and redundant responses than both control groups did, although the difference between the asthmatic and hyperactive children did not reach statistical significance.

Werry and Aman (in press) compared the performance of hyperactive and "psychiatrically normal" enuretic children on a CPT. Of three measures—omissions, commissions and response time—only the commission score yielded significant group differences.

Finally, Sostek, Buchsbaum, and Rapoport (1980) used signal detection techniques to study the vigilance performance of hyperactive and normal boys. They report group differences on a "perceptual sensitivity" or *d′* measure, which takes account of both "hit rates" and "false alarms." A second measure, "β," which is thought to reflect caution in reporting events, failed to yield group differences. As the authors point out, interpretation of these measures within the CPT paradigm is still problematic. With further work, however, signal detection methods may extend researchers' understanding of hyperactive children's difficulties on vigilance-type tasks.

Effects of Task and Treatment Conditions and Manipulations

Early reports of abnormal decrements in the performance of hyperactives over time on vigilance-type tasks have been replicated in recent studies; there also is some evidence that the children become more restless than controls do when tasks are repeated (Barlow, 1977; Douglas & Peters, 1979; Zahn, Little, & Wender, 1978). Interestingly, Barlow reports significant improvement when stimulation was added to the relatively dull materials used in his vigilance task. This finding is highly relevant to the "stimulation-seeking" hypothesis discussed earlier and should be pursued further.

That the children's performance deficit is not due to discrimination problems, or difficulty in making the necessary motor responses, is suggested by a study by Sykes, Douglas, and Morgenstern (1973) in which the performance of the same subjects was compared on the CPT, a choice reaction-time (CRT) task, and a serial reaction-time (SRT) test. The need to sustain attention is reduced in the CRT task by presenting the stimuli in discrete, announced trials; in the SRT test, the effect of attentional lapses is minimized by allowing the subject to pace the arrival of task stimuli. There were no group differences on the CRT task, or on the number of correct responses on the SRT test. Interestingly, the hyperactives did make significantly more incorrect responses on the SRT test, suggesting that impulsivity remains a problem, even within this paradigm.

There is general agreement that stimulant medication enhances the performance of hyperactive children on vigilance and reaction-time tasks (Aman, 1978; Rapoport, Buchsbaum, Zahn, Weingartner, Ludlow, & Mikkelsen, 1978; Sostek *et al.*, 1980; Werry & Aman, in press; Zahn, Rapoport, & Thompson, 1980). Some of the more recent studies, however, serve as a reminder that the effect of the stimulants on hyperactives is not unique; that is, it is not qualitatively different from the effect on normals. Nevertheless, Werry and Aman do suggest that the response of their hyperactive group may have differed quantitatively from that of the controls, in that it appeared more dramatic, although they refer to the statistical problems that arise in making such comparisons. Zahn *et al.* also report more pronounced drug effects in their hyperactive subjects, but attribute this to the significantly higher placebo values for this group.

It is noteworthy that findings from the two experiments by the National Institute of Mental Health (NIMH) group provide evidence that at least some of the differences between hyperactives and control groups remain in the drug condition. In the Sostek *et al.* study, for example, the *d′* difference between hyperactive and normal children was maintained under drug treatment.

Effects of reinforcement schedules on the performance of hyperactives on these measures also has been demonstrated (Douglas, 1980b; Douglas & Peters, 1979). In a study by Douglas and Parry (1983), for example, continuous reward reduced mean reaction times and reaction-time variability in both normal and hyperactive children on a DRT task. However, the behavioral intervention did not bring the hyperactives up to the performance level of a control group that also received positive feedback. In addition, the reaction times of the hyperactive group dropped more sharply than those of controls when extinction trials were introduced. These and other findings suggest that hyperactives may be strongly influenced by the withdrawal or withholding of rewards, whether this occurs during extinction trials, in response-cost procedures, or on partial reinforcement schedules.

Hyperactives also demonstrate other distinctive responses to reinforcement contingencies. The positive effects of reward during DRT tasks sometimes are accompanied by an abnormal increase in impulsive responding (Firestone & Douglas, 1975), which seems to be associated with increased arousal in the positive condition. It is particularly noteworthy that negative feedback also improved the ADD children's performance on the attentional measures, but did *not* lead to an increase in impulsive errors. In addition, Parry (1973) found that, although the performance of her normal sample benefited from the motivating effects of positive feedback even when it was delivered randomly (i.e., on a noncontingent schedule), the performance of hyperactives deteriorated in this condition. Thus, noncontingent positive feedback may increase arousal or distraction in ADD children, without guiding their attention to the specific qualities of the responses required. Another example of ADD children's atypical reactions to reinforcement occurred in a SRT paradigm used by Parry. She reports that reaction times of hyperactives dropped below those of normals on a partial (50%) schedule, whereas no group differences were found when the reinforcers were administered on a 100% schedule.

The results from these various studies do *not* support the notion that hyperactives are unresponsive to either positive or negative reinforcement (Wender, 1971, 1974). In fact, in the case of rewards, the opposite appears to be true; the children seem to be unusually sensitive both to the presence of rewards and to the loss of anticipated rewards.

Differential Reinforcement for Low-Rate Responding (DRL) Task

Although there are problems in obtaining independent concentration and impulsivity measures on vigilance and DRT tasks, the differential reinforcement for low-rate responding (DRL) paradigm provides a more direct measure of the ability of hyperactives to inhibit response tendencies. The paradigm does not involve correct versus incorrect stimuli, but requires the repeated withholding of responses over a series of time intervals. The task also introduces other elements, however, that are likely to be critical in hyperactive children. These are the presence of rewards and the frustration that is likely to accompany failure to obtain them.

Gordon (1979) compared the performance of hyperactive and nonhyperactive boys on a DRL task in which the children were required to withhold responding for brief time intervals (6 seconds) in order to obtain candy rewards. If the subjects responded before 6 seconds had elapsed, they had to wait another 6 seconds before a successful response could be made. There were highly significant group differences on three measures of DRL performance: total number of responses, number of reinforcements earned, and an efficiency score. The hyperactive boys responded more frequently but obtained fewer rewards than the controls.

Gordon also found that the hyperactive and normal boys used different strategies to help themselves wait during the delay intervals. The mediating behaviors employed by the hyperactives were more often observable (e.g., swinging the legs, hitting, tapping, or stomping), whereas a larger proportion of the normal boys reported the use of cognitive mediators.

Gorenstein and Newman (1980) report that deficits on DRL performance have been found in septal-lesioned animals, and they draw a parallel between the animals' failure to withstand delay in this paradigm and clinical and experimental findings suggesting that "psychopaths and antisocial adolescents are less disposed than normals to forego immediate gratification as a means of obtaining a larger reward later on" (p. 310). They also point out that the SHF animals' deficit can be overcome by providing an external stimulus to indicate the interval during which the response must be withheld. They believe that this suggests a "loss of normal ability to mediate temporal intervals." It is possible, however, that the animals are so highly motivated to obtain the reinforcers that little effort is directed toward mediation. The external stimuli may decrease the need for inner controls, much as having an authority figure monitor a hyperactive child's performance increases task-relevant behaviors. It is important that Gordon's experiment with hyperactive and normal samples be replicated. It would be interesting, too, to investigate the specific impact of the concrete rewards in Gordon's paradigm by administering the DRL task under both reward and nonreward conditions.

TASKS INVOLVING PERCEPTUAL SEARCH

There is a good deal of evidence that hyperactive children perform poorly on complex cognitive tasks requiring such visual strategies as scanning a visual field in an organized, purposeful manner, or conducting an exhaustive search for critical attributes of task stimuli. Although less information is available from tasks requiring careful listening, it appears likely that hyperactives also extract information from complex auditory stimuli less efficiently than normal children do. Since it is essential to differentiate between deficits resulting from ineffective perceptual-search strategies and those that stem from other perceptual deficits, such as impaired acuity, faulty memory, or visual–spatial problems, results from tasks tapping these abilities are contrasted here with findings from the perceptual-search tasks.

Matching Familiar Figures and Embedded Figures Tests

Differences between hyperactive and normal children on the Matching Familiar Figures Test of Reflection–Impulsivity (MFF) have been reported in several age groups, including preschool, elementary-school, and high-school samples (Aman, 1978; Douglas & Peters, 1979; Messer, 1976; Sandoval, 1977). A recent follow-up study by Hopkins, Perlman, Hechtman, and Weiss (1979) suggests that the children may not outgrow these difficulties. In addition, Firestone and Martin (1979) recently found that hyperactives made more errors than did both a normal and a clinical control group consisting of asthmatic children.

Earlier reviewers also have reported hyperactive–normal differences on the Embedded Figures Test of Field Dependence–Independence (EFT) (Aman, 1978; Douglas & Peters, 1979; Messer, 1976; Sandoval, 1977). Here, too, the differences continue into young adulthood. Perlman *et al.*'s hyperactive subjects took longer to isolate figures from embedding contexts, isolated fewer of the correct figures, and showed greater variability on both correct and incorrect responses.

There has been a good deal of debate about the nature of the processes assessed by the MFF and the EFT. After an extensive review of the literature, Messer (1976) concluded that the two tests share a demand for visual scanning and analysis, as well as careful decision making in situations of high response uncertainty. Messer based this argument on the similar patterns of findings obtained in research with the MFF and the EFT and on relatively consistent reports of significant correlations between the two instruments. It should be noted that this interpretation of the abilities assessed by the EFT differs from that of other authors, who have considered the poor performance of hyperactive children on the EFT as evidence of "distractibility" (Aman, 1978; Sandoval, 1977).

In the case of the MFF, much of the disagreement in the literature has centered on the response-time measure. Because of the close association drawn by Kagan and his associates (Kagan, Rosman, Day, Albert, & Phillips, 1964) between reflection–impulsivity and "conceptual tempo," several investigators, somewhat unthinkingly, have equated response times with impulsivity. Since findings on the latency measures have been less consistent than those obtained from error scores have been, some authors have expressed distrust of the MFF as a measure of impulsivity.

Interpretation of latency measures obtained from the MFF and similar instruments is difficult. Latency can be highly influenced by the manner in which individual examiners administer and score the tasks (Douglas & Peters, 1979). Equally important, findings from other tasks, as well as observations of the performance of hyperactives on the MFF, suggest that ADD children often do not use "looking times" as efficiently as normals do. As a consequence, they may require more time than controls do to obtain an equivalent amount of information from complex visual stimuli. Parry (1973), for example, carried out separate analyses of latency and error measures for the first and second halves of the MFF on data from hyperactive and normal control subjects. She found no group difference on the mean latency score during the first half of the test, but on the second half, the hyperactives responded more quickly than the controls did. Error scores, on the other hand, tended to be higher for the hyperactive group throughout. Parry suggests that the ADD children probably became progressively more frustrated as they received negative feedback for their frequent errors and consequently rushed to get through the test. She also questions the assumption that the hyperactive children's longer latencies during the first half reflected care in approaching the task. She reports that "many of the children glanced at the test items, then around the room, and then chose hastily" (p. 74).

Subject-Paced Viewing Tasks

Ain (1980) studied the performance of groups of hyperactive, reading-disabled, and normal children on subject-paced viewing tasks. Although the study was originally designed to investigate the stimulus-seeking hypothesis, it also provided information on the perceptual efficiency and perceptual discrimination of ADD children. The major experimental paradigm involved placing pictorial stimuli representing several levels of complexity, incongruity, or familiarity in a carousel projector and allowing subjects to self-pace the presentation of the pictures. Her experimental stimuli were modifications of materials developed by Berlyne (Berlyne, 1971; Berlyne & Parkam, 1968) and Faw and Nunnally (Faw & Nunnally, 1968a, 1968b; Nunnally, Faw, & Bashford, 1969) to study the effects of novelty on cognitive processes. Since viewing times were under the subjects' control, Ain was able to measure the extent to which stimuli of varying degrees of complexity, familiarity, or incongruity held the interest of children in the three subject groups.

Evidence for the stimulus-seeking hypothesis was ambiguous and difficult to interpret. In her study involving ordinary and incongruous stimuli, Ain's hyperactive group looked significantly longer than normal controls did at the incongruous stimuli during the first trial, whereas looking times for the two groups did not differ for the ordinary stimuli. In addition, the hyperactive group looked significantly longer at the incongruous stimuli than at the ordinary stimuli on the first trial. The fact that these differences occurred only on the first trial, however, suggests that any special attraction to novelty on the part of the ADD children was short-lived. It also is possible that the differences obtained were dependent on a "double" novelty effect, arising from the newness of the task itself, as well as from the novelty contained in the incongruous pictures. In her second study, in which "novelty" was defined as degree of familiarity with the stimuli, Ain found no support for the hypothesis that hyperactives have an unusual preference for novelty. In discussing her results, Ain suggests that further studies should be carried out in which novel elements are added to dull, routine tasks, such as the CPT employed by Barlow (1977). Although it is possible that the game-like quality of Ain's experimental procedures minimized the effects of manipulating novelty levels within the task stimuli, her findings can be considered as providing only limited support for the stimulus-seeking hypothesis.

An unannounced recognition task, administered at the end of her first two studies, yielded information about the children's efficiency in processing complex visual stimuli. Hyperactive children were less accurate than controls were in recognizing pictures of scenery they had viewed previously. Since there was no significant difference between the looking times of hyperactive and control children on this or a previous free-looking task, it appears that the hyperactive children were not using viewing times as effectively as controls were. Two further studies investigated the efficiency with which hyperactive children encode and match pictorial stimuli. The paradigm was changed from a free-looking procedure to one in which the children knew that the accuracy of their responses was being assessed. In both studies, ADD children apparently required longer encoding and matching times in order to obtain the accuracy levels of normal controls, suggesting again that they were not processing the stimuli as efficiently as the normal children were.

Ain also found that her hyperactive children were as sensitive as normal controls were to relatively minor changes, consisting of the addition of one, two, or three details to the pictures. Like the normal children, they extended their looking times as either ordinary or incongruous details were added. It is evident, therefore, that hyperactive children are capable of noticing and reacting appropriately to relatively subtle changes in perceptual stimuli.

Picture Recognition Task

Sprague and his associates (e.g., Sprague & Sleator, 1977) have completed several drug studies using a picture recognition task (PRT). Since this task sometimes has been designated a measure of "short-term memory," and since I am arguing that hyperactive children do not experience unusual difficulty with most memory tasks, it is important to consider the demands made by the PRT. In addition, before discussing drug studies in which the task was used, information regarding the performance of ADD children and controls in a nonmedicated condition is of interest.

The PRT involves the presentation of a series of arrays of 3 to 15 pictures. Each array is followed a few seconds later by a test picture, and the subject must decide whether or not the test picture appeared in the immediately preceding array. Measures are taken of accuracy of response and mean speed of responding. It is noteworthy that, along with the demands on visual memory, the PRT makes rather heavy attentional, inhibitory, and perceptual-search demands. Subjects must carefully scan a number of visual stimuli in order to perform relatively complex matching operations; furthermore, they must remain continuously vigilant and involved in the task over periods of several minutes.

Werry and Aman (in press) report results from a study in which they compared the performance of hyperactive and enuretic children on the PRT. The hyperactives performed more poorly than their enuretic peers did and also had faster response times. The latter finding was interpreted by the investigators as indicating greater impulsivity. It is of interest to note that, in the same study, hyperactive–enuretic group differences also were obtained on the CPT. Thus, it is difficult to judge the relative contributions of problems involving sustained attention, inhibitory control, the application of sophisticated perceptual-search strategies, and the memory demands mentioned by the investigators.

Videotaped Lessons

Barkley (1977) showed brief videotapes of an adult female teaching school lessons about fictional characters to normal and hyperactive boys. Subjects were forewarned that they might be asked questions about the lesson later. Thus, accuracy scores on the retention test reflected the children's success in processing the visual and auditory information contained in the lessons. The hyperactive group made more mistakes than controls did on the retention test. In addition, the ADD children spent less time observing the film and also were more active while it was being shown. Again, the evidence points to less efficient use of "looking times" by ADD children.

In attempting to understand the perceptual-search deficits of hyperactive children, it is important to note that their poor performance on such tasks cannot always be explained by observable "off-task" behaviors, as in the Barkley (1977) and Parry (1973) studies. Ain (1980) took particular care in her study to score looking times only when the children's gaze appeared to be fixed on the task stimuli. Thus, both gross nonlooking behaviors and more subtle perceptual-search deficiencies appear to be implicated.

PERCEPTUAL DISCRIMINATION AND RETENTION

In ruling out possible causes for hyperactive children's performance deficits, it is important to stress that there are many indications that the children are capable of perceiving visual and auditory stimuli clearly and accurately. It also appears that neuronal representations of perceptual stimuli persist over considerable periods of time, *provided* the children have concentrated sufficiently during the period when neural traces of such images were being established.

Visual and Auditory Acuity

Early evidence that hyperactive children are capable of noticing small discrepancies in auditory stimuli was obtained from a comparison of the performance of ADD and normal children on the Wepman Test of Auditory Discrimination (Douglas, 1972). In addition, no significant hyperactive–normal differences were found on the picture completion subtest of the Wechsler Intelligence Scale for Children (WISC), indicating that ADD children are aware of relatively subtle discrepancies in pictures. It is noteworthy that on both of these tasks the child must process only one item or one pair of items at a time. Consequently, demands for self-regulated, organized search strategies are minimized.

A study by McIntyre *et al.* (1978) also provides convincing evidence of the ability of hyperactive children to detect small differences in visual stimuli, even when the stimuli are exposed for very brief intervals. McIntyre *et al.* report that the spans of apprehension of normal and hyperactive boys were affected equivalently by variations in signal–noise similarity and noise redundancy of letters presented tachistoscopically. A previous study (Denton & McIntyre, 1978) had shown that spans of apprehension of ADD boys were much smaller than those of normal boys in the presence of "noise" (nonsignal) letters. Since no group differences were found when no noise letters were present, they at first suspected that the hyperactive boys were more distracted than the controls were by the noise letters. However, McIntyre *et al.* believe that the equal sensitivity of hyperactive and normal boys to signal–noise similarity and noise redundancy in their second study disproves the distractibility hypothesis, since some of the noise conditions would be expected to be considerably more distracting than others.

These investigators offer two alternative hypotheses to explain the consistently poor performance of the hyperactive sample in the presence of noise letters: Either the afterimage of the letter arrays must decay more rapidly in the hyperactive boys, or their pickup of information from the decaying afterimage must be slower. Since evidence from the next study to be discussed suggests that hyperactives have good immediate, short-term, and long-term memory, it seems unlikely that afterimages of hyperactives are subject to unusually fast decay, provided the images have been established accurately and fully. On the other hand, the weight of the evidence just summarized points to McIntyre *et al.*'s second hypothesis; that is, the pickup of information from the decaying afterimage is less efficient in hyperactive children. This hypothesis also concurs with Ain's findings.

Visual and Auditory Retention

Benezra (1980) employed a wide range of measures to study verbal and nonverbal memory in hyperactive, reading-disabled, and normal boys. She found few hyperactive–normal differences on her visual and visual–spatial memory tasks. The hyperactives did not differ significantly from controls in their reproduction of visual–spatial sequences demonstrated by an examiner (Corsi, 1972), or on a task requiring recall of the positions of small circles placed at a number of positions along straight lines (Posner, 1966). The hyperactive boys also experienced no particular difficulty in recognizing recurring geometric and nonsense figures that they had been shown previously (Kimura, 1963). Finally, although the ADD group had some difficulty copying and reproducing a complex geometric figure (Osterrieth, 1944; Rey, 1941), their memory of the figure 45 minutes later had not deteriorated any more than that of the normal control group had.

Benezra obtained equally convincing evidence of the ability to ADD children to retain verbally presented stimuli over both brief and extended time intervals. She used tasks requiring the repetition of digits or letters (Kimura, 1964); the repetition of letters after either "unfilled" delay intervals of 3 to 30 seconds or "filled" intervals in which subjects performed verbal counting tasks (Peterson & Peterson, 1959); and the recall and recognition of word lists and acoustically related word pairs (Kintsch, 1970; Wechsler, 1972).

These findings agree with earlier studies in which no hyperactive–normal differences were found on tasks involving immediate memory (Douglas, 1972), and they extend the findings to tasks involving retention over longer periods. The children's ability to retain information in memory is particularly evident in the case of the Posner (1966) visual–spatial task and the verbal paired-associates task; there was no evidence of greater decay of the memory traces in hyperactive children up to periods of 45 minutes. Although these results provide strong evidence of the verbal and nonverbal recall abilities of hyperactives, it should not be concluded that the children will do well on all memory tasks. As will be discussed shortly, hyperactive–normal differences *have* been found on tasks in which deliberate, organized effort and sophisticated strategies are necessary for the efficient acquisition of the material that must be remembered.

Effects of Treatment Manipulations on Tasks Involving Perceptual Search

The application of treatment manipulations sometimes makes it possible to differentiate between deficits arising directly out of self-regulatory problems and those that result from an earlier failure to learn essential search strategies. For example, if a child spontaneously begins using a particular strategy when he is given medication, the researcher or clinician can avoid the wasteful and sometimes alienating experience of trying to teach the child knowledge he already possesses and can concentrate, instead, on helping him make more consistent use of acquired skills.

If the child does not demonstrate the skill, even when a variety of manipulations are applied, further diagnostic testing and teaching may reveal why he has failed to learn it previously. A youngster who can be taught the strategy readily may simply not have received proper instruction, whereas failure to master the new learning may result from a number of more complex causes. Douglas and Peters (1979) have postulated that a likely cause in hyperactive children is past failure, because of attentional and inhibitory problems, to develop the organized cognitive structures on which such learning depends. If this reasoning is correct, a carefully programmed course of instruction in which the missing information is taught in a hierarchically structured manner becomes essential. Another question may then arise: How do the various treatment manipulations influence the acquisition of new learning of this kind? Regrettably, although there have been numerous treatment studies with hyperactives, researchers know little about the impact of treatment manipulations (such as medication and contingency management) on the acquisition and maintenance of *new learning*.

Most of the available information on treatment effects is limited to *production* deficiencies. As in the case of the more simple reaction-time tasks discussed earlier, it appears that these interventions can have either positive or negative impact on the application of perceptual search strategies. Some reviewers have suggested that any positive action of the stimulants is limited to relatively simple, repetitive tasks, and a few have argued that effects on complex cognitive processes are likely to be detrimental (Douglas & Peters, 1979). Recent findings from tasks requiring perceptual-search strategies make it clear that an additional variable—dosage level—also must be taken into account.

Effects of Stimulants and Major Tranquilizers on Perceptual-Search Tasks

There are several reports of improvement in MFF scores of hyperactive children as a result of administration of stimulant medication (Aman, 1978; Douglas & Peters, 1979; Sandoval, 1977). In the first investigation of the effects of different dosage levels of methylphenidate on the MFF, Brown and Sleator (1979) found that a relatively low dose (.3 mg/kg) markedly decreased errors made by ADD children on the test, in contrast to both placebo and a high dose (1.0 mg/kg), neither of which affected the error score significantly. No differences occurred between any of the drug conditions on the latency measure.

An earlier study by Sprague and Sleator (1977) involving the PRT lends support to the argument that higher levels of the stimulants may actually impair the children's performance on cognitive tasks. They found that accuracy of performance on the PRT was markedly enhanced at .3 mg/kg of methylphenidate, whereas performance at 1.0 mg/kg fell somewhat below the level achieved under placebo. It is of interest to note that significant drug effects were obtained only on the 15-item matrices, which presumably made heaviest demands on concentration and on the application of perceptual search and memory strategies.

In discussing their results, Sprague and Sleator draw attention to the fact that although their higher dosage produced deterioration on the PRT, this same medication level resulted in greatest improvement on teachers' ratings of the children's social behavior. Unfortunately, questions arise regarding the comparability of findings on the behavioral and cognitive measures used by Sprague and Sleator, because data from the PRT and the teachers' ratings were collected at different points along the time–response curve. Nevertheless, the results highlight the importance of comparing dosage effects on cognitive and behavioral measures.

One further point should be raised regarding the Sprague and Sleator study. These investigators refer to the PRT as a "learning" task and thus interpret the drug effects as effects on learning. Although the PRT might be considered a prototype of some learning situations, it is important to differentiate between changes that reflect more effective use of already learned search strategies and changes that result from mastering new, more sophisticated problem-solving strategies. The drug effects obtained by Sprague and Sleator most clearly reflect alleviation of production deficiencies.

A study by Werry and Aman (1975), which also involved the PRT, underscores the importance of investigating relationships among drug type, dosage level, and task complexity. These investigators studied the effects of a low dose of methylphenidate (.3 mg/kg) and both a high (.05 mg/kg) and a low (.025 mg/kg) dose of haloperidol, a major tranquilizer, on the performance of hyperactive and unsocialized aggressive children. Their test battery included the PRT and a CPT. Werry and Aman point out that, in all of the significant results obtained on the two tests, the rank order of the mean scores was the same. Subjects performed best on the low dosage of methylphenidate, followed by the low dose of haloperidol, the placebo, and the high dose of haloperidol. There was some evidence, as well, that the high dose of haloperidol caused deterioration of performance. It should be noted that the dosage Werry and Aman considered high (.05 mg/kg) is well within levels recommended in pediatric manuals. A significant interaction on the PRT suggested that the high dose of haloperidol exerted its greatest depressant effect at a moderate level of task difficulty, while methylphenidate (low dose) improved performance at the most difficult task level.

Werry and Aman tentatively suggest that the hyperactive child comes into the test situation slightly overaroused, and that the "slight slowing" produced by a low dose of haloperidol is "just enough for him to catch a little more of what is going on around him" (p. 794), whereas the higher dose presumably impairs attention. They attribute the positive effects of the low dose of methylphenidate to "a true physiological increase in efficiency" (p. 794).

Finally, Barkley (1977) reports that the administration of methylphenidate (10 mg to each subject) resulted in improved performance in his hyperactive group on the videotaped lessons described earlier. While on medication, the ADD children spent more time viewing the movie and also improved their scores on the retention test.

The Effects of Reinforcers on Perceptual-Search Tasks

Studies of the effects of reinforcing "impulsive" (the subjects were not diagnosed as hyperactive) children for delaying responding on the MFF have not resulted in significant improvement on error scores. On the other hand, the introduction of response costs for incorrect responses has been shown to produce significant changes on both the latency and the error measures (Errickson, Wyne, & Routh, 1973; Messer, 1976). Again, the essential question appears to concern *how the children use their viewing time.*

If similar improvements are obtained with children diagnosed as hyperactive, these, together with the improvements found in the drug studies, would suggest that a substantial proportion of ADD children's performance deficit on the MFF is attributable to production deficiencies, as opposed to mediation deficiencies. That is, it could be concluded that the children ordinarily do not make full use of perceptual-search strategies they already know. However, this does not preclude the possibility that, in addition, the strategies available to hyperactives are less efficient than those of normal children.

The Effects of Cognitive Training on Perceptual-Search Strategies

Douglas, Parry, Marton, and Garson (1976) investigated the effects of cognitive training techniques on the performance of hyperactive children on a large battery of measures that included the MFF. Modeling, self-verbalization, self-reinforcement, and self-monitoring techniques were used to teach the children both general problem-approach ("metacognitive") skills and the more specific operations required for efficient matching and comparison of visual stimuli. The training methods also were geared toward helping the children combat their concentration and inhibitory problems. Substantial improvements were obtained on both error and latency measures, and these persisted over a 3-month follow-up period. In addition, since materials other than MFF stimuli were used in the training sessions, the changes found on the MFF constitute evidence of generalization of training effects. Proof of generalization or maintenance of therapeutic effects has been extremely rare thus far in both drug and contingency-management studies with hyperactive children (Douglas, 1980b). The size, generalization, and maintenance of the improvements found by Douglas *et al.* raise the possibility that the changes produced may not have been limited to the correction of production deficiencies, but involved, as well, the learning of superior perceptual-search and metacognitive strategies. However, this matter requires further study.

TASKS INVOLVING LOGICAL OR CONCEPTUAL SEARCH

A few investigators have studied the performance of hyperactive children on cognitive tasks in which the solution of relatively complex problems depends on the discovery of underlying concepts, meanings, or relationships. Successful mastery typically also involves arriving at an accurate understanding of the nature of the problem, giving careful consideration to several alternative solutions, and applying appropriate strategies and knowledge in order to arrive at the correct solution.

It is probably on tasks of this kind that the impact of past learning is most evident. If a child has approached earlier opportunities for perceptual and conceptual learning in an impulsive and inattentive manner, neural representations ("schemata") of those experiences are likely to be less rich, elaborated, and organized than those of other children of similar intellectual potential. In addition, mastery of sophisticated problem-solving strategies, both general and specific, is likely to be less complete.

Memory Tasks

Although hyperactive children seem to have no particular difficulty in storing information so long as it has been adequately processed, there is evidence that the processing skills and effort required to establish clear, well-organized neuronal representations of new learning frequently are inadequate in ADD children. They appear to have less mastery than normal children do of the more sophisticated mnemonic devices. Effective use of mnemonic skills probably also is limited by a less complete network of images and ideas on which the kinds of associations that facilitate memory can be developed. Again, however, difficulties arise in attempting to differentiate between production and mediation deficiencies. As on other cognitive tasks, ADD children are likely to employ even familiar strategies and knowledge in a haphazard, inconsistent manner.

There have been a few instances in which increasing or manipulating task demands has exposed deficiencies in hyperactive children on tasks on which their performance previously was considered adequate. Spring, Yellin, and Greenberg (1976), for example, obtained significant group differences using an extended form of the digit span test that involved administering the spans at each level three times, using different digit sequences. When Benezra (1980) used 12-word lists, she found no differences on any of her measures (including primacy and recency effects) in the ability of hyperactive and normal children to memorize the material. Peters's (1977) hyperactive group, on the other hand, experienced significantly more difficulty than controls did with a 34-word list. It seems likely that these differences are attributable to increased demands for sustained, strategic effort.

Studies with paired-associates and related tasks provide additional insight into the difficulties ADD children have with some memory tasks. Kinsbourne, Swanson, and their associates have completed several studies using a Categorization Learning Task (CLT), in which the subject is shown pictures of several animals and is told that each of the animals is to be assigned to one of four zoos. The subject's job is to learn, over repeated trials, the particular zoo with which each animal is associated (Kinsbourne, 1977). Kinsbourne reports little difference between the performance of hyperactives and controls on initial trials, but "the rate of further gain of information by the hyperactives is more gradual than that of control subjects" (p. 296). It appears likely that the diminished effectiveness of the ADD children over learning trials is related to a disinclination to continue struggling with this rather tedious task.

Further evidence that hyperactives fail to apply themselves fully and efficiently to the task of forming associations on the CLT can be found in a study by Dalby, Kinsbourne, Swanson, and Sobol (1977) involving hyperactives who were favorable responders to stimulant medication. Performance on the CLT at three presentation rates (4, 8, and 12 seconds per item) was compared in a methylphenidate–placebo double-blind crossover design. Unfortunately, no normal control group was included. Instead, the investigators refer to the "total time hypothesis," which states that, in normal subjects, a fixed amount of time is necessary to learn a fixed amount of material, regardless of the number of trials into which that time is divided. Performance of the drug-responsive hyperactives conformed to the "fixed-time hypothesis" only when the children were on stimulant medication. In the placebo state, the slower presentation rates were not used effectively. Dalby *et al.* attribute the children's inferior performance while receiving placebo to inattention. Thus the improvement on methylphenidate is seen as resulting from the effects of the stimulant on attentive processes. In discussing their results, Dalby *et al.* suggest that repeated brief presentations of material to be processed might constitute another way of minimizing the impact of ADD children's attentional deficits on tasks of this kind. However, two earlier attempts to test the hypothesis that hyperactives would benefit from fast presentation rates of task stimuli provided little support for the hypothesis (Freibergs & Douglas, 1969; Sykes, Douglas, Weiss, & Minde, 1971). It appears that a number of factors, including the nature of task demands and the children's reactions to novelty and to repetition, interact in complex ways to influence their response to such procedural manipulations.

Although detailed data on dosage effects are not included, Kinsbourne (1977) reports that, typically, the difference between drug and placebo increases as the dose of stimulant medication is increased to an optimal level. He states that further increase beyond this point, however, "narrows and even abolishes the advantage" (p. 297). Swanson and Kinsbourne (1976) have raised another complex issue regarding stimulant effects on the CLT. They had hyperactive and nonhyperactive children perform the task while on and off stimulant medication. The subjects were later tested for retention of the material in either the same drug condition or in the alternate condition. These investigators are convinced that their findings demonstrate "symmetrical state-dependent learning" in those hyperactive children who are positive responders to stimulant medication. Clearly, this issue should be pursued further (see Chapter 18 of this volume).

The paired-associates tasks used by Benezra (1980) provide additional clues regarding the nature of hyperactive children's memory difficulties. Benezra's ADD subjects did not differ significantly from normal controls on a paired-associates tasks, so long as the pairs of words to be associated in memory were either acoustically or semantically related. They were less proficient than controls were, however, at associating word pairs in which there was no obvious relationship between the two words (arbitrary association condition). Benezra's data also provide partial support for Kinsbourne's (1977) contention that hyperactives demonstrate diminishing improvement on tasks of this kind during later trials. Significant hyperactive–normal differences occurred in her study only on the last two (third and fourth) learning trials. It also should be noted, however, that all subject groups, including the hyperactives, continued to show significant improvement over most of the learning trials. An analysis of the kinds of errors made by the subjects revealed that the youngest ADD children made more "intrusion errors" than their normal age-mates did. These errors reflect interlist interference, and thus may suggest poorer organization and inhibition in the young ADD sample.

Interviews at the end of testing revealed that Benezra's hyperactive subjects made less use than controls did of elaborate mnemonic strategies while attempting to link the arbitrarily associated pairs in memory. Besides requiring familiarity with specific mnemonic devices, the employment of these strategies entails effort, deliberation, and relatively deep processing of the meaning of the stimulus words (Craik & Lockhart, 1972). Further evidence that the control children might have been processing the material more deeply than the hyperactive children derives from a recognition task that Benezra employed following her recall procedure. A multiple-choice format was used, in which subjects were asked to select the correct associates of the target words from among four choices: the original response member of the pair, a word that was acoustically related to the correct word, a semantically related word, and an unrelated word. Although the pattern of errors reveals that the hyperactives were engaging in some semantic processing, they made more acoustic errors than either the normal or the reading-disabled control group did.

A paradigm used by Weingartner, Rapoport, Ebert, and Caine (1980) also points to differences in the depth of processing of hyperactive and normal children. Their subjects were asked to listen to 20 sets of three words; 10 of the sets contained two words that were semantically related and one word that differed in meaning, while the other 10 sets contained two words that sounded alike (acoustically related) and one word that did not rhyme with the other two. There was both an uncued "free-recall" procedure and a cued recall procedure. Both groups were administered dextroamphetamine (.5 mg/kg) and placebo on two different days in a double-blind crossover design.

There were several differences between the hyperactive and normal boys in the placebo condition. Although free recall of acoustically processed words did not discriminate between the two groups, hyperactives recalled significantly fewer meaningfully processed words. Also, "the tendency to recall related words together was far greater in normal than in hyperactive children" (p. 30). When clustering was evident in the recall of hyperactive children, "it was more likely to involve words that were related on the basis of the way they sounded, rather than on the basis of meaning" (p. 30). Interestingly, on the less demanding cued-recall procedure, there were no group differences in the placebo condition on recall of either the semantically or the acoustically processed words.

Following amphetamine treatment, Weingartner *et al.* found an increase in the free recall of hyperactives and controls on both the semantically and acoustically processed words. They stress, however, that "while normal children showed a particularly marked increase in recall of semantically processed words, the most marked amphetamine response in hyperactive children was for acoustically processed words" (p. 28). Furthermore, in the cued-recall procedure the hyperactive group demonstrated a significant increase in the recall of acoustically processed information, but did not significantly increase the recall of semantically processed words.

In discussing their results, Weingartner *et al.* stress that the acoustic strategies favored by their hyperactive subjects are less likely to "assure the formation of well-organized, meaningful (and perhaps strong) trace events in memory." They believe that, as a result, events "may be less likely to be stored in . . . permanent memory . . . and may be more susceptible to postprocessing interference" (p. 36). With regard to their drug findings, they point out that amphetamine seems primarily to enhance the kinds of cognitive operations an individual child typically uses to encode information in the unmedicated state; that is, improvement in the normal boys was found on "semantic processing and clustering based on semantic relationships," whereas in hyperactive boys the drug served mainly "to enhance acoustical processed information" (p. 34).

They suggest that effective learning in the classroom may not be facilitated by stimulants because they enhance mainly acoustic processing, and "processing of this kind is less relevant than are aspects of cognition involved in meaningful encoding and organized retrieval" (p. 36). Consequently, they conclude that they can be corrected only by teaching the children more effective processing strategies, although they appear hopeful that this teaching could be facilitated by concurrent use of stimulant medication.

Concept-Discovery and Rule-Learning Tasks

Most concept-discovery and rule-learning tasks require an exhaustive and penetrating search for underlying concepts, rules, or relationships on which stimuli can be classified. The available evidence suggests that hyperactive children encounter difficulty with tasks of this kind (Douglas, 1980a; Douglas & Peters, 1979; Tant & Douglas, 1982).

The problem of differentiating between production and mediation deficiencies is very apparent on these tasks. As in the case of memory skills, hyperactive children sometimes seem to have developed a partial or incomplete grasp of some concepts or strategies. This makes it particularly difficult to judge the extent to which increased attention and effort, in the absence of additional teaching, would result in improved performance. Certainly production deficiencies appear to diminish performance on many tasks where several solutions must be considered and weighed. On the other hand, evidence strongly suggests that ADD children simply do not possess some of the knowledge and skills available to other children of similar age and IQ.

Parry (1973) studied the performance of matched groups of hyperactive and normal children on the Wisconsin Card-Sorting Task, which provides information on a number of factors, including the ability to discover predetermined underlying dimensions on which stimuli can be ordered; the inclinations of individual subjects to group the stimuli into unique or unusual categories; and "perseveration," as reflected in an inability to change set when instructions necessitate shifts to different sorting categories. Some evidence of the validity of the Wisconsin perseveration measure is found in the work of Milner (1963), who reported high perseveration scores on the Wisconsin in patients with dorsolateral frontal brain damage.

When Parry (1973) employed the usual methods for scoring the Wisconsin, she found that her hyperactive subjects made fewer correct choices, more "perseverative" errors, and more "unique" responses than her control group did. A more careful examination of the data revealed, however, that one-third of the hyperactive children were using only one of the three possible sorting categories, a fact that artificially inflated their perseveration scores. A second analysis, excluding those children who failed to discover all three categories, no longer yielded a significant group difference on the perseveration measure.

The fact that a substantial proportion of the hyperactive sample did not discover a third sorting category probably represents another example of the children's failure to examine problem situations thoroughly. This interpretation is supported by Parry's observation that her ADD subjects often did not look carefully at the cards or pay close attention to feedback. It also should be noted, however, that, depending on one's definition of perseveration, the failure of some of the children to discover a third sorting category could, in itself, be considered evidence of perseveration, since it might involve "overfocusing."

Interestingly, the significant difference between the hyperactive and normal groups on "unique" or "illogical" sorting responses remained in Parry's more exacting statistical analysis. At McGill, we have repeatedly noted this tendency of hyperactive children to develop their own atypical responses on sorting tasks. Although their responses occasionally appear bizarre, we believe that they reflect the children's impulsive, unconforming approach to problems, rather than pathological thought processes.

Concept-Identification Tasks Involving Reinforcers

Two studies (Freibergs & Douglas, 1969; Parry, 1973) seem to demonstrate that the frustrative effects of failing to receive expected awards disrupt the performance of hyperactive children on concept-discovery tasks. The performance of hyperactives and normal controls did not differ on a concept-identification task when the subjects were reinforced on a continuous (100%) schedule for choosing correct exemplars of concepts. Under a partial (50%) schedule, however, the performance of the hyperactives was significantly inferior to that of control children. Thus, the poor performance of hyperactives on partial schedules described in the earlier discussion of simple reaction-time tasks is also evident in complex problem-solving situations. It should be noted that researchers seem to be dealing here with a production deficiency, since the hyperactive subjects had no particular difficulty discovering the correct concepts, so long as they were receiving an optimal schedule of reinforcement; in addition, Parry ruled out reduced feedback as an explanation of their poor performance in the partial condition.

These studies provided other information about the performance of hyperactives on tasks of this kind. First, Freibergs and Douglas (1969) failed to find evidence of perseveration in the hyperactive group. When the concept-discovery problems were reversed, so that previously incorrect stimuli became correct, the hyperactive children had no more difficulty than controls did in discovering the new "rules" and adapting their responses to them. These investigators also found no evidence of systematic position preferences in their hyperactive group. Secondly, hyperactive children on schedules of continuous reinforcement showed good transfer of learning from one concept identification problem to the next. The children's improvement was probably facilitated by the intrinsic interest of the tasks and the presence of immediate and continuous rewards (Douglas & Peters, 1979). It is noteworthy that transfer was dramatically absent under conditions of partial reinforcement. Freibergs (1965) reports that hyperactive–normal differences in this condition were even more marked on later problems than on earlier ones.

Freibergs also discussed several interesting characteristics of the performance of her hyperactive subjects on precriterion trials. Although hyperactives in the continuous-reward condition did not differ from normal subjects on criterion measures, analyses of learning curves revealed differences in the precriterion data. The precriterion curve of the hyperactive group on the first concept administered, for example, showed highly significant fluctuations around the chance level. Freibergs suggests that this may reflect "fluctuations in attention from task-relevant to task-irrelevant stimuli" (p. 95). Secondly, the mean proportion of errors was "slightly but consistently higher" in the hyperactive sample, a finding that she believes may indicate "a large number of irrelevant hypotheses in a subject's repertoire" (p. 96). These interpretations are supported by observations of the children's behavior during testing, which revealed that they were spending considerable time engaging in task-irrelevant activities.

Interestingly, Dykman, Ackerman, and Oglesby (1979) give similar accounts of the task behaviors of a hyperactive sample. The children were performing on a complex version of the Yerkes multiple-choice apparatus. Dykman *et al.* report that although the hyperactives gained insight into the features of the "game" somewhat more quickly than a learning-disabled control group did, the hyperactive children "did not use this information consistently." In addition, they more frequently wanted to quit before the session ended, and it became evident that they no longer were "playing the game in a straightforward way." Dykman *et al.* sum up these behaviors as revealing "lack of tolerance for a problem."

Matrix-Solution and Rule-Learning Tasks

Tant and Douglas (1982) used a series of matrix-solution tasks to compare hyperactive, reading-problem, and normal boys. These tasks belong to a group of games and situations in which solutions must be reached by a process of involving "diagnostic problem solving" (Niemark & Lewis, 1967). Like the popular "20 Questions" games, the tasks involved formulating questions about arrays of multidimensional stimuli in order to discover a designated "correct" stimulus in each array, while asking as few questions as possible. These tasks are more complex than any thus far discussed. Besides discovering the underlying dimensions on which the stimuli can be classified, subjects must choose those dimensions that will yield most information at any given point in the problem-solving process, organizing their questions sequentially so as to make most efficient use of the feedback provided by the examiner.

The performance of Tant's ADD subjects differed from that of the two control groups in a number of ways. As on the Wisconsin, they were less likely than the normal or reading-problem subjects were to perceive all of the dimensions on which the items on the matrix could be classified. Significantly, later questioning revealed that the hyperactives were capable of discovering the other dimensions; they apparently did not focus sufficiently on doing so without additional prompting. The ADD group also obtained lower scores than either the normal or the reading-problem group did on a number of measures reflecting the efficiency of the questions posed and the problem-solving strategies used. Tant was able to show that their inferior performance was not due only to their failure to discover all of the possible dimensions that could be used in posing questions. The hyperactive children did not make effective use of many of the dimensions they *did* discover. An analysis of the relationship between response latencies and efficiency of questioning strategies also ruled out the possibility that the hyperactive children's poor performance could be explained by an inclination to ask their questions more quickly than the normal group. Indeed, in summarizing the findings from her overall study, Tant points out that inferior responses often were associated with *longer* response times.

Tant made considerable effort to discover the reasons for her hyperactive subjects' poor performance. As she mentions, special care was taken to maintain the children's interest. Subjects were tested individually; the tasks were colorful and game-like; and her method of administering the matrices ensured that subjects would "solve" the problems within a fairly brief time. In addition, Tant introduced two experimental conditions designed to minimize the effects of inattention, low motivation, carelessness, and forgetfulness. In one condition, items eliminated by the subjects' questions were actually removed from the matrix so that they did not have to remember which stimuli they had already eliminated. In the other, a response-cost procedure was introduced for inefficient or poor questions; it was thought that this might encourage the children to reflect more carefully on the importance of asking questions that eliminated as many alternatives as possible. These manipulations were relatively ineffective. Experimental–control group differences remained in both conditions. In an effort to discover whether hyperactive children could recognize efficient questions if they were formulated for them, Tant administered a "recognition task" in which she presented a series of matrix problems and asked subjects to choose which of two questions would help solve the games faster. Even with this help, the hyperactive children failed to recognize the superiority of questions about groups of items, and their preference for "guesses" about single items remained.

The failure of these various attempts to improve the performance of the hyperactive subjects convinced Tant that the children probably "lacked a basic understanding of how to go about solving the matrices effectively" (p. 132). She also suggests that the hyperactives were less able than controls were to coordinate their separate questions into an overall strategy. Although the children's performance was probably impeded by unfamiliarity with some of the specific strategies required by the matrices' tasks, it seems likely that a more general failure to assume the problem-solving ("metacognitive") postures essential for successful coping with the problems was also involved. As in the case of the particular tasks within Benezra's (1980) battery that placed heaviest demands on "metamemory" skills, the hyperactive children in Tant's study showed impaired ability to adopt the role of "problem solver."

Tant obtained evidence that hyperactive children's problem-solving deficits are not limited to the specific strategies tapped by matrix-solution tasks. She administered a series of conceptual rule-learning tasks to her three subject groups, and again found significant differences between her hyperactive subjects and the normal and reading-problem groups. The format and operations involved in the rule-learning tasks differed considerably from those of the matrix problems. The children were required to discover conjunctive, disjunctive, and alternate-denial rules governing the assignment of patterns varying on four dimensions to positive and negative categories. As with the matrix tasks, it appears that the hyperactive children's performance deficits were attributable to both ineffective metacognitive strategies and unfamiliarity with the specific skills and strategies assessed by these tasks.

It is important to note, that, as in the concept identification tasks discussed earlier, the hyperactive children seemed to "settle in" as they gained experience in the matrix and rule-learning tasks. It appears that the children were able to use the feedback provided on the tasks to acquire some of the skills they apparently lacked; trial-to-trial transfer on both tasks was roughly comparable to that of normal children. Again, however, except where ceiling effects were encountered, the extent of improvement in the ADD group was never sufficient to eliminate experimental–control group differences.

TASKS REQUIRING MOTOR OR PERCEPTUAL-MOTOR COORDINATION

There is an extensive literature showing that hyperactive children have difficulty on a large number of tests involving motor or perceptual–motor coordination (Aman, 1978; Benezra, 1980; Douglas, 1972, in press-a, in press-b; Knights & Hinton, 1969; Sandoval, 1977). These include the Benter Visual–Motor Gestalt Test, the Rey–Osterrieth Figure, the Lincoln–Oseretsky Schedule of Motor Development, the Porteus Mazes, electronic stylus-type mazes, tapping tasks, the Goodenough–Harris Draw-a-Person Test, the Frostig Test of Visual Perception, and the Graduated Holes Test of Motor Steadiness. In the case of the Lincoln–Oseretsky and the Bender–Gestalt tests, the children's difficulties are known to extend into the adolescent years (Hoy *et al.*, 1978).

It is difficult to differentiate between primary motor deficits in hyperactive children and deficits that result from a failure to expend the effort and concentration required to guide, synthesize, and organize complex motor and perceptual–motor sequences (Douglas, 1972). Consequently, it is also difficult to identify the processes affected when treatment interventions result in improved performance. It seems likely, however, that effects on self-regulatory mechanisms are at least partially responsible.

TASKS INVOLVING AVOIDANCE LEARNING, INHIBITORY CONTROL, AND THE PULL OF IMMEDIATE REWARD

Gorenstein and Newman (1980) evaluated evidence from a number of investigations that have been interpreted as demonstrating that psychopathic individuals and animals with lesions involving the SHF system have an avoidance-learning deficit. Recently, Freeman (1978) used two of the paradigms from studies with psychopaths to assess the response of hyperactive children to punishment and the threat of punishment.

Freeman used a design favored by Kinsbourne, Swanson, and their associates. Children referred for hyperactive symptoms were divided into two groups consisting of "favorable responders" and "nonresponders" or "adverse responders" to stimulant medication. The performance of the two subject samples was studied in a double-blind, crossover, drug versus placebo design. The rationale for choosing subjects in this manner is based on the contention of Kinsbourne and his colleagues that a positive drug response identifies "true" hyperactives and that nonresponsive children demonstrating similar hyperactive symptoms constitute the most appropriate control sample (Freeman, 1978).

Lykken Maze Test

Freeman (1978) used a Lykken Maze Test consisting of four vertical rows of lights, each row of a different color. Thus, looking at the rows horizontally, each horizontal row contains a green, a yellow, a blue, and a red light. The subject's task is to push buttons corresponding to the colored lights in the horizontal row in order to discover an arbitrarily set sequence of lights by which he or she can progress from the top to the bottom of the maze. The subject proceeds by making guesses at each of the horizontal rows, obtaining feedback, and using the feedback to discover the correct sequence, row by row.

Lykken-type mazes contain an additional feature. Besides providing positive feedback for correct choices, they associate punishment with one of three incorrect lights in each of the horizontal rows. In the version used by Freeman, subjects were told that, sometimes, when they pressed a wrong button, they would hear a loud noise over earphones. In each of the horizontal rows, one of the wrong lights always was associated with punishment. Thus, the maze involved the "manifest" task of finding the predesignated route through the maze via the correct lights, and the "latent" task of avoiding the particular lights associated with punishment.

Freeman was interested in the performance of hyperactive children on this task because previous studies with psychopaths (Lykken, 1957; Schachter & Latané, 1964; Schmauk, 1970) had revealed that, unlike controls, psychopaths exhibit no improvement in the ratio of shocked errors to unshocked errors as they gain experience with the maze. These findings have been interpreted as support for the hypothesis that psychopathy is associated with "a disinclination to alter one's behavior to avoid discomfort" (p. 303). Freeman carried out three studies using the favorable versus unfavorable responder design described above. In one study, he also included a "quasi-control sample" of unmatched normal children of atypically high intelligence and social status.

Although Freeman's major focus was on the "latent" avoidance-learning aspect of the task, it is interesting to note that none of his results suggested that the favorable responders had difficulty with the "manifest" task. This might be considered surprising, since the job of learning the correct sequence of choices is moderately difficult. Freeman attributes the ADD children's success to the colorful, engaging format of the maze.

Group differences did occur on the avoidance-learning measure. Favorable responders on placebo ("true hyperactives" by the experimenter's definition) made significantly more errors than the "quasi-normal" group did, whereas adverse responders on placebo did not differ from the quasi-normal children. Freeman uses these findings to argue for an avoidance deficit in hyperactive children. Although he acknowledges studies in which hyperactives have been shown to respond to punishment and negative feedback (Firestone & Douglas, 1975; Worland, 1976), he finds these investigations unconvincing because of the relatively simple demands made on the subjects. He stresses that, on the Lykken, the child must cope with the manifest and latent tasks concurrently, and he sees this as a more adequate paradigm for revealing defective avoidance learning. Certainly, it seems likely that the presence of the manifest task influenced the results obtained on the latent task. Another hypothesis regarding the role played by the manifest task, however, must be considered. It is possible that the interesting and exciting "game" of finding their way through the maze so absorbed the attention and motivation of the "true hyperactives" that they were either less aware of the specific cues provided by the unpleasant noise or were less influenced by them.

Risk-Taking Situations

Interestingly, other data from Freeman's dissertation appear to show that hyperactives are capable of demonstrating avoidance behaviors, so long as certain crucial conditions are met. Freeman studied the behavior of favorable and adverse responders using two different risk-taking paradigms. In the first, subjects were told that they could win pennies each time they pressed a trigger on a dispensing machine. They were warned, however, that, after an arbitrarily set number of presses (a "magic number" secretly set in the machine), they would receive an electric shock, delivered through an electrode on their finger. A fake demonstration was held to convince the children that the shock was painful. The second paradigm was identical, except that, instead of threatening an electric shock, the experimenter told the children that when the secret number was reached they would lose all the money they had earned up to that point. In both paradigms the subjects were informed that they could press as many times as they wished and could stop whenever they wanted. The number of times a subject chose to press the trigger was regarded as an indicator of the degree of risk he was willing to take.

The two risk-taking paradigms yielded quite different results. Under the threat-of-shock condition, the favorable responders on placebo took significantly greater risk than the nonresponders on placebo did, whereas when the threat involved loss of monetary reward, there was no significant difference between the number of risks taken by the two groups in the placebo condition.

These results are in close agreement with findings from a similar study conducted with psychopaths. When Schmauk (1970) substituted loss of money for shock as punishment for errors on the Lykken Maze, he found that psychopaths were capable of learning to avoid the response button associated with loss of monetary reward. The question to be answered, therefore, is why psychopaths could learn the appropriate avoidance responses when loss of reinforcement was involved, but failed to learn them in response to punishment.

In interpreting findings from his three studies, Freeman seems to place most emphasis on his results on the Lykken Maze and the risk-taking situation involving threat of shock. He uses these findings to argue for "a disorder of impulse control, the basis of which may be a deficit in the neurochemical mechanism of avoidance" (p. 110). In addition, he uses drug findings from his dissertation demonstrating that methylphenidate improved the avoidance learning of favorable responders on the Lykken Maze and also reduced their risk-taking behavior in the threat-of-shock condition, to argue that the stimulants work to correct this inhibitory deficit. Again, however, it is necessary to explain why the children did not demonstrate a lack of impulse control when they were threatened with loss of monetary reward.

Gorenstein and Newman take an approach different from Freeman's. They use the findings from the Schmauk study and a number of other experiments discussed in their review to argue that, in order to understand the peculiar pattern of response deficits found in psychopaths and SHF-syndrome animals, we must "look to the irresistible and exaggerated hold that . . . immediate reward has gained on the organism's attention" (p. 313). This hypothesis is similar to the one advanced by Douglas and Peters (1979) to explain the unique response to reinforcement by hyperactives found by members of our research group at McGill (Cohen, 1970; Douglas & Parry, 1983; Firestone & Douglas, 1975; Freibergs & Douglas, 1969; Parry, 1973; Parry & Douglas, 1983). We concluded that hyperactive children may be unusually sensitive to rewards, and, consequently, to both the loss of reward and the failure of expected awards to appear. This same explanation could account for Freeman's findings. It also could go a long way toward accounting for the phenomena reviewed in the present chapter, including the children's vulnerability to reward-associated distractors, their failure to invest attention and effort in nonrewarding situations, their failure to modulate arousal levels in keeping with task demands, and their impulsive behavior on the DRL task. If one accepts this reasoning, the primary effect of stimulant medication would not be seen as "increasing . . . the degree to which negative events come to govern the behavior of these children" (Freeman, 1978, p. 95), but, rather, as decreasing the impact of immediate reward on their behavior.

Certainly, this line of reasoning has considerable appeal. However, it must be considered highly speculative until the response of hyperactive children to reward and the loss of reward has been more fully studied. Equally important, it should now be possible to design experiments that will help clarify the nature of the relationship between the children's reward-seeking tendencies and the attentional, inhibitory, and arousal phenomena that have been discussed.

SOCIAL AND ACADEMIC TASKS

This review has been mainly limited to the performance of hyperactive children on "attentional" and cognitive measures. It is important to note, however, that recent research on the academic and social functioning of ADD children is yielding similar answers to the questions posed in the present chapter (for a more complete review, see Douglas, in press-a, in press-b).

There is evidence, for example, that, in neutral situations, hyperactive children have considerably greater capacity to understand the perspective of others (Paulauskas & Campbell, 1979) than they normally exhibit under the pressure of real-life situations (Milich & Landau, 1982), on exciting interpersonal laboratory tasks (Whalen, Henker, Collins, McAuliffe, & Vaux, 1979), or in response to life-like stories involving frustrating events caused by peer or authority figures (Parry, 1973). As in the case of some of the more complex cognitive skills discussed in the present chapter, treatment and task manipulations suggest that the children's inadequate social interactions result from a combination of production and mediation deficiencies (Barkley & Cunningham, 1979; Douglas, in press-a, in press-b; Henker & Whalen, 1980; Kinsbourne, 1977). Also, as in the case of the MFF, there is evidence that cognitive training may be the most effective means of improving performance. The methods used in training have involved teaching a thoughtful, metacognitive approach to problem solving, social skills training, and the judicious use of reinforcers. Improved interpersonal responses have been reported both in laboratory situations (Pelham, 1980) and on the frustrating-stories task (Douglas, 1980b; Douglas *et al.*, 1976). Results from the frustrating stories also revealed generalization and maintenance of treatment effects, suggesting that the children had acquired new skills for dealing with interpersonal situations.

In addition, in spite of several pessimistic reviews in the literature on the effects of stimulant medication on the academic performance of ADD children, there is reason to believe that the stimulants can help correct production deficiencies on academic tests (Douglas, in press-a, in press-b; Douglas & Peters, 1979; Sprague & Berger, 1980). Limited and temporary improvement on academic measures also has been reported with carefully chosen behavior modification techniques (Ayllon, Layman, & Kandel, 1975; Wolraich, Drummond,

Salomon, O'Brien, & Sivage, 1978). Again, however, the cognitive-training approach has provided the only evidence of generalization and maintenance of treatment effects (Cameron & Robinson, 1980; Douglas, 1980b; Douglas *et al.*, 1976).

CONCLUDING REMARKS

Although it is difficult at the present time to decide whether one of the four postulated mechanisms discussed here is more basic than the others, there is considerable evidence that defective attentional, inhibitory, arousal, and reinforcement processes have both immediate and long-term impact on the behavior and cognitive functioning of hyperactive children. The therapeutic potential of reducing negative effects of the children's primary deficits on the acquisition of higher-order schemata, the development of sophisticated metacognitive processes, and effectance motivation can hardly be exaggerated.

If one accepts the premise that past learning guides new learning, then any success in combatting the children's primary deficiencies should reduce their impact on the development of secondary problems and the spiraling sequelae posited by Douglas and Peters (1979). The fact that stimulant medication and some reward schedules diminish the children's production deficiencies suggests that these treatments have positive effect on some or all of the underlying attentional, inhibitory, arousal, or reward processes (Barkley, 1977; Conners & Wells, 1979; Douglas, 1972; Douglas & Peters, 1979; Freeman, 1978; Henker & Whalen, 1980; Kinsbourne, 1977; Rosenthal & Allen, 1978; Wender, 1971; Zahn *et al.*, 1980).

It is also important, however, to stress that the interaction between primary and secondary deficits would be expected to work *in both directions* (see Figure 14-1). Consequently, it should be possible to modify the primary defective processes by interventions that help develop higher-order schemata, metacognitive strategies, and motivation for mastery. It is here that cognitive

Figure 14-1. Interaction of primary and secondary processes.

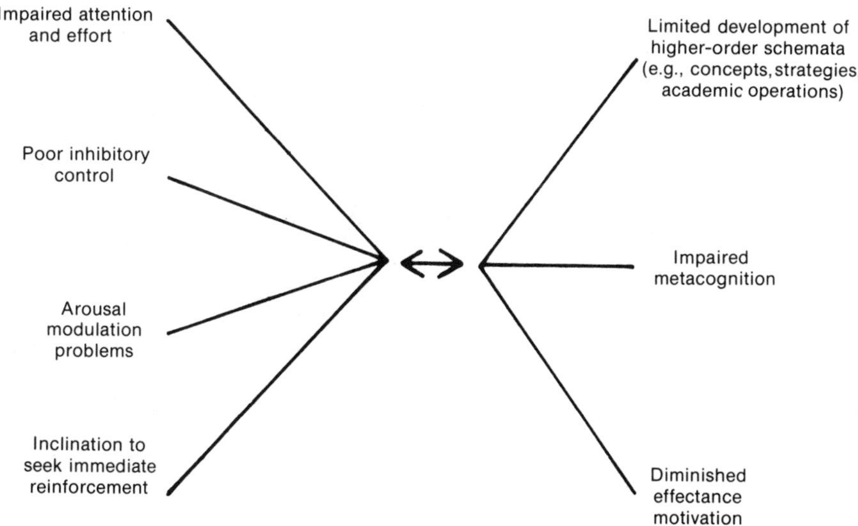

training can play the greatest role (Douglas, 1980b, in press-a, in press-b). In addition, when researchers have learned more about the effects of stimulant medication on *new learning*, it may be possible to use the stimulants along with carefully considered reinforcement schedules to facilitate and enhance cognitive-training programs.

References

Ackerman, P. T., Elardo, P. T., & Dykman, R. A. A psychosocial study of hyperactive and learning-disabled boys. *Journal of Abnormal Child Psychology*, 1979, *7*(1), 91–99.

Ain, M. *The effects of stimulus novelty on viewing time and processing efficiency in hyperactive children.* Unpublished doctoral dissertation, McGill University, 1980.

Aman, M. G. Drugs, learning, and the psychotherapies. In J. S. Werry (Ed.), *Pediatric psychopharmacology: The use of behavior-modifying drugs in children.* New York: Brunner/Mazel, 1978.

American Psychiatric Association. *Diagnostic and statistical manual of mental disorders* (3rd ed.). Washington: Author, 1980.

Anderson, R., Halcomb, C., & Doyle, R. The measurement of attentional deficits. *Exceptional Children*, 1973, *39*, 534–540.

Ayllon, T., Layman, D., & Kandel, H. A behavioral–educational alternative to drug control of hyperactive children. *Journal of Applied Behavior Analysis*, 1975, *8*, 137–146.

Barkley, R. A. The effects of methylphenidate on various types of activity level and attention in hyperkinetic children. *Journal of Abnormal Child Psychology*, 1977, *5*, 351–369.

Barkley, R. A. Specific guidelines for defining hyperactivity in children (attention deficit disorder). In B. Lahey & A. Kazdin (Eds.), *Advances in clinical child psychology.* New York: Plenum Press, 1982.

Barkley, R., A., & Cunningham, C. E. The parent–child interactions of hyperactive children and their modification by stimulant drugs. In R. Knights & D. Bakker (Eds.), *Treatment of hyperactive and learning disordered children.* Baltimore: University Park Press, 1979.

Barlow, A. *A neuropsychological study of a symptom of minimal brain dysfunction: Distractibility under levels of low and high stimulation.* Unpublished doctoral dissertation, Ontario Institute for Studies in Education, 1977.

Benezra, E. *Verbal and nonverbal memory in hyperactive, reading disabled, and normal children.* Unpublished doctoral dissertation, McGill University, 1980.

Berlyne, D. E. Attention as a problem in behavior theory. In D. I. Mostofsky (Ed.), *Attention: Contemporary theory and analysis.* New York: Appleton-Century-Crofts, 1970.

Berlyne, D. E. *Aesthetics and psychobiology.* New York: Appleton-Century-Crofts, 1971.

Berylne, D. E., & Parham, L. C. Determinants of subjective novelty. *Perception and Psychophysics*, 1968, *3*, 415–423.

Bindra, D. *A theory of intelligent behavior.* New York: Wiley, 1976.

Boder, E. Developmental dyslexia: Prevailing diagnostic concepts and a new diagnostic approach. In H. R. Mykelbust (Ed.), *Progress in learning disabilities* (Vol. 2). New York: Grune & Stratton, 1977.

Bremer, D. A., & Stern, J. A. Attention and distractibility during reading in hyperactive boys. *Journal of Abnormal Child Psychology*, 1976, *4*, 381–387.

Broadbent, D. E. The hidden preattentive process. *American Psychologist*, 1977, *32*, 109–119.

Brown, A. L. The development of memory: Knowing, knowing about knowing, and knowing how to know. In H. W. Reese (Ed.), *Advances in child development and behavior* (Vol. 10). New York: Academic Press, 1975.

Brown, R. T., & Sleator, E. K. Methylphenidate in hyperkinetic children: Differences in dose effects on impulsive behavior. *Pediatrics*, 1979, *64*, 408–411.

Cameron, M. I., & Robinson, M. J. Effects of cognitive training on academic and on-task behavior of hyperactive children. *Journal of Abnormal Child Psychology*, 1980, *8*, 405–419.

Campbell, S. B. *Dichotic listening in hyperactive and normal children.* Unpublished honours dissertation, McGill University, 1964.

Chapman, L. J., & Chapman, J. P. Problems in the measurement of cognitive deficit. *Psychological Bulletin*, 1973, *79*, 380–385.

Cohen, N. J. *Psychophysiological concomitants of attention in hyperactive children.* Unpublished doctoral dissertation, McGill University, 1970.

Cohen, N. J., & Douglas, V. I. Characteristics of the orienting response in hyperactive and normal children. *Psychophysiology*, 1972, *9*, 238–245.

Conners, C. K. Minimal brain dysfunction and psychopathology in children. In A. Davids (Ed.), *Child personality and psychopathology: Current topics* (Vol. 2). New York: Wiley, 1975.

Conners, C. K., & Wells, K. C. Method and theory for psychopharmacology with children. In R. L. Trites (Ed.), *Hyperactivity in children.* Baltimore: University Park Press, 1979.

Corsi, O. M. *Human memory and the medial temporal region of the brain.* Unpublished doctoral dissertation, McGill University, 1972.

Craik, F. I. M., & Lockhart, R. S. Levels of processing: A framework for memory research. *Journal of Verbal Learning and Verbal Behavior*, 1972, *11*, 671–684.

Cruikshank, W. M., Bentzen, F. A., Ratzeburg, F. H., & Tannhauser, M. T. *A teaching method for brain-injured and hyperactive children.* Syracuse: Syracuse University Press, 1961.

Dalby, J. T., Kinsbourne, M., Swanson, J. M., & Sobol, M. Hyperactive children's underuse of learning time: Corrected by stimulant treatment. *Child Development*, 1977, *48*, 1448–1453.

Davidson, E. M., & Prior, M. R. Laterality and selective attention in hyperactive children. *Journal of Abnormal Child Psychology*, 1978, *6*, 475–481.

Denton, C. L., & McIntyre, C. W. Span of apprehension in hyperactive boys. *Journal of Abnormal Child Psychology*, 1978, *6*, 19–24.

Douglas, V. I. Stop, look and listen: The problem of sustained attention and impulse control in hyperactive and normal children. *Canadian Journal of Behavioural Science*, 1972, *4*, 259–282.

Douglas, V. I. Sustained attention and impulse control: Implications for the handicapped child. In J. A. Swets & L. L. Elliot (Eds.), *Psychology and the handicapped child.* Washington, D.C.: U.S. Office of Education, 1974.

Douglas, V. I. Are drugs enough?: To treat or to train the hyperactive child. In R. Gittelman-Klein (Ed.), *Recent advances in child psychopharmacology.* New York: Human Sciences Press, 1975.

Douglas, V. I. Perceptual and cognitive factors as determinants of learning disabilities: A review chapter with special emphasis on attentional factors. In R. M. Knights & D. J. Bakker (Eds.), *The neuropsychology of learning disorders: Theoretical approaches.* Baltimore: University Park Press, 1976.

Douglas, V. I. Higher mental processes in hyperactive children: Implications for training. In R. M. Knights & D. J. Bakker (Eds.), *Rehabilitation, treatment, and management of learning disorders.* Baltimore: University Park Press, 1980. (a)

Douglas, V. I. Treatment approaches: Establishing inner or outer control? In C. K. Whalen & B. Henker (Eds.), *Hyperactive children: The social ecology of identification and treatment.* New York: Academic Press, 1980. (b)

Douglas, V. I. Attention deficit disorder in children: Are we any further ahead? *Canadian Journal of Behavioural Science*, in press. (a)

Douglas, V. I. The psychological processes implicated in attention deficit disorder. In L. M. Bloomingdale (Ed.), *Attention deficit disorder.* Jamaica, N.Y.: Spectrum, in press. (b)

Douglas, V. I., & Parry, P. A. Effects of reward on delayed reaction time task performance of hyperactive children. *Journal of Abnormal Child Psychology*, June 1983.

Douglas, V. I., Parry, P., Marton, P., & Garson, C. Assessment of a cognitive training program for hyperactive children. *Journal of Abnormal Child Psychology*, 1976, *4*, 389–410.

Douglas, V. I., & Peters, K. G. Toward a clearer definition of the attentional deficit of hyperactive children. In G. A. Hale & M. Lewis (Eds.), *Attention and the development of cognitive skills.* New York: Plenum Press, 1979.

Doyle, R. B., Anderson, R. P., & Halcomb, C. G. Attention deficits and the effects of visual distraction. *Journal of Learning Disabilities*, 1976, *19*, 48–54.

Dykman, R. A., Ackerman, P. T., Clements, S., & Peters, J. E. Specific learning disabilities: An attentional deficit syndrome. In H. R. Mykelbust (Ed.), *Progress in learning disabilities* (Vol. 2). New York: Grune & Stratton, 1971.

Dykman, R. A., Ackerman, P. T., & Oglesby, D. M. Selective and sustained attention in hyperactive, learning-disabled, and normal boys. *Journal of Nervous and Mental Disease*, 1979, *167*, 288–297.

Errickson, E. W., Wyne, M. D., & Routh, D. K. A response-cost procedure for reduction of impulsive behavior of academically handicapped children. *Journal of Abnormal Child Psychology*, 1973, *1*, 350–357.

Faw, T. T., & Nunnally, J. C. The influence of stimulus complexity, novelty, and affective value on children's visual fixations. *Journal of Experimental Child Psychology*, 1968, *6*, 141–153. (a)

Faw, T. T., & Nunnally, J. C. A new methodology and finding relating to visual stimulus selection in children. *Psychonomic Science*, 1968, *12*, 47–48. (b)

Ferguson, H. B., & Pappas, B. A. Evaluation of psychophysiological, neurochemical and animal models of hyperactivity. In R. L. Trites (Ed.), *Hyperactivity in children: Etiology, measurement and treatment implications.* Baltimore: University Park Press, 1979.

Feuerstein, M., Ward, M. M., & Le Baron, S. W. Neuropsychological and neurophysiological assessment of children with learning and behavior problems: A critical appraisal. In B. B. Lahey & A. E. Kazdin (Eds.), *Advances in clinical child psychology* (Vol. 2). New York: Plenum Press, 1979.

Firestone, P., & Douglas, V. I. The effects of reward and punishment on reaction times and autonomic activity in hyperactive and normal children. *Journal of Abnormal Child Psychology*, 1975, *3*, 201–215.

Firestone, P., & Martin, J. E. An analysis of the hyperactive syndrome: A comparison of hyperactive, behavior problem, asthmatic, and normal children. *Journal of Abnormal Child Psychology*, 1979, *7*(3), 261–273.

Flavell, J. H. Developmental studies of mediated memory. In H. W. Reese & L. P. Lipsitt (Eds.), *Advances in child development and behavior* (Vol. 5). New York: Academic Press, 1970.

Freeman, R. J. *The effects of methylphenidate on avoidance learning and risk taking by hyperkinetic children.* Unpublished doctoral dissertation, University of Waterloo, Waterloo, Ontario, 1978.

Freibergs, V. *Concept learning in hyperactive and normal children.* Unpublished doctoral dissertation, McGill University, 1965.

Freibergs, V., & Douglas, V. I. Concept learning in hyperactive and normal children. *Journal of Abnormal Psychology*, 1969, *74*, 388–395.

Gibson, E. J. *Principles of perceptual learning and development.* Englewood Cliffs, N.J.: Prentice-Hall, 1969.

Gibson, E., & Rader, N. Attention: The perceiver as performer. In G. A. Hale & M. Lewis (Eds.), *Attention and cognitive development.* New York: Plenum Press, 1979.

Gordon, M. The assessment of impulsivity and mediating behaviors in hyperactive and nonhyperactive boys. *Journal of Abnormal Child Psychology*, 1979, *7*, 317–326.

Gorenstein, E. E., & Newman, J. P. Disinhibitory psychopathology: A new perspective and a model for research. *Psychological Review*, 1980, *87*(3), 301–315.

Hagen, J. W. The effect of distraction on selective children. *Child Development*, 1967, *38*, 685–694.

Hastings, J. E., & Barkley, R. A. A review of psychophysiological research with hyperkinetic children. *Journal of Abnormal Child Psychology*, 1978, *6*, 413–448.

Hebb, D. O. *Organization of behavior.* New York: Wiley, 1949.

Henker, B., & Whalen, C. K. The changing faces of hyperactivity: Retrospect and prospect. In C. K. Whalen & B. Henker (Eds.), *Hyperactive children: The social ecology of identification and treatment.* New York: Academic Press, 1980.

Hiscock, M., Kinsbourne, M., Caplan, B., & Swanson, J. M. Auditory attention in hyperactive children: Effects of stimulant medication on dichotic listening performance. *Journal of Abnormal Psychology*, 1979, *88*, 27–32.

Hopkins, J., Perlman, T., Hechtman, L., & Weiss, G. Cognitive style in adults originally diagnosed as hyperactives. *Journal of Child Psychology and Psychiatry*, 1979, *20*, 209–216.

Hoy, E., Weiss, G., Minde, K., & Cohen, N. The hyperactive child at adolescence: Cognitive, emotional, and social functioning. *Journal of Abnormal Child Psychology*, 1978, *67*, 311–324.

Kagan, J. Reflection–impulsivity: The generality of dynamics of conceptual tempo. *Journal of Abnormal Psychology*, 1966, *7*, 17–24.

Kagan, J., Rosman, B. L., Day, B., Albert, J., & Phillips, W. Information processing in the child: Significance of analytic and reflective attitudes. *Psychological Monographs*, 1964, *78*(1, Whole No. 578).

Kahneman, D. *Attention and effort.* Englewood Cliffs, N.J.: Prentice-Hall, 1973.

Kimura, D. Right temporal-lobe damage. *Archives of Neurology*, 1963, *8*, 264–271.

Kimura, D. Cognitive deficit related to seizure pattern in centrencephalic epilepsy. *Journal of Neurology, Neurosurgery and Psychiatry*, 1964, *27*, 294–295.

Kinsbourne, M. The mechanism of hyperactivity. In M. E. Bow, Q. Rapin, & M. Kinsbourne (Eds.), *Topics in child neurology*. New York: Spectrum, 1977.

Kintsch, W. *Learning, memory, and conceptual processes*. New York: Wiley, 1970.

Klein, D. F., & Gittelman-Klein, R. Problems in the diagnosis of minimal brain dysfunction and hyperkinetic syndrome. *International Journal of Mental Health*, 1975, *4*, 45–60.

Knights, R. M., & Hinton, G. G. The effects of methylphenidate (Ritalin) on the motor skills and behavior of children with learning problems. *Journal of Nervous and Mental Disease*, 1969, *148*, 643–653.

Lahey, B. B., Stempniak, M., Robinson, E. J., & Tyroler, M. J. Hyperactivity and learning disabilities as independent dimensions of child behavior problems. *Journal of Abnormal Psychology*, 1978, *87*, 333–340.

Lambert, N. M., & Sandoval, J. The prevalence of learning disabilities in a sample of children considered hyperactive. *Journal of Abnormal Child Psychology*, 1980, *8*(1), 33–50.

Laufer, M. W., Denhoff, E., & Solomons, G. Hyperactive impulse disorder in children's behavior problems. *Psychosomatic Medicine*, 1957, *19*, 38–49.

Loiselle, D. L., Stamm, J. S., Maitinsky, S., & Whipple, S. C. Evoked potention and behavioral signs of attentive dysfunctions in hyperactive boys. *Psychophysiology*, 1980, *17*, 193–201.

Loney, J., Langhorne, J. E., & Paternite, C. E. An empirical basis for subgrouping the hyperkinetic/minimal brain dysfunction syndrome. *Journal of Abnormal Psychology*, 1978, *87*, 431–441.

Lykken, D. A study of anxiety in the sociopathic personality. *Journal of Abnormal and Social Psychology*, 1957, *55*, 6–10.

Mattis, S., French, J. H., & Rapin, I. Dyslexia in children and young adults: Three independent neuropsychological syndromes. *Developmental Medicine and Child Neurology*, 1975, *17*(2), 150–163.

McIntyre, C. W., Blackwell, S. L., & Denton, C. L. Effect of noise distractibility on the spans of apprehension of hyperactive boys. *Journal of Abnormal Child Psychology*, 1978, *6*(4), 483–492.

Meacham, J. A. The development of memory abilities in the individual and society. *Human Development*, 1972, *15*, 205–228.

Messer, S. B. Reflection–impulsivity: A review. *Psychological Bulletin*, 1976, *83*, 1026–1052.

Milich, R., & Landau, S. Socialization and peer relations in hyperactive children. In K. D. Gadow & I. Bialer (Eds.), *Advances in learning and behavioral disabilities* (Vol. 1). Greenwich, Conn.: JAI Press, 1982.

Milich, R., & Loney, J. The role of hyperactive and aggressive symptomatology in predicting adolescent outcome among hyperactive children. *Journal of Pediatric Psychology*, 1979, *4*, 93–112.

Milner, B. Effects of different brain lesions on card sorting: The role of the frontal lobes. *Archives of Neurology*, 1963, *9*, 90–100.

Moray, N. *Attention: Selective processes in vision and hearing*. London: Hutchinson Educational, 1969.

Neimark, F. D., & Lewis, N. The development of logical problem-solving strategies. *Child Development*, 1967, *38*, 107–117.

Neisser, U. *Cognition and reality: Principles and implications of cognitive psychology*. San Francisco: W. H. Freeman, 1976.

Nunnally, J. C., Faw, T. T., & Bashford, M. B. The effect of degrees of incongruity on visual fixations in children and adults. *Journal of Experimental Psychology*, 1969, *81*, 360–364.

Odom, R. D., & Guzman, R. D. Development of hierarchies of dimensional salience. *Developmental Psychology*, 1972, *6*, 271–287.

Osterrieth, P. A. Le test de copie d'une figure complex. *Archives de Psychologie*, 1944, *30*, 206–356.

Parry, P. *The effect of reward on the performance of hyperactive children*. Unpublished doctoral dissertation, McGill University, 1973.

Parry, P. A., & Douglas, V. I. Effects of reinforcement on concept identification in hyperactive children. *Journal of Abnormal Child Psychology*, June 1983.

Paulauskas, S. L., & Campbell, S. B. Social perspective taking and teacher ratings of peer interaction in hyperactive boys. *Journal of Abnormal Child Psychology*, 1979, *7*(4), 384–493.

Pelham, W. E. *Peer relationships in hyperactive children: Description and treatment effects*. In R. Milich (Chair), *Peer relationships among hyperactive children*. Symposium presented at the annual meeting of the American Psychological Association, Montreal, September 1980.

Peters, K. G. *Selective attention and distractibility in hyperactive and normal children.* Unpublished doctoral dissertation, McGill University, 1977.

Peterson, L. R., & Peterson, M. S. Short-term retention of individual verbal items. *Journal of Experimental Psychology*, 1959, *58*, 193–198.

Posner, M. I. Components of skills performance. *Science*, 1966, *152*, 1712–1718.

Posner, M. I. *Chronometric explorations of mind.* Hillsdale, N.J.: Erlbaum, 1978.

Posner, M. I., & Boies, S. J. Components of attention. *Psychological Reports*, 1971, *78*, 391–408.

Radosh, A., & Gittelman, R. The effect of appealing distractors on the performance of hyperactive children. *Journal of Abnormal Child Psychology*, 1981, *9*(2), 179–189.

Rapoport, J. L., Buchsbaum, M. S., Zahn, T. P., Weingartner, H., Ludlow, C., & Mikkelsen, E. J. Amphetamine: Cognitive and behavioral effects in prepubertal boys. *Science*, 1978, *199*, 560–563.

Rey, A. L'examen psychologique dans les cas d'encephalopathie traumatique. *Archives de Psychologie*, 1941, *28*, 215–285.

Rosenthal, R. H., & Allen, T. W. An examination of attention, arousal, and learning dysfunctions of hyperkinetic children. *Psychological Bulletin*, 1978, *85*, 689–715.

Rosenthal, R. H., & Allen, T. W. Intratask distractibility in hyperkinetic and nonhyperkinetic children. *Journal of Abnormal Child Psychology*, 1980, *8*(2), 175–187.

Ross, A. O. *Psychological aspects of learning disabilities and reading disorders.* New York: McGraw-Hill, 1976.

Ross, A. O., & Pelham, W. E. Child psychopathology. *Annual Review of Psychology*, 1981, *32*, 243–278.

Ross, D. M., & Ross, S. A. *Hyperactivity: Research, theory, and action.* New York: Wiley, 1976.

Rosvold, H. E., Mirsky, A. F., Sarason, I., Bransome, E. D., & Beck, L. H. A continuous-performance test of brain damage. *Journal of Consulting Psychology*, 1956, *20*, 343–352.

Sandoval, J. The measurement of hyperactive syndrome in children. *Review of Educational Research*, 1977, *47*, 293–318.

Schachter, S., & Latané, B. Crime, cognition, and the autonomic nervous system. In M. Jones (Ed.), *Nebraska Symposium on Motivation* (Vol. 17). Lincoln: University of Nebraska Press, 1964.

Schmauk, F. J. Punishment, arousal, and avoidance learning in sociopaths. *Journal of Abnormal Psychology*, 1970, *76*, 325–335.

Solley, C. M., & Murphy, G. *Development of the perceptive world.* New York: Basic Books, 1969.

Sostek, A. J., Buchsbaum, M. S., & Rapoport, J. L. Effects of amphetamine on vigilance performance in normal and hyperactive children. *Journal of Abnormal Child Psychology*, 1980, *8*(4), 491–500.

Sprague, R. L., & Berger, B. D. Drug effects on learning performance: Relevance of animal research to pediatric psychopharmacology. In R. M. Knights & D. J. Bakker (Eds.), *Treatment of hyperactive and learning disordered children.* Baltimore: University Park Press, 1980.

Sprague, R. L., & Sleator, E. K. Methylphenidate in hyperkinetic children: Differences in dose effects on learning and social behavior. *Science*, 1977, *198*, 1274–1276.

Spring, C., Yellin, A. M., & Greenberg, L. M. Effects of imipramine and methylphenidate on perceptual-motor performance of hyperactive children. *Perceptual and Motor Skills*, 1976, *43*, 459–470.

Steinkamp, M. W. *Relationships between task-irrelevant distractions and task performance of normal, retarded hyperactive, and minimal brain dysfunction children.* Unpublished doctoral dissertation, University of Illinois, 1974.

Swanson, J. M., & Kinsbourne, M. Stimulant-related state-dependent learning in hyperactive children. *Science*, 1976, *192*, 1354–1357.

Swanson, J. M., & Kinsbourne, M. The cognitive effects of stimulant drugs on hyperactive children. In G. A. Hale & M. Lewis (Eds.), *Attention and cognitive development.* New York: Plenum Press, 1979.

Swets, J. A., & Kristofferson, A. B. Attention. *Annual Review of Psychology*, 1970, *21*, 339–366.

Sykes, D. H., Douglas, V. I., Weiss, G., & Minde, K. K. Attention in hyperactive children and the effect of methylphenidate (Ritalin). *Journal of Child Psychology and Psychiatry*, 1971, *12*, 129–139.

Sykes, D. H., Douglas, V. I., & Morgenstern, G. Sustained attention in hyperactive children. *Journal of Child Psychology and Psychiatry*, 1973, *14*, 213–220.

Tant, J. L. *Problem solving in hyperactive and reading-disabled boys.* Unpublished doctoral dissertation, McGill University, 1978.

Tant, J. L., & Douglas, V. I. Problem solving in hyperactive, normal, and reading-disabled boys. *Journal of Abnormal Child Psychology*, 1982, *10*(3), 285–306.

Wechsler, D. *Wechsler Memory Scale* (2nd ed.). New York: Psychological Corporation, 1972.

Weingartner, H., Rapoport, J. L., Ebert, M. H., & Caine, E. D. Cognitive processes in normal and hyperactive children and their response to amphetamine treatment. *Journal of Abnormal Psychology*, 1980, *89*(1), 25–37.

Wender, P. *Minimal brain dysfunction in children.* New York: Wiley, 1971.

Wender, P. H. Some speculations concerning a possible biochemical basis of minimal brain dysfunction. *Life Sciences*, 1974, *14*, 1605–1621.

Werry, J. S., & Aman, M. G. Methylphenidate and haloperidol in children: Effects on attention, memory and activity. *Archives of General Psychiatry*, 1975, *32*, 790–795.

Werry, J. S., & Aman, M. G. Methylphenidate in hyperactive and enuretic children. In B. Shopsin & L. Greenhill (Eds.), *The psychology of childhood: Profile of current issues.* Jamaica, N.Y.: Spectrum, in press.

Whalen, C. K., & Henker, B. Psychostimulants and children: A review and analysis. *Psychological Bulletin*, 1976, *83*, 1113–1130.

Whalen, C. K., Henker, B., Collins, B. E., McAuliffe, S., & Vaux, A. Peer interaction in a structured communication task: Comparisons of normal and hyperactive boys and of methylphenidate (Ritalin) and placebo effects. *Child Development*, 1979, *50*, 388–401.

Wolraich, M., Drummond, T., Salomon, M. K., O'Brien, M. L., & Sivage, C. Effects of methylphenidate alone and in combination with behavior modification procedures on the behavior and academic performance of hyperactive children. *Journal of Abnormal Child Psychology*, 1978, *6*(1), 149–161.

Worland, J. Effects of positive and negative feedback on behavior control in hyperactive and normal boys. *Journal of Abnormal Child Psychology*, 1976, *4*, 315–326.

Zahn, T. P., Little, B. C., & Wender, P. H. Pupillary and heart rate reactivity in children with minimal brain dysfunction. *Journal of Abnormal Child Psychology*, 1978, *6*(1), 135–147.

Zahn, T. P., Rapoport, J. L., & Thompson, C. L. Autonomic and behavioral effects of dextroamphetamine and placebo in normal and hyperactive prepubertal boys. *Journal of Abnormal Child Psychology*, 1980, *8*(2), 145–160.

CHAPTER FIFTEEN

Monoaminergic Mechanisms in Hyperactivity

SALLY E. SHAYWITZ / BENNETT A. SHAYWITZ
DONALD J. COHEN / J. GERALD YOUNG

INTRODUCTION

Attention deficit disorder (ADD) with hyperactivity designates a syndrome characterized by disturbances in attention and impulsivity, as well as by hyperactive motor behavior. Historically, not only has ADD been known for decades under a variety of rubrics, including "the hyperactive child syndrome" and "minimal brain dysfunction" (MBD), but its etiology and pathogenesis have remained equally confusing. Thus, the physicians of an earlier era ascribed the symptoms of hyperactivity, short attention span, and impulsivity to "brain damage" from such factors as encephalitis or head trauma, while a successive generation believed that these symptoms arose from "reproductive casualty." This latter view, championed by Knobloch and Pasamanick (1959), suggested that difficulties arising during the perinatal period (e.g., maternal eclampsia, placenta previa) may result in profound damage to the central nervous system (CNS)—damage that might be manifest as a severe static encephalopathy (cerebral palsy) or severe epilepsy. According to the theory, lesser degrees of perinatal difficulty, so minor that the mother might not even be aware that any problem existed, would result in less severe CNS insults—"minimal" brain damage. Although intuitively attractive, this theory has not been supported by large prospective epidemiological studies such as the Perinatal Collaborative Project sponsored by the U.S. National Institutes of Health, which evaluated the long-term outcome in 55,000 pregnancies (Nelson & Ellenberg, 1979).

Most recently, evidence from epidemiological, pharmacological, and clinical studies in children, as well as investigations employing animal models of ADD, has led some investigators to suggest that perturbations in brain neurotransmitter function may be central to the symptom generation in these affected children. The acceptance of such a notion necessitates a critical examination of the evidence suggesting that brain catecholaminergic mechanisms may be involved in the pathogenesis of ADD. Our purpose in this chapter is to review that evidence and to discuss its potential relevance.

Sally E. Shaywitz, Bennett A. Shaywitz, Donald J. Cohen, and J. Gerald Young, Departments of Pediatrics, Neurology, and Psychiatry, and the Yale Child Study Center, Yale University School of Medicine, New Haven, Connecticut.

Before examining evidence supporting the important role of brain catecholaminergic mechanisms in ADD, the biochemistry of these neurotransmitters is briefly reviewed (Cooper, Bloom, & Roth, 1978). Tyrosine is the amino acid precursor of the catecholamines, dopamine (DA) and norepinephrine (NE). Tyrosine is ingested in the diet, and the first rate-limiting step in catecholamine synthesis within the neuron is hydroxylation of tyrosine by the enzyme tyrosine hydroxylase. The product of this reaction is L-dihydroxyphenylalanine (L-DOPA), which is quickly converted to DA by an enzyme with high activity, aromatic amino acid decarboxylase (AAAD). The final step in the formation of NE occurs through the action of dopamine-β-hydroxylase (DBH). In the adrenal medulla, and in small cellular systems in the brain stem, an additional catecholamine, epinephrine, is synthesized from NE via the enzyme phenylethanolamine-*N*-methyltransferase (PNMT).

Catabolism of the catecholamines is regulated by two enzymes, monoamine oxidase (MAO) and catechol-*O*-methyltransferase (COMT); the order in which they act determines which of two intermediate compounds is formed, dihydroxyphenylacetic acid (DOPAC; through deamination) or 3-methoxytyramine (MTA; through *O*-methylation). Each of these compounds is then converted to homovanillic acid (HVA) by the other of the two catabolic enzymes. The combined actions of COMT and MAO on NE result in the formation of two principal products, the proportions of each differing in the two major divisions of the nervous system: vanillylmandelic acid (VMA; the predominant product in the periphery) and 3-methoxy-4-hydroxyphenylethyleneglycol (MHPG; the predominant product in the brain).

The indoleamine, serotonin, is derived from the amino acid tryptophan; the availability of tryptophan and the activity of tryptophan hydroxylase (which converts tryptophan to 5-hydroxytryptophan, or 5-HTP) are the two determinants of the rate of formation of serotonin. The final step in the synthetic pathway is decarboxylation of 5-HTP to 5-hydroxytryptamine (5-HT, serotonin). Degradation by MAO produces the major metabolite of serotonin, 5-hydroxyindoleacetic acid (5-HIAA).

Methodological Considerations

The investigation of brain monoaminergic mechanisms in children presents both theoretical and practical obstacles. For obvious reasons, the strategies employed to assess monoamine metabolism in the human CNS have in common a dependence upon indirect estimates of neurotransmitter function. While it is now possible to obtain a small amount of tissue and culture it (e.g., fibroblasts taken from a skin biopsy; see Giller, Young, Breakefield, Carbonari, Braverman, & Cohen, 1980), the usual clinical method for metabolic studies will continue to be the assay of cerebrospinal fluid (CSF), blood, or urine samples. The concentration of neurotransmitter can be measured directly; alternatively, levels of precursors, metabolites, or related enzymes can be determined to estimate the function of the neuronal system (Cohen & Young, 1977).

The most logical approach to clinical measurement of brain monoaminergic mechanisms utilizes determinations of monamines or their metabolites in the CSF, which allow a direct assessment of central function. The rationale and limitations of this methodology have been described previously in detail (Cohen, Shaywitz, Young, & Bowers, 1980; B. A. Shaywitz, Cohen, & Bowers, 1980).

Several problems have complicated the direct measurement of neurotransmitters in peripheral fluids. The rapid reuptake and degradation of catecholamines, for example, results in very low levels in the plasma that cannot be measured by older analytical methods. New methods are now capable of determinations of several neurotransmitters in concentrations below 20 pg/ml of fluid; the principal techniques are high-performance liquid chromatography (HPLC) with electrochemical or fluorometric detection (Anderson & Young, 1981), radioenzymatic assays (Henry, Starman, Johnson, & Williams, 1975), combined gas chromatography and mass fragmentography (Muskiet, Jeuring, Korf, Sedvall, Westerink, Teelken, & Wolthers, 1979), and radioimmunoassay (Keeton, Krutzch, & Lovenberg, 1981). The clinical interpretation of the "meaning" of plasma levels of the free neurotransmitter is complicated by their responsivity to a range of transient (state) influences.

Determinations of 5-HT indicate other difficulties with this strategy. Approximately 90% of the serotonin in the body is in the gastrointestinal tract; lesser amounts are located in the platelets (8–10%) and CNS (1–2%). Nearly all of whole-blood 5-HT is stored in the platelets, so that the functional significance of blood serotonin levels has been unclear. Similarities between the structural and functional characteristics of 5-HT nerve endings and blood platelets, however, have suggested that the platelet might serve as a peripheral model of some aspects of central 5-HT metabolism (Stahl, 1977). Many further studies are necessary before this extrapolation can be made with confidence.

The measurement of neurotransmitter metabolites is attractive because the inactive metabolites are usually not degraded so quickly in peripheral fluids, and tend to indicate the function of a neuronal system over a longer time period (with improved test–retest stability). Recent evidence suggests that plasma levels of MHPG and HVA might provide an index of the activity of central noradrenergic and dopaminergic neuronal systems, respectively (Maas, Hattox, Greene, & Landis, 1979; Maas, Hattox, Landis, & Roth, 1977; Roth, Bucopoulus, & Heninger, 1978). For example, the plasma concentration of HVA appears to be increased following the administration of haloperidol (Roth *et al.*, 1978), supporting the concept that plasma concentrations of HVA parallel brain levels and are responsive to functional changes.

Enzymes related to the neurotransmitters usually function intracellulary, so that they are not present in samples of extracellular fluids (e.g., tyrosine hydroxylase). There are exceptions, however, as indicated by blood measures of DBH and MAO. DBH, the final enzyme active in the synthesis of NE, is contained with NE in the presynaptic vesicles; NE and DBH are extruded into the circulation, where DBH can be assayed in the serum (Goldstein, Freedman, Ebstein, Park, & Kashimoto, 1974; Weinshilboum, Raymond, & Weidman, 1973). However, the great range of DBH activities found in the normal population, due to genetic differences, makes clinical interpretation of such measurements difficult (Weinshilboum, 1979; J. G. Young, Kyprie, Ross, & Cohen, 1980).

The blood platelet contains substantial MAO activity. Different forms of this enzyme are designated as Type A MAO (which preferentially acts on serotonin and other compounds) or Type B MAO (which is specific for phenylethylamine and other related substances) (Cawthon & Breakefield, 1979; Domino, 1980; Edwards, 1980; Singer, Vonkorff, & Murphy, 1979; Sourkes, 1980). Some substrates, such as DA, are nonspecifically deaminated by both forms of MAO, while for others the specificity is not yet clear (e.g., NE appears to be either a type A specific or nonspecific substrate; see Domino, 1980; Edwards, 1980). In clinical studies, MAO is usually measured in the blood platelet, where it is uniformly Type B MAO (Edwards, 1980). Genetically based differences in platelet MAO activity have been investigated as markers for vulnerabilities to several human disorders (Murphy & Kalin, 1980; Wyatt, Potkin, Bridge, Phelps, & Wise, 1980), once again using the platelet as a model for the function of central nerve endings.

ANIMAL MODELS OF HYPERACTIVITY

Animal studies have provided strong evidence to suggest that perturbations of central DA mechanisms significantly influence the development of hyperactive motor behavior and cognitive difficulties, a thesis developed more fully in a recent review (Iversen, 1977). Their relevance to a clinical disorder such as ADD is enhanced if the animal model exhibits similar phenomenology, similar etiology, and similar response to treatments known to be effective in the clinical disorder. Those criteria we believe should be satisfied if the animal model is to be considered as a suitable one for ADD include the following:

1. Production in a developing animal, rather than the neurologically mature adult. Furthermore, the behaviors should follow the same developmental course in the animal model as in the clinical disorder. For example, hyperactivity in the adult animal does not correspond to the symptom in children, since the hyperactivity in ADD, while common in early childhood, abates with maturity.
2. Replication of particular cardinal features of ADD in the animal model. Such features may include hyperactive motor activity, cognitive difficulties, and difficulty in habituating to a new environment.
3. Production of the animal model by methods that are believed to bear some relationship to the presumed pathogenesis of the clinical disorder.
4. A response to medications that parallels the response to those same pharmacological agents in children with ADD. This would include the response to stimulants such as amphetamine and methylphenidate, as well as the response to agents such as phenobarbital.

Although a number of animal models have been suggested (S. E. Shaywitz, Cohen, & Shaywitz, 1978), the model that most closely parallels the clinical disorder is that described initially in 1976 (B. A. Shaywitz, Yager, & Klopper, 1976; B. A. Shaywitz, Yager, Klopper, & Gordon, 1976) and now confirmed by investigators throughout the world (Eastgate, Wright, & Werry, 1978; Erinoff, MacPhail, Heller, & Seiden, 1979; Heffner, Miller, Kotake, Heller, & Seiden, 1980; Sorenson, Vayer, & Goldberg, 1977; Stoof, Dijkstra, & Hillegers, 1978). It is produced in the developing rat pup by depletion of brain DA via the intracisternal administration of the neurotoxin 6-hydroxydopamine (6-OHDA).

Such treatment results in rapid and permanent reduction of brain DA to concentrations of 10 to 25% of that in controls, while brain NE and 5-HT remain unaffected. Furthermore, the developmental pattern of DA-depleted rat pups has many parallels with the clinical syndrome of ADD. Thus, animals treated with 6-OHDA are significantly more active than their litter-mate controls during the period of behavioral arousal that occurs between 2 and 3 weeks of age. However, with maturation, the hyperactivity disappears, a finding that corresponds to ADD, where hyperactivity is often pronounced until 10 to 12 years of age but then abates. Their associated cognitive difficulties persist, however, and this corresponds to the persistent deficits in avoidance learning shown by 6-OHDA pups in maze tasks. Still other parallels with the clinical syndrome are found in the stimulant induced reduction in activity observed in 6-OHDA pups with both amphetamine (B. A. Shaywitz, Yager, Klopper, & Gordon, 1976) and methylphenidate (B. A. Shaywitz, Klopper, & Gordon, 1978) and the exacerbation of hyperactivity produced by administration of phenobarbital (B. A. Shaywitz & Pearson, 1978). For the child with ADD, any change in milieu may result in an exacerbation of both hyperactivity and distractibility, a finding that has its experimental counterpart in the impaired ability of 6-OHDA pups to modulate their activity when placed in a novel environment, an effect described experimentally as "impaired habituation of activity" (B. A. Shaywitz, Gordon, Klopper, & Zelterman, 1977).

Most recently, we have utilized the 6-OHDA model to examine the interaction between biological factors (represented by preferential depletion of brain DA) and environmental influences (embodied in alterations in litter composition) upon locomotor activity and avoidance performance (Pearson, Teicher, Shaywitz, Cohen, Young, & Anderson, 1980). Both the hyperactivity and avoidance-learning deficits observed in the 6-OHDA pups were significantly improved by allowing the DA-depleted pups to be reared with normal littermates, rather than confined solely with other damaged animals—findings in a way comparable to clinical reports suggesting that particular modifications of the environment may be therapeutic in children with ADD (O'Leary & Pelham, 1978; Satterfield, Cantwell, & Satterfield, 1979).

The value of an animal model may be considered on a number of levels. In one sense, it may serve heuristic value in generating principles and generalizations about human behaviors. From a practical vantage point, it may be useful in deciding upon newer therapies or in studying particular pharmacological relationships that are not possible to achieve because of ethical and methodological restrictions imposed by human investigations. In this section, we have used animal models to illustrate and support the notion that disturbances in brain monoaminergic systems may be linked to the behaviors observed in ADD. In the following sections, we pursue this thesis in clinical investigations.

ONTOGENY OF BRAIN MONOAMINES

Most investigators believe that in ADD they are dealing with a developmental disorder, characteristic symptoms of which change with maturation. For example, hyperactive motor behavior, a cardinal symptom of the disorder, is most usually observed in the kindergarten and early school years, but tends to abate with maturity. It is uncommon to see teenagers with ADD whose primary presenting complaint is hyperactivity. A reasonable explanation for this phenomenon is an alteration in the CNS mechanisms believed to influence motor activity. As we discuss below, good evidence suggests that these involve brain monoaminergic, and particularly central dopaminergic, mechanisms. The alterations of brain monoamines with age provide a reasonable correlate of the behavioral changes, and if researchers are to understand the postulated variations of brain monoamines in disease states, it is mandatory that they utilize a developmental perspective, and do not simply describe a normal age-related change when investigating brain monoaminergic mechanisms in ADD.

The present understanding of the ontogeny of brain monoamines in humans is fragmentary, but the results of investigations of monoamines, their metabolites, or the enzymes involved in their synthesis and degradation has provided evidence to suggest significant variations in both catecholaminergic and indoleaminergic mechanisms with maturation (J. G. Young, Cohen, Anderson, & Shaywitz, in press).

Although the data are not totally consistent, the results of recent investigations support the belief that NE mechanisms tend to increase with maturation. For example, serum DBH increases with age, particularly over the first few years of life (Freedman, Ohuchi, Goldstein, Axelrod, Fish, & Dancis, 1972; Weinshilboum *et al.*, 1973; J. G. Young, Kyprie, Ross, & Cohen, 1980) as does plasma NE (Ziegler, Lake, & Kopin, 1976). However, examination of brain tyrosine hydroxylase (TH) activity at autopsy indicates that it decreases with age (McGeer & McGeer, 1973; McGeer, McGeer, & Wada, 1971); another study using autopsy tissue indicates that there is no change in TH activity with age, although the wide age range (4 to 33 years) and small numbers of subjects may have obscured changes during specific developmental periods (Robinson, Sourkes, Nies, Harris, Spector, Bartlett, & Kaye, 1977). A recent study of CSF concentrations of the activity of the cofactor believed necessary for the function of tyrosine and tryptophan hydroxylase activity indicates that this cofactor declines with age in an adult population (Williams, Ballenger, Levein, Lovenberg, & Calne, 1980). However, no information is available for childhood and adolescence. Studies of the degradative enzymes involved in brain catecholamines indicate that platelet MAO decreases during childhood and adolescence (J. G. Young, Cohen, Waldo, Feiz, & Roth, 1980), though data indicate that the activity of this enzyme increases again during later adult years (Belmaker, Ebbesen, Ebstein, & Rimon, 1976; Robinson *et al.*, 1977), a pattern that holds true for brain autopsy tissue as well (Robinson & Nies, 1980). A decrease in MAO during the first two decades could result in a reduced degradation of NE and thus an increase in its concentration. Further support for an increase in NE during childhood is found in studies of urinary excretion of NE metabolites. Thus, VMA, a principal metabolite of peripheral NE, increases in urine throughout childhood and into puberty (McKendrick & Edwards, 1965). In addition, MHPG, the principal metabolite of brain NE, has been found to be correlated with age in a recent study (J. G. Young, Cohen, Caparulo, Brown, & Maas, 1979). However, the concentration of this metabolite in CSF does not change with age.

In contrast to the ontogeny of NE, the development of DA activity appears to decrease as the organism matures. Using the probenecid method, we found a significant decrease with age in CSF concentration of HVA in 34 neuropsychiatrically disturbed children (Cohen, Shaywitz, & Johnson, 1974) and extended these observations in a study involving 154 psychiatric patients between the ages of 2 and 67 years (Leckman, Cohen, Shaywitz, Caparulo, Heninger, & Bowers, 1980). These findings have been corroborated by other research groups (Seifert, Foxx, & Butler, 1980) and extended to children with epilepsy and other neurological disorders (B. A. Shaywitz, Cohen, & Bowers, 1980; B. A. Shaywitz, Cohen, Leckman, Young, & Bowers, 1980). Thus the finding that children with a broad range of neuropsychiatric disorders have higher CSF accumulations of HVA compared to adult psychiatric patients is compatible with the earlier reports that the brains of children release more HVA into the blood than do the brains of adults (Fryo, Settergie, & Sedvall, 1978).

The development of the serotonergic system is difficult to characterize. Whole-blood serotonin levels decrease over childhood and adolescence (Ritvo, Yuwiler, Geller, Plotkin, Mason, & Faeger, 1971), while platelet MAO activity also decreases (see above). However, CSF concentrations of 5-HIAA are stable throughout the life cycle (Leckman *et al.*, 1980; B.A. Shaywitz, Cohen, & Bowers, 1980; B. A. Shaywitz, Cohen, Leckman, Young, & Bowers, 1980; S. N. Young, Gauthier, Anderson, & Purdy, 1980), though one investigation found a reduction in this metabolite with age (Seifert *et al.*, 1980). No relationship was observed between age and either serotonin or 5-HIAA in human brain autopsy tissue (Gottfried, Oreland, Wiberg, & Winblad, 1975; Gottfries, Roos, & Winblad, 1974; Grote, Moses, Robins, Hudgens, & Croninger, 1974; Robinson, 1975).

In summary, the most reasonable interpretation of the available information suggests that concentrations of NE tend to increase during childhood and adolescence. On the other hand, 5-HT either declines or stays relatively constant, and DA probably declines with maturation.

Sex Differences and Brain Catecholamines

Few studies have examined sex differences in central monoamines in children. In one study of 34 male and 9 female neuropsychiatric patients, we found that girls tended to have lower accumulations of DA metabolites than boys did (Cohen, Caparulo, Shaywitz, & Bowers, 1977), a finding replicated in a larger study of psychiatric patients aged between 3 and 20 years (Cohen, Shaywitz, Young, Carbonari, Nathanson, Lieberman, Bowers, & Maas, 1979; Cohen, Young, Nathanson, & Shaywitz, 1979). Recently we have extended these observations to 18 children with epilepsy (10 boys, 8 girls), and 20 children with other neurological disorders (14 boys, 6 girls). Compared to boys, girls tend to have lower accumulations of DA metabolites and higher accumulations of 5-HT metabolites. We would speculate that these findings suggest that girls tend to have a relatively more mature or modulated CNS functioning, particularly in relation to central inhibitory mechanisms (Aghajanian, Haigler, & Bennett, 1975). These differences are especially interesting because of the markedly greater vulnerability of boys to major neuropsychiatric disorders of childhood. Thus childhood autism, Gilles de la Tourette syndrome, and ADD all occur three to four times more frequently in boys, and it is possible that the variation in disease prevalence might relate to the observed differences in monoamine concentrations.

EARLY CLINICAL STUDIES

During the early part of this century, physicians were frequently confronted with children exhibiting hyperactivity and behavioral disturbances believed to be the sequelae of the great pandemic of von Economo encephalitis (Bond & Partridge, 1926; Ebaugh, 1923; Hohman, 1922). A relationship between von Economo encephalitis and Parkinson disease has been long established, as has the relationship between parkinsonism and damage to nigroneostriatal dopaminergic pathways. Thus, these findings led Wender (1971) to speculate that when the virus presumed to cause von Economo encephalitis infected adults, it produced damage to brain DA systems resulting in Parkinson disease. Presumably the virus similarly affected brain DA systems in children, but the behavioral effects in the developing nervous system were hyperactivity, impulsivity, and attentional deficits.

This imaginative suggestion is difficult to substantiate, however, since methodology for viral isolation was not developed at the time of the pandemic, and the virus of von Economo encephalitis was never isolated. However, recent animal investigations lend support for this notion. Thus, Lycke and Roos (1974, 1975) have demonstrated that if mice are inoculated with herpes simplex virus they exhibit not only hypermotility and behavioral excitation, but also an increased turnover and synthesis of brain DA and 5-HT.

Observations of the effects of stimulant drugs on hyperactive children provided still another bit of evidence linking brain catecholamines to ADD. As early as 1937, Bradley noted that administration of amphetamines to children with hyperactivity, attentional disorders, and impulsivity produced a remarkable ameliorative effect, reducing activity and improving attention without producing drowsiness. Numerous studies over the past two decades have confirmed these effects (Barkley, 1977; Whalen & Henker, 1976), though the long-term effects of stimulants remain controversial (Rie, Rie, Stewart, & Ambuel, 1976). Pharmacological studies in both animals and humans have documented that the stimulants, amphetamine and methylphenidate, exert their actions via central catechoaminergic mechanisms, though minor differences exist between these agents. Amphetamine acts on a reserpine-resistant pool of newly synthesized DA, whereas methylphenidate facilitates the impulse-mediated release of a reserpine-sensitive pool of DA (Clemens & Fuller, 1979); however, both act to increase the concentration of catecholamine, primarily DA, in the synaptic cleft. Because either amphetamine or methylphenidate often ameliorates the symptoms of ADD, and since both agents exert their effects via central catecholaminergic pathways, this commonality between ADD and the stimulants prompted Wender (1971, 1978) to suggest that brain catecholamines are influential in the genesis of ADD.

GENETIC INFLUENCES IN ATTENTION DEFICIT DISORDER

The demonstration of an hereditary pattern for a clinical syndrome is often the first clue to an underlying biochemical disturbance in that disorder. Though it does not point directly to an abnormality in brain monoamines, the finding of a genetic influence in ADD provides strong suggestive evidence that disordered biochemical processes (which could involve central monamine systems) play a role in this disorder. Such evidence has been obtained utilizing several diverse but complimentary research strategems, employing family studies, twin populations, and adoptee and foster-rearing methods.

Investigations of the parents of children with ADD provided the first suggestion of a genetic influence in the disorder. Morrison and Stewart (1971) noted hyperactivity during childhood in 12 out of 59 parents of hyperactive children, compared to only 2 out of 41 in the parents of controls, a finding corroborated by Cantwell (1972) in the fathers of hyperactives. Furthermore, these studies documented the increased prevalence of the triad of hysteria, sociopathy, and alcoholism in the families of affected children. Although such studies may implicate familial transmission of certain symptoms, they fail to differentiate genetic from environmental influences.

The relative contribution of each of these factors could be clarified utilizing other strategems, such as twin studies, and results of the one investigation employing this method supports the notion of a genetic component for activity levels in general and for hyperactivity in particular. Willerman (1973) examined hyperactivity levels (based on the Werry–Weiss–Peters Activity Scale) in 93 sets of twin girls. Monozygotic twins exhibited a high concordance for hyperactivity, while that in dizygotic twins was minimal, suggesting that genetic factors overshadowed environmental considerations. A major limitation of this investigation was its use of a population with a relatively low incidence of hyperactivity (girls), and thus it is difficult to extrapolate to the usual population of ADD, with its preponderance of boys.

More compelling data supporting the hypothesis of a genetic transmission in ADD are those provided by adoption studies (Morrison & Stewart, 1973; Cantwell, 1975). Both studies reported that the prevalence rate for ADD in the nonbiological relatives of adopted children with ADD was not significantly different from that observed in a control group. Thus the results would suggest that environmental factors are not as important in the genesis of ADD as is heredity. The complementary study, to demonstrate an increased prevalence of ADD in the adopted children's biological families, has yet to be performed. However, Safer (1973) was able to examine both the full and half siblings in a small cohort of adopted children with ADD. A diagnosis of ADD was made in 9 out of 19 full siblings but in only 2 out of 22 half siblings, results again suggesting that genetic influences in ADD are significant.

MONOAMINES, RELATED ENZYMES, AND METABOLITES IN ATTENTION DEFICIT DISORDER

While the findings of the investigations just reviewed are suggestive, documentation of an abnormality in the amines, their metabolites, or the enzymes concerned with their formation and degradation in populations of ADD children would provide considerably more convincing evidence for a relationship between central monoaminergic mechanisms and the behaviors exhibited in the clinical disorder. Utilizing urinary concentrations of HVA and 5-HIAA as indexes of central DA and 5-HT respectively, Wender, Epstein, Kopin, and Gordon (1971) failed to detect any differences in either metabolite in children with hyperactivity as compared to controls. Because such urinary concentrations undoubtedly reflect monoamine metabolism in not only CNS but peripheral (including autonomic) nervous systems, it is probable that urinary concentrations of these particular metabolites reflect not simply alterations of their parent amines in the brain, but rather the net activity from monoaminergic mechanisms throughout the body. In contrast, recent evidence suggests that the urinary concentration of MHPG might be a useful index of brain NE metabolism. Thus studies in both dogs and monkeys demonstrate that perhaps 60% of urinary MHPG originates in the brain (Maas *et al.*, 1977), and that this percentage probably holds true for humans as well. Based upon this data, Shekim, Dekirmenjian, Chapel, Javaid, and Davis (1979) reported reduced concentrations of MHPG in a cohort of 23 hyperactive boys; the concentrations were further reduced by administration of amphetamine. These results suggest a disturbance in central NE mechanisms in some children with ADD.

As noted earlier, concentrations of monoamine-related enzymes in plasma have potential utility in assessing brain monoaminergic systems. However, Rapoport, Wuinn, and Lamprecht (1974) failed to detect any relationship between plasma DBH and activity levels in 72 hyperactive boys. We have examined DBH concentrations in a cohort of 30 boys with ADD, both before and during administration of the stimulant methylphenidate. We did not observe any differences between mean DBH levels in this group compared to a contrast population with pervasive developmental disturbances; nor did we observe any alteration of DBH with methylphenidate, findings consonant with those of Rapoport *et al.* However, serum DBH levels have not generally proven to be a useful clinical measure, largely due to the more than 100-fold range of its activity in normal subjects (Weinshilboum, 1979; J. G. Young *et al.*, 1979). Serum DBH activity will be most informative clinically when examined in well-designed genetic studies that employ within-subject repeated-measures designs and novel approaches responsive to the findings of a decade of clinical studies.

In contrast, preliminary findings in our study suggest that platelet MAO activity might be reduced in certain subgroups of the ADD population. Since DA is a substrate for the Type B MAO found in platelets, this finding might reflect an abnormality in central DA mechanisms in certain ADD subgroups (Youdim, Collins, Snadler, Beven-Jones, Pare, & Nicholsom, 1972).

Investigations of amines and their metabolites within CSF have provided a window on brain metabolism that may more accurately reflect CNS monoaminergic function than measures in urine or plasma may. Not only have recent techniques enabled the examination of nanogram concentrations of the amine metabolites in CSF, but considerable evidence indicates that the concentrations of these metabolites reflect the activity of the parent amines in the brain (Cohen, Shaywitz, Young, & Bowers, 1980; B. A. Shaywitz, Cohen, & Bowers, 1980). In a study of 23 hyperactive children and 6 controls, Shetty and Chase (1976) reported that although baseline concentrations of each metabolite were similar in both hyperactive and control groups, administration of amphetamine resulted in a significant reduction in CSF HVA but not in 5-HIAA in the hyperactives. Amphetamine was not given to normal children, so whether this effect was in fact a function of amphetamine or reflected an actual disturbance in brain catecholaminergic activity due to the clinical disorder is difficult to determine. Thus, although the authors interpreted their findings as supporting an alteration in central DA function in children with hyperkinesis, such an interpretation is difficult to reconcile with the known actions of amphetamine, an agent whose administration should result in an increase in DA and a concomitant elevation of its metabolite, HVA, irrespective of the hyperactivity of the subject. Utilizing the technique of probenecid loading, we have examined a group of six boys aged 5 to 9 years, all of normal intelligence, who were referred from local schools because of cognitive difficulties, short attention span, hyperactivity, and impulsivity. Although at the time of the study criteria from the third edition of the *Diagnostic and Statistical Manual of Mental Disorders* (DSM-III) were not available, subsequent reexamination of their histories indicates that they all satisfied the diagnosis of ADD. Our control group comprised 20 children aged 2 to 16, evaluated for a variety of neurological difficulties such as headache, muscle weakness, back pain, or personality disorder. None had a learning disability or were hyperactive, and in contrast to the children described by Shetty and Chase, none were receiving amphetamine or methylphenidate, nor had they received such stimulants for at least 4 months prior to investigation. Concentrations of HVA relative to probenecid were significantly reduced in lumbar CSF of the hyperactive children, compared to the concentrations in controls. Furthermore, levels of 5-HIAA were not altered. Our findings are consistent with the notion that brain DA systems, but not 5-HT systems, may be abnormal in some children with ADD (B. A. Shaywitz, Cohen, & Bowers, 1977).

RECENT ADVANCES IN THE CLINICAL INVESTIGATION OF ATTENTION DEFICIT DISORDER

Although the strategies described in previous sections continue to be employed, most recently an entirely new kind of investigation has emerged that potentially may provide far more information about the functional characteristics of brain monoaminergic systems in ADD. The basis of this new research strategy is the utilization of pharmacological "probes" that act to stimulate particular monoaminergic systems in children with ADD. The stimulant methylphenidate is an example of such a probe, since good evidence from animal investigations suggest that this agent acts to stimulate the impulse-mediated release of a reserpine-sensitive pool of DA (Clemens & Fuller, 1979). We have recently examined the effects of both acute and chronic administration of methylphenidate in ADD (S. E. Shaywitz, Hunt, Jatlow, Cohen, Young, Pierce, Anderson, & Shaywitz, 1982). In our first experiment, we examined the effects of both low (.34 mg/kg) and high (.65 mg/kg) doses of methylphenidate in 14 boys ranging in age from 7 to 12 years, all of normal intelligence, and satisfying DSM-II criteria for ADD with hyperactivity. We found that peak concentrations occurred within 2 to 3 hours and that the plasma half-life averaged 2½ hours, findings consistent with the "behavioral half-life" of 2 to 4 hours reported by Swanson, Kinsbourne, Roberts, and Zucker (1978). However, in addition to clarifying the pharmacokinetics of methylphenidate in boys with ADD, we also documented a significant and consistent elevation in serum growth hormone and reduction in serum prolactin concentrations that followed the time course of methylphenidate (see Figure 15-1). These effects are most reasonably understood as the actions of methylphenidate on DA pathways,

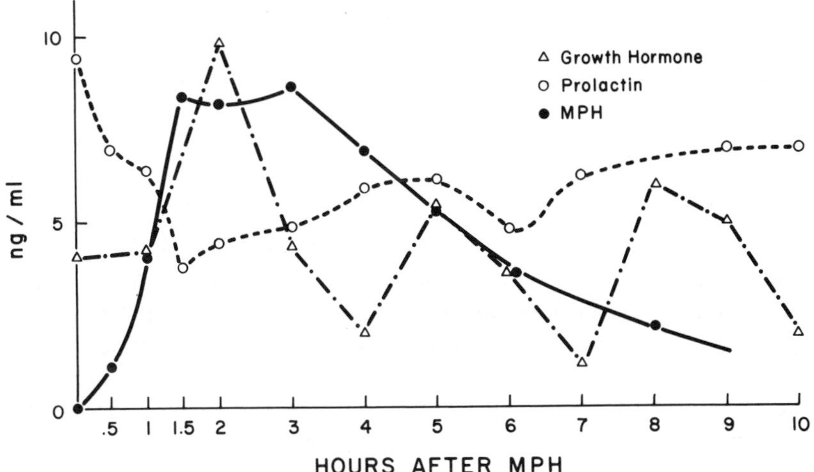

Figure 15-1. Mean concentrations of growth hormone, prolactin, and methylphenidate (MPH) in children who received .3 mg/kg of MPH. From "Psychopharmacology of Attention Deficit Disorder: Pharmacokinetic, Neuroendocrine and Behavioral Measures following Acute and Chronic Treatment with Methylphenidate" by S. E. Shaywitz, R. D. Hunt, P. Jatlow, D. J. Cohen, J. G. Young, R. N. Pierce, G. M. Anderson, and B. A. Shaywitz, *Pediatrics*, 1982, *69*, 688–694. Copyright 1982 by the American Academy of Pediatrics. Reprinted by permission.

most likely within the tuberoinfundibular DA system, and provide an index of DA function within this pathway. By comparing these effects with those observed after administration of a probe believed to affect primarily NE mechanisms, such as clonidine (Cohen, Detlor, Young, & Shaywitz, 1980), we may be able to discriminate particular subtypes of monoaminergic dysfunction in children with ADD. However, such a procedure will not permit the differentiation of children with ADD from normals; this process would require similar kinds of studies to be performed in normal children, something that at this time we do not believe to be reasonable or proper. It is, however, possible to compare their responses with those observed in other childhood neuropsychiatric disorders, such as Tourette syndrome (Cohen, Detlor, Young, & Shaywitz, 1980; Cohen, Shaywitz, Young, Carbonari, Nathanson, Lieberman, Bowers, & Maas, 1979; Cohen, Young, Nathanson, & Shaywitz, 1979). Such contrast groups have been utilized in a number of our previous studies, and provide a strategy that circumvents the ethical dilemma presented by the administration of stimulants to normal children.

In addition to effects on growth hormone and prolactin, we also measured plasma concentrations of DA, NE, and epinephrine after administration of methylphenidate. At this time, it is unclear to us whether such measures will prove helpful in elucidating monoaminergic mechanisms in ADD.

In our second study, we investigated the effects of chronic administration of methylphenidate to a similar group of boys with ADD. In this group, "spot" levels of methylphenidate after 2 hours agreed closely with those obtained in the acute studies just described, suggesting to us that the 2-hour concentration might be a useful clinical index of peak methylphenidate concentration and could be of practical importance, particularly in children who fail to respond to methylphenidate. Single samples of prolactin and growth hormone were not helpful, as might be expected, but it is too soon to know whether other measures of monoaminergic function (plasma MAO, DBH, HVA, DOPAC) might be useful in documenting abnormalities in children with ADD (see Figures 15-2 and 15-3).

SUMMARY

This review has attempted to give the reader an overview of the monoamine theory of ADD. We have provided some background on the chemistry and methodology so that the reader can more knowledgeably decide on their limitations and evaluate some of the more controversial notions so prevalent in the literature of ADD. Most importantly, we hope to have provided a framework to enable the reader to comprehend and place in perspective the voluminous and often conflicting literature relating to ADD. We believe that such a perspective is mandatory if we are to understand this pervasive and complex disorder better and manage it more appropriately.

Acknowledgments

The research described in this chapter has been supported by USPHS Grants NS 12384 and AA 03599; Mental Health Clinical Research Center Grant No. 1 P 50 MH-30929; Clinical Center Grant No. RR 00125; the state of Connecticut; and the Thrasher Research Foundation.

Figure 15-2. Mean concentrations of methylphenidate (MPH) after oral administration of .3 and .6 mg/kg. The figure also indicates concentrations of MPH 1½ and 2 hours after administration in patients receiving the drug chronically. From "Psychopharmacology of Attention Deficit Disorder: Pharmacokinetic, Neuroendocrine and Behavioral Measures following Acute and Chronic Treatment with Methylphenidate" by S. E. Shaywitz, R. D. Hunt, P. Jatlow, D. J. Cohen, J. G. Young, R. N. Pierce, G. M. Anderson, and B. A. Shaywitz, *Pediatrics*, 1982, *69*, 688–694. Copyright 1982 by the American Academy of Pediatrics. Reprinted by permission.

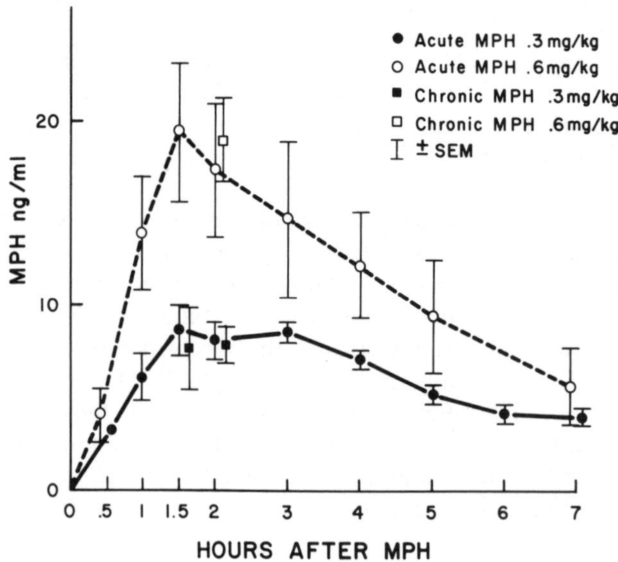

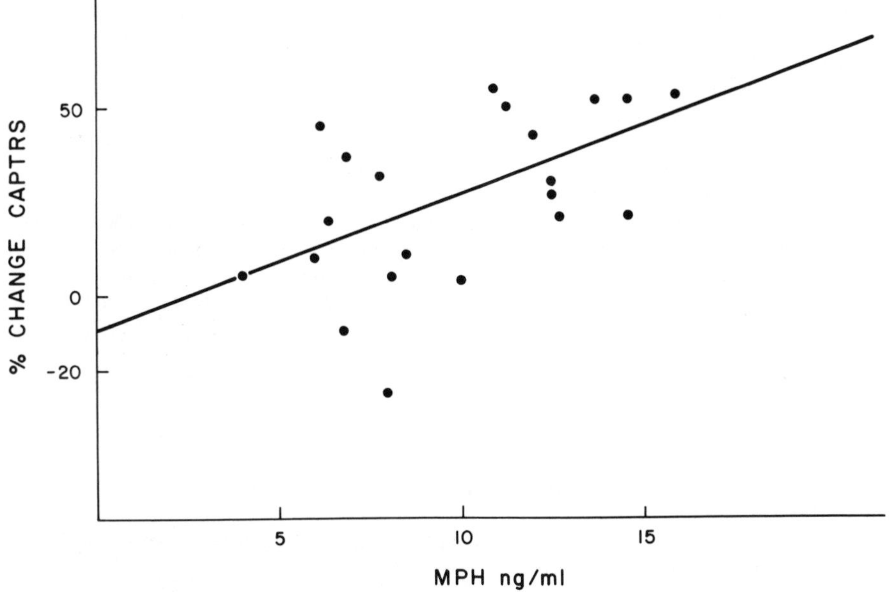

Figure 15-3. Relationship between the improvement on the Conners Abbreviated Parent-Teacher Rating Scale and methylphenidate (MPH) concentration at 2 hours. From "Psychopharmacology of Attention Deficit Disorder: Pharmacokineteic, Neuroendocrine and Behavioral Measures following Acute and Chronic Treatment with Methylphenidate" by S. E. Shaywitz, R. D. Hunt, P. Jatlow, D. J. Cohen, J. G. Young, R. N. Pierce, G. M. Anderson, and B. A. Shaywitz, *Pediatrics*, 1982, *69*, 688-694. Copyright 1982 by the American Academy of Pediatrics. Reprinted by permission.

References

Aghajanian, G. H., Haigler, H. J., & Bennett, J. L. Amine receptors in CNS: III. In L. L. Iversen, S. D. Iversen, & S. H. Snyder (Eds.), *Handbook of psychopharmacology* (Vol. 6). New York: Plenum Press, 1975.

Anderson, G. M., & Young, J. G. Minireview: Applications of liquid chromatographic–fluorometric systems in neurochemistry. *Life Sciences*, 1981, *28*, 507–517.

Barkley, R. A. A review of stimulant drug research with hyperactive children. *Journal of Child Psychology and Psychiatry*, 1977, *18*, 137–165.

Belmaker, R. H., Ebbesen, K., Ebstein, R., & Rimon, R. Platelet monoamine oxidase in schizophrenia and manic–depressive illness. *British Journal of Psychiatry*, 1976, *129*, 227–232.

Bond, E. P., & Partridge, C. E. Postencephalic behavior disorders in boys and their management in a hospital. *American Journal of Psychiatry*, 1926, *6*, 25–103.

Bradley, C. The behavior of children receiving benzedrine. *American Journal of Psychiatry*, 1937, *94*, 577–585.

Cantwell, D. Psychiatric illness in the families of hyperactive children. *Archives of General Psychiatry*, 1972, *27*, 414–417.

Cantwell, D. P. Genetic studies of hyperactive children: Psychiatric illness in biologic and adopting parents. In R. R. Fieve, D. Rosenthal, & H. Brill (Eds.), *Genetic research in psychiatry*. Baltimore: Johns Hopkins University Press, 1975.

Cawthon, R. M., & Breakefield, X. O. Differences in A and B forms of monoamine oxidase revealed by limited proteolysis and peptide mapping. *Nature*, 1979, *281*, 692–694.

Clemens, J. A., & Fuller, R. W. Differences in the effects of amphetamine and methylphenidate on brain dopamine turnover and serum prolactin concentrations in reserpine-treated rats. *Life Sciences*, 1979, *24*, 2077–2081.

Cohen, D. J., Caparulo, B. K., Shaywitz, B. A., & Bowers, M. B., Jr. Dopamine and serotonin metabolism in neuropsychiatrically disturbed children. *Archives of General Psychiatry*, 1977, *34*, 545–550.

Cohen, D. J., Detlor, J., Young, J. G., & Shaywitz, B. A. Clonidine ameliorates Tourette's syndrome. *Archives of General Psychiatry*, 1980, *37*, 1350–1357.

Cohen, D. J., Shaywitz, B. A., & Johnson, W. T. Biogenic amines in autistic and atypical children: Cerebrospinal fluid measures of homovanillic acid and 5-hydroxyindoleacetic acid. *Archives of General Psychiatry*, 1974, *31*, 845–853.

Cohen, D. J., Shaywitz, B. A., Young, J. G., & Bowers, M. B., Jr. Cerebrospinal fluid monoamine metabolites in neuropsychiatric disorders of childhood. In J. Wood (Ed.), *Neurobiology of cerebrospinal fluid*. New York: Plenum Press, 1980.

Cohen, D. J., Shaywitz, B. A., Young, J. G., Carbonari, C. M., Nathanson, J. A., Lieberman, D., Bowers, M. B., Jr., & Maas, J. W. Central biogenic amine metabolism in children with the syndrome of chronic multiple tics of Gilles de la Tourette: Norepinephrine, serotonin, and dopamine. *Journal of the American Academy of Child Psychiatry*, 1979, *18*, 320–341.

Cohen, D. J., & Young, J. G. Neurochemistry and child psychiatry. *Journal of the American Academy of Child Psychiatry*, 1977, *16*, 353–411.

Cohen, D. J., Young, J. G., Nathanson, J. A., & Shaywitz, B. A. Clonidine in Tourette's syndrome. *Lancet*, 1979, *2*, 551–553.

Cooper, J. R., Bloom, F. E., & Roth, R. H. *The biochemical basis of neuropharmacology* (3rd ed.). New York: Oxford University Press, 1978.

Domino, E. F. Monoamine oxidase substrates and substrate affinity. *Schizophrenia Bulletin*, 1980, *6*, 292–297.

Eastgate, S. M., Wright, J. J., & Werry, J. S. Behavioural effects of methylphenidate in 6-hydroxydopamine-treated rats. *Psychopharmacology*, 1978, *58*, 157–159.

Ebaugh, F. G. Neuropsychiatric sequelae of acute epidemic encephalitis in children. *American Journal of Diseases of Children*, 1923, *25*, 89–97.

Edwards, D. J. Molecular properties of the monoamine oxidases. *Schizophrenia Bulletin*, 1980, *6*, 275–281.

Erinoff, L., MacPhail, R. C., Heller, A., & Seiden, L. S. Age-dependent effects of 6-hydroxydopamine on locomotor activity in the rat. *Brain Research*, 1979, *164*, 195–205.

Freedman, L. S., Ohuchi, T., Goldstein, M., Axelrod, F., Fish, I., & Dancis, J. Changes in human serum dopamine-β-hydroxylase activity with age. *Nature*, 1972, *236*, 310–311.

Fryo, B., Settergre, G., & Sedvall, G. Release of homovanillic acid from the brains of children. *Life Sciences*, 1978, *17*, 387–402.

Giller, E. L., Young, J. G., Breakefield, X. O., Carbonari, C. M., Braverman, M., & Cohen, D. J. Monamine oxidase and catechol-*O*-methyltransferase activities in cultured fibroblasts and blood cells from children with autism and the Gilles de la Tourette syndrome. *Psychiatry Research*, 1980, *2*, 187–197.

Goldstein, M., Freedman, L. S., Ebstein, R. P., Park, D. M., & Kashimoto, T. Human serum dopamine-β-hydroxylase: Relationship to sympathetic activity in physiological and pathological states. In E. Usdin (Ed.), *Neuropsychopharmacology of monoamines and their regulatory enzymes: Advances in biochemical psychopharmacology*. New York: Raven Press, 1974.

Gottfries, C. G., Oreland, L., Wiberg, A., & Winblad, B. Lowered monoamine oxidase activity in brains from alcoholic suicide. *Journal of Neurochemistry*, 1975, *25*, 667–673.

Gottfries, C. G., Roos, B., & Winblad, B. Determination of 5-hydroxytryptamine, 5-hydroxyindoleacetic acid, and homovanillic acid in brain tissue from an autopsy material. *Acta Psychiatrica Scandinavica*, 1974, *50*, 496–507.

Grote, S. S., Moses, G., Robins, E., Hudgens, R. W., & Croninger, A. B. A study of selected catecholamine metabolizing enzymes: A comparison of depressive suicides and alcoholic suicides with controls. *Journal of Neurochemistry*, 1974, *23*, 701–802.

Heffner, T., Miller, F., Kotake, C., Heller, A., & Seiden, L. Transient or permanent hyperactivity following neonatal 6-hydroxydopamine: A function of brain dopamine depletion. *Neuroscience Abstracts*, 1980, *6*, 108.

Henry, D. P., Starman, B. J., Johnson, D. G., & Williams, R. H. A sensitive radioenzymatic assay for norepinephrine in tissues and plasma. *Life Sciences*, 1975, *16*, 375–384.

Hohman, L. B. Postencephalitic behavior disorders in children. *Johns Hopkins Hospital Bulletin*, 1922, *380*, 372–378.

Iversen, S. D. Brain dopamine systems and behavior. In L. L. Iversen, S. D. Iversen, & S. H. Snyder (Eds.), *Handbook of psychopharmacology* (Vol. 8). New York: Plenum Press, 1977.

Keeton, T. K., Krutzch, H., & Lovenberg, W. Specific and sensitive radioimmunoassay for 3-methoxy-4-hydroxyphenylethyleneglycol (MOPEG). *Science*, 1981, *211*, 586–588.

Keller, R., Oke, A., Mefford, I., & Adams, R. N. Liquid chromatographic analysis of catecholamines: Routine assay for regional brain mapping. *Life Sciences*, 1981, *19*, 995–1004.

Knobloch, H., & Pasamanick, B. The syndrome of minimal cerebral damage in infancy. *Journal of the American Medical Association*, 1959, *70*, 1384–1386.

Leckman, J. G., Cohen, D. J., Shaywitz, B. A., Caparulo, B. K., Heninger, G. R., & Bowers, M. B., Jr. CSF monamine metabolites in child and adult psychiatric patients: A developmental perspective. *Archives of General Psychiatry*, 1980, *37*, 677–681.

Lycke, E., & Roos, B. F. Influence of changes in brain monoamine metabolism on behavior of herpes simplex-infected mice. *Journal of the Neurological Sciences*, 1974, *22*, 277–289.

Lycke, E., & Roos, B. F. Virus infections in infant mice causing persistent impairment of turnover of brain catecholamines. *Journal of the Neurological Sciences*, 1975, *26*, 49–55.

Maas, J. W., Hattox, S. E., Greene, N. M., & Landis, D. H. 3-methoxy-4-hydroxyphenylethyleneglycol production by human brain *in vivo*. *Science*, 1979, *205*, 1025–1027.

Maas, J. W., Hattox, S. E., Landis, D. H., & Roth, R. H. A direct method for studying 3-methoxy-4-hydroxyphenylethyleneglycol (MHPG) production by brain in awake animals. *European Journal of Pharmacology*, 1977, *46*, 221–228.

McGeer, E. G., & McGeer, P. L. Some characteristics of brain tyrosine hydroxylase. In A. J. Mandell (Ed.), *New concepts in neurotransmitter regulation*. London: Plenum Press, 1973.

McGeer, E. G., McGeer, P. L., & Wada, J. A. Distribution of tyrosine hydroxylase in human and animal brain. *Journal of Neurochemistry*, 1971, *18*, 1647–1658.

McKendrick, T., & Edwards, R. W. The excretion of 4-hydroxy-3-methoxymandelic acid in children. *Archives of Disease in Childhood*, 1965, *40*, 418–425.

Morrison, J., & Stewart, M. A family study of hyperactive child syndrome. *Biological Psychiatry*, 1971, *3*, 189–195.

Morrison, J., & Stewart, M. The psychiatric status of the legal families of adopted hyperactive children. *Archives of General Psychiatry*, 1973, *28*, 888–891.

Murphy, D. L., & Donnelly, C. H. Monoamine oxidase in man: Enzyme characteristics in platelets, plasma, and other human tissues. In E. Usdin (Ed.), *Neuropsychopharmacology of monoamines and their regulatory enzymes: Advances in biochemical psychopharmacology*. New York: Raven Press, 1974.

Murphy, D. L., & Kalin, N. H. Biological and behavioral consequences of alterations in monoamine oxidase activity. *Schizophrenia Bulletin*, 1980, *6*, 355–367.

Muskiet, F. A. J., Jeuring, H. J., Korf, J., Sedvall, G., Westerink, B. H. C., Teelken, A. W., & Wolthers, B. G. Correlations between a fluorometric and mass fragmentographic method for the determination of 3-methoxy-4-hydroxyphenylacetic acid and two mass fragmentographic methods for the determination of 3-methoxy-4-hydroxyphenylethyleneglycol in cerebrospinal fluid. *Journal of Neurochemistry*, 1979, *32*, 191–194.

Nelson, K. B., & Ellenberg, J. H. Apgar scores and long-term neurological handicap. *Annals of Neurology*, 1979, *6*, 182. (Abstract)

O'Leary, S. G., & Pelham, W. E. Behavior therapy and withdrawal of stimulant medication in hyperactive children. *Pediatrics*, 1978, *61*, 211–217.

Pearson, D. E., Teicher, M. H., Shaywitz, B. A., Cohen, D. J., Young, J. G., & Anderson, G. M. Environmental influences on body weight and behavior in developing rats after neonatal 6-hydroxydopamine. *Science*, 1980, *209*, 715–717.

Rapoport, J. L., Wuinn, P. O., & Lamprecht, F. Minor physical anomalies and plasma dopamine-beta-hydroxylase activity in hyperactive boys. *American Journal of Psychiatry*, 1974, *131*, 386–390.

Rie, H. E., Rie, E. D., Stewart, S., & Ambuel, J. P. Effects of Ritalin on underachieving children: A replication. *American Journal of Orthopsychiatry*, 1976, *46*, 313–322.

Ritvo, E., Yuwiler, A., Geller, E., Plotkin, S., Mason, A., & Faeger, K. Maturational changes in blood serotonin levels and platelet counts. *Biochemical Medicine*, 1971, *5*, 90–96.

Robinson, D. S. Changes in monoamine oxidase and monoamines with human development and aging. *Federation Proceedings*, 1975, *34*, 103–107.

Robinson, D. S., & Nies, A. Demographic, biologic, and other variables affecting monoamine oxidase activity. *Schizophrenia Bulletin*, 1980, *6*, 298–307.

Robinson, D. S., Sourkes, T. L., Nies, A., Harris, S., Spector, S., Bartlett, D. L., & Kaye, I. S. Monoamine metabolism in human brain. *Archives of General Psychiatry*, 1977, *34*, 89–92.

Roth, R. H., Bucopoulus, N. G., & Heninger, G. Provenecid enhances haloperidol-induced HVA accumulation in CSF and plasma. *Neuroscience Abstracts*, 1978, *4*, 451. (Abstract)

Safer, D. J. A familial factor in minimal brain dysfunction. *Behavior Genetics*, 1973, *3*, 175–186.

Satterfield, J. H., Cantwell, D. P., & Satterfield, B. T. Multimodality treatment: A 1-year follow-up of 84 hyperactive boys. *Archives of General Psychiatry*, 1979, *36*, 965–974.

Seifert, W. E., Jr., Foxx, U. L., & Butler, I. J. Age effect on dopamine and serotonin metabolite levels in cerebrospinal fluid. *Annals of Neurology*, 1980, *8*, 38–42.

Shaywitz, B. A., Cohen, D. J., & Bowers, M. B., Jr. CSF monoamine metabolites in children with minimal brain dysfunction: Evidence for alteration of brain dopamine. *Journal of Pediatrics*, 1977, *90*, 67–71.

Shaywitz, B. A., Cohen, D. J., & Bowers, M. B., Jr. Cerebrospinal fluid monoamine metabolites in neurological disorders of childhood. In J. H. Wood (Ed.), *Neurobiology of cerebrospinal fluid*. New York: Plenum Press, 1980.

Shaywitz, B. A., Cohen, D. J., Leckman, J. F., Young, J. G., & Bowers, M. B., Jr. Ontogeny of dopamine and serotonin metabolites in the cerebrospinal fluid: Epilepsy and neurological disorders of childhood. *Developmental Medicine and Child Neurology*, 1980, *22*, 749–754.

Shaywitz, B. A., Gordon, J. W., Klopper, J. H., & Zelterman, D. The effect of 6-hydroxydopamine on habituation of activity in the developing rat pup. *Pharmacology, Biochemistry, and Behavior*, 1977, *6*, 391–396.

Shaywitz, B. A., Klopper, J. H., & Gordon, J. W. Methylphenidate in 6-hydroxydopamine-treated developing rat pups. *Archives of Neurology*, 1978, *35*, 463–469.

Shaywitz, B. A., & Pearson, D. E. Effects of phenobarbital on activity and learning in 6-hydroxydopamine-treated rat pups. *Pharmacology, Biochemistry, and Behavior*, 1978, *9*, 173–179.

Shaywitz, B. A., Yager, R. D., & Klopper, J. H. Selective brain dopamine depletion in developing rats: An experimental model of minimal brain dysfunction. *Science*, 1976, *191*, 305–308.

Shaywitz, B. A., Yager, R. D., Klopper, J. H., & Gordon, J. W. Paradoxical response to amphetamine in developing rats treated with 6-hydroxydopamine. *Nature*, 1976 *261*, 153–155.

Shaywitz, S. E., Cohen, D. J., & Shaywitz, B. A. The biochemical basis of minimal brain dysfunction. *Journal of Pediatrics*, 1978, *29*, 179–187.

Shaywitz, S. E., Hunt, R. D., Jatlow, P., Cohen, D. J., Young, J. G., Pierce, R. N., Anderson, G. M., & Shaywitz, B. A. Psychopharmacology of attention deficit disorder: Pharmacokinetic, neuroendocrine and behavioral measures following acute and chronic treatment with methylphenidate. *Pediatrics*, 1982, *69*, 688–694.

Shekim, W. O., Dekirmenjian, H., Chapel, J. L., Javaid, J., & Davis, J. M. Norepinephrine metabolism and clinical response to dextroamphetamine in hyperactive boys. *Journal of Pediatrics*, 1979, *95*, 389–394.

Shetty, T., & Chase, T. N. Central monoamines and hyperkinesis of childhood. *Neurology*, 1976, *26*, 1000–1002.

Singer, T. P., Vonkorff, R. W., & Murphy, D. L. (Eds.). *Monoamine oxidase: Structure, function, and altered functions*. New York: Academic Press, 1979.

Sorenson, C. A., Vayer, J. S., & Goldberg, C. S. Amphetamine reduction of motor activity in rats after neonatal administration of 6-hydroxydopamine. *Biological Psychiatry*, 1977, *12*, 133–137.

Sourkes, T. L. Some current matters of monoamine oxidase biochemistry. *Schizophrenia Bulletin*, 1980, *6*, 289–291.

Stahl, S. M. The human platelet. *Archives of General Psychiatry*, 1977, *34*, 509–516.

Stoof, J. C., Dijkstra, H., & Hillegers, J. P. M. Changes in the behavioral response to a novel environment following lesioning of the central dopaminergic system in rat pups. *Psychopharmacology*, 1978, *57*, 163–170.

Swanson, J., Kinsbourne, M., Roberts, W., & Zucker, K. Time–response analysis of the effect of stimulant medication on the learning ability of children referred for hyperactivity. *Pediatrics*, 1978, *61*, 21–29.

Weinshilboum, R. M. Serum dopamine-β-hydroxylase. *Pharmacological Reviews*, 1979, *39*, 133–166.

Weinshilboum, R. M., Raymond, F. A., & Weidman, W. H. Serum dopamine-β-hydroxylase activity: Sibling–sibling correlation. *Science*, 1973, *181*, 943–945.

Wender, P. *Minimal brain dysfunction in children*. New York: Wiley, 1971.

Wender, P. Minimal brain dysfunction: An overview. In M. A. Lipton, A. DiMascio, & K. F. Killam (Eds.), *Psychopharmacology: A generation in progress*. New York: Raven Press, 1978.

Wender, P. M., Epstein, R. S., Kopin, I. J., & Gordon, E. K. Urinary monoamine metabolites in children with minimal brain dysfunction. *American Journal of Psychiatry*, 1971, *127*, 1411–1415.

Whalen, C. K., & Henker, B. Psychostimulants and children: A review and analysis. *Psychological Bulletin*, 1976, *83*, 1113–1130.

Willerman, L. Activity level and hyperactivity in twins. *Child Development*, 1973, *44*, 288–293.

Williams, A., Ballenger, J., Levein, R., Lovenberg, W., & Caine, D. Aging and CSF hydroxylase cofactor. *Neurology*, 1980, *30*, 1244–1246.

Wyatt, R. J., Potkin, S. G., Bridge, T. P., Phelps, B. H., & Wise, C. D. Monamine oxidase in schizophrenia: An overview. *Schizophrenia Bulletin*, 1980, *6*, 199–207.

Youdim, M. B. H., Collins, G. G. S., Snadler, M., Beven-Jones, A. B., Pare, C. M. B., & Nicholsom, W. J. Human brain monoamine oxidase: Multiple forms and selective inhibitors. *Nature*, 1972, *236*, 225–228.

Young, J. G., Cohen, D. J., Anderson, G. M., & Shaywitz, B. A. Neurotransmitter ontogeny as a perspective for studies of child development and pathology. In B. Shopsin & L. Greenhill (Eds.), *The psychobiology of childhood: A profile of current issues.* New York: Spectrum, in press.

Young, J. G., Cohen, D. J., Caparulo, B. K., Brown, S. L., & Maas, J. W. Decreased 24-hour urinary MHPG in childhood autism. *American Journal of Psychiatry*, 1979, *136*, 1055–1057.

Young, J. G., Cohen, D. J., Waldo, M. C., Feiz, R., & Roth, J. A. Platelet monoamine oxidase activity in children and adolescents with psychiatric disorders. *Schizophrenia Bulletin*, 1980, *6*, 324–333.

Young, J. G., Kyprie, R., Ross, N., & Cohen, D. J. Serum dopamine-β-hydroxylase activity: Clinical applications in child psychiatry. *Journal of Autism and Developmental Disorders*, 1980, *10*, 1–14.

Young, S. N., Gauthier, S., Anderson, G. M., & Purdy, W. C. Tryptophan, 5-hydroxyindoleacetic acid, and indoleacetic acid in human cerebrospinal fluid: Interrelationships and the influence of age, sex, epilepsy, and anticonvulsant drugs. *Journal of Neurology, Neurosurgery, and Psychiatry*, 1980, *222*, 112–115.

Ziegler, M., Lake, C. R., & Kopin, I. J. Plasma noradrenaline increases with age. *Nature*, 1976, *261*, 333–335.

CHAPTER SIXTEEN

Drug Response and Diagnostic Validation

ERIC TAYLOR

Studies on the actions of drugs involve many research goals, quite apart from the immediate question, "Is drug *x* helpful in condition *y*?" Drugs offer a powerful tool for altering complex behavior, and hence for understanding it. Findings on drug response may also have important implications for the classification of disorders.

There is now a substantial literature on the drug responsiveness of overactive children (Barkley, 1977; Cantwell, 1977b; Cantwell & Carlson, 1978; Gittelman-Klein & Klein, 1975; Shaffer, 1977; see also Chapter 18 of this volume). In this chapter, I consider the results of this research, with special reference to a trial now in progress, in terms of the question of whether a characteristic drug response validates the diagnostic concept of "hyperkinetic syndrome." The problems inherent in this diagnosis are considered elsewhere in this volume (see Chapter 13). A broad and inclusive concept of "overactive behavior" is of limited value (Taylor, 1980a), is in many ways similar to the concept of "conduct disorder," and does not at present appear to carry specific etiological implications about brain dysfunction (Cantwell, 1977a; Sandberg, Rutter, & Taylor, 1978; Sandberg, Wieselberg, & Shaffer, 1980; Werry, 1968). A narrower concept may be of more value (Ounsted, 1955; Schachar, Rutter, & Smith, 1981; Taylor, 1980a), but it is much less researched and much less used. Studies of course and outcome also fail to demonstrate that overactivity is in any way a specific condition (Shaffer & Greenhill, 1979). The drug responsiveness of overactivity is therefore at the very heart of claims on the validity of the syndrome, and is a central reason for wishing to make the diagnosis.

There are, of course, limitations to the use of response to any kind of treatment as the validation of one's clinical concepts. The strongest objection is that treatments typically have multiple effects. Thus, the response of nocturnal enuresis to tricyclic antidepressants does not indicate that bedwetting should be classed as a form of depression. Nevertheless, a specific and unique response to a particular drug would constitute a strong argument for the theoretical and practical value of diagnosing a particular condition. This is the claim that has been made for hyperactivity. Very many trials attest the short-term efficacy of amphetamine and other stimulants (Taylor, 1979). There is, as I point out,

Eric Taylor. Department of Child and Adolescent Psychiatry, University of London Institute of Psychiatry, London, England.

more dispute about the uniqueness and specificity of the response. The strongest claim is that (1) the action of drugs on hyperkinetic children is different in kind from that on other people. Even if their action were the same in everyone, it would still be possible to argue that (2) only children with a syndrome of hyperkinesis, or attention deficit, or minimal brain dysfunction (MBD) are beneficially affected. If this were not sustained, it could still be that (3) only a hyperactive dimension of behavior is affected by the drug. These three claims need to be considered separately. In the process of doing so, problems are encountered in defining a "beneficial response" and variations in concepts of "hyperactivity."

QUALITATIVELY DISTINCT DRUG RESPONSE?

The strongest form of the hypothesis is also the easiest to disprove. It asserts that *the action of drugs on hyperkinetic children is qualitatively different from that on others.* More particularly, it says that stimulant drugs have a paradoxically sedative effect, reproducible in animals with certain kinds of brain damage (Grahame-Smith, 1978; Wender, 1971). The notion has become influential in clinical practice, but has rather little to recommend it.

Effects on Behavior and Cognitive Performance in Hyperactives and Normal Controls

The hypothesis of paradoxical effect was always difficult to sustain in the face of the undoubted fact that the unwanted effects of amphetamine-like drugs are just the same in the hyperkinetic individual as in anyone else. Insomnia and anorexia, frequently reported in drug trials (Barkley, 1977), are important markers of the stimulating central effect. Furthermore, it has long been clear that many of the main effects of these drugs are to be found in normal adults to the same extent as in hyperkinetic children. Weiss and Laties (1962), in an important review, stressed the effects of amphetamines on reducing reaction time, enhancing athletic performance, counteracting fatigue, and improving performance on certain cognitive tasks. Other researchers have argued for an introverting effect of stimulants (Eysenck, 1967), which can be seen as very much akin to its effect of diminishing outgoing and disinhibited behavior, and of diminishing the frequency with which activities are changed. The described effects in normal adults are therefore rather similar to the effects in "hyperkinetic" children. This is not, however, the end of the matter. In the first place, the measures used with normal adults and disturbed children have often been rather different; their responses therefore cannot be considered identical, and it is quite possible that subtle but important differences in response could be overlooked. In the second place, it is only one kind of psychological test performance that has been compared, and the psychiatrically important effects of drugs on mood, interpersonal behavior, and high-level cognitive processes are much less clear. In the third place, diagnosed children and normal adults might share a mechanism of response that is not seen in normal children or in children with other kinds of psychological disorder. Therefore, several other lines of evidence concerning the mechanism of stimulant drug actions need to be considered.

Pride of place should go to a study by Rapoport, Buchsbaum, Weingartner, Zahn, Ludlow, and Mikkelsen (1978) that directly addressed the question by comparing the effects of single doses of dextroamphetamine and placebo in normal children as well as in some hyperactive children for whom the drug was intended to be therapeutic. This is further described in Chapter 18 of this volume; the point of most interest to this argument is that normal, intelligent children and hyperactive children shared a similar pattern of cognitive and behavioral change. *Both* groups became less restless and more attentive as judged by the description of their teachers; both improved their scores on tests of attention and cognition. This does not, of course, mean either that stimulants are of no value or that everyone should have them. It was of no benefit to the normal children to have their activity level lowered, and it might even have been harmful to have their attention narrowed into an unduly small range of stimuli. Similar changes in overactive children might well be beneficial. Indeed, if it were the case that only the overactive were benefited, that would justify the diagnosis. The study, however, provides strong evidence against the idea that drugs act on the hyperkinetic in a radically different way; and therefore it lends no comfort to those who maintain that hyperkinetic children are different in any important way from children with other disorders of behavior.

However, not even this study is quite conclusive. It is based upon the acute response to a single dose of a drug. This is a reasonable design for testing effectiveness, particularly for a short-acting drug such as amphetamine; indeed, it is a necessary limitation, for ethical considerations would rule out any longer-term administration of stimulant drugs to normal children. Nonetheless, it is known that in other areas the chronic use of amphetamine has characteristics that differ from the acute response of a naive subject to a single dose. For example, the psychotogenic action of amphetamine is far more commonly seen in chronic administration than with single doses; while the anorectic effect is a function of acute administration, and commonly diminishes with long-term use. It therefore remains possible that the mechanism of response to *chronic* drug administration could be different in the hyperkinetic. It also remains possible that the response in hyperkinetics and in intelligent normals takes place for different reasons and through different mechanisms.

Comparisons of Hyperactivity and Other Psychiatric Conditions

Wender, Reimherr, and Wood (1981) have argued that the response to more chronic treatment does indeed validate the diagnosis of MBD (attention deficit disorder). They treated adults, all of whom showed antisocial and personality problems, and found that pemoline was helpful only in those whose parents' recollections were of hyperactivity shown during the patients' childhood. These recollections were formalized by completing a Conners Parent Rating Scale retrospectively, but could not be validated against anything other than treatment response. Superficially, this seems to contradict Rapoport *et al.*'s findings, and there could be many reasons for this: the grounds for diagnosis were quite different; adults may be different from children in their responses; pemoline may differ from dextroamphetamine; persisting treatment is quite different from single doses; and normal, intelligent controls are very different from Wender *et al.*'s normoactive psychiatric controls. Even if any or all of these reasons explained the discrepancy, some biological validation of a syndrome akin to hyperactivity would still have been achieved if the study were replicated. However, the results are not in direct contradiction to Rapoport *et al.*'s work. The *mechanism* of action could have been the same in Wender *et al.*'s previously hyperactive and previously normoactive groups, even though the action was *therapeutic* only in those previously hyperactive.

Another challenge to the view that drugs act identically in hyperactives and others comes from the work of Swanson and Kinsbourne (1976). It has been noted already that the overall similarity of behavioral response might conceal subtle but profound differences of action. Swanson and Kinsbourne's work suggests that hyperactive and nonhyperactive children differ in that only the hyperactives show the pattern of state-dependent learning. That is to say, the hyperactive children learned a set of associations more readily when on methylphenidate than on placebo, but could recall them better only if they were *still* taking methylphenidate. If the testing of recall was done under placebo, then it was actually a disadvantage for the initial learning to have taken place under methylphenidate. No such effect was found in the nonhyperactive. Now there may be uncertainty about the interpretation of this finding,[1] but if it were to be replicated, then it would seem to argue for a difference in *mechanism* between the diagnostic groups. It is therefore important to note that their definition of hyperactivity includes the requirement of a favorable response to methylphenidate. Accordingly, if they have demonstrated state-dependent learning, they have established it as a feature of methylphenidate action, not as a phenomenon that distinguishes different clinical patterns of presentation.

The uncertainties in the literature on the nature of drug response make it desirable to compare drug effects on hyperactive children with those on children who have other psychiatric diagnoses. Some preliminary data on this is available from a trial in progress at the University of London Institute of Psychiatry,[2] which is briefly described below. The English diagnostic and clinical practice in which hyperkinesis is a rare diagnosis constitutes the background to this trial. It is likely that there is some overlap between the *Diagnostic and Statistical Manual of Mental Disorders*, third edition (DSM-III) concept of "attention deficit disorder with hyperactivity" and the *International Classification of Diseases*, ninth edition (ICD-9) concept of "conduct disorder" (Taylor & Sandberg, 1982); and the indications for drugs are therefore uncertain. The main purpose of the trial was the examination of the clinical prediction of response to methylphenidate; the double-blind, crossover design followed from this. Methylphenidate was given in a flexible dosage scheme to find the optimal dose within the range of 5 mg to 30 mg a day. Each child received a 3-week trial of methylphenidate and a 3-week trial of placebo; the order was varied and not known to children, families, teachers, therapists, or assessors; a 1-week washout period was interposed between treatments. A full assessment was carried out before starting treatment and after each treatment period. The battery of measures included the Conners Parent and Teacher Rating Scales; ratings of target symptoms; a detailed and structured interview with parents to obtain

1. For instance, the number of initial learning trials was presumably not kept constant, and a facilitating effect of drug on initial performance might impair later performance by reducing the number of times the stimuli were presented in the initial learning sessions.

2. This was carried out by Taylor, Schachar, Wieselberg, and Thorley, and was partially supported by a grant from CIBA.

accounts of the children's behavior; direct observational measures of the children's activity and attention in structured situations; interview measures of family relationships and parental coping skills (Rutter & Brown, 1966); psychiatrists' interviews with the children (Rutter & Graham, 1968); a continuous-performance test of sustained attention and resistance to distraction; a test of memory for digits with competing input, as an index of selective attention; a paired-associates learning test (Swanson & Kinsbourne, 1976); and the Porteus Maze test (Porteus, 1967). In addition to these assessment measures, baseline information was obtained on possible biological and psychosocial adversity and on general cognitive abilities.

Some of these measures have needed to be developed for the purpose of the trial, and are to be reported in detail elsewhere. Six main scales are used for the results mentioned here. The first is a composite scale of attention, derived by summing the scaled scores on the tests of the psychometric battery. The second is a scale of hyperactive behavior at home, based upon items from the parental interview that load significantly upon a factor (the first to emerge in the factor analysis, accounting for nearly one-third of the total variance) of "restless, fidgety, inattentive behavior." The third is a scale of "antisocial, defiant conduct at home," also based upon a factor extracted from the results of the parental interview. The fourth and fifth measures are the "hyperactivity" and "defiance" factors of the Conners teacher questionnaire, calculated according to norms for the local population described by Taylor and Sandberg (1982). The sixth scale is the sum of items from the psychiatric interview relating to disinhibition, overactivity, and inattention, and of scores from direct observation of task-irrelevant behaviors during psychometric testing.

For some purposes, it may be misleading if only the drug actions are considered on scales such as these, which are intended to measure different aspects of behavior problems. It is possible for a drug to exert a definite action that nevertheless is not therapeutic in that it does not contribute to overall adjustment. Accordingly, target symptom ratings and overall judgments of severity of problems by parents and clinicians are included in the study as separate outcome measures.

The subjects were 32 boys aged 6 to 10 years, attending primary schools, who were referred to any of three different child psychiatry or child guidance units in South London because of antisocial, disruptive, or overactive behavior. They also met the conditions of living in family homes and not in institutions, of having measured IQs greater than 50, of not showing autistic features, of having problems of sufficient severity to warrant psychiatric treatment, of being free of contraindications to stimulant medication (such as tics or cardiovascular disease), and of having parents willing for such treatment to be tried. This last condition in practice excluded nearly three-quarters of otherwise suitable cases, and it is therefore important to note that the children treated were similar (in social class, IQ, and teacher and parent questionnaire ratings of severity of symptoms) to a consecutive series of boys seen at one of the three clinics before this study started (and reported by Sandberg, Rutter, & Taylor, 1978).

This is not the complete series to be treated in this study; the results to be described are a preliminary and interim account of work in progress and need to be read with corresponding caution. Some findings, however, are already clear.

Table 16-1. Percentages of children in different overall clinical response categories

CATEGORY	WORSE	NO CHANGE	SOMEWHAT IMPROVED	MUCH IMPROVED
Methylphenidate ($n = 32$)	12.5%	15.6%	34.4%	37.5%
Placebo ($n = 32$)	15.6%	56.2%	21.9%	6.3%

Note. χ^2 for repeated measures (McNemar, 1955) with Yates's correction = 8.45; $p < .01$.

The distribution of diagnoses in this series is very different from that of the many American trials of amphetamines and other stimulants. Of the 32 boys, 22 were given the ICD-9 (Axis I) diagnosis of "conduct disorder," 6 of "hyperkinetic syndrome," and 4 of "adjustment reaction" or "emotional disorder." (By contrast, our attempt to apply DSM-III criteria of diagnosis yielded 22 cases of hyperactivity.) The distribution of responses to drug and to placebo, by contrast, is rather similar to those of American studies: Table 16-1 shows the significantly larger percentage of positive responses in the "methylphenidate" category. The measure of change here is the overall clinical rating made by the study assessors, synthesizing information from home, school, and clinic, while still blind to the drug condition.

Measures not dependent upon the exercise of global clinical judgment are reported in Table 16-2. It can be seen that active drug treatment (by comparison with placebo) produced a marked fall in levels of hyperactive behavior at home, at school, and at the clinic, and a consistent fall in the errors made on tests of attention. Its effect on defiant, unruly behavior at home was less marked, and fell short of statistical significance. These effects are, of course, in line with those reported in trials on hyperactive subjects. A very similar pattern can be seen in Table 16-3, which includes only those children given a diagnosis of conduct disorder. Again, the major effects were on restlessness, impulsiveness, and inattention.

Table 16-2. Responses on different measures of whole group

MEASURE	MEAN (*SD*) BASELINE (B) ($n = 32$)	PLACEBO (P) ($n = 32$)	METHYLPHENIDATE (M) ($n = 32$)	*F* TEST	*t* TESTS*
Parent hyperactivity rating	1.00 (.73)	.83 (.73)	.39 (.48)	*	M < B, M < P
Parent defiance rating	1.04 (.58)	1.01 (.67)	.79 (.51)	ns	M < B
Teacher hyperactivity rating	7.77 (3.87)	6.32 (4.59)	2.96 (4.11)	*	M < B, M < P, P < B
Teacher defiance rating	10.32 (9.80)	9.75 (11.18)	4.47 (8.81)	*	M < B, M < P
Attention test scale	173 (60)	178 (74)	152 (70)	*	M < B, M < P
Psychiatric interview scale	6.98 (5.87)	8.21 (6.04)	4.62 (5.58)	*	M < B, M < P

*$p < .05$.

On the face of it, this is evidence against a drug response that is specific to hyperkinetic subjects. However, it could be that differences in diagnostic practice have simply resulted in a sample of hyperactive subjects' being given a different name. It is difficult to compare results across different cultures, but Table 16-4 shows the results for those children diagnosed as having a conduct disorder who did *not* show hyperactivity in that they scored less than the cutoff point of 18 out of 30 on the Hyperkinesis Index, which is derived from 10 items of the Conners scale. (It is reasonable to use this in view of the similarity of the scores of English and American children on those items; see Taylor & Sandberg, 1982.)

Numbers are small after this progressive whittling down, and accordingly fewer comparisons reach statistical significance; but the trend remains that the hyperactive behaviors are predominantly affected even in this nonhyperactive group. To put it another way, a fall in the parental hyperactivity rating between baseline and drug periods of 30% or more was shown by 56.3% of the total group and 44.4% of the nonhyperactive conduct-disordered group; for the teacher rating, the comparable figures are 65.6% and 66.7%; for the attention test scale, a fall of 15% or more was shown by 53.1% of the total group and 55.5% of the nonhyperactive conduct-disordered group. The trend of this study is therefore to emphasize the *similarity* of hyperactive patients and psychiatric controls in their response to drugs in behavior and performance.

Comparisons Using Physiological Measures

The physiological level of analysis does not add much weight to the notion that the mode of action of drugs is different in the hyperkinetic. Physiological studies are somewhat conflicting, but on the whole they argue that stimulant drugs do indeed stimulate (Hastings & Barkley, 1978), even in the overactive.

Paradoxical sedation, then, is an idea that has to be abandoned. It remains quite plausible that drugs should have differential effects depending upon the initial state of the organism. There is, for instance, evidence in the literature both that oversmall averaged evoked responses are increased by stimulants

Table 16-3. Responses on different measures of those diagnosed as having conduct disorders

MEASURE	MEAN (*SD*) BASELINE (B) ($n = 22$)	MEAN (*SD*) PLACEBO (P) ($n = 22$)	MEAN (*SD*) METHYLPHENIDATE (M) ($n = 22$)	*F* TEST	*t* TESTS*
Parent hyperactivity rating	.88 (.75)	.63 (.63)	.31 (.42)	*	M < B, M < P, P < B
Parent defiance rating	1.11 (.62)	.96 (.72)	.79 (.57)	ns	M < B
Teacher hyperactivity rating	7.21 (3.96)	6.11 (4.40)	3.86 (4.01)	*	M < B, M < P
Teacher defiance rating	12.60 (10.39)	10.75 (10.48)	8.02 (9.31)	ns	M < B
Attention test scale	161 (46)	170 (67)	148 (63)	*	M < B, M < P
Psychiatric interview scale	5.29 (3.24)	6.62 (4.84)	4.44 (6.27)	*	M < B, M < P

*$p < .05$.

(Prichep, Sutton, & Hakerem, 1976) and that overlarge evoked responses are decreased by some stimulants (Buchsbaum & Wender, 1973). Although investigators disagree about the central neurophysiological changes to be found in the overactive (Taylor, 1980c)—and, given the unsatisfactory nature of the clinical diagnosis, this is not surprising—there is some agreement on the normalizing effect of drugs by comparison with placebo. (Even here there is dispute; Zahn, Abate, Little, & Wender, 1975, for instance, found diminished electrodermal responses to be further diminished by stimulants; but this result could be accounted for by a change in the baseline skin resistance, potentially attributable to a peripheral action of the drug.) Robbins and Sahakian (1979) have argued that the effect of amphetamine on behavior is determined by the baseline frequency of that behavior; high-rate activities are diminished, and low-rate activities are increased. A drug effect on the central nervous system may be translated into behavior in a way that is determined by the animal's initial state. It is, however, a far cry from this proposition to the position that one pathological condition is characterized by a qualitatively different response. Rapoport's evidence (Rapoport *et al.*, 1978) seems to argue that global overactivity—at least as measured in her group's study—is not an important feature of the initial state. Individual behaviors still might be.

Comparisons Using Measures of Emotional Changes

Another suggestion that drugs may act differently in hyperkinetic children derives from clinical observations on their emotional responses. Misery and agitation are common results of giving stimulant drugs, mentioned in all clinical accounts. On the face of it, this is a rather startling contrast with the euphoria expected by adult users and abusers of the amphetamines. Rapoport (see Chapter 18 of this volume) has described a considerable distinction between children and adults given single doses of the drug. For the most part, the adults reported that they felt elated or cheered. The self-descriptions by the hyperkinetic children were much less clear, and typically referred to feeling "strange." This may be a difference between adults and children, rather than between diagnostic groups. Even so, it raises the interesting possibility of fundamental differences in drug action, depending upon the developmental level of the brain on which the drug acts.

Table 16-4. Responses on different measures of those having conduct disorder without hyperactivity

	MEAN (*SD*)				
MEASURE	BASELINE (B) ($n = 9$)	PLACEBO (P) ($n = 9$)	METHYLPHENIDATE (M) ($n = 9$)	*F* TEST	*t* TESTS*
Parent hyperactivity rating	.99 (.69)	.72 (.55)	.55 (.62)	*	M < B
Parent defiance rating	1.10 (.60)	.84 (.79)	.79 (.55)	ns	—
Teacher hyperactivity rating	4.45 (4.62)	4.12 (4.03)	2.04 (3.86)	*	M < B
Teacher defiance rating	10.45 (3.98)	9.98 (8.99)	9.76 (9.01)	ns	—
Attention test scale	172 (57)	185 (56)	161 (75)	ns	—
Psychiatric interview scale	5.88 (5.15)	5.30 (4.44)	2.80 (3.38)	*	M < B

*$p < .05$.

When one considers the general topic of how amphetamines affect mood, one has to recognize that the complexity of their action is much underrated by the view that they produce euphoria in adults and dysphoria in hyperkinetic children. They do not always produce euphoria in adults, but misery and tension are recognized complications of their use. The results depend in part upon the way in which they are taken. Schachter and Singer's (1962) well-known experiment is relevant here: An amphetamine dose in naive student subjects produced emotional effects that were determined by the social setting which the subjects entered, and by their knowledge of what they had been given. The intensity of the emotion was affected by the drug, but its form was determined by the individual's understanding. It is very likely that the understanding of the situation is very different for a disturbed child given a drug as treatment and a normal person volunteering for a laboratory experiment.

Just as adults' mood is sometimes worsened by stimulants, children's mood is sometimes lifted. A single case report (Goyer, Davis, & Rapoport, 1979) described a child who abused prescribed medication for pleasure. More to the purpose, it is clear from early descriptions of amphetamine treatment that it sometimes served to cheer up miserable and neurotic children. Bradley (1937) and Bender and Cottington (1942) did not confine treatment to the hyperactive, but administered it with considerable success to a large range of children with different problems. The four children in Bender and Cottington's series who had been diagnosed as having an emotional disorder all improved.

Table 16-5 shows comparisons of baseline, drug, and placebo scores on the scale of emotional disorder that is extracted from the parental accounts of their children's symptoms; no drug effect is seen. It seems likely that the affective response to a drug is determined by the initial state of the individual receiving it, and by his or her comprehension of what it is and why it is given. Much remains to be learned about this aspect of psychopharmacology, and it does not yet either confirm or disconfirm the hypothesis that hyperactive children react differently to drugs.

Differential Drug Effects as a Guide to Mode of Action

Evidence so far has been taken wholly from the studies of stimulant drugs. These are not, however, the only drugs that can ameliorate hyperactive behaviors. Imipramine, chlorpromazine, and haloperidol have all been shown superior to placebo in short-term trials. Such a finding would not be in keeping with an extreme view that hyperkinesis is validated by the uniqueness and specificity of the stimulant drug action. However, it does not bear with any strength on the question at issue of the mechanism of drug action. It is likely

Table 16-5. Effects of methylphenidate and placebo on children's symptoms of emotional disorder in Institute of Psychiatry trial

	EMOTIONAL DISORDER SCALE	
TEST PERIOD	MEAN	*SD*
Baseline	.65	.56
Placebo	.51	.59
Methylphenidate	.55	.48

Note. One-way analysis of variance shows no significant difference between test periods at .05 level.

that chlorpromazine and haloperidol act in different ways from stimulants. Imipramine has been shown to have an effect on cognition comparable to amphetamine (Werry, Aman, & Diamond, 1980), and that may reflect a similarity of biochemical action. While it cannot be concluded that dissimilar biochemical actions have similar antihyperactivity results (which would argue against any specificity of response), the variety of different ways through which hyperactivity can be reduced can legitimately be emphasized.

Summary

The hypothesis that drugs have a different action in hyperkinetics to others has not been sustained. Rather, drugs have a somewhat nonspecific action on a range of symptoms related to hyperkinesis—an action that is similar in normally active normal controls and in normally active children with conduct disorder. Their practical value in conduct disorder remains to be assessed.

ARE ONLY CHILDREN WITH THE SYNDROME BENEFITED?

A further hypothesis states that only children with one particular syndrome (variously termed "hyperkinetic syndrome," "MBD," or "attention deficit disorder") are benefited by stimulant medication. This hypothesis would be compatible with the evidence cited so far. If it survived experimental challenge, it would go far toward validating the syndrome. It is, of course, to be tested in the arena of studies that examine the factors predicting responsiveness to drugs.

Prediction by Overactivity

The conventional wisdom in this area is probably best expressed in the view that hyperactivity is the major clinical indication for prescribing stimulant drugs (O'Malley & Eisenberg, 1973; Safer & Allen, 1976) and that "attention deficit disorder with hyperactivity" is the DSM-III diagnosis giving "the best example of a specific indication in pediatric psychopharmacology" (Cantwell & Carlson, 1978). Certainly the vast majority of clinical trials have been carried out on children falling within the general description of inattentive overactivity. But one must not suppose, because the effect has been sought chiefly in one diagnostic group, that it will not be found in others. Indeed, what evidence there is suggests that a beneficial response to drugs is obtained in a wide range of behavior disorders (Bradley, 1937) as well as in delinquent youths (Eisenberg, Lachman, Molling, Lockner, Mizelle, & Conners, 1963) and possibly some psychopathic young adults (Hill, 1947).

If a good response were largely confined to overactive children, then one would expect that even within a group of children diagnosed as overactive, their degree of overactivity would predict the extent of their response. This is all the more to be expected, since hyperactivity is a frequent diagnosis in the United States and Australia, where most of the drug trials have been undertaken (Safer & Allen, 1976); is probably diagnosed in different ways in different places (Taylor, 1980a); and is generally agreed to be a heterogeneous collection of different kinds of problems (Cantwell, 1977a). If the group is large and heterogeneous, then one might indeed expect to find within it a subgroup of the most overactive whose drug response is greatest. Yet this is not the finding. Parental ratings of overactivity do not, on the whole, predict drug responsiveness (Rapoport, Abramson, Alexander, & Lott, 1971; Rapoport, Quinn, Bradbard, Riddle, & Brooks, 1974; Rie, Rie, Stewart, & Ambuel, 1976; Werry & Sprague, 1974; Zahn *et al.*, 1975), and neither do teacher ratings (Hoffman, Engelhardt, Margolis, Polizos, Waizer, & Rosenfeld, 1974; Rapoport *et al.*, 1971, 1974; Rie *et al.*, 1976; Satterfield, 1975; Werry & Sprague, 1974).

Occasional studies have argued that the most hyperkinetic as rated by their teachers have the best outcome (Denhoff, Davids, & Hawkins, 1971; Steinberg, Troshinsky, & Steinberg, 1971). In these studies, however, the teacher rating was also the measure of outcome. Great methodological difficulties exist when a variable is used to predict change in itself. One may, for example, expect that a more deviant score will show more change than a less defiant one will, simply because there is, so to speak, more room for improvement. The difficulties are sufficient to invalidate the method. Nevertheless, Schleifer, Weiss, Cohen, Elman, Cvejic, and Kruger (1975) showed differences between "extreme" hyperactives and "moderate" or "low" hyperactives; the extreme group showed greater improvement with drugs in an observational measure of the frequency with which they left their chairs. The correlation of this measure with the teacher rating exposes it to the criticism made above. Furthermore, a problem arises in the use of multiple measures of outcome, and of initial baseline, since chance alone will produce a few statistically significant correlations. Replicability must be the guiding principle in interpretation, and it has so far been lacking. Indeed, some workers (Hoffman *et al.*, 1974) seem to show a worse response to treatment among the children rated most hyperkinetic.

Prediction by Attentiveness

Overactivity, then, is not necessarily predictive of treatment response. However, it is only one part of the concept of hyperactivity in both the ICD-9 and the DSM-III classifications; and indeed motor overactivity is only one part of the descriptions of behaviors that make up the "hyperactivity" factor on rating scales. Inattention may be just as central to the concept. An influential review by Barkley (1976) concluded that measures of attention are the most useful predictors of the response to stimulants, and that the major effect of such drugs is on attention span. This conclusion is of course confined to children diagnosed as hyperkinetic, albeit in a variety of different ways. Can this conclusion be accepted? Not securely. To appreciate the uncertainties that exist, it is necessary to consider something of the range of measures that are subsumed into the very broad concept of "attention" (Taylor, 1980b).

First of all come the ratings of behavior related to concentration—for instance, the degree to which a child persists in a limited number of activities. This source of evidence gives a clear answer: Ratings of inattention do not predict drug response (Hoffman *et al.*, 1974; Rapoport *et al.*, 1971, 1974; Rie *et al.*, 1976; Satterfield, 1975; Werry & Sprague, 1974), and neither do observational measures of activity (Rapoport *et al.*, 1971, 1974; Schleifer *et al.*, 1975). Perhaps one should follow up the suggestion (Rapoport *et al.*, 1971) that the number of changes in toy play is predictive; but this kind of test does not imply cognitive impairment.

Next come psychometric studies, in which performance on a particular psychological test is taken to reflect the power to concentrate. Perhaps the most sensitive of such tests to drug treatment is the continuous-performance test, in which there is the requirement of an accurate response to a small fraction of a large number of stimuli successively presented. There is no evidence that it predicts treatment response. Nor is there any evidence that tests of selective attention are related to drug responsiveness (Buchsbaum & Wender, 1973; Satterfield, Cantwell, Lesser, & Podosin, 1972; Zahn *et al.*, 1975). What is one left with? Only with weak associations between longer reaction times and better drug responses (Porges, Walter, Korb, & Sprague, 1975; Zahn *et al.*, 1975), and between the latter and poor performance on the Porteus Mazes (Epstein, Lasagna, Conners, & Rodriguez, 1968) and Matching Familiar Figures Test (Rapoport *et al.*, 1974). If much weight is to be attached to these, weight should also be attached to the absence of relationships with other, better-established measures of attention used by the same investigators. One should also emphasize the lack of predictive power of a battery of tests supposedly related to attention (Barkley & Cunningham, 1979).

It therefore appears that the ability of such studies to validate attention deficit as a specific problem comes almost entirely from psychophysiological measures of bodily events believed to be associated with information processing, but certainly reflecting many other influences as well. Yet even here, results are contradictory. Visual and auditory average evoked responses have been reported as greater in responders than in nonresponders (Buchsbaum & Wender, 1973; Satterfield *et al.*, 1972), but also as smaller (Prichep *et al.*, 1976). The skin conductance response to stimuli in responders can be interpreted as showing underarousal (Satterfield *et al.*, 1972) or overarousal (Zahn *et al.*, 1975); however, a smaller response to a signal stimulus was a common feature. Good responders have showed slower heart rates (Porges *et al.*, 1975) and faster heart rates (Barkley & Jackson, 1978), and heart rate deceleration as an index of responsiveness to a stimulus is not a useful predictor (Porges *et al.*, 1975; Zahn *et al.*, 1975). Electronic pupillography suggests that both the underaroused and the overaroused respond significantly to drug treatment (Knopp, Arnold, Andras, & Smeltzer, 1973).

Methodological Problems in Prediction

I do not intend to be nihilistic about attempts to predict drug response. Diminished physiological responsiveness to simple stimuli has been repeatedly described by Satterfield's group (Satterfield, 1975), and may prove a useful predictor. One possible reason would be that anxious children tend to do badly. My point is simply that the weak and contradictory evidence at present linking attentional measures with the response to drugs is in no way sufficient to support the view that overactivity and inattention are of key importance in determining what happens in treatment. Indeed, there are many methodological difficulties in the way of demonstrating or disproving this. It may be convenient briefly to summarize some of these:

1. The available measures of overactive and inattentive behaviors, and of attention deficit, leave a good deal to be desired. While they are capable of showing differences between drug and placebo, it is possible that they are too unreliable to be sensitive to genuine differences between individuals.

2. Choosing as "responders" all the children who do well with an active drug is not a good strategy. It causes a confounding of the pharmacological response with the placebo response, since some children responding to drug

would also have improved with placebo. The effect is to obscure predictors, since different factors are probably involved in the two kinds of response. Examination of this issue will require that each child be assigned to periods of both drug and placebo treatment, and that "responders" to a drug must also be nonresponders to placebo.

3. The measurement of drug response is very variable between different investigations, and often is subjective in quality. I have discussed the problems associated with using the same variable both as predictor and outcome measure, as well as the problems with using large numbers of measures from which a few correlations are extracted and interpreted (but not replicated). The grounds for judging the degree of response should be detailed.

4. Compliance in the taking of medication is a notorious hazard for drug trials, not least in this area. The prediction of pharmacological effect can be confounded with the prediction of who will take medication. The efforts made to secure compliance, and the degree to which these efforts were effective, should therefore be described.

5. Different drug doses may have differential effects on psychological processes (Werry & Sprague, 1974). It is therefore a problem if different doses are used for different children, since initial state may be confounded with drug dose. On the other hand, it is also a problem if the same dose is used for all children, since effectiveness may then be largely determined by absorption from the gut and differences in metabolism. Individual differences in dose requirements certainly exist, both in humans and animals. The development of reliable methods of assay for levels of drugs in body fluids would be a real methodological advance in examining predictors of effect.

6. The common design of testing drug responders during a brief holiday from medication is to be deprecated. Measures at such a time may be very different from baseline measures (due to rebound effects, changes induced by drug that are not immediately reversible, and the passage of time); they should not be used as predictors.

Even bearing these issues in mind, one must conclude that research so far has failed to find a core syndrome of hyperactivity that is uniquely responsive to drugs. It could be argued that this is not a matter of too much moment, because all the children studied were hyperactive and a very high proportion of them were drug-responsive. In fact the subjects were distinctly heterogeneous, and the absence of factors of high predictive power does speak against the ability of drug studies to define a condition. Nevertheless, it is clear that the issue of whether the hyperkinetic syndrome is validated by treatment results must be addressed by including children to whom that diagnosis is not applicable.

Diagnostic Prediction in Institute of Psychiatry's Current Trial

I have already indicated that the antihyperactivity action of stimulants is better described as a nonspecific effect on a range of processes than as a unique action on a specific biochemical defect. It follows that potentially there is a very large variety of outcome measures which can be used to examine diagnostic distinctions. Table 16-6 shows the proportions of children who responded more beneficially to a drug than to placebo in the different diagnostic categories

Table 16-6. Percentages of children responding in each diagnostic category

DIAGNOSIS	CLINICAL RATING OF IMPROVEMENT[a] I	II	III
Conduct disorder ($n = 22$)	36.4%	36.4%	27.2%
Hyperkinetic syndrome ($n = 6$)	16.7%	0%	83.3%
Other ($n = 4$)	75%	25%	0%

[a]I, no superiority of drug over placebo; II, "somewhat improved" with drug, less with placebo; III, "much improved" with drug, less with placebo.

used. The outcome measure is the overall clinical judgment of change. When "Clinical Rating of Improvement" categories I and II are combined in order to focus on "much improvement," there is a significant difference in outcome between the group diagnosed with hyperkinetic syndrome and the group diagnosed with conduct disorder (Fisher's exact test, $p = .02$). This suggests that the narrower diagnosis of the hyperkinetic syndrome has some utility, since it has the effect of predicting the important result of a marked clinical improvement that is not achieved by a mere placebo. The ICD-9 diagnosis of "hyperkinetic syndrome" receives some support from this, but it is clear that many of the children who showed so marked a response did not have this diagnosis.

It is also clear that a broader diagnostic definition of "hyperactivity" is not helpful in prediction. Table 16-7 shows that the ratings of the presence or absence of the behaviors of hyperactivity (regardless of ICD-9 diagnosis) is not useful. Neither is the DSM-III diagnosis of "hyperactivity." While that diagnosis was made much more frequently than the ICD-9 diagnosis was, it fails to associate significantly with this global outcome measure.

Table 16-7. Outcome categories[a] in drug study, based upon global clinical rating

INITIAL MEASURES	I ($n = 12$)	II ($n = 9$)	III ($n = 11$)
Percentage of children with DSM-III diagnosis of "hyperactivity"	58.3%	66.7%	81.8%[d]
Percentage of children with hyperactive behavior judged present	75%	66.7%	90.9%[d]
Percentage of children with antisocial behavior judged present	75%	88.9%	63.6%[d]
Percentage of children with emotional disorder judged present	91.7%	44.4%	45.5%[b]
Mean psychiatric interview score on hyperactivity scale (*SD*)	4.7 (4.0)	5.8 (3.5)	10.8 (7.2)[c]
Mean score on attention test scale (*SD*)	147 (55)	157 (41)	246 (40)[c]
Mean score on parental hyperactivity ratings (*SD*)	.73 (.67)	1.28 (1.01)	1.29 (.76)[d]
Mean score on teacher hyperactivity ratings (*SD*)	6.77 (4.51)	7.66 (2.38)	9.25 (3.96)[d]

[a]I, no superiority of drug over placebo; II, "somewhat improved" with drug, less with placebo; III, "much improved" with drug, less with placebo.

[b]Significant differences between groups ($p < .05$) by χ^2 test.

[c]Significant differences between groups ($p < .05$) by one-way analysis of variance.

[d]No significant difference found between groups.

Tables 16-8 and 16-9 use outcome measures based respectively upon parent and teacher hyperactivity ratings. Each index the extent to which methylphenidate was superior to placebo for each child (i.e., the placebo score minus the methylphenidate score). While there are trends favoring the ICD-9 diagnosis of "hyperkinetic syndrome," the figures do not reach significance; the broader definitions of "hyperactivity" are even less helpful. It is interesting that the presence of symptoms of emotional disorder predicted the *failure* of treatment, even within this group of children with predominantly hyperactive and antisocial problems.

This is not to say that prediction is impossible. There are, in fact, a number of measures taken at baseline that seem to associate well with treatment outcome. The strongest are the psychometric scale of attention tests and the psychiatric assessment of hyperactivity-related behavior in the clinic. These are to be fully reported elsewhere. The conclusions to be drawn from these preliminary attempts at diagnostic prediction are that a narrow (ICD-9) definition is to some extent supported; that a wide American-type (DSM-III) definition is not; and that markedly beneficial treatment outcomes are by no means restricted to the hyperkinetic—however they are defined.

Prediction by Neurological Status

If it is agreed that a restricted concept of "hyperkinetic syndrome" is a useful means of description, and that it predicts at least some kinds of drug response, then it might be argued that it is therefore a physical condition. Obviously this would not be a sound argument. The problem need not be organically based merely because an organic treatment is successful—not, at any rate, in any useful sense of the word "organic" that will exclude some kinds of psychological problems as "not organic." One would, however, be on firmer ground in using

Table 16-8. Outcome categories[a] in drug study, based upon parental hyperactivity ratings

INITIAL MEASURE	I ($n = 11$)	II ($n = 14$)	III ($n = 7$)
Percentage of children with ICD-9 "hyperkinesis"	9.1%	14.3%	42.9%[d]
Percentage of children with DSM-III "hyperactivity"	54.5%	78.6%	71.4%[d]
Percentage of children with hyperactive behavior judged present	63.6%	78.6%	100%[d]
Percentage of children with antisocial behavior judged present	72.7%	78.6%	57.1%[d]
Percentage of children with emotional disorder judged present	90.9%	50%	42.9%[b]
Mean psychiatric interview score on hyperactivity scale (*SD*)	5.4 (4.0)	5.5 (3.7)	13.3 (7.3)[c]
Mean score on attention test scale (*SD*)	154 (56)	166 (57)	218 (59)[c]
Mean score on parental hyperactivity ratings (*SD*)	.50 (.53)	1.12 (.72)	1.94 (.66)[c]
Mean score on teacher hyperactivity ratings (*SD*)	7.14 (4.71)	7.31 (3.51)	9.90 (2.01)[d]

[a]I, drug ratings equal to or worse than placebo; II, drug ratings better than placebo by up to 30% of total scale; III, drug ratings better than placebo by more than 30% of total scale.

[b]Significant differences between groups ($p < .05$) by χ^2 test.

[c]Significant differences between groups ($p < .05$) by one-way analysis of variance.

[d]No significant difference found between groups.

Table 16-9. Outcome categories[a] in drug study, based upon teacher hyperkinesis index

INITIAL MEASURE	I ($n = 11$)	II ($n = 14$)	III ($n = 7$)
Percentage of children with ICD-9 "hyperkinesis"	0%	21.4%	42.9%[d]
Percentage of children with DSM-III "hyperactivity"	45.5%	78.6%	71.4%[d]
Percentage of children with hyperactive behavior judged present	72.7%	85.7%	71.4%[d]
Percentage of children with antisocial behavior judged present	63.6%	78.6%	71.4%[d]
Percentage of children with emotional disorder judged present	90.9%	57.1%	28.6%[b]
Mean psychiatric interview score on hyperactivity scale (*SD*)	5.3 (3.7)	7.0 (5.1)	10.5 (8.2)[d]
Mean score on attention test scale (*SD*)	145 (36)	182 (70)	207 (63)[d]
Mean score on parental hyperactivity ratings (*SD*)	.65 (.65)	1.36 (.76)	1.20 (.99)[c]
Mean score on teacher hyperactivity ratings (*SD*)	5.73 (4.66)	8.50 (3.15)	9.95 (1.26)[c]

[a]I, drug ratings equal to or worse than placebo; II, drug ratings better than placebo by up to 30% of total scale; III, drug ratings better than placebo by more than 30% of total scale.

[b]Significant differences between groups ($p < .05$) by χ^2 test.

[c]Significant differences between groups ($p < .05$) by one-way analysis of variance.

[d]No significant difference found between groups.

drug response as a pointer to a physical cause if it could be shown that only those with signs of neurological dysfunction are responsive to stimulant drugs.

The evidence on this is seriously limited by the infirmity of the measures of brain function that are now available (see Chapter 12 of this volume). The strength of neurological predictors of response has several times been reviewed (e.g., by Barkley, 1976, and Cantwell, 1977b). I do not quarrel with the conclusion that the results are conflicting; they are likely to remain so until more reliable measures can be used. When the measure is the clinically judged electroencephalogram (EEG), the bulk of studies find no predictive power (Knights & Hinton, 1969; Lytton & Knobel, 1958; Rapoport *et al.*, 1974; Weiss, Werry, Minde, Douglas, & Sykes, 1968). The measures taken from the EEG by those who find that it predicts success (e.g., Satterfield, Cantwell, Saul, Lesser, & Podosin, 1973) seem to be rather similar to those of other investigators who find that it predicts failure of treatment (e.g., Burks, 1964).

Minor degrees of neurological incoordination have been found by some to predict a successful outcome of treatment (Satterfield *et al.*, 1973; Steinberg *et al.*, 1971); others have found no association between "soft signs" and responsiveness (Rapoport *et al.*, 1974; Weiss *et al.*, 1968). It is hard to find any methodological reason for this difference, unless it be that the studies finding positive prediction both used a rather conservative measure of outcome; the one required a 30% fall in teacher ratings, the other a change in ratings greater than the greatest change produced by placebo in their series. It may well be that genuine predictors are obscured if a generosity of judgment includes all but a small minority as "responders."

Judgments of "organicity" applied to medical and developmental histories have also been pressed into service as predictors of drug effect. Epstein *et al.* (1968) and Conrad and Insel (1967) found them to be successful in this role; Knights and Hinton (1969) did not. One has to note that the lack of consensus among clinicians on the grounds for this kind of diagnosis militates against the likelihood of finding robust associations of any kind. For the present, it cannot be concluded that drug response is a pointer to organicity. Indeed, drug responders seem to comprise a heterogeneous group that should not be elevated to the status of a separate diagnostic category.

Summary

Since drug response is not unitary, single predictors will have limited power. Present evidence gives some support to a narrow diagnostic concept of "hyperkinesis" and to the construct of attention; like other evidence, it fails to delineate anything specific about milder degrees of overactive behavior.

DO STIMULANTS BENEFIT ONLY OVERACTIVITY AND INATTENTION?

Nevertheless, a weak form of validation might remain. Even if no categorical *syndrome* is validated by treatment response, it could be that certain *dimensions* of behavior are uniquely affected. The third form of the hypothesis, therefore, is that *the beneficial actions of stimulants are on overactivity and attention deficit only*. The point need not be labored, since abundant evidence indicates that this is not so. Defiant or antisocial behavior, as described by questionnaires, is affected as well as overactivity. Questionnaire measures, however, may confound these behaviors.

Observational studies, though generally less sensitive to drug effects, show a reduction in disruptive and disobedient activity, rather than in activity per se (Arnold, Huestis, Smeltzer, Scheib, Wemmer, & Colner, 1976; Gittelman-Klein & Klein, 1976; Rapoport *et al.*, 1974; Schleifer *et al.*, 1975; Sprague, Barnes, & Werry, 1970). It is clear that both disruptive behavior and inattention are ameliorated by drugs, but it is not at all clear that the two processes are affected together. The one may improve without the other (Gittelman-Klein & Klein, 1975), and they may have different dose–response curves (Werry & Sprague, 1974). In the Institute of Psychiatry study to which I have referred, there is preliminary evidence that both sustained attention and rated behavior are improved by methylphenidate. They are, however, affected *independently*, and the association between the two falls short of statistical significance (see Table 16-10).

Table 16-10. Intercorrelations of different responses ($n = 32$)

	ATTENTION TEST SCALE	PSYCHIATRIC INTERVIEW	PARENT HYPERACTIVITY RATING	PARENT DEFIANCE RATING	TEACHER HYPERACTIVITY RATING	TEACHER DEFIANCE RATING
Psychiatric interview	.20	1				
Parent hyperactivity rating	−.03	.39*	1			
Parent defiance rating	−.09	.19	.57*	1		
Teacher hyperactivity rating	−.07	.64*	.34*	.004	1	
Teacher defiance rating	−.17	.36*	.21	−.07	.73*	1

Note. Each response is calculated as (placebo score − methylphenidate score) for each individual.

*$p < .05$; Pearson product–moment correlations.

The general finding is one of several independent actions of stimulant drugs. This is, of course, very much in line with what is known of the pharmacology of amphetamine. It is a workhorse molecule, with many useful actions that have been refined by the drug industry. This multiplicity of effects is one of the key difficulties for predictive studies. An approach to solving the problem is that by Conners (1972), who has used factor analysis and cluster analysis to define subgroups with characteristic profiles of psychological response and of scores on baseline psychometric tests. The profiles obtained were not immediately recognizable to clinicians, and the range of tests used was not wide—most of them being psychometric assessments of abilities related to classroom learning. One subgroup is of particular note, in view of the above finding that impairment of concentration may predict treatment response: A small set of children with predominantly normal scores on performance tests showed little change with medication. However, the logic of the method requires that it be replicated before any judgment can be made about the validity of the subgroups. There are serious practical difficulties in the path of such research, which demands a large series of subjects and sophisticated analytic techniques. Nonetheless, it is disappointing that attempts to confirm or disconfirm this interesting approach have not, apparently, been made in the intervening decade. It may prove to be the case that the major contribution of drug trials to neurological understanding is that they suggest finer classifications, rather than that they reverse a pathology specific to one condition.

CONCLUSIONS

Stimulant drugs have multiple actions, and the problems of hyperkinetic children are also multiple. The evidence does not yet favor any specific effects of drugs on the hyperkinetic syndrome. There is some evidence that the concept of "impairment of attention," when objectively measured or part of the narrow ICD-9 definition of "hyperkinesis," is partly validated by its prediction of drug action. But the complexity of treatment effects, and their value for the understanding of the bases of behavior, are not sufficiently served by the simple view that stimulants treat hyperactivity.

References

Arnold, L. E., Huestis, R., Smeltzer, D., Scheib, J., Wemmer, D., & Colner, G. Levoamphetamine versus dextroamphetamine in minimal brain dysfunction. *Archives of General Psychiatry*, 1976, *33*, 292–301.

Barkley, R. Predicting the response of hyperkinetic children to stimulant drugs: A review. *Journal of Abnormal Child Psychology*, 1976, *4*, 327–348.

Barkley, R. A review of stimulant drug research with hyperactive children. *Journal of Child Psychology and Psychiatry*, 1977, *18*, 137–166.

Barkley, R., & Cunningham, C. E. Stimulant drugs and activity level in hyperactive children. *American Journal of Orthopsychiatry*, 1979, *49*, 491–499.

Barkley, R., & Jackson, T. Hyperkinesis, autonomic nervous system activity and stimulant drug effects. *Journal of Child Psychology and Psychiatry*, 1978, *18*, 347–358.

Bender, L., & Cottington, F. The use of amphetamine sulfate (benzedrine) in child psychiatry. *American Journal of Psychiatry*, 1942, *99*, 116–121.

Bradley, C. The behavior of children receiving benzedrine. *American Journal of Psychiatry*, 1937, *94*, 577–585.

Buchsbaum, M., & Wender, P. Average evoked responses in normal and minimally brain dysfunctioned children treated with amphetamine: A preliminary report. *Archives of General Psychiatry*, 1973, *29*, 764–770.

Burks, H. Effects of amphetamine therapy on hyperkinetic children. *Archives of General Psychiatry*, 1964, *11*, 604–609.

Cantwell, D. Hyperkinetic syndrome. In M. Rutter & L. Hersov (Eds.), *Child psychiatry: Modern approaches.* Oxford: Blackwell Scientific Publications, 1977. (a)

Cantwell, D. Psychopharmacologic treatment of the minimal brain dysfunction syndrome. In J. M. Wiener (Ed.), *Psychopharmacology in childhood and adolescence.* New York: Basic Books, 1977. (b)

Cantwell, D., & Carlson, G. A. Stimulants. In J. S. Werry (Ed.), *Pediatric psychopharmacology: The use of behavior modifying drugs in children.* New York: Brunner/Mazel, 1978.

Conners, C. K. Stimulant drugs and cortical responses in learning and behavior disorders in children. In W. L. Smith (Ed.), *Drugs, development and cerebral function.* Springfield, Ill.: Charles C Thomas, 1972.

Conrad, W., & Insel, J. Anticipating the response to amphetamine therapy in the treatment of hyperkinetic children. *Pediatrics*, 1967, *40*, 96–99.

Denhoff, E., Davids, E., & Hawkins, R. Effects of dextroamphetamine on hyperkinetic children: A controlled double-blind study. *Journal of Learning Disabilities*, 1971, *4*, 491–498.

Eisenberg, L., Lachman, R., Molling, P., Lockner, A., Mizelle, J., & Conners, C. A psychopharmacologic experiment in a training school for delinquent boys. *American Journal of Orthopsychiatry*, 1963, *33*, 431–447.

Epstein, L., Lasagna, L., Conners, C., & Rodriguez, A. Correlation of dextroamphetamine excretion and drug response in hyperkinetic children. *Journal of Nervous and Mental Disease*, 1968, *146*, 136–146.

Eysenck, H. J. *The biological basis of personality.* Springfield, Ill.: Charles C Thomas, 1967.

Gittelman-Klein, R., & Klein, D. Are behavioral and psychometric changes related in methylphenidate-treated, hyperactive children? *International Journal of Mental Health*, 1975, *4*, 182–198.

Gittelman-Klein, R., & Klein, D. Methylphenidate effects in learning disabilities: Psychometric changes. *Archives of General Psychiatry*, 1976, *33*, 655–664.

Goyer, P. F., Davis, G. C., & Rapoport, J. L. Abuse of prescribed stimulant medication by a 13 year old hyperactive boy. *Journal of the American Academy of Child Psychiatry*, 1979, *48*, 170–175.

Grahame-Smith, D. G. Animal hyperactivity syndromes: Do they have any relevance to minimal brain dysfunction? *Advances in Biological Psychiatry*, 1978, *1*, 84–95.

Hastings, J. E., & Barkley, R. A. A review of psychophysiological research with hyperkinetic children. *Journal of Abnormal Child Psychology*, 1978, *6*, 413–447.

Hill, D. Amphetamine in psychopathic states. *British Journal of Addiction*, 1947, *44*, 1–5.

Hoffman, S., Engelhardt, D., Margolis, R., Polizos, P., Waizer, J., & Rosenfeld, R. Response to methylphenidate in low-socioeconomic hyperactive children. *Archives of General Psychiatry*, 1974, *30*, 354–359.

Knights, R., & Hinton, G. The effects of methylphenidate (Ritalin) on the motor skills and behavior of children with learning problems. *Journal of Nervous and Mental Disease*, 1969, *148*, 643–653.

Knopp, W., Arnold, L. E., Andras, R., & Smeltzer, D. Predicting amphetamine response in hyperkinetic children by electronic pupillography. *Pharmakopsychiatrie*, 1973, *6*, 158–166.

Lytton, G., & Knobel, M. Diagnosis and treatment of behavior disorders in children. *Diseases of the Nervous System*, 1958, *20*, 1–7.

McNemar, Q. *Psychological statistics* (2nd ed.). New York: Wiley, 1955.

O'Malley, J., & Eisenberg, L. The hyperkinetic syndrome. *Seminars in Psychiatry*, 1973, *5*, 95–103.

Ounsted, C. The hyperkinetic syndrome in epileptic children. *Lancet*, 1955, *2*, 303–311.

Porges, S., Walter, G., Korb, R., & Sprague, R. The influence of methylphenidate on heart rate and behavioral measures of attention in hyperactive children. *Child Development*, 1975, *46*, 727–733.

Porteus, S. *The Porteus Maze test manual.* London: Harrap, 1967.

Prichep, L., Sutton, S., & Hakerem, G. Evoked potentials in hyperkinetic and normal children under certainty and uncertainty. *Psychophysiology*, 1976, *13*, 419–428.

Rapoport, J., Abramson, A., Alexander, D., & Lott, I. Playroom observations of hyperactive children on medication. *Journal of the American Academy of Child Psychiatry*, 1971, *10*, 524–534.

Rapoport, J., Buchsbaum, M., Weingartner, H., Zahn, T., Ludlow, C., & Mikkelsen, E. Dextroamphetamine: Behavioral and cognitive effects in normal prepubertal boys. *Science*, 1978, *199*, 560–563.

Rapoport, J., Quinn, P. O., Bradbard, G., Riddle, K. D., & Brooks, E. Imipramine and methylphenidate treatments of hyperactive boys. *Archives of General Psychiatry*, 1974, *30*, 789–793.

Rie, H., Rie, E., Stewart, S., & Ambuel, J. Effects of methylphenidate on underachieving children. *Journal of Consulting and Clinical Psychology*, 1976, *44*, 250–260.

Robbins, T. W., & Sahakian, B. J. "Paradoxical" effects of psychomotor stimulant drugs in hyperactive children from the standpoint of behavioural pharmacology. *Neuropharmacology*, 1979, *18*, 931–950.

Rutter, M., & Brown, G. W. The reliability and validity of measures of family life and relationships in families containing a psychiatric patient. *Social Psychiatry*, 1966, *1*, 38–53.

Rutter, M., & Graham, P. The reliability and validity of the psychiatric assessment of the child: I. Interview with the child. *British Journal of Psychiatry*, 1968, *114*, 563–579.

Safer, D., & Allen, R. *Hyperactive children: Diagnosis and management*. Baltimore: University Park Press, 1976.

Sandberg, S. T., Rutter, M., & Taylor, E. Hyperkinetic disorder in psychiatric clinic attenders. *Developmental Medicine and Child Neurology*, 1978, *20*, 279–299.

Sandberg, S., Wieselberg, M., & Shaffer, D. Hyperkinetic and conduct problem children in a primary school population: Some epidemiological considerations. *Journal of Child Psychology and Psychiatry*, 1980, *21*, 293–311.

Satterfield, J. Neurophysiological studies. In D. Cantwell (Ed.), *The hyperactive child: Diagnosis, management, current research*. New York: Spectrum, 1975.

Satterfield, J., Cantwell, D., Lesser, L., & Podosin, R. Physiological studies of the hyperkinetic child: I. *American Journal of Psychiatry*, 1972, *128*, 1418–1424.

Satterfield, J., Cantwell, D., Saul, R., Lesser, L., & Podosin, R. Response to stimulant drug treatment in hyperactive children: Prediction from EEG and neurological findings. *Journal of Autism and Childhood Schizophrenia*, 1973, *3*, 36–48.

Schachar, R., Rutter, M., & Smith, A. The characteristics of situationally and pervasively hyperactive children: Implications for syndrome definition. *Journal of Child Psychology and Psychiatry*, 1981, *22*, 375–392.

Schachter, S., & Singer, J. E. Cognitive, social and physiological determinants of emotional state. *Psychological Review*, 1962, *69*, 379–399.

Schleifer, M., Weiss, G., Cohen, N., Elman, M., Cvejic, H., & Kruger, E. Hyperactivity in preschoolers and the effect of methylphenidate. *American Journal of Orthopsychiatry*, 1975, *45*, 38–50.

Shaffer, D. Drug treatment. In M. Rutter & L. Hersov (Eds.), *Child psychiatry: Modern approaches*. Oxford: Blackwell Scientific Publications, 1977.

Shaffer, D., & Greenhill, L. A critical note on the predictive validity of 'the hyperkinetic syndrome.' *Journal of Child Psychology and Psychiatry*, 1979, *20*, 61–72.

Sprague, R., Barnes, K., & Werry, J. Methylphenidate and thioridazine: Learning, reaction time, activity, and classroom behavior in disturbed children. *American Journal of Orthopsychiatry*, 1970, *40*, 615–628.

Steinberg, G., Troshinsky, C., & Steinberg, H. Dextroamphetamine responsive behavior disorder in school children. *American Journal of Psychiatry*, 1971, *128*, 174–179.

Swanson, G., & Kinsbourne, M. Stimulant related state-dependent learning in hyperactive children. *Science*, 1976, *192*, 1354–1356.

Taylor, E. The use of drugs in hyperkinetic states: Clinical issues. *Neuropharmacology*, 1979, *18*, 951–958.

Taylor, E. Brain damage: Evidence from measures of neurological function in children with psychiatric disorder. In E. F. Purcell (Ed.), *Psychopathology of children and youth: A cross-cultural perspective*. New York: Josiah Macy, Jr., Foundation, 1980. (a)

Taylor, E. Development of attention. In M. Rutter (Ed.), *Scientific foundations of developmental psychiatry*. London: Heinemann Medical Books, 1980. (b)

Taylor, E. Psychophysiology of childhood disorders. In H. M. van Praag, M. H. Lader, O. J. Rafaelson, & E. J. Sachar (Eds.), *Handbook of biological psychiatry* (Part 2). New York: Marcel Dekker, 1980. (c)

Taylor, E., & Sandberg, S. *Classroom behaviour problems and hyperactivity: A questionnaire study in English schools*. Manuscript submitted for publication, 1982.

Weiss, B., & Laties, V. Enhancement of human performance by caffeine and the amphetamines. *Pharmacological Review*, 1962, *14*, 1–36.

Weiss, G., Werry, J., Minde, K., Douglas, V., & Sykes, D. Studies on the hyperactive child: V. The effects of dextroamphetamine and chlorpromazine on behaviour and intellectual functioning. *Journal of Child Psychology and Psychiatry*, 1968, *9*, 145–156.

Wender, P. *Minimal brain dysfunction in children*. New York: Wiley, 1971.

Wender, P. H., Reimherr, F. W., & Wood, D. R. Attention deficit disorder ("minimal brain dysfunction") in adults: A replication study of diagnosis and drug treatment. *Archives of General Psychiatry*, 1981, *38*, 449–456.

Werry, J. S. Studies on the hyperactive child: IV. An empirical analysis of the minimal brain dysfunction syndrome. *Archives of General Psychiatry*, 1968, *19*, 9–16.

Werry, J. S., Aman, M., & Diamond, E. Imipramine and methylphenidate in hyperactive children. *Journal of Child Psychology and Psychiatry*, 1980, *21*, 27–35.

Werry, J. S., & Sprague, R. Methylphenidate in children: Effect of dosage. *Australian and New Zealand Journal of Psychiatry*, 1974, *8*, 9–19.

Zahn, T. P., Abate, F., Little, B. C., & Wender, P. H. Minimal brain dysfunction, stimulant drugs and autonomic nervous system activity. *Archives of General Psychiatry*, 1975, *32*, 381–387.

CHAPTER SEVENTEEN

Nosological Issues and Biological Validation

H. BRUCE FERGUSON / JUDITH L. RAPOPORT

NOSOLOGICAL ISSUES

No aspect of neuropsychiatry has evidenced more confusion and inconsistency in nosology than those behavioral syndromes supposedly related to brain damage or dysfunction in children. Historically, children of normal intelligence with disorders of behavior and cognition have been labeled as having "brain damage" (Strauss & Lehtinen, 1947), "hyperkinetic reaction of childhood" (*Diagnostic and Statistical Manual of Mental Disorders*, second edition, or DSM-II), or, most recently, "minimal brain dysfunction" (Clements, 1966; Wender, 1971). The new diagnostic nomenclature of the American Psychiatric Association (DSM-III) has separated the various symptoms formerly grouped under "hyperkinesis" into "attention deficit disorder" (ADD) with or without hyperactivity, and two distinct behavior disorders, "oppositional disorder" and "conduct disorder." This DSM-III taxonomy reflects the continuing move away from the circularity inherent in the assumption of underlying but not necessarily demonstrable brain damage and toward the establishment of specific behavioral criteria for diagnosis. The purposes and practical advantages of this new system have been discussed elsewhere (B. A. Shaywitz, 1979; Spitzer, Williams, & Skodol, 1980).

There are several important issues surrounding the establishment of ADD. These include whether there is a distinct cluster of symptoms separate from the conduct disorders; whether ADD is indeed the core aspect of the disorder; and whether a common etiology, follow-up course, treatment response, and/or biological correlates will validate the disorder.

Past attempts to define a syndrome via statistically derived symptom clusters have been inconsistent in their attempts to find evidence for a syndrome concept within the broad categories of children in their samples (see Achenbach, 1980; Rutter, 1977; and G. Weiss, 1980, for reviews). Furthermore, in the Collaborative Perinatal Project of the National Institute of Neurological and

H. Bruce Ferguson. Department of Psychology, Carleton University, Ottawa, Ontario, Canada.

Judith L. Rapoport. Section on Child Psychiatry, National Institute of Mental Health, Bethesda, Maryland.

Communicative Disorders and Stroke (NINCDS), Nichols and Chen (1981) examined neurological and psychological test data from over 3000 7-year-olds. They reported that "the symptoms said to be characteristic of minimal brain dysfunction do not associate enough to warrant the designation of a syndrome" (p. 51). While these results have been discouraging, one widely recommended direction for future research is the classification of children into more homogeneous subgroups before attempting studies to establish their validity (Satz & Fletcher, 1980; G. Weiss, 1980). Acceptance of DSM-III diagnostic criteria provides a widely applicable basis for such an approach.

A frequently raised point regarding nosological validity queries the low prevalence rate of "hyperkinetic syndrome of childhood" (the term used in the *International Classification of Diseases*, ninth edition, or ICD-9, produced by the World Health Organization) in Britain and European countries, while apparently the same diagnosis is commonly made in the United States under a variety of different labels. A simple answer may reside in the intense research interest in the use of stimulant drug medication in the United States, which has proliferated awareness of these symptoms in child populations. Recently Glow (1980) tested the hypothesis that the conflicting incidences may be accounted for by the differences in diagnostic definitions and severity criteria. She applied typical British and American definitions to the same data set of teacher ratings of 2475 Australian schoolchildren and obtained disparate prevalence rates characteristic of those reported on the two continents. Thus Glow concluded that reported differences reflect artifacts of the diagnostic decision process, rather than true differences in incidence. While Glow's work provides an important first step, there is likely to be a continuation of such American–European conflicts unless DSM-III and ICD-9 criteria are reconciled systematically. For instance, the ICD-9 (312) diagnosis "disturbance of conduct" specifies only "aggressive and destructive behavior" and abnormal behavior that "gives rise to social disapproval." DSM-III, on the other hand, specifies that children with (312) "undersocialized aggressive conduct disorder" must have either (1) physical violence against persons or property or (2) thefts outside the home involving conflict with the victim, or both. Such differences between ICD-9 and DSM-III nosologies may predispose American psychiatrists to diagnose ADD for a large fraction of children for whom disturbance of conduct would be diagnosed in Europe.

Other causes for confusion include the lack of accepted objective measures of attention, hyperactivity, and impulsivity. As well, there remain the inconsistent guidance with respect to situational specificity of "inattentive and restless behavior" and the difficulty of separating out effects of inattention and impulsivity from those of "cognitive impairment." Diagnostic confusions are not, of course, unique to the American–European axis. A recent review of over 200 published studies (Barkley, 1982) indicated that, even in those cases where subject selection procedures were specified, neither inclusion nor exclusion criteria were consistent among researchers. This being the case, it is not surprising that such investigations have produced conflicting research findings.

There are additional potential problems in the official nosology of DSM-III. For example, the use of "oppositional disorder" includes a mild form in which only two of the following are required: (1) violation of minor rules; (2) temper tantrums; (3) argumentativeness; (4) provocative behavior; (5) stubbornness. Fortunately, this category has been neglected to date, but it is possible that it may be used instead of ADD, and may be overdiagnosed where no other disorder exists. A final source of confusion in DSM-III concerns the inclusion of "ADD, residual state." This may be a premature move, as the identity and validity of the disorder in childhood is not clearly established. Follow-up studies have not delineated a clear residual syndrome. Moreover, genetic studies (see below) have linked ADD symptoms with a variety of "adult" disorders, including alcoholism, schizophrenia, and hysteria. As the unique identity of ADD has not yet been established in childhood, and as the need for separation of the disorder from conduct disorders is not yet clear, the continuation of the label into adulthood seems premature.

DSM-III has extracted the behavioral symptoms (inattention, restlessness, impulsivity, etc.) without involving learning disabilities, neurological signs, or emotional problems, and has attempted to create a unified category that eventually would be considered nosologically valid. Widespread use of the specified criteria may allow definition of homogeneous subgroups for evaluation of biological markers or treatment regimens. However, when all the behaviors are considered together (ADD with or without hyperactivity, as well as oppositional and conduct disorders), it is possible that an alternative, broadly defined concept such as "impulsive–conduct disorder" syndrome will be supported by biological measures. Such potential validation studies are discussed in this review, which focuses on what we refer to as the "hyperkinetic syndrome."

BIOLOGICAL VALIDATION

Two issues are central to the notion of biological validation of the hyperkinetic syndrome. First, are there "biological" measures that correlate with inattentive, overactive behavior or with changes in these behaviors secondary to drug treatment, and what is the strength of such associations? Second, is there any evidence for the *specificity* of such a relationship? The thesis of this discussion is that (1) there are some measures, such as minor physical anomalies, that show statistically significant correlations with deviant behavior in selected populations; (2) there are powerful effects of stimulant drugs on deviant behaviors and probably measurable biological correlates of drug effects and clinical change. However, these demonstrated relationships are behaviorally nonspecific, are of low sensitivity, and do not "validate" a hyperkinetic syndrome. Finally, there is the issue of how one approaches the question of validation of what is undoubtedly a heterogeneous disorder.

Various strategies are used for examining biological factors in a "behavioral disorder." Genetic studies or studies of perinatal trauma have both been used to support some biological transmission of hyperactivity. There are, for example, adoption studies of hyperactives, as well as "high-risk" studies of adopted-away offspring of alcoholics. In addition, the effects of dietary or environmental toxins, such as lead, have been implicated in some populations of hyperactive children. Drug response has been proposed as a biologically validating feature, as have psychophysiological studies and, to some extent, animal models.

Pre- and Perinatal Risk as Antecedents to "Hyperkinetic Syndrome"

Pasamanick and Knobloch (1960) suggested that certain pre- and perinatal risk factors, such as bleeding in pregnancy or low birth weight, showed significant associations with learning and behavior problems exhibited by children at school age. Historically this study was important, since it shifted the existing overemphasis on purely psychological and environmental variables. Sameroff and Chandler (1975) summarized behavioral prediction from perinatal complications. They reported that there is some success in predicting "problems" in *infancy* from pre- and perinatal risk measures. But if the effects of perinatal complications are examined at school age, only the extreme disabilities, such as mental retardation or physical handicaps, can be predicted to any significant degree. The main points are that pre- and perinatal measures tend to "wash out" over time, and that socioenvironmental factors are of relatively greater importance.

A second point that emerges from surveys of infant prediction is that univariate analysis is too simplistic to generate useful clinical information. Two large epidemiological studies illustrate this point.

The Kauai study followed more than 1000 pregnancies prospectively for almost two decades (Werner, Berman, & French, 1971; Werner & Smith, 1977), collecting data on both school behavior and home support systems. When severity of perinatal stress was examined alone in relation to school achievement or hyperkinetic behavior disorders at age 10, there were no significant relationships, except for those with mental retardation or significant physical handicaps. Including social variables in the analysis, however, produced powerful relationships between severity of perinatal stress and a variety of behavioral measures for those with lower socioeconomic status, and/or those with below-average emotional support in the home. A "hyperkinetic syndrome" per se was predicted only by a measure of "educational stimulation" of the home. On the other hand, school achievement and "emotional problems" as a whole *were* well predicted at age 10 when social factors were taken into consideration. The point is that there is a group of vulnerable children whose environment may not make up for "insults" during the prenatal period.

The Collaborative Perinatal Project of NINCDS followed over 50,000 pregnancies from the time of the mothers' first missed periods until the children reached the age of 7. Both pre- and perinatal data were collected prospectively, as were repeated developmental measures. The project also included academic and neurological testing and behavioral ratings by psychologists during testing. The study lacked behavior ratings by teachers, and, although there were socioeconomic measures, no measures of emotional support or of educational stimulation in the home were included.

Behavioral, cognitive, perceptual, motor, academic, and neurological measures were examined for a group of 30,000 as established at the exam at age 7. Some associations between behavioral and neurological scores were found, with (interestingly enough) the weakest association between the cognitive and the neurological measures. Overall, Nichols and Chen (1981) have shown that *prenatal* predictors increased the likelihood of "minimal brain dysfunction" (MBD) from 2 to 5%, whereas the Kauai study showed that a lack of social and emotional support systems may increase the likelihood of such pathology by 200 to 400%. Thus, pre- and perinatal measures support only some complex, multivariate notion of "risk" in association with diverse pathology, rather than a specific behavioral profile.

Neurological "Soft Signs" and the Hyperkinetic Syndrome

There is a common assumption that the presence of neurological "soft signs" is diagnostically helpful in evaluating children with MBD, and that furthermore there may be some predictive usefulness in these measures. Theories postulating a maturational lag in hyperactive children have pointed to the presence of "soft signs" as supportive. Unfortunately, the value of "soft signs" for either diagnosis or screening is limited. Rutter, Graham, and Yule (1970) found up to five abnormal signs in 16% of children who had no other evidence of neurological disorder. The value of "soft signs" for screening is questionable, because these occur in a sizable proportion of children with normal behavior and abilities. Thus it has been reported (Adams, Kocsis, & Estes, 1974) that 10% of 9- to 11-year-olds showed mirror movements, and that choreiform movements could be elicited in 11% of normal children (Wolff & Hurtwitz, 1966).

While some studies have shown a slightly greater total number of neurological "soft signs" in hyperkinetic children, others have not (Camp, Bialer, Press, Suerd, & Winsberg, 1977; Werry & Aman, 1976; Werry, Minde, Guzman, Weiss, Dogan, & Hoy, 1972). Yet others found them to be associated with behavioral disturbance in only a nonspecific way (Mikkelsen, Brown, Millican, & Rapoport, 1982). Moreover, there is only a rather weak relationship between the number of "soft signs" in middle childhood and follow-up status in late adolescence; also, the associations tend to concern affective disorders rather than hyperactivity (see Chapter 8 of this volume).

The extent to which "soft signs" simply reflect initial cooperativeness and/or attention to a task remains an unresolved issue. If they are influenced to a considerable degree by motivational and/or attentional state, and some data suggest that ratings of "soft signs" correlate with the interview rating of cooperativeness (Mikkelsen *et al.*, 1982), then this examination is not adding to a "biological" understanding of this disorder. Certainly any association between "soft signs" and psychopathology is weak and nonspecific, and will not support validation of a syndrome.

Minor Physical Anomalies and the Hyperkinetic Syndrome

Recent studies have found an association between the number of minor physical anomalies (MPAs) of hands, feet, head, ears, face, and mouth, and behavior and/or learning problems originating in early childhood (Quinn & Rapoport, 1974; Waldrop & Halverson, 1971; Waldrop, Pedersen, & Bell, 1968). These MPAs are found in children with Down syndrome, but also are associated with other genetic defects, and occur within presumably normal populations as well (Smith, 1970). Quinn and Rapoport (1974) reported that hyperactive grade-school-age boys with high anomaly scores (weighted score of 5 or more) were more likely to have had an early onset of hyperactivity (before age 3) than were the hyperactive boys in the same study who had a total score of 3 or less for these anomalies.

A genotype–phenocopy model was proposed to account for the varied factors that are known to influence the formation of these features in the first trimester of fetal development (Rapoport & Quinn, 1975; Smith, 1970). The finding of higher MPAs in populations of hyperactive children has been replicated by Firestone and coworkers (Firestone, Lewy, & Douglas, 1976; Firestone, Peters, Rivier, & Knights, 1978) while others (Campbell, Geller, Small, Petti, & Ferris, 1978; Links, Mastronardi, Agichiandani, & Simeon, 1978; Walker, 1977) have found a higher incidence of anomalies for other behaviorally deviant pediatric populations. Recently, Waldrop, Bell, McLaughlin, and Halverson (1978) reported a significant association between high newborn anomaly scores and nursery school measures of inattentive, hyperactive behaviors for 23 males. Other studies continue to document the relationship between MPAs and inattentive, impulsive behavior in preschool populations (O'Donnell, O'Neill, & Staley, 1979; O'Donnell & Van Tuinan, 1979). Together these studies indicate that, at least for males, there is a relationship suggesting a congenital contribution to these behaviors. The question of the clinical usefulness and relevance of these relationships, chiefly obtained with "normal" preschool populations, remains.

In a longitudinal study by Rapoport and her coworkers (Burg, Hart, Quinn, & Rapoport, 1978; Burg, Quinn, & Rapoport, 1979; Burg, Rapoport, Bartley, Quinn, & Timmins, 1980; Quinn, Renfield, Burg, & Rapoport, 1977; Rapoport, Pandoni, Renfield, Ziegler, & Lake, 1977), the newborn score of MPAs and behavior at ages 1, 2, and 3 were examined in a subsample of 136 infants selected from a large newborn screening population. An association between high anomaly scores and some "difficult" behaviors was found for both males and females. A 3-year follow-up was carried out for 136 3-year-olds selected from the total newborn screening sample of 933 newborns on the basis of "high" or "low" anomalies. As reported elsewhere (Burg *et al.*, 1980), high-anomaly infants were somewhat more likely to have problem behaviors than were low-anomaly infants. The relationship between anomaly score and hyperactive, distractible, oppositional behavior held only for males and not for females. Classification on the basis of anomaly score led to many false positives and false negatives, and thus the anomaly score by itself is not a clinically useful indicator of high risk for hyperactivity.

Theoretically, the relationship between a measure of congenital developmental deviation and problem behaviors is particularly interesting. What is validated is not a "hyperactivity" syndrome, but a more general spectrum of difficulties including what might be (in DSM-III terms) "oppositional disorder," or what others consider "difficult temperament." Moreover, this relationship is not specific to behavior disorder, as several studies (Campbell *et al.*, 1978; Steg & Rapoport, 1975; Walker. 1977) have shown an increased frequency of MPAs in learning-disabled and autistic children. There is an interesting biological relationship to pursue with many aspects of this relationship, such as sex differences, that remain to be understood.

Genetic Studies

Evidence for a biological basis for hyperkinesis might come from the study of relatives of hyperkinetic children to see if there is a consistent pattern of disorders associated with this syndrome. Using this approach, parents of hyperactives have been found to show increased prevalence rates for alcoholism, sociopathy, and hysteria relative to control parents (Cantwell, 1972; Morrison & Stewart, 1971) or families adopting hyperactives (Morrison & Stewart, 1973). As the problem of separating adverse environmental effects from genetic influences is considerable, it is most useful to examine adopted-away offspring to obtain these data.

The only adoption study (Cantwell, 1975) compared the adopting families of 39 hyperactive children, 50 biological families of referred hyperactive children, and a control group of 50 children undergoing pediatric evaluation. Adopting families of hyperactive children were referred by pediatricians, while biological parents were referred by psychiatrists. Biological fathers had a much higher incidence of alcoholism and sociopathy, and biological mothers a considerably higher incidence of hysteria, than did the adopting parents or controls. These results are intriguing, but are flawed in two respects. First, alcoholism, sociopathy, and hysteria usually are manifested during young adulthood, and therefore psychiatrically disturbed adopting parents would be screened by agencies for these disorders. The second issue raised by the Cantwell study is that of referral bias. With increasing familiarity with medication for hyperactive children, pediatricians tend to refer to psychiatrists chiefly those cases who have either atypical drug response or, more pertinent here, difficult parents. Thus, this criticism implies that the cases referred to psychiatrists were more severe than the pediatric samples were. These factors would operate to increase the pathology in the parents of "ordinary" hyperactive children seen in a psychiatric clinic, relative to adopting parents (who were sought for) with children treated by pediatricians. An improved study would be one that compared prospectively the biological parents of adopted nonhyperactive children with biological parents of adopted hyperactive children. Such a study is logistically difficult, but it is a crucial comparison that is required in order to control for bias in parent selection.

Twin studies that compare monozygotic and dizygotic twins are a relatively practical approach to the study of hereditability of activity. Two studies have addressed this issue. Lopez (1965) reported data on 10 twin sets that cannot be interpreted, as four of the dizygotic twin pairs were of different sexes. Activity level of 93 pairs of same-sex twins was studied by Willerman (1973). Intraclass correlations for activity levels in monozygotic twins were substantially higher than those for dizygotic twins. Furthermore, among twin sets where one twin scored in the hyperactive range on the questionnaire (upper 20%), monozygotic twins showed a high correlation for activity level, while dizygotic twins showed no such correlation.

These family studies suggest a genetic link for problem behavior, but implicate a general hyperactive–conduct disorder entity, rather than a hyperactivity syndrome. None of the researchers systematically differentiated between restlessness–inattentiveness and conduct disorder, and their retrospective data suggests that usually both were present. Furthermore, the data suggest a genetic factor in the relationship between childhood hyperactivity and later alcoholism, sociopathy, and hysteria. As El-Guebaly and Offord (1977) have pointed out, future studies will be necessary to determine whether hyperactivity or conduct disorder or both are related to specific poor adult psychiatric outcome.

Psychophysiological Studies of Hyperactive Children

Study of psychophysiological variables has reflected attempts to test "arousal" hypotheses proposed as the organic basis of hyperactivity. The motor restlessness, attention problems, and other performance deficits shown by these children (Douglas & Peters, 1979) all are amenable to explanations involving hypothetical central nervous system (CNS) arousal systems. To date, hypotheses have been of two types: overarousal and underarousal. Overarousal could result either directly from excitatory processes (Buckley, 1972; Freibergs & Douglas, 1969; Laufer, Denhoff & Solomons, 1957) or indirectly from underactive inhibitory processes (Dykman, Ackerman, Clements, & Peters, 1972; Wender, 1971). Underarousal hypotheses implicate underactive excitatory processes (Bradley, 1937; Satterfield, Cantwell, & Satterfield, 1974; Werry, 1970). The latter proposals represent an especially attractive theoretical position, since both the behavioral symptoms and the seemingly "paradoxical" response of hyperactive children to stimulant drugs could be explained. The apparent testability of these contradictory theoretical proposals has produced a large number of studies having two goals: (1) to assess predicted differences between hyperactive and normal children in basal (tonic) and reactive (phasic) arousal; (2) to examine the effects of stimulant drugs on the arousal mechanisms of hyperactive children.

The majority of psychophysiological studies have measured peripheral autonomic nervous system indexes of arousal, but a growing number of investigations have examined cortical measures. This literature has been exhaustively surveyed recently in three critical reviews (Ferguson & Pappas, 1979; Hastings & Barkley, 1978; Yellin, 1978). Despite an array of methodological concerns, there is general agreement by these reviewers that the accumulated data support the hypothesis of CNS underarousal for at least a subgroup of hyperactive children. This difference has emerged most clearly when the children are engaged in tasks requiring attention to external signal stimuli.

Since the above reviews have been published, a series of studies has addressed directly the purported "paradoxical" response of hyperactive children to stimulants (Rapoport, Buchsbaum, Weingartner, Zahn, Ludlow, Bartko, & Mikkelsen, 1980; Rapoport, Buchsbaum, Zahn, Weingartner, Ludlow, & Mikkelsen, 1978). The remarkable similarity of the behavioral and physiological responses of normal and hyperactive children to the drug argues against any diagnostic usefulness of drug response. While the decreased motor activity and improved cognitive performance permit one still to regard the effects of this stimulant drug as "paradoxical," there is as yet no obvious basis in any aspect of the data to support a biological basis for hyperactivity or any aspect of the syndrome. A nonspecific drug effect, however, holds out the potential for future research to uncover validating biological correlates of behavioral change.

The results of a decade of psychophysiological study leave investigators with the suggestion that at least some subgroup of hyperactive children may be centrally underaroused. At this time, there is no hint of what behavioral criteria define this subgroup, if indeed systematic selection is possible. Diagnostically a crucial study would be the physiological examination of attentive, nonfidgety sociopaths. Hypoarousal in such delinquent young adults would suggest a more general correlation between hypoarousal and impulsive–deviant behavior. Certainly many adult studies reporting hypoarousal in criminals did *not* systematically select for inattentive subjects (Hare, 1970; Schalling, Lidberg, Levander, & Dahlin, 1973).

Toxic Substances and Hyperactivity

Another source of implied evidence for biological bases for hyperactivity resides in studies of acute or chronic effects of various substances acting as neurotoxins on the developing brain. Best known of such suggestions is the case study material of Feingold (1975), who asserts that ingestion of artificial food additives (colors and flavors) and naturally occurring salicylates in foods results in hyperactivity and learning disabilities in children. Initial experimental tests of this hypothesis (Cook & Woodhill, 1976; Salzman, 1976) provided encouraging results. Unfortunately, the findings of subsequent carefully controlled studies with appropriate selection and evaluation criteria (Conners, Goyette, Southwick, Lees, & Andrulonis, 1976; Harley, Ray, Tomasi, Eichman, Matthews, Chun, Cleeland, & Traisman, 1978) indicate that only a small subgroup of hyperactive children show improvement on the diet and that such efficacy may be restricted to the younger age group (under 6 years).

On the other hand, while the weight of the evidence argues against Feingold's hypothesis as a pervasive cause of hyperactivity, recent challenge tests with food dyes (Swanson & Kinsbourne, 1980; B. Weiss, Williams, Margen, Abrams, Caan, Citron, Cos, McKibben, Ogar, & Schultz, 1980) clearly suggest that ingestion of these substances can cause behavioral symptoms characteristic of hyperactivity, and they further indicate that the challenge dose of dyes tested in previous studies may have been too low. In addition, controlled studies (Rapp, 1979; Trites, Ferguson, & Tryphonas, 1980) have provided inconsistent evidence regarding the proposal of specific food allergies as a basis for hyperactivity. Thus, neither diet-related hypothesis currently holds much promise as a general explanation of hyperactivity. Moreover, even such positive results as do exist implicate only the broad hyperactivity–conduct disorder entity.

A less widely tested explanation implicates high levels of lead in the body as a causative factor in hyperactivity (David, Clark, & Voeller, 1972; David, Hoffman, Sverd, Clark, & Voeller, 1976; David, Hoffman, & Clark, 1977). Reducing body lead levels has revealed encouraging relationships to improved behavior. In addition, an interesting animal model of hyperactivity has been induced in mice by chronic low-level exposure to lead during early development (Silbergeld & Goldberg, 1974). Although the lead-level model presents an attractive etiological basis for lower-class urban children, it would appear to have limited explanatory value to the general problem of hyperactivity unless a recent report (Settle & Patterson, 1980) suggesting relatively high general levels of body lead is substantiated.

An intriguing relationship is that between maternal alcohol intake and numerous dysmorphic features, called the "fetal alcohol syndrome." As the fetal alcohol syndrome has become an accepted entity (Ulleland, Wenneberg, & Igo, 1970), and since there is an association between minor dysmorphic features and at least a subgroup of hyperactive children (Rapoport & Quinn, 1975), a possible vehicle by which behavioral disturbance is transmitted is suggested for cases of maternal alcoholism. Even adopted-away offspring have been subjected to early fetal toxicity of alcohol if *maternal* alcohol abuse occurred during pregnancy. If this influence were important, the offspring of alcoholic mothers would be dysmorphic, hyperactive, impulsive children, while those of alcoholic fathers would not. Indeed, it has been reported that maternal alcohol abuse may produce a continuum of teratogenic effects on morphology and the CNS. In screening a population for possible fetal alcohol syndrome, 15 cases of normal intelligence showing only mild dysmorphic features, but hyperactivity and persistent school difficulties, were isolated. These findings have led S. E. Shaywitz, Cohen, and Shaywitz (1980) to propose that the concept of "fetal alcohol syndrome" be expanded to include behavior and learning problems as manifestations of CNS involvement resulting from fetal exposure to ethanol.

Stimulant Drug Effects in Hyperactive–Impulsive Children

The question of clinical specificity of stimulant drug response remains open, since uncontrolled studies report therapeutic success for the entire spectrum of pediatric problems. Earlier investigators (Bender & Coddington, 1942) have reported cases of "anxiety neurosis" for which amphetamines were considered useful! No controlled studies have been carried out of stimulant drug treatment for pediatric conditions other than hyperkinetic and/or conduct disorders. As "neurotic" disturbances respond to other treatment and have better prognosis, there has been little impetus for drug studies with such populations, but the theoretical issue remains. Since the normal child's response is qualitatively similar (Rapoport *et al.*, 1978, 1980) to that of hyperactive children, it is probable that drug response has little diagnostic significance. Moreover, initial reports of stimulant drug efficacy described aggressive destructive behavior disorders more than "hyperkinesis" as drug-responsive (Bradley & Bowen, 1941; Conners & Eisenberg, 1963), as do later studies (Sprague, Barnes, & Werry, 1970). Therapeutically, a study of considerable practical significance would be to examine the stimulant drug response of attentive, motorically calm, but conduct-disordered children. ADD has become a separate diagnostic entity in DSM-III. However, inattention as a symptom is nonspecific in its associations. In the major pediatric behavioral epidemiological study on the Isle of Wight (Rutter *et al.*, 1970), both parent and teacher ratings of poor concentration were significantly and equally associated with both emotional disturbance and conduct disorder (70–80%, compared with 20–35% of the general population). Thus, the clinical response of "inattentive" children to stimulants says little about diagnosis in the traditional sense.

Clinically, the nonspecificity of stimulant drug "responders" has been well summarized by Taylor (1979). Reservations about his observation of a broad spectrum of stimulant drug response in his clinic sample are based only on the fact that the crucial study, yet to be done, is one that selects for child patients who are *clearly not* "hyperactive." For example, nonfidgety, highly attentive, but conduct-disordered children might be chosen from the larger pool of children who have both impulsive, antisocial behaviors and restless, inattentive behaviors. Such a group of conduct-disordered children would most probably be good responders to stimulants. Until such "pure" groups are selected and tested, however, studies of "diagnostic specificity" of clinical response to stimulants will remain inconclusive. In summary, the clinical effects of stimulants in the hyperkinetic syndrome have not yet been demonstrated to be specific to this disorder, and thus in themselves will not validate the syndrome. Such validation will require research with subgroups having clearly defined sets of symptoms, as proposed above. Silbergeld (1977) suggested an even broader approach, that of testing behaviorally defined subgroups of children for response to different classes of drugs. Work such as this may illuminate the broader issue of the developmental biology of overactivity, attention, and impulse control. Implicit in such a research strategy is the assumption that particular behavioral patterns result from dysfunction in specific neural systems or pathways, and that advances in the specificity of drug action will allow us to psychopharmacologically "dissect" out the involved behavior–mechanism relationships.

CONCLUSIONS

Historically, the hyperkinetic syndrome evolved from follow-up of children with known insult to the CNS (Strauss & Lehtinen, 1947; Strecker & Ebaugh, 1924). Although the pathophysiology of this syndrome has remained undefined, the assumption of underlying organicity is evidenced by the frequent interchangeable use of the label "MBD." Past examination of evidence for biological bases have produced both negative (Dubey, 1976) and positive (Goetz, Kramer, & Weiner, 1978; S. E. Shaywitz, Cohen, & Shaywitz, 1978) conclusions on this issue. In our judgment, the literature suggests general agreement for a broad concept of biological underpinnings of problem behavior. In no research area, however, have studies been done that would enable one to assign any of the observed biological deviations to a *specific* deviant behavior or clinical symptom. Moreover, the strongest evidence for biological factors is relevant only for a small fraction of children presenting as "hyperactive." Shaffer and Greenhill (1979) have argued that the lack of postdictive, concurrent, and particularly predictive validity weakens the clinical usefulness of the "hyperkinetic syndrome" as a diagnostic concept. The critical studies remain to be done wherein children carefully subgrouped according to behavioral criteria are the subjects of psychopharmacological, psychophysiological, and genetic study as well as careful follow-up. Apart from subject selection, acceptable methodological criteria for such studies are now widely established (Dubey, 1976). A set of behavioral criteria for subgrouping children previously labeled only as having "hyperkinetic syndrome" and/or "MBD" are established in the taxonomy of DSM-III. Utilization of the proposed criteria will provide a basis for systematic research examining possible biological underpinnings of the various groups. Furthermore, the relative validity and utility of empirically derived syndromes (Achenbach, 1980) can be assessed concurrently. Alternately, children having specific biological "risk" factors should be examined to see the spectrum of behavioral disturbance in such populations, a strategy expounded by Buchsbaum, Coursey, and Murphy (1976).

Unlike Shaywitz *et al.* (1978) and Goetz *et al.* (1978), we do not propose a central dopaminergic system mediation of hyperkinetic or MBD behavior. The strongest evidence for such a proposal derives from just one of several available animal models. At this time, it appears of doubtful value to base a proposal for the human hyperkinetic syndrome on these data alone. Suggestions such as ours that future progress in all research areas—drug response, genetic, psychophysiological—depends upon research with subject groups carefully selected for symptomatology will make it even more difficult for animal modeling to be illuminating with regard to mechanism. However, inasmuch as behavioral parallels can be established between species, such models can provide valuable tools for assessing efficacy and specificity of new drugs.

From pharmacological, physiological, and anatomical evidence, there are general correlates between "biological alteration" and deviant behaviors. Genetic data suggest that there are hereditary factors in behavior and learning problems and that childhood problems may be linked to adult psychopathology. Typically these relationships have been noted for males, as Omenn (1973) has noted; perhaps because of ease of measurement, the evidence also seems to favor links with conduct disorder (impulsive, aggressive behavior), although similar patterns have been found for other disturbances.

Some would argue that it is unreasonable to expect that biological correlates of deviant behavior be highly specific. In general psychiatry, for example, alterations of platelet monoamine oxidase (MAO) have been described for schizophrenia as well as for personality subtypes within a relatively normal college population (Buchsbaum *et al.*, 1976). Similarly, the idea of a graded characteristic with more and less severe manifestations (e.g., a gradual spectrum of severity from mild hyperkinesis to severe conduct disorder) is well recognized in family and genetic studies of schizophrenia, affective disorder, sociopathy, and so on. Therefore this review, rather than making a "negative" statement, may be providing as strong support for a "biological validation" of a syndrome as is to be found in modern biological psychiatry! If this is the case, then we should reassess what is meant by "validation." When a "risk" factor is demonstrated almost ubiquitously, it loses explanatory value. When we imply "biological validation," it suggests that some underlying measure would distinguish one syndrome from another—that it would predict treatment response or follow-up status.

This current nonspecific finding is still of general interest. There may be a final common path of biological disturbance (catecholamine depletion, receptor hyposensitivity) resulting from exposure to toxins, fetal brain damage, genetic transmission, and even early social deprivation. Such a relationship would be of considerable importance for understanding the biological basis for behavior, even if a particular syndrome cannot be delineated. Alternatively, the weak associations and lack of specificity relating biological factors and hyperactivity may reflect the fact that the hyperkinetic syndrome is not etiologically and biologically a unitary disorder. This hypothesis has been proposed to account for similar situations in adult psychiatry (Buchsbaum & Rieder, 1979), and certainly it is compatible with the data we have reviewed. If indeed this is the case, then the research goals and strategies for identifying meaningful subgroups are clearly indicated for future work in this area.

References

Achenbach, T. M. DSM-III in light of empirical research on the classification of child psychopathology. *Journal of the American Academy of Child Psychiatry*, 1980, *19*, 395–412.

Adams, R. M., Kocsis, J. J., & Estes, R. E. Soft neurological signs in learning-disabled children and controls. *American Journal of Diseases of Children*, 1974, *128*, 614–618.

American Psychiatric Association. *Diagnostic and statistical manual of mental disorders* (3rd ed.). Washington, D.C.: Author, 1980.

Barkley, R. A. Guidelines for defining hyperactivity in children. In B. Lahey & A. Kazdin (Eds.), *Advances in clinical child psychology* (Vol. 5). New York: Plenum Press, 1982.

Bender, L., & Coddington, F. The use of amphetamine sulfate (benzedrine) in child psychiatry. *American Journal of Psychiatry*, 1942, *99*, 116–121.

Bradley, C. The behavior of children receiving benzedrine. *American Journal of Psychiatry*, 1937, *44*, 577–585.

Bradley, C., & Bowen, M. Amphetamine therapy of children's behavior disorders. *American Journal of Orthopsychiatry*, 1941, *11*, 92–103.

Buchsbaum, M., Coursey, R., & Murphy, D. L. The biochemical high-risk paradigm: Behavioral and familial correlates of low platelet monoamine oxidase activity. *Science*, 1976, *194*, 339–341.

Buchsbaum, M., & Rieder, R. Biological heterogeneity and psychiatry research. *Archives of General Psychiatry*, 1979, *36*, 1163–1169.

Buckley, R. E. A neurophysiological proposal for the amphetamine response in hyperkinetic children. *Psychosomatics*, 1972, *13*, 93–99.

Burg, C., Hart, D., Quinn, P., & Rapoport, J. Newborn minor physical anomalies and prediction of infant behavior. *Journal of Autism and Childhood Schizophrenia*, 1978, *8*, 427–439.

Burg, C., Quinn, P., & Rapoport, J. Clinical evaluation of 1-year-old infants: Possible predictors of risk for the "hyperactivity syndrome." *Pediatric Psychology*, 1979, *3*, 164–167.

Burg, C., Rapoport, J., Bartley, L., Quinn, P., & Timmins, P. Newborn minor physical anomalies and problem behavior at age 3. *American Journal of Psychiatry*, 1980, *137*, 791–796.

Camp, J., Bialer, I., Press, M., Suerd, J., & Winsberg, B. *Pediatric norms for the NIMH Physical and Neurological Examination for Soft Signs* (*PANESS*). Paper presented at Early Clinical Drug Evaluation Unit Meeting, Key Biscayne, Fla., 1977.

Campbell, M., Geller, B., Small, A., Petti, T., & Ferris, S. Minor physical anomalies in young psychotic children. *American Journal of Psychiatry*, 1978, *135*, 573–575.

Cantwell, D. Psychiatric illness in the families of hyperactive children. *Archives of General Psychiatry*, 1972, *70*, 414–417.

Cantwell, D. Genetic studies of hyperactive children: Psychiatric illness in biological and adopting parents. In R. Fieve, D. Rosenthal, & H. Brills (Eds.), *Genetic research in psychiatry*. Baltimore: Johns Hopkins University Press, 1975.

Clements, S. D. *Minimal brain dysfunction in children* (NINCDS Monograph No. 3, U.S. Public Health Service Publication No. 1415). Washington, D.C.: U.S. Government Printing Office, 1966.

Conners, C. K., & Eisenberg, L. The effects of methylphenidate on symptomatology and learning in disturbed children. *American Journal of Psychiatry*, 1963, *120*, 458–464.

Conners, C. K., Goyette, C. H., Southwick, D. A., Lees, T. M., & Andrulonis, P. A. Food additives and hyperkinesis: A controlled double-blind experiment. *Pediatrics*, 1976, *58*, 154–166.

Cook, P. S., & Woodhill, F. M. The Feingold dietary treatment of the hyperkinetic syndrome. *Medical Journal of Australia*, 1976, *2*, 85–90.

David, O. J., Clark, J., & Voeller, K. Lead and hyperactivity. *Lancet*, 1972, *2*, 900–903.

David, O. J., Hoffman, S. P., & Clark, J. Lead and hyperactivity: Lead levels among hyperactive children. *Journal of Abnormal Child Psychology*, 1977, *5*, 405–416.

David, O. J., Hoffman, S. P., Sverd, J., Clark, J., & Voeller, K. Lead and hyperactivity. Behavioral response to chelation: A pilot study. *American Journal of Psychiatry*, 1976, *133*, 1155–1158.

Douglas, V. I., & Peters, K. G. Toward a clearer definition of the attentional deficit of hyperactive children. In G. A. Hale & M. Lewis (Eds.), *Attention and the development of cognitive skills*. New York: Plenum Press, 1979.

Dubey, D. R. Organic factors in hyperkinesis: A critical evaluation. *American Journal of Orthopsychiatry*, 1976, *46*, 353–366.

Dykman, R. A., Ackerman, P. T., Clements, S. D., & Peters, J. E. Specific learning disabilities: An attentional deficit syndrome. In H. R. Myklebust (Ed.), *Progress in learning disabilities*. New York: Grune & Stratton, 1972.

El-Guebaly, N., & Offord, D. R. The offspring of alcoholics: A critical review. *American Journal of Psychiatry*, 1977, *134*, 357–365.

Feingold, B. F. *Why your child is hyperactive*. New York: Random House, 1975.

Ferguson, H. B., & Pappas, B. A. Evaluation of psychophysiological, neurochemical, and animal models of hyperactivity. In R. L. Trites (Ed.), *Hyperactivity in children*. Baltimore: University Park Press, 1979.

Firestone, P., Lewy, F., & Douglas, V. Hyperactivity and physical anomalies. *Canadian Psychiatric Association Journal*, 1976, *21*, 23–26.

Firestone, P., Peters, S., Rivier, M., & Knights, R. M. Minor physical anomalies in hyperactive, retarded, and normal children and their familes. *Journal of Child Psychology and Psychiatry*, 1978, *19*, 155–160.

Freibergs, V., & Douglas, V. I. Concept learning in hyperactive and normal children. *Journal of Abnormal Psychology*, 1969, *74*, 388–395.

Glow, R. A. A validation of Conners TQ and a cross-cultural comparison of prevalence of hyperactivity in children. In J. S. Werry & G. D. Burrows (Eds.), *Advances in human psychopharmacology* (Vol. 1). Greenwich, Conn.: JAI Press, 1980.

Goetz, C., Kramer, J., & Weiner, W. J. Pharmacology of minimal brain dysfunction. In H. L. Klawans (Ed.), *Clinical neuropharmacology* (Vol. 3). New York: Raven Press, 1978.

Hare, R. D. *Psychopathy: Theory and research.* New York: Wiley, 1970.

Harley, J. P., Ray, R. S., Tomasi, L., Eichman, R. L., Matthews, C. G., Chun, R., Cleeland, C. B., & Traisman, S. Hyperkinesis and food additives: Testing the Feingold hypothesis. *Pediatrics*, 1978, *61*, 818–828.

Hastings, J. E., & Barkley, R. A. A review of psychophysiological research with hyperkinetic children. *Journal of Abnormal Child Psychology*, 1978, *6*, 413–448.

Laufer, M. W., Denhoff, E., & Solomons, S. Hyperkinetic impulse disorder in children's behavior problems. *Psychosomatic Medicine*, 1957, *19*, 38–49.

Links, P., Mastronardi, M., Agichiandani, F., & Simeon, J. *Minor physical anomalies in autism: Their relationship to pre- and perinatal complications.* Paper presented at the meeting of the Canadian Psychiatric Association, Halifax, Nova Scotia, October 1978.

Lopez, R. Hyperactivity in twins. *Canadian Psychiatric Association Journal*, 1965, *10*, 421–426.

Mikkelsen, E., Brown, G., Millican, F., & Rapoport, J. Neurologic status in hyperactive enuretic, encopretic, and normal children. *Journal of the American Academy of Child Psychiatry*, 1982, *21*, 75–81.

Morrison, J., & Stewart, M. A family study of the hyperactive child syndrome. *Biological Psychiatry*, 1971, *3*, 189–195.

Morrison, J., & Stewart, M. The psychiatric status of the legal families of adoptive hyperactive children. *Archives of General Psychiatry*, 1973, *28*, 888–891.

Nichols, P., & Chen, T.-C. *Minimal brain dysfunction: A prospective study.* Hillsdale, N.J.: Erlbaum, 1981.

O'Donnell, J., O'Neill, S., & Staley, A. Congenital correlates of distractibility. *Journal of Abnormal Child Psychology*, 1979, *7*, 465–470.

O'Donnell, J., & Van Tuinan, M. Behavior problems of preschool children: Dimensions and congenital correlates. *Journal of Abnormal Child Psychology*, 1979, *7*, 61–75.

Omenn, G. S. Genetic issues in the syndrome of minimal brain dysfunction. *Seminars in Psychiatry*, 1973, *5*, 5–17.

Pasamanick, B., & Knobloch, H. Brain damage and reproductive casualty. *American Journal of Orthopsychiatry*, 1960, *30*, 298–305.

Quinn, P., & Rapoport, J. Minor physical anomalies and neurological status in hyperactive boys. *Pediatrics*, 1974, *53*, 742–747.

Quinn, P., Renfield, M., Burg, C., & Rapoport, J. Minor physical anomalies: A newborn screening and 1-year follow-up. *Journal of the American Academy of Child Psychiatry*, 1977, *16*, 662–669.

Rapoport, J. L., Buchsbaum, M. S., Weingartner, H., Zahn, T. P., Ludlow, C., Bartko, J., & Mikkelsen, E. J. Dextroamphetamine: Cognitive and behavioral effects in normal and hyperactive boys and normal adult males. *Archives of General Psychiatry*, 1980, *37*, 933–943.

Rapoport, J. L., Buchsbaum, M. S., Zahn, T. P., Weingartner, H., Ludlow, C., & Mikkelsen, E. J. Dextroamphetamine: Cognitive and behavioral effects in normal prepubertal boys. *Science*, 1978, *199*, 560–563.

Rapoport, J., Pandoni, C., Renfield, M., Ziegler, M., & Lake, C. R. Newborn dopamine-β-hydroxylase, minor physical anomalies, and infant temperament. *American Journal of Psychiatry*, 1977, *134*, 676–678.

Rapoport, J. L., & Quinn, P. O. Minor physical anomalies (stigmata) and early developmental deviation: A major biological subgroup of "hyperactive children." *International Journal of Mental Health*, 1975, *4*, 29–44.

Rapp, D. Food allergy treatment for hyperkinetics. *Journal of Learning Disabilities*, 1979, *12*, 608–616.

Rutter, M. Brain damage syndromes in childhood: Concepts and findings. *Journal of Child Psychology and Psychiatry*, 1977, *8*, 1–21.

Rutter, M., Graham, P., & Yule, W. *A neuropsychiatric study in childhood* (Clinics in Developmental Medicine Nos. 35–36). London: Spastics International Medical Publications/Heinemann Medical Books, 1970.

Salzman, L. K. Allergy testing, psychological assessment, and dietary treatment of the hyperactive child syndrome. *Medical Journal of Australia*, 1976, *2*, 248–251.

Sameroff, A., & Chandler, M. Reproductive risk and the continuum of care-taking casualty. In F. Horowitz (Ed.), *Review of child development research*. Chicago: University of Chicago Press, 1975.

Satterfield, J. H., Cantwell, D. P., & Satterfield, B. T. Pathophysiology of the hyperactive child syndrome. *Archives of General Psychiatry*, 1974, *31*, 839–844.

Satz, P., & Fletcher, J. M. Minimal brain dysfunctions: An appraisal of concepts and methods. In H. Rie & E. Rie (Eds.), *Handbook of minimal brain dysfunctions*. New York: Wiley, 1980.

Schalling, D., Lidberg, L., Levander, S., & Dahlin, Y. Spontaneous autonomic activity as related to psychopathy. *Biological Psychology*, 1973, *1*, 83–97.

Settle, D. M., & Patterson, C. C. Lead in albacore: Guide to lead pollution in Americans. *Science*, 1980, *207*, 1167–1176.

Shaffer, D., & Greenhill, L. A critical note on the predictive validity of "the hyperkinetic syndrome." *Journal of Child Psychology and Psychiatry*, 1979, *20*, 61–72.

Shaywitz, B. A. New diagnostic terminology for minimal brain dysfunction. *Journal of Pediatrics*, 1979, *95*, 734–736.

Shaywitz, S. E., Cohen, D. J., & Shaywitz, B. A. The biochemical basis of minimal brain dysfunction. *Journal of Pediatrics*, 1978, *92*, 179–187.

Shaywitz, S. E., Cohen, D. J., & Shaywitz, B. A. Behavior and learning difficulties of children of normal intelligence born to alcoholic mothers. *Journal of Pediatrics*, 1980, *96*, 978–982.

Silbergeld, E. K. Neuropharmacology of hyperkinesis. In W. B. Essman & L. Valzelli (Eds.), *Current developments in psychopharmacology*. New York: Spectrum, 1977.

Silbergeld, E. K., & Goldberg, A. M. Lead-induced behavioral dysfunction: An animal model of hyperactivity. *Experimental Neurology*, 1974, *42*, 146–157.

Smith, D. *Recognizable patterns of human malformation*. Philadelphia: W. B. Saunders, 1970.

Spitzer, R. L., Williams, J. B. W., & Skodol, A. E. DSM-III: The major achievements and an overview. *American Journal of Psychiatry*, 1980, *137*, 151–164.

Sprague, R. L., Barnes, K. R., & Werry, J. S. Methylphenidate and thioridazine: Learning, reaction time, activity, and classroom behavior in disturbed children. *American Journal of Orthopsychiatry*, 1970, *40*, 615–628.

Steg, J., & Rapoport, J. Minor physical anomalies in normal, neurotic, learning-disabled, and severely disturbed children. *Journal of Autism and Childhood Schizophrenia*, 1975, *5*, 299–307.

Strauss, A. A., & Lehtinen, L. E. *Psychopathology and education of the brain-injured child*. New York: Grune & Stratton, 1947.

Strecker, E. A., & Ebaugh, F. Neuropsychiatric sequelae of cerebral trauma in children. *Archives of Neurology and Psychiatry*, 1924, *12*, 443–453.

Swanson, J. M., & Kinsbourne, M. Food dyes impair performance of hyperactive children on a laboratory learning test. *Science*, 1980, *207*, 1485–1486.

Taylor, E. *Clinical significance of stimulant drug response*. Paper presented at the International Symposium in Child Psychiatry, Paris, November 1979.

Trites, R. L., Ferguson, H. B., & Tryphonas, H. Diet treatment for hyperactive children with food allergies. In R. M. Knights & D. Bakker (Eds.), *The rehabilitation, treatment, and management of learning disabilities*. Baltimore: University Park Press, 1980.

Ulleland, C., Wennberg, R., & Igo, R. The offspring of alcoholic mothers. *Pediatric Research*, 1970, *4*, 474. (Abstract)

Waldrop, M., Bell, R., McLaughlin, B., & Halverson, C. E. Newborn minor physical anomalies predict short attention span, peer aggression, and impulsivity at age 3. *Science*, 1978, *199*, 563–565.

Waldrop, M., & Halverson, C. E. Minor physical anomalies and hyperactive behavior in young children. In J. Hellmuth (Ed.), *The exceptional infant*. New York: Brunner/Mazel, 1971.

Waldrop, M., Pedersen, F., & Bell, R. Q. Minor physical anomalies and behavior in preschool children. *Child Development*, 1968, *39*, 391–400.

Walker, H. Incidence of minor physical anomaly in autism. *Journal of Autism and Childhood Schizophrenia*, 1977, *7*, 165–176.

Weiss, B., Williams, J. H., Margen, S., Abrams, B., Caan, B., Citron, L., Cos, C., McKibben, J., Ogar, D., & Schultz, S. Behavioral responses to artificial food colors. *Science*, 1980, *207*, 1487–1488.

Weiss, G. MBD: Critical diagnostic issues. In H. Rie & E. Rie (Eds.), *Handbook of minimal brain dysfunctions*. New York: Wiley, 1980.

Wender, P. H. *Minimal brain dysfunction in children*. New York: Wiley–Interscience, 1971.

Werner, E., Berman, J., & French, F. *The children of Kauai: A longitudinal study from the prenatal period to age ten*. Honolulu: University of Hawaii Press, 1971.

Werner, E., & Smith, R. *Kauai's children come of age*. Honolulu: University of Hawaii Press, 1977.

Werry, J. S. Some clinical and laboratory studies of psychotropic drugs in children: An overview. In W. K. Smith (Ed.), *Drugs and cerebral function*. Springfield, Ill.: Charles C Thomas, 1970.

Werry, J. S., & Aman, M. The reliability and diagnostic validity of the Physical and Neurological Examination for Soft Signs (PANESS). *Journal of Autism and Childhood Schizophrenia*, 1976, *6*, 253–263.

Werry, J. S., Minde, K., Guzman, D., Weiss, G., Dogan, K., & Hoy, R. Studies in the hyperactive child. *American Journal of Orthopsychiatry*, 1972, *42*, 441–450.

Willerman, L. Activity level and hyperactivity in twins. *Child Development*, 1973, *44*, 288–293.

Wolff, P. H., & Hurwitz, J. The choreiform syndrome. *Developmental Medicine and Child Neurology*, 1966, *8*, 160–165.

Yellin, A. M. Recent advances in psychophysiology: Psychophysiological studies in hyperkinesis. *Research Communications in Psychology, Psychiatry, and Behavior*, 1978, *3*, 237–255.

CHAPTER EIGHTEEN

The Use of Drugs: Trends in Research

JUDITH L. RAPOPORT

INTRODUCTION

This chapter provides an *updated* overview of drug treatment of the hyperkinetic syndrome, rather than a general appraisal of pediatric psychopharmacology. Three recent excellent texts (Klein, Gittelman, Quitkin, & Rifkin, 1980; Weiner, 1977; Werry, 1978) provide that general background, and the issues are not considered here. Instead, this review focuses on recent clinical contributions to drug treatment of the hyperkinetic syndrome.

The topic of drug treatment of minimal brain dysfunction (MBD) has a special importance, in view of the fact that much of the current interest in this syndrome stems from the dramatic behavioral improvement of many of the "MBD" symptoms following stimulant drug treatment. The optimism and sense of clinical acumen and potency that such dramatic response brought to clinicians and researchers has spurred several fledgling investigators into the full-time study of these children and the clinical phenomenology of drug treatment response in hyperactivity.

Over the past 20 years, drug treatment of hyperactive–impulsive behaviors in children has gained acceptance; to date, there have been over 100 controlled studies demonstrating the short-term efficacy of stimulants for such behavior (Barkley, 1977). The more recent and controversial issues to be reviewed here include the choice of alternative medications; the importance of side effects (particularly on growth); the effects of stimulant drugs on learning; the effects on mood and interpersonal functioning; pharmacokinetics; the relative merits of medication and of behavioral treatments; the possible long-term benefits from drug treatment of hyperactivity; and the diagnostic specificity of clinical benefits.

STIMULANT DRUGS AND LEARNING

When stimulants were first studied in adult subjects, there was considerable controversy over what kind of cognitive function, if any, was helped by these

Judith L. Rapoport. Section on Child Psychiatry, National Institute of Mental Health, Bethesda, Maryland.

agents (B. Weiss & Laties, 1962). With pediatric populations, the initial improvement in hyperkinetic, inattentive behavior at school led to the expectation that there would be concurrent improvement in academic performance. This assumption has been increasingly questioned. Rie (Rie, Rie, Stewart, & Ambuel, 1976a, 1976b) indicated that, in a naturalistic setting, children receiving stimulants for up to 6 months did not improve differentially in academic performance, compared with their performance during a control period on placebo. Gittelman-Klein and Klein (1976), using a more careful and extensive design, made a 12-week study of 61 children with learning problems alone (i.e., without behavior disorder), using random assignment to placebo or methylphenidate. While stimulants improved many laboratory psychological tests, achievement measures did not change. The question remains, of course, whether stimulant drugs could improve academic achievement only in conjunction with appropriate remedial educational help (this issue is discussed further in Chapter 27 of this volume). Some hyperactive children may have attention-deficit-based, drug-responsive learning problems, but such a subgroup remains to be demonstrated (Douglas & Peters, 1979).

A second question that bears on stimulant drug effects on learning is whether state-dependent learning occurs—that is, if learning and recall should be in the same state for best retention. State-dependent learning has attracted a great deal of interest, both as to its mechanism and as to the possible practical implications. Nowhere is this question so important as with drugs used on school-age children. In 1976, Swanson and Kinsbourne published a report of a state-dependent learning effect in a group of 32 hyperactive children on methylphenidate (10–20 mg). In contrast with this report, Aman and Sprague (1974) had found no such effect of *d*-amphetamine (.2 mg/kg) and methylphenidate (.5 mg/kg), but as these researchers did not obtain an initial drug effect on learning, it may have been difficult to demonstrate state dependency. Our own data (Weingartner, Langer, Grice, & Rapoport) also do not indicate state dependency, so this question is far from settled.

As children receiving stimulants typically do homework during evening hours when stimulants have worn off, the phenomenon of state dependency has important practical implications, particularly in light of the negative findings cited above. It is uncertain whether state dependency could account for the "academic failure" of stimulants in the Gittelman-Klein and Klein (1976) and Rie *et al.* (1976a, 1976b) studies, but it seems unlikely that it did so. It is clear, however, that as yet psychopharmacology has no clear contribution to the treatment of learning disabilities. It remains to be seen whether there is a subgroup of children with an "attention-deficit"-based learning difficulty who would benefit academically from drugs. However, it would be simplistic to assume any single deficit in such a heterogeneous population.

EFFECTS ON MOOD AND INTERPERSONAL FUNCTIONING

The clinical efficacy of stimulant drugs is usually operationally defined by a decrease in motor restlessness and impulsivity as measured by the Conners Teacher Rating Scale (Conners, 1969), and by improvement on some vigilance task such as a reaction-time task or a continuous-performance test (CPT).

More recently, relatively subtle drug effects have been demonstrated; these were prompted by clinical reports that children on stimulants may be less sociable and even unduly serious or sad. Two reports concerned the effects of methylphenidate on mother–child interaction, and one concerned peer functioning. Barkley and Cunningham (1979) examined 20 hyperactive boys who were interacting with their mothers during free play and a task period (the mothers had the children pick up toys, copy designs, complete math problems and puzzles). While the boys on methylphenidate (usually 10 mg) were more compliant with maternal instructions than they were when on placebo, the children initiated fewer social interactions during free play. It has been observed frequently that hyperactive children are less talkative during drug treatment, but the long-term social consequences (good or bad) from this drug effect are unclear. Similarly, Humphries, Kinsbourne, and Swanson (1978) found more positive and less controlling interaction between mothers and their hyperactive children when the latter received methylphenidate than when they were on a placebo.

In a similar vein, Whalen, Henker, Collins, McAuliffe, and Vaux (1979) examined the interpersonal functioning of normal and hyperactive boys and the effects of methylphenidate on peer functioning in a "structured communication task." In this study, 23 hyperactive boys were observed and videotaped during a game with peers in which team work in a space game with dyadic roles of "mission control" and "astronaut" was important for completion of the task. A variety of behaviors was coded, including positive and negative statements about each child's own performance, appearance of mood (not relying on introspective reports of mood), and initiation of social interaction. While on placebo, the hyperactive children seemed happier, gave more positive feedback to their partners, and were less self-derogatory (in spite of superior task performance on the drug). These interpersonal effects are relatively subtle, and their clinical significance is unknown; moreover, other studies suggest more "positive" interpersonal effects (Humphries *et al.*, 1978). It may be that some socially isolated children will show these drug effects more strongly than others. Perhaps a sensitive clinical evaluation of such children's interpersonal functioning may indicate that medication should not be used for them. In view of the deficits in social function that have been documented in hyperactive children, these findings assume great clinical importance.

GROWTH EFFECTS OF STIMULANTS

The marked decrease in appetite experienced by most children receiving stimulants was formerly considered a side effect that was sometimes disturbing but not a serious impediment to continuing medication. A report in 1972 by Safer, Allen, and Barr, however, described a dose-related decrement in weight velocity and, more disturbingly, in height velocity in children receiving methylphenidate or dextroamphetamine over the school year. Decrements in height were estimated to be as much as 4 cm per year. Drug holidays and decreased dose could permit "catch-up" growth. Recent studies have not definitively resolved the issue, but have put it into better perspective. A special committee from the FDA Psychopharmacological Drugs Advisory Committee, including consultants in the growth and development area, reviewed all of the current reports on long-term adverse growth effects of stimulants (Roche, Lipman, Overall, & Hung, 1979). Most of the studies were retrospective and/or did not use meticulous measures of height and weight. One study that is exceptional in its care for detail of measurement (McNutt, Boileau, & Cohen, 1977) used unusually small doses (10–15 mg of methylphenidate per day), and thus their findings may not be applicable to usual practice.

Recently, Greenhill (1979), in an open prospective study, found a greater weight and height decrement following amphetamine treatment than following methylphenidate. Of particular interest is the apparently greater effect of amphetamine on mean sleep-related prolactin, while an actual *increase* in mean sleep-related growth hormone was found with methylphenidate. However, the difference between the drugs may relate to the difference in dose. If the relatively smaller growth decrement on methylphenidate is replicated, it provides another basis for making this the drug of choice in hyperkinesis.

Taking all of these studies and reports into consideration, the consensus is that there is a clear effect of stimulants on weight gain (about 1.5 kg less than might be expected over the first 2 years) with a small effect on height gain (about .9 cm). However, tolerance to this effect seems to develop about the third year, and longer-term effects than this appear much smaller, with no apparent effect on adult stature or weight.

It is not clear whether an "ideal" prospective study can ever be done to provide a final answer to this problem. As any such studies would be conducted at reputable academic pediatric care facilities, and as good practice demands that growth be monitored prospectively for any child on stimulant and drug holidays and that dose be regulated accordingly, it is unlikely that a scientifically acceptable study could actually be carried out. However, the unimpressive long-term effects on growth from those few studies in which children who received stimulants were followed prospectively (G. Weiss, Kruger, Danielson, & Elman, 1975) suggest that there will not be the impetus for the extraordinary effort required to attempt the "right" study.

The mechanisms for the decrease in growth are at this point unknown. Certainly the most obvious mechanism, that of decreased caloric intake secondary to the anorectic effect of the drugs, needs to be examined. Unfortunately, this has not been done, probably because of the difficulty in carefully following intake even on an inpatient unit, and because such a study would need to be conducted over a relatively long time period to be meaningful. At this point, it is agreed that more careful retrospective data are in order before any more extensive long-term studies should be done.

Other mechanisms have been studied in greater detail because of the feasibility (although by no means simplicity) of these measurements. Specifically, in humans treated over 6 to 8 months with methylphenidate, the growth hormone response to L-dihydroxyphenylalanine (L-DOPA) is delayed, but there is a higher level of growth hormone after fasting. *d*-Amphetamine appears to have different effects (i.e., not stimulating growth hormone) from methylphenidate (W. A. Brown, Van Wort, & Ambani, 1973; Greenhill, Puig-Antich, & Sassin, 1977). Blood prolactin has been shown to be suppressed with stimulant drug medication (Greenhill *et al.*, 1977), but the relationship between prolactin and growth in humans is not established.

Clinically, anorexia is often striking and seems likely to be an important mechanism. While tolerance to the anorectic effect is well known in adults, the tolerance is by no means so clear in hyperactive children. A study in which children are fed during periods of drug wear-off (e.g., later in the evening than most family suppers) would be useful.

DIAGNOSTIC SPECIFICITY OF STIMULANT DRUGS

The supposed diagnostic specificity of stimulant drug response constitutes an issue of theoretical and practical importance. It is important to separate this issue from any endorsement or objection to drug treatment. Many useful drugs are nonspecific; that is, agents such as insulin, diuretics, and analgesics act similarly on persons in the well and ill states. Moreover, their mechanism of action may be on a physiological process at a separate point from that where a "diagnostic" defect can be demonstrated. A good example is that of the diuretics, which act on the healthy kidneys of cardiac patients, to alleviate the fluid retention secondary to congestive heart failure.

A series of studies at the National Institute of Mental Health (NIMH) has addressed the question of specificity of stimulant drug response, both with respect to diagnosis (e.g., hyperactive children vs. normal children) and to age (normal children vs. normal adults). A particular issue was the commonly held view that the calming effect of stimulants had a quasi-diagnostic status for the hyperkinetic syndrome. Clinicians and teachers have believed that a child must have "MBD" if he or she becomes less restless and more attentive on stimulant. Theoretically, as the drugs are known to alter neurotransmitter function, demonstration of a different drug effect between patients and controls might be used to support a model of the hyperactivity syndrome that relies on an altered drug response following a chemical or surgical brain lesion.

In spite of the speculations that age and diagnostic differences provide important clues to the pathophysiology of the hyperactive child syndrome, until recently there had been no comparison of stimulant drug effects in normal children, hyperactive children, and normal adults using the same experimental conditions.

In a study that extended over a 2-year period at the NIMH (Rapoport, Buchsbaum, Weingartner, Zahn, Ludlow, Bartko, & Mikkelsen, 1980; Rapoport, Buchsbaum, Zahn, Weingartner, Ludlow, & Mikkelsen, 1978), the response to a single dose of *d*-amphetamine was compared for normal prepubertal boys, hyperactive boys, and college-age males. The latter were divided into two groups: One was given the same per-weight dose and the second was given half the per-weight dose, approximating the absolute total dose given the children. The differences and similarities between the groups' response to medication are of interest. First, of course, there was considerable difference between the groups off medication; the hyperactive children were most restless and most inattentive, the adults the least restless and most attentive, with the normal children falling somewhere in between. Drug effects on these groups showed both similarities and differences.

The measures of greatest interest here are those most commonly used in clinical studies with hyperactive children—ratings of motor activity (actometer), vigilance (a reaction-time task and a CPT), behavior during interview, and mood. Activity was measured for the 2-hour period during the (sedentary) task, using an activity monitor worn in a vest pocket located in the small of the back. Reaction time was measured by having the subjects release a telegraph key when they heard a tone. The CPT used requires a subject to push a button when a certain combination of letters or numbers appears. The failure to do so is an omission error; pressing the button for a number outside the critical sequence (in our task, a 6–4), is a commission error. In order to permit adult–child comparisons, the task was a variable one that got faster as the subject performed accurately and slower if errors were made. In addition, observations were made on behavior during testing, and subjects completed a self-rating mood scale.

The effect of stimulants on motor activity is shown in Table 18-1. Both the groups of children had a significant decrease in activity on amphetamine; the "low-dose" group of adults had a significant decrease in motor activity. Drug–placebo activity ratio differed between hyperactive children and adults, but not between hyperactive and normal children. On the other hand, the absolute difference (i.e., change in absolute amount of activity on drug) was markedly greater for the hyperactive children, and, of course, this was the only group for which there would be expected to be clinical benefits from this action.

Drug effects on reaction time are given in Table 18-2. On placebo, hyperactive children had a longer reaction time than the other three groups. While both groups of children and the low-dose adults showed decreased reaction time on the stimulant, this change was greater for the hyperactive boys for the short preparatory interval (PI) (i.e., the task requiring only a short period of attention), and also occurred for the hyperactive children for the long PI (which did not change significantly for normal children). The CPT, a second standard vigilance measure, improved significantly for both groups of children (see Table 18-3). However, while normal children improved on omission errors (with no change in commission errors), the reverse was true for the hyperactive children. Nevertheless, as the scores were so variable on this task, there was no significant difference between the children's groups in the drug–placebo ratio.

Children and adults gave different self-report accounts of stimulant drug

Table 18-1. Amphetamine effects on motor activity (counts/2 hours)

	PLACEBO (MEAN ± *SD*)	DEXTRO-AMPHETAMINE (MEAN ± *SD*)	*F*	*df*	*p*	DRUG–PLACEBO RATIO (MEAN ± *SD*)
Normal boys	421 ± 133	284 ± 88	16.92	1, 1	< .002	.76 ± .19
Hyperactive boys	731 ± 233[b]	431 ± 204	21.98	1, 13	< .0001	.56 ± .21[c]
Adult males (high dose)	225 ± 88	222 ± 93	.14	1, 14	ns	1.03 ± .48
Adult males (low dose)[a]	134 ± 40	116 ± 27	6.64	1, 11	< .03	.91 ± .15

[a]Different activity monitor was worn by this group, so data from these subjects are not comparable to data from first three groups.

[b]Significantly different from all other placebo groups ($p < .05$).

[c]Hyperactives were significantly different from high-dose adults but *not* significantly different from normal children.

effects (see Table 18-4). In general, adults on the high or low dose experienced euphoria, while the children did not report this and, in fact, reported feeling "funny" or "tired." Whether this latter reflects a side effect of acute dosage, dysphoria, or poor skills at labeling affective states is unknown.

A summary of similarities and differences across groups indicates that while all groups tended to decrease motor activity and increase vigilance, differences in drug response across groups were also prominent. Specifically, hyperactive groups made many commission errors on the CPT off the drug (in contrast to the other groups), and it was these errors that decreased when these children were on the drug. Similarly, hyperactive children were particularly poor at the reaction-time task with the long PI (i.e., the one requiring sustained attention), and this measure improved selectively in this group and did *not* improve significantly for the other three groups. As discussed, there is an apparent difference between children and adults in the mood state induced by the drug.

The simplest conclusion is that any clear "paradoxical" effect of amphetamine, either by diagnostic group or by age, does not occur. The differences are interesting, however, and deserve to be explored further.

The lack of diagnostic specificity of stimulant drug effects raises practical and theoretical clinical questions. For example, a group of conduct-disordered children *without* motor restlessness and with age-adequate attention span may well be candidates for stimulant drug treatment. An important study waiting to be undertaken is the selection of such a group and systematic examination of it in a double-blind crossover design of clinical efficacy of a stimulant drug. As the early studies with stimulants were often of unselected delinquent populations (Eisenberg, Lachman, Molling, Lockner, Mizelle, & Conners, 1963), it seems most likely that the "pure" behavior-disordered group would, in fact, also benefit from the drug.

Table 18-2. Effects of dextroamphetamine on mean reaction time (RT) and amplitude of skin conductance response (SCR) to RT stimuli

GROUP	MEASURE	PLACEBO (MEAN ± *SD*)	DEXTRO-AMPHETAMINE (MEAN ± *SD*)	*F*	*df*	*p*	DRUG–PLACEBO RATIO (MEAN ± *SD*)
Normal boys	RT, short PI (msec)	309 ± 84[a]	278 ± 75	9.30	1, 12	.02	.92 ± .12
	RT, long PI (msec)	323 ± 102[a,b]	309 ± 102	1.29	1, 12	ns	.97 ± 10[a]
	SCR (10^{-3} mho)	.49 ± .31	.31 ± .23	6.30	1, 12	.03	.64 ± .54
Hyperactive boys	RT, short PI (msec)	425 ± 201[b,c,d]	328 ± 95	11.08	1, 13	.01	.83 ± .16[b,c,d]
	RT, long PI (msec)	445 ± 153[b,c,d]	358 ± 157	24.39	1, 13	.001	.81 ± .13[b,c,d]
	SCR (10^{-3} mho)	.45 ± .23	.46 ± .37	< 1	1, 13	ns	1.05 ± .56
Adults (.5 mg/kg)	RT, short PI (msec)	201 ± 24	199 ± 31	< 1	1, 13	ns	.99 ± .08
	RT, long PI (msec)	206 ± 28	211 ± 33	< 1	1, 12	ns	1.03 ± .08
	SCR (10^{-3} mho)	.57 ± .46	.37 ± .26	3.11	1, 13	ns	.82 ± .84
Adults (.25 mg/kg)	RT, short PI (msec)	221 ± 26	216 ± 38	< 1	1, 14	ns	.98 ± .12
	RT, long PI (msec)	242 ± 34	226 ± 37	5.59	1, 14	.03	.94 ± .10
	SCR (10^{-3} mho)	.49 ± .34	.38 ± .27	4.24	1, 14	.06	1.18 ± 1.35

[a]Different from hyperactive boys ($p < .05$).

[b]Different from high-dose adults ($p < .05$).

[c]Different from low-dose adults ($p < .05$).

[d]Different from normal boys ($p < .05$).

PHARMACOKINETIC STUDIES OF STIMULANT TREATMENT OF HYPERACTIVE CHILDREN

The increasing sophistication of psychopharmacologists with respect to basic issues in pharmacology has led to an appreciation of the fact that how a medication works may be understood better through a knowledge of how a drug is handled by the body. For example, if a drug is absorbed in an idiosyncratic or highly variable manner, then prediction of clinical response from behavioral variables alone will probably not be fruitful, unless plasma concentration and/or drug half-life is known.

Recent studies describing some of the absorption–elimination characteristics of *d*-amphetamine have been conducted by G. Brown, Ebert, and coworkers at the NIH (G. Brown, Ebert, Mikkelsen, & Hunt, 1979, 1980; G. Brown, Hunt, Ebert, Bunney, & Kopin, 1979). Of greatest clinical interest is that unlike, for example, tricyclic antidepressants or phenothiazines, amphetamine has a relatively homogeneous plasma concentration for a given per-weight dose (one- to two-fold difference across children); and that the half-life (about 7 hours) is considerably greater than the time of important clinical effects that seem to occur during the 2- to 3-hour absorption phase (i.e., during the time that plasma concentration is on the rise), but is not correlated with specific plasma levels of the drug. Speculations about this phenomenon include a decreased clinical response to the drug over time due to depleted catecholamine stores, replacement by a false neurotransmitter, or alteration in receptor sensitivity.

Of clinical interest is the study by G. Brown *et al.* (1980), in which sustained release capsules of amphetamine were studied pharmacokinetically. The authors did *not* find a greater or more prolonged clinical response than that with regular tablets. The observations were made on only nine children and in a setting where school took place only in the mornings. If this finding can

Table 18-3. Dextroamphetamine effects on vigilance task (CPT)

GROUP	MEASURE	PLACEBO[a] (MEAN ± *SD*)	DEXTRO-AMPHETAMINE[a] (MEAN ± *SD*)	*F*	*df*	*p* (2-TAILED)	DRUG–PLACEBO RATIO (MEAN ± *SD*)
Normal children	Commission errors	6.7 ± 6.0	6.5 ± 2.7	.50	1, 13	ns	1.43 ± .88
	Omission errors	7.5 ± 4.9	5.9 ± 2.9	4.94	1, 13	< .05	.84 ± .28
	Interstimulus interval	404 ± 194	340 ± 67	2.44	1, 13	ns	.92 ± .20
Hyperactive children	Commission errors	47.7 ± 70.9[b,c,d]	17.5 ± 29.4	6.91	1, 14	< .05	.85 ± 1.22
	Omission errors	12.6 ± 7.4[c,d]	11.1 ± 7.1	4.20	1, 14	< .10	.89 ± .25
	Interstimulus interval	702 ± 308[b,c,d]	547 ± 272	7.28	1, 14	< .02	.82 ± .24[d]
Adults (.5 mg/kg)	Commission errors	3.9 ± 2.2	4.2 ± 2.1	.51	1, 14	ns	1.21 ± .73
	Omission errors	5.4 ± 2.7	4.2 ± 2.2	7.07	1, 14	< .02	.77 ± .33
	Interstimulus interval	331 ± 114	290 ± 31	4.21	1, 14	< .10	.90 ± .15
Adults (.25 mg/kg)	Commission errors	4.1 ± 3.2	4.7 ± 3.8	.59	1, 15	ns	1.12 ± .60
	Omission errors	4.6 ± 2.2[b]	4.8 ± 2.1	.02	1, 15	ns	1.25 ± .84
	Interstimulus interval	291 ± 27[b]	311 ± 88	.59	1, 15	ns	1.07 ± .31

[a]Drug–placebo analyses of variance (ANOVAs) done on log-transformed data.

[b]Different from normal children ($p < .05$).

[c]Different from high-dose adults ($p < .05$).

[d]Different from low-dose adults ($p < .05$).

be replicated in a more naturalistic setting, it will have considerable practical importance, as spansules are more expensive and not available at all in some public dispensaries.

Methylphenidate is generally considered the drug of choice in hyperactive children (see below), and therefore perhaps of greatest interest are those pharmacokinetic studies of this drug. Recently, Greenhill (1979) has reported that the maximal clinical effect of methylphenidate, as measured by a perceptual–motor task, corresponded to the absorption phase of the drug rather than to peak plasma concentrations. This finding is analogous with that of Brown and coworkers, again suggesting that catecholamine *release* mediates the clinical action of the stimulants.

Perel, Winsburg, and coworkers (Hungund, Perel, Hurwic, Sverd, & Winsberg, 1979) have reported relatively low binding to protein of methylphenidate, which may account for the brief duration of action, with peak effects being reported for methylphenidate at 1 to 2 hours after ingestion of the drug. Hungund *et al.* found an even more brief half-life for methylphenidate in the four case studies (2–3 hours), but this has not been replicated elsewhere. Clinically, there is no consensus as to whether amphetamine or methylphenidate

Table 18-4. Significant effects of dextroamphetamine on self-report mood scale (child version)

GROUP	ITEM	PLACEBO (MEAN ± *SD*)	DEXTRO-AMPHETAMINE (MEAN ± *SD*)	*F*	*df*	*p*
Normal boys	Feel funny, not like myself	.50 ± .94	1.64 ± 1.08	8.21	1, 12	< .02
Hyperactive boys	Feel tired or cranky	.73 ± .88	1.27 ± 1.03	5.69	1, 13	< .04
	Feel funny, not like myself	.40 ± .83	1.00 ± 1.13	6.26	1, 13	< .03
Adult males (.5 mg/kg)	Feel tired or cranky	.87 ± .92	.13 ± .35	8.24	1, 13	< .013
	Feel restless	.29 ± .47	1.40 ± 1.12	18.50	1, 13	< .008
	Feel like I don't want to play with anyone	.60 ± .74	.07 ± .26	7.19	1, 13	< .02
	Feel like talking more than usual	.20 ± .41	1.54 ± .92	29.00	1, 13	< .0001
	Feel happy	1.60 ± .83	2.20 ± .56	9.45	1, 13	< .008
	Feel funny, not like myself	.13 ± .35	.80 ± .86	8.18	1, 13	< .013
	Feel like my thoughts are going fast	.33 ± .49	1.20 ± .94	7.87	1, 13	< .014
	Feel like I have a lot of energy	.40 ± .63	1.73 ± 1.03	17.84	1, 13	< .0009
	Feel tired and slow	.93 ± .88	.07 ± .26	15.41	1, 13	< .001
	Feel like I'm doing a pretty good job	1.27 ± .80	2.13 ± .74	13.64	1, 13	< .002
	Feel friendly	1.53 ± .74	2.27 ± .59	17.47	1, 13	< .001
Adult males (.25 mg/kg)	Feel tired or cranky	1.37 ± .80	.56 ± .62	13.75	1, 14	< .002
	Feel in a good mood	1.31 ± .60	1.94 ± .77	7.12	1, 14	< .02
	Feel like I have a lot of energy	.25 ± .44	1.00 ± .96	5.71	1, 14	< .03
	Feel like my thoughts are going fast	.12 ± .34	.68 ± 1.08	6.08	1, 14	< .03
	Feel like talking more than usual	.18 ± .40	.81 ± .65	10.95	1, 14	< .005
	Feel tired and slow	1.43 ± .96	.62 ± .95	8.68	1, 14	< .01
	Feel happy	1.25 ± .77	1.75 ± .44	6.32	1, 14	< .02

acts for the longer time period. The immediate and brief action of methylphenidate also suggests that the main effects may take place during the absorption phase, rather than in relation to peak plasma concentration.

COMPARISON OF STIMULANT DRUG TREATMENT WITH BEHAVIORAL THERAPIES

Initial decisions about medication are made with respect to short-term gains. Long-term benefits of medication have not been demonstrated, and the ideal study to compare different treatments may not be ethically or strategically feasible.

There have been several studies, therefore, designed to compare the short-term effects of medication in comparison with those of behavioral treatment (see also Chapters 19 and 21 of this volume). These questions arose both from a natural preference for nondrug treatment of children, as well as from the claims for changes in impulsive–hyperactive behaviors at home and at school with the use of behavioral reinforcements (O'Leary, Pelham, Rosenbaum, & Price, 1976; Patterson, Jones, Whittier, & Wright, 1965) similar to that achieved by stimulants.

There have been several individual case reports demonstrating efficacy of behavioral treatment, but only a few group treatment reports in which behavioral and drug treatment were compared, which are of more general clinical interest.

Wolraich, Drummon, Salomon, O'Brien, and Sivage (1978) studied 20 hyperactive 6- to 9-year-olds. Half were placed on placebo and half on methylphenidate (.3 mg/kg). During the 6 weeks of the study, there were 2-week baseline, treatment, and reversal periods. The study is unique in that a special class and teacher were organized for the purpose of the study, thus insuring homogeneity of teacher response to the study (although thereby making the study less naturalistic and possibly less clinically relevant). Classroom procedures included token economy, with awards for attentive, nondisruptive behavior as well as for academic achievement. Teachers and coders were not blind as to period of behavior modification or nontreatment. Results were equivocal, as such behaviors as inappropriate vocalization and nonattending did not decrease as a function of behavior modification but worsened when behavior modification stopped. More tangible benefits resulted from medication. Behavior modification alone affected the "academic" measures (copying letters on blackboard and correct responses on an "insert" class task). The authors found that group work was most affected by behavior modification while seat work was most affected by the drug; there were no interactions between the treatments.

Loney, Weissenburger, Woolson, and Lichty (1979) studied a small number of hyperactive boys—four on methylphenidate (20–40 mg/day) and eight during behavioral treatment. On- and off-task behaviors were recorded in the subjects and in three classmates who were overactive, average, and "model." Behavioral intervention was in the form of consultation with the classroom teacher to increase approval of on-task behaviors, ignore off-task behaviors, and so on. Results suggested that behaviorally treated children showed a change comparable to that of the drug-treated group, and that this effect spread to other classmates as well, while pharmacological effects did not.

Gittelman, Abikoff, Pollack, Klein, Katz, and Maltes (1980), in the most extensive comparison to date, studied a total of 61 children who were treated for 8 weeks with methylphenidate, or with behavior modification and placebo. The study approximated the most widely used behavioral approach, that of home and school consultation, with additional support and discussion of family problems ongoing throughout. Moreover, in addition to parent and teacher ratings, extensive classroom observations were made by observers blind to the treatment groups of the children. The three groups all improved when pre- and posttreatment ratings were compared. However, all ratings favored drug treatment; behavioral treatment added to the family and teacher perception of change, but this perception was out of proportion to the actual change documented by direct observation.

None of these studies is ideal; all are limited in time and to the particular type of behavioral intervention. Moreover, drug dose varied considerably among the studies. The impression from these studies is, however, that methylphenidate is probably a more powerful short-term treatment, while the long-term advantages of either treatment cannot be assessed from present data.

ALTERNATE MEDICATIONS TO STIMULANTS

In view of concern about side effects, the availability of addicting drugs to children and their families, and the number of nonresponders to stimulants, there is continual interest in alternate drugs to use with hyperactive children. Perhaps the most interesting and "acceptable" substance has been caffeine, as this is a "natural" dietary ingredient felt to be less toxic than stimulants.

Caffeine

Since Schnackenberg's report in 1973 (see Table 18-5), there has been a steady interest in the use of caffeine for hyperactive children. This issue has broad appeal, as a "diet" rather than a pharmacological manipulation is invoked. The studies of caffeine in pediatric populations are summarized in Table 18-5. Two of these studies are with normal children, while the others are with hyperkinetic populations. The main point from the studies reviewed in Table 18-5 is that the clinical effects at low to moderate doses are lacking or insignificant, while at slightly higher doses (e.g., 10 mg/kg) there seems to be an actual *increase* in motor restlessness. There is considerable theoretical interest in the latter finding, as increased vigilance is usually thought to lead to decreased motor restlessness (during sedentary tasks), while the study employing the higher dose (Elkins, Rapoport, Zahn, Buchsbaum, Weingartner, Kopin, Langer, & Johnson, 1981) demonstrated that increased vigilance and increased restlessness could be brought about simultaneously by the same pharmacological agent.

As there is little margin between the dose of approximately 6 mg/kg (which shows little or no clinical effect) and the dose of 10 mg/kg (which produced increased restlessness and anxiety in a normal population), it seems unlikely that caffeine will prove useful in the hyperactive child syndrome. This stimulant effect is of considerable general interest, however, as the amount of caffeine that many children (both normal and disturbed) consume in cola beverages, tea, chocolate, and so forth, borders on the dose known to produce CNS disturbance (Life Sciences Research Office, 1978). Only chronic studies will be useful in answering the question of such dietary influences on behavior. It is conceivable, however, that some individual cases of hyperactivity are related to excessive dietary caffeine intake in children.

Tricyclic Antidepressants

Of the wide variety of other medications that have been tried in the hyperkinetic syndrome, some of the most careful work has been with the tricyclic antidepressants. Shortly after tricyclics began to be used for enuresis, reports on the use of the drugs in hyperactive and/or aggresive children claimed similar therapeutic effects to those found with stimulants (Krakowski, 1965, Rapoport, 1965). More recently, controlled trials have generally confirmed these initial

Table 18-5. Caffeine: Behavioral studies with child populations

AUTHOR(S)	*n*	SAMPLE	DRUG/DOSE	DESIGN	MEASURES	RESULTS AND COMMENTS
Firestone, Davey, Goodwin, & Peters (1978)	21	Hyperactive	Caffeine, 300 + 500 mg; M-P, 20 mg; placebo	Crossover (3-week period)	MFF, Porteus Maze, reaction-time test, Conners Rating Scale (Parent + Teacher) (Abbrev.)	No difference between caffeine and placebo on any measure for either dose; M-P superior to placebo.
Campbell, Reichard, & Elder (1977)	12	6 normal, 6 hyperactive	Caffeine, single dose, 6 mg/kg; upper limit of 200 mg; placebo	Crossover	Reaction-time test	No difference for normal sample on (1) mean reaction time; (2) initial reaction time; (3) number of correct responses per block of trials. Hyperactives' rate for (3) was *higher* for caffeine than placebo.
Schnackenberg (1973)	11	Hyperactive	Regular coffee, 200–300 mg/day; M-P, 20 mg/day	Crossover, uncontrolled	David's Scale, interviews	On parent and teacher interviews and David's Scale, caffeine superior to placebo ($p < .01$).
Gross (1975)	25	Hyperactive	Caffeine, 100–400 mg/day; placebo; Tofranil; M-P; *d*-amphetamine	1 week on each of 5 drugs; single-blind, no control for order effect	Parent reports	No benefit from caffeine. Stimulants superior to placebo.
Garfinkel, Webster, & Sloman (1975)	8	Hyperactive, aged 6–12	Caffeine, 160 mg; M-P, 20 mg; placebo	Crossover (10-day sessions)	Conners Scale (Abbrev.), Bender-Gestalt, Frostig, MFF	No difference between caffeine and placebo; M-P superior to placebo.
Huestis, Arnold, & Smeltzer (1975)	18	Hyperactive	Caffeine, 300 mg; M-P, 40 mg; *d*-amphetamine, 20 mg; placebo	Crossover (2 weeks)	David's Scale, Conners Scale (Parent + Teacher) (Abbrev.)	No difference. M-P + amphetamine superior to placebo.

open studies and demonstrated the beneficial effect of tricyclics in doses from 2 to 5 mg/kg for restless, antisocial behavior (Greenberg, Yellin, Spring, & Metcalf, 1975; Kupietz & Balka, 1976; Rapoport, Quinn, Bradbard, Riddle, & Brooks, 1974; Waizer, Hoffman, Polizos, & Engelhardt, 1974; Werry, Aman, & Diamond, 1979; Winsberg, Bialer, Kupietz, & Tobias, 1972; Yepes, Balka, Winsberg, & Bialer, 1977). This response is immediate and, in some cases, dramatic; most of these studies, however, have shown methylphenidate or amphetamine to be superior to tricyclics. The controlled clinical trials are summarized in Table 18-6.

Inasmuch as all of these controlled studies are short-term (4 weeks or less), the long-term usefulness of tricyclics for these disorders remains controversial. In an open study, Gittelman-Klein (1974) indicated that an initial response to a daily dose of 150 to 300 mg of imipramine seen at 2 weeks was not maintained at 12 weeks. Similarly, in a 1-year follow-up (Quinn & Rapoport, 1975), significantly more hyperactive children had discontinued tricyclic medication than methylphenidate, even when both groups had shown an initial response

Table 18-5. (Continued)

AUTHOR(S)	*n*	SAMPLE	DRUG/DOSE	DESIGN	MEASURES	RESULTS AND COMMENTS
Conners (1975)	8	Hyperactive	Caffeine, 3–12 mg/kg over 3-week period; placebo	Crossover (3 weeks)	Conners Scale (Parent + Teacher) (Abbrev.), reaction-time test, CPT	No statistical analysis, but no advantage for caffeine seen over placebo for individual children. Side effects negligible.
Firestone, Poitras-Wright, & Douglas (1978)	20	Hyperactive, aged 6–12	Caffeine, 300 mg/day; placebo	Crossover (2 weeks)	Conners Scale (Parent + Teacher) (Abbrev.), reaction-time test, Porteus Maze, MFF	*Caffeine superior to* placebo for parent and teacher ratings, but for *only one order*. Fewer "false starts on reaction-time task; otherwise, no difference in reaction time or tests.
Arnold, Christopher, Huestis, & Smeltzer (1978)	29	Hyperactive	Caffeine, 200–300 mg/day; placebo; amphetamine, 5–30 mg/day; M-P, 10–60 mg/day	Crossover (3 weeks per drug period)	David's Scale, Conners Scale (Parent + Teacher)	No difference between caffeine and placebo on most reusers. Caffeine superior to placebo on one parent rating.
Conners (1979)	17	Hyperactive	Caffeine, 3 mg/kg; placebo, 6 mg/kg	Crossover (single dose)	Actometer vigilance task	No significance found for improvement on caffeine.
Elkins, Rapoport, Zahn, Buchsbaum, Weingartner, Kopin, Langer, & Johnson (1981)	19	Normal	Caffeine, 3–10 mg/kg; placebo	Crossover (single dose)	CPT interview, activity	High dose of caffeine *increased* activity and *increased* vigilance. Low dose had no significant effect.

Note. Clarification of abbreviations: M-P, methylphenidate; MFF, Matching Familiar Figures Test; CPT, continuous-performance test.

after 6 weeks. It is my experience that long-term treatment of conduct-disordered or hyperkinetic children with tricyclics is unsatisfactory; this point deserves further study. Attempts to predict imipramine response in hyperactive children on the basis of clinical examination or history were unsuccessful (Rapoport *et al.*, 1974). For example, while about 25% of the sample of hyperactive boys showed some depressive symptomatology, this subgroup was not differentially responsive to tricyclic medication; also, a positive family history of depressive disorder was not predictive of response.

Because of the extensive work relating plasma tricyclic concentration to clinical effect with adult depression, it is of natural interest if such relationships could be demonstrated for hyperactive child populations treated with tricyclics.

Winsberg, Perel, Hurwiz, and Klutzch (1974) first presented data from a single case of a hyperactive boy for whom plasma tricyclic concentration (imipramine + desmethylimipramine) was followed serially with classroom and ward observational data over an 11-day period. There seemed to be some relationship between the continued change in behavior and plasma concentration over time. However, the authors stress (as noted previously) that the clinical effect of tricyclics are immediate, within 1 to 2 hours of the initial dose, and detailed studies of single-dose pharmacokinetics have not been reported in children.

Winsberg *et al.* (1974) then reported a wide range of values (from 50 to 500 ng/ml) in children receiving the same per-weight dose. One study of seven hospitalized aggressive prepubertal boys indicated that clinical improvement (i.e., decreased deviant behavior on the ward and increased attentiveness in the hospital school) correlated with plasma tricyclic concentration (Winsberg, Perel, Yepes, & Botti, 1977).

Linnoila and coworkers (Linnoila, Linnoila, Gaultieri, Jobsonik, & Staye, 1979) have shown that with chronic imipramine treatment of hyperactive children, tolerance to the clinical effect of tricyclics occurs in spite of adequate plasma–drug concentrations. Tolerance to tricyclics is unknown in adult psychopharmacology and occurs at about the time when an antidepressant effect of

Table 18-6. Tricyclic antidepressants: Controlled clinical trials with hyperactive–aggressive children

AUTHORS	*n*	AGE	DRUG	DOSE	DURATION	COMMENTS
Winsberg, Bialer, Kupietz, & Tobias (1972)	32	9.1	IMI Amphetamine	150 mg/day 20 mg/day	10 days	IMI > PL; amphetamine > IMI for hyperactivity.
Rapoport, Quinn, Bradbard, Riddle, & Brooks (1974)	IMI, 29 PL, 18 M-P, 29	9	IMI M-P	80 mg/day 20 mg/day	6 weeks 6 weeks	IMI > PL; trend for M-P > IMI; M-P > PL.
Waizer, Hoffman, Polizos, & Engelhardt (1974)	19	10	IMI	100 mg/day	2 weeks	IMI > PL on teacher and parent ratings.
Greenberg, Yellin, Spring, & Metcalf (1975)	IMI–PL, 25 M-P–PL, 25	9	IMI M-P	100 mg/day 40 mg/day	2 weeks	IMI > PL; M-P > PL; IMI = M-P.
Kupietz & Balka (1976); Yepes, Balka, Winsberg, & Bialer (1977)	22	9.2	AMI M-P	92 mg/day 40 mg/day	2 weeks	AMI > PL on attentional measures and AMI = M-P on behavior ratings (CPT).
Werry, Aman, & Diamond (1979)	30	8.5	IMI M-P	1 or 2 mg/kg .4 mg/kg	4 weeks	IMI > PL; M-P > PL; M-P > IMI. Clinical global impression favored IMI.

Note. Clarification of abbreviations: AMI, amitriptyline; IMI, imipramine; M-P, methylphenidate; PL, placebo.

the drug might occur. This "inverse" relationship, (i.e., of immediate response with frequent "wear-off") is of considerable theoretical interest and should be studied pharmacodynamically. While of great theoretical appeal, tricyclics are not likely to play an important role in the treatment of the hyperkinetic syndrome.

A series of studies over the past 12 years has demonstrated some efficacy for Thorazine (Werry, Weiss, Douglas, & Martin, 1966; G. Weiss, Werry, Minde, Douglas, & Sykes, 1968), thioridazine (Gittelman-Klein, Klein, Katz, Saraf, & Pollack, 1976), and haloperidol (Werry & Aman, 1975); that is, there is a decrease in activity and in impulsive behaviors following phenothiazine treatment of hyperactive children. However, in general, beneficial effects of phenothiazines on attention and learning have been lacking.

On the other hand, Werry and Aman (1975) demonstrated a beneficial effect of haloperidol on both attention and behavior when a quite low dose (.05 mg/kg) was used rather than a high one (.25 mg/kg). As there has been growing recognition that tardive dyskinesias can and do occur in children (Winsberg & Yepes, 1978), and as stimulants are generally regarded as more effective, the phenothiazines have been used less and less in recent years.

When a child appears to have continued evening behavior problems, however, for which stimulants might not be appropriate because of the stimulant side effects, it is still common for clinicians to add a phenothiazine as a second drug. In a large outpatient study addressing this issue (Gittelman-Klein *et al.*, 1976), it was shown that the combination of thioridazine and methylphenidate was better than either drug alone was for behavior problems that occur at home, although the benefits on laboratory tests of cognition seen with methylphenidate were not found with thioridazine. Presumably, the preference by parents for the antipsychotics is due to the longer duration of action of these drugs, in contrast to the action of the stimulants, which have usually worn off by the time a child returns home from school.

In general, with the growing concern about tardive dyskinesia and the lack of facilitation of learning, these drugs should be regarded as secondary and supplementary to stimulants in their usefulness in the hyperactivity syndrome.

LONG-TERM BENEFITS OF STIMULANT DRUG TREATMENT

A final and most important question in relation to drug treatment of the hyperkinetic syndrome is whether or not there are long-term benefits from drug treatment.

It would seem that with such a clear short-term effect—an effect that has kept children in regular classes, in good foster homes, and in relative control of aggressive, antisocial behavior—that there might be some consensus on the long-term benefit of stimulant drug treatment. In fact, this is not the case. Follow-up studies range widely in their reported pathology of hyperactive children as adults. This is probably due to the variety of children described as "hyperactive" for whom associated aggression, "borderline" symptoms, and degree of social deprivation may well be more important prognostic features than their "restless, inattentive" core problems. As follow-up studies are discussed in detail in Chapter 20, they are not considered further here. The main point, however, is that there is no agreed-upon outcome against which to assess treatment.

A second and more important problem in assessing long-term effects of stimulants is that of adequate controls, with random assignment to treatment or to a long-term placebo control. It is obvious that ethical and logistical reasons prevent such a study. However, the only study to come to grips with long-term treatment comparisons is that of G. Weiss *et al.* (1975), in which the 5-year outcome was compared for three groups of children who had been treated with either methylphenidate, chlorpromazine, or no medication. Subjects had received drug treatment for from 18 months to 5 years of this period. No statistically significant differences were found on measures of emotional adjustment, delinquency, intelligence, and academic performance. It is difficult to reconcile the difference between the short-term and long-term results. It is certainly not that tolerance to behavioral effects takes place, as even after several years cessation of drug treatment brings immediate protests from school and family.

It is important that short-term benefits not be dismissed even if long-term benefits are not demonstrated. The reduction in discomfort of families and children has evident inherent merit. Tricyclic antidepressants do not alter future course of (untreated) depression, but are still an important tool in the treatment of depression. It may be that the inherent limitations of impulsivity, inattentiveness, and learning disability are so pervasive in their effects that temporary symptomatic change is insufficient to alter long-term adjustment.

CONCLUSIONS

It is now generally accepted that stimulant drugs are efficacious in decreasing restless, impulsive behaviors and improving attention span in hyperactive/behavior-disordered children. More recent concerns are with the relative lack of effect of stimulants on academic achievement and on interpersonal functioning. Initial concerns about the effects of stimulants on growth have been somewhat eased by the knowledge that drug holidays may reduce long-term growth effects and that there is apparent tolerance to drug effect on growth with long-term usage.

There is increasing question about the diagnostic significance of stimulant drug efficacy, and this may lead to even broader use of the drugs on a more empirical basis. Specifically, it may be that other impulsive groups without accompanying restlessness or inattention will benefit from the drugs.

Whether or not a stimulant drug effect is "specific," the question of the mechanism of drug action is still important for understanding the biology of behavior. A new approach to this question has been provided by the study of the pharmacokinetics of stimulants. The short-term action of stimulants suggests that acute catecholamine release may be crucial for their effect. Future studies of the efficacy of metabolites of amphetamine or methylphenidate may provide cues to their mechanism of action.

Stimulant drugs remain clearly the drugs of choice, and usually the treatment of choice, for hyperkinetic children. Both in comparison with behavior therapies and in comparison with other agents, stimulants seem superior. These consistent results make the apparent lack of long-term benefit puzzling; continued research into this question should be a high priority for the field.

Aman, M., & Sprague, R. The state-dependent effects of methylphenidate and dextroamphetamine. *Journal of Nervous and Mental Disease*, 1974, *158*, 268–279.

Arnold, L. E., Christopher, J., Huestis, R., & Smeltzer, M. Methylphenidate vs. dextroamphetamine vs. caffeine in minimal brain dysfunction. *Archives of General Psychiatry*, 1978, *35*, 463–473.

Barkley, R. A review of stimulant drug research with hyperactive children. *Journal of Child Psychology and Psychiatry*, 1977, *18*, 137–165.

Barkley, R., & Cunningham, C. The effect of methylphenidate on the mother–child interaction and hyperactive children. *Archives of General Psychiatry*, 1979, *36*, 201–208.

Brown, G., Ebert, M., Mikkelsen, E., & Hunt, R. Clinical pharmacology of *d*-amphetamine in hyperactive children. In L. A. Gottschalk (Ed.), *Pharmacokinetics and clinical response*. New York: Spectrum, 1979.

Brown, G., Ebert, M., Mikkelsen, E., & Hunt, R. Behavior and motor activity response in hyperactive children and plasma amphetamine levels following a sustained release preparation. *Journal of the American Academy of Child Psychiatry*, 1980, *19*, 225–239.

Brown, G., Hunt, R., Ebert, M., Bunney, W. E., Jr., & Kopin, I. J. Plasma levels of *d*-amphetamine in hyperactive children: Serial behavior and motor response. *Psychopharmacology*, 1979, *62*, 133–140.

Brown, W. A., Van Wort, M. H., & Ambani, L. M. Effect of apomorphine on growth hormone release in humans. *Journal of Clinical Endocrinology and Metabolism*, 1973, *37*, 463–465.

Campbell, C., Reichard, M., & Elder, T. The effects of caffeine on reaction time in hyperkinetic and normal children. *American Journal of Psychiatry*, 1977, *134*, 144–148.

Conners, C. K. A teacher rating scale for use in drug studies with hyperactive children. *American Journal of Psychiatry*, 1969, *126*, 884–888.

Conners, C. K. A placebo crossover study of caffeine treatment of hyperkinetic children. *International Journal of Mental Health*, 1975, *4*, 132–143.

Conners, C. K. The acute effects of caffeine on evoked response, vigilance and activity level in hyperkinetic children. *Journal of Abnormal Child Psychology*, 1979, *7*, 145–151.

Douglas, V. I., & Peters, K. G. Toward a clearer definition of the attentional deficit of hyperactive children. In G. Hale & M. Lewis (Eds.), *Attention and the development of cognitive skills*. New York: Plenum Press, 1979.

Eisenberg, L., Lachman, R., Molling, P., Lockner, A., Mizelle, J., & Conners, C. A psychopharmacologic experiment in a training school for delinquent boys. *American Journal of Orthopsychiatry*, 1963, *33*, 431–447.

Elkins, R., Rapoport, J., Zahn, T., Buchsbaum, M., Weingartner, H., Kopin, I., Langer, D., & Johnson, C. Acute effects of caffeine on normal prepubertal boys. *American Journal of Psychiatry*, 1981, *138*, 178–183.

Firestone, P., Davey, J., Goodwin, J., & Peters, S. The effects of caffeine and methylphenidate on hyperactive children. *Journal of the American Academy of Child Psychiatry*, 1978, *17*, 445–456.

Firestone, P., Poitras-Wright, H., & Douglas, V. Caffeine as a therapeutic agent for hyperactivity. *Journal of Learning Disabilities*, 1978, *11*, 133–141.

Garfinkel, B., Webster, C., & Sloman, L. Methylphenidate and caffeine in the treatment of children with minimal brain dysfunction. *American Journal of Psychiatry*, 1975, *132*, 723–728.

Gittelman, R., Abikoff, H., Pollack, E., Klein, D., Katz, S., & Maltes, J. A controlled trial of behavior modification and methylphenidate in hyperactive children. In C. Whalen & B. Henker (Eds.), *Hyperactive children: The social ecology of identification and treatment*. New York: Academic Press, 1980.

Gittelman-Klein, R. Pilot clinical trial of imipramine in hyperkinetic children. In C. Conners (Ed.), *Clinical use of stimulant drugs in children*. The Hague: Excerpta Medica, 1974.

Gittelman-Klein, R., & Klein, D. F. Methylphenidate effects in learning disabilities. *Archives of General Psychiatry*, 1976, *33*, 655–664.

Gittelman-Klein, R., Klein, D., Katz, S., Saraf, K., & Pollack, E. Comparative effects of methylphenidate and thioridazine in hyperkinetic children. *Archives of General Psychiatry*, 1976, *33*, 1217–1231.

Greenberg, L., Yellin, A., Spring, C., & Metcalf, M. Clinical effects of imipramine and methylphenidate in hyperactive children. *International Journal of Mental Health*, 1975, *4*, 144–156.

Greenhill, L. *Growth and hormone responses in hyperkinetic males treated with methylphenidate.* Paper presented at the meeting of the American Academy of Child Psychiatry, Atlanta, October 1979.

Greenhill, L., Puig-Antich, K., & Sassin, J. Hormone and growth response in hyperkinetic children on stimulant medication. *Psychopharmacology Bulletin*, 1977, *12*, 33–34.

Gross, M. Caffeine in the treatment of children with minimal brain dysfunction or hyperkinetic syndrome. *Psychosomatics*, 1975, *16*, 26–27.

Huestis, R., Arnold, L. E., & Smeltzer, D. Caffeine versus methylphenidate in hyperkinetic children. *American Journal of Psychiatry*, 1975, *132*, 868–870.

Humphries, T., Kinsbourne, M., & Swanson, J. Stimulant effects on cooperation and social interaction between hyperactive children and their mothers. *Journal of Child Psychology and Psychiatry*, 1978, *19*, 13–22.

Hungund, B., Perel, J., Hurwic, M., Sverd, J., & Winsberg, B. Pharmacokinetics of methylphenidate in hyperactive children. *British Journal of Clinical Pharmacology*, 1979, *8*, 581–576.

Klein, D. F., Gittelman, R., Quitkin, F., & Rifkin, A. *Diagnosis and drug treatment of psychiatric disorders: Adults and children.* Baltimore: Williams & Wilkins, 1980.

Krakowski, A. Amitriptyline in treatment of hyperkinetic children: A double-blind study. *Psychosomatics*, 1965, *6*, 355–360.

Kupietz, S., & Balka, E. Alterations in vigilance performance of children receiving amitriptyline and methylphenidate pharmacotherapy. *Psychopharmacology*, 1976, *50*, 24–33.

Life Sciences Research Office. *Evaluation of health aspects of caffeine as a food ingredient, 1978* (prepared for the Bureau of Food, Federal Drug Administration). Bethesda, Md.: Federation of American Societies for Experimental Biology, 1978.

Linnoila, M. Personal communication, 1979.

Linnoila, M., Gaultieri, T., Jobsonik, V., Staye, J. Characteristics of the therapeutic response to imipramine in hyperactive children. *American Journal of Psychiatry*, 1979, *136*, 1201–1203.

Loney, J., Weissenburger, F., Woolson, R., & Lichty, E. C. Comparing psychological and pharmacological treatments for hyperkinetic boys and their classmates. *Journal of Abnormal Child Psychology*, 1979, *7*, 133–143.

McNutt, B., Boileau, R., & Cohen, M. The effects of long-term stimulant medication on the growth and body composition of hyperactive children: II. Report of 2 years. *Psychopharmacology Bulletin*, 1977, *13*, 36–37.

O'Leary, K., Pelham, W., Rosenbaum, A., & Price, G. Behavioral treatment of hyperkinetic children: An experimental evaluation of its usefulness. *Clinical Pediatrics*, 1976, *15*, 274–279.

Patterson, G., Jones, R., Whittier, J., & Wright, M. A behavior modification technique for the hyperactive child. *Behaviour Research and Therapy*, 1965, *2*, 217–226.

Quinn, P. O., & Rapoport, J. A 1-year followup of hyperactive boys treated with imipramine or methylphenidate. *American Journal of Psychiatry*, 1975, *132*, 241–245.

Rapoport, J. Unpublished data, 1964.

Rapoport, J. Childhood behavior and learning problems treated with imipramine. *International Journal of Neuropsychiatry*, 1965, *1*, 635–642.

Rapoport, J., Buchsbaum, M., Weingartner, H., Zahn, T., Ludlow, C., Bartko, J., & Mikkelsen, E. J. Dextroamphetamine: Cognitive and behavioral effects in normal and hyperactive boys and normal adult males. *Archives of General Psychiatry*, 1980, *37*, 933–943.

Rapoport, J., Buchsbaum, M., Zahn, T., Weingartner, H., Ludlow, L., & Mikkelsen, E. Dextroamphetamine: Behavioral and cognitive effects in normal prepubertal boys. *Science*, 1978, *199*, 560–563.

Rapoport, J., Quinn, P., Bradbard, G., Riddle, K., & Brooks, E. Imipramine and methylphenidate treatment of hyperactive boys. *Archives of General Psychiatry*, 1974, *30*, 789–794.

Rie, H., Rie, E., Stewart, S., & Ambrel, J. Effects of methylphenidate on underachieving children. *Journal of Consulting and Clinical Psychology*, 1976, *44*, 250–260. (a)

Rie, H., Rie, E., Stewart, S., & Ambuel, J. Effects of Ritalin on underachieving children: A replication. *American Journal of Orthopsychiatry*, 1976, *46*, 313–322. (b)

Roche, A., Lipman, R., Overall, J., & Hung, W. The effects of stimulant medication on the growth of hyperkinetic children. *Pediatrics*, 1979, *63*, 647–650.

Safer, D., Allen, R., & Barr, E. Depression of growth in hyperactive children on stimulant drugs. *New England Journal of Medicine*, 1972, *257*, 217–221.

Schnackenberg, R. Caffeine as a substitute for schedule II stimulants in hyperkinetic children. *American Journal of Psychiatry*, 1973, *130*, 796–798.

Swanson, G., & Kinsbourne, M. Stimulant related state-dependent learning in hyperactive children. *Science*, 1976, *192*, 1354–1356.

Waizer, J., Hoffman, S., Polizos, P., & Engelhardt, D. Outpatient treatment of hyperactive school children with imipramine. *American Journal of Psychiatry*, 1974, *131*, 587–591.

Weiner, J. (Ed.). *Pediatric psychopharmacology*. New York: Basic Books, 1977.

Weingartner, H., Langer, D., Grice, J., & Rapoport, J. Acquisition and retrieval of information in amphetamine treated hyperactive children. *Psychiatry Research*, 1982, *6*, 21–29.

Weiss, B., & Laties, V. Enhancement of human performance by caffeine and the amphetamines. *Pharmacological Reviews*, 1962, *14*, 2–36.

Weiss, G., Kruger, E., Danielson, U., & Elman, M. Effect of long-term treatment of hyperactive children with methylphenidate. *Canadian Medical Association Journal*, 1975, *112*, 159–165.

Weiss, G., Werry, J., Minde, K., Douglas, V., & Sykes, D. Studies on the hyperactive child: V. The effects of dextroamphetamine and chlorpromazine on behavior and intellectual functioning. *Journal of Child Psychology and Psychiatry*, 1968, *9*, 145–156.

Werry, J. (Ed.). *Pediatric psychopharmacology: The use of behavior modifying drugs in children*. New York: Brunner/Mazel, 1978.

Werry, J., & Aman, M. Methylphenidate and haloperidol in children: Effects on attention, memory, and activity. *Archives of General Psychiatry*, 1975, *32*, 790–795.

Werry, J., Aman, M., & Diamond, E. Imipramine and methylphenidate in hyperactive children. *Journal of Child Psychology and Psychiatry*, 1979, *20*, 1–9.

Werry, J., Weiss, G., Douglas, V., & Martin, J. Studies on the hyperactive child: III. The effects of chlorpromazine upon behavior and learning ability. *Journal of the American Academy of Child Psychiatry*, 1966, *5*, 292–312.

Whalen, B., Henker, B., Collins, B., McAuliffe, S., & Vaux, A. Peer interaction in a structured communication task: Comparison of normal and hyperactive boys and of methylphenidate (Ritalin) and placebo effects. *Child Development*, 1979, *50*, 388–401.

Winsberg, B., Bialer, I., Kupietz, S., & Tobias, J. Effects of imipramine and dextroamphetamine on behavior of neuropsychiatrically impaired children. *American Journal of Psychiatry*, 1972, *128*, 1425–1432.

Winsberg, B., Perel, J., Hurwiz, M., & Klutzch, A. Imipramine protein binding and pharmacokinetics in children. In I. Forrest & E. Usdin (Eds.), *The phenothiazines and structurally related drugs*. New York: Raven Press, 1974.

Winsberg, B., Perel, J., Yepes, L., & Botti, E. Personal communication, 1977.

Winsberg, B., & Yepes, L. Antipsychotics. In J. Werry (Ed.), *Pediatric psychopharmacology: The use of behavior modifying drugs in children*. New York: Brunner/Mazel, 1978.

Wolraich, M., Drummond, T., Salomon, M., O'Brien, M., & Sivage, C. Effects of methylphenidate alone and in combination with behavior modification procedures on the behavior and academic performance of hyperactive children. *Journal of Abnormal Child Psychology*, 1978, *6*, 149–161.

Yepes, L., Balka, E., Winsberg, B., & Bialer, I. Amitriptyline and methylphenidate treatment of behaviorally disordered children. *Journal of Child Psychology and Psychiatry*, 1977, *18*, 39–52.

CHAPTER NINETEEN

Behavior Modification and Educational Techniques

ROBERT L. SPRAGUE

INTRODUCTION

In most cultures children are expected to attend school and to gain academic, social, and motor skills. Exceptional children, such as hyperkinetic children, are also expected to learn these skills, although allowances are made for slower progress (Kauffman & Hallahan, 1981). One of the primary tasks of professionals of all disciplines working with exceptional children is to plan and monitor the effects of therapeutic programs that will enhance their school functioning. Nevertheless, there is little research to guide the therapist in this endeavor. The sparse available literature is spotty, haphazard, methodologically inadequate, and overemphasizes tangential questions. One of the aims of this chapter is to stimulate thought and research on the multimodal treatment of the hyperkinetic child, with an emphasis on educational approaches.

REVIEWS ON THE EDUCATION OF HYPERKINETIC CHILDREN

On the whole, educational issues have received little attention in discussions of the hyperkinetic child; similarly, hyperactivity has received little attention in reviews of special education. For example, in Cantwell's (1975) book on the hyperactive child, only one of the 12 chapters deals with education (Forness, 1975), and Haslam and Valletutti's (1975) book on the medical problems of children in school includes just one chapter on hyperkinesis—under the heading of "minimal brain dysfunction" (Johnston, 1975). Neither chapter deals with teaching techniques or curriculum. On the other hand, Ross and Ross (1976) provide a much more thorough discussion of the educational problems of hyperkinetic children.

One of the first organized educational approaches to hyperkinetic children is represented by the reduced-stimulation approach suggested by Strauss and coworkers (Strauss & Kephart, 1955; Strauss & Lehtinen, 1947). Although the

Robert L. Sprague. Institute for Child Behavior and Development, University of Illinois at Urbana–Champaign, Champaign, Illinois.

classroom cubicles derived from this approach received much publicity, the technique generally has not been supported empirically (Cruickshank, Bentzen, Ratzeburg, & Tannhauser, 1961). A comprehensive educational program designed primarily for the behaviorally disturbed child was also developed by Hewett (1968); this placed a great deal of emphasis upon engineering the classroom and on developing educational strategies for exceptional children.

Safer and Allen (1976) discuss educational problems of hyperkinetic children, assuming a behavior modification approach to these problems. They estimate that it would cost about $35 per year for stimulant medication, exclusive of the cost for the physicians' time, whereas behavioral therapy might cost $200 to $900 per year.

In Bosco and Robin's (1977) book, Johnson, Kenny, and Davis (1977) outline a school policy for the use of medication for hyperactive children. This constitutes one of the very few discussions (perhaps the only one) of the policy implications for schools that arise from the use of psychoactive medication. Another chapter (Sprague & Gadow, 1977) discusses the role of the teacher in psychoactive drug treatment, with attention devoted to estimates of the number of children receiving drug treatment in public schools. Alabiso and Hansen's (1977) book focuses explicitly on the hyperactive child in the classroom situation.

M. J. Cohen's (1979) book about psychoactive drugs in special education includes only one chapter devoted to treatment of hyperactivity (Weithorn, 1979). In Gadow's (1979) much more comprehensive book for teachers, the chapter on hyperactivity is concerned only with drug treatment, but considerable emphasis is given to the educational problems of hyperactive children.

In stark contrast, a few authors, representing a medical–nihilistic point of view, assert that the diagnosis and treatment of hyperactivity is unrelated to educational problems. S. A. Cohen (1973) calls his position EBD: "We call this the Etiology Be Damned (EBD) point of view" (p. 251). He claims, in dramatic prose, that schools should be in the business of developing educational programs and not in that of medical and behavioral treatment. Taking an even stronger position, but using less colorful rhetoric, Bateman (1973) states that diagnosis is irrelevant to school and that trait descriptions such as "hyperactivity" and "short attention span" have no educational implications.

Several books, such as those by Greenblatt (1975), Trites (1979), Gadow and Loney (1981), and Lahey (1979), review psychosocial treatment programs. In a book (Whalen & Henker, 1980) emphasizing the point of view of social ecology, Keogh and Barkett (1980) describe the educational analysis of hyperactive children's problems.

REVIEWS OF BEHAVIOR MODIFICATION WITH HYPERACTIVE CHILDREN

Although studies of behavior modification with hyperactive children are less numerous than psychoactive drug studies are, there have been several recent reviews of this approach, the most thorough of which is by Mash and Dalby (1979). They start their review with an enumeration of 11 reasons why psychoactive drugs may be inappropriate; many of their points are valid, but behavior modification should stand on its own feet without reliance on the limitations of psychoactive drug treatment. They cite an earlier paper of mine with Werry (Werry & Sprague, 1970) as offering a "conceptual rationale" for behavior modification, but seem to overlook our argument that pharmacotherapy can be effective and that neither drugs nor behavior modification, either alone or in combination, solve all the problems of hyperactive children. Mash and Dalby discuss classroom interventions, but it is primarily from a standpoint of behavioral therapy. They do not discuss educational and curricular interventions that might be appropriate with the hyperactive child.

One of the largest sections of their chapter deals with issues in behavioral intervention and represents one of the best analytical critiques of the state of the art in this area. Among the points they criticize in behavioral studies are (1) the small numbers of subjects, often single-subject cases; (2) the poor diagnosis and lack of standardized rating scales that have become accepted in the area; (3) the lack of adequate follow-up studies; and (4) the lack of adequate information to allow behavior modification procedures to be assessed from a cost–benefit standpoint. I would add another point: There are few behavioral modification studies that evaluate the outcome of treatment programs for hyperactivity by using multidimensional assessments of behavior in the classroom and at home, or assessments of learning as evidenced by poor school work and scholastic achievement.

Brundage-Aguar, Forehand, and Ciminero (1977), unfortunately, also pit psychopharmacological treatments against behavioral therapy, concluding on the basis of a less than adequate review that "the indiscriminant use of the psychopharmacological approach may constitute an infringement on the child's rights" (p. 7). Of course, others have maintained just as forcefully that behavior modification approaches may do so, too.

In a review written primarily for pediatricians, Wolraich (1979) has included 157 behavior modification studies that dealt with 3079 hyperactive children. One of the problems with this review, as with the field as a whole, is that many of the studies (probably 77 of the 157) were conducted with children who were either primarily aggressive as well as hyperactive, or aggressive and psychotic. He noted that academic assessments were made in only 39 of the 157 studies; in 36 (83%), academic improvement was noted. Phillips and Ray (1980) have reviewed behavior therapy with children in a survey of more than 200 studies published since 1974. They comment that design improvements are beginning to appear in the areas of (1) follow-up, (2) better diagnostic descriptions, and (3) multiple outcome measures.

Two brief reviews have dealt with the combination of behavior modification and psychopharmacological treatment. Backman and Firestone (1979) have selected four studies that involved both drugs and behavior modification. Buechin (1979) has reviewed all of the studies that had been published using both medication and behavior modification.

Long-term follow-up (1 year or more) of drug treatment of hyperactive children has become a topic of considerable interest. There are some long-term studies of psychoactive medication, but scarcely any of behavior modification (Keeley, Shemberg, & Carbonell, 1976). Mash and Terdal (1977) come to the same conclusion, but present a useful conceptual framework in which studies could be analyzed, dealing at length with the problem of differential subject dropout in long-term studies.

The issues involved in the combination of behavior modification techniques and psychoactive medication in the treatment of hyperactive children have best been described in an article by K. D. O'Leary (1980) with the provocative title of "Pills or Skills for Hyperactive Children." It is quite unsatisfactory to investigate the effects of treatments on only one, or even a few, target symptoms in just one behavioral domain. "Long-term treatment research comparing behavioral and pharmacological interventions and combinations thereof with multiple dependent measures in the school and home is critical if we are to address many questions raised in this manuscript. A multiclinic study of the scope of the NIMH depression study to start in 1980 is certainly in order" (K. D. O'Leary, 1980, p. 201). As O'Leary sees it, any study of psychoactive drugs and behavior modification should involve at least these four aspects: (1) academic performance of the child; (2) family changes as assessed by parent ratings and observations and an assessment of family discord; (3) detailed cost analysis; and (4) consumer satisfaction with the treatment. I would add a fifth—namely, the use of self-reports of the child in an attempt to assess his or her opinions and the dysphoric effects, if any, of the treatment (particularly the psychoactive drug treatment). Although previous research has typically been unsuccessful in attempting to obtain meaningful self-ratings from children under drug treatment, a recent dissertation in our laboratory at the University of Illinois, using a self-report of mood, found significant effects consistent with the clinical impression that stimulant medications—particularly higher doses—create dysphoria (Walker, 1980).

A Major Study of Behavior Modification and Psychoactive Drugs

Of the four studies investigating the combined effects of behavior modification and psychoactive drugs, that by Gittelman and her associates represents the best and largest attempt to study these treatments in combination (Gittelman, 1977; Gittelman, Abikoff, Klein, & Mattes, 1979; Gittelman, Abikoff, Pollack, Klein, Katz, & Mattes, 1980; Gittelman-Klein, Felixbrod, Abikoff, Katz, Gloisten, Kates, & Saraf, 1975; Gittelman-Klein, Klein, Abikoff, Katz, Gloisten, & Kates, 1976). They conclude that medication is the most effective treatment of hyperactivity, but that behavior therapy may be added if medication is not enough. Mash and Dalby (1979), in their critique, comment that the study was noteworthy in its careful attention to the design, selection of subjects, and use of observational measures for evaluating change. However, they also criticize the study because the children were treated with large doses of stimulant medication; because the study was conducted over a short period of time; because prestudy medication status was not included; because it was not clear whether the methylphenidate dosage was similar across two drug conditions; and because the amount and quality of behavior therapy was not specified as the same for the two groups. Nevertheless, Mash and Dalby concur with Gittelman's guarded conclusion that, in general, medication is more effective than behavior therapy is.

The most recent report of this study (Gittelman *et al.*, 1979) involved 83 hyperactive children. The children were carefully selected and cutoffs were established on the Conners Teacher Rating Scale, on parent reports, and on classroom observations before they were considered eligible to enter the study. After entering the study, the children were randomly assigned to one of three 8-week conditions: behavior modification plus placebo, behavior modification plus methylphenidate, and methylphenidate alone. Behavior modification procedures involved both the parents and the teacher. A number of pre- and posttreatment measurements were taken, including teacher rating scales, teacher evaluations of academic performance, observational data from the classroom, global improvement ratings from the psychiatrist and teacher, and parent ratings. The authors concluded: "A consistent pattern of treatment effects was obtained. The combination of methylphenidate and behavior therapy was regularly the best treatment; methylphenidate alone was next, and behavior therapy with placebo was the least effective. There was no exception to the above order." The authors cautioned that "the results are generalizable only to hyperactive children who are relatively *severely disruptive* . . . [and] to children who receive comparable methylphenidate dosage" (italics added).

Gittelman *et al.* also pointed out that there was no limit set on the amount of direct contact between the therapist, parents, and teachers, and thus that in the practical setting the cost of behavioral treatment would be undoubtedly much higher than the cost of stimulant medication alone would be. Because it was a research project, they obtained informed consent prior to entering any child and family into the study. They point out that this was a major problem, because in a large bureaucratic school system such as in New York City, it is difficult to obtain the necessary teacher cooperation to accept instruction and training from outsiders, to cooperate with the extensive amount of paperwork and request for additional time, and to permit outside observers to come into the classroom. Some pressing questions, however, remain unanswered. In particular, it is necessary to assess the effects, if any, of these various different treatments on academic performance.

Other Studies of Drugs and Behavior Modification

A series of other studies in the 1970s, which varied greatly in methodological soundness, also investigated the combined effects of behavior modification and psychoactive drugs in hyperactive children. One of the earliest studies was conducted on a group of 12 hyperactive children in a special experimental class (Christensen & Sprague, 1973). The only measure was seat activity during 20 minutes of class, and it was found that the drug significantly reduced the seat activity in comparison with the placebo condition. There was an interaction of drug and conditioning that became statistically significant on the third day of combined treatment, at which point drug plus conditioning reduced seat activity more than conditioning alone did. In another study of hyperactive boys in an institution for the mentally retarded, an experimental classroom was devised so that a number of measures could be taken. Methylphenidate was used in conjunction with behavior modification in a crossover design; thus all of the subjects received the same treatment, differing only in sequences, which were randomly assigned. A number of measures were taken, including teacher ratings, classroom observations, and an assessment of academic productivity and accuracy on tests given at the end of each class day. A number of significant effects were found, but the data were not strongly in support of medication; "the data showed that the substitution of active stimulant medication for placebo in the presence of the classroom management program produced little measurable enhancement of the effects of the environmental procedures" (Christensen, 1975, p. 274). Most important was the fact that overall there was a significant effect of the treatments on academic productivity; when this overall effect was subjected to post hoc tests for differences between conditioning and conditioning plus drug, a trend ($p = .06$) was noted for drug plus conditioning to increase academic performance more than conditioning alone did in the first half of the experiment. This result has been interpreted as a failure of medication to show effects on academic achievement (Barkley & Cunningham, 1978), but I have disagreed with this interpretation in a paper with Berger (Sprague & Berger, 1980). It seems that interpreting a $p = .06$ result simply as a failure is splitting hairs, because a $p = .05$ result is traditionally accepted as statistically significant.

Stableford, Butz, Hasazi, Leitenberg, and Peyser (1974) reported a case study of two boys who were receiving methylphenidate and dextroamphetamine and also behavior modification. Since there were no clear diagnostic data or rating scale information to indicate that the boys were hyperactive, it is not possible to interpret the results of this case study. Another case study of one child was reported by Wulbert and Dries (1977). The child received both behavior modification and methylphenidate. Both treatments were situation-specific (i.e., the reduction in repetitive behavior by conditioning in the clinic did not generalize to the home, and vice versa for aggression treated by drug in the home).

As has been cogently pointed out by S. G. O'Leary and O'Leary (1980), there are hundreds of studies describing how hyperkinetic children should be put on medication or how the medication should be used but almost no studies describing how the drug should be withdrawn. S. G. O'Leary and Pelham (1978) withdrew psychoactive medication from seven children and studied them for 4 months after withdrawal. After medication withdrawal, instructions from therapists were given to the family and the teacher about handling the children. Although the hyperactive children were significantly more off task compared with cohort children when they were initially taken off medication, this difference disappeared at follow-up. The authors interpreted this result to mean that behavior modification is an effective alternative for children who may be receiving stimulant medication.

In a 6-week study of 20 hyperactive children in two special classes, Wolraich, Drummond, Salomon, O'Brien, and Sivage (1978) studied the effects of behavior modification and a standardized dose of methylphenidate at .3 mg/kg per day. This is the first study in this series that used a standardized dose, and dosage is of interest, since it has been reported to influence learning (Sprague & Sleator, 1977). A number of measures were taken during this study. The classroom observations of social behavior generally favored behavior modification, but there were no significant differences between behavior modification and the drug. Interestingly, these authors attempted to measure academic performance. There was a significant triple-order interaction on academic measures of drug, behavior modification, and class group. The interaction makes interpretation difficult and less interesting than if there were a straightforward difference between behavior modification and medication. The authors concluded, however, that behavior modification significantly influenced academic performance.

Loney, Weissenburger, Woolson, and Lichty (1979) studied for 8 to 12 weeks 12 boys, some who were assigned to a psychiatrist who prescribed psychoactive medication, and some who were assigned to a psychiatrist who would not use medication. The eight boys not on medication were entered into a behavior modification program developed for and administered by the teachers. Both the drug and behavior modification treatments improved on-task behavior over the course of the study, but only the behavioral program had a "spillover" to other students in the same class; that is, not only the hyperactive target but also the nontarget children improved. This is the first report on "spillover" effects, and it should be studied further because it may be an important consideration in planning a behavior therapy program in the classroom.

Pelham, Schnedler, Bologna, and Contreras (1980) conducted a methodologically important study of behavior therapy and stimulant drug in the classroom and at home over 18 weeks with 8 children. Both a low (.25 mg/kg) and a moderate (.75 mg/kg) dose of methylphenidate were administered, and the drug was given briefly before behavior therapy started and at two times during the behavior therapy period. Both before behavior therapy and 3 weeks after the start of therapy, the moderate dose improved on-task behavior significantly more than the low dose did, but after 13 weeks of therapy there was no difference on this measure between the two doses. "These results suggest that low to moderate dosages of methylphenidate may be of incremental benefit to some and perhaps most hyperactive children being treated with a behavioral intervention" (p. 230). Although there was a significant increase in the number of math problems solved correctly from pre- to posttest sessions over the course of the experiment, academic performance was not monitored separately for drug and behavior therapy conditions.

BEHAVIOR MODIFICATION AS THE ONLY TREATMENT

The numerous studies in which behavior modification has been used as the only treatment modality for hyperkinetic children have been reviewed by Wolraich (1979). Most involved very small subject groups, often a single subject, and most of the designs utilized within-subject or crossover designs. The majority of the studies showed positive results, particularly when direct behavioral observation was utilized as the dependent variable (129 studies). Of the 39 studies that measured academic achievement, 36 of them showed improvement, which is dramatically different from the results indicated by the review of similar studies with stimulant medication (Barkley, 1979; Barkley & Cunningham, 1978). In the 10 studies using teacher rating scales as a dependent measure, 7 showed positive results.

From the 157 studies Wolraich reviewed, 11 have been selected for further discussion here. Patterson (Patterson, 1965; Patterson, Jones, Whittier, & Wright, 1965) was probably the first person to write about the effects of behavior modification on the hyperactive child. These early case studies suffer from a lack of clear diagnosis (no rating scales with cutoffs were used) and did not involve multidimensional assessment of the effects of behavior modification. A year later, Doubros and Daniels (1966) discussed behavior modification and token rewards with six mongoloid mentally retarded children who were also classified as hyperactive.

Quay, Sprague, Werry, and McQueen (1967) studied five children in their classroom who were classified as conduct problems. As opposed to the relatively few experimental sessions that were obtained in previous and subsequent studies, this study was conducted over 130 school days. The only dependent measure was orientation of the child to the teacher, who was sitting in front of the class and reading to the class as a whole. Conditioning procedures using a flashing light as reinforcement, backed up with candy at the end of the session, significantly increased the orientation during this lengthy period of time, with extinction resulting in decrease of orientation. Pihl (1967) studied two cases, one an epileptic and the other brain-damaged, and reported that behavior modification increased sitting in a chair. In the only study to investigate whether seat activity could be increased as well as decreased, Edelson and Sprague (1974) studied 16 hyperactive, educable retarded boys who were living in a facility for the mentally retarded. They were seen in an experimental classroom, which contained chairs with stabilmetric cushions that monitored seat activity and desks with lights that flashed reinforcement when activity contingencies were met. Significant effects were found. At the end of each of the 12 classroom sessions, a brief examination was given, and the number of correct answers were counted. There was a correlation of −.447 between the number of correct responses and the amount of seat movement during that day. Since the seat movements were increased as well as decreased, this correlation can be taken as an indication that some of the variance in the accuracy on the examinations was accounted for by wiggling during the classroom sessions. Alabiso (1975) studied eight institutionalized retarded individuals. Behavior modification contingencies were established to have the individuals remain seated. Although no data were given, the author interpreted his results to mean that behavior modification was successful.

Ayllon, Layman, and Kandel (1975) criticized previous behavior modification studies for not examining the academic performance of the subjects. They studied three children who were diagnosed as hyperactive and were also receiving psychoactive drugs. They found that behavior modification improved academic performance.

In the first behavior modification study to select children using a teacher rating scale and a cutoff level, Rosenbaum, O'Leary, and Jacob (1975) studied 10 hyperactive children who were very similar on the Conners Teacher Rating Scale to the hyperactive children typically studied on psychoactive drug studies. The children were divided into two groups; one received individualized reinforcement whereas the other received group reinforcement. Although there was no difference between the groups, there was a significant treatment effect over time as measured by the Conners Teacher Rating Scale. In a similar study (K. D. O'Leary, Pelham, Rosenbaum, & Price, 1976), 17 hyperactive children identified on the Conners scale were placed in a behavior modification study in which the rewards were administered at home by the parents after receiving daily teacher report cards over 10 weeks. Although both experimental and control groups improved significantly over the time, there was a significant interaction between the groups and time, indicating that the behavior modification group improved significantly more than the control group did.

The two final studies contain important aspects that should be described in more detail. Of 104 children referred to Kent and O'Leary (1976), 32 were selected as hyperactive. They were randomly assigned to experimental and control groups and followed for 9 months after the study. Although there was a significant difference noted at the end of the short-term study, with the behavior modification group showing more improvement than the control group, this difference disappeared by 9 months. It appeared that although short-term improvement could be induced with behavior modification, it did not persist. Worland (1976) studied 16 boys designated as hyperactive by a rating scale and 16 controls, using symbol encoding and spelling tasks as dependent measures. Both positive and negative reinforcement were given as the treatment conditions. During the task, the hyperactive children spent more time off task than the controls. But they showed significantly *less* off-task behavior at natural breaks, such as turning the page, which means that they were off-task more during study time when it was appropriate for them to be on-task. There was a significant difference found between the hyperactives and the controls on academic achievement—significantly more correct spelling obtained under positive-reinforcement conditions than negative.

COGNITIVE-BEHAVIOR MODIFICATION

Meichenbaum and Goodman (1971) introduced cognitive approaches to behavior modification in a group of 15 hyperactive children who had poor self-control. Unfortunately, they obtained no assessments of the academic performance of the children, but those children who received cognitive training in self-control improved more on an intelligence test, on the Matching Familiar Figures Test of impulsivity, and on the Porteus Maze Test of ability to plan ahead.

Douglas, Parry, Marton, and Garson (1976) used the Meichenbaum approach of cognitive-behavior modification with 29 hyperactive boys; there were 3 months of active training, and a follow-up evaluation was administered 6 months later. Ten different dependent measures were used in the assessment battery given at three different times, including the Durrell Reading Test and the Wide-Range Achievement Test (WRAT). Of the four variables that were measured in these two tests, only one showed a significant improvement—listening comprehension of the reading test (a difference due to an improvement in the group receiving cognitive-behavior modification). No educational variables showed significant differences on the follow-up measures 6 months later, although other variables did so.

A recent study by Friedling and O'Leary (1979) questions the efficacy of this form of cognitive training. Four hyperactive children were identified and given self-instruction sessions for only 2 days and then tested on easy and hard reading and mathematics tests. No effects of the self-control training were observed in on-task performance and quantity of work, but when the same subjects were subsequently given token reinforcement for on-task behavior, significant effects were obtained for that behavior. It may be that procedures of cognitive-behavior modification are useful but weak techniques with hyperkinetic children. Another possibility is that self-control instructions work best in combination with other approaches as part of a multimodality program.

The lack of reviews on the effects of educational procedures on the academic performance of hyperactive children reflects a serious neglect of this issue. There is, however, a recent review on the effects of psychoactive medication on learning of the hyperactive child (Aman, 1978). Aman agrees with Barkley and Cunningham (1978) that stimulant medication has little or no effect on the academic performance of hyperactive children, but I believe this to be a premature conclusion (Sprague & Berger, 1980; Ward, 1979). Barkley (1979) states that the situation is a paradox: "The stimulants appear to make substantial improvements in classroom attention and behavior but produce little or no effect on academic achievement or productivity" (p. 420). He then states four reasons why this may be true, but fails to state the most obvious—namely, that children who are seriously behind in academic skills should not be expected to make up these deficits when pills are placed in their mouths, or perhaps even to keep going at their usual slow pace, *unless remedial, appropriate educational training is given* (as noted above). This, then, is the issue: Studies have not been conducted to investigate the effects, if any, of remedial education in combination with stimulants and/or behavior therapy. The situation is equally dismal with regard to the impact of behavior modification treatment upon academic performance.

One of the best studies involving educational procedures with hyperactives was that by Conrad, Dworkin, Shai, and Tobiessen (1971). From a population of 1350 first- and second-graders, they selected 262 with the highest scores on a rating scale for hyperactivity. Parental approval was obtained for further research on 106 of these 262 children. Eventually only 68 children were randomly assigned to four groups: placebo with prescription tutoring, placebo without tutoring, dextroamphetamine without tutoring, and dextroamphetamine with tutoring. Double-blind conditions were maintained. Prescription tutoring was given twice a week for the 20-week experiment. A large number of dependent measures were taken, including motor coordination tests, visual–perceptual tasks, activity and distractability tasks, the Bender–Gestalt and Frostig tests, and the Wechsler Intelligence Scale for Children (WISC), giving a total of 34 dependent variables. Most of the significant differences were found between the placebo and drug groups, and also between the placebo-without-tutoring and drug-plus-tutoring groups. A significant difference was found in the information subtest of the WISC, with the drug-plus-tutoring group showing the greatest gain, the placebo-plus-tutoring group showing the next greatest gain, the drug-without-tutoring group showing some loss, and the placebo-without-tutoring group showing the greatest loss. There were no significant differences observed on either the reading or arithmetic parts of the WRAT.

However, there was one artifact militating against obtaining statistical significance in this study. When these researchers investigated whether the children in the drug groups were regularly taking the medication, it was discovered that 50% of the children were taking the medication irregularly. The problem of compliance (i.e., taking medication as prescribed by the physician) is a difficulty that plagues most psychoactive drug studies. This problem is usually ignored, but sometimes it is addressed in a variety of ways (e.g., by counting the number of pills remaining in a jar when the parent and child return for evaluation; by using an envelope system with individually dated envelopes and checking how many unopened envelopes are brought back; and, most recently, by conducting a urinalysis on the day the child comes back for evaluation). None of these methods is entirely satisfactory. Perhaps the most important aspect of compliance is that failure to take the medication reduces the possibility of finding a significant effect (Steinkamp, 1980).

Rie (1974) investigated tutoring in 13 children with minimal brain dysfunction; there was no control group. In 13 weeks the children received an average of 14.7 sessions, averaging 42.3 minutes of tutoring per subject. On the WRAT, there were significant improvements in reading, spelling, and arithmetic. However, the finding is uninterpretable in the absence of a control group.

Zentall, Zentall, and Booth (1978) investigated spelling accuracy in a group of hyperactive children who were given two kinds of training: one with traditional printed letters, and the other with words printed in color in large type in an attempt to attract the wandering attention of hyperactive children. There were five spelling tests given containing 10 words each. Contrary to the experimenters' expectation, there was a significant treatment × groups effect due to the fact that the hyperactive groups did *worse* on the experimental words. Rather than attracting and holding their attention as expected, the color and large size distracted the hyperactive children.

In an elaborate study of 61 children containing 22 hyperactive and 39 control subjects, Whalen, Collins, Henker, Alkus, Adams, and Stapp (1978) and Whalen, Henker, Collins, Finck, and Dotemoto (1979) investigated the effects of methylphenidate, self-pacing, noisy environments, and quiet environments on an experimental classroom setting. A large number of dependent measures were taken. The hyperactive children showed less attention to the task on placebo than on medication. A noisy environment produced less on-task behavior (previous literature is contradictory on the effects of external distraction; see Douglas & Peters, 1979, and also Chapter 14 of this volume). More importantly, the difference in off-task behavior between noisy and quiet conditions was greater for hyperactive than for control children. The hyperactive children also showed significantly more disruption.

Significant correlations were found between teacher ratings and behavior observations in a number of categories; also, teacher ratings were sensitive to medication-related changes in behavior. From a cost–benefit approach to research, classroom observations are time-consuming and expensive; if teacher ratings can be used as a substitute, efficiency is generally gained.

MULTIMODALITY TREATMENT

A logical interpretation of the above findings is that no one single treatment works successfully with all hyperkinetic children and that no single treatment shows much promise when subjected to long-term evaluation. Thus, researchers are turning to multimodality or "total push" treatment in an attempt to find some combination of treatments that will show both a higher percentage of improvement and effects that will last for months or years. Undoubtedly, the concern about side effects of psychoactive drug treatment and the cost of behavior modification have contributed to this search to find the right combination of treatments.

Feighner and Feighner (1974) discuss multimodality treatment of the hyperactive child but provide no systematic appraisal of the approach. A recent large study by Satterfield, Cantwell, and Satterfield (1979) is somewhat more informative. From 124 hyperactive children referred to their clinic, 117 were selected to participate in a 1-year follow-up study, and 84 remained in the study for the entire year. Methylphenidate treatment and various kinds of psychotherapy for each child and/or child and family were tried. Although all the children were administered medication, 89% of the families received some kind of psychotherapy during the course of the year. A large number of dependent measures were used. Unfortunately, the study did not have a control group, and in the words of the authors, "The absence of an untreated control group for comparison usually makes it difficult, if not impossible, to attach clinical significance to such outcome findings" (p. 972).

Using derived scores (expected grade level scores based upon the Peabody Individual Achievement Test and chronological age), expected achievement scores improved more in 1 year than did average growth in achievement based on a typical school year. There were significantly greater changes in expected achievement scores over the year on mathematics, reading recognition, and reading comprehension than anticipated. All of the teacher and parent rating scale factors showed significant improvements over the year, and all of the seven areas of psychosocial adjustment as rated by the psychiatrist showed significant improvement over the year.

But the study raises more questions than it answers:

1. How does one interpret these improvement data when there is no control group selected from the same population receiving the same amount of intensive attention and testing and retesting during the course of the year?

2. What is the effect on the findings of a 28% dropout during the course of the year?

3. What precisely occurred in the interventions termed "individual educational therapy," "individual psychotherapy," "group therapy," and "family psychotherapy"? In order to replicate such studies at other laboratories, it is necessary to have some detailed description of the kind of treatment that was administered.

4. What is the cost–benefit ratio of such intensive psychotherapy? Investigators in the behavioral sciences must be particularly sensitive to recommending expensive therapies that may have limited value. When the outcomes do not involve life and death, the cost–benefit ratio takes on an added significance.

5. What is the availability across the country of the kinds of psychotherapy and "total push" treatments recommended in the study? Even if the cost–benefit ratio question is entirely satisfactory, the question of availability of resources in the real world of competition for those resources must be addressed.

From the evidence currently available, it seems likely that no single treatment for hyperkinesis will be successful in the long run, so it is expected that researchers rightly will turn to multimodal approaches. But these raise many major questions, including those of cost–benefit, possibility of replication, and availability of resources at the clinical level.

Teaching and Curriculum Largely Ignored

It is evident from this review that teaching techniques and the curriculum have been ignored in the vast literature concerning psychoactive drug treatments, behavior modification, and other treatments. The teacher has been used extensively as a source of information, and, in fact, teacher rating scales are now almost standard for any psychoactive drug study and are used as standards in many of the behavior modification studies. Yet, although teachers provide information about the social behavior of hyperactive children in the classroom, they are seldom asked to comment on the academic performance of these children and are usually left on their own to develop appropriate teaching strategies and curriculum material for them. Nevertheless, those researchers with backgrounds in special education take a different approach. For example, Keogh and Margolis (1976) discuss these problems in relation to attention. They theorize that attention is not a unitary function and subdivide it into three parts: (1) coming to attention, (2) decision making, and (3) sustained attention. They suggest educational practices that could be used to aid a child in each of these three attention problem areas. But it is rare to find statements that address the issues of curricula for and teaching of these children.

Research into hyperactivity has largely ignored the effects of treatment on academic performance, and has seldom investigated the effects of educational practices such as tutoring, prescriptive teaching, special class placement, and kinds of curriculum material. The large literature in psychopharmacology has generally focused either on one single target (activity or, more recently, attention) or on one target dimension (e.g., the troublesome social behavior of children as seen by significant adults in their environment). Focus on one particular target dimension is largely attributable to the kind of schema the researcher uses when designing the investigation. This usually reflects the philosophical beliefs of the researcher. Often in medicine this is a biomedical model, but such a model may not be viable in the behavioral sciences (Engel, 1977). It has been suggested that a more appropriate model would be a biopsychosocial model, which would take into account the biological aspect of a child, the psychological context in which he or she is functioning, and the social and cultural demands placed upon him or her. As has been suggested by Loney (1980), measures are needed that have SCOPE (i.e., that are systematic, complete, objective, practical, and empirical). Although it will be difficult to design clever experiments that will accurately ensure the impact of treatment on all these dimensions, it seems clear that the field is moving in this direction. This trend represents one of the major issues.

New Approaches

Whalen and Henker (1976) have raised the possibility that the orientation of children in regard to the way they perceive themselves as either having power over events or not having power would lead to their attributing control largely to external forces or largely to internal self-control. They have suggested that treatment with psychoactive drugs might lead children to attribute significant aspects of their lives to external forces beyond their control—namely, to medication. This approach needs further study to evaluate the magnitude of attributional effects on eventual outcome.

At least on the American scene, there are new trends afoot with regard to classification of these children. With the coming of the new *Diagnostic and Statistical Manual of Mental Disorders*, third edition (DSM-III), the diagnostic focus is shifting from activity level to that of attention problems (Gittelman-Klein, Spitzer, & Cantwell, 1978).

K. D. O'Leary (1980) has called for changes in the way hyperactive children are evaluated, and he suggests large-scale, multicenter research. Such studies would clearly depart from traditional methods of evaluating the effectiveness of treatment. Closely related to the suggestions of O'Leary is the call for multimodal treatment and assessment, as represented by a recent study by Satterfield *et al.* (1979). Finally, theory is moving into the area, as shown by Douglas's theory of higher mental processes (Douglas, 1972, 1974, 1977, 1980a, 1980b; Douglas & Peters, 1979; see also Chapter 14 of this volume).

It is uncertain where these new directions and approaches will lead this field. It is clear that there are no simple answers, and, in fact, there are no simple questions. It does seem apparent, however, that these new approaches will heavily involve the educational system.

Rather than jumping on the bandwagon, if there is such a wagon in the vicinity, a cautious approach is suggested. The behavioral sciences are notoriously prone to fads and fashions, and some of these new approaches may represent faddishness that will pass in the sunlight of empirical data. It is certain that the educational problems of these children will not pass away. The children will be expected to stay in school and will be expected to function at least within the limits of their capability. So whatever treatments are designed will need to take this practical aspect into account and build systems of treatment that will work readily within the framework of the public (i.e., state) school. It goes without saying that treatment programs for use in the public schools will need to be cost-effective, because the schools operate under severe financial strain.

In summary, it seems that a cost-effective treatment that is multimodal in nature and multidimensional in assessment will be the system to be adopted in the long run, if it can, indeed, be proven cost-effective, and can be packaged to be readily available and usable by teachers and families.

References

Alabiso, F. Operant control of attention behavior: A treatment for hyperactivity. *Behavior Therapy*, 1975, *6*, 39–42.

Alabiso, F. P., & Hansen, J. C. *The hyperactive child in the classroom*. Springfield, Ill.: Charles C Thomas, 1977.

Aman, M. G. Drugs, learning, and the psychotherapies. In J. S. Werry (Ed.), *Pediatric psychopharmacology: The use of behavior modifying drugs in children*. New York: Brunner/Mazel, 1978.

Ayllon, T., Layman, D., & Kandel, H. J. A behavioral-educational alternative to drug control of hyperactive children. *Journal of Applied Behavior Analysis*, 1975, *8*, 137–146.

Backman, J., & Firestone, P. A review of psychopharmacological and behavioral approaches to the treatment of hyperactive children. *American Journal of Orthopsychiatry*, 1979, *49*, 500–504.

Barkley, R. A. Using stimulant drugs in the classroom. *School Psychology Digest*, 1979, *8*, 412–425.

Barkley, R. A. Hyperactivity. In E. Mash & L. Terdal (Eds.), *Behavioral assessment of childhood disorders*. New York: Guilford, 1981.

Barkley, R. A., & Cunningham, C. E. Do stimulant drugs improve the academic performance of hyperkinetic children? *Clinical Pediatrics*, 1978, *17*, 85–92.

Bateman, B. D. Educational implications of minimal brain dysfunction. *Annals of the New York Academy of Sciences*, 1973, *205*(1), 245–250.

Bosco, J. J., & Robin, S. S. (Eds.). *The hyperactive child and stimulant drugs*. Chicago: University of Chicago Press, 1977.

Brundage-Aguar, D., Forehand, R., & Ciminero, A. A review of treatment approaches for hyperactive behavior. *Journal of Clinical Child Psychology*, 1977, *3*, 3–9.

Buechin, N. *Treating hyperactivity: Drug therapy, behavior modification, or both?* Student paper, University of Illinois, December 1979.

Cantwell, D. P. *The hyperactive child*. New York: Spectrum, 1975.

Christensen, D. E. Effects of combining methylphenidate and a classroom token system in modifying hyperactive behavior. *American Journal of Mental Deficiency*, 1975, *80*, 266–276.

Christensen, D. E., & Sprague, R. L. Reduction of hyperactive behaviors by conditioning procedures alone and combined with methylphenidate (Ritalin). *Behaviour Research and Therapy*, 1973, *11*, 331–334.

Cohen, M. J. (Ed.). *Drugs and the special child*. New York: Gardner Press, 1979.

Cohen, S. A. Minimal brain dysfunction and practical matters such as teaching kids to read. *Annals of the New York Academy of Sciences*, 1973, *205*(1), 251–261.

Conrad, W. G., Dworkin, E. S., Shai, A., & Tobiessen, J. E. Effects of amphetamine therapy and prescriptive tutoring on the behavior and achievement of lower class hyperactive children. *Journal of Learning Disabilities*, 1971, *4*, 45–53.

Cruickshank, W. M., Bentzen, F. A., Ratzeburg, F. H., & Tannhauser, M. *A teaching method for brain-injured and hyperactive children*. Syracuse: Syracuse University Press, 1961.

Doubros, S. G., & Daniels, G. J. An experimental approach to the reduction of overactive behavior. *Behaviour Research and Therapy*, 1966, *4*, 251–258.

Douglas, V. I. Stop, look, and listen: The problem of sustained attention and impulse control in hyperactive and normal children. *Canadian Journal of Behavioural Sciences*, 1972, *4*, 259–282.

Douglas, V. I. Sustained attention and impulse control: Implications for the handicapped child. In J. A. Sivets & L. L. Elliott (Eds.), *Psychology and the handicapped child* (DHEW Publication No. (OE) 73-0500). Washington, D.C.: U.S. Government Printing Office, 1974.

Douglas, V. I. Are drugs enought?: To treat or to train the hyperactive child. In R. Gittelman-Klein (Ed.), *Recent advances in child psychopharmacology*. New York: Human Sciences Press, 1977.

Douglas, V. I. Higher mental processes in hyperactive children: Implications for training. In R. M. Knights & D. J. Bakker (Eds.), *Treatment of hyperactive and learning disordered children*. Baltimore: University Park Press, 1980. (a)

Douglas, V. I. Treatment and training approaches to hyperactivity: Establishing internal or external control. In C. K. Whalen & B. Henker (Eds.), *Hyperactive children: The social ecology of identification and treatment*. New York: Academic Press, 1980. (b)

Douglas, V. I., Parry, P., Marton, P., & Garson, C. Assessment of a cognitive training program for hyperactive children. *Journal of Abnormal Child Psychology*, 1976, *4*, 389–410.

Douglas, V. I., & Peters, K. G. Toward a clearer definition of the attentional deficit of hyperactive children. In G. A. Hale & M. Lewis (Eds.), *Attention and the development of cognitive skills*. New York: Plenum Press, 1979.

Edelson, R. I., & Sprague, R. L. Conditioning of activity level in a classroom with institutionalized retarded boys. *American Journal of Mental Deficiency*, 1974, *78*, 384–388.

Engel, G. L. The need for a new medical model: A challenge for biomedicine. *Science*, 1977, *196*, 129–136.

Feighner, A. C., & Feighner, J. P. Multimodality treatment of the hyperkinetic child. *American Journal of Psychiatry*, 1974, *131*, 459–463.

Forness, S. Educational approaches with hyperactive children. In D. P. Cantwell (Ed.), *The hyperactive child*. New York: Spectrum, 1975.

Friedling, C., & O'Leary, S. G. Effects of self-instructional training on second- and third-grade hyperactive children: A failure to replicate. *Journal of Applied Behavior Analysis*, 1979, *12*, 211–219.

Gadow, K. D. *Children on medication: A primer for school personnel*. Reston, Va.: Council for Exceptional Children, 1979.

Gadow, K. D., & Loney, J. (Eds.). *Psychosocial aspects of drug treatment for hyperactivity.* Boulder, Colo.: Westview Press, 1981.

Gittelman, R. Preliminary report on the efficacy of methylphenidate and behavior modification in hyperkinetic children. *Psychopharmacology Bulletin*, 1977, *13*(2), 36–38.

Gittelman, R., Abikoff, H., Klein, D. F., & Mattes, J. *A controlled trial of behavior modification and methylphenidate in hyperactive children.* Paper presented at the annual meeting of the American Academy of Child Psychiatry, Atlanta, October 1979.

Gittelman, R., Abikoff, H., Pollack, E., Klein, D. F., Katz, S., & Mattes, J. A controlled trial of behavior modification and methylphenidate in hyperactive children. In C. K. Whalen & B. Henker (Eds.), *Hyperactive children: The social ecology of identification and treatment.* New York: Academic Press, 1980.

Gittelman-Klein, R., Felixbrod, J., Abikoff, H., Katz, S., Gloisten, A., Kates, W., & Saraf, K. *Methylphenidate versus behavior therapy in hyperkinetic children.* Paper presented at the annual meeting of the American Psychiatric Association, Anaheim, California, May 1975.

Gittelman-Klein, R., Klein, D. F., Abikoff, H., Katz, S., Gloisten, A. C., & Kates, W. Relative efficacy of methylphenidate and behavior modification in hyperkinetic children: An interim report. *Journal of Abnormal Child Psychology*, 1976, *4*, 361–379.

Gittelman-Klein, R., Spitzer, R., & Cantwell, D. P. Diagnostic classifications and psychopharmacological indications. In J. S. Werry (Ed.), *Pediatric psychopharmacology: The use of behavior modifying drugs in children.* New York: Brunner/Mazel, 1978.

Greenblatt, M. (Ed.). *Drugs in combination with other therapies.* New York: Grune & Stratton, 1975.

Haslam, R. H. A., & Valletutti, P. J. *Medical problems in the classroom.* Baltimore: University Park Press, 1975.

Hewett, F. M. *The emotionally disturbed child in the classroom.* Boston: Allyn & Bacon, 1968.

Johnson, R. A., Kenny, J. B., & Davis, J. B. Developing school policy for use of stimulant drugs for hyperactive children. In J. J. Bosco & S. S. Robin (Eds.), *The hyperactive child and stimulant drugs.* Chicago: University of Chicago Press, 1977.

Johnston, R. B. Minimal cerebral dysfunction: Nature and implications for therapy. In R. H. A. Haslam & P. J. Valletutti (Eds.), *Medical problems in the classroom.* Baltimore: University Park Press, 1975.

Kauffman, J. M., & Hallahan, D. P. (Eds.). *Handbook of special education.* Englewood Cliffs, N.J.: Prentice-Hall, 1981.

Keeley, S. M., Shemberg, K. M., & Carbonell, J. Operant clinical intervention: Behavior management or beyond? Where are the data? *Behavior Therapy*, 1976, *7*, 292–305.

Kent, R. N., & O'Leary, K. D. A controlled evaluation of behavior modification with conduct problem children. *Journal of Consulting and Clinical Psychology*, 1976, *44*, 586–596.

Keogh, B. K., & Barkett, C. J. An educational analysis of hyperactive children's achievement problems. In C. K. Whalen & B. Henker (Eds.), *Hyperactive children: The social ecology of identification and treatment.* New York: Academic Press, 1980.

Keogh, B. K., & Margolis, J. Learn to labor and wait: Attentional problems of children with learning disorders. *Journal of Learning Disabilities*, 1976, *9*, 276–286.

Lahey, B. (Ed.). *Behavior therapy with hyperactive children.* New York: Oxford University Press, 1979.

Loney, J. Hyperkinesis comes of age: What do we know and where should we go? *American Journal of Orthopsychiatry*, 1980, *50*, 28–42.

Loney, J., Weissenburger, F. E., Woolson, R. F., & Lichty, E. C. Comparing psychological and pharmacological treatments for hyperkinetic boys and their classmates. *Journal of Abnormal Child Psychology*, 1979, *7*, 133–143.

Mash, E. J., & Dalby, J. T. Behavioral interventions for hyperactivity. In R. L. Trites (Ed.), *Hyperactivity in children: Etiology, measurement and treatment implications.* Baltimore: University Park Press, 1979.

Mash, E. J., & Terdal, L. G. After the dance is over: Some issues and suggestions for follow-up assessment in behavior therapy. *Psychological Reports*, 1977, *41*, 1287–1308.

Meichenbaum, D. H., & Goodman, J. Training impulsive children to talk to themselves: A means of developing self-control. *Journal of Abnormal Psychology*, 1971, *77*, 115–126.

O'Leary, K. D. Pills or skills for hyperactive children. *Journal of Applied Behavior Analysis*, 1980, *13*, 191–204.

O'Leary, K. D., Pelham, W. E., Rosenbaum, A., & Price, G. H. Behavioral treatment of hyperkinetic children. *Clinical Pediatrics*, 1976, *15*, 510–515.

O'Leary, S. G., & O'Leary, K. D. Behavioral treatment for hyperactive children. In R. M. Knights

& D. J. Bakker (Eds.), *Treatment of hyperactive and learning disordered children.* Baltimore: University Park Press, 1980.

O'Leary, S. G., & Pelham, W. E. Behavior therapy and withdrawal of stimulant medication in hyperactive children. *Pediatrics*, 1978, *61*, 211–217.

Patterson, G. R. An application of conditioning techniques to the control of a hyperactive child. In L. P. Ullmann & L. Krasner (Eds.), *Case studies in behavior modification.* New York: Holt, Rinehart & Winston, 1965.

Patterson, G. R., Jones, R., Whittier, J., & Wright, M. A. A behavior modification technique for the hyperactive child. *Behaviour Research and Therapy*, 1965, *2*, 217–226.

Pelham, W. E., Schnedler, R. W., Bologna, N. C., & Contreras, J. A. Behavioral and stimulant treatment of hyperactive children: A therapy study with methylphenidate probes in a within-subject design. *Journal of Applied Behavior Analysis*, 1980, *13*, 221–236.

Phillips, J. S., & Ray, R. S. Behavioral approaches to childhood disorders. *Behavior Modification*, 1980, *4*, 3–34.

Pihl, R. O. Conditioning procedures with hyperactive children. *Neurology*, 1967, *17*, 421–423.

Quay, H. C., Sprague, R. L., Werry, J. S., & McQueen, M. Conditioning visual orientation of conduct problem children in the classroom. *Journal of Experimental Child Psychology*, 1967, *5*, 512–517.

Rie, H. E. Therapeutic tutoring for underachieving children. *Professional Psychology*, 1974, *5*, 70–75.

Rosenbaum, A., O'Leary, K. D., & Jacob, R. G. Behavioral intervention with hyperactive children: Group consequences as a supplement to individual contingencies. *Behavior Therapy*, 1975, *6*, 315–323.

Ross, D. M., & Ross, S. A. *Hyperactivity: Research, theory, and action.* New York: Wiley, 1976.

Safer, D. J., & Allen, R. P. *Hyperactive children: Diagnosis and management.* Baltimore: University Park Press, 1976.

Satterfield, J. H., Cantwell, D. P., & Satterfield, B. Multimodality treatment. *Archives of General Psychiatry*, 1979, *36*, 965–974.

Sprague, R. L., & Berger, B. D. Drug effects on learning performance: Relevance of animal research to pediatric psychopharmacology. In R. M. Knights & D. J. Bakker (Eds.), *Treatment of hyperactive and learning disordered children.* Baltimore: University Park Press, 1980.

Sprague, R. L., & Gadow, K. The role of the teacher in drug treatment. In J. J. Bosco & S. S. Robin (Eds.), *The hyperactive child and stimulant drugs.* Chicago: University of Chicago Press, 1977.

Sprague, R. L., & Sleator, E. K. Methylphenidate in hyperkinetic children: Differences in dose effects on learning and social behavior. *Science*, 1977, *198*, 1274–1276.

Stableford, W., Butz, R., Hasazi, J., Leitenberg, H., & Peyser, J. *Sequential withdrawal of stimulant drugs and behavior therapy with two hyperactive boys.* Paper presented at the meeting of the Association for Advancement of Behavior Therapy, Chicago, November 1974.

Steinkamp, M. W. *The problem of children's failure to take medication during psychotropic drug trials.* Unpublished manuscript, University of Illinois, 1980.

Strauss, A. A., & Kephart, N. C. *Psychopathology and education of the brain-injured child* (Vol. 2, *Progress in theory and clinic*). New York: Grune & Stratton, 1955.

Strauss, A. A., & Lehtinen, L. E. *Psychopathology and education of the brain-injured child.* New York: Grune & Stratton, 1947.

Trites, R. L. (Ed.). *Hyperactivity in children: Etiology, measurement, and treatment implications.* Baltimore: University Park Press, 1979.

Walker, M. K. *Repeated acquisition behavior in hyperkinetic children.* Unpublished doctoral dissertation, University of Illinois, 1980.

Ward, L. C. Comment on "Recall, retention, and Ritalin." *Journal of Consulting and Clinical Psychology*, 1979, *47*, 975–976.

Weithorn, C. J. Perspectives on drug treatment for hyperactivity. In M. J. Cohen (Ed.), *Drugs and the special child.* New York: Gardner Press, 1979.

Werry, J. S., & Sprague, R. L. Hyperactivity. In C. G. Costello (Ed.), *Symptoms of psychopathology.* New York: Wiley, 1970.

Whalen, C. K., Collins, B. E., Henker, B., Alkus, S. R., Adams, D., & Stapp, J. Behavior observations of hyperactive children and methylphenidate (Ritalin) effects in systematically structured classroom environments: Now you see them, now you don't. *Journal of Pediatric Psychology*, 1978, *3*, 177–187.

Whalen, C. K., & Henker, B. Psychostimulants and children: A review and analysis. *Psychological Bulletin*, 1976, *83*, 1113–1130.

Whalen, C. K., & Henker, B. (Eds.). *Hyperactive children: The social ecology of identification and treatment*. New York: Academic Press, 1980.

Whalen, C. K., Henker, B., Collins, B. E., Finck, D., & Dotemoto, S. A social ecology of hyperactive boys: Methylphenidate (Ritalin) effects and medication by situation interactions in systematically structured classroom environments. *Journal of Applied Behavior Analysis*, 1979, *12*, 65–81.

Wolraich, M. L. Behavior modification therapy in hyperactive children. *Clinical Pediatrics*, 1979, *18*, 563–569.

Wolraich, M., Drummond, T., Salomon, M. K., O'Brien, M. L., & Sivage, C. Effects of methylphenidate alone and in combination with behavior modification procedures on the behavior and academic performance of hyperactive children. *Journal of Abnormal Child Psychology*, 1978, *6*, 149–161.

Worland, J. Effects of positive and negative feedback on behavior control in hyperactive and normal boys. *Journal of Abnormal Child Psychology*, 1976, *4*, 315–316.

Wulbert, M., & Dries, R. The relative efficacy of methylphenidate (Ritalin) and behavior modification techniques in the treatment of a hyperactive child. *Journal of Applied Behavior Analysis*, 1977, *10*, 21–31.

Zentall, S. S., Zentall, R. T., & Booth, M. E. Within-task stimulation: Effects on activity and spelling performance in hyperactive and normal children. *Journal of Education Research*, 1978, *71*, 223–230.

CHAPTER TWENTY

Long-Term Outcome: Findings, Concepts, and Practical Implications

GABRIELLE WEISS

A REVIEW OF SOME FOLLOW-UP STUDIES

The relationship between behavior problems of childhood and adult psychopathology is of more than theoretical interest. Knowledge in this area is essential for the planning of appropriate treatment programs for deviant children and for a better understanding of adult psychiatric disorders. The follow-up studies of O'Neal and Robins (1958) indicated that many disturbed children do not outgrow their problems; this applied particularly to those who showed antisocial behavior.

The etiology of the hyperactive child syndrome is unknown, and many clinicians and investigators consider the condition to be a final common pathway by which a variety of biological, psychological, and social influences are expressed. Considering, then, that the etiology of the condition is probably multiple and that more than a single etiology may be operating for any one child, it is of utmost clinical importance to determine which of the many variables assessed when the diagnosis is made are influential with respect to the final outcome. Unfortunately, predictors of outcome are only now beginning to receive adequate attention, and at the end of this chapter I discuss this aspect of follow-up studies. I also attempt to assess whether the body of findings from follow-up studies are sufficiently in agreement with one another to enable investigators to draw firm conclusions on the expected outcome of this condition. If such conclusions can be drawn, then researchers will have established that there exists a fair degree of predictive validity to the syndrome of the hyperactive child—an important issue, since the existence of this syndrome as a specific entity has recently been challenged (Shaffer & Greenhill, 1979).

Laufer and Denhoff (1957), who have had extensive clinical experience with hyperkinetic children, wrote: "In later years this syndrome tends to wane spontaneously and disappear. We have not seen it persist in those patients whom we have followed to adult life" (p. 464). In a later study, Laufer (1971) used a parental questionnaire, completed when the patients were aged 15 to 26 years (mean 19.8). Sixty-six of 100 completed the questionnaire. Some form

Gabrielle Weiss. Department of Psychiatry, The Montreal Children's Hospital, Montreal, Quebec, Canada.

of special schooling had been needed for 50 of the subjects. Overdoses with drugs, drug abuse, and suicide attempts were rare. Fourteen of 37 subjects had entered college. Of the 10 subjects who received military training, one had a bad conduct record. Hyperactivity had disappeared in 61% of the cases. Some kind of trouble with the police was described by 30% (16 subjects), but none was in jail. While these findings give valuable data, they are difficult to interpret because no control group was used. It is possible that there was a bias toward a relatively favorable outcome by the portion of the subject population that agreed to complete the questionnaire.

Recently, the same group of workers reported a 5-year follow-up study of 81 children diagnosed earlier as having minimal brain dysfunction or hyperkinetic impulse disorder (Feldman, Denhoff, & Denhoff, 1979). At follow-up the mean age of the subjects was 21 years, and a group of 32 older siblings of the subjects was evaluated as a comparison group. The subjects had received various forms of treatment, including stimulant therapy when necessary. Results indicated that about half of the group had no further symptoms or sequelae of the original syndromes. The use of stimulant medication was not associated with increased drug or alcohol use in adolescence or young adulthood. A higher percentage of the subjects than of the controls had used marijuana, and their self-esteem was lower than that of their siblings. Among the subjects, 91% were either at work or at school, and 10% were considered to have significant emotional or behavior problems. It is not clear whether all of the subjects included in the study were "hyperactive." The inclusion of any nonhyperactive subjects would provide a bias toward a more favorable outcome.

Menkes, Rowe, and Menkes (1967) studied 18 patients in a 25-year retrospective follow-up study. All 18 had had hyperactivity and learning difficulties at the time they were seen at the Johns Hopkins Child Psychiatry Outpatient Clinic, Baltimore, between 1937 and 1946. At the time of follow-up, they were interviewed and had a neurological evaluation. Four patients diagnosed as psychotic were in institutions; two were clearly retarded and leading dependent lives with their families. Eight were self-supporting, but four of these eight had spent some time in an institution. Three subjects complained that they still suffered from hyperactivity: "They felt restless and had a hard time settling down to anything." Menkes and colleagues included subjects with IQs at any level over 70, and it could well be that the poor outcome of the 14 subjects was related to low intelligence as well as or rather than hyperactivity. Unfortunately, no group was used to control for the intelligence factor.

Wood, Reimherr, Wender, and Johnson (1976) selected 15 adults from a patient group whose predominant symptoms were impulsivity, poor attention, restlessness, and emotional lability. The parents of these patients completed the abbreviated Conners Parent Rating Scale based on their memories of their children when they were 6 to 10 years old. Two-thirds of these parent ratings placed the adult patient in the 95th percentile for hyperactivity during their childhood, indicating that these adult psychiatric patients were still manifesting continued problems of the hyperactive child syndrome. The limitation of this interesting study is the lack of a control group, such as psychiatric patients with different problems, and the uncertain validity of parents' scoring the childhood behavior of their now adult children.

Shelley and Riester (1972) described 16 young adults serving in the U.S. Air Force who, as a result of difficulties in performing certain tasks expected of them, developed anxiety and self-depreciation, and reported difficulties in impulse control and concentration. The tasks they found difficult were tasks requiring fine and gross motor skills such as marching properly, learning judo, and so on. On neurological evaluation, most were found to be clumsy, and half of the group had dysdiadochokinesia or finger apraxia. Their mean performance IQ on the Wechsler Adult Intelligence Scale (WAIS) was 22 points below their verbal IQ. Their parents said that, as children, most of the subjects had been regarded as overactive and had experienced difficulties at school; during their adolescence they had improved until, on entering the Air Force, they were required to perform tasks that they found difficult. The findings of this clinical study are quite similar to that of Wood *et al.* (1976), already described, with the same drawbacks—namely, the problem of selective memory of parents' rating the childhood of their offspring more than 10 years later, and the lack of a control group.

Hans Huessy's (Huessy, Marshall, & Gendron, 1972) 7-year follow-up study of 501 children attending several rural Vermont schools is of great interest. Teachers completed a questionnaire on each child that tapped social maturity, academic performance, general attitude and behavior, and neuromuscular development. Raw scores were scaled into percentile scores, and the upper (i.e., the worst) 20% were designated as hyperkinetic. All children were rated in second, fourth, and fifth grades. Various checkback procedures asking teachers to identify problem children in their classes showed that children thus identified had scores above the 80th percentile. It was found that those children who were identified in second grade only, and not in fourth and fifth grades, while frequently repeating a grade, had a good prognosis (assessed in ninth grade). Those children whose mean percentiles in second, fourth, and fifth grades fell above the 80th percentile had the worst prognosis in high school, and 70% of them had poor or very poor social adjustment in their adolescence. In contrast, none of those children who scored below the 30th percentile in second, fourth, and fifth grades had any social problems in ninth grade. This study confirms the fact that academic performance and behavior in elementary school has high predictive value for adolescence. All children in this study who had had behavior and academic problems in high school first showed these difficulties when they were in elementary school. The study, however, has limitations because of the method of identifying hyperkinetic children. It is likely that the particular method chosen, which relied solely on a teacher rating scale, identified a mixed group of problem children that included a large percentage of children with the hyperactive child syndrome.

Borland and Heckman (1976) carried out a 20- to 25-year retrospective study of 20 men who in their childhood had conformed to diagnostic criteria for the hyperactive child syndrome. Brothers of these subjects were interviewed as a control group. The investigators found that the majority of men who had been hyperactive were now steadily employed and self-supporting. However, half of the subjects continued to show symptoms of the hyperactive syndrome. In addition, the hyperactive subjects had not attained the socioeconomic status of their brothers. This difference had declined slightly between the time of their first job and the time of the interview, but was significantly lower for the hyperactive subjects even at the time of interview.

Findings from our own 5-year follow-up studies at The Montreal Children's Hospital indicated that the prognosis of this group of children as they matured into adolescence was relatively poor. Despite a decrease of ratings of hyperactivity over a period of 5 years, as adolescents the subjects continued to be distractible, emotionally immature, and unable to maintain goals, and also had developed poor self-images (Minde, Weiss, & Mendelson, 1972; Weiss, Minde, Werry, Douglas, & Nemeth, 1971). The school records of the hyperactive adolescents showed a greater incidence of failed school grades and lower ratings on all subjects on report cards compared to matched control children in the same school (Minde, Lewin, Weiss, Lavigueur, Douglas, & Sykes, 1971). They continued to use impulsive rather than reflective approaches to cognitive tasks (Cohen, Weiss, & Minde, 1972), and over a period of 5 years they showed no improvement on tests of intelligence or visuomotor tasks and a decrement of performance on motor skills. About 25% of a group of 64 engaged in delinquent behavior, a far higher percentage than that of matched controls.

Similar findings regarding adolescent hyperactives were obtained by Mendelson, Johnson, and Stewart (1971) in a retrospective study, and by Dykman and Ackerman (1980) in a prospective study. Dykman and Ackerman reevaluated 62 learning-disabled children and 31 controls a few years after initial assessment, when both subjects and controls were 14 years old. Of the 62 learning-disabled subjects, 23 were initially diagnosed as being also hyperactive. At follow-up, about half of the hyperactive learning-disabled subgroup presented with fairly severe adjustment problems, mainly of an antisocial nature. Social deviancy was found to be infrequent among both the normal controls and the nonhyperactive learning-disabled adolescents. It is clear from this study that the presence of hyperactivity in learning-disabled children predicts poor social adjustment in adolescence.

SUMMARY OF THE 10- TO 12-YEAR CONTROLLED PROSPECTIVE FOLLOW-UP STUDY AT THE MONTREAL CHILDREN'S HOSPITAL

This study reports on a series of outcome variables from 76 hyperactive subjects aged 17 to 24 years (mean 19.5 years) and 45 control subjects aged 17 to 24 years (mean 19.0 years). The two groups were matched with respect to age, sex, socioeconomic class, and IQ (WAIS).

All the hyperactive subjects included in the study were initially assessed in the Department of Psychiatry at The Montreal Children's Hospital, 10 to 12 years previously (1962 through 1965), at which time they were 6 to 12 years of age. Children were admitted into the study if they met the following criteria: (1) Restlessness and poor concentration were their main complaints, and had been present since their earliest years; (2) the complaints were a major source of problems both at home and at school; (3) all children had IQs above 85 (Wechsler Intelligence Scale for Children [WISC]—full scale); (4) none of the children was psychotic, borderline psychotic, epileptic, or had cerebral palsy; and (5) all children were living at home with at least one parent.

A total of 104 hyperactive children were initially included in the study (1962 through 1965) and took part in a series of drug studies determining the efficacy of chlorpromazine (Werry, Weiss, Douglas, & Martin, 1966) and dextroamphetamine (Weiss, Werry, Minde, Douglas, & Sykes, 1968). While the presenting problems of these children were markedly similar, they differed from one another with respect to the socioeconomic class and degree of healthy functioning of their families, as well as the degree of conduct disorder associated with the primary behavioral symptoms of the hyperactive syndrome (Langhorne, Loney, Paternite, & Bechtoldt, 1976). They also differed with respect to the severity of the primary behavioral symptoms. Variations in these initial measurements were expected to have prognostic significance for later adolescent and adult adjustment.

Of the original 104 children, 91 were reevaluated in a series of follow-up studies during their adolescence 5 to 6 years after initial assessment (Minde *et al.*, 1971; Minde *et al.*, 1972; Weiss, Minde, Douglas, Werry, & Sykes, 1971). In the recent 10- to 12-year follow-up study, 76 of these 91 subjects agreed to participate once more.

The control group was first selected at the time of the 5-year follow-up study of the hyperactive children. A group of 35 children was matched with the group of hyperactive children on age, sex, IQ (WISC), and socioeconomic class. Criteria for inclusion in the study required that the control children have no significant academic or behavioral difficulties in the home or at school. This control group was expanded to 45 subjects at the time of the 10-year follow-up study, using the same matching variables and criteria for inclusion.

The results of our 10- to 12-year follow-up study are summarized here in the following categories: (1) biographical data; (2) psychiatric assessment; (3) physiological measures; and (4) psychological tests.

Biographical Data

The biographical data (Weiss, Hechtman, Perlman, Hopkins, & Wener, 1979) indicated that fewer hyperactive subjects than controls were still living with their parents (76% vs. 95%), and that hyperactives had made significantly more geographic moves during the 5 years before follow-up assessment. They had significantly more car accidents (mean 1.3 vs. .07), although the number of subjects in each group who had car accidents was not significantly different.

The hyperactives' school history indicated that they had completed less education, and more were still in high school at the time of the follow-up evaluation. Their average marks were lower, and more hyperactives discontinued participation in high school for this reason. They failed more grades in elementary and in high school, but no one particular subject or subjects was responsible for the failure.

Their work history indicated no difference in job status on the Hollingshead Scale (Hollingshead & Redlich, 1958) between the subjects working full-time in the two groups, at this age. It should be mentioned that this finding is not in agreement with that of Borland and Heckman (1976), and the discrepancy can probably be accounted for by the fact that our subjects were much younger than the subjects in Borland's retrospective study, and in this respect, time may well be on the side of the control subjects.

There was also no difference between the two groups with respect to discrepancy between the fathers' work status and that of the subjects. The vocational plans (or work aspirations) were not different between the groups as judged on the Hollingshead Scale, and there was no difference between the groups as to whether the vocational aspirations were judged by the psychiatrist to be realistic.

With respect to court referrals, there was a trend for the hyperactive subjects to have had more court referrals during the 5 years preceding follow-up (47% vs. 32%), but there was no difference between the groups as to the number of subjects who had had court referrals during the year before follow-up. A separate analysis, taking into account both the number and seriousness (on a single 3-point scale) of different kinds of court referrals, showed no difference between the groups regarding the seriousness of such offenses as disturbing the peace, theft, aggression, nonmedical drug possession (or selling), or traffic offenses committed within the 5 years prior to follow-up.

A significantly greater percentage (74% vs. 54%) of hyperactive subjects had tried some form of nonmedical drug (mostly marijuana or hashish) in the 5 years preceding follow-up, but there was no difference between the groups with respect to nonmedical drug use in the year preceding follow-up. Interestingly enough, significantly more controls had used hallucinogens in the prior 5 years. There was no significant difference between the groups with respect to severity of drug use (3-point scale: mild, moderate, or abusive) in the 5 years preceding follow-up.

Psychiatric Assessment

The psychiatric evaluation (Weiss *et al.*, 1979) indicated that more hyperactive subjects were diagnosed as having personality trait disorders, the two most frequent types being impulsive and immature–dependent personality traits. Two hyperactive subjects were diagnosed as borderline psychotics (this was not significant), but no subject in either group was diagnosed as being psychotic. Significantly more hyperactive subjects than controls felt restless, and significantly more were observed to be restless by the psychiatrist during their assessment, although actual getting up from their chair was rare. Hyperactive subjects rated their childhood as unhappy more often than did controls. When asked what helped them most, the commonest spontaneous response was one particular parent or teacher who believed in them or the development of a talent. "Family fights," "feeling dumb," and "being criticized" were the most frequent spontaneous responses as to what made their childhood the hardest.

Physiological Measures

There was no difference between the groups with respect to height, weight, blood pressure, or pulse rate (Hechtman, Weiss, & Perlman, 1978). Serial comparison of electroencephalograms (EEGs) of both groups at the 10-year follow-up revealed no significant difference. Comparison of EEGs of hyperactive subjects at initial evaluation, 5-year follow-up, and 10-year follow-up indicated that normalization of the EEG tended to occur during adolescence (Hechtman, Weiss, & Metrakos, 1978).

Psychological Tests

In the course of psychological testing (see Hopkins, Hechtman, & Weiss, 1979; Weiss, Hechtman, & Perlman, 1978), subjects rated themselves on the California

Psychological Inventory (Gough, 1957), designed to tap cultural ideals of self-esteem and social interaction; the SCL-90 (Derogatis, Lipman, & Lovi, 1973), designed to tap classical psychopathology; and tests of self-esteem (Davidson & Lang, 1960; Hoy, Weiss, Minde, & Cohen, 1978; Ziller, Hagey, & Smith, 1979). On both the California Psychological Inventory and the tests of self-esteem, hyperactives rated themselves as significantly inferior to controls. However, on the SCL-90, the ratings of the two groups did not differ, indicating that hyperactives did not see themselves as having classical symptoms of psychopathology. However, they did see themselves as functioning less optimally than did controls.

On social skills tests, hyperactives were worse only on oral tasks and performed as well as controls on written tasks. The social skills tests used were the Situational Social Skills Inventory (SSSI) in written and oral form (Clark, 1974) and the Means–End Problem-Solving (MEPS) test (Platt, Spivack, & Bloom, 1971).

Rating scales sent to employers and to teachers, containing almost identical items to be rated, showed that teachers rated hyperactives as inferior to controls on all items, whereas employers' ratings were identical for the two groups. This indicated that the demands of the social setting in which hyperactives are evaluated significantly influence the degree to which they are considered deviant.

Cognitive-style tests—Matching Familiar Figures (MFF) Test (Kagan, 1964); Embedded Figures Test (EFT) (Witkin, Dyk, Goodenough, & Karp, 1962), and the Stroop test (Stroop, 1935)—indicated that the problems hyperactives had had during their childhood and adolescence persisted into adult life (Hopkins *et al.*, 1979). It is difficult to know whether any bias was introduced into the results from the 27% of the original sample not reevaluated 12 years later.

Conclusions

This outcome study suggests that while few hyperactive children become grossly disturbed or chronic breakers of the law and none were diagnosed as being psychotic or schizophrenic, the majority continue as young adults to have various continued symptoms of the hyperactive child syndrome. For example, lower educational achievement, poorer social skills, and lower self-esteem than controls, as well as impulsivity and restlessness continued to be present. At the same time, unlike the delinquency of the antisocial children in one study (Robins, 1966/1974), in our study the majority of hyperactives who as adolescents had committed delinquent acts had gained sufficient control by the time they were young adults that they did not have significantly more court referrals than normal controls had.

This study left us with two important challenges:

1. To identify the minority of hyperactive subjects destined to have poor outcomes so that special attention can be given to those at risk.
2. To determine the types of intervention that would significantly reduce the continued morbidity of this condition. In other words, how are clinicians to modify or prevent the poor self-esteem, poor socialization, lower educational level, and impulsivity which are seen in most hyperactives even in adulthood?

Over the past two decades, it has been demonstrated beyond any reasonable doubt in a series of well-designed controlled acute drug studies, that dextroamphetamine and methylphenidate are effective by comparison with placebo in reducing many of the symptoms of the hyperactive syndrome. These studies taken together suggest that 70–80% of a group of hyperactive children respond favorably to stimulants, while the remainder of children are unimproved and a few become worse. It has been established that stimulants have the following effects:

1. Concentration (as measured by continuous-attention tasks) is improved (Conners & Rothchild, 1968; Sykes, Douglas, & Morgenstern, 1972).
2. Purposeless activity becomes more goal-directed (Conners & Eisenberg, 1963; Denhoff, Davis, & Hawkins, 1971; Weiss, Minde, Douglas, Werry, & Sykes, 1971).
3. Classroom behavior is improved (Sprague, Barnes, & Werry, 1970).
4. Aggressive behaviors are reduced (Winsberg, Bialer, Kupietz, & Tobias, 1972).
5. Fine motor activity (Knights & Hinton, 1969), rote learning (Conners, Eisenberg, & Sharpe, 1964), and discrimination of foreground from background (Campbell, Douglas, & Morgenstern, 1971) are facilitated.
6. Impulsivity as measured on a laboratory task is decreased (Campbell *et al.*, 1971).

It is not clearly established whether stimulants have a direct effect on motor skills, perception, memory, and learning, or whether all these are improved as a result of the increase of attention and reflectivity.

Because no evidence appeared to the contrary, it was taken for granted that the stimulants that were found to be so effective in all these short-term drug studies would be equally effective given over the years and would, therefore, in all likelihood improve the prognosis of children with the hyperactive syndrome.

Unfortunately, over time, both clinical experience and research findings have cast some doubts over this optimistic therapeutic prediction. Clinicians treating large numbers of hyperactive children who were receiving adequate amounts of stimulants and whose medication was well monitored found that over the years, in spite of medication, many problems continued. By adolescence, these stimulant-treated hyperactives were still failing in school and continued to be behavior problems; many had developed antisocial behaviors, as well as experiencing social ostracism. It was recognized that while the stimulants continued to reduce symptomatology, the children continued to be in various degrees of trouble, and that other methods of management as well as (or instead of) stimulants were required.

Four long-term drug studies (Blouin, Bornstein, & Trites, 1978; Riddle & Rapoport, 1976; Sleator, Neumann, & Sprague, 1974; Weiss, Kruger, Danielson, & Elman, 1975) tended to confirm this clinical finding of the relative lack of efficacy of stimulants used for many years. In one study, Sleator *et al.* (1974) found that in a group of 42 hyperactive children who were treated with methylphenidate, when placebo was substituted for 1 month in the year (unknown to teachers, parents, and the children themselves), only 17 out of the 42 children were rated as being worse by their teachers, and even a smaller number were rated as being worse by their mothers. This indicated that more than half the children who had initially responded so favorably to methylphenidate either required the drug less or were benefiting from it less 1 or 2 years later.

In a second study (Weiss *et al.*, 1975), it was found that a group of 26 hyperactive children treated with methylphenidate for 3 to 5 years did not have a more favorable outcome in their adolescence than did two matched groups of hyperactive children, one of which groups received no medication and the second of which received chlorpromazine for 1½ to 3 years. No differences among these three groups of hyperactive adolescent children were found in the following outcome measures: reduction in hyperactivity; emotional adjustment; antisocial behavior; school performance (measured by report cards and numbers of grades failed); mothers' view of overall improvement. While these measures of outcome were relatively crude, so that subtle differences might have been undetected, the authors concluded that methylphenidate continues to reduce the symptomatology of the syndrome in various degrees when given over several years, but that in the absence of a more comprehensive treatment program, the medication could not be demonstrated to have a significant effect on outcome as measured in adolescence.

In a third study, Riddle and Rapoport (1976) followed for 2 years 72 hyperactive middle-class children who were treated with stimulants or tricyclic antidepressants. After careful reassessment, the authors concluded:

> This 2-year follow-up study of relatively homogeneous "optimally treated" population of hyperactive boys indicates that, as in other studies, this population is at high risk for continuing academic and social difficulties. As 55% of the group were still receiving a stimulant and 9% were taking tricyclic antidepressants after 2 years, and a large number also had other academic and psychiatric aid, this outcome is disappointing. This study provides indirect support for the idea that the medication's long-term effect is mainly suppression of impulsive and hyperactive behaviors. (p. 131)

Trites and his coworkers (Blouin *et al.*, 1978), in their recent 5-year follow-up study of hyperactive children and children with school difficulties without hyperactivity, found that as adolescents the hyperactive group had more conduct problems and drank more alcohol than the adolescents who had school difficulties did. Regarding the effect of methylphenidate therapy on outcome of the hyperactive children, these authors concluded:

> Generally, clinical treatment with Ritalin was found to have no beneficial effect, and there was some evidence to suggest a poorer behavioral outcome for the drug-treated group. Even when good and poor responders were examined separately, no beneficial effects of the drug were detected on academic achievement, intellectual tests, or behavioral measures of hyperactivity and conduct disorders, although good responders were found to use less alcohol. The implications of these findings are that hyperactives are at a higher risk for conduct disorders and teenage alcohol use than children who have specific learning difficulties. Additionally, Ritalin as currently administered was found to have little or no beneficial effect on the intellectual, academic, or behavioral outcome of hyperactive children. (p. 193)

Investigators can ask themselves why their original optimism has not so far been confirmed in the long-term stimulant drug studies. However, the answer is at the present time a matter of guesswork based on common sense. It is very likely that some of the problems experienced by children having this behavioral syndrome are not affected by stimulants. This is certainly true for those hyperactives who have concomitant learning disabilities that require specific remediation with or without the adjunct of stimulants. It may also be true that subtle aspects of the syndrome such as socialization skills are not significantly affected by stimulants, or, as Loney's work suggests (Milich & Loney, 1979), that aggressive symptoms do not respond to stimulant therapy. Finally, the matter of tolerance developing over time to symptom responsiveness to stimulants has not been adequately investigated. Researchers, therefore, do not know whether tolerance takes place, and, if it does, whether it affects all symptoms to the same degree.

It can only be concluded that a condition with such a broad spectrum of difficulties as the hyperactive child syndrome requires a wide range of therapeutic input and can only rarely be managed by medication alone. This conclusion is supported by Satterfield and coworkers (Satterfield, Satterfield, & Cantwell, 1981), who have recently conducted a 3-year multimodality follow-up study of 100 hyperactive boys initially aged 6 to 12 years. Each child in this study, after a careful evaluation, was treated by various therapies determined by the individual child's needs. The treatments included family, individual, or group therapy; remedial education; and medication. The outcome for boys who had completed 3 years of treatment was compared with that of those who had received 2 years or less of treatment. It was found that those who received more treatment had a better outcome with respect to educational achievement and antisocial behavior than did those who had received less treatment. The authors also note that their group of adequately and comprehensively treated hyperactive boys had an unusually favorable outcome, compared to other groups of hyperactive children described in the literature.

Most researchers would agree that there is a strong likelihood that a comprehensive treatment plan (which includes stimulant therapy but does not rely on medication alone, and which addresses itself to all the various disabilities exhibited by the hyperactive child) will favorably influence outcome. Satterfield *et al.*'s study provides evidence that this is the case. Unfortunately, in this study children were not randomly assigned to a multimodality treatment group and some other comparison treatment group, such as a group receiving medication alone. Some researchers are awaiting the results of a controlled treatment study, which, although ideal, is unfortunately extremely difficult to carry out. Random assignment of children for long periods of time, such as 3 years, to different treatment groups has both ethical and practical difficulties. The possibility of carrying out this kind of research, which may require inter-university collaboration, was the subject of a National Institute of Mental Health (NIMH) conference in Washington in June of 1980.

Finally, from a clinical point of view, it is worth pointing out that although the long-term efficacy of stimulant medication for hyperactives has not yet been established in a controlled study, several prominent researchers in the field—for example, Paul Wender, Leon Oettinger, and Hans Huessy—have found that, based on their wide clinical experience, the need for stimulants and/or the tricyclic antidepressant medication does not automatically disappear with puberty, and that these drugs may be beneficial for treating adult hyperactives.

PREDICTIVE VALIDITY OF THE HYPERACTIVE CHILD SYNDROME

What conclusions can investigators draw from the body of literature on follow-up of hyperactive children? At first glance, there is little agreement among authors, and the studies suffer from various problems of methodologies. The study that is most out of line in terms of final outcome is that of Menkes *et al.* (1967). This study can be separated from all others in that retarded children were included. All other studies have, in fact, a high degree of agreement of outcome. For example, the studies of Laufer (1971), Borland and Heckman (1976), and Feldman *et al.* (1979), and our own study (Weiss *et al.*, 1979)—while quite different in the methodology used (the first relying on questionnaires, the second being a retrospective study, and the third and fourth being prospective studies)—all have essentially similar findings. These are as follows:

1. The majority of hyperactive children grow up without major psychopathology either of an antisocial or a psychotic nature. No children in the four studies were found to be psychotic.
2. In all four studies, half or more of hyperactives had varying degrees of continuing symptoms of the hyperactive child syndrome.

Not many investigators have as yet established the initial variables that affect outcome. Our own study of outcome measures in adolescence assessed those factors that predicted (1) satisfactory school performance (defined as not repeating any grades and achieving average or above-average marks at time of follow-up); (2) antisocial behavior; (3) good emotional adjustment (defined as not having inadequate, aggressive, socialized delinquent, and psychotic traits).

The children who at follow-up were succeeding in school (20%) differed from the rest only on the WISC IQ. While there was a trend for this 20% to have lower scores on distractibility and hyperactivity, this did not reach significance. Aggressivity scores, socioeconomic class, and family disturbance did not significantly distinguish the 20% who did well at school from the others.

Those who had overt antisocial behavior at follow-up were predicted by having higher initial scores on aggression and poorer overall family ratings. Within the latter, poor mother–child relationships, poor mental health of parents, and punitive child-rearing practices predicted antisocial behavior at adolescence. Hyperactivity, distractibility, socioeconomic class, and IQ failed to predict antisocial behavior.

None of the measures examined predicted emotional adjustment. We have not completed the prognostic indicators from the 10- to 12-year follow-up study.

Loney and her coworkers (Loney, Kramer, & Milich, 1981) have now carried out careful predictive studies using multivariate techniques. Their findings indicate that socioeconomic class and aggression, which are correlated at referral (Langhorne *et al.*, 1976), contribute to adolescent symptoms and delinquency. Treatment variables, childhood achievement, and hyperactivity, which are also correlated at initial assessment (Loney, Langhorne, & Paternite, 1978), predict achievement in adolescence. Family variables predicted delinquent behavior, aggressive symptoms, and achievement in adolescence. In this model, childhood aggression and childhood hyperactivity are assumed to have different correlates both at referral and at follow-up.

This model would explain why stimulant therapy does not lead to improved adolescent behavior or reduced delinquency. Although drug treatment reduces hyperactivity, it will not necessarily affect aggression and is unlikely to affect family variables. Loney *et al.* postulate that child hyperactivity itself is not the first link in a chain that leads to teenage delinquency and deviant behavior.

Although the last word has not been heard on this issue of prognostic indicators, Loney and her coworkers' multivariate studies have clarified the issue. Taken together, all these studies indicate that the outcome of hyperactive children has a fair level of predictability and that those hyperactive children who have more aggression initially have more chance of showing antisocial behavior in adolescence. The role of family variables as affecting measures of outcome is also established.

PRACTICAL IMPLICATIONS

1. Long-term follow-up studies of hyperactive children, whether prospective or retrospective, have shown a fair degree of similarity in their findings. In my view, this provides predictive validity for the existence of the syndrome of the hyperactive child. A skeptic could argue that the only fact that emerges from these follow-up studies of hyperactive children is that as adults they continue to be different from controls. The specificity of the adult outcome of hyperactive children can only be ascertained by a study that simultaneously follows matched children of other diagnostic categories. Such a study has not been done. In the meantime, it is of interest that while at different stages in the life history of a hyperactive child different complaints are predominant, all problems found in the adult life of hyperactives are nevertheless detectable early and are already present in the preschool years.

2. In all the outcome studies cited, the majority of hyperactive children in adult life had some continuing difficulties characteristic of the hyperactive syndrome; in particular, impulsivity, restlessness, and poor social skills continued to be present. It is, therefore, important to provide special treatment programs for young hyperactive children that emphasize impulsivity control and social skills training. In addition, since a minority of hyperactive children become chronic offenders of the law and/or seriously disturbed (although not psychotic), it is most important to find the predictors for this kind of poor outcome, so that this minority can be identified early and can receive special attention.

3. The high rate of antisocial behavior seen in groups of hyperactive subjects during adolescence (25–50%) diminishes as they reach young adult life. This seems in contrast to the outcome of "antisocial children," where follow-up indicates that over 50% continue antisocial behavior throughout their 20s and 30s (O'Neal & Robins, 1958). If this finding is confirmed, it will be of important practical significance for hyperactive children, their parents, and treating physicians, since the antisocial behavior of most (though not all) hyperactive adoles-

cents seems to be transitory. Final confirmation awaits controlled, simultaneous follow-up studies of both antisocial children (without hyperactivity) and hyperactive children. These have not yet been carried out.

4. Hans Huessy's study of 500 children has shown us that the social adjustment of hyperactive adolescents can be clearly predicted from behavior and academic records taken in second, third, and fifth grades, but not from second grade alone. Loney *et al.*'s study and Weiss *et al.*'s study have shown that antisocial behavior in hyperactive adolescents can be predicted from aggressive behavior in early childhood, and both Loney *et al.* and Weiss *et al.* found that family factors predicted adolescent antisocial behavior.

5. Long-term stimulant medication does little to improve the outcome of hyperactive children. Other modalities of treatment must be sought if researchers and clinicians hope to affect the adult outcome. At the same time, stimulants seem to be effective for symptom suppression of some but not all of the symptoms of the syndrome.

References

Blouin, A., Bornstein, R., & Trites, R. Teenage alcohol use among hyperactive children: A 5-year follow-up study. *Journal of Pediatric Psychology*, 1978, *3*, 188–194.

Borland, B., & Heckman, H. Hyperactive boys and their brothers: A 25-year follow-up study. *Archives of General Psychiatry*, 1976, *33*, 669–675.

Campbell, S., Douglas, V., & Morgenstern, G. Cognitive styles in hyperactive children and the effect of methylphenidate. *Journal of Child Psychology and Psychiatry*, 1971, *12*, 55–67.

Clark, K. *Evaluation of a group social skills training program with psychiatric inpatients: Training Viet Nam veterans in assertion, heterosocial, and job interview skills.* Unpublished doctoral dissertation, University of Wisconsin, 1974.

Cohen, N., Weiss, G., & Minde, K. Cognitive styles in adolescents previously diagnosed as hyperactive. *Journal of Child Psychology and Psychiatry*, 1972, *13*, 203–209.

Conners, C., & Eisenberg, L. The effects of methylphenidate on symptomatology and learning in disturbed children. *American Journal of Psychiatry*, 1963, *120*, 458–464.

Conners, C., Eisenberg, L., & Sharpe, L. Effect of methylphenidate (Ritalin) on paired-associate learning and Porteus Maze performance in emotionally disturbed children. *Journal of Consulting Psychology*, 1964, *28*, 14–22.

Conners, C., & Rothchild, G. Drugs and learning. In J. Hellmuth (Ed.), *Learning disorders* (Vol. 3). Seattle: Special Child Publications, 1968.

Davidson, H., & Lang, G. Children's perceptions of their teachers' feeling towards them related to self-perception, school achievement and behavior. *Journal of Experimental Education*, 1960, *29*, 107–116.

Denhoff, E., Davis, A., & Hawkins, R. Effect of dextroamphetamine on hyperactive children: A controlled double blind study. *Journal of Learning Disabilities*, 1971, *4*, 27–34.

Derogatis, L., Lipman, R., & Lovi, L. An outpatient psychiatric rating scale: Preliminary report. *Psychopharmacology Bulletin*, 1973, *9*, 13–28.

Dykman, R., & Ackerman, P. Long-term follow-up studies of hyperactive children. In B. W. Campbell (Ed.), *Advances in behavioral pediatrics* (Vol. 1). Greenwich, Conn.: JAI Press, 1980.

Feldman, S., Denhoff, E., & Denhoff, J. The attention disorders and related syndromes: Outcome in adolescence and young adult life. In E. Denhoff & L. Stern (Eds.), *Minimal brain dysfunction: A development approach.* New York: Masson, 1979.

Gough, H. *California Psychological Inventory.* Palo Alto, Calif.: Consulting Psychologists Press, 1957.

Hechtman, L., Weiss, G., & Metrakos, K. Hyperactive individuals as young adults: Current and longitudinal electroencephalographic evaluation and its relation to outcome. *Canadian Medical Association Journal*, 1978, *118*, 919–921.

Hechtman, L., Weiss, G., & Perlman, T. Growth and cardiovascular measures in hyperactive individuals as young adults and in matched normal controls. *Canadian Medical Association Journal*, 1978, *118*, 1247–1250.

Hollingshead, A., & Redlich, F. *Social class and mental illness: A community study*. New York: Wiley, 1958.

Hopkins, J., Hechtman, L., & Weiss, G. Cognitive style in adults originally diagnosed as hyperactives. *Journal of Child Psychology and Psychiatry*, 1979, *20*, 209–216.

Hoy, E., Weiss, G., Minde, K., & Cohen, N. The hyperactive child at adolescence: Emotional, social, and cognitive functioning. *Journal of Abnormal Child Psychology*, 1978, *6*, 311–324.

Huessy, H., Marshall, C., & Gendron, R. Five hundred children followed from grade 2 through grade 5 for the prevalence of behavior disorder. *Acta Paedopsychiatrica*, 1972, *39*, 301–309.

Kagan, J. Information processing in the child: Significance of analytic and reflective attitudes. *Psychological Monographs*, 1964, *78*(1, Whole No. 578).

Knights, R., & Hinton, G. The effects of methylphenidate (Ritalin) on the motor skills and behavior of children with learning problems. *Journal of Nervous and Mental Disease*, 1969, *148*, 643–653.

Langhorne, J., Loney, J., Paternite, C. E., & Bechtoldt, H. Childhood hyperkinesis: A return to the source. *Journal of Abnormal Psychology*, 1976, *85*, 201–209.

Laufer, M. Long-term management and some follow-up findings on the use of drugs with minimal cerebral syndromes. *Journal of Learning Disabilities*, 1971, *4*, 55–58.

Laufer, M., & Denhoff, E. Hyperkinetic behavior syndrome in children. *Journal of Pediatrics*, 1957, *50*, 463–474.

Loney, J., Kramer, J., & Milich, R. The hyperactive child grows up: Prediction of symptoms, delinquency, and achievement at follow-up. In K. Gadow & J. Loney (Eds.), *Psychosocial aspects of drug treatment for hyperactivity*. Boulder, Colo.: Westview Press, 1981.

Loney, J., Langhorne, J., & Paternite, C. E. An empirical basis for subgrouping the hyperkinetic/minimal brain dysfunction syndrome. *Journal of Abnormal Psychology*, 1978, *87*, 431–441.

Mendelson, W., Johnson, N., & Stewart, M. Hyperactive children as teenagers: A follow-up study. *Journal of Nervous and Mental Disease*, 1971, *153*, 273–279.

Menkes, M., Rowe, J., & Menkes, J. A 25-year follow-up study on the hyperactive child with minimal brain dysfunction. *Pediatrics*, 1967, *39*, 393–399.

Milich, R., & Loney, J. The role of hyperactive and aggressive symptomatology in predicting adolescent outcome among hyperactive children. *Journal of Pediatric Psychology*, 1979, *4*, 93–112.

Minde, K., Lewin, D., Weiss, G., Lavigueur, H., Douglas, V., & Sykes, E. The hyperactive child in elementary school: A five-year controlled follow-up. *Exceptional Children*, 1971, *38*, 215–221.

Minde, K., Weiss, G., & Mendelson, N. A five-year follow-up study of 91 hyperactive school children. *Journal of the American Academy of Child Psychiatry*, 1972, *11*, 595–610.

O'Neal, P., & Robins, L. The relation of childhood behavior problems to adult psychiatric status. *American Journal of Psychiatry*, 1958, *114*, 961–969.

Platt, J., Spivack, G., & Bloom, N. *Means–End Problem Solving (MEPS) manual and tentative norms*. Philadelphia: Department of Mental Health Sciences, Hahnemann Medical College and Hospital, 1971.

Riddle, K., & Rapoport, J. A 2-year follow-up of 72 hyperactive boys. *Journal of Nervous and Mental Disease*, 1976, *162*, 126–134.

Robins, L. N. A sociological and psychiatric study of sociopathic personality. In *Deviant children grow up*. Baltimore: Williams & Wilkins, 1966. (Reprinted, Huntington, N.Y.: Krieger, 1974.)

Satterfield, J., Satterfield, B., & Cantwell, D. Three-year multimodality treatment study of hyperactive boys. *Journal of Pediatrics*, 1981, *98*, 650–655.

Shaffer, D., & Greenhill, L. A critical note on the predictive validity of "the hyperkinetic syndrome." *Journal of Child Psychology and Psychiatry*, 1979, *20*, 61–72.

Shelley, E., & Riester, A. Syndrome of minimal brain damage in young adults. *Diseases of the Nervous System*, 1972, *33*, 335–338.

Sleator, E., Neumann, H., & Sprague, R. Hyperactive children: A continuous long term placebo controlled follow-up. *Journal of the American Medical Association*, 1974, *229*, 316–317.

Sprague, R., Barnes, K., & Werry, J. Methylphenidate and thioridazine: Learning reaction time, activity, and classroom behavior in emotionally disturbed children. *American Journal of Orthopsychiatry*, 1970, *40*, 615–628.

Stroop, J. Studies on interference in serial verbal reactions. *Journal of Experimental Psychology*, 1935, *18*, 643–662.

Sykes, D., Douglas, V., & Morgenstern, G. The effect of methylphenidate (Ritalin) on sustained attention in hyperactive children. *Psychopharmacologia*, 1972, *25*, 262–274.

Weiss, G., Hechtman, L., & Perlman, T. Hyperactives as young adults: School, employer and self-rating scales obtained during 10-year follow-up evaluation. *American Journal of Orthopsychiatry*, 1978, *48*, 438–445.

Weiss, G., Hechtman, L., Perlman, T., Hopkins, J., & Wener, A. Hyperactives as young adults. A controlled prospective ten-year follow-up of 75 children. *Archives of General Psychiatry*, 1979, *36*, 675–681.

Weiss, G., Kruger, E., Danielson, U., & Elman, M. Effect of long-term treatment of hyperactive children with methylphenidate. *Canadian Medical Association Journal*, 1975, *112*, 159–165.

Weiss, G., Minde, K., Douglas, V., Werry, J., & Sykes, D. Comparison of the effects of chlorpromazine, dextroamphetamine, and methylphenidate on the behavior and intellectual functioning of hyperactive children. *Canadian Medical Association Journal*, 1971, *104*, 20–25.

Weiss, G., Minde, K., Werry, J., Douglas, V., & Nemeth, E. Studies on the hyperactive child: VII. Five-year follow-up. *Archives of General Psychiatry*, 1971, *24*, 409–414.

Weiss, G., Werry, J., Minde, K., Douglas, V., & Sykes, D. Studies on the hyperactive child: V. The effects of dextroamphetamine and chlorpromazine on behavior and intellectual functioning. *Journal of Child Psychology and Psychiatry*, 1968, *9*, 145–156.

Werry, J., Weiss, G., Douglas, V., & Martin, J. Studies on the hyperactive child: III. The effect of chlorpromazine on behavior and learning ability. *Journal of the American Academy of Child Psychiatry*, 1966, *5*, 292–312.

Winsberg, B., Bialer, I., Kupietz, S., & Tobias, J. Effects of imipramine and dextroamphetamine on behavior of neuropsychiatrically impaired children. *American Journal of Psychiatry*, 1972, *128*, 1425–1431.

Witkin, H., Dyk, R., Goodenough, D., & Karp, S. *Psychological differentiation*. New York: Wiley, 1962.

Wood, D., Reimherr, F., Wender, P., & Johnson, G. Diagnosis and treatment of minimal brain dysfunction in adults: A preliminary report. *Archives of General Psychiatry*, 1976, *33*, 1453–1460.

Ziller, R., Hagey, J., & Smith, M. Self-esteem: A self-social construct. *Journal of Consulting and Clinical Psychology*, 1969, *33*, 84–95.

CHAPTER TWENTY-ONE

Hyperkinetic Syndrome: Treatment Issues and Principles

RACHEL GITTELMAN

The parent or therapist confronted with a hyperactive child is concerned about the clinical value of treatment in the child's real world—that is, at home with the immediate family and other relatives; in the community with peers and neighbors; and in school. Those who are the recipients of, and those who deliver, treatments are not interested in statistically significant changes detected in laboratory tasks or situations, unless these reflect clinically meaningful advantages in the here and now, and in the future.

WHICH SYMPTOMS RESPOND TO WHICH TREATMENTS?

As earlier chapters of this volume document, several treatment strategies have been applied to hyperactive children. Stimulants have been found to make a consistently significant impact on symptoms of hyperactivity (see Chapter 18), and both behavior modification and cognitive training have also been utilized (see Chapter 19). In view of the marked differences among these interventions, it would seem reasonable to expect that each would make an impact on different aspects of these children's behavior. One would predict that stimulants would improve attention and motor activity, but have little impact on social skills—a complex set of learned responses. Furthermore, if attention improves, it is reasonable to anticipate changes in academic performance. Therefore, stimulants would be expected to modify activity level, attention, and school performance. In contrast, it would seem that behavioral treatments should be effective in providing means for change in social behavior, with little short-term impact on attention and motor activity. Finally, cognitive training aims at correcting the manner in which information is processed, whether stimuli are cognitive or social, by providing hyperactive children with strategies that enable them to identify (1) the demand characteristics of a task, (2) the alternatives possible for the solution of these demands, and (3) the consequences for each set of alternatives. As a result, the children should become less impulsive, more self-critical, and more selective in their behavioral repertoires. The children are believed to learn a new style for coping, and changes in many behavioral

Rachel Gittelman. College of Physicians and Surgeons, Columbia University, New York, New York; New York State Psychiatric Institute, New York, New York.

domains can therefore be expected. An alteration in the children's mode of thinking, or cognitive style, should be reflected in better attention, with consequently improved academic performance as well as less impulsivity, which should lead to less hyperactivity and better social function.

Thus, the three treatment approaches most commonly evoked for treating hyperkinesis have seemingly different potential impact, with cognitive training providing the most hopeful expectations.

The empirical data do not conform to these reasonable presumptions. As it turns out, cognitive training has not been found to improve the behavior of hyperkinetic children (Abikoff & Gittelman, 1982; Douglas, Parry, Morton, & Garson, 1976). The finding by Douglas *et al.* (1976) that achievement was improved is weakened by the fact that academic remediation was included as part of the cognitive training. Furthermore, there is no evidence to support the claim that the hyperactive children's "cognitive styles" were altered by the training. That is, it is not apparent that the children acquired a new set of problem-solving strategies and that their way of processing external and internal pressures and needs was altered by cognitive training.

The stimulants, which hold great promise for modifying attention and academic performance (but not social behavior), do not live up to expectations either. Though stimulants improve the ability to focus and sustain attention, it does not appear that academic progress goes along with these changes. However, unexpectedly, the social behavior of hyperkinetic children is markedly improved by stimulant treatment.

The third type of treatment applied to hyperactive children, behavior therapy, can be designed to alter various aspects of behavior. In studies that have selected a single, discrete behavioral measure (such as "on-task" behavior), modification of the specific behavior has been observed. Unfortunately, all such studies have been done in very small study groups. More important to the clinician, the range of behaviors targeted for modification has been extremely narrow. As noted by several authors, and clearly stated by Sprague (see Chapter 19), multiple sources and types of assessments are necessary for an estimate of clinical efficacy. As things stand now, there is no adequate study of behavior modification in hyperactive children, since none has included controls for the professional attention received during treatment. However, from the clinical information obtained in studies comparing behavior therapy and methylphenidate in cross-situationally hyperkinetic children, it is clear that methylphenidate induces change in a greater variety of behaviors, and that the magnitude of the improvement is much greater with the medication than with behavioral intervention. My associates and I have found that in groups of hyperactive children treated either with stimulants or with behavior modification, there was no area of functioning—whether social, academic, or cognitive—that showed even a trend in favor of behavior therapy over drug therapy (Gittelman, Abikoff, Pollack, Klein, Katz, & Mattes, 1980). When behavior therapy seemed to have an effect, it was on the same behaviors as those modified by drug treatment.

Therefore, the reasonable expectancy that different treatments should alter contrasting aspects of dysfunction in hyperactive children is not supported by the data. At the same time, some youngsters, though improved to a meaningful degree with stimulant treatment, continue to have social or academic difficulties. For partial stimulant responders, the addition of behavioral treatment seems to have a positive impact. Residual problems in stimulant-treated hyperactive children respond to behavioral interventions (Gittelman *et al.*, 1980), but not to cognitive training (Abikoff & Gittelman, 1982).

The current status of therapeutic knowledge indicates that there are no subgroups of hyperkinetic children that respond better to one type of treatment than another. Consequently, it is not possible to claim that some hyperkinetic children are more effectively treated with one treatment than with another.

There are claims that special dietary conditions can affect the symptomatology of hyperkinetic children, but there are no systematic data to support this contention (Conners, 1980; Mattes & Gittelman, 1981).

IS THE BEHAVIOR OF HYPERKINETIC CHILDREN NORMALIZED WITH TREATMENT?

Stimulants improve the behavior of hyperactive children, but how well are the children when successfully treated? Are they still in difficulty, albeit improved? Examining the whole literature on stimulant effects in hyperkinetic children, one is impressed by the fact that all studies report a significant advantage for stimulant-treated children over those given a placebo. However, the extent of the change is considerably less impressive. The size of treatment effects is poorly communicated by levels of significance. The latter are crucial information, but insufficient for an understanding of the clinical implications of results. Scrutiny of the research on stimulant effects in hyperactive children leads to the observation that, though statistically significant, the magnitude of clinical improvement ranges widely, with the bulk of the studies showing rather mediocre clinical gains with treatment (Klein, Gittelman, Quitkin, & Rifkin, 1980). Can it be concluded that stimulants are useful, but not to a great degree? Not really. The studies on the topic of stimulant treatment have used different criteria for diagnosis: Some have used vague, imprecise, and unquantifiable concepts such as "minimal brain dysfunction" for selecting children; others have used objective criteria for hyperactivity, but have ignored the issue of pervasiveness, so that children included may have been considered hyperactive only in school and not in other settings; still other investigators have required that hyperactivity be present at home and in school for children to enter studies. In addition, dosage schedules have also varied. Thus, some studies have used mean doses of 10 mg/day of methylphenidate, others 50–60 mg. To assume that these two regimens represent similar treatment is inaccurate.

It is my impression that when dosage has been higher and diagnostic criteria have been more objective and stringent, so that children treated experimentally have had higher hyperactivity scores and cross-situationality has been present, greater stimulant effects have been noted. If so, a weak drug effect can be expected if doses are low, and if children do not present with high rates of the behaviors targeted to assess change (such as hyperactivity ratings). This belief does not imply that the stimulants are useful for hyperactive children only. It merely points to the fact that if one is concerned with a reduction in a specific set of behaviors, one stands a better chance of finding it if the behaviors are well represented in the sample.

Only a few studies have examined the degree to which hyperactive children were or were not perceived as being different from normal children. Whalen and associates (Whalen, Collins, Henker, Atkins, Adams, & Stapp, 1978) reported significant differences in attention, motor movement, noisiness, disruption, and inappropriate behavior between hyperactive and normal children observed in an experimental classroom. With methylphenidate treatment of the hyperactive children, these differences disappeared.

Conners and Taylor (1980) asked mothers to rate the degree to which their hyperactive children were different from normal children after treatment with placebo or methylphenidate. Ninety percent of the parents rated their methylphenidate-treated children as no different from, or better than, other children, whereas only 37% of the placebo-treated children were thus rated.

Abikoff and associates (Abikoff, Gittelman, & Klein, 1980; Abikoff, Gittelman-Klein, & Klein, 1977) found a marked distinction between the rate of problematic behavior in hyperactive and normal children in their regular classrooms. All the behaviors of an observation measure significantly distinguished the two groups. After treatment, the children on methylphenidate remained significantly more inattentive than their normal classmates, but were indistinguishable from them on measures of interference, motor activity, and demands from teachers (Gittelman *et al.*, 1980). Interestingly, the children who received *both* methylphenidate and behavior modification were not rated as different from normal children on any measure. In contrast, those who received only behavior modification continued to be significantly different from the normal children on all behavior ratings. In conclusion, short-term methylphenidate treatment normalizes many, but not all, aspects of symptomatology. Short-term behavior modification does not normalize behavior, but the combination regularly does.

It should be noted that the above pattern was obtained in groups of children and that their results are expressed in terms of group mean scores. There are individual hyperactive children whose behavior is completely normalized by short-term methylphenidate treatment in moderately high doses (30–60 mg/day). However, this magnitude of effects cannot be expected on a regular basis, whereas it can when behavioral treatment is added to the drug treatment. Thus, many hyperkinetic children treated with stimulants are no longer different from normal children; however, they do not maintain this improvement when the drug is withdrawn. The ameliorative effects of drugs occur during the active phase of treatment and not beyond. It is remarkable that so little carryover occurs from the treatment period since much of the change consists of social behavior. One would reasonably expect that once the stimulant-treated children have experienced a change in teacher and parent attitudes (Barkley & Cunningham, 1979; Humphries, Kinsbourne, & Swanson, 1978; Whalen, Henker, & Dotemoto, 1980), they would retain some of the behaviors that were instrumental in eliciting more positive social feedback. Yet, no such transfer seems to take place. There is little doubt that this represents a limitation of stimulant medication. Unfortunately, no alternative therapeutic intervention has been shown to alter the behavior of hyperactive children beyond the period of treatment.

Therefore, the answer to the question of whether the behavior of hyperactive children can be normalized is this: Yes, for some children, but only for as long as they are treated. Does this then imply that stimulant treatment needs to be extended and, in some caşes, to be lifelong?

HOW LONG DOES STIMULANT TREATMENT NEED TO BE CONTINUED?

The answer to the question posed above depends on how long symptoms remain and, if they do, whether they continue to respond to stimulant treatment.

It has been shown that some children who respond well to stimulants can be withdrawn from treatment (Sleator, von Neumann, & Sprague, 1974). Therefore, treatment with stimulants is not always an uninterrupted event throughout childhood. For children who do not function successfully when removed from stimulant treatment, reinstitution of medication seems, in the majority, to reestablish previous improvement. Whether this effect continues into adolescence and later is less clear.

The best information regarding the persistence of behavioral difficulties in hyperactive children has come from the group of investigators at The Montreal Children's Hospital. They have conducted the only prospective study of children diagnosed by consistent clinical practices (Weiss, Minde, Douglas, Werry, & Sykes, 1971; Werry, Weiss, Douglas, & Martin, 1966). Others have used clinic records for selecting hyperactive children. This approach is much less desirable since, in the absence of uniform chart recording, it is impossible to ascertain retrospectively what influenced the type of clinical information obtained, or the diagnostic decisions made, by the staff.

The results of the work done by Weiss and her team are presented in Chapter 20. The children diagnosed as hyperkinetic when younger continued to have multiple difficulties in adolescence, with poor school performance and social problems dominating. Antisocial behavior became more prominent during adolescence. Furthermore, the youngsters were judged still to have significant attentional problems (Hoy, Weiss, Minde, & Cohen, 1978). The picture that emerged as the children reached adulthood was somewhat different. Once out of school, social and work adjustment appeared much improved over that of adolescence. However, impaired cognitive performance (compared to normals) persisted (Hopkins, Hechtman, & Weiss, 1979). This suggests that stimulant treatment might be a plausible therapy for some previously hyperactive children, and that even in adulthood this might be the case. Some have argued that, in many instances, the disorder is lifelong, and that adults with symptoms believed to reflect late manifestations of early hyperactivity respond to stimulant treatment (Wender, Reimherr, & Wood, 1981; Wood, Reimherr, Wender, & Johnson, 1976).

To date, there are no empirical data from which one can safely estimate the value of stimulants in symptomatic adolescents or adults who were hyperactive as children. Generalizing from clinical experience (a risky exercise) suggests that some adolescents improve with stimulants, but that the positive drug effects are less frequent and less dramatic than those in younger children. Though improved, many retain social and academic problems. A complicating factor in using stimulant treatment (at least in our clinic at Hillside Hospital) was the very strong resistance of adolescents to medication, since they viewed this form of intervention as defining them as deviant, sick, or maladjusted. In general, these youngsters have tended to be difficult to engage in a treatment plan.

Long-term medication might become unnecessary if treatment during childhood protected children from experiencing difficulties in the years thereafter. Here again, there are no satisfactory data on which to come to tentative, let alone firm, conclusions regarding the ultimate impact of stimulant treatment. Weiss and her associates (Weiss, Kruger, Danielson, & Elman, 1975), who attempted to evaluate the adjustment of treated and untreated hyperactive children 5 years after referral, did not find differences between those who stayed on methylphenidate, those who received chlorpromazine, and those who had discontinued drug treatment (untreated children) because of poor response. As is apparent, the design cannot provide definitive answers, since there were clinical differences among the groups to begin with. However, the execution of carefully controlled longitudinal experiments dealing with the issue of treatment effects on the natural history of the disorder is not possible.

At this time, it does not appear justified to claim that stimulant treatment in childhood places children at an advantage later in life. Therefore, it may be overoptimistic to hope that this treatment protects hyperactive children against the development of antisocial behavior patterns later on, as some believe (Satterfield & Cantwell, 1975).

WHO SHOULD BE TREATED WITH STIMULANTS?

Stimulants have been studied in poorly defined samples of children with behavior problems, and significant effects have been found. Furthermore, normal children and children with pure learning disorders have been shown to improve on several types of tasks with these drugs (Gittelman-Klein & Klein, 1976; Rapoport, Buschsbaum, Weingartner, Zahn, Ludlow, Mikkelsen, Langer, & Bunney, 1978). Therefore, the attention-enhancing effect of stimulants is not specific to a diagnostic group. Does this imply that the treatment is appropriate to a great variety of childhood conditions?

With regard to the data on children with pure learning disorders—that is, children with impaired academic performance in spite of adequate intelligence and no behavior problems—the evidence suggests that, though attention is improved with stimulants, global aspects of academic performance are unaffected. Furthermore, the magnitude of the improvement on attention is not all that great, or functionally meaningful, in spite of statistical significance. The efficacy of stimulants with these children is discussed in Chapter 27 of this volume. The conclusion drawn is that there is no basis upon which to consider stimulants as a routine intervention in children with pure learning disorders.

How about normal children? Since they also perform better while on stimulants, should they be considered candidates for stimulant administration? No one has made such a claim—a laudable omission.

The most difficult problem is to define the limits of the efficacy of stimulant treatment in children with behavior disorders. It is clear that hyperactive children benefit from this intervention. But even with them investigators have noted a lack of information concerning the continued efficacy of stimulants over extended time. It is also unclear how early one can expect good responses to stimulants among hyperactive preschool children, since all but two drug studies have been restricted to the primary school ages (6 to 12 years). Hyperactivity is a disorder that is thought to begin during a child's early development. As a matter of fact, it has been suggested that the diagnosis is probably suspect if no history of difficulties is present before school age (Klein *et al.*, 1980). The two studies that have focused on preschoolers have produced conflicting results (Conners, 1975; Schleifer, Weiss, Cohen, Elman, Cvejic, & Kruger, 1975). One reported significant improvement for methylphenidate compared with placebo only on parent ratings, but not on the ratings of nursery school teachers of 4-year-olds whose parents considered them hyperactive (Schleifer *et al.*, 1975). In contrast, Conners (1975) reported marked improvement as perceived by parents *and* teachers in children under 6 (average age, 4.8 years) in a placebo-controlled methylphenidate study. The discrepancy between the two studies may be due to the fact that the first study included children under 5 years of age only; the second, under 6. It appears more likely that the diagnostic procedures account for the conflicting results. The sample in the negative study was identified by parents; in the positive study, by physicians. Parents may be more inaccurate in their evaluation of the diagnostic significance of their young children's behavior. Overactivity is an extremely common complaint of parents of normal children, especially boys (Shepherd, Oppenheim, & Mitchell, 1971). It is conceivable that by having a physician review the clinical information, a more judiciously selective procedure ensued. The data base to be used in the diagnosis of hyperactivity is not established. Should children be considered as having the disorder, no matter the source of complaint? Klein and I (Klein & Gittelman-Klein, 1975) found that, among cases diagnosed as hyperactive according to objective criteria, only a quarter were unanimously perceived as hyperactive by their teachers, parents, and clinic staff. It was further noted that in a number of cases, the parents failed to report hyperactivity, in spite of the latter's obvious presence in the clinic and its clear report by teachers. Rapoport and Benoit (1975) reported that ratings of hyperactivity by teachers and observers in the home were significantly correlated; parent ratings of activity, however, were not so correlated with either of the two other measures. Therefore, a diagnostic dilemma occurs when parents are the only source of information, since they appear to be poor judges of their children by virtue of the fact that they seem to confound objective behavior with subjective distress.

Apart from cases where parents are inaccurate informants, there are children who may be hyperactive in only one setting, such as school or home. Should these youngsters be considered diagnostically distinct for purposes of treatment? Investigators of drug treatment either have ignored this issue by requiring only one source of complaint for study inclusion (e.g., teachers), or have excluded children who were not cross-situationally hyperactive. No one has compared systematically the drug response of youngsters with and without cross-situational hyperactivity. It is not clear that children considered hyperactive in only one milieu exhibit mild forms of one condition—the extreme of which is exhibited by youngsters who are in difficulty in all settings. In view of reported differences in cognitive performance and in outcome between the two types of hyperactive children (Campbell, Schleifer, Weiss, & Perlman, 1977; Schachar, Rutter, & Smith, 1981), it seems likely that the cross-situationally affected children represent a separate diagnostic entity. This distinction may be an important one for prediction of treatment response and long-term prognosis. Only two sets of investigators in the field of hyperactivity have restricted their field of inquiry explicitly to children who were hyperactive in several settings.

TREATMENT COSTS

All treatments entail costs—financial costs, time costs, and, in the case of medication, possibly physical costs. In addition, it has been claimed that, because of state-dependent learning effects associated with stimulant treatment, the cognitive capacity of hyperactive children may be compromised when treatment is terminated. It is clear that the psychosocial treatments are much more burdensome economically than stimulant treatment is. However, this differential cost would be relatively minor, were it shown that the effectiveness of behavior therapy and cognitive training was in some way superior to that of stimulants. In the short run, the nonmedical treatments are significantly inferior to medication, no matter what aspects of the child's function are assessed. The long-run benefits remain a mystery. However, it is unusual for treatments with weak immediate effects to induce significant long-term benefit. This possibility is a most unlikely one, unfortunately.

In spite of its financial advantage, stimulant treatment entails costs not associated with other interventions. Side effects do occur. For the most part, they are not troublesome; but on occasion, they may be, to the point of having their use precluded. Among over 100 hyperactive children who were treated with methylphenidate in moderately high doses in our studies (Gittelman *et al.*, 1980; Gittelman-Klein, Klein, Abikoff, Katz, Gloisten, & Kates, 1976) only one could not be kept in treatment because of intolerable side effects (tachycardia). Among the rest, about 15% and 20% experienced moderate appetite and sleeping difficulties, respectively. As far as is known, these effects do not represent a medical liability. Of more concern is the occurrence of sadness, touchiness, and interpersonal sensitivity in about 3 to 5% of hyperactive children treated with methylphenidate. This reaction typically distresses parents, who feel that the spark has gone out of their children. But, as with the side effects of anorexia and delayed sleep, the mood changes are not dangerous, and are reversible either with dosage reduction or drug withdrawal. (For a detailed review of side effects, see Klein *et al.*, 1980.)

The most worrisome side effects concern the possible growth-reducing effects of stimulants. The large literature on this topic presents conflicting results. Some report no effect of stimulants on growth (Satterfield, Cantwell, Schell, & Blaschke, 1979); others report significant decrements in height over time (Safer, Allen, & Barr, 1972); still others claim height increases (Gross, 1976)! High doses of stimulant have been incriminated, whereas low doses have not; and dextroamphetamine appears more likely to induce growth velocity decrement than other stimulants (Safer & Allen, 1973). Among children we treated with methylphenidate for 4 years (Mattes & Gittelman, 1983), a significant decrement in height percentile was found over time. However, it is difficult to estimate the magnitude of the drug-induced effect, since several patient characteristics that are unrelated to drug treatment were correlated with the growth decrement. Thus, the children's initial height and age account for much of the change. When the effects of these pretreatment characteristics were controlled, methylphenidate explained only 5% of the variance in the height percentile decrement.

Therefore, we conclude that there is a significant effect on growth with methylphenidate. In groups, it is not large; but it might be in any one child. Consequently, the height of treated children should be monitored and drug holidays instituted if growth seems affected, since drug withdrawal has been found to induce significant gains in height in a controlled study (Gittelman, Mattes, Klein, Katz, & Landa, 1982).

The other potential long-term risk is substance abuse. The basis for this concern rests upon the expectation that pill taking may become an innocuous, routine event in children treated with drugs, leading to their easy adoption of drug-culture values. If true, this danger would invalidate the usefulness of the treatment, but the clinical evidence so far indicates that this risk is not present (Beck, Langford, Mackay, & Sum, 1975; Denhoff, 1973; Weiss, Hechtman, Perlman, Hopkins, & Werner, 1979).

It has been argued that, besides physical risks, there are psychological risks associated with drug treatment. The latter is suspected of inducting a state of helplessness and of interfering with children's ability to cope (Whalen & Henker, 1976), since they may attribute their improvement to the medication, rather than to themselves. This view has not been documented and makes many perhaps unwarranted assumptions about children's abilities to generate complicated hypotheses about their behavior.

Of great concern is whether the learning that occurs during treatment is accessible to children when they are removed from the drug. The issue of state-dependent learning has troubled some clinicians, since it is conceivable that special teaching efforts could be compromised by drug treatment (Douglas, 1980). This concern is reasonable, since one study of a single methylphenidate dose found that a rote learning task was recalled better off medication by children who had learned it while off medication than while on medication (Swanson & Kinsbourne, 1976). However, the study included a single dose of the drug and only one task of rote memory. The results may not be applicable to effects of chronic treatment and to complex academic skills. In a study of children with reading disorders, Klein, Feingold, and I (Gittelman, Klein, & Feingold, 1983) found no evidence for state-dependent learning on several tests of reading achievement (see Chapter 27). Hyperactive children were not included, but since the cognitive effects of stimulants are nonspecific, it is unlikely that only hyperactive children would be susceptible to a state-dependent effect of stimulants.

In addition to financial costs, side effects, and so forth, there are practical problems associated with each form of treatment. Behavior therapy is not the simple-minded, mechanical, cold procedure its "humanistic" critics would lead people to believe; nor is it the easily applied, smoothly undertaken procedure described in the clinical literature. We have found that a great many practical and interpersonal problems arise in applying operant techniques with hyperactive children. Some parents have difficulty giving rewards for behavior that they feel should occur without any special recompense. Others believe that their children's difficulties are due to underlying conflicts, and, unless one gets to the "root" of the children's problems, they cannot be helped in any fundamental sense. Such parents resist an application of behavioral techniques. Some over-indulgent parents have great difficulty regulating their reward-giving behavior, and feel guilty if they are not indiscriminately giving. Still others cannot resist the temptation to punish, and have difficulty changing their pattern of negative behavior toward their children. Also, marital conflict may impair the ability to institute a fully efficient program of behavior modification. These problems, as well as others, are discussed more fully elsewhere (Pollack & Gittelman, 1981).

The dispensing of medication has its own associated problems. Parents may disagree about the necessity for medication, and their child may become a pawn between the marital pair. This issue may become especially salient for children of divorced parents. Some parents may fail to follow instructions and may regulate dosage without prior consultation; others let their children decide when and how to take medication. Others use pills to punish the children when they misbehave. Some conceal and distort the purpose of treatment to the children and cannot bring themselves to discuss the issue in an open, matter-of-fact manner because of guilt feelings about the medication. Still other parents abdicate their role and expect the pills to take care of all problems, even normal developmental ones, and perceive ordinary conflicts as indicative of treatment failure.

Thus, there is no intervention that can be said to entail no effort on the part of the clinician, above and beyond the direct treatment application. In this sense, all modalities seem equivalent.

COMMENT

The stimulants are remarkably effective in ameliorating the laboratory test performance, social behavior, and other symptoms of hyperactive children. Yet, they cannot be said to ameliorate academic achievement, or to prevent the development of antisocial behavior patterns, or to alter the natural history of the disorder. Are researchers and clinicians therefore to indict this treatment approach as useless? Doing so would be to throw out the baby with the bath water. Since hyperactive children are referred and accepted for treatment because of behavior problems, the elimination of the latter cannot be viewed as a trivial accomplishment. It would be preferable, of course, if the secondary dysfunctions could be modified as well. The failure to do so is unfortunate, but hardly deserves condemnation. The same argument holds for the possible lack of medication effect on long-term outcome.

It seems that investigators are placing unusual expectations on a treatment: first, it should reverse symptoms that are the primary diagnostic signs; second, it should ameliorate all secondary complications; and third, it should improve eventual functioning. No psychiatric treatment has been shown to have such a rich therapeutic impact. In other branches of medicine, the only treatments that fulfill this ideal are those that reverse ongoing etiological provocations. It must be conceded that there is presently no cure for hyperkinesis. Until one is found, alleviation of dysfunction and pain is not a bad bargain. At the same time, efforts to develop new treatments are to be applauded, since they offer the hope that different outcomes may be provided. So far, the new treatments for hyperkinesis, such as diet and cognitive training, have failed to meet this goal. New forms of cognitive training are being developed that have a more modest objective: Rather than attempting to modify hyperactive children's cognitive style, they aim at instructing them on how to approach academic tasks in optimal fashion. This type of work is reminiscent of academic tutoring, which provides children with specific skills and means to apply them. It is possible that by combining stimulant treatment with an academically oriented remedial program, the school problem of hyperactive children can be altered, both in the short and long runs.

Behavior therapy can serve a valuable role in the treatment of hyperactive children, since, when it is combined with stimulants, excellent clinical results are obtained—superior to those of stimulants alone, in some cases.

There is no apology necessary for the use of stimulants in hyperactivity. It is the most effective treatment available. Its costs—social, psychological, and physical—are not prohibitive, given current knowledge. However, those who wish to communicate to children, parents, or school personnel that, through the use of medication, children will learn better and have a greater chance of success in life are misrepresenting the known treatment effects. The only established justification for the use of medication in hyperactive children is for the amelioration of current behavior problems. The same is true of other modalities—the efficacy of which is even less well established.

References

Abikoff, H., & Gittelman, R. *Cognitive training effects in hyperactive children maintained on stimulants.* Unpublished data, 1982.

Abikoff, H., Gittelman, R., & Klein, D. F. Classroom observation code for hyperactive children: A replication of validity. *Journal of Clinical and Consulting Psychology*, 1980, *48*, 555–565.

Abikoff, H., Gittelman-Klein, R., & Klein, D. F. Validation of a classroom observation code for hyperactive children. *Journal of Clinical and Consulting Psychology*, 1977, *45*, 772–783.

Barkley, R. A., & Cunningham, C. E. The effects of methylphenidate on the mother–child interactions of hyperactive children. *Archives of General Psychiatry*, 1979, *36*, 201–208.

Beck, L., Langford, W. S., Mackay, M., & Sum, G. Childhood chemotherapy and later drug abuse and growth curve: A follow-up study of 30 adolescents. *American Journal of Psychiatry*, 1975, *132*, 436–438.

Campbell, S. B., Schleifer, M., Weiss, G., & Perlman, T. A two-year follow-up of hyperactive preschoolers. *American Journal of Orthopsychiatry*, 1977, *47*, 149–162.

Conners, C. K. Controlled trial of methylphenidate in preschool children with minimal brain dysfunction. In R. Gittelman-Klein (Ed.), *Recent advances in child psychopharmacology.* New York: Human Sciences Press, 1975.

Conners, C. K. *Food additives for hyperactive children.* New York: Plenum Press, 1980.

Conners, C. K., & Taylor, E. Pemoline, methylphenidate, and placebo in children with minimal brain dysfunction. *Archives of General Psychiatry*, 1980, *37*, 922–930.

Denhoff, E. Natural history of children with minimal brain dysfunction. *Annals of the New York Academy of Science*, 1973, *205*, 188–205.

Douglas, V. I. Treatment and training approaches to hyperactivity: Establishing internal and external control. In C. K. Whalen & B. Henker (Eds.), *Hyperactive children: The social ecology of identification and treatment.* New York: Academic Press, 1980.

Douglas, V. I., Parry, P., Morton, P., & Garson, C. Assessment of a cognitive-training program for hyperactive children. *Journal of Abnormal Child Psychology*, 1976, *4*, 389–410.

Gittelman, R., Abikoff, H., Pollack, E., Klein, D. F., Katz, S., & Mattes, J. A controlled trial of behavior modification and methylphenidate in hyperactive children. In C. K. Whalen & B. Henker (Eds.), *Hyperactive children: The social ecology of identification and treatment.* New York: Academic Press, 1980.

Gittelman, R., Klein, D. F., & Feingold, I. Children with reading disorders: II. Effects of methylphenidate in combination with reading instruction. *Journal of Child Psychology and Psychiatry*, 1983, *24*, 193–212.

Gittelman, R., Mattes, J., Klein, D. F., Katz, S., & Landa, B. *Assessment of drug holidays in methylphenidate-treated children.* Unpublished data, 1982.

Gittelman-Klein, R., & Klein, D. F. Methylphenidate effects in learning disabilities. *Archives of General Psychiatry*, 1976, *33*, 655–664.

Gittelman-Klein, R., Klein, D. F., Abikoff, H., Katz, S., Gloisten, A. C., & Kates, W. Relative efficacy of methylphenidate and behavior modification in hyperkinetic children: An interim report. *Journal of Abnormal Child Psychology*, 1976, *4*, 361–379.

Gross, M. Growth of hyperkinetic children taking methylphenidate, dextroamphetamine, or imipramine/desipramine. *Pediatrics*, 1976, *58*, 423–431.

Hopkins, J., Hechtman, L., & Weiss, G. Cognitive style in adults originally diagnosed as hyperactives. *Journal of Child Psychology and Psychiatry*, 1979, *20*, 209–216.

Hoy, E., Weiss, G., Minde, K., & Cohen, N. The hyperactive child at adolescence: Emotional, social, and cognitive functioning. *Journal of Abnormal Child Psychology*, 1978, *6*, 311–324.

Humphries, T., Kinsbourne, M., & Swanson, J. Stimulant effects on cooperation and social interaction between hyperactive children and their mothers. *Journal of Child Psychology and Psychiatry*, 1978, *19*, 13–22.

Klein, D. F., Gittelman, R., Quitkin, F., & Rifkin, A. *Diagnosis and drug treatment of psychiatric disorders: Adults and children.* Baltimore: Williams & Wilkins, 1980.

Klein, D. F., & Gittelman-Klein, R. Problems in the diagnosis of minimal brain dysfunction and the hyperkinetic syndrome. *International Journal of Mental Health*, 1975, *4*, 45–60.

Mattes, J., & Gittelman, R. Effects of artificial food colorings in children with hyperactive symptoms. *Archives of General Psychiatry*, 1981, *38*, 714–718.

Mattes, J., & Gittelman, R. Growth of hyperactive children on maintenance regimen of methylphenidate. *Archives of General Psychiatry*, 1983, *40*, 317–321.

Pollack, E., & Gittelman, R. Practical problems encountered in behavioral treatment with hyperactive children. In M. Gittelman (Ed.), *Strategic interventions for hyperactive children.* Armonk, N.Y.: M. E. Sharpe, 1981.

Rapoport, J., & Benoit, M. The relation of direct home observations to the clinic evaluation of hyperactive school-age boys. *Journal of Child Psychology and Psychiarty*, 1975, *16*, 141–147.

Rapoport, J., Buchsbaum, M., Weingartner, H., Zahn, T., Ludlow, C., Mikkelsen, E., Langer, D., & Bunney, W. E. Dextroamphetamine: Cognitive and behavioral effects in normal and hyperactive boys and normal men. *Archives of General Psychiatry*, 1980, *37*, 933–943.

Safer, D., & Allen, R. Single daily dose methylphenidate in hyperactive children. *Diseases of the Nervous System*, 1973, *34*, 325–328.

Safer, D., Allen, R., & Barr, E. Depression of growth in hyperactive children on stimulant drugs. *New England Journal of Medicine*, 1972, *287*, 217–220.

Satterfield, J. H., & Cantwell, D. P. Psychopharmacology in the prevention of antisocial and delinquent behavior. *International Journal of Mental Health*, 1975, *4*, 227–237.

Satterfield, J. H., Cantwell, D. P., Schell, A., & Blaschke, T. Growth of hyperactive children treated with methylphenidate. *Archives of General Psychiatry*, 1979, *36*, 212–217.

Schachar, R., Rutter, M., Smith, A. The characteristics of situationally and pervasively hyperactive children: Implications for syndrome definition. *Journal of Child Psychology and Psychiatry*, 1981, *22*, 375–392.

Schleifer, M., Weiss, G., Cohen, N., Elman, M., Cvejic, H., & Kruger, E. Hyperactivity in preschoolers and the effect of methylphenidate. *American Journal of Orthopsychiatry*, 1975, *45*, 38–50.

Shepherd, M., Oppenheim, B., & Mitchell, S. *Childhood behaviors and mental health.* New York: Grune & Stratton, 1971.

Sleator, E. K., von Neumann, A., & Sprague, R. L. Hyperactive children: A continuous long-term placebo controlled follow-up. *Journal of the American Medical Association*, 1974, *229*, 316–317.

Swanson, J. M., & Kinsbourne, M. Stimulant-related state-dependent learning in hyperactive children. *Science*, 1976, *192*, 1354–1357.

Weiss, G., Hechtman, L., Perlman, T., Hopkins, J., & Wener, A. Hyperactives as young adults: A controlled prospective ten-year follow-up of 75 children. *Archives of General Psychiatry*, 1979, *36*, 675–681.

Weiss, G., Kruger, E., Danielson, U., & Elman, M. Effect of long-term treatment of hyperactive children with methylphenidate. *Canadian Medical Association Journal*, 1975, *112*, 159–165.

Weiss, G., Minde, K., Douglas, V., Werry, J., & Sykes, D. Comparison of the effects of chlorpromazine, dextroamphetamine, and methylphenidate on the behavior and intellectual functioning of hyperactive children. *Canadian Medical Association Journal*, 1971, *104*, 20–25.

Wender, P. H., Reimherr, F. W., & Wood, D. R. Attention deficit disorder ("minimal brain dysfunction") in adults: A replication study of diagnosis and drug treatment. *Archives of General Psychiatry*, 1981, *38*, 449–456.

Werry, J., Weiss, G., Douglas, V., & Martin, J. Studies on the hyperactive child: III. The effect of chlorpromazine on behavior and learning ability. *Journal of the American Academy of Child Psychiatry*, 1966, *5*, 292–312.

Whalen, C. K., Collins, B. E., Henker, B., Atkins, S. R., Adams, D., & Stapp, J. Behavior observations of hyperactive children and methylphenidate effects in systematically structured classroom environments: Now you see them, now you don't. *Journal of Pediatric Psychology*, 1978, *3*, 177–187.

Whalen, C. K., & Henker, B. Psychostimulants and children: A review and analysis. *Psychological Bulletin*, 1976, *83*, 1113–1130.

Whalen, C. K., Henker, B., & Dotemoto, S. Methylphenidate and hyperactivity: Effects on teacher behaviors. *Science*, 1980, *208*, 1280–1282.

Wood, D., Reimherr, F., Wender, P., & Johnson, G. Diagnosis and treatment of minimal brain dysfunction in adults: A preliminary report. *Archives of General Psychiatry*, 1976, *33*, 1453–1460.

SECTION FOUR

Learning Disabilities

CHAPTER TWENTY-TWO

The Similarities and Differences between Reading and Spelling Problems

UTA FRITH

CHANGING ATTITUDES TOWARD READING AND SPELLING

In educational practice and research, more and more value has been put on reading achievement and word recognition, with an increasing tendency to belittle spelling achievement and word production. Getting words right on a letter-by-letter basis appears to be of minor importance compared with recognizing what words mean. However, a century or so earlier these values were almost reversed (Venezky, 1980). School children had "spellers," "spelling books," and "ABC books," rather than "readers." "Literacy" might have been defined as being able to spell competently, and someone's level of education was often assessed by his or her ability to spell strange words. This made it convenient for novelists to indicate a character's educational status by allusion to his or her spelling. In the "Letters on the Conduct of a Gentleman" written by Lord Chesterfield in the middle of the 18th century, we find the following passage (quoted from Scragg, 1974): "I must tell you that orthography, in the true sense of the word, is so absolutely necessary for a man of letters, or a gentleman, that one false spelling may fix a ridicule upon him for the rest of his life; and I know a man of quality, who never recovered [from] the ridicule of having spelled *wholesome* without the *w*." In contrast, today, the ridicule is often directed at taking spelling seriously at all. Someone's education would certainly not be assessed by how well he or she can spell.

There are various social, cultural, and historical reasons for the changing values of different educational achievements. Although this is not the place to analyze them, investigators should bear in mind that these values directly influence research interests. Thus, children who have problems with both reading and writing are called "dyslexic," not "dysgraphic," even though, as a group, dyslexic children have consistently lower spelling achievement than reading achievement (e.g., Boder, 1973). There are countless books and articles on reading retardation, reading acquisition, reading strategies, word recognition, and so forth, but very few on spelling problems, spelling strategies, or writing production in general. This constitutes an imbalance, since it does not correspond to the relative difficulty or practical importance of the skills, nor to

Uta Frith. Medical Research Council Developmental Psychology Unit, London, England.

the relative extent of reading and spelling problems. Spelling is generally considered a more difficult task, since active word production as opposed to passive word recognition is required. It has been recognized that almost every child who has a reading problem also has a spelling problem. Yet it is often ignored that not every child who has a spelling problem has a reading problem. It follows that spelling problems are far more frequent than reading problems are.

The fact that some "dyslexic" children have no reading problems, only very severe spelling problems, comes as a surprise to many people, even though clinicians have long known about this. However, with notable exceptions, even clinicians have not been very concerned with the problems of "spelling retardates," a term used by Naidoo (1972) and Nelson and Warrington (1974). These children probably make up a subgroup of dyslexic children who have managed to overcome initial reading problems but who still suffer from severe spelling problems. There is, however, yet another group of children who never had a reading problem at any stage of their development but yet have persistent spelling problems. These have not been of much interest to either clinicians or researchers, but this is not surprising, in view of recent popular attitudes regarding spelling as a trivial matter. However, the existence of pure spelling problems without reading problems clearly demonstrates that there must be differences between reading and spelling; each deserves to be considered in its own right. The questions to which investigators need to address themselves are these: Is spelling really trivial? Is being a good speller simply being good at rote learning? Is being a bad speller just an endearing lack of pedantry? Are all these problems due to an illogical and now obsolete system of orthography?

The Importance of Being Earnest about Spelling

George Bernard Shaw is identified with the last spirited attempt at a spelling reform in English. His proposed British alphabet of 48 characters (shown in Figure 22-1) was intended to allow a direct and straightforward sound–letter correspondence. As is well known, the existing English orthography reflects speech sound very imperfectly. One reason for this is that speech sound is surprisingly ephemeral, while orthography is stable. It is partially this problem that also vitiates Shaw's attempt. In his will, Shaw asked that one of his plays, *Androcles and the Lion*, should be transliterated on the basis of the pronunciation of King George V. When this was finally published by Penguin in 1962, the chosen standard for pronunciation was already out of date, and many would agree that pronunciation (and hence transliteration) would have to be adapted for the many different dialects of the English-speaking world. Clearly, the enterprise was a failure, and no other serious attempt has been made since.

English orthography is not particularly concerned with the reflection of speech sounds. There can be gross discrepancies between spelling patterns and sound. Sometimes letters are used that actually misrepresent speech sounds. This is not necessarily a disadvantage. In intriguing experiments, Baker (1980) asked naive subjects to act as spelling reformers and found that they actually sometimes preferred nonphonetic spellings over phonetic ones. For example, people systematically preferred jump*ed*, hopp*ed*, and the like, over jump*t*, hop*t*, even though the latter are more accurate phonetic renderings. An obvious reason for this preference is that the *-ed* spelling pattern conveys *directly* (that

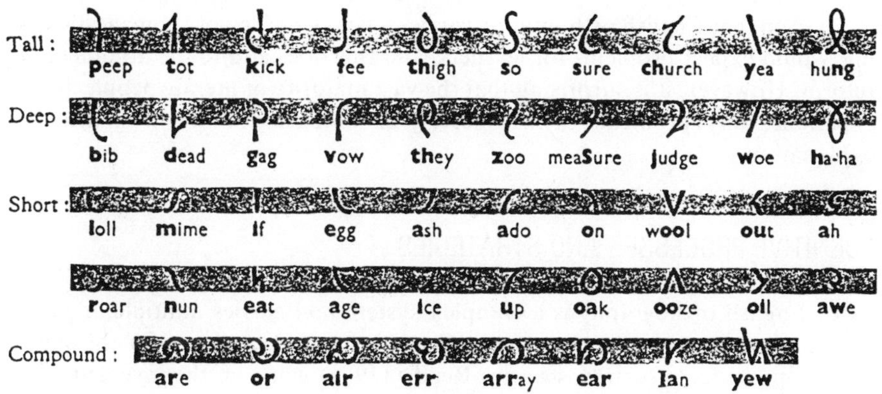

Figure 22-1. The Shaw alphabet reading key. From *Androclese and the Lion*. The Shaw Alphabet Edition, By G. B. Shaw, Harmondsworth, Middlesex, England: Penguin Books, 1962. Reprinted by permission of The Society of Authors on behalf of the Bernard Shaw Estate.

is, without mediation through sound) that the word in question is a verb in the past tense. Important linguistic information is often conveyed better by the written than by the spoken word. Sometimes this is syntactic information, as in the *-ed* forms just mentioned, or in plural *-s* (e.g., plea*s* and not plea*z*). However, semantic information also can be conveyed directly in writing, as in so-called homophones (e.g., *seem* vs. *seam*). This sort of information would be lost with a purely phonetic orthography.

A similar argument for the importance of factors other than speech sounds in spelling can be made on the basis of word relationships and derivations. The origin of English words from Latin, Norse, Anglo-Saxon, French, or other languages is often surprisingly transparent in their spelling. P. T. Smith (1980) has provided a theory and experimental evidence specifically on the use of final *-e* spellings. Thus people can differentiate *roll* from *role* or *loot* from *lute* directly by their spelling, distinctions that also contain information as to their origin in Germanic or Romance languages. A brief glance at the dictionary suffices to indicate the diversity of language sources for even everyday words as manifested in their orthographic patterns. For example, the correct spelling is *telephone*, with *ph* commemorating its Greek origin, and not *telefone*; *autumn* and not *autem*, from the Latin word *autumnus*; *parole* and not *paroll*, preserving the French spelling; *knight* and not *night*, or *nite*, since it was once pronounced not too differently from the German *K-necht*. As P. T. Smith (1980) and Baker (1980) have shown, even if people are not consciously aware of these aspects, they make use of them unconsciously.

However, all these interesting relationships of letters, sounds, and meanings cannot be readily reduced to a system of rules. Thus, English orthography is very complex (Haas, 1970) and more like an organic growth than a logical system. During the course of time there have been changes in vocabulary, changes in writing style, changes in printing practices, and changes due to orthographic reforms. For all these reasons, orthographic rules are complex and inconsistent (Scragg, 1974). It is, however, remarkable that orthography tends to be a strongly conservative element in the pattern of language change (Levitt, 1978).

Given that English orthography carries a heavy burden of language history, one would expect problems for learners, and this does add to the argument for reform. However, it is surprising that the vast majority of literate people do not experience any problems. Thus success, as much as failure, is in need of explanation.

COGNITIVE PROCESSES AND STRATEGIES

Since English orthography is a complex system and carries multiple linguistic information, there is more to spelling knowledge than memory for the superficial appearance of words. Charles Read's (1971) work on the invented spellings of preschool children was a breakthrough in the reconceptualization of spelling production. Just as remarkable creativity can be found in speech production, where children are capable of generating and using phonological rules, similar creativity can be observed in spelling production. Read, and also Chomsky (1971), showed that very young children who knew just a little about the names and sounds of the letters of the alphabet were able to make systematic and rule-governed guesses about the representation of speech sounds by letters. Thus, *sugar* was *SHGR*, *police* was *POLES* (Read, 1978).

One highly interesting finding was that children could not usually read what they themselves had written. Thus, although the children showed themselves capable of using a strategy of sound-to-letter translation, they did not use a strategy of translating the letters back into speech sounds. Bryant and Bradley (1980) found the same split between applying phonological rules in the writing but not in the reading of young schoolchildren. They demonstrated that a child might spontaneously read a particular word in look-and-say fashion and spontaneously write the same word in phonetic fashion.

Strategies in Reading

The well-known contrast between methods of teaching reading—namely, between look-and-say and phonics—is a useful starting point for understanding the handling of visible language. The methods correspond to two reading strategies: Words can be recognized instantly even without having to analyze full letter details; words can also be laboriously analyzed via letter-to-sound correspondence rules. One difference between these strategies is that one moves directly from print to meaning; the other moves indirectly, from print to sound and then to meaning. Hence one is also called a "visual" route, the other a "phonological" route. However, the instant recognition of familiar words is not concerned with visual shapes, since it can also work when the word is written or printed in totally unfamiliar script (Snowling & Frith, 1981). What is instantly recognized is not the shape of the letters, but their identity and position. Thus, the process of direct recognition is not using a "visual" route in the sense of shape perception, but rather an "orthographic" route.

The indirect or phonological route, on the other hand, needs full letter cues. It can be used for decoding unfamiliar or nonsense words in piecemeal fashion by translating individual graphemes into phonemes and finally synthesizing the sound of the word. This strategy is not normally used by skilled readers, as it is full of ambiguities and pitfalls. Even with very regular words, there are difficulties of placing correct stress and finding the appropriate segmentation if they have to be built up in piecemeal fashion (e.g., *trinitrotoluene*). However, this strategy may have to come into operation when letter strings to be read just cannot be recognized, simply because they are not represented in the "internal lexicon." Thus, one can also contrast nonlexical and lexical routes. This dual route theory has been elaborated and discussed by Coltheart, Davelaar, Jonasson, and Besner (1977) and Marcel and Patterson (1978), and criticized by Marcel (1980a).

The theoretical concept of the internal lexicon (Morton, 1964, 1969) has been highly fruitful in reading research (see discussions by Coltheart, 1979; Seymour & Porpodas, 1980; Shallice & Warrington, 1980). Baron and McKillop (1975) and Baron and Strawson (1976) developed a theory of individual differences in terms of direct or indirect strategies. Thus, there are people, termed "Chinese," who prefer the direct route—namely, instant word recognition (as in reading logographs). In contrast, there are people, termed "Phoenicians" (after the inventors of the alphabetic principle of sound represented by letters), who prefer the indirect route—namely, the translation of letters to sound. The "Chinese" excel at reading irregular words where letter-to-sound correspondence is poor. The "Phoenicians" excel at reading unfamiliar or nonsense words, which, at least partially, have to be decoded into sound.

These individual differences are preferences, not inabilities, and most skilled readers are flexible enough to adopt either strategy as the occasion demands (Barron, 1980). On the whole, fast reading of text can be done efficiently by relying on the direct lexical route. At least, there is very little evidence to the contrary (Frith, 1978).

Strategies in Spelling

In spelling, the same two routes might operate (e.g., Ellis, 1982; Nelson, 1980). Thus a highly practiced word may be present for writing directly (i.e., without breaking it up into components of phoneme-to-grapheme correspondence). Thus the correct letter-by-letter sequence of a word can be produced independently of its correspondence to sound, as is the case with irregular words, for example (as in *Leicester*). A letter-by-letter program may be available for all familiar words in the internal lexicon. In contrast, new, rare, and nonsense words that are not in the lexicon and for which no such program exists would have to be spelled by an indirect route—namely, by breaking up the word into constituent sounds and translating these sounds into plausible letters. From the earlier discussion, it is immediately obvious that this poses severe problems in English. Misspellings that are phonetically accurate but fail to use the precise letters required (e.g., *reign* vs. *rein* vs. *rain* vs. *rane* vs. *rayn* vs. *rayne*, etc.) are inevitable with this indirect route.

Good spellers, by definition, make few errors, and this must indicate an efficient use of the direct lexical route. Sloboda (1980) showed that what distinguishes highly skilled spellers is that they can readily spell words such as *label*, *whistle*, *hostel*, *table*. For these words, no consideration of sound–letter correspondence and no generally known rule would help to decide between *-el* and *-le*. Unlike reading, spelling by the direct route does need *full* cues: All the letters must be available in correct sequential order for correct production of a word, while correct recognition can proceed with *partial* cues (Frith, 1980; Henderson & Chard, 1980). For this short-cut process, not all letters need to be analyzed, nor does their exact order.

In the well-stocked internal lexicon, letter-perfect spellings are available. These can be conceptualized as memory images. However, they should really be thought of as abstract sequences. They are programs that can be put into various spelling actions, such as writing, typing, oral spelling, or visualizing words. Such programs are automatic and inaccessible to introspection.

In summary, it can be hypothesized that two strategies exist for reading as well as writing words correctly: one orthographic or lexical; the other phonological or nonlexical. Which of these strategies is used would depend on various factors: the stage of learning (i.e., whether automatic spelling programs are available), individual preferences, and demands of the task at hand. It would also depend on whether there is any impairment that affects availability or use of these two strategies.

LEARNING TO SPELL AND FAILING TO LEARN

Different stages of learning and different types of schooling have different manifestations of spelling problems. This is due mainly to the slow and lengthy process of acquisition of different aspects of English orthography. Nevertheless, one can talk about a common pattern in the normal learning process. At an early stage of learning, the main concern will often be with small units of sound–letter correspondences. The child, for instance, has to learn that the sound /ʃ/ is written *sh*. At a later stage, the concern will be with more general sound–letter rules. For example, rules are taught for doubling consonants with special affixes (as in *sit–sitting*). At all stages, however, the child has to learn the exact and often idiosyncratic letter-by-letter sequences of specific words (e.g., *two*, *to*, *too*). This will remain a target for learning even at a later stage where all sound–letter rules available have been mastered. Of course, different methods of teaching will influence the acquisition of spelling knowledge, how long it takes, how well it is practiced, and what strategies are adopted in case of an unknown word. Peters (1967) demonstrated that look-and-say, phonetic, and initial-teaching-alphabet teaching systems yielded marked and predictable effects in children's spelling errors at age 8. Interestingly, there was no effect on level of spelling achievement, only on the quality of spelling errors.

For all these reasons, one will encounter different problems when one is identifying spelling difficulties at different stages and types of schooling. It is another question whether the same child will be picked up as a poor speller at different stages.

There is some evidence for an unusual persistence of severe spelling problems. Rutter, Tizard, Yule, Graham, and Whitmore (1976) retested their sample of retarded readers and spellers after a 4-year interval (from age 10 to age 14). The children showed the same degree of reading retardation as before, but they lagged even further behind in their spelling than they did in their reading. This finding is the more remarkable, as some remedial intervention had taken place in the meantime. Rourke and Orr (1977) found that after a 4-year interval (from age 7 to age 11), retarded readers had increased their Wide-Range

Achievement Test (WRAT) reading ability relative to their age group, namely from the 27th to the 41st percentile, while their WRAT spelling remained the same at the 29th percentile. Their comparison group of normal readers held their places in reading and spelling at about the 80th percentile.

The persistence of spelling problems up to school-leaving age argues against developmental lag theories and for a deficit theory. Rourke (1981), in a useful review of the pitfalls of diagnosing learning problems at different ages, points out that at older ages poor spellers are more sharply discriminated from good spellers on a large variety of neuropsychological tests than they are at younger ages. It appears therefore that severe and specific spelling problems are not a transient phenomenon for which the blame can be put on poor teaching methods or lack of learning effort. Many poor spellers are unlikely to catch up with their age group as they get older. Some of them may even fall further and further behind.

THE SIGNIFICANCE OF DISSOCIATIONS BETWEEN READING AND SPELLING

Since a dual-route strategy theoretically applies to reading as well as spelling, more similarities than differences between these skills might be expected. Poor readers are usually poor spellers; good readers are usually good spellers. Correlations in surveys reported by Malmquist (1958) and by Horn (1969) vary between .50 and .80. On the whole, it can be expected that a child will acquire knowledge about orthography while learning to spell, and would apply this knowledge in both situations, when recognizing and when reproducing a word.

In view of this, it is odd that a child may be able to spell a particular word that he or she cannot read, and vice versa (Bryant & Bradley, 1980). This sort of dissociation between reading and spelling in the normal young child throws doubt on a straightforward and direct relationship between reading and spelling skills. It raises the possibility that a child may acquire orthographic knowledge and be able to apply it in one situation but not in another. This may be so because the reading situation is an input process, while the spelling situation is an output process. Input and output stages in highly practiced skills have very different, sometimes incompatible, requirements (Frith & Frith, 1980). Thus, both stages can fail independently of each other. Reading and spelling dissociations are by no means a rare occurrence. They are seen in specific spelling failure in seemingly normal schoolchildren and adults, and also in patients suffering from specific brain lesions. In this area, too, reading failure has attracted more interest than spelling failure, even though each can occur as an isolated failure, with the other apparently remaining intact (e.g., Beauvois & Dérouesné, 1979; Weigl & Fradis, 1977).

A concrete example for the extent of dissociation even in a normal primary school sample can be taken from a recent study in Germany (Valtin, Jung, & Scheerer-Neumann, 1981) with 291 pupils in the third grade, aged around 8 years. These children were given both reading and spelling tests and were classified as having problems if their scores fell below the 15th percentile of their group. By this definition, 49 children had reading problems and 93 had spelling problems. Only 35 children had both problems together; while 14 might be considered to have just reading problems, 58 had just spelling problems. Thus only 38% of all the children with severe spelling problems also had reading problems. In addition, a quarter of the poor spellers (i.e., below the 15th percentile) showed reading performances that were above average.

Through a series of experiments, I studied possible dissociations between reading and spelling in children in the middle period of their school years, and concentrated especially on children with specific spelling impairment without reading impairment. The results have been reported in some detail (Frith, 1978, 1979, 1980). Despite the theoretical possibility that there are children whose reading problems are more severe than their spelling problems, such children are in practice difficult to find. They can be found apparently quite readily in languages where orthography is regular, such as Spanish. For instance, Carbonell de Grompone (1974) found that 31% of 118 third-graders in Uruguay spell better than they read. These children are said to read in letter-by-letter fashion, which makes them slow, though usually accurate.

The independence of reading and spelling skills and problems presents a challenge to cognitive theorists. It suggests that if a dual-route strategy applies to both reading and spelling, the two routes are not shared entirely. Complex modifications of the theory have thus become necessary (Morton, 1980); Seymour & Porpodas, 1980).

DEVELOPMENTAL DYSLEXIA VERSUS DEVELOPMENTAL DYSGRAPHIA

Obviously, different children with equally low educational achievement may nevertheless differ in their strategies, in the cause of their difficulties, and in the treatment that they should receive. Rutter and Yule (1975) and Rutter (1978) have pointed out that children with general retardation (backwardness) in educational subjects (expectedly low achievement) must be distinguished from children with specific retardation (unexpectedly low achievement in some subjects but not others). This differentiation can be accomplished according to the pattern of cognitive and neuropsychological testing.

Given that dissociations between reading and spelling exist in many different groups, it is important to see if "specific" spelling retardation can be distinguished from "specific" but combined reading and spelling retardation. A shorthand label for this latter handicap is "dyslexia," and it may be useful to label the supposed contrast group as having "dysgraphia." There is indeed evidence to show that the distinction is valid and has interesting theoretical and practical implications.

Naidoo (1972) studied in depth a large group of boys aged 8 to 13 years and was able to differentiate a subgroup with a spelling retardation of 2 to 3 years whose reading retardation was only 5 to 14 months. Nelson and Warrington (1974) also described a large group of dyslexic children of the same age range. Like Naidoo, they were able to contrast two subgroups—one with severe reading and spelling retardation of about 3 to 4 years; the other with a 3-year spelling retardation, but an almost negligible amount of reading retardation. The dyslexic group performed significantly worse than the dysgraphic group did on the verbal scale of the Wechsler Intelligence Scale for Children (WISC). They also made qualitatively different kinds of spelling errors. Sweeney and Rourke (1978) distinguished two groups of retarded spellers on the basis of the quality of their spelling errors. Just as one would expect from the Nelson and Warrington study, they found that one group suffered from more general verbal deficits and additional reading retardation, while the other suffered from specific spelling deficits. Differences were especially clear-cut at age 13, while at age 10 the two groups were somewhat less differentiated in this respect.

The degree of the spelling problems in those children whose reading shows little, if any, retardation may vary from very poor to quite good performance. Investigators can still talk about spelling *problems*, since children with average spelling performance may be said to show specific spelling impairment if their actual reading performance and expected spelling performance are well above average. Similarly, reading performance might vary from poor to excellent. The particular group I studied (Frith, 1980) had below-average spelling ability and average reading ability. The mean reading age for the group on the Schonell Reading Test was 12.2; the spelling age on the Schonell Graded Word Test was 10.8. Children with average reading ability and this degree of spelling retardation were relatively easy to find. However, the overall incidence is as yet unknown. In any case, it must be concluded from all these studies that specific spelling retardation can be usefully contrasted with more general impairment in both reading and spelling.

The Evidence from Neuropsychological Studies

Specific and persistent learning problems are caused by a multitude of factors (cf. Rutter, 1978). Some of the most obvious causes are lack of instruction and lack of motivation, and these are often found in disadvantaged environments. However, apart from environmental factors, internal causes must also play a role.

Dalby (1979) and Jorm (1979) review research relating to cerebral involvement of reading disorders and find much evidence for brain dysfunction in children with reading problems. Evidence of brain damage can be established quite readily when reading disability is part of a pattern of general backwardness in both language and motor skills (e.g., Rutter & Yule, 1975). Interestingly enough, in the case of very specific disability, such evidence is more difficult to obtain. Mattis, French, and Rapin (1975) demonstrated that dyslexic children showing signs of damage closely resembled those dyslexic children who lacked any signs of brain damage on a variety of neuropsychological tests. On the other hand, both these groups differed from a third control group that was not dyslexic, but did have known brain damage. The diagnosis of brain damage was made on the following basis: (1) history of an encephalopathic event and subsequent abnormal development; (2) significant abnormality on electroencephalogram (EEG) or skull X-ray; (3) abnormality on special neuroradiographic study. Thus, presence or absence of brain damage judged on these criteria was irrelevant. Nevertheless, the hypothesis that some specific brain dysfunction is at the root of dyslexia and/or dysgraphia is not ruled out. Such dysfunction would have to be different from, and sometimes in addition to, the kind of brain damage seen in the Mattis *et al.* samples.

Rourke (1975, 1978) has argued convincingly that specific learning disabilities can be linked to cerebral dysfunction. In various studies, he applied neuropsychological test batteries and was able to classify specific subtypes. A reading disability subgroup could be shown to do poorly on the kind of tests that concern left-hemisphere functions. Especially relevant is that his two subgroups of poor spellers could also be clearly discriminated in terms of their performance on neuropsychological tests.

Genetic studies of dyslexia have yielded strong evidence that this problem does run in families. Recent studies (e.g., Finucci, Guthrie, Childs, Abbey, & Childs, 1976; Lewitter, DeFries, & Elston, 1980) have not been able to pinpoint the mode of inheritance, but this may partly be due to the lack of differentiating subgroups, such as, for example, dyslexia versus dysgraphia. As yet, as nobody has looked, it is unknown whether specific spelling problems, too, have a genetic basis, and if they also show the highly typical sex ratio of three or four boys to one girl in the distribution patterns. Only the Nelson and Warrington (1974) sample of a clinic population of children between 8 and 14 permits an estimate of the sex ratio. Their reading-plus-spelling group (i.e., dyslexic) had 33 males and 6 females, while their spelling-only group (i.e., dysgraphic) had 62 males and 20 females. This would lead one to expect a higher incidence of dysgraphia in females.

The Evidence from Spelling Errors

One of the first systematic attempts to relate spelling errors and reading disability was provided by Boder (1973). She was able to distinguish three atypical reading–spelling patterns with problems in either visual or phonological attack, or both, corresponding to three subgroups of dysphonetic, dyseidetic, and alexic children. Boder's work has been very influential and has also been applied to normal schoolchildren (Camp & Dolcourt, 1977). A critique of Boder's approach has been provided by Vellutino (1979).

The most important and consistent feature to differentiate dyslexic from dysgraphic children (Frith, 1980; Nelson & Warrington, 1974; Sweeney & Rourke, 1978) concerns the pattern of spelling errors. Briefly, children with specific spelling problems often make phonetically accurate errors (e.g., "I *offen* visited the *galerey*"), but only rarely make phonetically inaccurate errors (e.g., "I often *visen* the *garely*"). This is also true for the spelling errors that good spellers make and very different from the errors produced by poor spellers who have an associated reading problem (i.e., dyslexics). In that group one finds a high proportion of phonetically inaccurate errors. This group would correspond to the "dysphonetic" subgroup in Boder's classification.

For my own samples (Frith, 1980), using the Schonell Spelling Test and relying on two judges to classify errors, I found that dysgraphic children made twice as many phonetic as nonphonetic errors, but that dyslexic children made about equal amounts of each. This difference was significant at the .01 level and is especially interesting, since in terms of quantity of errors the two groups were equal.

Unfortunately, different investigators use somewhat different scoring criteria. Also, the score is dependent on the actual words used for testing spelling (Nelson, 1980). This is so because some words, by their spelling pattern, are extremely likely to result in phonetic errors (e.g., *ommit*, *omitt*, or *omett* for *omit*), whereas other words are extremely likely to result in nonphonetic errors (e.g., *specl*, *specal*, or *speical* for *special*). It is probably for this reason and also for differences in scoring methods and categories used that there are some apparently contradictory findings on the quality of spelling errors. Thus it is difficult to know whether errors made by learning-disabled children are the same as those of younger children, matched for spelling age. This is suggested by the studies of Holmes and Peper (1977) and Nelson (1980). Yet it cannot be ruled out that some types of errors made by dyslexic children are different from those made by beginners, just as some types of errors distinguish dyslexic and dysgraphic children.

In spite of these uncertainties and of having to make a rough-and-ready distinction of phonetic and nonphonetic misspellings, it seems possible to differentiate children according to the quality of their spelling errors into those who have spelling problems only and those who have both spelling and reading problems. It can be concluded from the studies quoted and also from a number of carefully conducted experiments by Perin (1980) with normal school leavers and adult illiterates that the level of reading ability predicts quite well the quality of spelling errors. High reading level appears to be associated with phonetic ("good") spelling errors, regardless of whether there are few errors (good spellers) or many errors (unexpectedly poor spellers).

Phonetic Misspellings and the Phonological Route

From the evidence of spelling errors, the nonlexical or phonological route must be intact in dysgraphic children and impaired in dyslexic children. Given that dysgraphic children make errors that are phonologically plausible, it must be the case that they have no problem in analyzing speech sound into phonemes. Furthermore, the translation of phonemes into graphemes cannot be a problem for them. In contrast, dyslexic children may well have problems in both these processes.

This conclusion is confirmed by results from a test in the spelling of nonsense words (Frith, 1980). In this type of task, use of the phonological route is tested as directly as possible. Spelling nonsense words in a phonetically acceptable way presumably means that the phonological route is used competently. Indeed, the results showed that the dysgraphic children can achieve a high proportion of phonetically correct renderings (85%) not statistically different from that achieved by good spellers (93%). The dyslexic children, on the other hand, differed significantly from both groups by producing only 67% phonetic versions.

Phonetic Misspellings and the Lexical Route

As already discussed, skilled spelling must rely on a lexical route. That is, in order to spell irregular words and homophones correctly, it is indispensable to have the letter-by-letter sequence stored in some internal lexicon, and this also applies to many other regular words that could be spelled in several ways (e.g., *hate*, *hait*, *hayt*). It is this route that appears to be deficient in some way in dysgraphic children who predominantly make phonetic misspellings. The test in the spelling of nonsense words just mentioned also provided some evidence for a failure of the lexical route. Paradoxically, even in this situation, lexical information as to the exact letter-by-letter structure of the strings was used. This means that nonwords were spelled as if they had lexical entries. Especially, the good spellers produced spellings that were closely based on similar regular words. Thus *rekind* was spelled like *remind* and not *rekyned*; *rituated* was spelled like *situated* and not *ritchuated.* Dysgraphic and dyslexic children, on the other hand, produced a certain amount of quite unconventional but nevertheless phonetically plausible responses. These responses are likely to be true examples of a phonological but nonlexical route. The conventional responses, on the other hand, are likely to show the operation of the lexical route even with the spelling of nonsense words.

THE TWO ROUTES AND SOME EXPLANATIONS OF SPELLING PROBLEMS

From the few spelling errors made by normal (good) spellers, we can hypothesize that whenever the lexical route fails (i.e., when the automatic program for spelling the letter-by-letter sequence of a word is not available), the spellers can fall back on the phonological route. This failure may happen only rarely in good spellers, but quite frequently in dysgraphic children. In terms of phonetic misspellings, there is a difference in the quantity but not the quality of spelling errors. Thus it should be the case that the groups are indistinguishable on a spelling test of entirely regular words without spelling ambiguity (e.g., *top*, *dig*, *pen*), and also in languages with regular orthography. It also follows that a difference can be detected when comparing performance on regular and irregular English words. There should be an enormous discrepancy in error rates for dysgraphic children, but only a small discrepancy, if any, for good spellers, as they can use the lexical route efficiently. These predictions could readily be tested.

For dyslexic children, on the other hand, it appears that when there is a failure of the lexical route, the phonological route cannot be used successfully as a backup strategy. In other words, they have a double impairment. Predictions from such a hypothesis have been tested by Seymour and Porpodas (1980). They elaborated and used the dual-route model to test differences between dyslexic and reading-age-matched normal readers. They compared the incidence of misspellings in regular and irregular words, as well as in common and rare words. They found that dyslexic children made many more errors on rare regular words than the normal children did, but were equal on rare irregular words. This lends support to the notion of a problem in the phonological route, since this route is presumably responsible for good performance on rare words with regular sound-to-letter relationships. However, dyslexic children also made significantly more errors with very common irregular words. They therefore have a problem in the lexical route also, since this route presumably handles words that cannot be spelled correctly by using a phonological route.

Thus dyslexic spellers differ from normal spellers by being deficient in two strategies. However, they differ from dysgraphic spellers in only one strategy. On the other hand, dysgraphic spellers also differ from normal spellers in one strategy only.

Failure of the Phonological Route

Failure of the phonological route discriminates dyslexic from dysgraphic children. Dyslexic children apparently find it difficult to pass the hurdles of phoneme analysis and of phoneme-to-grapheme translation. Could this be explained by a basic phonemic deficit?

Vellutino (1979), in a comprehensive review of dyslexia research, provides convincing arguments for specific deficits in one or more aspects of verbal processing in dyslexia. Several investigators (Bradley & Bryant, 1978; Snowling, 1980; Tallal, 1980) have all found converging evidence on problems with phoneme analysis in dyslexic children. This difficulty can be diagnosed in speech, not just in written language. There is thus a possibility of seeing dyslexia in close relation to dysphasia in childhood. Such a connection has also been suggested by Denckla and Rudel (1976), who found that dyslexic children were very slow at naming pictures.

Tallal (1980) found some low-level auditory perceptual dysfunction, at least in one subgroup of reading-disabled children. Snowling (1981) showed that dyslexic children compared to younger children of the same level of reading ability were relatively impaired in "repeating back" (i.e., in saying long nonsense words but not in repeating back closely similar real words; thus they could say *visitor* but not *fizidor*, *magnificent* but not *bagmivishent*). She explains this in terms of a phonemic deficit that is shown up with novel words, which need a great deal of phonemic processing, while words already in one's repertoire need only a very small amount of processing. Similar arguments have been put forward by Dérouesné and Beauvois (1979) to account for similar findings in adult alexia. If dyslexic children cannot cope easily with the processing demands involved in saying novel words, it is not surprising that they have difficulties in language learning. Delay in early language acquisition is consistently reported for dyslexic children (Ingram, 1963; Rutter, Tizard, & Whitmore, 1970/1981; Warrington, 1967).

An interesting approach toward understanding the nature of the deficit that leads to nonphonetic spelling errors has been provided by Marcel (1980b). Marcel has identified a certain type of spelling error that is characterized by omission of nasals and liquids in consonant clusters (e.g., *thoat* for *throat*; *poblam* for *problem*; *diffecot* for *difficult*; *groud* for *ground*; *gasse* for *glass*; *fide* for *find*). This type of error is highly characteristic of some individuals. These can be found in various groups, such as adult illiterates, neurological patients, and schoolchildren with reading and spelling problems. In some of the people this error does not occur in real words, since they spell them correctly by the direct lexical-orthographic route. Sometimes they only spell them partially correctly. Instead of omitting the liquid or nasal consonant in question, they misplace it (e.g., *fiurt* for *fruit*; *scienec* for *science*). However, the characteristic omission can readily be elicited by testing with nonsense words.

One fascinating fact about this type of error is that it occurs also in normal children's speech in early stages of language acquisition (N. V. Smith, 1973). Thus young children reduce consonant clusters and especially tend to omit nasals and liquids. Marcel was able to show subtle difficulties in phonetic segmentation in his deviant spellers. He also showed that they differed in their linguistic awareness. In particular, it appeared that, like young children who also lack this awareness, they did not code speech in terms of "phonemes" but in terms of "distinctive features." This work shows that the causes of failure in phonemic processing could be extremely complex.

Failure of the Lexical Route

The problem most closely descriptive of the spelling of dysgraphic children is the failure of the lexical route. Only in this do they differ from good spellers. It is important to point out that no such failure was in evidence in the reading of these children (Frith, 1978, 1980). On the contrary, only when they read by a lexical route was their reading performance equal to that of good spellers. Whenever phonological processing was demanded, such as in reading aloud, judging rhymes, and reading misspelled text with intact grapheme-to-phoneme relationships, their performance was significantly poorer than that of the good spellers. On the other hand, whenever reading without phonological processing was possible, such as silent reading for meaning or reading text with disturbed grapheme-to-phoneme relationships, the two groups were equal.

One explanation of the failure of the lexical route in spelling is that the lexical entries themselves are not letter-perfect. If dysgraphic children always avoid full cues when reading, then there might be little chance for good spelling programs to be developed. One could argue that the only way perfect spellings will be entered into the internal lexicon is through having looked at them, or analyzed them in their exact letter-by-letter sequence. Thus full details (i.e., all the letters in their correct order) have to be scrutinized. This is different from recognizing words by a direct visual route, for which full letter-by-letter detail is unnecessary. It is possible to recognize a word correctly by minimal cues, but it is not possible to reproduce a word correctly unless one has full cues.

Thus, there is no puzzle in finding that people can be good readers and at the same time atrocious spellers. A partial-cue strategy is excellently suited for recognizing words but poorly suited for recalling them. However, one would expect that good spellers would be able to use the full-cue strategy that is so essential for building up a spelling lexicon, and also for reading, if required. For poor spellers, on the other hand, this full-cue strategy should be difficult to adopt. Indeed, differences between the group in terms of their ability to use full cues and similarities between the groups in terms of their reliance on partial cues, have been shown in several studies (Frith, 1980).

As is discussed at the beginning of this chapter, the full letter-by-letter representation of words is not a trivial accomplishment. It opens up a rich source of many different kinds of linguistic information.

An Experiment on the Nature of the Partial-Cue Strategy

Relying on partial cues for reading is only possible because of the redundancy contained in the written word. If one had to read not words but random letter strings, then full cues would be necessary to process them. Since it is hypothesized that poor spellers who are good readers do not use full cues, they should do less well on such a task than good spellers should. On the other hand, they should equal the good spellers on redundant strings. This should be true not only for reading, but also for scanning letter strings. In order to test this hypothesis, I carried out an experiment where the task was finding a particular letter string embedded in similar strings. Attention to letter-by-letter detail was necessary in one condition, as all the letter strings were random, and not necessary in another, where they were redundant. Examples of two such lists are shown in Figure 22-2.

One type of list contained only highly redundant letter strings; that is, the letter strings were very much like words. The letter strings in the nonredundant lists were unpronounceable and hence did not at all resemble English words. A total of 10 normal spellers and 10 dysgraphic children, about 12 years old (with

eague	eaeug
EPhEw	EhPWe
eRElY	eeYLr
SPeCT	SCtpE
enCil	suOHg
iGHtS	iHTsg
EugEa	eUaEg
UNdOW	uDNwO
ennEL	eNLcI
EaGuE	EAeUG
aRcEL	uEnDd
auCEr	aECrL
ARlEY	rEocR
rAUsE	iGNrE
RoKEn	RoeKN
alKEd	aeUcR
REasE	uETnN
eAGuE	EAeUg
EReLy	aEYLr
EpHeW	ilBbE
eNcIl	sEUtm
ENneL	eENLn
eUGea	eUaEG
RAdLe	eEyLR
souGh	ENlCi
eAGuE	eAeUg
InGer	aeYlr
IBblE	SuOGh
sPeCT	aEUcR
aucEr	EEnlN
ArLEy	EhpwE

Figure 22-2. Example of the visual-search task with redundant and nonredundant letter strings.

equivalent reading age), had to scan as fast as possible through each list, marking the target word with a pencil whenever it occurred. Each child was given two practice trials and four test trials, using a different word each time. The target words used for high- and low-redundancy conditions were these: *encil/enlci*; *eague/eaeug*; *undow/udnwo*; and *tormy/tyomr*. In each list, one of these targets was embedded three times at quasi-random positions in the list, which was 30 items long. The last target always appeared in positions 24 to 29. For each pair of high- and low-redundancy target words, the two lists were identical as to position of the target words. Also, the actual letters used in the distractor words were the same (e.g., *udden/uendd*). These various controls ensure that the two conditions to be compared *only* differed in their degree of redundancy.

A special precaution was taken to prevent the children from simply scanning for a single letter in a specific position to find the target word. This would have meant that the two redundancy conditions, which were entirely defined by letter context, were effectively nonexistent. To avoid such a disaster, it was therefore necessary to induce a strategy that was less extreme in its use of partial cues. This was done simply by typing the letters in mixed case. The target word might have a little *e* or big *E* at the beginning, and so forth. In addition, the first letter was placed at different positions in the column. The sample lists in Figure 22-2 show this typographic manipulation. There were two trials for each condition, and the time taken to find the three targets was recorded. Errors were very infrequent.

The average times taken per list are shown in Table 22-1. Only the interaction between groups and conditions was significant ($F = 4.79, p < .05$). This means that the poor spellers were significantly slower than good spellers were with nonredundant strings, but equally fast with redundant ones. Thus, just as hypothesized, they can make good use of redundancy. However, they are at a disadvantage when the opposite strategy is required—namely, paying full attention to all letters. This is closely analogous to previous results demonstrating the similarity of the groups in reading real words and relative impairment of the poor spellers in reading nonwords (Frith, 1978).

It is interesting to note that the poor spellers' performance cannot be explained by poor images in visual memory. Their memory image for the wordlike targets was just as good as that of good spellers. Only the random strings gave them problems—while good spellers were hardly affected by the implied increase in attention demand.

Since paying full attention to all letters is necessary for acquiring the letter-by-letter representation of words, and since this strategy is not necessary for normal reading, it is not surprising then that good readers can be poor spellers. Those who always avoid paying full attention to letter-by-letter detail in reading obviously will acquire poor knowledge of letter-by-letter detail of words. It could therefore be stated that specific spelling difficulties in good readers originate in a strategy problem.

CONCLUSIONS AND IMPLICATIONS

An important requirement for the differentiation of subgroups of dyslexic and dysgraphic children is that of new diagnostic tests. The studies reported suggest that it would be useful to compare the written spelling of regular and irregular words, and also of real words and nonsense words.

A simple analysis of errors into phonetic and nonphonetic misspellings is already very helpful in pinpointing the problem. Nonphonetic misspellings,

Table 22-1. Average time taken to find three targets

GROUP	HIGH REDUNDANCY (*eague*)	LOW REDUNDANCY (*eaeug*)
Good spellers ($n = 10$)	12.97 sec	13.74 sec
Poor spellers ($n = 10$)	14.97 sec	18.54 sec

especially of nonsense words, can be indicative of phonological problems. Those with consonant cluster reduction are of particular interest, as they may define a special subgroup with subtle problems of phoneme perception and awareness. Phonological problems in spelling appear always to be associated with reading problems. It may well turn out that these cases are better defined as speech problems with inevitable repercussions in reading and writing. No such problems are apparent in dysgraphic children.

Phonetic misspellings, especially of irregular words and homophones, can be indicative of an impairment in the lexical (or "visual") aspect of spelling. This aspect refers to the specific letter-by-letter structure of words, which enables a differentiation over and above their sound (e.g., *to*, *too*, *two*). It is this aspect alone that appears to be impaired in dysgraphic children.

Those children who are poor spellers but nevertheless good readers show a failure of the lexical "visual" route in their spelling. This may be because these children when reading always use a lexical strategy based on partial cues. Good spellers, by contrast, can use a full-cue strategy if required. Thus, when looking at words, the dysgraphic children pay attention to some letters but not to others. Clearly this strategy is inadequate for acquiring and producing precise letter-by-letter spelling patterns.

The research reported permits some boldly concrete suggestions, which would of course need to be tested in an experimental remedial setting. *Dyslexic* children appear to need a new kind of speech therapy that would tackle their basic problems with phonological analysis. This may seem odious to many dyslexia teachers, since their speech is usually perfectly normal. The dyslexic children might nevertheless benefit from certain specific speaking and listening exercises. This training would have to be based on the concept of phonemes as they are represented by graphemes. Such training would be wasted, however, on dysgraphic children with good reading ability. They, instead, would need training that would ensure their paying attention to the letter-by-letter detail of words. Ways of doing this would include pointing to each letter, naming each letter, or writing each letter in a word in the proper sequence with equal emphasis on all. The acquisition of accurate automatic spelling programs would be the aim of this training. Various effective methods to achieve this aim have already been worked out by many teachers.

While these specific suggestions are debatable, the general implications of the research for remedial education are uncontroversial: Spelling needs to be looked at in its own right as a separate skill from reading, with important differences in optimal strategies. Poor spellers have to be distinguished according to whether lexical or nonlexical processing or both are impaired. They require different teaching programs. Whether to teach to the strength or to the weakness is, however, an unsolved question that cannot even be attempted to be answered in the present context.

References

Baker, R. G. Orthographic awareness. In U. Frith (Ed.), *Cognitive processes in spelling*. London: Academic Press, 1980.

Baron, J., & McKillop, B. J. Individual differences in speed of phonemic analysis, visual analysis, and reading. *Acta Psychologica*, 1975, *39*, 91–96.

Baron, J., & Strawson, C. Use of orthographic and word-specific knowledge in reading words aloud. *Journal of Experimental Psychology: Human Perception and Performance*, 1976, *2*, 386–393.

Barron, R. W. Visual and phonological strategies in reading and spelling. In U. Frith (Ed.), *Cognitive processes in spelling*. London: Academic Press, 1980.

Beauvois, M. F., & Dérouesné, J. Phonological alexia: Three dissociations. *Journal of Neurology, Neurosurgery and Psychiatry*, 1979, *42*, 1115–1124.

Boder, E. Developmental dyslexia: A diagnostic approach based on three atypical reading-spelling patterns. *Developmental Medicine and Child Neurology*, 1973, *15*, 663–687.

Bradley, L., & Bryant, P. Difficulties in auditory organization as a possible cause of reading backwardness. *Nature*, 1978, *271*, 746–747.

Bryant, P., & Bradley, L. Why children sometimes write words which they do not read. In U. Frith (Ed.), *Cognitive processes in spelling*. London: Academic Press, 1980.

Camp, B. W., & Dolcourt, J. L. Reading and spelling in good and poor readers. *Journal of Learning Disabilities*, 1977, *10*, 300–307.

Carbonell de Grompone, M. A. Children who spell better than they read. *Academic Therapy*, 1974, *9*, 281–288.

Chomsky, C. Write first; read later. *Childhood Education*, 1971, *47*, 296–299.

Coltheart, M. Lexical access in simple reading tasks. In G. Underwood (Ed.), *Strategies of information processing*. London: Academic Press, 1979.

Coltheart, M., Davelaar, E., Jonasson, J. T., & Besner, D. Access to the internal lexicon. In S. Dornic (Ed.), *Attention and performance* (Vol. 6). New York: Academic Press, 1977.

Dalby, J. T. Deficit or delay: Neuropsychological models of developmental dyslexia. *Journal of Special Education*, 1979, *13*, 239–264.

Denckla, M., & Rudel, R. Naming of object-drawings by dyslexic and other learning disabled children. *Brain and Language*, 1976, *3*, 1–15.

Dérouesné, J., & Beauvois, M. F. Phonological processing in reading: Data from alexia. *Journal of Neurology, Neurosurgery and Psychiatry*, 1979, *42*, 1125–1132.

Ellis, A. W. Spelling and writing (and reading and speaking). In A. W. Ellis (Ed.), *Normality and pathology in cognitive functions*. London: Academic Press, 1982.

Finucci, J. M., Guthrie, J. T., Childs, A. L., Abbey, H., & Childs, B. The genetics of specific reading disability. *Annals of Human Genetics*, 1976, *40*, 1–23.

Frith, U. From print to meaning and from print to sound, or how to read without knowing how to spell. *Visible Language*, 1978, *12*, 43–54.

Frith, U. Reading by eye and writing by ear. In P. A. Kolers, M. Wrolstad, & H. Bouma (Eds.), *Processing of visible language* (Vol. 1). New York: Plenum Press, 1979.

Frith, U. Unexpected spelling problems. In U. Frith (Ed.), *Cognitive processes in spelling*. London: Academic Press, 1980.

Frith, U., & Frith, C. D. Relationships between reading and spelling. In R. L. Venezky & J. F. Kavanagh (Eds.), *Orthography, reading and dyslexia*. Baltimore: University Park Press, 1980.

Haas, W. *Phonological translation*. Manchester, England: Manchester University Press, 1970.

Henderson, L., & Chard, J. The reader's implicit knowledge of orthographic structure. In U. Frith (Ed.), *Cognitive processes in spelling*. London: Academic Press, 1980.

Holmes, D. L., & Peper, R. J. An evaluation of the use of spelling error analysis in the diagnosis of reading disabilities. *Child Development*, 1977, *48*, 1708–1711.

Horn, T. D. Spelling. In R. L. Ebels (Ed.), *Encyclopedia of educational research* (4th ed.). New York: Macmillan, 1969.

Ingram, T. T. S. Delayed development of speech with special reference to dyslexia. *Proceedings of the Royal Society of Medicine*, 1963, *56*, 199–203.

Jorm, A. F. The cognitive and neurological basis of developmental dyslexia: A theoretical framework and review. *Cognition*, 1979, *7*, 19–33.

Levitt, J. The influence of orthography on phonology: A comparative study (English, French, Spanish, Italian, German). *Linguistics*, 1978, *208*, 43–67.

Lewitter, F., I., DeFries, J. C., & Elston, R. C. Genetic models of reading disability. *Behavior Genetics*, 1980, *10*, 9–30.

Malmquist, E. *Factors related to reading disabilities in the first grade of the elementary school.* Uppsala: Almquist & Wiksells, 1958.

Marcel, A. J. Phonological awareness and phonological representations: Investigation of a specific spelling problem. In U. Frith (Ed.), *Cognitive processes in spelling*. London: Academic Press, 1980. (a)

Marcel, A. J. Surface dyslexia and beginning reading: A revised hypothesis of the pronunciation of print and its impairments. In M. Coltheart, K. Patterson, & J. S. Marshall (Eds.), *Deep dyslexia*. London: Routledge & Kegan Paul, 1980. (b)

Marcel, A. J., & Patterson, K. E. Word recognition and production: Reciprocity of clinical and normal studies. In J. Requin (Ed.), *Attention and performance* (Vol. 7). Hillsdale, N.J.: Erlbaum, 1978.

Mattis, S., French, J. H., & Rapin, I. Dyslexia in children and young adults: Three independent neuropsychological syndromes. *Developmental Medicine and Child Neurology*, 1975, *17*, 150–163.

Morton, J. A preliminary functional model for language behaviour. *International Audiology*, 1964, *3*, 216–225.

Morton, J. The interaction of information in word recognition. *Psychological Review*, 1969, *76*, 165–178.

Morton, J. The logogen model and orthographic structure. In U. Frith (Ed.), *Cognitive processes in spelling*. London: Academic Press, 1980.

Naidoo, S. *Specific dyslexia*. London: Pitman, 1972.

Nelson, H. Analysis of spelling errors in normal and dyslexic children. In U. Frith (Ed.), *Cognitive processes in spelling*. London: Academic Press, 1980.

Nelson, H., & Warrington, E. K. Developmental spelling retardation and its relation to other cognitive abilities. *British Journal of Psychology*, 1974, *65*, 265–274.

Perin, D. *Spelling difficulty in school leavers and adults*. Unpublished doctoral dissertation, University of Sussex, 1980.

Peters, M. L. The influence of reading methods on spelling. *British Journal of Educational Psychology*, 1967, *37*, 47–53.

Read, C. Preschool children's knowledge of English phonology. *Harvard Educational Review*, 1971, *41*, 1–34.

Read, C. Writing is not the inverse of reading for young children. In C. H. Frederikson, M. F. Whiteman, & J. F. Dominic (Eds.), *Writing: The nature, development, and teaching of written communication* (Vol. 1, *Writing process, development and communication*). Hillsdale, N.J.: Erlbaum, 1978.

Rourke, B. P. Brain–behavior relationships in children with learning disabilities: A research program. *American Psychologist*, 1975, *30*, 911–920.

Rourke, B. P. Reading, spelling, arithmetic disabilities: A neuropsychologic perspective. In H. R. Myklebust (Ed.), *Progress in learning disabilities* (Vol. 4). New York: Grune & Stratton, 1978.

Rourke, B. P. Reading and spelling disabilities: A developmental neuropsychological perspective. In U. Kirk (Ed.), *Neuropsychology of language, reading and spelling*. New York: Academic Press, 1981.

Rourke, B. P., & Orr, R. R. Prediction of the reading and spelling performances of normal and retarded readers: A 4-year follow-up. *Journal of Abnormal Child Psychology*, 1977, *5*, 9–20.

Rutter, M. Prevalence and types of dyslexia. In A. L. Benton & D. Pearl (Eds.), *Dyslexia: An appraisal of current knowledge*. Oxford: Oxford University Press, 1978.

Rutter, M., Tizard, J., & Whitmore, K. (Eds.). *Education, health, and behaviour*. London: Longman, 1970. (Reprinted, Huntington, N.Y.: Krieger, 1981.)

Rutter, M., Tizard, J., Yule, W., Graham, P., & Whitmore, K. Research report: Isle of Wight Studies, 1964–1974. *Psychological Medicine*, 1976, *6*, 313–332.

Rutter, M., & Yule, W. The concept of specific reading retardation. *Journal of Child Psychology and Psychiatry*, 1975, *16*, 181–197.

Scragg, D. G. *A history of English spelling*. Manchester, England: Manchester University Press, 1974.

Seymour, P. H. K., & Porpodas, C. Lexical and non-lexical spelling in dyslexia. In U. Frith (Ed.), *Cognitive processes in spelling*. London: Academic Press, 1980.

Shallice, T., & Warrington, E. K. Single and multiple component central dyslexic syndromes. In M. Coltheart, K. E. Patterson, & J. C. Marshall (Eds.), *Deep dyslexia*. London: Routledge & Kegan Paul, 1980.

Sloboda, J. A. Visual imagery and individual differences in spelling. In U. Frith (Ed.), *Cognitive processes in spelling*. London: Academic Press, 1980.

Smith, N. V. *The acquisition of phonology: A case study*. Cambridge, England: University Press, 1973.

Smith, P. T. Linguistic information in spelling. In U. Frith (Ed.), *Cognitive processes in spelling*. London: Academic Press, 1980.

Snowling, M. The development of grapheme–phoneme correspondence in normal and dyslexic readers. *Journal of Experimental Child Psychology*, 1980, *4*, 294–305.

Snowling, M. Phonemic deficits in developmental dyslexia. *Psychological Research*, 1981, *43*, 219–234.

Snowling, M., & Frith, U. The role of sound, shape, and orthographic cues in early reading. *British Journal of Psychology*, 1981, *72*, 83–87.

Sweeney, J. E., & Rourke, B. P. Neuropsychological significance of phonetically accurate and phonetically inaccurate spelling errors in younger and older retarded spellers. *Brain and Language*, 1978, *6*, 212–225.

Tallal, P. Auditory temporal perception, phonics, and reading disabilities in children. *Brain and Language*, 1980, *9*, 182–198.

Valtin, R., Jung, U. O. H., & Scheerer-Neumann, G. *Legasthenie in Wissenschaft und Unterricht*. Darmstadt: Wissenschaftliche Buchgesellschaft, 1981.

Vellutino, F. *Dyslexia: Theory and research*. Cambridge, Mass.: MIT Press, 1979.

Venezky, R. L. Spelling instruction and spelling reform: From Webster to Rice to Roosevelt. In U. Frith (Ed.), *Cognitive processes in spelling*. London: Academic Press, 1980.

Warrington, E. K. The incidence of verbal disability associated with reading retardation. *Neuropsychologia*, 1967, *5*, 175–179.

Weigl, E., & Fradis, A. The transcoding process in patients with agraphia to dictation. *Brain and Language*, 1977, *4*, 11–22.

CHAPTER TWENTY-THREE

Subtypes of Reading and Arithmetical Disabilities: A Neuropsychological Analysis

BYRON P. ROURKE / JOHN D. STRANG

SUBTYPES OF READING DISABILITY

Background

The results of several investigations carried out in our laboratory at the University of Windsor and Windsor Western Hospital Centre have suggested rather strongly that learning-disabled children do not constitute a homogeneous population (see Rourke, 1975, 1978b, 1983). For example, it has become abundantly clear that learning-disabled children with different patterns of verbal–performance IQ discrepancies on the Wechsler Intelligence Scale for Children (WISC; Wechsler, 1949) exhibit strikingly disparate patterns of neuropsychological abilities and deficits, as well as quite distinctive patterns of academic handicap (Rourke & Telegdy, 1971; Rourke, Young, & Flewelling, 1971). It is also apparent that these relationships vary considerably as a function of age (Rourke, Dietrich, & Young, 1973).

In the case of reading disability, a similar situation obtains. For example, in one longitudinal investigation of reading-disabled children, we found that some (approximately a quarter) of a reading-disabled sample made appreciable progress in reading over the 4-year period studied (ages 7–8 years to 11–12 years), whereas the remainder of the sample made little or no progress over this same time period (Rourke & Orr, 1977). This finding alone, of course, would not be sufficient to suggest that there are two subtypes of reading-disabled children (i.e., one that "recovers" from reading disability and one that does not do so). However, we also found that the performances of these two groups of children differed markedly on some subtests of the Underlining Test (Doehring, 1968; Rourke & Gates, 1980; Rourke & Petrauskas, 1978), a complex test designed to tap speed of visual perception, which had been administered to all of the reading-disabled children during their initial examination in the 4-year study. If these results are confirmed by cross-validation, this would suggest that one or

Byron P. Rourke and John D. Strang. Department of Psychology, University of Windsor, Windsor, Ontario, Canada; Department of Neuropsychology, Windsor Western Hospital Centre, Windsor, Ontario, Canada.

more of the ability dimensions tapped by the discriminating subtests of the Underlining Test are crucial differentiating features for these two groups (subtypes) of reading-disabled children.

Our clinical experience (see Rourke, 1976, 1981) has also suggested strongly that children at different age levels who are severely deficient in the ability to read (in spite of apparently normal motivation and emotional stability, adequate sensory acuity, normal levels of psychometric intelligence, and adequate educational opportunity) can differ markedly in their neuropsychological ability structure. More generally, recent reviews of the clinical and research evidence relating to the neurobehavioral dimensions of reading disability (Benton, 1975; Rourke, 1978a) have garnered a host of evidence consistent with the view that reading disability of this type is a far from homogeneous entity. With these findings and conclusions as background, we set out to determine whether subtypes of reading disability at one particular age level (i.e., 7 years, 0 months to 8 years, 11 months) could be isolated in an empirical fashion. The results of this study are reported in some detail, so that the similarities and differences among subtypes of reading-disabled children can be highlighted.

The Petrauskas and Rourke (1979) Study

In this study, we employed a large number of measures of sensory–perceptual, motor, psychomotor, linguistic, and concept-formation abilities that bear close resemblance to those that have been shown to be deficient in reading-disabled children in a number of previous studies (Benton, 1975; Rourke, 1978a). In addition, our aim was to include a representative breadth of measures that are known to be sensitive to cerebral impairment in children at this age level (Reitan, 1974; Rourke, 1975, 1978b).

The total sample of 7- and 8-year-old children contained 160 subjects, of whom 133 were retarded readers and 27 were normal readers. All of the subjects met the stringent set of criteria for learning disabilities (in this case, reading disability) that has been employed in this series of investigations (Rourke, 1975, 1978b). All of the children in the group of disabled readers obtained a centile score of 25 or below on the reading subtest of the Wide-Range Achievement Test (WRAT; Jastak & Jastak, 1965). Subjects in the group of normal readers obtained a centile score of 45 or above on the WRAT reading subtest.

The initial pool of 44 dependent measures was classified into six categories (tactile–perceptual; sequencing; motoric; visual–spatial; auditory–verbal; and abstract–conceptual). This pool of 44 test measures was reduced to 20 measures in terms of the following criteria: (1) correlations between variables in each skill area were to be as low as possible; (2) a similar number of variables from each skill area would be included; and (3) the variables included, when taken together, would provide information of clinical significance.

The total sample of 160 subjects was divided into two subsamples of 80 subjects each, with the only restriction being that a similar number of normal readers was assigned to each subsample. The data matrices for these two subsamples were then subjected to a series of analyses involving correlations and the application of the *Q* factor-analysis procedure. Those profiles emerging in one subsample of data that yielded significant correlations with profiles in the other subsample constituted the reliable subtypes of disabled readers. In addition, an overall *Q* factor analysis was carried out for all 160 subjects. The profiles emerging from this overall analysis that correlated significantly with the reliable subtypes in the two subsamples of data constituted the subtypes.

A general comparison of performances of the normal readers and retarded readers with age-based norms revealed, as expected, that the normal readers exhibited better performances than did the retarded readers on the majority of the test measures that were employed. Of particular interest was the fact that the profile of test scores for the normal readers was rather flat and, for 17 of the 20 measures, was within one-half of one standard deviation about the mean of the norms for these tests. By way of contrast, the profile for the retarded readers contained a number of "peaks" and "troughs." This would suggest, among other things, that the retarded readers as a group exhibited much more variability in performance than did the normal readers as a group.

In the overall analysis, 119 of the 160 subjects exhibited single-factor loadings of .50 or greater. The number of subjects with factor loadings greater than or equal to .50 on two or more factors was relatively small. Those few subjects who exhibited loadings of .50 or greater on two or more factors and those who did not obtain factor loadings of .50 or greater for any single factor were not considered in the determination of subtypes. The small number of subjects who exhibited factor loadings of opposite polarity were also excluded for further consideration.

With these constraints in mind, three reliable subtypes of reading-disabled children were identified. In addition, a factor emerged that was comprised principally of normal readers.

The largest subtype of reading-disabled children that emerged (Subtype 1) contained an approximate ratio of three males to one female, which is about the same as that for the total sample of disabled readers. These subjects exhibited the largest discrepancy between WISC verbal IQ and performance IQ (favoring performance IQ) of any of the subtypes. In addition, their scaled scores on the WRAT reading and spelling subtests were somewhat poorer than were their arithmetic subtest scores. In general, they exhibited their most marked difficulties on tests that were primarily verbal in nature (such as tests for verbal fluency and sentence memory). Their abilities in the tactile–perceptual, motoric, visual–spatial, and abstract–conceptual areas were usually within normal limits. Relatively low scores on such tests as the WISC digit span subtest and the Matching Pictures Test (which involves a substantial amount of verbal coding) were consistent with the other rather specific psycholinguistic deficiencies exhibited by children of this subtype. This subtype of reading-disabled child was the largest subtype found in the study. This would suggest that these children "contribute" most to the very common finding that undifferentiated groups of reading-disabled children tend to exhibit (1) a WISC verbal–performance IQ discrepancy favoring performance IQ, and (2) significant auditory–verbal and language-related problems. This pattern of performances exhibited by Subtype 1 is quite similar to that of the group described by Mattis, French, and Rapin (1975) as evidencing "language disorder," and to that often observed in adults with actively debilitating lesions of the temporal lobe within the left cerebral hemisphere (Luria, 1973; Reitan, 1966).

The second reliable subtype that was identified (Subtype 2) exhibited a very small WISC verbal–performance IQ discrepancy. In addition to the so-called ACID pattern (i.e., outstandingly poor arithmetic, coding, information, and digit span subtest performances on the WISC), they exhibited uniformly poor performances on the WRAT reading, spelling, and arithmetic subtests. In general, their auditory–verbal and language-related problems were somewhat less severe than were those of Subtype 1. Their outstanding deficiencies were evident on tests for finger agnosia with the right and left hands and on a measure involving immediate memory for visual sequences. There were indications that this particular subtype of reading-disabled children may have a more general "sequencing" difficulty, and it is also interesting to note that this group of children, together with a less reliable subtype (Subtype 5), comprised almost half of those classified in the reading-disabled group. For this reason, it is not surprising that several investigators have suggested that sequencing difficulties may account for reading failure, at least in some reading-disabled children (Bakker, 1967; Spreen, 1978).

The evidence of difficulties in finger localization would also suggest that this subtype of retarded readers may be similar to at least some of those that have been identified by Satz and his colleagues (Fletcher & Satz, 1980). The combination of linguistic, sequencing, and finger-localization deficiencies, within a context of the other relatively intact abilities exhibited by Subtype 2, would be consistent with compromised functional integrity of the posterior (temporo-parieto-occipital) regions of the left cerebral hemisphere. However, it should be emphasized that this study was not designed as a test of this particular hypothesis, and, at this stage, there is little in the way of corroborative evidence to support it.

Another feature of Subtype 2 that differentiates it from Subtype 1 was the fact that Subtype 2 contained a ratio of approximately 12 males to 1 female. In this connection, it should also be pointed out that the less reliable subtype (5), which bore some similarity to Subtype 2, was found to contain a ratio of 20 males to 1 female.

The smallest reliable subtype identified (Subtype 3) contained 11 disabled readers and two normal readers. This subtype could be characterized as having average visual–spatial abilities, no clear deficiency in verbal comprehension, some difficulties in psychomotor skills, and problems on some tasks involving the generating of verbal information and verbal coding. Children in Subtype 3 exhibited some evidence of greater difficulty with the right than with the left hand on both the Tactual Performance Test and on the Finger-Recognition Test. They also appeared to have particular difficulty in conceptual flexibility, especially when linguistic coding was involved. Children in this group exhibited a lower verbal IQ than performance IQ on the WISC, and their lowest WISC verbal subtest scaled scores were obtained on the arithmetic, information, and digit span subtests (the so-called AID pattern).

Subtype 3 differed from Subtypes 1 and 2 particularly in the rather consistent evidence of relatively better performance on the left than on the right side of the body. In addition, their auditory–verbal and language-related abilities tended to be somewhat better than were those of Subtypes 1 and 2. For these reasons, it is clear that a parallel can be drawn between Subtype 3 and the group described by Mattis, French, and Rapin (1975) as displaying articulation and graphomotor discoordination. There is also some similarity between the pattern of neuropsychological abilities and deficits exhibited by this group and the pattern that is rather typically found in adults with lesions confined principally to the anterior (frontal) regions of the left cerebral hemisphere. Once again, however, it must be emphasized that this similarity in patterns of performance and its relationship to patterns of brain-related impairment is quite speculative at this point. Much more research will have to be conducted to ascertain to what extent and degree such a relationship exists.

Another subtype identified (Subtype 4) was comprised principally of normal readers and did not emerge reliably from the classification procedure. Seven of the 27 subjects in the group of normal readers and only one of the 133 reading-disabled children loaded on this factor. For the most part, the profile described for the normal readers as a group (see above) was evident for this group. However, the fact that the majority of the normal readers did not load on this subtype would suggest the possibility that there are different subtypes of normal readers. Nevertheless, this result does emphasize that differences between normal readers and reading-disabled children are probably qualitative rather than quantitative in nature (see Rourke & Gates, 1981).

The results of the Petrauskas and Rourke study (1979) have been discussed in some detail in order to show that the neuropsychological dimensions of the group of clinical disorders known as "reading disability" are quite complex. At the very least, this analysis should serve to indicate that reading-disabled children do not constitute a homogeneous group. Nevertheless, it is also clear that deficiencies in psycholinguistic skills play a major role in reading difficulties at this age level. In this connection, it should be pointed out that we have also found psycholinguistic disabilities to be major sources of problems for different subtypes of learning-disabled children at ages ranging from 9 to 14 years (Fisk & Rourke, 1979).

The potential clinical applicability of findings such as those just described should be clear. For example, what we need to know now is whether these various subtypes of reading-disabled children will respond differentially to forms of teaching and intervention that emphasize various styles and content areas. Investigations designed to reveal possible differential responses by each of the subtypes to different types of treatments constitute the next phase of this research strategy.

Finally, the conclusions that can be drawn from studies such as this one speak to issues of considerable theoretical interest. For example, the models of reading disability presented by Wiener and Cromer (1967) and those evaluated by Doehring (1976, 1978), varying as they do from simple univariate explanations to complex multivariate ones, can be evaluated within the context of the results of classification research in this area. The results of our own investigations would certainly coincide more with the multifactorial theories and models presented by these investigators, with the attendant implication that different types of reading disability are probably the results of quite different sets of etiologies. In addition, our speculations regarding the likelihood of dysfunction maximally involving different systems within the temporal (Subtype 1), temporo-parieto-occipital (Subtype 2), and frontal (Subtype 3) regions of the left cerebral hemisphere speak to the issue of differential locus—a dimension that may or may not relate in a simple way to etiology.

SUBTYPES OF ARITHMETICAL DISABILITIES

Background

Children who have problems with arithmetic are seldom found to be in the forefront of educational concern. It is much more likely that children with reading or spelling difficulties will receive the special attention of teachers and other professionals involved in the educational process.

There would appear to be a number of reasons for this particular state of affairs. Well-developed language abilities of the sort that relate to reading and spelling skills are often associated with intellectual prowess in Western culture. Hence, educators tend to emphasize the learning of reading and spelling. In addition, arithmetic skills are viewed by many as a type of language activity. Therefore, difficulties in this subject area are seen only as an offshoot of more fundamental difficulties with other language skills. For example, since most children who experience difficulty with arithmetic also obtain somewhat deficient scores in reading and spelling on standardized measures of academic achievement, it is often assumed that training in linguistic skills will have the effect of increasing performance in all three of these academic areas.

In this connection, we have found that some younger learning-disabled children exhibit a pattern of academic achievement that includes centile scores above 50 on the WRAT arithmetic subtest and centile scores on the WRAT reading and spelling subtests that are quite deficient. However, the number of children with this pattern of academic achievement appears to decrease with age. One factor contributing to this particular state of affairs involves the type of education afforded some learning-disabled children. In the later grades, typically, the identified reading- and/or spelling-disabled child becomes subject to remedial educational efforts that are focused specifically on the development of reading and spelling abilities. This type of special educational program serves to strengthen reading and spelling skills in many cases, while little attention is directed toward the development of mathematical abilities.

The marginal concern that most educational authorities have for arithmetic difficulties in school-age children is also reflected in the research literature dealing with learning disabilities in children. The number of studies of children with arithmetic disabilities is far outweighed by those dealing with children with spelling and, in particular, reading retardation. The relative dearth of information that has arisen from investigative studies of children with arithmetic disabilities has, of course, done little to alter the attitude of educators regarding the importance of such disabilities.

Although there have been a number of approaches adopted by investigators concerned with the elucidation of factors contributing to arithmetic disabilities in childhood, none has met with unequivocal success. However, it would seem worthwhile to present a general overview of this research in order to provide the reader with a context for evaluating our own investigations in this area.

It is not surprising to find that some researchers have attempted to study the arithmetic performances of brain-impaired children, since it has been well established that many children who have sustained damage to the central nervous system (CNS) perform poorly in mathematics. For example, Cohn (1971) conducted a retrospective investigation of a rather heterogeneous group of children who exhibited signs of brain impairment. These children had been tested on a number of occasions over approximately a 10-year period, and their competence in mathematics was evaluated at each testing session. He found little similarity in the types of calculation errors that the individual children were making, although it appeared that the mathematical abilities of these children improved, as did their abilities in other academic areas. He concluded that difficulties with mathematics were part of a more pervasive language deficit.

One of the most useful points that Cohn raised in his investigation was his suggestion that the more difficult and complex mathematical calculations (such as multiplication questions in which the numerator is a two-digit number) were much more likely to elicit mathematical difficulties. We have also found this to be the case in our own clinical analyses of the arithmetic performances of learning-disabled and normal children, although it would appear that there is no single best technique or calculation for identifying the specific central processing difficulties that children with arithmetic disabilities might be experiencing.

Another approach utilized in clinical and research efforts that have attempted to identify children who are arithmetic-disabled has involved a search for common "symptoms" that form a particular constellation. This "syndrome analysis" approach has proven to be an effective method for characterizing the symptomatology of a number of clinical disease entities. However, this particular identification and classification strategy has met with much more limited success within the realm of behavioral disorders.

Nevertheless, some researchers (e.g., Kinsbourne & Warrington, 1963) have investigated the significance of the developmental Gerstmann syndrome for children with arithmetic disability. The Gerstmann syndrome, first investigated in adults, includes the symptoms of dyscalculia, dysgraphia, finger agnosia, and problems with right–left discrimination. Kinsbourne and Warrington found that few children exhibited all four of these "symptoms" in combination and, in many cases, other "symptoms" were also present. Consequently, this approach has met with limited success with children, although it has served to demonstrate that there may be other brain-related disabilities correlated with arithmetic retardation.

The cognitive–educational approach to the analysis of arithmetic difficulties has become quite popular during recent years. Typically, in this approach, the errors of any child having difficulty with arithmetic are analyzed in an effort to discover underlying problems. The interpretation of these difficulties is then made within an established theoretical framework. In most cases, inadequate language skills are seen as being the limiting feature of the child's arithmetic performance.

An obvious limitation of this research strategy is the failure to use carefully defined criteria in selecting arithmetically disabled children for study. Consequently, rather heterogeneous groups of children with arithmetic problems have been examined. Results from such efforts serve to becloud rather than to elucidate the difficulties in arithmetic that various subtypes of learning-disabled children may experience. This has certainly been found to be the case in investigations of reading disability, as we have attempted to demonstrate earlier in this chapter. Furthermore, when studying children with arithmetic disabilities, the researcher must be especially careful with subject selection, since children with primary emotional disturbance often have outstanding difficulties in arithmetic (Slade & Russell, 1971).

In summary, investigations to date with arithmetic-disabled children have been somewhat deficient in one or more of the following areas: (1) careful selection of the population sample; (2) employment of an adequate theoretical framework; (3) utilization of a wide variety of measures that will provide information for the determination of the cognitive strengths and weaknesses of these children; and (4) systematic study of the limiting characteristics of a child's arithmetic performance.

In our own investigations at the University of Windsor and Windsor Western Hospital Centre, we have attempted to circumvent the limitations of this previous research. The dominant feature of our approach includes the use of measures that have been shown to be sensitive to the abilities thought to be subserved by the two cerebral hemispheres. This neuropsychological approach has proven to be effective in the identification of various subtypes of learning-disabled children. That is, we have found that it is possible to divide learning-disabled children into meaningful groups on the basis of their neuropsychological characteristics (e.g., Fisk & Rourke, 1979; Sweeney & Rourke, 1978).

As suggested above, the neuropsychological assessment that we utilize incorporates a wide range of measures, the vast majority of which can be fitted into one or more of the following categories: tactile–perceptual measures; visual–perceptual and visual–spatial measures; auditory–perceptual and verbal measures; motor and psychomotor measures; conceptual measures; and measures of academic achievement (see Rourke, 1981). Since psychometrists are employed to test the children, there is a minimum of experimenter bias present in the test results. The assessment is characterized by standardized behavioral measurement, as every child is tested in exactly the same fashion, completing the same tests under roughly the same conditions.

Utilizing data gathered in this fashion, studies at our laboratory (Rourke & Finlayson, 1978; Rourke & Strang, 1978) have demonstrated that children with similar levels of performance in arithmetic on standardized achievement tests can be vastly different in their neuropsychological structures of adaptive ability. That is, it would appear that one child may have difficulties with arithmetic for one set of reasons, while another may be having difficulties with arithmetic for an entirely different set of reasons. However, before discussing the implications of this research, it is first necessary to consider the complexity of arithmetic as an area of study.

Some Abilities Required for Arithmetical Calculation

It is quite conceivable that certain aspects of mathematical calculation (e.g., remembering multiplication tables) require different abilities than do other aspects of calculation (e.g., deciding on directionality). This particular state of affairs may have far-reaching implications for differences in the ability characteristics that may limit performance in arithmetic for various subtypes of learning-disabled children.

When approaching an arithmetic question, it is first necessary for children to be able to interpret what is required of them. At the simplest level, this involves reading numbers and mathematical signs correctly or, in the case of a question with a problem component, reading words correctly. Children who are unable to perform one or more of these operations will be limited from the outset in their ability to complete the problem.

If the children can interpret successfully what is required in the question, it is then necessary to be able to implement various procedures to arrive at a correct solution. Some of these procedures would appear to be rather simple, while others are clearly more complicated.

Simple abilities necessary for success with arithmetical computation include copying and writing numbers and mathematical signs. Children must also be able to align columns of numbers correctly, such as is required in complex multiplication questions. More complicated procedures include "carrying" and "borrowing" numbers. Furthermore, in very complex mechanical arithmetic calculations, a fairly large number of procedures must be employed in a systematic fashion in order to arrive at a correct solution. In a question involving complex multiplication, for example, remembering multiplication tables, carrying numbers, adding columns of numbers, and inserting necessary commas or other signs are all important at different stages in the question if one is to arrive at a correct solution. The knowledge of these procedures and the ability to implement them in a particular order can prove to be quite difficult for some children who have problems with arithmetic.

Another set of abilities that are important for the development of adequate arithmetic abilities are somewhat more obscure. These involve the ability of children to generate an adequate conception of what is required in the calculation. At the more elementary levels of mathematical calculation, it is sometimes found to be the case that children are able to obtain a correct solution to an arithmetic calculation without actually understanding the operation. However, when calculations become more complex and there are many numbers or procedures with which to deal, it is important for the children to keep in mind the relevant operation involved (e.g., whether it is subtraction or multiplication). Among other things, this provides the children with information necessary for checking the adequacy of the solution.

Typically, children who have problems with the conceptual aspects of mathematical calculation generate solutions that are entirely implausible in view of task requirements. (For example, the solution of a subtraction question might be greater than the minuend.) When children begin to use fractions, the understanding of fundamental mathematical concepts becomes especially important if these kinds of difficulties are to be avoided. Such understanding provides children with a basis for evaluating their answers and, in some cases, directs them to the most probable sources of error.

Our Investigations of Arithmetical Disabilities

The remaining discussion in this section focuses on our investigations of groups of 9- to 14-year-old children who obtained centile scores of less than 25 on the WRAT arithmetic subtest. The first group serves to illustrate how deficient language skills can interfere with the development of adequate arithmetic abilities (Group 2 in the Rourke & Finlayson, 1978, and Rourke & Strang, 1978, studies). These children exhibited a pattern of much better WRAT arithmetic subtest scores than reading and spelling subtest scores. The degree of discrepancy between the WRAT arithmetic performances of Group 2 children, on the one hand, and their WRAT reading and spelling performances, on the other, is not commonly found with learning-disabled children.

In addition to having better arithmetic abilities than reading and spelling abilities, it was found that these Group 2 children performed well on measures of visual–spatial and visual–perceptual abilities and performed poorly on most measures of verbal and auditory–perceptual abilities (Rourke & Finlayson, 1978). In a subsequent study, these children also performed well on measures of complex psychomotor abilities and on tests for tactile–perceptual skills (Rourke & Strang, 1978).

When the WRAT arithmetic performances of these children were examined, it was found that, for the most part, fewer mistakes were made by this group than is generally the case for children who are deficient in this area. As a group, these children appeared to have a tendency to avoid unfamiliar arithmetic operations or those about which they were uncertain. An exception to this state of affairs was sometimes seen in younger (9- to 10-year-old) children who seemed to find ways to calculate correctly without being entirely familiar with the standard procedure (e.g., they counted on their fingers because they did not remember a multiplication table). On the whole, the errors made by these children usually reflected some difficulty in remembering mathematical tables or perhaps in remembering (some step in) the correct procedure for solving a problem. Questions that involved the reading of printed words were often avoided by them.

It would seem that the disability that these children had in interpreting the requirements of some questions was the result of two factors: (1) disability in reading, and (2) inexperience with the subject material. As with younger children, their inexperience may have been a reflection of the fact that they were repeating a grade to help remediate deficient reading and spelling abilities, and consequently had not yet been exposed to age-appropriate levels of mathematics. Many of the older learning-disabled children in this group were in special programs for learning-disabled students. Typically, in these programs, reading and spelling activities were emphasized, while attention to the development of mathematical abilities was somewhat minimal.

It is suspected that many of these children had difficulty with the implementation of correct procedures because of a (verbal) memory impairment. There is no doubt that relative inexperience was also a factor contributing to their difficulties in this area.

It is difficult to ascertain the degree to which conceptual problems with mathematics contributed to the impairment of these children's arithmetic skills. However, there were some indications that these children actually had a good understanding of the requirements of many questions and some notion of what would constitute reasonable solutions to them. Their tendencies to make relatively few errors, to generate correct solutions to some questions without employing (or perhaps, having access to) standard procedures, and to avoid questions that were completely beyond their realm of competence would all suggest that these Group 2 children had an adequate appreciation of the conceptual underpinnings of mathematical operations.

It appears that the identified neuropsychological strengths and weaknesses of these children are quite consistent with problems that may underlie their arithmetic calculation difficulties. Clearly, they represent one group of children who are retarded to some degree in arithmetic abilities. However, it would seem that, with better developed verbal and auditory–perceptual abilities and age-appropriate instruction, they would have at least a reasonable degree of success with mathematics.

The group of children of most special interest for us are those children found to have average or above-average abilities in reading and spelling but outstanding deficiencies in arithmetic performance. (These children constitute Group 3 in the Rourke & Finlayson, 1978, and Rourke & Strang, 1978, studies.) It should be kept in mind that these Group 3 children and the Group 2 children described above actually exhibited impaired levels of performance in arithmetic that were indistinguishable.

Contrary to the widely held assumption that all children with arithmetic difficulties perform poorly for the same reasons, the markedly divergent patterns of academic performance of these two groups (Group 2 had much better developed arithmetic abilities and more poorly developed reading and spelling abilities; Group 3 had well-developed reading and spelling abilities and poor arithmetic abilities) should suggest that their difficulties with arithmetic might be a reflection of quite different patterns of central processing abilities and deficiencies.

The differences that we found in the neuropsychological ability structures of these two groups of children serve to illustrate this point. Group 3 children (who appear to exhibit a rather "specific" arithmetic disorder) were found to have well-developed auditory–perceptual and verbal skills and poorly developed visual–spatial and visual–perceptual abilities (Rourke & Finlayson, 1978). It was further demonstrated that these children exhibited very poor performances on complex psychomotor tests and rather poorly developed tactile–perceptual abilities (Rourke & Strang, 1978). These difficulties were reflected in performances with both right and left hands on most measures; outstandingly poor left-hand performances were also in evidence on some measures.

A qualitative analysis of the arithmetic errors of the Group 3 children revealed a far different picture from that obtained for the Group 2 children. In general, we found that Group 3 children attempted calculations for which they had little understanding of the task requirements or limited means for accomplishing the task. Although there was a tendency for children such as these to misread mathematical signs, it appeared that the most pervasive of their limitations in mathematics involved an impoverished understanding of mathematical concepts.

From a visual–spatial standpoint, the calculation work done by these children was quite disorganized. For example, written calculations for one question would sometimes "crowd" or "overlap" written numbers belonging to another question. Misinterpretation of task requirements occurred in cases in which signs were misread (e.g., a child would add when the sign required that multiplication be performed). Some seemingly simple tasks also caused difficulty for some of these children. For instance, printing numbers correctly and lining up rows and columns of numbers properly were sometimes found to be characteristics that contributed to their limited performances. Questions that involved procedures requiring some directional capabilities (e.g., up, down, left, right) were troublesome; the more complex subtraction and multiplication questions fit this category. In some cases, complete steps were omitted in the calculation procedure.

There were a number of indications that the concepts underlying some mathematical operations were not well understood by these children. For instance, in the case of subtraction questions involving several steps, it was sometimes found that such children ended up with a product that was something in excess of the minuend, even though some numbers had been subtracted. This kind of difficulty would suggest at least a limitation in the children's ability to check the adequacy of their solutions. Certainly, an impoverished understanding of fairly routine mathematical concepts has rather direct implications for the learning of more complex mathematical concepts (e.g., the use of fractions). In view of this, it was not surprising to find that even the 14-year-old children in Group 3 did quite poorly on questions involving fractions.

In summary, the difficulties that children in Group 3 exhibited with mechanical arithmetic calculations involved one or more of the following: (1) reading the calculation signs; (2) forming numbers; (3) aligning the columns of numbers corectly; (4) dealing with all of the numbers in a question instead of only a subset of them (in some cases numbers seemed to be visually neglected); (5) adding, subtracting, and multiplying in the proper direction; (6) carrying out standard procedures in a systematic and orderly fashion; (7) generally organizing their work; (8) employing an adequate procedure for checking answers; (9) understanding completely the concept underlying a particular arithmetic operation.

It is strongly suspected that the limiting characteristics of the arithmetic performances of Group 3 children are related directly to their neuropsychological deficiencies. Visual–spatial and visual–perceptual deficiencies such as those exhibited by these children can contribute to problems with reading similar-looking calculation signs, forming numbers, aligning columns of numbers, attending to all numbers in the operation, directionality, carrying out procedures in a systematic fashion, and generally organizing the work. The psychomotor deficiencies characteristic of these children (e.g., problems with motor steadiness in the kinetic disposition) can also contribute directly to many of the arithmetic difficulties that the Group 3 children exhibited.

The failure of these children to employ adequate checking procedures to evaluate their answers would appear to be related to an impoverished understanding of fundamental mathematical operations. On the surface, one is hard put to explain this aspect of their problems with arithmetic strictly in terms of visual–spatial, visual–perceptual, and psychomotor deficiencies. However, since these kinds of difficulties have probably contributed to a great deal of unprofitable experience with arithmetic drills and exercises, it might be argued that Group 3 children have failed to consolidate mathematical concepts because of this unfruitful experience.

A more plausible explanation of the problems with mathematical concepts exhibited by Group 3 children requires consideration of the neuropsychological deficiencies of these children within a developmental framework. As outlined above, these neuropsychological deficiencies included visual–spatial and visual–perceptual problems, bilateral psychomotor deficiencies, and bilateral tactile–perceptual difficulties.

It would seem probable that these kinds of difficulties were present since birth and were more exacerbated at the time of testing for most, if not all, of the Group 3 children in our studies. If this were the case, it would stand to reason that defective visual perception, defective tactile perception, and impaired psychomotor abilities, in combination with adequate auditory perception and verbal expressive capacities, would alter substantially normal progress in the development of sensorimotor skills for these children. This, in turn, might contribute to considerable developmental deviation with respect to "normal" cognitive capacities.

Many developmental theorists consider the adequacy of sensorimotor experience (particularly in the first 2 years of life) an important determinant of a child's potential for later concept formation abilities. Jean Piaget (e.g., Piaget, 1928) was a strong proponent of this particular position. Following this line of reasoning, it may be the case that concepts that are predominantly nonverbal in nature are generally deficient for Group 3 children. The suspected inability of these children to establish cause-and-effect relationships on a physical, concrete basis during infancy and early childhood (one of the supposedly principal intellectual achievements of the first 2 years of life) may, in turn, have limited their abilities to develop more abstract levels of thought. This would seem to have rather direct implications for the learning of mathematics, since the understanding of even rather simple mathematical operations requires some degree of nonverbal abstract conceptualization.

The conceptual difficulties that these children experience with mathematics also appear to extend into other realms of their academic development and everyday life. School subjects that involve logical nonverbal reasoning abilities, such as science, prove to be quite difficult for them unless lessons are taught in a step-by-step, "rote" fashion. In addition, it is almost always found that reading comprehension is much less well developed than are word-analysis skills in such children. By way of contrast, children who have a pattern of relatively better developed arithmetic abilities and more poorly developed reading and spelling abilities often can comprehend the meaning of sentences or passages while having decoded correctly only a small proportion of the words in the phrase(s).

In everyday life, it is not uncommon to find that learning-disabled children with "specific" difficulties in mathematics have interactional problems with their peers. Often, such children become rather withdrawn in novel social situations or seem somewhat "out of place." One factor possibly contributing to this situation is their somewhat deficient (nonverbal) logical reasoning abilities, particularly under novel conditions (Strang & Rourke, 1983). New social situations pose such a problem for them, in that there are a large number of cues that must be interpreted properly in order to understand fully the social interactions that are proceeding and the specific requirements demanded from or for each individual in them. Another factor that seems to contribute to their social inadequacies is their difficulty in attending to nonverbal cues and/or providing these cues. Facial expressions, hand movements, body posture, and other physical gestures are forms of nonverbal communication that are important for success in novel social situations. All of these seem to be deficient in such youngsters (Ozols & Rourke, in press; Rourke & Fisk, 1981).

These research results and clinical observations should be sufficient for the purposes at hand. They serve to illustrate that these two groups of children, who do not differ significantly with respect to their level of impairment in arithmetic, are quite radically different with respect to their central processing abilities and deficiencies. In addition, they suggest rather strongly that the ramifications of these differences in neuropsychological ability structure are not confined to tasks of an academic nature. Indeed, it would seem quite reasonable to infer that virtually all aspects of these children's personal and social lives are influenced by the disparities evident in their neuropsychological makeup (Rourke, 1982).

CONCLUSIONS

In this chapter, we have attempted to present some of the new challenges and possibilities associated with the determination of subtypes of reading and arithmetic disabilities. It should be clear that the subtypes of reading disability that we have identified at the 7- to 8-year-old level are similar to one another with respect to their sharing of some sort of psycholinguistic deficiencies. At the same time, the type and degree of such deficiencies are quite variable among the three reliable subtypes of disabled readers, and the presence of other fairly distinct deficiencies (e.g., sequencing difficulties, right-sided motor problems, and tactile–perceptual problems) also serve as differentiating features.

With respect to arithmetic disabilities, it should be clear that the same levels of poor performance in this skill area can be attributed to quite different sets of deficiencies in central processing skills. In fact, it seems that the two subtypes of children afflicted with problems in this area that have been highlighted in this chapter have almost nothing in common with respect to their patterns of neuropsychological abilities and deficits. Among other things, this would certainly argue for the application of quite different modes of educational and therapeutic intervention for these two subtypes of disabled learners.

The most important conclusion that emerges from this type of analysis is that the group of clinical disorders known as "learning disabilities" must be appreciated for the diversity of patterns of neuropsychological strengths and weaknesses that obtains within it. Failure to appreciate these taxonomic intricacies leads, inevitably, to conundrums in social planning, to clinical confusion, and to theoretical chaos.

Acknowledgments

Our studies that are reported in this chapter were supported by grants from the Ontario Mental Health Foundation (#195 and #933) and from the Ontario Ministry of Education Grants-in-Aid Educational Research and Development Programme.

References

Bakker, D. J. Temporal order, meaningfulness, and reading ability. *Perceptual and Motor Skills*, 1967, *24*, 1027–1030.

Benton, A. L. Developmental dyslexia: Neurological aspects. In W. J. Friendlanger (Ed.), *Advances in neurology* (Vol. 7). New York: Raven Press, 1975.

Cohn, R. Arithmetic and learning disabilities. In H. R. Myklebust (Ed.), *Progress in learning disabilities* (Vol. 2). New York: Grune & Stratton, 1971.

Doehring, D. G. *Patterns of impairment in specific reading disability*. Bloomington: Indiana University Press, 1968.

Doehring, D. G. The evaluation of two models of reading disability. In R. M. Knights & D. J. Bakker (Eds.), *Neuropsychology of learning disorders: Theoretical approaches*. Baltimore: University Park Press, 1976.

Doehring, D. G. The tangled web of behavioral research on dyslexia. In A. L. Benton & D. Pearl (Eds.), *Dyslexia: An appraisal of current knowledge*. New York: Oxford University Press, 1978.

Fisk, J. L., & Rourke, B. P. Identification of subtypes of learning-disabled children at three age levels: A neuropsychological, multivariate approach. *Journal of Clinical Neuropsychology*, 1979, *1*, 289–310.

Fletcher, J. M., & Satz, P. Developmental changes in the neuropsychological correlates of reading achievement: A six-year longitudinal follow-up. *Journal of Clinical Neuropsychology*, 1980, *2*, 23–37.

Jastak, J. F., & Jastak, S. R. *The Wide-Range Achievement Test*. Wilmington, Del.: Guidance Associates, 1965.

Kinsbourne, M., & Warrington, E. K. The developmental Gerstmann syndrome. *Archives of Neurology*, 1963, *8*, 490–501.

Luria, A. R. *The working brain*. New York: Basic Books, 1973.

Mattis, S., French, J. H., & Rapin, I. Dyslexia in children and young adults: Three independent neuropsychological syndromes. *Developmental Medicine and Child Neurology*, 1975, *17*, 150–163.

Ozols, E. J., & Rourke, B. P. Dimensions of social sensitivity in two types of learning-disabled children. In B. P. Rourke (Ed.), *Learning disabilities in children: Advances in subtype analysis*. New York: Guilford, in press.

Petrauskas, R. J., & Rourke, B. P. Identification of subtypes of retarded readers: A neuropsychological, multivariate approach. *Journal of Clinical Neuropsychology*, 1979, *1*, 17–37.

Piaget, J. *Judgement and reasoning in the child*. London: Routledge & Kegan Paul, 1928.

Reitan, R. M. A research program on the psychological effects of brain lesions in human beings. In N. R. Ellis (Ed.), *International review of research in mental retardation* (Vol. 1). New York: Academic Press, 1966.

Reitan, R. M. Psychological effects of cerebral lesions in children of early school age. In R. M. Reitan & L. A. Davison (Eds.), *Clinical neuropsychology: Current status and applications*. Washington, D.C.: V. H. Winston & Sons, 1974.

Rourke, B. P. Brain–behavior relationships in children with learning disabilities: A research program. *American Psychologist*, 1975, *30*, 911–920.

Rourke, B. P. Issues in the neuropsychological assessment of children with learning disabilities. *Canadian Psychological Review*, 1976, *17*, 89–102.

Rourke, B. P. Neuropsychological research in reading retardation: A review. In A. L. Benton & D. Pearl (Eds.), *Dyslexia: An appraisal of current knowledge*. New York: Oxford University Press, 1978. (a)

Rourke, B. P. Reading, spelling, arithmetic disabilities: A neuropsychologic perspective. In H. R. Myklebust (Ed.), *Progress in learning disabilities* (Vol. 4). New York: Grune & Stratton, 1978. (b)

Rourke, B. P. Neuropsychological assessment of children with learning disabilities. In S. B. Filskov & T. J. Boll (Eds.), *Handbook of clinical neuropsychology*. New York: Wiley–Interscience, 1981.

Rourke, B. P. Central processing deficiencies in Children: Toward a developmental neuropsychological model. *Journal of Clinical Neuropsychology*, 1982, *4*, 1–18.

Rourke, B. P. Reading and spelling disabilities: A developmental neuropsychological perspective. In U. Kirk (Ed.), *Neuropsychology of language, reading, and spelling*. New York: Academic Press, 1983.

Rourke, B. P., Dietrich, D. M., & Young, G. C. Significance of WISC verbal–performance discrepancies for younger children with learning disabilities. *Perceptual and Motor Skills*, 1973, *36*, 275–282.

Rourke, B. P., & Finlayson, M. A. J. Neuropsychological significance of variations in patterns of academic performance: Verbal and visual–spatial abilities. *Journal of Abnormal Child Psychology*, 1978, *6*, 121–133.

Rourke, B. P., & Fisk, J. L. Socio-emotional disturbances of learning disabled children: The role of central processing deficits. *Bulletin of the Orton Society*, 1981, *31*, 77–88.

Rourke, B. P., & Gates, R. D. *Underlining Test (preliminary norms)*. Unpublished manuscript, University of Windsor, 1980.

Rourke, B. P., & Gates, R. D. Neuropsychological research and school psychology. In G. W. Hynd & J. E. Orbzut (Eds.), *Neuropsychological assessment and the school-age child: Issues and procedures*. New York: Grune & Stratton, 1981.

Rourke, B. P., & Orr, R. R. Prediction of the reading and spelling performances of normal and retarded readers: A 4-year follow-up. *Journal of Abnormal Child Psychology*, 1977, *5*, 9–20.

Rourke, B. P., & Petrauskas, R. J. *Underlining Test (revised)*. Unpublished manuscript, University of Windsor, 1978.

Rourke, B. P., & Strang, J. D. Neuropsychological significance of variations in patterns of academic performance: Motor, psychomotor, and tactile–perceptual abilities. *Journal of Pediatric Psychology*, 1978, *3*, 62–66.

Rourke, B. P., & Telegdy, G. A. Lateralizing significance of WISC verbal–performance discrepancies for older children with learning disabilities. *Perceptual and Motor Skills*, 1971, *33*, 875–883.

Rourke, B. P., Young, G. C., & Flewelling, R. W. The relationships between WISC verbal–performance discrepancies and selected verbal, auditory–perceptual, visual–perceptual, and problem-solving abilities in children with learning disabilities. *Journal of Clinical Psychology*, 1971, *27*, 475–479.

Slade, P. D., & Russell, G. F. M. Developmental dyscalculia: A brief report on four cases. *Psychological Medicine*, 1971, *1*, 292–298.

Spreen, O. *Prediction of school achievement from kindergarten to grade five: Review and report of a follow-up study* (Research Monograph No. 33). Victoria, British Columbia: Department of Psychology, University of Victoria, 1978.

Strang, J. D., & Rourke, B. P. Concept-formation/non-verbal reasoning abilities of children who exhibit specific academic problems with arithmetic. *Journal of Clinical Child Psychology*, 1983, *12*.

Sweeney, J. E., & Rourke, B. P. Neuropsychological significance of phonetically accurate and phonetically inaccurate spelling errors in younger and older retarded spellers. *Brain and Language*, 1978, *6*, 212–225.

Wechsler, D. *Wechsler Intelligence Scale for Children.* New York: Psychological Corporation, 1949.

Wiener, M., & Cromer, W. Reading and reading difficulty: A conceptual analysis. *Harvard Educational Review*, 1967, *37*, 620–643.

CHAPTER TWENTY-FOUR

Auditory Organization and Backwardness in Reading

PETER E. BRYANT / LYNETTE BRADLEY

Faced with a child whose intelligence is perfectly normal but who nonetheless has great difficulty in learning to read and write, it is quite natural to turn to the possibility that there may be something the matter with his or her perception. After all, if the child's intelligence is adequate, his or her cognitive faculties should be intact, and that seems to leave two broad possibilities: one, that the problems are emotional; and the other, that they have something to do with the way in which the child processes visual and auditory information. Both possibilities, of course, have been pursued (Gibson & Levin, 1975; Vernon, 1971), and it is perhaps fair to say that on the whole the latter—the perceptual hypothesis—has met with very little success so far. Indeed, there have been many recent suggestions that investigators should abandon that hypothesis altogether (Vellutino, 1979).

But perhaps the reason why there is no very good evidence for it might have something to do with the way in which it has been tested, rather than with the intrinsic merit of the hypothesis itself. There are at least two reasons why the difficulties involved in the perceptual hypothesis might be the result of the ways in which it was investigated.

The first is the preoccupation of psychologists and of neurologists with visual, rather than with auditory, perception. By and large, ever since Orton (1937) suggested that backward readers might have particular difficulty with mirror-image letters and words, by far the greatest number of studies of perception in backward readers have concentrated on the possibility either that they do not make visual discriminations properly or that somehow they do not link effectively what they see with what they hear. These are the studies that have produced so little (Jorm, 1979). Most studies of visual discrimination or of coordination of visual with auditory information point to the conclusion that backward readers manage as well as their more fortunate peers do. But what about hearing?

It is very easy to make the case that hearing might be a more sensitive area than vision might be. After all, it is quite clear that when children come to learn to read, they have to analyze what they hear in a new way. Up to that point, the

Peter E. Bryant and Lynette Bradley. Department of Experimental Psychology, University of Oxford, Oxford, England.

natural auditory units have been the syllable and the word (Elkonin, 1973; Fox & Routh, 1975; Goldstein, 1976; Golnikoff, 1978; Savin & Bever, 1973). But when they have to deal with written language, they are faced with units (such as phonemes) that are much smaller than that. By and large, letters correspond to these smaller units, and if children are to grasp the principle of the alphabetic code they must begin to break the words and syllables into those smaller units that the letters signify. Any child who cannot reorganize what he or she hears in this way will have great difficulty with at least some aspects of the task of reading and writing.

But this brings up the second major weakness of most attempts to find evidence for the perceptual hypothesis. Probably because they had in mind a clear distinction between cognitive and perceptual activities, most of the people looking at perception in backward readers have stuck very much to the periphery. The commonest question has been whether the children can make this or that discrimination, rather than how they organize their discriminations. If one takes this point of view, then the possibility that backward readers have an auditory problem immediately seems very remote. After all, they can hear the words that they so dismally fail to read and spell. They can distinguish them from other words. So why should their difficulty have anything to do with auditory perception (Wallach, Wallach, Dozier, & Kaplan, 1977)?

The argument is insuperable, but only if it is put in this way. In fact, it is really not very impressive, because there are few psychologists nowadays who would think it possible to study any aspect of perception without taking into account a great deal more than basic discrimination. Organization, selection, and inference seem to play a crucial role in human perception.

Certainly, once one admits the possibility of perceptual organization, the hypothesis that backward readers might have a particular difficulty with auditory perception becomes a great deal more attractive. Investigators know, for example, that practically every backward reader can discriminate the words *hat* and *cat* as well as the next child. But what about realizing at the same time that these words have sounds in common? To appreciate that they both end in *-at* is obviously essential for any child who is learning how sounds are written. But, in order to do this, he or she must be able to break up each monosyllabic word into at least two components—the opening and the ending sounds—and then work out that the two words have different opening sounds but end in the same way. Obviously the fact that the child can distinguish the two words tells us nothing about his or her ability to cope with this level of phonological analysis.

It is, of course, very easy to look at this type of auditory organization. A child who perceives that *cat* and *hat* rhyme demonstrably knows that, though they are different, the two words do have a sound in common. So investigators can ask whether backward readers are any worse than other children are at spotting rhymes. If they are, they may very well be bad at the kind of auditory analysis that quite plainly is necessary for anyone who wants to learn how to use an alphabet. This has been demonstrated (Calfee, Chapman, & Venezky, 1972). It is also possible to ask children—poor readers and others—to identify either how many phonemes there are in a syllable (Liberman, Shankweiler, Liberman, Fowler, & Fischer, 1977) or what these phonemes are (Newton, Thomas, & Richards, 1979; Venezky, 1978). The message of all these studies is consistent: Backward readers are very ill at ease with this sort of auditory organization.

However, on the whole, these studies are rather unconvincing. They suffer, as we have pointed out elsewhere (Bradley & Bryant, 1978) from an empirical weakness that has beset far too many studies of backwardness in reading. How do investigators find out whether backward readers have a particular difficulty with some psychological task or other? Obviously they compare them to children who read as well as might be expected for their age; if the backward readers, but not the other children, mismanage the task, the investigators can conclude that they have shown something about reading difficulties.

So far there is nothing wrong with this course of action. The problem arises with the question of who should be the normal readers in the comparison group. With hardly an exception, the comparisons have been between backward and normal readers whose age, IQ, and therefore mental age are the same, and who differ apparently in only one respect—namely, that the backward readers cannot read or write nearly so well as the children in the other group. Now it is indeed true that, if backward readers are compared to other children in this way, they appear to be more inept with the kind of auditory organization that we have just described. They cannot rhyme so well, and they cannot divide words up into their constituent phonemes so well. Can it be concluded that they really do have a serious auditory problem?

No, it cannot be. This all too common comparison is not at all compelling, because it makes no attempt to distinguish cause from effect. Suppose that an investigator finds that 10-year-old backward readers who only read at a 7-year-old level are worse at spotting rhymes than are 10-year-olds who read normally; this might mean that the first group has not learned to read properly because of its inability to break up words into their constituent sounds. But there is another possibility, which is that the difference is the result, not the cause, of the two groups' very different levels of success with written language. It is possible that because the normal readers have forged ahead with reading and writing, they have been led into experiences that have made them more sensitive to rhyming words. There is nothing implausible about this alternative; the two groups definitely will have had quite different experiences at school, because they have reached different reading levels.

There is a simple solution, which is to change the design and make a different comparison. The investigator might take a group of backward readers, who read at a certain level, and compare them to another group who read at exactly the same level. Then, any difference between the two could not possibly be the result of the groups' being at different levels, because the levels now are the same. So if the backward readers are 10 and read at the level of 7-year-olds, they should be compared to 7-year-olds who have no reading problem.

It was the combination of these two factors—the importance of the question of auditory organization of words into their constituent parts; and the weakness of the design of most studies of perception in backward readers, and of all the studies of their auditory perception—that made us decide to carry out a large-scale study of backward readers' sensitivity to rhyme. The first thing to note about this study is the kind of comparisons that we made. Our backward and normal readers, all normal in intelligence, were at the same level of reading, and this meant that the normal readers were considerably younger, as Table 24-1 shows. We carried out two experiments with these children. In the first, we spoke out loud to each child a series of sets of four words. In every case, three of the words had a sound in common that the other did not share. Sometimes the relevant sound was the opening consonant (*sun*, *see*, *sock*, *rag*); sometimes the vowel (*nod*, *red*, *bed*, *fed*); and sometimes the closing consonant (*weed*, *peel*, *need*, *deed*) of these single-syllable words. At the same time, we checked whether the children could speak and distinguish and remember the words in question, and found no signs that the backward readers were any worse at taking them in and storing them. So they could perceive them satisfactorily, but they foundered on the main task. As Table 24-2 shows, they were much worse than the normal readers were at detecting the odd word out, despite the fact that their mental age was of course considerably higher.

In our second experiment, we tackled the question of rhyming a different way. This time the children had to *produce* a rhyme rather than *recognize* one. They were given 10 simple single-syllable words successively, and each time were asked to produce a word that rhymed with each of these words. Once again the backward readers were worse than the others were, even though their age and intellectual ability were higher; 38% of the backward readers and only 7% of the other group failed to produce any rhyming words at all, and the overall numbers of rhymes produced by the latter group was much higher. Here, then, is convincing evidence to support a number of people's intuitions that backward readers hear the difference between words reasonably well, but have remarkable difficulty when it comes to breaking them up phonologically.

But it is one thing to isolate a psychological weakness among backward readers and quite another to describe exactly how it affects their reading and writing. It is, of course, quite easy to demonstrate that a proper understanding of the alphabet must depend on an ability to see how words and syllables can be broken up into smaller units. But a more precise statement than this is needed. What exactly is the role of phonological analysis in reading and writing? Is it in fact always necessary, and is it necessary for all aspects of written language?

The answer to the second question is almost certainly "No." Teachers and psychologists have always recognized the possibility that words—at least some words—are read as wholes, without any attempt to break them up into their individual letters. Take, for example, *something*—a word that most children read unerringly quite early on. We have observed that many of those who do read it cannot manage to read either the word *some* or the word *thing*, and sometimes even fail to read both of them. It is obvious that at least these children are not breaking the larger word into its constituent parts.

There is strong evidence that children in the early stages of learning to read adopt a visual strategy that takes them straight on to the meaning of the word without any phonological intervention. Barron and Baron (1977) worked with

Table 24-1. Details of the two groups

GROUP	n	AGE MEAN	AGE RANGE	IQ (WISC) MEAN	IQ (WISC) RANGE	READING AGE (NEALE) MEAN	READING AGE (NEALE) RANGE	SPELLING AGE (SCHONELL) MEAN	SPELLING AGE (SCHONELL) RANGE
Backward readers	60	10 yr, 4 mo	8 yr, 4 mo–13 yr, 5 mo	108.7	93–137	7 yr, 7 mo	6 yr–9 yr, 4 mo	6 yr, 10 mo	5 yr–8 yr, 9 mo
Young normal readers	30	6 yr, 10 mo	5 yr, 8 mo–8 yr, 7 mo	107.9	93–119	7 yr, 6 mo	6 yr–9 yr, 2 mo	7 yr, 2 mo	5 yr, 1 mo–10 yr, 2 mo

Table 24.2. Mean error scores (out of 6) in the three conditions

		BACKWARD READERS ($n = 60$)		YOUNG NORMAL READERS ($n = 30$)	
SERIES	ODD WORD	MEAN	*SD*	MEAN	*SD*
1	Last letter different	1.15	1.43	.17	1.11
2	Middle letter different	1.49	1.58	.37	.99
3	First letter different	2.62	2.26	.67	1.188

children whose ages ranged from 6½ to 13½ years, giving them two tasks. In one (the sound task), the children were given a list of written words, and each word was paired with a picture. Some, but not all, of the pictures were of objects whose name rhymed with the word with which they were paired (e.g., a pair consisting of the word *horn* and a picture of corn), and the children had to mark the rhyming pairs. Obviously, this was a task that involved attending to the sound patterns of the words being read. In the other task (the meaning task), they were again given word–picture pairs in which the word and picture meant the same thing. The word and picture were, in fact, not identical, but were in the same category (*shirt–trousers*).

The children were given various kinds of interference during these tasks, one of which must have effectively blocked out all other phonological and articulatory activity. The children were required to say the word "double, double, double" aloud very quickly, and the experiment was arranged so that they did each task sometimes with this interference and sometimes without. If the task involved some kind of phonological strategy, then the children's performance should have been hindered by this interference. If the task was done purely visually, this inteference should have had little or no effect.

The interference did spoil the children's performance in the sound task, but not in the meaning task. Even the youngest children could indicate whether the picture–word pairs had the same "meaning," both during the "double, double" interference and during the period of no interference. These results imply that, right from the start, children can read words without having to build them up from their constituent phonological elements—and, it seems, without translating them into sounds at all.

Here, then, is a puzzle. Backward readers have difficulty with phonological analysis; yet normal readers seem to be able to read without the benefit of phonological analysis. How is one to explain it?

One could, of course, get around the difficulty by saying that the Barron and Baron study is a special case. They only used single words, and probably quite familiar ones at that. There is something to this objection. It is certainly possible, as we point out later, that phonological analysis is much more important for new words than for familiar ones. But there is a more radical solution, which raises a distinction that is a relatively new one in the study of the way children come to grips with written language. It is the distinction between learning to read and learning to spell (Frith, 1980).

Until recently, most psychological studies concerned with written language seemed to assume that both aspects of it were much the same thing. They both involved the same code—the alphabetic code—and they both made much the same demands on a child. Spelling, of course, was acknowledged to be the more difficult of the two skills, but this was no surprise. To spell a word is to produce it, while to read a word is to recognize it, and it is almost a commonplace in psychology that production is more difficult than recognition, output than input.

But we have recently found evidence for a qualitative difference between the two activities among young children. We should like to argue that children adopt rather different strategies when they read and when they spell, and that the kind of auditory organization that has been discussed plays a far greater role in spelling than in reading.

To us, the first sign that this might be so was a study carried out by Bradley with the same large group of backward readers mentioned in the study of rhyming. She had the simple idea of asking these children (and the same control group) to read a list of words that she showed them on one occasion, and on another occasion to spell exactly the same words, which this time she read out to them (Bradley & Bryant, 1979). What is the point of this?

If reading and spelling make much the same demands on children, then one would expect them to be able to read and to spell much the same words and to be unable to read and spell much the same words. Naturally, they would probably also read rather more than they could spell, so that there would be words that they could read but not spell properly. But one would not expect it the other way around. One would not expect them to be able to spell words that they could not read.

This was not what happened. Both groups certainly read words that they could not spell, but they also spelled words that they could not read. So the discrepancy went both ways, which argues that there is indeed a qualitative difference between the way children deal with reading and the way they deal with spelling. What is more, this difference is probably more marked among backward readers, as Table 24-3 shows. Both the discrepant categories (words read but not spelled, and words spelled but not read) were more common among backward readers.

But if there is a qualitative difference, what form does it take? We should like to advance the hypothesis that children beginning to read and write tend to treat words or clusters of letters as patterns, and thus to depend largely on visual codes when they read; and that they tend to apply phonological analysis much more to spelling. We also argue that this initial separation between the two activities is stronger and goes on longer in backward readers than in other children.

Here are our reasons for formulating this hypothesis:

1. In later studies, we have found evidence for a difference between words that young children read and do not spell and those that they spell but do not

Table 24-3. Mean number of words (out of 18) in four possible categories

GROUP	*n*		WORDS READ AND SPELLED	WORDS NEITHER READ NOR SPELLED	WORDS READ BUT NOT SPELLED	WORDS NOT READ BUT SPELLED
Backward readers	62	Mean	7.7	4.9	3.1	2.3
		SD	5.1	5.2	2.3	2.1
Young normal readers	30	Mean	10.6	3.9	2.1	1.4
		SD	6.1	5.8	2.1	1.9

read. The latter are phonologically regular, by which we mean they can easily be constructed from the sounds that characterize their constituent letters—words like *bun*. The former are not usually so easily constructed—words like *school*.

2. We have repeated the Barron and Baron (1977) interference technique and have found, as they did, that it does not make reading words more difficult for young children. But we have also found that the interference really does interfere with spelling. Children find it very hard to spell words when their phonological processes are impeded by having to repeat a word over and over again while spelling. Interestingly enough, we have confirmed this pattern (phonological interference impairing spelling but not reading) with Chinese children in Singapore when the language they are dealing with is English. However, something different happens when they read and write Chinese. Chinese, of course, is written in ideograms, not in alphabetic letters, and so requires no phonological analysis in the sense in which we have used the term. The Singapore children, who behaved in exactly the same way as English children did when the language was English, showed a different pattern with Chinese. Here the phonological interference did not impair their writing. Presumably because Chinese does not require them to break words into phonemes, the interference did not impair their writing of Chinese words at all.

3. Recent work by Uta Frith (1976) with children older than the ones whom we saw suggests a similar separation between reading and spelling among those who have very great difficulty with spelling. She found, for example, that their spelling errors tended to be reasonable phonological approximations of the word they were trying for—*nite* for *night*—but that in reading they were much less likely to notice that words that looked like the real one (*nght*) were wrongly spelled than words that sounded like it (*nite*). Her conclusion that they were using a visual strategy in reading and a phonological one in spelling is a convincing one.

We feel that experimental work with backward readers should go hand in glove with detailed histories of the particular difficulties of individual backward readers. This should help investigators to clarify the relation between different specific weaknesses and to explain the way in which they may operate singly or together in causing severe reading difficulties.

One such study reported the case of Mark, a 13-year-old boy of normal intelligence, who was backward in reading and had associated difficulties in verbal expression, auditory sequential memory, and visual association. The primary difficulty, however, seemed to be an inability to recall appropriate words. This did not seriously affect his memory for visually presented sequences, but meant that he did not learn the spoken counterparts of written words. Thus, he could reproduce complex visual sequences, such as *laugh* or *ceiling*, but as he did not know what they were called he could not learn to generalize from one written word to another. Phonemic analysis proved difficult too; it must be hard to analyze and take apart a word that itself is elusive (Bradley, Hulme, & Bryant, 1979).

Without appropriate help, such children leave school illiterate and subsequently join those vulnerable adults described by Saunders and Barker (1972). Their report deals with psychiatric disturbance in adults of normal intelligence who have hitherto unrecognized difficulties in reading, writing, and spelling that appear causally related to their psychiatric disturbance and result in subsequent referral to a psychiatrist. Characteristically, these patients are often very sensitive about this disability, and marital friction is common. They are also often noticeably resistant to remedial help.

One such patient for whom remedial help was sought was B.P. It was suggested that her psychiatric referral had probably been provoked by her inability to cope with the forms required for her divorce. Remedial help was sought for her. Aged 25 years, of normal intelligence (her IQ on the Wechsler Adult Intelligence Scale was 100), with a reading age of only 7 years (Neale Analysis), she was pessimistic about her chances of learning to read. She could write only three words correctly: *and*, *went*, and *the*. Teachers, although helpful up to a point, "just gave her more books." Again, a basic problem seemed to be this inability to categorize words aurally and visually, and thus an inability to generalize from one word to another. But Bradley has found that diagnostic and remedial techniques developed to encourage such skills in younger children have proved equally effective in cases of adult psychiatric referral. The method that had been so successful for Mark proved effective once again. On the basis of her own language and everyday experiences, B.P. was taught to generalize from one word that she knew (e.g., *and*) to other words that sounded alike (e.g., *hand*, *stand*, *standing*), using plastic script letters.

A particular problem for backward readers when they try to categorize words that sound alike is the abstract and transitory nature of speech. Although they can repeat the words (e.g., *and*, *hand*, and *stand*), there is nothing tangible or concrete to help them discern the element common to the group of words. But when the stimulus word is made with the plastic letters, the common element in the words remains constant (e.g., the plastic letters *a*, *n*, *d*) while the new words are formed around it. The connection between the auditory and visual elements of the words is thus made clear. These methods are fully described by Bradley (1980).

B.P. was soon writing her own letters and reading books to her young daughter. But why does one method work with such diverse subjects when previous remediation has proved ineffective? Using words of personal interest to the subject will aid retrieval of the spoken counterparts of the written word. Bringing the visual and auditory strategies together through the medium of the plastic letters makes categorization tangible.

We have, then, identified a major difficulty among backward readers, and we have tried to identify the detailed implications of this difficulty. However, our conclusions about the initial specialization of visual and phonological skills need some qualifying. Though at first the signs of specialization—visual reading and auditory spelling—are impressive among all children, later both major strategies (visual and phonological) must apply to both activities. It is fairly obvious that adults use visual memories, among other things, when they are trying to remember how to spell a word, and indeed there is good empirical evidence that they do so. We should also like to suggest that older children and adults begin to use phonological strategies when they read, and particularly when they encounter new words whose pattern is unfamiliar and whose meaning is not given away by the context of the passage. The backward reader's major difficulty in auditory perception might be partly a weakness in auditory organization and partly a tendency to confine his or her auditory strategies within one skill, spelling, and not the other, reading. It follows in our view that the most effective remedial techniques are likely to be those that, on the one hand, concentrate on teaching children how to generalize from one word to another phonologically, and that, on the other, encourage them to intermingle phonological and visual strategies when reading and spelling (Bradley, 1980).

References

Barron, R., & Baron, J. How children get meaning from printed words. *Child Development*, 1977, *48*, 594–598.

Bradley, L. *Assessing reading difficulties: A diagnostic and remedial approach.* Basingstoke, England: Macmillan Education, 1980.

Bradley, L., & Bryant, P. E. Difficulties in auditory organisation as a possible cause of reading backwardness. *Nature*, 1978, *271*, 746–747.

Bradley, L., & Bryant, P. E. The independence of reading and spelling in backward and normal readers. *Developmental Medicine and Child Neurology*, 1979, *21*, 504–514.

Bradley, L., Hulme, C., & Bryant, P. E. The connexion between different verbal difficulties in a backward reader: A case study. *Developmental Medicine and Child Neurology*, 1979, *21*, 790–795.

Calfee, R. C., Chapman, R., & Venezky, R. How a child needs to think to learn to read. In L. W. Gregg (Ed.), *Cognition and learning in memory.* New York: Wiley, 1972.

Elkonin, D. B. USSR. In J. Downing (Ed.), *Comparative reading.* New York: Macmillan, 1973.

Fox, B., & Routh, D. K. Analyzing spoken language into words, syllables, and phonemes. *Journal of Psycholinguistic Research*, 1975, *4*, 331–342.

Frith, U. *How to read without knowing how to spell.* Paper presented at the meeting of the British Association for the Advancement of Science, Lancaster, 1976.

Frith, U. Unexpected spelling problems. In U. Frith (Ed.), *Cognitive processes in spelling.* London: Academic Press, 1980.

Gibson, E. J., & Levin, H. *The psychology of reading.* Cambridge, Mass.: MIT Press, 1975.

Goldstein, D. M. Cognitive and linguistic functioning and learning to read in pre-schoolers. *Journal of Educational Psychology*, 1976, *68*, 680–688.

Golnikoff, R. Phonemic awareness skills and reading achievement. In F. B. Murray & J. J. Pilkuski (Eds.), *The acquisition of reading.* Baltimore: University Park Press, 1978.

Jorm, A. F. The cognitive and neurological basis of developmental dyslexia. *Cognition*, 1979, *7*, 19–33.

Liberman, J. Y., Shankweiler, D., Liberman, A. M., Fowler, C., & Fischer, F. W. Phonetic segmentation and recoding in the beginning reader. In A. S. Reber & D. L. Scarborough (Eds.), *Towards a psychology of reading.* Hillsdale, N.J.: Erlbaum, 1977.

Newton, M. J., Thomas, M. E., & Richards, I. L. *Readings in dyslexia* (Learning Development Aids). Wisbech, England: Bemrose (U.K.), 1979.

Orton, S. T. *Reading and writing and speech problems in children.* London: Chapman & Hall, 1937.

Saunders, W. A., & Barker, M. G. Dyslexia as a cause of psychiatric disorder in adults. *British Medical Journal*, 1972, *4*, 759–761.

Savin, H. B., & Bever, T. G. The nonperceptual reality of the phoneme. *Journal of Verbal Learning and Verbal Behaviour*, 1973, *9*, 295–302.

Vellutino, F. R. *Dyslexia: Theory and research.* Cambridge, Mass.: MIT Press, 1979.

Venezky, R. L. Reading acquisition: The occult and the obscure. In F. B. Murray & J. J. Pilkuski (Eds.), *The acquisition of reading.* Baltimore: University Park Press, 1978.

Vernon, M. D. *Reading and its difficulties: A psychological study.* Cambridge, England: Cambridge University Press, 1971.

Wallach, L., Wallach, M. A., Dozier, M., & Kaplan, N. E. Poor children learning to read do not have trouble with auditory discrimination but do have trouble with phoneme recognition. *Journal of Educational Psychology*, 1977, *69*, 36–39.

CHAPTER TWENTY-FIVE

Hemispheric Specialization and Specific Reading Retardation

DIRK J. BAKKER

INTRODUCTION

Whereas "alexia" refers to the loss of the ability to read, specific reading retardation, or "dyslexia," concerns the impaired acquisition of that skill. The impediment could be due either to a deficit (i.e., some sort of cerebral dysfunction), or to a developmental lag in brain maturation (Rourke, 1976). The latter theory is more optimistic, in that it predicts that dyslexic children may eventually catch up with their age-mates in skills basic to reading or even in reading proficiency itself. Rourke (1976), in reviewing longitudinal investigations into reading retardation, found that the age relationships of some reading-related skills support a model of developmental lag, but that those of some others do not, indicating that a preference for either model would be premature.

Several neuropsychological theories have been proposed to clarify the etiology of dyslexia (Bakker, 1981). A short description of two of these models serves as a background for the discussion of my own thoughts and observations regarding this issue.

MODELS OF DYSLEXIA

Satz's Model

The most elaborated neuropsychological model of dyslexia has been presented by Satz and associates. Following a proposal of the World Federation of Neurology, Satz and Sparrow (1970) define developmental dyslexia as failure "to acquire normal reading proficiency despite conventional instruction, socio-cultural opportunity, average intelligence, and freedom from gross sensory, emotional, or neurological handicap" (p. 17). The failure is held by them to be due to a functional delay of left-hemispheric specialization. The left hemisphere

Dirk J. Bakker. Subfaculty of Psychology, Department of Developmental, Educational, and Physiological Neuropsychology, Pedological Institute and Free University, Amsterdam, The Netherlands.

is said to specialize in the control of fine motor skills at about 5 years of age, followed by the lateralization of perceptual and linguistic functions at about the ages of 8 and 11 years, respectively. Young normal and disturbed readers are consequently predicted to differ on lateralized motor and perceptual performance, since such behaviors at young primary-school ages will be controlled by the left hemisphere in normals but not yet in disturbed readers. Between-group comparisons at older ages, conversely, would reveal differences in linguistic proficiency: Language by then will be lateralized in normals but not yet in dyslexics. The attractiveness of Satz's model is that it accounts for age-linked differences between normal and retarded readers. Visual–motor deficits, for instance, are predicted for younger but not for older dyslexics (Satz & van Nostrand, 1973). The contradictory findings of investigations on the relationship between perceptual performance and reading, as noted by Benton (1962), could thus partly be explained by the neglect of the age factors.

Masland's Model

Masland (1975) has formulated a different theory of dyslexia that stresses the impact of left-hemispheric dysfunctioning. He argues that reading requires the analysis of visually presented, spatially ordered graphemes, in which there is an association with a temporally ordered linguistic structure. It is thought that the right hemisphere is prepared to deal with the first part and the left hemisphere with the second part of this process. Reading thus seems to be an interhemispheric process. Masland argues, however, that connections *within* hemispheres are more easily effected than connections *between* hemispheres. He presumes that "the specific task of analysis of symbolic visually presented material is at some time transferred from the right to the left hemisphere" (1975, p. 4). The kernel of this theory is that dyslexics have difficulty with the interhemispheric transfer of function. Why should they? In answering this question, Masland (1975, p. 28) cites evidence (Kershner, 1974) to suggest that the development of one function may hamper the growth of another one: "The development of a strong spatial skill might interfere with language function and especially might interfere with the ability of the brain to transfer spatial functions to the left hemisphere." He goes on to state that "for some individuals with superior spatial functions, especially where there is a high degree of hemispheric specialization for such functions, this transfer may be resisted" (1975, p. 30). Boys have generally been the victims; Masland cites evidence that the visuospatial systems, as well as their subserving mechanisms, are more often "overdeveloped" in males than in females. Thus, more males than females will meet difficulty with the right–left cerebral transaction of visuospatial functions, which in turn would explain the fact that more boys than girls become dyslexic.

Masland has tried to explain why the left hemisphere may fail: Overdevelopment of the right hemisphere impedes the functional development of the left one. He notes, incidentally, that the reverse may also happen: "The marked development of a function such as language . . . may interfere with the development of the spatial skills" (1975, pp. 27–28). Masland disregards the possible consequences of such a development. Assuming, however, that visuospatial analysis is a prominent aspect of reading, one could predict that weakened visual abilities (caused by linguistic overdevelopment) should have a negative impact on learning to read. The existence of two etiological subtypes of dyslexia would then be plausible: dyslexia caused by overdevelopment of right-hemispheric visuospatial functioning and subsequent depression of left-hemispheric linguistic functioning; or dyslexia caused by overdevelopment of left-hemispheric linguistic functioning and subsequent depression of right-hemispheric visuospatial functioning.

The existence of two hemisphere-tied variants of dyslexia may be plausible, therefore, in view of the arguments to follow. To begin with, however, it must be shown that reading is primarily mediated by the right hemisphere, under conditions to be discussed.

RIGHT-HEMISPHERIC INVOLVEMENT IN READING

Cerebral locus of reading control depends on the perceptual complexity of script and the hemispheric side of speech mediation. The degree of perceptual complexity is related to the degree of acquaintance with script. One may need tricks to make letters complicated for adult readers, whereas all script is perceptually demanding for novice readers.

Perceptual Complexity

Faglioni, Scotti, and Spinnler (1969) compared adult patients, with either left- or right-hemispheric lesions, on letter-matching tasks. A letter on top of a card had to be matched with one of 10 alternatives. The target letters were printed either in a conventional or a nonconventional way; in the latter case, they were masked by curlicues. The authors found a group × condition interaction: Patients with left-hemispheric lesions did relatively poorly in matching the conventional letters, while patients with right-hemispheric lesions had greatest difficulty in matching the *non*conventional ones. Thus the right hemisphere seems to be the primary processor of perceptually demanding letters.

A similar conclusion can be drawn from a variety of psychological investigations. Using the so-called "visual half-field technique," investigators may flash stimuli at the left and/or the right side of the fixation point. Given that the subject keeps gazing at this point, the information presented to the left and right visual fields is relayed to the right and left hemispheres, respectively. Bryden and Allard (1976) flashed different typefaces to the hemifields of normal adults. These letters had to be named aloud. The authors found conventional letters better processed if presented to the right field, and non-conventional ones if presented to the left field. Hatta (1977) and also Sasanuma, Itoh, Mori, and Kobayashi (1977) flashed Japanese *Kanji* and *Kana* words to the visual hemifields of normal adults. (*Kanji* words are logographic; *Kana* words are more phonetic in nature.) These investigators found *Kanji* and *Kana* better processed if presented to the left and right visual fields, respectively.

From the results of these and other investigations, one may conclude that script that is made perceptually difficult requires right-hemispheric processing strategies in adults. Initial reading, in contrast to advanced reading, will similarly appeal to right-hemispheric strategies, since normal script is perceptually complex for novice readers but not any more for older ones.

Carmon, Nachshon, and Starinsky (1976) did a visual half-field study with first-, third-, fifth-, and seventh-grade normal children. They used letters, words, and numbers for hemifield stimulation. Clear-cut right-field advantages were reported in higher-grade children; lower-grade children, on the other hand, tended either to absence of field asymmetry or to left-field advantage (single letters). In a recently reported investigation (Silverberg, Bentin, Gaziel, Obler & Albert, 1979) Hebrew and English words were flashed to the hemifields of Israeli adolescents who were in their second, fourth, and sixth year of study of English as a second language. All groups showed better right- than left-field performance for Hebrew words. However, English words were processed better when flashed to the left field, except in the oldest group. The findings from a recent study by Silverberg, Gordon, Pollack, and Bentin (1980) also suggest that the right cerebral hemisphere is primarily involved in the processing of script during initial phases of learning to read. They presented second- and third-grade children with concrete words in either the left or right visual field. Left-field advantage was found in second-graders, right-field advantage in third-graders.

Such findings suggest that script is primarily processed by the right hemisphere during early stages of learning to read but by the left hemisphere in later stages, namely, when the subject gets acquainted with the reading material. The perceptual complexity of script may be called an *external* factor conditioning its primary control by the right hemisphere.

Cerebral Locus of Speech Control

The hemispheric side on which speech is mediated may be an *internal* conditioner of cerebral locus of reading control. Speech is an intrinsic aspect of reading (aloud). Those who have the reception of speech mediated in the left hemisphere may be biased to generate left-hemispheric reading strategies. Right-sided or bilateral speech mediation may be a matrix for the generation of right-hemispheric reading strategies. A series of investigations has been carried out at the Pedological Institute and Free University of Amsterdam in an effort to uncover two types of hemisphere-specific reading strategies. The differential hemispheric involvement in reading of left- and right-ear-dominant children has recently been demonstrated in an electrophysiological experiment (Bakker, Licht, Kok, & Bouma, 1980). Primary-school children who consistently showed either left- or right-ear advantage subsequent to the presentation of dichotic digit series were required to name monosyllabic meaningful words that were flashed at the point of fixation. Event-related potentials (ERPs) were recorded from the left (T_3, P_3) and right (T_4, P_4) temporal and parietal areas. The amplitudes of the P300 and N400 waves were analyzed in relation to earedness and hemispheric side of diversion. Significant ear advantage $\times$ hemispheric side interactions were found, both for the temporal and parietal areas, indicating that left- and right-ear dominants process printed words quite differently at the cerebral level of functioning (see Figure 25-1).

Children who show right- and those who show left-ear advantage, moreover, appear to differ in the way they read. Right-ear dominants tend to read

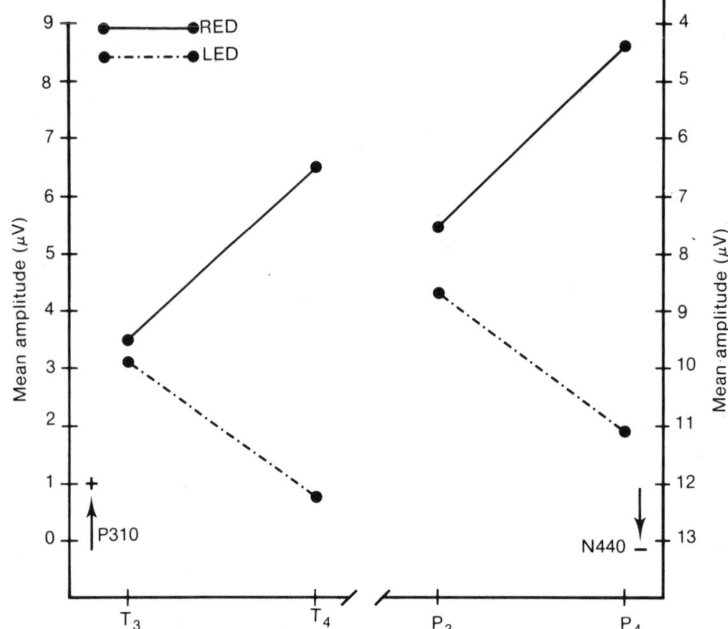

Figure 25-1. Positivity (P310) and negativity (N440) to word reading, by temporal (T_3 vs. T_4) and parietal (P_3 vs. P_4) side of diversion in normal children showing right-ear advantage (RED) or left-ear advantage (LED). Adapted from "Cortical Responses to Word Reading by Right- and Left-Eared Normal and Reading-Disturbed Children" by D. J. Bakker, R. Licht, A. Kok, and A. Bouma, *Journal of Clinical Neuropsychology*, 1980, *2*, 1–12.

relatively fast and inaccurately; left-ear dominants slowly but accurately (Bakker, 1979b, 1979c). The two reading strategies were demonstrated to have a reflection in types of errors made. Left-ear dominants may make more "time-consuming" errors, such as fragmentations and repetitions, than children showing right-ear advantage may. There is a tendency for the reverse to hold with substantive errors, such as omissions, substitutions, and additions of letters and words. Thus, two types of readers may be distinguished: those showing left-ear preferences, who tend to read slowly and to make time-consuming errors (P-readers); and those who show right-ear preferences and who, while reading relatively fast, tend to make substantive errors (L-readers). P-readers, while supposedly being sensitive to the *perceptual* features of script, may have their reading primarily controlled by the right hemisphere. L-readers, on the other hand, may be sensitive to the semantic and other *linguistic* aspects of text. The left hemisphere may primarily subserve their reading.

Hemispheric side of reading control thus seems to be determined by the perceptual complexity of the script and by the left or right cerebral locus of speech mediation. How much each of these conditioners weighs in the balance is unknown at the moment.

HEMISPHERIC SUBSERVIENCE DURING LEARNING TO READ

A child entering the primary school and facing perceptually complex letters and words will tend to generate right-hemispheric strategies to process the script.

The propensity to do so will be even stronger if the child happens to have speech that is mediated by the right hemisphere. Such a child seems privileged, since accuracy of reading is stressed and slowness is initially accepted. However, fluency (i.e., speed and accuracy) is the ultimate aim of the process of learning to read. This stage will be reached when perceptual analysis becomes automatized and the semantic aspects of the text get primary attention. Left-hemispheric subservience of reading seems most appropriate at this stage of reading acquisition. Having speech controlled by the left hemisphere may then be beneficial as a means of promoting left-hemispheric reading strategies. The hypothesis may thus be derived that proficient reading is correlated with right-hemispheric speech control at an early age and with left-hemispheric speech control at later ages. At the Pedological Institute and Free University, we tested these predictions in a longitudinal study (Bakker, 1979b). Subjects were administered a dichotic digit test at kindergarten, as well as at the start and at the end of first grade. A reading test was given in fifth grade. The results (Figure 25-2) indicated that children who showed a left-ear advantage in kindergarten read better ultimately than children who showed right-ear advantage did. Left-ear advantage at the end of first grade, conversely, tended to correlate with poorer reading than right-ear advantage did. We subsequently demonstrated that children who

Figure 25-2. Fifth-grade reading performance in relation to ear advantage at kindergarten (KS), first-grade start (G1S), and first-grade end (G1E). Adapted from "Hemispheric Differences and Reading Strategies" by D. J. Bakker, *Bulletin of the Orton Society*, 1979, *29*, 84–100.

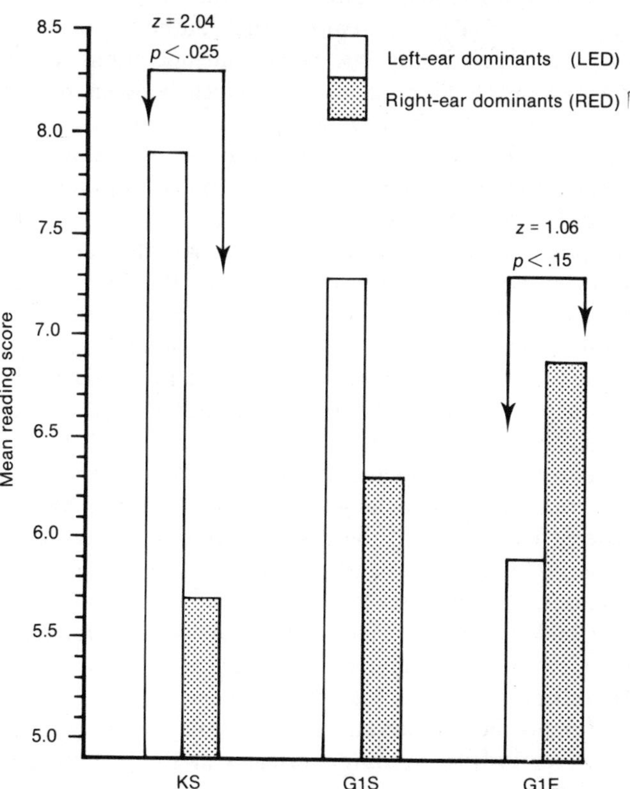

shifted from left-ear advantage at kindergarten to right-ear advantage one year later are the best fifth-grade readers, and that children who shifted reversely are ultimately the worst readers. As ear advantage is considered to reflect hemispheric side of speech control, one may conclude that the findings support the hypothesis. In order to shed some more light on the development of cerebral subservience of reading, we recently started a longitudinal investigation into the hemispheric correlates of word reading as reflected in lateralized electrophysiological parameters. The provisional results of the first probe seem to suggest that word reading by kindergarten children evokes somewhat more right- than left-hemispheric activity, in terms of certain amplitudes and latencies. How hemispheric involvement develops during subsequent reading acquisition remains to be seen, of course.

TWO TYPES OF DYSLEXIA?

Some children in learning to read may rely on left-hemispheric strategies at too early a stage (L-type dyslexics) or, conversely, may fail to adapt such a strategy in time (P-type dyslexics). The first group may show left-hemispheric mediation of speech, possibly along with a weak right-hemispheric specialization for the visuoperceptual functions. While perceptual analysis is required in an early phase of the process of learning to read, such readers may tend to overlook the perceptual features of script. They will read relatively fast, making many errors. This group may bear resemblance to Boder's (1973) dyseidetic readers, Kinsbourne and Warrington's (1966) Gestalt-weak readers, and Mattis's (1978) readers showing visuospatial perceptual disorder. Although reading has both visuoperceptual and linguistic aspects, perceptual operations are mostly required in early reading. A dipping of the balance between perceptual and linguistic analysis toward the perceptual approach would thus be useful at young reading ages. However, due to a *relative* overdevelopment of left-hemispheric functioning, the scale may be turned in favor of linguistic (semantic) approaches in L-type dyslexics.

While perceptual feature analysis is required in early reading and subsequent slowness is allowed, the ultimate aim of reading is fluency. Left-hemispheric mechanisms are most appropriate to subserve fluent reading. Thus readers should shift from a perceptual to a linguistic (semantic) reading strategy at some point during their development. Some of them may not be in a position to do so; they go on relying on right-hemispheric strategies (P-type dyslexics). Their problem may be due to relatively overdeveloped right-hemisphere functioning. This group bears resemblance to Boder's (1973) dysphonetics, Kinsbourne and Warrington's (1966) language-disturbed group, Mattis's (1978) language-disordered children, and the dyslexics who have been described by Satz and Sparrow (1970) and Masland (1975).

Two predictions can obviously be derived from what has been named the *balance* model (Bakker, 1979a). First, right- and left-ear preference will be greater in dyslexic than in normal readers, indicating a more pronounced hemispheric lateralization of speech to either left or right in dyslexics. These atypical left- and right-sided speech lateralizations may promote the premature generation of left-hemispheric reading strategies in L-type dyslexics and the prolonged generation of right-hemispheric reading strategies in P-type dyslexics. Gutezeit (1978), indeed, found ear asymmetries to be larger in dyslexics than in normals. Second, dyslexics showing left-ear preference will demonstrate strong left-field advantage for the processing of visuospatial information, which, while reflecting a definite right-hemispheric specialization for visuoperceptual functions, will promote the generation of right-hemispheric reading strategies. Dyslexics showing right-ear advantage, on the other hand, will demonstrate a weak lateralization of visuoperceptual functioning, a condition that is compatible with the generation of left-hemispheric reading strategies in these subjects. This prediction was recently supported in a study comparing left- and right-eared disturbed readers (Bakker, 1979b). Moreover, in the group of subjects showing left-ear and left-field preference, performances on word and form perception appeared to be correlated. These dyslexics (P-type) evidently handle letters the way they handle figures—primarily as visual shapes. No correlation was found in the group of subjects who showed right-ear preference along with a weak lateralization of visuospatial function. For them, shapes and words are different entities. While generating left-hemispheric reading strategies, they tend to disregard the visuoperceptual aspects of graphemes (L-type dyslexics). There is some evidence that left- and right-eared dyslexics can be distinguished on the basis of electrophysiological parameters. Bakker *et al.* (1980) found left-eared dyslexics to show less positive temporal and less negative parietal activity than right-eared dyslexics did.

The balance model, in summary, accounts for two types of dyslexia that originate from different etiologies. P-type dyslexia has its roots in the functional overdevelopment of the right hemisphere and/or underdevelopment of the left hemisphere. Reading may require the subservience of both hemispheres—the right one for feature identification, the left one for the derivation of meaning. Overdevelopment of the right hemisphere causes excessive sensitivity to the perceptual features of script. At first, a P-type dyslexic may not be recognized, as perceptual analysis is most required in early stages of the process of learning to read. Since reading progressively requires the application of semantic strategies, to be generated by the left hemisphere, one may expect the P-type dyslexic to encounter problems in subsequent stages of learning to read. P-type dyslexics, while stuck to the generation of right-hemispheric reading strategies, will show non-left-hemispheric speech control, definite right-hemispheric control of form perception, correlated form and letter perception, and time-consuming errors. Their pattern of strengths (visuospatial perception) and weaknesses (time-consuming errors) may or may not change over time, depending on the teaching methods they are exposed to and the requirements they meet. For instance, if a P-type dyslexic is forced to read fast, he or she may start to make substantive errors, as well as time-consuming errors.

The etiology of L-type dyslexia, conversely, is tied with the functional excess of the left hemisphere and/or weakness of the right hemisphere. L-dyslexics show a propensity to generate left-hemispheric (i.e., linguistic) strategies. They run into troubles from the very onset of the process of learning to read, since initial reading requires close attention to the perceptual features of the text, which they tend to overlook. They will consequently make many substantive (perceptual) errors. L-type dyslexics, while relying on left-hemispheric reading strategies, will show left-hemispheric speech control, ambivalent hemispheric control of form perception, noncorrelated form and letter perception, and substantive reading errors. Their difficulties may abate or change over time, due to the semantic demands of the evolving process of learning to read and the teaching methods used.

The percentages of P-type and L-type dyslexics within the population of specifically reading-retarded children remain to be established as yet.

References

Bakker, D. J. Hemisfeer-specifieke dyslexie-modellen in therapeutisch perspectief. In J. de Wit, H. Bolle, & J. M. van Meel (Eds.), *Psychologen over het Kind* (Vol. 6). Groningen, The Netherlands: Wolters Noordhoff, 1979. (a)

Bakker, D. J. Hemispheric differences and reading strategies. *Bulletin of the Orton Society*, 1979, *29*, 84–100. (b)

Bakker, D. J. A set of brains for learning to read. In K. C. Diller (Ed.), *Individual differences and universals in language-learning aptitude*. Rowley, Mass.: Newbury House, 1979. (c)

Bakker, D. J. Hemisphere-specific dyslexia models. In R. N. Matatesha & L. C. Hartlage (Eds.), *Neuropsychology and cognition* (Vol. 1). Alphen aan de Rijn, The Netherlands: Sijthoff & Noordhoff, 1981.

Bakker, D. J., Licht, R., Kok, A., & Bouma, A. Cortical responses to word reading by right- and left-eared normal and reading-disturbed children. *Journal of Clinical Neuropsychology*, 1980, *2*, 1–12.

Benton, A. L. Dyslexia in relation to form perception and directional sense. In J. Money (Ed.), *Reading disability*. Baltimore: Johns Hopkins University Press, 1962.

Boder, E. Developmental dyslexia: Prevailing diagnostic concepts and a new diagnostic approach. *Bulletin of the Orton Society*, 1973, *23*, 106–118.

Bryden, M. P., & Allard, F. Visual hemifield differences depend on typeface. *Brain and Language*, 1976, *3*, 191–200.

Carmon, A., Nachshon, I., & Starinsky, R. Developmental aspects of visual hemifield differences in perception of verbal material. *Brain and Language*, 1976, *3*, 462–469.

Faglioni, P., Scotti, G., & Spinnler, H. Impaired recognition of written letters following unilateral hemispheric damage. *Cortex*, 1969, *5*, 120–133.

Gutezeit, G. Neuropsychologische Aspekte zur Zentraler Organisation von Leselernprozessen. *Praxis der Kinderpsychologie*, 1978, *27*, 253–260.

Hatta, T. Recognition of Japanese Kanji in the left and right visual fields. *Neuropsychologia*, 1977, *15*, 685–688.

Kershner, J. R. Ocular-manual laterality and dual hemisphere specialization. *Cortex*, 1974, *10*, 293–301.

Kinsbourne, M., & Warrington, E. Developmental factors in reading and writing backwardness. In J. Money (Ed.), *The disabled reader*. Baltimore: Johns Hopkins University Press, 1966.

Masland, R. L. Neurological bases and correlates of language disabilities: Diagnostic implications. *Acta Symbolica*, 1975, *6*, 1–34.

Mattis, S. Dyslexia syndromes: A working hypothesis that works. In A. L. Benton & D. Pearl (Eds.), *Dyslexia: An appraisal of current knowledge*. New York: Oxford University Press, 1978.

Rourke, B. P. Reading retardation in children: Developmental lag or deficit? In R. M. Knights & D. J. Bakker (Eds.), *The neuropsychology of learning disorders*. Baltimore: University Park Press, 1976.

Sasanuma, S., Itoh, M., Mori, K., & Kobayashi, Y. Tachistocopic recognition of Kana and Kanji words. *Neuropsychologia*, 1977, *15*, 547–553.

Satz, P., & Sparrow, S. Specific developmental dyslexia: A theoretical formulation. In D. J. Bakker & P. Satz (Eds.), *Specific reading disability*. Lisse, The Netherlands: Swets & Zeitlinger, 1970.

Satz, P., & van Nostrand, K. Developmental dyslexia: An evaluation of a theory. In P. Satz & J. J. Ross (Eds.), *The disabled learner*. Lisse, The Netherlands: Swets & Zeitlinger, 1973.

Silverberg, R., Bentin, S., Gaziel, T., Obler, L. K., & Albert, M. L. Shift of visual field preference for English words in native Hebrew speakers. *Brain and Language*, 1979, *8*, 184–190.

Silverberg, R., Gordon, H. W., Pollack, S., & Bentin, S. Shift of visual-field preference for Hebrew words in native speakers learning to read. *Brain and Language*, 1980, *11*, 99–105.

CHAPTER TWENTY-SIX

Genetics, Epidemiology, and Specific Reading Disability

BARTON CHILDS / JOAN M. FINUCCI

Specific reading disability has been reported to be familial since its first description by Morgan in 1896, but its cause remains in dispute. Some say it is genetically determined, which implies that the gene effect is independent of experience; others believe in a cultural origin, which implies that the characteristic is uninfluenced by the genotype. These represent polar positions, each assuming an independent cause, both of which could produce familial aggregations of cases. And unless the aggregations fit some Mendelian expectation, there are no immediately obvious grounds upon which to base a choice. But such polar positions rarely prevail; gene effects are nearly always modulated by experience; and the more remote the phenotype is from the actual function of a gene, the greater is the chance of variability due to other causes. So it is a mistake at the outset to suppose that specific reading disability is going to prove to be either "genetic" or "cultural"; rather, it is more likely that a variety of genetic and environmental influences will account for this defect, and perhaps do so in different ways in different people. Indeed, Berger, Yule, and Rutter (1975) have given evidence favoring this idea in showing variation in prevalences of "specific reading retardation," depending upon geographical and socioeconomic factors.

Traditionally, the study of the genetics of human behavior has been dominated by attempts to partition the variation attributable to genes and to experiences (Ehrman, Omenn, & Caspari, 1972). This is expressed mathematically by a heritability coefficient, which represents the average degree to which the variance is assignable to heredity. When heritability is high, then most of the variance is genetic; if low, most variation is due to experience. Investigations of heritability have been useful in convincing doubters that disorders such as schizophrenia, manic–depressive disease, and alcoholism are not distributed at random, but are to be found among people whose genotypes make them likely subjects (Fieve, Rosenthal, & Brill, 1975). Heritabilities of IQ and many other cognitive properties, including reading, have also been shown to be high, again suggesting that the genes have something to do with the way groups of people deal with cognitive tasks (Ehrman *et al.*, 1972).

Barton Childs and Joan M. Finucci. Department of Pediatrics, Johns Hopkins University School of Medicine, Baltimore, Maryland.

But the heritability approach, while useful in a practical way in agronomy and animal husbandry, has limitations when applied to human populations. Heritabilities differ among populations and also change with time; therefore, they should not be used in human affairs for policy decisions. But the most telling objection is that the heritability coefficient, whether high or low, is representative of a population and indicates nothing at all about any individual. The only information that can be put to use by a remedial teacher, or by the parents of a reading-disabled child, is information that is characteristic of that child alone. Accordingly, an approach more suitable for characterizing individuals and their families must be employed. Such a method, which employs the techniques of both genetics and epidemiology, is outlined in Table 26-1.

THE GENETIC METHOD

Measurable Variables

The first and most desirable quality is some discrete and measurable property that allows investigators to quantify severity, as well as to say that one person is affected and another is not. When distributions of measurable properties are continuous, such designations may be straightforward for the occupants of the ends of the distributions, but must be arbitrary when a measurement falls into an indefinable band of values that represents the interface between normal and abnormal. Pedigree analysis—that is, the study of the distribution of affected persons in families—requires such classes, but the inevitable misclassification may be minimized by introducing a third class called "borderline." Such distinctions are made easier when the distribution is skewed, or when there is a bimodality. Such skewing has been shown by Yule, Rutter, Berger, and Thompson (1974) for distributions of reading scores.

Segregation Analysis

The next step is to consider segregation analysis; that is, to see whether the distributions of affected and unaffected persons in families fulfill any Mendelian expectation. Is the phenotype a dominant trait, a recessive trait, a sex-linked trait, and so on? Segregation analysis is most straightforward when the affected and the unaffected are easily discriminated, but there are methods to accommodate continuously distributed properties (Elston & Yelverton, 1975; Morton, 1977).

Genetic Heterogeneity

Many familial properties, when all cases are considered together, fail to segregate; and investigators must look for other explanations, the principal one being that of genetic heterogeneity. A phenotype is merely a description of a developmental end product that itself could be a result in different people of different mechanisms, both genetic and environmental. Mental retardation is an example of such a phenotype. It is a measurable property that is clearly associated with a variety of causes. Some mental retardation is nongenetic, the result of infections, trauma, or other adverse experiences. Many of the most severe kinds are due to

Table 26-1. Essentials of the method of genetic analysis

1. Assignment of phenotype
2. Pedigree and segregation analysis
3. Tests for heterogeneity
4. Linkage detection
5. Tests of physiological and biochemical phenotypes

inborn errors whose familial aggregations reveal them as recessives or, occasionally, as dominants with variable expression. Others are due to chromosome anomalies that are less likely to be familial. The milder forms are often familial and usually more complex in origin. The action of several or many genes acting in environments unfavorable for the development of normal IQ is assumed, and it is usually impossible in individual families to know either which factors are at work or how they are accomplishing their ends. In the absence of such insights, such cases are called "multifactorial." That is not to say that cases due to the effects of genes at single loci or to chromosomal anomalies are not lurking unidentified among those called "multifactorial," but rather that a more refined scrutiny of the clinical and epidemiological details of the latter may be required to cause the former to emerge. To accomplish this end, investigators start with the assumption that because relatives share genes, there should be intrafamily homogeneity of expression, while differences among families might be a result of quite different genetic mechanisms. That is, if there is genetic heterogeneity, relatives might be expected to share constellations of such properties as severity, age of onset, mode of inheritance, and many other aspects of clinical expression, even while members of different families are easily distinguishable in these ways.

Linkage, Physiological, and Biochemical Studies

Of course, familial properties might be the result of experiences shared in common by related persons, particularly if they live together. The genetic hypothesis can be more firmly grounded, therefore, (1) by showing that the property in question is linked with some other trait whose genetic origin is clearly known; or (2) by the discovery of physiological or biochemical properties that are clearly Mendelian traits not easily altered by special experiences and that show a strong causal association with the condition under scrutiny.

The possibilities for linkage are increasing with the rapid pace of gene assignment—that is, the discovery of the chromosomal position of genes that produce such measurable and easily characterized effects as enzymes or other proteins or diseases that are clearly Mendelian properties (Anonymous, 1983).

If it can be shown that the condition in question is strongly associated in families with a known genetic marker, both traits may be assumed to be the independent effects of genes located so close to each other in a chromosome as to be disassociated only rarely by recombination. Such association may be taken as evidence favoring the participation of a gene at a single locus in the production of the phenotype under study.

The discovery of a causal relationship between a clinical phenotype and an hereditary biochemical or physiological property makes the genetic hypothesis unassailable; and the value of biochemical techniques and chromosomal analysis in the elucidation of, for example, the many forms of mental deficiency is a familiar story. Everyone accepts a causal relationship between trisomy 21 and Down syndrome, and between a deficiency of activity of the enzyme phenylalanine hydroxylase and the mental retardation of phenylketonuria. The discovery of such relationships is the ultimate goal of all medical genetic study.

PAST AND CURRENT STUDIES OF FAMILIAL ASPECTS OF SPECIFIC READING DISABILITY

Although the context outlined above is one in which a test of the genetic hypothesis is best accomplished, most family studies reported in the past are of more limited scope, testing limited aims (Finucci, 1978). Some have been concerned with twin concordance, some with familial aggregation of cases, some with pedigree analysis, some with heterogeneity, and a few with neurophysiological testing. Although these reports differ widely in definition of reading disability, in the kinds of data collected, and in the ways in which they have been collected and analyzed, a compelling case has been made for the familial aggregation of cases and for the genetic origin of at least some forms of specific reading disability.

Twin Studies

Investigations of twins support the genetic hypothesis. When observations scattered through the literature were assembled, there was perfect concordance for dyslexia for 17 monozygotic twin pairs as opposed to 12 out of 34 dizygotic pairs (Zerbin-Rudin, 1967). In Bakwin's study of 31 pairs each of monozygotic and dizygotic twins ascertained by at least one dyslexic child per pair, concordance was 84% for the monozygotic twins and 29% for the dizygotic (Bakwin, 1973). Although biases of ascertainment in the assembly of twin pairs, as well as lack of rigor in diagnosis (hearsay evidence was accepted), undermine the value of these studies, they support the genetic idea when taken with everything else. Such high concordances for monozygotic twins are more often associated with monogenic traits than with multifactorial traits.

Family Studies

Many reported investigations have fulfilled the limited aim of demonstrating familial aggregations of cases of reading disability, often by inquiries about a family history rather than by tests (Drew, 1956; Eustis, 1947; Finucci, 1978; Symmes & Rappaport, 1972; Walker & Cole, 1965). A few report measurement of reading and spelling skills in parents or siblings; for example, Owen, Adams, Forrest, Stolz, and Fisher (1971) studied 76 quartets of children and their parents. The subjects consisted of 76 reading-disabled children and 76 same-sex siblings, as well as 76 academically successful children and 76 same-sex siblings. The reading-disabled and academically successful groups were matched on grade, sex, and intelligence. Siblings of the dyslexic children were, on the average, just below grade level in reading but were approximately 1 year retarded in spelling, while the siblings of the academically successful children were approximately a year above grade level in reading and not retarded in spelling. Fathers of the reading-disabled group were found to read significantly less well than fathers of academically successful children did, and both fathers and mothers of the reading-disabled group reported significantly poorer grades in high-school English courses than did the parents of the academically successful children.

In a series of papers, Foch, Lewitter, DeFries, McClearn, and others have demonstrated unequivocally a strong familial incidence of deficits in reading, spelling, and several other cognitive abilities in the families of 133 reading-disabled children (Decker & DeFries, 1980; DeFries, Singer, Foch, & Lewitter, 1978; Foch, DeFries, McClearn, & Singer, 1977). These investigators have compared the families of reading-disabled children with families of normal readers matched on the basis of sex, age, grade in school, school environment, and home neighborhood. All subjects were given a variety of achievement and ability tests, including reading, spelling, and intelligence tests, as well as various subtests of the Peabody Individual Achievement Test and the Illinois Test of Psycholinguistic Abilities. Significant differences were found in measures of performance for many of these tests between the families of the disabled readers and the controls. These investigators have done an immense amount of work, which, when added to other less definitive studies, establishes unequivocally the familial nature of specific reading disability and of the deficits of cognitive functions that characterize it. These studies, however, tell us nothing about what genes might be involved nor about whether there may be several mechanisms for reading disability. All of the results are reported as group differences and provide, therefore, no information as to individuals or distinctive families.

Pedigree Studies

The past literature reveals a number of reports of investigations in which attempts were made to describe the distribution of specific reading disability among members of families. In most of these, only one or two or a few families were studied (reviewed by Finucci, 1978). Various modes of inheritance, including recessive, dominant, sex-limited, and multifactorial, have all been proposed. What is certain is that no one of these modes fits all the cases.

Perhaps the most famous of these studies was that of Hallgren, who in 1950 studied 112 families ascertained through reading-disabled children in schools in Stockholm. He then studied as many of the relatives of these children as he could, but unfortunately the diagnosis for at least some of the children and most of the adults was based on historical evidence alone. Although there were some families in which the index case was the only affected person and others in which both parents read normally, Hallgren concluded that the condition was due to a gene at a single locus producing a dominant effect. Hallgren deserves a great deal of credit for this extensive study. If his genetic conclusions were somewhat naive, they are certainly compatible with the primitive state of human genetics in 1950. A conclusion similar to that of Hallgren was reached by Zahalkova, Vrzal, and Kloboukova (1972), who studied a sample of 29 dyslexics. Among many criticisms of this study, the principal one is that no definition of "dyslexia" was given.

Finucci and her colleagues (Finucci, Guthrie, Childs, Abbey, & Childs, 1976) studied 20 families in which all members of the families were tested. Their report confirmed the familial nature of the condition, but the transmission was so varied as to suggest heterogeneity. This study has been extended to 60 families; the distributions of affected persons in the families is shown in Table 26-2. The table shows a strong direct relationship between parental reading status and that of the remaining children after removing the index cases through which the families were ascertained. The idea of heterogeneity of cause is again borne out by examination of individual pedigrees, so a standard segregation analysis to test for a single mode of inheritance would be pointless.

On the assumption that small sample size, biases of ascertainment, and the arbitrariness of the designation of subjects as affected or unaffected might be confounding, Lewitter, DeFries, and Elston (1980) have applied the technique of Elston and Yelverton (1975) to their 133 families. This is a method of segregation analysis of continuously variable quantitative traits in which no diagnostic dichotomy is required. The results suggest that specific reading disability is etiologically heterogeneous; several hypotheses could not be rejected. For example, the analysis suggested that the most likely interpretation of the data from families of female index cases was that of recessive inheritance, while among the most severe cases, some form of nongenetic determination seemed the most plausible.

All of these studies make clear the necessity to perfect the diagnostic classification of dyslexia. When some specific subtypes have been identified, then investigators may expect segregation analysis to be a more rewarding exercise.

Phenotypic Heterogeneity

If mental retardation is a model for specific reading disability, it must be presumed that there are many causes; and there is much evidence that such variety exists (Benton, 1975). Table 26-3 shows that heterogeneity of phenotypes has been considered in the reading field for many years. The table shows that nearly all of these schemes have an auditory type, in which the reader is said to have trouble relating sound with visual symbols; a visual type, in which perception of or memory for the visual characters is thought to be wanting; and a mixture of these. There are, in addition, other types involving linguistic disorders, object and color naming, and so on (Denckla, 1972). With so many investigators arriving by different paths at common end points, it seems highly likely that subtypes of specific reading disability exist, but whether all of the "auditory" or "visual" types are the same is difficult to determine. For example, investigators have used their own sets of tests in each study; there is much variation in regard to diagnostic criteria, and, in general, quantitative variation

Table 26-2. Relationship between parental reading type and that of the siblings of index cases

		SIBLINGS OF INDEX CASES			
PARENTAL READING TYPE	NUMBER OF FAMILIES	NORMAL *n* (FREQ)	BORDERLINE *n* (FREQ)	DISABLED *n* (FREQ)	TOTAL
Both normal	24	26(.70)	8(.22)	3(.08)	37
One borderline	18	14(.41)	12(.35)	8(.24)	34
One affected	11	8(.40)	5(.25)	7(.35)	20
Total	60	48(.53)	25(.27)	18(.20)	91

Table 26-3. Subtypes of specific reading disability

SUBTYPES	INVESTIGATOR(S)
I. Visuospatial Audiophonic	Johnson & Myklebust (1967)
II. Auditory memory Visual memory Mixed	Bateman (1968)
III. Visuospatial Audiophonic Mixed	Ingram, Mason, & Blackburn (1970)
IV. Dysphonetic (audio) Dyseidetic (visual) Mixed	Boder (1971)
V. Language disorder Articulatory and graphomotor Visuospatial	Mattis, French, & Rapin (1975)
VI. Visual–perceptual Intersensory integration Naming Temporal ordering	Doehring & Hoshko (1977)
VII. Auditory predominance Visual predominance Mixed	Omenn & Weber (1978)

is ignored. Then, even accepting the proposition that there are at least two types of disabled readers—that is, visual and auditory—it is not certain that these are distinctive syndromes emanating from distinctive causes. They might be the consequences of the same cause imposed on different developmental substrates.

As we have indicated, the genetic method offers an opportunity to test the validity of these hypotheses. We have examined our data with heterogeneity in mind, using the severity of the reading disability and the kinds of qualitatively different spelling errors as criteria (Childs & Finucci, 1979). When scores of reading and spelling tests of siblings are considered in the light of the severity of reading disability of the case through which the family was ascertained, the distributions of siblings' scores differ, depending upon the severity of the index case. The reading scores of the siblings vary most widely when the index case is most severely affected and least when the index case is mildly affected. This is reminiscent of the various forms of mental retardation, in which the most severe defects are usually recessives and the families contain only defective or normal children, while the mildest are usually multifactorial and the siblings are either mildly affected or normal. This similarity is strengthened by looking at the distributions of reading scores of the parents of our index cases. Most of the parents of the most severely affected and of the most mildly affected children read normally, while those of cases in between are often themselves disabled readers. We are working on the hypothesis that the worst cases are recessives; that some of the moderately severe cases are dominants; that the mildest are nonfamilial cases (possibly associated with perinatal factors or other causes); and that the residue, of unknown proportion but probably large, are multifactorial, which is to say as yet undefined.

It remains to test this hypothesis by reference to other variables. One property that we and others have used is the quality of spelling mistakes, first suggested by Boder (1971). Omenn characterized subjects as "auditory" or "visual," depending in part on whether or not their spelling mistakes were "dysphonetic"; and although there was a high degree of within-family likeness for type, it is not clear precisely how the spelling mistakes were scored, or how the "typing" was done (Omenn & Weber, 1978). We have developed a scoring system in which a decision is made as to whether or not each word in the Wide-Range Achievement Test (WRAT) spelling subtest is misspelled in such a way as to indicate the use of phonetic rules—that is, phonetically or dysphonetically (Childs & Finucci, 1979). The subject is then given a score expressed as the percentage of dysphonetically misspelled words. Figure 26-1 shows that when the spelling of parents who are dyslexic is compared with that of their reading-disabled children, there is a strong correlation; dysphonetic misspellers are likely to have children who misspell in the same way, and the misspelling of the offspring of phonetic misspellers is also likely to mimic the parental type. It is improbable that this correlation could ever be perfect, because schoolchildren are taught that if they must misspell, they should misspell phonetically. It remains now to use other qualities, such as characteristics of language development, scores on subtests of the Wechsler and other cognitive tests, evidences of laterality, and the like, to refine the definition of these putative subtypes of specific reading disability. Once that is accomplished, it will be possible to test the genetic hypothesis with some rigor by subjecting the subtypes to pedigree and segregation analysis.

Genetic Linkage Analysis

Smith and her colleagues have evidence favoring a genetic linkage between at least one form of dyslexia and a frequent and innocuous structural variation of chromosome 15 (Smith, Pennington, Kimberling, & Lubs, 1979). The families they have studied were characterized by severe unexpected reading disability in the index cases (averaging four grades behind that expected) and evidence of dyslexia in three generations. In the families in which the chromosome variation was found to be segregating, its association with the reading disability was likely to be due to chance with a probability of only .001 (Smith, 1980). This important study is at once strong evidence favoring the idea in principle of a genetic origin of dyslexia, and an affirmation of the idea of heterogeneity, since it suggests that there is at least one dominant form. Efforts to relate this phenotype to one or other of those described by Mattis, however, have not been rewarding (Smith, 1980).

Neurophysiological Studies

In 1970, Conners reported a family in which several disabled readers showed anomalous recordings of visual evoked responses (VERs) when light flashes were used as a stimulus (Conners, 1970). Later, Preston reported average differences between the VERs of a sample of parents of disabled readers and normal controls using a more complex task (Preston, Guthrie, Kirsch, Gertman & Childs, 1977). This is indirect evidence that the VER variation associated with familial reading disability is also familial. The most important question, however, is whether the method can ever be refined to discover individual rather than group differences.

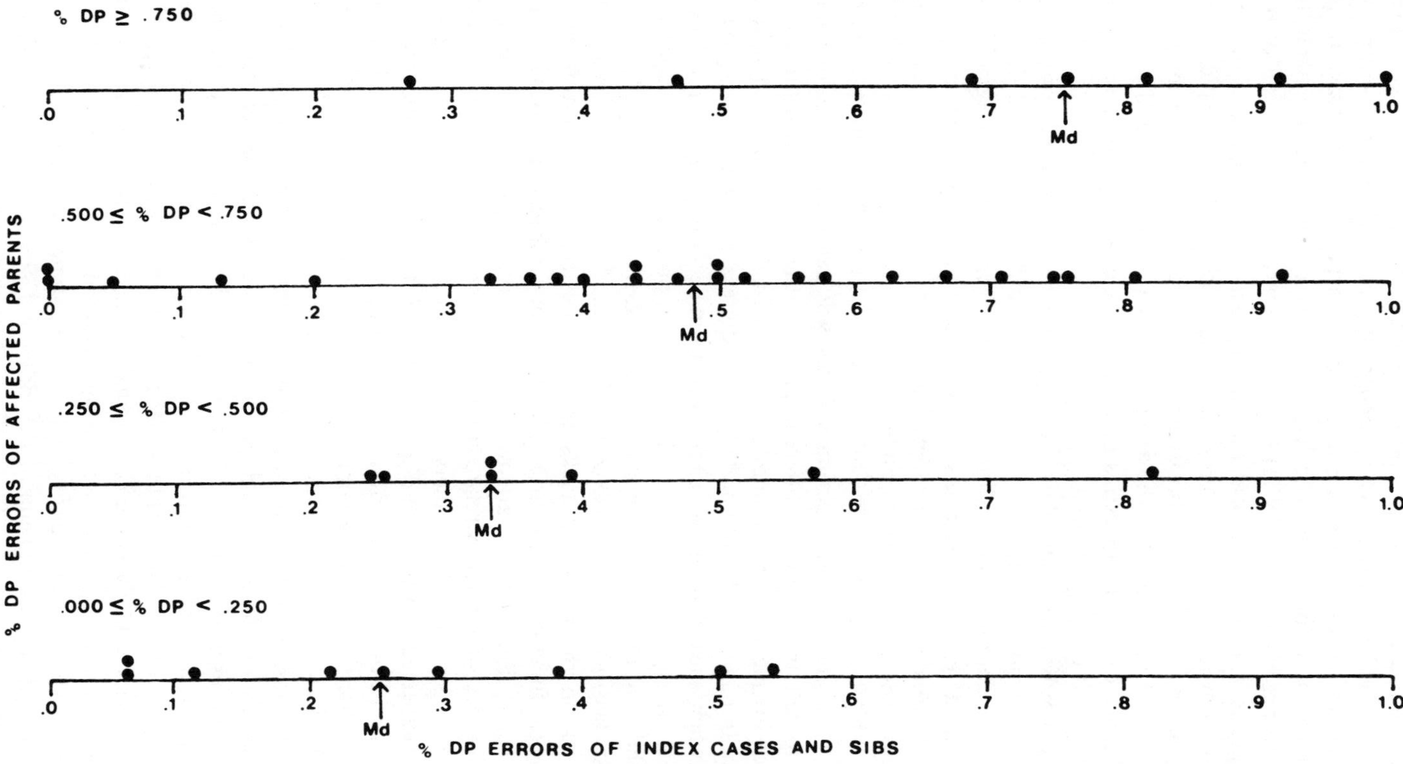

Figure 26-1. Proportion of dysphonetic spelling errors according to spelling type of parents. From "The Genetics of Learning Disability" by B. Childs and J. M. Finucci, in R. Porter and M. O'Connor (Eds.), *Human Genetics: Possibilities and Realities* (Ciba Foundation Symposium No. 66), New York: Excerpta Medica, 1979. Copyright 1979 by the Ciba Foundation. Reprinted by permission.

THE FUTURE

The evidence favoring the familial nature of dyslexia is overwhelming, but the factors that account for the aggregation of cases remain unclear. Some evidence that some kinds are strongly influenced by the genes has been outlined above, and it must be added that those who propose cultural hypotheses to account for *all* dyslexia rarely gather coherent evidence to support or refute their assertions. But definitive tests of the genetic hypothesis have been, and are likely to continue to be, handicapped by (1) the inconsistency and imprecision of the diagnosis; and (2) the categorical thinking by which it is supposed that all dyslexia, even while clinically diverse, has the same origin. These handicaps are not independent; diagnostic inconsistency and imprecision make for imprecise classification of subtypes, and the assumption that all dyslexia is due to the same influence causes the investigator to overlook clues that could refine the diagnostic precision.

It may not be altogether in error to say that in nearly every paper reviewed above, the diagnosis of dyslexia was based on different tests and different criteria. No doubt the results of different tests are correlated; the designation of "grades behind" expected performance correlates well with quotients based on IQ, age, and grade placement, or regression scores that use all these and more as predictors (Berger *et al.*, 1975, Finucci, Isaacs, Whitehouse, & Childs, 1982; Finucci, Whitehouse, Isaacs, & Childs, in press; Yule, 1973). But the use of different tests and different scoring systems will cause the scores of some subjects to fall in somewhat different parts of the several distributions—sometimes in one class, sometimes in another. Such variability can have a significant influence on the interpretation of pedigrees, always on shaky ground anyway when measures of the characteristic under study are continuously distributed. If so, then some sort of standard approach would enhance the comparability of the studies of numerous investigators.

Most classifications of dyslexia have been based on aspects of reading or spelling, or on the results of tasks that are presumed to be testing some psychological function—visual or auditory memory, for example, or visual or auditory perception. Too little attention has been given to demographic details or clinical aspects not directly related to reading or spelling skills. For example, one report suggests that the mothers and fathers of dyslexics are on the average older than expected (Jayaserkara & Street, 1978). But they are only older on the average; that is, there is a spectrum of parental age from young to old. If this interesting observation can be confirmed, it would be of great interest to see whether the dyslexic children of the older parents are different in any important detail from those of the younger parents. Severity of the dyslexia, family history, details of language development, presence or absence of perinatal problems, and even season of birth are all variables that come to mind that might help in such a test. Educational attainment, occupation, and other aspects of later life are also variables that can be used in the classification. Are familial dyslexics as likely as the nonfamilial to read for pleasure, go to college, or prosper in a wide variety of occupations? Outcome could also be used as a test of the validity of the auditory and visual subtypes. If these subtypes are rooted in the biological makeup of the individual, they might express themselves in ways other than reading, which, when combined with the residual aspects of dyslexia that persist into adult life, could be reflected in some aspects of the dyslexic's behavior, personality, or other expressions of living. This epidemiological approach could give promising leads for subtypes that could be validated by genetic tests and refined by psychological, physiological, and biochemical characterization. Once such a classification based on some agreed upon set of criteria is in place, pedigree and segregation analyses have some chance of sorting out the monogenic from the multifactorial types. The lesson of mental retardation suggests that the former will outnumber the latter in the proliferation of types, but that the latter will outnumber the former in number of individuals.

The virtues of this effort to sort out the varieties of dyslexia are two: (1) It may give valuable leads to the discovery of important nongenetic elements in the origin of particular cases; and (2) the elucidation of familial types can give parents and teachers valuable predictive information about individual children that can help in anticipating school problems and in suggesting appropriate teaching methods. These desirable ends are not unrelated. The discovery of nongenetic precipitating factors is a preliminary to preventing or minimizing the effects of the genetic propensity, and the distinction between familial and nonfamilial cases will help in focusing on those qualities of experience that must be adjusted so as to give each child the best opportunity to exploit his or her potential.

CONCLUSION

We have attempted in this chapter to show that the genetic–epidemiological method can be used to help in getting at fundamental questions about specific reading disability. What are the demographic, biological, and experiential qualities that distinguish individuals with specific reading disability from those with "general reading backwardness" (Yule *et al.*, 1974), and both of these types from normal readers? What are the qualities that distinguish individuals expressing the different forms of reading disability? And what distinguishes those disabled readers who surmount their reading handicaps from those who do not? It is not enough simply to state that specific reading disability is familial. It is more informative to use the familial quality and the mode of inheritance as a means of elaborating a classification with significant implications as to preventive and remedial actions.

Acknowledgments

This work was supported in part by grants from the National Institutes of Health (HD 00486) and the Gow School.

References

Anonymous. Human gene map. *American Journal of Human Genetics*, 1983, *35*, 134–156.

Bakwin, H. Reading disability in twins. *Developmental Medicine and Child Neurology*, 1973, *15*, 184–187.

Bateman, B. *Interpretation of the Illinois Test of Psycholinguistic Abilities*. Seattle: Special Child Publications, 1968.

Benton, A. L. Developmental dyslexia: Neurological aspects. *Advances in Neurology*, 1975, *7*, 1–47.

Berger, M., Yule, W., & Rutter, M. Attainment and adjustment in two geographical areas: II. The prevalence of specific reading retardation. *British Journal of Psychiatry*, 1975, *126*, 510–519.

Boder, E. Developmental dyslexia: Prevailing diagnostic concepts and a new diagnostic approach. *Progress in Learning Disabilities*, 1971, *2*, 293–321.

Childs, B., & Finucci, J. M. The genetics of learning disability. In R. Porter & M. O'Connor (Eds.), *Human genetics: Possibilities and realities* (Ciba Foundation Symposium No. 66). New York: Excerpta Medica, 1979.

Conners, C. K. Cortical evoked response in children with learning disorders. *Psychophysiology*, 1970, *7*, 418–428.

Decker, S. N., & DeFries, J. C. Cognitive abilities in families with reading-disabled children. *Journal of Learning Disabilities*, 1980, *13*, 53–58.

DeFries, J. C., Singer, S. M., Foch, T. T., & Lewitter, F. I. Familial nature of reading disability. *British Journal of Psychiatry*, 1978, *132*, 361–367.

Denckla, M. B. Performance on color task in kindergarten children. *Cortex*, 1972, *8*, 177–190.

Doehring, D. G., & Hoshko, I. M. Classification of reading problems by the *Q*-technique of factor analysis. *Cortex*, 1977, *13*, 281–294.

Drew, A. L. A neurological appraisal of familial congenital word blindness. *Brain*, 1956, *79*, 440–460.

Ehrman, L., Omenn, G. S., & Caspari, E. *Genetics, environment, and behavior*. New York: Academic Press, 1972.

Elston, R. C., & Yelverton, K. C. General models for segregation analysis. *American Journal of Human Genetics*, 1975, *27*, 31–45.

Eustis, R. S. Specific reading disability. *New England Journal of Medicine*, 1947, *237*, 243–249.

Fieve, R. R., Rosenthal, D., & Brill, H. *Genetic research in psychiatry*. Baltimore: Johns Hopkins University Press, 1975.

Finucci, J. M. Genetic considerations in dyslexia. *Progress in Learning Disabilities*, 1978, *4*, 41–63.

Finucci, J. M., Guthrie, J. T., Childs, A. L., Abbey, H., & Childs, B. The genetics of specific reading disability. *Annals of Human Genetics*, 1976, *40*, 1–23.

Finucci, J. M., Isaacs, S. D., Whitehouse, C. C., & Childs, B. A quantitative index of reading disability for use in family studies. *Developmental Medicine and Child Neurology*, 1982, *24*, 733–744.

Finucci, J. M., Whitehouse, C. C., Isaacs, S. D., & Childs, B. *Multiple-regression techniques for defining adult reading ability*, in press.

Foch, T. T., DeFries, J. C., McClearn, G. E., & Singer, S. M. Familial patterns of impairment in reading disability. *Journal of Educational Psychology*, 1977, *69*, 316–329.

Hallgren, B. Specific dyslexia: A clinical and genetic study. *Acta Psychiatrica et Neurologica Scandinavica*, 1950 (Suppl. 65), 1–287.

Ingram, T., Mason, A., & Blackburn, I. A retrospective study of 82 children with reading disability. *Developmental Medicine and Child Neurology*, 1970, *12*, 271–281.

Jayaserkara, R., & Street, J. Parental age and parity in dyslexic boys. *Journal of Biosocial Science*, 1978, *10*, 9–30.

Johnson, T. J., & Myklebust, H. *Learning disabilities: Educational principles and practices*. New York: Grune & Stratton, 1967.

Lewitter, F. I., DeFries, J. C., & Elston, R. C. Genetic models of reading disability. *Behavior Genetics*, 1980, *10*, 9–30.

Mattis, S., French, J. H., & Rapin, I. Dyslexia in children and young adults: Three independent neuropsychological syndromes. *Developmental Medicine and Child Neurology*, 1975, *17*, 281–300.

Morton, N. E. Some aspects of the genetic epidemiology of common diseases. In E. Inouye & H. Mishimura (Eds.), *Gene–environment interaction in common diseases*. Baltimore: University Park Press, 1977.

Omenn, G. S., & Weber, B. A. Dyslexia: Search for phenotypic and genetic heterogeneity. *American Journal of Medical Genetics*, 1978, *1*, 333–342.

Owen, F. W., Adams, P. A., Forrest, T., Stolz, L. M., & Fisher, S. Learning disorders in children: Sibling studies. *Monographs of the Society for Research in Child Development*, 1971, *36*, 1–77.

Preston, M. S., Guthrie, J. T., Kirsch, I., Gertman, D., & Childs, B. VERs in normal and disabled adult readers. *Psychophysiology*, 1977, *14*, 8–14.

Smith, S. D. Personal communication, 1980.

Smith, S. D., Pennington, B. F., Kimberling, W. J., & Lubs, H. A. Investigation of subgroups within specific reading disability utilizing neuropsychological and linkage analysis. *American Journal of Human Genetics*, 1979, *31*, 83a. (Abstract)

Symmes, J., & Rappaport, J. Unexpected reading failure. *American Journal of Orthopsychiatry*, 1972, *42*, 82–91.

Walker, L., & Cole, E. Familial patterns of expression of specific reading diability in a population sample. *Bulletin of the Orton Society*, 1965, *15*, 12–24.

Yule, W. Differential prognosis of reading backwardness and specific reading retardation. *British Journal of Educational Psychology*, 1973, *43*, 244–248.

Yule, W., Rutter, M., Berger, M., & Thompson, J. Over- and underachievement in reading: Distribution in the general population. *British Journal of Educational Psychiatry*, 1974, *44*, 1–12.

Zahalkova, M., Vrzal, V., & Kloboukova, E. Genetical investigation in dyslexia. *Journal of Medical Genetics*, 1972, *9*, 48–52.

Zerbin-Rudin, E. Congenital word blindness. *Bulletin of the Orton Society*, 1967, *17*, 47–54.

CHAPTER TWENTY-SEVEN

Treatment of Reading Disorders

RACHEL GITTELMAN

A great many treatment approaches have been advanced for the remediation of children with reading disorders, so that consumers find themselves with an apparent embarrassment of riches. The purpose of this chapter is to provide an overview of the empirical evidence for the efficacy of such interventions.

Unlike much medical treatment, which has evolved out of serendipity based on judicious clinical observations, the treatment of reading disability has been rooted in theoretical models that have preceded careful clinical observations and documentation of the validity of the postulated underlying causes. The theories fall into two broad classes: those that emphasize basic developmental perceptual factors as necessary prerequisites, and those that view spoken and written language skills as crucial to reading.

The first approach, sometimes referred to as the "basic factors" view of reading disability (Guthrie & Seifert, 1978), singles out the development of children's visual, auditory, and visual–motor abilities. Diagnostic materials are tailored to identify weaknesses and strengths. Remedial efforts are designed to teach children, using their stronger perceptual mode, while, at the same time, developing deficient sensory–motor abilities. The several variations of this model all share the basic characteristic of focusing on the development of sensory and sensory–motor skills while ignoring the reading task itself.

The second approach, which focuses specifically on the reading process, ignores perceptual–motor skills and instead aims at the identification of deficiencies in decoding ability. It is concerned with children's word-attack and word-analysis skills; assessment is geared to the identification of children's competence to analyze the phonetic characteristics of words, to understand the relationship between spoken and written language, to associate sounds with printed materials, and to apply phonological rules, as well as to the identification of their comprehension skills.

In addition to the perceptual and phonetic approaches to reading, some have viewed the acquisition of reading skills in an operant model, which posits a deficiency in children's previous learning experience, rather than in the basic cognitive skills required for reading.

Clearly, the various viewpoints are not mutually exclusive, so that the perceptual or decoding difficulties could interact with a deficient reward history

Rachel Gittelman. College of Physicians and Surgeons, Columbia University, New York, New York; New York State Psychiatric Institute, New York, New York.

to produce reading disorders; very different treatment strategies, however, ensue with each theoretical approach.

It is curious that there is no current view on the teaching of reading that cannot be dated back to the early 19th century. Heated arguments have raged in educational circles over the use of phonic versus "whole-word" or "look–say" approaches for over 150 years (Mann, 1979). The same is true of the concern over the role played by perceptual and sensory modalities in the reading process. As a matter of fact, the use of sensory cues to teach reading, such as kinesthetic ones where the child traces letters, is dated back to the 5th century (Fernald, 1943)! Diack (1965) points out that anyone wanting to find out about the theories of reading instruction in currency during the mid-1960s can obtain all relevant information from a text that appeared in 1908 (Huey, 1908). Given the extraordinary stability of theoretical approaches to reading development, it would be overoptimistic to expect a shift in theoretical understanding since Diack reviewed the field in 1965. The views of the 1980s largely reiterate earlier writings.

A historical review of theories of reading is beyond the scope of this chapter. No attempt is made to present them or their treatment implications in chronological order. Rather, the literature is arbitrarily divided between those approaches that focus on the teaching of reading without concern for other underlying causative factors, and those that aim at correcting putative underlying etiological dysfunctions without correcting reading directly. In addition, the study of motivational factors is discussed.

Before examining the merit of interventions in the treatment of childhood reading disorders, certain ubiquitous design issues deserve mention because of their pervasive influence on investigators' attempts to draw conclusions regarding treatment efficacy.

RESEARCH ISSUES

Diagnostic Considerations

There is no generally accepted set of criteria for establishing the presence of reading disorders. This lack of consensus plagues the field, since so much sample variation occurs. The only common feature is that children with mental retardation (IQs below 70) are not included. This exclusionary criterion represents the limit of consistency across investigations.

Obviously, objective assessment of reading achievement is crucial, but the standards for establishing the presence of reading deficiency are inconsistent. First, the definition of "reading lag" varies. Some use discrepancy between chronological age and reading level to determine reading disability. Others compare reading ability to mental age. The groups identified by each approach will overlap considerably, since mental and chronological age correlate highly, but the overlap will not be complete.

Second, the magnitude of discrepancy between age (whether mental or chronological) and reading level that is required to establish the presence of reading disorders, varies greatly. Some have used a 6-month decrement; others, a minimum of 2 years. These two standards are bound to yield very different samples of poor readers.

Third, expected levels for a child's local school community should be a consideration in the identification of reading disorders. This issue is always pertinent, but particularly so when a relatively short lag (e.g., 6 months) is used for diagnosis. This point is of lesser concern when children are identified as having reading disorders based on referrals from teachers—whom, it may be expected, are judging such children as needing special help in comparison with their peers. However, studies have not always relied on teacher referrals, and in no instance have investigators attempted to obtain estimates of local reading levels to determine the validity of their diagnostic criteria for defining children as being below their expected reading level.

There is no available rational resolution of this definitional dilemma, since there are no data to show the superiority of any criteria set. Nevertheless, it is disconcerting to come across studies where lags as minimal as 6 months are selected without consideration for mental age, and where scores are treated as precise measures, while psychometric issues such as standard error of estimate are ignored.

The above definitional limitations afford a glimpse of the difficulties encountered in coming to general conclusions concerning the treatment of reading disorders.

Treatment Characteristics

It is immediately obvious that any evaluation must consider the duration of treatment and the intensity of the intervention (usually defined as "contact frequency"). These vary tremendously, further limiting a straightforward interpretation of outcome.

Another complicating ambiguity is the use of the same term to refer to quite different techniques. Terms such as "visual–motor training" or "auditory training" seem to have little agreed-upon general usage, and often are used by different investigators to refer to different procedures. Therefore, detailed descriptions of treatment programs are essential, but not regularly provided, and their absence leads to further confusion.

Measures of Outcome

Proper outcome evaluation is crucial. Some measures may not be sensitive to change over relatively short periods of time, although these same measures may be useful for identification and definitional purposes. Most tests used in the assessment of treatment effects were devised for other purposes, and their ability to detect improvement over a few months or less is critical, but, in all cases, unestablished. Therefore, inferring a lack of treatment effect from such measures may be unjustified. In the absence of established instrumentation, the best way to protect against failing to detect treatment effects, should such effects truly occur, is to use a broad variety of reading tests, tapping different aspects of the reading process. Doing so may minimize Type II errors (i.e., not finding a treatment effect when there is one), but, unfortunately, it cannot be viewed as eliminating their likelihood altogether.

The above are only a few of the methodological issues that render overall treatment evaluation of reading disability problematic. Others also exist; they are discussed where particularly relevant.

The treatment tactics applied to children with reading disorders have been viewed as methods that enhance reading ability in all children, not only in those deficient in learning capacity. Therefore, many of these approaches have been investigated with normal kindergarten or first-grade children to determine whether they lead to more rapid reading proficiency than traditional teaching methods do. This literature is of great importance to educators, but it is not within the scope of this chapter, which is concerned with the treatment of children who have failed to master age-appropriate reading skills. Furthermore, this review includes only studies that can be considered as having satisfactory experimental designs—specifically, the inclusion of control groups. (A body of clinical literature provides anecdotal evidence for the efficacy of various interventions in children with reading disorders. The nature of these treatments and the clinical claims concerning their effectiveness are well summarized in a recent review by Johnson, 1978.)

Reading Remediation in the Treatment of Reading Disorders

Few reports have appeared on the effects of the teaching of reading skills in children with reading retardation.

Cashdan and Pumfrey (1973) compared the reading progress of 12 untreated controls with that of 24 children of low average mental ability, at least 2 years below grade level in reading, who received reading remediation. No group differences were found in reading ability on two individual reading tests after two terms of treatment. This study suffers from lack of random assignment, and very infrequent tutoring for 12 of the 24 children (a total of 14 sessions over 7 months).

From a total group of 66 reading-disabled children who participated in a treatment study in which children were randomly assigned to treatment or no treatment, Camp and van Doorninck (1971) were able to match only seven, from each treatment group, who had similar characteristics before treatment. Remediation, which consisted of word recognition, was extremely variable in the seven children treated (6 to 20 sessions). The treated children performed significantly better than the controls did on a vocabulary list, a task very similar to that used in the training, but not on the reading subtest of the Wide-Range Achievement Test (WRAT). The lack of control for the special attention received by the children in treatment precludes the interpretation that reading instruction per se led to superior vocabulary list reading.

In view of their very small samples, the above two studies represent inadequate tests of the efficacy of reading instruction in children with reading disabilities.

Barcai and associates (Barcai, Umbarger, Pierce, & Chamberlain, 1973) compared the effects of language training with those of art activity and of counseling in 62 underachieving 10- to 11-year-olds selected from schools in low socioeconomic areas and seen in groups of seven to eight children. The authors report treatment effects on some subtests of the Wechsler Intelligence Scale for Children (WISC), but not on reading proficiency.

A recent study (Gittelman & Feingold, in press) investigated the impact of an individual reading-remediation program that relied on individualized instruction of phonic principles, emphasizing word-attack skills and decoding skills. Whenever the children mastered adequate decoding skills, whole-word recognition was introduced, followed by sentences, and so on. However, most of the children did not reach the point of whole-word reading, since they were so deficient in word-attack skills. To enter the study, children had to be referred by schools because of poor academic performance, *not* behavior problems; they had to have verbal IQs of 85 or more, be native speakers of English, and obtain scores at least 1 year below their expected grade level on individually administered reading tests.

A total of 61 children were randomly assigned to receive reading remediation or nonspecific academic tutoring. The latter consisted of tutoring in school subjects other than reading, such as math and science. Both groups were reinforced for learning. Children were seen individually, three times a week, for 4 months (total, 54 sessions). Of the 61 children, 60 were reevaluated 2 months after treatment termination, and 53 were seen 8 months after treatment had ceased in order to evaluate whether treatment gains, if any, were sustained over time. No treatment occurred in the interim between experimental treatment and follow-up evaluation. Several reading and achievement tests were used to tap multiple aspects of reading: an oral word-recognition test (the WRAT); an oral paragraph-reading test (the Gray Oral Reading Test); a silent reading test (the Stanford Achievement Test); and a reading test with phonetic content only (the Daniels and Diack Test; see Daniels & Diack, 1973).

After 4 months of treatment, the children who had received reading remediation were markedly superior to the controls on tests of basic reading skills that reflect the ability to recognize various sounds, to blend sounds, to discriminate phonemes, and so forth. The children who had received reading tutoring read significantly better than the controls did on all the reading tests. The magnitude of the improvement was not trivial. Thus, on the Gray Oral Test, the children who received reading remediation had a 7-month superiority over the controls, and 6-month advantages on the Daniels and Diack Reading Test and on the word study skills subtest of the Stanford Achievement Test.

At 2 and 8 months after treatment, the remedial group continued to perform significantly better than the controls did on several measures of basic reading skills and on the phonetic Daniels and Diack Test. The word study skills subtest of the Stanford differentiated the two groups after 2, but not after eight, months of treatment. The other subtests of the Stanford Achievement Test did not show an advantage for the treated groups at follow-up. A trend in the Gray Oral Reading Test in favor of the reading group was found at the 2-month point. The reading subtest of the WRAT showed no sustained treatment differences at follow-up.

As expected, treatment effects were less consistent and marked as time passed. The fact that any carryover effects were found is encouraging and stimulates the hope that stable gains may be expected if vigorous, protracted attempts are made to reverse reading disabilities.

This study documents the value of an intensive remedial program that emphasizes training in decoding principles; it supports the prediction made by Guthrie (1978) that instruction in the decoding components of reading should lead to the acquisition of reading, and, furthermore that this process is important to all ages. Since the above investigation controlled all nonspecific aspects of treatment, such as the child–tutor relationship, reinforcement for learning, and so on, the gains found in the reading group can be interpreted as being due to the specific effects of the instructional effort. However, the study does not speak of the relative efficacy of this approach compared with other teaching methods.

In a British study (Lovell, Byrne, & Richardson, 1963), children with reading problems who had received full-time special teaching for an average of 1 year were reevaluated 3 years later. Controls, identified at the follow-up point, consisted of children who had similar ages, IQs, and reading ages as the treated group did at the time it was selected for treatment. No difference in reading level was obtained at follow-up. This study fails to indicate a long-term advantage for children who receive remedial reading, but the nature of the control group does not allow a definitive conclusion.

Though there have been other follow-up studies of children who had received reading tutoring, their contribution is limited by the fact that they had no control groups (Balow & Blomquist, 1965; Cashdan & Pumfrey, 1973; Franenheim, 1978; Kline & Kline, 1975; Lytton, 1967; Muehl & Forell, 1973; Preston & Yarrington, 1967; Rawson, 1968; Robinson & Smith, 1962). Some of these investigators report no maintenance of gains, while others report remarkable progress. However, the duration of treatment and the sample characteristics vary greatly across studies. In some, children received tutoring for a couple of months; in others, for several years. In addition, the reports that yielded the most favorable data with regard to eventual outcome included children with high IQ scores (e.g., median IQ in Rawson, 1968, equaled 131; mean IQ in Robinson & Smith, 1962, equaled 120).

Another consistent shortcoming of the long-term follow-up studies of children who received specialized reading instruction is the high attrition rate of the original cohort, which varies from 50 to 63%. Retrieval of less than half the children renders an estimate of clinical efficacy difficult. Nevertheless, the data indicate that the outlook for very bright children referred for reading remediation is not uniformly poor, and can even be very good. The degree to which treatment contributes to a favorable picture, when it occurs, is unclear, given the absence of untreated comparison groups.

NONREADING APPROACHES TO THE TREATMENT OF READING DISORDERS

There are several approaches to the treatment of children's reading disorders that do not instruct the children in reading, but offer training for other functions. The rationale is that the children have been unable to learn because of basic deficiencies, and that unless these hypothesized causal defects are altered, the children will not learn to read. Several etiological theories have generated models of treatment; these are arbitrarily classified as "perceptual," "attentional," and "motivational."

Perceptual Training

The impetus for altering perceptual function—visual, auditory, or tactile—rests on the assumption that proper sensory perception, intersensory integration, sensory–motor organization, and perceptual or perceptual–motor competence are the necessary foundations for the development of reading. Furthermore, it is assumed that improvement in these functions automatically leads to increased reading ability.

Many programs for perceptual training are commercially available. They overlap greatly, and differ only in emphasis, depending on the authors' view of the central perceptual mechanism responsible for reading. Perhaps the currently best known of the perceptual-training programs is Frostig's, which emphasizes the development of visual perception via eye–hand coordination exercises and training in form discrimination and spatial orientation (Frostig, 1969). Others include training in directionality (left–right discrimination) or in intersensory integration of auditory, visual, and kinesthetic modalities (Fernald, 1943; Hagin, Silver, & Beecher, 1978; Silver, Hagin, & Hersh, 1967). Some have used very similar perceptual and coordination training in combination with some teaching of verbal and language material, such as blending of words and analyzing sequences in stories (Tansley, 1967). Concern for sensory–motor and motor development is reflected in programs that also include training in "body awareness" or "body image" through physical exercises and balance training (Getman, Kan, Halgren, & McKee, 1964; Kephart, 1960).

In all cases, poor reading is viewed as the result of inadequate development of the neurophysiological substrates regulating perceptual and motor functions, believed to be cornerstones for the evolution of high-level cognitive functions. The exercises are viewed as replacement therapy (with ensuing cognitive development) for the lack of sensory–motor organization. Some have gone further in their claims, arguing that the training alters neurological development (Delacato, 1966).

The rationale for these theories is strikingly weak, since there is ample evidence that deficient visual perception or other sensory–perceptual dysfunctions are not well correlated with reading disorders. Some positive but mild association occurs between reading and visual–motor coordination in young children, but this association disappears in midchildhood. These results would suggest that an independent factor influences both visual–motor and reading performance early on, but that the regulating mechanisms change with age. If so, little benefit can be expected from altering sensory–motor development. The relationships between perceptual development and reading competence have been reviewed by Rutter and Yule (1977).

In spite of their weak theoretical rationale, perceptual programs have enjoyed great popularity, as shown by the plethora of commercially available kits and the vast number of articles published on their purported efficacy. Much of this literature does not meet minimum scientific standards, such as the inclusion of comparison groups, and therefore is not discussed in this review. "For instance" is not a binding argument. Limiting one's interest to properly controlled studies reveals a severely reduced body of relevant studies.

In the main, perceptual–motor training programs have been investigated in preschool and kindergarten children, normal or disadvantaged, for whom reading disorders were not a specific issue. Very little work has been done with children suffering from reading disorders.

McCormick and associates (McCormick, Schnobrick, Footlick, & Poetker, 1968) assigned 42 first-grade children to perceptual–motor training, to standard physical education, or to no treatment. The children were defined only as "underachieving." Children were seen twice a week in 45-minute sessions for a 7-week period. Perceptual–motor training included various exercises to train gross and fine motor control, directionality, and proprioception. Also, some attention exercises derived from Piaget's theory of cognitive development were included, as well as training in self-control, which required children to verbalize their activities (an application of one of Luria's principles of verbal mediation). No group differences were found among the three groups on the Lee–Clark reading test, using a rank test or analysis of variance. This study suffers from poor sample description: It is not clear that the children suffered from reading disorders. Furthermore, the use of a single atypical reading measure is unfortunate.

In another study of motor training, O'Donnell and Eisenson (1969) selected 60 children of normal IQ from a large population of second- to fourth-graders, chosen because of mixed lateralization and reading scores on the Stanford Achievement Test below the 25th percentile. They were randomly assigned to one of three experimental groups: One group received motor training consisting of cross-pattern creeping and walking and of visual pursuit (the Delacato training program); the second group received training in visual perception and engaged in physical education; the third engaged only in physical activity. Children were seen in groups for 30 minutes daily over a 20-week period. The rationale for selecting children without clear lateralization is related to the claim that it indicates immature neurological development, which is remediable through specific exercises (Delacato, 1963).

No differences were found among the groups at the end of treatment on the Gray Oral Test, on the seven reading tests of the Stanford Diagnostic Reading Test, or on the Developmental Test of Visual–Motor Integration; this was true whether data were analyzed by parametric group differences or nonparametric rank scores. As O'Donnell and Eisenson note, their study remedied shortcomings of previous reports: They evaluated treatment effects in especially selected poor readers, included younger children, provided longer treatment, and included more varied measures of outcome. Yet, in spite of these alterations, the programs in motor and visual training were no different in effect from a physical education program on tests of reading and visual–motor integration.

It could be argued that since training in motor coordination supposedly affects reading through its impact on neurological organization, much longer treatment periods would be required for a fair test. Though this point seems sensible, it is not pertinent, since proponents of the exercises in motor patterning claim dramatic effects on reading scores in children with reading disabilities after 6 and 8 weeks of treatment (Delacato, 1959, 1966).

Because they felt that children of low socioeconomic backgrounds were especially likely to have reading as well as auditory deficits, Feldman and associates (Feldman, Schmidt, & Deutsch, 1968) selected children from poor urban neighborhoods for study. Third-graders were targeted, since reading disorders can be diagnosed more reliably at that point than earlier, when reading disability may be confused with a temporary maturational delay in skill development. In addition, some association between auditory processing and reading proficiency had been reported for this age group, but not for older children. These considerations led to the expectation that third-graders would be the optimal age group for the investigation of the effect of auditory training on reading ability.

Third-graders with reading scores one standard error or less below the third-grade level were studied (but excluding those with subnormal intelligence, behavior problems in school, or gross neurological impairment). Four treatments were administered, in groups of three to four children, for a 5-month period (a total of 58 hours): (1) reading training alone; (2) auditory training alone; (3) reading plus auditory training; (4) no treatment. To control for the extra professional time given to children who received a combination of reading and auditory training, the other two treatment groups were seen for equivalent stretches of time in play sessions. A total of 57 children participated in the study. They were reevaluated 6 and 12 months after treatment.

Assessments consisted of four individual reading tests and 11 tests of auditory processing and auditory attention. The reading remediation is described only as "accepted remedial reading techniques," consisting of sight vocabulary, word-analysis skills, and comprehension. Auditory training focused systematically on four functional areas: recognition, discrimination, memory, and attention. No motor training was given. As the authors state, "It was expected that once the auditory skills were known, transfer of them to reading would occur automatically."

The results were altogether negative. No group differences were found at any time, and even more curiously, no significant within-group changes occurred, indicating that the children did not budge from the level of reading achievement and auditory ability they had achieved before treatment, despite the treatment received.

The authors make some puzzling statements in the report and omit much information. For instance, they state that "some effort was made to assign children randomly to treatment groups" (p. 469). It is difficult to understand the consequences of this comment on the study design. None of the patient scores are given; the report of results is limited to significance levels, which precludes an examination of the group characteristics. The number of subjects in each group is not specified. The fourth, "no-treatment," group is alluded to, but it is not certain that such a group existed at all or that it was included in the data analyses. It is most unfortunate that so much is ambiguous in this well-conceptualized study of auditory training.

It is obvious that the literature on the treatment of children with reading disorders through perceptual or perceptual–motor training is extremely limited. The little controlled evidence available fails to support the notion that such methods affect reading progress in children with reading disability.

There have been other studies with normal children or with children believed to be at risk for reading disorders. This literature has been well summarized elsewhere (Hammill, 1972; Hirsch & Anderson, 1976; Keogh, 1974; Lyon, 1977). Very few of the studies have any scientific merit. The weight of the evidence for the efficacy of perceptual programs is negative in normal groups as well, though the many clinical reports are remarkably enthusiastic.

A controlled study of children at risk for learning disorders, too recent to have been addressed in the reviews quoted above, is important because it claims not only that perceptual training prevents reading failure, but that it is preferable to the teaching of reading (Arnold, Barnebey, McManus, Smeltzer, Conrad, Winer, & Desgranges, 1977). This report indicates that the argument that teaching reading skills is beside the point for children at risk for reading disorders is not vestigial, but a persisting belief. The authors reported that children taught to read experienced a significant decrement in IQ, compared with those who received perceptual training. This is one of the very few studies to show apparent benefits from perceptual training, but it suffers from a reliance on a single word-recognition test to assess reading competence and from a failure to consider why their findings should differ from those of previous investigations (Gittelman, 1978).

Enhancement of Attention: Effects of Stimulant Medication

Attention has been claimed to be critical to the development of reading, and children with reading disorders are said by some to suffer from dysfunctional attentional processes. This view has linked reading disorders to other childhood conditions also purported to be due to poor attention, leading to the overall diagnostic rubric of "minimal brain dysfunction" (MBD) or "learning disabilities," under which hyperactivity (now called "attention deficit disorder with hyperactivity" in the United States; see American Psychiatric Association, 1980) and reading disorders are often lumped.

The concept of attention is not unitary, but comprises many component systems; therefore, the notion of attentional dysfunction without further refinement is vague. Experimenters have focused on reaction time and distractibility to operationalize the measure of attention. Several studies have shown that children with reading disorders are significantly more susceptible to the effects of experimental extraneous distractors than are normal controls, and that they are slower on reaction time (Douglas & Peters, 1979). However, it is apparent from the data that there is much overlap in attentional capacity between the two types of children, suggesting either that impaired attention is not a necessary condition for the development of reading disorders, or that the experimental paradigms have not been able to identify the attentional dysfunction specific to children with reading disorders, if such exist.

Since the psychostimulants are generally believed to enhance attention and facilitate its focus, the studies of stimulant treatment are interpreted as reflecting the consequences of attentional enhancement in children with reading disorders. Though many have reported on stimulant effects on achievement scores in hyperactive children or in children with nonspecific behavior disorders, few have singled out the effect of these drugs on youngsters with reading disability. The concern of this review is the impact of stimulant treatment on children with reading disorders—not of these drugs on cognition in general. Therefore, studies not restricted to reading disorders are not germane.

The length of treatment is crucial to one concerned about stimulant effects on the acquisition of reading skills. No one expects a pill to induce instant knowledge of complex academic tasks. Therefore, the way the stimulants would act in reading disorders, if effective, would be by enabling children to learn better because of a more efficient attentive focus and a more receptive capacity for instruction. This model of drug action, though simple, requires time, since adequate opportunity for developing the heretofore deficient reading skills is still necessary.

Stimulant treatment can vary, not only in time, but also in dosage. This issue is crucial to the use of this class of compounds in children with cognitive deficits, since it has been shown by Sprague and Sleator (1977) that low doses of methylphenidate have a significantly superior effect on a visual task of rote learning than higher doses do. Sprague and Sleator have claimed that higher doses may have a detrimental impact on children's learning ability. This has never been shown; if anything, the higher stimulant doses have been consistently reported to improve cognitive performance (see Klein, Gittelman, Quitkin, & Rifkin, 1980, for a review). However, if high doses impaired learning, the doses typically used for the clinical management of behavior problems would be expected to interfere with children's academic performance.

The first placebo-controlled study of stimulant effects on reading appeared in 1961 (Huddleston, Staiger, Frye, Musgrave, & Stritch, 1961). A total of 60 retarded readers (whose reading characteristics were not further specified), between elementary-school and college ages, received 150 mg/day of deanol or a placebo for 8 weeks. No clue is given concerning behavioral characteristics; age range of the subjects was extremely broad. No drug effect was noted on the Gates Reading Tests.

Deanol has very weak effects and is not as potent as other stimulants used in the management of children with behavior disorders (Klein *et al.*, 1980). It may be, therefore, that it was the wrong stimulant for the amelioration of reading disorders. No cognitive measures were reported to document that the drug enhanced attention. The time element may also have mattered; 8 weeks may be an insufficient length of time to evaluate the impact of a stimulant on reading.

Another study (Gittelman-Klein & Klein, 1976) included 61 children, referred by teachers because of poor academic performance, who were 2 years below grade level in reading achievement and who showed no signs of hyperactivity or other behavior disorders. The children were assigned to methylphenidate or a placebo for 12 weeks. A maximum dose of 60 mg/day was used (mean daily dose 52 mg) to match that administered to hyperactive children studied by the same team of investigators.

Compared with the placebo-treated group, the children on methylphenidate showed significant improvement on a number of psychometric measures: number of errors of commission on a continuous-performance test, Porteus Maze Test, and tests of visual–motor integration, visual sequential memory, and performance IQ. However, the academic achievement of the drug-treated children was no different from that of the placebo group. Therefore, over a 3-month period, stimulant treatment did not offer any advantage to children with reading deficits.

The treatment time span of 3 months might have been insufficient for reading improvement, but this was clearly not the case for drug effects on arithmetic, where a significant drug advantage was found after 4 weeks of treatment (though not after 12 weeks).

In the hope of finding a subgroup of children who might be methylphenidate responders, I (Gittelman, 1980) investigated whether, among the children with specific reading disorders studied previously (Gittelman-Klein & Klein, 1976), those with more neurological signs and those with poorer performance on cognitive tests (often used to infer neuropsychological integrity) improved more in reading skills than children without these characteristics. Essentially, the study examined whether the reading performance of children who had more evidence of MBD improved more on methylphenidate than the reading of children with less evidence did. The data failed to indicate that the reading of children with more salient signs of MBD was more likely to improve with methylphenidate than that of other children. Therefore, the notion that youngsters who have neurological deficits coupled with reading disorders are good candidates for stimulant treatment was not corroborated.

Thus, in spite of the drug-induced improvement on cognitive tasks, which was attributed to improved attention, no enhancement of academic skills ensued. It may be argued that improvement in attention is insufficient to induce significant changes in academic skills, since the children had developed a negative attitude toward classwork and did not take advantage of the drug-induced improvement in attention. Hence, stimulant treatment might contribute significantly to reading performance only when administered in conjunction with remedial instruction.

The earlier results (Gittelman-Klein & Klein, 1976) suggested that the attention of children with pure reading disorders is positively affected by methylphenidate, since significant improvement was found on cognitive measures with the drug compared with a placebo, but that such improvement does not automatically lead to gains in academic performance. It was conjectured that the drug-treated children could not take advantage of their better learning capacity because of possible negative attitudes toward school and its demands; and also because their reading skills were too rudimentary to provide them with a base from which to progress on their own, without special educational efforts.

A study was designed to test the above hypothesis. In a random-assignment, double-blind treatment study, children received reading remediation with placebo, or reading remediation with methylphenidate (mean, 44 mg/day) (Gittelman, Klein, & Feingold, 1983). A total of 61 children aged 7 through 12, with verbal IQs of 85 or more, whose primary language was English and whose reading was at least 1 year below expected grade level, were tutored three times a week for 4 months (total, 54 sessions). (This study is part of the study by Gittelman & Feingold, 1983, discussed in the section on effects of reading remediation. The clinical and other selection criteria are identical to those presented on p. 524.) At the end of treatment, children were evaluated on psychometric tests and standardized achievement measures. In addition, the children were reassessed 2 and 6 months after the end of treatment. None of the children received special instruction or medication during the interval between treatment cessation and follow-up evaluation.

The results on cognitive measures confirmed the attention enhancement of methylphenidate found in the previous study (Gittelman-Klein & Klein, 1976). Several of the tasks were performed significantly better by the drug-treated group (i.e., continuous-performance test, test of visual sequential memory, Raven's Matrices, Matching Familiar Figures Test, the Porteus Mazes, and the performance scale of the WISC-R).

There was no significant advantage for the drug-treated children on the word-recognition subtest of the WRAT, or on the Gray Oral Reading Test. However, on the Daniels and Diack Test (a British test with phonetic content exclusively), the methylphenidate-treated group scored significantly better than the placebo group did on one of the eight subtests (polysyllabic phonically simple words). Of the four reading subtests of the Stanford Achievement Test (vocabulary, comprehension, word study skills, and language), the methylphenidate group obtained higher scores than the placebo group did on one subtest (language; $t = 2{,}38$, $p < .02$).

The greatest methlphenidate-induced improvement was found on the other academic subtests of the Stanford Achievement Test. Thus, on the tests of computation and math application, on overall math scores, and in social studies, the drug group performed significantly better than the placebo-treated children did (*p* ranged from .04 to .0003 for these tests). These advantages were strictly due to the drug, since no tutoring was given in these subjects.

No measure yielded a significant difference in favor of the placebo-treated group. The results clearly indicated a significant beneficial methylphenidate effect on academic tasks in children with pure reading disorders who received individual reading instruction. However, if concern is restricted to reading performance, which was the area of function uniformly impaired in the sample and which brought the children for treatment, the clinical advantage induced by methylphenidate is ambiguous. Two of the reading tests were not affected (WRAT and Gray Oral). On the Daniels and Diack Test, which showed a drug effect, the magnitude of this effect was not impressive. However, the advantage of the drug group on the Stanford Achievement language subtest was .7 of a year (4.32 vs. 3.61 grade level); this difference does not seem inconsequential, especially since it occurred over a 4-month period.[1] We are conducting analyses to determine whether there are characteristics that predict which children, if any, among the overall group of pure reading disorders, were particularly likely to have benefited from methylphenidate. Undoubtedly, larger samples will be necessary to permit firm conclusions regarding the specificity of methylphenidate effects on reading performance in subgroups of children with uncomplicated disorders. Until such information is available, however, it would be premature and ill-advised to recommend the use of methylphenidate in this patient group. This is especially true since no significant differences occurred between the previously drug- and placebo-treated groups, 2 and 8 months after treatment. Therefore, even when drug-induced superiority on academic performance was found, it was not sustained beyond the treatment phase.

After cessation of treatment, there was no instance where the children who had received methylphenidate were significantly worse than those who had taken a placebo. This is an important finding, since it has been argued that a state-dependent phenomenon occurs with stimulant treatment (Swanson & Kinsbourne, 1976). Such an effect would lead to the expectation that children on methylphenidate (drug state) would perform less well after drug withdrawal (drug-free state) than would children who had never been on the drug. This pattern is clearly not valid when applied to the impact of methylphenidate in children with uncomplicated reading disorders. Since all evidence points to a lack of specific stimulant action in other nonpsychotic diagnostic groups, it also seems most improbable that a state-dependent learning phenomenon occurs in the performance of nonlaboratory academic tasks in other clinical groups, such as hyperactive children or those with conduct disorders.

In summary, the data suggest that, in the treatment of reading disorders, there is no justification for the use of methylphenidate alone, without concomitant tutoring; that the combined use of reading instruction and methylphenidate may induce significant gains over remediation alone; but that the drug-related advantage, over several months, is neither broad nor dramatic.

1. These values are controlled for pretreatment levels; therefore, their differences can be interpreted by direct comparison, without concern for group differences before treatment.

Therefore, until further refinements are developed concerning which types of children receiving remediation are particularly good responders to methylphenidate, it is premature to recommend the combination of instruction and stimulants in unselected groups of children with pure reading disorders.

Because of a concern over the high doses used in many studies reporting stimulant effects on achievement, Aman and Werry (1982) investigated the effects of low doses of methylphenidate (.35 mg/kg) in a crossover design that included three conditions: methylphenidate, diazepam (Valium), and a placebo. (The hope that diazepam would reduce anxiety and thereby facilitate performance was the basis for studying the drug.) Fifteen children with reading lags of at least 2 years for their mental ages received each treatment for only 6 days. The results were consistent with reasonable expectations: No treatment differences were found. As noted, time is necessary for the development of complex skills. The only way that brief stimulant treatment could quickly affect reading ability would be if the children had the necessary skills, but were not applying them because of poor attentive ability. In this view, impaired attention would not affect the acquisition of reading skills—only their expression. It seems that if this model of poor reading were accurate, it would be especially relevant to hyperactive children, for whom a good case can be made—at least based on unrefined clinical observations—that poor attention interferes with task performance. Yet the academic performance of hyperactive children has not been found to be affected by stimulants given over short periods of time in a wide dosage range. Therefore, an empirical or logical basis for the conjecture that very brief exposure to stimulants can be expected to affect the level of reading of disabled readers appears nonexistent.

Enhancement of Motivation: Effects of Reinforcement

The importance of motivation for the development of reading skills has been emphasized by many writers who view task interest as a factor affecting reading proficiency (Gaddes, 1980; Robinson, 1953; Vernon, 1972). Most view the poor motivation and negative attitudes of children with reading disorders as secondary to repeated failures, which, in turn, are due to the children's intrinsic limitations. It has now become platitudinous to note the necessity for developing better attitudes toward learning to read.

Another view, based on principles of learning theory, posits that motivational factors are primary causes of reading disorders, not secondary consequences. The development of reading is conceptualized as following the traditional stimulus-response (S-R) paradigm. If the response is not reinforced, it will be extinguished. In this model, cognitive development and motivational systems follow learning principles (Staats, 1968; Staats, Brewer, & Gross, 1970), and traditional behavioral principles are applicable to language development (Staats, 1971, 1975; Staats & Staats, 1963; Staats, Staats, Schutz, & Wolf, 1962). Following an S-R model, printed words elicit verbal responses. If appropriate responses are reinforced, they are acquired and reading occurs; if not, they drop out of a child's repertoire. Training or special teaching is viewed as necessary, since errors can be made by the child simply on the basis of stimulus generalization; the child must comprehend that closely similar spellings require different verbal responses. Under ideal conditions, teaching solidifies the verbal associations to stimulus words through positive reinforcement and enables the establishment of proper associations through assistance in discriminations. Reading failure is viewed as being due to very low rates of reinforcement received by the child in school. The classroom consequently becomes an aversive setting, and behaviors incompatible with academic progress occur (such as daydreaming, absences, etc.). These are reinforcing to the child, since they afford him or her an opportunity to leave the field (i.e., to avoid learning—an unpleasant experience). It is posited that the use of rewards immediately following the desired reading behaviors can prevent or reverse the learning of incompatible behaviors and make reading itself a reinforcing experience, which, in turn, should lead to rapid learning.

The first systematic attempt to use extrinsic tangible reinforcements to promote reading was conducted by Staats and his associates in a group of 4-year-olds (Staats *et al.*, 1962). In another small study, Staats, Minke, Finley, Wolf, and Brooks (1964) suggested that token reinforcement can sustain correct performance on a task of reading acquisition over many sessions better than social reinforcement alone can, and that variable ratios of reinforcement appear to maintain higher rates of performance than continuous reinforcement does.

A claim has been advanced through several case reports that the rate of reading progress may be facilitated by the systematic use of reinforcement during teaching. Lahey (1976) summarized these reports and correctly points to their limited scientific value since no controls were used, but notes that the results are encouraging.

Staats and associates (Staats, Van Mondfrans, & Minke, 1967) have published a system of reinforcement that is designed for use during academic remediation, and report that its application in an adolescent delinquent led to improvement in several social behaviors, as well as in reading (Staats & Butterfield, 1965). Staats and his associates (Staats, Minke, Goodwin, & Landeen, 1967) then applied the reinforcement method (called "motivated learning") to a group of 36 junior-high-school youngsters with reading problems. Eighteen were tutored by nonprofessionals—high-school students and housewives—daily for a mean of 38 hours over 4.5 months. The remediation consisted of training in word recognition, without teaching of phonic decoding skills. The control group received no special instruction or reinforcement. The careful design was unfortunately disrupted by the introduction of special reading programs in the classroom, so that halfway through the study, the control group obtained additional reading instruction in school. (However, this must also have been true of the experimental group.) Reading tests included the Iowa Test of Basic Abilities, Science Research Associates (SRA) Word Lists, the Lorge–Thorndike vocabulary test, and the California Achievement Test.

The only significant difference found between the groups after treatment was a significantly superior performance for the treated children on the SRA Word List. Since this test was used in the training procedures, it cannot be said to represent evidence for a general treatment effect on reading. The results of this study do not give support to the notion that "look–say" reading remediation, coupled with extrinsic reinforcement and performed by nonprofessionals, is a useful intervention in young adolescent poor readers. However, even if treatment differences had occurred, the design would not have permitted inferences to be drawn about the efficacy of "motivated" reading over ordinary, nonmotivated reading. The proper design for such a comparison is one including a control group that receives nonmotivated training, not a group that remains untreated.

Collette-Harris and Minke (1978) selected 12 children of normal IQ who were reading-retarded for study; six were defined as dyslexic and six as non-dyslexic poor readers, using idiosyncratic criteria for this controversial classification. Half received word-recognition training with the Staats reinforcement procedures, and half were seen in a reading clinic, for 2.5 months, four times per week. No group difference in reading progress was found. However, assignment was not random, and the reading program in the clinic was markedly different from that used in the "reinforced" group. Therefore, the results are uninterpretable.

Because no difference in treatment efficacy was obtained between the dyslexic and nondyslexic children, the authors conclude that the concept of dyslexia is invalid for treatment purposes. Given the fact that there were only three dyslexic and three nondyslexic children in each treatment group, the memberships of which were not random, the authors seem rather overconfident in their assertion of the null hypothesis.

It is striking that in spite of so much theoretical literature promulgating the merits of contingent reinforcement programs to facilitate reading progress, no controlled study of the approach has been conducted in children with reading disability.

Other Treatment Strategies

It is often thought that, in some children, emotional conflict is the origin of learning problems. At times, the failure to learn to read has been interpreted as a defense against knowledge, which is viewed as a symbolic representation of unconscious strivings. In cases where reading problems are viewed as secondary symptoms of underlying conflicts, psychotherapy is often believed to be the treatment of choice. So far, there has been no systematic attempt to investigate the value of interpretive or other forms of psychotherapy in children with learning problems. Though a controlled investigation by Barcai *et al.* (1973) studied the effects of group therapy in underachievers, the efficacy of this treatment on reading ability is not reported. The work of others, presented by Rutter and Yule (1977), does not provide clear evidence for the role of psychotherapy in the treatment of children with reading disorders. As Rutter and Yule point out, emotional distress, demoralization, and poor self-esteem are likely consequences of reading failure. Over time, they may, in turn, interfere with a child's progress by limiting self-application and inducing an unfavorable attitude toward academic pursuits. Whether emotional factors can play a primary etiological role in reading disorders is unclear.

What level of expertise is required from teachers to induce significant gains in children with reading disorders? Some work has been done on this point in the teaching of preschoolers, but not among children with reading disorders. Some have reported that parents of children with reading retardation can induce significant improvement in their children's reading achievement simply by offering social reinforcement for reading, without providing reading instruction (Morgan & Lyon, 1979); this proposition, however, has not been put to the test.

One study has been conducted of the difference between individual tutoring done by college students and the addition of a special reading program in the regular classroom teaching of children with deficient reading.

Using group test scores, Schwartz (1977) identified 260 high-school students (12 to 14 years of age) who had deficient reading performance, from a total population of 1265 children in four schools. In two of the four schools, children received, on a random basis, no treatment or weekly individual reading instruction with reinforcement, given by college students for 10 weeks. In the third school, five teachers were trained to use a similar reading program with contingent reinforcement, in addition to the regular curriculum. Five other teachers continued the regular teaching schedule without additional programs. In the fourth school, the poor readers were seen by college students, but were not given any reading instruction or contingent reinforcement.

The groups that received individual reading remediation performed better than did those that received similar instruction in the classroom. No difference was found between children whose teachers were trained to give their classes reading remediation and children who met with a college student without receiving any specific tutoring. Though a follow-up retest was conducted 6 months after treatment, which showed continued superiority for children individually treated, 36% of the original sample was not retrieved. This high rate of dropout from the total sample invalidates the results of the follow-up; however, this study suggests that individual tutoring is superior to classroom intervention.

No investigation of tutoring in small groups (three to four children) versus a one-to-one approach has been undertaken. It is my impression that with severely retarded readers, group instruction is distinctly inferior. There are serious difficulties encountered in efforts to maintain the children's interest and attention. Some studies have used group rather than individual training; the failure to obtain improvement may be the result of this treatment condition.

Cashdan and Pumfrey (1973) compared twice-weekly to once-weekly reading remediation. Assignment to treatment intensity was not random, and different types of teachers performed each treatment (university trainers for the more frequent treatment, regular community tutors for the other). No difference in outcome was obtained, after two terms of treatment, between the two treatment intensities.

COMMENT

It would seem reasonable to anticipate much activity in the empirical investigation of remedial teaching to children with reading retardation, since the problem of academically backward children who are not mentally retarded has been well recognized for a very long time; techniques for treating and studying it have been available for over a half century. It is therefore dismaying to confront the extraordinarily limited research done on this important issue, especially when one contemplates the enormous public resources allocated to remedial programs by school systems that, in their decision-making roles, essentially institutionalize ignorance. The dismay is accentuated when one considers the unfortunate children and their families who are consumers of current remedial practices.

Though tomes have appeared on sensory–motor training, the controlled studies are few. The little there is fails to support the clinical reports of this approach to ameliorate reading disorders, or, for that matter, to teach beginning readers (Robinson, 1972). It is unsettling that undocumented claims of efficacy for new sensory-training approaches still find their way into the literature (e.g., Schevill, 1978).

Similarly, in spite of extensive writings on the merits of contingent reinforcement in the teaching of reading, no systematic study has been undertaken to test these views.

The phonetic approach to teaching experienced an eclipse in the 1940s in favor of the whole-word or "look–say" approach, but has respectably reemerged. Neither has been well tested. Only one study (Gittelman & Feingold, 1983) has investigated the effect of the teaching of phonetic decoding in children with reading disorders. The results showed clear beneficial effects for this form of teaching; however, whether it is better than other instruction methods is unknown.

At this time, the usefulness of stimulant treatment in children with uncomplicated reading disorders appears limited. Whether this is also true for children with complicating behavior disorders, such as hyperkinesis, is not known.

The "linguistic" theory of reading has not been mentioned in this review. It has received much attention, probably attributable to the availability of the Illinois Test of Psycholinguistic Abilities (Kirk, McCarthy, & Kirk, 1968)—an instrument purported to assess linguistic skills. The reason for its omission is that the teaching program generated by the "linguistic" approach has not been investigated in children with reading disorders. Many studies have been done with normal school children. Hammill and Larsen (1974), who have reviewed this work, have concluded that the linguistic approach based on the Illinois Test has not been shown to be valid for diagnosing reading difficulties, or for the teaching of reading.

There have been refinements proposed in the classification of reading disorders (e.g., Boder, 1973; Kinsbourne, 1975; Mattis, French, & Rapin, 1975; Rourke, 1978; Satz, Friel, & Rudegeair, 1974; Satz, Rardin, & Ross, 1971); however, these have not generated specific treatment programs, despite the implicit (and at times explicit) claim that each form of reading disorder requires a different therapeutic strategy. Given the lack of empirical data concerning the interaction between diagnostic differentiations and treatment response, these classifications are not currently relevant to a discussion of treatment efficacy.

There is a very wide diversity of strategies for the treatment of reading disorders, such as the so-called Orton–Gillingham approach, which emphasizes the learning of letter sounds, blending, and decoding; the Fernald approach, in which tracing is a key component and teaching of whole words is pursued without consideration for the phonic components of written material; and the color phonics approach, in which different sounds are taught with the help of contrasting color codes. These techniques and others, as well as their respective shortcomings, are discussed by Johnson (1978) and Guthrie (1978). So far, no evidence exists indicating that any one method is best, either for groups of children, or for individual children with specific types of deficits. It cannot be argued that children with reading disorders are best helped with any of the therapies currently in vogue, nor that a child with impairment in auditory processing, for example, is best taught using the visual mode or any other form of treatment. There is a complete lack of evidence addressing the question of whether there exists an advantage of any one method over the others or whether certain children are more benefited by one teaching method than by others. Controlled studies concerning the issue of relative efficacy and specificity of various interventions are clearly needed.

The identification of discrete diagnostic subgroups of reading disorders is truly desirable. The overall group is most likely heterogeneous, and by generating a typology, chances of finding better specific treatments and possibly different antecedents may be enhanced. However, it is premature to imply that better treatment outcomes are possible with detailed diagnostic evaluation of the *type* of reading disorder (I am not referring to evaluation of reading ability or of decoding skills) based on performance on nonreading tests. Those who emphasize the need for the appraisal of skills other than reading (i.e., Bond & Tinker, 1973; Petrauskas & Rourke, 1979) for purposes of treatment have yet to demonstrate the merit of their views. Our recent study (Gittelman & Feingold, 1983) found improved reading performance with phonetic instruction, without regard to typology of the disorders.

Some investigators have urged the use of crossover ABAB designs to test the value of interventions in children with academic disorders (Barkley & Cunningham, 1978; Guralnick, 1978). The application of this design is especially inappropriate to the study of academic progress, since it is hoped that the treatment effects outlast the period of actual intervention, thereby making return to pretreatment levels unlikely. What are needed are random-assignment parallel-group designs, with large samples, that will allow a determination of interaction between type of reading disorders and treatment efficacy.

Anyone who approaches the field from previous experience in psychiatric research will have a thorough appreciation for how much costly professional behavior is perpetuated without critical concern for its efficacy or for the theories used to justify practice, and how mediocre much of what passes for research is. The literature on the treatment of children with reading retardation is full of opinionated practices devoid of even barely adequately controlled treatment research. In the field of psychiatric treatment, there are major methodological difficulties encountered in the assessment of patient characteristics (since one is often dealing with internal events), in the documentation of treatment procedures (especially for the psychotherapies), and in the evaluation of change. None of these impediments exist in the treatment evaluation of children with reading disorders. This realization is both depressing and encouraging—depressing, since in spite of these advantages, past performance is so poor; but encouraging, since it engenders the hope that well-executed treatment research is forthcoming.

Acknowledgments

This chapter was supported, in part, by United States Public Health Service Grant MH 18579.

References

Aman, M. G., & Werry, J. S. Methylphenidate and diazepam in severe reading retardation. *Journal of the American Academy of Child Psychiatry*, 1982, *21*, 31–37.

American Psychiatric Association. *Diagnostic and statistical manual of mental disorders* (3rd ed.). Washington, D.C.: Author, 1980.

Arnold, L. E., Barnebey, N., McManus, J., Smeltzer, D. J., Conrad, A., Winer, G., & Desgranges, L. Prevention by specific perceptual remediation for vulnerable first-graders. *Archives of General Psychiatry*, 1977, *34*, 1279–1294.

Balow, B., & Blomquist, M. Young adults ten to fifteen years after severe reading disability. *Elementary School Journal*, 1965, *66*, 44–48.

Barcai, A., Umbarger, C., Pierce, T. W., & Chamberlain, P. A comparison of three group approaches to under-achieving children. *American Journal of Orthopsychiatry*, 1973, *43*, 133–141.

Barkley, R., & Cunningham, C. Do stimulant drugs improve the academic performance of hyperkinetic children?: A review of outcome research. *Clinical Pediatrics*, 1978, *17*, 85–93.

Boder, E. Developmental dyslexia: A diagnostic approach based on three atypical reading–spelling patterns. *Developmental Medicine and Child Neurology*, 1973, *15*, 663–687.

Bond, G. L., & Tinker, M. A. *Reading diagnosis and correction*. New York: Appleton-Century-Crofts, 1973.

Camp, B. W., & van Doorninck, W. J. Assessment of "motivated" reading therapy with elementary school children. *Behavior Therapy*, 1971, *2*, 214–222.

Cashdan, A., & Pumfrey, P. D. Some effects of the remedial teaching of reading. In J. F. Reid (Ed.), *Reading problems and practices*. London: Ward Loch Educational, 1973.

Collette-Harris, M., & Minke, K. A. A behavioural experimental analysis of dyslexia. *Behaviour Research and Therapy*, 1978, *16*, 291–295.

Daniels, J. C., & Diack, H. *The standard reading tests*. London: Chatto & Windus, 1973.

Delacato, C. H. *The treatment and prevention of reading problems*. Springfield, Ill.: Charles C Thomas, 1959.

Delacato, C. H. *The diagnosis and treatment of speech and reading problems*. Springfield, Ill.: Charles C Thomas, 1963.

Delacato, C. H. *Neurological organization and reading*. Springfield, Ill.: Charles C Thomas, 1966.

Diack, H. *In spite of the alphabet: A study of the teaching of reading*. London: Chatto & Windus, 1965.

Douglas, V. I., & Peters, K. G. Toward a clearer definition of the attentional deficit of hyperactive children. In G. A. Hale & M. Lewis (Eds.), *Attention and the development of cognitive skills*. New York: Plenum Press, 1979.

Feldman, S. C., Schmidt, D. E., & Deutsch, C. P. Effects of auditory training on reading skills of retarded readers. *Perceptual and Motor Skills*, 1968, *26*, 467–480.

Fernald, G. M. *Remedial techniques in basic school subjects*. New York: McGraw-Hill, 1943.

Franenheim, J. G. Academic achievement characteristics of adult males who were diagnosed as dyslexic in childhood. *Journal of Learning Disorders*, 1978, *11*, 21–28.

Frostig, M. *Frostig move, grow, learn*. Chicago: Follett, 1969.

Gaddes, W. *Learning disabilities and brain function: A neuropsychological approach*. New York: Springer-Verlag, 1980.

Getman, G. N., Kan, E. R., Halgren, M. D., & McKee, G. W. *Developing reading readiness*. Manchester, Miss.: McGraw-Hill Webster Division, 1964.

Gittelman, R. Data do not always speak for themselves. *Archives of General Psychiatry*, 1978, *35*, 1394–1395. (Letter)

Gittelman, R. Indications for the use of stimulant treatment in learning disorders. *Journal of the American Academy of Child Psychiatry*, 1980, *19*, 623–636.

Gittelman, R., & Feingold, I. Children with reading disorders: I. Effects of reading instruction. *Journal of Child Psychology and Psychiatry*, 1983, *24*, 167–191.

Gittelman, R., Klein, D. F., & Feingold, I. Children with reading disorders: II. Effects of methylphenidate in combination with reading remediation. *Journal of Child Psychology and Psychiatry*, 1983, *24*, 193–212.

Gittelman-Klein, R., & Klein, D. F. Methylphenidate effects in learning disabilities. *Archives of General Psychiatry*, 1976, *33*, 655–664.

Guralnick, M. J. The application of single-subject research designs to the field of learning disabilities. *Journal of Learning Disabilities*, 1978, *11*, 415–421.

Guthrie, J. T. Principles of instruction: A critique of Johnson's "Remedial approaches to dyslexia." In A. L. Benton & D. Pearl (Eds.), *Dyslexia: An appraisal of current knowledge*. New York: Oxford University Press, 1978.

Guthrie, J. T., & Seifert, M. Education for children with reading disabilities. In H. R. Myklebust (Ed.), *Progress in learning disabilities* (Vol. 4). New York: Grune & Stratton, 1978.

Hagin, R. A., Silver, A. A., & Beecher, R. II. Teach: learning tasks for the prevention of learning disabilities. *Journal of Learning Disabilities*, 1978, *11*, 54–57.

Hammill, D. Training visual–perceptual processes. *Journal of Learning Disabilities*, 1972, *5*, 552–559.

Hammill, D. D., & Larsen, S. C. The effectiveness of psycholinguistic training. *Exceptional Children*, 1974, *41*, 5–14.

Hirsch, S. M., & Anderson, R. P. The effects of perceptual motor training on reading achievement. In R. P. Anderson & C. G. Halcomb (Eds.), *Learning disability/minimal brain dysfunction syndrome*. Springfield, Ill.: Charles C Thomas, 1976.

Huddleston, W., Staiger, R. C., Frye, R., Musgrave, R. S., & Stritch, T. Deanol as aid in overcoming reading retardation. *Clinical Medicine*, 1961, *8*, 1340–1342.

Huey, E. B. *The psychology and pedagogy of reading*. New York: Macmillan, 1908.

Johnson, D. J. Remedial approaches to dyslexia. In A. L. Benton & D. Pearl (Eds.), *Dyslexia: An appraisal of current knowledge*. New York: Oxford University Press, 1978.

Keogh, B. K. Optometric vision training programs for children with learning disabilities: Reviews of issues and research. *Journal of Learning Disabilities*, 1974, *7*, 36–48.

Kephart, N. C. *The slow learner in the classroom*. Columbus, Ohio: C. A. Merrill, 1960.

Kinsbourne, M. Cerebral dominance, learning, and cognition. In H. Myklebust (Ed.), *Progress in learning disabilities* (Vol. 3). New York: Grune & Stratton, 1975.

Kirk, S. A., McCarthy, J. J., & Kirk, W. D. *Illinois Test of Psycholinguistic Abilities*. Urbana: University of Illinois Press, 1968.

Klein, D. F., Gittelman, R., Quitkin, F., & Rifkin, A. *Diagnosis and drug treatment of psychiatric disorders: Adults and children*. Baltimore: Williams & Wilkins, 1980.

Kline, C., & Kline, C. Follow-up of 216 dyslexic children. *Bulletin of the Orton Society*, 1975, *25*, 127–144.

Lahey, B. B. Behavior modification with learning disabilities and related problems. In M. Hersen, R. M. Eisler, & P. M. Miller (Eds.), *Progress in behavior modification* (Vol. 3). New York: Academic Press, 1976.

Lovell, K., Byrne, C., Richardson, B. A further study of the educational progress of children who had received remedial education. *British Journal of Educational Psychology*, 1963, *33*, 3–9.

Lyon, R. Auditory–perceptual training: The state of the art. *Journal of Learning Disabilities*, 1977, *10*, 564–572.

Lytton, H. Follow-up of an experiment in selection for remedial education. *British Journal of Educational Psychology*, 1967, *37*, 1–9.

Mann, L. *On the trail of process: A historical perspective on cognitive processes and their training*. New York: Grune & Stratton, 1979.

Mattis, S., French, J., & Rapin, I. Dyslexia in children and young adults: Three independent neuropsychological syndromes. *Developmental Medicine and Child Neurology*, 1975, *17*, 150–163.

McCormick, C. C., Schnobrick, J. N., Footlick, S. W., & Poetker, B. Improvement in reading achievement through perceptual–motor training. *Research Quarterly*, 1968, *39*, 627–633.

Morgan, R., & Lyon, E. "Paired reading": A preliminary report on a technique for parental tuition of reading-retarded children. *Journal of Child Psychology and Psychiatry*, 1979, *20*, 151–160.

Muehl, S., & Forell, E. R. A follow-up study of disabled readers: Variables related to high-school reading performance. *Reading Research Quarterly*, 1973, *9*, 110–123.

O'Donnell, P. A., & Eisenson, J. Delacato training for reading achievement and visual–motor integration. *Journal of Learning Disabilities*, 1969, *2*, 441–447.

Petrauskas, R. J., & Rourke, B. P. Identification of subtypes of retarded readers: A neuropsychological, multivariate approach. *Journal of Clinical Neuropsychology*, 1979, *1*, 17–37.

Preston, R. C., & Yarrington, D. J. Status of fifty retarded readers eight years after reading clinic diagnosis. *Journal of Reading*, 1967, *11*, 122–129.

Rawson, M. B. *Developmental language disability: Adult accomplishments of dyslexic boys*. Baltimore: Johns Hopkins Press, 1968.

Robinson, H. M. Personality and reading. In A. E. Traxler (Ed.), *Modern educational problems*. Washington, D.C.: American Council on Education, 1953.

Robinson, H. M. Visual and auditory modalities related to methods for beginning readers. *Reading Research Quarterly*, 1972, *8*, 7–39.

Robinson, H. M., & Smith, H. K. Reading clinic clients: Ten years after. *Elementary School Journal*, 1962, *63*, 22–27.

Rourke, B. P. Reading, spelling, arithmetic disabilities: A neuropsychological perspective. In H. R. Myklebust (Eds.), *Progress in learning disabilities* (Vol. 4). New York: Grune & Stratton, 1978.

Rutter, M., & Yule, W. Reading difficulties. In M. Rutter & L. Hersov (Eds.), *Child psychiatry: Modern approaches*. Oxford: Blackwell Scientific Publications; Philadelphia: Lippincott, 1977.

Satz, P., Friel, J., & Rudegeair, F. Differential changes in the acquisition of developmental skills in children who later became dyslexic. In D. Stein, J. Rosen, & N. Butters (Eds.), *Plasticity and recovery of function in the central nervous system*. New York: Academic Press, 1974.

Satz, P., Rardin, D., & Ross, J. An evaluation of a theory of specific developmental dyslexia. *Child Development*, 1971, *42*, 2009–2021.

Schevill, H. S. Tactile learning and reading failure. In H. R. Myklebust (Ed.), *Progress in learning disabilities* (Vol. 4). New York: Grune & Stratton, 1978.

Schwartz, G. J. College students as contingency managers for adolescents in a program to develop reading skills. *Journal of Applied Behavioral Analysis*, 1977, *10*, 645–655.

Silver, A. A., Hagin, R. A., & Hersh, M. F. Reading disability: Teaching through stimulation of deficit perceptual areas. *American Journal of Orthopsychiatry*, 1967, *37*, 744–752.

Sprague, R. L., & Sleator, E. K. Methylphenidate in hyperkinetic children: Differences in dose effects on learning and social behavior. *Science*, 1977, *198*, 1274–1276.

Staats, A. W. *Learning, language, and cognition*. New York: Holt, Rinehart & Winston, 1968.

Staats, A. W. *Child learning, intelligence, and personality: Principles of a behavioral interaction approach*. New York: Harper & Row, 1971.

Staats, A. W. *Social behaviorism*. Homewood, Ill.: Dorsey Press, 1975.

Staats, A. W., Brewer, B. A., & Gross, M. Learning and cognitive development: Representative samples, cumulative-hierarchical learning, and experimental longitudinal methods. *Monographs of Society for Research in Child Development*, 1970, *35*(Serial No. 141).

Staats, A. W., & Butterfield, W. H. Treatment of nonreading in a culturally deprived juvenile delinquent: An application of reinforcement principles. *Child Development*, 1965, *36*, 925–942.

Staats, A. W., Minke, K. A., Finley, J. R., Wolf, M., & Brooks, L. O. A reinforcer system and experimental procedure for the laboratory study of reading acquisition. *Child Development*, 1964, *35*, 209–331.

Staats, A. W., Minke, K. A., Goodwin, W., & Landeen, J. Cognitive behaviour modification: "Motivated learning" reading treatment with sub-professional therapies by technicians. *Behaviour Research and Therapy*, 1967, *5*, 283–299.

Staats, A. W., & Staats, C. K. *Complex human behavior: A systematic extension of learning principles*. New York: Holt, Rinehart & Winston, 1963.

Staats, A. W., Staats, C. K., Schutz, R. E., & Wolf, M. The conditioning of textual responses using "extrinsic" reinforcement. *Journal of Experimental Analysis of Behavior*, 1962, *5*, 33–40.

Staats, A. W., Van Mondfrans, A. P., & Minke, K. A. *Manual of administration and recording methods for the Staats "motivated learning" reading procedure*. Madison: Wisconsin Research and Development Center for Cognitive Learning, 1967.

Swanson, J. M., & Kinsbourne, M. Stimulant related state-dependent learning in hyperactive children. *Science*, 1976, *192*, 1354–1357.

Tansley, A. D. *Reading and remedial reading*. London: Routledge & Kegan Paul, 1967.

Vernon, M. D. The effect of motivational and emotional factors on learning to read. In J. F. Reid (Ed.), *Reading: Problems and practices*. London: Ward Loch Educational, 1972.

CHAPTER TWENTY-EIGHT

Prognosis for Children with Learning Disabilities: A Review of Follow-Up Studies

STEVEN SCHONHAUT / PAUL SATZ

COMMON CLAIMS ABOUT THE PROGNOSIS OF LEARNING-DISABLED CHILDREN

Learning disabilities constitute a serious social problem of epidemic proportions. Prevalence rates in the United States are estimated to vary from 10 to 16% (Gaddes, 1976; Kline, 1972) and may be as high as 28% in urban populations (Eisenberg, 1966).

It is often thought that childhood learning disabilities represent just the beginning of lifelong difficulties. People claim that children with learning disorders are prone to become delinquent (Herjanic & Penick, 1972; Kline, 1972; Satz, Taylor, Friel, & Fletcher, 1978; Wright, 1974); to drop out of school (Herjanic & Penick, 1972; Kline, 1972; Satz *et al.*, 1978; Spreen, 1978); to develop emotional disorders (Eisenberg, 1966; Gaddes, 1976; Gates, 1968; Herjanic & Penick, 1972; Kline, 1972; Spreen, 1978); to have persistent academic problems (Carter, 1964; Dykman, Peters, & Ackerman, 1973; Gottesman, Belmont, & Kaminer, 1975; Hardy, 1968; Howden, 1967; Kline, 1972; Muehl & Forell, 1973; Rourke & Orr, 1977; Rutter, Tizard, Yule, Graham, & Whitmore, 1976; Satz *et al.*, 1978; Spreen, 1978; Trites & Fiedorowicz, 1976); and to end up in lower socioeconomic occupations (Eisenberg, 1966; Hardy, 1968; Howden, 1967; Spreen, 1978).

The strength of these views regarding poor prognosis is illustrated by the following quotations:

> Within the existing education systems across the nation . . . otherwise able students experience difficulty in learning to read. This difficulty is of sufficient severity to impair seriously the overall learning experience of these children and their ultimate usefulness and adaptability to modern society. . . . A student's initial failure in learning to read can have enormous consequences in terms of emotional maladjustment, tendency toward

Steven Schonhaut. Department of Clinical Psychology, J. Hillis Miller Mental Health Center, University of Florida, Gainesville, Florida.

Paul Satz. Neuropsychiatric Institute, University of California at Los Angeles, Los Angeles, California.

delinquency, likelihood of becoming a dropout, and difficulty in obtaining employment. The economic loss to the nation . . . is incalculable. (U.S. Department of Health, Education and Welfare, 1969, p. 8)

The Crime Study Commission in this report will attempt to go one step further in search for the cause of crime by postulating a theory which, simply stated, will argue that reading failure is the single most significant factor in those forms of delinquency which can be described as antisocial aggressive. (Wright, 1974, p. 4)

Studies have now shown that learning disorders which persist into late childhood and adolescence generally lead to serious emotional and behavioral disturbances which threaten the educational and social fabrics of our society. . . . Learning disorders, for example, now represent the major single cause of school dropouts in our educational system. . . . They also represent one of the major problems observed in referrals to clinics and juvenile courts. . . . It has been shown that many of the aggressive antisocial disturbances associated with learning disabilities, particularly in adolescence, may precede the development of schizophrenia in the adult. (Satz, 1977, p. 42)

The purpose of this chapter is to review the empirical evidence on the long-term outcome of learning disabilities. We include only studies focused on children with primary reading/learning problems. Those concerned with children labeled as having miminal brain dysfunction (MBD) or as hyperkinetic (e.g., Mendelson, Johnson, & Stewart, 1971; Menkes, Rowe, & Menkes, 1967) were excluded because of the secondary nature of the reading problems and the ambiguity concerning definition of the terms (Satz & Fletcher, 1980). Studies in which the primary purpose was to evaluate the effects of remedial treatment on learning-disabled children have also been excluded (e.g., Balow, 1965; Breuger, 1968; Knoppitz, 1971).

Some 18 follow-up studies, with a duration of 2 to 25 years, have been conducted on learning-disabled children. They vary markedly in terms of sample selection, sample size, criterion assessment measures, comparison groups, follow-up intervals, and outcome results (see Table 28-1).

The studies are evaluated in three ways. The first approach consists of a box-score count of outcome results (favorable, unfavorable, mixed) for all studies, independent of their scientific merit. The second approach involves a series of box-score counts for studies selected for merit on one of five methodological criteria (follow-up interval, sample size, sample representation, comparison group, criterion measure). The third approach represents an evaluation of outcome results for studies selected for merit, based on a composite scale derived from the preceding methodological criteria.

RESULTS

Overall Outcome Findings

The general outcome results, without weighing scientific merit, show that there were 4 favorable outcomes, 12 unfavorable outcomes, and 2 mixed outcomes. While the results show three times as many unfavorable outcomes, these findings could be misleading if the methodology of studies finding favorable outcomes is better than for those finding unfavorable outcomes. For this

Table 28-1. Follow-up studies

STUDY	SUBJECTS	*n*	FOLLOW-UP PERIOD	AGE OF SUBJECTS: AT INITIAL ASSESSMENT	AGE OF SUBJECTS: AT FOLLOW-UP
1. Robinson & Smith (1962)	Retarded readers	44	10 yr	Median age = 14; range 7–18	Median age = 24
2. Carter (1964)	Severely dyslexic readers	35	10–17 yr	Range 8–11	Mean age = 21.7
3. Silver & Hagin (1964)	Retarded readers; control group (with behavioral disorders)	Retarded, 24; control, 11	10–12 yr	Retarded, median age = 10; control, median age = 9	Mean age = 21
4. Balow & Blomquist (1965)	Disabled readers	32	10–15 yr	Median age = 11; range 7.7–13.5	Range 20–26
5. Howden (1967)	Poor readers; average readers; good readers	Poor, 22; average, 22; good, 9	Mean = 19 yr	Fifth or sixth grade	Range 29–35
6. Preston & Yarrington (1967)	Retarded readers	50	8 yr	Mean age = 12; range 6–17	Mean = 20; range 15–26
7. Hardy (1968)	Retarded readers	40	8 yr	Mean age = 11	Mean =19
8. Rawson (1968)	Dyslexic readers; average readers; superior readers	Dyslexic, 20; average, 16; superior, 20	18–35 yr	Range 6–8	Mean = 34.4; range 26–40
9. Dykman, Peters, & Ackerman (1973)	Learning-disabled readers; normal readers	Disabled, 31; normal, 21	2–4.5 yr	Mean = 10.5; range 9.5–12	14
10. Muehl & Forell (1973)	Retarded readers	43	5 yr	Mean = 11.5	Mean = 16.5
11. Gottesman, Belmont, & Kaminer (1975)	Disabled readers	58	3–5 yr	Range 7–14	Range 10–18
12. Kline & Kline (1975)	Treated dyslexics; untreated dyslexics	Treated, 140; untreated, 76	1–4 yr	Treated, range 5–17; untreated, range 5–17	Unknown for both groups

SOURCE OF SAMPLE	CONTROL GROUP	FOLLOW-UP MEASURES	OUTCOME RESULTS	EVALUATION OF GENERAL OUTCOME
Reading clinic	None	Interview or written questionnaire	Almost all graduated from high school; majority graduated from college; SES of occupations medium to high; adult reading—many above average.	Good
Reading clinic	None	Interviews	Two-thirds of the subjects were below class level in reading upon entering high school.	Poor
Mental hygiene clinic	Children referred to clinic for behavioral disorders	Neuropsychological tests; Wechsler Adult Intelligence Scale (WAIS); WRAT	Two-thirds of reading-retarded subjects became adequate readers; some neuropsychological differences between reading-disabled children and controls persisted in adulthood.	Mixed
Psychoeducational clinic	None	Interviews; Gates Reading Survey; MMPI	Most subjects graduated from high school; many held skilled jobs; slight evidence of emotional disturbance on MMPI.	Good
Springfield (Oregon) elementary school	Average and above-average readers	Interview; Gates Reading Survey	Poor childhood readers were worse adult readers, had lower-SES jobs, got less formal education, and dropped out of school at a higher rate.	Poor
Reading clinic	National averages	Interviews	Percentages of subjects graduating from high school, attending college, holding white-collar jobs, and being unemployed did not differ from national averages; more were left back a grade than national averages.	Good
Education clinic	None	Interviews; reading and spelling tests	Reading retardation at follow-up was worse than that at initial assessment; dropout rate was excessive; majority were in unskilled or semiskilled jobs; follow-up was best for young referrals.	Poor
School for Rose Valley (Pennsylvania)	Average and superior readers	Interviews	Of 20 dyslexic subjects, 18 graduated from college; years of education and adult SES were not significantly different for dyslexics and nondyslexics	Good
Learning-disabled children were identified by school guidance team; normal children were selected by teachers	Normal readers	WRAT; WISC; Gray Oral Reading; Bender–Gestalt; MCI; interviews	Learning-disabled children were behind in grade placement, had more failures, lower Gray reading scores, more neurological "soft signs," lower WISC, more signs of psychopathology on the MCI; teachers reported that learning-disabled children had more problems.	Poor
Reading clinic	None	Iowa Tests of Educational Development	Subjects were uniformly poor readers at follow-up; results at follow-up were somewhat better for younger referrals.	Poor
Medical clinic	None	WRAT reading subtest	Subjects fell further behind in percentile on WRAT reading test; children improved 3.8 months in reading level for every year.	Poor
Medical clinic	Untreated or school-treated dyslexics	WRAT; IOTA; parental telephone interviews	Some to dramatic improvement in 96% of dyslexics in Orton–Gillingham program; improvement in only 45% of dyslexics in untreated or school-treated programs. Parental telephone interviews yielded similar results for both groups. Orton–Gillingham treatment ranged from 3–36 months, with better outcome related to length of treatment.	Mixed

(continued)

Table 28-1. (Continued)

STUDY	SUBJECTS	*n*	FOLLOW-UP PERIOD	AGE OF SUBJECTS: AT INITIAL ASSESSMENT	AGE OF SUBJECTS: AT FOLLOW-UP
13. Rutter, Tizard, Yule, Graham, & Whitmore (1976)	Reading-retarded children; Reading-backward children; normal controls	Retarded, 86; backward, 155; normal, 184	5 yr	Range 9–10	Range 14–15
14. Trites & Fiedorowicz (1976)	Boys with specific reading disability; learning-disabled children with neurological impairment	Disability, 27; impairment, 10	Disability, mean = 2.5 yr; impairment, mean = 2.8 yr	Disability, mean = 11.6; impairment, mean = 11.5	Disability, mean = 14.1; impairment, mean = 14.3
15. Rourke & Orr (1977)	Retarded readers; normal readers	Retarded, 19; normal, 23	4 yr	Range 7.3–8.3	Mean = 12
16. Ackerman, Dykman, & Peters (1977)	Learning-disabled readers; normal readers	Disabled, 62; normal, 31	2–6 yr	Range 8–11.9	14
17. Satz, Taylor, Friel, & Fletcher (1978)	Severely disabled readers; mildly disabled readers; average readers; superior readers	Severe, 49; mild, 62; average, 252; superior, 63	3 yr	Second grade	Fifth grade
18. Spreen (1978)	Learning-disabled children with at least one neurological "hard sign" or at least three "soft signs"; learning-disabled children with one or two neurological "soft signs"; learning-disabled children with no neurological signs; average learners	Learning-disabled/damaged, 64; learning-disabled/"soft signs," 82; learning-disabled/no signs, 57; average, 52	At least 11 yr; mean = 10 yr	Range 8–10	Mean = 18.74; range 13–25

SOURCE OF SAMPLE	CONTROL GROUP	FOLLOW-UP MEASURES	OUTCOME RESULTS	EVALUATION OF GENERAL OUTCOME
Isle of Wight population	Average readers	Short WISC; Neale Analysis of Reading; Schonell Spelling; Vernon Math	At follow-up, almost all subjects in both reading-disability groups continued to be poor readers, as well as doing poorly in spelling and math.	Poor
Neuropsychological clinic	None	WISC; Peabody Picture Vocabulary Test (PPVT); WRAT; Halstead–Reitan tests	Subjects in all groups fell further behind grade level in reading, math, and spelling than they were at initial assessment.	Poor
Urban elementary school	Normal readers	Metropolitan Achievement Tests (MAT); PPVT; WISC; Underlining Test; WRAT reading and spelling subtests	Retarded readers at follow-up were worse on WRAT reading and spelling than they were initially.	Poor
Learning-disabled children were identified by school guidance team; normal children were selected by teachers	Normal readers	Grade placement WRAT; Gray Oral Reading; handwriting speed; silent reading speed; WISC	Learning-disabled children were behind in grade placement and had more failures, lower Gray reading scores, lower WRAT scores, lower WISC scores; slower writing speed; and slower silent reading speed.	Poor
Alachua County (Florida) schools	Average and superior readers	Fifth-grade classroom reading-level classification as severely disabled, mildly disabled, average, or superior readers according to strict criteria	Group membership in second grade strongly predicted group membership in fifth grade; few severely or mildly disabled readers improved, though a sizable number of average readers developed problems.	Poor
Learning-disabled children attended both a neuropsychological clinic and an education clinic; average learners were selected from classrooms by teachers	Average learners	Structured interviews with subjects and parents; permanent school record card; behavior rating scale filled out by parents; Personal Adjustment Inventory; rating of interview behavior of subjects	Average learners attended school longer and more went to college than all learning-disabled groups; more behavior problems reported for learning-disabled subjects; more learning-disabled subjects had seen a psychologist or psychiatrist; more learning-disabled children had been suspended from school at some time; job satisfaction was lower for average learners; more dating by average learners; no difference in amount of police contact by subjects; many trends toward worse outcomes by learning-disabled children with neurological signs (learning-disabled/damaged worse than learning-disabled/"soft signs" worse than learning-disabled/no neurological signs).	Poor

reason, it is important to identify a set of minimally sufficient criteria that should be employed in a follow-up study of learning-disabled children. These criteria could then be used in either of two ways: (1) to evaluate those studies that satisfied one of the methodological criteria (e.g., long follow-up interval or large sample size), or (2) to evaluate only those studies that satisfied a majority of the methodological criteria.

Outcome Findings from Studies Meeting Five Crucial Criteria

The five criteria considered crucial in follow-up research are these: (1) an adequate follow-up period, (2) a sufficiently large sample size, (3) a satisfactory method of sample selection, (4) an adequate comparison group, and (5) a valid and objective measure of reading/learning ability.

Follow-Up Interval

An adequate follow-up period should tell us the adult outcome of early school-age children with specific learning disabilities. Thus, a well-designed study should begin when a child enters elementary school and should extend at least until the child reaches age 20. Studies that start with children at a later age may be studying a biased sample (i.e., unremitting cases). Studies terminating before adulthood may provide limited information on ultimate adjustment.

A modified box score may be obtained by counting only those studies that had an adequate follow-up period. Considering only studies that followed children from age 8 to beyond age 20, there is just the Rawson (1968) report that gives a favorable outcome. Counting those studies that had a follow-up period of at least 10 years, the totals are three favorable outcomes (*1*, *4*, *8*), three unfavorable outcomes (*2*, *5*, *18*), and 1 mixed outcome (*3*). (The italicized numbers in parentheses following these outcome totals indicate which studies, using the numbers assigned in the left-hand column of Table 28-1, are counted in each total.) When all studies with a follow-up period of at least 5 years are counted, the score is four favorable outcomes (*1*, *4*, *6*, *8*), six unfavorable outcomes (*2*, *5*, *7*, *10*, *13*, *18*), and one mixed outcome (*3*). Thus, limiting the box counts to just those studies with extended follow-up periods reveals a balance between favorable and unfavorable outcomes.

Sample Size

There is no magic number of subjects necessary for a meaningful study. Nonetheless, a large sample does protect against some of the sampling artifacts inherent in small samples. Counting only studies with at least 100 subjects, we find there are no favorable outcomes, three unfavorable outcomes (*13*, *17*, *18*), and one mixed outcome (*12*). Including all studies with 50 or more subjects brings the total to two favorable outcomes (*6*, *8*), seven unfavorable outcomes (*5*, *9*, *11*, *13*, *16*, *17*, *18*), and one mixed outcome (*12*). Thus, larger studies show less favorable outcomes.

Method of Sample Selection

The sampling procedure by which subjects are selected determines the generality of results from a study. The ideal sample is an entire school population. Next best is a sample drawn from a large school population. Least desirable is a sample taken from a clinic, since this sample will probably be biased by the nature of the clinic. Counting only studies that used the population of an entire school reveals one favorable (*8*) and three unfavorable (*5*, *13*, *17*) outcomes. Inclusion of studies drawing their samples from a whole school population brings the totals to one favorable (*8*) and six unfavorable (*5*, *9*, *13*, *15*, *16*, *17*) outcomes. Thus, those studies that used the most representative samples found a majority of unfavorable outcomes.

Comparison Group

An adequate control group is a necessary yardstick for comparison. Only by knowing the relative outcomes of learning-disabled children, as measured against those of nondisabled children, can one make appropriate statements regarding the prognosis of learning-disabled children. Among studies that had an adequate control group of normal children, the box score is one favorable outcome (*8*) and seven unfavorable outcomes (*5*, *9*, *13*, *15*, *16*, *17*, *18*). Counting all studies that attempted to compare learning-disabled chilren to some sort of reference group, the totals are two favorable outcomes (*6*, *8*), seven unfavorable outcomes (*5*, *9*, *13*, *15*, *16*, *17*, *18*), and two mixed outcomes (*3*, *12*). Controlled studies show that outcomes for learning-disabled children tend to be unfavorable.

Valid Reading Learning Measures

Clear-cut definitional criteria for classifying a child as learning disabled are necessary for interpreting the meaning of results. Vague criteria make it impossible to determine the nature of samples, and thereby to interpret the meaning and generality of results. Particularly distressing is the complete absence of any formal criteria for classification, such as is found in many clinic samples that regard referral to the clinic as sufficient for diagnosis. Counting only studies with well-defined objective criteria provides no favorable outcomes, three unfavorable outcomes (*13*, *15*, *17*), and one mixed outcome (*12*). Including all studies that made some attempt at a systematic definition, the score is five unfavorable outcomes (*5*, *13*, *14*, *15*, *17*), three favorable outcomes (*4*, *6*, *8*), and one mixed outcome (*12*). Thus those studies that were most careful in their selection criteria showed a preponderance of unfavorable outcomes.

As a whole, these methodologically restricted box scores suggest that unfavorable outcomes for children with learning disabilities predominate. Large studies using well-chosen samples, adequate control groups, and clearly defined criteria for learning disabilities have usually found poor outcomes. The major limitation of the studies reporting poor outcomes is the inadequate length of the follow-up period. Thus, while the short-term prognosis for learning disabled children seems generally unfavorable, the long-term prognosis may be better.

It has been noted, however, that conclusions drawn from the box-score method are themselves limited. Important details of the studies are omitted. Methodologically weak studies may receive more weight than they deserve. Also, the box-score method treats results in terms of general criteria, without specifying the specific educational, occupational, social, and emotional outcome variables. As such, it is unclear whether learning disabilities lead to school dropout, delinquency, or psychiatric problems. Furthermore, even modified box scores do not give a full indication of the methodological merit of individual studies. To evaluate the outcome results separately for each of the methodological criteria could lead to misleading conclusions if there was significant variability within studies on each of the criteria (e.g., an adequate follow-up interval, but no control group or objective reading measure). Closer inspection of the better designed studies is necessary to make more definitive statements about the prognosis of learning-disabled children.

Findings from the Five Most Adequate Studies

Unfortunately, each of the follow-up studies is flawed on at least one of the methodological criteria mentioned above. They also vary considerably in overall quality of design. Thus, there is no definitive study to which one can turn for answers. To evaluate the aggregate methodological merits of each study, a crude scale, based on the five major criteria discussed in the previous section, was developed. Criteria for the scale are given in Table 28-2. While this scale is admittedly crude, it provides some notion of the overall merit of each of the 18 studies. The rating of each of the studies on this scale is presented in Table 28-3.

Five studies were shown to be methodologically superior to the rest. These five studies—Rawson (1968), Howden (1967), Spreen (1978), Rutter *et al.* (1976), and Satz *et al.* (1978)—are discussed here at some length. Close attention is paid to the specific findings, implications, and weaknesses in each of these studies. The box score for these five studies is one favorable outcome (*8*) and four unfavorable outcomes (*5*, *13*, *17*, *18*). If one compares these box-score outcomes with the remaining 13 studies, it can be seen (see Table 28-4) that unfavorable outcomes prevail, regardless of methodological merit. However,

Table 28-2. Scale of criteria for rating follow-up studies

CRITERIA	SCORE
I. Length of follow-up period	
A. Follow-up from before age 8 to after age 20	3
B. Follow-up period at least 10 years	2
C. Follow-up period at least 5 years	1
D. Follow-up period less than 5 years	0
II. Size of sample	
A. At least 100 subjects	2
B. At least 50 subjects	1
C. Less than 50 subjects	0
III. Adequacy of sampling procedure	
A. Population consisting of entire school class(es)	2
B. Sample drawn from an entire school class	1
C. Clinic sample	0
IV. Adequacy of control	
A. Matched control group of average readers	2
B. Some control group or means of comparison	1
C. No control group	0
V. Adequacy of criteria for defining learning disabilities	
A. Objective well-defined criteria	2
B. Some attempt at systematic definitional criteria	1
C. No attempt at systematic definitional criteria (e.g., vague criteria, diagnosis according to referral problem, etc.)	0

Table 28-3. Methodological rating of studies

STUDY	CRITERIA[a] I	II	III	IV	V	COMPOSITE TOTAL
1. Robinson & Smith (1962)	2	0	0	0	0	2
2. Carter (1964)	2	0	0	0	0	2
3. Silver & Hagin (1964)	2	0	0	1	0	3
4. Balow & Blomquist (1965)	2	0	0	0	1	3
5. Howden (1967)	2	1	2	2	1	8
6. Preston & Yarrington (1967)	1	1	0	1	1	4
7. Hardy (1968)	1	0	0	0	0	1
8. Rawson (1968)	3	1	2	2	1	9
9. Dykman, Peters, & Ackerman (1973)	0	1	1	2	0	4
10. Muehl & Forell (1973)	1	0	0	0	0	1
11. Gottesman, Belmont, & Kaminer (1975)	0	1	0	0	0	1
12. Kline & Kline (1975)	0	2	0	1	2	5
13. Rutter, Tizard, Yule, Graham, & Whitmore (1976)	1	2	2	2	2	9
14. Trites & Fiedorowicz (1976)	0	0	0	0	1	1
15. Rourke & Orr (1977)	0	0	1	2	2	5
16. Ackerman, Dykman, & Peters (1977)	0	0	1	2	2	5
17. Satz, Taylor, Friel, & Fletcher (1978)	0	2	2	2	2	8
18. Spreen (1978)	2	2	0	2	0	6

[a]I, length of follow-up period; II, size of sample; III, adequacy of sampling procedure; IV, adequacy of control; V, adequacy of criteria for defining learning disabilities.

an interaction seems to exist. Three of the four favorable outcomes involved weaker studies, and four of the five stronger studies revealed unfavorable outcomes.

Rawson (1968) is one of the most widely quoted follow-up studies on learning disabilities. The 56 subjects in this study represented all of the boys who attended the School for Rose Valley (Pennsylvania) for at least 3 years between 1930 and 1947. These subjects were rated by Rawson according to the Language-Learning Facility Scale, a largely subjective instrument developed by the author.

In 1964–1965, Rawson interviewed the subjects when they were aged 26 to 40. She reported that 18 of the 20 dyslexic children had graduated from college and had had an average of 6.02 years post-high-school education. This was slightly, but nonsignificantly, higher than the 5.45 years of post-high-school education obtained by the top 20 children on the Language-Learning Facility Scale.

The occupational achievement of Rawson's dyslexic subjects was also on a par with the average and above-average readers. The mean socioeconomic status (SES) of the dyslexics did not differ from the better readers; again, the difference was not significant. A majority of subjects in all of Rawson's groups fell into either SES Class I (professional or higher business) or Class II (subprofessional or middle business).

From these results, Rawson concluded that dyslexic children had a favorable prognosis. Several aspects of Rawson's study, however, restrict the gen-

Table 28-4. Outcome by methodological merit

STUDIES	OUTCOME GOOD	MIXED	POOR
Strong[a]	1		4
Weak	3	2	8
Total	4	2	12

[a]Composite score $\geq$ 6.

erality of her findings. First, Rawson's sample consisted of extremely bright children from upper-class and upper-middle-class families. The Binet IQs of the children ranged from 94 to 185, with a mean of 130.8. No fewer than 46 of the children had fathers in SES Class I. Moreover, Rawson's criteria for classifying a child as "dyslexic" are unclearly specified. Therefore, it is not known whether some of these children would have been labeled "dyslexic" on more objective criteria. It is clear that Rawson's subjects are not representative of the average dyslexic child; while the study was based on an entire school population, that population was unlike the population of schoolchildren at large.

One may conclude from the Rawson study that intelligent, middle-class elementary-school children with some degree of reading difficulties may, with adequate opportunities, become productive adults. The study, however, is limited in its generality, and as such does not tell us about the prognosis of less privileged dyslexic children.

Howden (1967) followed up 53 children who attended fifth- or sixth-grade classes in Springfield, Oregon, in 1942. The sample consisted of 22 "poor" readers, 22 "average" readers, and 9 "superior" readers. Classification into these categories was based on the relative reading performance of the students. Subjects more than 1 *SD* below the class mean were classified as poor readers, and those falling into the middle were considered average readers. Subjects were followed an average of 19 years later when they were from 29 to 35 years old. Follow-up assessment consisted of an interview and the Gates Reading Survey.

Results showed that the poor readers did not do as well on the Gates as the average and superior readers did. They also received fewer years of formal schooling and were more likely to have dropped out prior to graduating from high school. Likewise, the occupational status of the poor readers was below that of the average and superior readers. Howden's results apparently argue for a poor prognosis for reading-disabled children. There are, however, some reservations concerning this conclusion. For one, the SES of Howden's poor readers as *children* was lower than that of his average and superior readers. This is a serious confound. If high SES predicts good outcome (Rawson, 1968), then low SES may predict bad outcome, independent of childhood reading ability. What may be concluded, then, from this study is that children of lower SES who are also poor readers will tend to have poorer outcomes than higher-SES students who are better readers—which does not say very much.

The longitudinal project by Spreen (1978) provides the most extensive data gathered at follow-up. Subjects in this study were learning-disabled children who were referred to the University of Victoria (British Columbia) Neuropsychology Clinic and the Nanaimo School District Educational Clinic. The mean age of these children when they were first seen was 9, and the average length of the follow-up period was 10 years.

Spreen divided the learning-disabled children into three groups, depending on the presence and severity of neurological signs. The first group contained children with at least one neurological "hard sign" or at least three "soft signs"; the second group was comprised of children with one or two neurological "soft signs"; the third group consisted of children with no neurological signs. These three groups of learning-disabled children were compared with a control group of normal achievers, who were randomly selected by teachers. Structured interviews were conducted with both the subjects and their parents. Additional information was gathered from the Permanent (School) Report Card, a behavioral rating scale filled out by parents, the Personal Adjustment Inventory, and ratings of subjects' interview behavior.

It was found that in most aspects of educational, occupational, social, and psychological adjustment the outcome of learning-disabled children was worse than that of control-group children. For instance, Spreen reported that control-group children had attended school longer, had liked school better, had higher salaries, dated more often, and were less likely to have received psychological or psychiatric help than learning-disabled children were likely to have done. There were many significant trends toward better outcomes for learning-disabled children with less neurological involvement.

The major limitations of the study are that it used a clinic sample, and that it lacked strict criteria for classifying children as "learning disabled." Because of this, the external validity of Spreen's findings is limited; since the composition of the sample is unclear, it is difficult to generalize its findings to learning-disabled children at large. Despite those limitations, the study is valuable because it provides information on many areas of adjustment lacking in most other follow-up studies. In addition, it suggests that the presence and degree of neurological signs in learning-disabled children may be an important factor relating to prognosis.

Rutter *et al.* (1976) conducted a survey of children aged 9–10 who lived on the Isle of Wight in 1964–1965. These subjects were classified as "reading-backward," "specifically reading-retarded," or "normal" readers. Children were considered "reading backward" if they were at least 28 months below age-level reading, while they were labeled "reading retarded" only if they were 28 months below their expected age level and mental level (based on IQ). There was considerable overlap between the two reading-disabled groups, with 76 of the 86 reading-retarded children also being counted amongst the 155 reading-backward children. The control group of 184 normal 9- to 10-year-old readers was a random sample selected from the remainder of the Isle of Wight population.

These children were followed up 5 years later at ages 14–15. Follow-up measures included a short form of the Wechsler Intelligence Scale for Children (WISC), the Neale Analysis of Reading Ability, the Schonell Spelling Test, and the Vernon Arithmetic–Mathematics Test. It was found that 56% of the backwardness group and 58% of the retarded group were more than 2 *SD* below the mean in reading achievement. Also, only 4% of the backward readers and 2.5% of the retarded readers were at or above the age-level mean. The mean reading level for the combined group of disabled readers was that of the average 9-year-old, and spelling scores were even worse. Mathematics achievement of the disabled readers was also significantly below that of controls, although it was somewhat higher than the reading and spelling levels of these subjects. Compared to the reading-backwardness group, children with specific reading retardation showed (from ages 9–10 to 14–15) less improvement in spelling and reading, but more improvement in mathematics.

This landmark study appears to provide solid evidence that children who are severely disabled readers in middle childhood will continue to be disabled readers in adolescence. Indeed, the disabled readers fell, over the course of the follow-up period, even further behind grade-level reading than they were at the outset of the study. The Rutter *et al.* study also provides evidence that reading disability may not represent an isolated deficit and may be associated with deficits in related academic areas, such as spelling and math. Similar observations have been reported in the Florida Longitudinal Project (Satz & Morris, 1981; Satz *et al.*, 1978). The differences at follow-up in the Rutter *et al.* study between the reading-backward and the reading-retarded subjects indicate that subtyping of learning-disabled subjects may provide useful prognostic information (i.e., the outlook for all learning-disabled children may not be the same). In summary, it may be concluded from this study that the academic prognosis for severely disabled readers aged 9–10 is poor.

The major weakness of the Rutter *et al.* study is the length of the follow-up period. Children with learning disabilities who are younger than 9 or 10 may have a better prognosis. Also, the adult prognosis for disabled readers may be better than the adolescent academic status would indicate. While it is reasonable to speculate that 14-year-old children reading at a 9-year-old level may tend to avoid college or drop out of school, it is still speculation. Moreover, with regard to the adult occupational, emotional, and social adjustment of these children, even less can be said. Despite these limitations, the Rutter *et al.* study provides valuable data on the prognosis of learning-disabled children.

Satz *et al.* (1978) conducted a longitudinal study on the entire population of white male students entering kindergarten in Alachua County (Florida) public schools in 1970. Satz *et al.* obtained objective measures of second-grade classroom reading achievement and, based on these measures, classified subjects as "severely retarded" readers, "mildly retarded" readers, "average" readers, or "superior" readers. Out of a total of 426 students, 49 were considered severely retarded, 62 mildly retarded, 252 average, and 63 superior readers.

Follow-up of these children was conducted 3 years later at the end of fifth grade. Again, objective measures of classroom reading were obtained, and children were classified as severely retarded, mildly retarded, average, or superior readers. Of the 49 children classified as severely retarded readers at the end of second grade, only 6% were average or above-average readers at the end of fifth grade. Also, only 17.7% of the mildly retarded readers were average or above in the fifth grade. Meanwhile, 30% of the average second-grade readers were mildly or severely disabled readers by the end of fifth grade. Only 3% of the superior second-grade readers were at all disabled in fifth grade. Similar findings were also reported using Wide-Range Achievement Test (WRAT) reading level scores as criteria; children who did poorly on the WRAT in second grade continued to do poorly in fifth grade.

Results of the Satz *et al.* study suggest a grim prognosis for children having reading problems as early as second grade; very few children who had difficulty reading in second grade reached grade level by fifth grade. In contrast, several children who were average readers in second grade developed reading problems by fifth grade.

The major limitation of the Satz *et al.* study is the short follow-up period. However, in conjunction with the Rutter *et al.* results, the Satz *et al.* study suggests that children who encounter reading problems in second grade may often have serious academic problems, encompassing reading, spelling, and mathematics, as adolescents.

CONCLUSIONS

Socioeconomic Status

One reasonably firm conclusion from this set of studies is that SES is a powerful variable, related both to the initial probability of developing learning problems, and to academic prognosis when learning disabilities do develop. Lower-class youngsters are more likely to experience learning difficulties, and when they do develop learning difficulties, their academic prognosis is worse than that of middle- and upper-class children.

Evidence for the conclusion that SES is strongly related to learning disabilities is widespread. The SES variable may explain the superior outcome of Rawson's (1968) dyslexic subjects. Also, Satz and Morris (1981) reported that children in the Florida Longitudinal Project, classified as learning-disabled on the basis of a cluster analysis of fifth-grade WRAT scores, came from significantly lower-SES backgrounds than did children classified as non-learning-disabled. Similarly, Muehl and Forell (1973) found that higher parental occupation was associated with better follow-up reading scores among initially disabled readers. In a large-scale epidemiological study, Eisenberg (1966) reported that 28% of the public-school children in sixth grade in an urban American city were reading 2 or more years below their expected level. By comparison, only 3% of children in a nearby suburban school system and none of the children in private schools in the same city suffered from a reading lag of 2 or more years. From this data, Eisenberg concluded that sociopsychological factors were a major cause of reading disability. The data seem clear on the SES factor—it is a powerful variable moderating the reading potential of children. As such, future researchers are advised to report the SES status of disabled readers, and to control carefully for or take statistical account of the confounding effect of SES on follow-up outcome.

A second finding with considerable support is that early learning disabilities signal a poor prognosis for future academic studies. However, high SES may attenuate this prediction (Rawson, 1968; Robinson & Smith, 1962). This means that the average child with learning difficulties in elementary school will tend to have persistent academic problems (Carter, 1964; Dykman *et al.*, 1973; Gottesman *et al.*, 1975; Hardy, 1968; Howden, 1967; Muehl & Forell, 1973; Rourke & Orr, 1977; Rutter *et al.*, 1976; Satz *et al.*, 1978; Spreen, 1978; Trites & Fiedorowicz, 1976). Moreover, academic troubles are generally not limited to one subject area (Dykman *et al.*, 1973; Fitzsimmons, Cheever, Leonard, & Macunovich, 1969; Rourke & Orr, 1977; Rutter *et al.*, 1976; Satz *et al.*, 1978; Trites & Fiedorowicz, 1976).

With respect to the long-term follow-up on academic skills, there is evidence that reading-disabled children who are successful as adults may still have lifelong problems in using language. Rawson (1968) noted that despite occupational and educational success, dyslexic children as adults were poorer in reading and spelling than their peers who were average to superior readers as children were. Furthermore, Thompson (1971) reported that prominent individuals who achieved eminence as adults despite being dyslexic as children had persistent language difficulties in adulthood, especially in spelling. From this, it may be speculated that childhood learning disabilities, even when they do not hinder adult success, rarely are fully overcome. Naturally, anecdotal reports of this kind suffer from the bias of excluding unremitting cases or individuals who, because of occupational failure (and reading problems), never attained eminence.

School Dropout

While children with learning disabilities appear to have persistent academic problems, the question of whether they drop out of school more often (and if so, how much more often) is a separate issue. Inferentially, one would expect a strong association between academic difficulties and school dropout. There are, however, few data on the subject. Rutter *et al.* (1976) conducted a cross-sectional survey of 14- to 15-year-olds on the Isle of Wight. It was reported that twice as many poor readers as good readers *intended* to drop out of school at the first opportunity. While this provides some support for the connection between early learning disabilities and school dropout, it does not actually tell us what the relative dropout rates are for learning-disabled and normal children. One might expect, once again, that SES would be a strong moderating variable interacting with academic achievement in predicting dropout. For this reason, Howden's (1967) finding that lower-SES poor readers dropped out of school more frequently than higher-SES average and superior readers did is not particularly informative. At the present time, the contention that early learning disabilities lead to dropout appears to depend on the indirect evidence that links early learning disorders to persistent academic problems.

Occupational Achievement

Evidence on the occupational status of learning-disabled children is sparse. All of the studies that have followed learning-disabled children into adulthood have limitations. The inferential leap from academic failure at ages 14–15 to occupational failure in adulthood is a long one.

One approach to the question of the occupational prognosis of learning-disabled children has been through the use of testimonials. For instance, Thompson (1971) reported outstanding adult achievements among a very special subgroup of reading-disabled children—a subgroup that included Albert Einstein, Thomas Edison, and Woodrow Wilson. From this, Thompson inferred that the outlook for dyslexic children may be hopeful. However, testimonials are inferentially biased, and, as such, they do not tell us anything about the prognosis of the average learning-disabled child. Well-controlled follow-up studies, not testimonials, are needed to determine the occupational prognosis of learning-disabled children.

It may be speculated from the high-school academic failure of learning-disabled children that, despite the testimonials of Thompson (1971), most learning-disabled children will not enter careers demanding intellectual excellence. Current evidence, however, on the occupational status achieved by learning-disabled children is inconclusive. Only three follow-up studies with control groups have examined occupational status. Rawson (1968) found that upper-class dyslexic children attained occupational standing equal to that of nondyslexic children. Howden (1967) reported that poor readers from lower-SES backgrounds ended up in lower-SES jobs than did good readers from high-SES backgrounds. Finally, Spreen (1978) found no significant differences in job status between learning-disabled subjects and average readers.

In evaluating the overall occupational outcome of learning-disabled children, including SES, it is important to assess things such as job satisfaction, job salaries, and adult unemployment rates. The broadest assessment of occupational parameters, to date, has been that of Spreen (1978). In this study, it was reported that average readers had slightly higher salaries than learning-disabled subjects did. But, surprisingly, Spreen also found that self-reported job satisfaction was higher for learning-disabled subjects than for average readers.

One possible explanation for this paradoxical finding is that the average readers found their jobs less challenging than did the learning-disabled subjects; both held the same level of jobs. Perhaps with a mean age of $18^1/_2$ years at follow-up, there had been little time for the average readers to advance beyond low-level jobs. A demanding job for the learning-disabled subjects may have been quite boring for the average readers. This paradoxical finding on job satisfaction indicates the need to assess not only occupational status but also occupational adjustment. However, further research is needed both to replicate the findings and to test the suggested explanation.

Also, there is a need for longer follow-up periods to assess adult occupational prognosis. A follow-up period extending at least to ages 25–30 would appear to be necessary to get a meaningful assessment of long-range adult occupational outcome. By that age, many more subjects will have settled into permanent careers. As such, the differences in occupational status and job adjustment between learning-disabled and normal subjects will reflect lifelong trends better than they do at an earlier age. It is hoped that the Spreen project will eventually provide occupational data on its subjects at a later age.

Age of Diagnosis

Another undecided issue is whether early identification of learning disabilities leads to a better prognosis than does late identification. This question is essentially concerned with whether early treatment of learning-disabled children can improve their prognosis. Certainly, any optimist would like to believe so. SES data seem to provide some indirect evidence that early identification can benefit learning disabled children: this point assumes that the success of high-SES children with early learning problems is largely due to well-planned remediation. Additionally, two studies (Hardy, 1968; Muehl & Forell, 1973) have reported that the youngest children at the time of initial assessment showed the greatest amount of academic progress at follow-up—although Gottesman *et al.* (1975) and Kline and Kline (1975) found the opposite. Thus, there is some empirical evidence, some inferential logic, and much hope that early identification of learning-disabled children can lead to a better prognosis.

Treatment Effects

Virtually none of the studies have focused on the effects of treatment on follow-up outcome. Although presumably many of the learning-disabled children in these studies have been exposed to various remediation techniques, those treatments have varied in length, intensity, and method and have not been evaluated with respect to differential outcome. An exception is the study by Kline and Kline (1975), which compared the effects of the Orton–Gillingham method on a large sample of dyslexic children (140) with an untreated or school-treated sample of dyslexic children ($n = 76$). The treatment interval ranged from 3 to 36 months in each group (Orton vs. school treatment). Outcome results (WRAT, IOTA, parental telephone interviews) were obtained from 1 to 4 years after initial testing and/or intervention. The results were mixed and varied as a function of treatment. Improvement, ranging from slight to dramatic, was observed in 96% of the cases receiving the Orton–Gillingham program, whereas only 45% of the untreated or school-treated cases showed some improvement. The outcome was therefore poor in the majority of untreated or school-treated dyslexics. Despite the encouraging prognosis suggested for dyslexics exposed to the Orton–Gillingham program, the results may be misleading. All dyslexic cases were originally referred to the authors' clinic and were recommended for an intensive program using the Orton–Gillingham method. Those children who did not participate in the program following initial evaluation became the comparison group, some of whom remained untreated and some of whom received remediation in the schools. This represents a serious confounding in the comparison group. More serious, however, is the selection of the two groups. It is unclear as to why the parents of the comparison group refused to participate in the intensive private program. One possibility is that motivational and/or SES differences existed between groups, favoring the children in the Orton–Gillingham program. If so, it once again confounds good academic outcome with high SES (Rawson, 1968) and poor academic outcome with low SES (Howden, 1967). It is also not clear whether treatment length was controlled for between the group receiving Orton–Gillingham treatment and the group receiving school remediation.

Despite the improvement noted for children receiving the Orton–Gillingham program, 40% of them were still reading below grade level following treatment. The authors chose to classify these cases as "showing some improvement," thereby inflating their percentage of good outcomes. The preceding comments reflect some of the weaknesses that detract from an otherwise important study. It is hoped that future studies will attempt to isolate the treatment variable more rigorously in the investigation of academic outcome in learning-disabled children.

Antisocial Behavior

The reputed association between early learning problems and later antisocial behavior remains unclear. Follow-up studies have focused on academic and occupational prognosis. Moreover, even when follow-up studies have reported data on antisocial behavior, it has rarely been possible to determine whether the antisocial behavior preceded or followed the learning problems. Thus, evidence linking learning disabilities to antisocial behavior is essentially of a correlational nature (e.g., Kline, 1972; Rutter *et al.*, 1976).

Rutter *et al.* (1976) did, however, report some data relevant to the question of whether learning disabilities precede or follow antisocial behavior. They found that for conduct disorders first manifested between the ages of 10 and 14, the incidence of prior reading problems was no higher than for the general Isle of Wight population. However, there was a significant correlation between antisocial behavior that began prior to age 10 and reading problems. This relationship is strictly correlational, and, as such, does not tell us whether the reading problems or the antisocial problems came first. On the other hand, the study by Rutter *et al.* (1976) provides solid evidence that conduct disorders beginning after age 10 may not be the result of reading problems.

Offord, Poushinsky, and Sullivan (1978) investigated antisocial behavior preceded by learning problems. This study found that, among a random sample of juvenile boys placed on probation, half had learning problems prior to the onset of antisocial symptoms. Offord and Poushinsky (1981) conducted a parallel investigation with girls and reported similar findings. However, in comparing offenders who had prior learning problems with antisocial boys who did not have a history of prior school failure, it was found that the antisocial children with school failure came from lower-SES backgrounds and came from broken homes more often than the non-school-failure juvenile offenders did. Thus, it is not clear from Offord *et al.* whether learning problems caused antisocial behavior or whether deprived family backgrounds led to both school difficulties and antisocial behavior.

In sum, the available reports are insufficient to determine whether the elementary-school child with learning problems will become the delinquent adolescent or the adult criminal. It may be that antisocial adolescents become failures because of their antisocial tendencies, rather than the reverse; or it may be that both are a consequence of adverse family backgrounds. Follow-up studies starting prior to the age of onset for either learning problems or conduct disorders (i.e., no later than the beginning of first grade) are needed to determine whether any causal relationship exists between these variables.

Psychological Adjustment

Another unresolved issue is whether early learning disabilities lead to emotional and psychiatric problems. Balow and Blomquist (1965) reported that eight or nine learning-disabled children given the Minnesota Multiphasic Personality Inventory (MMPI) as adults showed some evidence of psychopathology. Dykman *et al.* (1973) found that learning-disabled children, followed up at age 14, showed more deviancy on the Minnesota Counseling Inventory (MCI) than did normal readers. Spreen (1978) reported that more learning-disabled children than control children had seen a psychologist or psychiatrist during the course of the follow-up period. However, in each of these studies no measures of emotional adjustment were made during the initial assessment period. As such, the psychiatric data are essentially cross-sectional. In sum, as with the delinquency issue, the psychiatric issue has not been explored in follow-up research.

Summary Critique

What conclusions, if any, can be drawn on the basis of the preceding review? First, the academic outlook for children with early learning problems is poor, unless a child happens to come from a high-SES family and/or is exposed to an intensive program such as the Orton–Gillingham program, in which case the outlook may be good. Second, children with early learning disabilities are probably more likely to drop out of school, but the seriousness of that risk is unknown. Third, it is probable that with the exception of high-SES children, few learning-disabled youngsters will enter occupations demanding extended education; however, what occupations these people enter and what level of job satisfaction they enjoy have not been determined. Fourth, whether early identification and treatment of learning disabilities improves prognosis (and, if so, to what extent) is still unanswered. Finally, the reputed connection between early learning disabilities and both later antisocial behavior and later emotional disorders is uncertain.

SUGGESTIONS FOR FUTURE RESEARCH

It is apparent from this review that more follow-up research on learning disabled children is needed. Many questions remain unanswered. Large-scale studies spanning the early school years to adulthood are needed.

The ideal follow-up study on learning-disabled children should use a longitudinal design, starting with children at an age prior to the development of learning disabilities (i.e., starting no later than the beginning of first grade). The advantages of this type of design have been well documented by research into schizophrenia (e.g., Garmezy, 1974; Mednick & McNeil, 1968). These advantages include (1) the absence of experimenter bias based on knowledge of which subjects are in the target group; (2) the availability of an ideal control group; (3) standardized measurement on selected variables of interest at the age of interest; and (4) optimal data for making causal inferences. The study by Satz *et al.* (1978) is an example of the power of this type of methodology.

Future follow-up studies should use a wide array of outcome measures to examine the prognosis of learning disabled children in a variety of areas (e.g., academic, occupational, social, emotional). Structured interviews may be used to collect a broad range of data. Spreen's (1978) procedure of interviewing both children and parents is recommended as a means of getting more information, and also as a check on data reliability. Variables such as school suspensions, arrests, convictions, and drug abuse need to be examined so that one can determine whether there is any empirical relationship between childhood learning problems and adolescent adjustment (e.g., antisocial behavior). Personality measures such as the MMPI, Cattell Personality Inventory (CPI), and Rorschach, as well as measures of inpatient and outpatient status, should be gathered to see whether learning-disabled children do have a high incidence of emotional problems as adults.

A major confounding variable in follow-up studies is the presence of various treatments for the learning-disabled children, which are either implied or inadequately assessed with respect to outcome. These interventions have varied in length, intensity, and method. Often the exact nature of the treatment method is not given at all. Ideally, it would be best to conduct follow-up studies on untreated children. However, to withhold treatment from children at risk could be questioned on ethical grounds. If treatment is given, studies should endeavor to identify variables such as the type and length of treatment(s), as well as the age at initial intervention. Of even greater importance are the selection criteria for the comparison group. Ideally, the investigator should have no particular investment in any particular treatment techniques, and the comparison group(s) should afford an unbiased evaluation of outcome with respect to the efficacy of treatment and/or type. Unfortunately, the Kline and Kline (1975) study failed to answer these questions.

A final recommendation for further research is the need for a more objective and reliable definition of the term "learning disability." All too often, this term is defined loosely and without operational specification. As such, it promotes ambiguity with respect to the nature of the sample under study. Terms such as "dyslexia," "specific reading disability," "specific learning disability," "MBD," and "hyperactivity" are often used, sometimes with reference to different children and at other times with reference to the same children—a counsel of despair, indeed. Moreover, attempts to define the target group (e.g., dyslexics) as a subset of the general population of learning disabilities suffer from the use of exclusionary criteria that focus on what the condition is not, leaving what it is unspecified and thus ambiguous (Ross, 1976; Rutter, 1978; Satz & Morris, 1981). More recently, attempts have been made to identify subtypes of learning-disabled children based on multivariate classification procedures (Darby, 1978; Doehring & Hoshko, 1977; Petrauskas & Rourke, 1979; Satz & Morris, 1981). These statistical approaches offer some promise for defining more homogeneous subtypes of learning-disabled children that could provide new insights into the etiology and treatment of these disabilities, as well as their differential prognosis along several outcome criteria.

It may be concluded that follow-up research on learning-disabled children is just beginning. The studies reviewed in this chapter leave unanswered many of the questions concerning the long-term outcome of these children. Although evidence points to a less favorable academic outcome in learning-disabled children, this conclusion should be viewed with caution until some of the preceding methodological recommendations are met. The outcome dimensions implied in any prognostic study must also be specified. An association between childhood learning problems and academic failure during adolescence does not speak to the issues of school dropout, occupational attainment, antisocial behavior, or emotional adjustment during this same period. These additional outcome questions still await more rigorous investigation.

Acknowledgments

The authors gratefully acknowledge the assistance of William Gaddes and Wayne Clark, University of Victoria, in the preparation of this chapter.

References

Ackerman, P. T., Dykman, R. A., & Peters, J. E. Learning-disabled boys as adolescents: Cognitive factors and achievement. *Journal of the American Academy of Child Psychiatry*, 1977, *16*, 296–313.

Balow, B. The long-term effect of remedial reading instruction. *The Reading Teacher*, 1965, *18*, 581–586.

Balow, B., & Blomquist, M. Young adults ten to fifteen years after severe reading disability. *Elementary School Journal*, 1965, *66*, 44–48.

Breuger, T. A. A follow-up of remedial reading instruction. *The Reading Teacher*, 1968, *21*, 329–334.

Carter, R. P. A. *A descriptive analysis of the adult adjustment of persons once identified as disabled readers*. Unpublished doctoral dissertation, Indiana University, 1964.

Darby, R. *Learning disabilities: A multivariate search for subtypes*. Unpublished doctoral dissertation, University of Florida, 1978.

Doehring, D., & Hoshko, I. M. Classification of reading problems by the *Q*-technique of factor analysis. *Cortex*, 1977, *13*, 281–294.

Dykman, R. A., Peters, J. E., & Ackerman, P. T. Experimental approaches to the study of minimal brain dysfunction: A follow-up study. *Annals of the New York Annals of Science*, 1973, *205*, 93–108.

Eisenberg, L. Reading retardation: I. Psychiatric and sociologic aspects. *Pediatrics*, 1966, *37*, 352–365.

Fitzsimmons, S. J., Cheever, J., Leonard, E., & Macunovich, D. School failures: Now and tomorrow. *Developmental Psychology*, 1969, *1*, 134–146.

Gaddes, W. Learning disabilities: Prevalence estimates and the need for definition. In R. Knights & D. J. Bakker (Eds.), *The neuropsychology of learning disorders: Theoretical approaches* (Proceedings of NATO Conference). Baltimore: University Park Press, 1976.

Garmezy, N. Children at risk—the search for antecedents of schizophrenia: I. Conceptual models and research methods. *Schizophrenia Bulletin*, 1974, *1*(8), 14–90.

Gates, A. I. The role of personality maladjustment in reading disability. In G. Natches (Ed.), *Children with reading problems*. New York: Basic Books, 1968.

Gottesman, R., Belmont, I., & Kaminer, R. Admission and follow-up status of reading disabled children referred to a medical clinic. *Journal of Learning Disabilities*, 1975, *8*, 642–650.

Hardy, M. E. *Clinical follow-up study of disabled readers*. Unpublished doctoral dissertation, University of Toronto, 1968.

Herjanic, B., & Penick, E. Adult outcome of disabled child readers. *Journal of Special Education*, 1972, *6*, 397–410.

Howden, M. E. *A nineteen-year follow-up study of good, average and poor readers in the fifth and sixth grades*. Unpublished doctoral dissertation, University of Oregon, 1967.

Kline, C. L. The adolescents with learning problems: How long must they wait? *Journal of Learning Disabilities*, 1972, *5*, 127–144.

Kline, C., & Kline, C. Follow-up study of 211 dyslexic children. *Bulletin of the Orton Society*, 1975, *25*, 127–144.

Knoppitz, E. M. *Children with learning disabilities*. New York: Grune & Stratton, 1971.

Mednick, S. A., & McNeil, T. F. Current methodology in research on the etiology of schizophrenia. *Psychological Bulletin*, 1968, *70*, 681–693.

Mendelson, W., Johnson, N., & Stewart, M. A. Hyperactive children as teenagers: A follow-up study. *Journal of Nervous and Mental Disease*, 1971, *153*, 273–279.

Menkes, M. M., Rowe, J. S., & Menkes, J. H. A twenty-five year follow-up on the hyperactive child with MED. *Pediatrics*, 967, *39*, 393–399.

Muehl, S., & Forell, E. R. A follow-up study of disabled readers: Variables related to high school reading performance. *Reading Research Quarterly*, 1973, *9*, 110–123.

Offord, D. R., & Poushinsky, M. F. School performance, IQ and female delinquency. *International Journal of Social Psychiatry*, 1981, *27*, 53.

Offord, D. R., Poushinsky, M. F., & Sullivan, D. School performance, IQ, and delinquency. *British Journal of Criminology*, 1978, *18*, 110–127.

Petrauskas, R., & Rourke, B. Identification of subgroups of retarded readers: A neuropsychological multivariate approach. *Journal of Clinical Neuropsychology*, 1979, *1*, 17–37.

Preston, R. C., & Yarrington, D. J. Status of fifty retarded readers 8 years after reading clinic diagnosis. *Journal of Reading*, 1967, *11*, 122–124.

Rawson, M. *Developmental language disability: Adult accomplishments of dyslexic boys*. Baltimore: Johns Hopkins University Press, 1968.

Robinson, H. M., & Smith, H. D. Reading clinic: Ten years after. *Elementary School Journal*, 1962, *63*, 22–27.

Ross, A. O. *Psychological aspects of learning disabilities and reading disorders*. New York: McGraw-Hill, 1976.

Rourke, B. P., & Orr, R. R. Prediction of the reading and spelling performances of normal and retarded children: A four-year follow-up. *Journal of Abnormal Child Psychology*, 1977, *5*, 9–20.

Rutter, M. Prevalence and types of dyslexia. In A. Benton & D. Pearl (Eds.), *Dyslexia: An appraisal of current knowledge.* New York: Oxford University Press, 1978.

Rutter, M., Tizard, J., Yule, W., Graham, P., & Whitmore, K. Research report: Isle of Wight studies, 1964–1974. *Psychological Medicine*, 1976, *6*, 313–332.

Satz, P. Reading problems in perspective. In W. Otto, N. Peters, & C. W. Peters (Eds.), *Reading problems: A multidisciplinary perspective.* Reading, Mass.: Addison-Wesley, 1977.

Satz, P., & Fletcher, J. M. Minimal brain dysfunctions: An appraisal of research concepts and methods. In H. Rie & H. Rie (Eds.), *Minimal brain dysfunctions.* New York: Wiley, 1980.

Satz, P., & Morris, R. Learning disability subtypes: A review. In F. Pirrozollo & J. Wittrock (Eds.). *Neuropsychological and cognitive processes in reading.* New York: Academic Press, 1981.

Satz, P., Taylor, H. G., Friel, J., & Fletcher, J. M. Some developmental and predictive precursors of reading disabilities: A six year follow-up. In A. Benton & D. Pearl (Eds.), *Dyslexia: An appraisal of current knowledge.* New York: Oxford University Press, 1978.

Silver, A. A., & Hagin, R. A. Specific reading disability: Follow-up studies. *American Journal of Orthopsychiatry*, 1964, *34*, 95–102.

Spreen, O. *Learning-disabled children growing up* (Finale report to Health and Welfare Canada, Health Programs Branch) Ottawa: Health and Welfare Canada, 1978.

Thompson, L. J. Language disabilities in men of eminence. *Journal of Learning Disabilities*, 1971, *4*, 34–45.

Trites, R., & Fiedorowicz, C. Follow-up study of children with specific (or primary) reading disability. In R. Knights & D. J. Bakker (Eds.), *The neuropsychology of learning disorders: Theoretical approaches* (Proceedings of NATO Conference). Baltimore: University Park Press, 1976.

U.S. Department of Health, Education and Welfare. *Reading disorder in the United States: Report of the Secretary's National Advisory Committee on Dyslexia and Related Disorders.* Washington, D.C.: U.S. Government Printing Office, 1969.

Wright, P. W. *Reading problems and delinquency.* Paper presented at World Congress on Dyslexia, Mayo Clinic, Rochester, Minn., 1974.

CHAPTER TWENTY-NINE

Outstanding Issues in Research on Learning Disabilities

BYRON P. ROURKE

Although learning-disabled children have been investigated on a fairly large scale during the past 20 years, it is obvious that there are several unresolved—and, perhaps, contentious—issues that require much further work. The six areas that seem to me to be of particular importance are as follows: definitions of learning disabilities; level-of-performance methodology; alternative methodologies; the determination of subtypes of learning disabilities; the prediction of high-risk children; and treatment considerations. In each of these areas, some representative research that has shown signs of coming to grips with these issues is mentioned.

DEFINITIONS

Ideally, any attempt to investigate a clinical disorder should be based upon an exact and unambiguous definition of the disorder. As any reading of the history of the investigation of human maladies will reveal, however, definitions of disorders that will enable research to proceed in a rational fashion are usually the *product* of extensive clinical investigation of a group of illnesses and forms of dysfunction, rather than their starting point. In other words, it is only *after* painstaking clinical observation and testing that reasonable definitions emerge. Having accomplished this, research on the disorders can proceed apace. The upshot of such research is often a redefinition of the disorders in question, as well as refinements in the pictures of presenting symptoms that serve to differentiate them from other illnesses or diseases.

In the field of learning disabilities, it would appear that the necessary phase of rigorous clinical investigation of the disorders in question was all but overlooked at its earliest stages. Instead, definitions of the disability were formulated prematurely and were forced upon the research and clinical communities with reckless disregard for scientific rigor.

A case in point is the World Federation of Neurology definition of "dyslexia." This definition has been criticized cogently by Rutter (1978), and has

Byron P. Rourke. Department of Psychology, University of Windsor, Windsor, Ontario, Canada; Department of Neuropsychology, Windsor Western Hospital Centre, Windsor, Ontario, Canada.

been subjected to empirical tests by Taylor, Satz, and Friel (1979). In the latter investigation, it was demonstrated that this definition is of little or no use, because reading-disabled children who met the criteria of this definition did not differ significantly from reading-disabled children who did not meet the criteria. In this sense, the definition does nothing to establish either the genus or the specific differences that are the very essence of a definition.

It would seem clear, then, that more information is needed before this disorder or group of clinical disorders can be defined with any degree of clarity. To this end, Rutter (1978) has proposed a distinction between "reading backwardness" and "specific reading retardation," and has presented evidence that would suggest rather strongly that this distinction is a valid one. Other dimensions of definitions of learning disabilities—ones that take into account distinct presenting characteristics, presumably reflecting underlying differences in brain dysfunction—are treated in subsequent sections dealing with subtype analysis. For present purposes, it is sufficient to note that much research is probably necessary if investigators are to arrive at consensually validatable definitions of children's learning disabilities. The fledgling attempts at taxonomy to be mentioned later in this chapter are the analogues of careful clinical observation and, in most cases, are direct results of it.

For the present, one thing that must be insured is that the groups of learning-disabled children who are investigated are very well defined with respect to their salient characteristics. For example, if investigators wish to exclude from consideration children with mental retardation, primary emotional disturbance, sociocultural deprivation, debilitating sensory impairments, and inadequate instruction (which many investigators, including myself, attempt to exclude), this must be done in a manner that can be replicated. This will, at least, allow the results of investigations within this area to be cross-validated. Of even more importance in the long run, however, is the fact that this will allow for programs of research to be mounted that can build upon findings of previous investigations in the field. Heretofore, this has been all but impossible, as the results of reviews of research in the area of dyslexia (e.g., Benton, 1975; Rourke, 1978a) have amply demonstrated. In my view, there are sufficient reliable research findings in this field at the present time for reasonable approximations of adequate definitions to be formulated. Not only has it been determined that "learning disabilities" constitute a group of clinical disorders; it has also been shown that subtypes of reading, spelling, and arithmetic disabilities appear to have quite different brain-related disabilities associated with them. These developments should have the effect of correcting the misconceptions created by the premature closure of inadequate definitions.

LEVEL-OF-PERFORMANCE METHODOLOGY

Many researchers have argued that, having adopted a "working definition" of a learning disability, it is then possible to proceed to do research relating to that disability. Typically, investigations in this area have taken the form of comparison of, say, reading-disabled and normal children on one or a very limited number of hypothesis-specific variables. Unfortunately, there are a host of problems associated with the use of this sort of methodology. For example, the degree of reading disability exhibited by the reading-disabled group very often determines whether significant differences will emerge favoring the performance of the normal controls. If the reading-disabled group is extremely deficient in reading, it increases the likelihood that they will be likewise deficient on almost any number of dependent variables that the investigator may wish to choose.

This state of affairs would suggest that one could support virtually any hypothesis or theory with respect to *the* disability that is "responsible" for reading disability by simply insuring that the normal and reading-disabled groups differ greatly in reading skills. This modus operandi becomes even less justifiable from a scientific standpoint when the investigator uses only one or two dependent variables, in addition to "stacking the deck" in favor of a particular result by following this strategy.

In general, there would seem to be little of benefit left to be gained from research strategies in this area which are confined to such simple-minded level-of-performance approaches to the problems in this field. There was a time when such investigations were necessary. For example, the largely ignored, but prodigious, study of Doehring (1968) demonstrated, among other things, that retarded readers could be differentiated in terms of scores of measures that are known to be sensitive to the effects of brain impairment. Little of value would have been lost had other investigators in this field simply acknowledged that this was the case, and then proceeded to specify with greater clarity the patterns of performance that can emerge within groups of reading-disabled children. Unfortunately, usually this was not done. Rather, the search for yet another variable upon which reading-disabled children could be shown to be deficient has proceeded virtually unabated.

However, there have been some recent examples of investigations that have offered more satisfactory solutions to some of the more pressing problems in this field through the use of more sophisticated research methodologies. Some of these are described in the next section.

ALTERNATIVE METHODOLOGIES

There are a variety of ways in which alternative methodologies in this area can be characterized. The one that I use here is based upon methods of clinical inference that are employed routinely in clinical neuropsychology. The first of these is one that attempts to exploit the "sign" approach.

A "sign" is considered to be an indication that a *particular* form of pathology is present, rather than a feature that can be present in any number of different forms of pathology. For example, if a 21-year-old person who has had normal educational opportunities looks at a picture of a fork and, when asked to name it, says the word "spoon," this is considered to be a sign that this person is suffering from aphasia (that is, a disorder of language resulting from a lesion of the brain).

Several investigators have attempted to design research projects in such a way that particular groups of learning-disabled children, defined in terms of the presence or absence of a particular sign, could be investigated. An investigation conducted by Sweeney and myself (Sweeney & Rourke, 1978) is an example of this. In this study, we constructed two groups of disabled spellers (who were equated for their level of impaired performance in spelling) in terms of a particular sign (phonetic inaccuracy of their misspellings): One group was dubbed "phonetically accurate" disabled spellers; the other, "phonetically inaccurate" disabled spellers. We then compared their performances to each other and to groups of normal-spelling children at two different age levels on a large number of hypothesis-specific variables. The results that emerged from this and subsequent studies of children so grouped (Sweeney & Rourke, in press) served to bolster the view that these were two very different subtypes of retarded spellers who, although they exhibited the same impaired levels of disabled spelling, had quite different profiles of neuropsychological ability. Furthermore, it would seem reasonable to suggest that these two types of disabled spellers would require rather different forms of remedial educational intervention in order to overcome their deficiencies in spelling. However, as Gittelman notes (see Chapter 27 of this volume), it has yet to be *demonstrated* that such subtypes of learning-disabled children do actually benefit differentially from programs designed specifically with their patterns of abilities and deficits in mind.

Other examples of the use of a type of "sign" approach to the investigation of learning-disabled children would include the very important work of Johnson and Myklebust (1967), the related investigations of Boder (1973), and the very interesting program of research outlined by Frith (see Chapter 22). There is good reason to believe that this mode of approach to research will become much more widely applied in the field of learning disabilities, and that it will prove to be a much more fruitful avenue to explore than will the level-of-performance methodology that has held sway in the field until rather recently.

Another mode of approach to the investigation of children with learning disabilities that has been used only sparingly until quite recently is one that is referred to as the "pattern analysis" or "configurational" approach. In this instance, the focus of interest in a child's performance is not the level of performance or any pathological signs that may be present, but rather the pattern of scores that is exhibited by the child. An example of this approach to research should illustrate its principal advantages over the level-of-performance strategy.

In two related studies (Rourke & Finlayson, 1978; Rourke & Strang, 1978), we compared children with learning disabilities who exhibited differing patterns of performance on the Wide-Range Achievement Test (WRAT; Jastak & Jastak, 1965). These studies are described in some detail in Chapter 23 of this volume. The generalizations suggested by the results of these two studies (both with respect to the patterns of neuropsychological abilities and deficits, and with respect to the possibility of differential hemispheric integrity) were made possible by the analysis of the three subtypes of learning-disabled children that had been constituted solely on the basis of three different *patterns* of performance on the WRAT. The groups had been equated for WISC full-scale IQ, and had been selected to coincide rigorously with our working definition of learning-disabled children (Rourke, 1975, 1978b).

The Rourke and Strang (1978) study was also an illustration of an attempt to capitalize upon another method of investigation that is an earmark of the neuropsychological approach to this field—namely, comparisons of performance on the two sides of the body. In this instance, systematic comparisons of sensory–perceptual, motor, and psychomotor performances are made on the two sides of the body (or within the left and right fields, in the case of vision and hearing) in an effort to elicit any asymmetries that may be present in a child's performance. Other examples of the application of this type of methodology would include the dichotic-listening studies of Bakker (see Chapter 25), the split-visual-field studies of Marcel (Marcel & Rajan, 1975), and the comparisons of groups of learning-disabled children with lateralized and nonlateralized psychomotor deficiencies that have been carried out in our laboratory (Rourke, Yanni, MacDonald, & Young, 1973). In all of these cases, the focus of concern was related to inferences that could be made regarding the relative integrity of the two cerebral hemispheres in children who manifested differing types of learning disabilities. Although the results of this type of research tend to be notoriously difficult to compare among laboratories (see Rourke, 1978a), there is good reason to believe that they will eventually lead to considerable advances in the understanding of learning disabilities in children.

These different types of methodologies have been outlined in some detail in order to illustrate and emphasize the importance of the issue of methodology in the field of learning disabilities at this time. The pessimism that has been expressed by many in the past in their reviews of research into learning disabilities has been largely justified because of the very simplistic methodological approaches that have dominated the investigative area of this field for so long. This fact, together with the almost dogmatic allegiance that various professional groups have given to such outmoded concepts as "minimal brain dysfunction" and "the brain-impaired child," would lead serious consumers or reviewers of the research in this area to throw up their hands in despair. Some of the more fruitful methodological approaches to research in this field have been explained briefly in order to indicate that all is not lost, and that there are investigators who have been taking paths to scientific understanding that are relatively free of the shortcomings of most of the (level-of-performance) research efforts in this field. Satz and Fletcher (1980) have provided a very good discussion of this issue from a somewhat different vantage point.

Finally, it should be clear that it is possible, with individual children, to derive much useful information from neuropsychological data organized to allow for methods of inference that make use of signs, configurations, and right–left comparisons. This, in turn, presupposes a comprehensive approach to neuropsychological assessment of learning-disabled children—one that goes much beyond the assessment of standard measures of educational achievement and psychometric intelligence, which, in themselves, provide little clinically relevant information. However, what may not be obvious is that this limited latter mode of assessment owes much of its rationale to the simplistic level-of-performance notions that generated research in this area for so many years. More extended discussions of this issue are provided in Rourke (1976a, 1981).

SUBTYPES OF LEARNING DISABILITIES

The importance of subtypes of learning disorders is discussed in an earlier chapter of this volume (see Chapter 23). Nevertheless, some methodological considerations in the research on this topic need emphasis here. Our studies in this area have taken two tacks: one, *a priori*; the other, *a posteriori*. In the *a priori* method (e.g., Rourke & Finlayson, 1978; Sweeney & Rourke, 1978), groups are composed beforehand on the basis of a particular sign or pattern of performance. They are then compared in terms of dependent measures that are known to be sensitive to cerebral dysfunction. In this way, preselected subtypes of learning-disabled children can be shown to differ in central processing deficiencies. The *a posteriori* procedures, in which subtypes are generated through the use of a grouping or cluster algorithm without invoking and utilizing prior classification procedures, are more complicated statistically. We have carried out this procedure with 7- to 8-year-old retarded readers (Petrauskas & Rourke, 1979) and with older learning disabled children (Fisk & Rourke, 1979). The procedures involved in clustering, as they apply in the neuropsychology of learning disabilities, are well discussed by Doehring, Hoshko, and Bryans (1979).

The determination of subtypes of learning-disabled children has considerable relevance for the issues discussed previously in this chapter. For example, the generation of definitions of learning disabilities becomes a much more complex—but, it may be hoped, more rewarding and scientifically justifiable—task when it can be shown that there are reliable subtypes of learning-disabled children. Even the few studies of reading, spelling, and arithmetical disabilities already mentioned in this chapter should make it clear, not only that there are such subtypes, but also that the differences in neuropsychological abilities and deficits they exhibit require specific "definitions." In addition, it is likely that more reliable (and, possibly, quite different) subtypes will emerge as research in this area develops. As a result, no *one* definition could encompass this degree of heterogeneity. Rather, a fairly substantial set of definitions will be required to encompass this degree of diversity.

The determination of subtypes should also sound the final death knell for the level-of-performance approach to research in this area. Research aimed at determining *the deficit* or *the cause* of learning disabilities will, quite simply, be irrelevant. The same should hold for research aimed at assessing the outcomes of various intervention techniques. Although it has not yet been demonstrated (see Chapter 27), it would seem highly probable that different subtypes of children with, say, arithmetical disabilities would respond quite differently to methods of remedial instruction that emphasize "verbal" as opposed to "visual–spatial" modes of information processing. Furthermore, it would seem likely that much of the intervention literature has yielded negative results largely because children with some subtypes have benefited from the procedure, whereas children with other subtypes were impaired by them. The *average* level of performance for a group composed of such diverse subtypes conceals this diversity and misleadingly suggests that the technique is ineffective for everyone, rather than that some children benefit whereas others become worse.

The delineation of the group of clinical disorders known as "learning disabilities" into some consensually validatable taxonomy is the most pressing issue in the field today. All other dimensions of this field are affected by it and, up to now, have suffered through a relative lack of attention to it.

PREDICTION OF CHILDREN WHO ARE "AT RISK" FOR LEARNING DISABILITIES

Those involved in the treatment of learning-disabled children have the very practical concern of determining those children who are most in need of intervention. That raises the question: Can investigators and clinicians predict (at or before school entry) which children are, as a result of a central processing deficiency, likely to experience considerable difficulty with standard educational instruction? There are several facets of this problem that have received attention, and there are a few issues that remain largely unresolved.

There is an abundance of literature on the long-range outcomes for learning-disabled children (e.g., Peter & Spreen, 1979; Rourke & Orr, 1977; Trites & Fiedorowicz, 1976). The conclusion to be drawn from almost all of this work is that a large proportion of learning-disabled children identified during the early school years do not have a very favorable prognosis for either academic success or social adjustment. There is also a body of longitudinal research (e.g., Rourke & Orr, 1977) intended to determine which subgroups of disabled readers are likely to make little or no progress in reading and spelling and which are likely to approach age-appropriate levels in these skills during the latter grades of school.

Satz and his colleagues (e.g., Satz, Taylor, Friel, & Fletcher, 1978) have sought to isolate some of the neuropsychological dimensions measurable in children of kindergarten age that predict reading failure. His exhaustive investigation of these so-called "developmental precursors" has been of theoretical and practical value. Some of the tasks that remain are (1) to refine the measuring instruments used for prediction; (2) to assess their reliability in various settings; (3) to render them fit for extensive application at, say, the preschool and early kindergarten levels; and (4) to determine their relative predictive accuracy in different sociocultural milieus. When these have been accomplished, two large further problems will remain; one concerns subtypes and the other concerns intervention.

If there are neuropsychologically differentiatable subtypes of learning-disabled children, it would seem reasonable to suppose that there would be different prognoses associated with one or more of these subtypes. Furthermore, since reading is not the only school-related performance of interest, it will be necessary to investigate the relative accuracy of various measures for the prediction of different subtypes of spelling, arithmetical, and other kinds of learning disabilities of concern to educators and parents. Most would claim that this task would be made much simpler by the fact that reading and spelling tend to be so intimately related, in the sense that children who are adept or poor at one tend to perform in similar ways on the other. However, the work of Frith (see Chapter 22) and our own studies of spelling (see Chapter 23) indicate that this is not the case for all reading- and spelling-disabled children. Arithmetic difficulties are only just beginning to capture the interest of serious investigators. Nevertheless, it seems clear that patterns of neuropsychological abilities and deficits that predict failure in arithmetic are likely to be quite different from those that predict reading and spelling disabilities.

Prediction is very important for intervention. The relevant questions include the following: Given a particular type of (educational) intervention, what is the likelihood that a child will read at an age-appropriate level when he or she leaves school? If a certain type of drug is administered in a certain dosage for a certain period of time, what is the probability that a child will remain at risk for this particular disability? These are important issues, since school systems engaged in the prediction of high-risk children must also provide remedial educational programming for children with learning disabilities. The efficient allocation of limited "special" services for school-age children is a necessary concern. School officials need to know which children will need a multifaceted —and probably expensive—program in order to make gains in academic performance, and which will require only very limited (inexpensive) ancillary assistance in order to develop to their full academic potential. Researchers have barely begun to address these issues, which probably will occupy the forefront of the investigative efforts for some time to come.

TREATMENT

Other unresolved issues in the treatment of hyperactive and learning-disabled children are well summarized in the recent monograph edited by Knights and Bakker (1980). The most significant issue concerns the individual response to treatment, another manifestation of the subtype problem. It is evident to anyone who observes the day-to-day behaviors of learning-disabled children that they vary in their response to different modes of intervention. Yet, still, there are those who would wish to search for—or, what is worse, argue for—*the* single best method of intervention for learning-disabled children. In view of the research findings already discussed, this does *not* appear to be a reasonable approach.

Another neglected issue concerns the possible *harm* from particular methods of intervention when applied to children with certain types of learning disability. Even after a particular intervention technique has been shown to be effective for a particular subtype of learning-disabled children, there remains the necessity of assessing the human "cost" (e.g., side effects) involved. Researchers have turned their attention to this issue only fairly recently, and, given the current public sensitivity to such issues, it is likely that increasing efforts will be directed toward assessing the possible social, emotional, and other side effects of intervention.

Another neglected facet of intervention is that of the generalizability of positive results. The problem here is no different from that in other areas of psychology—that is, do the results obtained in the laboratory have any impact upon a child's behavior in the classroom? Often, the root of this problem lies in the fact that the tasks or target behaviors used to test experimental hypotheses are not nearly as complex as (and sometimes, bear very little relation to) the demands of the classroom or the child's extraschool learning environment. Hence, very little, if any, "transfer of training" takes place between the laboratory and "real life." Efforts to remedy this situation have been appearing for some time, but the real issue of long-range outcome (another dimension of the problem of the generalizability of results) has yet to receive the attention that it merits.

The final issue with respect to treatment and intervention is that of the sequencing and timing of remedial programming. Both clinical experience and deductions from recent investigations in the literature on learning disabilities indicate that the sequencing of intervention strategies should receive much more attention. Were learning-disabled children to learn material in the same sequence as normal children do, the answer to this problem would be quite simple: Techniques based upon knowledge of how normal children acquire, say, reading proficiency should be applied to learning-disabled children. Unfortunately, teachers have been doing this since the time of Plato, apparently with little success. An example may serve to illustrate the point.

In our investigations of children who read and spell well, but who have outstanding difficulties in mechanical arithmetic, we have observed that, at about age 10, these children perform much better on tests of "class-inclusion" reasoning than they do on many types of "conservation" tests. If it is assumed that Piaget's views regarding class inclusion and conservation are correct, this rather marked difference in performance poses an interesting problem. According to Piaget, one must be able to "conserve" in order to "classify"; that is, successively developing levels of conservation abilities are prerequisites for class-inclusion reasoning. Thus, from a Piagetian standpoint, children with an arithmetical disability seem to perform in a manner that is qualitatively different from that of normal children. This could imply that the cognitive development of this type of child is qualitatively distinct from that of the normal child.

The point of interest in this example is that some learning-disabled children may not have progressed through a "normal" sequence of cognitive development. They may have "accomplished" certain developmental tasks in deviant ways. In consequence, they may have qualitatively distinct methods and styles for analyzing information. Accordingly, it could be advantageous to present learning materials in a sequence that differs from that most helpful for normal children. This hypothesis needs to be tested with different subtypes of learning-disabled children.

The timing of remedial intervention constitutes a related issue. Many children with a learning disability have more than one type of deficit. In the case of spelling disability, for example, Frith (see Chapter 22) might suggest that the "dyslexic" type of poor speller is deficient in the ability to follow both the phonological and the lexical "routes," whereas the "dysgraphic" poor speller is deficient only in the ability to follow or benefit from the lexical route. Hence, it would seem reasonable to propose that the former type of poor speller would require training in the use of the phonological route, followed by training in the use of the semantic route. If such be the case, it would also follow that probably one would have to decide at some time when there has been sufficient training in one skill area before passing on to the next. Other examples of the issue of timing are provided by questions on when to begin instruction in phoneme–grapheme matching, when to cease phonemic segmentation training and move to recognition of words as "wholes," and when to play down word recognition in favor of rapid reading with comprehension. All of these are difficult enough to decide in the case of normally developing children. The situation becomes much more complex when one has to consider the implications of disordered central processing skills, as appears to be the case in learning-disabled children.

CONCLUSION

In this chapter, some of the more salient "outstanding" issues in the neuropsychological investigation of learning disabilities in children have been noted. The principal conclusions are as follows:

1. The "standard" definitions of learning disabilities that held sway for some time are gradually giving way to definitions that take into account the diversity evident in this group of clinical disorders.

2. Outmoded methodologies still plague the field, but there has been a refreshing emergence of more sophisticated methods of study and analysis that are appropriate for addressing at least some of the complex issues in this field.

3. The determination of reliable subtypes of learning disabilities would appear to be the most pressing issue at this time. Its actual and potential impact upon such problems as definition, methodology, prediction, and treatment is pervasive.

4. The practical problems of prediction of children at risk for learning disabilities need much more attention. At present, it is clear that the "technologies" necessary to accomplish the aims of prediction are available, but that their widespread applicability and the modifications necessary for particular predictive purposes in particular milieus require more investigation.

5. The outstanding issues related to treatment of learning disabilities are legion. No one working in this field would have any great difficulty in specifying dozens of them. One hopeful sign in all of this is that investigators are on the verge of being able to submit to empirical test a variety of treatment × subtype interactions. The results of such studies may very well contribute substantially to the present state of understanding and clinical capabilities.

Other issues, such as the importance of developmental considerations (Rourke, 1981, 1983); the relevance of neuropsychological research for school psychology (Rourke & Gates, 1981); considerations regarding "developmental lag" versus "deficit" or "difference" positions (Rourke, 1976b); and socio-emotional dimensions of learning disabilities in children (Rourke & Fisk, 1981) could also have been discussed in this review. The number of unresolved issues, together with their very thorny nature, suggest that there is no shortage of problems to occupy investigators for some years to come.

References

Benton, A. L. Developmental dyslexia: Neurological aspects. In W. J. Friedlander (Ed.), *Advances in neurology* (Vol. 7). New York: Raven Press, 1975.

Boder, E. Developmental dyslexia: A diagnostic approach based on three atypical reading–spelling patterns. *Developmental Medicine and Child Neurology*, 1973, *15*, 663–687.

Doehring, D. G. *Patterns of impairment in specific reading disability*. Bloomington: Indiana University Press, 1968.

Doehring, D. G., Hoshko, I. M., & Bryans, B. N. Statistical classification of children with reading problems. *Journal of Clinical Neuropsychology*, 1979, *1*, 5–16.

Fisk, J. L., & Rourke, B. P. Identification of subtypes of learning disabled children at three age levels: A neuropsychological multivariate approach. *Journal of Clinical Neuropsychology*, 1979, *1*, 289–310.

Jastak, J. F., & Jastak, S. R. *The Wide-Range Achievement Test*. Wilmington, Del.: Guidance Associates, 1965.

Johnson, D. J., & Myklebust, H. R. *Learning disabilities*. New York: Grune & Stratton, 1967.

Knights, R. M., & Bakker, D. J. *Treatment of hyperactive and learning disordered children: Current research*. Baltimore: University Park Press, 1980.

Marcel, T., & Rajan, P. Lateral specialization for recognition of words and faces in good and poor readers. *Neuropsychologia*, 1975, *13*, 489–497.

Peter, B. M., & Spreen, O. Behavior rating and personal adjustment scales of neurologically and learning handicapped children during adolescence and early adulthood: Results of a follow-up study. *Journal of Clinical Neuropsychology*, 1979, *1*, 75–91.

Petrauskas, R. J., & Rourke, B. P. Identification of subtypes of retarded readers: A neuropsychological, multivariate approach. *Journal of Clinical Neuropsychology*, 1979, *1*, 17–37.

Rourke, B. P. Brain–behavior relationships in children with learning disabilities: A research program. *American Psychologist*, 1975, *30*, 911–920.

Rourke, B. P. Issues in the neuropsychological assessment of children with learning disabilities. *Canadian Psychological Review*, 1976, *17*, 89–102. (a)

Rourke, B. P. Reading retardation in children: Developmental lag or deficit? In R. M. Knights & D. J. Bakker (Eds.), *Neuropsychology of learning disorders: Theoretical approaches*. Baltimore: University Park Press, 1976. (b)

Rourke, B. P. Neuropsychological research in reading retardation: A review. In A. L. Benton & D. Pearl (Eds.), *Dyslexia: An appraisal of current knowledge*. New York: Oxford University Press, 1978. (a)

Rourke, B. P. Reading, spelling, arithmetic disabilities: A neuropsychologic perspective. In H. R. Myklebust (Ed.), *Progress in learning disabilities* (Vol. 4). New York: Grune & Stratton, 1978. (b)

Rourke, B. P. Neuropsychological assessment of children with learning disabilities. In S. B. Filskov & T. J. Boll (Eds.), *Handbook of clinical neuropsychology*. New York: Wiley–Interscience, 1981.

Rourke, B. P. Reading and spelling disabilities: A developmental neuropsychological perspective. In U. Kirk (Ed.), *Neuropsychology of language, reading, and spelling*. New York: Academic Press, 1983.

Rourke, B. P., & Finlayson, M. A. J. Neuropsychological significance of variations in patterns of academic performance: Verbal and visual–spatial abilities. *Journal of Abnormal Child Psychology*, 1978, *6*, 121–133.

Rourke, B. P., & Fisk, J. L. Socio-emotional dimensions of learning disabilities in children. *Bulletin of the Orton Society*, 1981, *31*, 77–88.

Rourke, B. P., & Gates, R. D. Neuropsychological research and school psychology. In G. W. Hynd & J. E. Orbzut (Eds.), *Neuropsychological assessment and the school-age child: Issues and procedures*. New York: Grune & Stratton, 1981.

Rourke, B. P., & Orr, R. R. Prediction of the reading and spelling performances of normal and retarded readers: A four-year follow-up. *Journal of Abnormal Child Psychology*, 1977, *5*, 9–20.

Rourke, B. P., & Strang, J. D. Neuropsychological significance of variations in patterns of academic performance: Motor, psychomotor, and tactile–perceptual abilities. *Journal of Pediatric Psychology*, 1978, *3*, 62–66.

Rourke, B. P., Yanni, D. W., MacDonald, G. W., & Young, G. C. Neuropsychological significance of lateralized deficits on the Grooved Pegboard Test for older children with learning disabilities. *Journal of Consulting and Clinical Psychology*, 1973, *41*, 128–134.

Rutter, M. Prevalence and types of dyslexia. In A. L. Benton & D. Pearl (Eds.), *Dyslexia: An appraisal of current knowledge*. New York: Oxford University Press, 1978.

Satz, P., & Fletcher, J. M. Minimal brain dysfunction: An appraisal of research concepts and methods. In H. Rie & E. Rie (Eds.), *Handbook of minimal brain dysfunctions: A critical view*. New York: Wiley–Interscience, 1980.

Satz, P., Taylor, H. G., Friel, J., & Fletcher, J. M. Some developmental and predictive precursors of reading disabilities: A six-year follow-up. In A. L. Benton & D. Pearl (Eds.), *Dyslexia: An appraisal of current knowledge*. New York: Oxford University Press, 1978.

Sweeney, J. E., & Rourke, B. P. Neuropsychological significance of phonetically accurate and phonetically inaccurate spelling errors in younger and older retarded spellers. *Brain and Language*, 1978, *6*, 212–225.

Sweeney, J. E., & Rourke, B. P. Subtypes of spelling disabilities. In B. P. Rourke (Ed.), *Learning disabilities in children: Advances in subtype analysis*. New York: Guilford, in press.

Taylor, H. G., Satz, P., & Friel, J. Developmental dyslexia in relation to other childhood reading disorders: Significance and clinical utility. *Reading Research Quarterly*, 1979, *15*, 84–101.

Trites, R. L., & Fiedorowicz, C. Follow-up study of children with specific (or primary) reading disability. In R. M. Knights & D. J. Bakker (Eds.), *The neuropsychology of learning disorders: Theoretical approaches*. Baltimore: University Park Press, 1976.

SECTION FIVE

Concepts of "Minimal Brain Dysfunction"

CHAPTER THIRTY

Issues and Prospects in Developmental Neuropsychiatry

MICHAEL RUTTER

Earlier chapters of this volume have outlined many of the recent advances in knowledge of the behavioral and cognitive sequelae of brain injury in childhood, together with the gains in understanding of some of the syndromes associated with organic brain dysfunction. It remains to reconsider the concept of "minimal brain dysfunction" (MBD) in the light of these empirical research findings and, more generally, to note some of the important outstanding issues and dilemmas in the field of developmental neuropsychiatry (see Rutter, 1982a, 1982b).

"MINIMAL BRAIN DYSFUNCTION"

It is clear that there is no one overriding concept of "MBD" (see Introduction); rather, there are a variety of somewhat disparate concepts. Nevertheless, the use of the term would seem to suggest that there *should* be some specific syndrome that is recognizedly different from all others. At one time it was thought that the behavioral manifestations of cerebral damage, whatever the cause, were fairly uniform (Bakwin & Bakwin, 1966). It is now apparent that this is far from the case; to the contrary, the manifestations are protean. Similarly, it was argued that the behavioral pattern characteristic of "MBD" is distinctive and easily recognized (Wender, 1971). Again, that has not proved to be the case, as shown by the continuing controversies over the diagnostic criteria for this hypothesized syndrome.

Of course, it is important to appreciate that uniformity in symptomatology does *not* constitute a necessary criterion for the validity of a syndrome, or even of a specific disease entity (Rutter, 1982b). There are many examples in medicine of conditions with highly diverse clinical pictures that nevertheless are known to represent some single pathological entity. A primary chancre, skin rashes, a gumma, tabes, and general paralysis of the insane seem to have little in common; moreover, they do not occur together at the same time in any one

Michael Rutter. Department of Child and Adolescent Psychiatry, University of London Institute of Psychiatry, London, England.

individual. Yet, because it is known that all of these disorders are caused by the same spirochete, investigators have no difficulty in grouping them together as part of the disease of syphilis. Or, again, a single genetic disorder may manifest itself in varied ways. Dystrophia myotonica may affect the eyes in some members of a single family, but yet the muscles in other members. Within psychiatry, too, it is generally recognized that manic–depressive illness has a unity, in spite of the fact that the excitement of mania and the retardation of depression look very different. The link is accepted because the two forms of the disorder often alternate over time, and because genetic studies suggest that mania and some forms of depression constitute different aspects of the same condition.

Cannot the same apply to "MBD"? Of course, it could, but with all the examples cited, the heterogeneous mixture of signs and symptoms are unified on the basis of evidence regarding a common etiology. Such evidence is lacking in the case of "MBD," and until it is forthcoming the concept of a syndrome is premature. For the hypothesis of an "MBD" syndrome to be at all convincing, let alone of any theoretical or practical relevance, there needs to be evidence that the clinical disorders thought to be due to "MBD" are recognizably different from other disorders in causation, course, response to treatment, or some other relevant feature. Such evidence is not yet available (Rie, 1980).

Naturally, that does not necessarily mean that in the course of time some such syndrome may not be identified, but that day has not yet arrived. Until it does, the notion of an "MBD" syndrome needs to be regarded as a somewhat speculative working hypothesis, which serves an important role as a guide to further research but which is not yet useful as a guide to clinical policy or practice. The way forward may lie in research into particular constellations of behavior or of cognitive features, but equally it may lie in the examination of the clinical correlates of specific biological features.

The Shaywitzes and their colleagues (see Chapter 15) argue that the basis of "MBD" syndromes may be some abnormality in brain monoaminergic systems. As they indicate, there are research findings that are consistent with that possibility, and certainly the matter warrants further serious investigation. However, in proceeding along that path, it will be necessary to determine whether such abnormalities are specific or nonspecific. Medicine is full of examples of laboratory findings that are useful in pointing to the likelihood that "something is wrong," but that are of little or no diagnostic importance in themselves. Just as a raised erythrocyte sedimentation rate or fever constitute nonspecific findings of this kind in general medicine, so there are parallels in neuropsychiatry. For example, a raised blood serotonin level is found in many cases of severe mental retardation and of autism ("Leader," 1978), but the finding does not seem to have any diagnostic importance with respect to a particular disease entity. With respect to many neurochemical findings, investigators have yet to discover which do and which do not carry specific diagnostic implications. Yet, there can be no doubt that the pinpointing of a specific neurochemical feature, if one can be found, may prove to be the best way of delineating an "MBD" syndrome.

It is also possible that a characteristic response to some specific drug might serve to identify the hypothesized syndrome. Although claims have been made that a favorable response to stimulant medication constitutes just such a diagnostic feature (Gross & Wilson, 1974; Wender, 1971), the claim runs ahead of the empirical evidence (see Chapters 16 and 17). There are three main problems in this use of drug response as a defining feature of the syndrome. First, in many respects, normal children show responses to stimulant medication that parallel those of children supposed to have an "MBD" syndrome (see Chapter 18). Second, the beneficial responses apply to drugs, such as imipramine and methylphenidate, with rather different pharmacological effects (see Chapter 18). Third, the effective drugs are known to have multiple pharmacological actions and to benefit obviously different psychiatric conditions. Thus, imipramine is an effective treatment for depression (Bielski & Friedel, 1976) and (at least in the short term) for nocturnal enuresis (Blackwell & Currah, 1973), as well as for attentional deficit syndromes. Research to investigate the possibility of a diagnostically specific drug response is worthwhile, but the issues are complex and the findings difficult to interpret.

Comparable problems apply to the use of genetic strategies for syndrome definition. Questions remain on the importance of hereditary influences in hyperkinetic and attentional deficit syndromes (see Rutter, Chadwick, & Schachar, in press). Nevertheless, it is quite likely that genetic mechanisms will prove to be of some relevance. However, even if that can be demonstrated, it will not necessarily help in validating the hypothesized "MBD" syndrome. After all, most human behavior is under genetic control to a greater or lesser extent. Rather, the issue is whether or not there are hereditary influences that are specific to the syndrome and that differentiate it from other psychiatric or psychological conditions. If the genetic component concerns temperamental variables or some general vulnerability to "stress," it may be of no diagnostic importance. On the other hand, genetic studies constitute a potentially powerful tool for the delineation of meaningful distinct syndromes, and the strategy requires further exploitation.

Clearly, it would be unwarranted to dismiss the possibility of some form of "MBD" syndrome that is biologically distinctive in terms of its etiology, its mechanisms, or its response to treatment. Further research to investigate that possibility is needed, but it is too early to predict what will be found.

HYPERKINETIC AND ATTENTIONAL DEFICIT SYNDROMES

In spite of its inclusion in the *International Classification of Diseases*, ninth edition (ICD-9; the World Health Organization classification), and in spite of the specific criteria laid down for its diagnosis in the *Diagnostic and Statistical Manual of Mental Disorders*, third edition (DSM-III; the American Psychiatric Association classification), the nosological status of the hyperkinetic or attentional deficit syndrome remains quite uncertain and lacking in empirical validation. Much of the difficulty stems from the very pervasiveness of the phenomena. Both epidemiological (Rutter, Tizard, & Whitmore, 1970/1981; Sandberg, Wieselberg, & Shaffer, 1980) and clinical studies (Sandberg, Rutter, & Taylor, 1978) have shown that a high proportion of children with psychiatric disorders of all kinds tend to be restless, fidgety, overactive, inattentive, and lacking in concentration. This is particularly striking in the cases of conduct disorders and of delinquency, which show a very substantial overlap with disorders of hyperactivity and inattention (Rutter & Giller, 1983). The available evidence suggests that, in and of themselves, the mere presence of overactivity or poor concentration is of no diagnostic importance. Both symptoms may have many quite different causes. Thus, for example, it is well recognized that high levels of anxiety may lead to restlessness and that depression tends to be accompanied by deficits in concentration.

The need is for some means to disentangle these different forms of hyperkinesis and inattention in order to determine whether there are some varieties that may be of diagnostic importance. Already there are some leads that suggest support for that possibility. It is widely thought that the form of overactivity specific to the supposed syndrome must be manifest already during the preschool years. While it cannot be said that this assumption has been put to the test in an adequate fashion, it would seem to follow from the hypothesized developmental nature of the disorder, and it is at least consistent with the available evidence (S. B. Campbell, Schleifer, & Weiss, 1978; Sandberg *et al.*, 1978). Also, however, it seems likely that it is hyperkinesis that is pervasive over situations and persistent over time (Schachar, Rutter, & Smith, 1981) that will prove to be of diagnostic importance. While empirical findings fail to support the validity of a very common, broadly based hyperkinetic syndrome, there are some pointers indicating that there may be a rarer, more narrowly defined condition that does have some validity. At present, the evidence is no more than suggestive but the possibility deserves further study.

But it may well turn out that the differentiating features concern inattention rather than overactivity. That supposition already constitutes the basis of the DSM-III concept of the syndrome, and, indeed, it led to the change in name (to "attentional deficit disorder"). The research findings well described by Douglas (see Chapter 14) amply document the importance of the study of attention. But, also, they indicate the complexity of the phenomenon of attention and the misleading character of some of the more simplistic notions that predominated a few years ago. It is abundantly clear that investigators need to differentiate between the several different varieties of attention and inattention. It remains to be established whether any specific type of attentional deficit serves to separate an "MBD" syndrome from other psychiatric conditions, but that possibility rightly constitutes the focus of much research on this topic.

The use of stimulant medication to treat children with hyperkinetic and attentional problems has been subject to more systematic research than has any other pharmacological treatment in child psychiatry. The results of well-controlled trials leave no doubt that stimulants constitute an effective form of short-term treatment (see Chapter 18). Moreover, it also appears that drugs are more powerful than are behavioral interventions, at least with respect to improvement in attentional problems over periods of a few weeks or months (see Chapters 19 and 21). But serious questions remain. It is not yet known whether a favorable drug response constitutes a consistent characteristic of individual children over time. It seems to be so over relatively short periods of time, but it is uncertain whether or not it remains so over a matter of years. It appears that it is possible to take some children off stimulants without loss (Charles, Schain, & Guthrie, 1979; Sleator, von Neumann, & Sprague, 1974), but the matter has been little investigated up to now. Investigators also lack knowledge on whether or not the use of stimulant medication improves the long-term prognosis. Comparisons of nonrandomly assigned groups show no apparent long-term benefit from medication (see Chapter 20), but methodologically adequate trials have yet to be undertaken. The prolonged treatment studies from the UCLA group (Satterfield, Satterfield, & Cantwell, 1980) are encouraging in showing a better prognosis than might have been expected; however, they lack a no-treatment control group, and the interventions were so complex and multifaceted that it is not possible to draw any conclusions on the specific effects of medication per se. It is apparent that there is still much to learn about the long-term effects of treatment and the factors that influence the long-term outcome (see Chapter 20).

LEARNING DISORDERS

Rather similar issues apply to the field of learning disorders. It is obvious that the term itself is far too broad to be of any diagnostic value. Children fail to learn for a host of different reasons—including generally low intelligence, inadequate schooling, and lack of family encouragement—quite apart from disorders associated with organic brain dysfunction or specific cognitive deficits. Moreover, these "nonorganic" factors are of very considerable importance, as shown, for example, by the studies of schooling (Rutter, Maughan, Mortimore, & Ouston, with Smith, 1979) and of the effects of children reading to their parents (Tizard, Schofield, & Hewison, 1982). It is apparent, too, that a distinction needs to be drawn between learning failures apparent from the outset of school and learning difficulties that develop only later in childhood (Rutter, 1974). However, in addition, as well documented in several chapters of this volume (see Chapters 22 and 23), very considerable progress has been made in delineating different varieties of learning disability according to the pattern of cognitive deficits shown. Not only are there major differences among reading difficulties, "pure" spelling difficulties, and arithmetical difficulties, but it has also proven possible to distinguish different varieties of reading disability (see also Boder, 1973; Mattis, 1978).

At present, this differentiation relies solely on the associations with patterns of cognitive disability. It is not known whether the various cognitive syndromes differ in their response to different forms of remediation, nor is it known whether they differ neurophysiologically or genetically. However, the means are now available to investigate these matters. Genetically, the question is *not* whether learning difficulties "run" in families (it is known that they do) but rather whether *specific* types of cognitive disability "breed true." The studies of Barton Childs and his colleagues (see Chapter 26), and also those of Harold Gordon (1980), provide leads in this connection. Similarly, neurophysiologically, the question is *not* whether electroencephalogram (EEG) abnormalities are associated with learning disabilities (possibly they are—see Hughes, 1978), but rather whether the pattern of regional brain activation during reading tasks differentiates "dyslexic" children from "normals" and differentiates among the various hypothesized specific varieties of learning disability (Galin, Johnstone, Yingling, Fein, Herron, & Marcus, 1982). The distinctive patterns of cognitive deficit found in some cases of learning disability suggest that there may be equally distinctive abnormalities in brain function that underlie the learning problems; however, these have yet to be demonstrated. Similarly, it seems reasonable to suppose that different types of learning disability might have a different course and outcome and might require different forms of specific remediation. Yet these linkages have still to be found. As Gittelman (Chapter 27) notes, present knowledge of the efficacy of the remedial methods in current usage is woefully inadequate. This constitutes a research area in need of development.

MEASUREMENT

As discussed in many chapters of this volume, questions of measurement continue to be of fundamental importance. It is obvious that investigators have an ever-increasing range of improved techniques at their disposal, but, in most cases, it remains unclear just what it is that is being measured (see Taylor's discussion of this point in Chapter 12). For example, the empirical evidence on neurological "soft signs" (see Chapters 7 and 8) indicates that such signs are related to cognitive dysfunction, learning difficulties, and psychiatric disturbance. Evidently, the signs are of some importance as indicators of malfunction. But what type of malfunction do the signs indicate? As Shaffer and his colleagues suggest (Chapter 8), it is likely that "soft signs" have many origins: Some may be a consequence of mild brain damage; some may represent genetically determined individual differences; some may reflect transient developmental phenomena that will pass as a result of neurological maturation; and some may be no more than behavioral epiphenomena that, like other forms of behavior, are subject to the influences of learning, motivation, attention, and anxiety. Investigations are needed to test these various possibilities more rigorously. To what extent do the individual signs show consistency over time and over situations? Which signs may be influenced by experimental modifications of the individual's state (as by drugs, "stressful" test conditions, or rewards to increase motivation)?

Closely comparable issues arise with the other measures of brain function and malfunction. Progress has been made in the development of improved neuropsychological measures. As a result of correlational, clustering, and factorial studies of different kinds, investigators now have a better appreciation of the extent to which different tests tap similar functions (see Chapter 10). This is helpful. However, researchers have a much more limited understanding of just what these functions mean in terms of brain processes. There has been an increasing tendency to speak of "left-hemisphere tests" and "right-hemisphere tests," as if the psychological measures were known to represent the operative efficiency of a particular cerebral hemisphere. But such knowledge is not available. Of course there are valid reasons for making such linkages (mainly based on work with adults) but, still, it has to be said that the assumptions that the tests reflect left- or right-hemisphere functioning are just that—assumptions and not facts. Moreover, even when there is evidence that, say, left-hemisphere damage leads to low scores on test *x*, that evidence cannot be used to justify the inference when expressed the other way round. That is, logically, it would not follow that low scores on test *x* therefore mean left-hemisphere damage. It does not follow, because there may be 101 other causes of low scores on test *x*. Lesions of the left motor cortex predictably lead to a right-sided limp, but not all limps are due to cortical injuries—they may stem from causes as diverse as a sprained ankle, a protruding nail in the shoe, an infection of the knee, or a peripheral nerve injury! Of course, there are well-established ways of determining the specific type of limp that is indicative of a pyramidal tract lesion. It may well be that this will prove to be possible, too, with neuropsychological measures, but investigators have not yet reached that point.

Sometimes it is thought that these considerations do not apply to physiological measures (such as the neurometric techniques described in Chapter 11) or anatomical measures (such as those provided by computer-assisted tomography). But, of course, they do. The discovery that normally the left parieto-occipital region is wider than the right (see Geschwind, Galaburda, & LeMay, 1979) was important, and the further suggestion that there may be *reversed* asymmetry in some cases of reading disability (Hier, LeMay, Rosenberger, & Perlo, 1978), if confirmed, is likely to have meaning. But what meaning? Obviously, it does not necessarily indicate any form of congenital or acquired "lesion"; rather, it opens up the possibility of biologically based differences in cognitive function that are not dependent upon some neuropathological abnormality (Geschwind *et al.*, 1979). But, of course, not only do investigators lack any adequate understanding of the biological correlates of anatomical asymmetry (is it paralleled by neurophysiological or neurochemical asymmetry?), but they also do not know the functional implications of the asymmetry.

Nevertheless, powerful new investigative techniques for the study of brain function and malfunction are beginning to open up fresh avenues of enquiry that carry high promise of providing some of the essential links so far missing in the present appreciation of the brain mechanisms that underlie learning disorders. For example, the combination of positron-computed tomography to measure the concentration of radioactivity in tissue *in vivo*, together with the use of physiologically active compounds labeled with positron-emitting isotopes and tracer kinetic models, allows the measurement of local physiological processes in human subjects (Phelps, Kuhl, & Mazziotta, 1981). These techniques have been used already to provide a metabolic mapping of the brain's response to visual stimulation, and presumably they carry the potential for studying other varieties of local cerebral metabolic function in a safe and noninvasive manner. Similarly, new neurometric techniques are being developed for the identification of dynamic spatiotemporal electrical patterns of the brain during purposive behaviors (Gevins, Doyle, Cutillo, Schaffer, Tannehill, Ghannam, Gilcrease, & Yeager, 1981). Patterns of correlation between electrical potentials have been found to differentiate visuomotor tasks, differing only in the type of mental judgment required (spatial or numerical). Both these techniques are still in their infancy, and much more work is required to validate the measures and to determine the relationships between neuroradiological, neurophysiological, and neuropsychological findings. Even so, for the first time, it appears that investigators may have available techniques for studying the dynamic associations between brain function and a person's cognitive performance and socioemotional behavior during life.

MATURATION AND DEVELOPMENT

Throughout the literature on "MBD," and on hyperactive or learning disorders more generally, there is frequent reference to concepts of "maturational lag" or "developmental delay." The notion, as expressed most simply, is both plausible and easy to understand. With almost all functions, there is wide variation among normal children in the age at which the usual developmental milestones are reached. Just as some children get their teeth early and others get theirs late, so some walk later than average or do not learn to speak until well past the usual age. It seems reasonable to regard some of the more extreme forms of developmental delay as no more than very marked exaggerations of this general trend for children to mature at different rates. Moreover, it seems equally tempting to link these variations in the development of language or motor coordination or reading skills to specific delays in the maturation of some specific part of the brain or some particular brain system. After all, just as some body organs mature early and some mature late, so some parts of the brain mature in advance of other parts. It is known, for example, that the lower, more primitive parts of the brain tend to develop earlier than the higher, more complex parts do (Marshall, 1968). The brain fibers for hearing develop early, but the regions concerned with the use and understanding of what is heard develop later. In short, it is normal for different brain systems to develop at different rates, with each system "out of step" with others. Accordingly, it might be suggested that, in some circumstances, unusually great variations in rates of brain maturation might be responsible for specific delays in the development of particular brain functions (such as speech or language). Hence the hypothesis of "maturational lag" (see Satz, Taylor, Friel, & Fletcher, 1978).

However, althought the concept is plausible, it is hypothesis rather than fact, and numerous difficulties surround the idea. Most fundamentally, investigators lack adequate direct measures of brain maturation that can be obtained during life, as well as understanding of the connections between brain maturation and brain functions, as reflected in the development of skills such as language, reading, attention, or motor coordination (Connolly & Prechtl, 1981). It may be that the availability of more sensitive and sophisticated neurophysiological markers (see Chapter 11) will provide the means to investigate these connections, but that remains to be seen. But questions also remain on the specific developmental disorders themselves. If the delay is a consequence of some "maturational lag," it might be expected that the course of psychological development should be normal in form, even if late in timing. But is this so? Studies of children with reading and spelling disabilities suggest that some use learning strategies that are *not* characteristic of normal children (see Chapters 22 and 24), and studies of children with specific language delays also suggest features showing deviance as well as delay (Menyuk, 1980). Does this mean *abnormal* brain maturation, rather than just a "lag"? Or have the deviant features arisen as responses or adaptations in children who are "out of step" with their peers and with educational expectations? If the delays are a result of a "maturational lag," one might also expect that the children should soon "catch up." But follow-up studies show that many do not (see Chapter 28). If normal children learn to read by, say, age 7 or 8, it is easy to believe that a lag in brain maturation might retard the acquisition of reading to age 9 or 10, or perhaps even age 11 or 12. But can such a hypothesis account for reading disabilities that still persist at age 17 or 18 or even at age 27 or 28? Is the brain still "immature" in late adolescence and early adult life; or is the persistence of reading problems due to some kind of "sensitive period" for learning effect; or are the continuing difficulties at older ages no longer due to "maturational lag" per se, but rather to a secondary feeling of failure or lack of adequate instruction at the time when the brain was "receptive" for the learning of the requisite skills?

SEVERE DEVELOPMENTAL REGRESSION OR DISINTEGRATION

The term "disintegrative psychosis" has come to be applied to disorders in which, following apparently normal development up to the age of 3 or 4 years, there is profound regression and behavioral distintegration (World Health Organization, 1978). Often there is a period of premonitory vague illness, and then the child becomes restless, irritable, anxious, and overactive. Over the course of a few months, there is an impoverishment and then a loss of speech and language. Comprehension of language deteriorates, and intelligence usually (but not always) declines; there is a severe loss of social skills, impairment of interpersonal relationships, a general loss of interest in objects, and the development of stereotypies and mannerisms (Rutter, 1977b).

This group of conditions was first described by Heller (1930/1969), using the diagnostic term "dementia infantilis." Although that term has fallen into disuse, there are obvious clinical parallels with the dementia seen in the chronic organic reactions of adult life. There are neuropathological parallels, too, in that in many cases the subsequent course of the disorders, together with postmortem studies, reveals some kind of organic cortical degeneration, such as that associated with the lipoidoses and leucodystrophies (Corbett, Harris, Taylor, & Trimble, 1977; Darby, 1976; Malamud, 1959; Rivinus, Jamison, & Graham, 1975).

Nevertheless, there are reasons for preferring the term "disintegrative psychosis," as this term recognizes both the differences from adult dementia and the unresolved issues regarding pathogenesis. In many cases, the initial psychiatric disturbance is chiefly characterized by bizarre and stereotyped behavior, delusional ideas, and inappropriate affect, rather than by intellectual decline. Although the course may be one of continuing deterioration, depending on the underlying pathology, in other cases a plateau seems to be reached—with severe handicap and a poor prognosis, but no further progression. Moreover, as shown by Evans-Jones and Rosenbloom's (1978) series of 10 patients, there are cases with closely similar symptomatology but no unequivocal evidence of neurological disease during a period of several years after the time of diagnosis. As they comment, it appears highly probable that there is an underlying basic neurological dysfunction in most (if not all) cases, but so far investigative tools have failed to identify the hypothesized neuropathological substratum.

THE APPARENT NONSPECIFICITY OF THE COGNITIVE SEQUELAE OF LOCALIZED BRAIN LESIONS IN CHILDHOOD

In turning from specific psychiatric and psychological disorders or conditions to the behavioral and cognitive sequelae of known brain lesions, further issues and dilemmas are evident. Perhaps the most surprising finding concerns the apparent nonspecificity of the sequelae of localized brain lesions in childhood. It is generally accepted that, in adults, the pattern of cognitive deficits after unilateral cerebral lesions differs according to which hemisphere is damaged (see Berent, 1981; Boll, 1981; McFie, 1975a). In general, verbal impairment is most characteristic of left-hemisphere lesions (even in the absence of dysphasia), and visuospatial impairment is most characteristic of right-hemisphere lesions. The effects of laterality are most marked in terms of the acute effects of deep intrinsic lesions (Fitzhugh, Fitzhugh, & Reitan, 1962; Newcombe, 1969) but laterality effects have been found to persist for as long as 20 years after the time of injury (Newcombe, 1969).

Why, then, was this laterality effect not found in our study of children with localized head injuries (see Chapter 5)? It could be suggested that this was because the lesions were too superficial, but this does not seem to explain the findings. McFie (1975b) found closely similar findings in his study of children with hematomas, abscesses, and tumors; and studies of hemidecortication (Kohn & Dennis, 1974) and hemispherectomy (Gott, 1973) have also shown rather minor laterality effects. Such effects have tended to be similar to those found in adults, but the differences have been both smaller and less consistent. Our own findings indicated that it was unlikely that contrecoup effects were responsible for the negative results, and such effects could not account for the similarly negative results in Lehmkuhl, Kotlarek, and Schieber's (1981) small-scale study of cerebral-palsied children in which the lesions were identified by means of computerized axial tomography (CT) scans. Of course, it could be that the laterality effects in all these studies of children were attentuated as a result of the (usually) long intervals between the time of injury and the time of testing. Certainly, it is possible that laterality effects might be more marked in the acute posttraumatic phase, but, as already noted, Newcombe's (1969) study of adults with localized injuries showed a persistence of laterality effects for two decades.

Other research has shown that the effects of aphasia-producing lesions in childhood differ from those in adult life (Alajouanine & Lhermitte, 1965; Guttman, 1942). At one time it was thought that aphasia in childhood always had a good prognosis and that the age differences in response argued for hemispheric equipotentiality in early childhood (Lenneberg, 1967). However, it is clear now that, although spontaneous recovery from language loss in childhood is often dramatic, it is not invariable, and some linguistic deficits may persist (Pirozzolo, Campanella, Christensen, & Lawson-Kerr, 1981; St. James Roberts, 1979; Satz & Bullard-Bates, 1981). Moreover, the better recovery in childhood does not necessarily indicate hemispheric equipotentiality. Nevertheless, even though some of the earlier claims were exaggerated, well-controlled studies have demonstrated that the effects of left-hemisphere damage on language functioning do indeed vary with age (Woods & Carey, 1979). Not only are the effects of such damage in early childhood *different*, in that the usual immediate result is impaired speech development rather than aphasic-type abnormalities of language; but also early damage to the left hemisphere is less likely to lead to permanent language impairment.

There are difficulties in drawing firm conclusions on age differences in laterality effects, if only because the types of lesions leading to focal brain damage and the conditions of testing tend to be different in childhood from those in adult life (Isaacson, 1975; St. James Roberts, 1979). Nevertheless, the evidence, when considered as a whole, certainly suggests that the cognitive deficits associated with lateralized brain injuries tend to be less specific in childhood than in adult life.

That conclusion seems to be reasonably well based, but it does raise difficult issues. In the first place, it would be unwarranted to assume from these findings that specific cognitive or language deficits do not occur in childhood. Obviously they do. For example, it is well established that children with learning disabilities not infrequently exhibit marked deficits in particular areas of cognitive functioning, in spite of normal levels of general intelligence (see Chapters 23 and 29). Similar, although less marked, patterns may also be seen in the relatives of "dyslexic" children (Gordon, 1980). Sometimes such specific deficits are used as the basis for inferences regarding malfunctioning in one or the other cerebral hemisphere. The studies of children *known* to have lateralized brain injuries suggest that such inferences are rather speculative. The links between specific learning disabilities and structural brain pathology have not been established, and the links with focal lesions even less so. Such links may exist (indeed, there are pointers to their possible presence in some cases), but they require empirical demonstration and testing, and that remains a task for the future.

The same applies to the specific developmental disorders of speech and language (Wyke, 1978) and to syndromes such as "the clumsy child" (Gubbay, Ellis, Walton, & Court, 1965). Both represent severe specific deficits. There are reasons for supposing that they are likely to be due to some type of organic brain dysfunction, but knowledge is lacking on just what form this dysfunction may take.

However, in addition to this broad range of specific disabilities for which the organic basis has yet to be delineated, there are also well-documented cases in which the links with brain pathology have been shown, or at least where there is strong circumstantial evidence that they exist. For example, this applies to those rare cases, first described by Worster-Drought (1964), in which children lose their speech entirely after a period of normal development. The loss of speech is often associated with gross but transient (usually bilateral) EEG abnormalities and epileptic fits occurring only for a short while after the onset. There are no motor abnormalities, and the intellect is usually unimpaired on nonverbal tasks. Most of these children remain permanently handicapped in their language, in spite of normal development in other respects. While the precise pathology remains unknown, the evidence suggests some form of *bilateral* damage. The same applies to many other cases of acquired aphasia in which severe language deficits persist. Accordingly, it may well be that in childhood bilateral brain lesions are required to produce *persistent* specific deficits. But this does not seem to be wholly the case (Satz & Bullard-Bates, 1981).

CT-scan studies also suggest that some cases of reading disability are associated with a reversal (Hier *et al.*, 1978) of the usual asymmetry in which the left parieto-occipital region is wider than the right (Geschwind *et al.*, 1979). This could be interpreted as implying a unilateral lesion; however, this is speculative, and the meaning of a reversed asymmetry remains obscure.

No closure is possible on this difficult question of the basis of specific cognitive deficits. Undoubtedly, further research is needed into the effects of localized or lateralized brain lesions in childhood, but, equally, it seems most unlikely that focal structural abnormalities will prove to be the cause of most specific developmental disorders. Investigators need to have a better understanding of the ways in which different brain systems operate, and this requires advances in neurochemical and neurophysiological studies even more than it requires improvements in the anatomical pinpointing of lesions.

Comparable issues arise with respect to brain–behavior relationships. There is some circumstantial evidence suggesting that, in adults, there may be links between right-hemisphere dysfunction and affective disturbance, and between left-hemisphere dysfunction and schizophrenia (Flor-Henry, 1979; Tucker, 1981; Wexler, 1980). However, it remains quite uncertain whether these associations apply in childhood, and, even if they do, it is evident that most of the child psychiatric disorders brought about by brain damage are nonspecific in type, with symptomatology that does not clearly differentiate them from functional psychiatric conditions.

But that conclusion should not be held to mean that there are no specific brain–behavior relationships, and certainly not to mean that there are no mental disorders of a characteristically different type that have an organic basis. Autism provides the most obvious example of just such a condition. The presence of some form of organic brain dysfunction in autistic children was first evident, perhaps, in the demonstration from follow-up studies that in about a quarter to a third of cases epileptic seizures develop during adolescence (Rutter, 1970). Subsequent epidemiological research (Deykin & MacMahon, 1979) has confirmed both the increased incidence of epilepsy and the fact that it is unusual in having its onset during the teenage years (most mentally retarded children with epilepsy first have seizures during early childhood). More recently, several studies have shown ventricular abnormalities either on pneumoencephalography (Hauser, DeLong, & Rosman, 1975) or on computer-assisted axial tomography (Damasio, Maurer, Damasio, & Chui, 1980). At first, it was thought that there might be a specific abnormality in the form of either dilatation of the left temporal horn (Hauser *et al.*, 1975) or reversed asymmetry of the parieto-occipital region similar to that supposed to be associated with reading disabilities (Hier, LeMay, & Rosenberger, 1979), but subsequent studies have not been able to confirm either as a consistent finding in autism (M. Campbell, Rosenbloom, Perry, George, Kricheff, Anderson, Small, & Jennings, 1982; Caparulo, Cohen, Rothman, Young, Katz, Shaywitz, & Shaywitz, 1981; Damasio *et al.*, 1980).

In a few cases, autism has been found to be associated with (and presumably due to) some medical condition giving rise to brain pathology. For example, infantile spasms with hypsarrthymia (Riikonen & Amnell, 1981; Taft & Cohen, 1971) and congenital rubella (Chess, Korn, & Fernandez, 1971) have both been linked with autism. Of course, these are medical syndromes that are also associated with general mental retardation. But it should be noted that the medical conditions that give rise to intellectual impairment differ strikingly in their links with autism. Some, such as the two just mentioned, fairly commonly lead to autism. Others, such as Down syndrome and cerebral palsy (Wing & Gould, 1979), rarely do so. At present, it is unknown just which are the neuropathological or cognitive features that differentiate these two rather heterogeneous groups—an issue that warrants systematic investigation.

Quite apart from associations with overt brain pathology of one type or another, or with perinatal factors that predispose to brain damage (Deykin & MacMahon, 1980; Finnegan & Quadrington, 1979), there is evidence from family studies (August, Stewart, & Tsai, 1981) and from twin comparisons

(Folstein & Rutter, 1977) of the importance of hereditary influences. However, the evidence suggests that it is probably not autism as such that is inherited, but rather some broader predisposition to language and cognitive abnormalities of which autism constitutes but one part. There is every indication that, ultimately, the study of the syndrome of autism should throw light on some specific mechanisms in brain–behavior relationships—but just what these will prove to be has yet to be determined.

Although autism constitutes the most obvious example in this connection, there are others. Thus, the Lesch–Nyhan syndrome is an X-linked central nervous system disorder associated with the overproduction of uric acid and dysfunction of brain neurotransmitters (Lloyd, Hornykiewicz, Davidson, Shannak, Farley, Goldstein, Shibuya, Kelley, & Fox, 1981). It is psychiatrically quite distinctive in terms of a most unusual compulsive form of self-mutilation (Nyhan, 1976). This begins when the teeth first erupt and characteristically leads to loss of tissue about the lips and partial autoamputation of the fingers. The mechanisms involved have yet to be identified, but it seems clear that there is some kind of specific brain–behavior association. Or, again, the Prader–Willi syndrome, a condition associated with deletion of chromosome 15, is characterized by an unusually voracious appetite and consequent severe obesity, as well as mental retardation, muscular hypotonia, hypogonadism, short stature, and other features (Ledbetter, Riccardi, Airhart, Strobel, Keenan, & Crawford, 1981).

The lesson here, as with cognitive deficits, is that if investigators are to make progress in elucidating neuropsychiatric mechanisms, they must approach the question from both ends. That is, there is a need for investigations that have as their starting point established brain pathology of some specific kind, but equally there is a need to study the processes underlying specific psychiatric disorders, when these disorders seem likely to be due to some form of organic brain dysfunction.

But it should not be thought that it is only the *specific* brain–behavior relationships that are of interest. There is a plethora of evidence that brain damage greatly increases the risk of emotional and conduct disorders of the same type that occur in children without structural brain pathology (see Rutter, 1981). But, *how* does this increase in psychiatric risk come about? For the reasons already given—especially the nonspecificity of the associations and the rather weak and inconsistent relationship with the severity of the brain damage—the effects seem likely to be indirect rather than direct. It should be noted, however, that it may well not be the *loss* of brain function that matters most in the genesis of psychiatric disturbance. The finding that epileptic children of normal intelligence and without any neurological condition also have a markedly increased risk of psychiatric disorder (Rutter, Graham, & Yule, 1970) suggests that it may be *abnormal* brain activity that plays the greater role. There are no very consistent correlations with EEG findings as ordinarily assessed (Harris, 1977), but the ordinary EEG is rather a crude diagnostic instrument.

If it is assumed that much of the effect of brain dysfunction is indirect, it might be expected that such dysfunction would operate through some general increase in children's susceptibility or vulnerability to psychosocial stresses. But that does not seem to be the case, in that there is no interaction between brain dysfunction and psychosocial adversity; both have an effect in predisposing to psychiatric disorder, but the effects are additive rather than interactive (Rutter, 1977a). Various possible mechanisms may be postulated, but evidence is meager on their relative importance, and this remains an issue requiring further study.

AGE EFFECTS

The possible importance of age effects in altering the impact of brain lesions constitutes a further matter of considerable theoretical importance as well as of controversy. The early experimental ablation studies in monkeys by Margaret Kennard (1942) gave rise to the general conclusion that brain lesions early in life lead to lesser deficits than do similar lesions at maturity. The studies of acquired aphasia due to unilateral lesions, showing the greater recovery in early childhood (Lenneberg, 1967), led to similar conclusions—usually expressed in terms of the greater "plasticity" of the developing brain (Chelune & Edwards, 1981). However, recent reviews of the evidence have included scathing attacks both on the hypothesis of better recovery with earlier brain lesions and on the concept of plasticity (St. James Roberts, 1979; Satz & Fletcher, 1981). Our own studies of children with head injuries (see Chapter 5) also showed no marked age effects on the frequency or severity of cognitive or behavioral sequelae. Should it be concluded, then, that developmental considerations are of no importance and that brain lesions at all ages have similar effects? Certainly not! There is a great deal of evidence to show that the effects of brain lesions *do* vary according to developmental level. It is *not* that the issue is of no importance, but rather that it is a highly complex one with several different mechanisms in operation, so that no simple statement is possible on whether it is better to have a brain lesion early or late.

So far as the cognitive and behavioral sequelae of brain injury are concerned, three rather different findings require emphasis. Firstly, in humans, the lesser deficits with early lesions largely applies to the effects on spoken *language*, and, even with language, to the effects of *unilateral* lesions. Thus, in Byers and McLean's (1962) study showing that acquired aphasias usually cleared up in childhood, not only did the hemiplegias remain, but also the children's school performance was impaired in many cases. Secondly, so far as cognition is concerned, it is not that early lesions lead to lesser or greater effects—rather, it is that the effects are *different*. As has been indicated, brain pathology in early childhood is *less* likely to lead to highly specific cognitive deficits, but it is probably *more* likely to lead to general intellectual impairment and to poor scholastic performance. Thirdly, the immediate and the long-term effects of brain injury are not necessarily the same. For example, the association between left-temporal-lobe epilepsy and schizophrenia concerns epilepsy with an onset in *childhood* but schizophrenia with an onset in *adult* life, many years later (Davison & Bagley, 1969; Taylor, 1975).

In interpreting these findings, attention needs to be paid to both neuropathological and cognitive mechanisms. Firstly, there is evidence that immature organs are more susceptible to injury than are mature ones, and that organs tend to be most vulnerable at the time of their most rapid growth, which, in the case of the brain, means the prenatal period and the first 2 years or so after birth (Dobbing, 1974). As a consequence of this increased susceptibility to damage (as well as the greater difficulties in early diagnosis in infancy), young infants are more likely than older children are to show serious intellectual impairment following meningoencephalities (see Rutter *et al.*, 1970) and therapeutic irradiation of the brain (Eiser, 1980). These considerations mean that early traumata tend to cause more damage than do similar traumata at a later age.

Secondly, experimental work with animals indicates that the earlier the brain damage, the greater the reorganization of the neuronal connections underlying behavior (see Lynch & Gall, 1979; Schneider, 1979; van Hof, 1981). That is to say, following brain injury, there is regrowth of neuronal axons and also sprouting of collateral axons. It has long been known that this process occurs following the cutting of peripheral nerves, but it is now well established that the same phenomenon takes place in the central nervous system. This regrowth occurs even in adults to some extent, but it is very much greater during the infancy period. To that extent, it is indeed correct to speak of the greater plasticity of the immature brain. The error comes in supposing that this "rewiring" of the brain necessarily leads to greater functional recovery or improved performance. In some circumstances, it may do so, but, on the whole, the evidence suggests that it is at least as likely to lead to a greater *mal*function as a result of the development of *anomalous* neuronal connections.

Thirdly, it seems that there is a greater potential for interhemispheric transfer of language functions in infancy. It is not, as once supposed, that there is equipotentiality of the two hemispheres in infancy (Witelson, 1977). Even in infancy, there is substantial hemispheric specialization. Nevertheless, the empirical findings indicate that there is a rather greater versatility of functioning in infancy and that, in particular, it is more readily possible for the right hemisphere to "take over" language functions when the left hemisphere is damaged. But, this effect has only been demonstrated at all clearly for *inter*hemisphere "transfer" of functions; it is dubious whether it applies to transfer within a single hemisphere. Hence, insofar as this versatility of the immature brain provides a potential for greater recovery, it is likely to do so only in relation to unilateral lesions. However, not only is very little known about "transfer" effects with bilateral lesions; there is also no precise understanding of the neurophysiological or neuropsychological mechanisms that underlie this apparent interhemispheric "transfer" or "take-up" of language functions (see Stein, Rosen, & Butters, 1974). In addition, it remains uncertain to what extent the effect applies to cognitive functions other than language.

Finally, the effects of brain injury are likely to be influenced by the stage of development of the cognitive or behavioral functions being considered. Forty years ago, Hebb (1942) suggested that brain damage had its greatest impact on *new learning*. It is not clear how far that is in fact the case, but, insofar as it is, the implication is that brain injuries may lead to greater impairments in young children just because they have more new learning to undertake, and less accumulated knowledge and established skills on which to rely (Rutter, 1981). Whereas brain injury in early childhood is likely to impede the learning of reading or arithmetic in a child who has yet to gain those skills, brain injury in the older child is less likely to cause a *loss* in those same skills, which are then well established. Much the same issues apply to social and emotional development. But, in addition, it is almost inevitable that the effects of brain injury on a skill yet to develop will be *different* (not necessarily worse or better) from those on an established skill. Thus, left-hemisphere lesions in infancy lead to a *delay* in speech development, rather than to aphasic-type *abnormalities* of language. There are likely to be parallels in other functions.

The issue of whether the effects of brain injury vary according to the child's developmental level is far from dead. There is much still to be learned, and the gaining of that knowledge should have both theoretical and practical implications. But the question is not just whether it is better or worse to have a brain lesion early; rather, it concerns the age-related neuropathological and psychological processes involved in the disabilities and the recovery that may follow different forms of brain injury at different phases of the developmental cycle. In that connection, it is particularly necessary that researchers investigate the *longitudinal course* of development following brain injury. The delayed onset of schizophrenia following left-sided temporal-lobe epilepsy has been mentioned already as an example of delayed effects that differ from the immediate sequelae. In that case the late sequelae are worse, but they can also be better. For example, the Lindsay, Ounsted, and Richards (1979) follow-up suggested that, apart from the onset of schizophrenia, the psychiatric disabilities associated with temporal-lobe epilepsy in adult life may be less than they were in the same individuals when younger. The suggestion remains speculative, in that it is unclear whether the measures in adult life were at all comparable with those in childhood, but the possibility warrants further exploration. The same applies to the question of changes in the characteristics of cognitive deficits as children grow older. For example, Fletcher and Satz (1980) in their general population follow-up study, found that whereas in younger children sensory–motor and perceptual skills were those most clearly associated with reading achievement, at an older age linguistic measures accounted for more of the variance in reading (although whether this age change in patterns of association applies to severe reading retardation is not known). Or, again, Ingram (1970), in his follow-up of speech-retarded children, found that many continued to have reading and spelling difficulties long after they had gained normal levels of spoken language. Neither study refers to brain-injured children, but comparable issues apply to the sequelae of brain injury; so far, they have been little studied.

THRESHOLD EFFECTS

The findings from our studies of children with head injuries (see Chapter 5) have suggested that there is a fairly high threshold for the cognitive and behavioral sequelae of brain injury. It seemed that for any persistent sequelae the head injury must have been sufficiently severe to have caused a post-traumatic amnesia (PTA) of at least 7 days. It appeared that mild brain damage had little long-term effect on psychological development. The conclusion that the threshold for sequelae is relatively high is in keeping with other studies of head-injured children and seems consistent with the results of follow-up studies of children suffering perinatal complications (Rutter, 1981). Once those with overt neurological handicaps are excluded, few sequelae are detectable by the time they reach middle childhood (Drillien, Thomson, & Burgoyne, 1980).

But a dilemma remains, in that there is other evidence suggesting a lower threshold. None of this evidence is clear-cut in its implications, but, taken as a whole, it raises some troubling questions. Firstly, in our study of children with localized head injuries (Chadwick, Rutter, Thompson, & Shaffer, 1981; Shaffer,

Bijur, Chadwick, & Rutter, 1980), the proportion of children with reading attainments at least 2 years below their chronological age was surprisingly high, even in the subgroup with the most minor injuries. Thus, among those with only slight local trauma and no generalized damage, 23% were 2 years or more backward in reading (in spite of a normal level of intelligence). The finding raises the possibility that there may be long-term scholastic difficulties, even if there is no effect on IQ. The increased rate of reading difficulties in epileptic children (Rutter *et al.*, 1970) suggests the same.

Secondly, there are the findings linking neurological "soft signs" with an increased risk of psychiatric disorder (Chapter 8) and those linking neurometric measures with learning disabilities (Chapter 11). The problem in the interpretation of both sets of findings lies in the uncertainty regarding the meaning of the clinical signs of neurodevelopmental impairment or the computer-analyzed neurophysiological measures (Chapter 12). Obviously, it cannot be assumed that they reflect brain dysfunction, but they may do so.

Thirdly, several studies have shown significant associations between low-level lead exposure and a slight increase in cognitive and attentional difficulties (reviewed in Rutter & Russell Jones, 1983). There are many problems in the interpretation of these associations (see Rutter, 1980), and it is difficult to be sure that they are not an artifact of some aspect of social disadvantage. Nevertheless, it seems that when social variables are taken into account, the links with lead exposure still remain. It is puzzling that the deficits associated with moderate lead exposure are no greater than those associated with low-level lead exposure. Inevitably, this lack of a consistent dose–response relationship raises doubts regarding the validity of the supposed biological effect. Yet, it would not be justified to dismiss the findings, and, if accepted, they argue for a much lower threshold than that suggested by the head injury findings. Of course, it may be that the mechanisms involved are different (after all, one represents the reaction to a severe acute trauma and the other the reaction to a mild but very chronic one). But that possibility only serves to emphasize the importance of the issues involved.

CONCLUSIONS

As I have indicated, there are very many real achievements in the field of developmental neuropsychiatry; the issues with which it deals are both theoretically and practically important, and the prospects for the future of the subject are highly promising. Nevertheless, as indicated in this final chapter, many areas of ignorance and uncertainty remain. The issues are susceptible to resolution, but for success to be achieved, it is clear that there must be a bringing together of expertise in diverse branches of the basic and clinical neurosciences. That constitutes the main goal for the future.

References

Alajouanine, T., & Lhermitte, F. Acquired aphasia in children. *Brain*, 1965, *88*, 653–662.

American Psychiatric Association. *Diagnostic and statistical manual of mental disorders* (3rd ed.). Washington, D.C.: Author, 1980.

August, G. J., Stewart, M. A., & Tsai, L. The incidence of cognitive disabilities in the siblings of autistic children. *British Journal of Psychiatry*, 1981, *138*, 416–422.

Bakwin, H., & Bakwin, R. M. M. *Clinical management of behavior disorders in children* (3rd ed.). Philadelphia: W. B. Saunders, 1966.

Berent, S. Lateralization of brain function. In S. B. Filskov & T. J. Boll (Eds.), *Handbook of clinical neuropsychology*. New York: Wiley, 1981.

Bielski, R. J., & Friedel, R. O. Prediction of tricyclic antidepressant response: A cortical review, *Archives of General Psychiatry*, 1976, *33*, 1479–1489.

Blackwell, B., & Currah, J. The psychopharmacology of nocturnal enuresis. In I. Kolvin, R. C. MacKeith, and S. R. Meadow (Eds.), *Bladder control and enuresis* (Clinics in Developmental Medicine Nos. 48–49). London: Spastics International Medical Publications/Heinemann Medical Books, 1973.

Boder, E. Developmental dyslexia: A diagnostic approach based on three atypical reading patterns. *Developmental Medicine and Child Neurology*, 1973, *15*, 663–687.

Boll, T. J. The Halstead–Reitan Neuropsychological Battery. In S. B. Filskov & T. J. Boll (Eds.), *Handbook of clinical neuropsychology*. New York: Wiley, 1981.

Byers, R. K., & McLean, W. T. Etiology and course of certain hemiplegias with aphasia in childhood. *Pediatrics*, 1962, *19*, 376–383.

Campbell, M., Rosenbloom, S., Perry, R., George, A. E., Kricheff, I. I., Anderson, L., Small, A. M., & Jennings, S. J. *Computerized axial tomographic scans in young autistic children*. Paper presented at the 134th annual meeting of the American Psychiatric Association, May 9–15, 1981.

Campbell, S. B., Schleifer, M., & Weiss, G. Continuities in maternal reports and child behaviors over time in hyperactive and comparison groups. *Journal of Abnormal Child Psychology*, 1978, *6*, 33–45.

Caparulo, B. K., Cohen, D. J., Rothman, S. L., Young, J. G., Katz, J. D., Shaywitz, S. E., & Shaywitz, B. A. Computed tomographic brain scanning in children with developmental neuropsychiatric disorders. *Journal of the American Academy of Child Psychiatry*, 1981, *20*, 338–357.

Chadwick, O., Rutter, M., Thompson, J., & Shaffer, D. Intellectual performance and reading skills after localized head injury in childhood. *Journal of Child Psychology and Psychiatry*, 1981, *22*, 117–139.

Charles, L., Schain, R. J., & Guthrie, D. Long-term use and discontinuation of methylphenidate with hyperactive children. *Developmental Medicine and Child Neurology*, 1979, *21*, 758–764.

Chelune, G. J., & Edwards, P. Early brain lesions: Ontogenetic–environmental considerations. *Journal of Consulting and Clinical Psychology*, 1981, *49*, 777–790.

Chess, S., Korn, S. J., & Fernandez, P. B. *Psychiatric disorders of children with congenital rubella*. New York: Brunner/Mazel, 1971.

Connolly, K. J., & Prechtl, H. F. R. (Eds.). *Maturation and development: Biological and psychological perspectives* (Clinics in Developmental Medicine Nos. 77–78). London: Spastics International Medical Publications/Heinemann Medical Books, 1981.

Corbett, J., Harris, R., Taylor, E., & Trimble, M. Progressive dysintegrative psychosis of childhood. *Journal of Child Psychology and Psychiatry*, 1977, *18*, 211–219.

Damasio, H., Maurer, R. G., Damasio, A. R., & Chui, H. C. Computerized tomographic scan findings in patients with autistic behavior. *Archives of Neurology*, 1980, *37*, 504–510.

Darby, J. K. Neuropathologic aspects of psychosis in children. *Journal of Autism and Childhood Schizophrenia*, 1976, *6*, 339–352.

Davison, K., & Bagley, B. R. Schizophrenia-like psychoses associated with organic disorders of the central nervous system: A review of the literature. In R. N. Herrington (Ed.), *Current problems in neuropsychiatry: Schizophrenia, epilepsy, the temporal lobe* (*British Journal of Psychiatry* Special Publication No. 4). Ashford, England: Headley Brothers, 1969.

Deykin, E. Y., & MacMahon, B. The incidence of seizures among children with autistic symptoms. *American Journal of Psychiatry*, 1979, *136*, 1310–1312.

Deykin, E. Y., & MacMahon, B. Pregnancy, delivery, and neonatal complications among autistic children. *American Journal of Diseases of Children*, 1980, *134*, 860–864.

Dobbing, J. Later development of the brain and its vulnerability. In J. A. Davis & J. Dobbing (Eds.), *Scientific foundations of pediatrics*. London: Heinemann Medical Books, 1974.

Drillien, C. M., Thomson, A. J. M., & Burgoyne, K. Low-birthweight children at early school age: A longitudinal study. *Developmental Medicine and Child Neurology*, 1980, *22*, 26–47.

Eiser, C. Effects of chronic illness in childhood: A comparison of normal children with those treated for childhood leukaemia and solid tumours. *Archives of Disease in Childhood*, 1980, *55*, 766–770.

Evans-Jones, L. G., & Rosenbloom, L. Disintegrative psychosis in childhood. *Developmental Medicine and Child Neurology*, 1978, *20*, 462–470.

Finnegan, J.-A., & Quadrington, B. Pre-, peri-, and neonatal factors and infantile autism. *Journal of Child Psychology and Psychiatry*, 1979, *20*, 119–128.

Fitzhugh, K. B., Fitzhugh, L. C., & Reitan, R. M. Wechsler–Bellevue comparison in groups with "chronic" and "current" lateralized and diffuse brain lesions. *Journal of Consulting and Clinical Psychology*, 1962, *26*, 306–310.

Fletcher, J. M., & Satz, P. Developmental changes in the neuropsychological correlates of reading achievement: A six-year longitudinal study. *Journal of Clinical Neuropsychology*, 1980, *2*, 23–38.

Flor-Henry, P. On certain aspects of the localization of the cerebral systems regulating and determining emotion. *Biological Psychiatry*, 1979, *14*, 677–698.

Folstein, S., & Rutter, M. Infantile autism: A genetic study of 21 twin pairs. *Journal of Child Psychology and Psychiatry*, 1977, *18*, 297–321.

Galin, D., Johnstone, J., Yingling, C., Fein, G., Herron, J., & Marcus, M. *Comparison of regional brain activation in dyslexia and control children during reading tasks: Probe event-related potentials.* Paper presented at the 10th annual meeting of the International Neuropsychological Society, Pittsburgh, February 3–6, 1982.

Geschwind, N., Galaburda, A., & LeMay, M. Morphological and physiological substrates of language and cognitive development. In R. Katzman (Ed.), *Congenital and acquired cognitive disorders* (Association for Research in Nervous and Mental Diseases, Vol. 57). New York: Raven Press, 1979.

Gevins, A. S., Doyle, J. C., Cutillo, B. A., Schaffer, R. E., Tannehill, R. S., Ghannam, J. H., Gilcrease, V. A., & Yeager, C. L. Electrical potentials in human brain during cognition: New method reveals dynamic patterns of correlation. *Science*, 1981, *213*, 918–922.

Gordon, H. W. Cognitive asymmetry in dyslexic families. *Neuropsychologica*, 1980, *18*, 645–656.

Gott, P. S. Cognitive abilities following right and left hemispherectomy. *Cortex*, 1973, *9*, 266–274.

Gross, M., & Wilson, W. C. *Minimal brain dysfunction: A clinical study of incidence, diagnosis and treatment in over 1000 children.* New York: Brunner/Mazel, 1974.

Gubbay, S. S., Ellis, E., Walton, J. N., & Court, S. D. M. Clumsy children: A study of apraxic and agnosic defects in 21 children. *Brain*, 1965, *88*, 295–312.

Guttman, E. Aphasia in children. *Brain*, 1942, *65*, 205–219.

Harris, R. The EEG. In M. Rutter & L. Hersov (Eds.), *Child psychiatry: Modern approaches.* Oxford: Blackwell Scientific Publications, 1977.

Hauser, S. L., DeLong, G. R., & Rosman, N. P. Pneumographic findings in the infantile autism syndrome: A correlation with temporal-lobe disease. *Brain*, 1975, *98*, 667–688.

Hebb, D. O. The effect of early and late brain injury upon test scores, and the nature of normal adult intelligence. *Proceedings of the American Philosophical Society*, 1942, *85*, 275–292.

Heller, T. About dementia infantilis [translation]. In J. G. Howells (Ed.), *Modern perspectives in international child psychiatry*. Edinburgh: Oliver & Boyd, 1969. (Originally published in German, 1930.)

Hier, D. B., LeMay, M., & Rosenberger, P. B. Autism and unfavorable left–right asymmetries of the brain. *Journal of Autism and Developmental Disorders*, 1979, *9*, 153–160.

Hier, D. B., LeMay, M., Rosenberger, P. B., & Perlo, V. P. Developmental dyslexia: Evidence for a subgroup with a reversal of cerebral asymmetry. *Archives of Neurology*, 1978, *35*, 90–92.

Hughes, R. Electroencephalographic and neurophysiological studies in dyslexia. In A. L. Benton & D. Pearl (Eds.), *Dyslexia: An appraisal of current knowledge.* New York: Oxford University Press, 1978.

Ingram, T. T. S. The nature of dyslexia. In F. A. Young & D. B. Lindsley (Eds.), *Early experience and visual information processing in perceptual and reading disorders.* Washington, D.C.: National Academy of Sciences, 1970.

Isaacson, R. L. The myth of recovery from early brain damage. In N. E. Ellis (Ed.), *Aberrant development in infancy*. London: Wiley, 1975.

Kennard, M. A. Cortical reorganization of motor function. *Archives of Neurology and Psychiatry*, 1942, *48*, 227–240.

Kohn, B., & Dennis, M. Patterns of hemisphere specialization after hemidecortication for infantile hemiplegia. In M. Kinsbourne & W. L. Smith (Eds.), *Hemispheric disconnection and cerebral function.* Springfield, Ill.: Charles C Thomas, 1974.

"Leader." Serotonin, platelets, and autism. *British Medical Journal*, 1978, *1*, 1651–1652.

Ledbetter, D. H., Riccardi, V. M., Airhart, S. D., Strobel, R. J., Keenan, B. S., & Crawford, J. D.

Deletions of chromosome 15 as a cause of the Prader-Willi syndrome. *New England Journal of Medicine*, 1981, *304*, 325–329.

Lehmkuhl, G., Kotlarek, F., & Schieber, P. M. Neurologische und neuropsychologische Befunde bei Kindern mit angeborenen umschriebenen. *Hirnläsionen Zeitschrift für Kinder und Jugendpsychiatrie*, 1981, *9*, 126–138.

Lenneberg, E. H. *Biological foundations of language*. New York: Wiley, 1967.

Lindsay, J., Ounsted, C., & Richards, P. Long-term outcome in children with temporal lobe seizures: III. Psychiatric aspects in childhood and adult life. *Developmental Medicine and Child Neurology*, 1979, *21*, 630–636.

Lloyd, K. G., Hornykiewicz, O., Davidson, L., Shannak, K., Farley, I., Goldstein, M., Shibuya, M., Kelley, W. N., & Fox, I. H. Biochemical evidence of dysfunction of brain neurotransmitters in the Lesch–Nyhan syndrome. *New England Journal of Medicine*, 1981, *305*, 1106–1111.

Lynch, G., & Gall, C. Organisation and reorganisation in the central nervous system. In F. Falkner & J. M. Tanner (Eds.), *Human growth* (Vol. 3, *Neurobiology and nutrition*). London: Balliere Tindall, 1979.

McFie, J. *Assessment of organic intellectual impairment*. London: Academic Press, 1975. (a)

McFie, J. Brain injury in childhood and language development. In N. O'Connor (Ed.), *Language cognitive deficits, and retardation*. London: Butterworths, 1975. (b)

Malamud, N. Heller's disease and childhood schizophrenia. *American Journal of Psychiatry*, 1959, *116*, 215–218.

Marshall, W. A. *Development of the brain*. Edinburgh: Oliver & Boyd, 1968.

Mattis, S. Dyslexia syndromes: A working hypothesis that works. In A. L. Benton & D. Pearl (Eds.), *Dyslexia: An appraisal of current knowledge*. New York: Oxford University Press, 1978.

Menyuk, P. Nonlinguistic and linguistic processing in normally developing and language-disordered children. In N. J. Lass (Ed.), *Speech and language: Advances in basic research and practice* (Vol. 4). New York: Academic Press, 1980.

Newcombe, F. *Missile wounds of the brain: A study of psychological deficits*. London: Oxford University Press, 1969.

Nyhan, W. L. Behavior in the Lesch–Nyhan syndrome. *Journal of Autism and Childhood Schizophrenia*, 1976, *6*, 235–252.

Phelps, M. E., Kuhl, D. E., & Mazziotta, J. C. Metabolic mapping of the brain's response to visual stimulation: Studies in humans. *Science*, 1981, *211*, 1445–1448.

Pirozzolo, F. J., Campanella, D. J., Christensen, K., & Lawson-Kerr, K. Effects of cerebral dysfunction on neurolinguistic performance in children. *Journal of Consulting and Clinical Psychology*, 1981, *49*, 791–806.

Rie, H. E. Definitional problems. In H. E. Rie & E. D. Rie (Eds.), *Handbook of minimal brain dysfunctions: A critical view*. New York: Wiley–Interscience, 1980.

Riikonen, R., & Amnell, G. Psychiatric disorders in children with earlier infantile spasms. *Developmental Medicine and Child Neurology*, 1981, *23*, 747–760.

Rivinus, T. M., Jamison, D. L., & Graham, P. J. Childhood organic neurological disease presenting as psychiatric disorder. *Archives of Disease in Childhood*, 1975, *20*, 115–119.

Rutter, M. Autistic children: Infancy to adulthood. *Seminars in Psychiatry*, 1970, *2*, 435–450.

Rutter, M. Emotional disorder and educational underachievement. *Archives of Diseases in Childhood*, 1974, *49*, 249–256.

Rutter, M. Brain damage syndromes in childhood: Concepts and findings. *Journal of Child Psychology and Psychiatry*, 1977, *18*, 1–22. (a)

Rutter, M. Infantile autism and other child psychoses. In M. Rutter & L. Hersov (Eds.), *Child psychiatry: Modern approaches*. Oxford: Blackwell Scientific, 1977. (b)

Rutter, M. Raised lead levels and impaired cognitive–behavioural functioning: A review of the evidence. *Developmental Medicine and Child Neurology*, 1980, *22*(1) (Suppl. No. 42).

Rutter, M. Psychological sequelae of brain damage in children. *American Journal of Psychiatry*, 1981, *138*, 1533–1544.

Rutter, M. Developmental neuropsychiatry: Concepts, issues and prospects. *Journal of Clinical Neuropsychiatry*, 1982, *4*, 91–115. (a)

Rutter, M. Syndromes attributed to "minimal brain dysfunction" in childhood. *American Journal of Psychiatry*, 1982, *139*, 21–33. (b)

Rutter, M., Chadwick, O., & Schachar, R. Hyperactivity and minimal brain dysfunction: Epidemiological perspectives on questions of cause and classification. In R. Tarter (Ed.), *The child at risk*. New York: Oxford University Press, in press.

Rutter, M., & Giller, H. *Juvenile delinquency: Trends and perspectives.* Harmondsworth, England: Penguin Books, 1983.

Rutter, M., Graham, P., & Yule, W. *A neuropsychiatric study in childhood* (Clinics in Developmental Medicine Nos. 35–36). London: Spastics International Medical Publications/Heinemann Medical Books, 1970.

Rutter, M., Maughan, B., Mortimore, P., & Ouston, J., with Smith, A. *Fifteen thousand hours: Secondary schools and their effects on children.* London: Open Books, 1979.

Rutter, M., & Russell Jones, R. *Lead versus health: Sources and effects of low level lead exposure.* Chichester, England: Wiley, 1983.

Rutter, M., Tizard, J., & Whitmore, K. (Eds.), *Education, health and behaviour.* Huntington, N.Y.: Krieger, 1981. (Originally published in London, 1970.)

St. James Roberts, I. Neurological plasticity, recovery from brain insult, and child development. In H. W. Reese & L. P. Lipsitt (Eds.), *Advances in child development and behavior* (Vol. 14). New York: Academic Press, 1979.

Sandberg, S., Rutter, M., & Taylor, E. Hyperkinetic disorder in psychiatric clinic attenders. *Developmental Medicine and Child Neurology*, 1978, *20*, 279–299.

Sandberg, S., Wieselberg, M., & Shaffer, D. Hyperkinetic and conduct problem children in primary school population: Some epidemiological considerations. *Journal of Child Psychology and Psychiatry*, 1980, *21*, 293–311.

Satterfield, J. H., Satterfield, B. T., & Cantwell, D. P. Multimodality treatment: A two-year evaluation of 61 hyperactive boys. *Archives of General Psychiatry*, 1980, *37*, 915–919.

Satz, P., & Bullard-Bates, C. Acquired aphasia in children. In M. T. Sarno (Ed.), *Acquired aphasia.* New York: Academic Press, 1981.

Satz, P., & Fletcher, J. M. Emergent trends in neuropsychology: An overview. *Journal of Consulting and Clinical Psychology*, 1981, *49*, 851–865.

Satz, P., Taylor, G., Friel, J., & Fletcher, J. Some developmental and predictive percursors of reading disabilities: A six year follow-up. In A. L. Benton & D. Pearl (Eds.), *Dyslexia: An appraisal of current knowledge.* New York: Oxford University Press, 1978.

Schachar, R., Rutter, M., & Smith, A. The characteristics of situationally and pervasively hyperactive children: Implications for syndrome definition. *Journal of Child Psychology and Psychiatry*, 1981, *22*, 375–392.

Schneider, G. E. Is it really better to have your brain lesion early?: A revision of the "Kennard principle." *Neuropsychologia*, 1979, *17*, 557–583.

Shaffer, D., Bijur, P., Chadwick, O., & Rutter, M. Head injury and later reading disability. *Journal of the American Academy of Child Psychiatry*, 1980, *19*, 592–610.

Sleator, E. K., von Neumann, A., & Sprague, R. L. Hyperactive children: A continuous long-term placebo-controlled follow-up. *Journal of the American Medical Association*, 1974, *229*, 316–317.

Stein, D. G., Rosen, J. J., & Butters, N. (Eds.). *Plasticity and recovery of function in the central nervous system.* New York: Academic Press, 1974.

Taft, L. T., & Cohen, H. J. Hypsarrhythmia and infantile autism: A clinical report. *Journal of Autism and Childhood Schizophrenia*, 1971, *1*, 327–336.

Taylor, D. C. Factors influencing the occurrence of schizophrenia-like psychosis in patients with temporal-lobe epilepsy. *Psychological Medicine*, 1975, *5*, 249–254.

Tizard, J., Schofield, W. N., & Hewison, J. Collaboration between teachers and parents in assisting children's reading. *British Journal of Educational Psychology*, 1982, *52*, 1–15.

Tucker, D. M. Lateral brain function, emotion, and conceptualization. *Psychological Bulletin*, 1981, *89*, 19–46.

van Hof, M. W. Development and recovery from brain damage. In K. Connolly & H. F. R. Prechtl (Eds.), *Maturation and development: Biological and psychological perspectives* (Clinics in Developmental Medicine Nos. 77–78). London: Spastics International Medical Publications/Heinemann Medical Books, 1981.

Wender, P. *Minimal brain dysfunction in children.* New York: Wiley, 1971.

Wexler, B. E. Cerebral laterality and psychiatry: A review of the literature. *American Journal of Psychiatry*, 1980, *137*, 279–291.

Wing, L., & Gould, J. Severe impairments of social interaction and associated anomalies in children: Epidemiology and classification. *Journal of Autism and Developmental Disorders*, 1979, *9*, 11–29.

Witelson, S. F. Early hemisphere specialization and interhemisphere plasticity: An empirical and theoretical review. In S. J. Segalowitz & F. A. Gruber (Eds.), *Language development and neurological theory*. New York: Academic Press, 1977.

Woods, B. T., & Carey, S. Language deficits after apparent clinical recovery from childhood aphasia. *Annals of Neurology*, 1979, *6*, 405–407.

Worster-Drought, C. An unusual form of acquired aphasia in children. *Folia Phoniatrica*, 1964, *16*, 223–227.

World Health Organization. *Mental disorders: Glossary and guide to their classification in accordance with the ninth revision of the International Classification of Diseases*. Geneva: Author, 1978.

Wyke, M. A. (Ed.). *Developmental dysphasia*. London: Academic Press, 1978.

Author Index

Subject Index